DRAMA

CRITICISM

Guide to Gale Literary Criticism Series

For criticism on	Consult these Gale series
Authors now living or who died after December 31, 1999	*CONTEMPORARY LITERARY CRITICISM (CLC)*
Authors who died between 1900 and 1999	*TWENTIETH-CENTURY LITERARY CRITICISM (TCLC)*
Authors who died between 1800 and 1899	*NINETEENTH-CENTURY LITERATURE CRITICISM (NCLC)*
Authors who died between 1400 and 1799	*LITERATURE CRITICISM FROM 1400 TO 1800 (LC)* *SHAKESPEAREAN CRITICISM (SC)*
Authors who died before 1400	*CLASSICAL AND MEDIEVAL LITERATURE CRITICISM (CMLC)*
Authors of books for children and young adults	*CHILDREN'S LITERATURE REVIEW (CLR)*
Dramatists	*DRAMA CRITICISM (DC)*
Poets	*POETRY CRITICISM (PC)*
Short story writers	*SHORT STORY CRITICISM (SSC)*
Literary topics and movements	*HARLEM RENAISSANCE: A GALE CRITICAL COMPANION (HR)* *THE BEAT GENERATION: A GALE CRITICAL COMPANION (BG)*
Asian American writers of the last two hundred years	*ASIAN AMERICAN LITERATURE (AAL)*
Black writers of the past two hundred years	*BLACK LITERATURE CRITICISM (BLC)* *BLACK LITERATURE CRITICISM SUPPLEMENT (BLCS)*
Hispanic writers of the late nineteenth and twentieth centuries	*HISPANIC LITERATURE CRITICISM (HLC)* *HISPANIC LITERATURE CRITICISM SUPPLEMENT (HLCS)*
Native North American writers and orators of the eighteenth, nineteenth, and twentieth centuries	*NATIVE NORTH AMERICAN LITERATURE (NNAL)*
Major authors from the Renaissance to the present	*WORLD LITERATURE CRITICISM, 1500 TO THE PRESENT (WLC)* *WORLD LITERATURE CRITICISM SUPPLEMENT (WLCS)*

ISSN 1056-4349

DRAMA CRITICISM

Criticism of the Most Significant and Widely Studied
Dramatic Works from All the World's Literatures

VOLUME 25

Jelena O. Krstović
Project Editor

THOMSON

GALE

Detroit • New York • San Francisco • San Diego • New Haven, Conn. • Waterville, Maine • London • Munich

Drama Criticism, Vol. 25

Project Editor
Jelena O. Krstović

Editorial
Jessica Bomarito, Kathy D. Darrow, Jeffrey W. Hunter, Michelle Lee, Thomas J. Schoenberg, Lawrence J. Trudeau, Russel Whitaker

Data Capture
Francis Monroe, Gwen Tucker

Indexing Services
Synapse, the Knowledge Link Corporation

Rights Acquisitions and Management
Margie Abendroth, Peg Ashlevitz, Lori Hines

Imaging and Multimedia
Dean Dauphinais, Leitha Etheridge-Sims, Lezlie Light, Mike Logusz, Dan Newell, Christine O'Bryan, Kelly A. Quin, Denay Wilding, Robyn Young

Composition and Electronic Capture
Kathy Sauer

Manufacturing
Rhonda Williams

Product Manager
Janet Witalec

LIBRARY OF CONGRESS CATALOG CARD NUMBER 76-46132

ISBN 0-7876-8109-1
ISSN 1056-4349

Printed in the United States of America
10 9 8 7 6 5 4 3 2 1

Contents

Preface vii

Acknowledgments xi

Literary Criticism Series Advisory Board xiii

Preface

*D*rama Criticism (*DC*) is principally intended for beginning students of literature and theater as well as the average playgoer. The series is therefore designed to introduce readers to the most frequently studied playwrights of all time periods and nationalities and to present discerning commentary on dramatic works of enduring interest. Furthermore, *DC* seeks to acquaint the reader with the uses and functions of criticism itself. Selected from a diverse body of commentary, the essays in *DC* offer insights into the authors and their works but do not require that the reader possess a wide background in literary studies. Where appropriate, reviews of important productions of the plays discussed are also included to give students a heightened awareness of drama as a dynamic art form, one that many claim is fully realized only in performance.

DC was created in response to suggestions by the staffs of high school, college, and public libraries. These librarians observed a need for a series that assembles critical commentary on the world's most renowned dramatists in the same manner as Thomson Gale's *Short Story Criticism* (*SSC*) and *Poetry Criticism* (*PC*), which present material on writers of short fiction and poetry. Although playwrights are covered in such Thomson Gale literary criticism series as *Contemporary Literary Criticism* (*CLC*), *Twentieth-Century Literary Criticism* (*TCLC*), *Nineteenth-Century Literature Criticism* (*NCLC*), *Literature Criticism from 1400 to 1800* (*LC*), and *Classical and Medieval Literature Criticism* (*CMLC*), *DC* directs more concentrated attention on individual dramatists than is possible in the broader, survey-oriented entries in these Thomson Gale series. Commentary on the works of William Shakespeare may be found in *Shakespearean Criticism* (*SC*).

Scope of the Series

By collecting and organizing commentary on dramatists, *DC* assists students in their efforts to gain insight into literature, achieve better understanding of the texts, and formulate ideas for papers and assignments. A variety of interpretations and assessments is offered, allowing students to pursue their own interests and promoting awareness that literature is dynamic and responsive to many different opinions.

Approximately five to ten authors are included in each volume, and each entry presents a historical survey of the critical response to that playwright's work. The length of an entry is intended to reflect the amount of critical attention the author has received from critics writing in English and from foreign critics in translation. Every attempt has been made to identify and include the most significant essays on each author's work. In order to provide these important critical pieces, the editors sometimes reprint essays that have appeared elsewhere in Thomson Gale's literary criticism series. Such duplication, however, never exceeds twenty percent of a *DC* volume.

Organization of the Book

A *DC* entry consists of the following elements:

■ The **Author Heading** consists of the playwright's most commonly used name, followed by birth and death dates. If an author consistently wrote under a pseudonym, the pseudonym is listed in the author heading and the real name given in parentheses on the first line of the introduction. Also located at the beginning of the introduction are any name variations under which the dramatist wrote, including transliterated forms of the names of authors whose languages use nonroman alphabets.

■ The **Introduction** contains background information that introduces the reader to the author and the critical debates surrounding his or her work.

■ A **Portrait of the Author** is included when available.

- The list of **Principal Works** is divided into two sections. The first section contains the author's dramatic pieces and is organized chronologically by date of first performance. If this has not been conclusively determined, the composition or publication date is used. The second section provides information on the author's major works in other genres.

- Essays offering **overviews and general studies of the dramatist's entire literary career** give the student broad perspectives on the writer's artistic development, themes, and concerns that recur in several of his or her works, the author's place in literary history, and other wide-ranging topics.

- **Criticism** of individual plays offers the reader in-depth discussions of a select number of the author's most important works. In some cases, the criticism is divided into two sections, each arranged chronologically. When a significant performance of a play can be identified (typically, the premier of a twentieth-century work), the first section of criticism will feature **production reviews** of this staging. Most entries include sections devoted to **critical commentary** that assesses the literary merit of the selected plays. When necessary, essays are carefully excerpted to focus on the work under consideration; often, however, essays and reviews are reprinted in their entirety. Footnotes are reprinted at the end of each essay or excerpt. In the case of excerpted criticism, only those footnotes that pertain to the excerpted texts are included.

- Critical essays are prefaced by brief **Annotations** explicating each piece.

- A complete **Bibliographic Citation,** designed to help the interested reader locate the original essay or book, precedes each piece of criticism. Source citations in the Literary Criticism Series follow University of Chicago Press style, as outlined in *The Chicago Manual of Style,* 14th ed. (Chicago: The University of Chicago Press, 1993).

- An annotated bibliography of **Further Reading** appears at the end of each entry and suggests resources for additional study. In some cases, significant essays for which the editors could not obtain reprint rights are included here. Boxed material following the further reading list provides references to other biographical and critical sources on the author in series published by Thomson Gale.

Cumulative Indexes

A **Cumulative Author Index** lists all of the authors that appear in a wide variety of reference sources published by Thomson Gale, including *DC*. A complete list of these sources is found facing the first page of the Author Index. The index also includes birth and death dates and cross references between pseudonyms and actual names.

A **Cumulative Nationality Index** lists all authors featured in *DC* by nationality, followed by the number of the *DC* volume in which their entry appears.

A **Cumulative Title Index** lists in alphabetical order the individual plays discussed in the criticism contained in *DC*. Each title is followed by the author's last name and corresponding volume and page numbers where commentary on the work is located. English-language translations of original foreign-language titles are cross-referenced to the foreign titles so that all references to discussion of a work are combined in one listing.

Citing *Drama Criticism*

When citing criticism reprinted in the Literary Criticism Series, students should provide complete bibliographic information so that the cited essay can be located in the original print or electronic source. Students who quote directly from reprinted criticism may use any accepted bibliographic format, such as University of Chicago Press style or Modern Language Association (MLA) style. Both the MLA and the University of Chicago formats are acceptable and recognized as being the current standards for citations. It is important, however, to choose one format for all citations; do not mix the two formats within a list of citations.

The examples below follow recommendations for preparing a bibliography set forth in *The Chicago Manual of Style,* 14th ed. (Chicago: The University of Chicago Press, 1993); the first example pertains to material drawn from periodicals, the second to material reprinted from books:

Morrison, Jago. "Narration and Unease in Ian McEwan's Later Fiction." *Critique* 42, no. 3 (spring 2001): 253-68. Reprinted in *Drama Criticism.* Vol. 20, edited by Janet Witalec, 212-20. Detroit: Gale, 2003.

Brossard, Nicole. "Poetic Politics." In *The Politics of Poetic Form: Poetry and Public Policy,* edited by Charles Bernstein, 73-82. New York: Roof Books, 1990. Reprinted in *Drama Criticism.* Vol. 20, edited by Janet Witalec, 3-8. Detroit: Gale, 2003.

The examples below follow recommendations for preparing a works cited list set forth in the *MLA Handbook for Writers of Research Papers,* 5th ed. (New York: The Modern Language Association of America, 1999); the first example pertains to material drawn from periodicals, the second to material reprinted from books:

Morrison, Jago. "Narration and Unease in Ian McEwan's Later Fiction." *Critique* 42.3 (spring 2001): 253-68. Reprinted in *Drama Criticism.* Ed. Janet Witalec. Vol. 20. Detroit: Gale, 2003. 212-20.

Brossard, Nicole. "Poetic Politics." *The Politics of Poetic Form: Poetry and Public Policy.* Ed. Charles Bernstein. New York: Roof Books, 1990. 73-82. Reprinted in *Drama Criticism.* Ed. Janet Witalec. Vol. 20. Detroit: Gale, 2003. 3-8.

Suggestions are Welcome

Readers who wish to suggest new features, topics, or authors to appear in future volumes, or who have other suggestions or comments are cordially invited to call, write, or fax the Product Manager:

Product Manager, Literary Criticism Series
Thomson Gale
27500 Drake Road
Farmington Hills, MI 48331-3535
1-800-347-4253 (GALE)
Fax: 248-699-8054

Acknowledgments

The editors wish to thank the copyright holders of the excerpted criticism included in this volume and the permissions managers of many book and magazine publishing companies for assisting us in securing reproduction rights. We are also grateful to the staffs of the Detroit Public Library, the Library of Congress, the University of Detroit Mercy Library, Wayne State University Purdy/Kresge Library Complex, and the University of Michigan Libraries for making their resources available to us. Following is a list of the copyright holders who have granted us permission to reproduce material in this volume of *DC*. Every effort has been made to trace copyright, but if omissions have been made, please let us know.

COPYRIGHTED MATERIAL IN *DC*, VOLUME 25, WAS REPRODUCED FROM THE FOLLOWING PERIODICALS:

Comparative Drama, v. 33, summer, 1999. Copyright © 1999 by the Editors of Comparative Drama. Reproduced by permission.—*Consciousness, Literature, and the Arts*, v. 3, August, 2002 for "Mirroring the Split Subject: Jean Genet's *The Balcony*" by Christine Boyko-Head. Reproduced by permission of the author.—*Dalhousie French Studies*, v. 44, 1998. Reproduced by permission.—*The French Review*, v. 63, May, 1990. Copyright © 1990 by the American Association of Teachers of French. Reproduced by permission.—*French Studies*, v. 50, October, 1996 for "Confused? You Will Be: Genet's *Les Nègres* and the Art of Upsetting the Audience" by Derek Connon. Copyright © The Society for French Studies 1996. All rights reserved. Reproduced by permission of Oxford University Press Journals and the author.—*Guardian (Manchester)*, April 17, 1987. Copyright Guardian Newspapers Limited 1987. Reproduced by permission.—*Medieval and Renaissance Drama in England*, v. 5, 1991. Reproduced by permission.—*Modern Drama*, v. 35, December, 1992. Copyright © 1992 by the University of Toronto, Graduate Centre for Study of Drama. Reproduced by permission.— *Modern Language Review*, v. 62, 1967. Copyright © Modern Humanities Research Association 1967. Reproduced by permission of the publisher and the author.—*Notes on Contemporary Literature*, v. 21, September, 1991. Copyright © 1991 by William S. Doxey. Reproduced by permission.—*Raritan*, v. 16, fall, 1996. Copyright © 1996 by *Raritan: A Quarterly Review*. Reproduced by permission.—*Renaissance Drama*, v. 9, 1966. Copyright © 1967 by Northwestern University Press. Reproduced by permission.—*Restoration and Eighteenth Century Theatre Research*, v. 11, winter, 1996. Copyright © 1996 Loyola University Chicago. Reproduced by permission./v. 16. 2003. Copyright © 2003 University of Denver. Reproduced by permission.—*Romance Notes*, v. 36, spring, 1996. Reproduced by permission.—*SEL: Studies in English Literature, 1500-1900*, v. 43, summer, 2003. Copyright © 2003 William Marsh Rice University. All rights reserved. Reproduced by permission of the Johns Hopkins University Press.—*The Seventeenth Century*, v. 2, July, 1987. Reproduced by permission.—*Studies in the Humanities*, v. 24, June-December, 1997. Copyright © 1997 by Indiana University Press of Pennsylvania. Reproduced by permission.—*Studies in the Literary Imagination*, v. 32, fall, 1999. Copyright © 1999 Department of English, Georgia State University. Reproduced by permission.—*Studies in Twentieth Century Literature*, v. 26, summer, 2002. Copyright © 2002 by *Studies in Twentieth Century Literature*. Reproduced by permission.—*Times Literary Supplement*, May 1, 1987. Copyright © 1987 by The Times Supplements Limited. Reproduced from *The Times Literary Supplement* by permission.—*The Wall Street Journal*, July 13, 1987 for "Shirley and Shakespeare" by Edwin Wilson. Copyright © 1987 Dow Jones & Company, Inc. All rights reserved. Reproduced by permission of the publisher and the author.—*Women's Writing*, v. 6, 1999 for "Too Theatrical? Female Subjectivity in Caroline and Interregnum Drama" by Sophie Eliza Tomlinson; v. 7, 2000 for "Is There a Whig Canon? The Case of Susanna Centlivre" by Brean S. Hammond. Copyright © Triangle Journals Ltd., 1999, 2000. All rights reserved. Both reproduced by permission of the publisher and the author.

COPYRIGHTED MATERIAL IN *DC*, VOLUME 25, WAS REPRODUCED FROM THE FOLLOWING BOOKS:

Bateson, F. W. From *English Comic Drama 1700-1750*. Oxford at Clarendon Press, 1929. Reproduced by permission of Oxford University Press.—Belsey, Catherine. From "Tragedy, Justice, and the Subject," in *1642: Literature and Power in the Seventeenth Century*. Edited by Francis Barker. Department of Literature, University of Essex, 1981. Reproduced by permission of the author.—Bradby, David. From "Blacking up—Three Productions by Peter Stein," in *A Radical Stage: Theatre in Germany in the 1970s and 1980s*. Edited by W. G. Sebald. Copyright © Berg Publishers Limited 1988. All rights reserved. Reproduced by permission.—Bratton, Jacky. From "Reading the Intertheatrical, or, the Mysterious Disappearance of Susanna Centlivre," in *Women, Theatre, and Performance: New Histories, New Historiographies*. Edited by

PHOTOGRAPHS APPEARING IN *DC*, VOLUME 25, WERE RECEIVED FROM THE FOLLOWING SOURCES:

Thomson Gale Literature Product Advisory Board

Susanna Centlivre
1669-1723

English dramatist and poet.

INTRODUCTION

In terms of number of performances, Centlivre could fairly be called the most successful English dramatist after William Shakespeare and before the twentieth century. Only three other pre-1750 playwrights—Shakespeare, Phillip Massinger and Colley Cibber—had plays still regularly staged in the nineteenth century. Like her more famous counterpart, the Restoration playwright Aphra Behn, Centlivre suffered the prejudices, slights, and outright attacks peculiar to the station of the woman writer, but her plays lasted much longer and were performed much more frequently than those of Behn. Because her works are better performed than read, she was long dismissed by critics. Recent recognition of her theatrical skill and interest in her unique perspective as a female Whig dramatist have returned Centlivre to prominence as a major playwright of the early eighteenth century.

BIOGRAPHICAL INFORMATION

The facts of Centlivre's birth remain in dispute, but the standard version of her origins identifies her as the child of William and Anne Freeman of Lincolnshire, baptized in 1669. According to some accounts, Mr. Freeman was a supporter of the Cromwellian party prior to the Restoration, placing the family in Ireland as exiles at the time of Centlivre's birth. A dissenting story of her parentage first appeared in an obituary written by a journalist personally known to Centlivre: Abel Boyer believed that Centlivre was born to a Mr. Rawkins, of lower estate than Mr. Freeman was thought to be. Documentary evidence exists to support both stories but confirm neither. Her early years are clouded by legend: Boyer refers provocatively to the "gay Adventures" of her youth ("over which we shall draw a Veil," he adds), and John Mottley includes in her biography a story in which a young Centlivre, fleeing a wicked stepmother, is picked up weeping at the side of a road by a Cambridge student. The young man, Anthony Hammond, secreted her away in his college rooms, according to Mottley's narrative—an arrangement that allowed her to get a brief, second-hand university education before venturing on to London to establish herself in

the theater. Mottley was also an acquaintance of the playwright, as was William Chetwood, who agreed that Centlivre fled her stepmother but wrote that she joined a troupe of traveling players.

Most scholars concur Centlivre was married, "or something like it," in Mottley's words, three times. Her first marriage was to the nephew of Sir Stephen Fox; it ended within a year, due to unknown circumstances. She soon married again, this time an officer of the army named Mr. Carroll, but she was widowed within a year and a half. The legitimacy of both marriages is a common problem for biographers; in Centlivre's day marriage laws were not clear and the common stereotype of the authoress as a loose woman made hers more suspect than usual in the eyes of her critics. Her third marriage, however, is fully documented. She wed Joseph Centlivre, a Yeoman of the Kitchen, on April 23, 1707, having already achieved a measure of success through what all her biographers agree was a large measure of skill and hard work.

1

Centlivre's journalist friend Boyer helped her launch her career in 1700, with the production of the tragicomic play *The Perjur'd Husband* at the Drury Lane Theatre. For the next two decades Centlivre worked steadily at playwriting, though she published her first several plays anonymously. Even her first major success was released without her name attached; *The Gamester* (1705) did so well at Lincoln's Inn Fields that it was used two months later to open the new Haymarket Theatre. In 1706 Centlivre offered her play *Love at a Venture* to Colley Cibber, who was managing the Drury Lane Theatre, but Cibber rejected it. When Cibber produced a very similar play, *The Double Gallants* (1707), under his own name, Centlivre had little recourse, but when Cibber's plagiarism was publicized he was roundly criticized. In the meantime, Centlivre had taken the play to the Duke of Grafton's servants, a troupe of strolling players then at Bath. Evidence suggests that she joined the troupe herself as a traveling performer. Legend holds that the players performed *Alexander the Great* (some say *The Rival Queens*) for the court at Windsor, with Centlivre herself taking the title role. It was as Alexander, the story goes, that Centlivre first attracted the notice of one of the Queen's cooks, Joseph Centlivre. After their wedding the couple lived at Buckingham Court, Spring Gardens, which was Centlivre's home for the rest of her life.

Although she was now financially secure, Centlivre continued to write plays, though not without difficulty. Her next play, *The Busie Body* (1709), was nearly rejected by Drury Lane, and contemporary newspapers document the actors' contempt for "a silly thing wrote by a Woman." Centlivre's confidence in pressing the play was well-founded; it became one of her most successful works, winning the praise of Richard Steele in *The Tatler* and enjoying command performances at court in the subsequent decade. Her next few plays were beset by further tensions with actors, exacerbated by remarks attributed to her in *The Female Tatler,* complaining of their lack of respect and gratitude. Centlivre denied ever making such statements, but the damage was done. Centlivre's Whiggish politics, about which she became increasingly open, further created problems for theater companies eager to avoid censure from Queen Anne's Tory government. In 1714 she dedicated her *The Wonder* to Prince George Augustus of the House of Hanover, Duke of Cambridge, in another show of Whig sympathies. Her faith was well-placed: the Duke soon became King George I, and the play became one of the most popular of the eighteenth century. She wrote two political satires in 1715, both of which were repressed by the Master of Revels, and a tragedy, *The Cruel Gift,* in 1716. Her Whig sympathies, anti-Catholic beliefs, and commercial success also made Centlivre a target for the era's keenest satirist, Alexander Pope. He alluded to her in his attacks on the publisher Edmund Curll, another member of the Whig literary circle, and lampooned her

in the character of the playwright Phoebe Clinket in the farce *Three Hours after Marriage* (1717), which he wrote with John Gay and John Arbuthnot; five years after her death he included her in his catalogue of dullards, *The Dunciad* (1728). Pope also accused Centlivre of participating in an attack on him in the poem *The Catholic Poet,* but this accusation is likely incorrect. Centlivre produced her final major comedy in 1718; *A Bold Stroke for a Wife* successfully played at Lincoln's Inn Fields that year, and continued to be a favorite actor's vehicle well into the next century. Her health began to decline in the next year, and she wrote only one more play, the stridently political comedy *The Artifice* (1722), which was not a popular success. Centlivre died on December 1, 1723, and was buried at St. Paul's in Covent Garden.

MAJOR DRAMATIC WORKS

The Busie Body, The Wonder, and *A Bold Stroke for A Wife* have long been regarded as Centlivre's major works. Comedies of intrigue, these are the plays that were longest lived and most frequently performed. As in many comedies of the time, they feature heroines crossed in marriage by their guardians and plots focused on tricking those guardians out of their plans. *The Busie Body* is unique in adding a comic central character as the focus of the action: Marplot, the "busy body" of the title, is a classic "humours" character, one whose absurdly exaggerated character traits are the source of his jests. Unlike the earlier humours comedy of Ben Jonson or Thomas Shadwell, however, Centlivre's treatment of Marplot is more gentle: Marplot is a friend to the lovers, and he retains many good qualities. His actions are laughable, but he is never the butt of satire; in many ways he is the hero of the play, making possible the happy resolution. *The Wonder* focuses more on the heroines and their lovers: Felix, the jealous hero whose sweetheart's father wants to place her in a nunnery, was a favorite role for David Garrick, one of the greatest actors of the eighteenth century. Set in Lisbon, the play gave Centlivre the opportunity to express her political views by contrasting the despotism of the southern nations with the liberty of England, and by addressing, through the tyrannical behavior of the heroines' fathers, the issue of the limits of authority. The theme of the despotic guardian is dramatized most fully in *A Bold Stroke for a Wife,* in which the suitor Fainwell faces the impossible tasks of winning the consent of four very different guardians for the hand of Ann Lovely. It is notable that although Centlivre's critics frequently accused her of excessive "borrowing"—a practice all playwrights participated in, but one that was easy to criticize in a woman—her most successful plays were her most original. She used stock comic situations and common "humors" characters but, as with the character of Marplot, she often used them in new ways and for different effects. Her treatment of familiar comic types shows her debt to Restoration comedy, but also points toward the sentimental comedy of the eighteenth century, making her a transitional figure in the development of English comic drama.

Critical opinion of Centlivre as a minor dramatist restricted the study of her works to *The Busie Body, The Wonder,* and *A Bold Stroke for a Wife* well into the twentieth century, but modern reassessments of her talent and importance have begun to increase the standard Centlivre canon. Two of Centlivre's earlier plays, *The Gamester* and its companion piece *The Basset Table* (1705), are now more widely read, especially because of their attention to women's relationship with money in the early eighteenth century. Her first popular hit, *The Gamester* is Centlivre's adaptation of Jean-François Regnard's *Le Joueur* (1696), with more substantial roles for the women and a happy ending in keeping with the fashion of "reform comedy." *The Gamester* is more didactic than Centlivre's other successful comedies: she makes the effort to correct a social vice through satire, an effort not evident in the comic roles of Marplot or the foolish guardians. *The Basset Table* was less successful, though very similar in plot, character, and intention. A significant difference in *The Basset Table* is Centlivre's emphasis on the "learned lady" character, typically the butt of comedy but here portrayed sympathetically. The restraint of the educated women towards gambling supports the value of women's education, while the folly of the uneducated women demonstrates the dangers of their ignorance to themselves and others.

CRITICAL RECEPTION

Centlivre struggled for acceptance as a dramatist despite—and in some cases because of—the popularity of her plays. Richard Steele's frequent admiration of her in *The Tatler* was a significant mark of success, but Steele's comments also underscore the difficulties she faced. His defense of her as a woman playwright obliquely points toward the very real prejudice she faced from critics, actors, theater managers, and others who felt that a woman had no place writing for the theater. F. W. Bateson contends that her comedies are the eighteenth-century equivalent of a "railway reading"—that is, without intellectual or literary significance. Whatever Centlivre's reputation as a literary figure, she was appreciated in the theaters well into the nineteenth century: in sheer number of performances, she outlasted all of her contemporaries, with plays still in repertory as late as 1887. Nonetheless, scholars tended to view her more as a curiosity than a serious dramatist. The first significant critical study of Centlivre is John Wilson Bowyer's biography of 1952, which continues to be a

primary reference on the author's life and works. Bowyer accepted much of the received legend of Centlivre's life uncritically, but defended her against the charges of plagiarism and unoriginality that had often been brought against her by earlier critics. As Bowyer notes, being a woman was repeatedly a disadvantage to Centlivre, making her more vulnerable to the common complaints of vulgarity and pandering to unsophisticated tastes. As scholars took more interest in rediscovering women authors, Centlivre gradually became better understood. Two early studies that further established Centlivre's importance are Thalia Stathas's 1968 edition of *A Bold Stroke for a Wife,* with a substantive introduction identifying Centlivre's strengths as a dramatic craftsperson, and F. P. Lock's updated 1979 biography. The late 1980s and 1990s, concurrent with the rise of gender studies, saw a significant increase in studies of Centlivre, most often focusing on her status as a female author in a male-dominated society. Centlivre's treatment of women is a primary theme of scholarship, especially her depiction of marriage and how women fare in finding and surviving a husband. Richard Frushell, Margo Collins, and Annette Kreis-Schink are among the critics who have discussed Centlivre's acute sense of marriage tensions; some scholars have even suggested that Centlivre's own life may have influenced her portrayals of gender relations. The topicality of her plays has inspired political criticism; Centlivre's outspoken support of Whiggish causes was matched, according to some readers, by Whiggish values permeating her plays. The intersection of gender and political themes has brought renewed attention to *The Gamester* and *The Basset Table,* which contain some of Centlivre's most progressive female characters. As Victoria Warren suggests, the unsettling combination of women and money in those plays spoke directly to Centlivre's predicament as a woman compelled for much of her life to write for her livelihood.

PRINCIPAL WORKS

Plays

The Perjur'd Husband; or, The Adventures of Venice 1700

The Beau's Duel; or, A Soldier for the Ladies 1702

The Stolen Heiress; or, The Salamanca Doctor Outplotted 1702

Love's Contrivance, or, Le Médecin Malgré Lui 1703

The Basset Table 1705

The Gamester 1705

Love at a Venture 1706

The Platonick Lady 1706

The Busie Body 1709
The Man's Bewitched; or, The Devil to Do about Her
  1709
A Bickerstaff's Burying: or, Work for the Upholders
  1710
Mar-plot: or, The Second Part of the Busie Body 1710
The Perplex'd Lovers 1712
The Wonder: A Woman Keeps a Secret! 1714
The Gotham Election. A Farce. 1715
A Wife Well Manag'd. A Farce. 1715; first performed
  1724
The Cruel Gift: or The Royal Resentment 1716
A Bold Stroke for a Wife 1718
The Artifice 1722

Other Major Works

*The Masquerade. A Poem. Humbly Inscribed to his
  Grace the Duke d'Aumont* (poetry) 1712
*An Epistle to Mrs. Wallup Now in the Train of Her
  Royal Highness, The Princess of Wales. As it was
  sent to her in the Hague* (poetry) 1715
*A Poem. Humbly Presented to His most Sacred Majesty,
  George, King of Great Britain, France, and Ireland.
  Upon His Accession to the Throne* (poetry) 1715
*An Epistle to the King of Sweden From a Lady of Great
  Britain* (poetry) 1717
*A Woman's Case: In An Epistle to Charles Joye, Esq;
  Deputy Governor of the South-Sea* (poetry) 1720

AUTHOR COMMENTARY

Susanna Centlivre (essay date 1703)

SOURCE: Centlivre, Susanna. "Preface to *Love's Con-
trivance.*" In *The Dramatic Works of the Celebrated
Mrs. Centlivre,* Vol. 2, 1872. Reprint. New York: AMS
Press, 1968.

[*In the follow essay, originally published in the 1703
edition of* Love's Contrivance, *Centlivre defends her
style of playwriting by pointing to her popular success
with audiences. The author also mentions her debt to
Molière.*]

Writing is a kind of Lottery in this fickle Age, and
Dependence on the Stage as precarious as the Cast of a
Die; the Chance may turn up, and a Man may write to
please the Town, but 'tis uncertain, since we see our
best Authors sometimes fail. The Criticks cavil most
about Decorums, and cry up *Aristotle*'s Rules as the
most essential part of the Play. I own they are in the
right of it; yet I dare venture a Wager they'll never
persuade the Town to be of their Opinion, which relishes

nothing so well as Humour lightly tost up with Wit, and
drest with Modesty and Air. And I believe *Mr. Rich* will
own, he got more by the *Trip to the Jubilee,* with all its
Irregularities, than by the most uniform Piece the Stage
cou'd boast of e'er since. I do not say this by way of
condemning the Unity of Time, Place, and Action; quite
contrary, for I think them the greatest Beauties of a
Dramatick Poem; but since the other way of writing
pleases full as well, and gives the Poet a larger Scope
of Fancy, and with less Trouble, Care, and Pains, serves
his and the Player's End, why should a Man torture,
and wrack his Brain for what will be no Advantage to
him. This I dare engage, that the Town will ne'er be
entertained with Plays according to the Method of the
Ancients, till they exclude this Innovation of Wit and
Humour, which yet I see no likelihood of doing. The
following Poem I think has nothing can disoblige the
nicest Ear; and tho' I did not observe the Rules of
Drama, I took peculiar Care to dress my Thoughts in
such a modest Stile, that it might not give Offence to
any. Some Scenes I confess are partly taken from *Moliere,* and I dare be bold to say it has not suffered in the
Translation: I thought 'em pretty in the French, and
cou'd not help believing they might divert in an English
Dress. The French have that light Airiness in their
Temper, that the least Glimpse of Wit sets them a laughing, when 'twou'd not make us so much as smile; so
that when I found the stile too poor, I endeavoured to
give it a Turn; for whoever borrows from them, must
take care to touch the Colours with an English Pencil,
and form the Piece according to our Manners. When
first I took those Scenes of *Moliere*'s, I designed but
three Acts; for that Reason I chose such as suited best
with Farce, which indeed are all of that sort you'll find
in it; for what I added to 'em, I believe my Reader will
allow to be of a different Stile, at least some very good
Judges thought so, and in spite of me divided it into
five Acts, believing it might pass amongst the Comedies
of these Times. And indeed I have no Reason to
complain, for I confess it met a Reception beyond my
Expectation. I must own myself infinitely obliged to the
Players, and in a great Measure the Success was owing
to them, especially Mr. *Wilks,* who extended his Faculties to such a Pitch, that one may almost say he out-
play'd himself; and the Town must confess they never
saw three different Characters by one Man acted so
well before, and I think myself extremely indebted to
him, likewise to Mr. *Johnson.* who in his way I think
the best Comedian of the Age.

Susanna Centlivre (essay date 1709)

SOURCE: Centlivre, Susanna. "Epistle Dedicatory." In
The Busie Body. Los Angeles: Augustan Reprint Society,
William Andrews Clark Memorial Library, 1949.

[*In the following essay, originally published in the 1709
edition of* The Busie Body, *Centlivre seeks the patron-*

age of Lord Sommers, a highly prominent Whig who had recently been made president of Queen Anne's Privy Council upon the Whigs' return to power in 1708.]

To the Right Honourable John Lord
Sommers, Lord-President of Her Majesty's
Most Honourable Privy-Council.

May it please Your Lordship,

As it's an Establish'd Custom in these latter Ages, for all Writers, particularly the Poetical, to shelter their Productions under the Protection of the most Distinguish'd, whose Approbation produces a kind of Inspiration, much superior to that which the *Heathenish* Poets pretended to derive from their Fictitious *Apollo:* So it was my Ambition to Address one of my weak Performances to Your Lordship, who, by Universal Consent, are justly allow'd to be the best Judge of all kinds of Writing.

I was indeed at first deterr'd from my Design, by a Thought that it might be accounted unpardonable Rudeness to obtrude a Trifle of this Nature to a Person, whose sublime Wisdom moderates that Council, which at this Critical Juncture, over-rules the Fate of all *Europe.* But then I was encourag'd by Reflecting, that *Lelius* and *Scipio,* the two greatest Men in their Time, among the *Romans,* both for Political and Military Virtues, in the height of their important Affairs, thought the Perusal and Improving of *Terence*'s Comedies the noblest way of Unbinding their Minds. I own I were guilty of the highest Vanity, should I presume to put my Composures in Parallel with those of that Celebrated *Dramatist.* But then again, I hope that Your Lordship's native Goodness and Generosity, in Condescension to the Taste of the Best and Fairest part of the Town, who have been pleas'd to be diverted by the following Scenes, will excuse and overlook such Faults as your nicer Judgment might discern.

And here, my Lord, the Occasion seems fair for me to engage in a Panegyrick upon those Natural and Acquired Abilities, which so brightly Adorn your Person: But I shall resist that Temptation, being conscious of the Inequality of a Female Pen to so Masculine an Attempt; and having no other Ambition, than to Subscribe my self,

My Lord, Your Lordship's Most Humble and Most Obedient Servant, Susanna Centlivre.

Susanna Centlivre (poem date 1714)

SOURCE: Centlivre, Susanna. "Prologue to *The Wonder! A Woman Keeps a Secret.*" In *The Dramatic Works of the Celebrated Mrs. Centlivre,* Vol. 3, 1872. Reprint. New York: AMS Press, 1968.

[*In the following poem, a prologue to the 1714 edition of* The Wonder, *Centlivre appeals to the ladies of the audience to support the work of a female playwright, urging them to regard the play as a common cause.*]

Our Author fears the Criticks of the Stage,
Who, like Barbarians, spare nor Sex, nor Age;
She trembles at those Censors in the Pit,
Who think good Nature shews a Want of Wit:
Such Malice, O! what Muse can undergo it?
To save themselves, they always damn the Poet.
Our Author flies from such a partial Jury,
As wary Lovers from the Nymphs of *Drury:*
To the few candid Judges for a Smile,
She humbly sues to recompense her Toil.
To the bright Circle of the Fair, she next
Commits her Cause, with anxious Doubts perplext.
Where can she with such Hopes of Favour kneel,
As to those Judges, who her Frailties feel?
A few Mistakes, her Sex may well excuse,
And such a Plea, No *Woman* shou'd refuse:
If she succeeds, a *Woman* gains Applause,
What *Female* but must favour such a Cause?
Her Faults,—whate'er they are—e'en pass 'em by
And only on her Beauties fix your Eye.
In Plays, like Vessels floating on the Sea,
There's none so wise to know their Destiny.
In this, howe'er, the Pilot's Skill appears,
While by the Stars his constant Course he steers:
Rightly our *Author* does her Judgment shew,
That for her Safety she relies on You.
Your Approbation, Fair ones, can't but move,
Those stubborn Hearts, which first you taught to love:
The Men must all applaud this Play of Ours,
For who dares see with other Eyes, than Yours.

OVERVIEWS

Anonymous (essay date 1760-61)

SOURCE: Anonymous. "To the World." In *The Dramatic Works of the Celebrated Mrs. Centlivre,* Vol. 1, 1872. Reprint. New York: AMS Press, 1968.

[*In the following essay, an introduction to the 1760-61 edition of Centlivre's collected works, the author emphasizes the difficulties the playwright faced because of her gender and uses Centlivre's career as the basis for a denunciation of women's oppression worldwide.*]

Be it known that the Person with Pen in Hand is no other than a Woman, not a little piqued to find that neither the Nobility nor Commonalty of the Year 1722, had Spirit enough to erect in *Westminster-Abbey,* a Monument justly due to the Manes of the never to be forgotten Mrs. *Centlivre,* whose works are full of lively Incidents, genteel Language, and humourous Descriptions of real Life, and deserved to have been recorded by a Pen equal to that which celebrated the[1] Life of *Pythagoras.* Some Authors have had a *Shandeian* Knack of ushering in their own Praises, sounding their own Trumpet, calling Absurdity Wit, and boasting when they ought to blush; but our Poetess had Modesty, the general Attendant of Merit. She was even asham'd to proclaim her own great Genius, probably because the Custom of the Times discountenanced poetical Excellence in a Female. The Gentlemen of the Quill published it not, perhaps envying her superior Talents; and her Bookseller, complying with national Prejudices, put a fictious Name to her *Love's Contrivance,* thro' Fear that the Work shou'd be condemned, if known to be Feminine. With modest Diffidence she sent her Performances, like Orphans, into the World, without so much as a Nobleman to protect them; but they did not need to be supported by Interest, they were admired as soon as known, their real Standard, Merit, brought crowding Spectators to the Play-houses, and the female Author, tho' unknown, heard Applauses, such as have since been heaped on that great Author and Actor *Colley Cibber.*

Her Play of the *Busy Body,* when known to be the Work of a Woman, scarce defray'd the Expences of the First Night. The thin Audience were pleased, and caused a full House the Second; the Third was crowded, and so on to the Thirteenth, when it stopt, on Account of the advanced Season; but the following Winter it appear'd again with Applause, and for Six Nights successively, was acted by rival Players, both at *Drury-Lane,* and at the *Hay-Market* Houses.

See here the Effects of Prejudice, a Woman who did Honour to the Nation, suffer'd because she was a Woman. Are these Things fit and becoming a free-born People, who call themselves polite and civilized! Hold! let my Pen stop, and not reproach the present Age for the Sins of their Fathers.

In antient Days the Men of France, urged by selfish and jealous Fear, made a Law called Salique, but that it has not always insured Safety to their Government my Sex have oft been witness, and particularly when the Statesmen of that Nation were obliged to seek Assistance from *Jane d'Arc,* who gained the Title of Maid of *Orleans,* from the Preservation she afforded that City, and could any old Woman act more indiscreet than their RULER now does with his Colonies, Ships, or Finances? The *English* Men, to give them their Due, have been more sensible of our natural Abilities, and not so barbarous as to exclude us from the Chance of Reigning, and during the Time it has fell to our Lot, as Mrs. *Centlivre* says, "What cannot *England* boast from Women? The mighty *Roman* felt the Power of *Boadicea's* Arm; *Eliza.* made *Spain* tremble; and *Anne,* the greatest of the three, has shook the Man that aim'd at universal Sway."

When I reflect on the French, I cannot forbear mentioning, with Anger, the *Spaniards,* who, since the Time their Kingdom was over-run by the Moors, have immured and shut up their Wives as it were, in Prisons. Is not this a barbarous Practice? Can the Nation be called civilized, that confines as wild Beasts that Part of the Creation, always acknowleged to be the most mild and gentle, and can it be expected that *Mahomet* shall find a Paradise, who has taught his Followers that Women come not there? These Doctrines are unreasonably inconsistent, and arise only from Prejudices which it is high Time should be exploded, and our Sex enjoy the Liberty which they have a natural Right to.

This Justice I must do the present Race of Mankind, their Eyes now seem open to Conviction, they acknowlege the real Merit of our Poetess, and of some other female Writers. The Nobility of Dublin lately went in Crowds to see the heretofore least regarded of her Plays, *viz. Marplot,*[2] and Miss *Macklin* has long shone in a Play of Mrs. *Centlivre*'s, called *The Wonder.*

A Poet is born so, not made by Rules; and is there not an equal Chance that this Poetical Birth should be female as well as male? Women are allowed to have a large Share of bodily Perfections, and if properly cultivated by Education, I believe those of the Mind would equally shine. Let both Sexes be placed at Quadrille, and see if Man has any Claim to Superiority; and are there not many Sciences easier learnt than that, and some other Games at Cards? Do not our Sex best understand the Art of Dress, and the Œconomy of Houshold Affairs; or are we deficient in other Matters which we have the same Opportunity of learning. To superficial Observers our Intellects may appear inferior to those of Men, but this can only be from a Comparison of our Skill in Things we have had no Experience in (such as War, Shipbuilding, &c.) with a Man's whose whole Employ has been in some one of these Branches—I could wish that some young Ladies of my Acquaintance, now in Boarding Schools, had classical Education, which would improve their Minds, furnish them with a more general Knowledge, and of course better fit them for Conversation, and the Management of Business. Have not Women Hearts largely filled with Humanity, and other social Virtues, Parts equally bright, a Discernment of Right and Wrong equally acute with those of Men? and of our Oratory, I call to Witness both *Europe* and *America* which have heard Mrs. DRUMMOND, with her *New Light,* leading Mankind from Darkness. We are allowed to have more native Modesty, that everlasting Charm, than the Sex that lords it over us, and I have oft observed, that the most ignorant amongst the Men are the most impudent, and from thence conclude that if our Sex had a better Education, it would decorate and add Charms to that Modesty. We have been depressed and taught to entertain an humble Idea of our Genius, which not being exerted, we lose the Influence we might have over our present Masters. Oft have I seen, in private Life, an illiterate churlish Fool of a Husband tyrannize over the Will, and with barbarous Insult, compel the Reason and good Sense of his Wife, to give Place to his Folly, and this on no better Foundation than Custom, established by Laws, the Handyworks only of Men.

Our Employment is chiefly in Retirement, and private Life, where our Actions, not being conspicuous, are little regarded; but the *present Days* have seen a Genius employed in translating, and illustrating *Epictetus,* and the Empress of *Germany* convinces the World that she is a Politician fearless even of the Horrors of War.

A pleasing Prospect I've lately had, *viz.* the Work of the ingenious Lord *Corke,* and the not less ingenious Mr. *Samuel Johnson,* who have took Pains to translate a large Part of Father *Brumoy's Greek* Theatre, and were not ashamed that their Labours should be joined to those of Mrs. *Lenox.* This convinces me that not only that barbarous Custom of denying Women to have Souls, begins to be rejected as foolish and absurd, but also that bold Assertion, that Female Minds are not capable of producing literary Works, equal even to those of *Pope,* now loses Ground, and probably the next Age may be taught by our Pens that our Geniuses have been hitherto cramped and smothered, but not extinguished, and that the Sovereignty which the male Part of the Creation have, until now, usurped over us, is unreasonably arbitrary: And further, that our natural Abilities entitle us to a larger Share, not only in Literary Decisions, but that, with the present Directors, we are equally intitled to Power both in Church and State. To reform the first, was our Author's latest Employ, and she shewed herself Mistress of the Subject in her Treatise which discloses and confutes the Errors of the *Church of Rome.*

In her early Days she was inclined to be very gay, being left an Orphan before she was twelve Years of Age, her Father, Mr. *Freeman,* of *Holbeach,* in *Lincolnshire,* having at that Time been dead, nine Years; thus was the Princess of Dramatic Poets left without a Guide, but her native Wit soon brought her into Fame. The Spirit of Poetry was born with her, for before she was seven Years old she wrote a very pretty Song, and adapted it to a sprightly Tune, which became a distinguished Country-Dance.

Her Education was such as the Place of her Nativity afforded; where tho' she had but small Instruction, yet by Application to Books, she soon became Mistress of the *Latin, Italian, Spanish,* and *French* Tongues. Before she attained the Age of fifteen she was married to the Nephew of Sir *Stephen Fox,* who left her a young Widow of sixteen, which State she was soon persuaded to change, in Favour of Captain *Carrol,* who was killed in a Duel about a Year and a half after his Nuptials. Soon after, *viz.* in the twentieth Year of her Age, she wrote her Play of the ***Perjured Husband,*** and in a short Time gained some Eminence in the literary World. Her

Wit procured her the Intimacy of the facetious Mr. *Farquhar,* and her theatrical Knowledge was the Cause of her great Intimacy with Mr. *Wilkes,* and Mrs. *Oldfield;* the latter distinguished our Poetess by speaking the Prologue to her first Play, and generally those great Actors filled the principal Characters in her Comic Performances.

At this Time an Intimacy was kept up betwixt her and the most esteemed Writers of the Time. Sir *Richard Steele,* speaking to the Public in his Tatler, thus mentions her ***Busy Body***; "The Plot and Incidents of the Play are laid with that Subtlety and Spirit which is peculiar to Females of Wit, and is very seldom well performed by those of the other Sex, in whom Craft in Love is an Act of Invention, and not as with Women, the Effect of Nature and Instinct." Mr. *Rowe* favour'd her with his Friendship, assisted her in composing the Tragedy called the ***Cruel Gift,*** and wrote the Prologue to her ***Gamester.***

After a Widowhood of about ten Years, Mrs. *Carrol* again ventured on the Marriage State with Mr. *Centlivre,* a *French* Gentleman, with whom she lived comfortably for many Years, rich in Fame and possessed of Plenty, which annually arose from her Poetical Skill; and at her Death, which happened in 1722, when she was near forty-five Years old, she left many and valuable Ornaments of Gold and Jewels, presented to her by the Royal Family, Prince *Eugene,* and Persons of distinction, but these Treasures her Husband did not long enjoy, for about a Year after he died, and was put into the same Grave, in the Parish Church of *St. Martin's in the Fields.* Thus drop'd she, Rara avis in Terris, after having by her own Works erected a Monument more lasting than that of Marble.

Notes

1. Madam *Dacier.*

2. Revived by Mr. *Woodward.*

F. W. Bateson (essay date 1929)

SOURCE: Bateson, F. W. "Mrs. Centlivre." In *English Comic Drama 1700-1750,* pp. 61-77. Oxford: Clarendon Press, 1929.

[*In the following excerpt, Bateson offers praise for Centlivre's ability to write to the taste of her audience, suggesting that her plays were commercially rather than artistically successful. Bateson also remarks on Centlivre's skillful use of disguise and mistaken identity in comic plots.*]

I

'What a Pox have the Women to do with the Muses?' exclaims the Critick of *A Comparison between the Two Stages.* 'I hate these Petticoat Authors; 'tis false Grammar, there's no Feminine for the Latin word, 'tis entirely of the Masculine Gender, and the Language won't bear such a thing as a She-Author.' The tirade typifies the attitude of the world of culture in the face of the invasion of literature by the 'fair sex' which had begun with the Restoration. An authoress was still a monstrosity. It was not only ridiculous, it was against the nature of things for a woman to write. The prejudice was, no doubt, a simple matter of sex antagonism. It may, however, have received some support in the characters and records of the few professional authoresses the period possessed. Aphra Behn, Mrs. Manley, Elizabeth Thomas, and Eliza Haywood could not boast of very savoury careers. They were the best possible argument against a 'Petticoat-Author'.

> The modest Muse a Veil with Pity throws
> O'er Vice's Friends and Virtue's Female Foes;
> Abash'd she views the bold unblushing Mien
> Of modern Manley, Centlivre, and Behn.

Susanna Centlivre, the once 'celebrated Mrs. Centlivre', was no better and no worse than the others. In her younger days she appears to have been something of an adventuress. 'She was inclined to be very gay', is the reluctant admission of a feminine admirer, and Boyer, another admirer, refers discreetly to 'several gay Adventures (over which we shall draw a Veil)'. It has been asserted that she was at one time the mistress of the poet Anthony Hammond and that she lived with him, when he was still an undergraduate at Cambridge, in boy's clothes. She was later 'married or something like it' to a Mr. Fox, then to a Mr. Carrol (who was killed in a duel), and finally and indisputably in 1706 to Joseph Centlivre, a Huguenot refugee who became Queen Anne's cook. A number of dates between 1667 and 1680 have been proposed for the year of her birth, and she has been provided with two fathers. It is certain that she died in London on the 1st of December 1723.

In spite of a somewhat disreputable youth we are told that Mrs. Centlivre later 'lived in a decent clean Manner, and could show (which I believe few other Poets could, who depended chiefly on their pen) a great many Jewels and Pieces of Plate, which were the Produce of her own Labour, either purchased by the Money brought in by her copies, her Benefit-Plays, or were Presents from Patrons'; and her acquaintances included 'a great Number of Gentlemen of Eminence and Wit, particularly, Sir Richard Steele, Mr. Rowe, Mr. Budgell, Dr. Sewel, Mr. Amhurst, &c.' It is to be noted that these 'Gentlemen of Eminence and Wit' were all Whigs. Mrs. Centlivre was an enthusiastic Whig herself, and this was probably the origin of these connexions. Like most of the Whig writers of the time she occupies a niche in *The Dunciad:*—

> At last Centlivre felt her voice to fail;
> Motteux himself unfinish'd left his tale;

> Boyer the State and Law the Stage gave o'er;
> Morgan and Mandevil could prate no more.

Pope also attacked her in two pamphlets, *Revenge by Poison on the Body of Mr. Edmund Curll* and its sequel, *The most deplorable condition of Mr. Edmund Curll,* and it has recently been suggested by Mr. George Sherburn (mistakenly, I think) that she may have been the original of Phoebe Clinket in *Three Hours after Marriage.* The ostensible origin of these attacks was 'a Ballad against Mr. Pope's Homer before he began it', called *The Catholick Poet; or, Protestant Barnaby's Sorrowful Lamentation,* of which Pope suspected Mrs. Centlivre. It is a scurrilous poem, but there is evidence that Pope was wrong in attributing it to her.

II

Mrs. Centlivre's nineteen plays include fourteen comedies, three farces, a tragedy, and a tragi-comedy, and range in date from 1700 to 1722. The farces, the tragedy, and the tragi-comedy, though the last has some amusing comic scenes, are almost completely worthless. It is upon the comedies, and not upon all of them by any means, that her reputation must rest. *The Beau's Duel, The Stolen Heiress, Love's Contrivance, The Platonick Lady, Mar-Plot, The Man's bewitch'd, The Perplex'd Lovers,* and *The Artifice,* may be mentioned only to be dismissed. *The Stolen Heiress* is a slovenly adaptation of a Caroline romantic comedy; *Love's Contrivance* is run together from two of Molière's farces; *The Man's bewitch'd* is a translation from the French dramatist Hauteroche; and *The Perplex'd Lovers* is admittedly only an English version of an unnamed Spanish play. *The Beau's Duel, The Platonick Lady, Mar-Plot,* and *The Artifice* are more or less original, but that is the only claim to consideration they possess. With the six comedies which remain—*The Gamester, The Basset-Table, Love at a Venture, The Busie Body, The Warder, A Bold Stroke for a Wife*—the position is different. They have all a certain vitality and technical *finesse,* and are as good examples as one can hope to find of the work of the professional dramatist of the eighteenth century. They have, it must be admitted, no intellectual or literary significance; the writing is never distinguished and the characterization, with the single exception of Marplot in *The Busie Body,* is conventional and superficial. But the purpose for which they were written is fulfilled, to a greater or less extent, in all of them. They amuse, they distract the mind. Mrs. Centlivre's comedies occupy the position in the literature of the eighteenth century that is now filled by a detective story. They are the railway reading of Georgian England.

* * *

The first of Mrs. Centlivre's plays to create something of a sensation was *The Gamester.* It is an experiment in the Cibberian manner with an abundance of ethical and sentimental motives, and as such is only moderately successful. The theme, however, is a picturesque one, and the local colour, with all the technicalities of the gaming tables, is worked up well. We hear the croupier calling the score. 'Seven's the Main', 'Four to Seven', 'Four Trae-Ace', 'Duce, Ace', 'Quator Duce', 'Cinque Duce'. We see the unsuccessful gambler 'with Arms a cross, down cast Eyes, no Powder in his Perriwig; a Steenkirk tuck'd in to hide the Dirt, Sword-knot unty'd; no Gloves, and Hands and Face as dirty as a Tinker'. We are introduced to the 'back-hand tip', and the 'Doctors' or false dice. We hear the box-keeper warning the players not to 'stay late for fear of the Press-masters, here was two Gangs last night before twelve a Clock'.

The gamester of the title is the younger Valere, who hesitates between his darling vice and the charms of Angelica, who will not marry him until he has abjured gambling. The climax comes when Angelica, disguised as a young beau, wins a portrait of herself, which she had recently given Valere and which he had promised never to part with. Finally, of course, Valere repents and reforms his ways, and Angelica forgives and marries him. The bulk of the play is based upon Regnard's *Le Joueur,* but the sentimental conclusion is Mrs. Centlivre's own invention. In the French version Valère, after losing his beloved by staking her gift at the tables, remains to the end the slave of his ruling passion, consoling himself with the hope that

> quelque jour
> Le jeu m'acquittera des pertes de l'amour.

The difference is a piquant illustration of the contrasting ideals of the classical comedy of Regnard and the sentimental comedy of Mrs. Centlivre.

* * *

The Basset-Table was written as a pendant to ***The Gamester,*** the gambler in this case being a woman and the reformer a man. The connexion between the two plays is similar to that between *The Careless Husband* and *The Lady's Last Stake* of Cibber. The hero and heroine are the virtuous Lord Worthy and the frivolous Lady Reveller, and their passages of arms are in the typically sentimental manner. In most of the scenes, however, the sentimentalism is obscured by the introduction of a number of the conventional types of Restoration Comedy. There is a Sir James Courtly, 'an airy Gentleman'; a Sir Richard Plainman, 'a great Lover of a Soldier, and an inveterate enemy to the French'; a bluff Captain Hearty; a Buckle and Alpiew, the pert footman and the perter waiting woman; and a Mr. and Mrs. Sago, a city couple who call each other 'Puddy' and 'Keecky' and indeed conduct all their conversation in a kind of baby language. The most original character is Valeria, who is described as a 'Philosophical Girl'.

She comes in running—'don't stop me, I shall lose the first Insect for Desection, a huge Flesh Fly'. A little later she is discovered in her study, 'with Books upon a Table, a Microscope, putting Fish upon it, several Animals lying by'. She is a great reader of 'Discartes' and the other philosophers, and is confident that 'Custom would bring them as much in Fashion as Furbeloes'. Her curiosity is indefatigable, and the moment she is introduced to Captain Hearty she begins to inquire 'if ever you had the curiosity to inspect a Mermaid—Or if you are convinced there is a World in every Star'. It is disconcerting to find that she has a lover, but their billing and cooing usually resolves itself into a discussion of the 'Lumbricus Latus' and the 'Lumbricus teres Intestinalis' and similar mysteries. Alternatively they fish for eels in vinegar. To the modern reader Valeria is a rather pathetic figure. She means no harm, and she is not by any means a fool. It is true she is a blue-stocking, that is her only crime; but the eighteenth century was curiously merciless to blue-stockings.[1]

The Basset-Table, though it was less successful, is a rather better comedy than ***The Gamester.*** Perhaps it is because the tone is more consistently that of a comedy of manners, less realistic; perhaps because the moralizing and the sentimental issues, never quite sincere with Mrs. Centlivre, are not so emphasized. The dialogue is written with spirit and an, 'atmosphere' is maintained with considerable skill. The opening scene is probably the most effective. It is four o'clock in the morning, and the footmen and porters ('with Chairs, Torches, and Flambeaux') are sleepily waiting for the gambling party to break up. At last the basset comes to an end. The servants are to be heard shouting within. 'Mr. Looseall's Man', 'Mr. Sonica's Servant', 'Ha, Hy, my Lady Gamewel's Chair ready there'. 'Where the Devil', cries one footman, 'is my Flambeaux?' The porter tells another, 'your Lady has gone half an hour ago'. 'The Devil she is', he grumbles, 'why did you not call me?' The shouting begins again. 'My Lady Umbray's Coach there.' 'Hey! Will, pull up there.'

* * *

Love at a Venture, Mrs. Centlivre's third important play, was acted in the New Theatre at Bath, probably in 1706, by a travelling troupe acting under the patronage of the Duke of Grafton. Mrs. Centlivre is said to have taken one of the parts herself. In *The Laureat,* a not very trustworthy authority, it is stated that Mrs. Centlivre had offered the play to Cibber at Drury Lane. Cibber, however, though he was later to appropriate many of its scenes for his own *The Double Gallant,* refused it with scorn. 'Why, Madam, said he, This would be putting upon the Audience indeed . . . 'tis extravagant, it is outraging Nature, it is silly, and it is not ridiculous.' If the episode is not fictitious, Cibber certainly made a mistake. *Love at a Venture* is a very pleasant comedy, at least as good and probably better than Thomas Corneille's *Le Galand Doublé,* upon which it is based. *The Gamester* and *The Basset-Table,* though primarily experiments in the fashionable sentimentalism, had shown that Mrs. Centlivre's real talent lay rather in a lively reproduction of the manners and atmosphere of contemporary society. The sentiment was false, but the animation was genuine and unquestionable. *Love at a Venture* is an advance upon the earlier plays because it has discarded sentiment altogether. It is definitely more in the Restoration mode than the majority of Mrs. Centlivre's comedies. The licence of Bellair, 'A Gentleman just come from Travel; an Airy Spark'; the snivelling senility of Sir Paul Cautious; the vapid fatuity of Wou'dbe—they are all more typical of the Restoration than of Queen Anne. And the dialogue, particularly that of Bellair and his friend Sir William, has a sparkle which was becoming rarer every year. An additional interest is the skill with which the intrigue is conducted. There is an admirable scene in which Bellair appears before Camilla and Beliza, at one moment as a Colonel Revell, the lover of Beliza and a man of the world just back from Portugal, at the next as a Mr. Constant, Camilla's lover and a steady-going country squire 'come up about a Law-Suit', and with such assurance and ingenuity that he ends by convincing them. The theme, Bellair's promiscuity in amour, is naturally sometimes a little audacious; but it is never gross, and the final impression the comedy leaves is one of gaiety, the gaiety of the inimitable and (in spite of his outrageous behaviour) very likeable Bellair.

* * *

Love at a Venture was the first of Mrs. Centlivre's plays to exhibit to the full her ingenuity in the manipulation of intrigue. In this it was an interesting forerunner of her masterpiece, indeed the only one of her comedies which is still almost readable, *The Busie Body.* It has been called the most remarkable comedy of intrigue in English, and its supremacy in this respect was recognized by Steele on its first appearance. 'The Plot', he wrote in a short notice in *The Tatler,* 'and Incidents of the Play are laid with that Subtilty of Spirit which is peculiar to Females of Wit, and is very seldom well performed by those of the other Sex, in whom Craft in Love is an Act of Invention, and not as with Women, the Effect of Nature and Instinct.' Unfortunately the best comedy of intrigue is apt to lose its savour when it comes down from the stage. The brilliance of its surprises and the excitement of its coincidences tend to evaporate on the printed page. A sympathetic imagination, quick to respond to the effectiveness of a situation in the theatre and willing to overlook occasional crudities and improbabilities of detail, is required for a thorough appreciation of *The Busie Body.* It is a play which demands the co-operation of the actor and the painted scene, and in their absence it may easily fall a little flat.

Two more or less parallel plots make up the play. Sir George Airy is in love with Miranda, but is at the mercy of her avaricious guardian, Sir Francis Gripe, who wishes to marry her himself. Sir Francis's son Charles and Isabinda are also in love, but Isabinda's father refuses to allow them to meet. There are plots and counterplots of considerable ingenuity. In the end both of the loving couples are successful, but their success throughout is always all but prevented by the well-intended but unlucky interferences of the busybody of the title, the unfortunate Marplot, another of Sir Francis's wards. Marplot is the real, if the unconscious, hero of *The Busie Body.* Hazlitt, in his telling way, has called him 'a standing memorial of unmeaning vivacity and assiduous impertinence'. He is one of the most attractive of literature's simpletons, a stepbrother, if not of Slender or Sir Andrew Aguecheek, at least of the gulls and ninnies, the Stephens and Fitzdottrels, of Ben Jonson's plays. Mrs. Centlivre has characterized him in the list of the *dramatis personae* as 'A sort of a silly Fellow, Cowardly, but very Inquisitive to know every Body's Business, generally spoils all he undertakes, yet without Design'; but that is both an understatement and unfair. It is true Marplot is not fond of fighting, but that is 'purely to be serviceable to my Friends'. There is no limit to his good-nature. Even the ungrateful Charles finds 'a thousand Conveniences in him, he'll lend me his Money when he has any, run of my Errands and be proud on't; in short, he'll Pimp for me, Lye for me, Drink for me, do anything but Fight for me'. He has his little weaknesses. He is something of a snob and would give ten guineas to be introduced to 'a Man of Wit'. 'Well', he reflects in his innocence, ''tis a vast Addition to a Man's Fortune, according to the Rout of the World, to be seen in the Company of Leading Men', and he assures Sir George that 'a Bow from the side Box or to be seen in your Chariot, binds me ever yours'. But his ruling passion is not snobbery but inquisitiveness. 'Business, and I not know it, Egad, I'll watch him,' 'why the Devil should not one know every Man's Concern?' 'I shall go stark Mad, if I'm not let into this Secret'—his curiosity is always wringing from him exclamations of this sort. 'Lord, lord,' he sighs (the reflection has a Pepysian ring), 'How little Curiosity some People have! Now my chief pleasure lies in knowing every body's Business.' It is a demon which possesses him, and the itch of his curiosity makes him the burden of his friends, while the goodness of his heart, reinforced by the weakness of his head, is always delivering him into the hands of their enemies. He is involved in a perpetual whirl of abuse and castigation, and the last we hear of him he is pitying himself, still blissfully unaware that he has only himself to thank for his misfortunes. 'So here's every body happy, I find, but poor Pilgarlick. I wonder what Satisfaction I shall have for being cuff'd, kick'd, and beaten in your Service.' Dryden's Sir Martin Marall must have been the model for Marplot. But Marplot is not by any means a mere copy. He wears his folly with a difference. He is absurd, but he is never, like Sir Martin, contemptible. He is, after all, a gentleman, and he is not altogether a nincompoop; even Charles has to admit that 'The Dog is diverting sometimes, or there wou'd be no enduring his Impertinence'. Sir Martin was never anything more than a walking vacancy.

The Wonder: A Woman keeps a Secret and *A Bold Stroke for a Wife* are two comedies which are often set by the side of *The Busie Bodie.* They belong to the same *genus* certainly, that of the comedy of intrigue. They exhibit similarly ingenious situations; they are bristling with parallel complications and misunderstandings. But they are *The Busie Body* without Marplot. Their characterization is conventional and superficial (Don Felix in *The Wonder* is a partial exception) and it is difficult, in the absence of the actors, to take much interest in the fortunes and misfortunes of such obvious puppets. The problems which beset the lovers in these plays become, in the reading, almost algebraic. Let *a* represent the heavy father, let *b* be the comic servant, let *c* be the passionate *jeune premier.* We can imagine Mrs. Centlivre working it out like a sum on the blackboard. There is no doubt, however, that the acting made all the difference. For one thing, *The Wonder* (with Wilks or Garrick in the role of Don Felix) was one of the most popular plays of the century. For another, Hazlitt, who could still see these plays at Covent Garden and Drury Lane, has praised *The Wonder* with an infectious enthusiasm the sincerity of which it is impossible to question. The passage is in the *Lectures on the English Comic Writers* and is too good not to be quoted.

> The *Wonder* is one of the best of our acting plays. The passion of jealousy in Don Felix is managed in such a way as to give as little offence as possible to the audience, for every appearance combines to excite and confirm his worst suspicions, while we, who are in the secret, laugh at his groundless uneasiness and apprehensions. The ambiguity of the heroine's situation, which is like a continued practical *equivoque,* gives rise to a quick succession of causeless alarms, subtle excuses, and the most hair-breadth 'scapes. The scene near the end, in which Don Felix, pretending to be drunk, forces his way out of Don Manuel's house, who wants to keep him a prisoner, by producing his marriage-contract in the shape of a pocket-pistol, with the terrors and confusion into which the old gentleman is thrown by this sort of *argumentum ad hominem,* is one of the richest treats the stage affords, and calls forth incessant peals of laughter and applause. Besides the two principal characters (Violante and Don Felix), Lissardo and Flippanta come in very well to carry on the underplot; and the airs and graces of an amorous waiting-maid and conceited man-servant, each copying after

their master and mistress, were never hit off with more natural volubility or affected *nonchalance* than in this enviable couple. Lissardo's playing off the diamond ring before the eyes of his mortified Dulcinea, and aping his master's absent manner while repeating—"Roast me these Violantes", as well as the jealous quarrel of two waiting-maids, which threatens to end in some very extraordinary discoveries, are among the most amusing traits in this comedy. Colonel Briton, the lover of Clara, is a spirited and enterprising soldier of fortune; and his servant Gibby's undaunted, incorrigible blundering, with a dash of nationality in it, tells in a very edifying way.

Although Hazlitt has omitted *A Bold Stroke for a Wife* from his survey, the case is much the same with it as with *The Wonder.* There can be no doubt that a play which has contributed to the language the once proverbial expression 'the real Simon Pure' must have been a popular favourite. But it is difficult now to recapture the first rapture of our ancestors. *A Bold Stroke for a Wife* is not absolutely unreadable, but it cannot be called a good play. It is, however, better written than *The Wonder* and the plot is easier to follow. The centre of all the intrigues is Mrs. Lovely. She has been provided by her father with four guardians. They are Sir Philip Modelove, 'an old Beau, that has May in his Fancy and Dress, but December in his Face and his Heels; he admires nothing but new Fashions, and those must be French; loves Operas, Balls, Masquerades, and is always the most tawdry of the whole Company on a Birth-day'; Periwinkle, 'a kind of Virtuoso, a silly, half-witted Fellow, but positive and surly; fond of nothing but what is Antique and Foreign, and wears his Cloaths of the Fashion of the last Century; doats upon Travellers, and believes Sir John Mandiville more than the Bible'; Tradelove, a merchant, 'a Fellow that will outlie the Devil for the Advantage of Stock, and cheat his father that got him in a Bargain'; and Obadiah Prim, a Quaker. The play is taken up with the various devices and disguises by which Colonel Fainwell, having already secured the affections of Mrs. Lovely herself, tricks the guardians, one by one, into consenting to the marriage. The interest of the piece is to a certain extent in the 'humours' of the guardians, but for the most part it consists in the constantly renewed, but somewhat mechanical, ingenuity of the intrigue.

III

Mrs. Centlivre, quite rightly, has not fared well at the hands of the critics. She was sneered at by Cibber and by Pope; she was patronized by the *Biographia Dramatica;* and more recently Mr. G. H. Nettleton has shaken a professorial head over the indecency of her plays. The only critics who have written of Mrs. Centlivre with some enthusiasm are Hazlitt and, rather surprisingly, A. W. Ward—and even Ward concludes his appreciation with the admission that 'in style and in the contrivance of situations she habitually sinks to the lowest level of our post-Restoration drama, exhibiting no trace of sympathy with the better and purer tone which was gradually gaining ground in English comedy'. Hazlitt, on the other hand, professed to discern in her plays 'a provoking spirit and a volatile salt' which 'still preserves them from decay'. He praised her 'intricate involution and artful *dénouement* of the plot'. He applauded 'the archness of the humour and sly allusion to the most delicate points'.

The indecency at which hazlitt hints and to which Professor Nettleton objects must be conceded. It is even objectionably present in the tragi-comedy of *The Perjur'd Husband.* But elsewhere it is of no importance; it is scarcely ever offensive or embarrassing, never merely gross. Indeed, in comparison with her predecessors and with many of her contemporaries Mrs. Centlivre is almost spotless. The suspicion of immodesty which remains, the vague aroma of *doubles entendres,* are far from objectionable. They impart a flavour to the plays; they are the spices in the comic soup.

Mrs. Centlivre was a professional dramatist, and her plays are specifically acting plays. Their effectiveness is one of action and of *ensemble,* not of detail. They are without the brilliance of dialogue and the sparkle of antithesis which a reading play possesses. Their language is sometimes, as the *Biographia Dramatica* complained, 'poor, enervate, incorrect and puerile'. It is almost always careless, abrupt, and without distinction. Like Dryden's Og, Mrs. Centlivre could 'doe anything but write'. But she had vivacity, vitality, and ingenuity. The characters in her comedies, though perhaps not one is original, are always to a greater or less extent animated. A few of them, Marplot certainly and perhaps Don Felix, are really alive. She was particularly successful in the depiction of impudence. The impertinence of her fine gentlemen is only excelled by that of their servants. Valere has no rival except Hector, or Britton except Gibby. And it is as much the impudent curiosity as the inanity of Marplot which appeals to us, just as it is the brazenness rather than the ingenuity of Bellair which is so attractive.

Hazlitt, writing of a performance of *The Wonder* at Covent Garden in 1816, speaks of it as a 'brilliant series of mis-timed exits and entrances'. It is an admirable definition of that quality in which Mrs. Centlivre is supreme. It is a genius for dove-tailing one laughable incident into another, for begetting ludicrous mistake upon ludicrous mistake. Mrs. Centlivre has no equal in the talent—though it may not be always appreciated in the reading—of disposing her *dramatis personae* into convenient closets and discovering them at inconvenient moments. She is without a rival in the possibilities she can detect in disguises, and in mistakes of identity. Indeed, to modern eyes, it often degenerates into a reckless defiance of realism. But within the conventions of her theatre she is a master-mechanic of dramatic construction. The prologue to *The Artifice* has put her merits not unfairly:—

> Ask not, in such a General Dearth, much Wit,
> If she your Taste in Plot, and Humor hit:
> Plot, Humor, Business, form the Comic Feast,
> Wit's but a higher-relish'd Sauce at best;
> And when too much, like Spice, destroys the Taste.

It is Mrs. Centlivre's justification that she did hit this taste, and her reward was that her comedies kept the stage much longer than many inherently better plays. They were popular throughout the eighteenth century, and *The Busie Body* and *The Wonder* survived well into the nineteenth. Etherege by that time was forgotten and Wycherley had beeen carefully 'doctored' into respectability, but Lamb and Hazlitt were able to laugh as heartily over the 'broad shining face, the orbicular rolling of his eye, and the alarming drop of his chin' of Munden as Marplot as their great-grandfathers may have done at the antics of Pack in the same part.

Note

1. It has been suggested that Valeria was intended to caricature a contemporary feminist, Mary Astell, who is also satirized in *The Tatler.*

John Wilson Bowyer (essay date 1952)

SOURCE: Bowyer, John Wilson. "'It Is a Woman's.'" In *The Celebrated Mrs. Centlivre,* pp. 41-91. Durham, N.C.: Duke University Press, 1952.

[*In the following excerpt, Bowyer discusses Centlivre's first period of success (1700-03), when the playwright began to attract public attention as an author. Bowyer highlights her adaptations of earlier plays and her efforts to establish herself as female author.*]

At the end of 1700 Mrs. Centlivre was well established in London. Her friends included Tom Brown, Abel Boyer, William Ayloffe, George Farquhar, Mrs. Jane Wiseman, Mrs. De la Rivière Manley, Mrs. Catharine Trotter, Mrs. Sarah Fyge Egerton, Mrs. Mary Pix, Lady Sarah Peirce. She probably had already met William Burnaby, John Oldmixon, Richard Steele, Nicholas Rowe, Charles Johnson, and others with whom she was to be associated later. These names may not seem important in the whole history of English letters, but they were not to be scorned in the year following Dryden's death. She also knew the actors and actresses of the time, and her close friendship with Anne Oldfield and Robert Wilks had probably already begun.

Susanna's first play had been acted with moderate success. Surprisingly enough, the Prologue boasted that it was a lady's:

And here's To-night, what doubly makes it sweet,
A private Table, and a Lady's Treat:

It had been printed also with her name on the title page. But the promise of an easy road to a professional literary career was illusory. She was to be allowed immediate credit for her second play, *The Beau's Duel: or, A Soldier for the Ladies,* which was acted at Lincoln's Inn Fields, about June, 1702,[1] but after that she would have to accept varying degrees of anonymity for some years.

Before 1700 women dramatists had sometimes found it to their advantage to represent their plays as the work of men when presented in the theater, but for the first two years of the eighteenth century there seems to have been some relaxation of the hostility toward women playwrights. Then the propaganda for improvement in the status of women increased, some even believing that Queen Anne could be persuaded to found a college for women. The reformers were usually rationalists, often members of the growing number of Cartesians in England. The writers of plays, letters, essays, and poetry of wit and gallantry toyed with ideas affecting the status of women, sometimes gallantly, sometimes scornfully, but with an astonishing demonstration of equality and freedom between the sexes. But the net result was that immediately following Anne's accession to the throne in 1702 the dislike of the traditionalists for women writers was stronger than before. For the time being, the decision remained securely with the conservatives—the clergy, the educators, and the moralists—who accepted woman's traditional inferiority of mind and character and feared what would happen if she were given an education, a more nearly equal position in marriage, and a more prominent role in society.

Throughout her literary career Mrs. Centlivre fought a woman's battle for recognition. Undoubtedly she used hostility toward women to excuse the failure of some of her works when a better explanation would have been lack of merit, but her desire to establish herself as a writer in a man's world was the governing idea of her life from 1700 until her marriage to Joseph Centlivre in 1707. During these seven years she wrote eight dramas. Part of the time she also acted in the provinces. Since making a living was her chief problem, she was primarily concerned with her plays, dedications, and benefits.

The cast for *The Beau's Duel* was stronger than for *The Perjur'd Husband,* though it is unlikely that the play had a very long run. Pack, as Ogle, a fortune hunter, was the most significant actor. Cory and Booth acted Colonel Manly and Captain Bellmein, two gentlemen paired with Clarinda and Emilia, acted by Mrs. Prince and Mrs. Porter, the distinguished tragic actress. Powell, notorious for his own drinking, was Toper, *"an*

Enemy to Matrimony, and a Friend to the Bottle," Bowman was Sir William Mode, a fop, and Fieldhouse was Carefull, the father. Mrs. Lee acted Mrs. Plotwell, a former mistress of Bellmein.

The comedy was repeated at Lincoln's Inn Fields in the autumn. It is advertised for October 21 in the *Daily Courant,* where it is called the last new comedy, "With the Addition of a New Scene, and a new Prologue and Epilogue, with a Whimsical Song Sung by Mr. Pack." Since all printed copies follow the first edition, there is no way to trace the additions.

The Beau's Duel was revived at Drury Lane on April 11, 1785, for the benefit of Baddeley, who took the part of Carefull, father of Clarinda. King, Dodd, Bannister, Jr., R. Palmer, Palmer, Miss Farren, Mrs. Brereton, Mrs. Ward, and Mrs. Wilson also participated. But except for the nonce presentation the play was dead within a year of its birth.

In the comedy Colonel Manly and Captain Bellmein both think themselves in love with Clarinda, whom her father, Carefull, wishes to marry to a foolish but wealthy fop, Sir William Mode. Sir William and Ogle, a conceited poet and beau who imagines every woman in love with him, are teased into a duel by Toper, but they arrange privately to fight with foils ("files"). Clarinda and her cousin, Emilia, with whom Bellmein is really in love, go to the duel disguised as men in order to get proof that Sir William is a coward. There they egg on the combatants, but they make off when Manly and Bellmein appear.

Carefull has meanwhile come upon a letter from Ogle to Clarinda, and, thinking his daughter in love with the beau, orders her to marry Sir William by six the following day or he will himself marry before twelve. Toper, a friend of Manly and Bellmein, offers his "cousin," really Mrs. Plotwell, whom he introduces as a highly virtuous Quaker, to be Carefull's wife.

At her request, Manly and Bellmein rescue Clarinda from Sir William as he is taking her to church, and Manly marries her. (The trick is as old as Dekker's *The Shoemaker's Holiday.*) Carefull thereupon marries Mrs. Plotwell. After the ceremony, however, she lays aside her Quaker demeanor and begins her persecution. (The situation suggests that in Jonson's *The Silent Woman.*) Finally, Carefull agrees to forgive his daughter for having married Manly if Bellmein and Toper will free him from his wife. Mrs. Plotwell returns her settlement, and, since Bellmein rather than a parson had performed the ceremony, it is revealed that there had really been no marriage. Bellmein is to marry Emilia.

According to Genest (II, 262) that part of *The Beau's Duel* relating to "Mrs. Plotwell's marriage and subsequent conduct is stolen from the City Match." Robert

Seibt[2] points out the chief scenes borrowed. The main distinction between the borrowed scenes and their originals is that Mrs. Centlivre writes as prose what Mayne had written as blank verse. Yet the characterization of Mrs. Plotwell as a reformed mistress and the brains of the plot is new. Also in *The City Match* (1639) it is the nephew rather than the daughter who is to be disinherited. The changes suggest that Mrs. Centlivre was giving more prominence to the nature and problems of women than Mayne had done.

The greater part of **The Beau's Duel** is Mrs. Centlivre's own. Her satire on beaux and fops is freshly handled, though the use of cowards who will not fight is not new, as readers of Shakespeare, Jonson, and Congreve know. In some respects the play reflects ideas and situations which had already appeared in her correspondence. For example, Sir William gives it as his opinion that the use of another man's oath is "as indecent as wearing his Cloaths." He is very proud of his "Affirmatives" like "Impair my Vigour," "blister me," and "enfeeble me." Bellmein says that he and his mistress pass for Celadon and Chloe, and Emilia, like Astraea in the letters, explains how she met Celadon and was so much entertained by his pretty discourse while sitting next him in the pit that she promised to write to him and could not help keeping her word if she was to be hanged for it. Also, Bellmein's description of himself to Emilia as the pale, wan, and skeleton-like lover is much like that of Celadon to Astraea. In short, similarities between the expressions in the letters and those in the comedy lead us to conclude that Mrs. Centlivre probably borrowed only the marriage of Carefull and Mrs. Plotwell.

Except that the various plots are never completely integrated, **The Beau's Duel** is an acceptable comedy, with realistic comments upon contemporary London life and allusions to popular topics like the prognostications of the astrologers and philomaths. The character of Mrs. Plotwell is well done, and the use of her to unify the action, though not completely satisfactory, shows a genuine dramatic sense. Three brief scenes are worth remembering: one in the first act where Sir William corrects Le Reviere, his supposed French valet, for speaking English without an accent ("Blister me if you don't speak plain *English!*"), another at the beginning of Act II where Sir William in a nightgown, before his mirror, conducts both parts of an imaginary conversation with a lord at the playhouse, and Act II, scene 2, in which Ogle describes his conquests over women's hearts, commenting on the fact that a tradesman fails to appreciate the honor a gentleman does him in making love to his wife and demonstrating how his mistress looks longingly down upon him from her window. These are not so crisp as similar scenes from Congreve,

but they are well above the Restoration average in the comedy of manners. Elsewhere the emphasis is predominantly on disguises, mistaken identity, and trickery.

One of the most interesting differences between **The Beau's Duel** and the Restoration comedy results from the new emphasis which Mrs. Centlivre puts on men and women of sense. Both a man and a woman of sense are capable of frankness, truth-telling, and genuine affection. The woman of sense is unlike her Restoration predecessor in that she does not make herself difficult and does not take pride in being pursued. In fact, she is as much the pursuer as the man, but only to learn whether her servant really loves her or to escape a second man who is being forced upon her against her will. She admits that she is in love and that she would like to be married, and she believes that no man of sense would take advantage of a virtuous woman. Men and women of sense would not think of marrying for money or of making love without feeling it regardless of the stakes, though they admit that riches are "the common Chance of Knaves and Fools" and "Fortune is rarely favourable to a Man of Sense." Clarinda and Emilia hesitate to don breeches as a means of showing up Sir William, for they fear that "this masquerade will not be reputable for Women of nice Honour," but they do it as a means of securing justice for themselves. Like the man of sense, the sensible woman is generous, courageous, judicious, and constant in love. She is capable of making her own decisions, and she regards love far more highly than obedience to her parents, a view very disagreeable to the moralists of the time.

The Prologue, by a gentleman, is interesting for showing the early eighteenth-century attitude of the dramatists toward their audience:

> What Hazards Poets run, in Times like these,
> Sure to offend, uncertain whom to please:
> If in a well-work'd Story they aspire,
> To imitate old *Rome*'s or *Athen*'s Fire,
> It will not do; for strait the Cry shall be,
> 'Tis a forc'd heavy piece of Bombastry.
> If Comedy's their Theme, 'tis ten to one
> It dwindles into Farce, and then 'tis gone.
> If Farce their Subject be, this Witty Age
> Holds that below the Grandeur of the Stage.

The dramatists sometimes, as here, charged the audience with a lack of taste and judgment and so accounted for the popular desire for farce, pantomime, and opera. In their view, the audience lacked a proper respect for the sober forms of tragedy and comedy and in its oversophistication condemned genuine emotion and poetry for flashy wit and superficial adornment. Undoubtedly the audience was changing. The people were becoming more interested in politics, science, and trade. In their interests they had been shifting from the court to the town, from court amusements to party controversies, from leisure to business. The small and select audience had given way to a larger but less cohesive one. Perhaps to this very fact was due the popularity of Mrs. Centlivre's busy comedies of intrigue.

Mrs. Centlivre had a third play ready for production before the year was out. *The Stolen Heiress: or The Salamanca Doctor Outplotted* was acted at Lincoln's Inn Fields for the first time on Thursday, December 31, 1702,[3] and was published anonymously on January 16, 1703,[4] with a dedication to Sir Stafford Fairborn, rear admiral of the fleet. The lady says that she is proud to be the first to make him an offering of this kind.

With *The Stolen Heiress* begins for Mrs. Centlivre the attempt to conceal the sex of the author. Her prologue, spoken by Mrs. Prince, begins:

> Our Author fearing his Success to Day,
> Sends me to bribe your Spleen against his Play, . . .[5]

Though, as we shall see, such deception rankled with her, she could do little to counter the demands of the players and the publisher.

The cast of *The Stolen Heiress* included several players who had acted in *The Beau's Duel.* But it was a far better cast than she had had earlier, for the younger players were becoming more experienced and better known, and, for the first time, Mrs. Barry took a part in one of her dramas. Powell had the part of Palante, the hero of the tragic plot, and Pack was Francisco, the protagonist of the comic plot. Dogget acted Sancho, a ridiculous scholar from the University of Salamanca. Mrs. Barry was Lucasia, the tragic heroine, and Mrs. Prince was Lavinia, the comic heroine. The Epilogue was spoken by Dogget, who, as Sancho, indicates his intention of burning all his books and using his shape, dress, and smiles to gain the ladies' favor.

The story of the play may be briefly summarized. Palante, foster son of Euphenes, is in love with Lucasia, daughter of Gravello. Gravello has circulated a false report of the death of his son Eugenio in order to make it appear that his daughter is an heiress, so that the rich Count Pirro will marry her. But Palante and Lucasia elope and are married. Thereupon Pirro uses his influence with his uncle, the governor of Palermo, to have Palante sentenced to death for stealing an heiress. Irus, really Eugenio himself in disguise, informs Gravello that Eugenio is alive, and then, suspecting the secrecy which his father enjoins upon him, gives the information also to Pirro, who employs him in writing to poison Eugenio. The Governor offers Lucasia Palante's life if she will marry his nephew, and, on her refusal, swears never to pardon him. Palante is discovered in the meanwhile to be the real son of Euphenes. As a last resort, Irus produces his contract with Pirro and then

discovers himself in order to free Palante. Pirro is exiled, and Palante and Lucasia are accepted by their fathers, who bury an old feud between the two families.

In the subplot Larich tries to marry his daughter Lavinia to Sancho, but by pretending unchastity she succeeds in getting her father's consent to marry Francisco, though at the expense of being disinherited. Then Francisco receives an estate as a result of his uncle's death, Lavinia convinces her father that she is really virtuous, and all are happy except Sancho, who takes a philosophical view of the events.

The Stolen Heiress was advertised and printed as a comedy. Jacob, however, calls it a tragicomedy, perhaps the best name for it. The comic and the tragic plots are better integrated than in *The Perjur'd Husband,* because Gravello and Larich, the fathers of the two girls, are brothers, and because both plots show fathers trying arbitrarily to dispose of their daughters. To some extent the play is propaganda against the Sicilian (and English) law making it a crime punishable by death to marry an heiress against her father's wishes. In the last scene the Governor of Palermo promises that he will "solicit earnestly the King to mitigate this cruel Law, and make the Thefts of Love admit of Pardon."

Although some writers say that *The Stolen Heiress* was probably taken from one of the old Spanish romances, Genest (II, 263) names the real source as Thomas May's *The Heir,* acted by the Company of the Revels in 1620 and printed in 1633.[6] Sometimes Susanna follows her source in the use of blank verse; at other times she writes the speeches, frequently with no other change, as prose. Nevertheless, she makes some alterations with the obvious intention of strengthening her original. She links the two plots somewhat more closely than May does. She also tries to motivate some of his unreal situations and to humanize his improbable characters. Thus, for instance, she replaces Shallow, who is stupidly persuaded that Lavinia is to bear him a child, with Sancho, who is willing to marry the girl but is under no illusions as to the child's parentage.

Philocles and Leucothoe in *The Heir* develop a sudden passion at first sight, but Palante and Lucasia are in love at the opening of the play. The rich count is also more plausible. The chief objection to Virro in *The Heir* is his age; in *The Stolen Heiress* it is Pirro's ugly passion, reflected in his appearance, that makes him distasteful.[7]

Much of May's play is in turn based on Shakespeare. The enmity between Polymetes and Euphues comes from *Romeo and Juliet,* as does the story of Philocles and Leucothoe's falling in love at first sight. Mrs. Centlivre shifts the emphasis, however, from the family feud to the stealing of the heiress. The offer of the

Governor to pardon Philocles if Leucothoe will give herself to him is from *Measure for Measure*.[8] The arrival of Leucothoe in the grove and her apprehension of ill comes from the Thisbe episode of *A Midsummer Night's Dream;* and the scene of the constable and the watch at the end of Act IV, from *Much Ado about Nothing.*

The Stolen Heiress seems not to have been revived, but Mrs. Cowley used the subplot, *The Salamanca Doctor Outplotted,* in *Who's the Dupe?,* a farce acted with considerable applause at Drury Lane in 1779 and the years following. There are no close verbal parallels. Doiley wants his daughter Elizabeth to marry a scholar named Gradus, but she prefers Granger. With her approval, Granger teaches Gradus the ways of the world and makes him drunk. Doiley, horrified, gladly considers another scholar for his daughter's hand. Following a word combat in which Granger, the new scholar, uses learned English and Gradus uses Greek, Doiley pronounces Granger the better Greek scholar and rewards him with his daughter. Gradus consoles himself with the witty servant Charlotte.

So far Mrs. Centlivre's plays had been presented at bad times of the year—very early or very late in the season or at vacation time. Her luck did not change with *Love's Contrivance: or, Le Medecin Malgre Lui,* which was first acted anonymously at Drury Lane on Friday, June 4, 1703. It was not unusual in the advertisements of a new play for no author to be mentioned, but when *Love's Contrivance* was published, on June 14, the initials "R. M." were signed to the Dedication. Two days later the following notice appeared in the *Daily Courant:*

> Whereas the last New Comedy, call'd, *Love's Contrivance, or, Le Medecin Malgre Luy,* has the two letters R. M. to the dedication. This is to give Notice, that the Name of the Author (who for some Reasons is not willing to be known at present) does not begin with those two Letters. The true Name will shortly be made known.

The real name of the author seems not to have been announced in the newspapers, but in the dedication of *The Platonick Lady* (1707) Mrs. Centlivre complains that the publisher of *Love's Contrivance,* realizing the contempt in which female authors were held, "put two letters of a wrong name to it; which tho' it was the height of injustice to me, yet his imposing on the Town turn'd to account with him; and thus passing for a Man's, it has been play'd at least a hundred times."[9] The only possible deduction is that Bernard Lintot, the publisher, played her a scurvy trick.

Mrs. Centlivre's embarrassment was no doubt due in part to the awkwardness of having her dedication falsely initialed. The inscription of a play was a recognized

source of income for the playwright, and she chose her patrons with some care. In this dedication to the old Earl of Dorset, who had a reputation for generosity to writers, she mentions "the courteous affability" with which his Lordship "once received a trifle" from her hand. But the style is so notoriously bad that one is tempted to charge the publisher with altering more than the signature.

The cast of *Love's Contrivance* was strong enough to please the dramatist herself. Wilks had the part of Bellmie, an attractive one for an actor because it provides him with three distinct roles—Bellmie, the "angry doctor," and the "doubting philosopher." Mills was Octavio, Bellmie's friend; Norris (better known as "Jubilee Dicky" from his astounding success in Farquhar's *The Constant Couple: or, A Trip to the Jubilee*) took the part of Martin, formerly the servant of Bellmie, now a fagot maker, and soon to pass for a famous doctor; Johnson played Sir Toby Doubtful, the superannuated lover of Lucinda; Bullock was Selfwill, father of Lucinda; Mrs. Rogers, Lucinda; Mrs. Oldfield, Belliza, her cousin; and Mrs. Norris, Martin's wife. Wilks probably spoke the Epilogue, since it refers to *"this Fortune-telling Play"* and suggests that he end it by telling the fortunes of the audience, presumably as he had told the fortune of Sir Toby.

The comedy ran for three nights, Susanna receiving her benefit on June 7. It was repeated on June 14 for the benefit of the boxkeepers, Lovelace, King, and White, with additions: "In which the Famous Gasperini will perform several Italian Sonatas. Entertainments of Singing by Mr. Leveridge and others, and Entertainments of Dancing by the Famous du Ruell and others, as express'd in the Bills at large." It was also repeated on June 18 and 22, on the second occasion for the benefit of Mrs. Campion and for the entertainment of the Envoy Extraordinary from the King of Denmark and several other foreign ministers and ladies of quality. On July 7 the last act, "the comical Scenes of The Angry Doctor, and, The Doubting Philosopher," was part of a hodge-podge entertainment at Drury Lane, including a comedy, *The Comical Rivals,* the fourth act of *The Old Bachelor,* and a variety of singing and dancing.

Our chief source of information about the early performances is Mrs. Centlivre's preface. She says that the play *"met a Reception beyond* [her] *Expectation"* and she attributes its success to the players:

> I must own myself infinitely obliged to the Players, and in a great Measure the Success was owing to them, especially Mr. *Wilks,* who extended his Faculties to such a Pitch, that one may almost say he out-play'd himself; and the Town must confess they never saw three different Characters by one Man acted so well before, and I think myself extremely indebted to him, likewise to Mr. *Johnson,* who in his way I think the best Comedian of the Age.

During the following season it was acted on October 20, February 16, and April 28. On the last occasion it was given at the desire of several persons of quality for the benefit of the author. This second benefit for what was no longer a new play seems unusual, but, since the author had to pay the charges of the house, the theater probably did not lose a great deal. In addition, the last act was used as an afterpiece on January 21, March 28 (for Mrs. Oldfield's benefit), and July 5, and again on June 7, 1705, and February 14, 1706. Tony Aston included it also in a medley which he produced in taverns about London in 1723 and 1724.

Lincoln's Inn Fields revived the full play on July 14 and 17, 1724, and twice in 1726. Apparently *Love's Contrivance* was never produced again. The presentation of Henry Fielding's *The Mock Doctor*, a rather close adaptation of *Le Médecin malgré lui*, in 1732, ended any further usefulness it may have had for the stage.

Yet the list of characters in *The Mock Countess*, an unprinted farce first presented at Drury Lane on April 30, 1733, shows that *Love's Contrivance* had not been forgotten. The farce probably included from Mrs. Centlivre's play the early scene in which Octavio gives Sir Toby advice about matrimony and the scenes between Sir Toby and the philosophers, and added the trick of the mock countess—Betty Kimbow in disguise—from *The Play's the Plot* (1718), by John Durant Breval.

The success of her comedy encouraged Mrs. Centlivre to write a preface in which she explained her method of working and her attitude toward the rules of the critics. It is her most fully developed statement of a dramatic theory:

> The Criticks cavil most about Decorums, and cry up *Aristotle*'s Rules as the most essential part of the Play. I own they are in the right of it; yet I dare venture a wager they'll never persuade the Town to be of their Opinion, which relishes nothing so well as Humour lightly tost up with Wit, and drest with Modesty and Air. . . . I do not say this by way of condemning the Unity of Time, Place, and Action; quite contrary, for I think them the greatest Beauties of a Dramatick Poem; but since the other way of writing pleases full as well, and gives the Poet a larger Scope of Fancy, . . . why should a Man torture, and wrack his Brain for what will be no Advantage to him.

For the time being, too, she acknowledged the necessity of modesty in style:

> The following Poem I think has nothing can disoblige the nicest Ear; and tho' I did not observe the Rules of *Drama,* I took peculiar Care to dress my Thoughts in such a modest Stile, that it might not give Offence to any.

Her last three plays, it must be admitted, are relatively clean in comparison with the drama that had gone before, but *Love's Contrivance* is far more objectionable than the other two.

Mrs. Centlivre says that she intended to write a farce and so divided her material into three acts, but *"some very good Judges,"* considering what she had added to the farcical scenes borrowed from Molière, divided it, in spite of her, into five acts, *"believing it might pass among the Comedies of these Times."* In her subtitle she acknowledges one of her sources, but Genest (II, 273) thinks that she tried to "conceal that she has borrowed the scenes, in which Sir Toby is concerned, from Molière's Forced Marriage." It seems unlikely, however, that she expected to hide borrowings from Molière; and, in any case, she deserves some credit for combining several plays into one.[10]

The opening scene of *Love's Contrivance* bears a close resemblance to the first scene in Molière's *Sganarelle, ou le cocu imaginaire,* where the father Gorgibus, asserting his absolute power over his daughter Célie, commands her to give her hand to the rich Valère, leaving her heart, if she pleases, with Lélie. But Mrs. Centlivre does not use any of Molière's language. Furthermore, Lucinda is much more impudent to her father than Célie, and Selfwill is much more tyrannical than Gorgibus. Here the Englishwoman is trying to bring her characters into accord with the contemporary types of the comedy of intrigue. A little later in *Sganarelle* Célie defends her lover from the doubts of her maid. Mrs. Centlivre, on the other hand, makes the maid into a friend, Belliza, whom she uses for her second pair of lovers.

Much of *Love's Contrivance* is literally translated from *Le Mariage forcé* and *Le Médecin malgré lui.* Mrs. Centlivre makes a characteristic alteration of the wife-beating scene from *Le Médecin malgré lui.* Molière's husband asks forgiveness of his wife and goes to the woods to make fagots for her. But Martin, despite his wife's plea not to spend the money for which her bones have suffered, starts for the alehouse:

MARTIN.

> But it was my Friend gave the Money tho'.

WIFE.

> But if I had not cry'd out, your Friend might not have come this way tho'.

MARTIN.

> That's right———well, Wife, I won't stand with you for little Matters, you shall beat me now, and I'll cry out, if you think that will get you a Guinea; if not, if you'll come to the Alehouse, I'll make you drunk; and so good b'w'ye.

Mrs. Centlivre again employs this method of turning the argument in the second act. There Belliza comes to Bellmie's lodgings with a message for him, finds a man reading, and strikes him on the shoulder with her fan.

She is surprised to find that he is not Bellmie, but she likes him at once. He addresses her as Bellmie's mistress, for whom he takes her. The scene is sprightly—the kind of thing Mrs. Centlivre could do well—with some sparkle, a bit of philosophizing, and a touch of the casuistry and lust of the Restoration rake in Octavio. The method is seen in these two selections of dialogue, which turn upon the current arguments for free trade:

OCTAVIO.

> Ah! Madam, he's the most generous Man in the World; his Mistress and his Pocket are still at his Friend's Service.

BELLIZA.

> Let his Friends share his Mistress! I'm afraid if his Friends applaud his Generosity, they condemn his Sense.

OCTAVIO.

> Quite to the contrary, Madam, they admire his Morals! he's a Wellwisher to his Country, and knows that the engrossing any Commodity ruins Trade.

But Octavio is so much taken with Belliza that he finds himself in love, and believes he will be to the end of his life.

BELLIZA.

> And how many Friends have you to share, pray?

OCTAVIO.

> Faith, Madam, none at all. I fancy I should play the Monopolist, were you once at my Disposal.

BELLIZA.

> But that would be a Ruin to Trade, you know; you would be reckoned an Enemy to your Country.

Mrs. Centlivre uses the Octavio-Belliza scenes to connect the borrowings from her two chief sources. Octavio, believing Belliza a jealous mistress of his friend, tells her that Bellmie does not really love Lucinda. It then becomes necessary for him to rectify his error. This he does by persuading Sir Toby to seek counsel on marriage from a learned doctor and a philosopher, both acted by Bellmie in disguise.[11]

During the summer of 1703 the players from Lincoln's Inn Fields went to Oxford for a period of vacation merrymaking called the "Act." It is satirically described in *The Players turn'd Academicks: or, a Description (In Merry Metre) of their Translation from the Theatre in Little Lincoln's-Inn-Fields, to the Tennis-Court in Oxford* (1703). Mrs. Centlivre (Carroll) would have liked to accompany them but could not afford the trip:

> The first that took Coach, and had often took———,
> Was the fam'd Mrs. *B*———with *P*——*x* at her *A*———,
> A Tool of a Scribe, and a Poetress great,
> Who was said to *Write* well, because well she could *Treat*,
> And for her sake had written her husband in *Debt*.
> While *Carrol*, her Sister-Adventurer in Print,
> Took her Leave all in Tears, with a *Curt'sie* and *Squint*,
> And would certainly take the same Journey as she,
> Had she not giv'n away *Medecin Malgre Lui.*

Mrs. *B*———is the unquestionably famed but notorious actress, Elizabeth Barry, and *P*——*x* is the fat ("great") Mary Pix. Susanna's squint, because of the wen on her left eyelid, was her hallmark among her enemies.

Mrs. Centlivre's giving away her play sounds like an ironical reminder of the false initials signed to the Dedication, but John Nichols in *Literary Anecdotes of the Eighteenth Century* (VIII, 294) notes that Bernard Lintot on May 14, 1703, paid Mrs. Knight ten pounds for **Love's Contrivance.** Apparently Susanna gave her friend the actress the publication rights. Ten pounds was a common but minimum fee for drama manuscripts at the time.

Notes

1. Advertised in the *Post Boy* for July 4-7, 1702, as to be published on the morrow.

2. "Die Komödien der Mrs. Centlivre," *Anglia,* XXXIII (1910), 83 ff.

3. *Daily Courant,* Dec. 29, 1702.

4. *Post Boy,* Jan. 16-17, 1703.

5. The prologue to Mrs. Pix's *The Conquest of Spain,* acted in May, 1705, is equally positive:

> How bold a Venture does our Author make?
> And what strange Measures do his Wishes take?
> How cou'd he hope the Tragick Scene shou'd please
> . . .

6. Hans Strube has made a textual comparison of the two plays in *S. Centlivre's Lustspiel "The Stolen Heiress" und sein Verhältnis zu "The Heir" von Thomas May* (Halle a. S., 1900).

7. Strube (*ibid.*) thinks that Mrs. Centlivre had Cibber's *Love Makes a Man* (acted at Drury Lane in Dec., 1700) in mind when she created Sancho. It is Cibber's scholar Carlos, however, who wins Angelina from his foppish brother despite the fact that the latter has the support of both their fathers. Cibber, who got the story of Carlos and Sancho from that of Charles and his servant Andrew in Fletcher's *The Elder Brother,* probably took the name of the servant from *Don Quixote,* and Mrs. Centlivre may have done the same, for at the end

of Act I she says that Sancho "makes as odd a Figure, Sir, as the famous *Don Quixot,* when he went in Search of his *Dulcinea.*"

At one point Mrs. Centlivre changed May's "As if 'twere writ in Gallobelgicus" to "as if they had been Spectators of his End." Disregarding dates, Strube suggests that here Mrs. Centlivre is punning on the title of Addison and Steele's *Spectator.*

8. In keeping with her attempt to make the character of the Governor more generally consistent, Mrs. Centlivre has him offer Lucasia a pardon for her lover if she will marry his nephew, apparently forgetting that Lucasia and Palante are already married.

9. The "hundred times" included acting in the provinces as well as in London.

10. Cf. Albert Wüllenweber, *Mrs. Centlivre's Lustspiel "Love's Contrivance" und seine Quellen* (Halle a. S., 1900), and Richard Ohnsorg, *John Lacy's "Dumb Lady," Mrs. Susanna Centlivre's "Love's Contrivance," Henry Fielding's "Mock Doctor" in ihrem Verhältnis zu einander und zu ihrer gemeinschaftlichen Quelle* (Rostock, 1900). Wüllenweber denies the charge of H. van Laun in "Les Plagiaries de Molière" (*Le Moliériste,* Jan., 1881, pp. 304-5) that Mrs. Centlivre was a pure and artless plagiary.

11. Wüllenweber *(ibid.)* believes than an incident about the middle of Act III may have been suggested by John Lacy's *The Dumb Lady, or the Farrier Made a Physician* (1672), a compounding of Molière's *Le Médecin malgré lui* and *L'Amour médecin.* In Act IV, scene 3, of *The Dumb Lady* Olinda says:

> And at the boot of your coach must be running an orange wench, presenting your lady a sweet lemon with a love letter in't.

This may have given Mrs. Centlivre the idea for the scene in which Martin enters Selfwill's house as a vendor of oranges, the cheapness of which attracts Sir Toby. When Martin insists that Lucinda try an orange and pretends to cut it for her, she strikes it down and a letter drops out.

John Loftis (essay date 1959)

SOURCE: Loftis, John. "The End of the War and Change in Comedy, 1710-1728." In *Comedy and Society from Congreve to Fielding,* pp. 77-100. Stanford, Calif.: Stanford University Press, 1959.

[*In the following excerpt, Loftis provides the political and social context for the increasingly favorable representation of merchant characters in early eighteenth century comedy. He groups Centlivre with Richard Steele and Colley Cibber as the leading playwrights of the era, observing that their artistic success correlates with their sympathy for the merchant classes and for Whiggish values in general.*]

In William III's reign and in the earlier years of Anne's, party politics had little discernible impact on the social themes of comedy. Before 1710 or thereabouts, playwrights sometimes expressed partisan political attitudes toward the war and related taxation and made topical allusions with political overtones, but they did not interpret class conflicts according to party principles. The reason is simple: it was not until the political debates preliminary to the Treaty of Utrecht that political rivalry was clearly and emphatically expressed by official propagandists in terms of the central social rivalry in comedy, that between gentry and merchant.

There is a connection between the Whig propaganda of Anne's last years and the shifting social relationships portrayed in comedy in the two decades after 1710. Some earlier plays had implicitly acknowledged the importance and dignity of great merchants, and some had been no more satirical of the merchants than of the gentry. Only after 1710, however, do we find comedies that openly and unequivocally take the side of the merchants.

As is well known, political rivalries in Queen Anne's reign turned on conflicting attitudes toward the war. Although the issues in dispute were far more than exclusively economic, the broad division, subject to many qualifications, between those who supported the war policy and those who opposed it corresponds to the division between the landed and the moneyed interests. The overseas traders and the financiers saw profits that were in the main rising; whereas the landed men (other than the great lords) were hard hit by wartime fluctuations in the price of agricultural products and the four-shilling land tax, so much so that some had to sell their land.[1] It is understandable that the squires should have grown insistent that the war be terminated.

In 1710, the Whig Ministry led by Godolphin, which was altogether sympathetic to Marlborough's war policy, was dissolved—for reasons personal, ecclesiastical, and economic—and was replaced by the Tory Ministry led by Harley and St. John. A general election gave the Tories an overwhelming majority in the House of Commons, a majority consisting mainly of country squires who were determined that the war should be brought to an end. The Ministry soon entered into negotiations with the enemy which, after long delays, terminated in 1713 in the Treaty of Utrecht.

But before a treaty could be negotiated, it was necessary for the Ministry to gain popular support for the idea of ending the war, no easy task in view of the personal popularity of Marlborough and the unprecedented series of victories the English armies under his command had won. The Tories accordingly undertook a major journalistic campaign, with Swift as their leading writer, to discredit Marlborough, the war, and the Whigs, and to reconcile the nation to the forthcoming peace. The Whigs countered with a barrage from their own spokesmen: an articulate and pugnacious group of journalists. The result was extended journalistic debate that canvassed fundamental issues of party policy, compelled individuals and parties to examine their political assumptions, and articulated the social and economic rivalries that had been caused by the war.

The antagonisms that pervaded these debates were the same that animated many of the comedies: the Tory journalists championed the squires and castigated the merchants and the "stock-jobbers"; the Whig journalists laughed at the squires and exalted the merchants as creators of the wealth of England. I shall take Swift and Addison as representative of the opposing positions.

Swift in the *Examiner* in 1710 and 1711 insists that landed interests should take precedence over mercantile interests. He regrets that the war has had the effect of enriching the latter at the expense of the former; he expresses sustained contempt for the financial community; and he emphasizes the value of high birth, adducing arguments that persons of gentle and noble birth usually have greater abilities than their social inferiors. His sentiments are summed up in the following passage (*The Examiner,* No. 13, November 2, 1710):

> It is odd, that among a free Trading People, as we call ourselves, there should so many be found to close in with those Counsels, who have been ever averse from all Overtures towards a Peace. But yet there is no great Mystery in the Matter. Let any Man observe the Equipages in this Town; he shall find the greater Number of those who make a Figure, to be a Species of Men quite different from any that were ever known before the Revolution; consisting either of Generals and Colonels, or of such whose whole Fortunes lie in Funds and Stocks: So that *Power,* which, according to the old Maxim, was used to follow *Land,* is now gone over to *Money;* and the Country Gentleman is in the Condition of a young Heir, out of whose Estate a Scrivener receives half the Rents for Interest, and hath a Mortgage on the Whole; and is therefore always ready to feed his Vices and Extravagancies while there is any Thing left. So that if the War continue some Years longer, a Landed Man will be little better than a Farmer at a rack Rent, to the Army, and to the publick Funds.

Although a prominent Whig and a celebrated author, Addison was not so active in the journalistic controversies as Swift. But he wrote enough on controversial subjects during the last four years of the Queen to establish his opposition to Swift on the issue of merchant-gentry rivalry. Two of the central characters

in the fictional circle of which Mr. Spectator is a member are embodiments—controversial embodiments—of the gentry and the merchants: Sir Roger de Coverley, who for all his benevolence is incompetent in practical affairs, and Sir Andrew Freeport, who, if socially deferential to Sir Roger, is clearly the more able of the two. (Addison portrayed Sir Roger more caustically, less sentimentally, than did Steele.)[2] Addison praised the merchants directly, in the *Spectator,* No. 69, eulogizing trade as the source of England's wealth—a theme that later in the century became commonplace but that in 1711 was still controversial. "There are not more useful Members in a Commonwealth than Merchants," Addison writes:

> They knit Mankind together in a mutual Intercourse of good Offices, distribute the Gifts of Nature, find Work for the Poor, add Wealth to the Rich, and Magnificence to the Great. Our *English* Merchant converts the Tin of his own Country into Gold, and exchanges his Wooll for Rubies. . . . Trade, without enlarging the *British* Territories, has given us a kind of additional Empire: It has multiplied the Number of the Rich, made our Landed Estates infinitely more Valuable than they were formerly, and added to them an Accession of other Estates as valuable as the Lands themselves.

A forceful statement, in opposition to the Tory view expressed by Swift, and one that was soon echoed in comedy.

Apart from the fundamental issue of ending the war, several lesser issues arose that helped to bring to focus the opposition between the landed and the moneyed interests. One was the Landed Property Qualification Bill of 1711, a bill which with the support of St. John passed both houses of Parliament and gained the royal assent to become law. A Tory measure, designed to keep moneyed men out of Commons and to perpetuate the majority of country squires, the bill provided that, except for the heirs of lords or the heirs of persons with £600 a year in land, no one could sit in Commons who did not have £600 a year in land if a knight of the shire, or £300 if representative of a borough.[3] The terms of Swift's praise of the bill in the *Examiner* establish succinctly the Tories' intent:

> The *Qualification*-Bill, incapacitating all Men to serve in Parliament, who have not some Estate in Land, either in Possession or certain Reversion, is perhaps the greatest Security that ever was contrived for preserving the Constitution, which otherwise might, in a little time, lie wholly at the Mercy of the *Moneyed* Interest.[4]

But the measure was not so effective as Swift and other Tories anticipated, for moneyed men found means of qualifying for Parliament through buying estates in fact, or through legal fictions. Addison himself bought an estate that made him eligible for Parliament—and thereby gained the social consequence which, despite all the Whig glorification of trade, went only with the possession of land in the eighteenth century.[5] The Landed Property Qualification Bill, then, failed to perpetuate the squires in Commons, the purpose for which it was intended. But for contemporaries the measure, both in itself and in the journalistic comment it evoked, helped to set in bold relief the opposition between landed men and moneyed men, between gentlemen and merchants.

An issue with similar implications was presented by one of the commercial clauses of the Treaty of Utrecht, by which it was proposed to resume trade with France, long since suspended for military and economic reasons. The French Commercial Treaty was sponsored by St. John, who hoped to gain partisan political ends by it as well as economic gains for the landed classes of which he was leader. The resumption of trade with France, he believed, would strengthen sentiment in England for the French-supported Pretender; and it would embarrass the English merchant classes by removing the protective tariffs that sheltered them and by interfering with their profitable trade with Portugal. The points at issue were complex, compounded of the economic self-interest of social classes and of political maneuvering in anticipation of the succession to the throne; but in general the Tories supported this clause of the peace treaty and the Whigs opposed it.

The issue occasioned a considerable journalistic debate, in which the principals were Defoe, supporting the measure in a ministerial periodical, the *Mercator,* and a group of prominent merchants opposing it in a periodical entitled *The British Merchant.* Addison, Steele, and others made intermittent contributions to the debate, in which opinion coincided with party affiliation. Despite the Tory majority in Commons, the Whigs ultimately defeated the measure—chiefly because they convinced a substantial body of the squires in Commons that it was unsound in terms of mercantilist economic theory.[6]

The political debates soon had their effect on dramatic criticism, notably in more frequent allusions to the exhaustion of the merchant stereotype. I have already mentioned Addison's complaints in the *Spectator,* Nos. 34 and 446, and the important anonymous one in the *Universal Journal,* July 4, 1724. There are others as well, among them an allusion in the epilogue of Addison's *The Drummer* (1716) to the triteness of jokes about "City-Cuckoldom" and one in the prologue of Charles Johnson's *The Country Lasses* (1715) to dramatists who "in threadbare Jests affront the City." The incongruity between the older dramatic patterns and contemporary fact was becoming apparent.

Hostile treatment of merchants in comedies by no means ceased, but the old stereotype became more and more the province of second-rate dramatists—men who

thought of their characters, consciously or otherwise, not as dramatic representations of contemporary life, but rather as literary conventions that could vary but slightly from a prescribed pattern. It has always been so. Not only is it far easier to be derivative than to be original—especially if one writes in haste, as many of the lesser dramatists did—but it is easier to see the virtues of the old dispensation than the emerging virtues of the new. The great Restoration dramatists had seen businessmen as avaricious, hypocritical, and lecherous fools; for their less imaginative successors, this was enough.

The longevity of the merchant stereotype in early-eighteenth-century comedy owes something to the concurrence of satirical intent with neoclassical emphasis on generalized characterization. Prefaces and prologues of the day reveal how steadily the dramatists tried to provide a satirical review of their times that should be at once comprehensive and corrective. They espoused a neo-Aristotelian theory of drama, holding that the didactic function of comedy was best fulfilled by ridiculing characters who embodied vices. The neoclassical principle of decorum—articulated by literary theorists like Rymer, Dennis, Gildon, and Pope—reinforced the tendency to see social and occupational groups in terms of uniform characteristics. The prologue of William Taverner's *The Maid The Mistress* (1708) sums up the comic dramatist's role:

> Instructive Satyr shall the Town Survey,
> And draw its Monsters in each artful Play:
> The Fop, the Rake, the Country Squire and Cit,
> The real Blockhead and conceited Wit,
> The Jilting Mistress and the Faithless Wife
> Shall see themselves all painted to the Life.

As the dramatists' hostility toward merchants declined, so also did their contempt for rustics. Farquhar's last two plays, as we have seen, depart from Restoration tradition so far as to portray rural life sympathetically— and other playwrights a few years later followed his precedent. This departure from dramatic tradition is remarkable since the tone of English literature around the turn of the century is intensely urbane—more so, perhaps, than during any other period: this was the time of the literary importance of the coffee houses, when Dryden held forth at Will's and Addison at Button's; and this was the time when the Kit-Cats (Whig poets and politicians) dined at Christopher Cat's, and when the Scriblerus Club met in Dr. Arbuthnot's apartment in St. James's Palace. But the trend was clear, and as early as 1715, we find signs in comedy of the preference for country over urban life that is common in English poetry of the 1740's.

* * *

The comedy that more than any other epitomizes the arguments of the Whig controversialists is Steele's *The*

Conscious Lovers, produced in 1722. The date of production, however, disguises the comedy's relation to the partisan debates of Anne's last years, for Steele had already planned it before the Queen died. As early as June 1710, he included in the *Tatler,* No. 182, what is in all probability an allusion to his plans for the play; and in January 1714, Swift described satirically the action of the projected play in such a manner as to suggest that Steele's plans for it had already been known about London for some time.[7] Certainly *The Conscious Lovers* as we know it is prefigured in Steele's series of major periodicals: the *Tatler* of 1709-10, the *Spectator* of 1711-12, the *Guardian* of 1713, and the *Englishman* (first series) of 1713-14.

It is in a special sense a comedy of ideas, of ideas that in dramatic form were in 1722 fresh and new. Whatever the ineptitudes and awkwardnesses of the play, it was in touch with lively political issues as few others were. Unfortunately, the ideas are not, for the most part, assimilated into dramatic action but are rather presented in conversation—with somewhat chilling results. Ponderous expository scenes, resembling *Spectator* papers put in dialogue, are interspersed with light and laughing scenes, but the juxtaposition never becomes a mixture. The plot, with its palpable absurdities, is too obviously a vehicle by which Steele can convey the opinions he formulated in the last years of Anne, when he was one of the chief Whig propagandists.

The Conscious Lovers attracted much contemporary comment from literary critics; for the play, the conspicuously successful work of a celebrity, embodies a theory of comedy evolved in protest against the comedy of the Restoration tradition. Most of the critical commentary, whether sympathetic or hostile to Steele, turned on principles of literary theory—on Steele's violation of the neoclassical doctrine of kinds by introducing into comedy pathetic incident and characters intended to arouse admiration.[8] But the play also presents the distinctively Whig view of the merchant and of the merchant's relation to the gentry. By way of satire as well as by the direct statements of normative characters, Steele insists on the hollowness of the gentry's assumption of superiority.

A memorandum he prepared while writing the play provides a firm indication of his satirical intent:

> That the Character of S[r.] John Edgar [Sir John Bevil] be Enlivened with a Secret vanity About Family, [And let M[rs.] Cœland, the March[.], Wife have the Same Sort of Pride, rejoicing in her own high Blood, Dispising her husbands Pedigree, and Effecting to Marry her Daughter to a Relation of her Own, to take of the Stain of the lowe Birth of her husbands Side, it is Objected, that in the Reign of Edw[d] the 3[d] A relation of her's was a Packer & lord Mayor of London.
>
> The only Scandal to her Family which She Ownes & Cant help, [make M[r.] Symberton, Such A Sort of

Coxcomb as at first Designd Still more Rediculous & Unsufferable from his talents & Improvements.[9]

The subjects of social satire in *The Conscious Lovers* are here suggested: not cuckolded aldermen but family-proud gentlefolk. Steele exploits the theme of social rivalry; he insists on it through repeated allusion; yet he does so with a reversal in satirical intent from that evident in the plays of Congreve, Vanbrugh, and Farquhar. Cimberton and Mrs. Sealand, his two contemptible characters, are of gentle birth; and a special reason for their absurdity is an affectation founded on an assumption of superiority.

The play's central action is provided by the effort of an exemplary young gentleman, Bevil, Jr., to reconcile the conflicting claims of filial devotion and love for a young woman, at first of unknown parentage but ultimately discovered to be the daughter of the rich merchant Sealand. Before the discovery of the young woman's parentage, Bevil's father wishes him to marry another, the known daughter of Sealand and the heiress to a vast fortune; but Sealand, having heard unfounded criticism of young Bevil, is reluctant to permit the marriage. The two fathers, one a landed gentleman and the other a great merchant, air their differences in opinion (IV):

SIR JOHN BEVIL:

> Oh Sir, . . . you are laughing at my laying any Stress upon Descent—but I must tell you, Sir, I never knew any one, but he that wanted that Advantage, turn it into Ridicule.

MR. SEALAND:

> And I never knew any one, who had many better Advantages, put that into his Account—But, Sir *John,* value your self as you please upon your ancient House, I am to talk freely of every thing, you are pleas'd to put into your Bill of Rates, on this Occasion—yet, Sir, I have made no Objections to your Son's Family—'Tis his Morals, that I doubt.

SIR JOHN BEVIL:

> Sir, I can't help saying, that what might injure a Citizen's Credit, may be no Stain to a Gentleman's Honour.
>
> . . . . .

MR. SEALAND:

> Sir, as much a Cit as you take me for—I know the Town, and the World—and give me leave to say, that we Merchants are a Species of Gentry, that have grown into the World this last Century, and are as honourable, and almost as useful, as you landed Folks, that have always thought yourselves so much above us; For your trading, forsooth! is extended no farther, than a Load of Hay, or a fat Ox—You are pleasant People, indeed; because you are generally bred up to be lazy, therefore, I warrant you, Industry is dishonourable.

The propagandist's willingness to suspend dramatic action in order to underline his points is all too evident in this humorless debate, in which the baronet mouths the clichés of his class, only to have them exposed by the strong sense of the merchant.

* * *

If the most celebrated dramatization of Whig argument, *The Conscious Lovers* is by no means the only one. In the larger number of comedies of the period 1710-28, merchant characters, when they appear, approximate the stereotype; but in other comedies merchant characters embody a bias resembling Steele's.

An insistence on the social consequence of the merchant animates a curious comedy entitled *The Beaux Merchant,* published in 1714 though never acted, written "by a Clothier" who has been identified as John Blanch[10]—an empty identification, however, since nothing is known of him. It is only by default of a more accurate term that *The Beaux Merchant* can be called a play, for it is a clumsy piece in which dramatic form is subservient to the intent of praising merchants in opposition to country gentlemen—and of insisting that merchants, too, have a fair claim to the pleasures of polite society. This play, subliterary in quality, is remarkable as the earliest openly propagandistic defense of the merchant in dramatic form: it antedates the production of, though not the preliminary plan for, *The Conscious Lovers.* In it there is a crude and forthright statement of ideas that were later assimilated and more capably expressed by competent dramatists. The play is about the business and love affairs of the "beaux merchant" Harpalus, a character presumably intended to represent an equivalent in mercantile life of the Congrevian man of fashion. There is much circumstantial detail about foreign trade, written, apparently, by someone who understood it very well; and extravagant praise, in terms that were becoming conventional, of the merchant's service to the nation. One of the characters refers, on a representative note, to the landed gentlemen and to "that bitter Edge of Envy, that too much Reigns in their Breast, at the Nice Living and Courtly Behaviour of the Merchant" (I). What the landed gentlemen can do, the author seems to say with a boyish boast, the merchants can do better—even enjoy the town more gracefully.

Mrs. Centlivre's later comedies show an assimilation of Whiggish views in her appreciative portrayal of merchants. A forthright and outspoken Whig even in the uncertain last years of Queen Anne, she avoids the stereotype of the merchant in her comedies of the second decade of the century (as she did not in those of the first),[11] except in one instance in which she presents satirically an exchange broker—as she could do without violating Whig doctrine, in which a distinction was made between speculators, considered to be parasites, and traders, considered to be productive.[12] Her growing emancipation from the traditionalism of her early comedies, evident in her turning away from the characters and situations of Restoration comedy, probably owes something to her increased command of her art. But the modification in implied social judgments can plausibly be associated with the Whig propaganda campaign.

In each of her two comedies of the second decade that were conspicuously successful, ***The Wonder; A Woman Keeps a Secret*** (1714) and ***A Bold Stroke for a Wife*** (1718), a young merchant who is socially accomplished appears as the confidant of the chief male character. In her earlier ***Busy Body,*** as we have seen, the children of merchants are appreciatively introduced as the gay friends of members of the gentry; but the two fathers are but lively versions of the stereotype. By contrast, the stereotype has disappeared altogether from ***The Wonder*** and occurs in ***A Bold Stroke*** only in the "Change Broker," who is one in a group of four contrasting social types, all guardians of a single young heiress.

The locale of ***The Wonder*** is Lisbon, and the characters are both English and Portuguese, the English having been drawn to Portugal by the necessities of commerce and war. The presence of the two nationalities provides an opportunity for contrasting national qualities. Characters make chauvinistic allusions to English freedom, several of them prompted by the observation that Portuguese ladies have much less liberty than their English sisters. There is an implied contrast between the Iberian conception of the importance of lineage and the more liberal English conception. Frederick, an English merchant who lives and conducts business in Lisbon, enjoys the friendship and confidence of the Portuguese grandees, though he is not, to his regret, treated as an equal. A conversation between Frederick and Don Lopez, one of the grandees, establishes the terms of his relationship with the Portuguese nobility, a matter of concern to Frederick; for were his status higher, he could hope to marry Don Lopez's daughter (I):

Don Lopez:

> I am not ignorant of the Friendship between my Son and you. I have heard him commend your Morals, and lament your Want of noble Birth.

Frederick:

> That's Nature's Fault, my Lord, 'tis some Comfort not to owe one's Misfortunes to one's self, yet 'tis impossible not to regret the Want of noble Birth.

Don Lopez:

> 'Tis pity indeed such excellent Parts as you are Master of, should be eclipsed by mean Extraction.

When he is left alone, Frederick in a soliloquy alludes to his love for the nobleman's daughter, concluding on a note of resignation: "But a Merchant, and a Grandee of *Spain,* are inconsistent names—" And with that remark the subject is permanently dropped. If, then, there is no insistence on the social deserts of the merchants, there is a favorable characterization of one, and an implied contrast between the inflexible social structure of Portugal and the more flexible one of England.

Cibber shows a change in attitude toward the merchants parallel to that of Mrs. Centlivre. He had been restrained in his use of the stereotype even in his early plays; yet in those written before the death of Queen Anne, he expends little sympathy on characters not members of the landed gentry or nobility. Among his characters in *The Refusal* (1721) is a rich citizen and South Sea director, Sir Gilbert Wrangle, a stereotype in some ways but essentially an attractive figure, aligned with, rather than opposed to, the gay young gallants in the love intrigue. Although *The Refusal* is an adaptation of Molière's *Les Femmes savantes,*[13] we can assume that the conception of Sir Gilbert Wrangle is Cibber's own because of the topical nature of the action in which he is central.

The time of the action is the peak of the South Sea Bubble—the summer, say, of 1720—when South Sea stock sold for a thousand pounds a share. It is indeed the immense inflation of the stock that has occasioned the complication of the love intrigue: when the stock was low Sir Gilbert, following an argument, became party to a wager with Witling, a fop, on what Sir Gilbert regarded as a certainty—that the stock would not reach a thousand. Witling, having won the wager as well as a huge fortune in stock, demands Sir Gilbert's compliance with the terms: Sir Gilbert's approval for his marriage with either of Sir Gilbert's handsome daughters. Bound by his sense of honor to observe the terms of the wager, Sir Gilbert can only hope that Granger and Frankly, two young gentlemen who are suitors for his daughters, will with the girls' contrivance be successful—as of course they are, one of the girls inducing Witling to give up Sir Gilbert's "promissory note."

Here is a merchant interpreted in an altogether new way. Sir Gilbert has through a foolish wager placed his daughters in a difficult position; but he made the wager as a man of spirit, in an effort to oppose folly. Having made it and lost, he feels bound to fulfill punctiliously the prescribed terms. In a conversation with Frankly (III), he explains his motives and congratulates himself on his status as a merchant—with borrowings from the Whig propagandists and anticipations of Mr. Sealand in Steele's *Conscious Lovers,* produced the next year:

SIR GILBERT:

. . . I have taken the Premium, and must stand to my Contract. For let me tell you, Sir, we Citizens are as tender of our Credit in *Change-Alley,* as you fine Gentleman are of your Honour at Court.

FRANKLY:

Sir, depend upon it, your Credit shall not suffer by me, whatever it may by your Comparison.

SIR GILBERT:

Why, what ails the Comparison? Sir, I think the Credit of the City may be compared to that of any Body of Men in *Europe.*

FRANKLY:

Yes, Sir; but you mistake me: I question if any Bodies may be compared to that of the City.

SIR GILBERT:

O! your humble Servant, Sir; I did not take you—. . . You'll find 'tis not your Court, but City-Politicians must do the Nation's Business at last. Why, what did your Courtiers do all the two last Reigns, but borrow Money to make War? and make War to make Peace, and make Peace to make War? And then to be Bullies in one, and Bubbles in t'other? A very pretty Account truly; but we have made Money, Man: Money! Money! there's the Health and Life-Blood of a Government: And therefore I insist upon't, that we are the wisest Citizens in *Europe;* for we have coin'd more Cash in an Hour, than the Tower of *London* in twenty Years.

FRANKLY:

Nay, you govern the World now, it's plain, Sir; and truly that makes us hope it's upon the mending hand: For since our Men of Quality are got so thick into *Change-Alley,* who knows but in time a great Man's Word may go as far as a Tradesman's?

SIR GILBERT:

Ah! a Wag! a Wag!

There is banter here, of course, and overstatement intended as mild irony. But the humor of the conversation serves to make palatable the praise of the merchants, which would otherwise seem intrusive in a gay comedy.

Sir Gilbert, even though a South Sea director, is portrayed sympathetically to the end. He is astonished and annoyed by the fever of stockjobbing, though he has profited from it, and he closes the play with the wise advice to all about him to sell their stock for ready money. Cibber, after all, produced the play several months after the crash.[14]

* * *

Steele, Mrs. Centlivre, and Cibber, the most distinguished playwrights in the interval between *The Beaux' Stratagem* (1707) and *The Beggar's Opera* (1728), were, then, thorough Whigs in their interpretation of the merchant. In contrast, almost all the petty dramatists of these years hewed to the old traditions. These dramatists, several of them actors by profession, who wrote one, two, or three indifferent comedies or farcical afterpieces, turned variations on the stereotype, making no dramatic acknowledgment of the distinctions between occupations and levels of attainment in business life. "Usurers," tradesmen, stockjobbers, bankers, merchants in domestic trade, and merchants in foreign trade all are introduced indifferently as variants in a character not much altered from Wycherley's time. Thus there seems to be some positive correlation between the literary merit of comedies produced during these years and the more liberal social views.

Newburgh Hamilton's *The Petticoat-Plotter* (1712), a farce in two acts that was popular enough to be acted for several years, has characters and action with a simplicity suggestive of the allegorical patterns of a morality play.[15] Mr. Thrifty, a merchant, is impelled by avarice to insist that his daughter Isabella marry Sir Simon Scrape-all, a seventy-year-old "usurer," rather than True-love, a worthy and resourceful, if poor, young man, with whom Isabella is in love. The course of True-love does not run smooth, but he prevails handily.

The outwitting of a foolish merchant provides the subject of another farce three years later, Benjamin Griffin's *Love in a Sack* (1715). Sir Arthur Addlepate, an old citizen now resident in Covent Garden, has fallen absurdly in love with the young wife of an officer, Captain Debonair. His servant cautions him about the danger of an amour (I):

> You know the Character you have about Town of a grave, sober, discreet Magistrate, an unweary'd Opposer of Lewdness and Debauchery; and then you, Sir, that have so often scoured the whole Parish of *Coventgarden* to clear it of Whores, and whipt all from the Velvet-Scarf to the three-penny Flat-Cap, to be catch'd at last in a Petticoat-Plot yourself, would ruin your Credit for ever.

Sir Arthur nevertheless pursues the young wife, who, urged on by her husband and friends (including a young man who loves Sir Arthur's daughter), leads him into a compromising position from which she releases him only when he agrees to let the young man marry his daughter.

William Taverner's *The Female Advocates; Or, The Frantic Stock-Jobbers,* first acted in 1713 though it was altered from an earlier, unacted play of 1705,[16] has a more fully developed though not much more subtle intrigue: a young couple in love scheme to frustrate the plan of the young woman's guardian to marry her to an old but rich citizen, so that they can themselves be married. Sir Charles Transfer, the young woman's guardian, and Sir Feeble Dotard, the husband her guardian has selected for her, are merchants whose avarice and hypocrisy occasion righteous denunciation, at length, by the young gentlemen of the play. Reinforcing the merchant-gentry antagonism, in this play which was produced the year of the Treaty of Utrecht, there is also a note of antagonism between soldier and civilian, between the officer, Captain Stanworth, who at high personal cost contributed to the victory, and the merchant, Sir Charles Transfer, who, having profited from the war, despises the soldiers who suffered for the nation.

Taverner again in *The Artful Wife* (1717) treats class rivalries and mutual resentments satirically, though this time with a certain subtlety. A lord's household is the scene of the action, and, with one exception, all of the principal characters are members of the nobility or gentry. The one exception is Ruth, the niece of the lord's wife, who notwithstanding her relationship (by her aunt's marriage) to a peer, is a City girl, by temperament and manners as well as by upbringing. Her presence provides occasion for extended talk about the rival merits of the east and west ends of London. "There's Lady *Harriet* and Mrs. *Ruth* engag'd in a warm Argument," observes Sir Francis Courtal (II), whose surname describes him. "St. *James*'s and the City are the Foundation. No two Councils at the Bar ever wrangled more to support their contrary Opinions." The portrait of Ruth is satirical yet not unsympathetic: she is absurd in her devotion to the City, and she is a hypocrite; but she is shown to be a wronged girl, seduced by the experienced and unscrupulous Courtal, whom she loves. Her loss of honor is ultimately amended by Courtal's enforced marriage to her. The qualified sympathy expended on Ruth, however, fails to alter the impression of contempt for the City conveyed by the sustained sarcastic comments of several characters.

All three of Charles Molloy's plays satirize the citizens. In *The Perplexed Couple; Or, Mistake upon Mistake* (1715) there are no fewer than three representatives of the avaricious old merchant: Morecraft, the heroine's father; Sterling, "an old Usurer" to whom Morecraft wishes to marry his daughter; and Sir Anthony Thinwit, "a Citizen," married to a young woman whose "Visitors are People of Fashion, fine bred Folks" (II). The main plot is provided by a young gentleman's successful stratagem to marry Morecraft's daughter over his objections; and the subplot by the marital misadventures of Sir Anthony Thinwit. *The Half-Pay Officers* (1720), a farce that is little more than a pastiche of several earlier plays (*Henry V, Much Ado About Nothing,* and Davenant's *Love and Honour*),[17] includes as one of several lines of action a competition between two absurd citizens, Meagre, "a Scrivener," and Loadham, "a *Hamburgh* Merchant," for a handsome young heiress, who laughs at them and will have neither of them. *The Coquet; Or, The English Chevalier* (1718), an intrigue play in the Spanish manner, has a French locale, a circumstance that permits the introduction of generalized conversation about England—some of it criticism of the business community.

James Moore-Smythe's *The Rival Modes* (1727), a "genteel" comedy given over to the love chase of two gay couples, includes class antagonism as a subsidiary theme, introduced not in dramatic action but rather in conversational allusion. The dramatist's social judgments, as they appear in the handling of characters, intrigue, and satire, are more subtle than usual, at times even ambiguous, but still fundamentally conservative. Of the two handsome young women who are pursued by suitors, the wittier and more attractive is the wealthy widow of a London merchant. Not herself a person of quality, as she freely acknowledges, she nevertheless avoids her late husband's merchant relatives; and she considers marriage to a titled husband. Her maid comments (II):

> Well, 'tis a Blessing upon your Ladyship's Endeavours, that you need not give yourself much Fatigue in finding out such a Person, tho' I don't doubt your Industry after you're set upon it;—but the Question is, whether you would chuse a Coach with a Coronet, or with Horses?

The jokes about the quality are reinforced dramatically by the inclusion among the characters of two foppish lords, father and son, old and young variants of the stock character of the beau. Their comments, again, turn to the theme of the poverty of the fashionable world. "A Person of Quality never pays ready Money but at a Turnpike," observes the father, Lord Late-Airs, on a familiar note (III).

The Rival Modes was produced at Drury Lane, but most of the other plays here described as embodying the older dramatic conception of the merchant were produced at Lincoln's Inn Fields (i.e., at the "new" theater which opened in 1714). During the years in question only one new play produced at Lincoln's Inn Fields, Elkanah Settle's *The Lady's Triumph* (1718) (about a young wife's duping a knight who attempts to seduce her), includes a sympathetic portrayal of a merchant—and this one includes also a pointed observation that a good and generous merchant is a rare exception. At Drury Lane, by contrast, the merchant stereotype was rarely in evidence in the new plays, and there were several sympathetic and original portrayals of merchants: in Mrs. Centlivre's **The Wonder** and **A Bold Stroke for a Wife,** Cibber's *Refusal,* and Steele's *Conscious Lovers.*

There are two reasons, I believe, for the difference in the theaters' records. First, Drury Lane during the reign of George I was ostentatiously Whiggish: as I have elsewhere argued, its managers, with Steele as titular head, attempted to identify the theater with the victorious Whigs and to identify their rivals at Lincoln's Inn Fields with the discredited Tories.[18] There seems in fact to have been some disaffection to George I at Lincoln's Inn Fields. It is scarcely plausible that at either theater political theory could have determined managerial policy to the extent that the managers would have been sympathetic or hostile to comedies depending on dramatized attitudes of social philosophy; but it is not implausible that Whig dramatists, whose social views influenced their comedies, would have been attracted to Drury Lane and Tory dramatists to Lincoln's Inn Fields. Second, during most of these years Drury Lane was the more prosperous theater: it had a better management and a stronger company of actors, and it usually was the more popular with the public. Thus, one season with another, the better plays were produced at Drury Lane and the poorer at Lincoln's Inn Fields; and among the poorer comedies certainly were those that included such stock situations as the outwitting of foolish merchants.

Notes

1. W. R. Ward, *The English Land Tax in the Eighteenth Century* (London, 1953), pp. 17-29; Habakkuk, "English Landownership," *Economic History Review,* X [1940], 2-17.

2. See Émile Legouis, "Les deux Sir Roger de Coverley: celui de Steele et celui d'Addison," *Revue germanique,* II (1906), 453-71.

3. George Macaulay Trevelyan, *England under Queen Anne* [London, 1930-34], III, 108; see also Keith Feiling, *A History of the Tory Party, 1640-1714* (Oxford, 1924), p. 432.

4. No. 44 (June 7, 1711).

5. Peter Smithers, *The Life of Joseph Addison* (Oxford, 1954), p. 248.

6. Jehan Maintrieu, *Le Traité d'Utrecht et les polémiques du commerce anglais* (Paris, 1909); Viner, *Studies in International Trade,* pp. 115-18.

7. See John Loftis, *Steele at Drury Lane* (Berkeley and Los Angeles, 1952), pp. 183-93.

8. See *ibid.,* pp. 195-213.

9. British Museum, Additional MS 5145 C, fol. 198. Printed by John Nichols in *The Epistolary Correspondence of Richard Steele* (London, 1809), p. 648n.

10. Nicoll, [*A History of*] *Early Eighteenth Century Drama* [3rd ed. (Cambridge, England, 1952)], p. 299.

11. See above, pp. 64-68.

12. Cf. Steele, *Englishman* (1st series), No. 4 (October 13, 1713).

13. Cibber's immediate source may have been Thomas Wright's *Female Virtuosos* (1693), which is itself an adaptation of *Les Femmes savantes*. See Barker, [*Mr. Cibber of Drurylane* (New York, 1939)], pp. 126-27; and William Henry Irving, *John Gay, Favorite of the Wits* (Durham, N.C., 1940), pp. 188-90.

14. For further discussion of the expression of Whig political views in eighteenth-century literature, see Cecil A. Moore, "Whig Panegyric Verse: A Phase of Sentimentalism" (first published in *PMLA*, XLI [1926]), in *Backgrounds of English Literature, 1700-1760* (Minneapolis, 1953), pp. 104-44; Clement Ramsland, "Whig Propaganda in the Theater, 1700-1742" (unpublished dissertation, University of Minnesota, 1940); Samuel Kliger, *The Goths in England: A Study in Seventeenth and Eighteenth Century Thought* (Cambridge, Mass., 1952), especially Introduction.

15. For an excellent discussion of farce in the eighteenth century, see Leo Hughes, *A Century of English Farce* (Princeton, N.J., 1956).

16. Nicoll, *Early Eighteenth Century Drama*, p. 210.

17. *Ibid.*, p. 214; the preface to the play.

18. John Loftis, "The London Theaters in Early-Eighteenth-Century Politics," *Huntington Library Quarterly*, XVIII (1955), 365-93.

Patsy S. Fowler (essay date winter 1996)

SOURCE: Fowler, Patsy S. "Rejecting the Status Quo: The Attempts of Mary Pix & Susanna Centlivre to Reform Society's Patriarchal Attitudes." *Restoration and Eighteenth Century Theatre Research* 11, no. 2 (winter 1996): 49-59.

[*In the following essay, Fowler interprets Centlivre's plays as feminist texts intended to advance the social status of women. Focusing on* The Basset Table *and* The Busie Body, *Fowler views Centlivre as the inheritor of a feminist agenda promoted earlier by Aphra Behn as well as the beneficiary of Behn's efforts to create a space for women playwrights.*]

Aphra Behn may have cracked the glass ceiling of the male-dominated Restoration theatre, but the patriarchal attitudes of English society continued to make survival and success difficult for early eighteenth-century female playwrights. As Paula Backscheider points out, "Who-ever controls representation controls identity, history and morality" (83), and until this point, men had been doing mostly all of the writing, thereby controlling cultural norms. Lawrence Stone agrees that decisions governing female behavior "have nearly always been made by men, and have mainly defined what is acceptable behavior by women" (484). Backscheider asserts that these early women writers "were seeking to wrest away man's power to define women's nature, needs, aspirations, and acceptable conditions of existence" (83). They were "re-negotiating elements of the patriarchal ideology such as 'woman' and woman's 'place' as well as things of crucial importance for women's lives such as 'satisfactory courtship,' 'good marriage,' and options for single women" (Backscheider 83). As Behn's successors, Susanna Centlivre and Mary Pix should be recognized for their attempts to reform society's attitudes and thus create a more *woman-friendly* culture. While producing popular plays that both appealed to their audiences and stayed within the conventional cultural boundaries of accepted drama, these two playwrights were attempting subtly to modify and reform established attitudes concerning accepted behavior for and the control of women.

Mary Pix is perhaps the more subtle of the two authors, yet her plays contain significant feminist views. Edna Steeves calls her "a feminist before feminism became trendy" (272). Steeves continues her description, "Although not stridently offensive in her feminism . . . she seizes every opportunity to defend women against attacks upon their character and intelligence" (272). Pix's play *The Beau Defeated* (1700) exhibits numerous feminist views seeping through the action of a typical comedy.

In this play, Pix ridicules the snobbery and extravagance of London society and satirizes the follies of money-hungry men looking for rich widows, but her more feminist agenda is hidden in the subplot surrounding Lady Landsworth. Pix's feminist criticism is evident in Lady Landsworth's description of herself: "I was married a mere baby to a very old man, who, in his youth, having been a debauchee, and dealing with the worst of our sex, had an ill opinion of all, kept me like a nun, broke off all commerce to London, or indeed with anybody" (168). Lady Landsworth continues, explaining that by being a good and faithful wife she was able to inherit her husband's estate, thereby reaching a level of freedom that can only be attained by widows. Here Pix criticizes the victimization of women through forced marriages, pointing out that their only means of escape is through the deaths of their husbands.

This point is reiterated through Mrs. Rich, who is also a wealthy, if somewhat foolish, financially independent widow. The second point Pix makes involving these widows is that although they have reached a level of independence it is only made possible through the men in their lives, and this independence is constantly threatened by other men who are wanting to take advantage of their wealth. Pix questions the merit of a society in which the quality of a woman's existence depends on the mercy of a man.

In Lady Landsworth, Pix creates a strong, intelligent woman who is more sophisticated than all the foolery going on about her. She is a young, wealthy woman with a title and the freedom to go after what she wants; in short, she has the type of lifestyle about which most eighteenth-century English women could only dream. Lady Landsworth says she intends to "participate in all the innocent liberty my youth, my wealth, and sex desires." She then reveals to the servant Betty that she has come to London to find a husband of her liking. "I am resolved to indulge my inclinations, and rather than not obtain the person I like, invert the order of nature, and pursue though he flies" (169). This resolution is probably not an unfamiliar fantasy for ladies of the day; however, the fruition of such a dream does represent an atypical reality. Through Lady Landsworth, Pix hopes to blur the lines separating radical feminine behavior from the conventional.

Pix throws in a second jab at England's patriarchal society during this same discourse between Lady Landsworth and Betty. Before answering a question from Betty, Lady Landsworth comments, "Why should we dissemble when we are alone?" (169). This may be interpreted to mean that no men are around, so the women can be honest, or that no other women are around who would be jealous of Lady Landsworth and try to thwart her plans. Either way, Pix implies that it is society that forces women's need to dissemble.

Pix makes another interesting point during this discourse. Lady Landsworth describes to Betty the characteristics of the man she is seeking:

> He should be genteel, yet not a beau; witty, yet no debauchee; susceptible of love, yet abhorring lewd women; learned, poetical, musical, without one dram of vanity; in fine, very meritorious, yet very modest; generous to the last degree . . . (and) mightily in love with me.
>
> (169)

Lady Landsworth is not just describing the kind of man *she* hopes to find; she is describing the kind of man *all* women should hope to find. Pix offers this description as an example that men should emulate and that women should seek out for marriage

Betty's reaction is not as surprising as it is important to Pix's feminist agenda. Betty laughs almost hysterically at Lady Landsworth and tells her that no such man exists. "Ha, ha, ha, to your romances again lady-fair, 'tis

only there you can converse with those heroes" (170). Yet it is Lady Landsworth who gets the last laugh, because she accomplishes her goal and marries just such a hero.

Pix accomplishes her goal as well; she produces a play with great audience appeal that also makes definite social comments. She exposes the injustices and the follies of London society in a humorous, nonthreatening way and ultimately creates a strong, intelligent, independent female character who admits to her desires and controls her own destiny, thus introducing an atypical yet successful woman to society in an attempt to make her more culturally acceptable.

In the years immediately following Pix, Susanna Centlivre continued to advance the feminist agenda of her predecessors. *The Basset Table* (1705) and *The Busybody* (1709) were produced almost twenty years after Behn's death and at least five years after Pix's *The Beau Defeated,* therefore allowing Centlivre to be somewhat more blatant in her chastisement of the English patriarchy. This, however, in no way implies that Centlivre enjoyed total freedom to express her dissatisfaction with society; she was still confined by the tastes and the acceptance of the theater-going public. Like Behn and Pix, Centlivre was aware of these limitations and used her pen to push their boundaries for the sake of womankind.

In **The Basset Table,** Centlivre provides a humorous and entertaining look at the follies of English society as a whole, yet her feminist ideas are undeniably evident throughout the play. Her most obvious social comments are centered around the forced marriage of Valeria, an educated young woman more interested in science than in silly coquettish games in spite of the opinions of those around her.

Valeria spends most of her time conducting and discussing her scientific experiments. She describes dissecting a dove, then offers to buy Lady Reveller's Italian greyhound for an experiment. While these comments about experiments and dissections have a great comedic effect and might be considered a spoof on the Royal Society, Centlivre invariably is making a more serious point concerning the education and intellectual abilities of women. Asked by Lady Reveller when she will tire of these whimsies (experiments), Valeria answers, "Whimsies! Natural philosophy a whimsy! Oh! The unlearned world!" (251). Valeria continues her argument, "Can animals, insects, or reptiles, be put to a nobler use than to improve our knowledge?" (252). Centlivre demonstrates an acute understanding of the educational needs of women and depicts the shortsighted perspectives of English culture.

During this same discourse, Lady Reveller sarcastically suggests that Valeria should, "bestow your fortune in founding a college for the study of philosophy, where none but women should be admitted" (251-2). What the foolish Lady Reveller offers facetiously, Centlivre, like Mary Astell in *A Serious Proposal to the Ladies,* ironically intends to be considered as a possibility. Valeria answers, "What you make a jest of I'd execute were fortune in my power" (252). Centlivre implies that women are capable of higher learning, but their lack of financial freedom, as well as society's patriarchal limitations, makes their education if not an impossibility, then an improbability. Jacqueline Pearson agrees: "She enters into some of the conventional debates about women, arguing, for instance, that women's apparent inferiority is the result not of nature but of custom" (214). This point is reasserted when Alpiew suggests that education is as unsuitable to women as jackboots, and Valeria replies, "Custom would bring them as much in Fashion as Furbeloes, and Practice would make us as valiant as e'er a Hero of them all" (251). To illustrate her point further, Centlivre hints at the male fear of educating women. Valeria asks her father, "Dear Father, save my Lumbricus Laetus," to which he replies, "I'll lamprey and latum You! . . . Where the devil got you names that your father don't understand?" (262). This interaction between father and daughter probably evoked much laughter from the audience; however, its deeper implications are obvious.

The cruelty of forced marriage is demonstrated by Centlivre in another interaction between Valeria and her father. Valeria attempts to show the strength and determination of her intellect by exclaiming her dissatisfaction with her father's decision to force her to marry a man she does not love: "Duty compels my hand, but my heart is subject only to my mind; the strengths of that they cannot conquer . . . I here protest my will shall ne'er assent to [another]" (274). Her father answers, displaying the true, patriarchal attitude of the day, also implying the physical domination of men over women:

> Aye, you and your will may philosophise as long as you please, mistress, but your body shall be taught another doctrine . . . Your mind and your soul quotha! . . . 'Tis the flesh, housewife, that must raise heirs, and supporters of my name.
>
> (274)

Here Centlivre portrays the strength of a woman's will, but demonstrates the futility and powerlessness of women to reject the imposed commands of men. This masculine lack of consideration for the wants and desires of women is presented as cruel and uncivil, and Centlivre attempts to create empathy for women suffering from such oppression.

Although Centlivre uses Valeria as a mouthpiece for many of her feminist ideas, other brief examples appear subtly throughout the play. In two instances Lady Revel-

ler exhibits what would be considered very masculine attitudes toward love. In the first, she asks Lady Lucy, "What pleasure is there in one lover? 'Tis like being seen always in one suit of clothes" (242). This seems a rakish attitude for a lady, but probably one privately possessed by many of the women in the audience. The second instance involves Lady Reveller's comment on Lord Worthy, her suitor, "I must not be friends with him, for then I shall have him at my elbow all night, and spoil my luck at the basset table" (269). Here Centlivre humorously satirizes gambling, but, more importantly, she depicts a woman who places her own interests above those of a man, indirectly implying that this is acceptable behavior for women.

Again, Centlivre's feminism seeps through the play's dialogue in a hilarious line from the servant, Alpiew, who quips, "Well, I shall have a husband one of these days, and be a widow too, I hope" (240). Even the servants knew that the only avenue of freedom for women was through widowhood. In the end, however, Alpiew turns down marriage, implying that it is acceptable for a woman to remain single by choice, a point that Centlivre reiterates in a later play *The Busybody.*

Probably one of the most amusing, yet subtly and ironically feminist, lines in *The Basset Table* is spoken by Sir James describing Lady Lucy's ability to debate, "'Tis a pity she were not a man, she preaches so emphatically" (276). Centlivre leaves the reader to ask, "And a penis would make her a better orator?"

Perhaps Centlivre's most blatant feminist ideology becomes apparent at the end of the play. Lady Sago and Lady Reveller are forced to abandon their vices, adultery and gambling, for love. There is, however, no insistence that Valeria give up science in order to find love. In fact, Centlivre allows her to have passion for both her husband and her philosophy, thus insisting that women can achieve both.

In *The Busybody,* Centlivre continues her chastisement of the male-dominated English culture through both covert and more overt methods, while still adhering to the dramatic conventions that assured success for the playwright. As Suz-Anne Kinney asserts, "many of the social conventions that solidify the oppression of women are critiqued by Behn and Centlivre" (90). By giving predominantly male attributes to female characters, Centlivre satirizes the conventional social behaviors of both genders, thus expanding the realm of accepted conduct for women. (Centlivre does give stereotypical female traits to male characters as well, but that should be addressed in another paper.)

According to Kinney, the two lead female characters in the play, Miranda and Isabinda, "actively (though sometimes covertly) rail against these treacherous oppressors and their ultimate weapon, marriage. Both women resist the marriages which Sir Francis and Sir Jealous have contrived for them, and both women succeed in achieving the marriages they desire" (90). Centlivre encourages women to oppose these forced marriages, while characterizing the men who propose such marriages as tyrants. She recognizes greed as the driving force behind many of these marriages, thereby denouncing a society that endorses a practice where a woman's happiness and well-being are sacrificed for wealth.

Miranda vividly expresses how it must feel to be forced to marry an old man when she describes Sir Francis, "What a delicate bedfellow I should have!" (327). Later, the old man comments that he is "all of a fire," to which Miranda mockingly replies, "'Tis a wonder the dry stubble does not blaze" (328). Even Sir George recognizes the lack of passion that Miranda can expect to endure should she marry Sir Francis, and he uses it in his attempt to woo her: "Can you prefer that old, dry withered sapless log of sixty-five, to the vigorous, gay sprightly love of twenty-four? With snoring only he'll awake thee, but I with ravishing delight would make thy senses dance in consort with the joyful minutes" (312). While this sexual innuendo would be amusing to the audience, it paints a clear picture of the sexual dysfunction inherent in such forced marriages. Also inherent in Sir George's statement is the implication that women should expect to receive sexual gratification from their husbands. Centlivre is insinuating that women should view sex as a pleasurable experience and not just as a conjugal duty. This theme is continued when Miranda tells Sir George, ". . . let the world see we are lovers after wedlock; 'twill be a novelty—" (344).

While both women rebel against their forced marriages, it is Miranda who controls the action of the play through her scheming and, more importantly, through her rhetoric. As Pearson points out, "Miranda's task is two-fold, for she must escape the domination not only of her oppressive guardian but also of the man she loves, Sir George Airy" (221). Miranda accomplishes the first by her clever use of language as she outwits Sir Francis; the second she accomplishes through silence: "George buys the right to speak to Miranda from her guardian, and she punishes him for treating her as a commodity by refusing to speak . . . It is only when he gives up his attempt to control her that she uses her powers over language to win him" (Pearson 221). She uses her mastery of masculine language to pursue and attain her goal.

Miranda's control of her situation is further exhibited when she proposes to Sir George in a brief proviso scene: "Do you think we can agree on that same terrible bugbear, Matrimony, without heartily repenting on both sides?" (343). It is again exemplified when Sir George wants to marry immediately, but she replies, "Hold, not so fast, I have provided better than to venture on dangerous experiments headlong" (344). Miranda has carefully planned her escape and will not abort her scheme. This displays the intellectual capabilities of women, demonstrating that they can think with their heads and not give in to the irrationalities of the heart. It also recapitulates that women, when given the opportunity, can govern their own lives. Miranda insinuates that her control will continue after her marriage to George when she answers Marplot's misguided question about whether the hiding monkey (Sir George) has a chain: "Not yet, but I design it one that shall last its lifetime" (346). While humorous, this dialogue attempts to bring a degree of female power into the conventional realm of the male-dominated marriage.

Through Miranda, Centlivre points out the powerless predicament that many women found themselves in because of marriage laws and what Kinney calls "the ultimate patriarchal institution" (90). Although she loves Sir George, and he declares his desire to marry her, "It has been my wish since first my longing eyes beheld ye," Miranda cannot help but question his motives by replying, "And your happy ears drank in the pleasing news, I had thirty thousand pounds" (344). Centlivre warns women that they can never be too careful where either their hearts or their purses are concerned. She further asserts that marriage can be a dangerous plight for women because they never know exactly what they are getting, and death is virtually the only escape. Miranda says of her decision to marry Sir George:

> . . . I have done a strange bold thing; my fate is determined, and expectation is no more. Now to avoid the impertinence and roguery of an old man, I have thrown myself into the extravagance of a young one; if he should despise, slight, or use me ill, there's no remedy from a husband but the grave; and that's a terrible sanctuary to one of my age and constitution.
>
> (350)

Miranda realizes that even though Sir George loves her, she will ultimately still be at his mercy.

In a more blatant comment on male oppression Miranda says of Sir Jealous, "Suppose he could introduce his rigid rules—does he think we could not match them in contrivance? No, no, let the tyrant man make what laws he will, if there's a woman under the government, I warrant she finds a way to break 'em" (301). This statement offers a triple interpretation. Not only does Centlivre challenge male authority, but she also insinuates that because women are not allowed to make the laws, they are forced to break them. Also present is the underlying message that women are capable of outwitting men. This line encompasses perhaps her most overt social criticism in the play.

A more positive aspect of Centlivre's feminist viewpoint is revealed in the true, caring friendship between Miranda and Isabinda. Miranda carefully plans Isabinda's escape from tyranny just as she does her own; she even provides her own trusted servant as a confidant and aide for Isabinda. Unlike many plays by men, *The Way of the World* and *The Beggar's Opera,* for example, where women exhibit false friendship, this play creates "a space where women can not only cease to be rivals, but actually understand, sympathize with, and respect each other" (Kinney 90). Centlivre presents true female friendship as a means for conquering, or at least improving, a society in which women must question the motives of each other almost as seriously as they question those of men. She asserts that through solidarity women can lessen their oppression.

In ***The Busybody,*** Centlivre takes her concept of female power a step farther than either Behn or Pix. Miranda rejects all attempts of male domination. Not only does she control her own future, but through her actions, she influences the destiny of every other character in the play. Her scheming provides Marplot and Charles with their inheritance, it allows both Isabinda and herself to marry men of their own choosing, and it foils the tyranical plans of the two domineering old men. Even the servants' lives are indirectly affected by her. Centlivre invents a strong, intelligent woman who seizes every opportunity and commands whatever power is available to gain dominion over her own fate. Centlivre reveals her feminist agenda neatly disguised in a play that met the expectations of the theater-going public and provided the customary *happy* ending culminating in the marriage of the hero and heroine.

Mary Pix and Susanna Centlivre were successful in writing popular plays that promoted their feminist ideology without offending or alienating a fickle public. This achievement is remarkable when one considers they were writing in a climate in which women writers were still considered a social taboo. Yet these women's need to express themselves through writing was greater than their need for personal acceptance. In describing the early eighteenth-century woman's need to write, Paula Backscheider quotes Cixous from "The Laugh of the Medusa":

> Cixous compared women's feelings about writing to their opinions about masturbation; both, she says, women allow themselves just enough "to attenuate the tension a bit, just enough to take the edge off. And as soon as we come, we go and make ourselves feel guilty."
>
> (102)

Luckily for women, Pix and Centlivre were able to overcome their feelings of guilt and write plays that attempted to improve female existence.

In reviewing *The Beau Defeated,* ***The Basset Table*** and ***The Busybody,*** I find similarities among the plays obvious, and a comparison of the playwrights seems inevitable. Both of these playwrights reveal carefully controlled feminist agendas which are expressed to various degrees through the dialogue and actions of their characters. Each criticizes a patriarchal society that strove to control and dominate women physically, emotionally, and financially. Each knew how much she could get away with, having her characters settle for a little oppression over total oppression, herself accepting a certain amount of constraint in order to meet accepted dramatic conventions, thereby assuring the success of her play. It is no surprise, then, that these two women were friends and, according to Paddy Lyons and Fidelis Morgan, possibly collaborated on ***The Busybody*** (xii). Following Behn's lead, these two early feminists wielded the only weapons they possessed—their pens—to criticize cultural injustice and force society to reevaluate accepted attitudes about women.

Perhaps Backscheider's statement about early women writers best summarizes the specific attempts of Mary Pix and Susanna Centlivre to reject the status quo and reform England's patriarchal society:

> Literature in these early women's hands became a hegemonic apparatus. As they wrote on subjects of crucial importance to women, they transformed them, represented them differently, and contributed to significant changes in the way the culture saw women, courtship, marriage, and family relations.
>
> (69)

Works Cited

Backscheider, Paula R. *Spectacular Politics.* Baltimore and London: Johns Hopkins UP, 1993.

Centlivre, Susanna. "The Basset Table." *Female Playwrights of the Restoration.* Ed. Paddy Lyons and Fidelis Morgan. London: Everyman, 1995. 235-292.

———. "The Busybody." *Female Playwrights of the Restoration.* Ed. Paddy Lyons and Fidelis Morgan. London: Everyman, 1995. 293-363.

Kinney, Suz-Anne. "Confinement Sharpens the Invention: Aphra Behn's *The Rover* and Susanna Centlivre's *The Busie Body.*" *Look Who's Laughing: Gender and Comedy.* Ed. Gail Finney. Langhorne, PA: Gordon and Breach, 1994. 81-98.

Lyons, Paddy and Fidelis Morgan. Introduction. *Female Playwrights of the Restoration.* Ed. Lyons and Morgan. London: Everyman, 1995. vi-xx.

Pearson, Jacqueline. *The Prostituted Muse.* New York: St. Martin's Press, 1988.

Pix, Mary. "The Beau Defeated." *Female Playwrights of the Restoration.* Ed. Paddy Lyons and Fidelis Morgan. London: Everyman, 1995. 161-234.

Steeves, Edna L. "Mary Pix." *Literature Criticism from 1400-1800.* Ed. Dennis Poupard. Detroit: Gale Research Co., 1984. Vol. 8. 270-274.

Stone, Lawrence. *The Family, Sex, and Marriage in England 1500-1800.* New York: Harper and Rowe, 1977.

Laura J. Rosenthal (essay date 1996)

SOURCE: Rosenthal, Laura J. "Writing (as) the Lady's Last Stake: Susanna Centlivre." In *Playwrights and Plagiarists in Early Modern England: Gender, Authorship, Literary Property,* pp. 204-42. Ithaca, N.Y.: Cornell University Press, 1996.

[*In the following excerpt, Rosenthal examines the gender issues involved in the authorial relationship between Centlivre and Colley Cibber, who was accused of plagiarizing from her. Rosenthal suggests that the limits placed on women as property holders affected contemporary interpretations of authorial ownership for men and women.*]

CENTLIVRE AND CIBBER: INTERTEXTUAL TENSIONS

Colley Cibber grew rich, famous, and powerful as a flamboyant hack, a position made possible by both his gender and the gender anxieties he provoked. Hostile fascination fed his career. Centlivre, however, did not become the most famous plagiarist of the eighteenth century, positioning herself instead as both a wife and a common hack who invented plots and contrivances with feminine skill. Cibber and Centlivre did not share the complex and documented history that Aphra Behn shared with Killigrew, nor did Cibber openly appropriate one of her plays the way Southerne did *Oroonoko.* Their intersecting careers, however, reveal both literal and symbolic tensions over their differing, gendered positions in relation to literary property. In one incident, Cibber seems to have plagiarized a play that Centlivre submitted to Drury Lane and that he rejected. In several others cases, however, he less directly rewrote Centlivre's plots, taking advantage of her acute ear for popular themes but revising her feminist individualist representation of property.

When Centlivre submitted her ***Love at a Venture*** to Drury Lane, she had no personal reason to satirize Cibber in particular as a fop author. She would soon acquire one. Cibber rejected *Love,* but produced *The Double Gallant*—a play with striking similarities—under his own name shortly thereafter. Centlivre's eighteenth-century biographer, in fact, reports that she "used to complain" that Cibber "had taken in the greatest Part of her Play."[1] Unlike Mary Pix, however, Centlivre found

some vocal supporters, perhaps as a result Cibber's reputation for plagiarism. Enemies leaped at the chance to charge Cibber once again with a violation of literary property, in spite of his greater power relative to Centlivre. Barton Booth wrote to Aaron Hill that "as soon as the good-natur'd Town found [Cibber] out, they resented his calling [*The Double Gallant*] a new Play, and *hounded* it in a most outrageous Manner."[2] Booth identifies Cibber's sources as plays by Burnaby and by Centlivre. Although such a response must remain in the context of Cibber's own self-positioning as a fop-author and the consequent eagerness to identify him with plagiarism, and although Cibber himself clearly did not respect Centlivre's capacity to own, she nevertheless appears to have achieved enough popularity to earn recognition for her ownership from others. Centlivre, in fact, did not invent the eponymous double gallant—a man who courts two women by pretending to be two men (played by Cibber himself in his *Double Gallant*)—for this device appears in Corneille's *Le Galant double* and Calderon's *Hombre pobre todo es trazas.* Booth, however, implicitly attributes this character to Centlivre.[3] Decades later, the anonymous author of *The Laureat* specifically represents the incident as the theft of Centlivre's property:

> There was at this Time a certain *Poetess* in *Rome,* called *Fulvia* [Centlivre], who had sometimes succeeded in Characters of Humour on the Stage; she offer'd a Play to the Perusal of *Aesopus* [Cibber]; in this Play she had drawn the Character of a very impudent Fellow, who in the same Play acted under his own Appearance two different Persons, and persuaded his Mistress to believe him not to be himself in Opposition to her Senses; this Character *Aesopus* scouted extremely. Why, Madam, said he, this would be putting upon the Audience indeed; they will never bear it; 'tis extravagant, it is outraging Nature, it is silly, and it is not ridiculous. The poor Lady was beat out of her Design; but as our Corrector had the Play left sometime in his Hand, he culled out this very Character, mix'd it with some other Felonies of the same Nature, which he had committed, and had it acted as his own the very next Year.[4]

Perhaps in response to such attacks, Cibber acknowledges his intertextuality several times but never mentions Centlivre. The prologue to *The Double Gallant* claims both originality and the lack of it, arguing that although "from former scenes some hints he [Cibber] draws / The ground-plot's wholly chang'd from what it was," hoping the audience will find "enough that's new, / In plot, in persons, wit, and humour too: / Yet what's not his, he owns in other's right."[5] In his autobiography, however, Cibber represents Centlivre's plot (without naming Centlivre) as waste matter and therefore open to salvaging efforts: *The Double Gallant,* he writes, "was a Play made up of what little was tolerable in two or three others that had no Success, and were laid aside as so much Poetical Lumber; but by collecting and adapting the best Parts of them all into one Play, the *Double Gallant* has had a Place every Winter . . . these Thirty Years."[6] While Restoration revisers represent earlier texts as raw material, Cibber here recognizes Centlivre's play as an artifact (not nature), but nevertheless as one whose low quality does not merit ownership. In his assumption that personal and socially contingent judgments of taste determine the proprietary status of a text, Cibber contributes to the emergent eighteenth-century distinction between the status of an artifact signified as an aesthetic object and one signified as "merely" commercial.

Having defined Centlivre's efforts as common (in both senses), however, Cibber immediately backs off from any claims to cultural capital, comparing himself to a cobbler who "may be allow'd to be useful though he is not famous: And I hope a Man is not blameable for doing a little Good, tho' he cannot do as much as another?" Cibber closes this case by returning to his self-representation as a hack, resigning himself to the fact that "Twopenny Criticks must live as well as Eighteenpenny Authors."[7] In spite of their profoundly entangled professional careers—Cibber, for example, acted in Centlivre's next play—the laureate never mentions Centlivre's name in regard to *The Double Gallant*, as if to reject the possibility that one could benefit from a woman writer. While he does not, like Southerne, rewrite the plot to disinherit his female precursor—in fact, he barely rewrites it at all[8]—his neglect witnesses a lack of obligation even to dispute borders.

It is tempting to speculate that Centlivre added the foppish, plagiarizing character of Wou'd-be to *Love at a Venture* in response to Cibber's appropriation.[9] Whether or not this character appeared in the version of *Love* that she first submitted, the upstart poet embodies many characteristics attributed to Cibber by his enemies. Centlivre commonly distinguishes her own works as more original and thus her own; Wou'd-be, however, trails around after gentlemen of fashion and literally takes notes on their clothes in order to have his tailor reproduce them. He even scribbles down their witty comments for the dialogue of his next play, a practice the gentlemen protest:

BELL[AIR]:

> I hope, you are not one of those Spungy-Brain'd Poets, that suck something from all Companies to squeeze into a Comedy, at Acting of which, the Pit and Boxes may laugh at their own Jests.

NED.:

> Where each may claim his share of Wit.

BELL.:

> And by my consent, shou'd claim a share of the Profits too, ha, ha.

WOU'D.

> This is a Gentleman of an intellectual Sublimity—No, Sir, I contemn the Terrene extraction of those poor Animals, whose Barren-Intellects thrusts such spurious Brats abroad; when I write, it shall be all my own, I assure you.

(27)

Wou'd-be's literary and sartorial plagiarism become parallel expressions of his limited capacity and resources; Wou'd-be's attempts at gentlemanly language ("Dear, Sir *William*," he says, "my Stars are superabundantly propitious, in administring the seraphick Felicity of finding you alone.") fail just as absurdly and foppishly as his attempts at gentlemanly appearance. Thus Bellair finally advises him to "leave off this foolish Whim of Mimicking" (the true gentleman) Sir William, who has a "plentiful Fortune. . . . you, whose slender Allowance from a Father's Hand, admits of no profuseness—to imitate him is Madness" (62). Centlivre's satire on the literary and cultural ambitions of some men differs from misogynist attacks on female authorship in that she argues against, rather than encourages, gender-based generalizations about the capacity to create literary property. Wou'd-be's fashions and authorship both appropriate transgressively—a point, as we have seen, that belongs to broader anxieties about the professionalization of authorship. But it is also important to Centlivre's feminist individualism to insist that paltry talents and overblown self-conception appear just as commonly among men as women. In the dedication to her next play, for example, she reminds audiences not to reject women authors out of hand since "we have had some Male-Productions . . . void of Plot and Wit."[10] In her most optimistic moments of feminist individualism, then, men and women share equal capacities to excel, appropriate, plagiarize, and scribble.

Cibber and Centlivre both thematized gendered literary property through the trope of the learned lady and gendered alienability through the trope of gambling. Ladies and fop authors, as it turns out, actually *were* in Cibber's case at odds, for learned or scribbling women became common objects of his satirical energy. As his prominent roles in *The Female Wits* and *Three Hours* suggest, Cibber's own exteriority to dominant masculinity did not create in him sympathy toward women writers (although he does seem to have been generous toward women actors).[11] Cibber's appropriation of *Love* provides the most obvious example of his unwillingness to recognize his female colleague's capacity to own; his revisions of Centlivre's liberal feminist plots elsewhere demonstrate their differing and complex relation to the position of ownership. Two sets of plays, possibly in dialogue with each other, reveal these differences. Centlivre's *Platonick Lady* appropriates and revises the popular trope of the learned lady, possibly responding to Thomas Wright's *Female Vertuoso's.* Centlivre, however, also satirized the learned man. In an echo of **The Platonick Lady** and *The Female Vertuoso's,* the problem of women who know too much later appears in Cibber's *Refusal.* Differences further become apparent in three gambling plays: Cibber's *The Lady's Last Stake* and Centlivre's **The Gamester** and **The Basset Table.**

The epilogue of Centlivre's **Platonick Lady,** written by Thomas Baker, represents the author not only as male but also as misogynistic: "What mighty pains our Scribling Sot has shown," an actress recites, "To Ridicule our Sex, and Praise his own." But in spite of Baker's epilogue, Centlivre actually represents her platonic lady quite sympathetically in a clear revision of the "learned lady" genre. More typical, and possibly providing a subtext and source for **The Platonick Lady,** is Thomas Wright's *The Female Vertuoso*'s, which satirizes learning as a sign of lust in women: "A Woman's Wit," Wright's Sir Maurice Meanwell complains, "was always a Pimp to her pleasures."[12] Meanwell insists that women should study only to please their husbands and instruct their children: "The Women of Old did not read so much, but lived better, Housewifry was all the Knowledge they aspired to; now adays Wives must Write forsooth, and pretend to Wit with a Pox."[13] Typically, Centlivre both repeats and attempts to refute cultural prejudices: she holds her platonic lady Lucinda up for admiration, but has this very same character satisfy the popular desire to ridicule learned women by joining in the scorn of Mrs. Prim, "the Poetical She-Philosopher, whose Discourse and Writings are fill'd with Honour and the strict Rule of Virtue" (17) that she does not follow herself. Lucinda, however, derides Mrs. Prim's hypocrisy, not her learning itself.

If in Locke full individuality, as Macpherson argues, is achieved at the expense of other men, full individuality in Centlivre is (temporarily) achieved by some women at the expense of other women. Even this individuality, however, often becomes compromised in some way by the end of the play. At the same time, however, **The Platonick Lady**'s Lucinda distinctly disrupts the trope of the learned lady. Combining a love of learning with a Platonism that recalls the earlier court culture in which Cavendish participated, Centlivre's Lucinda not only escapes the generic ridicule but also inadvertently prevents a disaster through her chaste philosophy. Belville loves and courts Lucinda, but she makes him swear only to "admire the Beauties of [her] Mind—without regarding those of [her] Person" (17). Meanwhile Isabella, who had been contracted by her father to marry Sir Charles (who loves Lucinda) but had also made her own contract to marry Belville, returns in various disguises to tempt Belville back into her arms. Lucinda's broad knowledge provides her with the first clue that Belville might have another love, for she recognizes the poem he courts her with: "what Lady

have you lavish'd your Wit upon this Morning," Lucinda demands, "that you are forc'd to Trade upon other Mens Stocks?" (16). In a curse that recalls Centlivre's Horatian epigram from **The Stolen Heiress,** Belville rails against "these Poetical Rogues, they publish every pretty Thought, that a Gentleman's forc'd to borrow to express his own Notions" (17). Belville's curse not only echoes the author's commitment to originality, but it also demonstrates one kind of usefulness of literary learning to a lady. Belville clearly did not expect Lucinda to recognize the lines. This scene, in fact, repeats an accusation that Centlivre herself makes to "Celadon" in one of her published love letters: "Let *Celadon* consider if I ought not to be angry after his affecting the wholsome food of Plaindealing, he should offer me the fragments of Flattery from the Table of another. . . . Learning, Wit, and Eloquence are your inseparable Companions; therefore borrowing is as unpardonable in you as in a Miser. You ought rather to enrich the Publick, than encroach upon it. . . . I must tell you there's not one word in that Letter could be apply'd to me."[14] Not only does Lucinda's learning make her a more savvy lover, but her platonism, which restrains her from offering Belville so much as a kiss, also saves them both from incest. When Lucinda's uncle, Sir Thomas, finally reveals Belville's true identity as Lucinda's *brother,* she platonically turns her affection into "a Sister's Fondness" (69) and recommends him to Isabella.

The risky efforts of Isabella, Lucinda's rival for Belville, suggest that Centlivre may even have had in mind a liberal feminist intervention not just into the learned lady in general, but into Thomas Wright's play in particular. In her desperation to win Belville, Centlivre's Isabella (disguised as Donna Clara) tells Lucinda that she had married, and been abandoned by, Belville, after which she gave birth to his son. In spite of her own love for Belville, Lucinda pities "Donna Clara" and vows to protect her. Isabella turns to this last resort out of love and resistance to her childhood betrothal to Sir Charles: "I own I have gone beyond my Sex and Quality," she confesses, "but it was to purchase Liberty, and break a forc'd Contract with that perfidious Man who paid his Vows to [Lucinda]" (66). In the process, however, she places her reputation in jeopardy. A similar device appears in *The Female Vertuoso's,* but in Wright's play a *servant* undertakes this risk *on behalf* of her lady. Here the maid Lucy fakes a pregnancy by Witless, an upstart pretender to both learning and numerous rakish conquests, as part of a plot to free the heroine Mariana for marriage to her true love Clerimont. Witless, however, uses Lucy "just as he do's his Books; for as he quotes every day Passages out of 'em, which he never read, so he boasts of Favours of mine he never enjoy'd" (4). Lucy takes pleasure in trapping Witless, who does not object even when he discovers Lucy's identity. Centlivre's rewriting, however, turns a servant's clever machinations into a lady's high-stake risk of her reputation. Wright's play has the servant scheme for her lady's sake, leaving Marianna herself relatively passive; in Centlivre's version, the lady herself risks her reputation and puts her faith in the good will of another woman.[15]

Thus, not only does Centlivre's **Platonick Lady** appropriate and rewrite the learned lady trope in feminist individualist terms, but it also represents Isabella as breaking a paternally arranged marriage contract and making one of her own choice. In order to accomplish this, however, she must adopt several disguises and plot to turn his affections away from another woman. And while we feel that poetic justice has nevertheless been served by the marriage of Isabella and Belville, the fate of the platonic lady herself remains enigmatic. Astonished at Belville's previous marriage to "Donna Clara" (Isabella), his apparent initial refusal to acknowledge this marriage *and* Isabella's deceit of *her,* Lucinda cries out, "What, am I then a Property, am I a Person fit to be Abus'd?" (67). In true platonic fashion, she vows to "renounce Mankind" (67). She does not, however, get away with this renunciation, even for a moment. Her uncle, Sir Thomas, insists, "Faith and Troth but thou shalt not" (67); soon after revealing Belville's identity, he and Belville agree to advance the interest of Sir Charles with Lucinda. Lucinda does not respond to this agreement between men, but the ending implies that between paternal insistence and fraternal coaxing, Lucinda will give in to marriage. At best, Centlivre's heroines negotiate for a better contract and greater individual choice. Unlike Cavendish, her more radical yet less liberal precursor, Centlivre does not imagine alternatives to marriage or even less traditional kinds of marriages. Perhaps the authority of aristocratic rank opens up these possibilities more readily. But whereas Thomas Wright, following his French source, represents women's learning as a hypocritical excuse for shrewishness, petty domineering, lust, and transgressive appropriation, Centlivre represents Lucinda's contemplative inclinations as dignified. Wright's Lady Meanwell and her friends, by contrast—the "Sappho's of our Age" (16)—seek power and have the audacity to set themselves up as the arbiters of literary value: "Our Society shall be as the Inquisition, a Tribunal without Appeal, or Mercy; where, with a Sovereign Authority, we shall Judge all Books that come out: No Authors shall write well, but those we approve of; and no body pretend to Wit, but we, and our Friends" (16). Lady Meanwell rejects Clerimont as a possible husband for her daughter because, among other reasons, he has failed to pay attention to her own literary accomplishment: she will not "admit into my Family a Despiser of Wit, one who knows well enough I'm an Author, and never had the manners to ask me to read any of my Works to him" (49). In Centlivre's play, however, Lucinda realizes that, in spite of her attempts to reject all

men in favor of philosophy, "a real Passion cannot be disguis'd" (67), which humanizes her and endears her to the audience. At the same time, the Platonism that prevents her from acting on this passion also saves her from incest.

Cibber's *Refusal* most distinctly repeats Wright's *Female Vertuoso's,* but it also engages Centlivre's portrait of female Platonism and the specter of women's authorship in general. In Cibber's *Refusal,* women's learning and/or writing only disguise hypocrisy or unbounded acquisitiveness. Cibber turns the awkwardly sympathetic and bookish lady in Centlivre into an expression of vicious misogyny, for Sir Gilbert suffers the torments of a wife far more learned than he. Lady Wrangle raises her daughter Sophronia "half mad with her Learning and Philosophy" (4:9); she resembles Centlivre's platonic lady in her apparent rejection of physical desire. Sophronia snobbishly considers sex fit only for "Cookmaids and Footmen" (4:28), while drifting off into rape fantasies. But Frankley, suitor to Sophronia's more willing sister Charlotte, reveals that Lady Wrangle has only trained the young women in Platonism out of her own desire to prevent their marriages and thus appropriate their fortunes. Female education in Cibber becomes a strategy for the mother to expand her possession of both language and money.

While Lady Wrangle's desire to educate her daughters may spring from unsavory motives, her enthusiasm for her own authorship proves genuine and perhaps even provides Cibber with the opportunity to ridicule his female competitors. But as in *The Female Wits,* the pretension to the highest cultural capital, not writing or reading in themselves, proves to be the genuine transgression: Charlotte's reading of the *Tatler* teaches her "natural" manners, while Sophronia's reading of Latin literature turns her into a harridan. Lady Wrangle, however, goes so far as to translate Latin poetry—an effort that the cook literally skewers ("what a Life's here about a Piece of foul Paper," the cook puns, 4:60). Lady Wrangle runs mad with provocation when she discovers the maid has given the cook her poems as scrap, and the cook will not return them for fear of burning his roast beef. Upon hearing his wife's exclamations of horror, Sir Gilbert Wrangle suspects a murder; he relaxes and dismisses her outrage upon learning that she only protests the loss of her literary property. Lady Wrangle probably does not satirize Centlivre or any other woman writer in particular, but she represents (like Phoebe Clinket) the mutually implicating literary and proprietary transgression of learned women. By contrast, her virtuous daughter Charlotte never falls for the trap of learning; even Sophronia, who at first indulges in learned literature, eventually gives it up for "plain, naked, natural Love" (4:93). Thus the play ultimately endorses Sir Gilbert's conclusion about Lady Wrangle's learning. Sir Gilbert locates Lady

Wrangle in the subordinated position of Prospero's Caliban when he implies the similarity of the wife's and the slave's relationship to language: "All the use I find of her Learning, is, that it furnishes her with more words to scold with" (4:62).

The satirized learned lady becomes a fixture in early eighteenth-century drama. And while a range of authors attack pedantry in general, Centlivre offers alternatives to the shrewish learned lady with both dignified learned women and with the absurd "learned man."[16] Attacks on male pedantry do not necessarily signal feminism; Centlivre's learned men, however, reveal their absurdity in gendered contexts. In her attack on the masculine learning to which she has no access, Centlivre once again echoes Cavendish. But whereas the duchess advances her aristocratic singularity, Centlivre opposes an elite masculine reliance on the authority of books to a savvy comprehension of the world that distinguishes many of her women characters and also describes her own authorial self-representation. Sancho in *The Stolen Heiress,* for example, represents Centlivre's elite scholar who knows nothing of human machinations.[17] Thus Francisco, who wants to marry the woman to whom Sancho has become engaged, tricks Sancho into pretending to know nothing of books and everything of the social world as a way to impress Lavinia. Lavinia's father and his stubborn insistence that his daughter marry a scholar, regardless of her affections, becomes the object of Centlivre's potent satire. Centlivre upholds the love between Lavinia and Francisco as more valuable than the father's hypocritical and elitist fascination with Sancho and his learning. Sancho earns some sympathy for his naive simplicity; he speaks an epilogue about the inadequacy of learning:

> Tho' the Learn'd Youth, can all the Sages Quote,
> Has *Homer, Hesiod,* and the rest by roat;
> Yet what's all this to Picquet, Dress or Play?
> Or to the Circle, on a Visiting-Day?[18]

Attached to a different play, these lines could read as yet another satire on a society too frivolous to honor learning. In the context of *The Stolen Heiress,* however, they leave genuine doubt about the superiority of Homer and Hesiod to visiting or the theater. Centlivre slyly opposes masculine rote learning of classical poets to the feminine world of fashion and drama.

The erudite Periwinkle cuts a similar figure in her *Bold Stroke for a Wife.* In order to marry Ann Lovely, Colonel Fainwell in this play must gather permission from each of three idiosyncratic guardians, including Periwinkle, "a kind of a silly *Virtuoso.*" Periwinkle cares only for "scientific" curiosities from the distant past and from around the world. As in *The Stolen Heiress,* however, the lover outsmarts the scholar: the Colonel pretends to share Periwinkle's interests and

earns his good will by offering him a girdle that he claims will render its wearer invisible. In both these plays of Centlivre's, the learned man blocks and thus structurally stands in opposition to a woman's happiness. Most of Centlivre's plays, in fact, feature young couples who plot against tyrannical fathers or guardians in order to marry. Her plays consistently protest fathers or guardians who treat women as property and celebrate the men and women who outmaneuver them. The marriage contract remains the goal; Centlivre's women, however, attempt to position themselves as makers rather than objects of this contract.

Cibber's and Centlivre's gendered relationships to property become perhaps most apparent, however, in their representations of gambling. Gambling attracted attention as a vice in the early eighteenth century,[19] but moralists and satirists expressed particular anxieties about women playing games of chance. Perhaps most memorably, the card game provides the scene of Belinda's jeopardy in Pope's *Rape of the Lock;* as in Pope's poem, most of the attacks on women and gambling represent the loss of chastity as the greatest danger to betting women. The sarcastic author of *The Womens Advocate* identifies the staking of virtue as every man's anxiety over his wife's gambling: "There she sits from after dinner, till one, two, three, four a clock i'the morning, day after day, night after night, consuming and wasting her fine Portion, till she begins to prey upon the main stock. And this is a parlous grievance. . . . One cries, *I think my wife will play away her A———.*"[20] *Mundus Mulierbris* identifies the same danger:

> To play at *Ombre* or *Basset,*
> She a rich *Pulvil* Purse must get,
> With Guineas fill'd, on Cards to lay,
> With which she fancies most to play:
> Nor is she troubled at ill fortune,
> For should the bank be so importune,
> To rob her of her glittering Store,
> The amorous Fop will furnish more.
> Pensive and mute, behind her shoulder
> He stands, till by her loss grows bolder,
> Into her lap *Rouleau* conveys,
> The softest thing a Lover says:
> She grasps it in her greedy hands,
> Then best his Passion understands;
> When tedious languishing has fail'd,
> *Rouleau* has constantly prevail'd.[21]

As *The Guardian* similarly concludes, "The husband has his lands to dispose of, the wife her person."[22] The trope of the female gambler takes on a life of its own, embodying more than the general concern for women's chastity. The lady in *Mundus Mulierbris* begins as a possessor and circulator of gold, but her body becomes a vessel for holding coins when she runs out. In the course of the poem, the gambler changes from a controller of property into property herself, as a prostitute but also as a body penetrated by and indistinguishable from money. So while satires against women gamblers warn against gambling's risk to chastity, they also repeat as a trope the fluidity of boundaries for women between circulating property and becoming property. For *The Guardian,* the possibility of circulating property without becoming property remains masculine; women who gamble thus earn sarcastic praise because they "acquire such a boldness, as raises them near the lordly creature man. . . . Their natural tenderness is a weakness here easily unlearned; and I find my soul exalted, when I see a lady sacrifice the fortune of her children with as little concern as a Spartan or a Roman dame."[23] The discourse of gambling thus reveals the ideology of post-Lockean representations of gender and ownership, for it consistently depicts female sexuality and self-possession not only as alienable, but also as constantly in danger of alienation. A lady's last stake differs from a gentleman's. Gambling *also,* however, potentially offers women the (temporary) position of possessor rather than possessed, although rarely in the drama can a woman keep from folding when a man calls her bluff.

Colley Cibber's gambling play, *The Lady's Last Stake, or, The Wife's Resentment* (1707), followed Centlivre's first two popular successes, **The Gamester** (1705) and **The Basset Table** (1705), to which I will return. Both of Centlivre's plays, as their titles indicate, address the issue of gambling. Although *The Lady's Last Stake* does not repeat Centlivre quite as explicitly as *The Double Gallant,* produced the same year, it certainly engages and responds to its Lincoln's Inn Field rivals. Cibber's rewriting of the learned lady reveals his patriarchal complicity; the unstable economy of gambling, however, prompts an exploration of the instability of gender. Like Centlivre's plays, but also like so many other texts at the time, *The Lady's Last Stake* locates money and sexuality in the same economy of risk: alienable sexuality is the lady's last stake, the ultimate prize she finds she must offer in order to pay off her debts. Cibber states his own purpose as exposing folly "to the Fair Sex in its most hideous Form, by reducing a Woman of Honour to stand the presumptuous Addresses of a Man, whom neither her Virtue nor Inclination would let her have the least Taste to" (2:196). Yet throughout the play and the dedication it becomes apparent that this promise of a moral for the ladies also becomes a vehicle through which Cibber expresses an array of anxieties over what Pocock calls the "mobility of property."[24] Cibber specularizes, with a combination of glee and horror, consumer culture's potential capacity to threaten naturalized gender differences. Locke's treatises may represent women as outside the position of ownership, but as Pocock points out, "a case might be made for the view that women could expect more mobility, and even active agency, from a commercially conceived society than from the alternative model of the masculine and self-contained classical patriots."[25] A gender ideology representing the

alienability of women's sexuality, as opposed to the inalienability of male sexuality, commonly emerges to offset this potential for equality. Cibber playfully and provocatively calls attention to this economy's potential "feminization" of men and "masculinization" of women. One would not have to see the play to guess the substance of the lady's "last stake"; in the dedication, however, Cibber represents *himself* as down to his last stake in the gamble of theater: "Great Sums have been ventur'd upon empty Projects, and Hopes of immoderate Gains; and when those Hopes have fail'd, the Loss has been tyranically deducted out of the Actors Salary" (2:196). Cibber's (not necessarily conscious) parallel between the actor/manager's and the lady's last stake further complicates the stated moral against women gamblers, for risky forms of financial circulation destabilize both gender positions and economies of desire that only differing capacities for self-alienation can reinscribe.

The creature to whom gambling unfortunately exposes Lady Gentle in *The Lady's Last Stake* is Sir George Brilliant, Cibber's nastiest fop. George Brilliant confesses to Lord Wronglove that he has reason to hope for the favors of the virtuous Lady Gentle because he has discovered her "over-fondness for play" (2:214). When she plays herself into debt she cannot repay, George tempts her into staking her body against all her losses. George, however, violates the gambling contract and cheats to ensure his victory. Further, when enough money mysteriously arrives to excuse Lady Gentle from her sexual obligation, George refuses to accept it and attempts to rape her. Once Lady Gentle enters the irrational economy of the gaming table, she, like the actors subject to the whims of managers and investors, becomes vulnerable.

On the one hand, then, Cibber counters Centlivre's gambling plays with a lesson about the extraordinary risk that women undertake once they enter such an unstable economy, but the play also suggests the danger of gambling to naturalized ideologies of masculinity. All of Cibber's fops, as Kristina Straub argues, express fluid sexual identities; George Brilliant, however, makes the most explicit declaration of homoerotic desire when he returns the greeting kisses of Lord Wronglove: "And kiss, and kiss again, my Dear," he responds, "By *Ganymede* there's Nectar on thy Lips."[26] As Straub further observes, at an historical moment of the emergence of bipolar oppositions between hetero- and homosexual identity, as well as the bipolar reification of masculine and feminine identity, Cibber's Brilliant comically destabilized both oppositions.[27] Like other fops, George's self-consciousness associates him with feminine consumer vanity. In intriguing gender-crossing symmetry, Lady Conquest, George's former lover, dresses up as her brother, John Conquest, in a bid to foil George's conquest of Lady Gentle. Mrs. Conquest accomplishes as a man what she cannot as a woman: s/he rescues Lady Gentle from George's advances and insists on fighting him to revenge the damage to his/her "sister's" reputation.

In the Mrs. Conquest plot, the gendered division between alienable and inalienable sexuality nearly collapses in the context of irrationally mobile finances. Mrs. Conquest ultimately makes a "conquest" of George Brilliant by putting him in the same financial and thus sexual position as he placed Lady Gentle. And while Lady Conquest achieves this by appearing to risk her own body and finances, she nevertheless takes this risk in male guise and uses it to manipulate Brilliant into marriage. When George arrives to fight "John" Conquest, robbers seize him and attempt to strip him of his clothes and money. They appear to wound "John" Conquest mortally, and when the surgeon reveals the gender of the injured patient, George promises to marry his former lover. Yet Lady Conquest has set up the whole plot, simultaneously staging her own vulnerability to the robbers *and* letting George think that *he* has become just as vulnerable to an illicit and violent economy as had Lady Gentle herself. Lady Conquest appropriates him as a husband just as he had tried to appropriate Lady Gentle as a lover. Gender *positions* remain the same, for Lady Conquest frightens George in male disguise and hires other men to help. *The Lady's Last Stake,* however, forces the feminized George himself down to his last stake: he gives himself (albeit in marriage) after a frightening encounter with men who would rob and strip him. Cibber's play thus raises the unnerving possibility that, in the context of an irrational economy, men might have a "last stake" as well.

While Cibber captures contemporary anxieties about gender difference and the mobility of property in the context of a lesson for women gamblers, Centlivre finds in this popular trope a range of feminist possibilities. In her successful *Gamester,* Centlivre uses gambling to suggest the alienability of male sexuality without, as in Cibber's play, "feminization"; in her *Basset Table,* she uses it to represent the related possibility of women as equally able to circulate property. Through the extreme mobility of gambling, Centlivre finds support for the very feminist individualism that Pocock suggests. At a time when the specter of the woman gambler embodied so many anxieties about gender and financial instability, Susanna Centlivre wrote her first big commercial success about a *man* who can't stop gambling. In *The Gamester,* Centlivre's Valere places himself in sexual danger by his gambling—not exactly in the same way as do women in so many representations, but enough to invite comparison. Valere loves Angellica, at least—as his servant Hector notices—when his luck turns down. Angellica loves him, but fears his bad gambling habit; her wealthy sister, however, loves him as well. Valere's

father has grown so impatient with his son's gambling that he threatens to disinherit him. Gambling, then, stands in the way of Valere's marriage to Angellica not only because she dislikes his addiction, but also because he becomes vulnerable to the advances of any woman who can offer him money.

With limited money from his father, Valere finds he can use his masculine charms to secure loans from women. In the first act, he flatters and flirts with Mrs. Security, but becomes indignant when she will not extend credit to him. Lady Wealthy, Angellica's rich sister, declares the profligate Valere unsuited to Angellica's small fortune, but thinks he would make a good match for her and the vast estate her dead husband left her. Both women offer gifts: Angellica seals her promise of love with her portrait; Lady Wealthy sends Valere money. Lady Wealthy represents herself as powerful, masculine, and sexually aggressive when she positions herself as Jove in this transaction: "I confirm my words," she writes, "in a Golden showr" (44). Valere knows that "when a Widow parts with Money, 'tis easie to read the valuable Consideration she expects"; he feels that his "Virtue's staggering." So although gambling does not expose Valere to literal rape, it turns him into a kind of prostitute and stands in the way of his affective choice in marriage.

Centlivre calls attention to her revisions of sexuality and commodification in part through her repetition and appropriation of Aphra Behn. Like Behn, she hangs out the sign of Angellica, who loves, as Lady Wealthy calls him, "the Gay, the Rover, the unconquer'd Rambler" (47). Centlivre, however, has collapsed the figure of the attractive prostitute and the marriageable lady in her Angellica. Like Hellena, she relentlessly pursues her rover, but like Angellica Bianca, she fully comprehends sexual commodification and attempts to establish a relationship outside of it. But whereas Behn's Angellica cannot escape the commodification of her sexuality in the Rover's eyes, Centlivre's Angellica directly intervenes to prevent Valere's temptation to cast her into the market. Armed with Angellica's picture and Lady Wealthy's hundred pounds, Valere heads to the gaming house and gradually begins to lose his money. At this point, both women have endangered their reputations by trusting him with symbols of their affection. Betting Lady Wealthy's money potentially commodifies *her,* and she becomes greatly distressed when she learns that rumors have begun to circulate about her payment. Angellica decides she must intervene before Valere can circulate the even more dangerous token of her affection, the picture that signifies the potential alienability of her sexuality. She appears at the gaming house disguised as a man, wins all Valere's money from him, and tempts him into staking her own portrait, which she wins as well. Through this intervention, Angellica insists that Valere cannot both have her and commodify her, for once he uses her picture as capital—in the way that he has been using their impending marriage as capital by borrowing against it—he no longer possesses proof of their constant love. Nevertheless, using Angellica's portrait as capital erases any difference between their relationship and Valere's potential prostitution to Lady Wealthy after accepting and losing her money. Further, he would have symbolically prostituted Angellica by staking her portrait to another man. Forced into this recognition by Angellica's trick and overcome with regret, Valere finally vows to leave off gambling. Lady Wealthy escapes commodification as well, for her admirer Lovewell falsely and gallantly claims that he had, out of jealousy, spread a spurious rumor that the lady had given money to Valere, compromising his own reputation to save hers. Centlivre, then, uses the symbolic economy of gambling to suggest the equal vulnerability of men and women to sexual alienability. In order to merit a happy marriage, Valere must learn not to commodify Angellica, but he must also escape commodification himself. In spite of the sexual vulnerability of both Angellica and Valere, however, the ending of the play, like so many "reformed rake" plots, creates as much ambivalence as it resolves. The end leaves us not so much with the specific anxiety that Valere will return to the gambling table, but with an uneasiness about Angellica's marriage to a man who was willing to stake her picture, her reputation, and thus her very self. Sexual commodification threatens both characters, but gender differences nevertheless remain apparent through Valere's capacity symbolically to "sell" Angellica. She can claim no property in him, and therefore has no such equivalent power. Angellica can rescue herself only by buying herself back, and she can do that only by temporarily inhabiting the position of masculine individual at the gaming table.

Following up on the success of **The Gamester,** Centlivre next wrote **The Basset Table,** a play that addresses the popular moral concern with women and gambling. **The Basset Table** resembles Cibber's *Lady's Last Stake* and may indeed have provided a source for it. Centlivre's Lady Reveller stays up all night gambling, eventually loses money, and must borrow from Sir James Courtly. Courtly then demands her body in exchange for his money, insisting that no woman can claim virtue who spends so much time at the basset table. Reveller's true love, Lord Worthy, apparently saves her from Courtly's rape attempt, and she swears off gambling thereafter. Cibber finds in Centlivre's plot the potential to specularize anxieties about the mobility of property and the instability of gender; **The Basset Table,** however, maintains confidence in possessive individualism, for her characters never truly face the bodily alienation that Cibber proposes. In this play Centlivre responds to the gendered positions of self-ownership by attempting to refute difference more optimistically: her lady cannot lose her "last stake."

Further, Centlivre includes in this play a subplot about the lady scientist Valeria, whose intellectual interests cheerfully, comically, yet somewhat ambivalently suggest the potential for women's equality and full individuality.

Cibber specularizes a mobile economy's potential destabilization of masculine selfhood in the context of assumptions that gambling endangers female virtue. From this perspective, women cannot fully inhabit the position of "individual" because they remain constantly available, willingly or not, to contracts of sexual (and self) subordination. In *The Lady's Last Stake,* then, it is not so much that gambling simply turns sexual access to Lady Gentle *into* a commodity; rather, sexual integrity is assumed to be alienable and open to contracts—her last piece of property, but one that is not even properly hers to stake.[28] In **The Basset Table,** however, Centlivre explores the possibility of women's sexual selves as inalienable: Lady Reveller and Valeria provide sharply and comically contrasting versions of femininity, but they nevertheless have in common a struggle over sexual self-ownership. Sir Richard Plainman, who battles to control his niece Lady Reveller and his daughter Valeria, swears that he will "find a way to humble" Reveller's insolence and berates her for gambling. Centlivre, however, gives Lady Reveller the most advantageous position from which to counter her uncle: that of a rich widow. "Widdows are accountable to none for their Actions," the lady's servant Alpiew declares (5). Lady Reveller laughs at her uncle's warning that "For she whose Shame, no good Advice can wake, / When Money's wanting, will her Virtue Stake" (6). Centlivre theatricalizes the pure pleasure Lady Reveller takes in manipulating money, and even though Sir James slips her extra money when she loses her own, Lady Reveller never actually gambles down to her "last stake." Cibber's Lady Gentle knows she has staked her virtue; Lady Reveller, on the other hand, refuses to recognize her virtue as vulnerable to being staked. She receives James's gift as the "Genteelest Piece of Gallantry" and becomes incredulous when he expects sex in return: "Basest of Men," she cries indignantly, "I'll have your Life for this Affront" (56). Sir James declares Lady Reveller's virtue a commodity that he now owns: he offers her another fifty guineas and insists, "You are mine; nor will I quit this Room till I'm Possest." Her lover Lord Worthy rescues her from the other man's advances, whereupon Lady Reveller accepts Worthy for her husband. In her understanding of the scene (which, as we will see, is not the only one available), Sir Richard never humbles her, she chooses her own husband, and her virtue remains inalienable.

In spite of Centlivre's clearly feminist intervention into the lady gambler trope, the ending of **The Basset Table** nevertheless reveals the inherent limits of her feminist individualism as the exchange of one form of patriarchy for another. Lady Reveller rejects the traditional patriarchalism represented by Sir Richard, but unwittingly embraces the fraternal patriarchalism of Sir James and Lord Worthy. When Sir Richard's bullying tactics fail to keep his niece away from the gambling table, Lord Worthy and Sir James hatch a plot of their own. Gambling alone stands in the way of Lady Reveller's acceptability as a wife to Lord Worthy. Thus the two men stage her loss at the table, the loan from Sir James, James's threat to her body, and Lord Worthy's opportunity to rescue her. What appears to her as a free choice to relinquish gambling and marry her lover appears to the audience as the successful manipulations of two men. With her marriage to Lord Worthy, she gives up the independence and self-ownership of a widow and subordinates herself (and her property) to a man in exchange for his protection of her from other men. True, Centlivre has Lord Worthy confess his manipulations, giving Lady Reveller the "choice" to marry him or not with full knowledge of his actions. Yet the threat that the two men stage persists, and individualism for Lady Reveller turns out to mean the willing exchange of obedience for protection.

Theatricalizing similar tensions between traditional patriarchy and liberal individualism, Lady Reveller's cousin Valeria openly defies her father. Though indulging in science rather than literature, Valeria represents the generic learned lady, who becomes an object of satire in the early eighteenth century. But just as Phoebe Clinket appears to invoke the woman author in general as well as Centlivre in particular, so Valeria bears a distinct resemblance to the duchess of Newcastle, with whom Centlivre shares, as argued earlier, authorial strategies. Centlivre creates in Valeria a female virtuoso consumed by a passion for science who nevertheless, like the duchess, loves a soldier who supports her intellectual endeavors. The other characters consider Valeria mad, but Centlivre draws this female eccentric with sympathy.[29] Valeria loves both her ensign and her experiments, which she will not leave even to run away with her lover. Sir Richard, in a gesture that expresses his refusal to believe that Valeria can own anything, smashes his daughter's specimens and orders the servants to clean out her laboratory. Sir Richard's patriarchalism remains ineffective in this household, however, for Valeria knows that the servants will not obey. Nevertheless, he has also taken the liberty to choose the rough-edged Captain Hearty for Valeria's husband, insisting that they produce a fleet of sons. Valeria, though, completely baffles the Captain with her learned language; she dismisses him as an "irrational creature," claiming the position of rational creature for herself.

Through Ensign Lovely, Valeria's true love, who tolerates her scientific projects, Centlivre not only suggests an alternative, more egalitarian relationship, but also finds the opportunity to satirize Sir Richard's conception of masculinity. When Lovely proves insufficiently manly for Sir Richard's approval, Captain Hearty helps him mimic virility: "mehap a Woman may not like me," the gentle Lovely declares, disguised as the manly Captain Match, "I am Rough and Storm-like in my Temper, unacquainted with the Effeminacy of Courts" (44). Centlivre's plot, however, ultimately allows Valeria to marry her lover without actually defying her father, for she weds "Captain Match" at Sir Richard's command. This plot, like the Lady Reveller plot, both parodies and reinscribes the alienability of women's sexuality, for the two men fool Sir Richard into believing that he owns Valeria, can trade on her sexual destiny, and can use her body as a vessel through which to produce grandsons. Once again the fraternal patriarchy triumphs over the traditional patriarchy, leaving Valeria both inside and outside of contractual relations.

Lady Reveller's self-ownership in widowhood provides the conditions for her circulation of money; similarly, Valeria struggles with her father for self-ownership as the foundation of her claim to intellectual property. While boastful of his daughter's immunity to the basset table, Sir Richard expresses extraordinary hostility to Valeria's philosophical interests. Centlivre, however, renders him powerless to stop either of these women. As in *The Platonick Lady,* Centlivre finds feminist possibilities in the same mind/body opposition that provides for Locke the basis for several forms of self-alienation. Sir Richard understands Valeria as a body that he owns, a mechanism for creating more men (implicitly under his command): "Oh! such a Son-in-Law—how shall I be Blest in my Posterity? Now do I foresee the Greatness of my Grand-Children; the Sons of this Man shall, in the Age to come, make *France* a Tributary Nation" (44-45). Valeria, however, insists on the inalienability of her heart and soul, distinct from her body:

VAL.

> . . . Oh my Dear *Lovely!*—We were only form'd one for another;—thy Dear Enquiring Soul is more to me—than all these useless Lumps of Animated Clay: Duty compels my Hand,—but my Heart is subject only to my Mind,—the strength of that they cannot Conquer; . . . I here protest my Will shall ne're assent to any but my *Lovely.*

SIR RICHARD.

> Ay, you and your Will may Philosophize as long as you please,—Mistress,—but your Body shall be taught another Doctrine,—it shall so—Your Mind,—and your Soul, quotha! Why, what a Pox has my Estate to do with them? Ha? 'Tis the Flesh Huswife, that must raise Heirs,—and Supporters of my Name.

(46)

From the perspective of paternal authority, Valeria can do anything she wants with her heart and soul. A husband's possession, however, must be more profound. When Sir James suggests to Lord Worthy that he merely carry Lady Reveller away, Lord Worthy refuses:

LORD.

> That Way might give her Person to my Arms, but where's the Heart?

SIR JAMES.

> A Trifle in Competition with her Body.

LORD.

> The Heart's the Gem that I prefer.

(42)

Although Cavendish and Centlivre both find feminist potential in versions of Platonism, the division of the true self from the body takes on a different meaning in Centlivre's post-Lockean individualism. By insisting that everyone owns his own body, Locke represents an owning self distinct from the body. The (masculine) ownership of the body provides the basis through which other forms of ownership become possible, but it also provides the capacity to alienate labor. In her feminist individualism, Centlivre insists that women possess themselves in this same way. Yet clearly in this play self-possession cannot be constructed in a gender-neutral way, for what part of Valeria would be left free if Sir Richard gave her to Captain Hearty to produce grandsons? Centlivre never truly challenges Sir Richard's ownership of Valeria, but merely allows the young men to trick him. For the husband, on the other hand, the sexual/marriage contract clearly has at stake more than a woman's body, for Lord Worthy responds to Sir James's suggestion to rape Lady Reveller not with indignation over the violation of her personhood, but with the observation that rape simply would not satisfy his desire.

Further, in Centlivre's liberal individualism, even the compromised potential self-ownership of Lady Reveller and Valeria does not extend to Mrs. Sago, the citizen's wife who keeps losing money that she does not have. Mrs. Sago functions in a similar way to George Brilliant: as an embodiment of the dangers and anxieties of finance capitalism. If Centlivre allows the unmarried, wealthy ladies various degrees of self-ownership, she also inscribes Mrs. Sago's body and wealth as the property of her husband. Mrs. Sago's unlucky gambling, in fact, parallels her affair with Sir James, for both steal from Mr. Sago. Mrs. Sago draws cash out of her husband through various underhanded manipulations of the credit system. In one instance, she leads her husband to believe that he has bought her a diamond ring, which she returns, keeping his note for basset. She cheats at cards (although it doesn't help her win) and gets credit against her husband's assets without his knowledge,

partly by sending herself gifts on his account and using those gifts to pay back her gambling debts. Thus she has "Imbezell'd," as Mr. Sago accuses her at the end, from the household accounts. Mrs. Sago clearly owns none of the marital property, nor does she have inalienable property in her sexuality: "For that Fair Face," Mr. Sago declares after he has been arrested for debt, "if I turn you out of Doors, will quickly be a cheaper Drug than any in my Shop" (62). Sir James pays Mr. Sago's debts, apparently out of generosity. But in doing so, James not only returns money he won from Mrs. Sago at cards, but also pays her off for her sexual services. Thus, Mrs. Sago's combined status as citizen's wife and married woman keep her from even the compromised individuality that Lady Reveller and Valeria achieve. Married women, which our heroines will soon become, have little to call their own.

In spite of Centlivre's feminist attempts to imagine some women as self-owners and consequently as owners of material and immaterial property, then, *The Basset Table* ultimately demonstrates the limits of Lockean individualism for feminists. Mrs. Sago can only manipulate property illegitimately. As Macpherson and Pateman have in various ways shown, Locke predicates his theory of property on the assumption of an unequal society. Centlivre's feminism allows her to reimagine the division between owners and non-owners somewhat differently from Locke, but her women characters still never truly achieve the equal status as individuals that they commonly insist upon for themselves. They defy tyrannical fathers for benevolent lovers, but remain both makers and objects of their marriage contracts. Those contracts themselves, even in Centlivre, usually exchange obedience for protection. Further, not all women can attempt even this level of autonomy. Perhaps, then, gambling becomes such a popular trope in Augustan drama not only because it dramatizes the risk of finance capitalism, but also because the basset table is literally a zero sum game. Mrs. Sago can never win, Lady Reveller can sometimes win, and Sir James Courtly can always win. In Locke as in basset, property is both finite and mobile: every time somebody wins, somebody else—ideologically inscribed as a non-owner—loses.

Authorship for Centlivre participates in this economy as well. In the dedication to the upholders (undertakers) prefacing *A Bickerstaff's Burying,* Centlivre represents her own ownership of literary property as made possible by the same material/immaterial split that allows Valeria to resist her father's attempts fully to appropriate her. "Gentleman," she comically declares, "I honour you tho' I have no Desire of falling into your Hands, but I think we Poets are in no Danger of that, since our real Estate lies in the Brain, and our personal consists in two or three loose Scenes, a few Couples for the Tag of an Act, and a slight Sketch for a Song, and as I take it, you are not over-fond of Paper-Credit, where there is no Probability of recovering the Debt: So wishing you better Customers, I expect no Return." Authorship consists of the ownership of immaterial property. Comically and morbidly, Centlivre locates her inalienable self-ownership in the brain; as for her body, a skimpy income provides little incentive for the upholders to look forward to possessing it. But even though writing generates immaterial property, authorship nevertheless resembles other games of chance:

> The Gamester Ventures, to improve his Store,
> And having lost, he Ventures on for more.
> The *London Punk,* in Garret shut all Day,
> At Night, with last half Crown she Ventures to the
>   Play.
> The Amorous Cully, meeting with the Miss,
> Ventures at Water-Gruel for a Kiss.
> Since every Man, Adventures in his way,
> Hither our Author ventur'd with her Play.
> And hopes her Profits will her Charge defray,
> If that bright Circle Ventures to adorn her Day.[30]

Everyone circulates what he or she has in the hope of accumulating more. In authorship as in gambling, some improve on their property, some find their estates in ruin, and others cannot get into the game in the first place.

Notes

1. John Mottley, *A List of All the Dramatic Authors, with some Account of their Lives; and of all the Dramatic Pieces ever published in the English Language to the Year 1747.* Appended to Thomas Whincop, *Scanderbeg, or, Love and Liberty* (London, 1747). Quoted in Bowyer, *The Celebrated Mrs. Centlivre,* 80.

2. Barton Booth to Aaron Hill, *A Collection of Letters, Never before printed: Written . . . To the Late Aaron Hill, Esq.* (London, 1751), 80. Quoted in Bowyer, *The Celebrated Mrs. Centlivre,* 82.

3. For Centlivre's foreign sources, see Bowyer, *The Celebrated Mrs. Centlivre,* 78-79.

4. *The Laureat: or, The Right Side of Colley Cibber* (London, 1740), 111-112; quoted in Bowyer, *The Celebrated Mrs. Centlivre,* 80.

5. *The Dramatic Works of Colley Cibber, Esq.,* 5 vols. (London, 1777), facsimile (New York: AMS Press, 1966), 3:5. Future references to Cibber's plays are from this edition and are cited in the text.

6. *An Apology for the Life of Mr. Colley Cibber, Written by Himself,* ed. Robert W. Lowe, 2 vols. (London, 1889; reprint, New York: AMS Press, 1966), 2:3.

7. Cibber, *Apology,* 2:4. Lowe points out that "eighteenpence was for many years the recognized price of plays when published."

8. See Bowyer, *The Celebrated Mrs. Centlivre,* 80-83, for an instructive comparison of passages.

9. Centlivre's *Love at a Venture* was first performed at Bath in 1706. According to eighteenth-century theater historian John Mottley, credited with writing the *List of All Dramatic Authors,* which was appended to Thomas Whincop's *Scanderbeg,* Centlivre acted in this play herself. See Bowyer, *The Celebrated Mrs. Centlivre,* 77-84.

10. Centlivre, dedication to *The Platonick Lady.*

11. See also Kristina Straub's chapter on Colley Cibber's daughter, Charlotte Charke, in *Sexual Suspects: Eighteenth-Century Players and Sexual Ideology* (Princeton: Princeton University Press, 1992), chap. 7.

12. Thomas Wright, *The Female Virtuoso's* (London, 1693), 26. Wright's play was itself inspired by Molière's *Femmes savantes,* which Centlivre and Cibber clearly knew also.

13. Ibid., 25.

14. Abel Boyer, "Letters of Wit, Politicks, and Morality" (London, 1701), 335-356. Nevertheless, "Astrea" adds a postscript, admitting that "I fear I shall go to the Play. I believe *Astrea* would be well enough pleas'd to find *Celadon* there."

15. Centlivre's plays stand out in this period for their positive representation of friendship between women. See also, for example, *The Wonder.*

16. Centlivre's satire of male literary and scholarly ambition has the most relevance here, but her comedies poke fun at a range of masculine foibles.

17. This opposition between knowledge of books and knowledge of the world became a central part of eighteenth-century thought, perhaps best articulated by Samuel Johnson in "The Vanity of Human Wishes." For a brilliant deconstruction of this division, see Joel Weinsheimer, *Imitation* (London: Routledge & Kegan Paul, 1984).

18. In fact, when Lavinia makes a desperate move to get out of marrying him by claiming pregnancy, Sancho generously takes public responsibility for the child to save her honor.

19. See, for example, *The Gamester Law* (London, 1708).

20. [M. Marsin], *The Womens Advocate; or, Fifteen Real Comforts of Matrimony . . . Written by a Person of Quality* (London, 1683), 107-108. The author comforts husbands: "there's the thing gone, which is many times the cause of all his fears, jealousies and disturbances. How many men are there, that curse their wives tayls? which if the women have a faculty to play away, there's a fair riddance of the mens discontent" (108).

21. *Mundus Mulierbris: Or, the Ladies Dressing-Room Unlock'd, and her Toilette Spread in Burlesque* (London, 1690), 4-5. Attributed to Mary Evelyn. The appended "FOP-DICTIONARY" defines "rouleau" as "Forty Nine Guineas, made up in a Paper Roll, which Monsiery F—— Sir J—— and Father B—— lend to losing Gamester, that are good Men, and have Fifty in Return."

22. *The Guardian,* 2 vols., London, 1714, no. 20, 2:193.

23. Ibid., no. 174, 2:503.

24. J. G. A. Pocock, "The Mobility of Property and the Rise of Eighteenth-Century Sociology," in *Virtue, Commerce, and History: Essays on Political Thought and History, Chiefly in the Eighteenth Century* (Cambridge: Cambridge University Press, 1985), 103-124. Although Cibber declared himself an adamant Whig in his *Apology,* the politics in his plays often theatricalize popular anxieties rather than stake out an explicit position. See John Loftis, *The Politics of Drama in Augustan England* (Oxford: Clarendon Press, 1963), 56. Loftis points out Cibber's dependence on Tory ministers in the early part of his career.

25. Pocock, *Virtue, Commerce, and History,* 118.

26. Straub, *Sexual Suspects,* 59. See also Susan Staves, "A Few Kind Words for the Fop," *SEL* 22 (Summer 1982): 413-428.

27. For a good discussion of the construction of feminine identity in the early eighteenth century, see Katherine Shevelow, *Women and Print Culture: The Construction of Femininity in the Early Periodical* (London: Routledge, 1989).

28. Perhaps this is why male chastity provides such a good joke for Fielding in *Joseph Andrews:* men have inalienable property in their bodies, and commodify nothing by violating their virtue.

29. Valeria differs from Cavendish in her interest in experimentation, as opposed to the duchess's preference for reason. Valeria's desire to establish a college for women also recalls Mary Astell. See Ruth Perry, *The Celebrated Mary Astell: An Early English Feminist* (Chicago: University of Chicago Press, 1986). As Perry argues elsewhere, however, Astell more fully recognized the place of women in possessive individualism. See her "Mary Astell and the Feminist Critique of Possessive Individualism," *Eighteenth-Century Studies* 23 (1990): 447-457.

30. Centlivre, prologue to *Love at a Venture* (1706).

Margo Collins (essay date summer 1999)

SOURCE: Collins, Margo. "Centlivre v. Hardwicke: Susannah Centlivre's Plays and the Marriage Act of 1753." *Comparative Drama* 33, no. 2 (summer 1999): 179-98.

[*In the following essay, Collins discusses the relationship between the Marriage Act of 1753 and the popularity of Centlivre's plays. According to Collins, the act, which attempted to prevent clandestine unions by emphasizing the written registration of a marriage, both responded to and raised questions about the power of women's guardians and the efficacy of language—issues that dovetailed with the marriage plots of Centlivre's* Busie Body *and* A Bold Stroke for a Wife.]

The years between 1700 and 1800 saw Susannah Centlivre's plays performed 1,227 times in London theaters. Two plays, *The Busie Body* and *A Bold Stroke for a Wife,* accounted for 822 of these performances.[1] *The Busie Body* was an immediate hit upon opening at the Drury Lane Theatre on 12 May 1709. After eighteen performances in its first season, it averaged more than six performances annually until 1800, thus becoming the most popular female-authored play of the century. The second spot belongs to Centlivre, too. *A Bold Stroke,* first performed on 3 February 1718 at Lincoln's Inn Fields Theatre, enjoyed a relatively successful run of six nights. Yet, unlike *The Busie Body,* this play was not consistently popular with early-century audiences; indeed, after the initial run, it was not produced again in London for ten years. But after 1750 the play's popularity increased markedly—so much so that by the end of the century it was performed almost as often as Centlivre's earlier play.[2]

Only a few critics have attempted to explain the popularity of these two plays. John Wilson Bowyer and Nancy Copeland both attribute the late-century success of *A Bold Stroke* to the popularity of the various actors who played the role of the hero, Colonel Fainwell. Thalia Stathis attributes the success to "cleverly wrought stage business," "plot intrigue," "amusing male roles," "structural unity," and "concentrated action." Jess Byrd credits *The Busie Body*'s popularity to Centlivre's "preference for laughing comedy with an improved moral tone" and characters and a plot that are "amusing but inoffensive, and . . . satisfy the desire of the growing eighteeth-century middle-class audience for respectability on the stage." Similarly, Fidelis Morgan asserts that Centlivre's comedies in general managed to please a "new and more po-faced audience," largely because "compromise and adaptation for the mealy-mouthed were in demand" in the latter half of the century.[3]

These critics are right, to some degree. However, the factors that they identify, either individually or combined, account only partially for the phenomenal popularity of *The Busie Body* and *A Bold Stroke,* particularly when the performance histories of these two plays are compared with those of Centlivre's other plays—plays which, like *The Busie Body* and *A Bold Stroke,* were "amusing but inoffensive."[4] Indeed, most of Centlivre's plays are typical of early eighteenth-century comedies. They trade in dramatic common-places of plots involving young lovers' attempts to marry against the will of the young woman's father or guardian; disguises and letters—misdirected, inter-cepted, or merely fraudulent; and characters that are designedly stereotypical. *The Busie Body* and *A Bold Stroke* are no exceptions. So Bowyer, Copeland, Byrd, and Morgan perhaps cast their claims a bit broadly.

What separates *The Busie Body* and *A Bold Stroke* from Centlivre's other plays, and what more fully explains the popularity of these plays, is their emphasis on the written legalities of marriage. Performed during a period of increasing literacy and legalism, these plays reflect the eighteenth century's anxiety about the gap between one's signature and one's intent, the gap between the written and the spoken word. The plays themselves simultaneously hinge on the idea of the written contract as more legally binding than the spoken contract—particularly when that contract involves mar-riage—and express the concern that the written contract is perhaps as mutable as the spoken contract. I argue that the thematic interest in the written legalities of marriage found in these plays contributed to their popularity because it tapped into a fund of anxiety about marriage that existed throughout the Restoration and eighteenth century but that became particularly perva-sive after the passage of Hardwicke's Marriage Act of 1753. Both the Marriage Act and Centlivre's plays elicited anxieties about the legal forms of marriage, and the tremendous popularity of the plays in the second half of the century suggests that their negotiations of marriage and legalism appealed to a theater-going population concerned with the new limits imposed on marriage.

By examining the congruency of the plays' reception and the shifting legal terrain of marriage, I hope to promote a clearer understanding of the social function-ing of plays that were once highly popular but have not yet proven susceptible to scholarly resuscitation. Ultimately, the curious rhythm of *A Bold Stroke*'s reception calls attention to important developments in social perceptions about youth and marriage brought into high relief by the passage of Hardwicke's Marriage Act in 1753. The play would have been received one way early in the century, another way later on, and it suited the latter part of the century better. A related claim may be made about *The Busie Body,* although its treatment of the marriage theme seems to have appealed more forcefully to pre-1753 audiences than did the same theme in the later play. Both plays are comedies, so both are about youth and marriage. But youth and mar-riage in 1710 weren't what they would be half a century later.

Both plays concern the conflict between desire and will, specifically a young woman's desire to marry against her guardian's will. In each of the two plays, this patriarchal will is embodied in the last will and testa-ment of the heroine's father and in the "blocking force" of one or more guardians.[5] In *The Busie Body,* Miran-da's father's will specifies that she will receive her inheritance when she turns twenty-five but will lose that inheritance if she marries before that time without her guardian's permission. Her guardian, Sir Francis Gripe, plans to marry her himself, thereby gaining permanent control of her inheritance. Thus, in order to marry the man of her choice, Sir George Airy, Miranda must trick Sir Francis into giving her written permission to marry without specifying a partner. Similarly, in *A Bold Stroke* Ann Lovely's father's will makes her marriage practi-cally impossible, as it requires that she have the consent of four very different guardians if she is to marry and keep her fortune of £30,000. The play follows Fain-well's attempts to trick Lovely's guardians into approv-ing her marriage to Fainwell. The plot depends upon the comic convention of disguise and upon each guardian's ability or inability to "read" Fainwell. However, Fainwell is unable to depend solely upon disguise because he must have the guardians' consent in writing, the only legally binding form of consent possible. As the play progresses, Fainwell increasingly relies upon written documents to support his disguises and to fool the guardians. This emphasis on written documentation allows Centlivre, as I shall demonstrate, to evoke her audience's anxieties about the incipient failure of oral promises as legally binding in the face of increasing literacy.[6]

In both plays, the conflict between desire and will is played out in a struggle between orality and literacy. An emphasis on the connection between writing and legal-ism is apparent from the first scene of *The Busie Body* that includes Miranda, who has gone in disguise to meet Sir George in the park. She overhears him negotiating with her guardian for the opportunity to speak to her:

SIR GEO.

Come to the Point, here's the Gold, sum up the Conditions———

SIR FRAN.

(*Pulling out a Paper.*) . . . *Imprimis,* you are to be admitted into my House in order to move your Suit to *Miranda,* for the space of Ten Minutes, without Lett or Molestation, provided I remain in the same Room.

SIR GEO.

But out of Ear shot———

SIR FRAN.

> Well, well, I don't desire to hear what you say, Ha, ha, ha, in consideration I am to have that Purse and a hundred Guineas.

(1.[1])

Sir Francis's reliance on a written contract indicates his belief in the stability of the written word—a belief that is underscored when Sir George comes to visit Miranda. Sir Francis insists upon a strict interpretation of the written contract he and Sir George had agreed upon. When Miranda enters and Sir George "Salutes her," Sir Francis steps between them and says "Hold, Sir, Kissing was not in our Agreement." When Sir George kneels before and Miranda *"gives him her Hand to Raise him,"* Sir Francis again refers to his written contract: "Hold, hold, hold, no Palming, that's contrary to the Articles." Sir George's response to these comments, however, reveals the impossibility of any literal interpretation of a written document. By saying that his kiss is "by way of Prologue," Sir George conflates writing, speaking, and acting, connecting the written contract to the verbal and physical medium of the stage itself. Sir George associates the action of kissing with the spoken element of a play's prologue, which in turn evokes the image of the written prologue to a play—or, for that matter, the written preamble of a legal document. Sir George further links writing, speaking, and acting when he tells Sir Francis to "Keep your Distance, or I'll write another Article in your Guts" and *Lays his Hand to his Sword"* (2.[1]).

However, Sir George himself is confounded by his own conflation of the verbal and the physical in the "dumb scene" with Miranda, who has promised Sir Francis that she will not speak to Sir George. Initially, she makes the promise in order to keep Sir George from discovering that she is the "Incognita" to whom he has previously spoken. Once Sir George says to her, "you must give me leave to make the best Interpretation I can for my Money, and take the Indication of your Silence for the secret Liking of my Person," and gives her a list of physical cues to use to answer his questions, though, Miranda determines to "fit him for Signs" and uses physical gestures not included in Sir George's instructions. By imposing his own interpretation upon the written contract, Sir George has opened a space for Miranda to interpret texts as well, including the "text" of physical "Signs." Although he is willing to use the inherent instability of the written word to his own advantage, Sir George is unable to admit that his own interpretation is as unstable as Sir Francis's.

Jacqueline Pearson has noted that in *The Busie Body,* men and women "fight to impose their own meanings, and questions about meaning are persistent." According to Pearson, "written documents, letters, deeds and will, are repeatedly used in the play to symbolise men's attempt to control women" and "women seek power over their own lives by gaining control over the 'Writings' of men."[7] Indeed, Miranda is the only character in the play who fully understands the importance of writing; moreover, she is the only character who recognizes the instability of interpretations, both of the written and of the spoken word, and she uses this knowledge to her advantage. She convinces Sir Francis that she wants his written permission to marry in order to keep "the malicious World" from claiming that she was tricked into marrying her guardian. Ultimately, she is able to fool Sir Francis because he believes in the reliability of both the written and the spoken word. She tells him that she will marry him but that she will "have everything according to form—Therefore when you sign an Authentick Paper, drawn up by an able Lawyer, that I have your Leave to marry, the next Day makes me yours" (3.[3]). Sir Francis does not realize that the spoken promise and the written permission will be in conflict; nor does he realize that once his "will" has been consigned to paper, he will be unable to control its interpretation. Thus Miranda is able to make promises that she knows she will not keep:

> I am so eager to have this Business concluded, that I have employ'd my Womans Brother, who is a Lawyer in the *Temple,* to settle Matters just to your Liking, you are to give your Consent to my Marriage, which is to your self, you know: But Mum, you must take no notice of that. So then I will, that is, with your Leave, put my Writings into his Hands; then to Morrow we come slap upon them with a Wedding, that no body thought on; by which you seize me and my Estate, and I suppose make a Bonfire of your own Act and Deed.

(3.[3])

Miranda's recognition that her "Writings" are "the most material point" (4.[3]) enables her to control her own life; she recognizes that although both the spoken word and the written word are inherently unstable, the person who controls written documents also controls the interpretation of those documents.

The subplot of *The Busie Body* also relies upon the instability of the spoken and the written word. Sir Jealous, having determined that his daughter Isabinda will marry his friend's son Seignior Diego Babinetto, evinces a simultaneous fear of and dependence upon the written word. In act 2, Sir Jealous sees Whisper, Charles's servant, outside his home, and demands to know if Whisper has a message for anyone in the house. Sir Jealous's fears that someone might be attempting to write to his daughter are of course justified, and the need to control the written word is emphasized when Isabinda's maid Patch drops the letter that Whisper has delivered. Sir Jealous picks it up; and because of his suspicions, Isabinda is unable to keep her appointment with Charles. The letter itself is in code, but Jealous's possession of the letter ensures that he will control its interpretation: "If this Paper has a Meaning I'll find it" (4.[1]). The fact that he interprets the letter correctly, if not exactly—it is indeed a love letter—is less important than the fact that he now owns both the letter and its interpretation. He is taken aback when Patch claims the letter for herself, exclaiming in an aside "What does she mean by owning it" (4.[1]). Once she has "owned" the letter, Patch is able to impose her meaning upon it, again revealing the instability of interpretation.

Sir Jealous's proprietary approach to written texts allows Charles to trick him. Because Sir Jealous has misplaced a letter of his own, Charles is able to disguise himself as Babinetto in the last act of the play. Equipped with a letter that is purportedly from Babinetto's father and that is counterfeited to look like Sir Jealous's friend's handwriting, Charles presents himself to Sir Jealous. Because Charles owns the letter, Sir Jealous does not question his interpretation of it, and allows Charles to marry Isabinda. Sir Jealous's vows that Isabinda would marry according to his will have been undermined by the written word.

A Bold Stroke contains a similar conflict between the written and the spoken word. It differs from Centlivre's earlier play, however, in its insistence upon the ultimate failure of orality. Although both plays question the stability of the written "will," *A Bold Stroke* more clearly demonstrates the inefficacy of the spoken word when compared to written texts. Colonel Fainwell begins his attempt to gain Ann Lovely by approaching her guardian Sir Philip Modelove, "an old beau." Modelove is a fop, and in order to gain his approval to marry Lovely, Fainwell dresses as a fop and approaches him in the park. Modelove, a character type concerned with appearance, is unable to see through Fainwell's disguise. In this scene, Centlivre immediately introduces the motif of the written word when Modelove says that he will "give it under [his] hand" that Fainwell is a gentleman (2.1.164). Not only does Modelove accept Fainwell's disguise at face value, but he is willing to swear in writing that Fainwell is who he pretends to be. Fainwell takes advantage of that compliance by saying "I wish you'd give me your consent to marry Mrs. Lovely under your hand, Sir Philip"—and of course Modelove agrees, saying "I'll do't, if you'll step into St. James's Coffee House, where we may have pen and ink . . ." (2.1.165-67).

Having gained one guardian's signature, Fainwell quickly finds his disguises and his verbal wit inadequate to the task of tricking the remaining three guardians. Indeed, Fainwell's next attempt at subterfuge is undone by a spoken word. When he meets Periwinkle in a tavern, he attempts to convince this "virtuoso" that he is a world traveler who has gathered a collection of fantastic items, including a girdle that causes invis-

ibility. He has almost succeeded (by use of a trap door) in persuading Periwinkle of the girdle's authenticity (thereby gaining Periwinkle's approval) when his disguise is undermined by a drawer in the tavern who calls him by his name. His elaborate disguise is destroyed by a single spoken word. Although Fainwell can, as the tavern proprietor Sackbut says, "lie with a good grace" (3.1.13), this verbal and physical subterfuge is not enough to fool Periwinkle, who, as the best reader of the four guardians, is the most difficult one to fool. Douglas R. Butler has noted that "[w]hen the Colonel tries to win Periwinkle, the motif is magic."[8] Butler specifically draws attention to Betty's choice of verbs, for example, when she says "I shall be the less surprised if the Colonel should conjure you out of the power of your guardians" (1.2.48-49); he claims that this is evidence of Fainwell's status as a magician figure. But the plan fails—as the inherent orality of the verb "conjure," with its connotations of invocation and incantation, almost certainly ensures it will in a play concerned with the written word.

Thus, in his attempt on the next guardian, Fainwell uses a fake letter to support his disguise as a Dutch tradesman, Timtamtirelereletta Heer van Fainwell. This letter, supposedly containing what we would now call "insider information" about the stock market, provides the "proof" that Tradelove needs to place a bet with Fainwell—a bet that he eventually pays off by writing a consent form for Lovely's marriage. Tradelove is undone by greed, and by his unwillingness to maintain control over his own writing. He writes his consent form and says to Fainwell, "you must insert your own name, for I know not how to spell it; I have left a blank for it" (4.4.54-55). Tradelove has left open a space for Fainwell's writing and has thus left his written "will" open to manipulation.

Because one letter works, Fainwell uses another in his next encounter with Periwinkle. Having learned that he needs written words to support his disguises, he adds other written texts to his disguise: a will and a lease. Periwinkle carefully reads both the will and the lease, then, thinking he is signing a lease based on the instructions in his uncle's will, signs his consent for Lovely's marriage to Fainwell. Periwinkle also fails to exert sufficient control over the documents that he signs. His mistake is looking away from the text even for an instance, since in a moment of inattention Fainwell switches the papers to be signed. Thus Centlivre highlights both the difficulty of transferring one's desires into writing and the mutability of the written word once it is in the world.

Fainwell also uses a letter in his encounter with the final guardian, the Quaker Obadiah Prim. This letter supports Fainwell's claim that he is Simon Pure, a preacher and co-religionist. Prim reads this letter carefully, noting that it "recommendeth a speaker," and he accepts Fainwell's spoken claim that he is the speaker mentioned, thus emphasizing Prim's belief that speaking is as legitimate as writing (5.1.53). Once convinced of the veracity of the letter, Prim does not again attempt to read it. He, too, loses control over the written word; he even allows Fainwell to write Prim's statement of consent. Fainwell then reads this statement aloud: "This is to certify to all whom it may concern that I do freely give up all my right and title in Anne Lovely to Simon Pure and my full consent that she shall become his wife, according to the form of marriage. Witness my hand" (5.1.410-13). Prim immediately signs it without reading it himself. The audience of the play is left to "read" the fact that Fainwell must have actually written his own name instead of "Simon Pure" in the consent form.

Repeatedly, those characters in the play who both read carefully and maintain control over the written word seem to have the advantage over those who do not read. For example, Fainwell learns of Simon Pure's visit to the house of Obadiah Prim and his wife because his ally Sackbut steals the original letter for him: "Looking over the letters our postwoman brought, as I always do to see what letters are directed to my house (for she can't read, you must know), I spied this, to Prim, so paid for't among the rest" (4.2.18-21). Fainwell has an advantage because Sackbut reads. Furthermore, Lovely almost ruins Fainwell's plans by refusing to read the letter that he attempts to give her; instead, she drops it on the floor (2.2.129-30). Although Lovely quickly recovers from her mistake by destroying the letter, she almost loses her chance to marry Fainwell because of her refusal to read.

However, Centlivre undermines the privileging of literacy by pointing to the instability of both the written word and the relationship between writing and intent. Tradelove believes that he has tricked the Dutchman into accepting a worthless payment for his debt, because all four guardians must consent to Lovely's marriage. Fainwell's friend Freeman tells Tradelove, "It is not your business to tell [Fainwell] that your consent will signify nothing" (4.2.126-27). Freeman is right. Fainwell already knows that Tradelove's signature signifies nothing—at least, nothing that Tradelove thinks it might signify. Ultimately, the guardians' signatures do not refer to the guardians' desires. Instead, the signatures are open to interpretation. Fainwell may "plead guilty" to tricking the guardians into signing the consent forms, but the law is on his side: he has the signatures (5.1.428). Given that the signed statements support Fainwell's right to marry Lovely, the guardians' desires are finally irrelevant. As in *The Busie Body*, control of written documents implies control of the interpretation of those documents.

The emphasis in both *The Busie Body* and *A Bold Stroke* on written documents pertaining to marriage would have registered differently for pre- and post-1754 audiences. The general concerns about the legalities of marriage that had been part of the *Zeitgeist* of English culture well before Centlivre wrote her two most popular plays became more pressing after the passage of the Marriage Act sponsored by Philip Yorke, Earl of Hardwicke.

The Act, which passed on 4 June 1753 and went into effect the following March, instituted a series of laws regulating ways in which a legally valid marriage could be performed. In effect, it codified marriage in a new, specifically written, way. According to the Act, banns had to be published upon "three Sundays preceding the Solemnization of Marriage during the Time of Morning Service, or Evening Service (if there be no Morning Service)" or a license had to be issued four weeks in advance of the wedding. Minors under the age of twenty-one had to have permission from a parent or guardian in order to marry. The wedding service had to be performed by a minister in front of two witnesses and then entered into a register and signed by the bride, the groom, the minister, and both witnesses.[9] Even the registers were subject to detailed rules, including legislation specifying the kind of paper that could be used and the method of pagination.[10] Any marriage that was not performed according to these requirements was declared void.[11]

The question of what, exactly, constituted legal marriage had been of general concern well before 1753. Indeed, marriage bills similar to Hardwicke's Act had been brought before Parliament in 1677, 1685, 1689, 1691, 1695, 1711, and 1735.[12] In 1686, Henry Swinburne published *A Treatise of Spousals, or Matrimonial Contracts,* a legalistic document that carefully outlines the differences between "spousals *de futuro*" (promises to eventually marry) and "spousals *de præsenti*" (promises that constitute a current, legally binding marriage).[13] Swinburne is careful to note that a couple's intent is more important than any formal ceremony: "Where two intend to Contract Spousals *de præsenti*, there is Matrimony always contracted, although the words import but future Consent only." Moreover, Swinburne claims that "we are not stand upon Terms, but upon truth, and any words will suffice to Contract Matrimony, so that the meaning do appear. . . . [But] how can we *know* a Man's meaning but by his words? Indeed if this meaning of the Parties may appear, namely; That they did *intend* to Contract Matrimony, then although the words import no more but Spousals *de futuro*, the Contract is no less than Matrimony." However, Swinburne's assertion that he values intent above from is undermined by the remainder of the treatise, which concentrates almost exclusively on the legally binding effect of one's spoken words, thereby emphasizing the period's concern over the differences between one's desire (or intent) and one's words. By publishing the *Treatise of Spousals,* Swinburne was in effect attempting to codify verbal promises through a written medium—an act that implies mistrust of the spoken word alone.

Most historians agree that the oral nature of spousals makes it almost impossible to determine how often they were used in place of more official ceremonies.[14] The value of Swinburne's treatise, then, is that it helps to illustrate and indeed probably contributed to what Stephen Parker calls the "moral panic over clandestine marriage."[15] Regardless of how often or even whether informal marriages actually existed, the publication of Swinburne's treatise and the passage of the Marriage Act suggest that many people in the eighteenth century believed that they occurred often enough to warrant concern.

This concern over informal marriages appears to have gathered force in the early decades of the eighteenth century, as cases involving the enforcement of spousals *de præsenti* came to the public's attention. Lawrence Stone notes that in the Consistory Court of Exeter alone, at least eighty-seven cases of this sort were tried between 1660 and 1730, and that "[b]y the 1730s elite public opinion was beginning to turn against the continued toleration of the clandestine marriage system, as shown by growing complaints in the London newspapers. The laity were becoming increasingly exasperated by these scandalous marriage procedures . . . ." Furthermore, Stone notes, "the judges were . . . exasperated by the unreliability of the evidence for clandestine marriages."[16] By 1753, it seems, lawmakers were exasperated enough to legislate against clandestine marriages.

Parker claims that the Marriage Act ensured that "at the very time when patriarchy wanted greater control over the marriage of children, the children wanted to be free of that pressure. . . . The victor was propertied patriarchy."[17] If the law was a victory for propertied patriarchy, however, it was an uncomfortable one, for the Marriage Act remained a source of public debate throughout the latter half of the century. The law was forcibly in the public consciousness for quite some time, as it was read aloud in all parish churches on specified occasions for two years after it was enacted in order to ensure publicity of the Act. The public did not respond particularly well, as one account from November 1753 suggests: "On *Sunday* the 4th, when the minister of *Kingston* in *Surrey,* began (after prayers were over) to read the marriage-act, almost all the congregation went out of the church." In March 1772, *Gentleman's Magazine* reported that

A cause of great consequence was lately determined in Doctors commons, where a marriage that had been solemnized in the church, by license, and consummated,

was declared null and void, in conformity to a clause in the late marriage act. It appeared, indeed, that the husband had obtained the license by swearing that the person, for whom the license was required, was of age, when she was not.—To bastardize the issue of such marriages, seems to have something in it repugnant to the sacred institution.

In 1780, Martin Madan asserted that "the *marriage-act,* by throwing the inclinations of children and wards, as well as their persons, under the absolute power of parents and guardians till the age of *twenty-one,* has, in many instances, proved fatal to their future peace." James Cookson claimed in 1782 that "what is, or is not, marriage, may be a question of no small importance," addressing the same issue that Swinburne had attempted to resolve in 1686.[18] Indeed, the Marriage Act continued to be debated well into the nineteenth century, when it was repealed and re-enacted (with several amendments) in 1823.[19]

A survey of Centlivre's plays indicates that she was almost certainly aware of the controversy surrounding clandestine marriage during her own lifetime.[20] In *The Platonick Lady* (1706), Centlivre signals her knowledge of canonical law with Isabinda's statement that her marriage contract with Sir Charles Richley was made by her father "in my Nonage, and the Barter's illegal" (1.2)—the contract, that is, is unenforceable because it was not ratified by Isabinda herself after she had reached twelve, the age of legal consent for women. Isabinda's own vows to Belvil, however, are presented as binding; in the final scene of the play, Belvil says of Isabinda, "this Lady is my Wife by Promise, five Years ago in *France* we plighted Faiths, and nothing now shall part us" (5.[1]). In fact, Centlivre's plays almost invariably present a verbal contract between adults— spousals *de præsenti*—as morally binding, regardless of its legal status. In *The Perjur'd Husband* (1700), Centlivre's first play and only tragedy, Alonzo clearly believes that Aurelia's spoken vows morally, if not legally, bind her to him:

[Aurelia]

. . . know base *Alonzo,*
That from this moment I resume my Freedom,
I disingage you from your former Vows,
And will henceforth be Mistress of my self.

[Alonzo]

. . . . Madam, I hope you do but try my Love:
I cannot think *Aurelia* would be false.
Besides, you can't recal what's registred in Heaven.

Aur.

Then stay till we come there—There you'll have witness.

Alon.

Witness!
Oh! Faithless, perjur'd Woman canst thou think,

Upon thy self and bid me call my Witness?
Yes, you are mine—By all the Gods, you are.

(3.1)

Moreover, the character Bassino—married to Placentia but in love with Aurelia—makes it clear that he also considers Aurelia's vows to Alonzo as binding as his own marriage vows when he says "Honour and Justice tell me I'm *Placentia*'s, / And that *Aurelia* is *Alonzo*'s Bride. / To him she gave her Virgin Vows" (4.1). Perhaps the most striking example of Centlivre's attitude toward spousals, however, occurs in Centlivre's last play, **The Artifice** (1721; printed 1723). In this play, Ned has exchanged vows with Louisa, then abandoned her in order to marry the wealthy Olivia. In the fourth act, Louisa pretends to have poisoned both herself and Ned because he has been unfaithful, and says to him:

> Call to Mind, who witness'd to your Vows;
> By whom your [*sic*] swore when first our Faiths were
>   plighted.
> It was by yon All-seeing Power Above,
> At whose Tribunal we shall soon appear.
> Death summons now our trembling Souls to Tryal;
> Stript of Excuses, Custom, and Evasion;
> This guilty Deed of mine will fall on Thee.
> There, there, our Marriage Contract is recorded;
> There is a Judge from whom you can't Appeal:
> Your Jury can't be Brib'd to save you:
> Your casting Witness is your broken Vows!

(4.[3])

Ned's reply—"Methinks, her Words pierce, like a Dagger, thro' me"—demonstrates his sense of guilt; he knows he has behaved inappropriately. His decision to marry Louisa before they die is rewarded at the end of the play with the revelation that Louisa has a fortune of £40,000, an indication that Ned's choice to honor his spousal vows was the right one, even though it was made when he thought he was dying. Centlivre's use of spousals can be explained in part, of course, as dramatic commonplace. Her consistent support of the validity of those vows, however, demonstrates an underlying conviction that consent, not ceremony, makes a marriage.

In **Love at a Venture** (1706), Centlivre presents a conversation between two young women:

[BELIZA]

> . . . you know your Father has dispos'd of you, and I'm affraid won't be prevail'd upon to alter his Mind.

[CAMILLA]

> Ay, there's the only Bar to all my wishes; why shou'd our Parents impose upon our Inclinations, in that one Choice which makes us ever Happy, or ever Miserable.

[BELIZA]

> 'Tis an unjust Prerogative Parents have got, from whence I see no deliverance without an Act of Parliament.

(2.[1])

When that Act of Parliament came in the form of the Marriage Act, however, it did not support children's right to choose a partner, but rather parents' right to constrain that choice, and the debates surrounding the Marriage Act throughout the century focused largely on the issue of children's obedience to parents. After 1754, the Marriage Act and Centlivre's plays were demonstrably evoking similar anxieties. In 1767, one pamphleteer asserted that "the late Marriage Act, *so wisely* calculated 'for the better preventing clandestine marriages,' and flattering the power of parents and guardians, has only served to stimulate the invention of their children and wards, to cast about how they might best elude the force of the act."[21] That same year, Arthur Bedford's *The Stage the High Road to Hell* criticized comedy in general, claiming that "disobedience to parents seems to be inculcated as a virtue by the comic authors, as, in most of their pieces, young women marry libertines against the consent of their parents and guardians, whose characters are always represented in the most ridiculous and disadvantageous light." He condemned *A **Bold Stroke** specifically for encouraging children to disobey their parents, asserting that Fainwell's success in tricking the guardians encouraged such actions "as laudable and praise-worthy."[22] In 1782, Cookson expressed his concerns about the Marriage Act's detrimental effects:

> When I consider the different situations of youth, as indulged in or opposed in their inclinations, I find myself inclined to declare, not against the laws of my country, but against *paternal* severity. . . . When youth are inconsiderately deprived of the object of their choice, consequences disagreeable and ruinous may be expected. On the side of the male, dissipation, folly and debauchery; on that of the female, if there is great delicacy of constitution, death; or else, equally lost to her friends and the public, she herds with those abandoned and wretched women, where *disease* soon puts a period to a disgraceful and hated life; and thus ends many a fine woman, who might otherwise have been ranked among the most *amiable of wives* and *of mothers*. This proceeds not from any defect in our system, but from the *abuse* of discretionary power lodged with parents and guardians.[23]

Centlivre's plays, while obviously not claiming that depriving children of the right to choose marriage partners might lead directly to prostitution, nonetheless advocate eliminating the possibility of abuse of parental discretionary power. Indeed, the plays advocate the elimination of the power itself.

Thus, the issue of parental power over children's marriages was inherent to both the Marriage Act and the plays. The fact that this power had been codified by the Act might well have made **A Bold Stroke** and **The Busie Body,** with their depictions of young couples using writing to subvert the written legalities of marriage, both more threatening to proponents of the Act and more appealing to its opponents. According to its framers, the Marriage Act would prevent clandestine marriages, bigamy, and "all commerce between the sexes except in Marriage."[24] Ultimately, the Marriage Act served to protect the landed, monied classes from fortune seekers. A male heir no longer had to fear that a pregnant woman might force him to marry her because he had promised to do so, and underage heiresses could no longer be seduced into marriage without paternal approval. As Eve Tavor Bannet points out, in practice the new law meant that a "couple's private verbal promises to live together as man and wife no longer had any force in law," whereas before 1754 verbal promises of marriage were often legally binding.[25] Indeed, the Marriage Act explicitly refuted Swinburne's earlier differentiations between spousals *de futuro* and spousals *de præsenti*: "No suit shall be had to compel a celebration of marriage upon pretence of any contract, whether the words of such contracts were in the present or future tense."[26]

In effect, the Marriage Act moved marriage from the realm of orality to the realm of literacy. The legal apparatus surrounding the enforcement of the law underscores the emphasis on literacy because it indicates that the registration of a marriage was considered more important than the marriage ceremony itself. Clergymen found guilty of performing marriage ceremonies without observing the law's basic requirements were subject to deportation to the colonies.[27] Anyone who engaged in any irregularities concerning the written elements of marriage was subject to more severe consequences: "False entry, license, or certificate, or destroying register books are felony, in principle and accessary, and to be punished with death."[28] As Bannet notes, "the Marriage Register acted very much like a copyright. . . . As copyright ensured that texts could be attached and attributed to authors, the Marriage Register ensured that women could be attached and attributed to a husband."[29] And like the copyright laws, the laws regarding the marriage register indicate a simultaneous reliance upon and fear of the written word.[30] Thus the Act, like *The Busie Body* and *A Bold Stroke*, privileges literacy while evincing concerns that literacy is no more stable than orality.

The Busie Body remained popular throughout the eighteenth century, and *A Bold Stroke*'s performance history indicates that it appealed more strongly to audiences in the latter half of the century than it had in the first half. The continuing popularity of these two admittedly conventional plays is in part a product of the different affective registers of pre- and post-1754 performances. The increased popularity of *A Bold Stroke* in the latter part of the century particularly points to heightened concerns about the written legalities of marriage after 1754. Butler correctly notes that Lovely's fortune "is basically a plot device to keep the lovers

from eloping, which would eliminate the problems of the guardians."[31] The same is true of Miranda's fortune in *The Busie Body.* At least, the fortunes are plot devices before 1754—in those earlier performances, the guardians' signatures were necessary so that the heroine of each play could keep her fortune. In 1709, during the first performances of *The Busie Body,* the audience would have recognized Miranda's desire to keep her fortune once she marries Sir George as the primary issue at stake. After the passage of the Marriage Act, however, marriage itself was at stake; in post-1754 performances of the two plays, the audience could interpret the guardians' signatures as inherently necessary for the young couples to marry at all, much less to retain their fortunes.

Furthermore, in 1718 performances of *A Bold Stroke,* when Fainwell says to Tradelove "This maiden is my wife . . . and thou hast no business with her" (5.1.461-62), he is possibly right—his statement that she is his wife, combined with her earlier comment that "[h]e promised to set me free, and I, on that condition, promised to make him master of that freedom," might be legally binding (1.2.43-45). According to the definitions in Swinburne's *Treatise,* Fainwell's use of the present-tense verb constitutes a "spousal *de præsenti,*" equivalent to a marriage. The same is true of the agreement between Miranda and Sir George. The audience of *The Busie Body* is given no indication that any formal marriage ceremony has taken place. Indeed, Miranda is still packing to leave when Sir Francis comes home. In the final scene of the play, however, Sir George takes Miranda by the hand and says to Sir Francis, "you [have] nothing to do with my Wife, Sir" (5.[4]). Patsy S. Fowler claims that "Centlivre points out the powerless predicament that many women found themselves in because of marriage laws." Furthermore, according to Fowler, "not only does Centlivre challenge male authority, but she also insinuates that because women are not allowed to make the laws, they are forced to break them."[32] However, before 1754 Miranda and Lovely might have had recourse to the ecclesiastical courts in order to force Sir George and Fainwell to keep their promises of marraige. After 1754, though, these promises would register as simply promises, not as contracts—would, in fact, almost certainly provoke a comparison with the terms of the Marriage Act and thus serve as a reminder that the verbal promise had become secondary to the written statements.

Ultimately, in its move from orality to literacy, the Marriage Act intersects meaningfully with *The Busie Body* and *A Bold Stroke,* given the plays' concern with the written consent of the guardians and the inefficacy of verbal discourse in general. And of course the Marriage Act, like Centlivre's plays, is predicated on a conflict between desire and will—the desire of a couple for marriage and the will of the courts that the marriage exist only under certain terms. In post-1754 performances, the plays would certainly have spoken to the anxieties that the Act elicited, particularly in young men and women concerned about their newly limited options for marriage. Paula R. Backscheider argues that female playwrights of the Restoration and early eighteenth century "were re-negotiating elements of the patriarchal ideology such as 'woman' and woman's 'place' as well as things of crucial importance for women's lives such as 'satisfactory courtship,' 'good marriage,' and options for single women. . . . Women were seeking to wrest away man's power to define women's nature, needs, aspirations, and acceptable conditions of existence."[33] And while the popularity of Centlivre's plays almost certainly resulted in part from their re-negotiation of patriarchal ideology, their continued success after 1754 had less to do with women "seeking to wrest away man's power" and more to do with the fact that the play appealed to both men and women whose definitions of marriage and courtship had been radically challenged by a new law. When they were performed in 1709 and 1718 respectively, **The Busie Body** and **A Bold Stroke** reassured young couples that they should have what the character Fainwell in **A Bold Stroke** calls the "liberty of choice" in marriage that "sweetnes life" for both husbands and wives (5.1.563-64). When performed after 1754, the plays acted as two of the "models" that Backscheider claims "tend to shape the possibilities and institutions open to human beings at a given moment in history and how those possibilities and opportunities are regarded."[34] They showed both women and men that the patriarchal will could be circumvented, even when that will had been legalized, codified, written down.

Notes

1. See *The London Stage, 1660-1800,* ed. William Van Lennep et al., 11 vols. in 5 parts (Carbondale: Southern Illinois University Press, 1960-68), in particular the Index volume (compiled by Ben Ross Schneider, Jr., 1979), 138-41, for a complete listing of performances.

2. See Judith Phillips Stanton, "'This New-Found Path Attempting': Women Dramatists in England, 1660-1800" in *Curtain Calls: British and American Women and the Theater, 1660-1820,* ed. Mary Anne Schofield and Cecilia Macheski (Athens: Ohio University Press, 1991), 333; Stanton ranks the plays by the number of years in which they were produced. See also Richard C. Frushell, "Marriage and Marrying in Susanna Centlivre's Plays," *Papers on Language and Literature* 22 (1986): 16; and John Wilson Bowyer, *The Celebrated Mrs. Centlivre* (Durham, North Carolina: Duke University Press, 1952), 217.

3. Bowyer claims that *A Bold Stroke* became particularly popular when the famous comedian

Shuter began playing the role of Fainwell in 1758 (216). Copeland follows Bowyer's lead, tracing the history of the actors who played Fainwell from 1763 through 1797; see introduction to *A Bold Stroke for a Wife,* ed. Nancy Copeland (Peterborough: Broadview, 1995), 28-31. Thalia Stathis, introduction to *A Bold Stroke,* xxiii; Jess Byrd, introduction to *The Busie Body* (Los Angeles: Augustan Reprint Society, 1949), i; Fidelis Morgan, *The Female Wits: Women Playwrights of the Restoration* (London: Virago, 1991), 329. All references to *A Bold Stroke* are to Stathis's edition; most of Centlivre's other plays can be found in *Three Centuries of Drama: English 1701-1750* (New York: Readex Microprint, 1960).

4. Of Centlivre's seventeen other plays, only *The Wonder! A Woman Keeps a Secret* enjoyed a similar level of popularity, with 239 London performances before 1800. During the same period, *The Gamester* (1705) was performed eighty-three times, *Love's Contrivance* (1703) was performed twenty-four times, and *The Man's Bewitch'd* (1709) was performed eleven times. Each of Centlivre's other plays was performed fewer than ten times before 1800.

5. For an analysis of Centlivre's use of "blocking figures," see Frushell, "Marriage and Marrying."

6. *A Bold Stroke* is not, of course, unique in this respect. See, e.g., John P. Zomchick's discussion of *Clarissa* in his *Family and the Law in Eighteenth-Century Fiction: the Public Conscience in the Private Sphere* (Cambridge: Cambridge University Press, 1993), 58-104.

7. Jacqueline Pearson, *The Prostituted Muse: Images of Women & Women Dramatists 1642-1737* (New York: St. Martin's, 1988), 221-22.

8. Douglas R. Butler, "Plot and Politics in Susanna Centlivre's *A Bold Stroke for a Wife,*" in *Curtain Calls,* 369.

9. Hardwicke's Marriage Act of 1753 was originally presented to parliament as the Clandestine Marriage Bill and enacted as Stat. 26 Geo. II. c. 33. For parliamentary debates surrounding its passage, see William Cobbett, *Parliamentary History of England,* 36 vols. (London: T. C. Hansard, 1806-20), 15:2-86. The Act itself is abstracted in a variety of eighteenth- and twentieth-century sources; see, e.g., "Some Account of the Statute to Prevent Clandestine Marriages" in *Gentleman's Magazine* 23 (1753): 399-400; R. B. Outhwaite, *Clandestine Marriage in England, 1550-1850* (London: Hambledon, 1995), 169-71; Stephen Parker, *Informal Marriage, Cohabitation and the Law, 1750-1989* (New York: St. Martin's, 1990),

29-31; and Eve Tavor Bannet, "The Marriage Act of 1753: 'A Most Cruel Law for the Fair Sex'," *Eighteenth-Century Studies* 30 (1997): 233-54.

10. Parker, *Informal Marriage,* 30.

11. It is important to note that even before the passage of the Marriage Act, English canonical law had required couples to publish banns or obtain a license and to participate in a public ceremony in the parish church between 8 a.m. and noon. However, failure to comply with these rules affected only the legality of a marriage, not its validity. A "clandestine marriage," as any irregular marriage was termed, was illegal, but valid nonetheless. Thus the Marriage Act differed from canonical law in that it invalidated marriages that did not follow the prescribed forms and required written documentation to prove that those forms had indeed been followed.

12. Randolph Trumbach, *The Rise of the Egalitarian Family: Aristocratic Kinship and Domestic Relations in Eighteenth-Century England* (New York: Academic Press, 1978), 102. Most of these bills passed in the Lords but failed in the Commons.

13. The *DNB* (*Dictionary of National Biography: from Earliest Times to 1900,* ed. Sir Leslie Stephen and Sir Sidney Lee, 22 vols. [since 1917; reprint London: Oxford University Press, 1937-38], vol. 19, 228-29) notes that Swinburne was trained in the law at Oxford, was a proctor in the ecclesiastical court at York, and eventually became commissary of the exchequer and judge of the consistory court at York. He is best known for his *Briefe Treatise of Testaments and Last Wills;* both this treatise and the *Treatise of Spousals* are "important from their intrinsic merit, and from being the first written in England on their respective subjects" (229). The following quotations come from the *Treatise of Spousals, or Matrimonial Contracts* (London: S. Roycroft, 1686), 63-64.

14. See, e.g., Parker, *Informal Marriage,* 33-36; Outhewaite, *Clandestine Marriage,* 2-22; and Roger Lee Brown, "The Rise and Fall of the Fleet Marriages" in *Marriage and Society: Studies in the Social History of Marriage,* ed. R. B. Outhewaite (New York: St. Martin's, 1981), 117-35. Cf. Lawrence Stone, *Uncertain Unions: Marriage in England 1660-1753* (Oxford: Oxford University Press, 1992), 16-17. Stone claims that clandestine marriages required the presence of two witnesses; what he does not acknowledge is that witnesses became necessary only when a marriage by spousals was contested. Any evidence of the overall use of spousals is anecdotal, given that the inherently oral nature of spousals precludes official records of any spousals that were not contested.

15. Parker, *Informal Marriage,* 34.

16. Stone, *Uncertain Unions,* 21, 29.

17. Parker, *Informal Marriage,* 31.

18. *Gentleman's Magazine* 23 (1753): 538; *Gentleman's Magazine,* 42 (1772): 149-50; Martin Madan, *Thelyphthora; or, a Treatise on Female Ruin* (London, 1730), 59n.; James Cookson, *Thoughts on Polygamy* (Winchester, 1782), 456.

19. Parker, *Informal Marriage,* 48.

20. Gellert Spencer Alleman notes that 69.2% of Centlivre's plays written before 1714 include a clandestine marriage, but does not differentiate between those marriages performed in the presence of clergy and those comprised solely of spouses. See Alleman, *Matrimonial Law and the Materials of Restoration Comedy* (Wallingford, Penn.: n.p., 1942), 82.

21. *A Scheme to Pay Off, in a Few Years, The National Debt, by a Repeal of the Marriage Act* (London, 1767), 13.

22. Bedford, *The Stage: The High Road to Hell* (London, 1767), 16.

23. Cookson, *Thoughts on Polygamy,* 448-449.

24. *Letter to the Public Containing the Substance of What Hath Been Offered in Late Debates upon the Subject of the Act of Parliament for the Better Preventing of Clandestine Marriages* (London, 1754), 18.

25. Bannet, "The Marriage Act," 235.

26. "Some Account of the Statute," 399.

27. At least two clergymen were convicted and transported under this law. In 1756, John Wilkinson and John Grierson were found guilty of performing marriages "without first Publication of Banns of Marriage in that Behalf, or without any Licence, first had and obtained of a Person having Authority to grant the same, in Contempt of our Lord the King, and against the Statute in that Case made and provided." The transcripts of these trials are interesting in that the prosecution focuses largely on the issue of written parental consent. See *Select Trials,* vol. 3 (London, 1764), 231-37, 245-53.

28. "Some Account of the Statute," 399. Although I have not found any cases involving actual executions under this law, the fact that the law existed at all points up the heightened concerns over the written legalities of marriage.

29. Bannet, "The Marriage Act," 240.

30. Given the severity of the penalties, the exact form the register entries should take was of major concern before the Marriage Act went into effect,

as the law did not initially offer specifications. For an example of one detailed suggestion, see "Forms of Registering Banns and Marriages," *Gentleman's Magazine* 24 (1754): 106-07.

31. Butler, "Plot and Politics," 366.

32. Patsy S. Fowler, "Rejecting the Status Quo: The Attempts of Mary Pix and Susanna Centlivre to Reform Society's Patriarchal Attitudes," *Restoration and Eighteenth-Century Theatre Research,* 11 (1996): 56.

33. Paula R. Backscheider, *Spectacular Politics: Theatrical Power and Mass Culture in Early Modern England* (Baltimore: Johns Hopkins University Press, 1993), 69, 83.

34. Ibid., 85.

Brean S. Hammond (essay date 2000)

SOURCE: Hammond, Brean S. "Is There a Whig Canon? The Case of Susanna Centlivre." *Women's Writing* 7, no. 3 (2000): 373-90.

[*In the following essay, Hammond considers Centlivre as a test case for the construction of a Whig school of literature that would stand in contrast to the Tory writers—including John Dryden, Alexander Pope, Jonathan Swift, and John Gay—who have traditionally dominated English studies. Hammond argues that Centlivre demonstrates Whig political sympathies with respect to specific political figures and events, but that she writes with a worldview correspondent with her Tory contemporaries.*]

Book the Second of Pope's *Dunciad* closes with a contest for would-be critics. They have to listen to the sentences of Henley and the verses of Sir Richard Blackmore without nodding off. The named contestants are a motley crew of atheists and Whigs. One of them is Susanna Centlivre—a child prodigy, Pope's note explains, whose prodigiousness, he snidely insinuates, seemed to become the gift of prophecy in later life:

> Mrs. Susannah Centlivre, wife to Mr. Centlivre, Yeoman of the Mouth to his Majesty. She writ many plays, and a song (says Mr. Jacob, vol. i. p. 32) before she was seven years old. She also writ a ballad against Mr. Pope's Homer, before he begun it.[1]

Centlivre had been a member of the Whig circle centred on the publisher Edmund Curll for many years and had first crossed Pope's path in 1716.[2] Her party politics were entirely at variance with Pope's, and the two writers certainly perceived themselves as at the opposite ends of a spectrum. Nevertheless, it can be argued, and has been by me, that artistically they were not worlds

apart. In chapter 6 of my book *Professional Imaginative Writing in England* [*PIW*], I contend that Pope's most important early poem, *The Rape of the Lock,* deploys a novelised *mise-en-scène* with which his readers would be already familiar. Centlivre's early plays **The Gamester** and **The Basset Table** (both 1705), contain scenes that interestingly pre-empt the climactic rape scene in Pope's poem, deploying a social geometry very similar to Pope's.[3] I go on to argue that both writers are caught in a dialectical double movement that enables Pope to take advantage of what Centlivre has to offer while drizzling ironically reconstructed epic conventions over the social ambience she so successfully represents. It is a seminal argument in *PIW* that Scriblerian satire capitalises on forms of energy that it simultaneously affects to despise. Perhaps the most spectacular example of this is that the central spatial metaphor of *The Dunciad,* the cave that is the dwelling-place for impoverished poets, had been deployed in 1715 by Lewis Theobald, Pope's much-maligned hero in the early *Dunciad,* in a poem called "The Cave of Poverty", to which Pope's imagination is undeniably indebted.[4] The point can be further illustrated by another example of Centlivre's work. In her **The Wonder: a Woman Keeps a Secret,** premiered in 1714 at Drury Lane, there is a scene in Act 3 in which Don Felix's servant Lissardo has just assured his inamorata, Inis, that he has not seen her rival, Flora, since he came to town, when—*enter Flora.* The scene quickly degenerates into trading of insults between the women and actual bodily harm, punctuated by moments at which they gather forces to attack Lissardo together, and by moments at which he assures each of them that he loves only her. At one point, Lissardo calls attention to the comparison between his predicament and that typical of heroic tragedy *à la* Dryden and Lee (specifically here to Lee's *The Rival Queens*), where the hero is torn between two lovers:

LISS.

> So! Now am I as great as the fam'd Alexander. But my dear *Statira* and *Roxana,* don't exert yourselves so much about me: Now, I fancy, if you wou'd agree lovingly together, I might, in a modest Way, satisfy both your Demands upon me.[5]

The emotional dynamic of this scene is precisely imitated by Gay in *The Beggar's Opera,* II.xiii, though transposed to the minor key of the condemned hold; and the comparison with heroic tragedy is rendered not by explicit allusion but by Polly Peachum's affected idiom. Gay captures the theatrical energy of this scene in Centlivre's well-known and hugely popular play and frames it in further layers of irony, so that the popular comic dramatist Centlivre's scalp is added to those of the seventeenth-century heroic tragedians.

What these examples suggest is that, however at variance Centlivre and the Scriblerians were in party affiliations, their horizons of cultural meaning were shared.

Recently, there have been powerful attempts to argue that in attending to what Louis Bredvold memorably called "the gloom of the Tory satirists", we have not listened to an equally important, and much more optimistic, chorus of Whig voices.[6] It was the historian Caroline Robbins who first presented the idea of a "Whig canon", which comprised, in her conception of it, the major seventeenth-century classical republicans: Milton, Marvell, Algernon Sidney, James Harrington and others. In a widely known essay, J. G. A. Pocock argued that the Augustan inheritors of this tradition are better comprehended under the rubric "Country" theorists or apologists.[7] My concern is not primarily with political theorists, however, but with imaginative writers. In the first section of this article, I will offer a contextualised account of the arguments made in my book, *Professional Imaginative Writing,* in the light of and partly in response to significant work on literary Whiggism being done in Oxford—work that amounts to the promulgation of a Whig canon to trump the older view that a Tory canon existed and had all the best writers. The focus here is on the word "canon" in my title. In the next section, I will suggest that the Whiggish thinking of this "Oxford school" presents some difficulties, and I will try to clarify the central terms of the debate about politics and cultural politics in this era: the focus is now on the word "Whig".[8] Finally, homing in on Centlivre, I will deploy her playwriting career as a test case for the positions taken in the earlier sections.

I

PIW was an extended meditation on Foucault's famous question, "what is an author?", arguing that our modern conception of proprietary authorship developed during the period that came under the book's investigation: 1670-1740. It was also an exploration of one of the most engrossing theoretical questions of the last twenty years: how are literary canons determined? The two questions are intimately related because competing models of authorship lie behind attitudes to literary evaluation that continue to split the academy. At the extremes are the views, on the one hand, that the ascription of literary worth is the most important task for literary analysis and that this is based on aesthetic qualities intrinsic to the text; and on the other, that all value is produced by culturally-determined criteria extrinsic to the work, recognition of which renders evaluation pointless. The former position is embarrassed by the charge of being a defence of vested interests, calculated to ensure that the same texts by the same (mainly male) authors are continuously recycled. The latter fails to explain why certain texts continue to present themselves for evaluation and seem to succeed no matter what cultural criteria are invoked, and is embarrassed by the charge that it rates the *Beano* as highly as the Bible. *PIW*'s foundational assumption was that a post-Kantian prejudice against commercial writing—writing that was

the product of a need to exploit emergent literary markets in the quest for a livelihood—had caused such writing to be relegated to the rubbish heap of literature by accepting the canonising fiats of powerful writers and texts: Dryden's *MacFleckno,* Swift's *A Tale of a Tub* and some later poems like "To Mr. Gay" and "On Poetry: a Rapsody", and pre-eminently, Pope's *Peri Bathous* and *Dunciad.* Women writers would suffer double jeopardy on this hypothesis, deriving from their gender and their supposed commercial greed and ambition. Whole genres, and especially prose fiction—the romance, in the process of mutating into the novel—would be written down, while others—heroic drama, the epic—would be sites of a doomed defensive rearguard action. Further, the real nature of the finest Augustan literary achievement was occluded by an approach to it that was of necessity purblind to its qualities.

Opening up the canon by giving a voice to writers who had been on the receiving end of summary justice, women writers prominent amongst them, was one of the book's endeavours, but this entails a very difficult methodological challenge. To characterise this, it is helpful to consider an important recent book that faces a similar challenge, though in a very different literary period and juggling different ideological counters. David Norbrook's *Writing the English Republic* argues that an entire corpus of Interregnum republican writing has been lost to us because history is written by the victors, and the Royalists won.[9] He redeems from obscurity several writers with whose work this reader, assuredly, was unfamiliar—but he keeps running into the problem of literary value. While writers like George Wither, Marchamont Nedham, Thomas May, Henry Marten, Payne Fisher and others do certainly help us to understand how the republican imagination played upon the events of the Civil Wars, the Regicide, the Commonwealth, the Protectorate and the Restoration, their main value can appear to be as pop-up illustrations for republican ideology. Those works that seem to have value independently of this are (a) the more familiar and expected texts, such as the poems of Marvell and the poems and prose of Milton, and (b) those in which the set towards republican ideology is most indirect and opaque. Marvell's early poems are fascinating because Norbrook can find in them no consistent ideological pattern; and he virtually concedes the inverse relationship between political directness and poetic subtlety at several points in the book. Thus, Marvell's *The First Anniversary* "is the most remarkable of Protectoral poems, an experiment whose very boldness and brilliance worked against its having an immediate political impact" (p. 339), and speaking of Satan in *Paradise Lost,* Norbrook presents it as a virtue that "Milton refuses his readers any easy position of identification, his iconoclasm extending even to potential republican heroes" (p. 445). My points are not made in the spirit of the ungenerous reviewer determined to pillory a book for its faults rather than to celebrate it for its virtues; on the contrary, I am deeply indebted to Norbrook's ideas in the later section of this article. Rather, I recognise in Norbrook's study very similar problems to those I faced and did not solve in *PIW*. A traditional account of literary value would hold that a clear distinction between "great" or "important" writers and those of the second rank lies in the extent to which the former transcend the specific issues of their gestation/publication period, and become available for polysemic interpretation in subsequent eras. To the extent that writers' interest is the ideology they mediate devoid of any independent "literary" value, this standard account runs, they deserve the oblivion to which they will undoubtedly be constrained. The surest way of demonstrating literary value is to find complexity in the ideology, which might derive from literary structure, and prevent ideology from being present in undigested form. To anyone uninterested in the English Civil War or republicanism, this account goes, writers like Payne Fisher are not interesting and cannot be.

The response to this implicit in Norbrook's work is that it is a crippling weakness to be uninterested in republicanism and the English Civil War, because the period is a seedbed for concepts that become very important in later literary history. *PIW* finds a similar route out of the impasse. Enabling Pope's Dunces to speak, the book encounters the objection that they have nothing valuable to say and no interesting ways of putting that nothing—Pope was right! I was reluctant to answer this by refusing to make any value judgements whatsoever. The New Historical strategy of juxtaposing texts from different epistemological domains and different artistic media was freighted with forms of political correctness that proscribed evaluation. One should not, on this dogma, *prefer* some texts to others. *PIW* did not, therefore, adopt the New Historicists' brand of interdisciplinarity and it was not abashed to make judgements. While the book "fearlessly" states its preference for Defoe over Haywood, for example, and for the Scriblerian satirists over many of those writers with whom they came into conflict, it conducts a parallel argument to Norbrook's in contending that all of the writers coming within the book's purview are caught up in forms of cultural politics in which it is vital to be engrossed, and a serious deficiency not to comprehend. "Cultural politics" has a broader sweep than, for example, a writer's opinion on the succession problem or the shortest way with dissenters, but it is more specifiable, one hopes, than "Zeitgeist". In *PIW*, it is specified with respect to a tranche of historical time in terms of writers and writing becoming professional, of the tendency of all imaginative literature towards the domestic and national agenda of the novel ("novelisation", in Bakhtin's term), and the development of a "bourgeois public sphere" first theorised by

Jürgen Habermas.[10] Armed with this conception, I am able to argue as I do, for example, in chapter 4, that the importance of certain writers may indeed be separable from their literary merit. In that chapter, I take a severe view of Blackmore's epic, *Prince Arthur* (1695), because it is all too easily reducible to a philistine, antiartistic ideology that reflects the climate of opinion so perfectly caught by Jeremy Collier in his *A Short View of the Profaneness and Immorality of the English Stage* (1698). Blackmore is an extremely *important* writer, whose vision of the epic figures very prominently in the Whig writing that publicised the emergent bourgeois public sphere—but he is not in my view a *good* writer. Pope's pot-shot in *The Dunciad* at one Whig, Eustace Budgell, attempting to interrupt another (Blackmore) but succumbing to the powers of Lethe, is well taken:

> Thrice Budgell aimed to speak, but thrice suppressed
> By potent Arthur, knocked his chin and breast.
>
> (*Dunciad* B, II.397-8)

In view of my book's argument that there is an important body of writing the cultural politics of which are tantamount to a legitimation of the bourgeois public sphere—is, indeed, the cultural arm of that Whiggish ideological project—I am somewhat surprised to be outflanked by David Womersley in his review of *PIW* published in the *Review of English Studies*.[11] Womersley's objection as stated is that I don't take Blackmore seriously enough, though he would have been more precise to say (because the book does take Sir Richard entirely seriously) that I don't *like* him enough:

> Literary whiggism is an important subject only now receiving the attention it deserves. When it has been properly studied one of the writers whose stock will surely rise is Sir Richard Blackmore. Blackmore marks the limits of Hammond's willingness to pass beyond Pope's view of literature, since for Hammond too Sir Richard is nothing more than a figure of fun. That eerie echo of Scriblerian tones in a book which was born out of a desire to escape from the Scriblerian perspective on the early eighteenth century indicates how much still needs to be done before we can say that we have forgotten *The Dunciad*.
>
> (pp. 359-360)

We will only escape the Scriblerian perspective, according to this, when we can say that Blackmore is as good a writer as Pope. Certainly, when we *can* say that, we *will* have forgotten *The Dunciad,* but that is not a desirable form of amnesia. Womersley's animus derives from the work he has done in compiling his anthology, *Augustan Critical Writing*—a valuable and important piece of work, though I must take issue with some aspects of the introduction he writes to position his selection.[12] Complementary to my own argument in *PIW*, Womersley contends that the period of English literature designated "Augustan" has been conceived in terms dictated by the writers who dominated it. Those dominant voices, he believes, comprise a "Tory" tradition including writers like Roscommon, Buckingham, Dryden, Atterbury and Pope, who have suppressed the voices of those Whig writers—Dennis, Blackmore, Gildon, Welsted and Oldmixon—that now need to be heard. I would not dissent from his characterisation of the emergent military-fiscal state that threw up a generation of money men unaffected by the high taxation imposed upon landowners, who developed a stake in society not grounded upon those values of civic humanism that motivated the landed elite. He goes on to say that there is a fundamental difference in aesthetic values, literary genres, themes and writing procedures between Whig and Tory writers by the first decade of the eighteenth century, because they are speaking for distinctly different sections of the social elite, who ground their authority with respect to different events—Tories to King Charles's Restoration in 1660 and Whigs to the Glorious Revolution in 1688—and who require their cultural products to do different kinds of ideological work. Whig writing celebrates native and domestic, rather than classical models; identifies with the exploits of William III's reign, especially the victory at the Boyne; and in its admiration for the trading, commercial and financial sectors is likely to applaud military success. There are three points that I would wish to make, and somewhat to amplify, about Womersley's analysis. First, I question the adequacy of the terms "Whig" and "Tory" to designate the cultural division that Womersley is indicating. Second, in so far as his argument depends on evaluation, on the claim that, for example, a poem like Blackmore's *Advice to the Poets* (1706) is a good poem—better, indeed, than Pope's *Essay on Criticism*—he may be barking up the wrong tree. Third, in liberating this suppressed canon of writing, Womersley has not emphasised sufficiently what its most persuasive claims to importance actually are.

II

On purely empirical grounds, there are some difficulties in calling the dominant tradition of Augustan writing "Tory". Dryden's first published poem was an elegy for Cromwell, and in his post-Restoration career, he occupied several positions that the label "Tory" is far too simple to designate. Edmund Waller is invoked as the main inspiration for this Tory tradition, but his name was a byword for a turncoat, a poet whose facility could be, and was, placed at the service both of monarchism and republicanism, author both of *A Panegyrick to my Lord Protector* and "To the King, upon his Majesties Happy Return". And did Pope, supposed apogee of this Tory writing, really ground all poetic authority upon the year 1660? *The First Epistle of the Second Book of Horace Imitated* gives at best a mixed impression of the Carolean Court and its effects upon poetry:

> I scarce can think him [the poet] such a worthless thing,
> Unless he praise some monster of a king;
> Or virtue, or religion turn to sport,
> To please a lewd, or unbelieving court.
> Unhappy Dryden!—In all Charles's days,
> Roscommon only boasts unspotted bays.

(ll. 209-15)

In the *Essay on Criticism,* the very poem that is adduced by Womersley as the Tory blueprint, there is a long passage devoted to the emasculating effect of Carolean patronage, in which Pope makes clear that the King's venality did not prepare a soil for great art to flourish:

> In the fat age of pleasure, wealth, and ease,
> Sprung the rank weed, and thrived with large increase;
> When love was all an easy monarch's care;
> Seldom at council, never in a war:
> Jilts ruled the state, and statesmen farces writ;
> Nay wits had pensions, and young lords had wit:
> The fair sate panting at a courtier's play,
> And not a mask went unimproved away:

(ll. 534-41)

Pope's ambivalence is epitomised in his attitude to Rochester and in the views on the period he expressed in several anecdotes recorded by Joseph Spence.[13] Later in his introduction, Womersley refers to the tradition that he wishes to discriminate as "Scriblerian": and it must surely be agreed that the term "Tory" is far too blunt an instrument to embrace the partisan allegiances of all the Scriblerians. For instance, the high point of Scriblerian writing in the late 1720s coincides with a point at which Bolingbroke's charismatic versions of history were persuading Pope's circle that party politics were obsolete. As another instance, recent accounts of Swift's politics have claimed that he is a crypto-Jacobite Tory, a moderate Whig and a radical Whig.[14]

The issue, however, is more conceptual than empirical. What bedevils the discussion, in my view, is the conflation of a particular, and a general understanding of the term "Whig", senses that require discrimination. The term "Whig" is widely recognised as part of a phrase, the "Whig interpretation of history", that refers to a Protestant, nationalist reading of events in the history of the British Isles. This reading, of which Macaulay was a seminal exponent, comes to full self-consciousness in the historiography of the twentieth century. Its ideological grip has been brilliantly expounded (and exposed) recently in Norman Davies's best-selling *The Isles: a History.*[15] The "Whig interpretation" concentrates on the landmark events in the development of Parliament and the English constitution, and is designed to show that Britain's characteristic strengths, those aspects of Britishness that have enabled us to achieve dominance over our European counterparts, depend on a very long, almost unbroken tradition of political liberty and representative government. Since the mid-sixteenth century when King Henry VIII sloughed off papal interference, this has extended also to freedom of worship. Erastian Parliamentary constitutionalism underwrites the British balance that has enabled trade, commercial prosperity, industrial progress, empire, all of which has ensured that even in post-imperial decline the British nation punches well above its weight in global terms. Of all the moments upon which such a reading might focus—the Anglo-Saxon Witenagemot, the Anglo-Norman *curia regis,* Magna Carta, Simon de Montfort's parliament of 1265, the Act of Supremacy of 1534; 1688 is perhaps the single most edifying. The period 1685-88 introduces us to the Whigs as those who ensure the triumph of Parliamentary constitutionalism and lay the foundations for Anglo-Scottish unity (the cornerstone of Britain) in the near future. The particular Whigs are those who enable the transmission of general Whig ideas at the historical juncture when all might have been lost.

The writing that Womersley valorises in the introduction to his anthology is writing that enshrines this way of seeing things, and he appears to argue that it is good writing *because* it does so—*because* his favoured writers obey this ideological imperative. His stance is that of a general Whig celebrating the achievements of the Whigs. Poets who celebrated William's exploits at the Boyne, as did Addison in *The Campaign* (1705), for example, and who rejected the classical tradition of epic writing, may not appeal to others as much as they do to Womersley. They are surely vulnerable to the charges of bellicosity, philistine Modernism (in the Swiftian sense of the term "modern") and Anglophilic Protestant-ascendancy triumphalism of which they were accused. Cited as a particular beauty is a passage from Blackmore's *Advice to the Poets* in which the bard discovers a sublimity adequate to the importance of his subject, Marlborough's campaign in the War of the Spanish Succession:

> 'Tis done. I've compass'd my ambitious Aim,
> The Hero's Fire restores the Poet's Flame.
> The Inspiration comes, my Bosom glows,
> I strive with strong Enthusiastic Throws.
> Oh! I am all in Rapture, all on Fire,
> Give me, to ease the Muse's Pangs, the Lyre.
> How can a Muse, that Albion loves, forbear
> To sing the Wonders of the glorious War?

And thus Blackmore continues on his flight towards the stars. In response to this one can only cite the line from Theobald's *Double Falshood* with which Pope had such sport in *The Dunciad:* "None but itself can be its Parallel". Pope's *Essay on Criticism* is compared unfavourably to this fustian because it can be read as rejecting the Whig manifesto embodied in Blackmore's lines. To pit Whig poetry against Tory to the disadvantage of the

latter is actually to readmit Pope's binarism and play his game, even if one is playing for the other side. It is emphatically not the way to go.

The teleological grand narrative of the Whig interpretation comprises a number of micro-narratives that relate the events of particular historical moments to the overarching pattern. Thus, the period from the accession of James II to the defeat of Jacobitism at Culloden can be framed as such a micro-narrative. And this micro-narrative can be read in different ways by individuals positioned differently with respect to it. Cultural historians are mainly interested, however, in the discourses that legitimised the linkage between the micro- and macro-narratives: in the discourses of liberty, progress and, to some degree explored in *PIW,* politeness and the sublime. Politeness as in Tobias Smollett's words, "the art of making oneself agreeable", was disseminated primarily in periodical writing undertaken by Whig writers, available to readers in newly constituted public spaces. Addison and Steele were forging a subjectivity based on new codes of social interaction and personal awareness. Aesthetic sensibility was crucial here. New vocabularies capable of democratising the discussion of art were central to the cultivation of the bourgeois public self. Womersley is absolutely correct to point to "moments of afflatus" in poems by writers like Blackmore and Montagu as generic elements in Whig poetry and to find them highly significant: but he does not educe this significance. David Norbrook has shown in *Writing the English Republic* that the origin of the English "sublime" is the Parliamentary poetry of the Interregnum. John Hall's translation of *Peri Hypsous, or Dionysius Longinus of the Height of Eloquence* was published in 1652, but prior to it, George Wither amongst others was developing a poetic style adequate to express the excitement of newly "democratic" modes of representation. Sublimity, in the sense of breaking through limits and boundaries, was located in the act of regicide, and an imaginative idiom equal to expressing the liberated self enraptured by access to public modes of debate was Milton's preeminent achievement. Something of this excitement is being recaptured by the Whig writers and theorists in the aftermath of the Revolution, in the constitutional monarchist rather than radical republican liberty that it underwrote. John Dennis is by far the most important theoretician of neo-sublimity in the early eighteenth century, even if Addison and Steele were very much more effective in packaging and disseminating it. The importance of Whig writing is not, in my view, that it is so much better than Scriblerian satire, but rather that it enabled the bourgeois subject by rediscovering Milton and promoting aesthetic canons like expressivity, natural beauty and sublimity, through print, behavioural codes and new spaces of public assembly. Whether or not one likes Blackmore, the cultural politics of this phenomenon are very important: and it is generally true that the

Scriblerians opposed them, even if that opposition should not be narrowly construed as "Tory". More accurately, it is an opposition to what they dimly discerned of the grand Whig narrative. Swift, Pope and Gay had this cultural outlook in common even if one can argue about the precise nature of their partisan commitments. The answer to the question, "is there a Whig canon?" is affirmative, therefore. Its central values are expressivity and the sublime in artistic creation, and appreciation of sublimity, especially in the natural world that for the first time becomes an object of aesthetic attention, in criticism of art. Radical republicanism is its ancestry, and Aaron Hill, George Lillo, James Thomson and the Whig poetry of the 1730s and 1740s are its short-term future.

III

What has already been said of Centlivre and the Scriblerians suggests that the vectors of influence between them are more complex than can be comprehended in the retrogressive style of argument that brands her as a Whig and them as Tories. Assuredly, Centlivre was a Whig. Fred Lock has accurately described her continuing support for Marlborough and the War of the Spanish Succession beyond the fall of the Whig administration in 1710, and the difficulty she experienced in licensing her 1712 play, *The Perplex'd Lovers,* with its epilogue in hero-worship of the now unpopular general.[16] The following words were printed in the preface to the published text:

> The sinking of my Play cut me not half so deep as the Notion I had, that there could be People of this Nation so ungrateful as not to allow a single Compliment to a Man that has done such Wonders for it. I am not prompted by any private sinister End, having never been oblig'd to the Duke of *Marlborough,* otherwise than as I shar'd in common with my Country; as I am an English Woman, I think myself oblig'd to acknowledge my Obligation to his Grace for the many glorious Conquests he has attained, and the many Hazards he has run, to establish us a Nation free from the Insults of a Foreign Power. I know not what they call Whigs, or how they distinguish between them and Tories: But if the Desire is to see my Country secur'd from the *Romish* Yoke, and flourish by a firm, lasting, Honourable Peace to the Glory of the best of Queens, who deservedly holds the Ballance of all *Europe,* be a Whig, then I am one, else not

> (2.252-3; italics reversed)

Anti-Catholic and anti-European jingoism are apparent in the final sentences, and even more so in the poem "To his Illustrious Highness Prince Eugene of Savoy" printed with the play. It dramatises the proclamation of Eugene's arrival in Britain by a Triton, and then Fame's announcement of his coming to an expectant London, and finally his presence in Anne's Court, where the poem becomes a paean to Marlborough and Eugene ut-

tered by "Britain's Genius". Those who oppose Marlborough and the war are said to be a Francophile faction. Centlivre's later plays, written in the wake of the "'15 rebellion[,] manifest a virulent dislike of nonjuring, dissenting Protestants and of Catholic Jacobites similar to Colley Cibber's in *The Non-Juror* (1717), where the central character, Dr Lopez, a wolf in sheep's clothing, is constructed to show that one can easily metamorphose into the other.[17] Indeed, she had represented Quakers as cowardly, unpatriotic hypocrites since her debut. In *The Beau's Duel,* Mrs Plotwell disguises herself as the Quaker, Anne, who is used to ridicule those who support peace with France, by implication cowards who are the objects of satire, just as are the play's cowardly fops:

PLOT.

> Verily I believe, if we are punish'd with Taxes again to carry on another War, 'twill be a just Judgment upon this sinful Land for their long Wigs, hoop'd Coats, Furbelows, false Teeth, and Patches.

> (1.105)

She returns to the stereotype of the lascivious Quaker in *A Bold Stroke for a Wife,* and the character of Obadiah Prim. Centlivre's unacted *A Gotham Election* (1715) culminates in the staging of an election that dramatises the excesses of Dissent and Catholicism, between which the reasonable Whiggish-English tolerance of Sir Roger Trusty mediates:

> *Enter Mob with their Candidates at the Head of each Party one bearing a Pope, and wooden Shoes, with Wool in their Hats; the other a Tub, with a Woman Preacher in it, and Laurel in their Hats; crying on one Side, A Tickup, a Tickup; on the other, A Worthy, a Worthy, huzza.*

With cries of "No *Pope;* no *Perkin*" on one side, and "No Tub-preaching; no Liberty and Property" on the other, the two factions set about one another and violence ensues.[18] To measure the distance in party terms between Centlivre and Pope, one need only read her dedication to Eustace Budgell in the published edition of her second tragedy, *The Cruel Gift* (1716). Well on the way to his watery, suicidal grave, Budgell would shortly be dismissed from the post, secured for him by Addison's influence, of accountant and controller general of the Irish revenues: and for the Tories, he represented the precise combination of bad politics and incompetent art that defined Whig men of letters at this time:

> FOR my Part, it has always been my Ambition to desire the good Opinion of Men of your Turn; and I never have, or shall be asham'd of publishing the Virtues of those who have been eminent in their Services for our KING, Country and Legal Constitution; and in this View (if any Thing of mine can reach so far) would I be look'd upon by Posterity.

IN the mean Time, I cannot but congratulate my Country for breeding such gallant free Spirits, who, like your Self, have rose up in Opposition to the two most implacable Powers that can be let loose upon Mankind, *Tyranny* and *Popery.* It is your Praise, Sir, to have acted a most noble Part on this Account, in the *Irish Senate,* a Country more than once the Scene of the most dreadful Massacres, but now, by the Actions of YOU and your fellow PATRIOTS, happily recover'd from the same threat'ning (and oh! too near) impending Persecution.[19]

If the character of Phoebe Clinket in the Scriblerian confection *Three Hours After Marriage* is, as I have argued, a personal satire against Centlivre, this dedication was assuredly more fuel to the fire.[20]

Yet, the cultural politics that operate in Centlivre's plays are not, as they have sometimes been said to be, straightforwardly Whiggish in supporting the capitalist aspirations of merchants, manufacturers and financiers.[21] There is not in fact a positive portrait of a merchant anywhere in her oeuvre prior to that of the sensible and decent Frederick in *The Wonder: a Woman Keeps a Secret* (1714). Her heroes are all military men, and although the relationship between the military interest and the trading interest might be thought complementary, it was at times considerably vexed. Centlivre formed one particularly important friendship with George Farquhar, than whom it was impossible to be more Whig. His home was looted at the Siege of (London)derry and he saw action in the Boyne. What Peter Dixon, one of Farquhar's recent editors, terms his "staunchly Protestant, Williamite and pro-Dutch stance, and a correspondingly deep hostility towards Catholics, Jacobites and the French" was assuredly absorbed by Centlivre along with her vast enthusiasm for Farquhar's *The Constant Couple; or a Trip to the Jubilee* (1699).[22] This play, however, was written in the shadow of the 1699 Act of Parliament to disband the army that resulted in a complete demobilisation by May 1699 and a very large number of impecunious military men without an occupation. The opening scene of *Constant Couple* brings a merchant, Smuggler, face to face with the intense, brooding Colonel Standard, whose regiment has been disbanded:

STANDARD.

Did not we venture our Lives, Sir?

SMUGGLER.

And did not we pay you for your Lives, Sir?—Venture your Lives? I'm sure we ventured our Money, and that's Life and Soul to me.[23]

A later scene (2.4) exposes Smuggler, one of Lady Lurewell's various suitors, as a hateful hypocrite, whose false religion and activity in the "Reformation of Manners" is powerfully exposed. In Act 4, Smuggler in drag has been lured into a closet by Lady Lurewell, where she has set his nephew Vizard to him. Vizard, who thinks he is making love to Lady Lurewell, exposes to Smuggler his plan to cheat the latter out of his estate; and as a whole the marriage of hypocritical religion and money-grubbing trading venality displayed by the pair indicates Farquhar's intense hatred of both.

Farquhar associates a combination of money-making and religious cant with the Society for Reformation of Manners and Jeremy Collier: and Centlivre's set towards both was entirely onside with Farquhar's. Collier's call for exemplary comedy is closely in tune with Blackmore's for an ethical, Christianised epic. Despite being a Non-Juror, Collier was far more in sympathy with Whig taste than were any of the playwrights who ranged themselves against him.[24] Here is a clear example of the oblique, non-reflexive relationship between partisan politics and cultural politics in the period. Centlivre's party affiliations should have brought her into the Collier fold; they did not because as a professional dramatist she could see that Collier's aesthetics were stultifying. Her successful play *The Busy Body* (1709) has a hero (Sir George Airy) modelled upon Farquhar's Sir Harry Wildair, whose aristocratic ease is very far from the Whig ideal.[25] In *The Busy Body,* again the parental generation of merchants, Sir Francis Gripe and Sir Jealous Traffick, are the villains of the piece, and the combination of nonconforming rhetoric and greedy accumulation is similar to that dramatised by Farquhar. Traffick's admiration for the Spaniards and Spanish customs is perceived to be dangerously anti-English. Centlivre's soldier-protagonists in plays like *The Beau's Duel: or, A Soldier for the Ladies* (1702) are constructed as anti-establishment figures whose personal honour and bravery contrasts with the cartel of professional interests profiteering from war.

A Bold Stroke for a Wife (1718) is the play most usually cited to illustrate Centlivre's Whig affiliations. Here is the plot. Mrs Anne Lovely, "a fortune of thirty thousand pound", is protected by four guardians: Sir Philip Modelove, an old beau, Periwinkle, "a kind of silly virtuoso", Tradelove, "a changebroker", and Obadiah Prim, a Quaker. To win her hand, Colonel Fainwell has to persuade all four such incompatible humours that he is an ideal husband; that is, that his disposition is similar to each of theirs. This he does using rhetoric, disguise and the good offices of his friend Freeman, who is called a merchant but who behaves throughout like a gallant in a Restoration comedy, eager to assist his friend in the "bite". Certainly, the play draws attention to the head-on collision between an older landed and a new trading interest that J. G. A. Pocock has argued is a structural characteristic of early-century ideology when he contrasts "a conception of property which stresses possession and civic virtue" and "one which stresses exchange and the civilisation of the passions".[26] *A Bold Stroke for a Wife* pits a Tory squire against a Whig stockjobber and sets a scene in Jonathan's coffee house, centre for the securities market—a scene as realistically notated as are the gaming scenes in the earlier plays, *The Gamester* and *The Basset-Table* (both 1705). The dialogism of drama has a habit of complicating clear dichotomies, however. Although, as we have seen, Centlivre moved in Whig circles and certainly espoused Whig principles, she comes down harder on Tradelove than on Modelove, between whom and the hero Fainwell there is considerable affinity. Again, the normative values would seem to be the military ones to which Colonel Fainwell's final speech attest:

> I have had the honour to serve his Majesty and headed a regiment of the bravest fellows that ever pushed bayonet in the throat of a Frenchman; and notwithstanding the fortune this lady brings me, whenever my country wants my aid, this sword and arm are at her service.[27]

Finally, however, the play's most recent editor, Nancy Copeland, is right to pick up on an article by Douglas R. Butler stressing the cultural dimension of Fainwell's suiting his manners to his customers like a tradesman.[28] Fainwell gains his ambition less through the deception devices of Restoration theatre (though he does resort to them) than through an ability to be liked: to oil the social wheels by playing back to the guardians a self-image of which they narcissistically approve. This is an eminently Addisonian way of being in the world. "Exchange and civilisation of the passions", social consensus, is the play's desired end.

IV

On the basis of the foregoing discussion, my conclusion would run along the following lines. Beyond doubt there were, from the 1680s onwards, writers whose partisan affiliations were Whig, and whose poetry was written to propagandise the political attitudes of that party. Following David Womersley's lead, Abigail Williams's excellent forthcoming work will demonstrate the continuities in this writing that give it coherence as a corpus, and she will also argue, partly as a riposte to my own neglect of this in *PIW,* that it was sustained by patronage networks just as much as by the literary market place.[29] To the writers whose names are already encountered in this article can be added those of Ambrose Philips, Thomas Tickell and Laurence Eusden, all of them deserving more attention than they have received. It cannot be argued, however, to rescue this group of writers from neglect, that they are good *because* they legitimise the Glorious Revolution and the War of Spanish Succession, presenting an image of William III as a warlike hero-monarch. Party allegiance is only one aspect of a much wider cultural programme that puts politeness, sublime self-expression and appreciation of art, including sublimity in the natural world, into a complex and at times near-paradoxical relationship. Within this programme, individual Whig writers contributed more or less effectively, and there should be no embargo on evaluating them as more, or less, effective. The backlash to this in Scriblerian writing was somewhat delayed, not getting under way until the 1720s, by which time it is probably anachronistic to term it "Tory". By zooming in on Susanna Centlivre, I hope to have demonstrated that her undeniable partisan affiliation was not straightforwardly reflected in her drama, but was mediated by the dialogic function of dramatic art in a complex and refracted cultural politics.

Notes

1. *Dunciad B,* II.41 1n. Quoted from *The Oxford Authors Alexander Pope,* ed. Pat Rogers (Oxford: Oxford University Press, 1993), p. 488. All subsequent quotations from Pope are taken from this edition.

2. For a fuller discussion of what Pope had against Centlivre—in particular, her membership of "the group of Whig writers centred on Edmund Curll"—see Valerie Rumbold, *Women's Place in Pope's World* (Cambridge: Cambridge University Press, 1989), pp. 165-167.

3. Brean S. Hammond, *Professional Imaginative Writing in England 1670-1740* (Oxford: Clarendon Press, 1997), ch. 6. Hereafter referred to as *PIW.*

4. See also Roger Lund's convincing account of Pope's indebtedness to Thomas Newcomb in "From Oblivion to Dulness: Pope and the Poetics of Appropriation", *British Journal for Eighteenth-Century Studies,* 14 (1991), pp. 171-190; and Harold Weber, "The 'Garbage Heap' of Memory: At Play in Pope's Archives of Dulness", *Eighteenth-Century Studies,* 33 (1999), pp. 1-19.

5. Quoted from *The Works of the Celebrated Mrs. Centlivre in Three Volumes* (London, 1761, repr. 1872), 3, p. 32. All subsequent quotations from Centlivre are taken from this edition.

6. Louis I. Bredvold, "The Gloom of the Tory Satirists", *Eighteenth-century English Literature,* ed. James L. Clifford (Oxford: Clarendon Press, 1959), pp. 3-20.

7. Caroline Robbins, *The Eighteenth-century Commonwealthman: Studies in the Transmission, Development, and Circumstances of English Liberal Thought from the Restoration of Charles II until the War with the Thirteen Colonies* (Cambridge, MA: Harvard University Press, 1959). This is discussed by J. G. A. Pocock in "Machiavelli, Harrington and English Eighteenth

Century Ideologies" (1965), reprinted in *Politics, Language and Time: Essays on Political Thought and History* (London: Methuen, 1972), ch. 4.

8. It is a little grandiose, perhaps, to refer to the work being done in Oxford as a "school", but not undeserved. David Womersley, Christine Gerrard and Abigail Williams recently organised a highly successful conference on Whig writing, and when the proceedings are in due course published, the school of thought will be properly launched.

9. David Norbrook, *Writing the English Republic: Poetry, Rhetoric and Politics, 1627-1660* (Cambridge: Cambridge University Press, 1999).

10. It is interesting to note that Norbrook joins those who wish to push the formation of the bourgeois public sphere back into the Civil War period: the constituting of "a space for the critical discussion of public issues independent of the traditional monopolies of discourse held by the church, the court and the professions", in his economical and elegant definition (p. 13). The weakness of this position is that Norbrook can point to very few *material* spaces, rather than discourse spaces, in which this project was forwarded.

11. David Womersley, review of Hammond, *Professional Imaginative Writing in England, 1670-1740,* in *Review of English Studies,* N.S., 49.195 (1998), pp. 358-360.

12. David Womersley, ed., *Augustan Critical Writing* (Harmondsworth: Penguin, 1997), pp. xi-xliv.

13. Joseph Spence, *Observations, Anecdotes, and Characters of Books and Men: Collected from Conversation,* ed. James M. Osborn, 2 vols (Oxford: Clarendon Press, 1966), No. 472, 1, p. 202.

14. Alan Downie has written a series of articles in which he has challenged prevailing views of the partisan affiliations of all the main Scriblerian writers. As an example, see his "Gay's Politics" in *John Gay and the Scriblerians,* eds Peter Lewis & Nigel Wood (London: Vision Press, 1988), pp. 44-61. Ian Higgins, in *Swift's Politics: a Study in Disaffection* (Cambridge: Cambridge University Press, 1994), argues that Swift was an extreme crypto-Jacobite Tory, whereas in *Faction's Fictions: Ideological Closure in Swift's Satire* (Newark: University of Delaware Press, 1991), Daniel Eilon has argued that he was a radical Lockean Whig!

15. Norman Davies, *The Isles: a History* (Basingstoke: Macmillan, 1999). Davis gives Paul Rapin de Thoyras's fifteen-volume *History of England* in Nicholas Tindale's translation (1726-31) as the

most influential exposition of the "Whig interpretation" prior to Macaulay (pp. 825-834), though John Kenyon considers that "it is arguable that Sir Walter Raleigh was the first Whig historian" in *The History Men: the Historical Profession in England since the Renaissance* (London: Weidenfeld & Nicolson, 1983; 2nd edn. 1993), p. 19.

16. F. P. Lock, *Susanna Centlivre* (Boston: Twayne, 1970), pp. 21-25.

17. The name "Lopez" is of course a reference to Queen Elizabeth's Jewish physician, who was convicted of attempting to poison her. Calling his villain Lopez enables Cibber to construct him as an identikit portrait of the "enemy of state".

18. "Perkin" is, of course, Perkin Warbeck, an earlier Pretender than James Stuart.

19. Quoted from the first edition, published by Edmund Curll, in 1717.

20. See *PIW*, pp. 203-204.

21. Nancy Copeland, in her recent valuable edition of *A Bold Stroke for a Wife* (Peterborough, Ontario: Broadview Press, 1995), plays a fairly straight bat in relating Centlivre's partisan and cultural politics: see pp. 11-12, 16-17, 22.

22. See the account given by Peter Dixon, ed., *George Farquhar, The Recruiting Officer* (Manchester: Manchester University Press, 1986), pp. 1-9.

23. *The Works of George Farquhar,* ed. Shirley Strum Kenny, 2 vols (Oxford: Clarendon Press, 1988), 1, pp. 115-116.

24. Robert D. Hume's recent article, "Jeremy Collier and the Future of the London Theatre in 1698", *Studies in Philology,* 96 (1999), pp. 480-511, is exceptionally lucid on the cultural conflict between Collier and the playwrights, and on the influence that Collier had (or in Hume's argument, did not have) on the English stage.

25. See Shirley Strum Kenny's discussion of this influence, *The Works of George Farquhar,* 1, pp. 136-137.

26. J. G. A. Pocock, *Virtue, Commerce and History: Essays on Political Thought and History, Chiefly in the Eighteenth Century* (Cambridge: Cambridge University Press, 1985), p. 115.

27. Susanna Centlivre, *A Bold Stroke for a Wife,* ed. Thalia Stathas (London: Edward Arnold, 1968), 5.549-54.

28. Copeland, ed., *A Bold Stroke for a Wife,* p. 22. The article cited is Douglas R. Butler, "Plot and Politics in Susanna Centlivre's *A Bold Stroke for*

a Wife", in *Curtain Calls: British and American Women and the Theatre, 1660-1820,* eds Mary Anne Schofield & Cecilia Macheski (Athens: Ohio University Press, 1991), pp. 357-370.

29. Abigail Williams, "Whig Literary Culture: Poetry, Politics and Patronage, 1678-1714", unpublished University of Oxford PhD dissertation. Just as significant an area of neglect is pointed out by Sarah Prescott in her study of Elizabeth Singer Rowe, who worked outside the "competitive, financially motivated and market-led" circles emphasised in *PIW.* See her chapter, "Marketing the Provinces: Elizabeth Singer Rowe and the Non-Metropolitan Context" in *Female Authorship in Early Eighteenth-century England* (forthcoming). One might regard the Whig-supported authors in Williams's account as residual, in Raymond Williams's sense, whereas those studied by Prescott would be "emergent".

Jacky Bratton (essay date 2000)

SOURCE: Bratton, Jacky. "Reading the Intertheatrical, or, the Mysterious Disappearance of Susanna Centlivre." In *Women, Theatre, and Performance: New Histories, New Historiographies,* edited by Maggie B. Gale and Viv Gardner, pp. 7-24. Manchester: Manchester University Press, 2000.

[*In the following essay, Bratton contends that Centlivre's diminished importance in the canon of eighteenth-century theater results from a ideological bias toward texts that correspond with traditional Western literary values, including the autonomy of the artist, the primacy of the text over the collaborative performance experience, and the distinction between the commercial and the artistic.*]

THE DISAPPEARANCE

Susanna Centlivre (1667-1723) published twenty plays and had nineteen of them staged between 1700 and 1720; adding up the number of years in which each of her plays was produced in London during the eighteenth century, Judith Phillips Stanton arrives at the remarkable figure of 289. They were published or republished 122 times.[1] The popularity of Centlivre's three most acted comedies, *The Busie Body* (1709), *The Wonder! A Woman Keeps a Secret* (1714) and *A Bold Stroke for a Wife* (1718) extended well into the nineteenth century; so that in terms of stage success, before the twentieth century, Centlivre is second only to Shakespeare.[2]

And yet she is more or less forgotten by modern audiences. In 1997 there was a website entitled 'Susanna Centlivre, The Forgotten Playwright of the Eighteenth

Century', which has itself now disappeared.[3] She wrote Garrick's favourite role, Don Felix in *The Wonder!,* in which he chose to take his farewell of the stage;[4] but, according to the critics, she never wrote a witty line. When her plays are mentioned in mainstream critical discourse,[5] it is as Whiggish Restoration-and-water, harmless but ultimately dreary fun, part of the deplorable reaction and decline initiated by Collier's attack upon the stage. His *Short View of the Immorality and Profanity of the Restoration Stage,* published two years before her first play was produced, was long supposed to have corrupted the sensibility and the playgoing habits of London society: the result was said to be an audience so misled as to prefer Mrs Centlivre, while the more sensitive genius of Congreve was driven from the stage. Critics from Elizabeth Inchbald in 1808 to Bonamy Dobree in 1924 attributed Congreve's failure, and Centlivre's success, to 'the degraded taste of the public'.[6] It was Byron who actually blamed Centlivre for Congreve's rout: 'I . . . know that Congreve gave up writing because Mrs Centlivre's balderdash drove his comedies off.'[7]

During the ensuing century her plays gradually ceased to be produced, at least in a form that had to be attributed to her. The critical exercise of canon-formation was able to exclude her work; in the twentieth century, accounts of the drama of the eighteenth century began to dismiss it completely, to extraordinary effect. The convention amongst summarising literary critics until the 1960s was to refer their readers only to Farquhar, who died in 1707, or straight to the unplayable sentimental comedies of Cibber and Steele, leaving the student of theatre baffled as to what the early eighteenth century thought was funny.[8] It is striking that the feminist recuperation of the female dramatists of the Restoration has focused on the work of Aphra Behn, who now finds a leading place in the literary canon; Centlivre does not. Many feminist commentators echo the emphasis on Centlivre's conformity to Whig, mercantile values and seem disappointed to discover her supreme technical skills: they prefer Behn, a complex writer whose work can be compared with that of male contemporaries, and discovered to be great literature.[9] Laura Rosenthal, in her book on the development of literary property as part of the commodification and professionalisation of Early Modern culture,[10] sees Centlivre as deliberately setting herself up to fail as a contender for literary honours. Pointing out that 'dramatic writing raises particular ambiguities of intertextuality and originality', she argues that Centlivre was acutely aware of the challenge her success might present to the male literary establishment. Rosenthal suggests that she deliberately avoided claiming originality or genius for her work, publishing her most popular, intertextual pieces anonymously or under a male name, and where she wrote as herself deliberately characterising her plays as trivial entertainments. She refrained from the publication of her collected plays so as to avoid any claim to literary prestige. The consequences of this gendered negotiation of power and submission were, I would argue, perpetuated in the emergent discourse of Romantic and post-Romantic aesthetics, and are still operative today; Centlivre is only one woman theatre worker to suffer from them.

Centlivre is heavily disadvantaged by hegemonic ideology. Her work can be—indeed, has to be—condemned as inferior three times over. In the first place, Centlivre's plays fail to fulfil the basic requirement of art in bourgeois society, that it be the unique product of the autonomous artist, the individual 'genius' at work alone, challenging and expanding the horizons of human experience.[11] Extending Rosenthal's observation, we may say that this is the case with all dramatists: none can operate fully without the co-operation of other creative artists, and their work will be not only added to, but transformed, by the actor, the scene-painter and others. When the aesthetic of autonomy was first articulated in Western literary and philosophical thought around 1800, there was a strong move to free the dramatic writer from what was perceived as the impediment of theatrical realisation. Coleridge and Charles Lamb insisted that the work of the great dramatists, especially Shakespeare, was best appreciated as literature, by the solitary reader. In the closet, Centlivre's work reads as incomplete, as indeed it is; she wrote for performance. Wrested from its context, it is impoverished and compromised, shown to be reliant upon what she takes from and gives to others. In artistic practice, as the aesthetic of autonomy gained ground in England, writers for the stage struggled to assert exclusive possession of their work and repudiate all theatrical involvement, until by the 1880s Arthur Wing Pinero could write his drama, having it 'laboriously thought out, every detail of it' and printed, complete with stage directions, before he entered the theatre, where, he said, 'rehearsal is not—or certainly should not be—a time for experiment'.[12]

Centlivre's failure to create literature is expressed from the first as a lack of 'wit', an essential tool for neutralising and converting theatrical pleasure to an acceptable aesthetic response. Wit is the rationalising abstraction of laughter by the exercise of mind, converting human relations into a play of language. Critics, from the writer who composed a study of her work for the *Morning Chronicle* in 1758 onwards, have agreed that Centlivre's language did not do this. Reviewing a production of *The Wonder!* he pronounces that 'the language is contemptible to the last degree'.[13] Most subsequent writers have agreed with him. Bertram Shuttleworth in 1953 speaks of her 'rather flat, but unexpectedly natural dialogue';[14] Nancy Cotton, who uses many superlatives in her discussion of Centlivre, is apparently self-contradictory over this issue. She says Centlivre 'is a

writer of small verbal distinction. She did, however, have a good ear for jargon, slang, religious cant, dialect, and foreign accent.' In other words she can write interesting realistic dialogue; what is lacking is the literary quality of wit. Even for Nancy Cotton, therefore, *A Bold Stroke for a Wife* 'has no depth but is an excellent stage play'.[15] Douglas R. Butler spells out the implications of this in the eyes of the literary critic. Writing in 1991 about the same play (under the extraordinary heading of 'Closet Drama'), he claims Centlivre has 'little wit', and deduces that she 'does not have a serious vision' because her ideas are 'not conveyed most effectively through her language'.[16]

The second barrier to Centlivre's being taken seriously is succinctly expressed by F. W. Bateson, in 1927. He states that all but six of her plays are 'almost completely worthless', but that these six comedies,

> all have a certain vitality and technical *finesse*, and are as good examples as one can hope to find of the work of the professional dramatist of the eighteenth century. They have, it must be admitted, no intellectual or literary significance; the writing is never distinguished and the characterization, with the single exception of Marplot in *The Busie Body*, is conventional and superficial. But the purpose for which they were written is fulfilled, to a greater or lesser extent, in all of them. They amuse, they distract the mind. Mrs Centlivre's comedies occupy the position in the literature of the eighteenth century that is now filled by the detective story. They are the railway reading of Georgian England.[17]

This attractive passage captures the evaluation of her work as 'entertainment' that asserts its essential difference from art. Such work amuses and distracts, serving to pass time when one has an excuse for self-indulgent avoidance of intellectual pursuits. It has no literary significance, however good of its kind it might be, because it has only the technical vitality of professional (paid) work, which can never be the life of art. Again, this remains an assumption in the work of recent critics. F. P. Lock, in the only current monograph about Centlivre, speaks dismissively of hers as 'the representative career of a prolific, professional dramatist'. Pointing out John Loftis's false opposition in calling Centlivre 'thoroughly professional, much concerned with the money to be made from her plays'. rather than with 'artistic consistency', even Jacqueline Pearson hastens to claim that *despite* being an 'accomplished practical playwright' Centlivre had 'her own consistent vision as an artist'.[18]

Pearson's anxiousness as a feminist to make the 'larger claim' of artistic integrity for Centlivre, like Bateson's vehement, sneering dismissal sixty years before, signals the third and most important ideological issue. The process of the elevation of plays into literature is part of a hegemonic move upon the theatre. To take Centlivre's work seriously, as we take that of her only theatrical rival, Shakespeare, would challenge the way in which plays are read as literature, and undermine the division between art and entertainment that protects literature from the market-place; it would also allow a woman's work to undermine the fundamental binary, the distinction between mind and body, upon which Western patriarchal culture rests. The feminist writer prefers the less radical option of asserting the literary value of her female subject; the masculine discourse, however, knows that this claim cannot be made without undermining the whole structure.

The purity of the aesthetic is guaranteed by its lack of *function,* and thus its distinction from the material and the mortal. Through our grasp of the aesthetic, our recognition of beauty in pure art, the power of Reason can be applied to the physical world that so delights our senses and bring the bodily under moral control. This has amounted to a 'programme of spiritual hegemony' whereby 'sensibility' became the foundation of moral life and the rational education of desire became 'an active, transformative force' that teaches us pleasure in the material world is wrong.[19] The peculiar dangers involved in finding art in the setting of the theatre are vividly described by Centlivre's contemporary, Jeremy Collier:

> The business of Plays is to recommend virtue . . . This design has been oddly pursued by the English Stage. Our poets . . . have in a great measure the Springs of Thought and Inclination in their Power. Show, Musick, Action and Rhetorick, are moving Entertainments . . . But . . . If delight without Restraint, or Distinction, without Conscience or Shame, is the supream Law of Comedy, 'twere well if we had less on't. Arbitrary Pleasure, is more dangerous than Arbitrary Power. Nothing is more Brutal than to be abandon'd to Appetite.[20]

Collier is less direct, but even more extreme, about the role of women in this dangerous business of theatre. He cites Dryden as censuring the Roman dramatists for 'making Mutes of their single women', not allowing them to speak. He himself feels this 'old Discipline would be very serviceable upon the Stage' in his own time.[21] He does not want to hear the voices of women. In the English theatre after the Restoration, the novel presence of women on stage contributed to the imperative that aesthetic distance be preserved, and that first wit, and later sensibility (the intellectualised response to feeling), should police the bodily. The outstanding and enduring success of a woman as writer is an unmanageable challenge to the masculine aestheticisation of the theatre's public space. Bateson begins his chapter on Centlivre with a quotation from an eighteenth-century source: 'What a Pox have women to do with the Muses?'[22]

THE INTERTHEATRICAL

To make a valuation of Centlivre's work that explains its success without simultaneously condemning it as dangerously second-rate we have, I would argue, to free our consideration of all plays in the theatre from the ideologically-driven aesthetics I have outlined. Rejecting these three grounds of condemnation—that her work is not literature because it is collaborative, that it is compromised by the populist and commercial creative processes of the theatre, and that it is morally and aesthetically suspect because it provokes and includes rather than suppresses bodily response from an audience—I want to offer a conceptualisation of her work that addresses and analyses its theatrical success. By analogy with a range of accepted terminology I want to call this concept 'intertheatricality'.

Some modern writers have begun to move towards reading Centlivre's work in its context. Her theatrical success is noted, sometimes quite enthusiastically, by modern writers. Nancy Cotton begins by announcing that she was 'the most successful of England's early women playwrights, perhaps the best comic playwright between Congreve and Fielding'[23] (this is not actually a very large claim). Jacqueline Pearson is self-consciously bolder: 'Her best comedies are the most brilliant of the century: I would not myself exclude even Goldsmith or Sheridan from this. [Their] disappearance from the stage . . . is a serious loss.'[24] Her theatrical artistry is suggested when Fidelis Morgan points out that in *The Wonder!* Centlivre achieved a 'brilliant compromise', a play with 'one foot in each century', 'finding a way to please the new and more po-faced audience with a distressing degree of vitality'.[25] I would argue that, in the first place, at the moment Centlivre was writing her ability to match the feeling of her audience was an outstanding, and a unique, achievement. The early eighteenth-century stage was reeling under the loss of fashionable patronage, the assaults of Collier and his followers, and the influx of audiences with different cultural imperatives and agendas; the successful dramatist had to negotiate and reconcile contradictory audience demands, delivering the bodily pleasure of laughter within the grip of repressive sensibility. What Fidelis Morgan sees in *The Wonder!* is an instance of this, an ingenious compromise between moral sentiment and rakish attitudes. Richard Frushell prefaces his edition of her plays—the first complete edition, published in 1982—with the confident assertion that 'there can be no doubt that Mrs Centlivre is one of the most . . . savvy playwrights of the first quarter of the eighteenth century. She was at once actively regardful of the Restoration comic traditions of plot and theme, mindful of textual and tonal fashions of her own day, and unwittingly prescient of what would please in generations after her.'[26]

Her success, then, is the entertainer's success, in matching her offering to the taste of the time. But Frushell's final clause troubles this simple formulation. It signals that there is a dimension of her success—its long duration—that cannot be accounted for as merely shrewdness and observation of her market; he is content to ignore the challenge this presents to his account, and dub her 'unwittingly prescient'. But performers and indeed writers whose skill is in echoing contemporary vibrations are just those whose work goes out of date. There are many examples of such transient success amongst Centlivre's contemporaries, including all the writers of the comedy of sensibility, and most of the satirists and poets of the time. But her best work requires no footnotes. It did not only succeed in those circumstances for which it was written: on the contrary, the extensive stage histories which Frushell provides demonstrate that her plays have an astonishing degree of flexibility and transferability across both space and time.

The huge figures for years of performance given at the head of this essay were computed by Judith Stanton from *The London Stage,* which details recorded performances in the capital. Frushell's net is cast more widely. He shows that even Centlivre's minor work had a busy life on the theatrical fringe; *The Man's Bewitched* (1709) was turned into a harlequinade and given at Bartholomew Fair, for example, and *Love's Contrivance* (1703), a pastiche of three plays by Molière, was a favourite in the tavern theatres of the day. Centlivre herself claimed a hundred performances for this play.[27] Her major plays were staged from Covent Garden to the Crown Inn, Islington, and then across Britain and the world. Sybil Rosenfeld records them as the staple of British provincial circuits and strolling companies;[28] Frushell documents that General Burgoyne's soldiers played her first in America, and the theatre in Sydney mounted her work as early as 1796; the records of theatres large and small in Ireland, Canada, Australia and the USA show her plays as standard repertoire well into the next century. Such a record is not simply accounted for as a capacity to respond to the passing fashion at the time the plays were first written; these texts are alive in stage entertainment.

Frushell's evidence offers some suggestive leads from which to begin a revaluation of Centlivre's work according to a different perspective. He remarks an extraordinary number of adaptations, shortened versions and rewritings of her plays. Some are selections or cut versions for small playhouses, some open adaptations by actors, while others are by dramatists who tried to pass off the results as their own, as in the case of Colley Cibber's *The Double Gallant* (1707), which is clearly taken from Centlivre's *Love at a Venture* (1706), which he had read and rejected in his role as manager.

Her texts lived on in twenty new versions, as well as in their original shapes. Bowyer's exhaustive work on the derivations and analogues of her writing similarly demonstrates that the plays had an ancestry as well as a rich and varied posterity.

They also existed in close relationship with their own generation of entertainments. All eighteenth-century plays were presented within a programme of entertainments, framed and punctuated by interludes of various kinds. F. P. Lock, producing a purely literary reading of Centlivre, explicitly chooses to pretend the plays did not suffer from such destructive interruptions.[29] Frushell reports, with a note of surprise, that 'Success in the theatre came also because her plays often had the good fortune to be accompanied by popular afterpieces, vocal and instrumental music, dancing, and interesting paradramatic entertainments otherwise—the total theatrical evening as much a draw as the plays that mainly constituted it.' He also shows that these theatrical successes were often command or benefit nights[30]—moments when someone, either powerful members of the audience, who could choose what would please them most, or a working performer who could predict what would bring in the biggest audience receipts, put together the best possible bill.

I suggest that the choice of Centlivre on these nights is not a matter of her good fortune; that her plays have a quality that made them especially suitable and likely to be selected for galas, benefits and evenings of choice entertainment, just as they were fruitful ground for the adapter and the theatrical thief. The last clue to the special value of Centlivre's work to be found in Frushell's stage history is that his account of their productions reads like a roll-call of major actors, all of whom founded a reputation on roles in these plays. They seem to have made the careers of a long succession of men. Frushell, in noting this, quotes Edward Shuter's critique of the dramatist from a performer's point of view:

> Mrs Centlivre's Comedies have a vein of pleasantry in them that will always be relish'd. She knew the Genius of this nation, and she wrote up to it; her ***Bold Stroke for a Wife,*** was a masterpiece that much increased her reputation: it establish'd that of Kit Bullock . . . a smart sprightly actor . . .[31]

The plays, then, belong to the theatre—they support it and are supported by it. They are precisely the kind of writing that refuses to be understood on the page, as 'Drama'; their capacity to please must therefore be challenged or obscured, lest the autonomy of art be undermined by it. Their excellence is not in spite of, but because of their multiple strands of connection, their place *within* their milieu, meshed to writing past and present, to actors and their strengths and needs, to music, dancing the audience's pleasures. They have to a high degree the quality of 'intertheatricality'.

By intertheatricality I mean that mesh of connections between theatre texts and between texts and their creators and realisers that makes up the moving, multi-dimensional, cross-hatched background out of which individual performances, nights at the theatre, regularly crystallise. The plays written and performed within a single theatrical tradition are all more or less interdependent. They are uttered in a theatrical code shared by writers, performers and audience which consists not only of language, but of genres, conventions and memory—shared by the audience—of previous plays and scenes, previous performances, the actors' previous roles and their known personae on and off stage. There is a collaboration, taking place not only over the period of the creation of a play in rehearsal, but anew, live, each night of its performance in front of an audience, that creates shared meaning out of the concatenation of theatre systems that is far more complex than any set of conventions deployed by a writer whose medium is print.

The extent to which this quality, especially when it is presented in the work of a woman, is perceived as threatening and needing to be critically put down is signalled by the charges brought against Centlivre. After she is denied the literary quality of wit, she is denied the other literary marker, originality; indeed she is accused of plagiarism. John Wilson Bowyer, writing in 1952 in a critical tradition that made the identification of sources and analogues its primary method, was nevertheless surprised at '[t]he extent to which scholars have sought sources for *The Busy Body* . . . They seem to have assumed that Mrs Centlivre could not write a play of her own. Except for the two scenes from Jonson, her borrowings are general and no discredit to her'.[32] The issue is control, integration and integrity: women lack integrity, they and their works are permeable, inadequately bonded and bounded; this is deprecated by classic dramatic theory which demands a defined shape, an integration of all parts subordinated to whole, a single forward drive, climax and closure. Feminist writers have sought to discover a female counter-tradition at work within the literary, tracing a line from Aphra Behn to Centlivre to Hannah Cowley, whose play *Who's the Dupe?* (1779) is based upon the subplot of Centlivre's *The Stolen Heiress* (1702). It would be more effective as a recuperative strategy to see these female writers as central to a different tradition—that of intertheatricality. They could be said to be leaders in a practice that they shared with countless other women and men, of making plays within, instead of at odds with, the context in which the theatre artist works. Centlivre explicitly acknowledged this when she dismissed literary prescriptions in her preface to *Love's Contrivance,* saying 'the criticks cavil most about Decorums, and cry up Aristotles Rules'. Tongue in cheek she owns they are in the right, but that 'the Town'—audiences—do not agree; so while 'the Unity of Time, Place and Action' are no doubt 'the greatest Beauties of a Dramatick Poem', successful *plays* are created by 'the other way of writing'. And this other, or Other, way is the procedure of the person who crystallises the successful moment—or string of moments—out of the intertheatrical chemistry of plots, players and expectations. The differences between Shakespeare's use of earlier dramatic sources, Cibber's casual appropriation of Centlivre's play as so much 'Poetical Lumber' handy for his use, the actors' conversion of *A Bold Stroke for a Wife* into a fairground droll, and Centlivre's translation and condensation of three plays by Molière, lie in the politics of public utterance and the construction of critical control.

Centlivre encapsulates a salient feature of her method when she goes on, in this same preface, to describe her construction of plays in a metaphor from her husband's realm, the kitchen.[33] She says her audience 'relishes nothing so well as Humour lightly tost up with Wit, and drest with Modesty and Air . . .'. The ingredients of a salad are not fixed; we may pick out the bits we like better, or tip the whole thing into a sandwich and add a piece of cheese. Entertainment is created like a salad, which may contain variable amounts of lettuce; *The Busie Body* may please one day as a main course, another as a three-act snack. Thalia Stathas is troubled by the 'tonal shifts and shifts in characterisation' that abound even in Centlivre's best plays. She prefers for that reason *A Bold Stroke for a Wife* which provides a fairy-tale structure, the wooing of four guardians who are strongly contrasting cartoonish humorous characters, to justify the comic shifts 'without making them incredible'. But it is this characteristic structuring to convince and amuse scene by scene, rather than according to an integrated unity of plan, that gives the plays their powerful malleability, and makes them—as Stathas herself concedes—ideal vehicles for the actor. Seeking the reason for Garrick's love of *The Wonder!,* she says 'The changing moods of Don Felix are said to have been a perfect vehicle for Garrick's skills, and the rapidity with which these changes occur itself demands a virtuosity in characterisation which few actors can achieve convincingly.'[34] Perhaps not, today; but for many decades such virtuosity was the actor's stock-in-trade. That is why the role of Fainwell in *A Bold Stroke for a Wife* was chosen by the great comic actors—Shuter, Woodward, Bannister, Charles Kemble, Charles Mathews, Robert Elliston—and by all the barnstormers of the provincial circuits, and of Ireland, Scotland, Australia and colonial America. It is a play that is about acting your way to success, the trickster's triumph, the apotheosis of impersonation; and every man who believed in the power of the stage—which must needs have been a powerful belief, to keep the strolling player on the flinty and unresponsive road, convinced of his personal ability to charm money out of Philistine pockets—would want to see himself in it.

The Busie Body

The best demonstration of the intricate mesh which is intertheatricality is a consideration of one play. Centlivre's most popular production was **The Busie Body** (1709), which Hazlitt said had been played a 'thousand times in town and country, giving delight to the old, the young, and the middle-aged'.[35] It was staged in London during eighty-seven years of the eighteenth century, with 475 known performances. There were doubtless many more, not only at unrecorded little theatres, but at the main houses, where it was the play of all others to be put on when the advertised piece for some reason failed: an actress ill, an actor detained in the country, and at an hour's notice Covent Garden could stage a successful performance of **The Busie Body**.[36] Into the next century this was still the case: John Philip Kemble kept a production in reserve, always ready in case of accidents.[37] From London the play was carried across the world by strollers, professionals and amateur gentlemen; it was a stock piece at the foundation of most anglophone theatres. Any pile of old playbills, from Devon to Virginia, will probably contain its name.

The rapid success of the play, despite the hostility of its original performers and a thin attendance on the first night, caused considerable critical unease. Richard Steele wrote a favourable notice in *The Tatler,* for which, according to Bowyer, Centlivre was for ever grateful. To the modern eye Steele's praise is lukewarm and patronising, and chiefly concerned, as most critics have been, to explain away a moral impossibility—the success of a woman dramatist:

> On Saturday last was presented **The Busie Body,** a comedy, written (as I have heretofore remarked) by a woman. The plot and incidents of the play are laid with that subtilty of spirit which is peculiar to females of wit, and is very seldom well performed by those of the other sex, in which craft in love is an act of invention, and not, as with women, the effect of nature and instinct.[38]

It is significant that Bowyer should assert that Centlivre was eternally indebted to Steele for disempowering her and allaying audiences' fears of an unnatural success by reducing her writing to 'the effect of nature and instinct'.

Many critics have since worked hard at explaining away her success by seeking to show which men she borrowed the play from. The first suggestions of sources appear in an early critical account of her work, David Baker's *Biographia Dramatica 1782,* and by the time Bowyer wrote borrowings from Francis Fane's *Love in the Dark* (1675), Dryden's *Sir Martin Mar-all* (1668), Molière's *L'Étourdi* (1653), John Dryden Jnr's *The Husband His Own Cuckold* (1696) had all been suggested as her sources. None of them bears anything but a slight general resemblance to her work. There is one significant analogue, however, and that is a scene in Ben Jonson's *The Divell is an Asse* (1616). This is clearly a rewriting on her part, interesting in the way in which Centlivre changed the balance of power in the important scene she borrowed from the male characters to her heroine Miranda. Modern feminist critics like Jacqueline Pearson and Suz-Anne Kinney find the controlling power of Miranda throughout the play attractive, reading her as a stand-in for the writer.[39] But theatre audiences have been less interested in her than in the eponymous Busy Body, Marplot, the one character in all Centlivre's writing that Bateson allowed to be original. (Even this is disputed by the source hunters, who find a tenuous resemblance to the ineffectual servant Pug in Jonson's play.) But the original creation Marplot is still strikingly successful because of his intertheatricality. Like many iconic creations—Falstaff, Pickwick, Dracula, James Bond, Superman—he takes on a life of his own, and exists within and beyond the play in his own right. Centlivre wrote a sequel to feature him again, **Marplot, or the Second Part of the Busie-Body** (1710). Woodward, for whom Marplot was a signature role, then adapted this into a farce afterpiece, *Marplot in Lisbon* (1755), which found its way into the first collected edition of Centlivre's works in 1760-61. By the early nineteenth century the character was ripe for further updating, and was transmogrified into Paul Pry, in a play written first by John Poole and then by Douglas Jerrold.[40] Poole acknowledged a French source for his subplot, but insisted the rest was all his own. It 'became one of the greatest theatrical hits of the age: it had one of the longest runs recorded since *The Beggar's Opera*'.[41] The farce was a star vehicle for John Liston, in which he was known to thousands and modelled in china by the Bloor Derby works.

So the text, transformed and redirected by Centlivre's work, was also deeply embedded in other writings; and on a second axis, in the performances of actors. Even more than Fainwell and Don Felix, Marplot was a comic actor's vehicle; the play was staged so that Edward Shuter could repeat his much-loved creation of the role, Henry Woodward could inject funds into the Covent Garden box office, or Garrick could challenge him in it.[42] The text became not only a pretext for the character, but a malleable vehicle for him. It was changed around him, giving him more prominence, presumably by the actor playing the role. Beginning as a five-act comedy, the play was cut to three acts by the exclusion of the second love intrigue, without cuts to Marplot's appearances or lines; and even the printed editions hint at the nature of the role, the spaces that were given to its performer for extemporisation and extra business. In 1776, after Woodward performed his famous Marplot for the last time, the printed editions[43] change markedly; one might speculate that they are changed to show or suggest his alterations to the text, now that they had ceased to be a trade secret of his. At the end of Act II, for example, the editions of 1776 onwards show a changed order of speeches, and violence is done to the sensible sequence of exits in order to give Marplot the tag, and a moment on stage when he is alone with the audience. No doubt these changes happened even more in the theatre than is recorded in print; Marplot is allowed out of the frame of the plot, into direct and conspiratorial relationship with the audience.

If Miranda is a surrogate for the writer, Marplot is perhaps the opposite: he is a kind of anti-dramatist; he conspires with the actor and the audience to disintegrate the play. His interference, with the best of intentions, spoils plots and ruins closures; he is not a gull, or the foppish, would-be wit of earlier plays, for he has no vanity or covetousness or sense of envy or emulation towards the lovers. He is indeed a virgin, a point which is more stressed in **Marplot** than the earlier play; and he is a coward, a desexualised innocent, a kind of wild child who just wants *to know what they are all doing*. A well-trained audience, with a proper sense of how a love-intrigue plot should be conducted, watches with horrified amusement as his well-meaning interference lays it in ruins over and over again.[44] He is in that sense an unruly member of the audience taking control, the disintegrative force outside of both the writer's text and the theatrical pact. And like both audience and comic performer, at the end of both **The Busie Body** and **Marplot** he remains outside the pattern of the fiction, resisting, or immune to, closure, the dance, the marriages. The writer is not helpless in this intertheatrical nexus, of course, but collaborates in it, actively creating a channel through which the work of others flows, and is enabled and developed. She participates in a process which is a manifestation of the female aesthetic discussed by Jane Marcus, 'in terms of repetition, dailiness and process':[45] the work of creation in collaboration.

It is too narrow to define intertheatricality simply as a female tradition. It is perhaps not a coincidence that group composition and devising were methods preferred by many feminist theatre groups in the 1970s and 1980s. But the point is not that only women do it, or might be argued to do it particularly well, or alternatively that they are critically assigned to consideration as parts of such groups so as to avoid giving them any higher status. I would rather regard collaborative practice as a model for understanding the creative process in the theatre that reflects, more nearly than the Aristotelian masculine metaphors of the drama do, what actually happened—'wie es eigentlich war'—and still happens now. If that is so then it should, by classic Rankean criteria, be the basis of theatre history. That it is not bespeaks the ideological structuring of the discourse.

The rejection of the intertheatrical model of creativity has been made necessary by the aesthetic of autonomy and its insistence upon the uniqueness of the text and the creative artist. It has been achieved by dubbing intertheatrical works commercial, entertainment, professional, feminine, and in all possible ways both inferior and dangerous to true art. To fight back, that tradition must assert that real plays are not inviolable, single-authored creations. Their collaborative and multiple creation is integral to them, and includes not only borrowing from play to play, rewriting night by night, but also many more dimensions: the non-verbal systems of spectacle and sound, the other items on the bill, who is in the audience, and the presence in performances of the actors and their own personae, with their remembered other performances in this role, their known other roles, their rumoured private lives. Intertheatricality, the co-operative operation of the theatre, is a feminine aesthetic, in the same way that entertainment is a feminised tradition; neither is really confined to women, but both are excluded and downgraded by that association, in the service of 'male' models of history and of genius.

Notes

1. Judith Phillips Stanton, 'This New-Found Path Attempting: Women Dramatists in England, 1660-1800', in Mary Anne Schofield and Cecilia Macheski, eds., *Curtain Calls* (Athens, Ohio University Press, 1991), pp. 325-54, 336.

2. John Wilson Bowyer, *The Celebrated Mrs Centlivre* (Durham, NC, Duke University Press, 1952), p.v.

3. http://www.mtsu.edu/-enghoodb/leighj.htm.

4. Drury Lane, 16 May 1776. See Thalia Stathas, 'A Critical Edition of Three Plays by Susanna Centlivre', Stanford University Ph.D., (Ann Arbor, University Microfilms Inc., 1966), pp. 475-8.

5. See for example the brief dismissal in Simon Trussler, *The Cambridge Illustrated History of British Theatre* (Cambridge, Cambridge University Press, 1994), p. 143, where her picture adorns a short essay on 'the female wits' safely cordoned off from the main text in a grey box; and Richard W. Bevis, *English Drama: Restoration and Eighteenth Century, 1660-1789* (London, Longman, 1988), p. 162, who discusses her work in a page under the unpromising heading 'Stagnation 1708-1720'.

6. Elizabeth Inchbald, 'Remarks on *A Bold Stroke for a Wife*', published in *The British Theatre 11* (London, Longman, Hurst, Rees & Orme, 1808), p. 4; and see Bonamy Dobree, *Restoration Comedy 1660-1720* (Oxford, Oxford University Press, 1924), in which he says (p. 140) that *The Way of the World* was 'too civilized for an age that revelled in the scribblings of Mrs Pix'. He does not mention any of Centlivre's plays except *The Gamester,* cited as an example of British drama-

tists' propensity to stage the obvious, where Frenchmen allow suggestion to work: p. 49.

7. Quoted in Bowyer, *The Celebrated Mrs Centlivre,* p. 97. The supposition that Congreve retreated from the stage jealous and Centlivre's success is recorded in Hazlitt, Lectures on the Comic Writers, 1819, Lecture VIII, 'On the Comic Writers of the Last Century', in *Complete Works,* ed. P. P. Howe, 21 vols (London, Dent, 1930-34), Vol. 6 (1931), pp. 149-68, p. 155.

8. For a summary of dismissive critical approaches see F. W. Bateson, *English Comic Drama, 1700-1750* (Oxford, Oxford University Press, 1929), pp. 61, 75-7; for the habit of omitting Centlivre altogether, see for example John E. Cunningham, *Restoration Drama* (London, Evans Brothers Ltd, 1966) and Oscar Brockett, *The Theatre, an Introduction* (New York, Holt, Rinehart and Winston, 1965).

9. See for example Marilyn L. Williamson, *Raising Their Voices: British Women Writers, 1650-1750* (Detroit, Wayne State University Press, 1990); Cheryl Turner, in *Living by the Pen: Women Writers in the Eighteenth Century* (London, Routledge, 1992), speaks of Centlivre only in lists; the index entry on her 'as dramatist' refers to a footnote to chapter two in which the author lists women whose achievements have remained obscure in comparison with Behn's. *An Annotated Bibliography of Twentieth-Century Studies of Women and Literature, 1600-1800* (New York and London, Garland, 1977) by Paula Backscheider, Felicity Nussbaum and Philip B. Anderson, has 75 entries under Behn and 33 under Centlivre, relying heavily on Bowyer, bibliographic notes and unpublished dissertations. Since then Centlivre has been included in general studies such as Nancy Cotton's *Women Playwrights in England, c.1363 to 1750* (Lewisburg, PA, Bucknell University Press, 1980), and Jacqueline Pearson's *The Prostituted Muse* (London, Harvester, 1988), and has been accorded a long descriptive entry by Jean Gagen in vol. 84 of the *Dictionary of Literary Biography* ed. Paula R. Backscheider (Detroit, Gale Research Inc., 1989. But all of these sources still see Centlivre as a successor to Behn, one of a group of lesser dramatists; and the only single-author study, F. P. Lock, *Susanna Centlivre* (Boston, Twayne, Publishers, 1979), is purely literary in its approach, and concludes that 'in the wider perspective of English drama as a whole, Centlivre can rank only as a minor figure' (p. 134).

10. Laura J. Rosenthal, *Playwrights and Plagiarists in Early Modern England: Gender, Authorship, Literary Property* (Ithaca and London, Cornell University Press, 1996), p. 7.

11. This formulation, and much of the following section, derive from Peter Burger, 'The Institution of Art as a Category of the Sociology of Literature' (1979), in P. and C. Burger, eds, *The Institutions of Art,* trans. Loren Kruger (Lincoln and London, University of Nebraska Press, 1992).

12. Pinero told this to his first biographer: see H. Hamilton Fyfe, *Sir Arthur Pinero's Plays and Players* (London, Greening, 1930), p. 259.

13. Quoted in Stathas, 'A Critical Edition', p. xi.

14. Review of Bowyer, *Theatre Notebook* 8, 20, cited in Rosenthal, *Playwrights and Plagiarists,* p. 133.

15. Cotton, *Women Playwrights in England,* pp. 144-5.

16. Douglas Butler, 'Plot and Politics in Susanna Centlivre's *A Bold Stroke for a Wife*', in Schofield and Macheski, *Curtain Calls,* pp. 357-70, p. 357.

17. Bateson, *English Comic Drama,* p. 64.

18. Lock, *Susanna Centlivre,* p. 134; Pearson, *The Prostituted Muse,* pp. 202-3.

19. See Terry Eagleton, *The Ideology of the Aesthetic* (Oxford, Blackwell, 1990), p. 21.

20. Jeremy Collier, *A Short View of the Immorality and Profaneness of the English Stage, 1698;* reprinted from the 3rd ed. (New York, AMS Press, Inc., 1974), pp. 163-4.

21. *Ibid.,* p. 21.

22. Bateson, *English Comic Drama,* p. 61; the quotation is from *A Comparison Between the Two Stages* (1702), attributed to Charles Gildon.

23. Cotton, *Women Playwrights in England,* p. 122.

24. Pearson, *The Prostituted Muse,* p. 228.

25. Fidelis Morgan, *The Female Wits: Women Playwrights on The London Stage 1660-1720* (London, Virago, 1981), p. 329; see also Marilyn L. Williamson, *Raising Their Voices: British Women Writers 1650-1750* (Detroit, Wayne State University Press 1990).

26. Susanna Centlivre, *The Plays of Susanna Centlivre,* edited with an introduction by Richard C. Frushell, 3 vols (New York and London, Garland Publishing Inc., 1982), Vol. 1, p. ix.

27. In her Preface to *The Platonick Lady* (1706).

28. Sybil Rosenfeld, *Strolling Players and Drama in the Provinces 1660-1765* (Cambridge, Cambridge University Press, 1939), *passim.*

29. Lock, *Susanna Centlivre,* p. 72.

30. Frushell, *Plays,* vol. 1, pp. xvii, xxviii; *The Busie Body* had 22 royal command performances, including the night, 22 October 1717, when the Prince of Wales demanded it instead of *Othello.*

31. Frushell, *Plays,* vol. 1, p. lxvii.

32. Bowyer, *The Celebrated Mrs Centlivre,* p. 103.

33. Joseph Centlivre was a cook in the royal household.

34. Stathas, 'A Critical Edition', pp. xxi, 477.

35. Quoted in Frushell, *Plays,* vol. 1, p. xxvii.

36. See examples given in *ibid.,* p. xciv, n. 68.

37. Morgan, *The Female Wits,* p. 59.

38. *The Tatler,* no. 19, 24 May 1709, quoted in Bowyer, *The Celebrated Mrs Centlivre,* p. 98.

39. Suz-Anne Kinney, 'Confinement Sharpens the Invention': Aphra Behn's The Rover and Susanna Centlivre's The Busie Body', in Gail Finney, ed., *Look Who's Laughing: Gender and Comedy* (New York, Gordon and Breach, 1994), p. 96; see also Pearson, *The Prostituted Muse,* pp. 220-1.

40. Haymarket, 1825; Coburg, 1827.

41. Jim Davis, *John Liston Comedian* (London, The Society for Theatre Research, 1985), p. 56.

42. See Frushell, *Plays,* p. xxix; he cites Arthur Murphy's story that Garrick took on the role because Woodward, confident of his drawing power in the part, refused to continue without a rise in his salary.

43. *Busie Body* is the first play in *The New English Theatre in Eight Volumes, Containing the most valuable plays which have been Acted upon the London Stage,* (London, Rivington *et al.,* 1776); it occurs in vol. 8 of *Bell's British Theatre,* also dated 1776; most editions from 1777 onwards reflect these same alterations.

44. See Pearson, *The Prostituted Muse,* p. 210, for an interesting interpretation of Marplot as a feminised figure, parodying stereotypes of female inquisitiveness and weakness - a notion which reinforces the tension his stage activity creates.

45. 'Daughters of anger/material girls', in Regina Barreca, ed., *Last Laughs,* Women's Studies Vol. 15 (New York, Gordon and Breach, 1988), pp. 281-308, 287.

Annette Kreis-Schinck (essay date 2001)

SOURCE: Kreis-Schinck, Annette. "'What pleasant Lives Women lead in *England,* where Duty wears no Fetter but Inclination': Dramatic Representations—Susanna Centlivre." In *Women, Writing, and the Theater in the Early Modern Period: The Plays of Aphra Behn and Suzanne Centlivre,* pp. 71-82. Madison, N.J.: Fairleigh Dickinson University Press, 2001.

[*In the following essay, Kreis-Schinck considers the nexus of Centlivre's gender politics and her Whiggish nationalism, finding the playwright inconsistent in her treatment of women and liberty. Kreis-Schink suggests that Centlivre's popularity owed much to her dramatization of the tension between progressive politics and conservative gender roles—a tension she could uniquely experience as a female dramatist.*]

It would be tempting to read cultural history and its implications in gender politics as a seamless story of progress and success, one that describes a linear development from the dark ages of women's oppression to the bright present or future of their liberation and emancipation. It would be equally tempting to create a genealogy of women dramatists in which Susanna Centlivre figures as Aphra Behn's natural daughter, her successor picking up the pen precisely where Behn had put it down some twenty years earlier. In fact the quotation from Centlivre's **The Wonder: A Woman Keeps a Secret** (1714) that forms the title of this chapter seems to suggest that such a streamlined version of cultural history could be manufactured from the history of women, marriage, the growth of the nuclear family, and the dramatic representations of all these, from the late seventeenth to the early eighteenth century—even if only for English theater.[1]

Yet in spite of a number of instances where Centlivre's plays do allude to concepts of liberty, no reading could be more reductive. Thus alongside her claims for women's freedom, enfranchisement, and authority there are deplorable representations of submissiveness, passive virtue, and uniform weakness and fallibility. One reason for such inconsistency could be the widening range of her female characters. Next to the usual blend of the young heiress, country gentleman's daughter, fashionable widow, and clever maid or confidante, new characters make their appearance, characters that demonstrate the eighteenth century's broadening interest in different strata of society. For a woman writer this move makes possible a fuller spectrum of female characters too: the political campaigner, the research scientist, the social reformer, the reformed mistress, as well as wives and daughters of merchants, tenant farmers, and stewards. Representing different social classes was nothing new on stage, but never before had the middle and lower classes reached so much prominence. One other temptation, therefore, would be to associate conservative attitudes toward gender politics in Centlivre's plays with those social and political classes that embodied and upheld past aristocratic ideals of behavior while conversely associating the emerging middle classes with more progressive and liberal convictions. Such a neat distinction would gain considerable weight in the light of Centlivre's personal allegiance to the social groups on the rise, her staunch support of mercantilism, Whig politics, and constitutional monarchy.

Unfortunately, no such coherent picture of Centlivre's attitude toward gender issues can be drawn. Political liberalism does not necessarily correlate with liberalism in respect to gender. It could be argued that her texts incarnate the divergent speaking voices I have discussed in connection with Mary Astell's essay on marriage. Little wonder, therefore, that Centlivre's lack of a "logical and consistent evaluation of life," and her "failure to forge separate elements into a coherent whole" have been stressed by two of her twentieth-century critics.[2] That she would express especially her gender-political viewpoints in an incoherent, polyvocal, amorphous way testifies on the one hand to the sexual dynamics inherited from an earlier, more radical, and more unsettled epoch—one that Behn exploited to the utmost. On the other hand, Centlivre's work points to the growing influence of what was to develop and to solidify, as the century progressed, into the dominant discourse of femininity, domesticity, and the sentimental family. Given that she wrote during the very first two decades of the eighteenth century, she can be squarely placed between competing sets of social and sexual value systems.

It will be the aim of the following chapter to pay particular attention to Centlivre's inconsistencies in respect to women who are, or are going to be, wives. From a gender-specific point of view, her dramatic work might be called a borderline case that displays a broader variety of speaking positions for both men and women, while at the same time fighting a rearguard action against inevitable changes and limitations within and beyond the world of drama. Yet fight she did, and her success was unquestionable: two of her comedies, ***The Wonder*** and ***The Busy Body*** (1709), became stock pieces through the nineteenth century. "Except for Shakespeare, this statement can be made for only four comedies . . . written before 1750—these two by Susanna Centlivre, *A New Way to Pay Old Debts* by Philip Massinger, and *She Would and She Would Not* by Colley Cibber."[3]

Contemporary public taste cherished Centlivre's plays. Any analysis of them, however, exposes a number of contradictory dramatic elements and goes some way to explaining why studying her work is less satisfactory than reading, for example, Behn. Yet to dismiss Centlivre on account of these inconsistencies would be all too facile, for it would mean neglecting the way in which social, cultural, and literary history interrelate. It is the very complexity of this relationship that has become a feature of literary criticism in recent years. Such critical sensitivity serves to show why Centlivre marked the end of a period during which women playwrights made an important contribution to the history of drama, and explains why in the second half of our century women dramatists have returned to prominence.

* * *

With very good reason Centlivre's plays may be described as studies in the concept of liberty,[4] which, significantly, often appears in conjunction with the notion of property and in almost every play represents an unbroken nationalist pride and a hearty faith in England's political, economic, and juridical systems. The opening moment of ***The Wonder*** is a case in point. Having recently returned to his native Lisbon, a young merchant is asked by an old grandee: "You have been there, what sort of People are the *English*?" The following panegyric is by no means atypical of Centlivre's work: "My Lord, the *English* are by Nature, what the ancient *Romans* were by Discipline, couragious, bold, hardy, and in love with Liberty. Liberty is the Idol of the *English,* under whose Banner all the Nation lists; give but the Word for Liberty, and straight more armed Legions wou'd appear, than *France,* and *Philip* keep in constant Pay" (3:8).

There is no doubt that this would have gone well with an audience keenly aware of the political and military questions of their day. The peace of Utrecht brought to an end a war against France that had lasted more than a decade. During the year in which the play was performed, George I became king, a political development wholly in accordance with Whig theories of limited kingship rather than Stuart absolutism. If a woman had been eligible for a poet laureateship, Susanna Centlivre would certainly have received this title, as she had already lent her unfaltering support to the house of Hanover for a very long time indeed.[5]

Critics have long recognized the effect contemporary sociopolitical ideas had on Augustan drama and on Centlivre's plays in particular.[6] It is interesting, however, that these same critics fail to read the lines immediately following those just cited from ***The Wonder.*** Reflecting upon the convictions of the English, the old grandee offers this comment: "I like their Principles; who does not wish for Freedom in all Degrees of Life? Though common Prudence sometimes makes us act against it, as I am now oblig'd to do, for I intend to marry my Daughter to *Don Guzman,* whom I expect from *Holland* every Day, whither he went to take Possession of a large Estate left him by his Uncle" (3:8).

So how far does the battle-cry liberty carry when employed in connection with women? Not very far, it seems. Like countless of her predecessors, a Centlivre daughter still has to labor under the patriarchal notion that obliges fathers and guardians to move these female objects from one destination to the other, joining one piece of property to another, even to Don Guzman, who is characterized as "Age, Avarice, and a Fool" (3:8). What distinguishes this highly stereotypical element from earlier dramatic and nondramatic literature is its proximity to the principle of freedom.

This proximity, it is clear, stems from a political rationalism outlined, for example, by Locke's *Two Essays on Government* (1690), that was applied by some writers to the authority that men exercise over women. Mary Astell, as we have seen, was such a writer, Elizabeth Singer Rowe another. Giving these ideas a patriotic twist, which Centlivre was later to use in her plays, Rowe in a 1696 work establishes a clear geographical distinction: "here's a plain and open design to render us meer *Slaves,* perfect TURKISH WIVES, without *Properties,* or *Sense,* or *Souls;* and are forc'd to Protest against it, and appeal to all the World, whether these are not notorious Violations on the *Liberties of Free-born English Women?*"[7] In distinguishing between a notoriously unfree country and proverbial English liberty, and by tying these differences to the question of a woman's status, Rowe gives her reader no choice but to answer her provocative question with a decisive "yes," which, at least linguistically, implies that women in England are "*Free-born*" and enjoy "*Liberties.*"

Another writer, the anonymous author of *The Hardships of the English Laws in relation to Wives* (1735), puts the case in less polemic and patriotic but in more jurisprudential terms when she (or is it he?) wonders whether "by the Nature of Societies, and established Rules of Government, all Parts of a Community have not a Right to a Degree of Liberty and Property correspondent to the Constitution under which they live?" The well-formed answer implies that the anonymous author would be convinced that female subjecthood is possible in legal as well as in religious terms: "'Tis nothing to the Purpose to say, we should make an ill Use of this Liberty, for if the Law of God, and the Rules of Equity allow it us, we have a Right to it, and must answer for the Misapplication of our Liberty (as Husbands do for theirs) to God alone."[8]

In their analyses of individual freedom in respect to women, these writers faced the limits of precisely that liberalism that enabled the construction of the autonomous subject during the eighteenth century. Increasingly, these limits made themselves felt as "women's benefitting from individualist ideas about equality was undercut by the very configuration the family was assuming."[9] The sentimental family, firmly closed off from the public world, came to be the only space deemed appropriate for women. This nascent discourse on a distinctive femininity posited an ideal according to which female characteristics could well be positive. Now no longer defined by the lack or the inversion of certain male qualities, the female-gendered self gradually assumed a position of its own, albeit one predicated upon the internalization of restraint, etiquette, and confinement. Consequently, women's role within the family was defined exclusively in terms of an idealized domesticity, in which children and servants and the care for the sick or needy certainly played a role, but in which the figure of the pater familias loomed larger than life:

> Every Moment of her Life brings me fresh Instances of her Complacency to my Inclinations, and her Prudence in Regards to my Fortune. Her Face is to me much more beautiful than when I first saw it; there is no Decay in any Feature which I cannot trace from the very first Instant it was occasioned, by some anxious Concern for my Welfare and Interests. . . . Oh! She is an inestimable Jewel. In her Executions of her Household Affairs, she shows a certain Fearfulness to find a Fault, which makes her servants obey her like Children; and the meanest we have, has an ingenious Shame for an Offence, not always to be seen in Children in other Families.

This exquisite household aria reaches its climax when the wife and mother dies, to the last "concealing the Pain's she endur'd, for fear of encreasing [her husband's] Affliction."[10]

Thus the *Tatler* in 1709. Thanks to Kathryn Shevelow's excellent study of early popular periodicals, it is now possible to assess in more detail the influence those publications had on the construction of the roles the genders were to play. Given the low price at which they sold, a measure that was intended to broaden their reading public to include women and the ever-increasing middle classes, periodicals were able to reach a far larger audience than the conduct books before them, and, consequently, contributed in no small part to shaping normative images of the family. With a reformist agenda geared in particular towards the "fair sex," the periodicals, in Shevelow's analysis, presented a continuum of intentions between "'learning' (the periodical as an informational tool in itself, as well as a force exhorting women to gain knowledge) and the modification of behavior (the periodical as social critic and conduct book, exposing vice and modeling virtue)." What is significant about this continuum, however, is the different topics on which it focuses. "These reformist agendas coexisted within the same periodical—indeed, they were inseparable—but in the space of twenty years between the major periodicals of Dunton and Steele, the emphasis shifted from reform-as-knowledge to reform-as-behavior-modification."[11] Thus the very first of these publications, John Dunton's *Athenian Mercury* (1691-97), presents a relatively loose definition of gender roles: this openness "permitted them occasionally to articulate the rationalist feminist arguments which were current in the later seventeenth century."[12] For a while radical arguments coexisted with the conservative ideal of domestic femininity slowly taking hold. A little over a decade later, with Richard Steele's *Tatler* (1709-11), and Steele's and Joseph Addison's *Spectator* (1711-13), "the desirable domestic woman became central" to the program of periodicals, whose most striking characteristic was the "creation of a consistent rhetoric to and about women that, self-consciously 'progressive,' claimed to defend and elevate women's status by defining femininity in a privileged way and designating an area of perception and experience as female."[13] It goes without saying that this female area of influence was under strict male control, and that household and family arrangements reinforced patriarchal relations of authority and submission between husband and wife.

* * *

In terms of Centlivrean drama, the discursive inheritance of late seventeenth-century rationalism leads to the creation of plain-speaking women of sense who negotiate their marriages not so much on the basis of passionate love but rather of reason and a careful consideration of social and material circumstances. It is these women characters who, at least temporarily, stress for themselves the notion of liberty and personal choice. On the other hand, Centlivre's work displays early examples of women of feeling and sentimentality who anticipate eighteenth-century middle-class female norms.

A note on definition is called for here: my use of "sentimental" and "sense" is, obviously, modern. In Centlivre's time sentimental could still have referred to someone able both to express thoughts, opinions, and ideas, and to make intellectual judgments. From roughly mid-century onwards the words "sentiment" and "sentimental" experienced considerable change and came to denote the refined, delicate, intense emotions that sometimes verge on the lachrymose. What, in theory, signified a combination of a feeling heart and a reflective mind was narrowed down and, from the following century onwards, suffered a distinct pejoration. According to Jean Hagstrum, the word "came to refer specifically to the gentle, tender, loyal, courteous emotions, precisely those most amenable to domestic needs and desires."[14] One of the effects of tenderizing and civilizing public and private discourse, of domesticating culture at large, was a growing feminization of this culture. Needless to say, this "impregnation by the feminine spirit" would in due course cause the pejoration of the term.[15] *Sentiment* and *sentimental* thus received the satirical treatment that became such a well-known feature of the epoch that followed. This development was also to bring about a dichotomization in terms of gender. While "sentiment" and "sentimental" from the following century onwards received a distinctly female connotation, the term "sense" slid in the opposite direction. In Richardson, a man of sense could still signify a man of passion. One hundred years later, common sense, rationality, and a cool analytic mind were what the phrase suggested, characteristics no longer available for women.

The sentimental woman owes her construction, I would propose, to the gender norms being established by the beginning of the eighteenth century. As a reaction against the licentiousness (or freedom?) of the Restoration years, the picture of the domestic woman, as painted by the *Tatler*, epitomized this change. Predictably, it was the sentimental woman who made more impact upon an audience or a reader. The demonstration of strong emotions could be portrayed far more easily than a dispassionate consideration of arguments—something that was especially unattractive in a female character. This is why I shall deal with some of Centlivre's sentimental heroines first, before having a look at their more sensible, but far less colorful, sisters.

* * *

On the whole, those of Centlivre's women of the reforming or reformed type are, more often than not, wives. This fact alone seems to indicate that the containment female conduct experiences throughout the century is first represented for those women who are placed under the regime of a husband. Fatherly authority may indeed be as despicable as it usually is in Centlivre's work, but in all her plays it is curtailed. Not so the regime of a husband. Once a wife, the character behaves in a way that approximates the sentimental model, without, however, endorsing the ideal of domesticity.

Let us start with the exception to the rule, Angelica, in ***The Gamester*** (1705), who does her best to rescue a thoroughly profligate fiancé from gambling. She trusts him when he claims he will mend his ways, in spite of the proof to the contrary that the play offers, and she agrees to marry him to prevent him from being disinherited. Louisa, the Dutch lady in ***The Artifice*** (1722), has contracted her marriage by vows, and now pursues her reluctant husband to England, where she rescues him from a purely mercenary and bigamous marriage.[16] In ***Love at a Venture*** (1706), Lady Cautious is kept from adultery by a morally stern brother who profits financially from her fidelity within an unsuitable marriage. She is brought to repent her flirtation and eulogizes this fact in embarrassingly eloquent terms. In a symmetrical move, the moral and sexual didacticism repeats itself in ***Marplot in Lisbon*** (1710), where a cross-dressing Isabinda has followed her husband to Portugal in order to protect him not only from the dangers of adultery but from the very real threat of being killed by a jealous local husband.

It is clear from these accounts that the term "wife" had undergone considerable change within the span of a generation. Patterns of female behavior that could not possibly have been represented in earlier pieces have now gained ground. Isabinda, whom I have just mentioned, is a case in point. Although her character is strongly reminiscent of the independent young heroine of earlier drama—moving alone from place to place, using male disguises in pursuit of her husband, and eventually winning him thanks to her contrivance—she must finally comply with the emerging norms of female etiquette. It is her clever scheming that rescues her husband from the house of a jealous grandee, whom Charles was about to cuckold and who had already prepared the scene for the murder of his wife and her lover. By assuming yet another male disguise, Isabinda prevents bloodshed. Yet instead of taking pride in her achievements, she offers these lines, which end the play:

> In vain we strive by haughty Ways to prove
> Our chaste Affections, and our duteous Love.
> To smooth the Husband's rugged Storms of Life,
> Is the Design and Business of a Wife;
> Men from Example more than Precept, learn,
> And modest Carriage still has Power to charm.
> After my Method, wou'd all Wives but move,
> They'd soon regain, and keep their Husband's Love:
> Our kind Indulgence wou'd their Vice o'ercome,
> And with our Meekness strike their Passions dumb.

(2:184)

Lip service to emerging norms? Irony, or even sarcasm? It is hard to take these lines at face value, given what we have seen of Isabinda and her comportment in the previous three acts, for wifely meekness and modesty are not exactly what she has represented on stage. This final text, however, slyly conceals a female independence that the play's plot has revealed throughout. In spite of its seemingly unequivocal call to submissiveness, the speech must be considered as an afterthought, one that idealizes the norms of a companionate, or rather, sentimental marriage, in which the wife's position is that of the healer of male evil. That the play from time to time strives in the opposite direction becomes apparent by a remark made earlier by Charles as he enters the room of his Portuguese beloved: "Suppose somebody shou'd be doing me the same Favour in *England* now with my Wife, cou'd I be angry? no Faith; if a man is born to be a Cuckold, 'tis none of his Wife's Fault" (2:142). Very much at odds with the final lines of the play, the kind of liberty that is put into discourse by Charles creates an indeterminacy challenging the period's urge to consolidate femininity.

Centlivre contrasts her more sentimental women, who, more often than not, are wives, with women of sense. Not yet married, they are personified by the young, self-assured, sensible daughter, who functions as the heiress to the concepts of the early Enlightenment. Confined and controlled by mercenary fathers on the one hand and by the demands of their suitors on the other, these women face a twofold struggle. In Centlivre's work it is principally the machinations of the young men that allow the women to outwit their fathers: female involvement in the intrigues is usually limited, especially in comparison to Behn's young heroines.[17]

On the other hand, they must educate their overtly passionate or simply unreasonable suitors in the kind of sensible behavior on which, for them, marriage must be based. Violante, in *The Wonder: A Woman Keeps a Secret,* fights such a twin battle. She must confront her father, who, eager to keep her fortune for himself, has destined her for a nunnery. And she must confront Felix, her possessive lover. At the same time she loyally hides Isabella in her apartment: the latter being on the run from her own father, whose views on female liberty I have discussed above.[18] Yet keeping the other woman's secret and mapping out some space for her own decision and actions proves increasingly difficult for Violante. Her loyalty to her friend drives her lover's jealousy to hysterical heights, as honor and free will stand in stark contrast to his notion of female accomplishments: "Honour, what hast thou to do with Honour, thou that canst admit plurality of Lovers, a Secret? Ha, ha, ha, his Affairs are wondrous safe, who trusts his Secret to a Woman's keeping, but you need give yourself no Trouble about clearing this Point, Madam, for you are become so indifferent to me, that your Truth, and Falsehood are the same" (3:27-28).

Despite this and similar verbal onslaughts, Violante comes into her own a little later when she confronts Felix with her well-reasoned analysis of love. Couched in a whole string of rhetorical questions, her strategy is to convince him with arguments, to prove her true feelings for him with the help of rational discourse:

> Cou'd I, think ye, cou'd I put off my Pride so far, poorly to dissemble a Passion which I did not feel? Or seek a Reconciliation, with what I did not love? Do but consider, if I had entertain'd another, shou'd I not rather embrace this Quarrel, pleas'd with the Occasion that rid me of your Visits, and gave me Freedom to enjoy the Choice which you think I have made; have I any Interest in thee but my Love? Or am I bound by aught but Inclination to submit and follow thee—No Law whilst single binds us to obey.

(3:38)

Even when her eloquent pleading climaxes with "Can you love without Esteem?" she does not succeed in convincing him as his answer shows: "Your Notions are too refin'd for mine, Madam." Demonstrably, the power to analyze and reason, to construct a logical argument, is not a woman's lot. *Persuadere*—the art of rhetoric is of no avail to a female character. The scene emphasizes that a reversal of linguistic strategies does not work either: male railing against female reasoning proves equally unsuccessful, so that communication between Felix and Violante breaks down. Only the intricacies of a complicated plot finally establish her fidelity. Only the comedy's business, the countless intrigues and counter-intrigues, put her on a par with Felix, whose jealousy—another word for hysterical fear of loss of control—interested Garrick so much that he chose Felix as his favorite role.[19]

The woman of sense, a contradiction in terms, is hard to represent. Yet Centlivre, as others, persists in attempting to do so. Exchanging eloquence for dumbness, Miranda in **The Busy Body** (1709) chooses the opposite strategy. Her lecherous old guardian, who covets her for himself, sells an hour's interview with his ward for 100 guineas to Sir George, who is in love with her. Policed by the two men—the ardent young lover and the disgusting figure of authority—she refuses to speak. This move seems to her in her exasperation to be the only one that will secure her integrity. In what is an extremely effective scene, Sir George then playacts both their roles, construing her "answers" to his declarations of love according to his own fancy and desire. Miranda thus emerges as the perfect willing mistress, eager to be taken in by his wooing. This play within the play, however, is deconstructed when she does finally speak to him after she has managed to get rid of the guardian. She immediately cuts him short: "What! beginning again in Heroics!—*Sir George,* don't you remember how little Fruit your last prodigal Oration produc'd?" While he continues in the same vein, Miranda insists on a sensible, matter-of-fact approach: "Prithee no more of these Flights; for our Time's but short, and we must fall to Business: Do you think we can agree on that same terrible Bugbear, *Matrimony,* without heartily repenting on both Sides!" (2:108).

She too, it becomes clear, is modeled on the reasonable type of woman. Rejecting the aristocratic rhetoric of courtship, she insists on the emerging bourgeois norms, where plain speech, material considerations, and a mutual acceptance of the conditions of marriage play an increasingly important role. Paramount in these negotiations is her securing her own fortune. "I have provided better than to venture on dangerous Experiments headlong," which means for Miranda tricking her guardian out of her "Writings," thereby guaranteeing her financial independence.

Marriage as a "Bugbear"? The *Oxford English Dictionary* defines the term as an "object of dread, esp. of needless dread; an imaginary terror," that is, something that loses its alarming quality when handled rationally. Can it ever be handled so? Jacqueline Pearson correctly draws attention to a number of Centlivre's female characters who choose to remain single and who recognize in more or less humorous terms that the institution of marriage is beyond their rational control. Pearson is equally right in stressing that none of them is a major character. Nonetheless, she fails to be more specific: of the six examples she gives, five are maids to the main female characters.[20] It is the heroine's alter ego who rejects marriage, a move impossible for middle- and upper-class daughters themselves. Thus Centlivre adapts another familiar pattern of Baroque

drama: while the main female character is restricted by social conventions, it is her pert maid who speaks and acts out much more freely against gender restriction.

There is, however, one instance in which Centlivre goes beyond this common class distinction. Lady Lucy in **The Basset-Table** (1705) is the interesting exception to the rule. Thoroughly upper-middle class, though decisively a minor figure, characterized in the dramatis personae as a "*sober Lady*" (1:202), Lady Lucy reacts with extreme caution to a proposal of marriage: "My Fault is Consideration you know, I must think a little longer on't" (1:256). Simultaneously disgusted and attracted by her suitor's gaming habits and profligacy, as well as by his generous evidence of friendship, she asks to be given time in which to consider the offer. For her, it becomes possible to maintain the ambiguous position of an unmarried woman of means, at least temporarily, thereby remaining outside the norms of her class, norms that stabilize the contemporary hierarchy of men and women. As chance would have it, Lady Lucy is part of a comedy whose plot questions social prescription for women in quite a different way: in the final part, I shall deal at some length with the problems involved by female learning and education as represented in **The Basset-Table.**

* * *

Although, in 1673, Poulain de la Barre declared that reason knew no sex, the implications of his dictum proved increasingly more complex and more contradictory.[21] It enabled some female writers to call in the debt due their sex and to present rational arguments with which they could underpin their claims. At the same time, a discourse on femininity developed that, by idealizing women's position, aimed at a strict observance of gender difference and gender hierarchies. Particularly in respect to the sensitive area of marriage and the home, a cultural practice emerged during the first half of the eighteenth century that disenfranchised, depoliticized, and essentialized protobourgeois women. By 1782, this discourse had firmly taken hold, and had been internalized so thoroughly that Elizabeth Griffith's *Essay, Addressed to Young Married Women* presented the relationship between husband and wife thus:

> A love of power and authority is natural to men; and wherever this inclination is most indulged, will be the situation of their choice. Every man ought to be the principal object of attention in his family; of course he should feel himself happier at home than in any other place. It is doubtless, the great business of a woman's life to render his home pleasing to her husband; he will then delight in her society, and not seek abroad for alien amusements. A husband may, possibly, in his daily excursions, see many women whom he thinks handsomer than his wife; but it is generally her fault if he meet with one that he thinks more amiable.[22]

Centlivre, writing at the start of the century, finds at her disposal two sets of assumptions, neither of which has become official gender doctrine. Thus the term "English wife," frequently found in her work, points in two mutually exclusive directions. It celebrates for women constitutional, that is, limited forms of patriarchal government and authority, access to the law, and the rational management of the affairs of daily life. On the other hand, it also alludes to libertine notions of sexual freedom, an inheritance from the previous century, which now have had to be contained by exposure through bawdy jokes. In her struggle with these competing discourses Centlivre splits woman and prospective wife into the two concepts I have shown here. The incoherence this step creates has to be studied in order to throw into relief the contradictions inherent in writing for an early eighteenth-century woman dramatist.

Women writers, it is obvious, are not alone in representing this central confusion of the period: Centlivre's contemporary, Daniel Defoe, faces the same double bind. In his conduct manuals—*The Family Instructor* (1715-18), *Religious Courtship* (1722), *Conjugal Lewdness; or, Matrimonial Whoredom* (1727)—he celebrates the internalization of rules guaranteeing familial harmony. Insisting upon justice and equality between the spouses, Defoe nonetheless ensures strict hierarchy with the help of providence and God's will: unruly wives and children are endlessly chastened and punished into appropriate behavior and moderation. These texts construct the companionate marriage as a purely spiritual and affective relation with no mention of the material and economic circumstances shaping it. In stark contrast, Defoe's fictional heroines, Moll Flanders and Roxana, cannot escape the material realities of their society. Time and again these women of sense experience their subordination to patriarchal authority in grossly realistic terms. Selling themselves, their bodies, and the lives of their children, they represent a material practice far removed from the sentimental ideal described in Defoe's conduct texts.[23]

* * *

In official representations of the public realm, and that includes the theater, sentimental woman reigned supreme for more than one-and-a-half centuries.[24] Centlivre's comedies, in their emphasis on reforming or reformed women characters, cater to this specific gender construct. This is why they held the stage for almost the entire period. When this construct began to lose importance, her plays were lost. Conversely, hers is the last attempt for the theater to combine sense and sensibility in her heroines. For reasons outlined above, the well-spoken, clear-thinking female character increasingly finds herself on the losing, that is, unattractive and therefore unrepresentable side. It is my contention that only with the reemergence of the chance to portray

women of sense and to make them visible even in the public domain, did female writers return to prominence in the history of drama. When it finally became possible to see and to hear women engage in rational as well as emotional discourse and to participate in social and political as well as private affairs, the female playwrights of the twentieth century began once more to play an important part in the theater.

Notes

1. *The Dramatic Works of the Celebrated Mrs. Centlivre,* 3 vols. (1761; reprint, New York: AMS Press, 1968), 3:13. References are to this edition and will be given parenthetically in the text by volume and page number. I do not use *The Plays of Susanna Centlivre,* ed. Richard C. Frushell, 3 vols. (New York: Garland Publishing, 1982) for the simple reason that Frushell's reproduction of the plays' first editions does not have continuous pagination.

2. John Wilson Bowyer, *The Celebrated Mrs. Centlivre* (Durham, N.C.: Duke University Press, 1952), 250; F. P. Lock, *Susanna Centlivre,* (Boston: Twayne Publishers, 1979), 31. Apart from these, only very few critics deal with Centlivre: Jacqueline Pearson dedicates a chapter to Centlivre in *Prostituted Muse: Images of Women and Women Dramatists, 1943-1737* (Hemel Hempstead: Harvester Wheatsheaf, 1988), 202-28, and Richard C. Frushell, the editor of her plays (see previous note), offers a stage history in his introduction to the edition. Frushell's further contributions to Centlivre criticism are "Marriage and Marrying in Susanna Centlivre's Plays," *Papers on Language and Literature* 22, 1 (winter 1986): 16-38, and "Biographical Problems and Satisfactions in Susanna Centlivre," *Restoration and 18th-Century Theatre Research* 7, 2 (winter 1992): 1-17.

3. Bowyer, *Celebrated Mrs. Centlivre,* v.

4. Pearson, *Prostituted Muse,* 222-28, discusses the restrictions of female liberty, without, however, accounting for them.

5. For an account of Centlivre's dedication of *The Wonder* to the Duke of Cambridge, later George II, before the question of succession was fully settled, see Bowyer, *Celebrated Mrs. Centlivre,* 152-54.

6. John Loftis, *The Politics of Drama in Augustan England* (Oxford: Clarendon, 1963), 154-61; Lock, *Susanna Centlivre,* 93-107.

7. Quoted in Vivien Jones, ed., *Women in the Eighteenth Century: Construction of Femininity* (London: Routledge, 1990), 144-45.

8. Ibid., 224.

9. Kathryn Shevelow, *Women and Print Culture: The Construction of Femininity in the Early Periodical* (London: Routledge, 1989).

10. Quoted in Shevelow, *Women and Print Culture,* 131-32.

11. Ibid., 4.

12. Ibid., 50.

13. Ibid., 95-99.

14. Jean H. Hagstrum, *Sex and Sensibility: Ideal and Erotic Love from Milton to Mozart* (Chicago: University of Chicago Press, 1980), 10.

15. Ibid., 163.

16. It is interesting that by 1722 "spousals" or marriage vows had lost importance in England: in the play, this form of marriage is moved abroad. In contrast to seventeenth-century practice and representation, only a dim cultural memory seems to have persisted, before, in 1753, the Marriage Act, which invalidated certain marriages, was passed.

17. The clearest example is found in *A Bold Stroke for a Wife* (1718), where a highly inventive Colonel Fainwell has to trick four guardians into giving their consent to his marrying Anne, who passively observes his scheming.

18. Another word on patriarchal authority as represented by fathers is necessary here. The number of outright despicable fathers (and sometimes guardians) in Centlivre is impressive. Each play contains one; a lot of plays, however, assemble two or more of them, as for example *The Stolen Heiress, The Busy Body, The Wonder.* Obsessed with their daughters' sexuality, these fathers sometimes go as far as wishing for their death or infertility in order to prevent their marriage (*The Busy Body, A Bold Stroke for a Wife*). Most disturbingly, these figures quite often refuse to join in the happy ending. Their plans for their daughters' future slighted, they often fail to accept the loss of their authority and leave the stage with bitter words or even a curse (*Love's Contrivance, The Busy Body, The Man's Bewitched, The Wonder*). Of course, old fathers who must be outwitted are a time-honored dramatic commonplace. What is striking about Centlivre's handling of this device is the excesses and the nastiness of many of these figures. It is here that the playwright focuses her fiercest criticism of social custom. As it was impossible within the discursive parameters of her time to criticize the institution of marriage and its forms of male control, it is between the generations, between a father and a daughter, that Centlivre highlights the

struggle. The abuse of the right to liberty and freedom of choice can be emphasized more clearly in such a father/daughter relationship than it can within marriage.

19. Bowyer, *Celebrated Mrs. Centivre,* 177-83.

20. Pearson, *Prostituted Muse,* 214-15; the sixth is an ex-mistress, who, as a result, cannot be placed in any particular social category.

21. *De l'égalité des deux sexes* (Paris, 1673) was published in England as *The Woman as Good as the Man: Or, the Equality of Both Sexes* (London, 1677). See Michael A. Seidel, "Poulain de la Barre's *Te Woman as Good as the Man*," *Journal of the History of Ideas* 35 (1974): 499-508.

22. Quoted in Cheryl Turner, *Living by the Pen: Women Writers in the Eighteenth Century* (London: Routledge, 1992), 44.

23. For a fuller discussion of these issues, see Carol Houlihan Flynn, "Defoe's Idea of Conduct: Ideological Fictions and Fictional Reality," in *The Ideology of Conduct: Essays in Literature and the History of Sexuality,* ed. Nancy Armstrong and Leonard Tennenhouse (New York: Methuen, 1987), 73-95.

24. To be sure, the case is quite different for the novel where fictional women of sense and their creators led a kind of invisible, only audible, underground life throughout. Yet until the beginning of our own century, even Virginia Woolf fought hard to throw out of her writing the alleged "angel in the house," the quintessential sentimental woman. For a discussion of the exaltation of woman as angel, see Jean H. Hagstrum, *Sex and Sensibility: Ideal and Erotic Love from Milton to Mozart* (Chicago: University of Chicago Press, 1980), 163-65.

THE BASSET-TABLE (1705) AND *THE GAMESTER* (1705)

CRITICAL COMMENTARY

LuAnn Venden Herrell (essay date fall 1999)

SOURCE: Herrell, LuAnn Venden. "'Luck Be a Lady Tonight,' or at Least Make Me a Gentleman: Economic Anxiety in Centlivre's *The Gamester*." *Studies in the Literary Imagination* 32, no. 2 (fall 1999): 45-61.

[In the following essay, Herrell reads The Gamester *in terms of the tension between the older land-based economy and the emergent cash-based economy. Her-*

rell traces the stability of honor alongside the stability of social class, eventually concluding that the play's critique of fluid status undercuts any interpretation of The Gamester *as a typical reform comedy.*]

John Dennis, in a 1704 response to yet another of Jeremy Collier's attacks on the immorality of the stage, criticizes Collier for neglecting to discuss what he sees as a more tangible and therefore more serious vice:

> But how does [Collier] propose to himself, to bring [reform] about? Why, not by suppressing Vice, but the Stage that Scourges and exposes it. For he meddles not with that Vice that is in the World, let it be never so flaming and outragious. For example, the crying Sin of England next to Hypocrisie, at this time is Gaming; a Sin that is attended with several others, both among Men and Women, as Lying, Swearing, Perjury, Fraud, Quarrels, Murders, Fornication, Adultery. Has not Gaming done more mischief in England within these last Five Years than the Stage has done in Fifty?
>
> (29)

Susanna Centlivre's dedication to her 1705 comedy *The Gamester,* an adaptation of Jean François Regnard's *Le Joueur* (1696), aligns Centlivre with Dennis in calling gambling one of the great vices of England and nods to Collier in its recommendation of morality "according to the first intent of Plays" (qtd. in Bowyer 59).[1] In so doing, Centlivre manages to associate herself both with the reformers of the stage led by Collier and with Dennis, who cagily asserted that the stage could be an amusing and palatable instrument of reform, rather than an evil. Modern readers have recognized the gambit. The few critics of the play agree with Jay E. Oney's analysis of Centlivre's sense of what the market would bear in her production of "a strong script on a timely topic with just the proper mixture of fun and moralization" (192-93).[2]

But the "moralization," in this case, is not merely an anti-gambling diatribe. Another topic very much in the minds of the contemporary audience was the fallout from the 1695-96 Recoinage Act, which inspired a flurry of debate that James Thompson characterizes as a questioning of the possibility of controlling or mastering money (47). *The Gamester*'s title character, Valere, is mastered by money and chance. By tracing this rake's progress, Centlivre explores a fundamental economic anxiety brought on by the shift from a system based on land to one based on ready money. In this new arrangement, social station could conceivably rise and fall as quickly—and randomly—as the roll of a gamester's dice. Most scholars who have commented on the play remark in passing that this story of a gamester's redemption is an exemplary comedy.[3] I would argue, however, that the play as a whole, including the epilogue and prologue, transcends the formulaic "reform comedy" structure. Rather, it is a cautionary and pessimistic portrayal of a social system struggling to come

to terms with the move away from the conservative Lockean model of the possessive individual to the more modern model of the economic subject. Ultimately, *The Gamester* rejects this proto-Marxian model, but not without raising doubts about the impossibility of returning to a more stable landed system.

Written as it was during the height of the "second" Collier controversy (1703-08), the play is often overtly didactic. Centlivre allows much on-stage time for the audience to witness the comic vagaries of Dame Fortune and the havoc she wreaks on the various hopeful couples before the rakish Valere is perfunctorily redeemed at the end of the play. Acting in contradiction to Collier's claim that "these Sparks generally Marry the Top-Ladies, and those that do not, are brought to no penance, but go off with the Character of Fine Gentlemen" (142), Centlivre portrays Valere's penance and remorse graphically, whether or not the audience—and the other characters—really believes that his repentance is sincere. But gambling within the play is not simply one of the obligatory plot devices providing the obstacle for the stock "young lover" characters. It is also a means of illustrating the tension caused by the changing notions of inherent or intrinsic value during the period after the Recoinage Act. This shift in value is capable of redefining the very nature of things; as Marx put it, "since money, as the existing and active concept of value, confounds and exchanges all things, it is the general *confounding* and *compounding* of all things—the world upside-down—the confounding and compounding of all natural and human qualities" (169). In Valere, *ancien regime* notions of gentlemanly behavior are confounded because of his gambling addiction, and the effects of his behavior ripple outward through his social circle.

During its fourteen-night run at Lincoln's Inn Fields, all the stalwarts of the Rebel Company appeared in *The Gamester* in their usual pairings. Valere the gamester (played by John Verbruggen) is in love with Angelica the heiress (Anne Bracegirdle), who loves him but despises his gambling. Also in love with Valere is Angelica's sister, the widowed coquette Lady Wealthy (Elizabeth Barry), who is in turn pursued both by the upright Mr. Lovewell (Thomas Betterton) and the Marquis of Hazard ([William?] Fieldhouse), who is a footman masquerading as a French nobleman. Valere's uncle, Dorante (John Corey), is in love with Angelica and has bribed her servant Favourite (Mrs. Hunt) to advance his cause. The plot concerns Valere's relationship with Angelica; Angelica banishes Valere each time she learns he is gaming. His reaction to this depends on his current streak of luck: at the beginning of the play, when informed that Angelica has cast Valere off yet again, his valet Hector (George Pack) pronounces, "If he has lost his Money, this News will break his heart" (1.1).

One of Valere's early speeches, given as he is riding high on a big pay-off, sets up his utopian idea of the gamester's milieu:

> Who is happier than a Gamester; who more respected, I mean those that make any Figure in the World? Who more caress'd by Lords and Dukes? Or whose Conversation more agreeable—Whose Coach finer in the Ring—Or Finger in the Side Box produces more Lustre—Who has more Attendance from the Drawers—or better Wine from the Master,—or is nicer serv'd by the Cook?—In short, there is an Air of Magnificence in't—a Gamester's Hand is the Philosopher's Stone, that turns all it touches into Gold.
>
> (3.1)

While Valere can think of nothing better than the gambling life, virtually all the other main characters condemn him for his profligacy, calling to mind Collier's general definition of a stage libertine: "A fine Gentleman that has neither Honesty, nor Honour, Conscience, nor Manners, Good Nature, nor civil Hypocrisie" (144). His long-suffering manservant, Hector, succinctly delivers the dominant opinion on the dangers of gaming; when Valere claims that he, as a gamester, has mastered alchemy with the Midas touch "that turns all it touches to Gold," Hector responds, "And Gold into Nothing" (3.1). This suspicion of such "alchemy" is particularly applicable to the era following the Recoinage Act. The play illustrates the change in the way wealth was judged and circulated, and takes up what Thomas Kavanagh calls the "increasingly ubiquitous phenomenon of money," specifically the question of "how different societal groups related to this circulation of money—how they responded to being redefined, at least within the context of the game, by the cards they drew and the points they threw" (29-30).

The points that Valere throws, or his luck with the dice, redefine his social group and dictate the complicated maneuvering of the other characters, with various potential pairings of couples appearing and disappearing rapidly. His actions at the gaming table redefine his peers; his dice throwing turns social relationships into a high-stakes game. A bejeweled portrait of Angelica serves as a marker of Valere's fortune and his heart; tracking its progress through various hands is a tangible warning of how, once she is invited in, Lady Luck can disorder a previously stable system. The game that Valere plays is not a mere diversion, nor does he play it as a gentleman should, with a disinterested air. Rather, his obsession threatens the stability of the larger culture in which he operates, undercutting the social strata.

Valere's emotional state is dictated by his luck throughout the play—he is unable to gamble in typical gentlemanly fashion, and both his honour and his love are subsumed by the quest for more cash to gamble away: "I promis'd to visit Angelica again to Night, but fear I shall break my Word," Valere airily tells Hector after his winning streak. "And will you prefer Play before that charming Lady?" Hector asks him. Valere's answer, "Not before her—but I have given my Parole to some Men of Quality, and I can't in Honour disappoint 'em" (3.1), comes not more than several hours after he has received Angelica's gem-adorned portrait as a token of his renunciation of gambling and vowed undying devotion to her in grand heroic style (2.1). If Valere has no money, his promises to Angelica are worthless; if he has cash and is ready to play, he follows the genteel code of honor. Valere's conduct is based on his economic status at any given moment. J. G. A. Pocock notes that "in the credit economy and polity, property had become not only mobile but speculative: what one owned was promises, and not merely the functioning but the intelligibility of society depended upon the success of a program of reification" (113). Because Valere's "investments," such as they are, are so overtly speculative, his promises, figuratively speaking, are not worth the paper they are printed on.

Valere's course of action reinforces Centlivre's attack on the intelligibility of society and traces the erosion of any notion of intrinsic value in his own character. He clashes with his father, Sir Thomas Valere, who has thrown him out of the house for his rakishness, and he bargains with his father for more cash as a tradesman might (1.1). He strikes up an association with Count Cogdie, in order that he may learn how to throw loaded dice (1.1). He refuses to pay off his considerable debts, except, as he says, those "honourable" ones incurred at play. He commands Hector to lie on his behalf, for which Hector is often beaten (1.1; 2.2; 3.1; 4.3; 5.1). He nearly capitulates to Lady Wealthy's proposition for his sexual favors in return for her cash, in blatant disregard of his friendship with Lovewell, Lady Wealthy's long-time suitor (4.1). All the while, Valere protests mightily that the other characters do not seem to place the same value on his honor, pledge, and word as he does. Hector comments wonderingly, "Ah, what a Juggler's Box is this Word Honour! It is a Kind of Knight of the Post—That will swear on either Side for Interest I find" (3.1). Valere is a graphic representation of the type portrayed by Dennis; in him, gambling coexists with the attendant sins of "Lying, Swearing, Perjury, Fraud, Quarrels, Murders, Fornication, [and] Adultery" (Dennis 29).

The persona of the gentleman gambler is still with us today, in sources as diverse as the obligatory casino scene in any James Bond film to Kenny Rogers's song "The Gambler." Castiglione's *Book of the Courtier* (1528) frames in the negative what becomes the long-standing precedent for gentlemanly gambling, in terms that describe Valere perfectly: gaming is not a vice for the courtier "unless he should do so too constantly and as a result should neglect other more important things, or indeed unless he should play only to win money and to cheat the other player; and, when he lost, should show such grief and vexation as to give proof of being miserly" (127). Valere violates all these rules of conduct—he doesn't know when to hold 'em or fold 'em, and he routinely makes the socially unacceptable mistake of counting his money while sitting at the table.

Centlivre takes care to establish Valere's violations of the gentleman gamester's code from the first and ultimately brings the audience to the realization that Valere is altogether without honor. Valere's violations spread to his entire social circle, indicating the virus-like power of the new economic system. The first lines in the play are from Hector, bemoaning his lot in serving a gamester. He supposes that Valere's luck has been bad, putting him "out of Humour" (1.1), so that Hector doesn't dare ask him for any dinner—the usual state of affairs while Hector has been in his service. Valere's acquaintances and all their servants are well aware of his obsession and the effect it has on him: when Hector tries to persuade Angelica's maid, Favourite, that he is at business, her response indicates the emotional involvement with gaming against which Castiglione warns: "Yes, yes, I guess the Business; he is at shaking his Elbows over a Table, saying his Prayers backwards, courting the Dice like a Mistress, and cursing them when he is disappointed" (1.1). An exchange between the two servants comparing the merits of Valere with old Dorante indicates the play's pessimistic view of the leveling effect of Valere's gambling. Favourite's description of Valere deliberately invokes an unkempt member of the lower class:

HECTOR:

Ay, but Women generally love green Fruit best: besides, my Master's handsome.

FAVOURITE:

He handsome! Behold his Picture just as he'll appear this Morning, with Arms across, down-cast eyes, no Powder in his Perriwig, a Steenkirk tuck'd in to hide the Dirt, Sword-knot untied, no Gloves, and Hands and Face as dirty as a Tinker. This is the very figure of your beautiful Master.

HECTOR:

The Jade has hit it.

FAVOURITE:

And Pocket as empty as a Capuchin's.

(1.1)

Indeed, the stage directions for his first entrance read "Enter Valere, in disorder"; an obvious sight gag would be to match his "disorder" to Favourite's description. And throughout the scene, "disorder" is keyed to violations of class and conduct, as we see when Hector chases his master around the stage.

Further action in the play illustrates Valere's abandonment, which seems to place Centlivre in agreement with Collier's assertion in *A Short View* that enslavement to one's passions is among the worst of crimes (164). In **The Gamester,** Centlivre is more closely aligned to Collier's *Short View* on the function of comedy than to the stance of her own earlier work, where she had repudiated Collier and asserted along with Dryden and others that the purpose of comedy was to entertain. Centlivre sets up a situation in which Valere's lack of control provides Lady Wealthy a way to satisfy her appetite for Valere—an appetite that Centlivre links to Valere's dissipation. After a comic scene in act 2 in which Angelica discovers Valere on his knees before Lady Wealthy—a posture that Lady Wealthy attempts to pass off as evidence that Valere is courting her rather than pleading for her help to win back Angelica's good graces—Lady Wealthy sets out to purchase Valere's sexual favours. "Oh, that I could once bring Valere within my Power," she fantasizes, "I'd use him as his ill Breeding deserves; I'd teach him to be particular. He has promised Angelica to play no more; I fancy that proceeds from his Want of Money, rather than Inclination" (3.2).

The letter she sends him, accompanied by a check for £100, underscores both his willingness to do anything for money and her lapse in moral behavior. She asks Valere to return her affections and makes it clear that Valere's greed provides the opportunity for her to pursue him: "I confirm my Words in a golden Shower—'Tis what I believe most acceptable to a Man of your Circumstances" (4.1). Both Valere and the audience know what Lady Wealthy is asking for. Lady Wealthy bypasses the standard mode of flirtation and turns instead to a straightforward financial transaction, in a singular moment of social disorder and a reversal of standard gender roles. An intuitive gambler herself, she has read Valere's hand correctly: despite his assertion to Hector in act 1, scene 1 that he detests the wealthy widow, the sight of what amounts to cash in hand is too much for him. He debates, "What must I do now? prove a Rogue, and betray my Friend Lovewell . . . But then Angelica, the dear, the faithful Maid—But then a Hundred Guineas, the dear tempting Sight!" (4.1).

The abstractions of honor, love, and friendship nearly lose out to Lady Wealthy's gift. Only Lovewell's expedient entrance saves Valere from accepting the solicitation—a scene in which Valere seems to recognize that his honor is not an inherent quality: "Ha, Lovewell! thou com'st in good Time; for my Virtue's staggering" (4.1). His response to Lady Wealthy objectifies his honor as a gentleman, to be purchased by the highest bidder; Lady Wealthy's money trumps the portrait of Angelica and all of Valere's worthless promises upon his receipt of it.

Another character in this sub-plot is corrupted by the gamester's vice. On the face of it, Lovewell appears to be the model of virtue, as he steadfastly refuses to game with Valere, moralizes on Lady Wealthy's coquettish tricks and the disreputable crowd of admirers surrounding her, remains her faithful and patient suitor, and triumphs by winning her hand in the end. But even this seeming contrast to Valere is redefined by Valere's economic irresponsibility. Although he has loved Lady Wealthy since before her first marriage, Lovewell is incapable of persuading her to accept his hand now that she is widowed: he freely admits that his "long success-less Love assures me I have no Power" (2.1). Even while she herself admits that he is the best of her suitors, Lady Wealthy fixes her mind on Valere. When Valere exposes her perfidy in act 4, Lovewell offers to duel with his friend for Lady Wealthy's nonexistent honor. Valere refuses, begging a previous engagement at the gaming-table (yet another indication that he is no gentleman), and Lovewell realizes that "Something must be done; but what I know not" (4.1).

His solution, as he informs Lady Wealthy, is to falsify the situation and manufacture honor in her where there is none: "I have since been with Valere, sworn to him the Letter was a Plot of mine, the Hand and Bill all counterfeit, to satisfy my jealous Scruple, if there were Affairs between ye, he believed it, and your Honour's free from all ill Tongues" (5.2). Essentially, he blackmails and purchases her by a falsehood, indicating that old notions of honor are ineffective in a system rendered economically chaotic. The new bond between them is a contract, but it is one based on deception and dishonor, giving the lie to Valere's description of Lovewell as "a Gentleman without Exception" (1.1).

Angelica also must find a way to move through this new economic landscape and to deal with the redefinition of her role necessitated by Valere's flirtation with Lady Luck. Lady Wealthy may have won the trick in act 4, but Angelica wins the round in act 5. She is aware that the odds are against her from the start. The "odds" are not entirely familiar, dramaturgically speaking: Centlivre's plot departs from the usual comic structure of young lovers thwarted by older characters. In fact, Sir Thomas sees Valere's love for Angelica as being his only redeeming quality: "I know your Love, and [it is] the only Thing I like in you: She's a virtuous Lady, and her Fortune's large" (1.1). The obstacle is framed in economic terms—it is Valere's gambling that comes between him and this virtuous lady. A commonplace repeated throughout the play is first stated by Favourite, as she and Hector argue the respective merits of Dorante and Valere: "For she that marries a Gamester that plays upon the Square, as the Fool your Master does, can expect nothing but an Alms-House for a Jointure" (1.1). This view, reiterated by almost every character in the play, is not only a contradiction of Valere's picture of

the gamester's life, but also a very real possible fate for Angelica if she does not redeem her occasional suitor. The difference in the women's estates ups the ante for Angelica, as an early conversation between them points out:

LADY WEALTHY:

> Believe me, Sister—I had rather see you married to Age, Avarice, or a Fool—than to Valere, for can there be a greater Misfortune than to marry a Gamester?

ANGELICA:

> I know 'tis the high Road to Beggary.

LADY WEALTHY:

> And your Fortune being all ready Money will be thrown off with Expedition—Were it as mine is indeed. . . .

> (2.1)

Although Lady Wealthy's motives are suspect at this point (we discover several lines later that she wants Valere for herself), her business sense is sound. When Angelica turns on her in shock and surprise at this disclosure, given her advice, Wealthy replies, "My Estate's intail'd enough to supply his Riots, and why should I not bestow it upon the Man I like?" (2.1).

Even though the immediate effect her advice has on Angelica is to cause her again to forgive Valere, Lady Wealthy reinforces Angelica's sense that she must hedge her bets as fully as she can. After castigating Valere in act 2 for playing false and breaking his vow to her yet again, Angelica reveals the steadfastness of her love for him and asks for what amounts to a business contract, framed conditionally: "I differ from my Sex in this, I would not change where once I've given my Heart, if possible—therefore resolve to make this last Trial—banish your Play for Love, and rest secur'd of mine" (2.1). Her rhetorical stance is similar to that taken by conservative theorists in the debates surrounding the Recoinage Act in the belief that contractual relationships could "maintain a monetary system which is stable and which will not reveal money to be yet another commodity" (Thompson 69). She attempts simultaneously to set a new standard of their love, replacing its current economic foundation, and to corner the market. She does so by a Lockean insistence on contract and trust, in which Thompson observes that "stability or security is dependent on each subject's observing his pledge" (58).

As a signifier of their bargain, she offers Valere a physical symbol of their business deal, the portrait set with diamonds, and stipulates that if he loses it "thro' Avarice, Carelessness, or Falshood," he loses her heart. Valere's unreliability is so obvious by this point that the foreshadowing is more than a bit heavy when he responds, "I agree; and when I do, except to yourself, may all the Curses ranked with your Disdain, pursue me—This, when I look on't, will correct my Folly, and strike a sacred Awe upon my Actions" (2.1).

All very well, as long as he keeps it, but the audience must observe sarcastically with Favourite that the portrait is "worth two hundred Pounds, a good Moveable when Cash runs low" (2.1). Joanna M. Cameron claims that the portrait "keeps the audience aware of Angelica's influence on Valere in scenes in which she does not appear" (36). I'd quibble with Cameron's wording and emphasize that what the portrait does is remind the audience of how little Angelica's influence matters; as soon as act 3 opens, we discover that Valere has borrowed five guineas from "Honest Jack Sharper" (3.1) and has won 557½ guineas. He has already broken the contract, although the portrait is still in his possession. In fact, the structure of the play suggests that he went immediately from Angelica's presence to the sharper.

Hector bets on Angelica when he urges Valere to marry her before his luck changes, but Valere, too taken by his streak of good luck, questions whether he should marry at all. Again, observes Hector, Valere's "Pocket and [his] Heart runs counter" (3.1). It is this state of affairs over which Angelica must triumph, and she ends act 3 with her assessment of the situation. She speaks in verse before her exit, marking the seriousness of the venture:

> For when from Ill a Proselyte we gain,
> The goodness of the Act rewards the Pain:
> But if my honest Arts successless prove,
> To make the Vices of his Soul remove,
> I'll die—or rid me from this Tyrant Love.
>
> (3.2)

Her "honest Arts" (a wonderful oxymoron, in this context, implying as it does the disguise and manipulation she is about to employ) further exemplify the social disorder and gender reversals caused by Valere's gambling fixation: in order to gain mastery over Love, the tyrant, Angelica must beat Valere at his own game. In act 4, scene 4, the game is Hazard, a French import and an early form of craps. Centlivre underscores the far-reaching effects of Valere's gambling addiction by featuring a high-stakes game in which, arguably, the only "skill" involved is in throwing loaded dice undetected.

Centlivre structures the discovery scene in order to display Valere in company with Count Cogdie, the gaming-table attendants, and a shady crowd of gamesters (4.4). Valere loses a vigorous round of Hazard and curses, blasphemes, accuses other players of cheating, and argues petulantly all the while. His emotions are at

the whim of Fortune; when his luck turns, he laughs and declares, "I have more Manners than to quarrel now I'm on the winning Side" (4.4), a shameful admission for a well-bred man. Into this atmosphere enters Angelica on her mission of redemption, disguised, pointedly, as a man. She further scandalizes and titillates the audience by joining in the game and acquitting herself more than admirably. Although she is perfectly well-mannered, she fits right into the company, strolling in and employing gaming terminology like a pro.

The argument that Angelica and Valere have near the end of the game again illustrates the parallel permutations of honor and economy. Valere, who has lost his entire stake and then some to Angelica, asks to set a hundred Guineas "upon Honour." Angelica's refusal—"I beg your Pardon, Sir, I never play upon Honour with Strangers" (4.4)—is both ironic and startling, showing as it does a fundamental change in social interactions. Earlier in the play, Valere tries to raise fifty Guineas from the pawn-broker, Mrs. Security, with nothing more than his good name. She refuses indignantly, her name of course the indication that something more substantial is required. She is quite right to do so; as Hector pronounces, "I'd have you to know, my Master's Note is as good as a Banker's—sometimes, when the Dice run well" (1.1). A gentleman's word, in this system, is no longer good enough; honor built on a foundation of chance is worth nothing. This chaotic economy is never more clear than when Valere, remembering Angelica's picture, appraises it as worth more than his life but offers it up as a stake after a minimum of persuasion from Angelica.

Moreover, after having lost the portrait fair and square, he regains not a shred of equanimity but, rather, threatens to cut Angelica's throat if she does not restore it to him. He threatens to challenge her to a duel, as well. A lover's display of affection, surely, but this is also a case of exceptionally poor sportsmanship combined with immorality. Fortunately, he is distracted, allowing her to run away before he can carry through. After calling himself a monster and enumerating his crimes (a far cry from his earlier assessment of his life), Valere exits the stage after a verse bemoaning, yet accepting, the justice of his fate (5.2). Angelica has won—but only through disguising her gender and blending in with a thoroughly rakish lot. Because of Valere's lack of honor, she is reduced to a disreputable masquerader.

"Where is the Immorality of Gaming," Valere asks disingenuously earlier in the play, "Now I think there can be nothing more moral—It unites Men of all Ranks, the Lord and the Peasant—the haughty Dutchess, and the City Dame—the Marquis and the Footman, all without Distinction play together" (3.1). Because Valere is cowed and discredited by the end of the play, not without some last-ditch efforts at bluffing, it is clear we are not meant to agree with his assessment but, rather, to recognize the startling negative effect of Valere's purchasable honor. Angelica gives him a scalding rebuke and is only persuaded to take him back through witnessing Sir Thomas's murderous rage at Valere's stupidity; after drawing his sword on his own son, Sir Thomas disowns Valere. Ironically, Angelica uses the terminology she earlier eschewed to extract yet another vow from Valere: "Valere, come back, should I forgive you all—Would my Generosity oblige you to a sober Life.—Can you upon Honour (for you shall swear no more) forsake that Vice that brought you to this low Ebb of Fortune?" (5.2).

This exchange, more than any other, underscores the fact that honor has become a hollow concept. If we've been paying attention to Valere's actions, the answer to Angelica's question is a resounding "No," leading us to wonder why she resorts to this useless terminology. She is falling back on old notions of honor rather than realizing that in this new society, as Kathy Strong frames the point in a somewhat different context, "pledges and promises necessitate a reliance on honesty, but invite the opportunity of illicit gain through falsehood" (1). Angelica asks Valere for a pledge based on honesty, despite the fact that he has failed her again and again. Through his dishonest pledge, then, Valere will gain Angelica's ready money.

Throughout the play, honor is consistently undermined and illustrated by the lack of honor, with little or nothing to take the place of honor. Centlivre advances her only stipulative definition in act 2, scene 2, when Hector presents Sir Thomas with a list of Valere's debts in the hope that Sir Thomas will settle the accounts. Sir Thomas refuses on moral grounds to pay the so-called "debts of honour" to Valere's mistress, his fellow gamblers, and his userers, and he revises the notion of honorable debts in favor of the new mercantile class: "He that makes no Conscience of wronging the Man—Whose Goods have been delivered for his Use, can have no Pretence to Honour—whatever Title he may Wear" (2.2). But tellingly, even here, while displaying Centlivre's Whiggish concern with "the increased importance of merchants in English society" (Loftis 65), the definition is framed in the negative, illustrating the anxiety produced by the move away from a landed economy. If there is no honor, then, the play allows very little hope that Valere's reclamation is in any way meaningful.

While Valere's lines in the last scene are downcast and penitent and while his father settles two thousand a year on him, the status of Angelica's fortune has not changed. Given Valere's previous lack of ability to keep his word, his debased notion of honor, and the play's repeated warnings about the danger of marrying a gamester, Valere's repentance is suspect. Underneath

the trappings of a standard comic denouement and a return to the status quo is the fear that ready money might be "a socially destructive threat to due respect for rank and privilege" (Kavanagh 52). Angelica may have won the round, but Valere is now in possession of more cash; and who knows what temptations may arise after the obligatory country dance?

* * *

In his curtain speech, Valere proclaims his complete redemption:

> Now Virtue's pleasing Prospect's in my View,
> With double Care I'll all her Paths pursue;
> And proud to think I owe this Change to you
> Virtue that gives more solid Peace of Mind,
> Than Men in all their vicious Pleasures find;
> Then each with me the Libertine reclaim,
> And shun what sinks his Fortune, and his Fame.
>
> (5.2)

But Valere, as we have seen, has resisted each reclamation that the play's plot twists have presented. Most critics of *The Gamester* agree with Robert D. Hume's remark that the piece is "a highly competent if entirely implausible exercise in reform and reclamation" and with his categorization of it as a "well-handled didactic play" among the period's "reform comedies" (469).

Critics also avoid discussing the prologue and the epilogue. While I am in general agreement with John Wilson Bowyer's claim that, for many works of this period, prologues and epilogues have little thematic connection to the plays themselves (63), I would argue that, in this case, the prologue and epilogue frame the play in a way that emphasizes the impossibility of Valere's reclamation. The play is not a reform comedy in the typical sense of the term: as the chances that Valere will relapse are so high, any reform must take place on the part of the audience, making *The Gamester* more didactic, and perhaps more realistic, than other reform comedies of the period. Hume further notes that "modern critics tend to find [*The Gamester*] self-delusory, or even dishonest" (470). However, an analysis of the framework provided by the prologue and epilogue authorizes a reading that maintains a consistently negative attitude toward the outcome of Angelica's marriage to Valere.

The prologue and epilogue, written by Nicholas Rowe and Charles Johnson, respectively, provide the audience with a plausible outcome of the young couple's marriage. Both pieces narrate a sort of rake's progress, leading to the deterioration of a marriage in which one of the partners is a gamester. Bowyer, the only critic to discuss anything about the pieces other than their authorship, mentions only the "sermonizing epilogue on the vicious effects of gambling for both men and women" (59). However, his comment that the play "asserts the goodness of ordinary human beings" (62) ignores the overall pessimistic tone of the play, which is substantiated by the monologues.

The first six lines of Rowe's prologue establish the controlling metaphor of the speaker as a young wife (the stage), who, while formerly "kept fine, caress'd and lodg'd" (9) by her new husband (the town), has discovered that the honeymoon is over. On the face of it, the metaphor plays out as a typical rant against the fickleness of the audience, which is weary of what it once enjoyed and is not so prone to attend the plays: "Sometimes, indeed, as in your Way it fell, / You stop'd, and call'd to see if we were well" (15). The speaker complains of her childbearing (playwriting) efforts and calls her progeny "Toads" (22), alludes to the gender of the playwright by mentioning a midwife (26), and threatens to abandon the current "toad," or play, to the parish if the neglectful audience forsakes it. Oddly, from a staging perspective, Centlivre's **Dramatic Works** (1872) lists Thomas Betterton as the speaker of the prologue, which bit of casting ignores the clear identification of both the "Plaintiff Stage" and "humble Wives" with the pronoun "we" in the first six lines. It is possible to assume that Betterton was given the speech as a nod to his managerial role at Lincoln's Inn Fields, thus making him a fitting "voice" for the stage, despite the gender mismatch. The speaker complains that the audience's "Love [has] dwindled to Respect" (14) but does not identify what new entertainment has taken the place of the playhouse.

I have observed that Favourite's first description of Valere, which occurs early in the first scene, pictures him "courting the Dice like a Mistress" (1.1). Given that the prologue would still be fresh in the audience's minds, it is reasonable to assume that they might imagine the charms of a wife paling beside those offered by a new amour. And, as I have shown, the play shows over and over again that Valere's inclination is toward gaming above all else, including his betrothed. This theme is borne out in the epilogue's sad words of advice about a young man ruined by gambling.

Throughout the play, several of the characters have uttered dire predictions about Valere's fate if he refuses to renounce gaming. In threatening to disown his son, Sir Thomas shouts, "then try if what has ruin'd you, will maintain you" (1.1); in refusing Hector the money to pay Valere's debts, he shouts, "Play, hang, or starve together, I care not" (2.2). Hector compares the lives of gamesters to those of highwaymen hanged for their crimes (3.1). Dorante points out to Angelica that Valere's "head-strong Courses and luxurious Life, will ruin both your Peace and Fortune" (3.2), and although she quibbles with him over his motives for informing on Valere, she does not argue with his conclusion. Sir

Thomas, delighted by the news that Angelica and Valere are finally to wed, announces that he plans to settle two thousand pounds a year on his son. "He shall make thee a swinging Jointure, my Girl" (5.2), he says exultantly to his future daughter-in-law.

The modern sense here, of course, is that Angelica is going to receive a jointure "to die for"—but the slang, given all the previous allusions to hangings and ruin, takes on a more ominous meaning when it culminates in the epilogue. "As one condemn'd, and ready to become / For his Offences past, a Pendulum," begins the speaker, who plays out the subject of the simile as one "Condemn'd . . . to play that tedious, juggling Game, a Wife" (1, 7-8). The speaker has long deliberated over the choice between the hangman's or the hymeneal knot and is giving the usual address to the crowd before being carted away for punishment (10). In contrast to Valere's euphoric picture of gambling utopia, the speaker in Johnson's epilogue shows the downward spiral of the gamesters, dismissed as "Fortune's sporting Footballs" (15). The speaker catalogues vignettes from the play itself: the gamester's hopes and fears, his inability to rule his passions, his loss of "his good Dad's hard-gotten hoarded Gain" (20), and his failure to raise more cash from the sharpers. But the epilogue goes beyond the scope of the play and follows the twists of Fortune to their logical conclusion: the gamester observed by the embittered wife becomes a sharper himself, is still unable to best Fortune, and at last must admit that "this itch for Play has likewise fatal been" (31).

There is some possible gender confusion in the casting of the epilogue as well as the prologue: Bowyer points out that there is uncertainty about whether John Verbruggen or his wife Susanna delivered the epilogue.[4] As the first gendered pronoun in the speech is "his," in the second line, it is understandable that one might assume that the dissolute gamester is the speaker. However, since there is such a strong thematic link between the monologues and the play itself, it would be odd for the actor playing Valere to deliver these lines; he has just ended the play with an edifying speech about his own redemption. When the speaker uses first person, the pronoun "I" refers to the noun "Wife," as noted above. Furthermore, there is a clear distinction established between the speaker/wife and the group of gamesters/ the audience, whom she addresses as "You roaring Boys" in the section of the epilogue beginning the "Word of good Advice" (11, 9). Given that the turning point of the plot calls for the actress playing Angelica to dress in men's clothing, and given that the syntax points toward a female speaker, it makes good dramatic sense for an actress originally to have delivered the epilogue.

The closing lines of the epilogue return to the metaphor established by the prologue: this wife is the same stage who no longer diverts the audience; but here the question of what entertainment has taken her place is answered:

> You fly this Place like an infectious Air,
> To yonder happy Quarter of the Town,
> You crowd; and your own fav'rite Stage disown;
> We're like old Mistresses, you love the Vice,
> And hate us only 'cause we once did please.

(39-43)

The stage has been abandoned for what Centlivre makes clear in her dedication is one of England's greatest vices; but it is not only the clever wordplay that matters here. The parallel to what has just occurred in the play—the marriage of Angelica and Valere—is clear as well and would be further enforced if the epilogue were delivered by the same actress playing Angelica. Pierre Bourdieu notes that "Marriage is the occasion for an (in the widest sense) economic circulation which cannot be seen purely in terms of material goods" (120); Thompson, in examining Bourdieu's concept of marriage as economic transaction, concludes that "those texts in which these two, the economic and symbolic (or, in our terms, the financial and the domestic), can be seen to touch are fraught with anxiety" (4). *The Gamester* produces anxiety because of the means by which Angelica's fortune is transferred. There would be far less tension, for instance, if the pairing were Valere and Lady Wealthy, as the play has made it clear that Lady Wealthy's fortune is entailed, thereby rendering Valere's obsession manageable. But nothing has changed about Angelica's money by the end of the play—all we are left with is Valere's unbelievable and unsubstantiated change of heart.

Rather than taking place in its rightful sphere, upon 'Change, in this case, economic circulation occurs amongst the gamblers out "upon the Square" (1.1) under conditions that are neither honourable nor productive. Although Bowyer points out how unlikely and unsatisfactory it is that Valere "eats his cake and has it too" (60), he assumes that the audience will join him in hoping "that [Angelica] is right in thinking that [Valere] has reformed forever" (62). But surely Centlivre's audience would have been just as skeptical of his eleventh-hour conversion, especially when it is so strongly linked with the despair and futility of the wife of the prologue and epilogue, who has made the mistake of marrying a gamester.

It is nonsensical to attempt to force the play into the reform model in this fashion. To do so is to disregard the hopeless scenario anticipated by the prologue, illustrated at Valere's every turn, and summed up in the epilogue. Valere has shown no inherent honor. He will not remain reformed but will succumb to the lure of Angelica's ready money. As the audience has seen, Val-

ere is irredeemable: "Few are his Joys, and small the Gamester's Rest" (5.2), which will perhaps inspire them, not Valere, to reform before they come to such a pass. "In this period of extreme social change and the transition to agrarian capitalism," says Thompson, "money and credit come to stand for the potential of liquid assets, to their dangerously enabling capacities" (35). In this reading of *The Gamester,* then, Centlivre has written a reform comedy only in the broadest of senses. If anything, the play offers a realistic portrayal of what damage an inveterate gamester can cause his social sphere when liquid assets are accessible. Hector's observation that Valere's fob is the barometer of his emotional state, which changes with his fortune, prefigures Marx's 1844 observation about the true alchemical properties of money:

> Money, then, appears as this *overturning* power against the individual and against the bonds of society, etc., which claim to be *essences* in themselves. It transforms fidelity into infidelity, love into hate, hate into love, virtue into vice, vice into virtue, servant into master, master into servant, idiocy into intelligence, and intelligence into idiocy.

(168-69)

Just how thoroughly these bonds of society have been overturned is illustrated by a minor character in the play, the Marquis of Hazard. He is chief of the foolish suitors who surround Lady Wealthy, whom he courts with stilted French and mismanaged posturing. He is actually Mrs. Security's nephew, a footman who is attempting to pass as a French nobleman in order to marry a rich woman of quality. While his social blunders seem to give validity to the notion that honor is an inherent quality, it is gaming that admits him into polite society in the first place. As Marx and Valere both claim, money has the power to obliterate former notions of class, as well as the potential for reconfiguring notions of value in both the public and private spheres. The Marquis is exposed as Robin Skip and ridiculed by the entire company in the last scene of the play, indicating a seeming return to the status quo further enforced by the predictable pairings of lovers and the usual triumph of youth over age. But because so many of the characters' virtues have been turned into vice by way of Valere's slavish adulation of Lady Luck, Robin Skip's lines— "Who once by Policy a Title gains, / Merits above the Fool that's born to Means" (5.2)—ring truer than Valere's last speech lauding his own reform.

The implausibility of that reform is not Centlivre's main point, ultimately, as it is certain that Valere's renewed luck will overturn the bonds of love and honor; rather, it is Angelica's plight, and the near-certain squandering of her non-landed fortune, to which the play anxiously returns. As a landed economy becomes ever more impossible off-stage, notions of inherent honor tied to that land become more and more suspect to timely writers like Centlivre, who resolves *The Gamester* in typical reform comedy fashion but introduces inescapable concerns about how the individual must function in the rapidly changing economic system of the day.

Notes

1. Cameron documents Centlivre's use of both Regnard and Charles Du Fresny's *Le Chevalier Joueur* (1697). See Bowyer for the most comprehensive bibliographic list of Centlivre's sources.

2. See also Hume 469-70, Loftis 65, and Rogers 161.

3. Criticism on *The Gamester* generally falls into two categories: a plot summary in the midst of biography (see, e.g., Bowyer and Lock), or a brief analysis as part of a larger work (see, e.g., Oney, Loftis, and Hume). Most criticism takes the form of Hume's, in that the play is mentioned in a line or two, while examining "exemplary," "reform," or "sentimental" comedies in general.

4. Bowyer compares the record in the *Diverting Post* of 27 Jan.-3 Feb. 1705, which identifies John Verbruggen as the speaker, with the 1725 edition, which identifies Susanna Verbruggen (59n. 13). That the complete works give the epilogue to Mrs. Santlow supports my reading of the speaker as female. As it is likely that an actress would have done the part in breeches, the audience might call to mind Angelica's appearance dressed as a boy in the pivotal gambling scene in act 4, thereby reinforcing the dramatic connection between the afterpiece and the play itself.

Works Cited

Bourdieu, Pierre. *The Logic of Practice.* Trans. Richard Nice. Stanford: Stanford UP, 1990.

Bowyer, John Wilson. *The Celebrated Mrs. Centlivre.* Durham, NC: Duke UP, 1952.

Cameron, Joanna M. "Susanna Centlivre's Satirical Retorts to Jeremy Collier: *The Gamester* and *The Basset-Table.*" M.A. Thesis. U of Houston-Clear Lake, 1992.

Castiglione, Baldesar. *The Book of the Courtier.* Trans. Charles S. Singleton. New York: Doubleday, 1959.

Centlivre, Susanna. *The Dramatic Works of the Celebrated Mrs. Centlivre, with a New Account of Her Life.* Vol. 1. London, 1872.

Collier, Jeremy. *A Short View of the Immorality and Profaneness of the English Stage.* New York: AMS, 1974.

Dennis, John. *The Person of Quality's Answer to Mr. Collier's Letter, Being a Disswasive from the Play-*

House. The English Stage: Attack and Defense 1577-1730. Collier Tracts 1703-1708. Ed. Arthur Freeman. New York: Garland, 1973.

Hume, Robert D. *The Development of English Drama in the Late Seventeenth Century.* Oxford: Clarendon, 1976.

Kavanagh, Thomas M. *Enlightenment and the Shadows of Chance: The Novel and the Culture of Gambling in Eighteenth-Century France.* Baltimore: Johns Hopkins UP, 1993.

Loftis, John. *Comedy and Society from Congreve to Fielding.* Stanford: Stanford UP, 1959.

Marx, Karl. *The Economic and Philosophic Manuscripts of 1844.* Ed. Dirk J. Struik. New York: International Publishers, 1964.

Oney, Jay E. "Women Playwrights During the Struggle for Control of the London Theatre, 1695-1710." Diss. Ohio State U, 1996.

Pocock, J. G. A. *Virtue, Commerce, and History.* Cambridge: Cambridge UP, 1985.

Rogers, Pat. *The Augustan Vision.* New York: Barnes & Noble Books, 1974.

Strong, Kathy. "'Give Credit Where It's Due': The Instability of Credit and Falsehood in Elizabeth Inchbald's *Such Things Are.*" Unpublished essay, 1999.

Thompson, James. *Models of Value: Eighteenth-Century Political Economy and the Novel.* Durham, NC: Duke UP, 1996.

Victoria Warren (essay date summer 2003)

SOURCE: Warren, Victoria. "Gender and Genre in Susanna Centlivre's *The Gamester* and *The Basset Table.*" *Studies in English Literature 1500-1900* 43, no. 3 (summer 2003): 605-24.

[*In the following essay, Warren disputes the categorization of Centlivre's comedies as "sentimental," maintaining that in such plays as* The Gamester *and* The Basset Table *the playwright undercuts sentimental morality and also draws an analogy between her learned ladies and the uneasy social status of the playwright herself.*]

> The play's the thing.
>
> —Shakespeare, *Hamlet* (II.ii.641)

Restoration theater—spanning the period from the Restoration of Charles II in 1660 through the reign of Queen Anne (1702-14)—covers a diversity of dramatic styles. In addition to conventional forms of "comedy" or "tragedy," other dramatic genres such as "heroic drama" and "tragicomedy" flourished as well. Moreover, within the category of "comedy" itself, critics—looking back in retrospect at the extant body of comic plays—have grouped the comedies into such subdivisions as "comedy of manners," "comedy of wit," "political satire," and "sentimental comedy." The last is the category to which *The Gamester* and *The Basset Table* by Susanna Centlivre (1667?-1723) have been assigned.[1] It is my contention that this categorization of Centlivre's plays as "sentimental comedy" is inadequate, inaccurate, and a distortion of the plays themselves. In this essay I examine the problematics of the term "sentimental comedy," interrogating its application to Centlivre's plays and analyzing the significance of the cultural context within which Centlivre wrote. At the same time, I look at the texts of the plays themselves, arguing that the concept of "play" within Centlivre's plays functions as a subversive counter-movement in the texts, deconstructing the dominant ideology of her audience and its demand for a comforting moral.

In labeling these plays "sentimental comedies," the critic distorts the plays in three principal ways. First, because of the twentieth century's negative connotations of the word "sentimental," the label has often been used as a means of segregating a playwright's plays from the so-called "wit" comedies and thereby assigning the plays a second-rate status.[2] One of the problems, then, lies in the terminology used to describe the new comedies. To call these plays "sentimental" is to cast them into an inferior position—a position that in the twentieth century was too often reserved primarily for the work of women writers. Although men wrote plays that have been called sentimental comedies, it is not surprising that earlier twentieth-century anthologies of Restoration and eighteenth-century comedies contain few or no works by women—despite the fact that women were among the most popular playwrights.[3] One solution to this problem would be to use a different term to describe the comedies. Shirley Strum Kenny has suggested that we call them "humane comedies," which provides a less negatively charged description of the works.[4]

This solution does not resolve the other problems, however. The critics' one-dimensional language in assigning labels to the plays overlooks the dialectic of the works—the tensions and contradictions within the plays. The designation "sentimental comedy," or even a substitute term, the purpose of which is to define and limit, forces the play into a preconceived mold, and in doing so, loses sight of the specific qualities that go to make up the play itself. A principal aspect of most definitions of sentimental comedy is the play's inclusion of a moral, and the term has often been used to suggest that the moral is the most important aspect of the play, that the play is important primarily as an ex-

emplum.[5] Moreover, the attempt to categorize constitutes an artificial separation of elements that are in fact blended together in the plays.[6] In looking at a play only in terms of the moral that it is supposed to convey, critics have overlooked or misunderstood other aspects of the play. Ultimately, the focus should not be on the label, but on the plays themselves; in other words, "The play's the thing."

An examination of Centlivre's *The Gamester* and *The Basset Table,* both of which were first performed in 1705, casts significant doubt on the appropriateness of the label sentimental comedy for these plays. First of all, can we say categorically that each of these plays is in fact prescribing a moral? In order to understand the "truths" that might be abstracted from the plays, we need to look at the economic and social factors that underlie the discourse, that is, the *context* within which the plays were written.[7] Second, even if we agree that there is a moral to be abstracted from the plays, can we be certain of what that moral is and do we know whether or not it is an unmixed dictum? If we deconstruct the text of the comedies, we find innumerable threads of difference that are in tension with the ostensible moral of the plays. Although most critics agree that a sentimental comedy portrays the characters' moral reformation, there are ambiguities and incongruities in these two plays that force us to ask questions about the nature of the characters' reform.

Before we proceed to a discussion of Centlivre's plays—and in order better to understand the problems inherent in the categorization of her plays—it is necessary to look at the historical evolution of the term "sentimental" as it has been applied to Restoration and eighteenth-century comedy. There are two principal debates concerning the term sentimental comedy. First, critics have not been able to agree on the definition of sentimental comedy. During the Restoration, the term was not used to describe the plays. The first significant mention of sentimental comedy does not appear until later in the eighteenth century. Oliver Goldsmith, in "An Essay on the Theatre" (1773), contrasts "laughing" and "sentimental" comedy, characterizing sentimental plays as "weeping comedy," in which the "virtues of private life are exhibited, rather than the vices exposed."[8] In the same period, William Cook, in *The Elements of Dramatic Criticism* (1775), expressed a similar contempt for sentimental comedy, calling it "a driveling species of morality."[9] These two works illustrate the difficulty of definition. For example, Goldsmith cites Colley Cibber as a good example of a playwright who does *not* write sentimental comedy; yet twentieth-century critics designated Cibber as the founder of sentimental comedy, citing his *Love's Last Shift* (1696) as the first of that genre.[10] Moreover, Cook and Goldsmith both maintain that sentimental comedy focuses on virtue rather than on ridiculing vice. Yet ridicule and satire play an important role in many plays that have been designated sentimental comedy.

Despite—or perhaps because of—the difficulties inherent in defining sentimental comedy, the question of definition formed a principal focus of twentieth-century criticism. In the long history of this debate in the last century, critics suggested various criteria.[11] Arthur Sherbo's *English Sentimental Drama* (1957) is an attempt to find a definition of the genre. Ultimately, however, Sherbo concludes that "attempts at rigid definition are fruitless"; there are too many exceptions and it is too difficult to ascertain the point at which a particular play becomes or avoids becoming "sentimental."[12] As Robert D. Hume notes in *The Rakish Stage,* "Sherbo's cautious and sensible investigation of the 'sentimental' shows that no clear-cut genre can be isolated."[13] Despite Sherbo's conclusion, however, critics continued to attempt to define sentimental comedy. Maureen Sullivan, in the introduction to her edition of Cibber's plays (1973), summarizes her discussion by listing five characteristics that she sees as inherent in sentimental comedy.[14] Frank H. Ellis, in *Sentimental Comedy* (1991), goes to extreme lengths to provide a detailed definition of sentimental comedy, analyzing eleven "primary elements" and four "secondary characteristics."[15] Yet after he has charted the elements he defines, he concludes that in the end one cannot be sure what is in fact sentimental because there is no way to chart "proportion."[16]

If there is no easy answer in the debate about definition, the second principal debate about sentimental comedy among critics of eighteenth-century drama is equally inconclusive: it centers on the question of whether or not sentimentality was the prevailing spirit of the age. The majority of twentieth-century critics maintained that in the period from the Restoration until the late eighteenth century the drama was increasingly dominated by the sentimental.[17] Other critics have disagreed with this portrait of eighteenth-century comedy. Richard Bevis, in *The Laughing Tradition* (1980), claims that the period was not dominated by sentiment, and concludes that earlier critics were mistaken in their conclusion because they did not have access to the full repertory of plays.[18] Hume in *The Rakish Stage* (1983) asserts that the sentimental was never dominant in eighteenth-century comedy and says that Goldsmith's lamentation "about the disappearance of humor from the stage is plainly nonsense."[19]

Although there is disagreement over the definition and prevalence of sentimental comedy, most critics agree that there was a shift in tone in the comedies during the 1690s. By the turn of the century, the rise of the "she" tragedies, which portrayed the suffering female victim, introduced a different flavor to the stage.[20] Many of the new comedies assumed a goodness in humanity that was reflected in the portrayal of character and in the as-

sumption of audience sympathy. This emphasis is clearly apparent in Centlivre's *The Gamester* and *The Basset Table.*

Centlivre, who wrote a total of nineteen plays between 1700 and her death in 1723, has been described as "an excellent craftsman for the stage, a precise observer of social trends."[21] Edward Burns in *Restoration Comedy* (1987) maintains that she wrote "more good plays than anyone between [George] Farquhar and [Oscar] Wilde."[22] *The Gamester,* which was first performed at Lincoln's Inn Fields Theatre on 1 February 1705, and published later that month, was Centlivre's fifth play and the most successful of her plays to that date; it continued to be performed regularly throughout the eighteenth century. *The Basset Table,* produced on 20 November 1705, and published later in November, had a much shorter run. Both plays deal with gambling and involve the reformation of at least two characters in each play. It is primarily because of this reformation that the plays have been labeled sentimental comedies. In the following pages I look at these two plays in relation to the question of the accuracy of the label sentimental comedy, a label that has not been applied to Centlivre's other plays. In order to understand the problematics of the label, we need to examine the economic and social context within which the plays were written as well as the texts of the plays themselves.

It is important to recognize that for most of her life, Centlivre, who had no literary or social connections except those that she formed herself, had no income but what she earned from her theatrical work.[23] Leaving home at a young age, and educating herself as she could, she earned her living as part of a company of traveling players and then came to London, where in 1700 she began to make her mark in the theater. Her first play, *The Perjur'd Husband,* was performed at the Drury Lane Theatre in October 1700. Writing with the necessity of earning her living, Centlivre did not have the luxury of disregarding what the audience wanted in theatre. As Samuel Johnson observed, "The Drama's Laws the Drama's Patrons give, / For we that live to please, must please to live."[24] That Centlivre was very conscious of her dependency upon the public is apparent in her preface to *Love's Contrivance* (1703), her fourth play (and the first to give her some success). "Writing," she said, "is a kind of Lottery in this fickle Age, and Dependence on the Stage as precarious as the Cast of a Die; the Chance may turn up, and a Man may write to please the Town, but 'tis uncertain, since we see our best Authors sometimes fail."[25]

Keeping in mind Centlivre's need to earn her living, and her awareness of the need to "please the Town," let us turn to a second aspect of the social context within which she wrote: the changing attitude toward women playwrights. As John Wilson Bowyer notes, the first two years of the eighteenth century marked an increased attention to the equality of women, and there was talk that when Queen Anne ascended the throne she might even open a college for women; however, soon after Anne became queen in 1702, there was an apparent backlash.[26] Although Centlivre had signed her name to her first two plays, when her third play, *The Stolen Heiress,* was performed in December 1702, the author's identity not only was not revealed, but the prologue was also written as though the author were a man, referring to "his" success and "his" play. Similarly, her name and gender were concealed when her fourth play, *Love's Contrivance,* appeared in June 1703. No name appeared on the playbills, and when the play was published, the initials "R. M." were signed to the dedication.

Centlivre's next two plays, *The Gamester* and *The Basset Table* (1705), also appeared anonymously. Finally, in 1707, having by then authored seven plays, Centlivre revealed that it was not she who had chosen to remain anonymous; in fact, she was angry and bitter at not receiving recognition for her plays. In the dedication to her eighth play, *The Platonick Lady,* published in February of 1707, she explained that her name and gender had been concealed because it was believed that it would be better for business if the public thought that a man had written the plays. The publisher of *Love's Contrivance,* she said, had deliberately "put two letters of a wrong Name to it; which, tho' it was the height of Injustice to me, yet his imposing on the Town turn'd to account with him; and thus passing for a Man's, it has been play'd at least a hundred times."[27] In the same dedication she said that her bookseller had told her of a "spark" who had bought a copy of *The Gamester,* but when he heard it was by a woman, he threw it down and said that he "was sure if the Town had known that, it wou'd never have run ten days."[28] *The Platonick Lady,* which was produced with Centlivre's name signed to it, was not a success. In the dedication Centlivre notes that her two most popular plays to date, *The Gamester* and *Love's Contrivance,* had been produced anonymously. She observes with bitterness that a play can make money if it is anonymous, unless by chance it is discovered to be "fatherless"; unless it is revealed that *"it is a Woman's."*[29]

It is clear that Centlivre agreed to remain anonymous because of her need to earn her living. In 1706 she was without funds and again joined a company of strolling players. However, after the financial security that came with her marriage in 1707 and the striking success of *The Busy Body* in 1709, she was no longer afraid to insist on using her own name. According to a contemporary, Centlivre initially had difficulty getting the actors to play their parts in *The Busy Body* because they knew it was by a woman. One actor is said to have thrown down the script in disgust. People who had heard about the play from the actors believed that "it

was a silly thing wrote by a Woman" and knew that the actors "had no Opinion of it."[30] The first-night audience was sparse, but although the audience began by not expecting to like the play, it ended by applauding loudly, and the play became an extraordinary success.[31] In two issues of *The Tatler* Richard Steele referred to the success of the play, and, noting that it was by a woman, criticized the audience who had prejudged the play. He went on to say that "Females of Wit" could write such a play better than a man.[32] Although his praise includes a stereotypical view of women, his notice of the play was of immense service to Centlivre.

Centlivre's struggle, then, was not only to make a living from her plays but also to do so in spite of the hostility toward women writers. Since *The Gamester* and *The Basset Table* were written at a time when she was most insecure about her ability to succeed—during the period when she had to conceal her identity and gender in order to make money from her plays—it is not surprising if her explicit comments about the plays seem to express what she believed the public wanted. This brings us to the third aspect of the social context within which Centlivre wrote: the increasing emphasis on morality in the theater.

At the beginning of her career Centlivre stated her ideas about the goal of comedy. She wrote in 1700, "I think the main design of Comedy is to make us laugh,"[33] and three years later she wrote in the preface to *Love's Contrivance* that the primary function of a comedy is to entertain (2:np[4]). However, in the dedication to *The Gamester* in 1705, Centlivre seems to contradict this opinion; she writes that it is her intention to correct a social vice and says that she hopes that her play will, "according to the first intent of Plays, recommend Morality."[34] Similarly, in her dedication to *The Basset Table* in the same year she says that poetry is designed to correct vice; her purpose in this play, she says, is to "Redicule and Correct one of the most reigning Vices of the Age."[35] In all of her plays that were performed before and after his one-year period, Centlivre demonstrated a belief in the opinion that she had stated at the outset of her career: that the end of comedy is to make us laugh. How can we account for her apparent deviation in 1705? F. P. Lock in his biography *Susanna Centlivre* (1979) concludes that the one-year period during which Centlivre was writing *The Gamester* and *The Basset Table* marks a break in the "theory and practice of comedy" of her twenty-three-year career, and Bowyer, in *The Celebrated Mrs. Centlivre* (1952), insists that these two plays have a "conscious moral purpose."[36] The question is, however, *why* should Centlivre have had such a break? And more important, do the plays in fact constitute a break?

At this point we need to examine specific historical events that were occurring at the time and analyze Centlivre's response to them. Of particular importance was

Jeremy Collier's 1698 call for morality in the theater, *A Short View of the Immorality and Profaneness of the English Stage*.[37] As John Loftis points out, Centlivre was responding to "the Collier controversy and its aftermath."[38] In fact, her writings reveal that she was in dialogue with the Collierites. In 1700, in a poetic tribute to Farquhar, she held that he had succeeded in answering Collier. She appears to accept the necessity of complying with what she apparently regards as the public's preference, and she praises Farquhar, who "without Smut, can make an Audience smile."[39] In the same year, in the preface to her first play, *The Perjur'd Husband,* Centlivre defends her play against the moralists who, following Collier's lead, had criticized the language used by one of the characters in her play. Although she accepted the call for morality, she nevertheless insisted on the need for realism: "I cannot believe that a Prayer Book should be put into the Hands of a Woman, whose innate Virtue won't secure her Reputation; nor is it reasonable to expect a Person, whose inclinations are always forming Projects to the Dishonour of her Husband, should deliver her Commands to her Confident in the Words of a Psalm" (1:v). In the preface to *Love's Contrivance* three years later, however, Centlivre notes that in this play she has been careful to avoid offensive language: "The following Poem I think has nothing can disoblige the nicest Ear; and tho' I did not observe the Rules of Drama, I took peculiar Care to dress my Thoughts in such a modest Stile, that it might not give Offence to any" (2:np[4]).[40]

That Centlivre's decision to "clean up" her language is motivated by her belief that this was what the audience wanted is apparent from her comments about the "unities" in the same preface. The critics, she says, "cry up Aristotle's Rules as the most essential part of the Play. I own they are in the right of it; yet I dare venture a Wager they'll never persuade the Town to be of their Opinion, which relishes nothing so well as Humour lightly tost up with Wit, and drest with Modesty and Air" (2:np[4]). If the town does not care about the unities, Centlivre says, she will not strive to adhere to them since she herself does not think they are important; but since the town does care about the language that she uses, she will make an effort to use language that the town approves.

Soon after *Love's Contrivance* appeared, other events occurred that reinforced Centlivre's impression that what the public wanted was moral plays. In December of 1703, Steele's emphatically moral play, *The Lying Lover,* was produced. Steele wrote in his preface that it was his "Ambition to attempt a Comedy, which might be no improper Entertainment in a Christian Commonwealth"; he hoped, he said, that "by being encourag'd in the Interests of Virtue," comedy would "strip Vice of the gay Habit in which it has too long appear'd."[41] That Centlivre paid attention to Steele's play is suggested by the fact that she followed his lead in her next play in two obvious ways. Both plays were adapted from the French: Steele's *The Lying Lover* from *Le Menteur* (1642) by Pierre Corneille; Centlivre's *The Gamester* from *Le Joueur* (1696) by François Regnard. Both plays condemned a social vice: Steele's play was a condemnation of dueling, Centlivre's a critique of gambling. Although these parallels suggest that Centlivre took notice of Steele's play, we cannot conclude that she shared his intention; it may be simply that she saw in Steele's adaptation and attack on a social vice an idea for a profitable play. Other events also played a role in inclining Centlivre toward making a moral statement in her 1705 plays, however. In January of 1704 Queen Anne issued two proclamations. One required that all plays be licensed by the Master of the Revels, and the second ordered the Master of the Revels to be careful "in the perusing and licensing of plays."[42] The town obviously was taking an interest in morality in the theater.

It was in this atmosphere that Centlivre was working on *The Gamester* and *The Basset Table.* In both plays she explicitly claims that her intention is to correct a social vice and asserts that the "first intent of plays" is to recommend morality. Given the events that were occurring in the theater, and given Centlivre's need to earn her living by her writing, combined with the prejudice against women playwrights that drove her into anonymity during the period that she was writing *The Gamester* and *The Basset Table,* it is not surprising that these two plays should contain such explicit claims.

The mistake of the critics is to accept the stated intention as the explanation of the plays. If we examine the texts of the plays themselves, looking at the dissonant strands that help us to read "against the authority of meaning,"[43] we will find important discrepancies between the stated intention and what Centlivre actually accomplishes in the plays. First of all, although critics have called these two plays sentimental comedies, the majority of the scenes and characters in the plays are antisentimental: they are realistic, satirical, and witty. These aspects of the plays undercut the seriousness of the stated moral. Second, there is nothing sentimental about the portrayal of the gamester. During play he is "shaking his Elbows over a Table, saying his Prayers backwards, courting the Dice like a Mistress, and cursing them when he is disappointed" (1:134). The "morning after" he has "down-cast Eyes, no Powder in his Perriwig, . . . and Hands and Face as dirty as a Tinker" (1:134). During the basset game the players defraud each other in any way they can. Satire and comic characters predominate in both plays. All of the characters' pretensions are undercut, and even the reformation scenes are primarily comic.

Less obvious than the antisentimental elements in the plays are the incongruities and ambiguities in the text that undermine the easy assumption that the plays are simply an expression of moral reform. There is no question that the plays portray the reform of characters; but, although critics have questioned whether or not the conversion in such comedies is permanent, few have questioned that the reform in these two plays is a *moral* one.[44] There are numerous indications in the plays that the reforms are not wholly moral. Valere's change of heart in *The Gamester* comes after he has gambled away Angelica's picture, and he declares that he was wrong to "follow Vice" (1:182). Despite this explicit statement, however, the reform is portrayed not as moral but as primarily expedient. Valere is not ready to give up gaming until he is penniless and his father threatens to disinherit him. At the end of the play, having renounced gaming, he appeals to members of the audience to reform as he has. The reasons he gives are certainly not moral reasons: "Then each with me the Libertine reclaim, / And shun what sinks his Fortune, and his Fame" (1:194). The message is not that gambling is morally evil, but that it prevents a man from getting ahead. Lady Wealthy in the same play also makes a pragmatic reform. She has been a coquette who seeks the admiration of many men. At the end of the play she agrees to marry Lovewell and promises to "banish from my House that senseless Train of Fop Admirers, which I . . . only kept to feed my Vanity" (1:186). Her reason, however, is not that she realizes that her flirtations are morally wrong; rather, she realizes how close she has come to destroying her reputation. She exclaims, "Am I become so wretched—I shall be sung in Ballads shortly" (1:174). The thought that she might become a public joke is a humiliating one.

The reforms in *The Basset Table* are similarly pragmatic. Lady Reveller renounces gambling, not because she realizes it is morally wrong, but because she is threatened with rape. Even when she learns that the rape was a trick, she vows that she will give up gambling because it has made her vulnerable. Mrs. Sago, the wife of a middle-class "cit," also reforms, but hers can hardly be called a moral reform. She renounces gaming because her husband threatens to leave her. As her final speech indicates, her motives are wholly practical. She declares that she is "bound to good Behaviour" because she almost lost her husband's "Favour" (1:258). She does not regret her decision, she says, because a woman who is separated from her husband has no social life: "Some Neighbours' Wives have but too lately shewn, / When Spouse had left 'em, all their Friends were flown" (1:258). Thus she gives up gaming so that she can retain her social position.

Not only is the conversion of character in the plays not a moral one, but it is also not an unmixed reformation. There is evidence in the plays that negative results are involved in the reforms. Each of the characters has to give up freedom when he/she reforms. Valere is not

anxious to marry and give up gaming until he is desperate and does not see any other solution. He recounts all of the advantages of the life of a gambler, and in spite of the ironic humor of some of his comments, which reflects Centlivre's social satire, he creates an appealing image of the life he leads: "I love Liberty . . . Who is happier than a Gamester; who more respected? . . . Who more caress'd by Lords and Dukes? . . . A Gentleman that plays is admitted every where—Women of the strictest Virtue will converse with him . . . Oh! The charming Company of half a Dozen Ladies, with each a Dish of Tea" (1:162-3). When Valere speaks of "Liberty," he means the liberty to pursue his "addiction" and the enjoyment of the lifestyle that accompanies it. We also know that he has a mistress, "Mademoiselle *Margaret de la Plant,* lately arrived from *France,*" whose bill for "four Guineas a week" appears on the list of creditors Hector draws up for Valere's father (1:156). Lady Wealthy characterizes Valere as "the Rover, the unconquer'd Rambler" (1:172). The libertine or rover was a popular figure on the Restoration stage,[45] and Centlivre's portrait of Valere before his reformation would have been an attractive one to the audience.

When the women in these two plays reform, the results of their reformation are even more ambivalent. However, with respect to the women, the ambivalence does not derive from the fact that the audience would have found their prereformation life attractive, for the women's reformation is consistent with the dominant ideology of the time. Rather, their reformation is ambivalent because, in spite of the fact that Centlivre portrays the reform as right and proper, there are numerous threads throughout the plays which run counter to the conventional view. Centlivre portrays all three of the women as having unusual freedom and independence prior to their reformation. Lady Wealthy in *The Gamester* is a rich widow who enjoys her independent status. When the constant Lovewell presumes to tell her what she thinks, she reprimands him: "How dare you suppose my Thoughts—and who gave you this Privilege in my House?" (1:150). At the end of the play, although she is grateful to Lovewell for salvaging her reputation and she esteems him for his merit, she is still reluctant to remarry. It is significant that, although Lovewell has been portrayed throughout the play as solicitous and nonaggressive, in the final scene his words express possession and appropriation. And it is this suggestion of the threat to Lady Wealthy's liberty that makes her reform ambivalent. There is something ominous about Lovewell's declaration that he will "fright the Fool Pretenders from approaching, and these fond Arms secure you ever mine" (1:186). Up to this point Lady Wealthy has control over who can come into her house; after marriage she will be answerable to her husband. Just how severely Lady Wealthy's freedom and independence will be curtailed is suggested by the way in which she is finally married to Lovewell, who, with the help of the servant Betty, practically forces her into it. "Nay, look not back," says Lovewell, as they pull her out to meet the chaplain, "your Eyes consent, and *I'll have no Denial*" (1:186; my italics).

Lady Reveller in *The Basset Table* is also an independent well-to-do widow. As her servant Alpiew tells Lady Reveller's uncle when he attempts to bully her: "My Lady's a Widow, and Widows are accountable to none for their actions" (1:206). Lady Reveller comments of her suitors: "*He that would gain my Heart, must learn the Way / Not to controul, but readily obey*" (1:236). She speaks assertively to Worthy and to her uncle when they try to tell her what to do. Worthy, she says, is only in her way in the gaming room: "I shall have him at my Elbow all Night, and spoil my Luck at the *Basset-Table*" (1:236). To make use of him, she gives him a book of poetry to read aloud in order to distract her opponent during play (1:217). Her aside about the other men also illustrates her independent spirit: "Who cou'd endure these Men, did they not lose their Money?" (1:247). On one level, these comments function to contribute to the piquant humor of the play. However, they also help to provide a picture of the autonomy that she enjoys, an autonomy that is completely destroyed with her reformation. Her self-assertion is quickly dispelled when she is threatened with rape (in a trick arranged by Worthy and Sir James), and she humbly turns to Worthy, who "saves" her. She weeps and says to him: "You've sav'd my Virtue . . . [I] hate myself for all my Folly. Oh! Forgive me" (1:250-1). Moreover, the author interweaves into the portrait of Worthy other threads which undercut his "worthy" image. Implicit in the play is the suggestion that Worthy's pursuit of Lady Reveller is not for her person and her heart. As Sir James points out, he is "a younger Brother" (1:258), and her fortune will compensate him for his humiliation. We also see his violent reaction when he is angry. When Worthy strikes his servant, Lady Reveller realizes that he is really striking out at her: "Where did you learn this Rudeness, my Lord, to strike your Servant before me? . . . The Affront was meant to me—nor will I endure these Passions" (1:236). The suggestions of crass motives and latent violence, combined with Worthy's willingness to join in the rape deception, undercut the romantic reformation in Lady Reveller's capitulation. She reforms, but she also loses her autonomy to a man who is less than "worthy," and the method of bringing her down is a rather dirty trick.

The other woman who reforms in *The Basset Table,* the citizen's wife, Mrs. Sago, steals from her merchant husband in order to fund her losses at the basset table. Her role is not an attractive one, and Centlivre's satiric portrait of her provides much humor. Yet when we examine the specifics of her situation, we find many signs that take us in another direction. First of all, Cen-

tlivre gives us a perceptive portrayal of class as well as gender distinctions. Both Mr. and Mrs. Sago are flattered that she is associating with "quality," but, as Lady Reveller says, Mrs. Sago is only welcome at the basset table because of her money (1:217). Moreover, Sir James has only been toying with her, as is clear when he says in an aside, "Now to what Purpose have I lyed myself into her good Graces, when I would be glad to be rid of her?" (1:232). Mrs. Sago, who is vulnerable to Sir James's trifling because of her class and gender, is portrayed as a person with no alternatives. She renounces gambling and plays the penitent wife because there is nothing else that she can do. When she is forced to swear to her husband that she will be "good," he demands that she be specific about her future activities, and she promises: "I won't come within the Air [of gambling halls], but take up with City Acquaintance, rail at the Court, and go twice a Week with Mrs. *Outside* to *Pinmakers-hall*" (1:255). It is this promise to fall back into the routine life of the wife of a bourgeois "cit" that convinces her husband to take her back. Mrs. Sago, too, has given up her freedom. Her reform is a positive one for her husband, but it represents a significant loss for her.

The sexual politics inherent in the ambivalence of the conversion of the women in these plays is confirmed by Centlivre's portrayal of the other female characters in the plays. Both of the plays affirm the independence of women, from the portrayal of nonreforming central characters to the portrayal of ladies' maids. Favourite and Betty, the maids in *The Gamester,* attempt to orchestrate events, and Alpiew, Lady Reveller's maid in *The Basset Table,* speaks assertively to Sir Richard. The character of Angelica in *The Gamester* is particularly significant. Neither passive nor ignorant, Angelica is sensible in her attempt to deal with Valere's addiction, and the action that she takes underscores her agency: she dons breeches, goes into the gaming rooms, and wins her picture from Valere in a dice game.[46] The most significant portrayal of female independence in these two plays, however, is the portrayal of Valeria, the scientist philosopher, in *The Basset Table.* She is regarded as mad because she attempts to speak to men as equals. She says to Captain Firebrand, the man her father wants her to marry: "The Converse I hold with your Sex, is only to improve and cultivate the Notions of my Mind" (1:220). He concludes that she is "fitter for *Moorsfields* [lunatic asylum] than Matrimony" (1:221) and refuses to marry her—leaving her free to marry the man she loves. In her "madness" there is much sense. Valeria's frankness and unconventional behavior, juxtaposed against the manipulations and game playing of the other characters, are clearly positive. Although Valeria is presented humorously (this is, after all, a comedy), she represents a rupture in the cultural binaries of the text. It is not insignificant that her name is the feminine of Valere, the "unconquered rover" of *The Gamester.*

Centlivre's portrayal of the independent women in the plays, like the ambivalence inherent in the characters' reformation, reflects the countermovement of the text and helps to undercut the ostensible moral, the result of which will be the destruction of the independence of the women who "reform." Elsewhere Centlivre is explicit with respect to women's status; she is particularly outspoken about the criticism of and contemptuous attitude toward women writers. Two years before she wrote *The Gamester* and *The Basset Table,* she wrote a poem to another woman writer, Sarah Fyge Egerton, which expresses her confidence in women's talents:

> Thou Champion for our Sex go on and show,
> Ambitious Man what Womankind can do:
> In vain they boast of large Scholastick Rules,
> Their skill in Arts and Labour in the Schools.
> What various Tongues and Languages acquir'd,
> How fam'd for Policy, for Wit admir'd;
> Their solid Judgment in Philosophy,
> The Metaphysicks, Truths, and Poetry,
> Since here they'll find themselves outdone by thee.[47]

Centlivre's most significant statement on behalf of women writers is contained in her dedication to her play *The Platonick Lady* (1707): "To all the Generous Encouragers of Female Ingenuity."[48] She says that she hopes "to find some Souls Great enough to protect her [woman] against the Carping Malice of the Vulgar World; who think it a proof of Sense, to dislike every thing that is writ by Women."[49] She was induced to write this application, she says, because of "the Usage I have met on all sides."[50]

In order to understand how Centlivre was able to accomplish her resistance to this "usage" and still earn her living from the theater, we need to understand the "play" within the structure of the plays. By decentering the text and identifying the supplementary meanings within the apparent reification of the dominant discourse of Centlivre's culture, we open the plays to the "play of signification."[51] Even the word "play" itself is significant. Centlivre plays with the word throughout both of these plays. "Play" means gaming (the French title of *The Gamester* was *Le Joueur* or "the player"); or acting on the stage (in these works Centlivre makes constant comparisons to "play-acting" in the theater); or dissimulation (the characters pretend or "play at" interpersonal relationships); or all of the above. Clearly, Centlivre's plays cannot be summed up in a label. Borrowing from Centlivre's play on the word "play," and remembering the importance of the play itself and the deconstructionist's identification of the "play" of signification, I contend that, in more ways than one, "The *play's* the thing."

To label *The Gamester* and *The Basset Table* sentimental comedies is to accept a limiting definition and thus to overlook the plays themselves. By examining the metatext of the plays—the context within which Centlivre wrote and the texts of the plays—the reader is able to recognize the discrepancies between the stated intention and the powerful subtext of the plays. It is this complexity that underscores the inadequacy of the genre label sentimental comedy. Centlivre fulfilled the expectations of the dominant ideology of her society while at the same time maintaining a resistance to it. Driven into anonymity during the writing of these plays, she expresses her resistance to her society's hostility toward independent women and conveys a cogent answer to those whose "Carping Malice" is responsible for the "Usage" she has "met on all sides."

Notes

1. Critics who have labeled the plays "sentimental comedies" include John Wilson Bowyer, who, in *The Celebrated Mrs. Centlivre* (Durham NC: Duke Univ. Press, 1952), describes *The Gamester* as Susanna Centlivre's "chief excursion into the realm of the sentimental drama" (p. 61). Richard Bevis, in *The Laughing Tradition: Stage Comedy in Garrick's Day* (Athens: Univ. of Georgia Press, 1980), characterizes *The Gamester* as "sentimental" (pp. 8-9); and Robert D. Hume, in *The Rakish Stage: Studies in English Drama, 1660-1800* (Carbondale: Southern Illinois Univ. Press, 1983), although he disapproves of simple labeling, groups Centlivre with Colley Cibber and Richard Steele as "sentimental" playwrights (p. 178). See also Hume, *The Development of English Drama in the Late Seventeenth Century* (Oxford: Clarendon Press, 1990), pp. 33-8. Only Arthur Sherbo, in his attempt to define sentimental comedy in *English Sentimental Drama* (East Lansing: Michigan State Univ. Press, 1957), questions the label for Centlivre's *The Gamester* (pp. 113-4).

2. As Hume observes in *The Rakish Stage,* the term sentimental has been "discredited" (p. 178).

3. In the years 1695-96, for example, as Paula R. Backscheider notes in *Spectacular Politics: Theatrical Power and Mass Culture in Early Modern England* (Baltimore: Johns Hopkins Univ. Press, 1993), one-third of all new plays were by women (p. xiii). Paddy Lyons and Fidelis Morgan point out in their introduction to *Female Playwrights of the Restoration: Five Comedies* (London: J. M. Dent, 1991), pp. xvi-xx, that more than fifty plays by women appeared in print between 1660 and 1710, noting that since publishers only printed those plays that had been successful, there probably were many others that were performed but were not published (p. xx). An

example of the femaleless anthology that I am referring to is the 1952 edition of *Eighteenth-Century Plays,* ed. Ricardo Quintana (New York: Modern Library), or its companion volume *Restoration Plays,* ed. Brice Harris (New York: Modern Library, 1953). The 1973 Norton Critical Edition of *Restoration and Eighteenth-Century Comedy,* ed. Scott McMillin (New York: W. W. Norton), contains no female playwrights, but Aphra Behn's *The Rover* has been added to the second edition (1997).

4. Shirley Strum Kenny, "Humane Comedy," *MP* 75, 1 (August 1977): 29-43.

5. As Richard Braverman notes in his discussion of the political dimension of Restoration comedy in "The Rake's Progress Revisited: Politics and Comedy in the Restoration," in *Cultural Readings of Restoration and Eighteenth-Century English Theater,* ed. J. Douglas Canfield and Deborah C. Payne (Athens: Univ. of Georgia Press, 1995), pp. 141-68, a too-narrow focus on one aspect of drama can cause the reader to undervalue or overlook other aspects of a work (p. 143).

6. For example, although the reformation of a character has been regarded as part of the definition of sentimental comedy, it appears in many of the "comedies of wit" also, as in the reformation of Dorimant in George Etherege's *Man of Mode* or Mirabell in William Congreve's *The Way of the World.*

7. If, as Michel Foucault has pointed out, concepts regarded as "truths" possessing the "universality of a meaning" are the result of society's protective control of the "production of discourse," one cannot understand discursive truths without examining their cultural context (*The Archaeology of Knowledge; and, The Discourse on Language,* trans. A. M. Sheridan Smith [New York: Pantheon Books, 1972], pp. 4, 216, 234).

8. Oliver Goldsmith, "An Essay on the Theatre; or, A Comparison between Laughing and Sentimental Comedy," in *Restoration and Eighteenth-Century Comedy,* pp. 489-92, 490-1.

9. William Cook, *Elements of Dramatic Criticism* (London: Kearsly, 1775), p. 142.

10. Critics who have cited Cibber's *Love's Last Shift* (1696) as the first sentimental comedy include Ernest Bernbaum, *The Drama of Sensibility: A Sketch of the History of English Sentimental Comedy and Domestic Tragedy, 1696-1780* (Gloucester: Peter Smith, 1915), pp. 1-2; F. W. Bateson, *English Comic Drama, 1700-1750* (Oxford: Clarendon Press, 1929), p. 20; Joseph Wood Krutch, *Comedy and Conscience after the*

Restoration (New York: Columbia Univ. Press, 1924; rprt. 1949), p. 202; Allardyce Nicoll, *A History of English Drama, 1660-1900,* 6 vols. (London: Harrap and Co., 1965), 2:189; and Bevis, *English Drama: Restoration and Eighteenth Century, 1660-1789* (London: Longman, 1988), p. 154.

11. Bernbaum identifies "confidence in the goodness of average human nature" as the "mainspring" of the sentimental and asserts that the essence of sentimental drama was to portray virtuous redemption in the "everyday world" through an appeal to the emotions (pp. 2, 10). Krutch cites as the principal aspect of sentimental drama the audience's jubilant response to the moral reformation portrayed in the play (p. 192); Bateson looks to the belief in "an abstract ideal of order" and a sensitivity to the needs of one's neighbors (p. 6); and Nicoll, in *A History of English Drama,* focuses on the "deliberate enunciation of a moral or social problem" (2:180).

12. Sherbo, p. 140.

13. Hume, *The Rakish Stage,* p. 321.

14. Maureen Sullivan, introduction to *Colley Cibber: Three Sentimental Comedies,* ed. Sullivan (New Haven: Yale Univ. Press, 1973), pp. xiii-li, xxvi.

15. Frank H. Ellis, *Sentimental Comedy: Theory and Practice* (Cambridge: Cambridge Univ. Press, 1991), p. 19.

16. Ellis, p. 120.

17. The dominance of sentimentality in the theater is asserted by Bernbaum and Krutch, as well as by Louis I. Bredvold, *The Literature of the Restoration and the Eighteenth Century, 1660-1798* (New York: Collier Books, 1962); James J. Lynch, *Box, Pit, and Gallery: Stage and Society in Johnson's London* (Berkeley: Univ. of California Press, 1953); Louis Kronenberger, *The Thread of Laughter: Chapters on English Stage Comedy from Johnson to Maugham* (New York: Knopf, 1952); Leonard R. N. Ashley, *Colley Cibber* (New York: Twayne, 1965); Allan Rodway, "Goldsmith and Sheridan: Satirists of Sentiment," in *Renaissance and Modern Essays: Presented to Vivian de Sola Pinto in Celebration of His Seventieth Birthday,* ed. G. R. Hibbard (London: Routledge, 1966), pp. 65-72; and A. N. Kaul, *The Action of English Comedy: Studies in the Encounter of Abstraction and Experience from Shakespeare to Shaw* (New Haven: Yale Univ. Press, 1970).

18. Bevis, *The Laughing Tradition,* pp. 246-7.

19. Hume, *The Rakish Stage,* p. 338. William Archer, in *The Old Drama and the New: An Essay in Re-Valuation* (London: W. Heineman, 1923), was

among the first to assert that one could not blame the decline of eighteenth-century drama on senti- ment (p. 222); and Nicoll, in *British Drama: An Historical Survey from the Beginnings to the Present Time* (New York: Thomas Y. Crowell, 1925), declares: "It must not be supposed, of course, that sentimentalism completely dominated the age" (p. 289). Bateson maintains that eighteenth-century drama was not predominantly sentimental; in fact, he says, sentimental comedies were an "aberration" (pp. 11-3). Sherbo compares the contemporary reception of comedies that have been categorized as sentimental and non-sentimental and concludes that there is no basis for the assertion that the eighteenth century represents the triumph of sentiment in comic drama (pp. 157-63).

20. In "Heroic Tragedy," in *Restoration Theatre,* ed. John Russell Brown and Bernard Harris (London: Edward Arnold Publishers, 1965), pp. 135-57, Anne Righter notes that by the end of the seven- teenth century, the emotion and pathos of tragedy began to be joined with comedy (p. 157).

21. Pat Rogers, *The Augustan Vision* (New York: Harper and Row, 1974), p. 161.

22. Edward Burns, *Restoration Comedy: Crises of Desire and Identity* (New York: St. Martin's Press, 1987), p. 231. Bevis, in *English Drama,* points out that Centlivre's plays were the "most popular of the period, and two of them (*The Busy Body* [1709] and *The Wonder* [1714]) survived the *nine- teenth* century" (p. 163).

23. For information about Centlivre's early life, see Bowyer, pp. 3-14; F. P. Lock, *Susanna Centlivre* (Boston: Twayne Publishers, 1979), pp. 13-8; and Nancy Cotton, *Women Playwrights in England, c. 1363-1750* (Lewisburg: Bucknell Univ. Press, 1980), pp. 123-4.

24. Samuel Johnson, "Prologue Spoken at the Open- ing of the Theatre in Drury-Lane, 1747," in *Poems,* ed. E. L. McAdam Jr., vol. 6 in *The Yale Edition of The Works of Samuel Johnson,* 16 vols., 1958- 90, ed. McAdam Jr. et al. (New Haven: Yale Univ. Press, 1964), pp. 87-90, 89, lines 53-4.

25. Centlivre, preface to *Love's Contrivance,* in *The Dramatic Works of the Celebrated Mrs. Centlivre,* 3 vols. (London: John Pearson, 1872), 2:np[4]. The preface to this play is unpaginated; the text of the play begins on page ten, and the page I have cited would be page four. All references to Cen- tlivre's plays, henceforth cited parenthetically in the text by volume and page number, derive from this edition. References to dedications, however, which are omitted from the 1872 edition, are to first editions.

26. Bowyer, p. 42.

27. Centlivre, dedication to *The Platonick Lady, A Comedy* (London, 1707), np.

28. Ibid.

29. Ibid.

30. John Mottley, *A Compleat List of All the English Dramatic Poets,* in Thomas Whincop, *Scander- beg: Or, Love and Liberty* (London: Reeve, 1747), p. 189.

31. Mottley, pp. 189-90.

32. Steele, *The Tatler,* 14 and 24 May 1709; rprt. in *The Tatler,* ed. Donald F. Bond, 3 vols. (Oxford: Clarendon Press, 1987), 1:129-30, 1:154-5. Steele's suggestion that a woman might be able to write a better play than a man suggests a reason for some of the hostility toward women play- wrights. This hostility continued into the nine- teenth century. The *Biographia Dramatica* (1812) marvels at the success of Centlivre's play com- pared to the relative failure of Congreve's *The Way of the World* (David Erskine Baker, Isaac Reed, and Stephen Jones, *Biographia Dramatica,* 3d edn., 3 vols. [London: Longman, Hurst, Rees, Orme, and Brown, 1812], 1:97-100); and in 1820- 21, when *The Busy Body* was still running, George Gordon, Lord Byron complained that Centlivre "drove Congreve from the theatre" (*The Works of Lord Byron: Letters and Journals,* 6 vols., ed. Rowland E. Prothero [New York: Octagon Books, 1966, 4:426-7, 5:218-9]).

33. Centlivre, "Letter to Abel Boyer, 1700," in *Letters of Wit, Politicks, and Morality,* ed. Boyer (London, 1701); rprt. in *The Complete Works of George Farquhar,* ed. Charles Stonehill, 2 vols. (London: Nonesuch Press, 1930; rprt. New York: Gordian Press, 1967), 2:259-60. In a more recent edition of Farquhar's works, Kenny makes reference to but does not reprint Centlivre's "Letter to Boyer" and her "Epistle to Mr. Farquhar" cited below. See *The Works of George Farquhar,* ed. Kenny, 2 vols. (New York: Clarendon, Oxford Univ. Press, 1988), 2:416, 420, 531.

34. Centlivre, dedication to *The Gamester, A Comedy* (London, 1705), np.

35. Centlivre, dedication to *The Basset Table, A Com- edy* (London, 1705), np.

36. Lock, p. 46; Bowyer, p. 61.

37. Jeremy Collier, *A Short View of the Immorality and Profaneness of the English Stage* (London, 1698; rprt. New York: AMS, 1974).

38. John Loftis, *Comedy and Society from Congreve to Fielding* (Stanford: Stanford Univ. Press, 1959), p. 65.

39. Centlivre, "Epistle to Mr. Farquhar upon His Comedy Call'd *A Trip to the Jubilee* [subtitle of *The Constant Couple*]," in *Complete Works of Farquhar,* ed. Stonehill, 2:261-2. Centlivre writes:

> For since the learned *Collier* first essay'd
> To teach Religion to the Rhiming Trade,
> The *Comick* Muse in *Tragick* posture sat,
> And seem'd to mourn the Downfall of her State.

40. As Nancy Copeland notes in her introduction to Centlivre's *A Bold Stroke for a Wife,* ed. Copeland (Peterborough ON: Broadview Press, 1995), pp. 7-39, the only concession Centlivre made to the Collierites was her use of more "'modest' language and situations" (p. 10).

41. *The Plays of Richard Steele,* ed. Kenny (Oxford: Clarendon Press, 1971), pp. 115-6.

42. Lock, p. 46.

43. In *Positions,* trans. Alan Bass (Chicago: Univ. of Chicago Press, 1981), Jacques Derrida writes: "I have attempted to systematize a deconstructive critique precisely against the authority of meaning" (pp. 49-50).

44. Even during the period itself, there were those who questioned the permanency of the reform in the reform comedies. See, for example, John Vanbrugh's play *The Relapse* (1696), which was a response to Cibber's *Love's Last Shift* (1696).

45. For discussions of the popularity of the libertine or rake in Restoration theater, see, e. g., Virginia Ogden Birdsall, *Wild Civility: The English Comic Spirit on the Restoration Stage* (Bloomington: Indiana Univ. Press, 1970), pp. 3, 5-8; and Susan Staves, *Players' Scepters: Fictions of Authority in the Restoration* (Lincoln: Univ. of Nebraska Press, 1979), pp. 296-302.

46. I would point out that Centlivre's choice of naming her heroine Angelica is a comment on the character Angellica in Behn's *The Rover* (1677). Whereas Behn's Angellica is a costly prostitute (thus not the play's heroine, who is the witty Hellena), Centlivre makes Angelica her main heroine who brings about the (pragmatic) reform of the libertine hero (Valere). Also significant is Centlivre's use of Angelica's picture. In Behn's play Angellica's picture was an item that Willmore appropriated, and in Centlivre's play Angelica's picture is taken by Valere—but in Centlivre's play it is through Angelica's own agency that she reclaims her image. The name Angelica is also used by Congreve in *Love for Love* (1695) and by Farquhar in *The Constant Couple* (1699) and its sequel *Sir Harry Wildair* (1701). In the latter Farquhar play, a comical French marquis uses a forged picture of Angelica fraudulently to claim a conquest and to obtain money.

47. Centlivre, "To Mrs. S. F. on Her Incomparable Poems," preface to Sarah Fyge, *Poems on Several Occasions* (1703); rprt. in Sarah Fyge Egerton, *A Collection of Poems on Several Occasions* (1705); cited in Bowyer, p. 67.

48. Centlivre, dedication to *The Platonick Lady,* np.

49. Ibid.

50. Ibid.

51. Derrida, *Of Grammatology,* trans. Gayatri Spivak (Baltimore: Johns Hopkins Univ. Press, 1976), pp. 49-50.

Antonella Rigamonti and Laura Favero Carraro (essay date 2003)

SOURCE: Rigamonti, Antonella and Laura Favero Carraro. "Women at Stake: The Self-Assertive Potential of Gambling in Susanna Centlivre's *The Basset Table.*" *Restoration and Eighteenth-Century Theatre Research* 16, no. 2 (2003): 53-62.

[*In the following essay, Rigamonti and Carraro contend that Centlivre's* Basset Table *likely failed as a follow-up to the more successful* Gamester *because the playwright posed a more direct challenge to accepted social norms for women. Comparing the play to similar works by male playwrights, the authors highlight Centlivre's unique take on the empowering possibilities offered to women at the gaming table.*]

Almost as a bet, Susanna Centlivre[1] wrote, in the same year (1705), two plays dealing with the same theme: gambling. The first, *The Gamester,* was also her first hit and established for her an identity as "the Author of The Gamester"; the following play, *The Basset Table,* was instead a flop, although its situations and characters were an improved version of the previous one.

The Gamester was largely derived from Jean Françoise Regnard's *Le Joueur* (1696), although Centlivre admits it only in part ("Part of it I own myself oblig'd to the French for, particularly for the character of the Gamester"[2]); she herself bases on it *The Basset Table*; either Regnard's or, more probably, Centlivre's work was to prompt Colley Cibber to write, a couple of years later, *The Lady's Last Stake* (1707). Much later, in 1750, Carlo Goldoni was to write for the Venetian Carnival *Il Giocatore,* which is also indebted to Regnard's play and which met with perhaps even less favor than Centlivre's *The Basset Table.*[3]

A clear line of continuity and orthodoxy runs through the plays directly based on the French comedy; apparently distinctive traits—some of the characters in Goldoni's play have names taken from the *commedia dell'arte;* in Venice faro (pharaoh) has replaced basset of which it is a simplified form—all but reinforce the common *topoi* of the servant's complaining about his master's callous behavior, of the fathers'/fathers-in-law's sermons against gambling and of the betrothed's self-delusion about the gambler's actual order of priorities. Along this straight line, however, the place ***The Basset Table*** finds is only apparently a comfortable one. Subtle deviances from established models and patterns of behavior make of the ***Basset Table*** a play in which gambling, more than the butt for customary reprimands, can be seen as the occasion for creating a social enclave in which ladies can venture into behaviors which are distinctively different from the dominant ones.

The cultural and social relevance of gambling cannot be underestimated. If one had only to judge by the number of laws which tried to regulate it, gambling would appear, in all its multifarious forms, as the common pastime of all layers of society, both high and low. We may wonder at the reason for this passion, but if we avoid the moral bait and give a closer look to the life of some famous gamblers, it can probably be discerned that as they mix their cards, gamblers seem to mix something more: social levels, genders and opportunities. They gamble because their own lives can receive an unforeseen spin from the gambling table. Carlo Goldoni, who was entering a steady career as a civil servant for the Republic of Venice, threw away this opportunity by forgetting his duty at a table around which four unknown men and a beautiful woman were playing hombre. Unwittingly or not, he staked more than his money. At that table, he staked his career against the chance of losing it so that he eventually could become what he really wished: *compositor di commedie* (playwright). As Giacomo Casanova (to whom we owe most for information on the games which were played all over Europe in the eighteenth century) witnesses in his *Histoire de ma vie,* (1789-98) gambling can well be considered as a condensed, symbolic version of the spirit of the century itself.[4] This resemblance that can be explained by what Roger Caillois describes as the ingredients that make a game worth playing, that is: *agon* (competition), *alea* (chance), *mimicry* (make-believe), and *ilynx* (vertigo)[5], so that one may wonder if it was exactly this mixture of rules and hazard, calculus and chance, theatricals and thrill that made gambling so attractive to people in the eighteenth century. Wasn't gambling a closet version of that speculative inclination to risk which made this century particularly prone to philosophical, political and financial hazards and speculations? And, can a *basset table* bear the burden of this all?

The Difference of the *Basset Table*

Mrs. Centlivre, neé Freeman, had already shown herself to be at stake when accepting the various turns of fortune that characterized her early years and with the ***Basset Table*** she tried to make, in the language of basset, a *paroli;* that is, she tried to double the win of ***The Gamester.*** She lost, however, as she had probably staked too high. As Katherine M. Rogers notes, "If women playwrights deviated from convention to express a distinctively female point of view, they took care to do it incidentally or indirectly."[6] (xiv). This is something Centlivre had done quite skillfully in the ***Gamester.*** Deviating from the French model, she changed Angelica from a rather passive bystander into an active "player": she is disguised as a man, goes to the gaming house and outwits her fiancé Valere. It is with the ***Basset Table,*** however, that the extent of Centlivre's deviation comes to the fore.

From the very title, it is clear that this play is somewhat different from its models, as attention is centered on the gambling table rather than on the single gamester. Moreover, notwithstanding Centlivre's programmatic assertion that her play's "main Drift" was "to Redicule and Correct one of the most reigning Vices of the Age,"[7] gambling (duly punished at the end of the play) seems rather to be the informing philosophy which governs the behavior of most characters—and of the ladies in particular. The table is the pivotal point around which Lady Reveller's enlarged and "whimsical" family revolves and from which a number of unforeseen spin-offs, in terms of gender definitions and social relations, are produced.

Mixing Moral Values: Lady Reveller Stakes Her Virtue

In both Regnard's and Goldoni's plays, gambling is shown from the opening scene as a personal obsession isolating the individual from even the simplest forms of social interaction: a sleepy servant awaits the return of his master, cursing his life and lamenting the loss of sleep and, perhaps, of good opportunities. His master arrives and is, invariably, in a foul mood, worn out, and dishevelled. It does not matter whether he has won or lost. Goldoni's Florindo, for instance, has won, but he can't stop thinking of the game, haunted as he is by his gambling demon. His servant, Brighella, observes "Gamesters are never satisfied. If they lose, they cry, if they win, they are dissatisfied because they might have won more. Thus, a gamester's life is always unhappy." Valere, both in the French original and in Centlivre's rendering, has lost, with his money, also his good looks: ". . . with Arms across, downcast Eyes, no Powder in his Perriwig, a Steenkirk tuck'd in to hide the Dirt, Sword-knot untied, no Gloves, and Hands and Face as dirty as a Tinker" (1.46-50).

In the **Basset Table** we find an apparently similar situation: the servants waiting for their masters (or rather mistresses, as the players seem to be mainly ladies) are tired and cursing their life, but the scene shows a world of social interaction, where footmen and porters enter into dialogue and call one another by proper names ("Robin," "Will"). The polyphonic nature of the opening scene emphasizes a change of perspective and introduces a different gambling figure, Lady Reveller. She has won "50 Pieces," is in perfect good humour and health, and says to her woman, Alpiew, "Pr'ythee, what shall we do, Alpiew? 'Tis a fine morning. 'Tis pity to go to bed" (1.41-2). Lady Reveller, far from being exhausted, would even consider a stroll in the park, were it not too early to meet any of the Beau-Monde.[8]

Her woman, Alpiew, unlike Brighella or Hector, is unswervingly supportive and clearly admires her. Thus Lady Reveller is in full control of herself and mistress of the game. She is not obsessed with gambling. She plays for pleasure and to follow her inclinations, as she makes clear both to her uncle, Sir Richard, and her cousin, Lady Lucy. Like their counterparts Pantalone and Rosaura in Goldoni's *Il giocatore* and Sir Thomas in **The Gamester,** Sir Richard and Lady Lucy start their reprimands by reminding the gamester of her social duties. However, whereas both Florindo and Valere try to divert the moralists' attention by swearing they will quit (in the meantime racking their brains as to how they might raise some money), Lady Reveller defies both her uncle and cousin, laughs at them and strikes back, hitting at their sore points: Sir Richard's "philosophic" daughter and Lucy's love for Sir James, the other unrepentant gamester of the play.

There is no guilt and, apparently, no compulsive drive in Lady Reveller's gambling, as there is in Valere, Florindo or Cibber's Lady Gentle. Wherein consists then the attraction of the basset table for Lady Reveller? Lady Reveller enjoys gambling: she enjoys the personal risk involved, she believes she is lucky, she enjoys competition, and the feeling that she can make people believe what she wants them to. Her parodic mastery of nautical and scientific jargon, of the language of literature and drama, and her competent use of the language of gambling enable her to have the upper hand in the most varied situations and are, by the way, amongst the best instances of Centlivre's own ability of imitating and exploiting linguistic varieties and registers.

Lady Reveller likes gambling because it offers her the possibility of exploiting her talents, "a Face, a Shape, an Air for Dress, and Wit and Humour," in order to subdue men, and strip other gamblers without losing her virtue. She has quite a clear and interesting notion of virtue. It is not what the "Town" commonly calls virtue, a mere "Name," she says (1.206), but an "innate Virtue" (5.68); that is, not the appearance, but the real substance of virtue. This distinction is rather more than a fine point to have the last word in a verbal skirmish. Whereas the moral stand of Goldoni's Florindo and Regnard's Valère is shaky to say the least, hers is quite firm.

The moral steadfastness of this concept becomes clear when she has to face Sir James. Although she is said to love money most of all, when Sir James dares her to barter her virtue for it, thus implying that no values exist outside those established by the cash nexus, Lady Reveller doggedly refuses and still boasts the possession and sole control of her "innate Virtue" to the point of being ready to face a social scandal—"Raise the House! I'll raise the World in my defence" (5.84-85), rather than keep quiet and cover up her loss under the appearance of virtue.

How far her stand is from the typical morals of the gamester can be seen by comparing this scene to the scene in which Florindo in *Il Giocatore* is ready to sell himself to an old lady ("*un cadavere,*" a corpse, he calls her) in order to obtain the money which will allow him to continue his game.[9]

MIXING GENDERS: GAMBLERS AND LOVE

Gamblers love, as Valere says: "Love her! I adore her!" . . . "Don't you imagine whatever passion I have for Play, that I have Power to forget that amiable Creature!" (I: 124-5), but they love their cards better. Loves goes bankrupt when the gamester's purse is replenished, and a lover can not compete with a gambling table; thus Valère's servant, Hector, dryly comments in Regnard's play: "*Ai-je tort quand je dis que l'argent de retour vous fait faire toujours banqueroute à l'amour? Vous vous sentez en fonds, ergo plus de maîtresse*" (Am I mistaken if I say that a replenished purse always entails love's bankruptcy? You're flush again, therefore, no more mistress) (200). Gamblers find it very difficult to reconcile their two passions. They generally pretend they are just about to quit gambling in order not to lose the woman they love, but when they get caught in their lies, this game of make-believe collapses and they have to admit their defeat.

Lady Reveller's relation with Lord Worthy is much more straightforward. She does not pretend she is not gambling. On the contrary, Lord Worthy is even asked to sit at the basset table and, being unable or unwilling to play, he has to entertain the other players by reading some poetry. If, at times, Lady Reveller seems on the point of admitting she loves Lord Worthy, she is however constantly aware that she "must not be Friends with him" (3.377). Being friendly with him would mean changing her priorities and eventually giving up gambling. Not that she would be unable to stop, as Florindo or Valere are, she simply does not want to, as gambling is the way she can assert herself.

As Richard Steele observed (although in an ironic context), the female gamester's "chief passion is to emulate manhood." (no. 174, 2:503).[10] It is in her relationship with Lord Worthy that Lady Reveller makes her clearest statement that she is the one who leads the game. In this relationship, roles are swapped; Lady Reveller defies Lord Worthy: "Dare you, the Subject of my Power . . . arraign my Pleasures," (3.370-1) and he, after some resistance, gives in: "Oh! You have tortur'd me enough, take Pity now dear Tyrant, and let my Sufferings end" (3.375-6). Mixing cards and roles, Lord Worthy ends up getting the role that, in the plays by Goldoni and Regnard was respectively Rosaura's and Angélique's; in fact, he assumes some traits which are generally considered typically feminine: the capacity of loving someone with total abandon to the point of forgetting oneself, and forgiving and justifying almost everything. Lord Worthy's feminization is noticed by various characters. To her husband, who asks what kind of man Lord Worthy is, Mrs. Sago answers, "a mere Woman, full of Spleen and Vapours" (2.467-8) and, later on, Lord Worthy's servant, Buckle, describes Lord Worthy's reaction to Lady Reveller's repeated rejections as an unmanly fit of hysterics. Lord Worthy is either made fun of or pitied, but there is one more voice which seems to hint at the possibility of judging him differently: Centlivre's own. Lord Worthy refuses Sir James's suggestion that he should try to "force" Lady Reveller; he refuses the suggestion as Lady Reveller's body is nothing to him without her heart. He therefore seems to be able to think of Lady Reveller as a person endowed with both a body and a mind/heart; moreover, he is also capable of putting everything he is at stake; that is, his social image as a man, to gain Lady Reveller's heart. He will be saved this ultimate stake by the intervention of Sir James, who keeps mixing his and the other players' cards with the competence and aplomb of the consummate player described by Mme de Sévigné in a letter written to her daughter on July 29 1676 after a day spent at Versailles: "*Je voyais jouer Dangeau; et j'admirois combien nous sommes sots auprès de lui. Il ne songe qu'à son affaire et gagne ou les autres perdent, il ne neglige rien, il profite de tout, il n'est point distrait; en un mot, sa bonne conduite défie la fortune* (II:155)[11] (I have seen Dangeau play; he makes us all look stupid in comparison. His attention never strays from the game, and he wins when all players are losing, he misses nothing, takes adavantage of everything, is never off his guard; in one word, he conducts himself so well that he seems to defy fortune itself).

Mixing Social Classes: Mrs Sago's Stake

Lady Reveller also enjoys the social risk gambling involves: getting in touch and dealing with mixed classes and people. As Valère says: "*Le jeu rassemble tout; il unit à-la-fois le turbulent marquis, le paisible bourgeois. La femme du banquier, dorée et triomphante, coupe orgueilleusement la duchesse indigente. Là, sans distinction, on voit aller de pair le laquais d' un commis avec un duc et pair; et quoi qu' un sort jaloux nous ait fait d' injustices, de sa naissance ainsi l' on venge les caprices*" (200). (The gambling table brings together all and sundry: the unruly marquise and the peaceful bourgeois; the banker's wife, bejewelled and triumphant proudly cuts for the impoverished duchess. There, the commissioner's footman mixes with the duke; there, if you have been unjustly treated by a jealous fate, you can avenge yourself of the arbitrariness of your birth). As Caillois observes, the basic rule of any game is that of creating an absolute, albeit fictitious, equality among the players, thus creating a world governed by rules that are different from those of the real world. This is, in a way, the same otherness Voltaire noticed when he visited the London Stock-Exchange, where investors divested themselves of their social or religious identity to enter the game as if they were all equals. It is, however, left to Sir Richard, a former merchant risen to the ranks of gentry thanks to his success in trade, to blame his niece for her lack of discrimination: ". . . your Apartment is a Parade for men of all Ranks, from the Duke to the Fidler; . . . every one has his several Ends in meeting here, from the Lord to the Sharper, and each their separate Interest to pursue" (1.66-71).

Sir Richard, like Pantalone, is the representative of a social group that has finally attained economical power and social esteem by professing such virtues as fairness, trustfulness, moderation and hard work. Money, as Pantalone says, is his "blood" and its increase is the tangible proof of the merchant's social worth. In the merchant's economy, strict obedience to rules is meant to minimize the risk element, but in the gambler's economy, risk maintains all its aleatory character. A fine example of the gambler's economy is given by Sir James when fending off Lady Lucy's tirade against gambling. It is true that "Coaches and Equipage [are] dismiss'd" because of cards, but, Sir James observes, "how many fine Coaches and Equipages have they set up?" (4.226-8). Unlike the merchant, whose economic goal is increase, the gambler's goal is a zero sum economy. It is the individual who is either impoverished or enriched, whereas the system itself registers neither loss nor increase. Moreover, gambling stands for the utopian dream of begetting money in pleasure, as Florindo in Goldoni's *Il giocatore* explains drawing up his economic plan: "If I can win ten thousand sequins, I'll play no more. Ten thousand sequins invested at 4% can yield an annuity of 400 sequins a year . . . This is what I call gambling like a man" (1.4.3-6).

In this "parade of men of all ranks" who strive to get a fortune, there are also those for whom becoming rich means, in the words of Regnard's Valere, "revenging the injustice of one's birth." In the ***Basset Table,*** it is a woman, Mrs. Sago, who is not "content with her present State." She is a drugster's wife but she has become acquainted with Lady Reveller and is Sir James's mistress. Apparently not noticing what his wife's social climbing involves, Mr. Sago is very proud of her social success. Mrs. Sago stakes high; she is staking her virtue and her husband's money to become part of Lady Reveller's world, but she will lose. However, the fact that Centlivre has a chastened Mrs. Sago close the play should not make us overlook the fact that while she is staging her defeat, Centlivre also shows how skilfully Mrs. Sago plays her cards and what deep awareness she has of the way a trading economy works.

Mrs. Sago has bought her admittance into Lady Reveller's circle—"she has sent . . . [her] . . . the finest cargo, made up of Chocolate, Tea, Montifiasco Wine" (2.194-5), but to keep the game going (Lady Reveller accepts her as a friend as long as she has money), she needs to "replenish her Purse" quite often. In order to do this, she sets up a maze of complex trade relationships with various people and what she does not actually own, she buys "on margin" for a value of a thousand Pounds. Her risky investment might have proved rewarding if she had won at the basset table, but, as in all commercial enterprises, failure is always possible. When trying to help Mrs. Sago convince her husband to buy a diamond ring which she will then resell, Alpiew explains: ". . . the Owner is my Relation and has been as great a Merchant as any in London, but has had the Misfortune to have his Ships fall into the Hands of the French, or he'd not have parted with it" (2.504-7), so, a few lines later, when Mrs. Sago (her purse full) pleads: "Oh! Cast me, Fortune, on the winning Shore: Now let me gain what I have lost before" (2.541-2) it is not easy to distinguish the merchant's from the gamester's fortune—a blurring of differences which Centlivre was to underline again in *A Bold Stroke for a Wife* (1718), in which stockjobbers at Jonathan's Coffee House are shown to trade indifferently "South Sea bonds" and "Class Lottery tickets."

The basset table is therefore, for Mrs. Sago, a sort of Jonathan's Coffee House, both the place where she can access Lady Reveller's world and the means by which she plans to recover the investment she made to enter that world. Her frantic desperation when she realizes she is losing everything can be fully understood only if we clearly have in mind the value of her investment. The risk she is running is astonishingly high: if her husband were to turn her out of doors, as he seems likely to do once he has discovered the amount of his loss, ". . . that fair face . . . will quickly be a cheaper Drug than any in my Shop" (5.384-6). Mrs. Sago would be reduced to survival by investing in the only thing she actually owns: herself, a commodity which devaluates rapidly. Luckily, she is saved (again) by Sir James, who pays for all her debts and, in so doing, also pays her off.

Mixing Learning and Gender: Valeria's Stake

In *The Basset Table* the daughter to be married is Valeria. In the criticism concerning the play, she is generally introduced as a character apart, as the "Philosophical girl" thanks to whom the issue of female education is brought to the fore in an unusually sympathetic way and at an early date. A more central position in the play's economy is given her by F. P. Lock, who counterpoints gambling and education, observing that "the educated either see nothing attractive in the card game, or if they do play they know when to stop" (54).[12] Detached though she may seem, however, she is still part of the game. Science is Valeria's stake, her own form of investment ("Where Fortune in my Power," she says, she would be ready to bestow her capital to found a college where women could study "Philosophy") towards sexual self-ownership and inalienable individuality. Like her cousin, Lady Reveller, she is thus trying to avoid the exploitation of patriarchal authority/ economy and to negotiate the terms of the fraternal one that the play shows as emerging. Beyond the superficial differences, Valeria, the serious philosophical girl, and Lady Reveller, the frivolous gambler, are linked by structural and cultural ties stronger than family. Was not science or "natural philosophy," as it was then called, condemned as a social deviation as much as gambling? Were not virtuosi criticised because they dissipated their money and their children's inheritance, forgot their familiar and social duties and neglected their personal appearance? Gamblers and scientists alike were considered social misfits because of the excessiveness of their passion. And were not female virtuosos abused because learning, besides making them unfit for wives and housewives, encouraged immoral behavior, providing them with occasions their devious natures could not resist?[13]

Besides thus evoking a general framework, Centlivre also suggests similarities within the play that become explicit when both Valeria and Lady Reveller have to resist the bullying—though inoffensive—methods of Sir Richard, who represents patriarchy[14] and who considers his daughter as a form of "future" investment (she will breed heirs for him). Valeria, like Lady Reveller, is also given supremacy in the gendered power relation, as when calling Captain Firebrand "an irrational creature" and claiming for herself the superior rational quality. "The Philosophical Gimcrack I don't value of a Cockle-Shell" (2.384) retorts the Captain, voicing the general opinion and highlighting the amount of Valeria's scientific stake. Since Molière's *Femmes Savantes* (1672), or its English version (Wright's *Female Vertuoso's*, 1693), no substantial variation seems to have intervened. The flesh and bone learned lady is still ambiguous and suspect: Centlivre's learning is attributed to illicit contacts with men; her successful plays are stolen or at best given her "by some Gentl'men"[15];

she is variously satirized in Pope's *Dunciad* and in *Three Hours after Marriage* by Gay, Pope and Arbuthnot (1717); Centlivre herself laments the meagre consideration learned ladies are given by even their own sex; even her character, Valeria, is sometimes seen as a satiric portrait of Mary Astell. Against this background, Centlivre projects the utopian coordinates of the basset world inhabited by all of Lady Reveller's "whimsical family." In the end, both the gambler and the virtuosa will be brought to more ordinary behavior but beyond the apparently orthodox conclusion we read Centlivre's painstaking enquiry into "A Lady"'s "proper Sphere of Activity."[16]

In conclusion, it is necessary to hint, at least, at another revealing characteristic of **The Basset Table**: it is an original play only indebted to a previous work, *Le Divorce,* again by Regnard (1688), for the marginal (sub-)plot line of one character, Mrs. Sago, who retains the negative behavioral traits (a sum of Molière's and Boileau's different satires) of the original Dame Sotinet, while the aristocratic status of the lady gambler gives rise to the new character of Lady Reveller. What matters here, however, apart from traditional debates over English theatrical indebtedness, or more recent gender questions (when writing incognito Centlivre seems readier to admit to borrowings), are the distinctive features of the resulting characters. Mrs. Sago is the one who has to bear the burden of the orthodox reform plot that the play seems to emphasize, especially in its conclusion. There is no real reform for Lady Reveller; instead, unlike Valere or Florindo, she is shown as thoroughly self-possessed, competent, and winning. Purposely paired with Valeria, the other character who defies accepted norms, Lady Reveller does not have to reform; her problem is that in comic as well as in social constraints, she has to get married before the play is over. Centlivre's "feminist individualism" is thus not limited[17]; it is enormously amplified by the absolute, albeit fictitious, equality created by the alternative rules of the basset table and all it stands for. Centlivre's awareness of its utopian dimension (shown also in her poem "A Woman's Case" (1720), where she deals with the limits her own marriage imposed), does not diminish the breadth of her own speculations and suggests, beautifully capturing the best spirit of play, an entirely different form of a lady's last stake.

Notes

1. Susanna Centlivre, *The Basset Table* and *The Gamester* in *The Dramatic Works of the Celebrated Mrs. Centlivre With A New Account of her Life,* 3 vols. (London: John Pearson, 1872); Jean-Françoise Regnard, *Le Joueur* in Document électronique, INALF, 1961 reproducing the 1820 edition of *Ouvres complétes de Regnard* (Paris: J. L.Briére, 1820); and Carlo Goldoni, *Il giocatore* (Venezia: Marsilio 1997). Subsequent references will be to these editions.

All translations from Italian and French into English are by the authors of the article.

2. Quoted in Laura J. Rosenthal, "Writing (as) the Lady's Last Stake: Susanna Centlivre," in *Playwrights and Plagiarists in Early Modern England: Gender, Authorship, Literary Property* (Ithaca and London: Cornell U.P., 1996), p.208.

3. The play ran but for one night and has been seldom performed ever since. Carlo Goldoni wrote in his *Mèmoires* that the "Piece tombée sans ressource" and that the reason was to be found in the fact that "C'étoit mal à propos de mettre à découvert les conséquences de cet amusement dangereux, et encore plus la mauvaise foi de certains joueurs, et les artifices des courtiers de jeu." Quoted from Goldoni's *Mémoires* in the introduction to *Il Giocatore,* p.82.

4. See Giancarlo Dossena, "Elogio dell'azzardo e del Casinò" in AA. VV., *Fanti e denari: Sei secoli di giochi d'azzardo* (Venezia: Arsenale, 1989), p. 11-34.

5. Roger Caillois, *Les jeux et les hommes, le masque et le vertige* (Paris: Gallimard, 1958).

6. Katherine M. Rogers ed., *The Meridian Antology of Restoration and Eighteenth-Century Plays by Women* (New York: Meridian-Penguin, 1994).

7. Unsigned Dedication to *The Basset Table* added to the 1706 edition.

8. Lady Reveller's dashing entrée is unusual even in comparison to other female gamblers. Lady Dealer in Etherege's *The Man of Mode* is, after a gambling session, as dishevelled as her male counterparts. "I have played with her now at least a dozen times, till she's worn out all her fine complexion and her tour would keep in curl no longer" (2.1. 95-97)

9. Florindo is in serious financial straits and Gandolfa (the elderly aunt of Rosaura, Florindo's fiancée) offers to help him. She wants him to marry her in exchange for a pension of 1,000 ducats a year. In his asides he curses her, hopes she will die soon, calls her a corpse, and, for a good measure, a stinking on his honour he will play no more and offers her his hand. "Here is my hand, if you want it" (3.18.19)

10. *The Guardian,* 2 vols., (London: J. Tonson, 1714).

11. Mme de Sevigné, *Lettres* (Paris: Bibliotheque de la Pleiade, 1960).

12. F. P. Lock, *Susanna Centlivre* (Boston: Twayne, 1979).

13. To remain within the genre, and to quote only some of the best known examples, a whole gallery of satirical portraits comes to mind, starting with

the three imported virtuosae of Molière's *Femmes Savantes* (1672), later adapted for the English stage by Thomas Wright as *The Female Vertuoso's* (1693); Sir Nicholas Gimcrack in Shadwell's *Virtuoso* (1676); Sir Formal Ancient in D'Urfey's *The Fool Turned Critic* (1676); Lady Knowell in Behn's *Sir Patient Fancy* (1678); the virtuoso imitation presented by Lawrence Maidwell in *The Loving Enemies* (1680), for which Shadwell wrote an epilogue; Doctor Boliardo of Behn's *The Emperor of the Moon* (1687); Sophronia in D'Urfey's *The Richmond Heiress* (1693); Bizarre in Farquhar's *The Incostant* (1702); Marsilia, Calista and Mrs. Wellfed in the anonymous *The Female Wits* (1704); Florida in Johnson's *The Generous Husband* (1711); Phoebe Clinket and Doctor Fossile in *Three Hours After Marriage* by Gay, Pope, and Arbuthnot (1717); Lady Wrangle and her daughter in Cibber's *The Refusal* (1721); Lady Science in Miller's *The Humours of Oxford* (1727).

14. Rosenthal, p.237.

15. "Some have arm'd themselves with resolution not to like the Play they paid to see; and if in spite of Spleen, they have been pleased against their Will, have maliciously reported it was none of mine, but given me by some Gentleman." Dedication to *The Platonick Lady* (1707).

16. The words pronounced by Frederick in D'Urfey's *The Richmond Heiress* (1693) reflect an increasingly common trope and are used by Centlivre herself when trying to understand men's dislike of women writers: "perhaps you'll answer, because they meddle with things out of their Sphere: But I say, no; for since the Poet is Born, why not a Woman as well as a Man?" Dedication to the *Platonick Lady*.

17. Rosenthal, p.206, p.240-1.

THE BUSIE BODY (1709)

CRITICAL COMMENTARY

Elizabeth Inchbald (essay date 1806)

SOURCE: Inchbald, Elizabeth. "Remarks." In *Remarks for the British Theatre (1806-1809)*, n.p. Delmar, N.Y.: Scholars' Facsimiles & Reprints, 1990.

[*In the following essay, first published in an 1806 edition of* The Busie Body, *Inchbald offers a brief biography of Centlivre, emphasizing the need for* unmarried or widowed women and mothers to earn a living and defending authorship as a legitimate profession for women. Critiquing The Busie Body, Inchbald contends that the character of Marplot, especially in the hand of an able comedian, made possible the long life of an otherwise mediocre play.]

When a man follows the occupation of a woman, or a woman the employment of a man, they are both unpleasing characters, if they are guided in their pursuits by choice; but, if necessity has ruled their destinies, they are surely objects of compassion and mercy should be granted to their want of skill in their irregular departments.

The female author of **The Busy Body** was driven to a poet's calling by the hardships of her fate.

Mrs. Centlivre's father was the possessor of a considerable estate at Holbeach, in Lincolnshire, at the time of the Restoration; but, as he was a zealous dissenter, he was, of course, persecuted for the political opinions which adhered to this church: his estate was at length confiscated, and he, with his family, obliged to seek refuge in Ireland.

The authoress of this play was, at twelve years of age, an orphan; and at fifteen, being persecuted on account of her poverty and her beauty, as much as her father had been for his religious and republican principles, she pursued his example; and, flying from her enemies, took shelter in England. England had not the virtue to protect her, either from want or from dishonour. A student of Cambridge met her, a forlorn traveller, on her way to London; and this young man, being of an engaging mind and person, prevailed on her (destitute as she was) to accompany him to the university in man's attire, as his companion and friend.

The haste with which this intimacy was formed was but the forerunner of as hasty a separation. She, however, remained long enough at the college to learn experience, and to improve her taste for literature.

The biographers of Mrs. Centlivre have not said where she met with her second lover; but it is certain she had the prudence to make him her husband: she had the affliction, likewise, to be a widow before she was eighteen.

Her deceased husband was a gentleman, and the nephew of Sir Stephen Fox. Her next husband was also a gentleman; for she married, not long after her widowhood, a Mr. Carrol, who was killed in a duel the year following;—and, once more, she became a widow.

It was now discreet to think on another support than such as had depended on the lives of two young husbands, who, having offended their family by a contract of marriage, the mere effects of love, had, on their demise, left their relict in the most indigent circumstances. Mrs. Carrol became an actress; but, notwithstanding her youth, her wit, and her beauty, she was unsuccessful in that profession.

To avoid the alternative, female profligacy, or domestic drudgery, she now encountered the masculine enterprise of an author. She wrote eighteen plays, of which three will preserve her memory:—these are, *The Wonder, Bold Stroke for a Wife,* and the present comedy.

In this period of her writing, (and, no doubt, its concomitant, fasting,) the reader will not be surprised that Mrs. Carrol should marry a third time.—She now united herself to a man, whose very title promised her protection from that ancient and modern visitation upon authors, denominated—hunger. Mr. Centlivre was "yeoman to the mouth," or principal cook to Queen Anne. Mrs. Centlivre's forecast in these her last nuptials, did her judgment more honour than her ambition. She died in 1723, of a disorder neither so lingering, nor so painful, as starving.

The comedy of *The Busy Body,* which has survived one hundred years, was, by the actors who performed in it, expected to die on the first night.

The foresight of actors, in regard to the success of new dramas, has been long out of credit—unjustly so—for, although their predictions are not infallible actors are as frequently prophetic upon the life and death of a play as the physician upon that of his patient.

The part of Marplot is the sole support of this comedy.—A most powerful protector in all, that original character can give. The busy curiosity, the officious good temper, and the sheepish cowardice of this mean atom of human nature, are so excellently delineated, that he allures the attention and expectation of the auditors, and makes them bear with patience, the dull and common-place dramatic persons which surround them.

Authors of the past time, and those of the present, have had very different notions of the ties which subsist between parents and children. It is shocking to see how tyranny on one part, and deceit on the other, disgrace most of our old play books. It is to be hoped that these portraits of unnatural vice have been daubed with such hideous colours, they have reclaimed all fathers, mothers, sons, and daughters, and left to the writers of these days, to paint from nature—parental and filial love.

F. P. Lock (essay date 1979)

SOURCE: Lock, F. P. "*The Busy Body.*" In *Susanna Centlivre,* pp. 63-77. Boston: Twayne Publishers, 1979.

[*In the following excerpt, Lock cites* The Busie Body *as an excellent example of Centlivre's style and method, emphasizing her careful construction of plot and skillful use of intrigue.*]

Two years elapsed between Centlivre's marriage in 1707 and the production of her next play. She put the interval to good use in writing what is probably her best play. *The Busy Body* remained popular with theatergoers on both sides of the Atlantic for over one-hundred-fifty years. Yet this success was not won without a struggle. Mottley tells us that "when it was first offered to the Players, [it] was received very cooly, and it was with great Difficulty that the Author could prevail upon them to think of acting it." During rehearsals Robert Wilks, who was to play the leading role of Sir George Airy, "had so mean an Opinion of his Part . . . that one Morning in a Passion he threw it off the Stage into the Pit, and swore that no body would bear to sit to hear such Stuff." The play was reported to be "a silly thing wrote by a Woman, that the Players had no Opinion of it."[1]

In these inauspicious circumstances, *The Busy Body* was produced at Drury Lane on May 12, 1709. Mottley describes the audience on the first night as "agreeably surprized" by the play.[2] Mottley's account can be confirmed from contemporary sources. In October 1709, the *Female Tatler* reported that at a rehearsal, Wilks had "flung his Part into the Pitt for damn'd Stuff, before the Lady's Face that wrote it."[3] In the *Tatler* for May 14, Steele wrote "this play is written by a lady. In old times we used to sit upon a play here after it was acted; but now the entertainment is turned another way."[4] Steele was obviously thinking of the preproduction prejudice that Mottley describes.

Steele returned to *The Busy Body* in a later *Tatler.* This time he did not merely ask for a fair hearing; he handed down a favorable judgment. The *Tatler* was an influential tastemaker. Steele's praise probably contributed to the play's success: "The plot and incidents of the play are laid with that subtlety of spirit which is peculiar to females of wit, and is very seldom well performed by those of the other sex, in whom craft in love is an act of invention, and not, as with women, the effect of nature and instinct."[5] Steele seems to mean that in *The Busy Body* the incidents and intrigues appear natural, not forced. A man writing the same kind of play would have had to invent the stratagems, which would consequently have appeared contrived. Steele's point is not very convincing. It is hard to believe that a man could not have written *The Busy Body.* But it was traditional to praise women writers for their natural talent rather than their acquired art. Dryden had used the same antithesis as Steele in his ode on Anne Killigrew:

Art she had none, yet wanted none:
For Nature did that Want supply,
So rich in Treasures of her Own,
She might our boasted Stores defy.[6]

Steele's praise may have gratified Centlivre as a woman: it can hardly have pleased her as a writer.

I PLOT AND MARPLOT

As with most of Centlivre's comedies, the plot of *The Busy Body* centers on the problems and intrigues of two pairs of lovers. But contrary to her usual practice, in this play Centlivre pairs sparkish hero with lively heroine and quiet heroine with serious hero. Sir George Airy wants to marry Miranda: her guardian (Sir Francis Gripe) wants to marry her himself. Charles Gripe wants to marry Isabinda: her father (Sir Jealous Traffick) wants her to marry a Spanish merchant. The business of the play is to outwit father and guardian.

The lovers are contrasted in circumstances as well as in character. Sir George is rich and rakish, but he is in some doubt as to whether his love for Miranda is returned. Charles is poor, but he is assured of Isabinda's love. Miranda is dependent on her guardian for her fortune, but she enjoys personal freedom of movement. Isabinda is virtually imprisoned in her father's house. Miranda inevitably appears more active and independent, Isabinda more timid and subdued. Sir George is engaged in a pursuit of Miranda; Charles in the rescue of Isabinda. This makes for greater variety of comic effects than in Centlivre's earlier plays.

The clever and resourceful Miranda is the most memorable of the lovers. It is she who makes the running, and Sir George has to follow where she leads. She is a consummate dissembler, as adept at playing the coquette as at acting the prude.[7] Yet she is neither of these. She is in love with Sir George from the beginning, although she is too prudent to admit as much to him at the outset. Perhaps Steele had her role particularly in mind when he spoke of "craft in love" as "the effect of nature and instinct."

In the subplot, the dominant role is played by Charles. This is necessarily so since Isabinda is immured in her father's house. Sir Jealous Traffick is a retired merchant who lived for many years in Spain. There he contracted an admiration for Spanish customs, especially their treatment of women. There is a similar character in Wycherley's *The Gentleman Dancing Master* (1672), in which James Formal renames himself Don Diego and prides himself on being "as grave, grum, and jealous, as any Spaniard breathing."[8] This is Sir Jealous's character in a nutshell. Centlivre presumably knew Wycherley's play, but she took from it no more than the idea of the Spanish humor. The Spanish treatment of women, especially of daughters before marriage, gives great scope for the writer of the comedy of intrigue. It makes even a lover's access to his mistress a problem of disguise and deception, surreptitious entry, and probably precipitate retreat. In later plays, Centlivre

exploited these possibilities more fully: *Marplot* and *The Wonder* are both set in Lisbon, where intrigue and jealousy seem more natural than in London.

Miranda and Sir Jealous are, after Marplot, the most notable characters in the play. The guardian, Sir Francis Gripe, is an avaricious and amorous old man. But he is more of a type, and less well individualized than Sir Jealous. Neither Sir George nor Charles has a very good part. Perhaps this was why Wilks "flung his Part into the Pitt"; only in the "dumb" scene does Sir George have a dominant role.

The Busy Body as described thus far is much like earlier Centlivre comedies. There is the usual quartet of lovers, although there are—untypically—two father figures. But it is the character of Marplot that is the really new and distinctive feature of *The Busy Body.* Marplot is the title character. His peculiar humor is his insatiable and usually unseasonable curiosity. Before *The Busy Body,* Centlivre had used characters like Marplot to provide broader comic fun than the stratagems of the lovers. They were often only minimally involved in the plot, but shown off in static satiric scenes that functioned chiefly to display them. A notable example is Wou'dbe in *Love at a Venture.* His principal scene (pp. 5-9) contributes nothing to the advancement of the action; it serves only to display Wou'dbe's foolishness. Characters like Wou'dbe were usually treated with amused or dismissive contempt.

This type of humor character is represented in *The Busy Body* by Sir Jealous Traffick and Sir Francis Gripe. But in Marplot, Centlivre created a new kind of sympathetic humor character. Nor is Marplot a static or subsidiary character: he is the mainspring of the greater part of the action of the play. There can be little doubt that the character of Marplot was the chief reason for *The Busy Body's* popular success.

Marplot was well calculated to appeal to an age which was beginning to distrust wit and the laughter that derived from what Hobbes had called a "sudden glory arising from some sudden conception of some eminency in ourselves, by comparison with the infirmity of others, or with our own formerly."[9] The triumph of good nature and sympathy over this laughter of "sudden glory" brought about a new kind of humor character, the "amiable humorist." Stuart Tave offers this distinction between the old humor and the new: "Humor is no longer the satirist's carrion, but the expression of good nature. People like Colley Cibber begin to appear, parading their foibles, happy and complacent. . . . This distinguishes [Sir Roger de Coverley, in the *Spectator*] from the humorous characters of Jonson and Shadwell; unlike them he has no directly didactic, satiric function as a comic character."[10]

Centlivre is a transitional figure in this progress from satiric to sympathetic humor. Her earlier plays are notably more astringent than her later ones. The treatment of the guardians in *A Bold Stroke for a Wife* is affable compared to the treatment of Ogle in *A Beau's Duel* or Wou'dbe in *Love at a Venture*. In *The Wonder*, Felix's jealousy is treated not satirically but sympathetically. But Marplot is Centlivre's best "amiable humorist."

Perhaps the crucial factor in the characterization of Marplot is that we are not invited or intended to feel superior to him. This is clear from comparisons with the notable busybodies in restoration comedy who have been proposed as prototypes of Marplot. The comparisons are interesting irrespective of the question of "source."[11] The two are Sir Martin in Dryden's *Sir Martin Mar-All* (1667) and Intrigo in Sir Francis Fane's *Love in the Dark* (1675). Intrigo is actually closer to Sir Politick Would-be in *Volpone* than he is to Marplot. He is a minor character, much occupied with ferreting out state secrets. His inquisitiveness gets him into several scrapes; but unlike Marplot, he is treated with contempt, not sympathy.

Sir Martin Mar-All is concisely described in the list of characters as a "Fool." He is less a busybody than a blunderer, who talks when he should be quiet and who will not listen to advice. There is nothing beguiling or sympathetic about Sir Martin's invincible stupidity. He is harshly treated by Dryden, losing his prospective wife to his clever servant Warner. John Downes recorded that Dryden wrote Sir Martin "purposely for the Mouth of Mr. Nokes."[12] Cibber's description of Nokes's acting gives us a good idea of how contemporary audiences saw Sir Martin: "he had a shuffling Shamble in his Gait, with so contented an Ignorance in his Aspect, and an aukward Absurdity in his Gesture, that had you not known him, you cou'd not have believ'd, that naturally he could have had a Grain of common Sense."[13] It is clear that we are intended to feel superior to Sir Martin; that the laughter he provokes derives from a "sudden glory."

Marplot's humor is his inquisitiveness: "Lord, Lord, how little Curiosity some People have! Now my chief Pleasure lies in knowing every Body's Business" (p. 28). It appears an amiable humor because it is so frank, active, and disinterested. Centlivre prevents Marplot appearing merely absurd or stupid by endowing him with a lively curiosity, an engaging lack of foresight, and an open good nature. He is also generous and anxious to help his friends. He often gets into scrapes through his misdirected efforts to do them a good turn. He is often tactless, impudent, obsessive, officious, and inept. But it is impossible to remain angry with him for long, as Sir George and Charles find at the end of the play:

SIR GEORGE.

Thou hast been an unlucky Rogue.

MARPLOT.

But very honest.

CHARLES.

That I'll vouch for; and freely forgive thee.

(P. 71)

The "amusing but inoffensive Marplot," as Jess Byrd calls him, is obviously "designed not for reform but for laughter."[14]

II ST. JAMES'S PARK

The Busy Body is worth examining in some detail as perhaps the best example of Centlivre's dramatic technique. One of her most enjoyable plays, it is also a triumph of construction, timing, and the disposition of comic business. Like all Centlivre's full length plays, *The Busy Body* is divided into five acts. But the construction and balance of *The Busy Body* are exceptional. Only *A Bold Stroke for a Wife* is as skillfully composed. *The Busy Body* consists of an act of exposition, three acts of complication, and a final act of unraveling. The two major comic scenes—the "dumb" scene and the "monkey" scene—are so placed as to balance each other, in the first half of Act II and the second half of Act IV. Proper attention is paid throughout the play to the provision of necessary "bridge" scenes, to the modulation of tension, and to the varying of the pace of the action.

The first act of *The Busy Body* takes place in St. James's Park at an unfashionable hour of the morning: an ideal time and place for both the chance encounter and the discreet appointment. Two friends, both on errands of love, meet accidentally. They compare notes on their situations and plans. Sir George Airy is a man of independent fortune: 4,000 a year. He is engaged in two affairs. He has made an assignation in the park with a masked *incognita* who is clever and witty; but he is more deeply involved with a woman whom he has admired by sight but not spoken with. The latter is Miranda, the ward of Sir Francis Gripe. Sir George's friend is Charles Gripe, Sir Francis's son. Charles is in love with Isabinda, the daughter of a rich merchant—Sir Jealous Traffick. She returns his love, but her father disapproves of Charles as a son-in-law. Instead, he is determined that she shall marry a Spanish merchant.

The characters and circumstances of the two men are rapidly developed (pp. 1-3). Marplot, who is to be the play's driving comic force, is introduced. We do not see him in action this early in the play, but Charles tells an anecdote that gives us some idea of what to expect in the way of comedy from Marplot: "I had lent a certain Merchant my hunting Horses, and was to have met his wife in his Absence: Sending him along with my Groom to make the Complement, and to deliver a Letter to the Lady at the same time; what does he do, but gives the Husband the Letter, and offers her the Horses" (p. 6). Charles's servant Whisper brings word that Isabinda has been prevented from meeting him in the park. The three men go their separate ways. The tone and social milieu of the play have been set, and we know what kind of comedy to expect.

The second scene combines development with further exposition. Miranda arrives in the park and meets Isabinda's maid, Patch. This second accidental rencontre parallels the first. Isabinda's plight is sketched in more detail and is graphically illustrated by her inability to come to the park as arranged. The comparative situations of the two women are discussed, as those of the men had been earlier. The action proper of the play begins with Sir George's reentry with Sir Francis Gripe (p. 9). Miranda and Patch withdraw out of sight but not out of earshot. Sir George is trying to arrange for Sir Francis to let him speak with Miranda. A hundred guineas is agreed on for an interview.[15] This clear breach of his trust as a guardian establishes Sir Francis as both venal and stupid. He can see in the proposal neither immorality nor danger to his own plans. He is foolishly deluded by Miranda's pretended fondness for him.

A notable feature of this scene is Miranda's succession of peeping asides. In about two pages of text (pp. 9-10), Miranda eight times peeps out of hiding and makes a remark aside. This convention may seem strange to modern readers, but Centlivre's contemporaries accepted it as a common dramatic technique. In this scene, the peeping asides function as comic punctuation. Some of Miranda's remarks are replies to Sir George or Sir Francis, others are serious statements of her real feelings about the two men. One aside is both comic and serious:

SIR FRANCIS

   . . . in sober Sadness she cannot abide 'em [young men].

MIRANDA.

   (Peeping.) In sober Sadness you are mistaken—.

(P. 9)

Here Miranda is obviously intended to mimic Sir Francis's intonation; but she is also telling the truth. This combination of jest and earnest is characteristic of her. Outraged by the bargain the two men are driving about her—as though she were some piece of property to be bartered—she promises to "fit you both" (p. 10). Thus, unexpected developments are foreshadowed in the approaching interview that Sir George has bought.

Sir Francis leaves with Sir George's guineas. Miranda and Patch come forward. Miranda is masked, and Sir George is therefore unaware that he is now enjoying gratis what he has just paid a hundred guineas to enjoy later. In this scene, Miranda plays the coquette (pp. 10-13). There is an amusing duel of wit as Sir George tries to persuade her to unmask. Finally she agrees to, if he will turn his back. He does so and Miranda and Patch promptly slip out. For about half a minute, Sir George keeps up a running commentary as though Miranda were still present; finally the suspicious silence prompts him to turn round. First Miranda was heard but not seen; then spoken to but not present. Both the concealment and the disappearing trick develop Miranda's character as resourceful and elusive. The act ends with Sir George abashed but determined to intensify his pursuit.

III THE "DUMB" SCENE

Act II begins with a short scene (pp. 14-15) between Sir Francis and Miranda. He tells her about his bargain with Sir George. Miranda affects to be amused and to think Sir George an "odious young Fop" (p. 14). In order to prevent Sir George discovering that she is his *incognita* of the park, she proposes to Sir Francis that she should remain dumb throughout the interview. Sir Francis agrees to the stratagem. Our curiosity about the interview is thus heightened. But instead of gratifying us at once, Centlivre suspends the issue for a few pages (pp. 15-19). Sir Francis is now shown to be an unnatural father as well as a venal guardian. Charles enters in a vain attempt to appeal to his father for financial support. The best that Sir Francis will do is suggest that Charles should find a wealthy wife—such as Lady Wrinkle (p. 18). He offers to introduce Charles to her for nothing, even though a matchmaker would charge twenty guineas for the service. Sir Francis's calm acceptance of this traffic in marriage is of a piece with his sale of an interview with Miranda.

Sir Francis is also Marplot's guardian. It is therefore no surprise when Marplot enters, having followed Charles from the park. Marplot is a static character, but Centlivre develops his role slowly. In Act I he was merely inquisitive; in this scene we find him actively running about after Charles. Only in Act III and later is comic capital made out of his humor. Consequently, we do not tire of him as we might have done if his blunders had been introduced too soon and repeated too often. The economy of Centlivre's construction is seen in the threefold purpose that his brief scene serves: it increases the tension, shows another side to Sir Francis's character, and develops the role of Marplot.

As soon as Charles and Marplot are disposed of, Sir George arrives for his interview (pp. 19-24). Sir Francis remains in the room but out of hearing. Sir George begins by declaring his love in some prepared speeches. Miranda's silence provides a test of his resourcefulness. First he gets Miranda to reply to his questions with a system of nods, shakes of the head, and sighs (p. 21). Then in a virtuoso improvisation, he asks his questions and answers them himself on Miranda's behalf (pp. 22-23). He even composes an extempore letter and a song to himself. The "dumb" scene is punctuated in two ways: by Miranda's asides and by Sir Francis's interruptions. Miranda's asides work in much the same way as in the scene in the park. Sir Francis is presumably stationed in a remote area of the stage; on three occasions he runs up to the couple, disturbed at the turn affairs appear to be taking, and has to be repelled by Sir George. The asides and the interruptions prevent the scene from becoming monotonous without dissipating the rising tension. When Sir George's time has expired, Miranda silently withdraws. Sir George and Sir Francis have a brief talk. Miranda's ascendency over both men has been confirmed: neither knows what she is really about. Sir George is baffled, but cannot really believe that she intends to marry Sir Francis. Sir Francis is complacent, seeing nothing strange in Miranda's declared preference for himself. Both men exit with sets of couplets (p. 24). The midact couplets serve to emphasize a pause and a break in the action as we move to Sir Jealous Traffick's house and the Spanish plot.

The "dumb" scene is a variant on a comic situation that had been used by both Boccaccio and Ben Jonson: in the fifth tale of the third day of *The Decameron,* and in Act I, Scene vi of *The Devil Is an Ass.* Ben Jonson's editors, Herford and Simpson, think that Centlivre used Boccaccio because "In Boccaccio the interview is not in the hearing of the husband; Jonson has changed this in order to make Fitzdottrel look a more consummate fool."[16] Actually, Centlivre's scene is a further refinement on Jonson's, not a return to Boccaccio's. Sir Francis's interruptions—which naturally have no counterpart in Boccaccio, where the husband is not in the room—parallel Fitzdottrell's intrusions into Wittipol's conversation with his wife. In *The Devil Is an Ass,* Fitzdottrell stands close by; Centlivre improved the theatrical possibilities of the scene by making Sir Francis run backwards and forwards.

In both Boccaccio and Jonson, the silence is enjoined by the husband. The moral point is that the husband thinks that the letter of imposing silence is more important than the spirit of pimping—for that is what it amounts to—for their wives. Jonson indeed makes Fitzdottrell "the more consummate fool," notably by allowing him to expose his own folly in a long speech of intended self-justification. Jonson makes the scene a searching critique of marital responsibility. Centlivre changed both the emphasis and the morality by giving the idea of not speaking to Miranda herself; in addition, Miranda is not the wife but the ward of Sir Francis. These changes complicate the intrigue while they simplify the morality. Sir George is engaged on a legitimate courtship, not on a cuckolding expedition.

The moral condemnation falls entirely on Sir Francis. At the same time, neither Sir George nor Sir Francis really knows what Miranda is up to. In Boccaccio and Jonson, the wife was a pawn between the two men. In *The Busy Body,* it is Miranda who is in control: she "fits" the two men as she had earlier promised herself that she would.

IV THE PLOT THICKENS

Contemporary audiences would have seen *The Busy Body* with brief intervals between each act. These intervals would have been enlivened by some musical or other entertainment. But for convenience of discussion, the middle part of the play—between the "dumb" scene and the "monkey" scene—can be considered as a whole. This central section comprises four main sequences and two bridge scenes. Sandwiched between the two major scenes involving Miranda and Sir George, this part of the play is primarily concerned with the Charles-Isabinda plot. Act II is completed by the first scene at Sir Jealous's house and a short bridge scene at Charles's lodgings. Act III consists of a second scene at Sir Jealous's, a scene at Sir Francis Gripe's, and a bridge scene in a tavern. Act IV begins with a third scene at Sir Jealous's, and is completed by the "monkey" scene. Centlivre's care in the construction of the play is evident from this summary.

The first scene at Sir Jealous's house is slow-moving, providing a change of pace from the bustling "dumb" scene. Its purpose is largely expository: it introduces us to Sir Jealous and his Spanish humor. Whisper and Patch arrange for Charles to visit Isabinda as soon as Sir Jealous has gone out. Unluckily Sir Jealous sees Whisper, and his suspicions are aroused. This prepares us for his later unexpected return. As so often in Centlivre, developments that surprise the characters in the play are foreseen by the audience. Centlivre generally prefers anticipation to surprise as a dramatic technique.

The scene in Charles's lodgings at the end of the act (pp. 27-29) has two functions. Whisper brings Charles news of the appointment with Isabinda. More importantly, it contributes to the characterization of Marplot. The scene shows him at his best and worst. It begins with Marplot advancing Charles a loan; this is one instance when he is genuinely serviceable to his friends. But the scene ends with Marplot's exasperating refusal to take no for an answer when Charles will not let him into the secret of his assignation with Isabinda. Marplot secretly determines to follow him; this will lead to the first comic disaster in the next act. Sir George also has a small part in this scene. His presence helps prevent the two parts of the play from moving too far apart.

Act III has two comic sequences, both involving Marplot and his blunders. Faster moving than Act II, it represents an increase in the play's momentum. The first sequence concerns Charles and Isabinda. Charles arrives at the street outside Sir Jealous's house. Patch lets him in. Marplot arrives just too late, but decides to wait about on the off chance of something interesting happening. The scene changes to the inside of the house for a brief scene between Charles and Isabinda—the first in the play (pp. 30-31). But their protestations of love are interrupted by Patch's news that Sir Jealous is coming back (p. 31). Patch conducts Charles out through the balcony. The scene changes back to the street.[17] Sir Jealous arrives, and Marplot overhears him threaten to "make Mince-Meat" of any man he finds in the house (p. 32). Marplot thinks he will do Charles a service by telling Sir Jealous that "the Gentleman you threaten is a very honest Gentleman" and not without friends. Of course this merely confirms Sir Jealous's suspicions. He beats Marplot for his pains and goes into the house. Charles drops down from the balcony and finds Marplot. Charles thinks that it was Marplot who alarmed Sir Jealous and exits in high dudgeon. But in fact Marplot did Charles a service by detaining Sir Jealous in the street. Here Marplot appears as, for once, more sinned against than sinning. His efforts get him nothing but hard blows from Sir Jealous and hard words from Charles. The whole episode is rounded off by a brief scene inside the house (pp. 33-34) in which Sir Jealous upbraids Isabinda and threatens her with an imminent Spanish husband. As in the middle of Act II (p. 24), a decisive break in the action is signaled by Isabinda's final speech in couplets (p. 34).

The scene changes to Sir Francis's house. Sir Francis and Miranda are discussing the "dumb" scene and their approaching—as Sir Francis thinks—marriage (pp. 34-36). Miranda uses Sir Francis's good temper to get him to promise her his written consent to marry whom she pleases. She tells him that this is merely to prove that she marries him freely. They are interrupted by Marplot (p. 36). As in the previous scene, Marplot combines good intention with inept execution. Here he acts as Sir George's advocate to Miranda; he has of course no inkling of her real feelings for Sir George. The resourceful Miranda puts Marplot to use, just as she has made Sir Francis her unwitting agent in the first part of the scene. She gives Marplot a message for Sir George: that his suit is hopeless and that he should "keep from the Garden Gate on the left Hand; for if he dares to saunter there, about the Hour of Eight, as he used to do, he shall be saluted with a Pistol or a Blunderbuss" (p. 38). Miranda hopes that Sir George will take the hint and come. Neither Marplot nor Sir Francis suspects her real purpose. Here again, as in the "dumb" scene, Miranda manipulates and makes fools of two men at the same time.

Act III, like Act II, ends with a bridge scene (pp. 39-42). This time the location is a tavern. Once again Sir George and Charles are engaged in a discussion of their affairs. Marplot is prudent enough to send a message to test his welcome from Charles before joining them (p. 40). He apologizes to Charles and gives Sir George the message from Miranda. Charles writes a letter to Isabinda and gives it to Whisper to deliver to Patch. Uncharacteristically, Charles offers Marplot his company home: the unwonted attention makes Marplot suspect that there is more to the affair of the garden gate than he had supposed. Charles, of course, hopes to be able to keep Marplot from spoiling Sir George's clandestine appointment. But Marplot determines to give Charles the slip and to follow Sir George. The mystery of the garden gate seems more attractive than the mystery of Charles's letter. Thus the act ends with a promise of rapid developments in both actions— Charles's new appointment with Isabinda, and Sir George's assignation at the garden gate. We can look forward to Marplot's unseasonable presence at one of these at least.

The first half of Act IV (pp. 43-51) is a more dramatic rerun of the earlier scene at Sir Jealous's (pp. 29-34). Again, there are rapid changes of scene between the street and the inside of the house. We begin in the street. Whisper brings Charles's letter and gives it to Patch. Patch unluckily drops it for Sir Jealous to pick up on his return (p. 43). Sir Jealous is alarmed, cancels his engagements, and orders his supper to be laid in Isabinda's room—the better to keep watch over her. There is no opportunity for the appointment with Charles to be canceled: no sooner is Patch's loss discovered that Sir Jealous arrives with it. Since the letter in in cipher, Patch makes a shift to pretend that it is her "Charm for the Tooth-ach" (p. 46). The immediate crisis is averted; but Sir Jealous's suspicions have not been totally allayed. The tension increases as we begin to watch for Charles's arrival. Sir Jealous has Patch sing and Isabinda accompany her on the spinet. They are nervous and therefore "horribly out of Tune." Just as Sir Jealous is losing his temper, Charles steps out of the closet, suspecting nothing (p. 48). He retreats at once when he sees Sir Jealous; Isabinda pretends to faint in front of the closet door. By the time Sir Jealous can get into the closet Charles is safely off. Sir Jealous summarily expels Patch from the house. Outside she meets Charles. As usual, out of the ashes of one plot another plot is born. Patch gives Charles the idea of impersonating the Spanish merchant that Sir Jealous is expecting. She and Charles go out on a happier note (p. 51).

V THE "MONKEY" SCENE

The second part of Act IV (pp. 51-58) begins outside the garden gate. Sir George has kept his appointment, and Miranda's maid Scentwell lets him in and conducts him to her mistress. We move into the house. Miranda has a brief soliloquy (p. 51) in which she justifies her actions to herself. Sir George arrives, and he and

Miranda have their first serious conversation (pp. 52-53). Their talk confirms that Miranda is neither a coquette nor a prude but a woman of sense. They are interrupted by Scentwell's news that Sir Francis (and Marplot) are coming into the house. Thus far—in the surreptitious entry, the serious conversation between the lovers, and the interruption—the scene parrallels the sequence in Act III with Charles and Isabinda (pp. 29-33). But here Centlivre develops the comedy along a different line.

Sir George does not leave as Charles had done: instead, he is hidden behind the chimneyboard. Sir Francis enters with Marplot. Sir Francis had been on his way to Epsom. He has returned at Marplot's behest to warn Miranda not to shoot Sir George if he should fail to disregard the warning (p. 54). Thus once again, it is Marplot who is responsible for the unseasonable interruption. The main comedy of the scene, however, develops from the fact that Sir Francis enters "peeling an Orange." The peel has to be disposed of and the fireplace—where Sir George is hiding—is the obvious spot. Scentwell tries to avert the discovery of Sir George by asking for the peel to eat. Sir Francis refuses, saying that she has the "Green Pip" already. The tension mounts as Sir Francis approaches the chimney. Miranda in turn tries to avert the crisis: she tells Sir Francis that she has a pet monkey shut up in the chimney. This is not so far from the truth. Sir Francis believes her and gives the peel to Scentwell to dispose of. But the crisis is prolonged: inquisitive Marplot wants to see the monkey, and it is all Sir Francis and Miranda can do to keep him away from the chimney. Eventually Sir Francis's coach is announced, and all seems to be well. But Marplot contrives to stay behind a moment and lifts up the chimneyboard. Discovering Sir George without seeing who he is, Marplot cries out "Thieves, Thieves, Murder!" and Sir Francis rushes back.

Luckily Marplot manages to save the awkward situation that he has precipitated. Before Sir Francis is back, Sir George runs out. On his way he breaks some china ornaments; Marplot invents a story that the "monkey" was responsible and has escaped through the window. Obviously, rapid pace and sharp timing are essential to the effectiveness of this scene, which is one of the best in the play. Each peak of tension must be greater than the last, and the speed of action must accelerate. Sir Francis finally leaves, and Sir George returns. The tension relaxes. Patch comes in with news of what has happened at Sir Jealous's. Marplot is anxious to meddle with Charles's affairs, but Miranda and Sir George keep him with them. This part of the scene (pp. 56-58), after the final exit of Sir Francis, has the same function as the bridge scenes that concluded Acts II and III. Future developments are foreshadowed but not revealed in detail. At the end of Act III Marplot was anxious to shadow Sir George; at the end of Act IV he is just as

keen to be after Charles. At this point, the outwitting of Sir Francis is virtually completed; the final act will concentrate once again on Sir Jealous.

VI THE UNRAVELING

By the end of Act IV, the resources of the comedy of concealment and inopportune entry have been exploited to the full. For the last act, Centlivre changes to a comedy of disguise. Between Acts IV and V, Sir George and Miranda are married. Act V begins with a sententious exchange between Miranda and Patch on the "strange bold thing" that Miranda has just done (p. 58). Patch voices Centlivre's modest but sensible approach to marriage: "it is impossible a Man of Sense shou'd use a Woman ill, indued with Beauty, Wit and Fortune. It must be the Lady's fault, if she does not wear the unfashionable Name of Wife easie, when nothing but Complaisance and good Humour is requisite on either side to make them happy" (p. 58). Miranda is congratulating herself on her escape from her guardian when Sir Francis himself enters. The momentary awkwardness passes; the resourceful Miranda soon adapts her plan to suit the unexpected event. She and Patch had been going to Sir Jealous's; Miranda simply determines to take Sir Francis with them. Miranda tells Sir Francis "positively this is my Wedding Day" (p. 60). The deluded knight supposes that Miranda intends to marry him after they have witnessed the wedding at Sir Jealous's.

The scene changes for the last time, to Sir Jealous's house. Charles and Sir George have disguised themselves as Don Babinetto and his friend Meanwell. Sir Jealous is deceived by the impersonation and drags in Isabinda to be married to the Spanish merchant without delay. Isabinda protests violently and implores pleadingly until Sir George whispers that Don Babinetto is Charles in disguise. Parson Tackum is announced; the party goes offstage for the wedding ceremony. But Marplot has a final plot to mar. He arrives outside Sir Jealous's (p. 56) and alarms a servant with his inquiries after Charles. Marplot is taken in to Sir Jealous, who recognizes him from the incident in Act III. Sir Jealous guesses at the imposture, but not quite in time. Sir George keeps him out with the point of his sword while the parson finishes the ceremony. Sir Francis and Miranda arrive (p. 69). All the plots and secrets come out, including Miranda's marriage to Sir George. A general reconciliation takes place. Only Sir Francis refuses to forgive and join in; he leaves with a "Confound you all!" (p. 71). Like Malvolio at the end of *Twelfth Night,* Sir Francis takes with him all the accumulated strife and bitterness of the play. His departure prepares the way for general concord. Sir Jealous accepts Charles with a good grace; Miranda gives him the papers—kept by Sir Francis—that make him master of his estate. Marplot is forgiven. Whisper and Scentwell are given the choice "to Marry, or keep their Services." Both choose the second option. Sir Jealous invites all to "a chearful Glass, in which we'll bury all Animosities' (p. 72).

The Busy Body is a successful amalgam of the comedy of humors with the comedy of intrigue. There are several memorable characters, and they are well integrated into the busy and bustling plot. The action of the play is certainly not probable, but it is well motivated according to the conventions of its genre. Its comic business is plausibly introduced and skillfully spaced out.[18]

Notes

1. Mottley ["Mrs. Susanna Centlivre." *A Compleat List of All the English Dramatic Poets.* Appended to Thomas Whincop, *Scanderbeg* (London, 1747), p. 189.

2. Mottley, p. 190.

3. *The Female Tatler,* No. 41 (October 7-10, 1709).

4. *The Tatler,* No. 15 (May 14, 1709); ed. G. A. Aitken, I (London, 1898), 135.

5. *The Tatler,* No. 19 (May 24, 1709); ed. Aitken, I, 163.

6. John Dryden, "To the Pious Memory of the Accomplisht Young Lady Mrs. Anne Killigrew, Excellent in the Two Sister-Arts of Poesie and Painting. An Ode," ll. 71-74; *Poems,* ed. James Kinsley (Oxford, 1958), I, 461.

7. *The Busy Body* (London, 1709), pp. 10-13, 19-23. Subsequent references are to this edition and will be given in the text.

8. William Wycherley, *Complete Plays,* ed. G. Weales (New York, 1967), p. 152.

9. Thomas Hobbes, *On Human Nature,* Chapter 9; in his *English Works,* ed. Sir W. Molesworth, IV (London, 1840), 46.

10. Tave, pp. 104, 105.

11. None of the "sources" are in fact very close. Bowyer discusses them (pp. 100-03) and sanely concludes that except for Jonson "her borrowings are general and no discredit to her" (p. 103).

12. John Downes, *Roscius Anglicanus* (London, 1706), p. 28.

13. Cibber [*An Apology for the Life of Colley Cibber.* Ed. B. R. S. Fone, Ann Arbor, 1968], pp. 84-86.

14. Jess Byrd, Introduction to *The Busy Body* (Los Angeles, 1949), p. ii.

15. The time is inconsistently specified. In Act I (p. 10) it is given as ten minutes, but later (pp. 14, 19, 23) as an hour.

16. Ben Jonson, *Works,* eds. C. H. Herford, Percy and Evelyn Simpson, X (Oxford, 1950), 230. Jess Byrd (p. ii) thinks Centlivre's scene "a close imitation" of Jonson, but "more amusing . . . perhaps because the characters, especially Sir Francis Gripe and Miranda, are more credible and more fully portrayed."

17. These would all have been actual changes of scene, effected by changing the sliding flat scenes at the rear of the stage. The staging of Centlivre's plays is outside the scope of this study. The standard account is Richard Southern, *Changeable Scenery* (London, 1952). Southern does not mention Centlivre, but his work gives the contemporary practices.

18. Since this account was written, Robert D. Hume has discussed *The Busy Body* as a type of "Augustan Intrigue Comedy" in *The Development of English Drama in the Late Seventeenth Century* (Oxford, 1976), pp. 116-21.

Suz-Anne Kinney (essay date 1994)

SOURCE: Kinney, Suz-Anne. "Confinement Sharpens the Invention: Aphra Behn's *The Rover* and Susanna Centlivre's *The Busie Body*." In *Look Who's Laughing: Gender and Comedy,* edited by Gail Finney, pp. 81-98. Langhorne, Penn.: Gordon and Breach, 1994.

[*In the following essay, Kinney discusses Behn and Centlivre as feminist pioneers in the theater, observing several similarities in the two playwrights' approaches to female characters, but suggesting that Centlivre's plays may reflect the increased conservatism of the early eighteenth-century theater.*]

Aphra Behn's contribution to the history of literature is, by now, well known. In 1929, in her study of women and literature *A Room of One's Own,* Virginia Woolf marks Aphra Behn's career as a "very important corner on the road," a turning point. With Behn, Woolf argues

> We leave behind, shut up in their parks among their folios, those solitary great ladies who wrote without audience or criticism, for their own delight alone. We come to town and rub shoulders with ordinary people in the streets. Mrs. Behn was . . . forced . . . to make her living by her wits . . . She made, by working very hard, enough to live on. The importance of that fact outweighs anything that she actually wrote, . . . for here begins the freedom of the mind, or rather the possibility that in the course of time the mind will be free to write what it likes. For now that Aphra Behn had done it, girls could go to their parents and say, You need not give me an allowance; I can make money by my pen.

(66-67)

While we have no way of knowing for certain the number of women who actually decided to make their livings as writers as a direct result of Behn's pioneering career, the connection between Susanna Carroll Centlivre's career and Behn's is perhaps the most direct. In 1700, eleven years after Behn's death, Susanna Centlivre wrote her first play, **A Perjur'd Husband.** From the mid-1680s to 1722—the years that Centlivre worked in the theatre as both playwright and player—Aphra Behn's works were performed on a regular basis. *The Rover,* for instance, was produced 70 times between 1700 and 1725. While we can only assume that Centlivre saw—perhaps even acted in—a number of Behn's plays, her general opinion of Behn was a matter of public record in 1701. In one of the letters included in *Familiar and Courtly Letters* (1700), Centlivre praises Behn's "genius" and wishes an equivalent talent for herself. In letters that she contributed to *Letters of Wit, Politicks and Morality* (1701), Centlivre's use of the *nom de plume* Astraea—the name that Behn was known by a generation earlier—is a defining gesture, not only a conscious act of homage, but a conscious act of appropriation as well.

For Centlivre, the act of appropriating Behn's poetic name implies her own desire to be like Behn, to share in the nominal and monetary rewards associated with being a successful woman playwright. Certainly, a need to identify with someone who had lived through similar experiences would not have been out of the question for Centlivre, for many of her experiences in the theatre were remarkably similar to Behn's. Chief among these similarities is the fact that the plays of Behn and Centlivre were attacked because they were written by women. Not surprisingly, they responded to this criticism in much the same way. In the Preface to *The Dutch Lover,* which was first produced in 1673, Behn writes:

> I printed this Play with all the impatient haste one ought to do, who would be vindicated from the most unjust and silly aspersion, Woman could invent to cast on Woman; and which only my being a Woman has procured me: *That it was Baudy,* the least and most Excusable fault in the Men writers, to whose Plays they all crowd, as if they came to no other end than to hear what they condemn in this: *But from a Woman it was unnaturall.*

Centlivre, in her dedication to **The Platonick Lady** (1707), expands upon this analysis when she chastises

> the Carping Malice of the Vulgar World; who think it a proof of their Sense, to dislike every thing that is writ by Women.

> A Play secretly introduc'd to the House, whilst the Author remains unknown, is approv'd by every Body: The Actors cry it up, and are in expectation of a great Run; the Bookseller of a Second Edition, and the Scribler of a Sixth Night: But if by chance the Plot's discover'd, and the Brat found Fatherless, immediately

it flags in the Opinion of those that extoll'd it before, and the Bookseller falls in his Price, with this Reason, *It's a Woman's.* Thus they alter their judgment, by the Esteem they have for the Author, tho' the Play is still the same. They ne'er reflect, that we have had some Male Productions of this Kind, void of Plot and Wit, and full as insipid as ever a Woman's of us all.

While these frontispieces show that Behn and Centlivre were capable of recognizing and exposing the absurd ideology of the dramatic criticism that was practiced upon their plays, the very criticisms they were protesting became the basis for much of what has been said about them in the last 250 years. In 1754, for instance, John Duncombe was expressing a popular attitude when he wrote *The Feminiad:*

> The modest Muse a veil with pity throws
> O'er Vice's friends and Virtue's foes;
> Abash'd she views the bold unblushing mien
> Of modern Manley, Centlivre, and Behn;
> And grieves to see One nobly born disgrace
> Her modest sex, and her illustrious race.
> Tho' harmony thro' all their numbers flow'd,
> And genuine wit its ev'ry grace bestow'd,
> Nor genuine wit nor harmony excuse
> The dang'rous sallies of a wanton Muse

This belief that the plays of Behn and Centlivre were dangerous lasted until well after the end of the Victorian era; in a 1905 edition of Behn's novels, for instance, Ernest Baker charged that Behn's plays were "false, lurid and depraved." As a result of this type of criticism, Behn was seen as a "colosal and enduring embarrassment to the generations of women who followed her into the literary marketplace" (Gallagher 23). It was not until 1929, when Woolf wrote *A Room of One's Own,* that the process of reclamation began.

As Susanna Centlivre understood when she took the name Astraea, the similarites between her career and Behn's were many. Perhaps the most ironic similarity given the criticisms they endured for being women is that both wrote immensely popular plays. Behn's *The Rover* (1677) was performed 158 times from 1700 to 1760 (Link xiii). Centlivre's **The Busie Body** (1709) was performed in London 475 times between 1709 and 1800 (Frushell 16). They were both accused of plagiarism, for although it was very common for dramatists to borrow from and rewrite the works of other playwrights, both Behn and Centlivre turned other playwrights' ideas to their own purposes and suffered virulent criticism as a result. Knowing that publication of their names could result in serious personal consequences, both—without success—tried to publish plays anonymously. Perhaps most interesting though is the fact that both were forced, due to the circumstances of their lives, to support themselves through the money they received from writing plays. In mid-1663, Aphra Behn's father was appointed Lieutenant General of Surinam, a commission which promised to make his fortune. On the voyage to South America, however, he became ill and died. Though Behn completed the journey and spent a short time in Surinam (a period in which she enjoyed unusual autonomy and had the experiences that would later contribute to her novel, *Oroonoko*), she had neither income nor prospect of income when she returned to London in 1664 (Goreau 71). Pressed by circumstance, she became a spy for Charles II during the second Anglo-Dutch War. But this occupation, far from making her self-sufficient, led to a substantial debt, and she may have spent time—from late 1668 to the middle of 1669—in a debtor's prison. It was only after these extraordinary experiences that Behn decided to become a writer. If Susanna Centlivre's life was less adventurous, it was no more secure financially. While the details of her early life are sketchy and difficult to substantiate, several accounts suggest that Centlivre left home before she was fifteen with little money and no connections (Bowyer 7; Lock 15-16). To support herself, she joined a company of strolling players. She was married twice before 1700, but neither marriage lasted much longer than a year and neither provided her with any financial security. In 1700, **The Perjur'd Husband** was produced, and she became a professional. Despite her early successes, however, she was forced to supplement her income by acting. While her marriage to Joseph Centlivre, one of the Queen's cooks, in 1707 provided Centlivre with a degree of financial security, she continued to write plays until 1722, a year before she died.

Other similarities emerge from a study of their writings. In "Aphra Behn and Sexual Politics: A Dramatist's Discourse with her Audience," for instance, Cheri Davis Langdell focuses on the addendum to the plays—the prologues, epilogues, and dedications. Because these writings were not governed by the conventions that the plays themselves were, Langdell argues, they were a place where Behn's views about her own role in the theatre could find fuller, more honest expression. As a result, Langdell concludes that Behn's "writing and her attitude toward it are acts of sexual politics": they exemplify "woman's resourceful exertion of whatever power she may have—sexual, social, economic, or political—so as to redress the social and psychosexual balance ever so slightly in her favour" (113). Langdell also points to the Centlivre's prologue to **The Platonick Lady** (the one which I have excerpted above) as a continuation of Behn's sexual politics, an illustration of the extent of Behn's legacy and her influence on Centlivre in both content and attitude.

I would like to suggest a reading of Aphra Behn's *The Rover* and Susanna Centlivre's **The Busie Body** in which these concerns—the sexual politics of both writers—are not marginalized, are not extrinsic to the plays. Within the texts of the plays, female experience, including the experience of female authorship, is dramatized.

Because of this unique perspective, Behn and Centlivre began to establish what Susan Carlson, in *Women and Comedy,* calls a "countertradition" to what was (and still is in many respects) a male-dominated theatre. Their plays, like all others, are governed by social and literary conventions, conventions that conform to established attitudes about appropriate behavior for women. And, as in all drama of these periods, these conventions erupt most forcefully into the plays' endings. As Rachel Blau DuPlessis says in *Writing Beyond the Ending,* "social convention is like a 'script,' which suggests sequences of action and response, the meaning we give these, and ways of organizing experience by choices, emphases, priorities" (2). These social scripts control the whole of narrative or plot, but the endings are the place where plot meets ideology most forcefully. Not surprisingly, the priorities of the seventeenth- and early eighteenth-century scripts demanded that the ending of the plots either deemphasized or completely silenced any potential for women characters beyond those conventions. For these reasons, my objective here will be to recover the narrative middle from these plays—to reclaim any possible revolutionary characterizations, attitudes, or structures—before they are sacrificed for the common good known as communal values. At the same time, I would like to recover from the endings any trace of ambiguity over the scripted resolution, for as DuPlessis says, "Any resolution can have traces of the conflicting materials that have been processed within it. It is where subtexts and repressed discourses can throw up one last flare of meaning; it is where the author may sidestep and displace attention from the materials that a work has made available" (3).

Early in her career, Behn saw herself and her work as outside the tradition of male playwriting. In the epilogue to *Sir Patient Fancy* (1678), for instance, Behn criticizes the traditionalists who are more concerned about unities than audience:

> Your way of Writing's out of fashion grown.
> Method, and Rule—you only understand;
> Pursue your way of fooling, and be damn'd.
> Your learned Cant of Action, Time and Place,
> Must all give way to the unlabour'd Farce.

In the prologue to her first play, *The Forc'd Marriage; or, the Jealous Bridegroom* (1671), Behn describes a different approach to drama. She outlines the differences she sees between female writers and their male counterparts:

> Women those charming Victors, in whose Eyes
> Lie all their Arts, and their Artilleries,
> Not being contented with the Wounds they made,
> Would by new Strategems our Lives invade.
> Beauty alone goes now at too cheap rates;
> And therefore they, like wise and Politick States,
> Court a new Power that may the old supply,
> To keep as well as gain the Victory.

> They'll join the force of Wit to Beauty now,
> And so maintain the Right they have in you.

Uttered by a male actor, this prologue warns the audience that playwriting, which requires the writer join a new weapon (her wit) to her old weapon (her beauty), has become a means of extending and exerting female power. As Catherine Gallagher says in "Who Was That Masked Woman? The Prostitute and the Playwright in the Comedies of Aphra Behn," Behn "creates the possibility of a woman's version of sexual conquest [in this prologue]. She will not be immediately conquered and discarded because she will maintain her right through her writing" (25).

Certainly, these prologues and epilogues are statements of intention, the place where Behn articulates her dramatic theory most directly. They point to the fact that her purpose in writing these plays was to carve out a countertradition in the theatre, one that would not only defy the classical unities, but would value both female writers and female experience as well. This feminist countertradition is one that still exists. Susan Carlson, for instance, sees the connection between Behn and contemporary feminist comedy in the following way:

> despite the qualified nature of her comic rebellion, in her controversial women and their unorthodox behavior Behn still manages to sketch the outlines of what I would like to call a "countertradition" of comedy. In her shaping of women characters and especially in her frank portrayal of women's sexuality, she prefigures contemporary British comedy by women, a comedy that still more clearly asserts a tradition of its own.
>
> (128)

If Aphra Behn first envisioned this countertradition, Susanna Centlivre certainly benefited from her vision. In her prologues, epilogues, and dedications, she too carried on the struggle to win legitimacy for the female voice and female experience in the early eighteenth-century theatre. In her preface to **Love's Contrivance,** Centlivre outlined her own method of writing plays, a method that she contrasts with traditional ones:

> The Criticks cavil most about Decorums, and cry up Aristotle's Rules as the most essential part of the Play. I own they are in the right of it; yet I dare venture a wager they'll never persuade the Town to be of their Opinion, which relishes nothing so well as Humour lightly tost up with Wit, and drest with Modesty and Air . . . I do not say this by way of condemning the Unity of Time, Place, and Action; quite contrary, for I think them the greatest Beauties of a Dramatick Poem; but since the other way of writing pleases full as well, and gives the Poet a larger Scope of Fancy, . . . why should a Man torture, and wrack his Brain for what will be no Advantage to him.

This statement of dramatic theory is similar to Behn's: Centlivre criticizes what Behn called "Cant of Action, Time and Place." Her "other way of writing," which gives the Poet "a scope of fancy" beyond the conventional, can be seen as the equivalent to Behn's "new Strategems": her "Humour tost up with Wit." Because too many rules confine the poet, they not only inhibit the playwright's creativity, but fail to produce entertaining drama as well. This final point is important, for throughout part of her career, Centlivre felt compelled (perhaps because she had learned from Behn's experience) to please her audience. The popularity of her plays proves this other way of writing was successful.

So, while both of these playwrights were inevitably constrained by the tradition of comedic drama that they inherited, they also both envisioned their work as being somehow distinct from this tradition. How successfully their feminist visions were translated into the texts of their plays, however, is a controversial issue. Many contemporary readers and critics have perceived a gap between the intentions that they articulated in their prologues, epilogues, and dedications and their ability to accomplish these intentions. In *Feminism in Eighteenth-Century England,* for instance, Katharine M. Rogers says that "[n]either Behn nor Centlivre . . . wrote plays distinguishable from men's. They might protest vigorously against sexual discrimination in their prefaces, but they followed literary forms that provided no scope for feminine perceptions or feminine experience" (100). While the plays of Behn and Centlivre certainly seem conservative to a modern reader, we must also acknowledge, as Moira Ferguson does in *First Feminists,* that the definition of feminism changes with time and place—what seems extreme or revolutionary in one age often becomes part of the mainstream culture in another (xi). For their respective historical periods, these plays were clearly viewed by audiences as nontraditional, as "dang'rous sallies of a Wanton Muse," a fact that becomes clear through a comparison of their early plays and their later plays. Over the course of their careers, due (we can only assume) to the increasing virulence of the criticism they received, both Behn and Centlivre began to conform to audience tastes for tradition in two ways: overall, fewer women appeared in their later plays, and the women who were in these later plays spoke fewer lines than their sisters in the earlier plays (Pearson 146, 209).

Aphra Behn's *The Rover* and Susanna Centlivre's **The Busie Body** are amazingly similar comedies. They both operate within the Spanish intrigue comedy tradition, and both focus primarily on two couples—the witty couple and the romantic couple—who are attempting to thwart the wishes of the father or male guardian of the woman. Both end in multiple weddings. They were also, as I noted above, extremely popular plays, so popular in fact that their writers subsequently penned sequels to them: *The Rover, Part II* (1681) and **Mar- Plot** (1710). Their most remarkable similarities, however, can be found in the ways they diverge from tradition. In both *The Rover* and **The Busie Body,** a critique of the way women are treated is an essential element of the plot. At the same time, both Behn and Centlivre attempt to create a positive space outide of that critique, a place where their women characters can have supportive friendships with one another, a place where strong women characters can make their own decisions and act on them, a place where their characters' actions do not have to be driven along a linear and unified path to a predetermined end such as marriage. Finally, in the characters of Angellica and Miranda, Behn and Centlivre inscribed images of the woman playwright into their plays. Because they wrote plays in a period that undervalued their abilities and their contributions, both of these dramatists attempted to create a positive space wherein the woman playwright could exist.

The Rover and **The Busie Body** begin—in keeping with traditional dramatic structure—by establishing a status quo. In *The Rover,* the "virtuous" women—Florinda and Hellena—are under the control of their father, who has planned their futures in advance: Hellena will take vows and enter a nunnery, and Florinda will make an advantageous marriage to an unattractive aristocrat. A critique of this position of authority is facilitated by the fact that the patriarch himself does not appear in the play. Instead, Don Pedro, the brother of Florinda and Hellena, is the patriarch's spokesperson in the scheme of the play; as a member of the younger generation, however, Pedro's ability to protect and sustain the status quo is ineffectual. Because there is no vocal, embodied representation of the view that women should submit to the law of their fathers, then, Behn's critique of patriarchal authority is achieved rather easily. Florinda, for instance, makes the following comment about her forced marriage to Pedro: "I hate Vicentio, sir, and I would not have a man so dear to me as my brother follow the ill customs of our country and make a slave of his sister" (I.i). Hellena sides with Florinda, of course; she comments on her father's choice of a husband for Florinda and—indirectly—on her own probable future as a nun: "Marry Don Vincentio! Hang me, such a wedlock would be worse than adultery with another man. I had rather see her in the *Hostel de Dieu,* to waste her youth there in vows, and be a handmaid to lazars and cripples, than to lose it in such a marriage" (I.i). In the course of the play, when both Florinda and Hellena extricate themselves from the control of their father and assert their love and sexual attractions to their respective prospective husbands, the audience approves their triumph.

This approval, of course, was not socially acceptable during the period. As Rogers points out, "Marriage was more or less forced on women, as their only way to a recognized position in society . . . [It] ranged from

mild subjection to virtual slavery" (7); "[w]omen who married contrary to their parents' wishes were apt to find themselves without portion or inheritance and with reputations damaged by such evidence of uncontrolled passion and willfulness" (11). In the play, the concept of forced marriage is often seen in terms of slavery (as Florinda points out). Often in Behn's play, relationships are viewed in terms of power struggles. In forced marriages—like the one Florinda is destined for at the beginning of the play—women usually lose this struggle. But in marriages of choice—like the Hellena/ Willmore match—women often win the struggle. Because of this differential in sexual politics, Behn takes on the institution of forced marriage in her plays in order to criticize its unjust control over women. As Jacqueline Pearson says in *The Prostituted Muse,* Behn often "attacks the control exerted on the young and un-moneyed, both male and female, by patriarchal authorities, fathers and guardians and husbands, but the emphasis most often falls on the suffering of women" (160).

Pearson's observations could just as easily apply to Susanna Centlivre, for a similar resistance to the status quo is represented in **The Busie Body.** Sir Francis Gripe and Sir Jealous Traffick, as the ruling patriarchs in the scheme of the play, have ultimate control over virtually all the characters. Whether it is for consent to marry (as is the case with Miranda and Isabinda), or for payment of an inheritance (as is the case with Marplot, Miranda, Isabinda, and Charles) most of the characters in this play must rely upon the protection and support of these two domestic tyrants. Because they appear in the play as actual characters, though, Centlivre can critique them in both their characterizations and the speeches of other characters. Both Sir Francis and Sir Jealous are depicted as insidious money-grubbers and foolish old lechers. Sir Francis' lack of good faith pervades the administration of all of his duties. Once he has convinced his brother patriarchs to place their estates in his control, he abuses his power. In one of his most insidious acts, he becomes Miranda's pimp; he sells her time—one hour for 100 pounds—to Sir George as if she were a prostitute. Not satisfied with a mere 100 pounds, however, Sir Francis sets his goal at nothing less than Miranda's money and body: "Some Guardians wou'd be glad to compound for part of the Estate, at dispatching an Heiress, but I engross the whole [by marrying her myself]" (III). Sir Jealous is only slightly better than Sir Francis. His obsession with Spanish customs makes him appear only foolish at first. But in his desire to make Isabinda live according to Spanish customs—"No Galloping abroad, no receiving Visits at home; for in our loose Country [England], the Women are as dangerous as the Men" (II)—Sir Jealous' actions are as motivated by monetary considerations as Sir Francis'. Deeply suspicious, he attempts to control all of Isabinda's actions: from her walks on the balcony to the choice of her husband. He is consistently locking her in her rooms in order to prevent "some sauntering coxcomb" from thinking that "by leaping into her arms, [he can] leap into my estate" (II).

The women in **The Busie Body**—Miranda and Isabinda—actively (though sometimes covertly) rail against these treacherous oppressors and their ultimate weapon, marriage. Both women resist the marriages which Sir Francis and Sir Jealous have contrived for them, and both women succeed in achieving the marriages they desire, an ending that is—like the ending of *The Rover*—approved in the scheme of the play. At the same time, however, Miranda resists the confines of marriage itself, first to Sir George in act I: "Matrimony! Ha, ha, ha; what Crimes have you comitted against the God of Love, that he should revenge 'em so severely to stamp Husband upon your forehead" (I). Later, Miranda tells Sir George during their scaled-down version of the proviso scene that marriage is a "terrible Bugbear" (IV); she knows that she is trading her dependence upon a *certain* tyrant for dependence upon a *possible* tyrant. Even though Sir George is a "man of sense" and not as unreasonable and disagreeable as Sir Francis, Miranda knows that "If he should despise, slight or use me ill, there's no Remedy from a Husband, but the Grave" (V). This attitude toward marriage—the ultimate patriarchal institution—is supported by the end of the play. There, Whisper and Scentwell (two people who because of their class would seem to have less control over their lives than their employers) are given the choice to marry or not. Given this choice by Charles, both Whisper and Scentwell claim an equal distaste for the "terrible Bugbear." They both opt for the benevolence and loyalty they have found in service over the forced servitude of marriage.

In both of these plays, many of the social conventions that solidify the oppression of women are critiqued by Behn and Centlivre. Yet, as dramatists, they do not settle for mere critique of social and dramatic conventions. One of the counter-strategies that they offer to these limited views and treatments of women characters is the possibility of female friendship. Unlike their counterparts in plays like *The Way of the World, The Man of Mode, The Tragedy of Jane Shore,* and *The Beggar's Opera,* where women only pretend friendship and later turn out to be rivals and enemies, the women in these two comedies create a space where women can not only cease to be rivals, but actually understand, sympathize with, and respect each other. One of the most remarkable aspects of *The Rover,* for instance, is its opening scene; this play is one of the few in Restoration drama that opens with a woman-only scene. This fact is significant, for it allows the audience to view the rest of the play—particularly the actions of men—through the perspective of the women who appear in the scene. A similar woman-only segment occurs in the

beginning of act III, scene i as well, before the men enter the scene. Pearson has surveyed all of Behn's plays and concludes that she is unusual "in allowing women to speak first in plays so often, and in including so many scenes in which only women appear, scenes which are often particularly vivid and convincing" (146). What is even more unusual in *The Rover,* though, is how women characters who are set up into rival positions react to one another. In act IV, scene ii, Angellica and Hellena (dressed in man's clothing) find themselves in the same room with Willmore. Instead of fighting each other, they both question Willmore's intentions and character. Hellena, who knows that Willmore is involved with Angellica, does not attack her rival, but warns her of Willmore's "inconstancy" (IV.ii). When Hellena tells her story, Angellica—while she does not know Hellena's true identity—immediately reacts by questioning Willmore—"Is't thus you pay my generous passion back?" (IV.ii)—and promises revenge not on Hellena but on Willmore—"I am resolved to think on a revenge / On him that soothed me thus to my undoing" (IV.ii).

While Susanna Centlivre does not use as many women-centered scenes as Behn does in *The Rover,* the friendship that is established between Miranda, Isabinda, and Patch is a much more thorough one. Miranda and Isabinda are genuinely friends in this play. Miranda works as hard to extricate her friend from the clutches of a controlling father and an unknown mate as she does to free herself from Sir Francis' grip. She arranges for Patch to act as Isabinda's servant, a sacrifice that helps Isabinda gain intermittent freedom to see Sir Charles. Patch, in effect, becomes the conduit of their friendship. Both Miranda and Isabinda receive news of each others' circumstances from the servant that they both love and trust. And the only woman-only segments that occur in the play are between Miranda and Patch, and later Isabinda and Patch. Ironically, Isabinda and Miranda, who appear in the same scene only at the end of the play, never speak to each other. At the same time, their sisterhood is an integral part of the play.

Another counter-strategy used by these two playwrights involves their characterizations of women. Consistently, Behn and Centlivre imagine strong, witty, and active women, women who are capable of setting goals and making them a reality. *The Rover*'s most effective character in fact is not the title character, who is represented as either passive, ineffectual, or drunk, but Hellena. From early in the play, Hellena knows that she does not want to take her vows and join the convent. She wants marriage, and not just any marriage: "I don't intend every he that likes me shall have me, but he that I like" (III.i). She pursues her desired mate, effectively using disguises both at the carnival and in the confrontation scene with Angellica and Willmore. Throughout the play, she is active and effective in a way that the the

Rover himself is not. As Pearson says, "Willmore is a passive centre of the intrigues of the women rather than, as they are, an active mover" (153). (Pearson's "they" is important here, for even the most passive woman character in the play—Florinda—acts with the purpose of escaping a forced marriage.)

Two other female characters in Behn's play help round out this pattern of behavior. The two prostitutes, Lucetta and Angellica, represent what Pearson calls the "most extreme examples of female power" and male powerlessness in the play. Both of these themes are demonstrated in the Lucetta/Blunt subplot. After luring Blunt to her home, she does not sleep with him, but instead robs him and has him dumped in the sewer. The most surprising aspect of this subplot is that it has no—realized—consequences. Lucetta is never punished for her treatment of Blunt, and Blunt's revenge—the attempted rape of Florinda—is thwarted as well. Angellica also provides an example of these themes when, in act V, she draws a pistol and threatens Willmore's life. This, according to Pearson, is the kind of sexual reversal that often occurs in Behn's plays. "Male sexuality in Behn is often an instrument of power, and she allows women to compete for this by allowing them to share the phallic power of swords, daggers, and pistols" (158). And while Angellica's revenge—like Blunt's—is never accomplished, this equality in representation is itself a mark of progress.

Representations of female power can also be found in **The Busie Body,** but they are representations of a kind of power that, like Hellena's, is often wielded indirectly—through disguise and manipulation—instead of directly as in the case of Lucetta and Angellica. Like Hellena, Miranda resists any attempt at masculine control. She is talking about Sir Jealous, for instance, when she tells Patch, "Suppose he could introduce his rigid Rules—does he think we cou'd not match them in contrivance? No, no; Let the Tyrant Man make the laws he will, if there's a Woman under the Government, I warrant she finds a way to break 'im" (I). Miranda's stratagem to free both herself and Isabinda from their respective dictators reflects a more comprehensive power than Hellena's, for while Hellena can only affect her own fate, Miranda's actions affect every character in the play. Through her actions—her providing Isabinda a loyal servant in Patch, her manipulation of Sir Francis, and her ability to procure the "authentick papers" at the end of the play—the two couples achieve the economic independence they need to marry. Her greatest achievement is her manipulation of Sir Francis. In spite of the fact that he has technical control of both her body and her money, Miranda manages to outwit his scheme to become her husband and permanent master. Her stratagem begins to take shape at the beginning of act 2, when she says to her guardian, "I am not to possess my Estate, without your Consent, till I'm

Five and Twenty; you shall only abate the odd Seven Years, and make me Mistress of my Estate to Day, and I'll make you Master of my Person to Morrow." In act 3, scene 4, Miranda's plan has been revised, her argument substantiated:

Sɪʀ Fʀᴀɴᴄ:

[W]hen shall we marry, ha?

Mɪʀᴀɴ:

There's nothing wanting but your Consent, Sir Francis.

Sɪʀ Fʀᴀɴ:

My Consent! what do's my Charmer mean?

Mɪʀᴀɴ:

Nay, 'tis only a Whim: But I'll have every thing acording to form—Therefore when you sign an Authentick Paper, drawn up by an able Lawyer, that I have your Leave to marry, the next Day makes me yours, Gardee.

Sɪʀ Fʀᴀɴ:

Ha, ha, ha, a Whim indeed! why is it not Demonstration I give my Leave when I marry thee.

Mɪʀᴀɴ:

Not for your Reputation, Gardee; the malicious World will be apt to say, you trick'd me into Marriage, and so take the Merit from my Choice. Now I will have the act my own, to let the idle Fops see how much I prefer a Man loaded with years and Wisdom.

Ultimately, this stratagem works, for Miranda escapes the confines of a marriage to that "delicate bedfellow" Sir Francis by manipulating him with language. She is not, however, above using the disguise of silence when it suits her purposes. In the dumb scene in act 2, Miranda uses silence to resist a similar type of control by Sir George Airy. After he purchases the right to speak with her, Miranda, in Pearson's words, "punishes him for treating her as a commodity by refusing to speak": "It is only when he gives up his attempt to control her that she uses her powers over language to win him" (221).

Because of their depictions of women, both as individuals and friends, *The Rover* and **The Busie Body** become dialogues about sexual politics. What Aphra Behn originated with Hellena and Angellica, Susanna Centlivre continued with her portrayal of Miranda. Yet, despite these considerable successes in creating a tradition of their own in comedy, there are, as I pointed out in the beginning of this essay, considerable problems as well. Despite their ground-breaking depictions of women in their courtship and marriage plots, the endings of these two plays are extremely conventional. Both follow linear plots constructed on the desire of two young couples to marry and focus on the ways that their desires are acheived. Behn's *The Rover* ends shortly after the marriage of Florinda and Belvile, shortly before the marriage of Hellena and Willmore. Centlivre's **The Busie Body** ends with the marriage of both couples—Miranda and Sir George Airy and Isabinda and Charles. Because of their conventional closings, many of the revolutionary aspects of these plays that I have outlined above—the critique of marriage and the strong, independent women—seem to be undercut by the total immersion into the patriarchal institution of marriage. They are as Elin Diamond says in "*Gestus* and Signature in Aphra Behn's *The Rover,*" "recuperated back into the economy they rebel against" (540). In effect, these endings trap the women they are about (and by) in the ideology of the times during which they were written. Carlson summarizes these concerns when she writes, "while a comic ending restores men to their power in the social heirarchy, it restores women to powerlessness" (22).

There are, in these two plays, however, traces of ambiguity over their endings, traces of ambiguity that highlight the concerns that I have outlined above. Much of this ambiguity can be found in the characterizations of Angellica and Marplot. Angellica and Marplot have been described by many critics as the most striking characters to take the stage in their respective plays. Both have also been the center of critical controversies because they seem to rattle around in their respective plays' marriage plots like loose cogs. Angellica disappears from the play half way through the final act. And Marplot, while he is forgiven by the other characters and receives control of his own estate at the end of the play, is the only character in the younger generation who does not get married. This failure to include these two powerful characters in their resolutions has often been seen as a sign of weakness. As Regina Barreca says in her introduction to Last Laughs, "The refusal to supply closure has been misread as an inability to do so, as a failure of imagination and talent on the part of the writer" (17). Instead of reading these two characters as failures as so many critics have in the past, I suggest we read them as examples of what Elin Diamond calls a feminist version of Brechtian *Gestus:* a moment in a feminist text where the contradictory meaning of both theatrical and social conventions "for female fictions and historical women" become apparent to the spectator or reader (524).

In this context, the character of Angellica can be seen as a symbol for the commodification of women. Because she is a prostitute, Angellica's body is, in Marx's terminology, a commodity. But, unlike the other more virtuous women in the play, Angellica has no owner, no father, husband, or brother to act as her trader. She sets her own price, and the market is then regulated only by whether or not a would-be purchaser can afford her price. Angellica, unlike the other women in these plays, is in control of her only commodity—her body. In a conversation at the end of act II, scene II, Angellica and Willmore exchange the following words about her value:

WILLMORE:

> Take heed, fair creature, how you raise my hopes,
> Which once assumed pretends to all dominion:
> There's not a joy thou hast in store
> I shall not then command.
> For which I'll pay you back my soul, my life!
> Come, let's begin th'account this happy minute!

ANGELLICA:

> And will you pay me then the price I ask?

WILLMORE:

> Oh, why dost thou draw me from an awful worship,
> By showing thou art no divinity.
> Conceal the fiend, and show me all the angel!
> Keep me but ignorant, and I'll be devout
> And pay my vows forever at this shrine.

ANGELLICA:

> The pay I mean is but thy love for mine.
> Can you give that?

WILLMORE:

> Entirely.

As Diamond says, "By eliminating her value-form [the fetishized, market form of the commodity which alienates the producer from the product], Angellica attempts to return her body to a state of nature, to take herself out of circulation" (533). But thematically, here, Angellica is more than just a symbol of Marxist political philosophy. Her character is, as Diamond points out, an example of Brechtian gestus, a place where the play itself (Angellica's characterization), the theatre apparatus (the actress and the female playwright), and the social struggle (an analysis of the commodification of women) intersect. Accommodating Angellica in the ending of the play, into the marriage plot, would have diminished her gestic significance. Angellica's function in the play is to reveal the contradictions inherent in a society which treats human beings as material objects and, as Laura Brown says in *English Dramatic Form,* reduces "human relationships to economic exchange" (62).

Marplot's character undergoes a similar symbolic transformation in **The Busie Body.** Like Angellica, his significance as a character can be seen as a result of his role in the sexual economy of the play. On one hand, Marplot is desexed in the play; he is a "curiously unmale figure, in some ways an embodiment and parody of stereotypical views of women" (Pearson 210). One the other hand, Marplot is like Willmore, the rake. He moves through this play in much the same way that Willmore moves through *The Rover*. Like Willmore, Marplot's chief pleasure is in knowing everybody's "business," a common pun for sex in Restoration drama. One of his primary functions is to "subvert male sexuality" (Pearson 210): he, like Willmore, continually interferes with the sexual intrigues of his friends. Furthering this ambiguity about Marplot's sexuality is his function in the plot. Marplot, more than any other character in *The Busie Body,* occupies the position of "Other" in this play. Throughout the play, he wants to be part of the action, part of the courtship plot; continually, however, he is marginalized by the other characters. Like Angellica, then, Marplot's characterization as Other becomes a gestic moment in the text. His ambiguous sexuality functions as comic relief in the play itself. Through his characterization, however, the theatre conventions of the rake and the Spanish intrigue comedy are parodied. Marplot is the rake who is actually desexed, no longer a potent force in the drama itself. Through his ineffectualness, he also parodies the male-originated form of the intrigue comedy, a form of drama that depends upon intelligence. Because he is not accommodated into the resolution of the play, Marplot also becomes a symbol of the contemporary social struggle over gender roles and exclusion, a subject that is very real to Centlivre as a woman writer in the eighteenth century.

In these two characters—Angellica and Marplot—Behn and Centlivre add gestic characters whose significance cannot be integrated into the conventional endings of the plays. But that fact does not undercut, I think, the importance of these characters within the schemes of the plays. In fact, this refusal to "supply closure" in these instances is one of the projects of feminist drama today. As Barreca points out, feminist drama depends "on the process, not on the endings" (17):

> Resolution of tensions, like unity or integration, should not be considered viable definitions of comedy for women writers because they are too reductive to deal with the non-closed nature of women's writings. As [Mary Ellmann in *Thinking About Women*] asserts, the woman writer cares less for what is resolved than for what is recognized in all its conceivable diversions into related or, for that matter, unrelated issues. Once rules are suspended, admirable and remarkable "exceptions are released," recognised, and embraced.
>
> (17)

Being confined by the dramatic conventions that limited the power of women in the theatre led Behn and Centlivre to create other possibilities in their plays. Because conventional comedy generally ended with marriage, and because Behn and Centlivre were writing for an audience that expected this type of ending, both of these writers gave their publics what they wanted. At the same time, this confinement, as Isabinda says in *The*

Busie Body, can "sharpen the invention." This sense of confinement that Behn and Centlivre inevitably felt writing in a male centered tradition accounts for the final innovation that can be found in these two plays. In *The Rover* and *The Busie Body,* Behn and Centlivre inscribe a space where women writers can exist, and in doing so, they release another exception to tradition. As Diamond says about *The Rover,* "As a woman writer in need of money, Behn was vulnerable to accusations of immodesty; to write meant to expose herself, to put herself into circulation; like Angellica, to sell her wares. Is it merely a coincidence that Angellica Bianca shares Aphra Behn's initials, that hers is the only name from *Thomaso* that Behn leaves unchanged?" (536). Similarly, in *The Busie Body,* Miranda—because of the way she orchestrates the action of the play through language—can be read as a stand-in for the writer.

There is a significant difference, though, between these two characterizations, an ambiguity that their conflicted endings highlights. Angellica, as I have noted above, does not participate in the ending of the play; at great personal cost, she succeeds in remaining outside the control of the communal values that try to define her. As a result, her creator achieves a similar degree of literary freedom. Miranda, on the other hand, has a place in the resolution of the plot, a *telos* which reasserts the status quo. Similarly, Centlivre as a playwright—because of the changes that had occurred between Behn's time and her own, in the theatre and its audience's expectations—had less control than the previous Astraea. In the early eighteenth century, the British theatre was more conservative than it was during the Restoration. When Behn began writing, a relaxation of moral strictures was occurring in both society in general and the theatre in particular, a laxity that provided an opening for a freer, more innovative, drama. By the beginning of the eighteenth century, though, an increased sentimentalism led to a demand for a more moral drama. As J. H. Smith says in *The Gay Couple* in *Restoration Comedy,* "In the first half of the eighteenth century it becomes the principal business of comedy (if this term may still be used to describe the plays) to empty . . . standard patterns, to repress rakishness and coquetry, and to recommend contrary ideals" (199).

This diminution in the acceptance of women in the theatre from Behn's time to Centlivre's was a precursor to what would happen to theatre in general—and specifically feminist theatre—in 1737 when the Licensing Act was passed. At this time, women writers in the theatre became even more rare. As Pearson says,

> The intention of this legislation was to bring the theatre under very firm government control and to 'limit the production of legitimate drama to two patent houses and place the licensing of plays under the Lord

Chamberlain.' The Act was particularly troublesome to women like Charlotte Charke who were working in 'alternative' theatres and dramatising anti-establishment views; but by increasing the legal control over drama, it may have offered a more general deterrent to women, who were already nervous about appearing in public as writers. The Act also discouraged risk-taking by theatre managers, which may also have hit women disproportionately.

(20)

Whatever the intention of the Licensing Act, its repercussions for women were long-felt: women playwrights were scarce between the periods when Behn and Centlivre wrote and the beginning of the twentieth century. And the prohibitions were not only institutional. Virginia Woolf was correct in pointing out that after girls began telling their parents they could make money by their pens, "the [parent's] answer for many years to come was, Yes, by living the life of Aphra Behn! Death would be better! and the door was slammed faster than ever" (67). By the beginning of the twentieth century, however, the lives of Behn and Centlivre—and their nascent visions of a dramatic countertradition—no longer seemed so dangerous. Between 1900 and 1920, some four hundred British women wrote plays (Carlson 164).

Works Cited

Baker, Ernest. "Introduction." *The Novels of Aphra Behn.* London, 1905.

Barreca, Regina. "Introduction," in: *Last Laughs,* ed. Regina Barreca. New York: Gordon and Breach, 1988, 3-22.

Behn, Aphra. *The Rover,* ed. Frederick M. Link. Lincoln: University of Nebraska Press, 1967.

Bowyer, John Wilson. *The Celebrated Mrs.* Centlivre. Durham: Duke University Press, 1952.

Brown, Laura. *English Dramatic Form, 1660 to 1760.* New Haven: Yale University Press, 1981.

Carlson, Susan. *Women and Comedy.* Ann Arbor: University of Michigan Press, 1991.

Centlivre, Susanna. *The Busie Body* (1709). Augustan Reprint Society 19. Los Angeles: University of California Press, 1949.

Diamond, Elin. "*Gestus* and Signature in Aphra Behn's *The Rover.*" *English Literary History* 56 (1989): 519-41.

DuPlessis, Rachel Blau. *Writing Beyond the Ending.* Bloomington: Indiana University Press, 1982.

Familiar and Courtly Letters Written by Voiture. London, 1700.

Ferguson, Moira. *First Feminists.* Bloomington: Indiana University Press, 1985.

Frushell, Richard C. "Marriage and Marrying in Susanna Centlivre's Plays." *Papers on Language and Literature* 22 (1986): 16-38.

Gallagher, Catherine. "Who Was That Masked Woman? The Prostitute and the Playwright in the Comedies of Aphra Behn." *Women's Studies* 15 (1988): 23-42.

Goreau, Angeline. *Reconstructing Aphra.* New York: Dial, 1980.

Hume, Robert D. *The Development of English Drama in the Late Seventeenth Century.* Oxford: Clarendon, 1976.

Langdell, Cheri Davis. "Aphra Behn and Sexual Politics: A Dramatist's Discourse with her Audience." *Drama, Sex and Politics.* Cambridge: Cambridge University Press, 1985. 109-128.

Letters of Wit, Politicks and Morality. London, 1701.

Link, Frederick M. "Introduction." *The Rover,* by Aphra Behn. Lincoln: University of Nebraska Press, 1967, ix-xxvi.

Lock, F. P. *Susanna Centlivre.* Twayne's English Authors Series, ed. Bertram H. Davis. Boston: Twayne-Hall, 1979.

Pearson, Jacqueline. *The Prostituted Muse.* New York: St. Martins, 1988.

Rogers, Katharine M. *Feminism in Eighteenth-Century England.* Urbana: University of Illinois Press, 1982.

Root, Robert L. "Aphra Behn, Arranged Marriage, and Restoration Comedy." *Women and Literature* 5 (1977): 3-14.

Smith, J. H. *The Gay Couple in Restoration Comedy.* Cambridge: Harvard University Press, 1948.

Woolf, Virginia. *A Room of One's Own.* New York: Harvest-Harcourt, 1929.

A BOLD STROKE FOR A WIFE (1718)

CRITICAL COMMENTARY

Elizabeth Inchbald (essay date 1808)

SOURCE: Inchbald, Elizabeth. "Remarks." In *Remarks for the British Theatre (1806-1809),* n.p. Delmar, N.Y.: Scholars' Facsimiles & Reprints, 1990.

[*In the following essay, first published in an 1808 edition of* A Bold Stroke for a Wife, *Inchbald commends Centlivre's skill as a dramatist but censures her for depicting licentiousness.*]

Susannah Centlivre, the writer of this play [*A Bold Stroke for a Wife*], says of it, in her dedication to the duke of Wharton,—

> All that I have to assert in favour of this piece is, that the plot is entirely new, and the incidents wholly owing to my own invention; not borrowed from our own, or translated from the works of any foreign poet; so that they have at least the charm of novelty to recommend them.

It would at present be more honourable to the authoress, that a reader should believe she had inconsiderately adopted the scenes of another, in the following play, than invented them herself. Still, in that supposition, much blame would attach to her taste and morality for the choice she had made in the adoption.

It is deeply to be lamented, that, at the time the most ingenious and witty of the English dramatists lived, there was no restraint, as at this period, upon the immorality of the stage. Plays would have come down to the present age, under such restrictions, less brilliant in humour and repartee, with fewer eulogiums from the admirers of wit, but with fewer reproaches from the wise and the good, upon the evil tendency of the dramatic art.

The happy effect of the moral dramas of this æra, in impressing those persons with just sentiments who attend no other place of instruction but a theatre, has not yet erased from the mind of the prejudiced former ill consequences from former plays.

Mrs. Centlivre, as a woman, falls more particularly under censure than her contemporary writers: though her temptations to please the degraded taste of the public were certainly more vehement than those of the authors who wrote at that time, for they were men whose fortunes were not wholly dependent on their mental exertions; yet the virtue of fortitude is expected from a female, when delicacy is the object which tries it; and the authoress of this comedy should have laid down her pen, and taken, in exchange, the meanest implement of labour, rather than have imitated the licentious example given her by the renowned poets of those days.

That Mrs. Centlivre was unfortunate from her birth, an orphan in her tender years, and a friendless wanderer at that age when most she required protection, has been already related in the sketch of her life affixed to her comedy of *The Busy Body*; the difficulties under which she had to struggle for subsistence, may plead some excuse to the indulgent for her having in this one production, out of those which now keep a place upon the stage, applied to that disgraceful support of her muse, to which her own sex of those times did not blush to attend as auditors. Nor can her offence be

treated with excessive rigour in reference to the present time, by those who consider that this very play of *A Bold Stroke for a Wife* is now frequently performed to an elegant yet applauding audience.

The authoress has displayed high dramatic talents in the conception and execution of the various characters and incidents with which this play abounds. Herein the genius of Mrs. Centlivre consisted—the dialogues of her dramas might be given by a common writer, but her fable and events are proofs of a very extraordinary capacity.

But, in this comedy, however fertile her imagination has been in forming a multiplicity of occurrences, and diversifying the whole exhibition by variety of character, probability is so often violated, that the effect, though powerful, is that of farce, and not genuine comedy.

To admire Mrs. Centlivre as her talents deserve, it is necessary to read, or to see, her *Wonder, or a Woman keeps a Secret.*

The following comedy was brought upon the stage in 1717, when the authoress was in her thirty-eighth year. She enjoyed at that time the intimacy and friendship of Farquhar, Rowe, Steele, and other men of letters, to whom her conversation was highly delightful; as it is said she had more wit and repartee in herself, than she ever gave to her dramatic characters.

Congreve, who lived in her time, is an exception among the literary men who courted her acquaintance, for he had the humility to be jealous of the favour with which her works were received by the public.

The *Bold Stroke for a Wife* is the drama on which the well-known predictions of Wilkes, the celebrated comedian, was delivered, upon his hearing it read previous to its rehearsal. As the first part of that prediction failed, so it is ardently to be hoped did the last.

Thalia Stathas (essay date 1968)

SOURCE: Stathas, Thalia. Introduction to *A Bold Stroke for a Wife,* edited by Thalia Stathas, pp. xi-xxvi. Lincoln: University of Nebraska Press, 1968.

[*In the following excerpt, Stathas discusses the stage history and sources for* A Bold Stroke for a Wife, *one of Centlivre's most successful plays. Stathas identifies plotting and realistic dialogue as the strengths of the play and links it to the gentler style of wit associated with sentimental comedy.*]

A Bold Stroke for a Wife was first produced at Lincoln's Inn Fields on February 3, 1718.[1] It was performed six times, almost consecutively, with

Christopher Bullock playing Fainwell, the comedy's most demanding part. Despite initial success, it was not performed again until 1724, and then not in London but on Epsom Walks by a company of strolling actors.[2] Lincoln's Inn Fields revived the play, "Not Acted these Ten Years," on April 23, 1728, with Milward as Fainwell. For the next decade, it was staged in London principally under Henry Giffard's management, at Goodman's Fields and then at Lincoln's Inn Fields. Unlike managers at the other theaters, he favored contemporary and recent works over those of the Restoration;[3] he frequently staged *A Bold Stroke for a Wife, The Wonder* (1714), and *The Busy Body* (1709), Mrs. Centlivre's most popular comedies. In *A Bold Stroke for a Wife,* Giffard presented such distinguished comedians as Huddy, Pinkethman, Bullock, Sr., and Norris. Often he produced the comedy with supplementary entertainments, ranging from dancing and singing to operas and other plays.

In the 1730's, *A Bold Stroke for a Wife* was also staged by Covent Garden, Drury Lane, the new theater in the Haymarket, and the theater at Southwark. On the Kentish circuit, Dymer's company played it at Margate in 1730.[4] In London, Mrs. Clive led the first cast at Drury Lane on January 13, 1739, with Milward as Fainwell and Woodward as Simon Pure. She was the most distinguished actress to take the role of Ann Lovely; at other London theaters, it had most often been played by Mrs. Berriman, Mrs. Hamilton, Mrs. Haughton, and Mrs. Younger. A new part was, apparently, added at Drury Lane, for cast listings regularly include Mrs. "Pickup," a role also listed by Goodman's Fields for a performance on October 16, 1741.[5]

During 1740 and 1741, Drury Lane continued to produce *A Bold Stroke for a Wife,* once "By His Majesty's Command" (March 5, 1741). Nevertheless, in the 1740's, the play's stage history is dominated by Goodman's Fields, where it was produced fifteen times between October, 1740, and March, 1747. The management evaded the Licensing Act by presenting it "gratis" during intermissions at concerts or with tumbling and dancing.[6] In this same period, theatrical booths at the fairs produced the comedy as a two-act droll, *The Guardians over-reached in their Own Humour: or, the Lover Metamorphos'd.*[7] In the provinces, a company visiting Ipswich staged the play in January, 1741, and the Bristol company performed it in 1745.[8]

By the middle of the century, *A Bold Stroke for a Wife* had been staged about eighty times in London theaters. Yet, as with *The Wonder,* one of Garrick's favorite plays, this comedy's greatest popularity came after 1750. During the season of 1757-1758, Edward Shuter first played Fainwell at Covent Garden; by 1762, he had performed this part almost as often as Garrick had Don Felix, in *The Wonder,* at Drury Lane. Having

earlier diverted audiences as Periwinkle, Shuter decided to attempt Fainwell in a benefit for himself on April 3, 1758. His advertisement of March 8 suggests the reasons for his choice: "Mrs. Centlivre's Comedies have a vein of pleasantry in them that will always be relish'd. She knew the Genius of this nation, and she wrote up to the spirit of it; her *Bold Stroke for a Wife,* was a masterpiece that much increased her reputation: it establish'd that of Kit Bullock. . . ."[9] Shuter's choice proved sound; the receipts for his benefit were the largest of the season.[10]

In 1762, Henry Woodward returned to London theater after an absence of several seasons. Thereafter, for more than a decade at Covent Garden, he appeared as Fainwell and Shuter as Periwinkle or Prim. During the last part of the century, the play continued to be produced, averaging six performances each year.[11] John Philip Kemble staged it often because of its reliability in pleasing his audiences. The comedy remained popular in the nineteenth century, when Charles Kemble, Charles Mathews, and Robert Elliston appeared in it, enhancing its reputation as an acting play. With these performers the stage history of *A Bold Stroke for a Wife* came to a close. No major company has produced it during the twentieth century; however, in a performance at Ealing in 1954, Questor's Theatre demonstrated that this comedy is still effective upon the boards.[12]

One apparently insoluble problem exists regarding the play's authorship. Although in the Dedication Mrs. Centlivre claims complete originality, one of her fullest and most accurate contemporary biographers states that she had a collaborator: "In this Play she was assisted by Mr. Mottley, who wrote one or two entire Scenes of it."[13] The anonymous biographer is generally assumed to be John Mottley himself. Unfortunately, no known evidence exists by which to test his statement. The anonymous Prologue announces that the comedy is entirely Mrs. Centlivre's, including neither foreign nor native borrowings. More specifically, the writer states that "not one single tittle [is] from Molière." This protestation may be conventional, for eighteenth-century prologues and epilogues often disclaim debts to foreign plays, especially French ones, boasting questionable originality for English authors.[14] On the other hand, Mrs. Centlivre's dedicatory remarks cannot be disregarded, particularly since this is the only play for which she claims complete originality. That the comedy is stylistically and thematically consistent from beginning to end tends to support her statement. Presumably, she reworked any contributions that Mottley may have made.

Sources for specific episodes in the comedy have been suggested. Genest says that Mrs. Centlivre imitated Newburgh Hamilton's *Petticoat Plotter* in creating Simon Pure, the visiting Quaker whom Fainwell impersonates in order to outwit Prim.[15] Like the Colonel, Hamilton's True-love poses as a Quaker, Ananias Scribe, to gain entrance to Thrifty's house in order to court his daughter. As in *A Bold Stroke for a Wife,* when the real Scribe arrives, he is deemed an impostor and treated rudely. Unlike Prim, however, Thrifty himself discovers the fraud. Mrs. Centlivre's satire on Quakers may also be indebted to Cowley's *Guardian* (V.vi and xi), especially for the seduction of Tabitha and Mrs. Prim's rationalization of it (II.ii.30-44).[16] Reminiscent of *The Guardian* (V.i), too, is the Colonel's vision predicting his marriage to Mrs. Lovely, a ruse by which he accomplishes his aim (V.i.160-413). Yet, unlike Cowley's Cutter, Fainwell does not even try to dupe his beloved through this trick. To outwit her mother, Tabitha cooperates with Cutter by being well deceived; but Mrs. Lovely aids the Colonel directly in overcoming the Prims. Regarding the general satire on Quakers, Bowyer notes similarities between the Prims and Mrs. Plotwell, a character in Mrs. Centlivre's earlier comedy *The Beau's Duel* (1702).[17] Referring to this resemblance and that which Genest observes, he states that *A Bold Stroke for a Wife* often draws on earlier comedies. Several other parallels to Restoration plays are, in fact, evident.

Both uses of disguise in the gulling of Periwinkle (III.i and IV.iii) recall *Sir Martin Mar-all*. In Dryden's and Newcastle's play the landlord attempts to dispose of Sir Martin's rival by impersonating a mail carrier and informing Sir John that his father has died (II.ii). Disguised as a steward, Fainwell uses similar tactics against Periwinkle in their second encounter. But in contrast to Sir Martin Mar-all, he undertakes this stratagem himself, and his opponent is a guardian, not a suitor for Mrs. Lovely. When Sir Martin impersonates a traveler in trying to gull the Swashbuckler of his daughter (V.i), his antics more closely parallel the Colonel's first venture against Periwinkle. This episode in *A Bold Stroke for a Wife* also recalls the satire on the Royal Society in *The Virtuoso*. Although Shadwell employs no disguises that anticipate Mrs. Centlivre's, Sir Nicholas Gimcrack is a guardian; like Mrs. Lovely, the virtuoso's two wards lament their fate (I.ii). Still other similarities to earlier plays exist in *A Bold Stroke for a Wife*. Yet no one work can be termed a major source for this comedy. Even in the episodes just described, Mrs. Centlivre uses materials which had become the common property of contemporary writers: satires on Quakers and virtuosos abound in this period, as does delight in disguise.[18] That Mrs. Centlivre reshapes such conventional subjects with freshness surely justifies her protestation of originality.

A Bold Stroke for a Wife draws on contemporary literary traditions in still other ways. All of the guardians and Mrs. Prim resemble character sketches of the period. A true descendant of Shadwell's Gimcrack,

Periwinkle also recalls stereotyped characters of virtuosos in *The London Spy* (Pt. 1), *The Tatler* (No. 216), and *The Spectator* (Nos. 21 and 275). Tradelove's sharp practices and manic-depressive reactions to their success and failure find counterparts in Ward's *London Terrae-filius* (No. 5), his *London Spy* (Pt. 16), and Defoe's *Anatomy of Exchange-Alley* (1719). The change-broker's admiration for Dutch management is paralleled by contemporary characters whom Ward entitles "The English Foreigners; or, The Whigs turn'd Dutchmen."[19] With his pocket mirror and French inclinations, Sir Philip Modelove is an even more familiar type, one recurring throughout *The Tatler* and *The Spectator;* his dedication to ease and bachelorhood recalls the predilections of "Sir Narcissus Foplin: or, the Self-Admirer" in *Hickelty Pickelty: or A Medley Of Characters Adapted to the Age* (1708). Prim's hypocrisy, belief in inspired visions, and advocacy of the inner light are reminiscent of Quakerish speakers in a group of pamphlets initiated by *Aminadab, or the Quaker's Vision* (1710).[20] His wife's allusions to Biblical figures in arguing for homespun feminine attire echo *The Scourge,* a contemporary periodical satirically characterizing Quakers.[21]

Although Mrs. Centlivre ridicules the guardians and Mrs. Prim, her primary aim is not didactic; unlike Shadwell, she does not even pretend to use humors characters to laugh men out of their follies. The guardians' eccentricities may be the butt of occasional satire; yet more often these characters serve merely to amuse, and Mrs. Centlivre's attack on them ends amiably. Despite their whimsicalities, we sense that everyone will live happily together after Fainwell succeeds in winning Mrs. Lovely. In any case, the guardians do not receive the lambasting essential to the Jonsonian tradition. Instead, their presence and function recall Sir William Temple's belief that the richness of English comedy derived from native humors types who were to be tolerated.[22] Far from being benevolent, the four guardians cannot evoke the affectionate laughter accorded to eccentrics in later eighteenth-century literature. Still, they are not the targets for merciless ridicule that they would have been in most earlier comedy.

To differentiate between late seventeenth- and early eighteenth-century comedy can, of course, lead to artificial generalizations which obscure the continuity of a tradition. Probably no single tendency within it can be isolated as an exclusively early or late one. Temple's attitude regarding humors, for example, indicates the relatively early origins of tolerant laughter; and, as Norman N. Holland observes, even the first Restoration comedies contain strains of sentiment from which sentimentality could develop.[23] Nevertheless, as Clifford Leech demonstrates in a study of Congreve, changes in comic perspective and emphasis had begun to occur within the Restoration tradition by the end of the seventeenth century.[24] In the eighteenth century, comedy became more "homespun" and "less marked by the obvious contrivances of wit" than it had been in the Restoration.[25] *A Bold Stroke for a Wife* manifests these changes as well as others associated with the turn of the century.

Mrs. Centlivre's treatment of merchants in this comedy is more ambivalent than her use of humors characters.[26] Tradelove is ridiculed, as are merchants' wives and daughters (II.i.116, and II.ii.190); yet Freeman is heroic, and Tradelove's praise of mercantile contributions to English welfare is not intended ironically (II.ii.200-201, V.i.94-95, and V.i.99-105). With few exceptions, earlier comedies consistently ridicule merchants. But before Mrs. Centlivre wrote *A Bold Stroke for a Wife,* Collier, Steele, Blackmore, and other reformers had effectively criticized dramatists for such derision.[27] In arousing laughter at the mercantile class, Mrs. Centlivre may recall Restoration attitudes; however, as a friend of Steele's, she also echoes his patriotic defense of merchants in *The Englishman* of 1713 (Nos. 3 and 4).

As a more significant result of the reform movement, her comedy is freer of profanity and sexual innuendo than are most earlier plays.[28] Dispensing with a love chase, the hero and heroine have decided upon matrimony before the action opens. Like their Restoration predecessors, Fainwell and Mrs. Lovely find love without money impractical, but unlike the gay couples of earlier comedy, they engage in no verbal sparring.[29] Bold as Fainwell may be, he is not a rake; nor is he referred to as a reformed rake. Saucy as Mrs. Lovely is, her prayer for his success (I.ii.66-70) is tinged with sentimentality. In their most pensive moods, a Millamant or Harriet would be reluctant to utter this plea or Mrs. Lovely's subsequent avowal to Fainwell, "Thou best of men, Heaven meant to bless me sure, when first I saw thee" (V.i.226-227).

The intrigue of the outwitting games which form the comedy's plot precludes frequent intrusions of such sentimentality. It also obscures the sentimentality of the situation which gives rise to the action. Like the heroines of popular romances, Mrs. Lovely is a damsel in distress whom a hero must rescue. This situation contrasts markedly with anti-heroic and harshly realistic attitudes about the sexes predominating in earlier Restoration comedy. Mrs. Lovely's plight is, in fact, reminiscent of fairy tales: her father hated posterity and therefore arranged to have his daughter permanently confined. Freeman terms this conduct "unnatural" (I.i.81), and Sackbut describes Lovely as "the most whimsical, out-of-the-way tempered man I ever heard of" (I.i.72-73). He was, apparently, even more eccentric than the guardians whom he appointed to govern his daughter. Just as their behavior causes more amusement than ridicule, so, too, do the events which originate in his last will and testament.

According to Dryden, a situation arising from such behavior is bound to create farce rather than comedy. In the Preface to *An Evening's Love; or the Mock Astrologer* (1671), he defines the difference between these genres with reference to natural and unnatural behavior: "Comedy consists, though of low persons, yet of natural actions and characters; I mean such humours, adventures, and designs, as are to be found and met with in the world. Farce, on the other side, consists of forced humours, and unnatural events. Comedy presents us with the imperfections of human nature: Farce entertains us with what is monstrous and chimerical."[30] Restoration comic theory and practice are too intricate to permit simple differentiation between comedy and farce; nevertheless, Dryden's comments are provocative in respect to *A Bold Stroke for a Wife.* Although the play is by no means pure farce, it abounds in farcical situations generated by Lovely's unnatural will.

In III.i, for example, we laugh not at the gulling of Periwinkle but at Fainwell's forced inventions and the operations of a trapdoor. Throughout the play, we are amused by the unlikeliness of the Colonel's disguises, as they interact with the guardians' unnatural capers. We do not laugh at a realistic Restoration outwitting match between the sexes or between young lovers and their parents. Here we are amused by a preposterous contest of incongruities, created and perpetuated by eccentrics. Yet once we accept the initial fiction of the humorous father and guardians, all else follows logically. The play's success emanates from this artistic consistency and from the sense of realism that it establishes within a basically unrealistic situation. When, for example, Mrs. Lovely feigns a Quaker conversion (V.i), her antics are farcical; however, the plot justifies this pose and its comic mode and thus makes both credible. Since the Colonel must impersonate a Quaker to gain Prim's consent to marry her, she must cooperate with his efforts. Mrs. Lovely's world is, after all, based on unnatural behavior.

If *A Bold Stroke for a Wife* is tolerantly humorous and often farcical, it is also witty; however, Mrs. Centlivre's wit is seldom rhetorical or fanciful.[31] She infrequently achieves the brilliantly racy repartee of earlier Restoration comedy with its witty similitudes and balanced parallelisms.[32] Rather, hers is the kind of wit that Corbyn Morris was to describe later in the century as "gay allusion."[33] In her dialogue, sound judgment does not create "What oft was thought, but ne'er so well expressed." Instead, it seeks out topical allusions that comment implicitly and aptly on the situation at hand. For this reason, Mrs. Centlivre's abundant references to social and political events require glossing to an extent that Congreve's witty comparisons do not.

The full humor and wit of Fainwell's first contest with Periwinkle (III.i) can unfold only if we know that his allusions to science and his smattering of Greek comment on projects of the Royal Society. His reference to "a learned physiognomist in Grand Cairo" (III.i.208) and Periwinkle's acceptance of this authority mock the Society for occasionally recognizing such charlatans as experimental scientists.[34] In IV.i, Tradelove's miscalculating efforts to manipulate the stock market allude wittily to contemporary scandals in which overreached sharpers had to flee the town when they could not make good their wagers (see too IV.ii.102-116).[35] Sir Philip's and the Colonel's allusions to Heidegger's entertainments (II.i.109-111) suggest, without specifying, reports about the license associated with masquerades.[36] As these examples may imply, range of allusion, rather than development of particular references, characterizes Mrs. Centlivre's wit. If her facility of allusion is an intellectual limitation, nonetheless, it creates as much pleasure as does her evident ease in manipulating the play's plot.

Although witty repartee is not Mrs. Centlivre's forte, her use of language in this play is workmanlike and lively. So realistic is her scene at Jonathan's Coffee House (IV.i) that a mid-eighteenth-century commentator on the stock market commends the accuracy and vividness of her dialogue.[37] More significant is Mrs. Centlivre's use of expressive neologisms. The compound *simon-pure,* meaning *genuine,* entered the language through her creation of a character in this play.[38] Her use of *put* in reference to stockjobbing (IV.i.22) is the first recorded occurrence of this term cited by the *OED.* More interesting is her yet unacknowledged use of the substantive *poluflosboio* (III.i.141), a Greek loan meaning *loud roaring.* Under the adjectival form of this word (*polyphloisboian* or *poluphloisboian*) the *OED* enters a noun, *polyphloisboioism,* crediting *Blackwood's Magazine* (1823) with its first appearance in English; the adjective is said to occur first in 1824. That Mrs. Centlivre employs this esoteric borrowing with wit and accuracy again suggests her deftness in manipulating language.

Significant as they may be, neither this kind of linguistic skill nor topical wit can explain the continuing success of *A Bold Stroke for a Wife* over two centuries. By the nineteenth century or even earlier, many of its topical allusions had become meaningless to audiences and readers. And a play is seldom if ever read by the general public or staged for its philological interest. More specifically dramatic achievements account for this comedy's popularity. In part, it must be attributed to cleverly wrought stage business, plot intrigue, and amusing male roles. However, structural unity and concentrated action contribute at least as much to the comedy's dramatic success. As Bowyer notes, all the play's incidents center on the protagonist, Fainwell, and a single concern which he announces as the comedy opens: his intention to win Mrs. Lovely.[39] Like tightly developed variations on a theme, the action employs

varied devices to convey a repeating motif, without monotony or extraneous complications. It presents a cycle of repetitive episodes and settings, modifying and embellishing them with new details.

Five times Fainwell attempts to overreach the guardians. Although each opponent presents a unique challenge, each challenge is directed to the same end: obtaining written consent for Fainwell to marry Mrs. Lovely. Determinedly individual as the guardians are, they are also unified, by their common ward and their fundamental eccentricity. Like a chameleon, the Colonel adapts himself to each man's foible, feigning friendship and kindred spirit toward the opponent at hand. In frequent tavern interludes, we preview all five disguises from a different perspective, as the real Fainwell and his real friend, Freeman, plan them. Freeman enters the action against the eccentrics in miniature outwitting games, gulling Periwinkle (III.i) and Tradelove (IV.i and iv) in acts of feigned friendship. His games bear on the main action, enabling the Colonel to complete his contests with these guardians. As the play draws to a close, the real world of tavern plots merges with that of deceptive appearances. To signal the merger, Freeman arrives at Prim's house with all the other guardians. In their presence, Fainwell assumes his true identity, after rapidly recapitulating all five contests.

To prevent monotony, Mrs. Centlivre varies the tempo of the outwitting games. The first, against Sir Philip, takes place in one uninterrupted episode, concluding successfully. The second, against Periwinkle, is also a single episode; however, it ends unsuccessfully, as chance intervenes and Periwinkle discovers the Colonel's real identity. Halfway through the play, this contest marks a turning point in Fainwell's fortunes, slowing down the action. Although the ensuing game against Tradelove is successful, it observes the retarded pace, going through three phases before reaching completion (IV.i, ii, and iv). As an added complication, it brings Freeman's outwitting match against Tradelove into action. Fainwell's third game is further complicated by being interwoven with the second against Periwinkle (IV.iii). Freeman initiates the latter before the third game commences, and the Colonel wins his second contest with Periwinkle while that with Tradelove is in progress. Through such contrapuntal treatment Mrs. Centlivre thickens the plot's texture, creating good-natured suspense.

Though a single episode, the Colonel's second match against Periwinkle introduces a significant variation on the basic pattern of outwitting games. In this venture, unlike any of the others, Fainwell disguises the marriage contract, presenting it as a lease in order to defeat his most troublesome opponent. Once he has brought Periwinkle to bay through this device, the action is again unimpeded; the match against Tradelove now moves rapidly to completion. As the action speeds forward, the gulling of the last guardian, Prim, takes place like that of the first, in one continuous episode which terminates successfully (V.i). As in the first game against Periwinkle, an outside party threatens to expose the Colonel's identity. But this time chance favors Fainwell, and he obtains the Quaker's signature before Simon Pure returns to disabuse Prim.

Despite their thematic repetitiveness, the outwitting contests create an impression of linear movement through space, as they take Fainwell to such varied settings as the Park and Exchange Alley. Nevertheless, two pivotal points exist to which the action always returns and on which it always turns, suggesting the motion of a cycle. They are the settings of the first act: the tavern, where Fainwell plots, and Prim's house, where Mrs. Lovely awaits him. Before Fainwell can claim his bride, he must successfully invade the Quaker's house. Twice he gains entry, and twice Mrs. Lovely almost upsets his plans because she fails to recognize him. Fainwell first arrives at Prim's after obtaining Sir Philip's consent (II.ii), and next when he returns as Simon Pure to gain the Quaker's. Although not identical, his two visits and Mrs. Lovely's responses to them reinforce the sense of repeating action observed in the gulling of Sir Philip and Prim. This impression is further strengthened because only in II.ii and V.i do all four guardians assemble. Three times they meet, always at Prim's house to discuss suitors for Mrs. Lovely. During Fainwell's first visit, their dissension quickly leads to his dismissal. Early in V.i, as if to blight his impending arrival, they reconvene to disagree, as in their first meeting. But by the end of Fainwell's second visit, when they last appear, he has resourcefully overcome their discord.

Fainwell's final triumph over the eccentrics marks the victory of concerted disguise. In V.i, Mrs. Lovely unwittingly dons her first deceptive costume and joins him in the game against Prim. Ironically, throughout the play she has scorned as hypocritical the Quaker garb that finally brings her liberation. Whenever we see her at Prim's house, she is as preoccupied by scorn for deceptive dress as Fainwell, in the tavern, is by plans for disguise. Before the guardians can be completely overreached, this difference in the hero's and heroine's attitude must be reconciled. Like Fainwell, Mrs. Lovely must realize that disguise is not necessarily a mark of affectation or hyprocrisy. When she first appears on stage, she debates whether or not to put on the Quaker habit she detests (I.ii). After her next entrance (II.ii), she berates Mrs. Prim's hypocritical dress, having resolved not to wear it herself; by contrast, Fainwell now arrives, disguised as a beau, a breed he abhors as much as Mrs. Lovely does Quakers. Guided by necessity and realistic aims, he in no way shares Sir Philip's affectation. At the opening of the last act, just before

his next arrival, Mrs. Lovely and Mrs. Prim echo their earlier conversation about clothing, but a significant change has occurred: for practical reasons, Mrs. Lovely has dressed as a Quaker. By altering her appearance, she hopes to silence Mrs. Prim's rebukes. During Fainwell's first visit, he has remarked, "How charming she appears" (II.ii.111-112). In his second visit to the Prims', he, too, echoes his earlier words, adding significantly to them: "How charming she appears, even in that disguise" (V.i.158-159). Once Mrs. Lovely discovers the full advantage of her dress, together she and Fainwell can play the final outwitting game to bring the action to a close.

Complication by disguise is a salient characteristic of Restoration comedy. It compliments the polite world's penchant for conducting intrigues and pranks in costumes and for attending masquerades. Accordingly, Holland interprets Wycherley's, Etherege's, and Congreve's use of this device as a mirror of court life.[40] He also believes disguise has more profound comic significance for these writers: it reflects the discrepancy between appearance and nature which the new science had disclosed.[41] In *A Bold Stroke for a Wife* disguise lacks this serious intellectual function. It simply fosters delight and a tightly developed plot. In a world of eccentrics where things are too much what they seem, only disguise can invert the orders of appearance and reality. And only disguise can place real people on an equal footing with humorous aberrations. That cleverly masked reality triumphs over unrealistic eccentricity is to be expected in the Augustan world to which this play belongs. In sentimental moments, Fainwell and Mrs. Lovely may feel that love conquers all things. But as intelligent people of fashion, they know that the god of love helps those who help themselves.

Notes

1. Unless otherwise noted, information regarding the play's stage history is based on Parts II, III, and IV of *The London Stage: 1660-1800*, ed. Emmett L. Avery, *et al.* (Carbondale, Ill., 1960-).

2. [John Wilson Bowyer, *The Celebrated Mrs. Centlivre.* (Durham, N.C., 1952)], p. 215.

3. See Arthur H. Scouten, *The London Stage: 1660-1800, Part Three: 1729-1747* (Carbondale, Ill., 1961), I, lxxxii.

4. Sybil Rosenfeld, *Strolling Players and Drama in the Provinces, 1660-1765* (Cambridge, England, 1939), p. 221.

5. I have not been able to determine the nature of this role or whether a printed text including it exists.

6. See *The London Stage: 1660-1800, Part Three: 1729-1747,* II, the entry for Goodman's Fields, April 16, 1745.

7. Bowyer, p. 216. This version of the play is included in *The Stroller's Pacquet Open'd* (London, 1742); the title page of the droll is dated 1741.

8. Rosenfeld, pp. 99, 207.

9. *The Public Advertiser;* quoted in *The London Stage: 1660-1800, Part Four: 1747-1776,* ed. George Winchester Stone, Jr. (Carbondale, Ill., 1962), II, the entry for April 3, 1758.

10. *Ibid.;* the receipts totalled £325 9*s.* 6*d.*

11. Bowyer, p. 217. For a detailed account of the play's late eighteenth- and nineteenth-century stage history, see Bowyer, pp. 217-218, on which my discussion is based.

12. [J. E.] Norton, "Susanna Centlivre," [*Book Collector* VI (1957)] p. 178.

13. *A Compleat List of all the English Dramatic Poets, and of all Plays ever printed in the English Language to the present Year 1747,* appended to Thomas Whincop's *Scanderbeg: or, Love and Liberty* (London, 1747), p. 191.

14. Mary E. Knapp, *Prologues and Epilogues of the Eighteenth Century* (New Haven, 1961), pp. 221-229, especially pp. 225-226; in discussing conventional protestations of originality, Miss Knapp refers to this Prologue, though she erroneously terms it the Epilogue.

15. *Some Account of the English Stage* (Bath, 1832), II, 498-499.

16. Professor James Sutherland has kindly called this possibility to my attention.

17. Bowyer, p. 215.

18. Regarding the period's preoccupation with disguise, especially in reference to comedy, see Norman N. Holland, chapter 6, "Disguise, Comic and Cosmic," *The First Modern Comedies: The Significance of Etherege, Wycherley and Congreve* (Cambridge, Mass., 1959). I discuss his thesis briefly below.

19. *The Poetical Entertainer* (1712), No. 3; see also No. 2.

20. The pamphlets prompted by this one also appeared in 1710: *A Reply to Aminadab: or an Answer to the Quaker's Vision; Aminadab's Declaration delivered at a General Meeting holden upon the first day of the Pentecost;* and *Azarias, a Sermon held forth in a Quaker's Meeting immediately after Aminadab's Vision.*

21. See No. 4, February 25, 1717.

22. *Of Poetry* (1690). For a discussion of the changing attitudes towards humors types, see Stuart M. Tave, *The Amiable Humorist: A Study in the Comic Theory and Criticism of the Eighteenth and Early Nineteenth Centuries* (Chicago, 1960), especially chapters 4 and 5.

23. Holland, pp. 85, 113, 160.

24. "Congreve and the Century's End," *Philological Quarterly,* XLI (1962), 275-293.

25. *Ibid.,* p. 284.

26. Regarding changing attitudes towards the mercantile class in Restoration comedy, see John Loftis, *Comedy and Society from Congreve to Fielding* (Stanford, Calif., 1959), especially pp. 33-35.

27. See Loftis, pp. 30-35.

28. Regarding these aspects of the reform movement, see Loftis, pp. 24-33.

29. John Harrington Smith traces changing attitudes towards love and marriage in Restoration comedy: *The Gay Couple in Restoration Comedy* (Cambridge, Mass., 1948).

30. *Essays of John Dryden,* ed. W. P. Ker (Oxford, 1900), I, 135-136.

31. For a discussion of the wit characteristic of early Restoration comedy, see Thomas H. Fujimura, *The Restoration Comedy of Wit* (Princeton, 1952), chapter 2.

32. Dale Underwood analyzes the nature of comic language and its relationship to wit in Restoration comedy: chapter 6, "The Comic Language," *Etherege and the Seventeenth-Century Comedy of Manners* (New Haven, 1957); see especially pp. 106-110.

33. *An Essay towards Fixing the True Standards of Wit, Humour, Raillery, Satire, and Ridicule* (London, 1744), p. 14.

34. See R. F. Jones, "The Background of the Attack on Science in the Age of Pope," *Pope and his Contemporaries: Essays presented to George Sherburn,* ed. James L. Clifford and Louis A. Landa (Oxford, 1949), pp. 111-112.

35. See John Francis, *Chronicles and Characters of the Stock Exchange* (London, 1849), pp. 58-65, especially pp. 61-62; see too [Daniel Defoe], *The Anatomy of Exchange-Alley: or, a System of Stock-Jobbing* (London, 1719), reprinted as an appendix by Francis, pp. 359-383.

36. See *Freeholder,* No. 44, *Guardian,* No. 154, and an advertisement in *Spectator,* No. 22.

37. [Thomas Mortimer], *Every Man his own Broker: or, a Guide to Exchange-Alley,* 2d ed. (London, 1761), p. 133.

38. Glosses for words and linguistic information in this edition are based on the *Oxford English Dictionary,* unless otherwise noted.

39. Bowyer, p. 212.

40. Holland, pp. 47-50.

41. Holland, pp. 54-58.

Douglas R. Butler (essay date 1991)

SOURCE: Butler, Douglas R. "Plot and Politics in Susanna Centlivre's *A Bold Stroke for a Wife*." In *Curtain Calls: British and American Women and the Theater, 1660-1820,* edited by Mary Anne Schofield and Cecilia Macheski, pp. 357-70. Athens: Ohio University Press, 1991.

[*In the following essay, Butler distinguishes Centlivre's style in* A Bold Stroke for a Wife *from Restoration comedy, suggesting that plot, rather than witty banter, is the center of her plays and of their political meaning.*]

Although she is generally recognized as England's most popular woman playwright, Susanna Centlivre has inspired relatively little critical attention and even less acclaim. The standard critical observation is that she writes highly theatrical plays, full of action, that are quite innocent of thought. Perhaps Centlivre does not have a serious vision, but she does seem to share certain assumptions with the Whiggish writers of her time, with those who believed that society should guarantee (in Locke's terms) a citizen's life, liberty, and property.

Centlivre's plays, particularly one of her best, *A Bold Stroke for a Wife* (1718), manifest her Whiggish perspective. If Centlivre has political and social ideas—and I think that she does—they are not conveyed most effectively through her language, the preoccupation of the twentieth-century critic. Centlivre gives us few images and little "wit." Except when they are endowed with broad accents, her characters sound much the same. Most are so busy hatching plots that they have little time for reflection or banter. Motivation, then, is a function of the character's type and not the character's psyche.

For critics who want to hold Centlivre to standards set by the best Restoration comedies, her inability to sustain a metaphor through dialogue is obvious. Sir George Airy, the "Gentleman of Four Thousand a Year" in Centlivre's *The Busy Body* (1709), is reputed to be a man of wit. The play's audience, however, must rely on the testimony of other characters since the evidence is too thin for us to judge. Sir George is in love with two women, he thinks: one, a witty vizard who frequents the park; the other, Miranda, a wealthy heiress (of thirty thousand pounds), whose fortune and person are held hostage by her greedy guardian, Sir Francis Gripe. Sir George, of course, does not know that the two ladies are indeed the same person, and therein lies the intrigue when the lovers meet in the first act. Sir George has just given Sir Francis a hundred pounds for the chance to woo Miranda for ten minutes:

Sɪʀ Gᴇᴏʀɢᴇ:

What tho' my Tongue never spoke, my Eyes said a thousand Things, and my Hopes flatter'd me hers answer'd 'em. If I'm lucky—if not, 'tis but a hundred Guineas thrown away. (Miranda *and* Patch *come forwards.*)

Mɪʀᴀɴᴅᴀ:

Upon what Sir *George:*

Sɪʀ Gᴇᴏʀɢᴇ:

Ha! my *Incognito*—upon a woman, Madam.

Mɪʀᴀɴᴅᴀ:

They are the worst Things you can deal in, and damage the soonest; your very Breath destroys 'em, and I fear you'll never see your Return, Sir *George,* Ha, Ha!

Sɪʀ Gᴇᴏʀɢᴇ:

Were they more brittle than *China,* and drop'd to pieces with a Touch, every Atom of her I have ventur'd at if she is but Mistress of thy Wit, ballances Ten times the Sum—Prithee let me see thy Face.

Mɪʀᴀɴᴅᴀ:

By no means, that may spoil your Opinion of my Sense—

(10-11)

Miranda, of course, does not wish to be discovered; if she is to win Sir George, it must be as Miranda and not as a vizard. Sir George wants to know who the shadowy woman is. These conflicting desires do not let the characters really explore the metaphor of woman as commodity. Neither character really tests or explores the other; the inspirations of intrigue, the character's designs, keep the subjects and metaphors moving. Thus, Sir George soon calls his mysterious lady a "Dish of Chocolate": according to the new metaphor, women are no longer bartered but consumed. Woman as china to woman as chocolate is an intellectually acceptable progression, but most of Centlivre's shifts in metaphor are not so felicitous.

In the best Restoration comedies, metaphors are often milked dry before they are abandoned. In Wycherley's infamous "china scene," the word "china" is worked hard, serving as a metaphor for sex organs, sex acts, and sexual potency. Part of the fun is that two characters,

Lady Fidget and Horner, understand the metaphor and two characters, Mrs. Squeamish and Sir Jasper Fidget, do not. Mrs. Squeamish's failure to see the innuendo does not keep her from adding life to the metaphor:

MRS. SQUEAMISH:

Oh, but it may be he may have some you could not find.

LADY FIDGET.

What d'y think if he had had any left, I would not have had it too? for we women of quality never think we have China enough.

(4.3-189-92)

The metaphor, here, is not merely a figure of speech, a medium for communication; it is also a dramatic device, showing us Mrs. Squeamish's inability to penetrate the surfaces. In effect, if the characters create the metaphor, the metaphor also creates the characters. This kind of dynamic relationship rarely occurs in Centlivre's drama. One often gets the feeling, for example, that in Etherege or Congreve characters meet just so the author can see what will happen, can watch the displays of wit. Centlivre's characters meet because they must—they meet to satisfy the demands of the plot. And the rapid pace of her plays does not leave much time for exhuberant displays of wit. What we have instead are language devices that move the plot or promote Centlivre's view of her society.

Most noticeable of these devices, perhaps, are the topical allusions, which Centlivre uses often. In act 4, scene 1 of **A Bold Stroke for a Wife,** Centlivre renders the stockjobbing at Jonathan's Coffee House in Exchange Alley, giving us highly realistic dialogue and an education in the business. The scene opens with stockjobbers (brokers) waving "rolls of paper and parchment" and trying to drum up buyers:

FIRST STOCKJOBBER:

South Sea at seven-eights! Who buys?

SECOND STOCKJOBBER:

South Sea bonds due at Michaelmas, 1718! Class Lottery tickets!

THIRD STOCKJOBBER:

East India bonds?

FOURTH STOCKJOBBER:

What, all sellers and no buyers? Gentlemen, I'll buy a thousand pound for Tuesday next at three-fourths.

COFFEE BOY:

Fresh coffee, Gentlemen, fresh coffee?

(1968, 4.1.1-7)

The litany of arcana includes references to the Sword Blade Company, the Civil List Lottery, bulls, bears, the Dutch Walk, cocoa beans, and Bohea tea.

By giving us such a close view of stock trading, Centlivre helps the credibility of her character Tradelove, whom we see trying to manipulate the market and win a fortune. Unfortunately, one of his intended victims is Jan van Timtamtirelereletta Heer van Fainwell, Dutch trader, actually Colonel Fainwell in disguise. Tradelove loses a large bet to Colonel Fainwell, but rather than lose the money, he gives up the hand of his ward, Mrs. Ann Lovely, instead. Obviously, Centlivre also uses the language of stockjobbers to poke fun at the profession.

The scene at Jonathan's shows us another feature of Centlivre's language—her fondness for accents. If Colonel Fainwell must impersonate a Dutch trader, he must sound like one, so Centlivre fits him with an accent: "Two duysend pond, mynheer; 'tis gedaen. Dis gentleman sal hold de gelt" (4.1.97-98). Accents can also create verisimilitude (the Dutch accent is part of the Colonel's disguise), but Centlivre never misses an opportunity to mock foreigners, and she likes the sheer fun of absurd speech. When the Colonel needs to trick Periwinkle, an experimental scientist and collector of curiosities (in eighteenth-century terms, a "virtuoso"), he shows off his own curiosities, among them a vial of "poluflosboio" water, which bore Cleopatra's vessel when she sailed to meet Anthony, and a belt:

COLONEL:

But here's the wonder of the world: this, sir, is called *zona,* or *moros musphonon;* the virtues of this is inestimable.

PERIWINKLE:

Moros musphonon! What in the name of wisdom can that be? To me it seems a plain belt.

(III.147-50)

These Greek-like neologisms are fun, of course, but they also allow Centlivre to satirize scientists, those who prize the flotsam and jetsam of ages past. Here, the corrupt language suggests the corrupt values of the world's Periwinkles.

Without denying Centlivre's linguistic ingenuity and her taste for the satirical thrust, we can see that her language serves her plot above all else. And so too with her characters. Centlivre created one original character—Marplot, the good-natured and nosey bungler of **The Busy Body.** The rest are basically stock characters, recognizable Restoration types refurbished for the prudish and fickle audiences of the Augustan stage. In **The Busy Body,** for example, Centlivre gives us two traditional "blocking" agents, Francis Gripe and Sir

Jealous Traffic. Sir Francis, a greedy curmudgeon, wants to marry his ward, Miranda, (and her money) and thus tries to thwart the suit of Sir George Airy. But Sir Francis, in comparison to stage guardians of the past, is not very oppressive. Aphra Behn's Sir Patient Fancy is splendidly lecherous, forever leering and plotting a way to get his victim into bed. Sir Francis, though, never gets near a bed, and his passion is never really very threatening:

SIR FRANCIS:

And then, Adod, I believe I am Metamorphos'd; my Pulse beats high, and my blood boils, me thinks— (*Kissing and Hugging Her.*)

MIRANDA:

O fye, *Gardee,* be not so violent; Consider the market lasts all the year.

(39)

This is mild stuff, but Centlivre never lets her characters get more passionate—at least among themselves. Absent from Centlivre's plays is Restoration comedy's exuberant portrayals of sexual encounters. We have neither bed tricks nor risque repartee. When Centlivre places her characters in situations where sex must be a motivation, she usually skirts the issue and writes only suggestively.

Centlivre does not use sex well in *A Bold Stroke for a Wife,* however, when she creates Obadiah and Mrs. Prim, hypocritical Quakers and guardians to Ann Lovely. The couple can't keep their eyes off Ann's revealing bodice, rebuking her for lewdness and demanding that she cover up temptation. Mrs. Prim tells Ann that "Thy naked bosom allureth the eye of the bystander, encourageth the frailty of human nature, and corrupteth the soul with evil longings" (1968, 2.2.26-29). Mr. Prim is less detached: "Verily, thy naked breasts troubleth my outward man; I pray thee hide 'em, Ann. Put on a handkerchief Ann Lovely" (2.2.48-50). Although Prim says that he wants Ann to cover up, he would actually like her to bare her bosom altogether. In fact, Ann is quite aware of his lechery and accuses him of molesting the maid: "Ah, you had no aversion to naked bosoms when you begged her to show you a little, little, little bit of her delicious bubby" (2.2.94-96). Mrs. Prim gives herself away when responding to Ann's scorn of Quaker dress: "Well, well make thy jests, but I'd have thee to know, Ann, that I could have catched as many fish (as thou call'st them) in my time as ever thou didst with all thy fool traps about thee" (5.9-12).

The Prims are engaging but utterly conventional. When *A Bold Stroke for a Wife* was produced, hypocritical puritans had long been a staple on the English stage.

All stage puritans, like the Prims, hide their own lust or greed by pointing out the sins of others. As a rule, the stage puritans get duped, so Centlivre found a convenient character to add to her stable of eccentric guardians—all of whom will lose to Colonel Fainwell's ingenuity. Centlivre's plot dictates the nature of her characters.

I have suggested that Centlivre's language and characters serve her plots, which, ostensibly, dominate her plays. But are the intrigue elements of Centlivre's plays so dominating that we worry only about what happens next? Does Centlivre give us plot for plot's sake? On the contrary, plot serves more than itself—plot helps suggest Centlivre's view of society.

Centlivre writes about social problems—arranged marriage, gambling—exploring only occasionally personal vice and not morality. Centlivre's interest in something elemental like love, for example, is almost logistical: how do we get this couple together? She really doesn't care about what love is, what it looks like, or what it feels like. Her characters do not discover their love in the plays—there is no courtship; rather, love is a given, and the action focuses on the plots and counterplots of the lovers and guardians, who have (of course) other plans. Intrigue, not romance, is the keynote.

Centlivre's plays do not argue for specific social reforms. Unlike Aphra Behn, for example, who made it quite clear (without writing social tracts) that she felt women were getting a raw deal from society, Centlivre uses forced marriage not as a subject but as a vehicle for stage business. Nevertheless, Centlivre does display enough concern for social issues to give her plays a Whiggish tenor. Centlivre's position that human beings should be free to marry whom they choose (and have free access to their inheritance) is a subset of the Whig point of view. As H. T. Dickensen has pointed out (1981), the Whigs believed that society should guarantee individuals the rights of life, liberty, and property. Although the Whigs do not believe in democracy (that would be chaos), they believe that the individual has the right to resist tyranny, to resist any government official or function that would deprive him or her of any of these rights. Individuals must have the power to create their own destinies, to make their existence in society less than miserable.

And given the chance, the citizen is capable enough to do it. There is power within, the power of reason. We are not depraved and irrational creatures whose survival is dependent solely upon the grace of God; we are good-natured, rational creatures who, more often than not, use our reason for the good of ourselves and society. And if society is working properly, than the interests of the individual and those of society are the same. The individual is both deserving and capable of the rights that the Whigs would grant.

In one sense, Centlivre's plays are a dramatic fulfill-ment of Whig philosophy. Sturdy, self-reliant characters win their fortunes and future mates by virtue of their own cleverness—and some good luck. It is the middle-class ethic in operation—work hard, be smart, and success in matters of love and money cannot be too far away, an ethic clearly in operation in Centlivre's *A Bold Stroke for a Wife.*

There is nothing new in the plot of this play: four traditional butts—a scientist, a businessman, a Puritan, and a fop—are duped in succession. Centlivre's audi-ences were used to seeing fops and fools suffer on-stage for their excesses, usually in the subplot of a play. Cen-tlivre, however, gives us four fools at once and makes them the main event. Naturally, the audience recognizes these refugees from plays of the past and anticipates their extravagant behavior and the just desserts they will eventually suffer. And the audience knows im-mediately who will dupe them (Colonel Fainwell) and why (to win Mrs. Lovely). Sackbutt, a tavern keeper, tells the Colonel in the first scene that Mrs. Lovely's father "died worth thirty thousand pounds, which he left to this daughter provided she married with the consent of her guardians. But that she might be sure never to do so, he left her in the care of four men, as opposite to each other as light and darkness" (1968, 2.1.82-86). After Sackbutt describes the humors of each guardian, no one doubts for a minute that the Colonel will claim the heiress. The only mystery left for the audience is how the dupes will be duped.

Centlivre's theater audience will certainly laugh at the fools, and to that extent, become engaged by the characters, but, primarily, the audience is engaged by the unfolding of events. In a play, we anticipate the ac-tions, but we also note the orchestration, that is, how Centlivre has arranged it all, what patterns she has cre-ated.

As Thalia Stathas has pointed out in the introduction of *A Bold Stroke for a Wife,* Centlivre's plot structure is unified by the character of the Colonel—his need to gull all the guardians is the play's single premise. Stathas believes this structure is efficient and harmoni-ous, suggesting that "Like tightly developed variations on a theme, the action employs varied devices to convey a repeating motif, without monotony or extraneous complications. It presents a cycle of repetitive episodes and settings, modifying and embellishing them with new details" (Centlivre 1968, xxiii). Indeed, the audi-ence (with some reflection) cannot miss the play's movement, which Stathas calls "contrapuntal."

In act 1, the premise of the play is established when the Colonel discovers the enormous labors facing any suitor wishing to win the hand of Ann Lovely. The Colonel, however, is undaunted, and we learn in the succeeding

scene that Ann will not marry and leave her fortune behind because "Loves makes but a slovenly figure in that house where poverty keeps the door" (1.2.30-31). The Colonel has an easy time with his first challenge, the fop; the Colonel puts on some French finery (including snuff box, watch, and pocket glass), and af-fects some French phrases (*les belles Anglaises!*), and easily wins Sir Philip's signed consent.

Perhaps the audience, at this point, expects the Colonel to move to the next guardian, but, instead, Centlivre gives us a preview of the challenges that lie ahead, as Sir Philip accompanies the Colonel (still in his fop gear) to the house of Obadiah Prim to get sanction from the rest of the guardians. The Colonel is readily dismissed, but is able to size up his labors and the audi-ence sees Ann for the first time and witnesses the abuse she suffers at the hands of the Prims, her current overseers. Centlivre has thus slowed the pace of her ac-tion and set up the Colonel's contest with the Prims which continues throughout the play.

The Colonel next tries Periwinkle at the beginning of act 3, disguising himself as another scientist. The Colonel has about won Periwinkle over with the powers of his bogus curios when his identity is revealed, which spoils the game. This forces the Colonel to find a new expedient for trying Periwinkle again later on. In the Periwinkle variation, then, instead of showing us suc-cess on the first pass, or spreading out the action, Cen-tlivre gives us two parts: the unsuccessful first try and the successful second, which comes later in the play.

Tricking Tradelove, the stockbroker, requires three parts—although the Colonel's plan, in this case, goes without a hitch. In the first part—beginning act 4—Tradelove is passed some false information, and he makes a large bet with the Colonel, who is disguised as the Dutch trader Jan van Timtamtirelereletta Heer van Fainwell. The Colonel's accomplice, Freeman, suggests in the following scene (4.2) that Tradewell relieve his debt by convincing the Colonel to accept Ann Lovely in lieu of the money, a trade which the Colonel agrees to in act 4, scene 4. Sandwiched between the second and third parts of the Tradelove affair is the second part of the Periwinkle plot, in which the Colonel uses the bait-and-switch maneuver to get Periwinkle to sign a marriage consent instead of a property lease. During this act, the Colonel also finds a means to trick the Prims. Thus, in act 4, Centlivre has interleaved three of the gulling plots.

With the signatures of the fop, the scientist, and the merchant in hand, the Colonel needs only to acquire the sanction of the Prims, which he wins in act 5. Tricking the Prims is the action that Centlivre spends the most time on, interlacing it with the other actions. Also, trick-ing the Prims is the only case wherein the Colonel faces the ruin of his plot and then manages to avoid it. This time he comes dressed as a "real" person, Simon Pure, a Quaker from Pennsylvania whom the Prims have never net. Predictably, the genuine Pure shows up at the Prim household, threatening to expose the imposture, but the crisis is averted, and the Colonel wins the Prims' approval.

Stathas is surely right in calling the movement of the play "contrapuntal," suggesting that each time a guardian is gulled, we see a variation on a theme. The four actions of tricking the four guardians are interwoven, and no two of the actions progress in the same way. The fop is duped in a single successful try; the first with Periwinkle is ruined, but the second succeeds; Tradelove is tricked in three parts; and gulling the Prims runs the duration of the play. Centlivre's audience (or reader) leaves the play with the impression that the play is busy, but artfully orchestrated; her plotting is a virtuoso performance, and we enjoy the order, the arrangement.

This is not to suggest, however, that the audience sees only structures. On the contrary, we delight in seeing the resourceful Colonel outwit the tyrannous guardians and steal Ann from their clutches. The delight springs first from our recognizing an old, familiar action. (The play has not developed the delight in us, but has elicited it.) Second, we delight in the Colonel's success because he is the most sympathetic character, and the play is written from his point of view. We see the guardians and Ann as he does—and we are automatically drawn to the character who, with or without our empathy, is the most attractive of the lot.

We are most tempted, of course, to compare the Colonel to the rake of the Restoration stage—but the comparison is abortive. Like a Horner or a Dorimant, for example, the Colonel tricks some foolish characters; however, the Colonel is much less the knave among fools. He enjoys the sport, but there is no evidence that he considers himself society's avenging angel, making sure that extravagant creatures suffer. There is no wasted motion, no gratuitous flagellation of fools. This is so because the Colonel's sole purpose is to marry Ann Lovely— and not merely to bed her. Even Ann's money seems to be of little concern. (Her fortune is basically a plot device to keep the lovers from eloping, which would eliminate the problem of the guardians.) Comparing the Colonel to Restoration rakes only reinforces our notions about how the tastes of theater audiences during the early 1700s differed from those of Restoration audiences.

Another way to view the Colonel is as a knight who works for both himself and society. In act 1, Ann Lovely's maid, Betty, makes us believe that the Colonel will need fantastic powers to rescue his mistress: "Well,

I have read of enchanted castles, ladies delivered from the chains of magic, giants killed, and monsters overcome; so that I shall be the less surprised if the Colonel should conjure you out of the power of your guardians. If he does, I am sure he deserves your fortune" (1.2.46-50). Like the knights of Betty's romances, the Colonel, with his retainer, Freeman, defeats the trolls who keep the maiden fair confined. He is, of course, a soldier, and thus, like knights, is physically capable, but like them too, he relies primarily on his native wit and the supernatural powers of kindly magicians and demigods. In describing the Colonel to Betty, Ann suggests his knightly function: "There's something so *jantee* in a soldier, a kind of *je ne sais quois* air that make 'em more agreeable than the rest of mankind. They command regard, as who should say, 'We are your defenders; we preserve your beauties from the insults of rude unpolished foes'" (1.2.53-58). In her next speech, Ann mentions the Colonel's mind and body, invoking supernatural powers for his aid: "But the Colonel has all the beauties of the mind, as well as person.—O all ye powers that favor happy lovers, grant he may be mine! Thou god of love, if thou be'st aught but name, assist my Fainwell' (1.2.65-68).

Calling up the powers of Cupid seems to work for the lovers, and Colonel Fainwell's final speech also suggests his martial prowess and his duty to his king, his religion, and his lady:

> I must beg Sir Philip's pardon when I tell him that I have as much aversion to what he calls dress and breeding as I have to the enemies of my religion. I have had the honor to serve his Majesty and headed a regiment of the bravest fellows that ever pushed a bayonet in the throat of a Frenchman; and not withstanding the fortune this lady brings me, whenever my country wants my aid, this sword and arm are at her service.
>
> (5.546-54)

The Colonel is, then, a good knight and a good Whig.

Although Colonel Fainwell's profession has no real bearing on the action of the play—he is resourceful, but he does not need to scale any walls or fight any duels— Centlivre's use of a soldier as the hero of her play, risked the irritation of the Tories in her audience. In the first two decades of the eighteenth century, the span of Centlivre's career as playwright, the Tories had an instinctive distrust of the soldier and the standing army. Many, like Swift, believed that keeping a standing army was "the first and great Step to the Ruin of Liberty" (Swift 1941, 146). The most compelling evidence for this proposition, of course, was the New Model army, which, created by Parliament in 1645, took on a life of its own as a political and military force, a force that resisted dissolution and helped put Charles I to death in 1649.

Swift, who hated a mob in any form, never had to witness the dismantling of England's political institutions by angry brigades of political and religious radicals. On the contrary, the army helped to maintain the status quo, suppressing French imperialism in the War of Spanish Succession and defeating the Jacobite invasions of 1715 and 1745. Nevertheless, the Tories, around 1708, began to oppose the war with France, arguing that the Whigs and the Duke of Marlborough, general of the English army, had already beaten the French and were pursuing the war only for personal advantage.

The Tories won this debate, and Anne's Whig ministers were replaced by Harley, Earl of Oxford and St. John, Viscount Bolingbroke. According to Geoffrey Holmes, the number of soldiers was reduced after the war from about 100,000 to under 30,000 by 1714, but the army by now was a fixture (1982, 265). So too was the career officer, who, if he held a king's commission, could be discharged and still draw half-pay—by a House of Commons resolution in 1713 (Holmes 1982, 264). Thus, it is no surprise that Swift sees soldiers overrunning the streets of London and threatening a way of life:

> It is odd, that among a free Trading People, as we call ourselves, there should so many be found to close in with those Counsels, who have been ever averse from all Overtures towards a Peace. But yet there is no great Mystery in the Matter. Let any Man observe the Equipages in this Town; he shall find the greater Number of those who make a Figure, to be a Species of Men quite different from any that were ever known before the Revolution; consisting either of Generals and Colonels, or of such whose whole Fortunes lie in Funds and Stocks: So that *Power,* which, according to the old Maxim, was used to follow *Land,* is now gone over to *Money;* and the Country Gentlemen is in the Condition of a young Heir, out of whose Estate a Scrivener receives half the Rents for Interest, and hath a Mortgage on the Whole; and is therefore always ready to feed his Vices and Extravagancies while there is any Thing left. So that if the War continue some Years longer, a Landed Man will be little better than a Farmer at a rack Rent, to the Army, and to the publick Funds.
>
> (1941, 5)

Swift's assertion that the army officer is a new breed—in the profession for status and money—is supported by Holmes, who notes that "Except during the Interregnum there were few, in [*sic*] any, periods . . . when the self-made man flourished in the army to the extent that he did for the quarter-century after the 1688 Revolution" (269). And some of these "Species of Men" did use their position to become quite wealthy. No longer did the Tory land-owner dominate the profession. Thus, Centlivre, in making the hero of her piece a soldier, risks alienating the Tories, who believed that the army had become a Whiggish institution and a symbol of the Whigs' increasing influence in government and society at large. As a soldier for the Crown, the Colonel resists

the tyranny that the Jacobites would impose on England. As a magician/artist figure, the Colonel also resists tyranny—the tyranny of those who would block the progress of romantic love. Consider Betty's verb when she says "I shall be the less surprised if the Colonel should *conjure* you out of the power of your guardians" (1.2.48-49; emphasis mine). The Colonel does not lay siege to the guardians' fortress, overwhelming them with force. He sneaks in and beats them with guile and craft. He is a protean being, artfully changing his disguise as the situation warrants. When the Colonel tries to win Periwinkle, the motif is magic. Periwinkle is impressed by the Colonel's Egyptian dress and his vial of *poluflosboio,* but he finds the *moros musphonon*—the girdle—stunning. When Periwinkle puts on the girdle, the Colonel and his accomplice, Sackbut, pretend that they can't see him. When the Colonel dons the girdle, he too disappears—through a trap door—and Periwinkle is amazed: "Ha! Mercy upon me! My flesh creeps upon my bones—this must be a conjurer, Mr. Sackbut" (3.193-94).

Like Prospero, the Colonel finds an appropriate means to trick each quarry. He appears as a scientist to the scientist and as a fop to the fop. All of the Colonel's victims are vain; all prey on society in some way. Tradelove manipulates the economy to extort money; the fop imports French customs; the scientist dwells in the past and in the fantastic; the puritans advocate, hypocritically, retirement from society. All of these creatures either corrupt or leech from society. In the context of the play, all are tyrants keeping Ann Lovely from her fortune and her lover. But through the white magic of the play's central force, the Colonel, order is restored, and love is allowed to run its course.

As the chief arranger and author of the guardians' travails, the Colonel may also remind us of Centlivre herself. The didactic function of Centlivre's plays is never too far below the surface. Although the prime business of her drama is good-natured fun, she is always aware that her audiences seemed to demand (at least from new plays) that virtuous characters find reward and vicious characters punishment. Art helps to redeem society from squalid people. And to this end, Centlivre shows tyrannies—whether the tyranny of vice as in *The Basset Table* (1705) or the tyranny of parents as in *The Wonder* (1714)—thrown off through the devices of resourceful characters. Society is restored through rearrangements effected by Centlivre—and the Colonel.

Whether we see the Colonel as magician, knight, or author, he embodies the middle-class dream and sanctions Whig values. Faced with impossible odds, the Colonel uses his own wit to rescue Ann Lovely from the clutches of her guardians. The Colonel has a confederate in his merchant friend, Freeman, and gets some eleventh-hour assistance from Ann herself, but, essentially, he is alone in his labors. God and government are not around. The Colonel's self-reliance is supported, of course, by his industry and resourcefulness, both important qualities for any middle-class hero. Thus, the Colonel seizes every opportunity and finds ways to overcome obstacles. He never gives up and is thereby successful in his quest, winning a clever but graceful woman and her fortune.

If Centlivre's plays are dominated by intrigue, if wit and character are only subordinate elements, this does not make the plays second rate or rob them of meaning. In Centlivre's case, the intrigue is the point—the intrigue in **A Bold Stroke** is the method of a man who frees a woman from her oppressive guardian. Society, the play suggests, needs to accommodate the basic right of all people in freedom. Perhaps Centlivre's plays are best described as good fun, but her Whiggish assumptions resonate through the laughter.

Works Cited

Centlivre, Susanna. 1968. *A Bold Stroke for a Wife.* Ed. Thalia Stathas. Lincoln: Univ. of Nebraska Press.

———. 1981. *The Busy Body: A Comedy.* London [1709].

Dickinson, H. T. 1981. "Whiggism in the Eighteenth Century." In *The Whig Ascendancy: Colloquie on Hanoverian England.* Ed. John Cannon. London: Edward Arnold, 28-44.

Holmes, Geoffrey. 1982. *Augustan England: Professions, State and Society, 1680-1730.* London: George Allen & Unwin.

Swift, Jonathan. 1941. *The Examiner and Other Pieces Written in 1710-11.* Vol. 3 of *The Prose Writings of Jonathan Swift.* Ed. Herbert Davis. 14 vols. London: Basil Blackwell.

Wycherley, William. 1979. *The Country Wife.* Ed. Arthur Friedman. Oxford: Clarendon.

FURTHER READING

Criticism

Frushell, Richard C. "Marriage and Marrying in Susanna Centlivre's Plays." *Papers on Language and Literature* 22, no. 1 (winter 1986): 16-38.

Links Centlivre's treatment of marriage to the concerns and mores of Restoration comedy, calling the playwright a "barometer" of changes in the drama in the early eighteenth century.

Jerrold, Walter. "Susanna Centlivre: 'The Cook's Wife of Buckingham Court'." In *Five Queer Women,* pp. 139-99. New York: Brentano's, 1929.

Chiefly biographical study of Centlivre as one of five professional female authors, relying heavily on legend and conjecture; emphasizes her struggle for legitimacy.

Morgan, Fidelis. "Susannah Centlivre." In *The Female Wits: Women Playwrights of the Restoration,* pp. 51-61. London: Virago Press, 1981.

Brief biography of Centlivre, emphasizing the stage history of her works and her popularity throughout the eighteenth century.

Pearson, Jacqueline. "'In Love with Liberty': Women, Whigs, and Freedom in the Plays of Susanna Centlivre." In *The Prostituted Muse: Images of Women and Women Dramatists, 1642-1737,* pp. 202-28. New York: St. Martin's Press, 1988.

Examines Centlivre's career with a focus on feminism and politics, judging the playwright moderately—and sometimes covertly—progressive. Pearson defends Centlivre's works from critiques of them as inferior or vulgar, concluding that early sexist evaluations of her plays unduly influenced later scholars.

Sutherland, James R. "The Progress of Error: Mrs. Centlivre and the Biographers." *Review of English Studies* 18, no. 70 (April 1942): 167-82.

Examines the legends proliferating about Centlivre's biography, concluding that very little can be known with certainty; traces the accretion of multiple embellishments by a series of biographers.

Wallace, Beth Kowaleski. "A Modest Defense of Gaming Women." *Studies in Eighteenth-Century Culture* 31 (2002): 21-39.

Contends that the physical presence of the female actor undercuts the generally patriarchal values of "gambling" plays including Centlivre's *The Basset Table.*

Additional coverage of Centlivre's life and career is contained in the following sources published by Thomson Gale: *Dictionary of Literary Biography,* **Vol. 84;** *Literature Criticism from 1400 to 1800,* **Vol. 65;** *Literature Resource Center***; and** *Reference Guide to English Literature,* **Ed. 2.**

Jean Genet
1910-1986

French novelist, playwright, and poet.

INTRODUCTION

Genet is best known for his surreal poetic dramas in which he utilizes the stage as a communal arena for enacting bizarre fantasies involving dominance and submission, sex, and death. Genet, whom Jean Cocteau dubbed France's Black Prince of letters, is linked to such amoral, antitraditional writers as the Marquis de Sade and Charles Baudelaire by his use of rich, baroque imagery, his deliberate inversion of traditional moral values, and his belief that spiritual glory may be attained through the pursuit of evil. Although Genet first won international recognition for his lyrical novels about prison life, most critics contend that his dramas represent the most refined synthesis of his characteristic style and themes.

BIOGRAPHICAL INFORMATION

Genet was born in Paris on December 19, 1910. He never knew his father, and he was abandoned by his mother, a prostitute, when he was just a few months old. He spent his early years in an orphanage before being sent to live with a peasant family in the Morvan region of France. The foster parents, who were paid by the state to raise him, accused him of theft, and sometime between the ages of ten and fifteen he was sent to the Mettray Reformatory, a penal colony for adolescents. After escaping from Mettray and joining and deserting the Foreign Legion, Genet began a period of wandering throughout Europe, making his living as a thief and male prostitute. It was during this time that Genet gleaned the experiences of the French underworld he later detailed in his dark autobiographical novel, *Journal du voleur* (1949; *The Thief's Journal*). From 1938 to 1942 Genet's life was marked by a series of petty thefts and subsequent short imprisonments, during which he began to write poetry as well as his first novel *Notre-dame-des-fleurs* (1944; *Our Lady of the Flowers*), all based on his criminal encounters. Quickly catching the attention of such literary figures as Jean Cocteau and Jean-Paul Sartre, Genet's writing ultimately earned him the support of intellectual circles for his early release from prison in 1948 and a pardon for his crimes by French authorities. Genet thereafter abandoned his

criminal activities in favor of his literary career, producing four novels, five plays, and numerous poems over the next two decades. In 1964, upon the sudden suicide of his long-time lover, he ceased his literary activities and destroyed all his manuscripts. He spent the remainder of his life engaged in social and political causes. Diagnosed with throat cancer in 1979, Genet died on April 15, 1986, in Paris, and was buried in Larache in Morocco.

MAJOR DRAMATIC WORKS

While his earliest literary productions were poems and novels, for Genet, drama offered the most effective literary form for the incantatory expression of dream and ritual. His early plays, although true to the inverted universe he depicts in his novels, reflect the influence of Sartre's drama *No Exit* and his dictum, "Hell is other people," in their stylized and abstract portrayals of inescapable personal rivalries. Genet's first produced play, *Les bonnes* (1947; *The Maids*), was based on the actual murder of an upper-class mistress by her female servants. In this ritualistic drama of uncertain identities, two sisters assume the roles of sadistic employer and submissive maid in enacting their fantasies of power and revenge. When their attempts to kill their real mistress fail, the sisters must satisfy themselves with killing her image, and the play ends with the dominant sister committing suicide as her submissive counterpart reads a eulogy. This conclusion echoes Genet's contention, expressed in *The Thief's Journal,* that acts must be carried through to their completion. Whatever the point of departure, the end will be beautiful. Genet blends naturalism and fantasy in *Haute surveillance* (1949; *Deathwatch*), about the ritualistic efforts of a petty criminal, trapped in a cell with two killers, to achieve the saintly designation of murderer. Because, unlike his cellmates, he has not killed without reason or motive, he is ridiculed for his immoral inferiority.

Genet's later plays center increasingly on the illusory nature of social roles as well as on the rituals of the theater and their relationship to reality. These works, which are generally regarded as Genet's masterpieces, reveal the influence of Antonin Artaud's Theater of Cruelty in their emphasis on violence and sadism and make use of such theatrical devices as mirrors, masks, exaggerated costumes, and choreographed gestures to reveal symbolic meaning. The protagonist of *Le balcon* (1957; *The Balcony*), is Madame Irma, the opportunistic proprietress of a brothel known as the Grand Balcony, where clients act out their fantasies of authority, sex, and power. As a revolution occurs offstage, Irma's clients assume the roles of bishop, judge, general, and police chief; they are subsequently persuaded by government officials to assume their fantasy roles in public to restore order among the populace. As the old regime retains its power through these new leaders, Madame Irma's establishment comes to represent a microcosm of society in which her clients' fantasies emerge as reality. Uncertain and changing identities are again central to *Les nègres: Clownerie* (1959; *The Blacks: A Clown Show*). In this drama, fantasies of racial revenge are enacted by Black actors, half of whom, painted in whiteface and occupying the stage's highest point, represent white society as Blacks view them—pompous, hypocritical, and repressive. The remaining Blacks are positioned at the stage's lowest point to reflect how they regard themselves and how white society views them. As a revolution rages offstage, the Blacks enact the ritualized rape and murder of a white woman and escape to a cannibalistic existence in the jungle. Although the Blacks overthrow their white oppressors, they finally reinstate the major authority figures of the previous government, illustrating that repressiveness and hypocrisy are not racially defined qualities. Genet's last play, *Les paravents* (1961; *The Screens*), his longest and most ambitious work for the theater, utilizes colonialism in North Africa as a metaphor for humanity's worst traits. Although Genet indirectly condemns France's involvement in the Algerian War, the drama is nonrevolutionary in intent. The major contribution of *The Screens* to contemporary drama lies in its innovative staging technique. As the scenes progress, settings are suggested by camera projections onto a series of folding screens or are sketched on canvases by actors.

CRITICAL RECEPTION

Recognized by his contemporaries for his artistic originality and subversive view of current issues, Genet was continually lauded in academic circles. However, at the time of publication, many of Genet's works were considered disturbing and scandalous. His works sparked controversies and censorship throughout Europe, and many of his dramas were banned from public playhouses. *The Balcony,* his first commercially successful play, was originally staged in London, as it was prohibited in France. The play was well received and three years later its American debut earned Genet an Obie Award. The playwright became an acknowledged icon for the radical Beats of the 1950s, as his works defied conventional literature and inspired revolutionary insights into the possibilities of dramatic illusion and distortion. His work eventually earned him the Grand Prix des Arts et Lettres in 1983. Today Genet's works are generally recognized as masterpieces for their ingenuity. However, his plays often prove difficult to stage as a result of their reliance on surrealism and illusion. Similarly, untrained audiences struggle to comprehend much of his abstract, enigmatic approach to plot development and characterization. Nevertheless, Genet's ingenious, surreal literary revelation has secured his reputation in the modern theater.

PRINCIPAL WORKS

Plays

Les bonnes [*The Maids*] 1947
Haute surveillance [*Deathwatch*] 1949
Le balcon [*The Balcony*] 1957
Les nègres: Clownerie [*The Blacks: A Clown Show*] 1959
Les paravents [*The Screens*] 1961

Other Major Works

Notre-dame-des-fleurs [*Our Lady of the Flowers*] (novel) 1944
Miracle de la rose [*Miracle of the Rose*] (novel) 1946

Pompes funèbres [*Funeral Rites*] (novel) 1947
Querelle de brest [*Querelle of Brest*] (novel) 1947
Journal du voleur [*The Thief's Journal*] (novel) 1949
Oeuvres complètes. 5 vols. (novels, plays, and poetry) 1951-79
The Complete Poems of Jean Genet (poetry) 1981
Treasure of the Night: The Collected Poems of Jean Genet (poetry) 1981
Un captif amoureux [*Prisoner of Love*] (novel) 1986

OVERVIEW

Leslie Katz (essay date fall 1996)

SOURCE: Katz, Leslie. "Jean Genet: 'Une Solitude Mortelle.'" *Raritan* 16, no. 49 (fall 1996): 65-85.

[*in the following essay, Katz explores Genet's personal involvement in his work, providing a comprehensive background on the author's perspective.*]

In the art of the tightrope walker, Jean Genet discovered a metaphor for a particular kind of theatricality: at once grand and furtive, flamboyant and private. In his essay, "Le Funambule," he writes, "It was not a whore we went to see at the circus, but a solitary lover in pursuit of his own image. . . . It was Narcissus who danced." Through the reference to Narcissus, Genet may wish to capture the performer's radical and necessary absorption in his art, the placement of the foot and, by extension, the weight of the entire body on the wire; a level of concentration that, second by second, averts the possibility of the performer falling to his death. But it is not only the tightrope walker who, "in pursuit of his own image," diverts his focus from the audience. The crowd averts its eyes as well, Genet says, and not because the onlookers are concerned for the funambule's safety. On the contrary. His exotic appearance, his outré makeup, his costume (especially the brocade dragon stitched at the crotch of his leotard, calling attention to his balls)—his whole grotesque flirtation with mortality offends their sensibilities, makes them look down, and thus protects him in his work from their hostile (literally, rigid) gaze. This immunity, however, is symptomatic of a prior, unlocatable rejection, something in his origins that compels him to *be* a tightrope walker. In adulation, Genet writes, "At the first of your turns on the wire, one understands that you, this monster with the mauve eyelids, could only dance there." Then in the voice of an affronted audience member: "Those painted cheeks, those gilded nails . . . *oblige* him to be there [on the wire] . . . where we (thank god) will never go." Genet sees in the tightrope spectacle, as in his own

writing, a need to court the audience's hatred, to reject them before they can reject him, and finally to do so by participating in a rite that marks him, makes him incommensurable with them. The funambule rejects everything other than his own image, which is equally "la mort elle-même." To the tightrope artist, Genet says: "You are the residue of a fabulous age. . . . Your ancestors ate broken glass and fire, charmed serpents . . . juggled with eggs, made a council of horses talk." Like the funambule, the poet lives his theatrical existence in quarantine, in a "solitude mortelle."

This is the paradigm from which Genet constructs his everyday persona. Edmund White, in the biography, talks about Genet's personal powers of seduction, especially his compulsive self-theatricalization: theatricalizing his criminal activities for friends in the Paris intelligentsia, and in a more intimate context, theatricalizing his experience as a gay male prostitute for the wives of those friends. "Once Olga [Barbezat] asked him how he picked up boys. Genet instantly set up the scene and invited her to play the boy." This act of objectifying, maybe grotesquing, the predatory gay male is partly self-mocking: for Barbezat's amusement, Genet turns himself into a caricature, a type. But it is also aggressive, in that through the exhibition he is mocking *her* bourgeois naivete, trying to shock and titillate her with the "mysterious" rituals of a subculture she knows nothing about. Moreover, by placing Barbezat in the boy's role, Genet reminds her that she is a mere stand-in for the object of desire, at once implicating her in and distancing her from what the performance really represents. He thus turns the entire game into a greater erotic tease.

Lola Moloudji also remembers Genet's demonstrations. "He played the cruiser to perfection. It was killingly funny. He had extremely lively eyes that moved all the time." Genet betrays himself and his kind to the bank of eyes that make up the straight world. But this betrayal, he counters, is the mark of the pederast, a drive, under the guise of seduction and solicitation, to turn against others and, so doing, to dehumanize himself. This, he concludes (in a 1956 interview for *Bulletin de Paris*), is preferable to the alternative, for "[it] follows that if the homosexual accepts more or less to play a role in [the social] comedy, like Proust or like Gide, he's cheating, he's lying: everything he says becomes suspect." For Proust, the world is a universal closet in which everyone actively conceals their homosexuality; Genet, by contrast, refuses to accept *any* normalization of gay desire. For him, the homosexual is a pariah, whose purity comes from existing beyond societal redemption. "The sentence passed against thieves and assassins can be revoked, but not our sentence." In homage, Genet says that the homosexual "by his very nature . . . refuses to enter into the system that organizes the entire world."

"Le Funambule," Genet's *ars poetica,* intersects with his personal *ars erotica,* or his queering of solipsistic desire: they coincide in their systematic assertion of un-assimilable difference. As narrator of the prose fiction, Genet represents himself as expelled from the world, immersed in the highly private activity of constructing a hermetic anti-universe. Even though he had first-hand experience of the institutions he writes about (reform school, the military, the French prison system, and so on), his aesthetic and erotic reformulations of those institutions depend on the ecstatic images of someone who, like a cloistered monk, lacks direct knowledge of the "real" world. This heremetic stance underscores Genet's insistence that "homosexuality cuts each homosexual off from the world—even from the world of other pederasts." While Genet rhapsodizes his exile as an absolute repudiation of the social order, it is important to emphasize that his antithetical system depends largely on *words.* Even here there is a catch. "Because language," Genet says, "is built on a sense of shared human community," and because pederasts do not belong to that community, they "can do nothing more than mock language—alter it, parody it, dissolve it." The image of the funambule's radical inwardness captures the stakes of Genet's own self-absorption as he appropriates words and puts them on the page. Through this physical activity, he spurns the world in a way that is the same as coupling with death, as in the funam-bule's pas de deux with "la mort elle-même." Elsewhere Genet writes that "these funereal themes will come back in fags' behaviour." The undercurrent of homo-sexuality is always there, brushing up against the theme of mortal solitude.

"Your leaps, your bounds, your dance steps—you execute them not so that *you* can sparkle, but so that a steel wire that was dead and voiceless can finally sing." Genet says that the funambule's isolation entails absolute surrender to the tyranny of an inanimate object—the wire—which he must invest with imaginary power so that it will consent to keep him aloft. Rhetori-cally, Genet muses, "Who before you understood the wistful memory that dwells immured in the soul of a seven-millimeter steel wire?" The wire acquires an antithetical life, as it draws into itself chains of associa-tion, fantasy, and desire. While rummaging through his lover's wallet (and here, we realize that the funambule and Genet's actual lover, Abdallah, are one and the same), Genet finds a piece of paper covered with "curi-ous signs," signs like ciphers in a magic spell. "Along a straight line which represents the wire, he's put oblique marks to the left and right—these are his feet, or rather the place his feet will tread, these are the steps that he'll take." To Genet's eye, the markings become a blueprint or private formula for Abdallah's art. Genet declares that the funambule will "emerge victorious" because he brings the rigors of magic to bear on this poetic act ("in which the training is usually haphazard

. . ."). This is the same rigor that Genet brings to the art of writing, a "discipline of numbers" that organizes words in magical sequence, so that each—like a poetic image, only more demonic—can unleash its private *and* anonymous contents: anonymous, because Genet so fully lends his "soul" to the word that its chain of metaphoric association comes back, as foreign as death, to claim him. Genet's prose structures, the narrative connections *between* words, are as spectral as the tightrope walker's achievement, while the word itself, like the high wire, sustains a tense division, keeping "reality"—a lapse in consciousness, an intrusion of the world—successfully at bay.

The funambule is, for Edmund White, at once "a toreador, a medieval juggler before the statue of the Virgin, a monk, a sacrificial wonder-working victim." At any given moment on the wire, his body is seized in mid-declension. As long as it remains suspended, Ab-dallah's body can be wedded to the instability of Genet's fantasy, to the fluidity and indeterminacy of interpretation. Afterward, however, the spell breaks like a fever. Watching Abdallah perform his aerial routine, Jean Goytisolo, one of Genet's coterie, writes, "when he finishes and jumps on the carpet under the corbelled ceiling of the unfriendly banquet hall where he rehearses, I suddenly see the tension and the strain, the sweat that bathes his face, the fragility of his fine smile." The body, submitting to gravity, rematerializes in the world rather than the mind, as an object rather than a trope. The strain, the sweat, and above all the fragility of the smile testify to the unstable relation that exists at the intersection of absolute and material being. At this moment of crisis, Abdallah also takes shape as an object of carnal desire, his vulnerability serving as a lure that draws other men toward him: with the hope of possessing him, as the wire has possessed him.

Genet's fascination with the theater is connected to this aspect of the high wire act: that the danger is renewed and reinvented with each performance. The forces that maintain the illusion, the tense balance between real and imaginary event, are invisible and present each time Genet surrenders to the word; each time Abdallah, mounting, succumbs to the wire; each time the actor, in costume, resubmits to the stage. The act, ideally, allows all three to break free momentarily of physical laws and to vault beyond the claims of a social order. In a letter to Roger Blin, Genet writes, "If . . . life and the stage are opposites, it is because . . . the stage is a site closely akin to death." The actors' makeup and altered voices, "by transforming them into 'others,' enable them to try any and every audacity."

In what follows, I will begin by talking about the act of meaning in Genet's prose fiction—a submission to the word, understood as a talismanic entity, that enforces the author's solitude. But then, against the example of the fiction, I will go on to address what I take to be Genet's dissatisfaction with the literary fact of the word, that is, with its static and overly concrete existence on the page. Confined to print, poetry need not rise repeatedly to meet the myriad complications posed by the physical world. What drives Genet is the precise and strenuous labor of poetic acts that, in seeking to unite body with word, require endless physical repetition. To Blin again, he writes: "All of us—you, me, the actors—must steep ourselves for a long time in the shadows, we must work until we are utterly worn out, so that one evening we come to the brink of the final act." The final act would mean utter absorption into an alternative realm, analogous to death, homosexuality, or whatever locks the final barrier in place between self and world, whatever finalizes the state of solitude.

. . . . .

> Sous le drap, ma main droite s'arrête pour caresser le visage absent, puis tout le corps du hors-la-loi que j'ai choisi pour mon bonheur de ce soir. La main gauche ferme les contours, puis arrange ses doigts en organe creux qui cherche à résister, enfin s'offre, s'ouvre, et un corps vigoureux, une armoire à glace sort du mur, s'avance, tombe sur moi, me broie sur cette paillasse tachée déjà par plus de cent détenus. . . .
>
> [Beneath the sheet, my right hand stops to caress the absent face, and then the whole body, of the outlaw I have chosen for that evening's delight. The left hand closes, then arranges its fingers in the form of a hollow organ which tries to resist, then offers itself, opens up, and a vigorous body, a wardrobe, emerges from the wall, advances, and falls upon me, crushes me against my straw mattress, which has already been stained by more than a hundred prisoners. . . .]

Genet prefaces the text of *Notre Dame des Fleurs* with this joint allegory of writing and masturbation. The "right hand" which stops to caress an imaginary face is connected to Genet's desire: thus, he calls it "*my* right hand." But note the shift from personal pronoun to definite article: "*the* left hand closes." Genet takes a piece of his own body, makes it stand for something unconnected to him and, so doing, turns that piece against himself. Cupped to form a hollow space, a phantom cock, the left hand becomes pleasurably alien or "other," potentially adversarial and capable of treating Genet as an inanimate object. The empty space created by the closed hand, and signified by the phrase "hollow organ," becomes the subject of its own clause: "qui cherche à résister, enfin s'offre, s'ouvre . . ." as if this "other," the "organ creux," served as an alienated image of the narrator's own mounting arousal. A highly private and idiosyncratic set of connections seems to emerge out of the accidental puns and phonic half-rhymes of his prose: thus a subtle shift in sound from *off-* to *ouv-* underlines, even coincides with the shift in meaning from *s'offre* (in the sense of intentional surrender or self-sacrifice) to *s'ouvre* (an involuntary unlocking, spreading, and submission to sexual

pleasure). Suddenly the phantom organ vanishes and in its place "un corps vigoureux . . . sort du mur"—a vigorous body emerges from the wall—as if the verb *sort* had grown out of the tonal progression: *s'offre, s'ouvre, sort*. The vigorous body, marked by its own capacity, but failure, to open, becomes, through a final and particularly radical metaphoric substitution, "une armoire à glace," a wardrobe with mirrored doors—a ruthless, faceless, soulless object (also the parody of a tabernacle)—which advances on Genet, *becoming* the orgasm that overtakes and crushes him as if from outside, with overwhelming, pulverizing force.

Self-division makes masturbation and the entire trajectory toward orgasm possible. For Genet, it is a case of investing one's own body with the power to produce pleasure and secure lust, as if it were an other. *Most important in the prose fiction, this effect (the self crushed under the weight of its own alienated orgasm) is equivalent to the violence that rebounds upon the subject by, from, or through chains of metaphoric meaning.* The violence attributed to language emerges out of nowhere in particular, but impresses itself with a ferocity that perverts the symbolic order. Apparently harmless words become Pandora's boxes, containing the very stuff of unsocialized aggression. Genet explains, "When closed words, sealed, hermetic words, open up, their meanings escape in leaps and bounds that assault and leave us panting." We might map this description onto the earlier passage, correlating the hermetic words that open up with the opening of the narrator's left hand as it successfully incubates, then liberates the imaginary but vigorously erect organ. The written word, as medium, is volatile; it translates the author's sensations into unpredictable projectiles, chosen by him but beyond his control. Personal histories, imaginary psychodramas, the lives of his fictive characters, all spring from the word and its magical opening.

One example from *Notre Dame des Fleurs* will suffice. The scene is set in an imaginary version of the author's own childhood, with Genet's part played by the semifictive character, Lou Culafroy. "The first time Culafroy had asked his mother [Ernestine] to buy him a violin, she had winced. She was salting the soup." The word *violin* sets off a complex chain of response: the cleft holes carved on either side of the violin's imagined soundboard become the shape of serifed letters *f* and *l*. Out of this metonymic association springs a pageant of words—sinister hieroglyphs—beginning with or incorporating the fatal letters: "une fleuve, des flammes, des oriflammes écussonnées . . ." ("a river, flames, escutcheoned oriflammes"). From "oriflammes écussonnées" proceeds "un talon Louis XV" ("a Louis XV heel"), echoing the shape of the violin itself. From the homologous curves of escutcheon-heel-violin issues a secondary chain of courtly emblems, including "un page à maillot bleu" ("a page in blue tights"). In anticipation of the word *torturées,* as in the tortured lines of the violin, the list culminates with "l'âme torse, retorse du page" (literally, the soul, like a column, turning in a spiral, the crafty soul of the page). In sum, from the single word *violin,* an external and agentless drama unfolds: of lines that archly turn, return, torture, and re-torture, whose recurring curves encode an entire history of courtly coils, cunning, and intrigue.

"*None* of the preceding images . . . appeared before [Ernestine's] eyes with any precision." I take Genet's "none" ("aucune") to signal, not that this parade of images belongs to Ernestine's unconscious, but that it does not properly belong to Ernestine at all. Again, Genet makes a set of eccentric associations, germane to his private fantasy, look like the bastard offspring of the word-image *violin,* the demonic sperm spilled by the "organ creux" or the "corps vigoreux." "The disturbance that each created within Ernestine . . . held her for a moment between life and death." Each shock, Genet says, was "a plunge into an ink-black lake," a moment of epileptic oblivion. The passage gives no hint of, for Genet has no interest in, the psychic origins of the trauma—how the shape of the violin, for example, might itself have been evoked by the archetypal contours of the mother's body. Everything there is to say about the moment is contained in the word itself, in the scope and reverberation of its assault. "When two or three seconds later, [Ernestine] came to herself ("elle revint à elle"), a nervous shudder made the hand salting the soup tremble." A connection has been forged between Culafroy and the word, so that to Ernestine it feels as if the child, instead of the word, is the source of disturbance. For each time she blacks out, the murderer in her flares up. ("She wept with rage at being unable to kill her son.") The word, or Culafroy's bad luck in speaking it, transforms him, without his comprehending why, into an object of his mother's loathing: unknown to him, "violins" are connected to her dreams of dangerous, sleazy, cat-infested quartiers, the neighborhoods of La Bastille or Montmartre where murders happen. "Violins moved about in her dreams in the company of lithe cats, at corners of walls, under balconies where thieves divide the night's loot . . . on stairways that squeak like violins being skinned alive." Cat = violin = Culafroy. As Ernestine goes about her business of preparing the soup, she is visited by an urge that dwells not in her, but in the shrill, high-strung sound of the violin itself, an urge to skin all three, in one, alive.

Words in the prose fiction are able, by virtue of their overheated associations, to get under characters' skin. Likewise, the most idiosyncratic reactions to particular words can coincide with the harshest expressions of desire. *Violin,* once uttered here, short-circuits or swallows up the space of give-and-take between mother and son. Culafroy is not only ashamed of having spoken it, but afterwards becomes tainted with a sense of unworthiness at asking for or receiving anything from Ernestine. He is thrust into the position of having to construct, for himself and by himself, imaginary substitutes for what the world withholds. Genet portrays the child "in his vatican, a sovereign pontiff"—oppressively alone, in other words, wedged between the remains of his ancestors ("torn and dog-eared picture albums, a shaggy teddybear"). "From that bed of darkness . . . he pulls out a grayish violin *which he himself has made.*" The act of making is not only Culafroy's way of giving form to his loss (what Ernestine will not provide), but of recreating the source of his mother's hatred—of trying, perhaps, to discover what, in the word or in himself, has moved her to despise him. He slips, or regresses, into an archaic attachment to the object. The "violin" is his semblable . . . just as the fictive Culafroy is Genet's.

In imagining the two-dimensional instrument, constructed almost entirely out of household scraps (the cardboard binding of the picture albums, a piece of broom handle, four white threads), Genet seems to be thinking of Picasso's *papiers collés:* objects literally "cut out" of and abstracted from the world. However, its constituent parts carry their own material history—their own connection to the mother's domicile—and thus exert a sinister, even malignant, opposition to Culafroy's need (specifically, the need to know something about violins or, at least, about the mysteries locked inside the shape of that hermetic word). The cardboard object resists his efforts to play it. "The disappointing squeak that the bow tore from the strings gave his soul gooseflesh." He reacts to the disappointing squeak, an inhuman noise with origins outside of himself, as though the cry of frustration were his own. "His heart was drawn out fine and unravelled into strained silences—ghosts of sounds." In his attempt to animate the violin, Culafroy lends it enough transformative power to commandeer his soul. He makes the object sing in a displaced and wounding way. In the likeness of the object, his fragility becomes that of paper; he is able to be torn in two. The violin, "which he himself has made," violates him: "He drew the bow from the point to the base, slowly, magnificently; this final laceration sawed his soul apart." (We can almost imagine Abdallah lacerated by the wire he makes love to.)

. . . . .

Culafroy's, like Genet's, is a chain of encounters with the world, each of which impresses upon him the unnatural character of his desires. His internalization of shame gives rise to a repertoire of gestures that he rigorously repeats. For example, his infatuation with a village no-good named Alberto, combined with the power of the word *Nijinsky* ("the rise of the N, the drop of the loop of the j, the leap of the hook of the k, and the fall of the y"), cause him to dance every night "on the grass in black wool slippers, with his hands clinging to the low branches." His dance, like the funambule's, is performed with eyes trained inward, but with only himself for an audience. ("He was very much afraid of being discovered, especially by Alberto. 'What would I say to him?'") To avoid detection, he hides his dance inside of other movements: with something like a magician's sleight of hand, he conceals the "entrechats" and "jetés-battus" (which engender a "host of figurines . . . in white tulle tutus"), so that to an unsuspecting eye his silhouette remains that of a schoolboy gamboling about the countryside in search of mushrooms or dandelions.

As if word and gesture partook of the same inorganic animacy—rise, drop, leap, fall—Genet places them on an equal plane where they become things in their own right, inscrutably alive and at play. "One evening, Culafroy made a broad, extravagant, tragedian's gesture. A gesture that went beyond the room, entered into the night, where it continued on to the stars, among the Bears, and even farther. . . ." No less than the word, the gesture is a fetish, stolen from the category of the naturalized or conventional and reinvested with strangeness. In its trajectory, as in the word's opening, a version of lust and violation looms. Its magnitude alone imports the depth of Culafroy's surrender. "Like the snake that bites its tail, [the gesture] returned to the shadow of the room, and into the child who drowned in it." Culafroy resembles a sleepwalker, cut off from, yet immersed in his own movements. The gesture, circling back on him, hides both its homoeroticism and its tragic content. In its grandeur and opacity, it is analogous to the word, whose volatile contents have been sealed under high pressure.

In playacting, one becomes by doing, by performing a set of repeatable actions. This is different, however, from what happens when Culafroy, by producing a certain gesture, unlocks its powers and the full extent of association repressed within it. This species of gesture has its own momentum, moves along its own sequential chain, and unfolds its own narrative. Like the talismanic word, it does not belong to the referential system of the living, but to something presocial. Culafroy's gesture removes him from the world and prefigures his death. As with the adult transvestite, Divine, he will drown in his own pool of vomited blood: "as s/he expired, she had the supreme illusion that this blood was the visible equivalent of the black hole [in] a gutted violin." In his third novel, *Pompes Funèbres,* Genet takes this notion further: he indicates how, by conforming to the contours of a particular pose, it is actually possible to strike the nerve of the dead. The energy thereby released is potent, aggressive, and "gives greater vigor" to unsocialized desire.

Pompes Funèbres is about finding the gestures appropriate to mourning, not the conventional, false ones given by the symbolic order, but the as-yet-undiscovered ones that the dead find satisfactory. In the course of the novel, certain iconic gestures surface from the narrative, presenting themselves to Genet with enigmatic force. Looking from his hotel window, for instance, he sees "two bare arms [that] stood out . . . against the dark sky, on the rooftop. . . . Joined at the hands, one of the arms was pulling the other toward it." In the ensuing scenes, Genet tries to catch in his own movements and the movements of others echoes of this fragmentary gesture. Throughout the novel, there is a drive on his part to see how far the fact of embodiment will carry and toward what denouement, whether for instance it is possible in the bodies of the living to realize the logic and the "language" of the dead. By tracing a succession of parallel gestural images—"joined hands" and "parted lips"—Genet eventually arrives at the threshold of a rite of passage, a way out of the symbolic world. Guided by the hand of death, he becomes the instrument of execution in the murder of a child, or rather, in the imaginary rendering of the murder, since it is the act of writing the scene that literally brands him.

"The reader will not be surprised that I wanted to be helped in my first murder." By an act of poetic decomposition, Genet-as-narrator breaks the event into a series of bracketed stills (a stop-frame day-dream), projecting himself into the sequential gestures of a handsome young SS official named Erik. A stone hurled by a fifteen-year-old boy happens to graze the bottom of Erik's trousers—that is, the trousers worn by Genet-in-Erik's body. "My hand flew to my revolver. I was immediately on guard. . . . I bent one knee and spun around." The pose is that of a militiaman in action, but equally the stuff of boys' adventure novels, of cops-and-robbers games. Because it is so stagey, the pose also provokes for Genet the shame of exposure: "Fear and then anger of having been afraid and reacting with fear in sight of a child's innocent eyes . . . made me grab the grip of my revolver and tear it from my holster." Under the killer's obelisk gaze, the child continues to play in pastoral twilight: "He straightened up with a laugh. Snow fell. Before my eyes, such gentleness descended upon the woebegone landscape to soften the ridges of things, the angles of gestures, the thorny crown of the stones." The killer's vantage point perverts the elegiac tableau. The combination of twilight and snow, an ironic contrivance on the part of nature or the author to shroud the child in a cinematic wash of sentiment and tranquillity, serves to magnify Erik's rage. Consequently, a perfect emotional polarity is set in motion. The alternating swells of gentleness and hatred are like the battle of competing cosmic fronts: the one, without meaning to, pleading mercy, the other, in response, sharpening its gleaming barrel for destruction.

Following the architecture of Erik's responses, Genet's identification spirals, enlarging at a furious pace, so that in a flash he outgrows and overshadows the scenario: "the swift, shoreless rivers of green anger [flowed] within me, from north to south. . . . My gaze was fixed in a set, grim, and yet sparkling face, for rays from all the features converged around the bridge of the nose." (Note again, the shift from possessive pronoun to indefinite article: "*my* gaze fixed in *a* set, grim, and yet sparkling face.") With terrific energy, the fantasy melds Genet to the external structure of Erik's grandiose and formidable rage; but each transformation likewise joins with, contributes to, and finds confirmation in a preexisting narrative structure. The story of murder is already coded in Erik's statuesque and Aryan physique. This is Genet speaking: "I envisage theft, murder, and even betrayal as emanating from a bronzed, muscular, and always naked body that moves in the sun and waves."

The growth of the killer proceeds like a phallic gorging, until suddenly the gargantuan murderer pauses and, as if instinctively, in an act of ritual mimicry, mirrors the gestures of the child: "The boy's lips were parted, and I parted mine in the same way, but without smiling." Earlier in the novel, the image of parted lips gives rise in Genet's mind to the word *âme* (soul), from the embryo of which evolves the phrase *âme d'un fusil* (bore of a gun), as if the word itself could stand in for, then collapse the distinction between life and death. Via the synecdoche (parted lips = soul), the narrator arrives at a transverse, metaphoric emblem. The soul is "the inner wall of the gun," then "less than the wall itself . . . the gleaming, steely, icy vacuum," then not even a void, just its properties, "the vacuum and the coldness of the metal." Gesture and word fuse in a moment of poetic combustion.

Around the killer's actions, Genet's imagination festers, with the "I" projecting itself not only inside the stages of the murder as it unfolds but into the fragmented details of the body that performs it. The "I" does not probe the killer's mind (you cannot compass the mind of a colossus), but rather burrows, like a crab, into the groin of the statuesque body, the chiselled pubic hairs. "What is the soul?" Genet asks, reprising the question that constitutes the novel's obsessive core: "It is that which emerges from the eyes, from tossed hair, from the mouth, from the curls, from the torso, from the member." The point of the fantasy is to wrest the phallus, like the word, from the purely symbolic register, where it exists as an empty image of power, and to reinvest it, as literal member, with transformative, sacred, and destructive power. The punch line of the slaying is the narrator's discovery of the fatal link—the icy vacuum—that runs between the phallus and the soul, between the killer's steely cock and the victim's "parted lips." The subtle accommodations by which Erik synchronizes his gestures to those of the victim prepare for the moment when both will be caught up, or

possessed, by the ideal, and absolute, form of an event. For something *happens* whenever a bullet enters a body, or a dick plunges into another man's mouth: these are actual, unalterable, and, in Genet's mind, polluting events.

Within the rigid structure of ritual time, a "column of darkness or pure water" pours into the inhuman, self-mirroring space between killer and victim, "contained by the shape of our lips, circulating from my open mouth to the open mouth of the child sixty feet away." Released from, or immersed in, simultaneous taboos against murder and sodomy, the "I" experiences the displacement of itself (its cravings?) into the weapon: "I felt that the gun was becoming an organ of my body, an essential organ whose black orifice . . . was, for the time being, my own mouth, which at last was having its say." Genet materializes *inside* of his own fictive narration. His identification with the gun is complete, as he finds himself levelled at the victim, somewhere in the space between infantile reverie and state-sanctioned murder. If the child were Jewish, or a defector, or someone who had very simply broken the law, the murderer could justify his act inside the terms of a social contract, but to become a thing, to discharge (to express) through the mouth of an object, means to perform a purer type of murder, an absolute act for which the killer claims sole responsibility. "I fired three shots." In the aftermath, Genet's words become cooler, more porous. A concluding phrase glides from him— words, like a final postlapsarian and profane caress of the cock: "A boy as pretty as that can make me shoot three times." This phrase, spoken in the context of a purely imaginative scenario, becomes increasingly offensive, as it reverberates at the boundary of the reader's ethical assumptions. First, it culminates the sequence of gestures through which the author mourns the death of his lover. Then, it seals the author's hatred of France. The novel is full of this zeal to offend. Genet revels in the German occupation and glorifies those French citizens who, out of self-interest, sided with the enemy and betrayed the motherland—as he likes to think his own books betray the mother tongue. We are thus steeped in the climate of scandal, a scandal that Genet says elsewhere is as fresh as a virginal breeze.

. . . . .

Genet says that he would like his play, **Les Paravents,** to create a scandal, and through this act of scandalizing the public, to illuminate the world of the dead. From 1946 to 1966, he began to devote more time to revising drafts of his plays and preparing them for production. His letters to director Roger Blin give a concrete idea of how he imagined his work mounted on stage. We might take this development as evidence that the imaginary or inward realization of fantasy was wearing thin for him, that the challenge and the risk were no longer enough to absorb him. At any rate, Genet gives new emphasis to the importance of coming up against a live audience, of meeting the frontal resistance of an actual other. Among the shifts that mark the dramatic works and lend them a more public flavor, I would list: 1) the change to an external viewpoint (a vista outside the self); 2) a Brechtian separateness of character from audience, which corresponds to the separateness of the characters from their own fantasies; 3) the failure of characters, especially in **Les Bonnes** and **Le Balcon,** to *make* things happen (to perform actual, transformative rites). But there is also the shift in medium: Genet is no longer working with the picture of the word or gesture on the page, but with its apparition in the flesh. The stakes of the medium are highest in **Les Paravents,** where Genet says that he wants the audience to fall in love with the smallest gesture, and to suffer a broken heart when the most peripheral character disappears into the wings.

To realize Genet's ideal in a stage version of **Les Paravents,** the body of the actor must be wrenched free of its conventional postures and welded to the movement of an alien spirit, like Madani, who consents to lie down on the earth and become a dead man's mouth "full of earth and roots and gravel" ("pleine de terre, de racines, et de graviers"). Or Said's Mother, who admits that her faults are not native to her but to the nettle family, as if she were claiming an old Parisian bloodline: "la famille des Orties," or better put, to the ancient family of associations that springs from the word *nettle* ("growing near the ruins . . . their bushes were my cruelty, my hypocritical meanness that I kept, with one hand behind my back, in order to hurt the world!"). The gestures that guide the actor do not have their source in the body but, as is the case with the characters in the fiction, in the imaginary shapes and power of words. To make way for these incarnations, to free the body to receive them, Genet says that all recourse to prescribed symbols and signs must be suppressed. For the gesture to realize its poetic fullness, the body has to become something unmoored from the human and the living, something radically absorbed into fantasy.

Although **Les Paravents** is about the French war in Algeria, Genet insists that the director draw not on recent history but on his own "wildest ravings." "You must call upon your dreams . . . not upon your observations, unless they are mad and make you see velvety fleece around the Arabs' eyes." Elsewhere he tells Blin, "Real paratroopers have given me a hard-on; I've never had an erection over stage paratroopers." Desire is connected for Genet to the freedom to appropriate, reconceive, and exoticize things external to him. To simulate this effect on stage, he demands that facial expressions, cultural tics, even the "colors of poverty" have to be reinvented. Ommu, a mad village outcast, appears in the last scene of the play, carrying herself, in her sublime decrepitude, on crutches. Genet tells Blin

that "it would be a good idea to cover [the crutches] with bright red velvet . . . and for Ommu to use them like knitting needles, as though she were knitting on the ground." The gesture produces a fantastic way of walking, and at the same time it corresponds to the radical isolation of the character who is caught between the world of the living and the dead. Genet says that when Ommu, stinking, raving, and delirious with fever, calls for "as . . . prin," it should be "the way an addict calls for heroin."

To Blin: "When we first started rehearsals, I forbade anyone to make the slightest gesture, however simple, with their body or their little finger. . . . The fact is that actors are always prone to 'finding spontaneously' gestures which help the words to emerge from the mouth." The gesture is a way of "hamming it up," displacing self-consciousness into awkward extravagance, a way of calling attention to the self that is the same as being "dead to shame." But for Genet, the point of theater is to recapture the shame of speaking, to set off time and again the wounding process of being caught in a floodlight, cut off from the accepted repertoire of public pantomime. Genet declares that *only* the presence of an audience can confer genuine solitude. "To the same degree that waves mount—like the cold, which begins at your feet, then overtakes the legs and thighs . . . the coldness [of the crowd] seizes your heart and freezes it." It requires an act of will for the actor to accept the public gaze as food for his shame, but once the "other's" frigidity has passed like hemlock through his body, it seals the shame inside and makes it indistinguishable from temerity. "It seems to me that each character is nothing but a wound concealed under his accoutrements."

In **Les Paravents,** Genet has a gathering of Arab villagers quake—or pretend to quake—in the presence of a colonial landowner and his son.

SIR HAROLD:

  (*Au Chef arabe*)

  Tu trembles?

LE CHEF:

  Yes, Sir Harold, je tremble au nom de tous.

LE FILS:

  Oui, qui t'a enseigné le tremblement?

LE CHEF:

  La droiture de votre regard et notre nature servile.

[SIR HAROLD:

  (*to the Arab chief*)

  You're trembling?

THE CHIEF:

Yes, Sir Harold, I tremble in the name of the people.

THE SON:

Who has taught you the art of trembling?

THE CHIEF:

Your unswerving gaze and our servile nature.]

The Chief's irony is that of a Caliban, pretending servility to a would-be monarch whose claim to authority is transparently groundless. But Genet is not interested in the mimesis of mutual or self-deception. He is only concerned with defining the gesture by which the assembled Arabs reinforce the Chief's speech. He tells Blin that "every actor must practice making all his limbs tremble . . . from head to toe, from their shoulders to their hands, and the trembling should be carried to trancelike lengths but should [also] evoke the image of a field of rye swayed by a strong wind, or the flight of a flock of partridges." In a play that exalts the stupidity of the French colonists as well as the cowardice and treachery of the colonized, Genet says that the gesture is meant to instantiate a "painful vision" of impotence and fear. (The fear that the French imagine they have instilled in the Algerians? The colonists' impotence to inspire genuine rather than fake fear?) The theatrical representation has been purposely stylized, allegorized, and lifted from its moral context, so as to reveal—I imagine Genet would say—the beauty intrinsic to fear itself. To Blin, he writes, "The attitude and the word which in real life seem abject, in the theatre must fill the audience with wonder." (It is interesting, even moving, to note the echo of Aristotle.)

But there is something else. Like the funambule, the actors' bodies have become the physical loci for Genet's metaphors (trembling limbs = swaying rye = flock of partridges in flight). Like the tremors of an epileptic fit, the gesture ideally plunges the actors beyond consciousness, their bodies becoming the site of a sourceless violence (and here it is fitting to remember the trembling that seizes Ernestine's hand as she stirs the soup). Genet asks each actor to withdraw into a privately imagined wound, until his or her "absence à la salle" becomes palpable to the audience. The actor does not perform for the public, but against it. Genet does not mean for any particular action on stage to offend the audience so much as the fact of the actor's truancy. In translating his art to the stage, however, Genet risks not being able to represent the violent and phantasmatic possession which occurs in the fiction, risks not being able to get the actor's body to hold such a representation in palpable, breathing form. That is the danger and the thrall of the body, its susceptibility to fantasy, yet its instability as a vessel for poetic form.

· · · · ·

Do you know the amusing physical experiment in which a ring that hangs from a thread is supported after the thread is burned? The thread is soaked in very salty water. The ring is then tied to it. Then you burn the thread with a match. The ring stays up, supported by the delicate cord of salt.

Genet interrupts the narrative of *Pompes Funèbres* to describe this party trick, a metaphor for what the self experiences as it passes from the rigors of a poetic act back into the material of the body. The image is one to which he obsessively returns: it is Abdallah dismounting from the wire; it is also Erik returning to the barracks, following the murder of the child in *Pompes Funèbres.* "At the roots of the hair above the forehead were delicate beads of sweat. He felt he was borne up by fear itself . . . a very fragile framework of salt that was supporting the undamaged head." Sweat = salt = fear = the residue of an ephemeral glory, literally the only thing that holds the body together following the enormous and consuming strain of lending imaginary significance to its actions. In the theater, the strain comes from working against the collective will of the audience, a focused and highly physical instance of working against the claims of a symbolic order.

This ellipsis of word and body, of iconic gestures and physical presence, resembles the style of French neoclassical drama, in which the actors deliver their lines from a repertoire of stock rhetorical poses. But here the dramatic strategy, for turning people into allegories of action, works in the service of Genet's own antipolitical aesthetic vision. If transformative events in the novels take place in a detemporalized and denaturalized space, transformative events are rarely, if ever, represented on stage in Genet's plays. For instance, when Roger castrates himself at the end of **Le Balcon,** his action fails either to invest the phallus with or to divest it of deep meaning. From the viewpoint of the onstage characters, he merely succeeds in cutting off his balls and getting blood all over Irma's carpets. To the offstage audience, his actions—however grandiose in their intent—look like the parody of going through a rite. In **Les Paravents,** however, the fact of being unable to disturb the symbolic structure of the human world provokes neither anxiety nor displeasure. Characters pass from the world of the living with bodies (wounds, lice, odor, and so on) intact. Raised to the world of the dead, they enjoy better, more elevated seats for watching the play; perched above the stage, they are freer to laugh, writhe, and curse. They await Said's arrival as a hero, *because* his attempt to betray the Algerian forces to the French army has failed (he strikes the pose of a traitor, says the words, leaks the information, but no one hears him). The play—satirical, irreverent, and topical—remains a bacchanal of inaction.

"Everything should work together to break down whatever separates us from the dead." In *Pompes*

Funèbres, Genet watches as an assistant screws the lid on his lover's coffin; he remarks that the only thing separating him from the deceased is "a hypocritical, light, porous board that a more depraved soul than Jean's could dissolve." The real action of *Les Paravents* lies in approaching this fragile barrier, making sure that the actors do not fall back on conventional gestures or the familiar inflections of the living. In his letters to Blin, Genet calls this "procedure, a refusal of natural sham," and describes its goal as making heard "what *generally* passes unperceived." When the actors walk, run, or charge across the stage, they must do it silently, the better that Genet can fill this auditory blankness with new, unnatural noises. "I should like the actors to make no sound with their feet in order to replace it, if I may suggest, by a ringing sound similar to that made by my cane one day in Maria Cesares' living room, when it struck the slender leg of a metal table." Through this relentless displacement of the natural, Genet hopes to arrive at "a new joy, a new festivity, and God knows what besides." In his letter to Abdallah, he ends by apologizing: "This is vain, clumsy advice that I offer you. No one would know how to put it into practice." But the theater, by constantly resurrecting the threat of failure—of not being able to put "it" into practice—renews the desire, in all of its fresh, insane hopefulness, of achieving an encounter with the absolute. Genet's final words to Blin are less gentle, less conciliatory: "The fact is that we still have a long way to go . . . we are in no danger of death, nor has poetry *come* the way it should."

THE MAIDS (1947)

CRITICAL COMMENTARY

Cynthia Running-Johnson (essay date May 1990)

SOURCE: Running-Johnson, Cynthia. "Genet's 'Excessive' Double: Reading *Les Bonnes* through Irigaray and Cixous." *French Review* 63, no. 6 (May 1990): 959-66.

[*In the following essay, Running-Johnson examines Genet's use of the principle of duality throughout* The Maids, *incorporating Luce Irigaray's and Hélène Cixous's feminist interpretations of the work.*]

Critics discussing Jean Genet have named the configuration of the double as one of the major elements of his work. They have examined the form as it appears in the

relationships between characters, in the dual narrative structures of his writing, and in the thematic organization of his texts, with their paradoxical pairing of good and evil, masculine and feminine, and illusion and reality. Certain writers—Jean-Paul Sartre, and critics Richard Coe and Jean-Marie Magnan—have linked the form to existential theory. Others, including Lewis Cetta and Robert Hauptman, have examined it from a more specifically psychological perspective. Sociological approaches such as that of Lucien Goldmann and the formalist perspective of Camille Naish are also inspired by the double in Genet's texts.

In investigating Genet's dualities, critics have often simplified them unnecessarily, not stopping to examine the complex workings of the double in particular texts. They have viewed the sets of oppositions in his works as evidence that strict duality is the texts' ruling principle of organization.[1] In my reading of Genet, however, words such as "strict" and "principle" do not apply. His work overflows boundaries, incarnates transgression. Genet's use of the double in fact moves past opposition and into the realm of the multiple.[2] I will examine Genet's expansion of the double in light of two critical theories that take account of such multi-valence: Hélène Cixous's concept of feminine writing and Luce Irigaray's related idea of the "feminine." Appropriately enough, Cixous has named Genet as one of a small number of French authors in whose work "femininity" is inscribed (42).

Genet's "excessive" double is particularly evident in his play, *Les Bonnes.* This play highlights the form, especially in the interrelationship of its characters, the structuring of the action, and the interplay of reality and illusion at work in the text. The duality most obvious in *Les Bonnes* is formed by the two main characters, the sisters Claire and Solange. They are the maids of Madame, who also appears on stage. During much of the play, the two sisters act out the roles of "Madame" and "Maid." In reality, Claire and Solange have had their mistress's lover, Monsieur, imprisoned through false accusatory letters that they have written to the police, and they are planning to kill off Madame. Monsieur is provisionally set free, however. In the final scene, as the maids await the discovery of their wrongdoing, Solange murders "Madame"—though here "Madame" is being played by Claire. In one interpretation of this ending,[3] Solange, in poisoning her "mistress," thereby destroys "madame-ness" and assumes the evil of both herself and her sister.

Though Madame is on stage during part of *Les Bonnes,* it is Claire and Solange who occupy most of the performance time and whose interaction constitutes the major interest of the play. The relationship between them is largely one of similarity. The sisters resemble each other in personality and function, neither one more important than the other nor basically different from her counterpart. Possible distinctions between them are blurred by the fact that, in the characters' play-within-the-play, each one is capable of acting out different roles, including (in the case of Solange) that of the other sister. The acting is imperfectly done, with the two slipping in a dizzying fashion from role to "true identity" and on to a mixture of the two modes.

Part of the resemblance between Claire and Solange consists in their shared sexual ambiguity. Through the characters' actions and words, one is led to believe that their relationship is an incestuous one. Erotic currents flow both during tender moments (such as when, after a particularly exhausting tirade by Claire, Solange calms her sister by kissing her feet and caressing her) and during violent episodes (when, for example, near the end of a round of play-acting, Solange places her hands on Claire's neck, ready to strangle her). Yet both sisters express heterosexual desire as well, in their longing to be with Monsieur, Madame's lover, and in their discussion of past and future liaisons with Mario, the milkman.

The fact that one sister is a mirror reflection of the other is constantly stated in the dialogue and underscored by the presence of mirrors, both in fact and through reference. The maids often gaze at themselves in the looking glass that is on stage. This action, frequently mentioned in the spoken text, finds itself reflected in the maids' language as they discuss the likeness between them: "Je peux me regarder dans ton visage" (36), says Claire to Solange. Even the characters' names contain reflected elements: The "Sol-" in "Solange" and the name "Claire" are both etymologically related to "light."

Claire and Solange are united not only by their physical similarity but by their feelings toward Madame: "Nous sommes enveloppées, confondues dans nos exhalaisons, dans nos fastes, dans notre haine pour vous" (26), says "Claire" to her "mistress." Yet it is their likeness which serves as the source of the venomous outbursts between them. Claire, for example, says to her sister at one point, "Je n'en peux plus de notre ressemblance" (47). During both play-acted scenes between ruling "Madame" and oppressed "Maid" and "normal" ones between the "real" Solange and Claire, the two often take turns in becoming aggressor and victim of the aggression. Moments of intense hatred are balanced, however, by the surges of incestuous tenderness mentioned earlier.

The relationship between Solange and Claire reflects in certain respects that between self and "other" in Jacques Lacan's theory of the mirror stage. Lacan's concept, as explained in this article, "Le Stade du miroir comme formateur de la fonction du Je," serves as a metaphor for the beginning of identity formation, when the (male)

child first "sees himself" as unified. This coherent image is a fiction which contrasts with the child's true incoherence—his lack of motor control—at the time (six months of age). It establishes a relation between him and his reality, permits him to begin acting in the world. The child sees not only a total image, but one that resembles the others whom he sees around him—most significantly, the mother. Simultaneously and more importantly, however, the mirror image prefigures his "destination aliénante" (95); for a fundamental division exists between the child's inner incoherence and the ideal image of unity that appears in the glass. And, although he is similar to the mother, the two are not one. Thereby is established the never-ending cycle of lacking and desire that underlies the formation of the subject in relation to the symbolic and the workings of the symbolic itself. In Lacan's model, then, the fact that the "other" resembles the self is reassuring; but at the same time, as the other is *not* the self, a sense of loss and separation also obtains.

So far in our discussion of *Les Bonnes,* this ambiguous type of relationship—the mixture of attraction to and alienation from the "other"—has been visible in the love/hate relationship between the two characters, Claire and Solange. Lacan's concept thus initially seems appropriate for discussing Genet's universe of reflections. But, as I have also indicated, the two sisters' emotions transgress the bounds of the normal. Their feelings of both like and dislike are exaggerated. The especially intense interaction between Solange and Claire—the continual reflection of one by the other—that constitutes the movement of the play is created by the *excess* of similarity between the two sisters. It is for these reasons that I propose as more appropriate theoretical constructs for discussing *Les Bonnes,* Hélène Cixous's concept of "écriture féminine" and Luce Irigaray's theory of feminine sexuality.

Cixous views feminine writing as precisely that which goes beyond the limits of oppressive hierarchical doubles, which has the potential to subvert the pairings such as active/passive and ruler/ruled that are part of the symbolic and societal realms. In her article, "Le Rire de la Méduse," Cixous describes feminine writing as that done by the "New Woman," who emerges from her traditional position as the excluded, as the "excess"-ive, and uses the power of her profuse libidinal energies to disrupt repressive and oppressive structures. Cixous suggests as a metaphor of this force the figure of the Medusa. The writhing snakes on the Medusa's head embody the movement and multiplicity of the "feminine." It is this strength and energy that appear in the continuous interaction between the maids in Genet's play.

The "excessive" nature of the exchange between Solange and Claire relates even more specifically to Luce Irigaray's notion of the "feminine." Irigaray presents her ideas as a critique of Lacan's concept of the mirror stage in her book, *Ce Sexe qui n'en est pas un*.[4] In this collection of essays and narratives, she moves beyond Lacan's idea of identity formation. His concept is based upon a male model and defines the female as more "lacking" than the male: in the woman's mirror image, the male genitals are "missing." Irigaray refuses this depiction of woman as absence. In the chapter entitled, "La 'Mécanique' des fluides," she speaks of the way in which Lacan's model wrongly subsumes woman under the heading of the male, "recourant à la nécessité de l'intrication 'des deux' dans 'le même'" (114). Irigaray sees woman as present, but suppressed in the Lacanian metaphor, in the "turbulence de mouvements" (Lacan 95) that characterizes the young child before the mirror. In his concept, woman is the "incoherence" that seeks the unified masculine image. Irigaray, on the other hand, gives value to this feminine "turbulence" and dissymmetry. She writes: "[J]amais nous ne sommes finies. . . . [N]otre plaisir est de nous mouvoir, émouvoir, sans cesse. Toujours en mouvements. . . ." (209). In her view, the emphasis in Lacan's mirror stage on the division of self and on the consequent striving for internal unity has nothing to do with the affirmation of inner plurality and constant change that characterize the "feminine."

In "Le Miroir, de l'autre côté," the first section of her book, Irigaray borrows from Lewis Carroll's *Through the Looking Glass* to describe the "feminine" as Alice's space on the "other side" of the mirror. In this space, hierarchical pairings—presence and absence, possessing and lacking, controlling and being controlled—are not valid. The relationship between two characters in this chapter, Alice and Anne, exemplifies the traits that she associates with the "feminine." The characters form a pair that cannot be reduced to the sum of its two individual parts. The boundaries between them dissolve, and they move into the realm of the multiple, where the concepts of division and addition no longer apply. She describes them as "[l]une, ou l'autre, les deux, ou aucune des deux . . . encore plus (qu')elle" (19). In *Les Bonnes*, Solange and Claire approach this kind of blending of character through their heightened similarity.[5] Face to face, one character mirrors the other, and the reflections continue *ad infinitum* to form a "feminine" space that surpasses both.

Not only is there an overabundance of similarity in the relationship between the two sisters in Genet's play; the double that they form is further expanded through the addition of a third term—their mistress. They are closely connected to this third character. The sisters most often gaze at themselves in the mirror when they are dressed as Madame. The image that they see is therefore not exactly that of one maid or the other, but of their mistress. The extent to which the identities of Claire and Madame are blended appears, for example, in the ambiguity of the subject and object pronouns in the following lines of the play. Solange is speaking to Claire as she gazes into the mirror after the first part of their "cérémonie": "Tu te regardes encore. . . . Qu'est-ce que tu as? Tu peux te ressembler maintenant" (28-29). The pronoun "te" does not have a clear referent in the first statement. It may either represent Claire or "Madame." In the last sentence, the pronoun refers more clearly to Claire, but the difference made between "you" and "yourself" in the use of the reflexive verbs accentuates the idea of play-acting, and thus reinforces the character's multiplicity of identity.

The maids' linking to Madame is effected largely by Claire's assuming the role of her mistress. This blending is underscored by the use of the word "bonne" which, appearing as the adjective "good" as well as the noun "maid," is used to describe both madame and the maids. Play on the word through frequent reference to Madame as "bonne" culminates in Solange's comment on the difficulty of being "bonne quand on est bonne" (34). The play's title is therefore connected to all three characters who make up its configurations of the double. It also comments ironically on their "bonté": that of Madame, who is in actuality the oppressor, and that of the maids, whose betrayal of Monsieur and efforts to kill their mistress hardly evidence goodness.

The constant presence—stated, acted or actual—of Madame thus serves to enlarge the dual relationship of Claire and Solange, moving it further into the polyvalent, Medusean space located beyond the mirror. Solange's remark in reference to madame's fur cape that "la doublure est déchirée" (60) describes the expansion of the double formed by Solange and Claire, as well. As doubles of Madame and of each other ("la doublure" means both "lining" and, appropriately enough for this play, "understudy"), they are thus split ("déchirée(s)") into more than two parts. But they are part of the same cloth, remaining in contact with each other. This image of diverse yet connected elements brings to mind Irigaray's representation of feminine sexuality, in which the two lips of feminine genitalia touch: "[Ce sont] deux lèvres qui s'embrassent continuellement. Ainsi, en elle, [la femme] est déjà deux—mais non divisibles en un(e)s—qui s'affectent" (24).

The web of dual relationships that connect Solange, Claire and Madame is constructed, as mentioned earlier, through intense verbal exchanges between the sisters. The directness of the communication between them, manifested in the prevalence of the pairing of first- and second-person pronouns in the dialogue ("Je te hais," "Vous nous confondez"), contributes to the extreme and bonding nature of these interactions. In the introduction to the 1963 version of the play, Genet speaks of how "tous les soirs [les bonnes] se masturbent et déchargent en vrac, l'une dans l'autre, leur haine de Madame" (8).

Indeed, the play consists of build-ups toward the moment of final "décharge," metaphorically represented by the image of the "crachat" that is frequent in *Les Bonnes.* In the first movement,[6] the maids' "ritual" ends with the warning ring of the alarm clock just at the moment when Solange (playing Claire) is about to strangle her sister (who is playing Madame). At that point the two move physically against each other and then apart. The tension has been broken without the maids having completed their "vidage." The next "scene," to the point of the telephone call from Monsieur, repeats this movement, culminating in Claire's describing the glorious future of the two sisters as criminals, and ending in the characters' momentary collapse. In the next scene, beginning with Madame's entry on stage, the action builds up to another barely-missed event: that of Madame's poisoning. The last movement results in the killing of Claire ("Madame"). The endings of the five "scenes" constitute a series of climaxes that formally mirrors Cixous's and Irigaray's definitions of a multiple, "feminine" sexuality.

In the last scene, the divisions that characterize the maids' interrelationship seem to be resolved. The two project a future in which Solange, the glorious murderess, will "contain" the poisoned Claire: "Nous sommes Mlle Solange Lemercier, . . . la fameuse criminelle" (90), intones Solange from the window to the imagined crowds below her. Claire says to her sister, "Nous irons jusqu'à la fin. Tu seras seule pour assumer nos deux existences" (91). Madame, too, is assumed by Solange, since Claire is playing the part of their mistress as she drinks the poisoned tea. The various reflections at work in *Les Bonnes* thus merge, as Solange, now a multiple form, moves beyond the reflecting mirror to the "other side." Irigaray's evocation of this space as one that literally and metaphorically permits the two labial lips to touch finds its echo in the posture of Solange that closes the play: she stands with her two wrists touching, crossed. The stage directions indicate that she stands as though handcuffed. But as evident in the maids' previous dialogue, we may see this attitude as emblematic of an ultimate freedom in glorious criminality.[7]

The play between "reality" and "illusion" at work in the maids' relationship with each other forms another duality in the text, this time on a thematic level. The "real" rapport between Solange and Claire mirrors the "acted" one in its similar movements of antagonism. The two levels remain distinguishable until near the end of the play (85), when Solange, speaking to her sister, begins to address Claire and "Madame" alternately, and finally in a manner that blends the two personas. Solange says to Claire: "Ne bougez pas! Que Madame m'écoute. Vous avez permis qu'elle s'échappe. Vous!" (85). The "elle" refers to Madame, whom Claire was unable to entice to drink the poisoned tea. Normally the "vous" is

used to mean Madame; here, however, it must refer to Claire, too, who has let Madame ("elle") escape. "Elle" and "vous" have thus become one. Finally, in the last scene, "reality" and "illusion" are definitively united through the poisoning of Claire/"Madame."

The true richness of this pairing of "truth" and "play" is effected, however, through the reference that it implicitly makes to the theatrical situation itself. Within the theatrical conceit in *Les Bonnes,* the two modes cross each other to form a multivalent combination by the end of the play. The performance of the work reflects this process. Theater blends the reality of a place—shared by spectators and actors—with the fiction of a text, and combines the physical ("real") presence of actresses and actors with the roles that they are playing. The combination of these considerations with the nature of the particular story being presented in *Les Bonnes* expands the meaning of "reality" and "illusion," both inside and outside the bounds of the play.

Genet's expansion of the double in this text is only one example of the ways in which his writing may be connected with Cixous's and Irigaray's concepts of the "feminine." A more extended discussion of his work would reveal other such meeting points: Genet's surging rhythms and series of alliterative and assonant sounds, resembling the bodily, libidinal nature of "écriture féminine" as Cixous describes it; his texts' returns and repetitions, which one may connect with the maternal, ever re-producing character of the "feminine"; and the metamorphosis of one character into another, one story line into another, one scene into another, manifesting the characteristics of acceptance and transformation that Cixous and Irigaray associate with feminine writing. This evidence of "femininity" may reflect the multiple ways in which the author himself occupied the position traditionally held by woman—the position of the excluded, the "other." He was not only homosexual (and so connected in a quite literal sense to the "feminine"), but also an outsider in his status as abandoned child, as thief and prisoner, and as author. In his writing, however, he was able to benefit from his position as "other," producing multivalent, "excessive" texts in the creative and creating space on the other side of the looking glass.

Notes

1. I have discussed this body of critical work on Genet, focusing on its reductive tendencies but also indicating its insights, in the introduction to my dissertation, "Jean Genet and Hélène Cixous: Reading Genet Through the Feminine" (Rowe, 1-28).

2. My perspective on the author complements the more recently-published Genet criticism which, influenced by post-structuralist theory, generally

takes greater account of his textual ambiguities than did previous work. See Henning, Savona, Chaudhuri and, most importantly, Derrida.

3. See, for example, McMahon (39).

4. I am indebted to Linda Gillman for her article, "The Looking Glass Through Alice," where she describes Irigaray's ideas in a way that first made them seem appropriate to my examination of *Les Bonnes.*

5. The resemblance between the sisters in *Les Bonnes* is seen by critic Joseph McMahon as a failed effort on Genet's part to establish individuation between the two (149). He also considers the author's confusion of reality and illusion as a detriment to his play (149-50). In light of Irigaray's theory, McMahon may be seen to be relegating Genet to the Lacanian region of female "lacking."

6. As Naish has also noted (134), *Les Bonnes,* though not formally divided into acts or scenes, can be seen to consist of five movements to be discussed.

7. Published versions of the play end in two slightly different ways. That published by Barbezat in 1963 has the ending just described. The 1954 version (Décines, Isère: L'Arbalète) finishes with no mention of the crossing of Solange's wrists, and includes an additional speech by Solange in which she sings the glories of life as a famous criminal in prison. The 1963 text does not end on such an obviously jubilant note, and includes in the preceding pages some reservations on the maids' part about the punishment that is surely in store for them; but the joyous anticipation of the future that is also expressed in the '63 edition seems to me to carry through to the play's last moments.

Works Cited

Bonnefoy, Claud. *Jean Genet.* Paris: Editions Universitaires, 1965.

Cetta, Lewis. *Profane Play, Ritual, and Jean Genet: A Study of His Drama.* University, AL: U of Alabama P, 1974.

Chaudhuri, Una. *No Man's Stage: A Semiotic Study of Jean Genet's Major Plays.* Ann Arbor: UMI Research Press, 1986.

Cixous, Hélène. "Le Rire de la Méduse." *L'Arc* 61 (1975): 39-54.

Coe, Richard. *The Vision of Jean Genet.* London: Peter Owen, 1968.

Derrida, Jacques. *Glas.* Paris: Galilée, 1974.

Genet, Jean. *Les Bonnes.* Décines, Isère: L'Arbalète, 1963.

Gillman, Linda. "The Looking Glass Through Alice." *Women and Literature: Gender and Literary Voice.* Ed. Janet Todd. New York: Holmes and Meier, 1980. 1:12-23.

Goldmann, Lucien. "The Theater of Genet: A Sociological Study." Trans. Pat Dreyfus. Ed. Richard Schechner. *Tulane Drama Review* 12.2 (1968): 51-61.

Hauptman, Robert. *The Pathological Vision of Jean Genet, Louis-Ferdinand Céline and Tennessee Williams.* New York: Peter Lang, 1984.

Henning, Sylvie Debevec. *Genet's Ritual Play.* Amsterdam: Rodopi BV, 1981.

Irigaray, Luce. *Ce Sexe qui n'en est pas un.* Paris: Minuit, 1977.

Lacan, Jacques. "Le Stade du miroir comme formateur de la fonction du Je." *Ecrits.* Paris: Seuil, 1966: 93-100.

Magnan, Jean-Marie. *Pour un blason de Jean Genet.* Paris: Seghers, 1966.

McMahon, Joseph. *The Imagination of Jean Genet.* New Haven: Yale UP, 1963.

Naish, Camille. *A Genetic Approach to Structures in the Work of Jean Genet.* Cambridge: Harvard UP, 1978.

Rowe, Cynthia Running. "Jean Genet and Hélène Cixous: Reading Genet Through the Feminine." Diss. U of Wisconsin-Madison, 1985.

Sartre, Jean-Paul. *Saint Genet.* Paris: Gallimard, 1952.

Savona, Jeannette. *Jean Genet.* London: Macmillan, 1983.

Thody, Philip. *Jean Genet: A Study of His Novels and Plays.* New York: Stein and Day, 1969.

Gene A. Plunka (essay date September 1991)

SOURCE: Plunka, Gene A. "A Source for Jean Genet's *Les Bonnes*: Jean Cocteau's 'Anna la bonne.'" *Notes on Contemporary Literature* 21, no. 4 (September 1991): 2-3.

[*In the following essay Plunka suggests an alternative source of inspiration for* The Maids.]

For years, critics have cited the 1933 murders committed by Christine and Léa Papin of their mistress and her daughter in Le Mans, France, as the source of Jean Genet's **Les Bonnes** (Décines: Marc Barbezat, 1947). Genet, an avid reader of *Détective*, would have acquired his information on the Papin sisters as a result of their appearance on the cover of that magazine (9 February 1933) during their notorious trial, which was widely publicized in France. Genet, however, in a 10 March

1949 interview with Hélène Tournaire in *La Bataille,* stated that he was not inspired by the trial of the Papin sisters ("Jean Genet, évadé de l'enfer cherche la clé d'un paradis défendu," 5). Yet critics persist in arguing that the Papin sisters are the precursors of Claire and Solange, Genet's protagonists.

A more likely source for **Les Bonnes** is Jean Cocteau's 1934 ballad, "Anna la bonne" (*Oeuvres complètes de Jean Cocteau,* vol. 8 [Geneva: Marguerat, 1949], 401-403). Cocteau exerted a strong influence on Genet in 1946, when Genet wrote the first draft of the play. Cocteau initially met Genet on 14 February 1943, when Genet impressed the poet-playwright by reciting the latter's poem, "Le Fils de l'air," by heart. Cocteau admired Genet's potential as a novelist and became his mentor, exhorting him to experiment with various genres, as Cocteau had done throughout his career. Cocteau immediately influenced Genet's work. Genet's first poem, "Le Condamné à mort," strongly resembled the 260-alexandrine style of Cocteau's "Plain-chant." Genet's first completed play, *Héliogabale* (no longer extant), was written for Cocteau's confidant, actor Jean Marais. Cocteau's personal secretary, Paul Morihien, signed a contract with Genet for five of his early works; in fact, Editions Paul Morihien was created for the sole purpose of publishing Gente's *oeuvre.* Meanwhile, Cocteau had been influential in reducing Genet's prison sentence for theft in 1943 by testifying in court that Genet was a future Rimbaud, one of the most promising literary talents in France. Furthermore, during 1944 and 1945, Cocteau was responsible for introducing Genet to Parisian literati, particularly Simone de Beauvoir, Jean-Paul Sartre, Louis Jouvet, and Marcel Jouhandeau. In addition, Cocteau's friends, Marc Barbezat and Roland Laudenbach, published Genet's first poems and prose. Finally, Cocteau urged Genet to tailor **Les Bonnes** to a one-act format to fit into the second half of a twin bill, accompanying Louis Jouvet's staging of Jean Giraudoux's *L'Apollon de Marsac* at the Théâtre de l'Athénée.

"Anna la bonne" is a sixty-four line *chanson parlée* about a hotel maid who poisons well-to-do guests out of jealousy. The motif is quite similar to the animosity shown by Claire and Solange towards Madame, their wealthy patronne. Madame refuses to drink the poisoned *tilleul*; instead, Claire-Madame drinks the tea, thereby canonizing Solange, who becomes the condemned murderer-saint (93). Cocteau eulogizes Mademoiselle Annabel Lee, whose spirit becomes eternal after she commits her ghastly crime (402). As she steps onto her balcony, Anna, the maid, imagines herself immortalized by princes, dukes, and counts (403). Similarly, Solange recites a speech before the imaginary masses huddled beneath her balcony (86-90). In Solange's fictitious scenario, butlers, footmen, valets, and chambermaids wear the finery of royalty to honor Mademoiselle So-

lange Lemercier (89). Mademoiselle Anna la bonne has become Mademoiselle Solange Lemercier, both maids glorified as criminal-saints. In short, Genet, when requested to appease Cocteau and Jouvet, impressed his mentors by choosing a motif that Cocteau previously had crafted in the form of a ballad twelve years earlier.

Gary Day (essay date 1994)

SOURCE: Day, Gary. "Artaud and Genet's *The Maids*: Like Father, Like Son?" In *Twentieth-Century European Drama* edited by Brian Docherty, pp. 146-61. New York: St. Martin's Press, 1994.

[In the following essay, Day considers the influence of Antonin Artaud on Genet with regard to The Maids.*]*

At least two commentators have claimed that Antonin Artaud was an important influence on Jean Genet. Ronald Harwood says this influence was 'enormous'[1] while John Russell Taylor classifies Genet as a 'follower'[2] of Artaud. Such views represent the received wisdom and, like all received wisdom, it needs to be questioned. The purpose of this essay is to examine the influence of Artaud on Genet with reference to **The Maids,**[3] and then to consider examples of other approaches to the play before finally problematising the whole question of 'influence' as a way of making sense of a text, especially when that text is a play.

Artaud's most influential text was *The Theatre and Its Double.*[4] It is a collection of essays which criticises the state of French theatre and proposes a new theatre, the Theatre of Cruelty. What Artaud disliked about his contemporary theatre was its emphasis on entertainment and its unwillingness to challenge the social and political order. He felt that it avoided danger and had too much respect for the past. It was a descriptive, narrative theatre, primarily concerned with defining character and with resolving its emotional and psychological conflicts. At times, Artaud referred to this theatre as psychological theatre, and he objected to psychology on the grounds that it made the unknown known, which resulted, though he does not explain how, in a loss of 'energy' (*TD* [*The Theatre and its Double,*] 'No More Masterpieces', p. 58), a characteristically loose term in a text brimful of poetry and gnomic utterances.

In addition to being 'psychological', French theatre was also representational, and its plots of 'money . . . social climbing [and] the pangs of love unspoilt by altruism (*TD,* 'No More Masterpieces', p. 58) were derided by Artaud as 'ridiculous imitation[s] of real life' (*TD,* 'On the Balinese Theatre', p. 42), since they turned the audience into mere 'Peeping Toms' (*TD,* 'Theatre and Cruelty', p. 84). His main objection, however, was to the dominance of dialogue. He called this a 'dictator-ship of words' (*TD,* 'Production and Metaphysics', p. 29) which pushed what he considered to be the truly theatrical elements, such as symbols, mimicry, mime and gestures, into the background. In Artaud's view, the script had to go, since it was implicated not just in the repression of everything that was properly theatrical, but also in some 'dark prodigious reality' (*TD,* 'On the Balinese Theatre', p. 43), the nature of which again remains unexplained. Words, he felt, were incapable of expressing strong or true feelings and it was for this reason that he preferred allegories or images, since by disguising what they were meant to reveal they brought more enlightenment to the mind. In this respect, Ar-taud's was an expressive, rather than representative, theatre.

The name he gave to this expressive theatre was the Theatre of Cruelty. As Artaud was at pains to point out, this had nothing to do with the cruelty individuals inflict on one another; on the contrary, it was intended to show 'the far more terrible, essential cruelty objects can practise on us. We are not free, and the sky can still fall in on our heads. And above all else, theatre is made to teach us this' (*TD,* 'No More Masterpieces', p. 10). It seems that the message of theatre is that man is in bond-age to the inanimate world, which contrasts strongly with another statement, that theatre should confront us 'with all our potential' (*TD,* 'Theatre and Cruelty', p. 66). This sort of inconsistency is not untypical of Ar-taud, and is indicative of his desire to move beyond rationality and so put himself, and us, in touch with vital forces and energies. In his theatre there is a 'reduced role given to understanding' (*TD,* 'Theatre and Cruelty', p. 66); and, while this may in some ways be welcome, in that it is an appeal to the senses and emo-tions as well as to the intellect, it is also dangerous, for it can lead to the worshipping of those vague but power-ful forces which Artaud wanted his theatre to com-municate and his audience to experience. Put like this, it is not too difficult to see his theatre as a form of fascist art which 'exalts mindlessness [and] glamourises death'[5] especially when he gives vent to such senti-ments as 'Violent . . . action is like lyricism' (*TD,* 'No More Masterpieces', p. 62).

If one meaning of cruelty relates to objects, another has to do with control; in Artaud's own words, 'cruelty means strictness, diligence, unrelenting decisiveness, ir-reversible and absolute determination' (*TD,* 'Letters of Cruelty', p. 79). Exactly what this determination and decisiveness are to be exercised on is not clear, but it seems reasonable to assume that it has to do with every aspect of a performance, since what Artaud admired in Balinese theatre was the 'loving, unerring attention to detail', the order and 'the deliberate accuracy directing everything, through which everything happens' (*TD,* 'On the Balinese Theatre', p. 46). Once more there

seems to be a contradiction between this statement, with its emphasis on control, and a view of theatre as releasing 'our repressed subconscious' (*TD,* 'Theatre and the Plague', p. 19) and liberating 'powers' which are most definitely 'dark' (*TD,* 'Theatre and the Plague', p. 21).

A third meaning of cruelty refers to creation, and here it has two aspects. The first is that it is 'a hungering after life' and the second is that it is 'a cruel need for creation', which has to be obeyed (*TD,* 'Letters of Cruelty', p. 80). Cruelty is thus both a desire and a command, something that is both within and without the self, and, as such, it overcomes the subject/object division, which has been one of the enduring problems of Western philosophy. Artaud is able to straddle this divide by altering the usual meaning of cruelty, and what he does in criticism is paralleled by what he is trying to do in the theatre, which is to liberate the sign, the sign being understood as every aspect of a produc-tion.

One of Artaud's main aims was to restore to theatre a sense of religious or mystical meaning, and one way of achieving this was by 'a return to ancient Primal Myths' (*TD,* 'The Theatre of Cruelty—Second Manifesto', p. 82). Through the poetry of stage language, that is, such things as gestures, postures, ritualistic costumes, master and puppets, all of which should overlap and intercon-nect, a kind of metaphysics is created which reveals the 'identity of the abstract and concrete' (*TD,* 'On the Ba-linese Theatre', p. 41). What Artaud means by this is that audiences become aware of the connection, or even unity, between themselves and the primal forces of nature. This is impressed upon them by the fact that the action of an Artaud play—which incidentally deals with universal cosmic themes, change, fate, creation, growth and chaos—takes place around them; the audience is in the centre and the 'play' is performed all around them in a space which admits no division between stage and auditorium. With this staging, together with the combined effect of its poetic devices, Artaud hoped to 'directly affect . . . the anatomy' (*TD,* 'No More Masterpieces', p. 61) of the audience. The language he uses to describe this process is, however, somewhat suspect—he calls it, on one occasion, a 'tangible laceration' (*TD,* 'Theatre and Cruelty', p. 65). Whether the audience is a body to be scarred by a sadistic dra-maturge, or whether it needs such violence for the mes-sage to get through, is a question that is never really answered, but it does again raise doubts about the ultimate direction of Artaud's work.

Once the audience is conscious of the primal forces of nature which, it should be stressed, are dark, and cannot be imagined 'aside from a mood of slaughter, torture and bloodshed' (*TD,* 'Theatre and the Plague', p. 21), it is then in a position to 'command . . . certain predominant powers, certain ideas governing everything; and since ideas, when they are effective generate their own energy, rediscover within [the audience's self] that energy which in the last analysis creates order and increases the value of life' (*TD,* 'No More Masterpieces', p. 60). To Artaud then, theatre is about release, a feeling of energy or even rapture which may then lead to the creation of a new order. This points to the revolutionary potential of Artaud's theatre, which is underlined by his view of stage poetry as anarchic, since it 'questions all object relationships or those between meaning and form. It [stage poetry] is also anarchic to the extent its occurrence is the result of disturbances leading us nearer to chaos' (*TD,* 'Production and Metaphysics', p. 32). Artaud's theatre is somewhere between chaos and a new order. In fact it is doubtful if we can talk about a new order, since Artaud talks mainly about *restoring* theatre to its proper state. Ultimately this means a return to its origins and, as such, betrays Artaud's romanticism. As his language makes clear, he has no real understanding of post-war France; in traditional fashion he rails against its materialism without having any real knowledge of its true material conditions. His writing is prescriptive and hyperbolic, rendering it incapable of producing a clear logical analysis either of theatre or of society. It is also full of contradictions, the most striking of which is between the obsessive desire for control and the longing to release those dark forces which Western society has, in his opinion, so long suppressed. Finding the West bankrupt, he turns to the East and proposes a theatre of ritual and ceremony, completely failing to realise that such a theatre is dependent on a certain stage of economic, political and social development which is not present in the West. Ritual and ceremony also assume shared values, and are closely akin to magic, again making them inappropriate forms for a sceptical society made up of competition.

Despite the criticisms that can be made against Artaud, there is no doubt that his ideas have had an impact on theatre practice. Certainly he was right to criticise the state of pre-war French theatre, and there is nothing wrong with his aim of appealing to the whole person or his desire to involve the audience. The Left is always going to be nervous about such approaches because it is uncomfortable both with pleasure and with the notion of a whole person, neither of which, as far as it is concerned, can exist in a capitalist society where everyone is alienated. Because of this theoretical straitjacket, supported by psychoanalysis, with its view of the divided subject, the Left tends to interpret moves towards regenerating the community and stimulating the emotions as a form of fascist aesthetics. Unfortunately Artaud's language would seem to support their case, but it is important to remember that Artaud was trying to find an alternative to what he considered to be the moral and intellectual bankruptcy of post-war

French society. The violence of his imagery is indicative of how radically he felt that society should be overhauled, and it also acts as a metaphor for a society and theatre built around more significant issues. His ideas were an expression not of bloodlust but of 'the value of life', which was intended, unlike fascism, to steer us away from 'chaos famine bloodshed, war and epidemics' (*TD,* 'No More Masterpieces', p. 60).

Turning now to Artaud's influence on Genet, the first thing to say is that it is overrated, at least where ***The Maids*** is concerned. Artaud's main idea, that 'theatre's production potential is wholly related to staging viewed as a language of movement in space' (*TD,* 'Production and Metaphysics', p. 34), has no bearing whatsoever on Genet's play. In fact, most of the techniques which Artaud suggests would constitute his Theatre of Cruelty cannot be found in ***The Maids.*** It does not call for the kind of acting area Artaud recommended, nor is it replete with shouts, groans, apparitions, surprises, symbolic gestures, masks, puppets, incantations, rare musical notes, movement exactly choreographed (as if for a dance), objects of strange proportion, or hieratic costumes. Neither is there any eye rolling, pouting lips, twitching muscles or anything else an actor may use to create the massive impersonality which Artaud so admired in Balinese Theatre. Nor is it possible to find in ***The Maids*** that fusion of sight and sound, intellect with sensibility, which again Artaud found in Eastern theatre. Nor is ***The Maids*** an example of a return to primal myths; and, while it may be possible to argue that it deals with a universal theme, here the master-servant relationship, so does any good play. Indeed, Artaud's theory may be at its weakest when talking about the subjects of his theatre, for, in one form or another, they have always been part of theatre—a farce is about chaos, though not in the same way as *King Lear,* so it is not a particularly discriminating term to use when prescribing subjects for a new kind of drama.

As has been noted, Artaud's chief objection to theatre was its subordination to the script, and for this reason alone ***The Maids*** cannot be considered a candidate for the Theatre of Cruelty. Genet's script is crucial for delineating the psychology of Madame and her maids and, to that extent, it is part of Western theatre, to which Artaud objected on the grounds that 'words are used solely to express psychological conflicts peculiar to man and his position in everyday existence' (*TD,* 'Oriental and Western Theatre', p. 65) Indeed, these words so exactly describe ***The Maids*** that it can almost be seen as a paradigm of everything Artaud loathed, rather than as exemplum of his ideas. Artaud believed that 'theatre's space is physical and plastic' (*TD,* 'Oriental and Western theatre', p. 52), not psychological, but ***The Maids*** suggests that theatre is a matter of mind rather than a radical innovation in the use of space.

If Genet's play is so different from how Artaud imagined a Theatre of Cruelty, how is it that so many critics have thought otherwise? Perhaps one answer lies in the actions of Solange and Claire, whose behaviour towards both their mistress and each other may be described as 'cruel'. 'I hate her! I loathe her!' (*M* [*The Maids*], p. 80), says Solange of Madame and, earlier in the play, she is delighted by the idea of dismembering her: 'Let's sing! . . . we'll cut her to bits by the light of the moon' (*M,* p. 65). Both maids, who incidentally are sisters, are also interested in crime.

MADAME:

Do you go to trials? You?

SOLANGE:

I read the crime news.

(*M,* p. 67)

When Madame expresses similar astonishment at Claire's knowledge of jurisprudence, Claire replies, comically 'I read *True Detective.* I know those things' (*M,* p. 73). This cruelty and interest in crime may be one reason why Genet is seen as a follower of Artaud. However, there may be some misunderstanding here, for, as we have seen, cruelty in Artaud's sense of the term, has nothing whatsoever to do with cruel behaviour. We are on safer ground with Genet's interest in crime, for Artaud believed that his theatre 'must present everything in love, crime, war and madness'. Furthermore, he wanted to centre his shows 'around famous personalities, [and] horrible crimes' (*TD,* 'Theatre and Cruelty', p. 65), and in this connection it is interesting to note that *The Maids* may very well have been based on the celebrated case of the murderous Papin sisters.[6]

Crime functions, in Artaud, like most of his 'subjects', to effect a kind of release which allows the audience to examine not just the outer world but their own inner one as well—to be facetious for a moment, it's a sort of thinking person's purge. Crime, in Genet, also produces a feeling of liberation:

CLAIRE:

We've read the story of Princess Albanarez who caused the death of her lover and her husband. . . . As she stood before the corpses, she saw only death and, off in the distance, the fleet image of herself being carried by the wind.

(*M,* p. 62)

In addition to this mystical release, crime offers a practical one, for to kill Madame would be to free the sisters from servitude. Earlier in the play Solange declares that 'I wanted to make up for the poverty of my grief by the splendour of my crime' (*M,* p. 57). Here crime is not just a compensation, it is also something dazzling and

magnificent that Solange believes will elevate her: 'The famous criminal . . . I'm not a maid. I have a noble soul' (*M,* p. 95) and turn her into an object of desire. 'The hangman's by my side! . . . He's trying to kiss me' (*M,* p. 94). This dazzling, magnificent conception of crime corresponds to Artaud's idea of grand subjects which not only reflect the unrest of the times but also tower above the utilitarian and technological considerations of contemporary society, putting us in touch with fundamental emotions. Moreover, Artaud values a theatre which intoxicates, restoring us to that sense of rapture we have lost, and this intoxication is to be found in Claire's remarks: 'We must be joyous. And sing. Let's sing. . . . Laugh!' (p. 65), as well as in Solange's 'We are beautiful, joyous, drunk and free!' (*M,* p. 100).

There is some justification, then, for seeing Genet's conception of crime as being influenced by Artaud. Crime, in *The Maids,* is surrounded by the ritual of Claire dressing up as Madame and Solange dressing up as Claire, and thus they act our their fantasies and frustrations but never quite reach the goal of their little drama, which is to kill Madame; as Solange says: 'The same thing happens every time. And it's all your fault, you're never ready. I can't finish you off' (*M,* p. 46). Ritual was important to Artaud, for he believed that it put an audience's sensibility into a more refined state of perception; but this is not the case with Solange and Claire, who use ritual as a rehearsal for real life, but they so confuse the two that they can no more kill Madame in one than in the other. Their conflation of ritual and reality is not something Artaud would approve of, for he makes a clear distinction between the two (*TD,* 'On the Balinese Theatre', p. 42).

If Solange and Claire do not have their sensibility enhanced, neither do the audience, the play remains a puzzle, an intellectual one too, which distances them even further from those forces Artaud wanted them to perceive. It is not enough, therefore, for Genet to use— even if he consciously did, Artaud's conception of crime, without also using the entire stage language which would make crime signify in an Artaudian way.

Another area where Artaud's influence maybe felt is in the attention Genet pays to gesture. For Artaud, gestures teach us 'the metaphysical identity of abstract and concrete' (*TD,* 'On the Balinese Theatre', p. 35), they bring out a truth that is otherwise hidden from us; they also, though he does not really explain how, 'keep us from chaos'. For Artaud, then, gestures are connected with revelation, true being and order, but this is not the case with Genet. In *The Maids* the gesture seems to be the only reality. Solange says she has made 'the gestures a servant must make' (*M,* p. 92), implying that, even though she is a servant, she has only been playing at being a servant; her 'real being', if she has one, is elsewhere and remains unexpressed. In Genet, therefore, the gesture points toward acting. What the audience is continually reminded of in this play, through the physical gestures as well as through the repetition of the word itself, is that what they are watching is indeed a play; gesture is both real and artificial, breaking down the distinction between those two terms, causing the same kind of confusion as there is between ritual and reality. Gesture, in *The Maids,* seems to have significance only within the paranoid psychology of the individual characters, 'The slightest gesture makes you feel like a murderer trying to slip away by the service stairway' says Claire to Solange (*M,* p. 51). The gesture has no objective, no public meaning. Furthermore, it is linked to crime, for, just as crime is a compensation for the constraints of servitude, so is gesture, elevated to drama, a compensation for a failure to act to change that situation:

SOLANGE:

She gets away and you just stand there!

CLAIRE:

What do you want to do? Make a scene . . .

SOLANGE:

Let's get on with it.

(*M,* p. 81)

Paradoxically, acting becomes a compensation for not acting. Gesture, organised into drama or fantasy, is also like crime in that it offers release or liberation. Both the sisters and Madame dream of accompanying or being accompanied by the loved one who is a criminal figure. Claire says to Solange that 'if I have to leave for Devil's Island, you'll come with me. . . . We shall be that eternal couple, Solange, the two of us, the eternal couple of the criminal and the saint' (*M,* p. 63), while Madame says that she would follow Monsieur 'to Devil's Island, to Siberia' (*M,* p. 67). In both instances crime becomes the basis of a new role, more abstract and absolute ('criminal and saint') than Solange or Claire, individualised by their names but not knowing how to play who they are.

Gesture in *The Maids,* then, has little in common with Artaud's use of the term, though both writers show an interest in it *per se.* However, there may be some common ground between them when it is remembered that Artaud reviled representational theatre, favouring an expressive one,[7] and gesture certainly functions in an expressive, non-representational way in Genet. However, to see Artaud's influence at work on Genet here may be rather misleading, for Artaud's thinking itself is a product of Symbolism and Surrealism, as indeed is Genet's, since both inherited the same cultural background. Artaud ultimately differs from the Surrealists in suggesting that symbols should have a public, as well

as private, dimension, whereas Genet shows the irreducible privacy of the gesture or symbol, and in that sense he is Surrealism's true inheritor. Despite this difference, it is interesting to note that both Artaud and Genet, in favouring a non-representational theatre, signal their lack of interest in society as it is. Artaud looks to renew it from the East and Genet from its own deviant groups. In the thirties, when Artaud was writing, societies were renewed by fascism, and, after the war, it was the turn of consumerism to obliterate those differences which Artaud found in the Balinese and Genet in his criminals and gays. The monolithic society they bemoaned and sought to change continues the same.

It should by now be fairly clear that Artaud's influence on Genet is, to say the least, problematic. It would be easier to make out a case for saying that Aristotle was more of an influence that Artaud, in that *The Maids* shows a unity of place and time, if not action, which, with its opening of the role-play between Claire and Solange, has more in common with the Elizabethan subplot, or even dumbshow, since it compresses, albeit with speech, most of the major themes and actions of the play. Aristotle's theory of catharsis is not entirely irrelevant either, for there is a sense of release at the end of the play, evident in Solange's 'we are beautiful, joyous, drunk and free!' (*M,* p. 100). However, Aristotle looked for this sense of release in the audience, and it is simply not possible to say whether this is their experience at the end of this play. In addition, Aristotle said audiences were purged, perhaps by and perhaps of, the emotions of pity and terror, but these emotions are not really relevant to *The Maids.* Furthermore, Aristotle said that this effect came about through our identification with the characters, but it is impossible to identify with characters in *The Maids* since, to a large extent, it is character which is in question. More joy may be had from seeing whether Aristotle's theory of catharsis surfaces in Artaud, as indeed it does when he writes that seeing something in a theatre so affects spectators that they are incapable of imitating what they have seen once they are outside the theatre (see 'No More Masterpieces', p. 62). This roughly corresponds to Aristotle's notion that tragedy purges us of destructive emotions and is therefore a force for good.

Of course it is possible to pursue this matter of who influenced whom further but, ultimately, that is not the point. Perhaps what we should really be asking is why is it important to understand one writer as being influenced by another? Why should we look at the history of drama, or, for that matter, literature, in such a light? What other approaches does this exclude? One approach is philosophical, for it is possible to use Hegel's model of the master-slave relationship as a way into *The Maids.*[8] This is not to say that the relationship between the maids and Madame is an illustration of Hegel's thesis, merely that there are some similarities which may increase our understanding of it. The master-slave relationship can be understood in two ways: as a relationship between two people in the evolution of self-consciousness, or as the development of self-consciousness within one person with consciousness taking the part of the master and unconsciousness the part of the slave. For Hegel, self-consciousness only exists when it is recognised as such by another self-consciousness. Self-consciousness begins when it is confronted by another self-consciousness and sees in that self-consciousness a quality of being that it has itself, yet which it is not completely aware of. Thus the first self-consciousness is not conscious, because it has not constituted the other self-consciousness as a self-consciousness, and because it has unwittingly projected onto that other self-consciousness its own qualities. Another way of saying this is that self-consciousness has discovered itself in another being and has therefore found itself as another being, which, of course, suggests that there is an 'otherness' in the heart of self-consciousness. In order to become truly self-conscious, it must destroy this otherness in the heart of itself, and it does this by constituting the other self-consciousness as a self-consciousness that is other than its own self.

It is not easy to relate this process to *The Maids* in any systematic way. To begin with we need to distinguish between Solange and Claire acting out their relationship with Madame, and their actual relationship with her. The basic difference between the two is that, in the former, Solange is able to rebel against her mistress and say what she thinks of her:

SOLANGE:

> Yes, my proud beauty. You think you can always do just as you like. You think you can deprive me forever of the beauty of the sty, that you can choose your perfumes and powders, your nail polish and silk and velvet and lace and deprive me of them? . . . Solange says: to hell with you!
>
> (*M,* p. 44)

whereas in the latter she's grateful and deferential: 'Oh! Madame . . . never. . . . Madame is "too kind"' (*M,* p. 71). However, fantasy and reality do overlap, for, just as Solange attempts to control Claire, the fantasy Madame, so she endeavours to guide and advise the real Madame: 'Madame mustn't get such ideas into her head. You must rest' (*M,* p. 68). There are other blurred boundaries too, and, together, they suggest that Madame's existence in the play, even when she is on stage, is in fact no more than the maids' mental projection. If this is the case, then she is not encountered as a self-consciousness who can confer recognition on the self-consciousness of Claire and Solange. Indeed, Madame is presented by Genet as being little more than a collection of clothes and jewelry, a costume rather than a consciousness. As a result she cannot, as

Madame, authenticate Claire and Solange as maids. 'I want', says Solange at one point, 'to be a real maid' (*M,* p. 82). It is because they are not maids that they are dissatisfied; they are not dissatisfied because they are maids. Because of this situation, they are condemned to see in Madame their own deepest desires, without actually being conscious that that is what they are doing. As Madame, Claire asserts that 'Monsieur will be led from prison to prison, perhaps even to Devil's Island, where I, his mistress, mad with grief, shall follow him' (*M,* p. 39) and, as herself, she declares to Solange that 'if I have to leave for Devil's Island, you'll come with me'. In both cases there is a yearning to escape into degradation through crime. Because the maids see themselves in Madame without recognising themselves as such, they cannot be constituted as self-consciousness; a problem aggravated by the fact that, since Madame herself is encountered more as an object than a self-consciousness, she cannot underwrite Claire and Solange's existence. Consequently, the maids have no full self-consciousness nor, it follows, knowledge of themselves, and that perhaps explains their inconsistencies, repetitions and fractured, often illogical, conversations.

Even if Madame were a self-consciousness it would be doubtful whether either she or her maids would achieve that state of self-possession which is implied in Hegel's view of full self-consciousness. The reason for this is that certain *social* requirements are needed for the complete development of self-consciousness, and they are freedom, work and discipline, the latter referring to how the self must submit to certain external rules. Hegel argues that these can only be found in the right measure in a free society, but that if the social order is one of domination and submission, as it is in *The Maids,* then the experience of self-consciousness is divided between the master and the slave. This takes the form of the self being aware of its divided nature, experiencing one part of itself as changing and the other as unchanging. Certainly the sisters have an unchanging part, which Claire identifies as 'the eternal couple of the criminal and the saint' (*M,* p. 63), and their changing part has to do with their constant role-swapping, 'it's my turn to be Madame' (*M,* p. 81) which constitutes both their fantasy and their reality. Madame, too, has a dual view of herself: first of all as Madame, with all her changing moods, and then as the loyal, steadfast lover of Monsieur. Given their internal divisions, neither Madame nor the maids can recognise one another as a fully developed self-consciousness. Hegel suggests a number of ways of compensating for this condition, and the one that most approximates to Claire and Solange is a withdrawal inwards, which corresponds to the sisters' almost psychotic—in the clinical sense of that term—world. It is important to note, in this context, how Solange incorporates Claire, through her death. 'I call upon you to represent me', Claire says to Solange (*M,*

p. 97). In this way, Claire dies but remains alive; it is the ultimate movement inwards.

Indeed, a case can be made for saying that what happens in ***The Maids*** is an internalisation of an external conflict, and that that conflict only partly concerns Madame, for it takes place mainly between the two sisters. 'I hate you', says Claire to Solange (***M,*** p. 55). It is difficult to pinpoint all the causes of this conflict, but one lies in the sisters being so alike: 'I can't stand our being so alike', says Solange (***M,*** p. 60), and Claire adds 'I'm sick of seeing my image thrown back at me by a mirror, like a bad smell. You're my bad smell' (***M,*** p. 61). One way of avoiding this sameness is for one of them to pretend she is Madame, and thus the sisters' play is a response not so much to their relationship with Madame as to the mirror image they have of each other. Their relationship is a constant struggle for mastery and, even though it is Claire who dies, she is in the dominant position, ordering Solange to command her to drink the poisoned tea.

CLAIRE:

> (*holding her by the wrists*) You bitch! Repeat. Madame must have her tea.

SOLANGE:

> Madame will have her tea.

> (***M,*** p. 98)

There are two possible resolutions to this problem. The first has already been mentioned, which is to become that eternal couple, the saint an the criminal; this offers an escape, from the facticity of being, into the absolute. The second is to contain the other within the self, 'I myself am both the thief and his slavish shadow', cries Solange (***M,*** p. 88). The thief is obviously the criminal of the eternal couple, but the 'slavish shadow' is more ambiguous. It could refer to the saint, since the saint, by being associated with the criminal, is his shadow; but shadow also refers to darkness, which is the dwelling place of maids and servants generally, and it is described as dangerous (***M,*** p. 45). However we choose to interpret this, though, one thing is a clear: Solange's cry represents a desire to be double, and this can only be achieved by incorporating the other, Claire, who is double to the extent that she is the same as Solange. To mention the double echoes the title of Artaud's work *The Theatre and its Double,* but he never quite makes clear what this mysterious double is; actor, costume, or audience, it could be any or all of these or something else entirely. Solange's incorporation of Claire also resolves the relationship with Madame, for Claire does not die as Claire but as Madame, and in the guise of Madame she takes upon herself all the new and imagined slights that the maids have suffered. To that extent she is also a sacrificial figure: her death allows

Solange to be Madame, so that the 'real' one will no longer be able to humiliate her. Literally, at the end of the play, acting is equated with death and theatre is consumed in the moment it is performed.

If the relationship between Madame and her maids benefits from a Hegelian approach, so would the relationship between the maids benefit from a psychoanalytic one.[9] The fact that they see in one another a mirror image encourages the critic to examine their relationship in terms of Lacan's account of the mirror stage. This is an attempt to answer the question as to why the paranoid attacks himself in the image of another. Lacan's view is that he projects onto another something unacceptable in himself, and, according to Freud, what that unacceptable thing is, is homosexuality. Here it is important to remember that Genet was a homosexual and that the parts of ***The Maids*** are to be played by men. ***The Maids*** would seem to offer support for such a view, not just because of the mirror-like relationship between Claire and Solange, but also because of their paranoia, 'Listen, we're being spied on', says Claire (***M,*** p. 83), and Solange adds, 'It's God who's listening to us' (***M,*** p. 84); and because of the erotic way in which they perceive each other: Claire says to Solange that she has lovely hair (***M,*** p. 64), while Solange tells Claire that she has a lovely throat (***M,*** p. 85). If ***The Maids*** is about paranoia and therefore homosexuality, it is important not to forget the mechanism of paranoia: projection—for that, in a sense, is what constitutes the theatrical experience. Literally, the actor has to project him/herself into the character and then project that character to an audience. The audience, too, have to project themselves into what is happening on stage. So it is clear that projection is an essential part of theatre, which, because of this, is always, potentially, paranoia.

Artaud's strictures on theatre as psychology would discourage both a philosophical and psychoanalytic approach to Genet's ***The Maids,*** despite the fact that the play deals with a repressed force, which is what Artaud expects theatre to do. Hegel's master-slave relationship is essentially dramatic, as is the mirror stage with all its ramifications. Both philosophy and psychoanalysis not only offer readings of the play: they, as part of the culture, may also be seen as an influence upon it; an influence, moreover, incompatible with the views of Artaud. What still remains to be explained is why critics persist in explaining one author in terms of another. Perhaps there is something patriarchal about it; an influence being tantamount to a form of paternity, which names an legitimises a work. It is a search for origins and therefore stability, but what happens in the process is that the work loses some of its power; by being placed in a tradition, continuity and hierarchy are stressed at the expense of the real nature of the work. This is especially true of drama, which for too long has been regarded as a sub-species of literature. By being assimilated into literature, drama is seen as something written rather than something that is performed. This has the effect of turning drama into an antiseptic activity for a cultural elite who, by approaching it as a text within literary history, rob it of its power to disturb them.

The radical potential of Genet's **The Maids** lies not in its being influenced by Artaud (which in any case is questionable) but in its excessive concern with role-playing; the maids are sisters, mother and daughter, lovers, would-be murderers and a host of other things as well. These multiple roles challenge conventional ideas of character, nowhere more so than in Solange's long speeches at the end which, among other things, point forward to the breakdown of Cartesian rationalism found in Lucky's speech in Samuel Beckett's *Waiting for Godot*. The ceaseless changing of roles suggests a kind of freedom; we live in a society where we move, almost unconsciously, from one role to another; **The Maids** celebrates that fact and shows how we can manipulate it. However, the radical potential of the script is curtailed by its being framed within a realistic set, and by the fact that it is tied to private obsessions, which makes the play inward rather than outward-looking. This, however, is to see **The Maids** as a text, but it is not a text in the same way that a novel is; this is a text that has to be performed and it is through its productions that **The Maids** names itself again and again, each time as something different, not at all like the dutiful son that critics would like it to be.

Notes

1. R. Harwood, *All the World's a Stage* (London: Methuen, 1984) p. 287.

2. J. Russell Taylor, *Dictionary of the Theatre* (London and New York: Penguin, 1984) p. 113.

3. J. Genet, *The Maids and Deathwatch,* trans. B. Frechtman (London and Boston: Faber and Faber, 1989). All quotations are from this edition, with page references given in the main body of the essay as '(*M,* p.)'.

4. A. Artaud, *The Theatre and its Double,* trans. V. Corti (London: John Calder, 1985). All quotations from Artaud are from this edition, with the name of the essay and page references given in the main body of the text as '(*TD,* title, p.)'.

5. S. Sontag 'Fascinating Fascism', in *A Susan Sontag Reader* (London and New York: Penguin, 1987) pp. 305-25 and p. 316.

6. See B. Benvenuto and R. Kennedy, *The Works of Jacques Lacan* (London: Free Association Books, 1986) p. 33.

7. Although Artaud rejected a representational theatre, it is important to remember that he was talking about a particular kind of representational theatre. Ultimately, his view that theatre should reconcile us to the universe implies some form of representation, as indeed does his view that theatre should reveal repressed forces and energies. This is not, as it at first seems, a theory of expression, which has to do with the unique and personal, for the forces and energies he is talking about are profoundly impersonal.

8. For a useful introduction to Hegel's theories, see R. Norman, *Hegel's Phenomenology: A Philosophical Introduction* (Brighton: Sussex University Press, 1976).

9. For a more detailed view of these ideas, together with Hegel's 'influence' on Lacan, see W. Ver Eecke, 'Hegel as Lacan's Source for Necessity in Psychoanalytic Theory', in J. H. Smith and W. Kerrigan (eds), *Interpreting Lacan* (New York: Vail Ballou Press, 1983) pp. 113-39.

Brian Gordon Kennelly (essay date spring 1996)

SOURCE: Kennelly, Brian Gordon. "The Unknown Role of Madame in Genet's *Les Bonnes.*" *Romance Notes* 36, no. 3 (spring 1996): 243-52.

[*In the following essay, Kennelly examines the role of Madame in* The Maids, *specifically noting discrepancies in the text and Madame's differing character in two versions of the drama.*]

> "«Madame», il ne faut pas l'outrer dans la caricature. Elle ne sait pas jusqu'à quel point elle est bête, à quel point elle joue un rôle, mais quelle actrice le sait davantage, même quand elle se torche le cul?"
>
> "Comment jouer *Les Bonnes*"

The text of Jean Genet's **Les Bonnes** that is taught and performed most regularly is the shorter of the two versions[1] of the play published side by side by Jean-Jacques Pauvert in 1954. It is considered the third and final acting script used in the first production of the play. Material from the earlier versions of the play, unused by Louis Jouvet who first directed it at the Théâtre de l'Athénée in Paris in 1947, went unperformed and is, some fifty years after the premiere of **Les Bonnes,** essentially unknown. The first version of the play dates from 1943 and includes the roles of the milkman Mario and Monsieur in addition to those of the sister-maids Claire, Solange, and their mistress, Madame. It is jealously guarded by a private collector.[2] The longer version of the play published by Pauvert is considered the second acting script used during rehearsals for Jouvet's production.

Housed at the Bibliothèque de l'Arsenal in Paris, the Jouvet typescripts of the play shed light on how Genet's first performed drama evolved during rehearsals and especially on how Genet earlier conceived of the ending to his play. Catalogued with the call number LJMS 22, there are seven available for consultation, the eighth being only a recent acquisition.[3] They include: the second version of the play, which is actually the first version received by Jouvet (typescript one); the second-last version of the play (typescript two); the first "Relevé de la mise en scène" of Marthe Herlin (typescript three); a version incorporating those changes noted in typescripts two and three (typescript four); the second "Relevé de la mise en scène" of Marthe Herlin (typescript four *bis*); the "livre de conduite" of the stage manager René Besson (typescript five); the text of the prompter Suzanne Pougaud (typescript six); and the last uncorrected text prepared for the staging of **Les Bonnes** (unnumbered). These typescripts—in particular typescripts two and three—contain material not published by Pauvert and thus represent two different unpublished and unperformed stages of the play.[4]

In his *From Writer to Reader: Studies in Editorial Method,* Philip Gaskell points out that any work of literature intended to be communicated primarily by spoken performance rather than by a written text characteristically goes through three textual stages. (245) The first might be called the "script," or the written version of what was originally intended to be "said." The second could be considered the "performance text," or what was actually said in one or more performances. The third, one could call the "reading text," or the version subsequently published by the author or the author's publisher as a record of what might have or what should have been said.[5] Of the unpublished sequences of the Jouvet typescripts of **Les Bonnes,** or the "scripts" of the play—the written version of what was originally intended to be *said*—, a sequence at the end of the third typescript of the play in which Madame returns (unnoticed by Solange and Claire?) to witness their/her demise and that shows how the play once ended has to-date been ignored by critics. Just as her two maids role-play in her absence without her knowledge (they think), in one of these sequences (unknown to Claire and Solange) Madame appears to take on a role herself: as gatekeeper to the crowds, as witness, and guarantor of their/her suicide/murder. "Que personne n'approche d'elles," she warns the crowds that she imagines are gathering to witness the climax to Solange and Claire's ritual of hatred, "Restez. Je vous redirai tous les détails." (footnote on back of page 59 73) Because of cuts made during rehearsals, these details remained, as they still do today, untold, "unsaid," as Madame's final role—like those of Monsieur and Mario—was eliminated from the play.[6] It is our intention to give Madame her say at last.

Marcel Oddon has carefully detailed in his "Essai d'analyse de l'œuvre dramatique" how in the published versions of **Les Bonnes,** the second person singular and plural personal pronouns "tu" and "vous" measure the confusion of roles, indeed of the identities of Solange and Claire—where their identity is in large part determined by role. One of the values of the Jouvet typescripts of the play is that they further demonstrate the absolute interchangeability of Solange and Claire and thus amply justify what is to be Madame's confusion of her two maids. On page ~~52~~ 66 of the third typescript, for example, second person singular personal pronouns become second person plural pronouns, at the same time that "Claire" becomes "Madame":

CLAIRE:

> Je suis malade . . .

SOLANGE:

> On ~~te~~ vous soignera là-bas.

CLAIRE:

> Je suis malade . . . je . . . je vais mourir (*elle semble avoir des nausées*).

SOLANGE:

> (*elle s'approche et, avec compassion*)
>
> Vraiment? ~~Tu es~~ Vous êtes très mal? ~~Claire~~ Madame ~~tu es~~ vous êtes vraiment très mal?

CLAIRE:

> Je suis au bord . . .

SOLANGE:

> Pas ici, ~~Claire, retiens—toi~~ retenez-vous. (*Elle la soutient*) Pas ici, je ~~t'~~ vous en prie. ~~Viens~~ Venez. ~~Appuie-toi~~ Appuyez-vous sur moi. Là. Marche doucement [. . .]

Similarly, on page 9 of the first typescript, the words of Claire become those of Solange and then those of Claire again. Likewise, Solange's words become Claire's and then those of Solange again:

CLAIRE:

> (*ironique*)
>
> [. . .] Sans moi, sans ma lettre de dénonciation tu n'aurais pas eu ce spectacle: l'amant avec les menottes et Madame en larmes.

~~CLAIRE SOLANGE~~ CLAIRE:

> Elle peut en mourir. Ce matin elle ne tenait plus debout.

~~SOLANGE CLAIRE~~ SOLANGE:

> Tant mieux. Qu'elle en claque! Et que j'hérite, à la fin! Ne plus remettre les pieds dans cette mansarde sordide, entre ces imbéciles, entre cette cuisinière et ce valet de chambre.

Claire Solange CLAIRE:

Moi je l'aimais notre mansarde.

Solange Claire SOLANGE:

Ne t'attendris pas sur elle. Et surtout pour me contredire. Moi qui la hais, je la vois telle qu'elle est, sordide et nue. Dépouillée. Mais quoi, nous sommes des pouilleuses.

And in the fourth typescript, on pages 31 and 32, Solange's words become Claire's words:

CLAIRE:

Le gardénal! Ne fais pas cette tête [. . .] (*En riant, Solange ferme la fenêtre.*) L'assassinat est une chose . . . inénarrable!

SOLANGE:

Chantons!

CLAIRE:

Nous l'emporterons dans un bois.

SOLANGE:

Et sous les sapins, au clair de lune.

CLAIRE:

Nous la découperons en morceaux.

SOLANGE:

Nous chanterons! [. . .]

Besides the changes of pronouns and names that are clearly evident in the typescripts and that show how Claire and Solange were, in *Genet*'s mind at least, interchangeable while he was still writing the play, the combination of a second person singular pronoun with a second person plural verb that Genet uses in the definitive published version of his play (or what we will call the "dysfunctional" verb form of this version)[7] underlines *Madame*'s confusion of her two maids. Because such a combination is twice rehearsed in the Jouvet typescripts, it also merits attention. Madame's "Et vous ne disiez rien! Une voiture. Solange, vite, vite, une voiture. Mais dépêchez-toi. (*Le lapsus est supposé.*) Cours, voyons. (*Elle pousse Solange hors de la chambre.*)" from the definitive published version of the play (165) is echoed in an unpublished sequence from the typescripts where Solange is playing Claire and where Claire is playing Madame. This sequence, changed in the definitive edition of the play to

SOLANGE:

Madame me comprend à merveille. Madame me devine.

CLAIRE:

Tu sens approcher l'instant où tu ne seras plus la bonne. Tu vas te venger. Tu t'apprêtes? Tu aiguises tes ongles? La haine te réveille? Claire n'oublie pas. Claire, tu m'écoutes? Mais Claire, tu ne m'écoutes pas?

(143-4)

contains another dysfunctional verb form, "tu aiguisez," on page 7*bis* of the second typescript:

SOLANGE:

Madame me comprend à merveille. Madame me devine.

CLAIRE:

. . . m'approcher l'instant où cessent d'être une bonne tu deviens la vengeance elle-même. Tu t'apprêtes? Tu aiguisez tes ongles. La haine te réveille? [. . .][8]

Likewise, a sequence published in the definitive edition of *Les Bonnes* as

SOLANGE:

Je vous écoute.

CLAIRE: (*elle hurle*)

C'est grâce à moi que tu es, et tu me nargues! Tu ne peux savoir comme il est pénible d'être Madame, Claire, d'être le prétexte à vos simagrées! Il me suffirait de si peu et tu n'existerais plus. Mais je suis bonne, mais je suis belle et je te défie. Mon désespoir d'amante m'embellit encore!

(144)

retains the dysfunctional form of the verb "narguer" on page 8 of the second typescript:

SOLANGE:

Je vous écoute.

CLAIRE: (*elle hurle*)

Tu existes grâce à moi. Chacun de mes gestes t'accomplit. Je porte la responsabilité de ton existence. Et tu me narguez. Claire, si tu pouvais savoir comme c'est pénible d'être Madame [. . .][9]

By cutting these two dysfunctional verb forms from the play, Genet must have felt that he could draw attention in the definitive published version of *Les Bonnes* to the one moment when the "real" Madame couples a second person singular pronoun with a second person plural verb. Had he retained the additional two dysfunctional verb forms, he would have reduced the dramatic impact of Madame's "dépêchez-toi." Moreover, because neither the transitional verb "aiguiser" nor "narguer" are reflexive, to have "normalized" their verb form was to rely only on the verb meaning "to hurry up" to dramatize how Madame, in her haste to rejoin Monsieur at the *Bilboquet,* gets ahead of herself and fuses her two maids as one before the gardenal is consumed.

If changes of pronouns and names show the interchange-ability of the two maids for Genet and changes in verb form anticipate the fusion of the two maids by Madame, in *all* versions of the play (including the published versions) Claire (playing "Claire")'s promise to Solange (playing "Solange") that "Ce soir, Madame assistera à notre confusion" (156) remains unchanged. As a result, it leaves a fundamental and to-date overlooked question unresolved in the play: *when* or *where* in the play does this occur?

There is certainly little doubt that Madame confuses or interchanges her two domestics. Besides the dysfunc-tional "dépêchez-toi" to Solange that we have noted, she slips, for example, from a second person singular to a second person plural pronoun when she donates a dress to Claire. "Ma belle «Fascination»", she says, "La plus belle. Pauvre belle. C'est Lanvin qui l'avait dess-inée pour moi. Spécialement. Tiens! Je *vous* la donne. Je *t'*en fais cadeau, Claire!" Her seemingly out-of-place "vous" is confirmed when Claire reacts by asking: "Madame *me* la donne vraiment?" (163, emphasis added) Furthermore, when Madame leaves the room, Claire bitterly remarks: "Madame nous a vêtues comme des princesses. Madame a soigné Claire ou Solange, car Madame nous confondait toujours" (167).

But if Madame has confused her two maids in the past and continues to do so, is she ever present to witness the role-playing, or confusion, of her two maids—a confusion in which she herself is indicted?

By the end of the final tirade by "Solange," when So-lange and Claire become—or "lose" themselves as—the singular "mademoiselle Solange Lemercier," "la femme Lemercier," "la Lemercier," "la fameuse criminelle" (175), Madame has, one assumes, long since left in a taxi to rejoin the recently liberated Monsieur at the *Bil-boquet* and thus cannot possibly witness this so-called confusion of her two maids. During the tirade of "So-lange," just as after it when the gardenal is consumed, Madame is surely at the *Bilboquet* plotting with Monsieur over how best to punish or avenge her maids, as she will have learned from him of their role in the handwritten denunciation of him to the police.

This is at least what the published versions of **Les Bonnes** lead us to assume. To fully understand Claire (playing "Claire")'s promise that Madame *will* witness, or be present for the confusion that we have described, we must turn to the third typescript of the play where Madame does indeed witness the confusion of her two maids with herself.

In this third typescript, after Solange's final tirade, in the final sequence of role-playing between the two maids Madame reappears and thus shows how radically different an ending Genet had envisioned for his play. On page ~~57~~ 71, after Claire (or Claire as "Madame") warns, "Solange, tu me garderas en toi. Fais bien atten-tion," Genet writes in blue ink: "(*Madame apparaît à la porte par où elle est sortie. Elle reste immobile. Très visible du public.*)" On an unnumbered page that is inserted between page ~~57~~ 71 and page ~~58~~ 72 after Claire (still as "Madame") points out, "Nous sommes au bord. Solange, il y a une heure que les fenêtres sont ouvertes et que les voisins sont attentifs. Nous ne pouvons plus reculer," again in blue ink Genet adds the stage direc-tion: "(*Madame fait le geste d'arrêter une foule de gens qui voulaient assister au spectacle.*)" With Madame's presence apparently unnoticed by her two maids, So-lange then asks "Alors?", Claire reacts "Nous irons jusqu'à la fin", and Solange declares "Ils vont venir . . ." At this point in the drama Genet crosses out in pencil Madame's imperative and noble: "Que personne n'approche. J'ai seule le droit d'être présente. N'entrez pas" and replaces it with Madame's more reasoned "Que personne n'approche. Moi-même je m'aventure trop près. N'entrez pas. Elles ont encore besoin de beau-coup de solitude [. . .] Priez qu'elles réussissent." On the back of the page that is inserted between page ~~57~~ 71 and ~~58~~ 72 of this same typescript, Madame continues: "Elles m'arrachent d'elles-mêmes. Elles m'extirpent de leurs gestes. Elles s'élèvent. Je n'ai plus peur pour elles . . ." Finally, on page ~~59~~ 73 before Claire (playing "Madame") authorizes her sister to continue, Genet footnotes: "MADAME (*entrant dans la pièce à reculer*): Que personne n'approche d'elles. Regardez-les de loin mais n'approchez pas [encore] d'elles. Restez où vous êtes. Restez. Je vous ~~réciterai~~ redirai tous les détails. Priez ensemble!"[10]

In this unperformed early version of the play, Solange (still playing "Claire"?) is wrong, then, in assuming that the real Madame is at this time celebrating Monsieur's release at the *Bilboquet* and in believing that Madame has been permitted to escape in a taxi.[11] Rather than celebrate the liberation of Monsieur, as she is assumed to in the later versions of the play, in this typescript version Madame plays the role of gatekeeper to the crowds, guarantor of the suicide of her maid/s and the end of their ceremony of hatred. In playing this role, she moreover takes on one final role: as spokesperson, witness, reporter—possibly even as manipulator—of the truth.

Her sudden return to witness the demise of her maids raises troubling questions, however: Has she abandoned Monsieur at the *Bilboquet*? Was her excitement at learn-ing that he had telephoned during her absence merely play-acting on her part too, so that she could convince her maids that it was safe for them to continue their ritual to its end for once and for all? Did she plan her return in order to witness it? Or did she never really take the taxi to the *Bilboquet* at all? In her final role as witness to a tragedy, does she really enjoy alone the spectacle of the true confusion of roles that goes beyond Claire (as "Madame") drinking the gardenal and killing herself, beyond Solange as surviving maid carrying her sister within her to prison, beyond her being the unsuspecting dupe of her domestics to where *they* are the duped, the pawns, and *Madame* the true queen?

Perhaps Genet felt that the questions raised by Madame's return at the end of the play were so numerous that they warranted his elimination of her final and seemingly ambiguous role from the play altogether. Whatever the reason, he seems to have overlooked Claire (playing "Claire")'s promise of Madame's return. A footnote that he added to the definitive version of *Les Bonnes* suggests that he might have been preoccupied with the large number of cuts that he had already made. In this footnote he writes:

> Il est possible que la pièce paraisse réduite à un squelette de pièce. En effet, tout y est trop vite dit, et trop explicite, je suggère donc que les metteurs en scène éventuels remplacent les expressions trop précises, celles qui rendent la situation trop explicite par d'autres plus ambiguës. Que les comédiennes jouent. Excessivement.

(158)

Future directors hoping to flesh out the version of *Les Bonnes* that Genet left us with before his death in 1986 might be wise not to replace Genet's words with their *own* but rather to add to *Genet*'s words, or those he originally gave to Madame at the end of the play. Should they in such a way restore Madame's final role, they would revest this play so intensely concerned with its own theatricality with all of its earlier ambiguity and that, some twenty years after its first performance when preparing his play for publication in his complete works, Genet appears to have yearned for once more. After all, if Madame's return is anticipated, as Claire (playing "Claire")'s promise would suggest, the two maids surely *expect* her to spy on them. By pretending not to notice her when she reappears at the doorway, they (as Madame thinks only she does) most surely push their own role-playing to its excessive limit.[12]

Notes

1. The second version was performed at the Théâtre de la Hachette in 1954.

2. Actress Monique Mélinand, who played Solange in Jouvet's production of *Les Bonnes,* confirms this in an interview with Alain Ollivier. After he tells her "Je crois qu'il y avait trois versions: un premier manuscrit dont le propriétaire ne veut pas qu'il soit mis à la disposition de quiconque, et dans ce premier manuscrit, on pouvait lire le rôle de Monsieur et celui du laitier Mario," Mélinand responds: "Oui, je m'en souviens très bien. Je sais que c'est certainement Jouvet qui a convaincu Genet de supprimer le rôle de Monsieur et celui du laitier, Mario." ("Les Premières 'Bonnes'" 61) However, in his "Jean Genet's Mentor: Jean Cocteau," Gene Plunka notes that the first version included eight characters instead of five. (54)

3. Claire Saint-Léon refers to the original five in "*Les Bonnes* de Jean Genet: Quelle version faut-il jouer?" A description of the eighth typescript can be found in the *Revue de la Bibliothèque Nationale* (49): 63. For more on Jouvet's production of the play, see: Bettina Liebowitz Knapp's *Louis Jouvet: Man of the Theatre* (New York: Columbia University Press, 1957); Alain Ollivier's "Les Premières 'Bonnes': Entretiens d'Alain Ollivier avec Monique Mélinand et Yvette Étiévant" (*Alternatives théâtrales* 43): 60-66; Richard C. and Suzanne A. Webb's *Jean Genet and His Critics: An Annotated Bibliography, 1943-1980* (Metuchen: The Scarecrow Press, 1982); and Edmund White's *Genet: A Biography* (New York: Knopf, 1993).

4. Typescript 3 is a carbon copy of typescript 2, but the annotated changes made in one were not always duplicated in the other. Where in typescript 2 (the original) there is nothing marked, for example, in typescript 3 (the carbon copy) there is an annotation in ink by Genet on the back of page 4̶8̶ 62. Moreover, in typescript 2 (the original) there is again nothing marked, where in typescript 3 (the carbon copy) there is an annotation in pencil on the back of an unnumbered page that is stuck between pages 5̶7̶ 71 and 5̶8̶ 72.

5. As summarized by T. H. Howard-Hill in his "Playwrights' Intentions and the Editing of Plays" and published in the fourth volume of *Text. Transactions of the Society for Textual Scholarship* (New York: AMS Press, 1988): 274.

6. How much was Genet influenced by Jouvet? While to consider the question of whether *Les Bonnes*—as we know the play—was more Jouvet's than Genet's play is beyond the scope of this article (note), it is certainly a relevant question worth further consideration. Actress Yvette Étiévant, who played Claire in Jouvet's production notes that Genet (then unknown as a dramatist) was at the same time most happy to have his play produced by the famous director but also found much of what Jouvet made of the play—or turned the play into—disagreeable. She tells Ollivier: "[Genet] avait écrit une pièce en trois actes enfin, je crois que c'était trois actes, en tout cas, quelque chose de vraiment tout à fait différent [. . .] je

crois qu'il n'était pas content. Il n'avait pas vu ça comme ça [. . .] je crois qu'il n'était pas content et en même temps, c'était compliqué. En même temps, il était aussi fasciné par Jouvet. Et puis Jouvet avait une autorité formidable . . . alors il était persuadé. Mais je n'ai jamais eu le sentiment d'un vrai accord, non jamais." ("Les Premières 'Bonnes'" 66)

7. Here, we refer to the definitive version published in his complete works, for all dysfunctional verb forms have been cut from both versions of the play published in the Pauvert edition of *Les Bonnes.*

8. Within this same typescript Claire (playing "Madame")'s words are changed by hand to: "Tu sens approcher l'instant où tu ne seras plus la bonne. Tu vas te venger. Tu t'apprêtes? Tu aiguisez tes ongles? La haine te réveille?"

9. Like the previously cited sequence, however, it also undergoes a handwritten change by Genet. Claire's words thus shorten to: "Et tu me narguez. Claire, si tu pouvais savoir comme c'est pénible d'être Madame [. . .]"

10. The text of the footnote is on the back of page 59 73. Besides the sequences by Madame that we have noted, on page 59 73 after Claire's prompting of Solange ("Madame prendra son tilleul"), Genet pencils in the words of the "real" Madame: "Ni pour moi-même."

11. She has told Claire (playing "Madame"—but who tries to drop this role and be herself again): "Ne bougez pas! Que Madame m'écoute. Vous avez permis qu'elle s'échappe. Vous! Ah! quel dommage que je ne puisse lui dire toute ma haine! que je ne puisse lui raconter toutes nos grimaces. Mais, toi si lâche, si sotte, tu l'as laissée s'enfuir. En ce moment, elle sable le champagne!" (172)

12. An earlier version of this paper was presented at the 1995 NEMLA conference in Boston in the session entitled "The Silence of the Text: the 'Unsaid.'"

Works Cited

"Les Acquisitions présentées par les conservateurs de la Bibliothèque Nationale: Département des Arts et du Spectacle." *Revue de la Bibliothèque Nationale* 47 (1993): 61-64.

Gaskell, Philip. *From Writer to Reader: Studies in Editorial Method.* Oxford: Clarendon Press, 1978.

Genet, Jean. *Les Bonnes.* Sceaux: Pauvert, 1954.

———. *Les Bonnes.* Fonds Jouvet. Bibliothèque de l'Arsenal, Paris.

———. "Les Bonnes." *Œuvres complètes.* Tome IV. Paris: Gallimard, 1968. 137-76.

———. "Comment jouer *Les Bonnes.*" *Œuvres complètes.* Tome IV. Paris: Gallimard, 1968. 265-70.

Howard-Hill, T. H. "Playwrights' Intentions and the Editing of Plays." *Text: Transactions of the Society for Textual Scholarship.* Vol. 4. Ed. D. C. Greetham & W. Speed Hill. New York: AMS Press, 1988. 269-78.

Oddon, Marcel. "Essai d'analyse de l'œuvre dramatique." *Les Voies de la création dramatique.* Tome IV. Paris: Éditions du Centre National de la Recherche Scientifique, 1975. 111-42.

Ollivier, Alain. "Les Premières 'Bonnes': Entretiens d'Alain Ollivier avec Monique Mélinand et Yvette Etiévant." *Alternatives théâtrales* 43 (1993): 60-66.

Plunka, Gene A. "Jean Genet's Mentor: Jean Cocteau." *New England Theatre Journal* 4 (1993): 49-63.

Saint-Leon. "*Les Bonnes* de Jean Genet: Quelle version faut-il *jouer?*" *Studies in Foreign Language and Literature: The Proceedings of the 23rd Mountain Interstate Foreign Language Conference.* Ed. Charles L. Nelson. Richmond: Eastern Kentucky University, 1976. 513-16.

Webb, Richard C. & Suzanne A. *Jean Genet and His Critics: An Annotated Bibliography, 1943-1980.* Metuchen, N.J.: The Scarecrow Press, 1982.

White, Edmund, *Genet: A Biography.* New York: Alfred A. Knopf, 1993.

Paula Kamenish (essay date June-December 1997)

SOURCE: Kamenish, Paula. "The Theory of Games and Dramatic Behavior: Uncovering Patterns of Dominance in *Les Bonnes.*" *Studies in the Humanities* 24, nos. 1-2 (June-December 1997): 85-99.

[*In the following essay, Kamenish analyzes the psychological strategies of both the characters and audience of* The Maids *in terms of game theory.*]

. . . play is a voluntary activity or occupation executed within certain fixed limits of time and place, according to rules freely accepted but absolutely binding, having its aim in itself and accompanied by a feeling of tension, joy and the consciousness that it is "different" from "ordinary life."

(Huizinga 28)

Jean Genet's *Les Bonnes,* based on the actual 1933 murder of Madame and Mademoiselle Lancelin by their maids, Christine and Léa Papin, is more than a mere 1947 theatrical rendition of the infamous crime. Genet freely explores the murderous motivations of the malevolent maids in a contest in which these sisters are first pitted against their mistress, then face off against each other. Genet recognizes that the theatre is the perfect arena for a game of scheming and dominance: the artifice of his stage is capable of sustaining characters whose passionate opposition inspires the spectator or critic to enter the game. Although his notion of play includes elements of *alea* [chance], mimicry, and *ilinx* [vertigo], echoing Callois' well-delineated categories of play, Genet, like Huizinga, overwhelmingly stresses the supremacy of *agon,* the competitive spirit of play. The dramatic situation of **Les Bonnes** takes the form of a competition; players, be they within or (as members of the audience) outside the physical confines of the stage, are cleverly induced to pursue strategies that result in either victory or defeat.

In *Saint-Genet: comédien et martyr* (1952), Jean-Paul Sartre stresses that it is the sham, the artificiality of the theatre that seduces Genet, the artist (561). Indeed, no other medium can provide such opportunities for the master riddler: **Les Bonnes** relies solely upon theatrical techniques such as disguise, role-playing, volte-face *and coup de theatre* to design its puzzle, to set its trap. The play, vertiginous for reader or spectator thanks to the ever-shifting nature of its plot and characterization, easily lures the audience into the game. At first self-assured and eager to play from a safe aesthetic distance, the spectator soon becomes what Jeffrey Malkan refers to as Genet's "betrayed victim," a contestant compelled to play opposite a self-proclaimed liar/criminal who seems to delight in his opponent's dilemma (101).

The dramatic conflict inherent in Genet's game and the ludic role he forces on the audience invite a structural analysis of play in **Les Bonnes** as provided by game theory. The problem-solving techniques set forth by mathematician John von Neumann and economist Oskar Morgenstern in their 1944 work *The Theory of Games and Economic Behavior* have been applied over the past 50 years to many disciplines (military strategy, social behavior, product marketing, voting strategies, plea bargaining, etc.). Game theory is equally effective when used in the study of Genet's drama, especially in the case of his most agonistic play, **Les Bonnes.** Within the realm of game theory, the play invites comparison with the two-person, non-zero-sum game which, like **Les Bonnes,** proposes a complex pattern of strategies and has no single, predictable outcome. The players pick their strategies simultaneously; neither player knows her opponent's choice. The best-known example of the two-person, non-zero-sum game is indisputably the Prisoner's Dilemma. In brief, Albert Tucker's original Prisoner's Dilemma (see also the diagram below) postulates the following:

> Two men suspected of committing a crime together are arrested and placed in separate cells. . . . Each suspect

may either confess or remain silent, and each one knows the possible consequences of his action. These are:

> 1. If one suspect confesses and his partner does not, the one who confessed turns state's evidence and goes free and the other one goes to jail for twenty years.

> 2. If both suspects confess, they both go to jail for five years.

> 3. If both suspects remain silent, they both go to jail for a year for carrying concealed weapons—a lesser charge.

(Davis 108)

Of course, the bilaterally satisfying option is for both men to refuse to confess (and serve one year), but if we presume that there is no "honor among thieves," that each man will make a choice based on his own self-interest, and if we take into account that each suspect must predict his partner's options and foresee the effect of each option upon himself, then there is only one safe answer: each man is better off confessing so as to avoid the chance of being double-crossed by his partner and serving the twenty-year sentence. Yet, a paradox exists: consider two naive prisoners, too ignorant to weigh the alternatives, who simply remain silent and each serve one year in prison, while the more sophisticated thinkers, employing their knowledge of game theory and realizing their chance to lose their freedom for twenty years, confess and are subsequently rewarded with five-year prison terms!

		SUSPECT A	
		CONFESS	DO NOT CONFESS
SUSPECT B	CONFESS	5 yrs, 5 yrs	go free, 20 yrs
	DO NOT CONFESS	20 yrs, go free	1 yr, 1 yr

Indeed, studies show that the cooperative strategy is not the one commonly favored by most players. In an experiment conducted by Alvin Scodel and J. Sayer Minas as a variation of the Prisoner's Dilemma, only two of the 22 pairs of college student subjects collaborated in the game while none of the 36 prison inmates in the experiment displayed a cooperative strategy. Scodel and Minas conclude that there is an underlying "unwillingness to engage in collaborative behavior" that is demonstrated in both college and prison populations. It seems that both groups of test subjects choose to play in an "unreasonable" way because of their overwhelming desire to receive the maximum reward (136-137).

The reluctance of players to cooperate is further explained by Philip Straffin, who contends that there is an absolute conflict between "individual rationality" and "group rationality." According to Straffin, when individuals rationally pursue their own best interest, the outcome is unfortunate for both players as a matter of course (73). One wonders if, by some law of human nature, individuals would rather risk a negative payoff than relinquish the opportunity to defeat an opponent. Clearly, the Prisoner's Dilemma reveals complications that depend upon players' motivations and their ability to plot and choose. Intellectual aptitude, emotional stability, and general personality traits, all influence the outcome of a game.

The central "game" in **Les Bonnes** demands that the players, Solange and Claire, choose a strategy that will lead to a result, the players' payoff, i.e. either punishment or reward. The maids' professed goal is the murder of Madame. During the course of the play, the two sisters repeatedly playact the killing of their mistress, with Claire playing Madame and Solange playing Claire. Behind these rehearsals, however, lurk darker purposes that lead ultimately to an unanticipated death. To analyze the underlying motives of the murderers, one may turn to the Prisoner's Dilemma vector. By examining the following matrices, we can observe the maids' most favorable options, the alternatives they must consider, and the anticipated payoffs. (Start at the top left rectangle of the diagram below and work around it counter-clockwise.) If Claire and Solange work cooperatively to murder Madame, they will receive equal payoffs, sharing the possible 10 points. Award 5 points to Solange and 5 points to Claire. If, however, Claire cooperates but Solange double-crosses her sister, Claire will receive a negative payoff (her own death by strangulation or a negative 10-point value), while Solange will exult in her new role as murderess (gaining 10 points). If both maids refuse to cooperate to act against their common enemy, neither will receive a payoff, and they will continue their lives imprisoned by Madame. The final scenario is an inversion of the second quadrant, with Solange acting cooperatively this time while Claire takes control and double-crosses her sister. Solange will be condemned for a murder she does not commit. Consequently, Claire will force her sister to a negative 10-point punishment and claim a 10-point reward for herself in her glorious suicide.

	CLAIRE	
	GOAL=MURDER	COOPERATIVE	UNCOOPERATIVE
SOLANGE COOPERATIVE	Madame is murdered	Solange jailed for murder. Claire commits suicide.
UNCOOPERATIVE	Solange overcomes Clair\. Claire is dead?	The maids remain enslaved.

	CLAIRE	
	GOAL=10 POINTS	COOPERATIVE	UNCOOPERATIVE
SOLANGE COOPERATIVE	5, 5	10, 10
UNCOOPERATIVE	10, -10	0, 0

It is important to remember when viewing the pattern of the Prisoner's Dilemma that neither player can possibly know her opponent's strategy while she makes her own choice. Each player must guess, based on the payoffs, which choice her sister will make and then select either the least harmful option for herself or risk

punishment in trying to increase her payoff. The element of chance naturally lends suspense to the game, and to the play.

Although it is in the interest of both Solange and Claire to cooperate to reach their goal, the studies by Scodel and Minas (among others) suggest an instinctive preference of human subjects for competition instead of cooperation. In the case of Claire and Solange, there is a certain point of panic at which time the law of the jungle overrides any feeling of identification with the other, and at this juncture the sisters reject their roles as self-sacrificing team players in favor of a confused self-interest.

How can Genet's two maids *collaborate* to rid themselves of Madame when their devotion and loyalty to each other is tinged with mistrust, hate, and jealousy? The stress of their dramatic situation allows no semblance of group solidarity that might take precedence over individual interests. Furthermore, as Morton Davis points out, "as a rule, when analyzing a game, you are content if you can say what rational players should do and predict what the outcome will be" (113). But what of Genet's dangerously irrational characters whose passionate obsessions drive them to find an available victim? What new factors must be taken into account when examining the game of Claire and Solange?

First of all, there is the unpredictable element of Madame, the intended murder victim. Madame is the chosen object of vilification, an unwitting scapegoat whom the maids condemn for hyperbolic crimes. Paradoxically, the sisters who blame her for the sordid lives they have been born to also deify their mistress: ". . . comme elle souffre en beauté. La douleur la transfigure!" (50) [How she suffers in beauty. Suffering transfigures her!]. But the deification of the beautiful object soon turns obsessive and destructive: "Tu l'as vue? Sa peine étincelante des feux de ses bijoux, du satin de ses robes, des lustres! Claire, la beauté de mon crime devait racheter la pauvreté de mon chagrin. Après, j'aurais mis le feu." (51) [Did you see her? Her grief sparkling with the fire of her jewels, with the satin of her dresses, with the chandeliers! Claire, the beauty of my crime was supposed to make up for the poverty of my sorrow. Afterward, I would have set it all on fire.]

The actions of the two women gradually reveal an uncomfortable mixture of worship with violence, and of demonstrations of love with those of hate. This combination of contradictory emotions, instead of confusing their plans, fuels the sisters' passions and fortifies their resolve to kill. From the outset of the play, the maids seem to be in perfect agreement: they must poison Madame. If the Prisoner's Dilemma demonstrates that the most beneficial solution for both players at this point is to cooperate to perpetrate their crime against Madame, then why are the sisters unable to choose the obvious strategy, the one that will cause them both to win? One problem is the volition of Madame, for she too must cooperate in order for the game to play out according to the strategy of its players.

Although she is oblivious to everything but Monsieur's misfortune, Madame nevertheless plays a pivotal role in the game. She serves as a kind of wild card, the possession of which is necessary to win the hand. Without access to their mistress, the maids cannot possibly choose the strategy that will yield an equally shared reward. Madame's failure to drink the poisoned tea before her departure from the scene arrests the initial scheming and forces the maids to consider alternative behaviors. Genet disallows the possibility of mutual cooperation between the sisters. When they can no longer dedicate themselves to the destruction of their common enemy, they must choose another strategy, another victim. Hence, the ersatz Madame of the interrupted strangulation scene (a mere rehearsal for the up-and-coming "murder"?) is reincarnated.

In the scene depicted in the bottom left quadrant of the matrix, Claire will risk her life (as she did unknowingly in the opening of the play) if she acts cooperatively and submits to Solange's furious will: "Et cette fois, je veux en finir avec une fille aussi lâche" (104) [And this time I want to be finished with such a cowardly girl]. Solange envisions the glory of her role as murderess; she will finally be Madame's equal and walk with her head held high. Furthermore, Solange adopts her sister's point value insofar as she has absorbed her sister's identity into her own: "Maintenant nous sommes Mademoiselle Solange Lemercier" (109) [Now we are Mademoiselle Solange Lemercier]. In her role as murderess she is so convincing that the spectator actually imagines that Claire lies dead in a corner of the stage. Here, Genet entices the play-goer, his opponent in the larger on-going game of the play, with a cogent bait that makes possible a second *coup de théâtre* when Claire returns to the stage to contemplate her assassin-sister. Visible only to the audience, Claire supports herself against the jamb of the kitchen door and listens to her sister. Once more, the game does not play out as we were led to expect; the audience (not Claire's opponent, Solange) is up-uprooted from the comfort of assumed assurances. We have been duped by Genet the prankster.

Yet another choice open to the maids is the option to abandon the plot altogether. (Bottom right quadrant of matrix.) Although the sisters voice their frustration and fear, demonstrate their uncertainty, or show signs of hesitation at one time or another, they do so alternately. Whenever one flinches from her sworn duty to kill Madame, the other draws upon her passionate abhor-

rence for her mistress and all she represents to rally her sister and force the game to continue. The sisters' patterns of coercion vary according to the target of their anger at the moment; Solange's sarcasm is characteristically colored with the malevolence she feels towards Madame, and then towards her sister. To Claire's claim that Madame is good, that Madame loves them, Solange displays her wrath by accusing the mistress of loving the maids as she loves her armchairs or her bidet!

It is morbidly interesting to note that in the Papin sisters' murder of their mistresses, the victims were objectified, reduced to everyday objects. Lynda Hart reveals that "the sisters testified to cutting little marks in the women's thighs like the ones French bakers make in their loaves, a detail that suggests the maids' desire to manipulate their mistresses' bodies as objects, common objects that the women contacted daily" (134). In Hart's opinion, the Papin sisters "reversed the authoritative gaze of the Lancelins who viewed the maids as ordinary household objects" (134). Genet perceptively echoes the objectification of the subservient body, and, as illustrated in the above scene, the fact of being reduced to a mere bathroom fixture becomes the impetus behind Solange's murderous hate of her mistress.

In scene after scene, the sisters prod one another with disguised threats and innuendoes in order to prolong their deadly game. Ultimately, Claire and Solange cannot consciously elect to dissolve their pact; it has become their obsession. Throughout the play, the sisters take turns reminding each other that they are committed to a murderous scheme to emancipate themselves, whatever the cost. Quitting the game is not a viable option.

Unable to abandon their vengeful plotting and incapable of retaining Madame for the murderous ceremony, the sisters must reexamine their options. Consequently, the audience is led to anticipate the displacement of aggression; the maids will redirect their rancor toward the substitute victim they find in one another. Taking into account their previous conduct and their obsessive compulsion to discharge their anger, it is logical to conclude that the maids will not both act cooperatively; rather, as long as the sisters are lured by the promise of the larger reward, glory and renown, one of them will always be willing to gamble and risk punishment. Moreover, the sisters will not both act uncooperatively: while one will submissively collaborate, yielding to her sister's wishes, the other will invariably double-cross her opponent. (Bottom left and top right quadrants.)

This psychological pattern of passive versus active behavior is documented in Jacques Lacan's 1933 study of Genet's source murder, "Motifs du Crime Paranoïaque: Le Crime des Soeurs Papin." Lacan judges that the Papin women were suffering from a paranoid disorder that he labels *délires à deux* (double delirium). He postulates that this form of psychosis relies upon an unequal relationship between the two parties: a more powerful partner influences a weaker, suggestible one. Simone de Beauvoir concurs that this was the generally accepted diagnosis as reported by the newspapers and the court. She reports one popularized rendition: "l'aînée était atteinte d'une paranöia aiguë, et la cadette épousait son délire" (137) [the elder sister suffered from acute paranoia, and the younger sister shared her delirium]. In Genet's version of the crime, Solange firmly asserts her control over her sister in most scenes; nevertheless, the maids occasionally reverse roles to comfort or encourage one other. The Prisoner's Dilemma matrix illustrates the possible fluctuations in the power dynamics between the two sisters. In the case of Claire and Solange, declarations of their growing hostility toward each other reinforce our understanding of the sisters' ongoing struggle for dominance: "Je ne te crains pas. Je ne doute pas de ta haine, de ta fourberie, mais fais bien attention. C'est moi l'aînée" (48). [I'm not afraid of you. I know you hate me, that you're a cheat, but watch out. I'm the older sister.] With taunts about the milkman and accusations of misplaying roles, the maids' dialogue consists of a strategic set of moves and countermoves.

Ultimately, Solange's warnings begin to echo, this time in Claire's voice. The latter has already glimpsed the danger of cooperating with her murderous sister: "Quand nous accomplissons la cérémonie, je protège mon cou. C'est moi que tu vises à travers Madame, c'est moi qui suis en danger" (48). [When we complete the ceremony, I'm protecting my neck. You're aiming for me through Madame. I'm the one in danger.] After this realization Claire proclaims her new-found strength: "Je suis capable de tout, et tu le sais" (56) [I can do anything, and you know it]. She hints at her strategy and calls herself the winner: "J'aurai ma couronne. Je serai cette empoisonneuse que tu n'as pas su être. A mon tour de te dominer" (59). [I shall have my crown. I shall be the poisoner that you failed to be. It's my turn to dominate you.] Claire, taking her cue perhaps from Solange's earlier triumphant soliloquy, merges the forces of the two opponents, and their point values in the game, into one "couple éternel, du criminel et de la sainte" (60) [eternal couple, of criminal and saint].

Paradox though it seems, Claire wins the game by authoritatively commanding her sister to serve the poisoned tea, thereby selecting suicide as her winning move. Genet's design to have Solange submit to her sister's will at this point in the play supports William Poundstone's theories as set forth in his *Prisoner's Dilemma*: on the third attempt, he says, the subject will endeavor to cooperate. This is Solange's third murder attempt.

At the climactic moment in which Claire-Madame voluntarily swallows the tainted brew, she metaphorically defeats her sister by abandoning Solange to a solitary life of punishment for a crime that the maids were, in actuality, too ineffectual to commit. (Top right quadrant of the matrix.) When Claire says to her sister, "Tu seras seule pour vivre nos deux existences (111) [You shall be alone to live out our two lives], a triumphant double-entity promises to emerge, but Solange's former strength is undercut by the fact that the soon-to-be-celebrated murderess recognizes she has failed in her attempt on Madame's and her sister's life. Solange has fallen short of her duty and is consequently deflated. (See her submissive, contracted body language as the curtain falls: "Solange, face au public, reste immobile, les mains croisées comme par des menottes." [Solange stands facing the audience, her hands crossed as if in handcuffs.])

Although critic Cynthia Running-Johnson finds Solange's final posture "emblematic of an ultimate freedom in glorious criminality" (964), the formerly dominant sister is actually defeated in her bid for fame in criminality. There can be no victorious rejoicing by a bogus criminal. In addition, Solange will remain "seule," condemned to live without her double and mirror, without the companionship of a malleable co-star in the sisters' fantasy-world play-acting. If we view the sisters as indispensable partners and competitors in a fatal game, we comprehend Solange's solitary punishment as her defeat and Claire's freedom from Madame and dominance over her sister as the winner's pay-off.

It is ironic that, simply by a shift of dominance, the same result (the death of Claire) awards the dead sister the winning points that she would have lost to her opponent had she met her death in the first scene. Opposing strategies yield truly mirror-opposite results, and the Prisoner's Dilemma matrix demonstrates this particular form of mirroring in the structure of ***Les Bonnes.*** If the line that separates cooperative from uncooperative behavior becomes a looking glass, the two sides clearly reflect each other, uncovering the parallels, but displaying them in an inverted order.

The mirror is perhaps the most obvious and meaningful of symbols in the play. Richard Coe argues that "the mirror is the most obsessive symbol in Genet's thought; . . . [it] is the symbol of the whole of Genet's world" (7). Coe suggests an image of two mirrors facing one another, "each reflecting an eternal emptiness in infinite repetitions of Nothing" (7). This mirrored world provides no certainty, no tangible realities, "but only appearances and voids: reflections alternating with panels of plain glass, both equally baffling and impenetrable" (7). The fantastic and deceptive quality of this funhouse hall of mirrors purposely, but playfully, distorts reality. Genet's theatre embraces the grotesque as human bodies are refigured or contorted to conform to new roles: Claire as Madame, Solange as Claire, sister as lover, and (at the request of Genet, his final *coup de théâtre*) male actors playing female characters, all to mirror the sisters' distorted images (in the eyes of Madame, Monsieur, and audience—the judgmental eyes of the bourgeois) or to clarify their pitiful self-images: "La crasse n'aime pas la crasse" [Filth hates filth].

Not only do the maids catch their reflections in Madame's vanity mirror (and in her well-polished shoes) from time to time, but they perceive their likeness in each other and in Madame herself. Indeed, some critics argue that characterization in the play relies on a technique of multivalence, a kind of "mirrors mirroring mirrors." In "Genet's 'Excessive' Double: Reading *Les Bonnes* through Irigaray and Cixous," Running-Johnson points out numerous instances of doubling, including Genet's conscious and exaggerated duplications between Claire and Solange (960-961).

But it is not only in the creation of character that the mirror motif appears. The Prisoner's Dilemma matrices prove that the written or performed text actually reflects itself. structurally, *Les Bonnes* is composed of a series of repetitious, frustrating scenes that continually set up the same game, seemingly between the same players. These players, however, fail to carry their strategies to a satisfying culmination, to a final determining act. Maria Paganini documents the sometimes virulent condensation of Genet's spectators: "ils accusent Genet d'avoir eu entre les mains tous les éléments permettant la production d'une véritable tragédie mais de ne pas avoir su les exploiter jusqu'au bout" (470) [they accuse Genet of having had in his hands all the elements of a true tragedy but of never having known how to use them to their best advantage]. Running-Johnson likens this building-up of tension on stage to "a series of climaxes that formally mirrors Cixous's and Irigaray's definitions of a multiple, 'feminine' sexuality" (964).

One may debate whether or not Genet delves into the "écriture féminine" in *Les Bonnes,* but one thing is certain: if there is evidence of this "écriture féminine," the playwright uses it as part of the deception, part of the ambiguity that characterizes his art. Whether the repetitions in *Les Bonnes* signal a conscious or unconscious connection with reproducing the nature of feminine writing, no one can dispute Genet's deliberate use of mirroring to set up the game motif of the play. Lucien Daenbach's description of the reflected narrative seems applicable to Genet's text in that there is clearly an "internal mirror that reflects the whole of the narrative in simple, repeated or 'specious' (or paradoxical) duplication" (43). We have only to compare the second and fourth quadrants in the matrix to observe the purposefully inverted repetition of scenes and of character dominance. Indeed, Genet's *Les Bonnes* is

like most games, inherently specular, pitting competitors against one other in a symmetry mediated by play.

Moreover, the play in its entirety proves to be a sort of mirror, tilted and warped according to Genet's seeming plan to force spectators to encounter themselves as they examine their own prejudices. Baffled by distorted and contradictory reflections, the audience moves without guidance through Genet's hall of mirrors where things are often not what they seem. Unlike traditional mirroring techniques that clarify themes (as in, for example, *Hamlet's* play-within-a-play scene), the specular structure of *Les Bonnes* skews and disfigures meaning.

Toward the end of the drama, spectators take pleasure in unearthing what they believe to be Genet's game, namely, that the entire plot to kill Madame is merely a subterfuge, a ruse to distract the audience from the main contest, the conflict between the two sisters. The first scene, instead of a dress rehearsal for the murder of the mistress, is truly a game of power between the maids that, without the alarm clock or the intrusion of Madame's presence, would have been played to the end, to the capitulation (in this case, death) of the weaker opponent.

There is, however, a larger game of supremacy being played in *Les Bonnes,* one that neatly frames the struggle between the maids and Madame, and between Claire and Solange. It should finally dawn on the spectator, after viewing the various distracting machinations of the play, that Genet has purposefully set up a contest with the audience as his opponent. Genet has been, all along, the game master. He has cleverly established an adversarial relationship in which we do not have the pleasure of choosing a strategy. Genet sets up the game, invites the spectator's participation, but double-crosses the spectator by thwarting all his rival's efforts to play.

Thus, his strategy of deception extends from the sisters' deliberate confusion of pretended and actual staged murder scenes to the playwright's deceptive game which engages and tricks the spectator. The maids' successive mirages of murder become mirrored by Genet's illusive game-playing, thereby underlying the true mirroring distortion of the play: the inability to distinguish reality from fiction in and outside *Les Bonnes.* This looking glass technique echoes the Gidean *construction en abyme* and Cocteau's mirrors, but introduces a twist: Genet turns the mirror to reflect his audience. While we watch his players, we also watch ourselves. The multi-layering of mirrored realities affects the reader or spectator of *Les Bonnes* by simulating sensations of depth, infinity, vertigo, and falling. Our aesthetic pleasure resulting from the unraveling of the successive plays within the play is short-lived, undercut by our sudden discomfort at realizing our place within the mirror's frame.

At the conclusion of the performance, the audience formulates a final matrix that includes the playwright and the spectator, locked in their own version of the Prisoner's Dilemma. Depending on whether we choose to cooperate with the playwright or try to double-cross him, the possible outcomes include (from upper left and circulating counterclockwise):

> 1. Genet and the audience collaborating to produce and find lazy satisfaction in an unsuspenseful and trite theatrical event.

> 2. Genet offering a comfortable, predictable drama during which the unengaged spectator uncooperatively falls asleep.

> 3. The playwright impertinently challenging the audience, who, in turn, abandons him by walking out during the play.

> 4. Genet frustrating the play-goer's expectation to procure suitable entertainment between dinner and bed.

It is likely that, as proven by empirical studies of prisoners, college students, and fictional characters in **Les Bonnes,** the game between Genet and his audience will culminate in uncooperative behavior on the part of one of the players. The spectator readily suspects Genet of refusing to collaborate, based on his proven history of uncooperative and deceitful conduct. (See, for example, his fabrication of "autobiographical facts" in the *Journal d'un voleur* as dissected by Stewart and McGregor.)

Genet

	GOAL=GOOD THEATRE	COOPERATIVE
YOU	COOPERATIVE	You enjoy a trite, predictable, unsuspenseful play.
	UNCOOPERATIVE	Genet writes a predictable play; you fall asleep.

	GOAL=GOOD THEATRE	COOPERATIVE
YOU	COOPERATIVE	You want to be entertained, but Genet makes you think and feel.
	UNCOOPERATIVE	Genet taunts the audience. You don't care so you leave the theatre.

Moreover, Genet is hardly known as a playwright who caters to the boulevard mentality that mandates a comfortable piece of entertainment to fill the evening hours; thus, we can rule out his willingness to write a gentle, pleasing piece that relaxes (and sedates) the bourgeois spectator. Quite to the contrary, Genet never fails to jolt his audience awake with his audacity. His theatre invariably takes risks. Consequently, we must assume that the only options available in the matrix lie in the third and fourth quadrants in which the playwright remains uncooperative. In both cases Genet is uncollaborative; hence, he is simultaneously granted the possibility of double-crossing his opponent. These facts would seem to place Genet at an advantage. Nevertheless, the audience is ultimately left to decide whether to accept Genet's challenge or simply ignore it.

Does this privilege of decision place us finally in a position of dominance over Genet? Since the audience can walk out of a theatre or interrupt the reading of a play simply by putting it down, perhaps Genet's initial manipulation only appears at first to be the winning strategy. Couldn't his plan prove to be ineffectual when faced with an uncooperative opponent?

Clearly, it is preferable to remain an ever vigilant rival when sitting down to play opposite a game-master such as Genet. Does a forewarned playgoer's preparation for the game assure a favorable outcome? Not necessarily. We are reminded of the story of the scientist who, in his experiments on primates, places a monkey in a closed room for observation. Just when the scientist ventures to peer through the peephole to observe the monkey, what does the scientist encounter but the eye of the monkey, also at the peephole, regarding him! Likewise the audience mistakenly feels it has the upper-hand, holding Genet and his play up to scrutiny, but ultimately it is the playwright who is studying his spectator. Genet's metatheatrical **Bonnes** poses the question of what is reality and what is fiction, both on the stage and in the relationship between the play (*pièce/jeu*) and its viewers (as they become themselves *jouers*).

Plays such as **Les Bonnes** (or **Les Nègres** or **Les Paravents,** for that matter) demand a certain type of spectator, one who is willing to gamble. Whoever enters a playhouse to watch one of Genet's works agrees to join his game at the risk of being implicated in Genet's invented crimes. Surpassing his contemporaries in the establishment of such a problematic relationship with the audience, Genet's dramatic oeuvre educates the playgoer about the nature of theatre and about the spectator's role and responsibility vis à vis the theatrical event.

Works Cited

Beauvoir, Simone de. *La Force de l'Age.* Paris: Gallimard, 1960.

Caillois, Roger. *Les Jeux et les Hommes.* Paris: Gallimard, 1967.

Coe, Richard N. *The Vision of Jean Genet.* New York: Grove, 1969.

Dallenbach, Lucien. *The Mirror in the Text.* Trans. Jeremy Whiteley and Emma Hughes. Chicago: U of Chicago P, 1989.

Davis, Morton D. *Game Theory: A Nontechnical Introduction,* rev. ed. New York: Basic Books, 1983.

Genet, Jean. *Les Bonnes.* Paris: Folio, 1976.

———. *Journal d'un voleur.* Cambridge, MA: Schoenhof, 1966.

Hart, Lynda. "'They Don't Even Look Like Maids Anymore': Wendy Kesselman's *My Sister in This House.*" *Making a Spectacle: Feminist Essays on Contemporary Women's Theatre.* Ed. Lynda Hart. Ann Arbor: U of Michigan P, 1989. 131-146.

Huizinga, J. *Homo Ludens. A Study of the Play-Element in Culture.* Boston: Beacon, 1950.

Lacan, Jacques. "Motifs du Crime Paranoïaque: Le Crime des Soeurs Papin." *Minotaure: Revue artistique et littéraire* 3-4 (15 Feb. 1933): 25-28.

Malkan, Jeffrey. "Aggressive Text: Murder and the Fine Arts Revisited." *Mosaic* 23:1 (Winter 1990): 101-115.

Neumann, John von and Oskar Morgenstern. *The Theory of Games and Economic Behavior,* 3rd ed. Princeton: Princeton UP, 1953.

Paganini, Maria. "L'Inscription juridique dans *Les Bonnes* de Jean Genet." *Romanic Review* 80 (1989): 462-482.

Poundstone, William. *Prisoner's Dilemma.* New York: Doubleday, 1992.

Running-Johnson, Cynthia. "Genet's 'Excessive' Double: Reading *Les Bonnes* Through Irigaray and Cixous." *French Review* 63 (1990): 959-966.

Sartre, Jean-Paul. *Saint Genet: Comédien et martyr.* Paris: Gallimard, 1952.

Scodel, Alvin and J. Sayer Minas. "The Behavior of Prisoners in a 'Prisoner's Dilemma' Game." *Journal of Psychology* 50 (1960): 133-138.

Stewart, Harry E. and Rob Roy McGregor. *Jean Genet: A Biography of Deceit, 1910-1951.* New York: Peter Lang, 1989.

Straffin, Philip D. *Game Theory and Strategy.* Washington: Mathematical Association of America, 1993.

Tucker, Albert William. *Contributions to the Theory of Games.* Princeton: Princeton UP, 1959.

THE BALCONY (1957)

CRITICAL COMMENTARY

Carol Rosen (essay date December 1992)

SOURCE: Rosen, Carol. "The Structure of Illusion in Genet's *The Balcony.*" *Modern Drama* 35, no. 4 (December 1992): 513-19.

[*In the following essay, Rosen appraises the image of the brothel as a venue for political, philosophical, and symbolic commentary in* The Balcony.]

Although in fact a brothel is more likely to resemble a nondescript rooming-house than an ornate pleasure dome, popular literature favors fancy rather than reality. And the brothel, an institution of tabooed sexuality, is an especially inviting premise, promising to substantiate forbidden dreams. So in fiction, heroes have been regularly seduced into submission and then metamorphosed into creatures of degenerate lust by vile temptresses (who occasionally sport hearts of gold). The Circean nighttown episode of *Ulysses* may be seen as the apotheosis of this fictive standard, for in Joyce's novel the brothel suggests a modern sexual mythology.

On the stage, too, the brothel and its residents have been depicted more often as glazed stereotypes than as real subjects. Traditionally, the "fallen woman" has been a pathetic stereotype, a sensuous heroine hopelessly drawn—and drawing men with her—into the romantic quicksand of sin. Only the melodramatically repentant of this kind, typified for Victorian audiences by Pinero's suicidal second Mrs. Tanqueray and typified for depression era audiences by O'Neill's plucky Anna Christie, may be saved. The brazen of this kind, on the other hand, typified by Lulu, the malleable whore of Frank Wedekind's dramatic trilogy, by Esmeralda, the enterprising Gypsy's daughter of Tennessee Williams's dream-play, *Camino Real,* and by the "tarts" and earthy whores—notably *The Great God Brown*'s Cybele—fleshed out repeatedly in O'Neill's melancholy plays, endure only as protean extensions of male fantasies. With the notable exception of Shaw's *Mrs. Warren's Profession,* then, a play considered scandalous in its own time (considered scandalous, incidentally, *not* because its title character is a fallen woman, but because unlike the conventionally repentant stage courtesan of the nineteenth century, Shaw's Mrs. Warren, a *new* fallen woman, recognizes both the horrors and the hypocrisy of respectable society), the subject of prostitution tends to conjure up a perfumed purgatory even in the avant-garde theater.

Jean Genet's *The Balcony* (first published in 1956), however, singularly transcends such sensationalism. In this play, Genet reconstructs on-stage the kind of institution to which Shaw's Mrs. Warren could not even discreetly allude in the theater fifty years earlier. Further, the brothel serves Genet as an image of the revolution raging outside his House of Illusion. It is at once: (1) a naturalistic reconstruction of a brothel, (2) a structural analogue for society, (3) a symbolic reflection of grand illusions and larger-than-life desires, and, most significantly, (4) a metaphysical construct in a discussion play about the value of mimetic ritual, the transcendence possible in play, and the magical efficacy of the theater itself.

Genet's plays have all been described as taking place in "private hells (each a paradise to him) in which the Usual Order is interrupted." For Genet:

In these special places—prisons, barracks, the Mass—the real Game is played. . . . And yet these secret societies, these places of "difference," have an attraction: They are a terrain for art, microcosms of the wider outside world to which a Genet can apply special rules. They are places of secret languages; of shorthands by which like recognizes like; of accepted hierarchies. They are places from which the Alien is excluded; they are abstract, impersonal.[1]

The colossal whorehouse of *The Balcony* is just such a place. Here, the customer is given a private vision of another world of release and escape, and the audience is given the cruelest reflection imaginable—in the Artaudian sense of cruelty—of an underworld of sordid spectacle. Genet's *The Balcony* turns an elaborate whorehouse into an apocalyptic image of the society it mocks, and the play derives its theatrical power from its setting in one of Genet's "private hells," in Mme. Irma's House of Illusions.

Genet's Mme. Irma plays upon us the way Euripides' Dionysus toys with Pentheus. The first four scenes of *The Balcony* are performed in quick succession on a revolving platform beneath a single chandelier. Each studio is equipped with a trick mirror which seems to reflect an unmade bed located "in the first rows of the orchestra."[2] In these first four vignettes, we peer through an imaginary mirror stationed before us. On-stage, the "secret theatres" of sexual identity are reflected (p. 35); a "mode of being . . . in solitude, for appearance alone," is clarified (p. 12).

The play begins in the middle of an erotic enactment in one of the "secret theatres" of Mme. Irma's house. The Bishop, "obviously larger than life" and wearing "garish make-up" (p. 7), is dispensing absolution to a scantily dressed whore. Standing by is Mme. Irma, the director of this scenario in a studio of her brothel. When the Bishop's performance exceeds his allotted time, Mme. Irma abruptly ends this improvised scene and supervises the Bishop's transformation back to "the normal size of an actor" (p. 12). Other episodes immediately follow; a series of colorful fantasies unfold before us in an urgent rush and in a kaleidoscopic pattern. A Judge begs a whore in chains to confess that she is a thief; a General watches a whore parade as a circus horse in an imaginary procession; and a little old man dressed as a Tramp is whipped by a whore. In each of these preliminary scenes we witness intrusions of realistic concerns: the Bishop is hurried away by Mme. Irma; the Judge questions the acting ability of a novice whore and he is irritated by outside noises which interrupt his interlude; the General negotiates with Mme. Irma over price and over authentic details; and the Tramp's only line in his screened-off arena is "What about the lice?" (p. 28). These pragmatic concerns are demands for naturalism by customers *playing* at being a Bishop, a Judge, a General, a Tramp. By the time we in the audi-

ence realize just where this play is set, by the time we realize that those perfectionist demands are signals of intricate performances in a brothel, it is too late. Mme. Irma, Genet's Circe, has initiated us into voyeuristic participation in secret ceremonies and rituals of degradation reflected before us.

In its mirrors lurks both the theatrical and philosophical terrain of *The Balcony.* By means of Mme. Irma's peeping-tom apparatus (including buzzers and a "kind of switchboard with a view-finder and earphone" [p. 30] as well as trick mirrors), Genet focuses on props and devices that are: (1) naturalistic details true to the kind of elaborate brothel his play depicts; (2) references to the self-conscious theatricality of this House of Illusion, where Mme. Irma keeps tabs on the multiple diversions occurring simultaneously in her labyrinthian establishment by watching images transmitted to her on her closed-circuit screen; when, for example, she narrates a violent scene of a heroic Legionnaire, Mme. Irma seems to be an audience surrogate as well as a manipulative stage manager; and (3) sounding boards for philosophical speculation. Throughout the play, especially in discussion scenes such as Scene V, characters conceptualize their ideas and contemplate their roles using the image-in-the-mirror as an extroversion of the inner self. In *The Balcony,* the mirror is an emblem of the play's erotic dialectic.

The discussion of ideas begins in Scene V. Following the shock of the opening routines, this lengthy scene is expository. In the course of self-congratulatory remarks, Mme. Irma properly introduces herself; our observations about her domain, drawn from the first four episodes which bombarded us, are now unequivocally borne out. In her elegant quarters, Mme. Irma transcends the taboos of proper society as well as the polite conventions of staging. "Cat-house, whore-house, bawdy-house. Brothel. Fuckery. Call it anything you like" (p. 51), she tells her respectable business partner, the Chief of Police. Mme. Irma's establishment on the outskirts of society defies euphemism. Like a barker before a grotesque carnival mirror, Mme. Irma cajoles us into "The Grand Balcony . . . the most artful, yet the most decent house of illusions" (p. 34). The equation of the brothel with the theater is symbolized by Mme. Irma herself. She delights in spectacle, making our heads spin with her frenetic inventory of "chandeliers, mirrors, carpets, pianos, caryatids and . . . studios, girls, crystals, laces, balconies" (p. 37). She is an impresario determined to furnish the audience with whatever they want:

> They all want everything to be as true as possible. . . . Minus something indefinable, so that it won't be true. [. . .] it was I who decided to call my establishment a house of illusions, but I'm only the manager. Each

individual, when he rings the bell and enters, brings his own scenario, perfectly thought out. My job is merely to rent the hall and furnish the props, actors and actresses.

(p. 36)

But Mme. Irma is being modest. She is not just a caretaker in a bizarre warehouse; she does more than furnish props for amateur improvisations. She has exalted (as she herself rhapsodizes, "I've succeeded in lifting it from the ground" [p. 36]) the profession of the stage manager far beyond its theatrical place as a go-between in Thornton Wilder's *Our Town*. Rather, she casts, directs, and co-ordinates performances in a house of infinite mirrors and theaters; she considers the splendor of her productions to be a reflection of her own creative energy, and so she is determined to keep Appearance pure and "the Revels intact" (p. 36). For in *The Balcony,* like the mirrors that line its walls, the house itself is a negative reflection of the world crumbling around it. Here, forces of truth and illusion are each charged with the preservation of the other.

In addition to being a structural analogue for the society which surrounds it and which it reflects, the House of Illusion also functions symbolically. For Genet the brothel is an outpost of hell. Complaining about the English premier of *The Balcony,* Genet argued, "My play was set in a brothel of noble dimensions . . . Peter Zadek [the director] has put on the stage a brothel of petty dimensions."[3] Genet's objection to the naturalizing of his dream-vision makes sense when we see his brothel on his ontological terms. To Genet, the brothel is a combination whore-house, theater, and church, a place where ceremonies are performed "in the sense that the outside world says a mass is celebrated" (p. 49).

The magical value of mimetic ritual, central to the theatrical construct of *The Balcony,* is characteristic of Genet's Artaudian dramaturgy. In Scene V, Mme. Irma (Genet's spokeswoman here) emerges as a disciple of Artaud. She has conceived and realized a theater of cruelty where her "mirrors and orders and the passions" expressed (p. 41) bear what Artaud termed in *The Theater and Its Double* a "magical relation to reality and danger."[4] In Mme. Irma's bedrooms of mirrors, an image of the secret self—the double of Artaud's dark, metaphysical theater—is manifested. Her chambers are like the "essential theater" to which Artaud aspires in his essay on "The Theater and the Plague"; in these boudoirs occur "the revelation, the bringing forth, the exteriorization of a depth of latent cruelty by means of which all the perverse possibilities of the mind . . . are localized."[5] By localizing larger-than-life desires under a single roof, Genet transforms a specific locale into a cosmic landscape. Just as Mme. Irma's brothel is the intangible shadow of a real social phenomenon, her

closet dramas are the Artaudian double of their impotent bases in truth.

Once the revolution threatens the Balcony, the revolution, like all outer reality, loses itself to the hall of mirrors. It, too, is consumed by the structure of illusion. When Mme. Irma is approached by an envoy from the real palace with the news that the real queen, her real bishop, and her real general are dead, Mme. Irma and her clients agree to masquerade publicly in the roles they previously assumed only in private. After an off-stage procession through the war-torn streets, Mme. Irma as the Player Queen, *her* Bishop, *her* General, and *her* Judge appear briefly before the rabble. Costumed in torn and dusty ceremonial garments, they stand, gigantic and silent figures on the balcony itself, which "projects beyond the façade of the brothel" (p. 70). Now, a shot rings out, killing Chantal, who deserted Mme. Irma to join and then to symbolize the rebellion. According to Roger, the standard-bearer of the doomed rebellion, Chantal "embodies the Revolution. . . . In order to fight against an image Chantal has frozen into an image. . . . It's the combat of allegories" (p. 57). So Mme. Irma wins this combat. At the scene of the mysterious assassination of Chantal, the boundaries of illusion are extended, and the insurrection which raged like the plague is put down by a show of power. Even Chantal's image is incorporated into Mme. Irma's structure of illusion: the regime spreads rumors insinuating that Chantal was "playing a double game," she is canonized, and her image is blazoned on the state flag (p. 81).

Though Mme. Irma easily seizes the title of Queen, her customers are ill-suited to function with power. Mme. Irma's brothel is like the snapshot posed by the photographers in Scene IX. It is "a true image, born of a false spectacle" (p. 75). Exposed to the light of day, Mme. Irma shines like one of her mirrors. But her customers, rigged in their costumes, remain men of glass, incapable of reflecting real power. The consequences of their charade trap and terrify them.

Only the Chief of Police, Mme. Irma's business partner, shares her ability to function, to hold concrete power. Ironically, the Chief of Police yearns for the consecration of his power through ritual. This desire for the validation of function through form—a desire to take his place in the structure of illusion beyond reality—contrasts sharply with the longing for actual function felt by the other ministers of Mme. Irma's sham cabinet. The Chief of Police, however, filled with his own real power, ready with a scenario, and eager to descend forever into his well-stocked Mausoleum, now waits only for a sign of his transcendence, a sign that his maneuvers have been transformed into myths, a sign that his bureaucratic identity has been merged with the universal image of the Hero.

Finally, in the House of Illusion, Genet stages a showdown between appearance and reality, symbol and substance, form and function. The result of the show-down between opposite sides of a trick mirror is a draw: ideas are dramatically represented by characters, and their fusion is integrated into the action. The climax of the play—the union of revolution and ritual in a fatal gesture of castration—is a cruel resolution of the two-sided issue by means of quite literal *coup de théâtre*. With Artaudian "poetry of the senses" and "concrete physical language," Genet and his Mme. Irma reveal "to collectivities of men their dark power, their hidden force," and invite them "to take, in the face of destiny, a superior and heroic attitude they would never have assumed without it."[6]

The climax of *The Balcony,* reflecting the action of the play as a whole, fills the space between two figures in a mirror. Finally, someone comes to the brothel who wishes to imitate the Chief of Police. It is Roger, the leader of the failed revolt, the lover of the dead Chantal. As the leader of the revolution, Roger sought to supplant the Chief of Police in a new order to be symbolized by the image of Chantal. But Chantal's petrified image has been absorbed into that of Mme. Irma, and the insurrection has been quelled. Defeated now by shadows in a mirror, Roger seeks symbolic revenge. The triumph of the Brothel—the untarnished symbol—is signalled to us by Roger's appearance there. Even he succumbs to the lure of sympathetic magic, and he, too, seeks self-annihilation in a distortion of his own image. But Roger's inauguration of the Mausoleum Studio is highly unorthodox. In a gesture of self-defeat and projected retribution, Roger kills himself as he satisfies his obsession. Mutilating himself in an act of impersonation, he transcends the dimension of play, and he dies.

By merging his role-playing with his ruined self, Roger breaks the rules of the brothel. He reasons:

> If the brothel exists and if I've a right to go there, then I've a right to lead the character I've chosen to the very limit of his destiny . . . no, of mine . . . of merging his destiny with mine.
>
> (p. 93)

This collision of psychodrama and sympathetic magic not only destroys Roger, this violent synthesis simultaneously catapults the Chief of Police towards his own destiny. Finally consecrated into an image, the Chief of Police feels freed to descend permanently into his well-stocked tomb where he, like Mme. Irma, may endure interminably in a state of suspended animation. In Roger's real suicide and symbolic murder, as in Pirandello's *Six Characters in Search of an Author,* we are shown a real death set off from its surrounding stage-world, a stage-world constructed upon a foundation of playing. And in *The Balcony,* as in *Six Characters,* this climactic interruption of the game merely tests it. Though Roger dies, the structure of the brothel endures.

Genet's play ends with an affirmation of the structure. Hearing a renewed burst of gun-fire from the street and realizing that yet another revolution is at hand, Mme. Irma begins to extinguish her lights and to dismiss her bedecked Judge, Bishop, and General. Abruptly, she sends us home where, she assures us, "everything—you can be quite sure—will be falser than here" (p. 96). With her sudden direct address to us, Mme. Irma shatters the imaginary fourth wall, and like one of her ubiquitous mirrors, she reflects us. Her Balcony, then, is more than a naturalistically ordered stage brothel; it is more than real; it expresses conflicting ideas with the erotic nuances of a dream. Indeed, Genet's play—his theater and his brothel—is like a dream: a place where archetypal images are unhampered in their concrete expression. As in a dream, too, the pattern of action in *The Balcony* is composed of rapidly shifting images and strong visual signs.

In Mme. Irma's theater-brothel-universe, Genet presents us with an extraordinary microcosm. Like a shadow in a mirror, this play gives a mythic dimension to the dark side of the human soul; its conceit of whoredom finally burns "like an imperceptible light in . . . an imperceptible castle" (p. 34) in the darkest region of the imagination. Here, Genet realizes his dream of a pure theater in which communion is possible. Genet puts forth this dream of a pure theater in his **"A Note on Theatre."** He suggests:

> A clandestine theatre, to which one would go in secret, at night, and masked, a theatre in the catacombs, may still be possible. It would be sufficient to discover—or create—the common Enemy, then the Homeland which is to be protected or regained.[7]

The Balcony reconstructs just such a clandestine theater on the modern stage. Conceived in the image of a brothel, perceived as a structure of illusion, Genet's play is an elaborate game of deception and illumination. And like most magic, it is mostly done with mirrors.

Notes

1. Keith Botsford, "But He Writes Like an Angel," *The New York Times Magazine,* 27 February 1972, p. 70.

2. Jean Genet, *The Balcony,* revised edition, trans. Bernard Frechtman (New York, 1966), p. 7. Subsequent page references to this edition of *The Balcony* will appear in the text.

3. Quoted in Martin Esslin, *The Theatre of the Absurd,* revised edition (Garden City, NY, 1969), p. 180.

4. Antonin Artaud, *The Theater and Its Double,* trans. Mary Caroline Richards (New York, 1959), p. 89.

5. Ibid., p. 30.

6. Ibid., p. 37, p. 32.

7. Jean Genet, "A Note on Theatre," in *Genet/ Ionesco: The Theatre of the Double,* ed. Kelly Morris (New York, 1969), p. 21.

Christine Bokyo-Head (essay date August 2002)

SOURCE: Bokyo-Head, Christine. "Mirroring the Split Subject: Jean Genet's *The Balcony." Consciousness, Literature, and the Arts* 3, no. 2 (August 2002).

[*In the following essay, Boyko-Head investigates how characters in* The Balcony *fail to reconcile the split between their perceived images and their true identities.*]

Una Chadhuri defines avant-garde theatre as "performance under-erasure . . . a radical, total disunity. In semiotic terms . . . it is a fall into the abyss between signifier and signified" (1990, 39). Jean Genet's literary work celebrates the abyss as a parallel universe for the decentralized, and the socially subverse. While writing about this parallel world may negate its radical potential, Genet points to a necessary ironic tension co-existing between legitimate and subversive realms. According to Mark Pizzato, Genet's subversive creations mark an autobiographical reconstruction where "the sole purpose of his writing would then have been to read it himself, to re-read himself and his imaginings, and to re-imagine himself through his written fantasies" (1990, 116). In Genet's play *The Balcony* there is a continuous re-writing and re-reading of self by the characters. Genet shows that the individual's desire to (re)create oneself using an other image, and in Genet's case the desire to see his radical behaviour reflected in art, becomes the secret, collective dream of the masses.

The transformations that take place at the Grand Balcony are portraits of self-conscious disunity. Genet states in a letter to Roger Blin that "my books, like my plays, were written against myself . . . to expose myself" (Innes, 1993, 111). But they are also a post-modern manipulation of theatrical conventions exposing the audience to a self-reflexive, theatrical experience. Similarly, Jacques Lacan's psychoanalytical theories also pose a postmodern interpretation of development whereby individuals re-imagine, re-write and re-read their subject positions. Genet's avant-garde challenge to mimetic representation and Jacques Lacan's deconstruction of the Freudian Subject, which he makes using

theatrical metaphors and allusions, creates an interesting analogy between *The Balcony* and Lacanian psychoanalysis. Both show representation, on and off the stage, as a process determined by a discourse that is never truly one's own. *The Balcony*'s thematic and structural masquerade place the audience in a carnivalesque world where everything is theatrical, or nothing is. Genet's post-structuralist text parallels Lacan's observation that individuals are immersed in their own psycho-masquerades. Both visions expose a psycho-theatrical process determined by the subject's ability to 'try on' discourses. Genet and Lacan's positions undermine the concept of power by showing us, through their distinct works, how everything that is meaningful also has the clownish potential to slide into the abyss of meaninglessness. Discourse(s), then, become life's chief organizing principle while simultaneously destroying the boundaries between fantasy and reality, art and life, stage and audience, subject and ideal object.

The Balcony, in Genet's play of the same name, is a brothel, a house of illusions; it is also a stage. Its liminality, or decentralized sacred space, belongs to both a fictional and a referential reality where characters *and* audience participate in transformative experiences. The dramatized space and the playing space position theatricality in the audience's gaze; both performances require costumes, the creation of characters, the playing of roles. Inundated with mirrors, Genet's stage accentuates the theme of theatrical masquerade. In 1962, he writes that the play is a "glorification of the Image and the Reflection" (Knapp, 1968, 119). The mirrors reinforce Genet's challenge to subjectivity and assault on social theatricality by revealing that a "reflected image requires the pre-existence of a reflectable entity" (Chaudhuri, 1990, 46). According to Una Chaudhuri, the performance-as-mirror emphasizes the theatre's split subjectivity since it occupies two spaces—the fictive and the referential—and would no longer exist if this spatial duality were broken. While optic devices decorate the walls, flesh and cloth 'mirrors' walk upon the boards. Without the play's clients the fantasies would not exist; without the audience the performance would not exist.

The parallels between Genet's theatre and Lacan's psychology strengthens my reading of the play as a postmodern assault on society's theatricality. The clients come to the Grand Balcony to live out power fantasies by playing with the tools of domination and submission. Their action presents a strong analogy to Jacques Lacan's theories of subject-development. He asserts that all humans suffer from fragmented body-images, and desire to create a unified form even if it means acquiring "the assumption of the armour of an alienating identity" (Lacan, 1977,4). The clients' desires to enter the brothel's illusory satisfaction stems from their psychological need to move from an incomplete existence to one of unity. The elements required for Genet's stage—a mirror which reflects an unmade bed, a costume and a woman—manufacture the drama that results in the temporary actualization of the clients', and the audience's, psycho-fantasies. In Genet's world, according to Christopher Innes, "the usual equation between appearance and essence has been reversed. The artificial appearance is the essence" (1993, 109). The costume's effect is believed to be 'real' because the client desires to become an 'essential' archetype:

> The General: (He looks at himself in the mirror) Auster-litz! General! Man of War and in full regalia, behold me in my pure appearance. Nothing, no contingent trails behind me. I appear, purely and simply.
>
> (62)

In this case, the subject, the inadequate being from beyond the balcony's threshold, looks into the mirror and sees the object: the "pure appearance" of a general. The client gains a sense of completeness through masquerade. This pleasurable misidentification erases the separation between client and the ideal image, signifier and signified, referent and reference.

According to Lacan, the subject's desire to rediscover an ideal image is rooted in his/her primary narcissism. Entry into the world of language terminates the subject's blissful existence in the primal stage. The subject then displaces his narcissistic tendencies onto another, with the 'other' taking the form of a virgin or prostitute. But, while Genet's Bishop, Judge and General love that which Freud says we all "would like to be" (Freud, 1984, 84), the anaclitic theme also occurs at the Grand Balcony: "this time it's the baby who gets slapped, spanked, tucked in, then cries and is cuddled" (47). Here, the sought-after object is clearly a (m)other substitute. Since no sexual act is explicitly performed in the play, the brothel's conventions encourage sublimation whereby the clients displace their ego ideals onto the reflections they perceive in the mirror. Consider how theatre's conventions encourage audiences along the same path. Furthermore, the visual absence of sexual intercourse raises doubts to its actual occurrence. Genet's decision to not toy with the audience's morals by having the characters "perform" sexual acts introduces a more subversive message to the script. This gap in narrative expectations enables Genet to transform the Balcony's deviant space—as a house of sexual pleasures—into an acceptable arena performing empowerment rituals through the alienating techniques of the masquerade. And masquerade is neither deviant, nor against the Law. In essence, Genet's erotic pleasure of theatricality is shown to also be the same pleasures not only sought by average men, but necessary to their normal functioning in society.

Trying to escape society's decentring function, the clients re-create images that, nevertheless, are embroidered by social decorum and tradition and embossed by

the power of fantasy-specific discourses. In Lacanian terms, language and discourse characterizes the symbolic stage's fragmenting horror. Ironically, the Lacanian subject only recognizes the imaginary stage's gratification once he has come under the power of Language and the Name of the Father or Law. Alienated and fragmented in the world of signifiers and signifieds, the subject seeks the impossible: a return to the Imaginary's satisfaction. But satisfaction is known only upon "reflection", so subjects play, in earnest, at misidentifying who they are. This Hegelian paradox is, as Mark Pizzato observes, evident in Genet's life where in order to carry the identity of an outlaw, Genet subjected himself to the law's authority by being caught and imprisoned. According to Jeanette Savona, Genet understood the oppressive power of symbolic naming: "accepting the condemnation of others, he attempted to become what the world saw in him, someone bound to be bad" (1983, 3). But to say one is this or that is not enough. A disguise, costume, or prop becomes essential for the subject's meconnaissance. The men masquerade as active ideals; the women play at being passive slaves to the ideal images. Here, Lacan's definition of "masquerade" is useful in understanding the paradox of play at the Grand Balcony: "the masculine ideal and the feminine ideal are represented in the psyche by . . . the term masquerade . . . [which] is precisely to play not as the imaginary, but at the symbolic level" (1981, 93). Language's power to name, while being the cause of the subject's inadequate feelings, is the gateway to the subject's return to an imaginary completeness. Genet's characters willingly forfeit their everyday identities in order to focus on their ideal images. They want to experience their object-ideals in masturbating solitude: "I want to be general in solitude. Not even for myself, but for my image, and my image for its image, and so on. In short, we'll be among equals" (27). The client misperceives the representational process since "a reflected image requires the preexistence of a reflectable entity" (Chaudhuri, 1990, 46). He cannot be a General in solitude because identity requires the presence and validation of another even if that other is only a cloth replica.

Analogous to psychoanalytical transference, the illusion's construction is conveniently ignored by the client. Lacan points out that Freud "in touching on the feelings involved in the transference, insisted on the need to distinguish in it a factor of reality" (Innes, 1993, 109). Likewise, the play's women realize that certain props are necessary in creating the imaginary transference:

CARMEN:

And what'll the authentic detail be?

IRMA:

The ring . . .

CARMEN:

What about the fake detail?

IRMA:

It's almost always the same: black lace under the homespun skirt.

(35)

The Balcony inverts the categories of reality and fantasy with only the Chief of Police recognizing that "brothel tricks are mainly mirror tricks" (48). Being excluded from the imaginary order's satisfaction, the Chief arrogantly pronounces the brothel's function only to ignore the theatrical machinery once *his* misidentification is eminent.

Genet's other clients, the audience, undergo the same process. At the box office, they trade in their daily realities and willingly enter the rejuvenating, but illusional, space of the theatre. Not unlike the characters, they are confronted with inadequate reflections since their desire to enjoy the image in private can never be realized. For one, theatre is a collective art form. For another, the actors remind the audience that they are slaves to language and a discourse "in the universal movement in which their places are already inscribed at birth, if only by virtue of [their] proper names" (Lacan, 1977, 148). Life and art is inscribed by the tension between signifier and signified, the symbolic and the imaginary. So, while the audience enjoys their temporary fall into the imaginary, the authentic detail—the ticket stub—burns in their pockets.

The tension between the authentic and the inauthentic is evident in the clients appropriation of authoritative language in order to create their scenarios. While the sessions belong to the imaginary realm, they are controlled and organized by the symbolic. Scene two demonstrates that the sessions are scripted and proceed along a course determined by the language of an elusive Author. The clients agree to use these fantasy-specific discourses because their transformations rely upon naming that which they desire. "Ornaments! Mitres! Laces! You, above all, of gilded Cope, you protect me from the world" (13): naming the items that create the object of desire indicates a revolution in language that releases the client from his oppressive discourse by paradoxically (en)trapping him in another representational, discursive structure. Thus, Genet is not against theatricality; in fact, he revels in it. His attack is aimed at society's theatrical seriousness, or its inability to see its theatricality as anything but serious by depicting grown men playing "dress-up".

Genet's revolution in art, like Lacan's in psychology, positions language as Janus-faced. It is language that disrupts the euphoria of the imaginary bond between subject and object. It is language that also allows the imaginary to be named and re-entered by the subject through a fictitious chain of signifiers. However, the signifier is always already beyond reach; it is part of "an essential encounter—an appointment to what we are always called with a real that eludes us" (Lacan, 1981, 53). Dramatically, the clients want to participate in a perfect illusion, and for the session's duration, the image is not provisional. As the Envoy says: "It is a true image, born of a false spectacle" (75). The fantasy-specific discourse supports the improbable probability of the ideal image's stability by removing it from the symbolic world, and ritualizing language's metonymic function. This revolutionary stance toward language and subjectivity is reflected in the client/bishop's voiced desires:

A function is a function. It's not a mode of being. But a bishop—that's a mode of being. It's a trust. A burden. Mitres, lace, goldcloth and glass trinkets, genuflexions . . . To hell with the function! . . . The majesty, the dignity, that light up my person, do not emanate from the attributions of my function. No more, good heavens! than from my personal merits. The majesty, the dignity that light me up come from a more mysterious brilliance; the fact that the bishop precedes me . . . And I wish to be bishop in solitude, for appearance alone. . . .

(12)

The client wants to be the one and only Bishop because "priority in time is one of the very sources of the father's power" (Bleikesten, 1981, 118). According to Lacan, "it is in the name of the father that we must recognize the support of the symbolic function which, . . . has identified his person with the figure of the Law" (1977, 67). Since the client desires to be the Law's signifier, he is no longer subjected to Law's castrating power.

The men erase their subservience to the Law by performing the functions that give power to the Law's images. Twisting the priority principle, Genet takes the Hegelian master/slave relationship to its ultimate subversive end. The client-judge says:

We are bound together, you, he and I. For example, if he didn't hit, how could I stop him from hitting? Therefore, he must strike so that I can intervene and demonstrate my authority. And you must deny your guilt so that he can beat you.

(15)

The thief, not the judge, has claim to priority because "[his] being [a] judge is in emanation of [her] being a thief" (19). Not unlike an audience agreeing with theatrical conventions, a contract must be made between those who represent the script and those who are submissive to its authority. However, like the breach between *langue* and *parole,* this contract is not infal-

lible. Genet's performers, mimicing referential performances, illustrate the signifier's emptiness and the
individual's responsibility for impregnating the discourse with meaning; however, pregnancy is an illusion
at the Grand Balcony.

The women's refusal to name the clients as Law
emphasizes their position as the legitimizing (m) other.
As long as the client is in his studio his desires reign:
"here there's no possibility of doing evil" (10). Seeming to be the master of his own desires, the client
neutralizes the Law that precedes him through the
cooperation of the women who take pleasure in disrupt-
ing the imaginary chain of signifiers by using anal
language: a verbal simulation mirroring the psychological function of anal manipulation. The client's gratification is orgasmically heightened by the threat of reality:

THE WOMAN:

> Reality frightens you, doesn't it?

THE BISHOP:

> If your sins were real, they would be crimes, and I'd
> be in a fine mess.

(10)

The women defer the client's gratification by refusing
to accept the ideal object/ego's authority and only later
providing the client with their bodies' metaphorical
gifts. Delaying in telling the Chief of Police "the fact
that his image does not yet conform to the liturgies of
the brother" (47), the women derive erotic pleasure
through suspending "the subject's certainties until their
last mirages have been consumed" (Lacan, 1977, 43).
As archetypal mothers, the women nourish and sustain
the client's *jouissance* by epitomizing Lacan's "woman
as the possessor of man" (Lacan, 1982, 145). The
women also derive pleasure from participating, at a
distance, in the male's fantasy's. Carmen and Irma comment that "The revels that [we] indulge in . . . are to
forget theirs" (36).

Ironically, it the bought position of the women that
stimulates their own fantasies. Irma is "The Woman
. . . as an absolute category and guarantor of fantasy"
(Lacan, 1982, 48). Ultimately, her deceptive love
becomes narcissistic as she exerts her authority by
remaining "alone, mistress and assistant mistress of this
house and of herself" (95). As Jane Gallop points out,
"the whore gives man all he wants without ever being
broken, tamed, possessed" (1982, 89). Genet further
plays with society's patriarchal power structure by
revealing what Lewis Cetta calls the Chief's "ecstati-
cally transcendent figure" (1974, 54) to be nothing more
than *Madam Irma's* finest and most comical travesty.

Through self-reflexive doubling, Genet spreads this
narcissistic subversion onto the audience. The client
loves what he sees in the mirror because it reflects how

he wants to be seen: "Mirror that glorifies me! Image
that I can touch, I love you . . . (The general bows to
his image in the mirror . . . and bows to the audience)"
(18-19, 27). The general's bow to the audience draws
us into the narcissistic pool by exposing our pleasure in
quiet voyeurism. Like the women, the actors are props
initiating the audience's *meconnaissance*. However, the
audience becomes voyeurs not of elicit sexual acts, but
of the desire for such acts to occur. Thus, genet invites
us into the play's sacred ritual only to embarrass us for
being there. Once the sessions end, the women's indifference parallels representational art's dispassion toward
everything except its own perpetuation. Once the show
is over, actors do not often hobnob with the audience.
Through theatre's trick mirrors, Genet recognizes the
audience's authority only to thematically drain them of
power.

Genet completes his attack on realism through the
character of Roger. This ideal voyeur insists on loving
Chantel, the ideal whore. He exalts her as his sexual
ideal and transforms her into an exotic figure incapable
of physical love. Roger states his motivation for such
reverence: "If we behave like those on the other side,
then we *are* the other side. Instead of changing the
world, all we'll achieve is a reflection of the one we
want to destroy" (56). This self-reflexive statement
enhances the problematic ideology behind realist
representation. Audience identification with the other
confuses or nullifies social-consciousness by forcing
people to embrace false images. The psychological
reasoning behind Roger's castration can be explained in
Lacanian terms: "I love you, but because inexplicably I
love in you something more than you—the *objet petit
a*—I mutilate you" (1981, 268). Lacan's equation of
misidentified love leading to self-mutilation rather than
political violence reinforces Genet's vision of the
dangers of mimetic identification. Without phallic
power, Roger cannot mutilate the symbol; therefore, in
a sexually deviant act he mutilates the real object of his
love—himself. Genet's theatre suggests that realism
hides ideological conspiracies by encouraging false
identifications that lead to the audience's socio-psycho
self-mutilation. Such violence creates hollow subjects
stuffed with realist straw incapable of revolutionary
thought or action.

Psychological transference and the artistic transference
encouraged by realist theatre are parallel dangers since
both are based on false premises. In the psychological
transference the synchronic intersection of the diachro-
nic fantasy is, in Lacan's thinking, the "moment in
which the symbolic and real come together" (1977, 95).
In Genet's psycho-theatre, the client's donning of the
disguise unites his fragmented existence with the
fantasy's eternal power. The monetary exchange insures
the client the privilege of time to experience this
encounter with the desired object. However, the

symbolic does not play fair; it terminates the possible encounter with the real. At the play's beginning, Irma interrupts the bishop's fantasy: "It's time. Come on! Quick! Make it snappy!" (9). The client, like the audience, participates in the fantasy with the imposing foreknowledge of its termination. Michele Piemme observes that "the ceremony in the Grand Balcony does not have a chance to unfold as it should since everyone is preoccupied with events on the outside" (1979, 165). But while machine gun fire punctuates the fantasy it also intensifies the client's pleasure by reminding him of the situation he has temporarily escaped, and the titillating possibility of its intrusion. That is, if the machine-gun fire isn't merely a sound track!

Likewise, audiences can not ignore theatre's punctuating traces. No matter how perfect the spectacle, theatre/brothel is a business that requires a quick, patron turnover. Although Irma does limit the time, she does not rush the men. They are given time in relation to their scenarios' individual progress. The sessions' various lengths indicate that the Balcony does not adhere to routine time. Multiple time schemes are at work in the theatre and at the brothel, and are measured by the individual's capacity to uncover the scenario's truth: "Everything was carefully planned long ago. It's all been worked out. The rest is up to you" (88). This line places the responsibility of a successful encounter on the audience/client's deciphering capabilities and suspension of disbelief.

Each scenario brings the audience closer to Genet's revolution against representational art and language. Once the client inaugurates his fantasy, the significant points are scripted and the time limit determined. Exchanging one language system for another, the men reveal their desires through fantasy-specific discourses. Once Roger advances through the discourse, the session is over. Going beyond the allotted time is in accordance with Lacan's warning for the psycho-therapist: "The punctuation, once inserted, fixes the meaning; changing the punctuation renews or upsets it; and a faulty punctuation amounts to a change for the worse" (1977, 99). The brothel's statute book fixes the scenario's ritualized time and action. Once the ritual is complete, the client must get dressed and go home: "It's late. And the later it gets, the more dangerous it'll be . . ." (11) for the client.

Violating time is dangerous for the discourse because it introduces the unexpected into the scenario. This may take the form of love, a contradiction to the brothel's goals, or fixation. In *Ecrits,* Lacan discusses the transference in a manner that parallels the Balcony's situation:

> The indifference with which the cutting up of the 'timing' interrupts the moments of haste within the subject can be fatal to the conclusion towards which

his discourse was being precipitated, or can even fix a misunderstanding or misreading in it, if not furnish a pretext for a retaliatory ruse.

(1977 96)

Carmen's faulty punctuating allows Roger to rebel against his inadequacy by taking the scenario's discourse beyond the imaginary identification. He misrecognizes the transformation and believes he has merged with his ideal object/ego: "I've a right to lead the character I've chosen to the very limit of his destiny . . . no, of mine . . . of merging his destiny with mine . . . (93). In his case, he does attain the impossible: he makes the signifier, his castrated body, correspond to the signified that promotes the emptiness of all signifiers. Here too, Genet attack's bourgeois assumptions concerning sexual theatricality by showing power to reside in a mutilated sexual body. The scenario's complexity, mock-power, and faulty punctuation leads the discourse on a dangerous path by giving the client too much unchecked independence. Carmen says, "you wouldn't be the first who thought he'd risen to power" (93). Now it is too late to reverse the grammatical error. Once again, Lacan's description of the transference is helpful:

> We re-establish in the subject his original mirage in so far as he places his truth in us, and that if we then give him the sanction of our authority, we are setting the analysis off on an aberrant path whose results will be impossible to correct.

(1977, 96)

But Genet's doubling self-reflexivity complicates even this reading by suggesting that Roger's scenario, and its violent castration, is not his own, but the Chief of Police's script. The Chief's rise to power is part of the audience's script, and their script part of the realist conspiracy that is part of . . . and so on.

Nevertheless, the clients' inabilities to return to the symbolic 'on time' strand them as ideal object/egos. Disguised as the Queen, Irma tells the bishop that he "happens to be wearing that robe this evening simply because he was unable to clear out of the studios in time" (81). The men, trapped in their fantasy-specific discourses, should be in a euphoric state. But they are not:

> So long as we were in a room in a brothel, we belonged to our own fantasies. But once having exposed them, having named them, having proclaimed them, we're now tied up with adventure according to the laws of visibility.

(79)

The studios create a unifying pleasure between subject and object. According to Chaudhuri, a performance, like that enacted in Genet's text, does not offer an "absence from the self, [nor] escape into a center of pure otherness, but an experience of 'in-between-ness' of the *process* of self-loss" (1990,67). Unfortunately, once the narcissism is publicized the individual no longer enjoys the process because Law crystallizes the private process into a public product featuring collective escapism. The above speech parallels Lacan's theory that individual's enjoy the search for rather than the conquering of the desired object. The subject can never attain real, solitary power because power involves an inter-dependent dialectic between master and slave, ego and image, character and audience.

Genet's attack on representation and bourgeois society is furthered by the audience's reflection in the clients' dissatisfactions. Both Genet and Lacan recognize that the subject's submission to the system heightens his insignificance; the brothel's scenarios continue even in his absence: "If the gentleman doesn't fit the bill, then get a dummy" (Chaudhuri 1990, 67). The audience is forced to see the ideal image's impotence, especially when the clients voice their dissatisfaction with the game:

> We shall go back to our rooms and there continue the quest of an absolute dignity. We ought never to have left them. For we were content there, and it was you who came and dragged us away. Fore ours was a happy state. And absolutely safe . . . we were general, judge and bishop to the point of perfection and to the point of rapture!
>
> (79)

Dissatisfaction motivates rebellion; but, the clients' empowerment is based on the false premise that they can unite their inferior egos with their ideal object/egos. Using theatricality as a weapon, Genet shows power to be anti-thetical to the notion of self because it requires an *aphanisis,* or fading, of the subject. By extension, the psychoanalytical explanation is as follows:

> They simply exercise, in relation to one another, that function of being pure representatives and, above all, their own signification must not intervene . . . they are supposed to represent something whose signification, while constantly changing is, beyond their own persons.
>
> (Lacan 1981, 220)

When the client's persona still pokes through the image, the necessary fading is disrupted and the ideal ego looses its authority. Stripped of its exotic pleasure, the bishop states the banality of their new entrapment: "as for my lace, I no longer look forward to it—it's myself . . . I'm just a dignity represented by a robe. . . . By Jove, I no longer dream" (Genet, 1981, 364). Pure power, solitary authority and rebellion are impossible.

While the priority principle endows the roles with authority, it is the costume that signals that authority to the world. Likewise, in describing the acting process,

Bettina Knapp says the actor embodies the Creator and the incarnator, and is a "sign charged with signs" (90). The actor is a paradox: real and unreal, concrete and abstract, one yet multiple. In order to create a character, the actor must fade into the scenery; however, in Genet and Lacan's world the split between actor and character is always already present and visible, and a challenge to oppressive, ideological structures.

In effect, the clients become truly powerful only in the illusory misidentifications created by the women who cunningly transform themselves into tricks/mirrors. Irma says, "Their seed never ripens in you, and yet . . . if you weren't there?" (31). The female's sterility makes her the Mother-object and not a penetratable, sexual entity. The male's ecstasy is evoked through his false reunion with the object; the child with the mother; the masculine external with the feminine interior. According to the Lacan, the masquerade is the very definition of femininity because it is constructed with reference to a male sign. The clients masquerade as feminine ideals because they both desire and lack the phallus. To be the symbol of power, the phallus and the Other of themselves, is only possible in the illusory role of the Law. The masquerade connects them with the hidden power of their own interior femininity because it is the Mother gives the father power by naming him. This suggests that real power can only be achieved through the reunion of the feminine and the masculine. But how to achieve this?

The setting implies that sexual intercourse precedes the masquerade. The unmade bed is a reflection suggestive of the scenario's main focus: "The scenarios are all reducible to a major theme . . . Death" (87-88). Like the Surrealists, Genet and Lacan view the business of sex as the business of the mortuary. Lacan says "sex and its significations are always capable of making present the presence of death" (1981, 205). The clients play our their death scenes while also experimenting with the false possibility of producing bastard children, an idea that intensifies their lack to the point of ecstasy. By playing with a social death, the clients attempt to destroy their social egos and (re)produce the imaginary bond. However, the prostitute's sterility, as stated by Irma, makes the issue of sex and death a mockery that defers the subject's ecstasy to the scenario:

> If I went through wars without dying, went through sufferings without dying, if I was promoted, without dying, it was for this minute close to death . . . where I shall be nothing, though reflected ad infinitum in these mirrors, nothing but my image.
>
> (26)

Undoubtedly, death is linked to sex. However, while in the illusion, death is a fantasy because the general can die only figuratively. Irma's characters are immortal

Others. Likewise, Lacan's Other is immortal, thus making any risk for the subject inoperant since "death is present only in jest" (1971, 290). The general participates in his own funeral ritual and revels in the fact that as the client he can get up and go home.

Genet's ultimate challenge to realism's ideological construction comes in the form of the Chief of Police. While the other clients are ordinary men who desire to be Father archetypes, the Chief is always already a signifier of Law. Yet, even the Law desires an imaginary return: "for me, the Queen has to be someone. And the situation had to be concrete" (63). *His* need for validation undermines the existence of a pure Signifier. Once he is assured that his image will be perpetuated in men's fantasies the Chief becomes a symbol in waiting and wins the right to eternal life. He wins the right to die by provoking the image's ritualized death. The Chief stresses his independence by constantly asserting that the "people fear him more and more" (48).

Although the Chief continually asserts his power, the *meconnaissance* would be impossible without Irma. Like Genet, she transforms ordinary prostitutes into mother substitutes; she transforms empty spaces into theatrical dreamscapes. Everything she does is for the ultimate scenario, the Mausoleum Studio. For example, scene four's tramp prepares to be the Hero's slave. The Balcony's economical use of clients as employees strengthens Genet's thematic destabilization of self. Everything is theatrical in order to foreground "a becoming rather than a being" (Chaudhuri 1990, 71). Everything and everyone, including the audience, becomes part of the theatrical process. The Chief immortalizes his identity; however Roger's castration of the "Chief" emphasizes his powerlessness. Robert Brustein asserts "the mutilation bestows godhead upon the Chief of Police, for, like the ancient gods, 'he has been mutilated and remained whole'" (1964, 401). The Chief endorses this view by mistakenly thinking he can still separate himself from his image: "though my image be castrated in every brothel in the world I remain intact" (94). Earlier, he contradicts this idea by saying, "I'll know by a sudden weakness of my muscles that my image is escaping from me to go and haunt men's minds" (82). In fact, this discrepancy parallels the audience's fluctuating engagement between their total fading into the theatrical experience and their self-awareness of realism's artifice. I suggest that the castration, performed by one who plays the duo role of powerful father and power-seeking son is analogous to Lacan's interpretation that all individuals seek a return to an imaginary completeness with the Other while knowing such a return is impossible.

Ultimately, Genet's characters become playful shifting signifiers in a never-ending process of (re)discovery and loss. Una Chaudhuri states that Genet's theatrical world is a liminal time and space marked by make-believe. The literal activity of mirroring, and its metaphorical connection to art, is presented as a subconscious necessity in transgressing the symbolic's divisive power. Interestingly, it is Irma, not the Chief of Police, who exerts Genet's final blow against society and its privileging of representational ideology. Directly addressing the audience as she would a client, she says: "You must now go home, where everything—you can be quite sure—will be falser than here. . . . You must go now. You'll leave by the right, through the alley . . ." (96). Pointing to the theatre's sacred space and the audience's communion with its ritual offerings, Bettina Knapp enhances Genet's belief that the desires of the individual are not private and personal, but the collective dreams of the oppressed masses. Lacanian psychology also posits this notion. Knapp comments that the audience's participation in the theatrical ritual, even if it is a passive one, is one where "he renounces his individual existence and becomes part of the collective body (1968, 93).

Emphasizing theatre's scared function, Saint Genet's radical splitting of self through doubling self-reflexivity parallels the Lacanian, post-structural challenge of self and representation. Genet's theatre and Lacan's psychology invites audiences/clients to an aggressive carnival presented in a hall of mirrors where no one is real, all is theatrical, and everything reflects empty images drowning in narcissistic desires.

References

Bleikesten, A. "Fathers in Faulkner" in *The Fictional Father: Lacanian Readings of the Text.* Ed. Con Davis, Amherst: University of Massachusetts Press.

Brustein, Robert. (1964). *The Theatre of Revolt,* Boston: Little Brown.

Cetta, Lewis. (1974). *Profane Play, Ritual and Jean Genet: A Study of his Drama.* Alabama: University of Alabama Press.

Chaudhuri, Una. (1990). *No Man's Stage: A Semiotic Study of Jean Genet's Major Plays,* Ann Arbor: UMI Research Press.

Freud, Sigmund. (1984). "On Narcissism: An Introduction" in *On Metapsychology: The Theory of Psychoanalysis,* ed. A. Richards. New York: Penguin Books.

Gallop, Jane. (1982). *The Daughter's Seduction: Feminism and Psychoanalysis,* New York: Cornell UP.

Genet, Jean. (1962). *The Balcony,* trans. Bernard Frechtman, New York: Grove Press.

————. (1981) *The Balcony* in *Nine Plays of the Modern Theatre.* ed. H. Clurman, New York: Grove Press.

Innes, Christopher. (1993). *Avant Garde Theatre: 1892-1992,* London: Routledge.

Knapp, Bettina. (1968). *Jean Genet,* New York: Twayne Publishing.

Lacan, Jacques. (1977). *Ecrits,* trans. A. Sheridan, New York: W. W. Norton & Company.

———. (1981). *The Four Fundamental Concepts of Psychoanalysis,* trans. A. Sheridan. ed. J. A. Miller. New York: W. W. Norton & Company.

———. (1982). *Feminine Sexuality: Jacques Lacan and the Ecole Freudienne,* trans. J. Rose, ed. J. Mitchell, J. Rose. New York: W. W. Norton & Company.

Piemme, Michele. (1979). "Scenic Space and Dramatic Illusion in *The Balcony*" in *Genet: A Collection of Essays,* New Jersey: Grove Press.

Pizzato, Mark. (1990). "Genet's Violence, Subjective Split into the Theatre of Lacan's Three Orders" in *Journal of Dramatic Theory and Criticism* 5.1, 116.

Savona, Jeanette. (1983). *Jean Genet.* New York: Grove Press.

LES NÈGRES (1959)

PRODUCTION REVIEW

David Bradby (review date 1988)

SOURCE: Bradby, David. "Blacking Up—Three Productions by Peter Stein." In *A Radical Stage: Theatre in Germany in the 1970s and 1980s,* edited by W. G. Sebald, pp. 18-30. Oxford: Berg Publishers Limited, 1988.

[*In the following review, Bradby assesses three productions of* The Blacks *directed by Peter Stein.*]

'One evening an actor asked me to write a play for an all-black cast. But what exactly is a black? First of all, what's his colour?'[1] With these words Genet introduced his play ***The Blacks,*** adding a further note in which he insisted that the play must be performed to an audience of whites. If by chance there were to be no white person present, a white dummy or white masks would have to be used.

The reasons for Genet's insistence are clear enough: blackness is a social construct, something culturally determined, having its origin in the colonial encounter.

Biological factors such as ethnic origins and skin colour are quite unimportant by comparison with the power of one group of people to impose an identity on another group. Genet, who has always identified with the outlawed and criminal classes, has described himself as 'a black whose skin happens to be pink and white'.[2]

Genet wrote ***The Blacks*** for a group of black actors mostly from West Africa who called themselves 'Les Griots' (poet-musicians) and since its first production (by Roger Blin in 1959) the play has rarely been revived in Europe, though it is regularly performed by black theatre groups in America. The reason for this is simple: it is written in such a way as to demand performance by an all-black cast. So it was a bold move by Peter Stein and the Schaubühne to decide that they would undertake a production.

Bold, but not altogether surprising. Many of Stein's productions have involved his company identifying with a group quite different from themselves and spending a great deal of time and effort getting into their skins. They did this for the revolutionary sailors of Vishnevski's *Optimistic Tragedy* in 1972 and for the idle *datshniki* of Gorki's *Summerfolk* in 1974. In 1976 they spent a year transforming themselves into inhabitants of Elizabethan England for *Shakespeare's Memory.* If Stein did experience any doubts about the wisdom of getting his cast to transform themselves into blacks, he may have felt it was no different in kind from these earlier experiments. Stein has always claimed that he has no set working method, that he shapes his methods according to the demands of the plays he tackles. The one constant factor in his working practice is a preference for working as part of a collective: clearly ensemble work of a high order is needed for Genet's dramatic ritual to find adequate expression on stage, but is it the kind of ensemble work developed by Stein and his company? Does it in the end matter whether Genet's prescription about black actors playing for a white audience is or is not followed?

In order to answer this and to understand Stein's work in 1983 and 1986, it is necessary to consider briefly the nature of Stein's early work as a director of the Schaubühne in the early 1970s.[3] The strength of this work lay in the way he confronted the contradictions it involved, contradictions which may be reduced schematically to two: one internal to the company and the other external. The internal contradiction was that of having to impose his role of director within the structure of a democratically self-governing collective. The external contradiction was that of performing revolutionary works (such as *The Optimistic Tragedy*) in a West Berlin theatre heavily subsidised as a showcase for capitalist values. Stein's work at this time prompted questions about the relationships between the individual and authority, private satisfactions and the public good.

These questions were not confined to the subject matter of the plays he produced (such as *Prinz Friedrich von Homburg* or *Peer Gynt*); they permeated the processes of his work at every level. His role in the German theatre was not only to question all established practices, but openly to advocate the overthrow of the institutions that paid him. He was able to do this partly because of the peculiar state of cultural politics in West Berlin and partly because of his own qualities of vision, determination and commitment. One of his exceptional qualities was a sharp awareness of the contradictions involved in his own and his company's work, and his ability to turn this awareness into a significant element of his productions.

Stein at first appeared to welcome both contradictions, not seeking to eliminate them but harnessing the dynamic process of challenge and counter-challenge that they entailed. Where the 'external' contradiction was concerned, he could point to a successful record of exploiting his favoured position without being exploited by it. For a time, during the early 1970s, he consistently presented material that challenged the expectations of his audiences and could not be accused of selling out to his paymasters. With respect to the 'internal' contradiction, Stein's success with the Schaubühne company appears to have stemmed from his total commitment to the collective process, even when it worked to his own inconvenience, and his ability to command the loyalty of first-rate actors. He was able to do this because the group was united by a sense of political purpose. The discussion of their contradictions was made to fuel a learning process. From the outset Stein's working methods involved a strong element of research and discovery by all members of the company. In order to raise the general level of political consciousness and to inform the managerial discussions within the group, political seminars were arranged, which everyone attended in working hours. The artistic aims of the group were also defined in terms of a learning process:

> We wanted to concern ourselves with subjects not normally dealt with in the theatre, that is to say the history of revolution or revolutions and of the working class movement. That was our firm intention. And we were conscious of everything that implied: raising our political consciousness, studying the historical facts, etc. In short our need to learn not only about aesthetic matters, but also and especially about historical matters. That can only be a long-term undertaking. The other direction concerned the past and the history of the bourgeois class. There again, it seemed important to us to know more about it and to deal with it in our productions.[4]

This is unusual as a declaration of intent by a director of a theatre company because of its emphasis on what is to be learned rather than what is to be shown, on process rather than on product. It was informed by a clear belief that learning of this kind served a useful

purpose: to understand and hence to be able to change. Significantly, Stein expressed the company's project in terms of alternatives: history of revolutions on the one hand, history of the bourgeois class on the other. Together with this political aim went an aesthetic ambition to research and experiment with the alternative modes of representation available in a theatre such as his. In 1972 Stein talked about a planned production concerning the Paris Commune of 1871 (this never reached fruition). He explained that he had rejected both the existing plays on the subject by Brecht and Adamov and had sketched out a new idea in which the subject was to be 'the end of the bourgeois conception of revolution and the emergence of a different form of revolution, a different aesthetic, a different mode of representation and different metaphors since the Commune. That, I believe, is an interesting subject for the theatre'.[5] It can be seen that the focus of Stein's work was not just historical or political alternatives, but a reflection on the alternative modes of representation available for depicting historical events, and this in turn is closely connected to the nature of the raw material with which the director works—that is, a company. Speaking fifteen years later about his production of Verdi's *Otello*, Stein said: 'You have to persuade people you are right to be on stage—and that for me is always the central problem. That we can only achieve if everybody on stage knows exactly what is going on, what the play or opera is about, of course, but also *what the staging in itself means.*'[6]

It is in this spirit that Stein's production of **The Blacks** must be examined to determine how 'the staging in itself' became a bearer of meaning. Stein stated clearly that the choice of play corresponded to the Schaubühne's desire to work collectively and to pursue its reflection on modes of dramatic representation:

> We chose **The Blacks** because it opened up a subject having to do with the activity of theatre and one which we thought we could usefully explore and learn from. The subject was Africa, the European-African relationship, of course, as the play describes it. Moreover the actors were keen to work as a chorus and they are all on stage all the time.[7]

He added that the play also fitted the company's desire to follow up experiences not normally available to actors—in this case getting to know Africa. They made a brief trip to Africa, where they learned some basic African dance steps and these were put to good effect in the performance.

Genet's plays present any director with an unusual challenge since they are more ceremonies than stories, while nevertheless retaining close links to political realities. **The Blacks** presents not a story at all in the traditional sense, but a struggle between two languages. By imposing the French language on the Africans the colonisers have forced them to adopt all the hidden judgements enshrined in the European language. In the play a group of blacks face a white court, also played by blacks, wearing white masks. Beneath the horrified gaze of the court, the blacks re-enact the rape and murder of a white woman. The court appeals to Racinian purity, meta-phoric whiteness, images of light and spotlessness, the white man's civilising mission. The blacks respond with a 'litany of the livid', exploiting the unpleasant as-sociations of pallor, then they begin to develop a new set of value associations in which positive values are linked with notions of blackness. Genet's strategy here is not that of Senghor who, in developing his concept of negritude, used metaphors of blackness to which positive values have traditionally ascribed: mystery, fertility, power. Instead, Genet picked on all those things that have traditionally been used as insults by whites: smells, savagery, cannibalism. This is the language through which the white colonisers oblige the Africans to represent themselves—the only self-image available to them once they have adopted the French language. And so they develop and extend it, they celebrate it to a point of extremism, revel in it grotesquely. Genet's text prescribes the precise details of this ritual: the move-ments, the music, the use of masks, costumes and props. For example, he specifies a raised gallery running round the back of the stage from which the court looks down on the action, so that the ceremony of the blacks is caught between the facing ranks of white audience and white court: the gaze of one is reflected in the other. He also specifies that the play opens with the blacks danc-ing a minuet to a tune by Mozart.

Stein's production gave an extremely brilliant and very faithful representation of all this, adding very little that was not explicitly mentioned in Genet's directions. This in itself was remarkable since it had frequently been a hallmark of Stein's earlier works that he would reorder the text or add in extra material, the better to convey the kind of critical reflection on the play and its modes of representation alluded to in his remarks quoted above. In ***The Blacks*** scope for such additional work was reduced since the play is itself a reflection on modes of representation. The only changes or additions made by Stein appeared to be governed by political rather than aesthetic motives: they served to stress solidarity with the blacks rather than to reflect critically on representational images. But in so doing they undermined the very basis of Genet's theatrical ceremony. In order to understand how this happened it is necessary to consider the organisation of the performance in some detail.

The performance began with the audience viewing the process of blacking up by the actors. It was clearly important for Stein that the spectators should witness this complete transformation—i.e. should realise that they were to be faced, as nearly as possible, with a real

group of blacks performing for them. After this, the play unfolded almost exactly as specified by Genet. The opening minuet was exquisitely performed by the group, humming in Swingle-singer style and waltzing round the stage as they did so. This was dramatically inter-rupted by a detail not of Genet's invention: an African spear which fell from the flying gallery to embed itself with a splintering crash in the beautiful varnished black wood of the stage. The members of the court, all blacked up like the others, wore white masks over their black faces as specified by Genet. They watched the ritual from a balcony set above and behind the action, much as in Blin's original production, and their pale gaze was supplemented by hundreds of other white masks which descended on strings as Village protested his love for Vertu—a mass of white voyeurs gloating in their power over the blacks. This addition helped to underline the fact that in Genet's ceremony the blacks have to refuse love as something polluted by the way it has been annexed by white civilisation. Instead, the only hope for the blacks is in the cultivation of hatred and the difficulty of this was demonstrated with great clarity in the dialogue between Village and Vertu (performed by Peter Simonischeck and Jutta Lampe) as they tried to develop a verbal language of hatred while all their body language expressed desire for one another.

The production was remarkable for the intelligence and faithfulness which Stein brought to the realisation of Genet's intentions. Particularly successful was the chanting of Félicité's 'Dahomey, Dahomey' speech in which Miriam Goldschmidt (the only black member of the cast) built up an atmosphere of tremendous power. The ensuing sequence, too, in which Neige accuses Vil-lage of having been attracted to the white woman was performed by Martina Krauel as a wild possession dance with everyone on stage joining in. The use of move-ment and gesture was constantly illuminating and there were various ingenious *coups de théâtre,* such as the point where Diouf (dressed up as a white woman) and Village go behind the screen, ostensibly for the re-enactment of the rape and murder. When Ville de St. Nazaire folded up the screen, Diouf had disappeared: he was no longer on the same level as the other blacks but entered, suspended on a wire, flying like a grotesque angel above the head of the queen. Yet despite the faithfulness and clarity of the production, its overall ef-fect was not to disturb and challenge the audience as Genet had intended. The reasons for this can be ad-duced from an examination of Stein's additions, modest though they were.

The one aim of all his additions seemed to be to increase the political punch of the show, as if, to make up for the fact that they were not real blacks, the cast had to demonstrate special energy and commitment. This aspect of the production became progressively clearer towards the end. At the point where Ville de St.

Nazaire re-enters to announce the execution of a traitor off-stage in another place, Genet's stage direction specifies the sound of firecrackers going off and, on the black velvet of the set, the reflections of fireworks.[8] Not content with mere reflections, Stein provided a complete firework show which dazzlingly filled the whole stage space and led into a mood of common celebration as the court descended, removed their masks and pressed round Ville de St. Nazaire eager for information about the 'real' action taking place off-stage. For there are references throughout Genet's play to the effect that what we are being shown is not in itself of central importance: it is merely a diversion to keep its audience's mind off the 'real' action, taking place elsewhere, and involving the trial and execution of a black freedom fighter who has betrayed the cause, together with the commissioning of a new man to work in his place. Ville de St. Nazaire says: 'He's on his way. He's going off to organise and continue the fight. . . . As for you, you were only present for the display.' To which the one who played the valet replies curtly: 'We know. Thanks to us, they've sensed nothing of what's going on elsewhere.'[9] As this exchange makes quite clear, the function of Genet's play is somehow to disguise the reality of armed struggle, not to mobilise the audience for it. What is shown on stage can never have the force of an active revolt. Indeed, there are constant references to the suicidal nature of the enterprise the blacks are engaged on. In accepting the world of theatre, they have entered a de-realising space which robs them of any impact they might have had on the real world. This is spelled out by Archibald near the beginning of the ceremony: 'They tell us we're grown-up children. In that case what's left for us? The theatre! We'll play at being reflected in it and we'll see ourselves, big black narcissists, slowly disappearing into its waters.'[10] When Village protests that he wants to live Archibald snaps back at him:

ARCHIBALD:

> You're no exception! Nothing will remain of you but the foam of your rage. Since they merge us with an image and drown us in it, let the image set their teeth on edge!

VILLAGE:

> My body wants to live.

ARCHIBALD:

> You're becoming a spectre before their very eyes and you're going to haunt them.[11]

The necessary condition for transforming subservience into domination is first to cease to exist in the real world and turn into a spook, an 'image to set their teeth on edge'.

The political function of Genet's theatre is a subject on which he has spoken out forcefully. He has constantly said that the stage should not be used as a vehicle for resolving social problems. He insists that problems shown on stage should never be resolved on the imaginary plane because this will leave the audience with the comforting sense that the problem has been overcome and requires no further action: 'On the contrary, let evil explode on stage, let it show us naked, leave us haggard if possible, and with no other recourse than to ourselves.'[12] He wrote in a similar vein about *The Maids*: 'This is not an apologia on the lot of domestic servants. No doubt there exists a Trade Union for them—that does not concern us.'[13] The consequence of this attitude is that Genet's plays are not satirical in the common sense. Rather than cutting their characters down to size, they exalt them. The maids, the blacks do not represent the reality of servility or colonialism, but its image. They are reflections of images in the minds of their audiences. In so far as they represent social relations as they exist in the real world, Genet's *dramatis personae* become simple figures onto which the audience is invited to project its familiar images. Hence the importance for Genet of the play being performed *by* blacks *for* whites: what takes place on stage is created by the spectators as much if not more than by the actors. The play is a ritual designed solely to undermine and dissolve the status of the actors as 'blacks', i.e. people whose being is defined by 'whites' as being non-white, other, alien, inferior. The function of Genet's play is not to appeal to the spectators' sympathy for the plight of the oppressed but rather to trap them in an act of imaginative complicity that can then be turned against them. It aims to disturb, challenge and upset them—it cannot at the same time win their sympathy for the cause of black freedom fighters. Yet this was exactly what the last stages of Stein's production pointed towards, moving on from the celebratory fireworks and concluding with the display of an enormous map of Africa divided into those territories that are independent and those still under the colonial heel. In front of this, the cast performed not a Mozart minuet (as in Genet's stage direction) but an aggressive dance to African drums.

Stein was criticised by some reviewers for having introduced an excessively political note into his production.[14] This is surely wrong. The mistake was not to suggest a political dimension but to misunderstand the force of the work's political thrust, presenting it as a call to action instead of a play of image and reflection. It is perhaps surprising to find Stein slipping into this error in view of his earlier emphasis on modes of representation. But at the same time it is not difficult to see why Stein's production developed in this way: it was a natural consequence of his emphasis on the group process and on a theatrical form that allowed for exploration of group identity. Once having undertaken the almost impossible task of performing a play written for black actors, it is clear that the whole company found itself identifying strongly with the oppressed group they were trying to portray. It was this same emphasis on group work that lent such power to Stein's production of *Otello* in 1986. He had been attracted to the Welsh National Opera Company because of the outstanding quality of its chorus work.

This production was the story of far more than just the relationship between Otello and Desdemona. It was the account of a ruler's relationship with his people and the key to this was Stein's use of the chorus. In the first act, he explained, 'the microcosm of Cyprus society and the macrocosm of the universe are both threatened by chaos.' Theatrically, this was conveyed by the chorus filling and swirling around the stage. Otello entered and both the storm and the citizens of Cyprus were stilled. Later, when a drunken brawl erupted, Otello again restored order. Stein described Otello's relation to the chorus as that of a good father to his children and the first act successfully established the sense of a community governed on old-fashioned paternalist principles: so long as Otello was among his people, all was well. In the second act, as Iago began to poison Otello's mind, he drew across the stage an enormous red curtain, half shutting out the brilliant light of the Mediterranean exterior, symbolically separating Otello from the public life of his people. This in turn built up to the catastrophe of the third act when Otello, crazed by suspicion, rounded on the chorus and attacked them: in Stein's words, 'the head turns against the limbs'. Here Otello's private tragedy, as he accepts the apparent proof of Desdemona's guilt was expressed in public disintegration as he hurled himself at the chorus, scattering them in all directions. The fourth act followed, as Stein put it, 'like a sad private consequence of a public crime, like ritual fulfilment of its implications' and the logical conclusion to his production would have been to bring the chorus back on stage at the end, opening the tragedy out once more to show its double dimension, extending beyond the destruction of Otello's love for Desdemona to the destruction of the bond between Otello and his people. He did in fact plan to introduce something of this kind but, in the end, found that he was unable to make it work and so left the focus on the bodies in the bedroom.

Stein himself expressed what gave his production its force when he said that 'Verdi and Boito's great invention, which they do not find in Shakespeare's tragedy, is the sense of community on the stage participating in the action. The chorus themselves create the space for the protagonists to act in . . . They construct the stage.' It is striking how aptly these words would also serve to describe what happened in Stein's 1986 production for the Schaubühne of O'Neill's *The Hairy Ape*. In both productions the real centre of the dramatic action is located in the relationship between the hero (Otello or Yank) and the group which he both dominates yet longs to be part of. Like Otello's encounter with Desdemona,

the meeting in O'Neill's play between the coal-black Yank and the dazzling millionaire's daughter only acquires meaning in relation to the social and political forces in play. Such stark contrasts emphasising how an individual's existence only acquires meaning in relation to larger groupings had been a feature of Stein's work at the Schaubühne since its beginnings, but had previously been fuelled by an urgent sense of the need to discover alternative modes of understanding or of action in order to reconstruct the social order.

In Stein's 1986 productions however, that urgent search for alternatives seemed to give way to a crushing pessimism. His stage images repeatedly stressed the individual's inability to make sense of his life, either as an individual or as a member of society. *The Hairy Ape* revealed this *Weltanschauung* most clearly as it unfolded its powerful catalogue of alienation. Lucio Fanti's monumental set for the ocean liner placed Yank (the representative industrial worker) in a position literally squeezed between the vast voracious boilers that he had to stoke in the dark bowels of the ship and the inaccessible passenger deck where the light was bright and the rich were free to lounge. Although Yank began by proclaiming his faith in the liberating power of modern industrial progress, he gradually realised that his faith was misplaced and that for him there could be no source of pride or self-esteem, whether in class-consciousness or in personal strength.

The reasons for choosing this play were similar to those governing the choice of earlier Schaubühne work: the play has a strong choral or 'ensemble' element and it focuses clearly on working-class experience under capitalism. It is possible to go further and to interpret it as an anti-colonial play: the encounter between Yank and the millionaire's daughter reproduces exactly the terms of the colonial encounter underlying Genet's **The Blacks.** Stein explained in an interview that he had always sought out plays about working-class experience but that 'Brecht, who was so terribly keen on the working class, scarcely wrote *anything* directly about them', so that after *The Mother* in 1970 the Schaubühne had turned to other authors, such as Vishnevski.[15] But, unlike *The Mother* or *The Optimistic Tragedy, The Hairy Ape* offers no political solution to the troubles of the modern world. Instead it presents, in spectacular fashion, a series of images of exclusion, imprisonment and failure. For this play, written in 1921-2 at the height of the Expressionist Movement, Stein made unashamed use of the whole arsenal of Expressionist production methods. But in so doing, and in complaining that Brecht failed to write plays of this kind, he was overlooking the reason why Brecht (and other political dramatists) turned their back on Expressionist depictions of the working class. This was because Expressionist art favoured the presentation of stark images of alienation, tending not towards movement or analysis of alternatives, but rather towards fixity and fatalism. The more effectively group movement and stark visual contrast were employed, the more an image of hopelessness was reinforced, so that what might appear to be an art form sympathetic to mass experience in fact had the effect of suggesting that the lot of the working class was irremediably awful: sympathy tipped over into fatalism.

This experience is at the heart of O'Neill's play and was crystallised in one of the most successfully realised moments of the production. Travelling on the great ocean liner which forms the setting for the first part of the play is Mildred, the daughter of the millionaire president of the Steel Trust. Having trained as a social worker, she wants to visit the boiler hall in the depths of the ship and observe the conditions in which the stokers work. After a magnificently choreographed scene, in which the coal-blackened stokers shovel real fuel into the fiery furnaces, she appears, descending the ladder all in white, an alien being from a different world. The confrontation destroys both her and Yank. For her it is an experience of despair, since she was already aware of her superfluousness in her own world ('I'm a waste product in the Bessemer process') but had imagined that she might be able to enter sympathetically into the world of the exploited workers. Faced with the 'naked and shameless brutality' of the world of the stokers, she falls into a faint, muttering 'Oh, the filthy beast!'

Yank is destroyed because he suddenly sees himself through her eyes as nothing more than a beast of burden. His pride in himself has been destroyed and so he sets out to get even with Mildred and her class. In the second half of the play Yank is brought face to face with a circle of capitalists, a circle of union activists and finally a circle of apes in the zoo. With an equal lack of success, he tries to break into each of these circles in turn. His descent into a subhuman category is complete when he releases a gorilla from its cage; the animal crushes him to death before ambling off to enjoy a doubtless all-too-brief moment of freedom.

The strength of this production was in the extraordinarily powerful ensemble playing that Stein drew from the company, combined with the spectacular settings designed by Lucio Fanti (also the designer for *Otello*). At each point in the drama Yank's experience was echoed or contrasted with that of the whole group, who were on stage for most of the evening. This production confirmed the outstanding talent of Stein, who must rank as one of the most brilliant directors at work in the theatre today. But it also confirmed the reasons for the ultimate failure of **The Blacks**: Stein's willingness, in the early 1970s, to embrace contradictions, to mobilise them in the analysis of a social problem has given way in the 1980s to a coldness, even a fatalism, that finds

expression in overwhelmingly beautiful images of irremediable alienation. In 1985 Stein resigned his post as artistic director of the Schaubühne without giving any very clear reason for this unexpected decision. He had only recently moved into a new theatre, built to his own specifications; he could call on a virtually limitless budget and an ensemble of outstanding actors who had worked together for nearly two decades. What cause could he possibly have for discontent? It seems likely that both he and the company felt that they had reached the end of their abilities to produce work that was new and challenging. The production of *The Hairy Ape* was a near-perfect realisation of O'Neill's text, but its very perfection stressed the death of the belief that had fuelled the company's early work: that a process of learning could lead to the discovery of social and political alternatives strong enough to mount a real challenge to the status quo. *The Hairy Ape* suggests that for Stein this belief may have turned into despair.

Notes

1. Jean Genet, *The Blacks,* trans. Bernard Frechtman, London 1960, p. 5.

2. 'Jean Genet talks to Hubert Fichte', *The New Review* 37 (1977), 9-21.

3. For a full discussion of Stein's work in the 1970s see Michael Patterson, *Peter Stein, Germany's Leading Theatre Director,* Cambridge 1981, and David Bradby and David Williams, *Director's Theatre,* London (Macmillan) forthcoming.

4. Interview in *Travail Théâtral* (Paris) 9 (1972), 16-36.

5. Ibid.

6. Interview in the programme for the Welsh National Opera production of *Otello,* 1986. All subsequent quotations by Stein concerning *Otello* come from this interview.

7. Interview in *Théâtre en Europe* (Paris) 1 (1984), 24-9.

8. *The Blacks,* p. 84.

9. Ibid., p. 85.

10. Ibid., p. 31.

11. Ibid., p. 32.

12. (My translation) Jean Genet, *Oeuvres complètes IV,* Paris 1968, p. 35.

13. Ibid., p. 269.

14. E.g. Michael Stone in *The Guardian,* 24 June 1983: 'Genet did not really write a play about racial discrimination and its effects on its victims. *The Blacks* is only another expression of Genet's love of Mayhem.'

15. 'The Theatre of Peter Stein', Interview by Roy Kift, *Drama* 2 (1987), 5-7.

CRITICAL COMMENTARY

Derek F. Connon (essay date October 1996)

SOURCE: Connon, Derek F. "Confused? You Will Be: Genet's *Les Nègres* and the Art of Upsetting the Audience." *French Studies* 50, no. 4 (October 1996): 425-38.

[*In the following essay, Connon discusses the role of the audience in* The Blacks, *focusing on Genet's direct implication of its racial composition and his intentional creation of discomfort.*]

Whilst **Les Nègres** is the play which Genet wrote to be performed by black actors, this is really the only sense in which it is a play written *for* blacks. In every other sense it is a play written *against* whites, even if Genet's double question 'Qu'est-ce que c'est donc un noir? Et d'abord, c'est de quelle couleur?'¹ alerts us to the fact that the distinction between black and white is subject to symbolic as well as literal interpretation. Indeed, as J. P. Little puts it, by specifying that the intended public for the play is white 'Genet, as it were, wrote a "part" for the audience'.² He even felt that the work would make sense to a black audience only if it were made clear that it was aimed not at them, but at whites,³ and although the enormously successful off-Broadway run of 1961-64 paradoxically attracted a large proportion of black spectators, Edmund White confirms that their reaction to the action, in contrast to the disquiet of the whites present, was generally laughter.⁴

More than one critic has pointed out that the depiction of blacks by Genet is not in any sense realistic, but is rather an image of what whites expect blacks to be, an image which, in keeping with the Jungian concept of the Shadow, as Graham Dunstan Martin indicates, is a projection of white repressions and prejudices.⁵ The relationship between stage and audience is, consequently, fundamentally antagonistic. There is ample evidence that Genet's theatre, despite its depiction of oppressed minorities, has no intention of provoking social reform. In *Comment jouer 'Les Bonnes'* he writes: 'Une chose doit être écrite: il ne s'agit pas d'un plaidoyer sur le sort des domestiques. Je suppose qu'il existe un syndicat des gens de maison—cela ne nous regarde pas' (IV, p. 269), and despite both the more obviously political content of his last two plays and Genet's active participation in politics in the latter part of his life, the intention of his drama seems not to have changed. In the interview published in *Playboy* in 1964, for instance, he is quoted as saying:

I write plays in order to crystallize a theatrical, a dramatic emotion. I'm not concerned about whether, for example, **The Blacks** serves the Negroes. Besides, I don't think it does. I think that direct action, the fight against colonialism, does more for the Negroes than any play.⁶

Roger Blin was also able to say of him: 'Il ne cherche pas à corriger la société qu'il dénonce. Il n'essaie pas de substituer un ordre à un autre puisqu'il est opposé à toute forme d'ordre.'⁷

So Genet has no socially-conscious aim of the sort found in most drama dealing with the oppressed or the less fortunate, no intention of drawing the plight of its subjects to our attention and encouraging us to do something about it. Rather, as Graham Dunstan Martin puts it: 'The play is calculated, it seems, to offend its audience, or else frighten them, or else to stimulate their worst racial instincts.'⁸ And this aim of upsetting the audience is achieved in a number of ways, some quite obvious, others acting on a more subliminal level.

Most obvious of all is the ritual itself: the murder of a white woman reenacted by black 'actors' before a stage 'audience' of white caricatures played by masked blacks is hardly guaranteed to reassure the white theatre-goer. The act of provocation formed by the murder attacks the spectators in one way whilst the mockery provided by the parody of their own kind offends in another, and the implied threat is intensified when the stage 'audience' of whites enter into the ritual itself, only to be symbolically murdered in their turn.

The white audience in the auditorium will inevitably have a mixed response to the symbolic figures of the white Court, for although they will be alienated by the mockery of the parody of white attitudes they represent, they will also find that they are being linked with these caricatures as joint objects of black hatred: from the very beginning we are told that the introductory remarks of Archibald should be addressed 'tantôt au public, tantôt à la Cour' (V, p. 83), and this identification will continue.

The idea that the audience has a role within this play can be taken much further than Genet's specification of his audience's colour. There is one major difference between **Les Nègres** and Genet's other plays, indeed, most other plays. For while in his other works for the stage the actors play characters, be they maids, prisoners, prostitutes or whatever, in this play the actors play 'actors', 'actors' who are going to enact a ritual for the benefit of two audiences, the white Court on stage and the white audience in the auditorium. In this way, the audience finds itself playing an 'audience', and the fact of its participation in the action is underlined by the scene in which one of its number is invited up to hold the knitting of the victim in the ritual (V, pp. 120-23). However, to complicate matters, Genet multiplies the use of such layers of action in *Les Nègres.*

Genet's previous play, *Le Balcon,* has certain characteristics which shed light on the nature of *Les Nègres.* First is the discussion of the theme of reflection and reality. In this play, in which the clients in the brothel attain satisfaction from acting out their fantasies, it is claimed that someone who acts out a role captures better its essence than someone who does it as a job of work. This leads to a degree of confusion about the nature of reality:

IRMA:

> C'est le plombier qui s'en va.

CARMEN:

> Lequel?

IRMA:

> Le vrai.

CARMEN:

> Lequel est le vrai?

IRMA:

> Celui qui répare les robinets.

CARMEN:

> L'autre est faux?

> (IV, p. 70)

And whilst it is Irma who here expresses what we might regard as the common-sense viewpoint, at the end of the play she will suggest that what we see in the theatre/ brothel is more real, or at least less false, than what happens outside: 'Il faut rentrer chez vous, où tout, n'en doutez pas, sera encore plus faux qu'ici' (IV, p. 135). The aspect of this play in which the ambiguous relationship of illusion to reality is at its most pronounced is also the element which most closely prefigures *Les Nègres,* the revolution taking place in the wings. The revolution in *Le Balcon* gives a constant sense of threat, but there are both internal and external suggestions that its 'reality' is questionable. From the outset we hear the sound of machine guns off stage, and the revolution is discussed, but the first concrete evidence we have on stage is the death of Arthur, an event presented in such a way as to put its 'reality' in doubt without actually denying it. First of all, the fact that the character is shot just before he is due to play a corpse (which he goes on to play) seems almost too coincidental. Secondly, the *sang froid* of the other characters in the face of his death is surprising even in a play as stylized as *Le Balcon.* And lastly, Genet's very precise stage direction

requires the single bullet that we hear fired to break the window on its way in, but then to go on to perform the implausible feat of both breaking a mirror *and* shooting Arthur:

> *On entend un claquement sec. Une vitre de la fenêtre vole en éclats. Un miroir aussi, près du lit.*
>
> *Arthur tombe, frappé au front, d'une balle venue du dehors.*

> (IV, p. 91)

When the revolution apparently starts up again in the final pages of the play Irma has the following ambiguous exchange with the Envoy:

IRMA:

> Qui est-ce? . . . Les nôtres . . . ou des révoltés? . . . ou? . . .

L'ENVOYÉ:

> Quelqu'un qui rêve, madame. . . .

> (IV, p. 134)

'Les nôtres'? Our side? Or our people, in the sense of the employees of the brothel? More conclusive, however, than these internal ambiguities is the external evidence. In *Comment jouer 'Le Balcon'* Genet writes: 'L'existence des révoltés est *dans* le bordel, ou au-dehors? Il faut tenir l'équivoque jusqu'à la fin' (IV, p. 274, Genet's italics), and, in the same text, he also suggests the use of masks for the revolutionaries, which will also tend to undermine any sense of their 'reality'.

So, *Le Balcon* has shown us that 'reality' and 'real', loaded terms in any discussion of theatre, are even more problematic in the context of Genet's work in the medium. We will need to proceed with caution. In the most literal sense, there is a clear dividing line between reality and the fiction of a play. Our daily lives, the fact of buying a ticket and going into the theatre to watch actors is real, the story enacted by the actors is pure fiction, and no part of that action can be any more or less fictional than any other; the main action is no more real than a play within the play, a dream sequence or a story invented by one of the characters, since all elements of the work are inventions of the author. On the other hand, if we accept Coleridge's willing suspension of disbelief, we will also accept that the average spectator is unlikely to have such a literal-minded response to the theatrical experience (indeed, anyone who has, has probably wasted the money spent on the ticket). Whilst the intelligent and receptive spectator never confuses the internal 'reality' of the play with the external reality of the outside world, there is a temporary acceptance that the main action is 'real' and that elements like the play within the play, the dream sequence or similar inclusions are not. If we were to add a further level, then the play within the play would logically be less 'real' than the main action, but more 'real' than the play within the play within the play. The human instinct to sort out truth from falsehood, as evinced by the popularity of the detective-story structure in literature, means that spectators are anxious to keep the demarcations between various layers clear in their minds. Certainly Genet's concern to keep the status of the revolution in *Le Balcon* ambiguous indicates that he is exploiting his audience's preoccupation with what is 'real' and what is not, for if the audience does not care whether the revolution is taking place outside the brothel or is simply another of Irma's illusions, there is no point in keeping them in a state of confusion about it.

Which brings us back to *Les Nègres.* The multi-layering in this work is even more complex than that of *Le Balcon*: in *Les Bonnes* it is relatively easy to sort out one layer from another, even if the very opening of the play sets out to confuse us; with *Le Balcon* we have seen that the relationship between layers is deliberately ambiguous; in *Les Nègres* the layers proliferate and overlap to an alarming extent. We have already seen the problem posed by the relationship of the Court to the ritual: are they an 'audience' to the ritual, or a part of it? In other words, do they and the unmasked 'actors' represent two different levels of illusion, or the same one? Then there is the theme of the love between Vertu and Village: we are frequently told that this is not part of the ritual, but, if it is 'real', how 'real' is it? A third strand is apparently provided by a 'real' revolution taking place in the wings, but *Le Balcon* has taught us to beware of plays involving off-stage revolts. It is difficult to accept Jeanette L. Savona's remark that 'unlike the plot of *The Balcony* whose ambiguity was due to its lack of causal links, the three stories of *The Blacks* are individually clear cut'.[9] George B. Macdonald seems closer to the mark when he writes: 'A true paraphrasing of the entire work becomes not the labor of a lifetime, but of an eternity. Its levels are continually being shuffled, its juxtapositions become identities, its opposing forces fight on either side.'[10]

It is not surprising, given the complexities of the play, that critical opinion on the status of the revolution is not unanimous. Some are content to accept it as 'real' (or even real),[11] while for others its 'reality' is put in question by the problem of theatrical reality in general.[12] However, all accept that the basic situation being presented to us is this: the actors are playing 'actors', who, in order to distract the 'audience' (or even audience) from events taking place off stage, are enacting a ritual. But is the situation quite so simple?

If Genet is to suggest to us that the ritual is merely a blind to take away our attention from events happening off stage he clearly needs to give us some hint that those off-stage events are occurring, but those hints

must be subtle enough to suggest a serious attempt on the part of the characters to keep them secret. And yet what do we find in *Les Nègres*? Genet, the master of ambiguity, presents us with one of the worst-kept secrets in the history of drama. The very appearance of Ville de Saint-Nazaire, the character who provides the link between the on-stage and off-stage actions, will alert us from the outset that we should pay special attention to him, for his casual clothing contrasts with the elaborate formal dress of the others. So, we will be particularly interested when he is dismissed from the stage. This is what Archibald says to him:

> Et vous, monsieur, vous êtes de trop. Tout, étant secret, il faut foutre le camp. Allez, mais allez donc les prévenir. Dites-leur bien que nous avons commencé. Qu'ils fassent leur travail comme nous allons faire le nôtre. Tout se passera comme à l'accoutumée. Je l'espère.
>
> (V, p. 87)

We may already feel that Genet is being uncharacteristically heavy handed here, particularly in the use of the word 'secret'—the worst way to keep a secret is surely to begin by pointing out that there is a secret to be kept. But if this is heavy handed, it is as nothing compared to what will follow. Only a short time later Ville de Saint-Nazaire returns and we hear the following extended exchange:

ARCHIBALD:

> Eh bien? Est-ce qu'il y a déjà quelque chose?

VILLE DE SAINT-NAZAIRE:

> Il est arrivé. On l'a amené, menottes aux mains. *Tous les Nègres se groupent autour de Ville de Saint-Nazaire.*

NEIGE:

> Qu'allez-vous faire?

VILLE DE SAINT-NAZAIRE:

> (*il se baisse et ramasse le revolver posé sur la boîte de cireur*) Avant tout, l'interroger . . .

ARCHIBALD:

> (*l'interrompant*) Ne dites que ce qu'il faut dire, on nous épie. *Tous lèvent la tête et regardent la Cour.*

LE JUGE:

> (*criant*) Parce que vous êtes déguisés en chiens savants, vous croyez savoir parler, et déjà vous inventez des énigmes . . .

VILLAGE:

> (*au Juge*) Un jour . . .

ARCHIBALD:

> (*l'interrompant*) Laisse. Dans la colère tu vas te trahir et nous trahir. (*A Ville de Saint-Nazaire*) A-t-il dit quelque chose qui le justifie? Rien?

VILLE DE SAINT-NAZAIRE:

Rien. Je m'en vais?

ARCHIBALD:

Quand le tribunal sera en place, reviens nous prévenir. *Ville de Saint-Nazaire se détache du groupe et va pour sortir.*

DIOUF:

(*timidement*) Vous tenez vraiment à emporter cet objet? *Il montre le revolver que tient Ville de Saint-Nazaire.* [. . .]

ARCHIBALD:

(*impérieux*) Partez! Rentrez dans la coulisse. Emportez le revolver, et allez faire votre besogne.

VILLE DE SAINT-NAZAIRE:

Mais . . .

VILLAGE:

(*intervenant*) Pas de mais. Obéis à monsieur Wellington.

(V, pp. 95-6)

There is little more left to find out about this mysterious secret, and yet the ritual intended to prevent us from finding out has not yet even begun. And there will be more such discussions later on, both before and after the execution of the off-stage victim. Perhaps the hints concerning the ambiguity of the revolution in **Le Balcon** are too subtle, but if we are really intended to believe in the characters' attempt to keep this off-stage action secret from us, Genet has overplayed his hand.

And yet, spelling things out too much is so uncharacteristic of Genet's art in general that this alone should perhaps alert us to the possibility that we should not take this 'real' action at face value. But it is not the only clue. In the above extract it is not the audience, but the Court who the blacks think may be spying on them. The Valet also asks a question which both signals his own ignorance of the events and draws the attention of the audience to them: 'Auriez-vous la bonté de me renseigner? Car enfin j'ai choisi d'être compréhensif. Où est allé le Nègre avec son colt, tout à l'heure?' (V, p. 98). Later the Judge will comment that he suspects another crime is being judged elsewhere (V, p. 131). These details tend to suggest that the execution is more closely linked to the fiction of the ritual than to the play's internal 'reality'.

And then there is the sound and lighting effect representing the execution. Since the entire action played out in front of us in **Les Nègres** is part of the ritual performed by the blacks, the presentation is staunchly non-illusionistic—the sound effects are created by the ac-

tors, the lighting does not change. The only exception is the effect which signals the execution, and the use of an illusionistic effect for this event could be a strong confirmation of its 'reality'. And yet, Genet is quite specific in what he asks for, an effect which although realistic, is not a realistic representation of an execution, but rather a firework display:

Soudain, dans la coulisse, on entend une, puis plusieurs explosions de pétards, et, sur le velours noir des décors, les reflets d'un feu d'artifice.

(V, p. 146)

The fact that this is a real noise, but not the right real noise, undermines our belief in the off-stage action as much as it encourages it.

The nature of the trial itself is also of interest. J. P. Little comments:

And what of the act for which the off-stage black is being executed? It is, in fact, treason. But treason for Genet is not judged according to normal codes of morality. For him it is one of the most desirable of crimes—because one of the most terrible.[13]

To this we can add the fact that the accused is black. That the trial is being carried out by a revolutionary black organization certainly represents some threat to the white audience, as does the fact that, in meting out their own justice, the blacks are taking on themselves the role which the colonial system allocates to whites, but it remains an internal affair, blacks judging and executing a black, which must surely be less threatening to a white audience than the killing of a white woman which we are told has taken place as a prelude to the ritual. Surely if this off-stage action were intended as Genet's direct threat to his white audience he could have invented a more worrying attack on white supremacy. It may also seem odd that this sub-plot is resolved so long before the end of the ritual: if it is only this that is being concealed by the on-stage events, why do they need to continue for so long after it is over?

There are, however, other hints that something else is going on, hints so much more in keeping with the allusive nature of Genet's work that they seem to have gone undetected by critics. When Archibald first dismisses Ville de Saint-Nazaire this is what happens:

Ville de Saint-Nazaire s'incline et va pour sortir vers la droite, mais Village intervient.

VILLAGE:

Pas par là, malheureux. On vous avait dit de ne plus venir, vous gâchez tout.

VILLE DE SAINT-NAZAIRE:

Le mal . . .

ARCHIBALD:

> (*l'interrompant*) Plus tard. Sortez.
>
> *Ville de Saint-Nazaire sort à gauche.*
>
> (V, p. 87)

What are we to make of this? Genet does not provide any explanation, but he clearly wants to be sure that we have not missed the point, because at Ville de Saint-Nazaire's next exit we find a near repetition of this action:

> (*Résigné, Ville de Saint-Nazaire va pour sortir, à droite, mais Village intervient.*) Pas par là, malheureux!
>
> *Ville de Saint-Nazaire sort à gauche.*
>
> (V, p. 96)

During a later discussion between Ville de Saint-Nazaire and Archibald concerning the morality of the act of executing a fellow black, we find the following curious exchange:

VILLE DE SAINT-NAZAIRE:

> Mais, alors, cette comédie que nous jouons, pour vous, ce n'était qu'un divertissement?

ARCHIBALD:

> (*l'interrompant*) Tais toi.
>
> (V, p. 128)

'Cette comédie que nous jouons'. Does this refer to the ritual? It would appear not, since Ville de Saint-Nazaire uses the *nous* form, despite being the only character not directly involved in the ritual. But if it is not the ritual that he is referring to, it must be the off-stage action, an interpretation which is confirmed by Archibald's curt response; that the ritual is 'une comédie' is no secret and would not therefore explain why Ville de Saint-Nazaire should be silenced with such urgency and with no further explanation. The word 'divertissement', with its double meaning, suggests that this false off-stage action is present in order to divert our attention from something else. And there is Archibald's comment towards the end of the action: 'Mais peut-être soupçonne-t-on ce que peut dissimuler cette architecture de vide et de mots' (V, p. 155). If the emptiness of the ritual is still hiding anything it can hardly be the off-stage execution, since that is by now a thoroughly open secret. Perhaps the implications of the remark are metaphysical, perhaps not. Whilst this last remark is so ambiguous that it would be difficult to draw any specific conclusions from it, the other three seem to be intended as indications that another action is supposed to be taking place off-stage right, an action from which the audience is being diverted by both the fake execution off-stage left and the ritual on stage. In other words, there is another level of illusion between the external reality of the performance and the action that has generally been accepted as 'real', the execution of the black traitor. That is to say that the actors are playing 'actors', who, in order to distract our attention from events taking place off-stage right, are playing 'actors', who, in order to distract our attention from events taking place off-stage left, are enacting a ritual.

The situation is deliberately confusing. The audience will obviously be puzzled about what is meant to be 'real' and what is not, perhaps even about what is real and what is not, for the idea of actors playing to an audience is repeated on so many different levels that there is bound to be a degree of blurring in the mind of the spectator between the various levels, including, perhaps, even that of reality itself. And the off-right action, which must now be taken to be the 'real' action rather than the off-left action, has the additional threat of being unspecified, giving free rein to the imagination. So the multi-layering will cause the audience to feel both confused and threatened.

But this is not the only source of confusion in the play. One of the things that we expect of any work which has a narrative element is that we should be able to follow the story. At least in reading a novel we can read a complex narrative at our own pace, and if we become confused by certain details we have the option of going back to check over what we have already read. In the theatre there is no such possibility, and we depend on author, director and actors to provide us with an action which is both simple enough and clearly enough presented for us to be able to follow. The psychological response if we are unable to do so may vary, but certainly each time we are presented with a detail which contradicts what we thought was happening we will be puzzled. The more often this happens, the more confused we will become, and, whilst in the case of a very complex plot this confusion may well translate itself into impatience or even annoyance with the author, the more simple the plot is, the more likely we are to blame ourselves for not following and to begin to feel foolish or even stupid. And, once we cut our way through the complexities of the multi-layering of *Les Nègres,* the plot which is at its centre would seem to be simplicity itself. A white woman has been murdered, and the blacks are re-enacting her death in a ritual. Given the straightforwardness of this outline, it comes as a surprise that the ritual is so difficult to follow.

Clearly the improvisatory nature of the action provides one explanation for this: the re-enactment of the murder as well as the introductory explanations of what is about to happen are continually being interrupted both by the black 'actors' themselves, who argue about their roles or go back over parts of the ceremony that have been forgotten, and by the white Court, who question the blacks, discuss the action among themselves, and play out little scenes which parody white attitudes to blacks. However, although the fragmentation resulting from this approach means that the central narrative of the ritual requires rather more concentration, it is still obvious to an audience what is going on. The spectator will no doubt become frustrated at the failure of the 'actors' to get on with it and tell their story, for as Diderot shows in *Jacques le fataliste,* even the most banal of tales begins to exert an irresistible fascination when it is interrupted. However, it is not this particular aspect of the work which causes the confusion which undoubtedly results from any initial encounter with it, be it on the stage or on the page. On the other hand, this fragmentation does help Genet in his use of another technique, one which few other critics appear to have noted,[14] and this is the continual shifting in the details of the story. Without the fragmentation, it would be much more obvious that the contradictions in the narrative are not the result of our own failure to remember what has gone before, but have been placed there deliberately by the author. As it is, by keeping the whole structure of the play so fluid, by separating one detail of the narrative from another, Genet is able to trick us into blaming ourselves for the disquieting feeling that the details of the murder are shifting like a mirage. It is the identity of the victim which causes the greatest confusion, and, in order to increase the impact of that confusion, Genet begins with the sort of allusive remarks which are guaranteed to focus our interest on that particular detail: 'Vont-ils la tuer?' (V, p. 84) asks the Queen in the first intervention by the Court, and then has to repeat her question before the Missionary replies: 'Mais, madame . . . (*Un temps.*) elle est morte!' (V, p. 84). The theme of death is bound to arouse our interest (Genet was particularly scathing about the public's fascination with literary representations of crime),[15] and so the failure to specify the victim's identity will surely intrigue us too.

The next reference to the identity of the victim, the body in the coffin, is scarcely less vague, but suggests that for a long time before her death Neige has been jealous of Village's love for her:

NEIGE:

> Et sans ma jalousie à votre égard, Village . . .

VILLAGE:

> (*l'interrompant*) On le saura. Vous l'avez assez répété. Bien avant sa mort (*Il montre du doigt le catafalque.*) vous lui portiez une haine mortelle. Or, sa mort ne devait pas seulement signaler qu'elle perdît la vie. Tous, tendrement, nous l'avons couvée, et non dans l'amour.
>
> *Long sanglot de la Cour.*

NEIGE:

> Vraiment?

(V, p. 88)

This detail, however, is quite inconsistent with Village's description of the murder that we hear shortly afterwards, for it is clearly a random killing of someone previously unknown to either of them:

VILLAGE:

> Monsieur Hérode Aventure et moi, juste après le dîner, nous sommes passés sur les quais. Il faisait assez doux. Un peu avant l'entrée du pont, il y avait une vieille clocharde accroupie—ou allongée—sur un tas de guenilles. Mais je vous ai déjà tout raconté . . .

BOBO:

> Qu'elle s'estime heureuse, la clocharde. Elle aura des funérailles solennelles.

ARCHIBALD:

> (*à Village*) Mais dites encore. A-t-elle gueulé?

VILLAGE:

> Pas du tout. Pas eu le temps. Monsieur Hérode Aventure et moi, nous nous sommes approchés, carrément. Elle pionçait: elle s'est réveillée à demi. Dans le noir . . .

BOBO ET NEIGE:

> (*riant*) Oh! Dans le noir?

VILLAGE:

> Dans le noir elle a dû nous prendre pour des agents. Elle puait le vin, comme toutes celles qu'ils rejettent sur les quais. Elle a dit: "Je ne fais pas de mal . . ."

ARCHIBALD:

> Ensuite?

VILLAGE:

> Comme d'habitude. C'est moi qui me suis baissé. Je l'ai étranglée avec mes deux mains pendant que monsieur Hérode Aventure emprisonnait les siennes. Elle s'est un peu raidie . . . enfin elle a eu ce qu'ils appellent un spasme, et c'est tout.

(V, pp. 90-91)

So the victim, who was so drunk that at the approach of her murderers she only half woke up, did not even have the time to shout out before Village bent down and strangled her. How then, do we explain a detail that we are given shortly afterwards: 'Je vous dirai seulement que cette femme était blanche et qu'elle prenait prétexte de notre odeur pour me fuir' (V, p. 93)? Clearly this does not fit into the story as it was previously told to us, and, furthermore, shortly afterwards Neige confuses the issue even further by reiterating her conviction that Village was in love with the victim (V, p. 94), an accusation that she will continue to make.

There is a major shift in the identity of the victim when we move on to the ritual enactment of the crime, for she becomes a young woman serving behind a counter in a bar.[16] Or is she at her sewing machine? Neige claims that Village has said so earlier (V, p. 110), but if the audience has no recollection of this, it is because he has not said it during the course of the action.

There is a certain logic behind the idea that the identity of the 'real' body in the coffin does not determine the identity of the victim in the murder enacted in the ritual, but even here we find contradictions which mean that this shift in identity is unlikely to be clear to an audience seeing the play for the first time. A comment like that of the Judge: 'Vous nous avez promis la représentation du crime afin de mériter votre condamnation' (V, p. 93), tends to suggest that it will be the 'real' murder that will be enacted in the ritual, and, indeed, most discussion of both ritual and body tends to suggest that the 'real' and ritual victims are one and the same.

There is, however, one suggestion that the identity given to the victim in the ritual may not be the same as the identity of the corpse in the coffin: when the Valet asks if the victim has ever been a man, he receives the following reply from Bobo:

> Oui, cela nous est arrivé! Nous avons ramassé un ancien chanteur de charme tombé dans la misère et dans l'oubli: empaqueté, et en caisse. Là. (*Elle montre le catafalque.*) Trop heureux de lui prêter, pour la cérémonie, l'apparence d'un gouverneur-général, quand il fut tué sous les yeux de la foule—celle d'hier soir, messieurs-dames.
>
> (V, p. 102)

But even this comment, suggesting as it does that the ritual can change from evening to evening, is contradicted by others which imply that it never changes, such as Archibald's 'Vous n'avez pas le droit de rien changer au cérémonial' (V, p. 89). A similar implication can be found in Bobo's objection to a detail in Village's narrative: 'Vous mentez. Sournois, hier vous êtes entré avec circonspection. Vous déformez' (V, p. 115), a remark which is doubly confusing, for by suggesting that this ritual is intended to be absolutely identical to that of the previous evening, she contradicts not only her suggestion to the Valet that the identity of the victim in the ritual can change, but also the information contained in that same speech that the previous evening's victim, in 'reality' as well as in the ritual, was a man.

From this point, apart from a passage in which Village confuses the victim with Vertu (V, p. 119), the narrative proceeds relatively coherently until, in a scene in which the victim's talents and habits are being enumerated, there is a sudden lurch in her identity and, without any explanation, although she has just been rinsing glasses, she becomes Joan of Arc:

VILLAGE:

Un jour même elle grilla dans les flammes . . .

LA COUR:

(*sauf le Missionnaire*) Vite, racontez vite!

LE MISSIONNAIRE:

Vous oseriez rappeler cette méchante affaire?

LE VALET:

(*au Missionnaire*) Vous ne l'avez pas mise au ciel, depuis?

LA REINE:

Mais, que veulent-ils?

VILLAGE:

Sur son cheval, caracolant parmi les oriflammes, on la prit un jour, on l'enferma et on la brûla.

NEIGE:

(*montrant sa tête, et riant aux éclats*) Ensuite on mangea les morceaux.

LA REINE:

(*dans un cri déchirant*) Ma Sainte!

(V, p. 121)

And by Village's next speech she is a sort of symbolic mother of the whole white race, giving birth to dolls representing the members of the white Court. We are also told that when the victim's husband returns home he will find the body of his dead wife, murdered by Village, an obvious impossibility if the body is supposed to be in the coffin.[17] And was she murdered by strangulation (V, pp. 91, 120) or with a knife (V, pp. 108, 123)?

But then we will learn that there was not actually a body at all, or even a coffin (V, pp. 137-39), a development which mocks us by rendering all our previous attempts to establish the identity of the victim retrospectively futile. But is there really no corpse? The final gesture of the play, in which the back curtain is raised to reveal another catafalque, has generally been interpreted as an indication of the cyclic nature of the ritual which, as it ends, is already about to begin again, and so it is. But does it not also carry with it the threat that there might have been a 'real' body after all, a body which has lain here behind the stage while we were tricked into thinking that it was in the fake coffin at the front? One major detail confirms such an interpretation. Although Genet does not give us any advance warning of the *coup de théâtre* in which the catafalque is dismantled to provide chairs for the Governor and Missionary, that *coup de théâtre* itself clears up a mystery to which our attention has been drawn near the beginning of the action: what has become of the missing chairs belonging to the Valet and the Missionary? On one level this is yet another way of making the audience feel foolish: we were bound to wonder about the significance of the mystery of the chairs, and we find both that they have been right in front of us all along and that we have been tricked into believing in the reality of a fake catafalque. The sequence also, however, has the effect of drawing forcefully to our attention another detail: in order to construct their fake catafalque the blacks have been forced to steal two of the chairs belonging to the Court, but since only two chairs were missing, and these are now accounted for, what could a second fake catafalque be made from? The obvious conclusion is that the second catafalque cannot be fake and so must be 'real'.

So, is the victim an old beggar-woman too drunk to get up, or did she run away? Might she sometimes be a man even though the unchanging ritual would appear to demand a female victim? Is she serving in a bar or sitting sewing? Or then again, is she Vertu, or Joan of Arc, or the mother of the white races? Did her husband find her body, or is it in the coffin? But, in fact, there is no coffin and no body. Or is there? The ground is continually shifting beneath our feet, and it is clear that an audience will be confused: it takes at least a second viewing or reading to begin to become aware that all these inconsistencies are in the text rather than being the result of the spectator's inability to follow a simple story. As in the case of the equally confusing multi-layering of levels of illusion, the result will be a sense of disquiet, even of threat, which is part of the humiliation of his white audience undertaken by Genet in this play.

There remains, however, an important paradox, to which Edmund White draws attention in his discussion of Blin's first production: 'Audiences scarcely knew how to react—whether to applaud the beauty, hiss at the hostility or walk out in cold disapproval. In any event the Lutèce was packed every night and Genet had never received such brilliant notices.'[18] How are we to explain the success of this play if it sets out both to confuse and to threaten its audience? Why do we want to put ourselves through such an experience? The answers are surely related to the whole nature of the impact of theatre. We are able to appreciate the stage action, be profoundly moved, frightened or amused on one level, while never totally losing sight of the artificiality of the spectacle. Surely Joseph McMahon is underestimating the sophistication of the average audience when he writes: 'If [the audience] had understood the furtive undercurrents of revolt at the beginning of the play they would have done something about the situation.'[19] The notion of the audience storming the stage in order to prevent the execution of the black traitor, or even to put a stop to the more mysterious action off-stage right is just as ludicrous as the example cited by Philip Thody of the woman who shouts out to tell Othello that Desdemona is innocent.[20] Although I have spoken of the levels of this play blurring in such a way that we may

confuse illusion not just with 'reality' but with reality, that confusion will never be complete. As Richard Coe puts it: '[Our] reason and [our] emotion are forced into contradiction, and [we are] obliged to agree and disagree with [ourselves] simultaneously, to believe and not to believe in the actions [we are] witnessing.'[21] In the theatre as in all the arts of imitation, aesthetic pleasure may be derived from the depiction of events which, in reality, could not be considered enjoyable in any sense; were it not for this phenomenon, *King Lear* would hardly be good box-office. In the search for an ever wider range of aesthetic experiences, we find in Genet's plays, as in his novels, a unique way of looking at life. The experience of witnessing a performance of **Les Nègres** is harrowing because the audience is so much more directly implicated than in most theatre, and we are left feeling upset, confused, threatened. And yet, this is such an unusual and powerful experience in the theatre, that its novelty makes the play a unique source of aesthetic fulfilment.

Notes

1. Genet, *Œuvres complètes,* 5 vols ([Paris], Gallimard, 1951-79), V, 79. All references to Genet's works refer to this edition.

2. J. P. Little, *Genet: 'Les Nègres',* Critical Guides to French Texts, 80, (London, Grant & Cutler, 1990), p. 65.

3. See his elaborate instruction in the second introductory note, V, 79.

4. White, *Genet* (London, Chatto and Windus, 1993), pp. 506-07. See also Maurice Lecuyer, 'Les Nègres et au-delà', in *Obliques,* II (1972), 44-47, (p. 44).

5. Martin, 'Racism in Genet's *Les Nègres*', in *Modern Language Review,* 70 (1975), 517-25, (passim).

6. 'Interview with Jean Genet', in *Playboy,* IX (April 1964), 45-54, (p. 52).

7. Bettina Knapp, 'Entretien avec Roger Blin', in *Obliques,* II (1972), 39-43, (p. 39).

8. Martin, 'Racism in Genet's *Les Nègres*', p. 519.

9. Savona, *Jean Genet,* Macmillan, Modern Dramatists (London, Macmillan, 1983), p. 103.

10. Quoted in Richard N. Coe, *The Theatre of Jean Genet: A Casebook* (New York, Grove Press, 1970), p. 128. From 'The Blacks and Ritual Theater', first published in *Humanities* (Spring 1962), 32-44.

11. See for instance Joseph H. McMahon, *The Imagination of Jean Genet,* Yale Romantic Studies, 2nd series, 10 (New Haven-London, Yale University Press; Paris, PUF, 1963), p. 186; Jean-Marie Magnan, *Essai sur Jean Genet* (Paris, Seg-

hers, 1966), pp. 173-74; Philip Thody, *Jean Genet: A Study of his Novels and Plays* (London, Hamish Hamilton, 1968), p. 197; Edmund White, *Genet*, p. 500.

12. For Jean Decock this action is 'moins imaginaire que le rituel mais tout aussi factice', '*Les Nègres* aux USA', in *Obliques,* II (1972), 48-50, (p. 50), and Richard N. Coe (*The Vision of Jean Genet* (London, Peter Owen, 1968), p. 287) and Martin Esslin (*The Theatre of the Absurd* (London, Eyre and Spottiswoode, 1962), p. 172), while accepting the 'reality' of the revolution in the context of the fiction of the play, both point out that there is a sense in which the ritual which we see in front of us has more reality than an action merely reported from the wings.

13. Little, *Genet: 'Les Nègres'*, p. 26. Little is, to my knowledge, the only critic to draw attention to the deliberate ambiguity of the off-stage action, but although she writes that there are 'many indications that we are not to take the events off-stage as indicative of a serious political purpose', she cites only this and the 'bruit de pétard' (p. 26).

14. I have found references to the contradictory nature of the narrative in only two studies, those of J. P. Little and Martin Esslin. Little says that the plot is 'confused in various important details', but gives only one example, and goes on to conclude that 'the details do not matter, since the event never took place anyhow' (*Genet: 'Les Nègres'*, p. 47). I would contend that for an audience trying to follow the story, the details *do* matter, since thcy are unaware until the *coup de théâtre* of the absence of a victim. For Esslin's comments, see note 16.

15. See *L'Enfant criminel*: '*Votre* littérature, *vos* beaux-arts, *vos* divertissements d'après-diner, célèbrent le crime. Le talent de vos poètes a glorifié le criminel que dans la vie vous haïssez' (V, 390, Genet's italics).

16. It is this distinction between the identities of the body in the coffin and of the victim in the ritual which has been noted by Martin Esslin (*The Theatre of the Absurd*, p. 170).

17. It is this contradiction to which J. P. Little draws attention, see note 14 and Little, *Genet: 'Les Nègres'*, p. 47.

18. White, *Genet,* p. 499.

19. McMahon, *The Imagination of Jean Genet*, p. 187.

20. Thody, *Jean Genet,* p. 43. Of course, groups of spectators did storm the stage at French performances of *Les Paravents,* but this was because they objected to Genet's treatment of a politically sensitive issue, not because they were confused about the reality of the stage action.

21. 'Genet', in *Forces in Modern French Drama: Studies in Variations on the Permitted Lie,* ed. by John Fletcher (London, University of London Press, 1972), pp. 147-67, (p. 162).

Brian Gordon Kennelly (essay date 1998)

SOURCE: Kennelly, Brian Gordon. "Less or More Black and White? Reassessing Genet's *Les nègres* in Light of Both Published Versions." *Dalhousie French Studies* 44 (1998): 123-33.

[*In the following essay, Kennelly studies the changes Genet made to the text of* The Blacks *in its two versions, concentrating on the issue of ambiguity.*]

> Je suis furieux. Je me donne depuis 15 jours tant de mal pour corriger cette pièce et la rendre possible, et vous me compliquez tout. [. . .] Envoyez-moi le manuscrit. J'ai besoin de contrôler, mais avec cette imbécile manie de vouloir me conserver les manuscrits, je ne peux jamais corriger. À quoi jouez-vous? Je ne signerai pas une réédition des *Nègres* si je ne peux pas corriger ce texte, s'il est mal imprimé.[1]

Each of the five plays by Jean Genet performed before his death in 1986 exists in more than one published version.[2] Critics have discussed the differences between the various published versions of each play[3] with the exception of *Les nègres*: the drama commissioned by Raymond Rouleau, first published by Mare Barbezat in 1958, first performed in a production by Roger Blin at the Théâtre de Lutèce in Paris in 1959, and published in a revised edition the following year.

Why have the changes Genet made to *Les nègres* remained undiscussed? Perhaps the attention of critics, like that of the audience described by Bernard Frechtman, Genet's American translator, has been diverted by the ceremony at the heart of the drama (Frechtman 5). Could a study of the changes Genet made to the play lead to a better understanding of ambiguity in *Les nègres*? When Gent "cleaned up" the text in the late 1950s, "suppressing" everything, as Blin recalls he did, that "didn't work" (White 431), did the dividing line between the staged and the real in his complex work so intensely concerned with difference become less or more black and white?

A Framework of Confusion

Derek F. Connon's study of "confusion," of what he terms Genet's "art of upsetting" the audience in—and of—*Les nègres* usefully frames these questions. Picking up on Graham Dunstan Martin's observation that the play is calculated to offend its spectators, to frighten them, or stimulate their worst racial instincts (Martin 519), Connon notes that Genet achieves this in both obvious and subliminal ways. Among the more obvious ways, Connon lists the ritual murder of a white woman reenacted by black actors before a stage audience of white caricatures played by masked blacks, and the mixed response to the symbolic figures of the white Court by the white audience in the auditorium. Among the ways he sees as acting on a more subliminal level, Connon draws our attention on the one hand to the fragmentation of the ritual re-enactment of the murder at the heart of the play. He points out that it helps Genet trick us into blaming ourselves for the disquieting feeling we have—derived in part from questions that arose over the true identity of the victim—that the details of the murder are shifting like a mirage. On the other hand, Connon also explores the rich layering of action in the play, showing how it deepens the ambiguous relationship of illusion to reality in Genet's work. Comparing Genet's intentions in two of the plays he wrote before *Les nègres* to his intentions in this drama, Connon writes:

> The multi-layering in this work is even more complex than that of *Le balcon*: in *Les bonnes* it is relatively easy to sort out one layer from another, even if the opening of the play sets out to confuse us; with *Le balcon* we have seen that the relationship between layers is deliberately ambiguous; in *Les nègres* the layers proliferate and overlap to an alarming extent.
>
> (428)

As evidence of this layering, Connon notes: first, the problem posed by the relationship of the Court to the ritual; second, the theme of love between Vertu and Village; finally, Connon discusses at some length the third complicated strand in this dramatic work, which he sees as having been written deliberately to confuse: the real revolution taking place in the wings. Alluding to the studies of Joseph H. McMahon, Jean-Marie Magnan, Philip Thody, Edmund White, Jean Decock, Richard N. Coe, and Martin Esslin, Connon reminds us that critical opinion of the status of the revolution is not unanimous: McMahon, Magnan, Thody, and White accept it as "real"[4]; Decock, Coe, and Esslin put its reality into the same question as they do theatrical reality in general. Nonetheless, he summarizes, all accept the basic situation being presented to us: that of actors playing "actors," who—in order to distract the audience from events taking place off stage—are enacting a ritual. For Connon, however, this is a gross simplification. He writes:

> If Genet is to suggest to us that the ritual is merely a blind to take away our attention from events happening off stage he clearly needs to give us some hint that those off-stage events are occurring, but those hints must be subtle enough to suggest a serious attempt on the part of the characters to keep them secret. And yet what do we find in *Les nègres*? Genet, the master of ambiguity, presents us with one of the worst-kept secrets in the history of drama.
>
> (428-29)

Connon then goes on to explain that Ville de Saint-Nazaire, the only character in Genet's drama who provides a link between on-stage and off-stage actions, is distinguished from the other characters: attention is drawn to him when he is dismissed from the stage by Archibald, the master of ceremonies; and Genet is uncharacteristically heavy-handed in the attitude towards secrecy manifested in the dialogue of the play. "The worst way," Connon points out, "to keep a secret is surely to begin by pointing out that there is a secret to be kept." We should not, therefore, take this "real" action at face value, he argues. Critics have overlooked what is really going on, something "so much more in keeping with the allusive nature of Genet's work." To support his case, Connon points to where Ville de Saint-Nazaire exits the stage. On two different occasions, Ville de Saint-Nazaire wants to exit stage-right. But Archibald instructs him to exit stage-left. Connon suggests that the off-stage action serves to divert our attention:

> there is another level of illusion between the external reality of the performance and the action that has generally been accepted as "real," the execution of the black traitor. That is to say that the actors are playing "actors," who, in order to distract our attention from events taking place off-stage right, are playing "actors," who, in order to distract our attention from events taking place off-stage left, are enacting a ritual.

This situation, Connon believes, is deliberately confusing:

> The audience will obviously be puzzled about what is meant to be "real" and what is not, perhaps even about what is real and what is not, for the idea of actors playing to an audience is repeated on so many different levels that there is bound to be a degree of blurring in the mind of the spectator between the various levels, including, perhaps, even that of reality itself. And the off-right action, which must now be taken to be the "real" action rather than the off-left action, has the additional threat of being unspecified, giving free rein to the imagination. So the multi-layering will cause the audience to feel both confused and threatened.
>
> (432)

Could Genet's early (and to date unperformed) version of *Les nègres* shed light on what is happening stage-right? If performed instead of the later version (as the early version of *Les bonnes* often is), would it be liable to leave audiences as puzzled, confused, and threatened?

BEHIND THE DELETIONS

Other than peripheral changes made between the two editions of *Les nègres*—which include the deletion of one of the letters "c" in the cry of "coccorico" (1958:117, 144, 146; 1960:138, 171, 173), the addition of three footnotes referring to Blin's staging of the play at the Théâtre de Lutèce in the second edition (1960:64,

146, 176), and the integration of thirty-three photographs of Blin's production taken by Ernest Scheidegger into the second edition,[5] only four short sequences differ between the first and second editions of the play. The seeming superficiality of the changes is more likely the real reason critics have not compared the two versions. Except for one line (part of one of the four sequences in question) which is substituted for a gesture in the second edition, each change represents a deletion in the dialogue of the drama. One might thus also ask whether the relationship between Genet's cutting dialogue from the script and confusing the audience is parallel or inverse.

The least troubling change made between the first and second editions of *Les nègres* occurs in the lines Genet cut from the Black who played the Governor before the "lyrical" massacre of the Court. Still, these cuts do touch on the issues of certainty, ambiguity, and of what Connon terms "the clear dividing line between reality and the fiction of a play" (427).

First, from the answer of the Black who played the role of Governor to Archibald's question: "Jusqu'où acceptez-vous d'aller?" the line following his clearly bold "Jusqu'à la mort" has been cut. In the first edition of the play, the Black playing the Governor adds: "Et qu'on se rassure, chacun de nous *saura* choisir pour le Blanc qu'il incarne ce soir, l'arme *la plus sûre* et *la plus infâme*" (140; emphasis added). While not specifying the weapon each Courtmember will choose, this Black nevertheless presents it in categorical, no uncertain terms.

Second, from the speech he makes before being "shot dead" by Village—only immediately afterwards to be instructed by Archibald to die (center-stage rather than on the spot)—, Genet cuts the very section in which the Governor seems to fall apart, with the very "real" trembling that overtakes him seeming to undermine the resigned calm with which he faces his fate. But even more striking is the Governor's calling into question of "reality": both his trembling and the definitiveness of his fate. In the second edition, the Governor's interrogative "Quoi? Vous dites que je tremble? Vous savez bien que c'est la goutte militaire?" is directly followed by his commanding "Eh bien, soit, visez donc ce cœur indomptable. Je meurs sans enfants . . . Mais je compte sur votre sens de l'honneur pour remettre mon uniforme taché de sang, au musée de l'Armée. En joue, feu!" In the first edition, it is followed first by this sequence in which both his state of mind and the true aims of the Blacks become even harder to decipher:

> Eh bien, vous ne parlez pas? Oh, vous me reprochez les dix mille adolescents écrasés par mes chars? Eh quoi! un homme de guerre ne saurait faire mordre la poussière à des lurons qui grandissent? . . . ([Il

tremble de plus en plus fort]) . . . *Non, je ne tremble pas de plus en plus fort,* j'envoie à mes troupes des signaux d'alarme . . . Vous n'allez tout de même pas me tuer *pour de bon?* . . . *Si?* . . . *Non?* . . .

(1958:143-44; emphasis added)

A second sequence cut by Genet between editions of *Les nègres* is more closely related to the issue of distraction raised by Connon. This sequence directly precedes the showdown between Félicité and the white queen, who with her Court comes to judge the Blacks. As with the sequence involving the Governor, this sequence—while on one level seeming to bring to light that there was no crime and that in their distraction the Court members have been duped—also tends towards ambiguity. It gives Félicité's explosive "Eh bien, Dahomey! Dahomey! Nègres, venez m'épaulez. Et qu'on ne laisse pas escamoter le crime. ([À la reine.]) Personne n'aurait la force de le nier" (1958:125; 1960:146) a troubling context. It raises questions over what has really occurred in—and/or during—the ritual reenactment by the Blacks. In the second edition of the play, Genet juxtaposes the very adjective suggesting certainty in Village's "Madame, méfiez-vous. Vous êtes une grande Reine et l'Afrique *n'est pas sûre,*" which is directed at the white queen (1960:123; emphasis added), with Félicité's interruptive "Assez! Et reculez!", which is directed at all the Blacks. However, in the first edition of the play Genet inserts between them the following sequence in which Village underlines the reality of the Blacks' fear while justifying the ritual that has been played out before the Court as a substitute for a reality that never was:

VILLAGE:

> Puisqu'il est encore temps, rentrez. Reculez. Remontez. l'escalier. Rentrez chez vous. *Vraiment,* nous avons peur et nous tremblons, car vous êtes belle, mais . . .

LE JUGE:

> Nous avons entendu le récit, et la ferveur de votre chant nous a touchés: même le blanc de vos yeux en prenait un sale coup . . .

NEIGE:

> ([*humble*])

> C'était pour mieux l'exalter, monseigneur.

VILLAGE:

> Il faut m'écouter, et rentrer. Ou bien alors, doublez, triplez vos escortes. Nous vous sommes soumis et dévoués, mais . . .

BOBO:

> ([*obséquieuse*])

> Car vous êtes belle et vous sentez bon . . .

VERTU:

> ([*souriant*])
>
> Et finalement nous avions imaginé cette mise en scène pour offrir avec délicatesse des chaises à votre suite . . .

VILLAGE:

> . . . *puisqu'il n'y a pas eu de crime, madame* . . .
>
> (1958:123-24; emphasis added)

This brings us to the third sequence that Genet changed in rewriting **Les nègres.** It is the only sequence that can actually be considered part of the ritual. Here, goaded on by the other Blacks to the strains of the *Dies iræ,* Village is to enter the bedroom of his victim and kill her. While the first two portions cut from this sequence seem not really to remove—or add—much to the play, the effect of the elimination of the third portion is more troubling.

The first portion cut by Genet is the very militaristic, but uneven

> Un, deux, trois, quatre, cinq! / Un, deux, trois, quatre, cinq! / Un, deux, trois, quatre, cinq! / Un, deux, trois, quatre, cinq! / Six!

which is sung out as though during a strident march by the Court. Genet had originally inserted it as a jarring descant between Neige's softly encouraging

> Expire, expire doucement, / Notre-Dame des Pélicans, / Jolie mouette, poliment, / Galamment, laisse-toi torturer . . .

and Vertu's

> Endeuillez-vous, hautes forêts / Qu'il s'y glisse en silence. / À ses grands pieds, poussière blanche / Mets des chaussons de lisière.

The second portion cut by Genet is Neige's

> Étendez-vous sur son chandail / Votre coude sur son mouchoir / Vous ne reverrez plus le jour . . .

which directly follows Vertu's "À ses grands pieds, poussière blanche / Mets des chaussons de lisière" and which directly precedes the sequence in which the Judge asks the Governor what he can make out in his telescope.

Now if the second cut portion, sung out by Neige—as with the portions Genet did not cut, which are sung out by Neige and Vertu—, seems in some way designed to push Village to murder and is thus directly linked to the ritual at hand, the relationship of the beginning of the third portion cut by Genet to what is unfolding onstage and offstage is less clear. Indeed, this very relationship

is at the heart of the ensuing argument between Vertu and Neige, and through it are raised still more troubling questions over the nature of reality, referentiality, and the blurring of the boundaries between the layers or levels of truth and/or performance in the play.

VERTU:

> Et vous ma tendre abeille / O mon regard abeille d'or / Que ton vol direct le conduise / Jusqu'à mon cœur . . .

NEIGE:

> ([*hurlant*])
>
> Menteuse!

VERTU:

> J'ai dit la vérité.

NEIGE:

> Au moment qu'il nous trompe avec toute la pâleur du monde.

ARCHIBALD:

> Mesdames! Silence!

NEIGE:

> ([*accusant Vertu*])
>
> C'est elle! Elle a changé des mots et vous ne vous en aperceviez pas. Elle chantait son amour.

VERTU:

> J'ai le droit d'inventer. Les Nègres improvisent. Je ne pariais pas en mon nom, mais au nom de toute ma race amoureuse, non de Village, non d'un homme, mais . . .

NEIGE:

> De qui?[6]

As Neige claims, Archibald has been distracted in order not to notice that Vertu has changed the words of the drama to suit an undisclosed referent. How? And, more important, why? It could not have been by Ville de Saint-Nazaire who, while slowly making his way on-stage during Félicité's great tirade, has not been noticed by Archibald. For as the stage directions make clear, Ville de Saint-Nazaire is only noticed now:

ARCHIBALD:

> ([il s'aperçoit *soudain* de la présence de Ville de Saint-Nazaire, entré très lentement, alors que Félicité disait sa grande tirade])
>
> Vous! Je vous avais dit de ne venir nous prévenir que quand tout serait achevé. C'est donc fait? C'est fini?
>
> (1958:98; emphasis added)

By cutting this and the other two sequences, Genet eliminates from *Les nègres* the questions they might have raised. Likewise, in the changes he made between the first and second published version of *Les nègres* to a fourth section of the play, he seems to remove some of the mystery surrounding the backstage action(s). While the cuts made in this section are more scattered than in the first three, all relate in some way to the judgment at hand off-stage left.

Roughly in the middle of the exchange taking place between Archibald and Ville de Saint-Nazaire (after Ville de Saint-Nazaire surprises Archibald by appearing onstage earlier than expected), the strands of the confusing layers of this drama seem at once to intersect and overlap. And again, the issues of the measurability of certainty, reality, and the levels of audience are raised.[7] In both the first and second editions of the play, we have the following sequence:

ARCHIBALD:

> Vous êtes sûr qu'il soit coupable? Et surtout qu'il soit le coupable que nous cherchons?

VILLE DE SAINT-NAZAIRE:

> ([*un peu ironique*])
>
> Vous auriez tout à coup des soupçons?

ARCHIBALD:

> Réfléchissez: il s'agit de juger, probablement de condamner, et d'exécuter un Nègre. C'est grave. Il ne s'agit plus de jouer. L'homme que nous tenons et dont nous sommes responsables est un homme réel. Il bouge, il mâche, il tousse, il tremble: tout à l'heure il sera tué.

VILLE DE SAINT-NAZAIRE:

> C'est très dur, je le sais. Mais je sais que si la comédie peut être menée devant eux ([*il montre le public*]), nous ne devons plus jouer quand nous sommes entre nous. Il faudra nous habituer à prendre la responsabilité du sang—du nôtre. Et le poids moral . . .

ARCHIBALD:

> ([*l'interrompant*])
>
> Tais-toi.

(1958:98-99; 1960:115-16)

However, in the second edition of *Les nègres,* what follows Archibald's "Tu n'empêcheras pas, comme je te l'ai dit, qu'il ne s'agisse d'un sang vivant, chaud, souple, fumant, d'un sang qui saigne . . ." and Ville de Saint-Nazaire's "Mais, alors, cette comédie que nous jouons, pour vous, ce n'était qu'un divertissement?" (1960:116) is stripped of its mysterious shroud. In the first edition, we have:

ARCHIBALD:

> Tu n'empêcheras pas, comme je te l'ai dit, qu'il ne s'agisse d'un sang vivant, chaud, souple, fumant, d'un sang qui saigne, *en somme . . .*

VILLE DE SAINT-NAZAIRE:

> Mais, alors, cette comédie que nous jouons, pour vous, ce n'était qu'un divertissement? *Elle n'avait pas pour but de détailler . . .*

(1958:99; emphasis added)

In the first edition, the "précisions" of both men, Archibald's summation ("en somme . . .") and Ville de Saint-Nazaire's apposition ("Elle n'avait pas pour but de détailler . . ."), are left unfinished. Attention is drawn to them not by what they tell us but by what they leave unsaid, in the dark. And in the middle of the sequence directly following this one—in two lines also cut from the play—, after the Judge (referring to the Queen's understanding of what is unfolding on stage) asks the Valet, who has just reentered: "Elle sait ce qui se passe?" the Valet replies: "Les Nègres gueulent assez fort" (1958:100). It is as though he implies that everything has just been spelled out loud and clear.

SUPPRESSING THE TRUTH?

But what? And why then did Genet make these cuts? If, as Connon observes, the dramatist's goal was to leave audiences of *Les nègres* feeling upset, confused, and threatened (437), and if, as these cut sequences suggest, in the first edition of the play matters seem even more ambiguous than in the second, by making these cuts Genet surely lessens the potential upset, confusion, and threat of the audience.

Before writing the dozen paragraphs that constitute "Pour jouer *Les nègres*" Genet wrote a much longer, "windy" (White 274) introduction to his play. Perhaps the manuscript pages of this introduction hold clues to his true intentions. But as Genet's publisher, Barbezat convinced the dramatist to eliminate them. He considered such an introduction uncharacteristic of the dramatist who, Connon reminds us, was characteristically *ambiguous* (429).

Hoping to learn more about Genet's intentions in writing *Les nègres,* I wrote to Barbezat in October 1993, asking him about the suppressed introduction. As Barbezat had not yet responded at the time, I asked him publicly about it at the Centre Pompidou in Paris, where he had just spoken on a panel about his role as Genet's publisher (see Alphant). In response, Barbezat denied knowledge of such an introduction. But immediately after his claim of ignorance, the publisher's wife, Olga, arose from the front row of the auditorium where she had been sitting. She turned to me and confirmed that Genet had, indeed, written it. Olga Barbezat explained that this introduction was so unlike anything else the dramatist had written that her husband had convinced him never to publish it.

Some three weeks after this public confirmation of the existence of an unpublished introduction to *Les nègres,* I received the following letter—a written "confirmation"—from Barbezat himself:

Monsieur,

Je n'ai pas perdu de vue votre lettre du 16/10/93 et j'y réponds aujourd'hui.

Vous étiez présent, du reste, à la soirée du Centre Pompidou consacrée à Jean Genet et Olga Barbezat vous a répondu à la question que vous avez posée. Genet a pris la décision de ne jamais publier l'introduction aux *Nègres*; elle ne sera jamais publiée et vous pouvez considérer qu'elle n'existe pas.

Je vous prie d'agréer, Monsieur, mes salutations distinguées.

Marc Barbezat

Pages that at the same time exist but do not exist? Whether or not he intends the decidedly Genetian overtones, Barbezat makes his position—both as publisher and "conservateur" of Genet's works—unambiguous, very black and white. Indeed, coupled with this ironic afterword, the seeming reduction of the apparent upset, confusion, and threat of the audience through the lessening of ambiguity in the cuts made from the first to the second published version of *Les nègres* appears in retrospect counterbalanced in the shift between stages: from genesis to (self-) censorship, from performance to (non-) publication. As critics of Genet, privy for now, at least, only to what Barbezat feels is actually worthy of Genet and to what he has actually published, we are faced with—and inevitably frustrated by—the questions within the play and pertaining to it that are raised by Genet's (and Barbezat's?) cuts and the larger, more pressing question of the possible implication or implications these questions have on our past—and will have on our future—interpretations of the play. Perhaps we can accept this frustration at never being able to know the truth as a compromise solution. Like Vertu in her last, unfinished line to Village at the end of the play ("Ce qui est sûr, au moins, c'est que tu ne pourrais jamais enrouler tes doigts dans mes longs cheveux blonds . . ."), we might ultimately embrace an impossibility as the only certainty.[8]

Notes

1. Genet 1988b (letter of 9 October 1959 to Marc Barbezat).

2. *Les bonnes* 1947, 1954, 1968b; *Haute surveillance* 1949, 1965, 1968c, 1988a; *Le balcon* 1956, 1962, 1968a; *Les nègres* 1958, 1960; *Les paravents* 1961, 1976.

3. See for example Saint-Léon, Kennelly, Bougon, Walker 1982 and 1984, and Aslan 1972.

4. Although not mentioned by Connon, both Blin and Asian also consider this action "real, Blin recalls: "Tout dans le spectacle est faux. Des comédiens jouent le procès des Noirs par des Blancs, puis le procès des Blancs par des Noirs, et

ça c'est de l'ordre de la représentation. Mais pendant ce temps, en coulisse, se déroule la seule chose sérieuse et réelle, le jugement d'un Noir par d'autres Noirs. Ville de Saint-Nazaire, qui est chargé de rendre compte de ce qui se passe dehors, est le seul personnage qui soit hors du jeu" (137). Asian echoes Blin: "Spectateurs blancs conviés à constituer dans la salle l'audience nécessaire à tout cérémonial, nous n'assistons en réalité qu'à une partie de la cérémonie, à savoir un spectacle de parade dissimulant, masquant le véritable événement qui, lui, se passe derrière le rideau, un règlement de comptes qui ne nous regarde pas; il ne concerne que les Noirs" (1990:184).

5. 1960; cover and 9, 10, 11, 12, 21, 22, 39, 40, 49, 50, 67, 68, 77, 78, 79, 80, 89, 90, 107, 108, 117, 118, 119, 120, 129, 130, 146, 147, 148, 149, 167, 168.

6. 1958:97-98. Two—more superficial—changes in this sequence (on pages 100 and 102) also relate to the Vertu/Neige conflict.

7. It should be noted that the only other sequences cut by Genet—which occur later on in the play— further complicate the layering. They are:

VILLAGE:

([*insistant*])

Nous peser? Avec leurs balances d'or et de rubis? Et pensez-vous, s'ils s'en vont mourir, qu'ils me laisseront aimer Vertu—ou plutôt que Vertu pourra m'aimer?

VILLE DE SAINT NAZAIRE:

([*à Village*])

~~Tu as peur? Vous avez eu tort de vous avez comme comédiens.~~

ARCHIBALD:

~~C'est par honnêteté Nous nous donnions surtout comme Nègres.~~

VILLE DE SAINT-NAZAIRE:

([*souriant mais précis*])

Vous n'avez pas essayé de les négrifier? De leur greffer des narines et des lèvres bambaras? De leur crépeler les cheveux? De les réduire en esclavage? (1960:127)

and:

ARCHIBALD:

Tout acteur sait qu'à une heure fixe le rideau sera baissé. Et presque toujours qu'il incarne un mort ou une morte: Phèdre, Don Juan, Antigone, la Dame aux Camélias, monsieur le Docteur Schweitzer . . . ([*Un long silence.*])

DIOUF:

~~Nous le savons tous, que le seul événement qui pourrait nous arracher à ce jeu de miroir, c'est le sang qui coule.~~

([On entend un bruit de pas dans la coulisse. Diouf affolé remet son masque. Les autres Nègres paraissent apeurés. Ils vont tous, en masse, avec madame Félicité, se grouper à gauche de la scène sous le balcon où apparaissait la Cour. Le piétinement et le bruit deviennent plus précis. Enfin, de la coulisse de droite, semblant descendre un chemin, à reculons, sort d'abord le Valet. Il rote et titube. Manifestement, il est ivre.])

(1960:132-33)

8. An earlier version of this article was presented at the Fourteenth Annual International Colloquium on Twentieth-Century French Studies in Columbus, Ohio.

References

Alphant, Marianne, org. "Autour de Jean Genet." Paris: Centre Georges Pompidou, 21 October 1993.

Aslan, Odette. 1972. *"Les paravenis* de J. Genet." *Les voies de la création théâtrale* 3:12-107.

———. 1990. *Roger Blin: qui êtes-vous?* Paris: La Manufacture.

Blin, Roger. *Souvenirs et propos.* Paris: Gallimard, 1986.

Bougon, Patrice. "L'ultime version de *Haute surveillance.*" *Critique* 45.503 (1989):301-02.

Coe, Richard N. *The Vision of Jean Genet: A Study of His Poems, Plays and Novels.* New York: Grove Press, 1968.

Connon, Derek F. "Confused? You Will Be: Genet's *Les nègres* and the Art of Upsetting the Audience." *French Studies* 50.4 (1996):425-38.

Decock, Jean. *"Les nègres* aux USA." *Obliques* 2 (1972):48-50.

Esslin, Martin. *The Theater of the Absurd.* New York: Doubleday, 1961.

Frechtman, Bernard. *Showbill for* The Blacks. New York, 1961.

Genet, Jean. 1947. *Les bonnes.* Décines: L'Arbalète.

———. 1949. *Haute surveillance.* Paris: Gallimard.

———. 1954. *Les bonnes.* Sceaux: Pauvert.

———. 1956. *Le balcon.* Décines: L'Arbalète.

———. 1958. *Les nègres.* Décines: L'Arbalète.

———. 1960. *Les nègres.* Décines: L'Arbalète.

———. 1961. *Les paravents.* Décines: L'Arbalète.

———. 1962. *Le balcon.* Décines: L'Arbalète.

———. 1965. *Haute surveillance.* Paris: Gallimard.

———. 1968a. "Le balcon." *Œuvres complètes.* Paris: Gallimard. IV:33-135.

———. 1968b. "Les bonnes." *Œuvres complètes.* Paris: Gallimard. IV:137-76.

———. 1968c. "Haute surveillance." *Œuvres complètes.* Paris: Gallimard. IV:177-213.

———. 1976. *Les paravents.* Décines: L'Arbalète.

———. 1979. "Pour jouer *Les nègres.*" *Œuvres complètes.* Paris: Gallimard. V:77-78.

———. 1988a. *Haute surveillance (nouvelle version).* Paris: Gallimard.

———. 1988b. *Lettres à Olga et Marc Barbezat.* Décines: L'Arbalète.

Kennelly, Brian Gordon. "The Unknown Role of Madame in Genet's *Les bonnes.*" *Romance Notes* 36.3 (1996):243-52.

Magnan, Jean-Marie. *Essai sur Jean Genet.* Paris: Seghers, 1966.

Martin, Graham Dunstan. "Racism in Genet's *Les nègres.*" *Modern Language Review* 70 (1975):517-25.

McMahon, Joseph H. *The Imagination of Jean Genet.* New Haven: Yale University Press, 1963.

Saint-Léon, Claire. *"Les bonnes* de Jean Genet: quelle version faut-il jouer?" *Studies in Foreign Languages and Literature: The Proceedings of the 23rd Mountain Interstate Foreign Language Conference.* Richmond: Eastern Kentucky University, 1976. 513-16.

Thody, Philip. *Jean Genet: A Study of His Novels and Plays.* London: Hamish Hamilton, 1968.

Walker, David. 1982. "Introduction." *Le balcon,* by Jean Genet. London: Methuen Educational. 1-39.

———. 1984. "Revolution and Revisions in *Le balcon.*" *Modern Language Review* 79.4:817-30.

White, Edmund. *Genet: A Biography.* New York: Knopf, 1993.

Debby Thompson (essay date summer 2002)

SOURCE: Thompson, Debby. "'What Exactly Is a Black?': Interrogating the Reality of Race in Jean Genet's *The Blacks.*" *Studies in Twentieth Century Literature* 26, no. 2 (summer 2002): 395-425.

[*In the following excerpt, Thompson provides a broad discussion of race within* The Blacks, *arguing that the purpose of the play is not the determination of "blackness," but the dramatization of white guilt and how to embrace the issue of racial relations.*]

The Negro is not. Any more than the white man.

—Frantz Fanon, *Black Skin, White Masks*

Blackness exists, but "only" as a function of its signifiers.

—Henry Louis Gates, *The Signifying Monkey*

To be inauthentic is sometimes the best way to be real.

—Paul Gilroy, "'. . . to be real': The Dissident Forms of Black Expressive Culture"

On the dedication page of the Grove Press, English translation of *The Blacks: A Clown Show* Genet asks, "what exactly is a black?" This is a question which has been intensely engaged by African diasporic writers from Frantz Fanon to Henry Louis Gates, Jr. to Paul Gilroy and by African diasporic cultures generally. Yet when asked by a white Frenchman, the question seems to serve different ends. Fanon's denial of the ontological grounds of racial identity comes in a cultural context where crude racial stereotypes are still very much in place. Gates's and Gilroy's statements about the constructed or performative nature of racial identity are an attempt to retain the political power of black communal identity in an era of radical deconstruction of identity. All three writers are speaking primarily to black readerships. Genet's questioning, however, is directed first to white audiences in the presence of blacks, or perhaps, as Lorraine Hansberry claims, is "a conversation between white men about themselves"—and a conversation "haunted by guilt" and "steeped in the romance of racial exoticization" (Hansberry 42).

To some readers and audiences, the play *The Blacks,* Genet's incendiary satire on racism and colonialism, is itself innately racist and neo-colonialist. And yet, the question "What exactly is a black?" comes from a playwright who, around 1970, became involved with the Black Panthers, and later supported the Algerian revolution and the PLO. Genet's sympathy with the struggles of people of color against oppression led his translator to call Genet a "white Negro," and Genet himself to refer to himself as "a black man who happens to have white or pink skin."[1] Is Genet a "black" man in a "white" mask—an outsider to white culture even though he is himself white—or is he simply reviving American theater's horrendously racist tradition of blackface minstrelsy? Eric Lott, a cultural theorist of blackface minstrelsy, suggests a complication to my either/or question. Lott suggests that American blackface minstrelsy was itself a deeply ambivalent practice which reflected "a mixed erotic economy of celebration and exploitation" (or, more simply, "love and theft") of black culture by whites. That is, blackface minstrelsy presents "a dialectical flickering of racial insult and racial envy, moments of domination and moments of liberation, counterfeit and currency, a pattern at times amounting to no more than the two faces of racism, at

others gesturing toward a specific kind of political or sexual danger, and all constituting a peculiarly American structure of racial feeling." It is this dialectical structure of American racial feeling, though in a more contemporary form than that of nineteenth-century blackface minstrelsy, which I want to explore through a reading of *The Blacks.* This play both studies and enacts the dialectical structure of the white gaze—a study and a performance, I argue, that cannot, at least in the current and historical context of global politics, take place outside of white guilt.

The image of racial transvestism used to characterize Genet encapsulates a major ambivalence in his play: the phrase "white Negro" both essentializes the racial categories of "white" and "Negro" and shows them to be transgressable constructs. Combining incantations and demystifications of "blackness" (as well as of "whiteness"), Genet's play refuses to take "race" as a given, even as it dramatizes the impossibility of this refusal. At the same time, the politics of asking the question "what exactly is a black?" is complex, and it matters a great deal who is asking the question, and in what context. Who is empowered by the affirmation of racial authenticity? Who is empowered by its deconstruction? Do both racism and its overthrow hinge on beliefs in the reality or facticity of race? Does a derealizing of race throw racial politics into a crisis? Or can—and should—there be a racial politics divested of the reality of race? These are some of the questions Genet both poses and evades in *The Blacks.*

After *The Blacks*' successful run in Paris, it achieved a great deal of acclaim and popularity in its American run off-Broadway, and left a wave of dramatic responses to it, from playwrights as notable and diverse as Lorraine Hansberry, Amiri Baraka, Adrienne Kennedy, ntozake shange, and George C. Wolfe.[2] *The Blacks*' setting was originally read as Africa or the West Indies; however, Genet's play, written in France by a Frenchman, has been a disturbing and provocative text for many African American dramatists, and these dramatic responses in turn create a context of *American* racial politics, philosophy, and history (particularly the historical phenomenon of minstrelsy, the first theatrical tradition to be developed by whites on American soil) from which to reevaluate the play. While *The Blacks* was written during the time of the American civil rights movement's struggle for equality between blacks and whites in the 1950s, the struggle that *The Blacks* reflects on is one of a real crisis over the authenticity of "black identity"—a struggle more characteristic of later decades. *The Blacks*' insistence on the very real ways in which the identities of "black" and "white" are lived and socially enforced, and the play's simultaneous argument that these body-identities are ultimately fictional, prefigures major issues and paradoxes of current African American Cultural Studies and of the emerging field of

Whiteness Studies. Hence the play has new relevance to us now. Both *The Blacks* and current African American cultural studies grapple with the paradox that racial identity is real in that it is *realized*—that the reality of racial identity exists through performative constitution, or what Paul Gilroy calls "black vernacular self-fashioning, culture-making, play and antiphonic communal conversation" (Gilroy 13). Equally paradoxical, both the position that black identity has real ontological status and the opposite position, that black identity is only a function of signifiers, can serve both racist and anti-racist ends, depending on the specific situation of the assertion. Genet's play participates in current studies of the "technologies of race" operating in twentieth-century America. It looks not only at how race is made to be real, but also at how the deconstruction of racial constructions can still reinforce those constructions. Even more importantly, the play, in my reading of it, suggests that the assertion/deconstruction of the realness of racial identity is inherently a political and situational question. What I am arguing, then, is that Genet can never answer the question "what exactly is a black," or even whether or not blackness *is*. Instead, he dramatizes whites' investment in the question of racial ontology. Most radically, he offers up a form in which to entertain white guilt.

A brief plot outline of *The Blacks* will suggest some of the complexity and novelty of that form, and will make evident both Genet's refusal to take race—any race—as a given, and his devious pleasure in ferreting out and dis-playing the inherent theatricality of racial identities. Onstage, *The Blacks* presents a play-within-a-play—or rather a play-within-a-play-within-a-play. In the play most within, the "Negroes"—Archibald, Village, Bobo, Snow, Felicity, Virtue, and Diouf—ritualistically re-enact, before a "white" "Court," the rape and murder of a "white woman" by a "black" man. The "white Court" then travels to the "black jungle" to seek revenge. The "Court," however, is played by "black actors" (or black actors playing black actors) in White Masks. Masking goes beyond individual characters; the performance itself is a mask. The onstage *divertissement* diverts the audience from another act taking place beyond the wings, which is reported by Newport News: the Negroes' execution of a traitor and the simultaneous rise to power of a new leader. After this "offstage" drama is disclosed, the "Court"—the Governor, the Judge, the Missionary, the Valet, and the Queen—ceremoniously "die." The Court exits to Hell, stage right, while the Negroes exit stage left, leaving behind Village, who performed the rapist-murderer, and Virtue, a prostitute. The two are in love. Virtue challenges Village to invent new kinds of flirting, love-making, and love proper. The backdrop rises, and all the "Negroes" appear without their masks. Village and Virtue walk toward the "Negroes" and away from the audience as the curtain is drawn.

So to return to that seductive, promising yet withholding dedication page in the American Grove Press edition of *The Blacks.* Before readers encounter any characters or events, we read, under "To Abdallah": One evening an actor asked me to write a play for an all-black cast. But what exactly is a black? First of all, what's his color? (3). Before Genet can "write a play for an all-black cast," he must ask what it means to be "a black," and what "black" means. Is "black" innate? Is it internal? Is it worn on the skin like a mask? Is it a made-up role? A biological fact? A symbol? A metaphor or metonym? Is one born black? Does one achieve blackness? Is a black actor an actor first, and does he or she enact blackness? Or is he or she black first, before the acting starts? Is the all-black cast to be a group of actors all of whom are black, or a group of black actors whose blackness is all-black, pure, untainted by whiteness? And what is "whiteness"? These questions, and the many more implied by Genet's two simple questions about the color of "a black," precede all racially-marked bodies involved in *The Blacks*: bodies of the playwright, of the actors, of the characters, of the spectators.

THE WHITE GAZE AND SPECTACLES OF RACE

On the page directly following the dedication, Genet "repeat[s]" what he has not yet said: this play is "written . . . by a white man" and "intended for a white audience" (4). Genet feels that these "white" specifications repeat the "black" specifications of the previous page; the recognition of the "black" race implies that of the "white" race simultaneously, in that one race is not recognized as such except in opposition to another. White producers and white spectatorship seem to be implicit in the idea of a black spectacle. Furthermore, the white audience—or rather, the whiteness of the audience—is as much a player in *The Blacks* as the black(ness of the) actors. So salient is the structure of white spectators gazing at the spectacle of black actors to this production of color, that Genet will go to all lengths to achieve it:

> [I]f, which is unlikely, [*The Blacks*] is ever performed before a black audience, then a white person, male or female, should be invited every evening. The organizer of the show should welcome him formally, dress him in ceremonial costume and lead him to his seat, preferably in the front row of the orchestra. The actors will play for him. A spotlight should be focused upon this symbolic white throughout the performance.
>
> (4)

The symbolic presence of a white onlooker is more important than the presence of a real white person. (But what is a "real white person"? First of all, what is her or his color?) The staging of the "white gaze" here is a decade-before-the-fact parody of the trial of the "Soledad Brothers." Speaking of this and other trials of

Black men and women, Genet writes, "a minimum of courtesy toward justice would require that the majority of the jury be Black, whether they live in the ghetto or not, but that they had known at least once the humiliation of a white gaze" ("The Black and the Red"). Paralleling feminist film theory's still inchoate (at the time) concept of the "male gaze," Genet's "white gaze" suggests not only a theatrical/juridical audience, but a more thoroughly surveillant white overseer built into the very ideological structure of American culture.

The literal foregrounding and spotlighting of the token white foreshadows a play which foregrounds and spotlights skin color. In doing so, Genet exaggerates the black-white dialectic into absurdity. After he specifies that at least one white spectator must be present, Genet continues: "But what if no white person accepted? Then let white masks be distributed to the black spectators as they enter the theater. And if the blacks refuse the masks, then let a dummy be used." Although Genet prefers and anticipates white spectators, he presents people with "black skin, white masks" or white mannequins to be viable substitutes. Much of *The Blacks* suggests that skin is itself a mask in two contradictory senses: it implies a preceding and controlling subject, and it precedes and controls the subject. The actor wears the mask, but the mask also wears the actor. Traditionally, of course, masks have been used in theater not only physically and ritually, but also rhetorically, as tropes of a false surface covering a true identity. Genet's masks at times work this way. Each actor playing a member of the Court is conspicuously black under the mask: "The mask is worn in such a way that the audience sees a black band all around it, and even the actor's kinky hair" (8). The image of white power is created and supported by black characters embodied by black actors (and prescribed by a white writer); whiteness is defined in opposition to blackness. The white skin or white mask covers over its own dependence on blackness (just as, on a social level, European and American monuments rarely acknowledge the black slave labor and disproportionately black minimum wage underclass that build and mop and polish those monuments). But the many masks of *The Blacks* also suggest that a mask need not hide a true identity behind it; instead, the mask may make the underlying identity recognizable to itself, even as it encourages that identity to claim its distinctness from the mask.

Genet's "Negroes" exaggerate the mask-ness of their black skin by making it even blacker. If members of "the Court" create whiteness, "the Negroes" make up their blackness both with soot mixed with saliva and with language games. They apply black makeup to perform before the white Court and the white spectators:

> As you see, ladies and gentlemen, just as you have
> your lilies and roses, so we—in order to serve you—

shall use our beautiful, shiny black makeup. It is Mr. Deodatus Village who gathers the smoke-black and Mrs. Felicity Trollop Pardon who thins it out in our saliva. These ladies help her. We embellish ourselves so as to please you. You are white. And spectators. This evening we shall perform for you. . . .

(10)

Even their method of making their makeup is part of the blackface. Their crude charcoal and spit, contrasting with whites' flowers, are organic properties which show the races they encode to be social and theatrical manufactures. Archibald's description of the application of blackface plays off of and ridicules the binarism of white civility vs. black primitivism. Archibald's ridicule goes further: white spectators are pleased by blacks, perhaps want to see blacks only when they are deep-black, soot-black. In fact, the whiteness of the whites is a product of the blacking-up of the blacks. The fact that "you are white" comes only after "the blacks" make themselves contrastingly black. ("The blacks" are likewise not "black" before they make themselves "black.") Throughout the play, as in this speech, almost every reference to blackness is immediately contiguous to a reference to whiteness, and vice versa. The references are tellingly asymmetrical. As whites adorn themselves with flowers, blacks adorn themselves with black makeup. As blacks make themselves black, whites are pleased—and are white. Furthermore, their characterization as white immediately produces their characterization as spectators, as if "spectators" is the next unit along a chain of connotations. As whites are spectators, blacks are performers. . . . And what blacks perform is blackness, which makes whites white. The classificatory system circles in a tautological loop which never centers on reality—or rather, the loop of tautological performance *becomes* reality. The black makeup becomes black skin, that which makes blacks up, and makes them up to be black. This is of course not to deny the organic reality of skin color, but to suggest how skin color becomes perceptible, and to suggest further that *to white audiences* blackness seems more produced than whiteness, the "null" race.

Already blackened onstage once, Village is blackened even further in order to perform the "rape" and "murder" of a "white woman" before "the Court." Archibald directs Village to play blackness itself: "I order you to be black to your very veins. Pump black blood through them. Let Africa circulate in them. Let Negroes negrify themselves" (52). Both scenes of "blacking up" involve the application of both external and internal masks—masks which will then be worn as innate, bodily realities. "Let Negroes negrify themselves" ("Que les Nègres se nègrent," 66); this self-contradiction and/or tautological order encapsulates and generates a whole complex of questions about race. If "negrify" means "to make (into a) Negro," then what are "Negroes" before they "negrify themselves"? Can these pre-"Negroes" ever resist "negrifying" them-selves—and if so, what are they then? Maybe the "ne-grification" is unavoidable (as is "caucasification"). Maybe the pre-"Negro" can only be posited in retrospect after the "negrification" has occurred. The construction of the sentence implies that Negroes pre-exist and are agents of their own negrifying. Which comes first, the Negroes or the negrification? Or is such a causal structure even relevant to racial identity?

Village, under Archibald's direction, will "negrify" himself into stereotype:

> Let Negroes negrify themselves. Let them persist to the point of madness in what they're condemned to be, in their ebony, in their odor, in their yellow eyes, in their cannibal tastes. Let them not be content with eating Whites, but let them cook each other as well. Let them invent recipes for shin-bones, knee-caps, calves, thick lips, everything. Let them invent unknown sauces. Let them invent hiccoughs, belches and farts that'll give out a deleterious jazz. Let them invent a criminal paint-ing and dancing. Negroes, if they change toward us, let it not be out of indulgence, but terror.
>
> (52)

Negroes will "invent" and stage a primitivism and savagery which comes after and is already created by and demanded by whiteness and civility. Invention is offered up as a last-ditch form of agency within a hope-lessly prescribed discourse. Archibald's description plays off the stereotype of primitive jungle-dwellers as creatures of the body prior to social codes. But the seemingly artless bodily primitivism—the black body untainted by civilization—the cannibalism, the odor, hiccoughs, belching, farting, dancing—are invented in the society of "white" spectatorship according to the highly theatrical codes of colonialism, racism and artistic representation. This notion of Blackness Itself—the ebony black African savage, one with nature, endowed with animal instincts unfettered by conscience or reason—is created belatedly by a nostalgic civiliza-tion. The (white) Valet finds the Negroes "exquisitely spontaneous. They have a strange beauty. Their flesh is weightier . . ." (19). We know from Village's com-ments on his performance just before the Valet's intru-sion that Village is carefully pacing his performance, is modulating when "to speed up or draw out [his] recital and [his] performance" (18), and is adjusting his sighs for the greatest effect. The appearance of spontaneity is craftily cultivated. The Valet, speaking "very affect-edly," makes the unspontaneous (indeed highly prescribed) observation that Negroes are spontaneous. The observation, as well as the pronouncing of it, is af-fected by a tradition of negrification so pervasive that "blacks" and "whites" can no longer see each other

outside of its codes. In other words, colonial discourse is not simply dominating, but hegemonic. It does not simply repress individuals; it enables and creates identi-ties.

Hegemonic structures, further, operate most effectively through the production of desires and pleasures. In this way, the stereotype of "darkness itself" is not always expressly derogatory (at least not "intentionally" derogatory). The black male body of the white cultural imaginary can signify an intense physicality which is erotic and exotic as well as dangerous and terrifying. Eric Lott reads this phenomenon in blackface minstrelsy, whose performers and audiences may have found in blackface an erotic charge:

> [The] common white associations of black maleness with the onset of pubescent sexuality indicate that the assumption of dominant codes of masculinity in the United States was (and still is) partly negotiated through an imaginary black interlocutor . . . [W]hite male fantasies of black men undergird the subject posi-tions white men grow up to occupy. This dynamic is, further, one whose results are far from given; its ap-propriations of "black" masculinity may or may not have racist results. But in thus mediating white men's relations with other white men, minstrel acts certainly made currency out of the black man himself, that obscure object of exchangeable desire. The stock in trade of the exchange so central to minstrelsy . . . was black culture in the guise of an attractive masculinity.
>
> (53)

Technologies of race—combined inextricably with technologies of gender—produce a desired fantasy of "darkness itself." The desire for imaginary "darkness itself" becomes very difficult to classify as either racist or non-racist.

Furthermore, the stereotype of "darkness itself" is not always propagated by whites (or by blacks in the service of supreme white pleasure). It is also an ideal which "blacks" create for themselves, not necessarily out of "false consciousness," but perhaps necessarily in deeply ambivalent and problematic forms. The search of contemporary African Americans for their African roots, for example, can be a powerful source of pride, con-nectedness, and liberation from white ideology—when the Africanness sought is truly other to, not merely the opposite of, "the White Man" or "the Man" (to use the African American synecdoche). But when African primitivism is affected in order to shake off the "American" half of "African American" (a method hopelessly counterproductive to its aim), when African traditions are exoticized and performed as *refutations* or even *negations* of white cultural forms, then the reconstructed Africanism is complicit in the very white mythology it is talking back to. Similarly the perfor-mance of savagery in some forms of black militancy, while it threatens individual white people, actually serves and justifies white supremacy.

Felicity performs similar self-Africanizing rituals when she plays a jungle dweller whom the Court must punish for Village's crime:

> Beyond that shattered darkness, which was splintered into millions of Blacks who dropped to the jungle, we were Darkness in person. Not the darkness which is absence of light, but the kindly and terrible Mother who contains light and deeds.
>
> (105)

Felicity's desire to incarnate Mother Africa residing in an unshattered darkness, to be not only dark but "Darkness in person," to embody an abstract and disembodied essence, demands that she put on a mask, an African mask, not take one off.

Felicity's proud image of "Darkness in person" is, as she goes on to tell the Queen, created as a negation—almost a photographic negative—of white ideals:

> Look, Madam. Here it comes, the darkness you were clamoring for, and her sons as well. They're her escort of crimes. To you, black was the color of priests and undertakers and orphans. But everything is changing. Whatever is gentle and kind and good and tender will be black. Milk will be black, sugar, rice, the sky, doves, hope, will be black. So will the opera to which we shall go, blacks that we are, in black Rolls Royces to hail black kings, to hear brass bands beneath chandeliers of black crystal. . . .
>
> (105-06)

While this vision of black supremacy reverses and parodies white supremacist values, it fails to change—indeed it reinforces, albeit parodically—the reduction of identity and of heritage to skin colors, the reduction of skin colors to black and white (and the blindness to all those races for whom both of these two categories are inapplicable), the assignment of values to these colors, and the pervasion of these racialized values into all aspects of life. (Not to mention its conservation of the class system.) To say that in a system of black supremacy milk will be black is to reinforce a link between white milk (a nutritive good) and white supremacy. Earlier, Felicity summons up a similar personification of Africa:

> Are you there, Africa with the bulging chest and oblong thigh? Sulking Africa, wrought of iron, in the fire, Africa of the millions of royal slaves, deported Africa, drifting continent, are you there? Slowly you vanish, you withdraw into the past, into the tales of castaways, colonial museums, the works of scholars, but I call you back this evening to attend a secret revel.
>
> (77)

This embodying of Africa on the one hand offers a liberation from being a display for the white colonialist gaze, but on the other hand can only be accessed through such a gaze. It is a primitivism constructed belatedly, a conception of Africa as a unified whole which black Africans have possessed only in the contrasting presence of white non-Africans.

· · · · ·

RE-INVENTING THE REAL

If *The Blacks* is skeptical about reconfiguring black-white interactions, it more sanguinely gestures towards alternate scenarios for all-black casts. While the play-within-the-play theatricalizes the role-ness of all racial roles and the predominance of a prior script to which there is no outside-script, the presence of a play ontologically outside the play-within, and of blatant references to an audience and actors ontologically outside of the "outer" play, suggest (but also suspend) the possibility of alternatives to the ritual enacted. Perhaps even more importantly, I think, the play ultimately displaces the question of whether a real exists outside of representation to the question of who has power over representations of the real. The ultimate political power is the power to invent new ontologies, new realities.

If rituals and theatricality seem to engulf every attempt to subvert them, if all relationships between and within races, and indeed the very notion of "race," seem to be always already prescripted and staged, is there any outside-theater? Can we go beyond the Big Black Buck, the white princess, the Sambo, the Queen, the Judge, and the lot? While there is an outside (of sorts) to the individual play *The Blacks,* there may be no outside to theatrical phenomena such as acting, making-up, building a character, learning how to be authentic. So the references to the real lives of characters may ring false. Archibald, for example, tells white viewers that "when we leave this stage, we are involved in your life. I am a cook, this lady is a sewing-maid, this gentleman is a medical student, this gentleman is a curate at St. Anne's . . ." (14). White viewers "know" that the black actors are, in "real life," no more a cook, sewing-maid, medical student, curate, etc. than the catafalque is occupied by a "real" corpse of a white woman. (In fact, as viewers learn, the catafalque is empty.) White viewers of the American production "knew" that James Earl Jones, Roscoe Lee Browne, Louis Gossett, Cicely Tyson, and the rest of the cast were not cooks and sewing ladies playing black actors playing Negro savages, but black actors playing cooks and sewing-maids playing black actors playing Negro savages (in a kind of metastasized A-effect).

Nevertheless, the continuous references to many simultaneous ontological levels suggests that ontology itself is theatrically constituted, that "reality" is recognizable as such only in opposition to "fiction" or "performance." But even if all reality-effects are theatrically constituted, there still remain incontrovertible differences between theatrically-constituted realities and bald-faced lies. In **The Blacks,** Newport News's news of the "off-stage" execution of a Negro traitor provides such an ontological critique of the onstage ritual. All the other "Negroes" wear evening clothes except for Newport News, the emissary from the "real" drama, who is barefooted and wears a woolen sweater. The woolen sweater and even the bare feet are as much costumes bearing encoded meanings as are the evening suits and dresses. The bare feet, for example, signify or represent an intimacy with nature untainted by civilization: the noble savage, or the savage downright, once again. Then again (especially if the sweater is a color other than black or white), Newport News's costume breaks out of the exaggerated black-and-white motif which is artificially maintained on so many levels in this play, and to which the "black tie" dress of the other black men visually contribute, albeit satirically. Newport News's costume, then, gestures toward a less artificially black-and-white political struggle. This struggle is over both visual images and the bodies which embody these images—both over the images of white power and over the whites in power. Newport News explains that the blacks aim "not only to corrode and dissolve the idea they'd like us to have of them" but also to "fight them in their actual persons, in their flesh and blood" (112). The other onstage blacks have been "present only for display" (112). The real struggle of blacks against white supremacy entails *both* physical bodies *and* the representation of racial identities.

When Archibald interrogates Newport News on the traitor's guilt, Archibald explains,

> [I]t's a matter of judging and probably sentencing and executing a Negro. That's a serious affair. It's no longer a matter of staging a performance. The man we're holding and for whom we're responsible is a real man. He moves, he chews, he coughs, he trembles. In a little while, he'll be killed . . . it's a matter of living blood, hot, supple, reeking blood, of blood that bleeds. . . .
>
> (82)

The "real man" offstage has both more and less physical presence than the onstage characters performed by real actors. The audience "knows" that there is no traitor in the wings who is "really" executed offstage simultaneous to Diouf's symbolic execution onstage, nor is there a revolution geared for execution in the wings. The effect of an absolutely real act devoid of play-acting is a product of play-acting; in this case, "reality" is dramatically constituted. At the same time, however, the on-stage gesture toward an offstage reality within the theater also gestures toward yet another offstage reality outside of the theater, where killings mirror the onstage caricatured rituals but are performed on real people of flesh and hot, supple blood. This real revolution both re-enacts the ritual scripts and roles of racial relations and is no longer only "a matter of staging a performance."

Yet other theatrical gestures toward other actual acts occur which do not re-enact the same racially-cast rape-and-murder scenario as that represented onstage. For example we learn that "in real life" Virtue is a black "whore" for "[w]hite customers." Virtue reminds us that "[e]very brothel has its negress" and that "this evening's ceremony will affect [her] far less than the one [she] perform[s] ten times a day" (38). Whereas black women are left out of the onstage ritual in which white women figure as signifiers (or dead metaphors) in the establishment of power relationships between white men and black men, black women "in real life" are exploited and humiliated "ten times a day." The (white, male) customer—(black, female) prostitute relationship, so prevalent offstage and unrepresented onstage as well as in other media (including TV and newspapers), metonymizes colonialist and phallocratic relationships invisible to the "white gaze." (Even less visible and/or representable may be intra-racial rape.)

Perhaps even more unrepresentable yet to a white gaze is a *love* between two black people, especially a love that is not prescripted and formulaic. In what some have called uncharacteristic sentimentality, Genet ends the play with the fragile possibility of authentic love between Virtue and Village. The very possibility of this love is extremely threatening to the Court. When Village declares to Virtue: "Our color isn't a wine stain that blotches a face, our face isn't a jackal that devours those it looks at. . . . I'm handsome, you're beautiful, and we love each other!" (pre-wording the "Black is Beautiful" slogans soon to resonate in African American pop counter-culture), the Governor says "We've got to stop them. Right away" (43-44). Their creation of love is neither an escape from racial body-politics nor a liberatory return to the natural body. At first they can conceive of a "love" between them only as the opposite of the white heterosexual "love" typified by the idealization of a woman in white (such as the woman played by Diouf). Archibald tells Village that Negroes and performers can't "know love" (39), therefore Village must hate Virtue. As abstract absolutes, hate and love, fear and delight, black and white, spectacle and spectator, are mutually constitutive. When Village and Virtue want to live outside the "clown show," Archibald sends the lovers "out" into "the audience." Actually, "Archibald, Bobo, Diouf, Snow and Felicity turn away and, holding their faces in their hands, move off, when suddenly nine or ten white masks suddenly appear about the Court" (41). If Village and Virtue won't play black roles of hatred, if they insist on playing lovers, then, Archibald commands, they must "discolor [them]selves" and "be spectators"—that is, "if they'll [the white spectators, will] have you" (40). Virtue and Village can never be absolutely alone as two people who love each other. For love is a political matter; it is always under surveillance, if not external then internalized. The white masks which appear, representations of a panopticon-like white gaze, are empty; the white gaze is always present for Virtue and Village, even when individual white onlookers aren't. The Benthemite Panopticon functions even when no one is in the tower; the structure of surveillance remains intact, as Genet, who inhabited a literal Benthemite panopticon in his youth, must have well understood (White 55). Like the mannequin to be seated in the audience if no white spectators attend, the empty white masks are symbolic presences. Masks are generally used by *performers,* not spectators. The on-stage appearance of white masks which mirror the offstage audience suggests that white spectatorship is always a player in the performance whether or not it is embodied.

Village and Virtue, however, want to live outside of this performance. They attempt to break out of dead white expressions of love. But to exactly reverse a white mythology into a black one is also to ventriloquize white discourse:

VIRTUE:

> . . . I was already in bed, with your image. Other girls may guard the image of their beloved in their heart or eyes. Yours was between my teeth. I would bite into it . . .

VILLAGE:

> In the morning, I would proudly display the marks of your bites.

(120)

Are Virtue and Village breaking out of white love clichés? Virtue's violent biting certainly does violence to the ideal of virtuous, lily-white, gentle femininity. But it may perpetuate white myths of black primitivism. Furthermore, the ontological level of this exchange is unclear. It is just before—and may even be played as simultaneous with—the assassination of "the Court." Are Village and Virtue performing for an onstage audience? If so, is this audience black or white (or outside of this dialectic)? Are they performing for themselves, out of the pleasure of improvisation? Is this performance solely for the white offstage audience? Are Village and Virtue masking themselves? With the removal of white spectators from the stage, can Virtue and Village improvise a way to love which neither invokes ideals of white femininity and masculinity (as well as heterosexuality) nor sets itself in opposition to these ideals? A love which stands outside of binary racial and gender roles? Perhaps a more immediate question is, can a white playwright invent and represent such a relationship? And if so, given a theater with black actors and white spectators, can these spectators *see* such a love, or will their own racial and gender assumptions always engulf the stage?

The Blacks presents powerful jolts to existing body-politics, but is (necessarily) much weaker in presenting

alternatives. Genet leaves us not with a vision of black love outside of a white gaze (impossible for him to do so), but only a skeptical hope for such a loving relationship:

VILLAGE:

> But if I take your hands in mine? If I put my arms around your shoulders—let me—if I hug you?

VIRTUE:

> All men are like you: they imitate. Can't you invent something else?

VILLAGE:

> For you I could invent anything: fruits, brighter words, a two-wheeled wheelbarrow, cherries without pits, a bed for three, a needle that doesn't prick. But gestures of love, that's harder . . . still, if you really want me to . . .

VIRTUE:

> I'll help you. At least, there's one sure thing: you won't be able to wind your fingers in my long golden hair . . .
>
> (The black backdrop rises. All the Negroes—including those who constituted the Court and who are without their masks—are standing about a white-draped catafalque like the one seen at the beginning of the play. Opening measures of the minuet from Don Giovanni. Hand in hand, Village and Virtue walk toward them, thus turning their backs to the audience. The curtain is drawn.)

THE END

This closing dialogue may not denaturalize the use of heterosexual coupling as a figure for other political set-ups; rather, it potentially denaturalizes the classic choreography within this gesture of the man putting his arms around the woman. Furthermore, this closing dialogue exploits the traditional figurative use of heterosexual romance to suggest once again the co-imbrication of gender and racial systems of power and to suggest the immensity of the task of reinventing love, given how tightly and surreptitiously old political systems cling to rhetorical figures, and through them to emotions and objects (fruits, words, wheelbarrows, cherries, beds, needles, love). Virtue does not suggest that there is a real (hetero)sexuality prior to false choreography; she does not ask that Village step out of the cliché-ridden choreography to return to real-and-natural love-making movements. She asks, rather, that Village "invent something else." The solution to imitation is not "truth" but invention—invention which denaturalizes prior truths and indeed the notion of "truth" itself. *Invention* is the appropriate (and appropriating) form of *agency* for a (post)colonial subject whose very subjectivity is realized within colonial discourse. If colonial discourse defines the very categories of authenticity (black and white, male and female, primitive and civilized) within which the (post)colonial subject's subjectivity is born, then the seizing of agency by the (post)colonial subject must be a discursive event, one which involves not the reclaiming of authenticity but the invention of new identity categories.

Village's list of inventions suggests a general sense that things can be very different than they are. The specific images that he uses (all steeped in well-worn codes of sexual connotations), however, do not radically depart from the rhetorical figures of the old regime, but rather decenter these figures, most obviously in the pitless cherries. The two-wheeled wheelbarrow visualizes a shifting of the center of gravity and a redistribution of weight. The final two images decenter heterosexuality even within their context in a heterosexual courtship (in which the man brings gifts to the woman). The extra room in "a bed for three" would be superfluous for a man-woman binary coupling. The needle that pricks is a well-worn cliché for sexual penetration and embodies a phallocentric sex/gender system in which a man leaves a mark on the woman and in which the sexual act involves pain and violence. "Needles that don't prick" might metonymize a love-making without pain and violence, even if this figure does continue to metonymize the sexual acts of men and women in the pointed instrument of the men. These rhetorical figures suggest how deeply entwined sex/gender and race systems are, as well as how resistant they are to change. (As in the "Fuck Racism" T-shirts I recently saw, worn by an all-male black rap group.) Gestures of love may be so deeply naturalized as to be impossible either to purge, alienate, or disempower, even when the physical objects, such as needles, beds for two, and long golden hair are altered.

The promise that Virtue will help Village to rechoreograph love, and their departure hand-in-hand, present an almost Utopian image of mutuality and rebirth; that they turn their backs to the audience suggests, finally, a turn away from a performance before a white audience and toward one before a black audience, or perhaps even toward non-performance (is there such a thing?). The actors playing "the Court" have removed their masks; have they also removed the external and internalized white gazes from their self-presentations? Such a hoped-for performance, it seems, can only occur offstage, outside of a play written by a white man and intended for a white audience.

Perhaps *The Blacks* ultimately fails to imagine racial identities outside of white hegemony and white mythology. Certainly, Genet's *The Blacks* does not present "real" blacks, or even the possibility of "real" blacks, but rather presents, in all its ludicrousness and with relish, white mythologizing and eroticizing of "the Negro," and the mechanisms which encourage "blacks" to perform this role before a white gaze. To paraphrase Gilroy, sometimes to be grossly inauthentic is the best way to be honest. *The Blacks* candidly examines white mythology, and how this mythology may mask its whiteness and its mythological character both to "blacks" and to "whites."

In the end, Jean Genet is no "white Negro" or black man with pink skin (however much you complicate these terms, and however desirable such an identity might seem). Genet speaks "as a white" playwright. Ultimately, *The Blacks* participates not so much in Black or African American Studies as in Whiteness Studies. Or perhaps, while it may desire to question the boundaries between the two, *The Blacks* succeeds best in prefiguring the way that Black Studies would inevitably, necessarily, lead to Whiteness Studies as both its backlash and progressive complement. In asking "what exactly is a black?" and in examining white fears and resistances to asking, much less answering, such a question honestly, Genet is inevitably asking simultaneously "what is a white?"—and discovering only overdetermined and at the same time tautological answers to this question: a white is someone who plays the role of a white. *The Blacks'* satiric interrogation of all racial identities is so painfully ambiguous because it is permanently suspended not only in a dialectic of racism and antiracism, but also and more importantly in a dialectic of both reinforcing the black/white binary and invalidating it. *The Blacks* both asserts that "a black"—or "a white"—is, and simultaneously retorts that "a black"—or "a white"—is not.

Painful ambiguity, though, gave Genet immense pleasure. As a final statement on the play, I want to return to Ed Bullins's comment that "Jean Genet is a white, self-confessed homosexual with dead, white Western ideas—faggoty ideas about Black Art, Revolution, and people." Offensive as this comment is, it is insightful in that it suggests that Genet draws fundamentally on a gay sensibility and aesthetic in his treatment of racial relations. Genet is, I feel, drawing on a long tradition of gay camp, which uses radical laughter in questioning oppressive social structures and their imbrications in questions of ontology about gender and sexual identity. While the parallel is inexact, I suggest that Genet's theatrically self-conscious cross-racial casting in *The Blacks* is in the mode of gay camp's drag. Queer Theory has revalidated camp as a means of granting creative agency to subjects within a discourse that denies their subjectivity, and does so through the power of pleasure and laughter at the discourse itself. Perhaps what's most truly productive about *The Blacks* is that it offers a pleasurable (if painful and dangerous) form for blacks and whites in the same audience to take on the toughest issues of black-white relations through the use of radical laughter. Genet offers white spectators a mode of embracing the radical inauthenticity of race as a way to "get real" about race relations.

Notes

1. In an interview with Hubert Fichte in 1976, Genet stated, "I learned very young that I am not a Frenchman, that I don't belong to the village. . . . Subsequently I could only join all those suppressed colored peoples who revolted against the whites. Against all whites. Perhaps I am a black man who happens to have white or pink skin. I don't know my family" (Fichte 180).

2. Hansberry's 1970 play *Les Blancs* suggests by its very title a sarcastic reversal of *The Blacks*. Hansberry is highly critical of Genet for not representing "real" blacks or real revolt. LeRoi Jones/Amiri Baraka's 1966 *Great Goodness of Life,* subtitled "A Coon Show" in semi-sarcastic allusion to *The Blacks'* subtitle "A Clown Show," balances a sense of the absurdity of racism with a sense of its injustice, and implies that decentering parodies must be accompanied by militant action within the black-white binarism. Other plays seem to me to be indirect responses to *The Blacks*. See Adrienne Kennedy's *Funnyhouse of a Negro*; ntozake shange's *spell #7*; and George C. Wolfe's *The Colored Museum*.

Works Cited

Cleaver, Eldridge. *Soul on Ice.* New York: Bantam Doubleday Dell, 1968, 1992.

Fanon, Frantz. *Black Skin, White Masks.* Trans. Charles Lam Markmann. New York: Grove Weidenfeld, 1967.

Fichte, Hubert. "'I Allow Myself to Revolt': Jean Genet Interviewed by Hubert Fichte." *Genet: A Collection of Critical Essays.* Ed. Peter Brooks and Joseph Halpern. New Jersey: Prentice-Hall, 1979.

Gates, Jr., Henry Louis. *The Signifying Monkey: A Theory of African-American Literary Criticism.* New York: Oxford UP, 1988.

Genet, Jean. "The Black and the Red." *The Black Panther.* Saturday, September 11, 1971: 14.

———. *The Blacks: A Clown Show.* Trans. Bernard Frechtman. New York: Grove Press, 1960.

Gilroy, Paul. "'. . . to be real': The Dissident Forms of Black Expressive Culture." *Let's Get It On: The Politics of Black Performance.* Ed. Catherine Ugwu. Seattle: Bay Press, 1995. 12-33.

Hansberry, Lorraine. *Les Blancs. Les Blancs: The Collected Last Plays of Lorraine Hansberry.* Ed. Robert Nemiroff. New York: Random House, 1972. 35-188.

Jones, LeRoi. "Great Goodness of Life: A Coon Show." *Four Black Revolutionary Plays.* Ed. LeRoi Jones. New York: Bobbs-Merrill, 1969. 41-64.

Kennedy, Adrienne. "Funnyhouse of a Negro." *In One Act.* Minneapolis: U of Minnesota P, 1988. 1-23.

shange, ntozake. *spell #7. Three Pieces.* New York: Penguin, 1982. 1-52.

Smith, Valerie. "Split Affinities: The Case of Interracial Rape." *Conflicts in Feminism.* Ed. Marianne Hirsch and Evelyn Fox Keller. New York: Routledge, 1990. 271-87.

Webb, Richard C. *Jean Genet and his Critics: An Annotated Bibliography, 1943-80.* London: Scarecrow Press, 1982.

White, Edmund. *Genet: A Biography.* New York: Knopf, 1993.

Wolfe, George C. *The Colored Museum.* New York: Grove Press, 1988.

FURTHER READING

Criticism

Akstens, Thomas. "Representation and De-realization: Artaud, Genet, and Sartre." In *Antonin Artaud and Modern Theater,* edited by Gene A. Plunka, pp. 170-82. Cranbury, N.J.: Associated University Presses, 1994.

Offers an assessment of the similarities between Antonin Artaud and Genet and an examination of the influence of both on Jean-Paul Sartre.

Bradby, David. "Genet, the Theatre and the Algerian War." *Theatre Research International* 19, no. 3 (autumn 1994): 226-37.

Examines Genet's role in dramatizing and recording the Algerian War through *The Balcony, The Blacks,* and *The Screens*.

———. "Genet's *Splendid's.*" In *Flowers and Revolution: A Collection of Writings on Jean Genet,* edited by Barbara Read, pp. 145-55. London: Middlesex University Press, 1997.

Reviews Neil Bartlett's translation and production of Genet's play *Splendid's* in 1995.

Cazorla, Hazel. "The Ritual Theater of Luis Riaza and Jean Genet." *Letras Peninsulares* 6, nos. 2-3 (fall 1993-winter 1994): 373-81.

Compares the works of Luis Riaza to those of Genet, noting their similarities in metatheatricality, the grotesque, and irony.

Finburgh, Clare. "Facets of Artifice: Rhythms in the Theater of Jean Genet, and the Painting, Drawing, and Sculpture of Alberto Giacometti." *French Forum* 27, no. 3 (fall 2002): 73-98.
> Extensively studies the dynamic rhythms in Genet's prose as a reflection of Giacometti's sculpture.

Flenga, Vassiliki. "Jean Genet's Political Brothels: The Perfect Prostitute and 'l'érection tombe.'" *Text & Presentation* 22 (April 2001): 23-30.
> Analyzes the political role of the brothel in *The Balcony* and *The Screens*.

Frese Witt, Mary Ann. "Author(ity) and Constructions of Actress in the Drama of Pirandello and Genet." *Comparative Literature Studies* 32, no. 1 (1995): 42-57.
> Studies the role of the actress and "feminized" authorship in the dramas of Pirandello and Genet.

Kennelly, Brian Gordon. "Dissolving the Divine: The Tragedy of Identity in Genet's 'Elle.'" *Symposium: A Quarterly Journal in Modern Literature* 49, no. 4 (1996): 274-96.
> Considers Genet's fascination with the pope, as evidenced in "Elle," a one-act play staging an autobiographical poem by the pope.

Lane, Christopher. "The Voided Role: On Genet." *MLN* 112, no. 5 (December 1997): 876-908.
> Provides a commentary on previous criticism of Genet and inspects his role in dramatic literature.

Oswald, Laura. *Jean Genet and the Semiotics of Performance*. Bloomington: Indiana University Press, 1989, 169 p.

Offers a broad overview on the dramatic performance of Genet's work.

————. "Victor Turner and Jean Genet—Rites of Passage in *Les Nègres*." *Theatre Annual: A Journal of Performance Studies* 45 (1991-1992): 65-88.
> Summarizes and expands upon Victor Turner's extensive analysis of rites of passage in *The Blacks*.

————. *The Rites of Passage of Jean Genet*. Cranbury, N.J.: Associated University Press, 1992, 357 p.
> Examines rites of passage and their significance in each of Genet's major works as well as their presentation in theatrical productions.

Ross, Kristin. "Schoolteachers, Maids, and Other Paranoid Histories." *Yale French Studies* 91 (1997): 7-27.
> Considers the characterization of the title figures in *The Maids*.

Wallis, Mick. "Stages of Sadomasochism." *Paragraph: A Journal of Modern Critical Theory* 17, no. 1 (March 1994): 60-9.
> Reflects on Richard Schechner's production of *The Balcony* and examines sadomasochism as a staged sexuality.

Wilkerson, Donna. "Interculturality in Technicolor: History as Simulation in Jean Genet's *Les Paravents*." *Word & Image* 18, no. 1 (January-March 2002): 53-6.
> Remarks on Genet's use of aesthetics in *The Screens*.

Additional coverage of Genet's life and career is contained in the following sources published by Thomson Gale: *Contemporary Authors*, Vols. 13-16R; *Contemporary Authors New Revision Series*, Vol. 18; *Contemporary Literary Criticism*, Vols. 1, 2, 5, 10, 14, 44, 46; *Dictionary of Literary Biography*, Vol. 72; *Dictionary of Literary Biography Yearbook, 1986*; *DISCovering Authors 3.0*; *DISCovering Authors Modules: Dramatists*; *Drama for Students*, Vol. 10; *Encyclopedia of World Literature in the 20th Century*, Ed. 3; *European Writers*, Vol. 13; *Gay & Lesbian Literature*, Ed. 1; *Guide to French Literature, 1789 to the Present*; *Literature Resource Center*; *Literary Movements for Students*, Vol. 2; *Major 20th-Century Writers*, Eds. 1, 2; *Reference Guide to World Literature*, Eds. 2, 3; *Twayne's World Authors*; and *Twentieth-Century Literary Criticism*, Vol. 128.

James Shirley
1596-1666

English dramatist and poet.

INTRODUCTION

Shirley was the leading dramatist of the Caroline era, making his theatrical debut the same year that James I died and passed the throne to his son Charles. He wrote prolifically, producing comedies of wit and romantic tragedies with equal success. Especially in such comedies as *Hyde Park* (1632) and *The Lady of Pleasure* (1635), Shirley captured the essence of Caroline London and its social elite. Though some critics have found Shirley's work less original or intellectual than that of his great Elizabethan and Jacobean predecessors, his plays resonate with the turbulent times in which he wrote, addressing themes of social class, gender, marriage, tyranny, and liberty.

BIOGRAPHICAL INFORMATION

Shirley styled himself a gentleman, but the facts of his ancestral line remain obscure. Biographer Anthony Wood describes him as a descendent of a prominent family, and one of his students recalls him wearing a coat of arms, but no other details are available about his background. Shirley the playwright is assumed to be the James Shirley baptized September 7, 1596, in London, the son of James Shirley. As a youth he studied at the notable Merchant Taylor's school before either entering St. John's College, Oxford, or starting an apprenticeship as a scrivener in 1612. Here, too, the records are unclear, but Wood's account claims that while Shirley was at Oxford the master of the college, William Laud, discouraged him from preparing for the ministry because of a mole on his cheek. (Laud would later become the infamous Archbishop Laud, who is sometimes considered the basis of the title character in Shirley's *The Cardinal*.) If he did attend Oxford, he did not graduate, nor do records exist of his attendance. He did enroll in St. Catherine's College, Cambridge, where from 1615 to 1617 he pursued and earned his bachelor's degree. Shirley was ordained an Anglican priest in 1617 and may have pursued a master's degree for the next few years.

In 1618 Shirley married Elizabeth Gilmet and took a living in Wheathampstead, Lincolnshire; in 1619 the couple had a child. (Scholars further disagree on

whether the first child was a son or daughter; in all, Shirley seems to have had three daughters, Marie, Grace, and Mary, and two sons, Mathias and Thomas.) In 1620 or 1621 Shirley changed careers, leaving his parsonage and taking a position as a teacher at a grammar school in nearby St. Albans. According to some biographers, the change was occasioned by Shirley's conversion to Catholicism, although others suggest that Shirley did not convert until after he had been at St. Albans for some time. (Even the fact of Shirley's conversion is not clearly documented, but is assumed by a majority of scholars.) After five years of teaching, Shirley again took an abrupt turn, moving his family to London and beginning to work as a playwright. His first play, the comedy *Love Tricks,* debuted in 1625, the same year that Charles I married his French Catholic queen, Henrietta Maria. *Love Tricks* was a success and Shirley became a dramatist for the Queen's Men at the Cockpit and Phoenix theaters. He followed his first comedic success with an attempt at tragedy, *The Maid's Revenge* (1626), which was equally well received and remained in the theater's repertory for more than a decade.

At some point between 1625 and 1627 Shirley established a residence at Gray's Inn, where he connected with a circle of writers including John Ford, Thomas May, William Habington, Phillip Massinger, and others. The friends wrote commendatory verses for the publication of each other's works and likely provided advice and help with courtier patrons—a requirement for a professional playwright. Shirley wrote occasional verses for the nobility and dedicated his plays to important figures at court in his search for patronage; his industriousness in doing so has led some scholars to see him as excessively eager for social advancement. And he did advance: in the 1630s he wrote several of his most successful comedies, including *Hyde Park* and *The Lady of Pleasure,* and in 1632 he accepted a post in the household of Queen Henrietta Maria, a significant mark of his preferment. Shirley's unique position in the royal household and the Inns of Court gave him an opportunity to write the libretto for one of the most opulent masques presented at court, *The Triumph of Peace* (1634). At this same time, however, Shirley's greatest rival for the status of court dramatist returned to London. William Davenant excelled at the art of winning the patronage of important court insiders and was more than willing to write to the tastes and whims of the court. For his part, Shirley became increasingly pointed in his satire of courtly excess in such works as *The Ball* (1632) and *The Bird in a Cage* (1632-33). By the time Shirley left London because of an outbreak of the plague, Davenant had succeeded him as a royal favorite.

Shirley went to Dublin in 1636, where he wrote for John Ogilby's theater. Among the plays he wrote during his four years in Dublin are the "Irish" plays *St. Patrick for Ireland* (1637-40) and *The Doubtful Heir* (1638), and the comedies *The Gentleman of Venice* (1639) and *The Constant Maid* (1637-40). Shirley received the final proof of his loss of preferment when Davenant was chosen to succeed Ben Jonson for the office of poet laureate in 1638. If this was a mark of a decline in his status at court, it was no reflection on Shirley's popularity as a playwright: verses of the time suggest that Shirley was generally considered more worthy of the title. Upon returning to London in 1640, Shirley became the chief playwright for the King's Men at Blackfriars, succeeding his former Gray's Inn compatriot, Massinger. The post was short-lived, owing to the closure of the theaters by the Puritans in 1642, but Shirley wrote one of his best tragedies for the company—*The Cardinal* (1641).

From 1642 to 1644 Shirley served the royalist cause fighting under the Earl of Newcastle. When Newcastle fled for the continent, Shirley returned to London. In 1646 Shirley resumed his teaching career at Whitefriars, where he was generally admired as an instructor. He published occasional poems and three grammar texts in addition to publishing his dramatic works, including the new works *Cupid and Death* (1653), a masque, and *The Contention of Ajax and Ulysses for the Armor of Achilles* (1658). Shirley's plays were among the first to be performed at the reopening of the theaters in 1660 (often altered to suit the tastes of the new age), but Shirley never wrote for the stage again. He continued teaching at Whitefriars until October 1666, when he and his second wife, Francis, were driven from their home by the Great Fire of London. Both died from exhaustion in the aftermath of the fire and were buried at Shirley's longtime parish church, St. Giles in the Fields.

MAJOR DRAMATIC WORKS

Shirley was a terrifically prolific author who provided the Caroline theaters with a steady supply of reliable performance pieces. In the centuries since his death, however, his plays have been regarded as almost too well suited to his times, without strong interest for later audiences, readers, and scholars. Important exceptions are two of his city comedies, *Hyde Park* and *The Lady of Pleasure,* and his tragedy *The Cardinal. Hyde Park* is a complicated comedy tying together three separate love plots. The lovers Carol and Fairfield entertain with witty sparring that points toward the "gay couple" of early Restoration comedy. Other plots involve a widow on the last day of her mourning period and the surprise return of her husband, and a young woman whose fiancé plots to test the strength of her chastity by getting a notorious rake to seduce her.

For its intimate knowledge of the London elite at play, *Hyde Park* represents Shirley's own style of realism: an idealized version of a world that would be instantly recognizable to his aristocratic audiences, populated by characters who exhibit a high command of courtly manners and a few charming vices. A few years later, in *The Lady of Pleasure,* Shirley created a similar world, but with less emphasis on setting and more attention to manners and mores. Shirley is more satirical in the later play, taking aim at the extravagance and licentiousness of the upper classes, especially in the character of Lady Aretina Bornwell. Arriving in London, Lady Bornwell is quickly swept up in the thrill of flirtations and assignations, while her husband, Lord Bornwell, merely pretends to go along in order to eventually rein her in. In contrast to Lady Bornwell stands Celestina, a young widow determined to remain chaste who cleverly plays the game of courtship with several suitors but proves herself more than a match for any of them. In the final act, Lord Bornwell drives his wife to reform, while Celestina finds a pure and noble love with Lord A., after testing his honor by pretending to seduce him. The relationship between Celestina and Lord A. represents Shirley's caution to the court, for the high-flown love rhetoric the couple use mimics the language of Platonic love admired at court, especially by Queen Henrietta Maria.

One of Shirley's late plays, *The Cardinal* is often noted as the last of the Jacobean revenge tragedies, but it shows its Caroline origins as well. Where his earlier plays were bloodier, more macabre, and more baroque, Shirley's revenge tragedy uses plainer language. The title character is likely modeled on a contemporary villain, Shirley's old master Archbishop Laud, a wicked advisor to Charles I much like the Cardinal to the King of Navarre. Shirley may also have drawn inspiration from John Webster's popular tragedy *The Duchess of Malfi* (1614) for his own heroine, the duchess Rosaura. Rosaura, a widow, is betrothed to the nephew of the Cardinal, but secretly loves the Count d'Alvarez. Her efforts to extricate herself from a planned marriage eventually result in the murder of Alvarez. Rosaura feigns madness in order to advance her plans for revenge, but the Cardinal has also planned his revenge against her. He comes to her chamber to first rape and then poison her, but he hesitates after kissing her and falling in love with her. Rosaura calls for help, and Hernando, once a colonel in her betrothed's army, comes to save her, already incensed at the Cardinal for his political interference. At the denouement, the Cardinal, believing himself mortally wounded by Hernando, confesses his plan and warns Rosaura that she has been poisoned, offering an antidote and drinking a portion first to prove his honesty. Rosaura drinks, and the Cardinal reveals the extent of his malice: he has actually poisoned himself in order to kill her as well. The action of *The Cardinal* is familiar, but the themes of authority applied specifically to the late Caroline era, as the use and abuse of monarchical power became an increasingly tense issue.

CRITICAL RECEPTION

When Shirley lost his court preferment, verses and broadsides proclaimed him the true poet laureate, and at the time of his death he was widely celebrated as a brilliant dramatist. Yet even in the early years of the Restoration, his plays did not do well at the theater. Samuel Pepys, the diarist who logged his frequent visits to the theater, disliked several of the productions he saw, and Restoration poet laureate John Dryden named Shirley one in the line of dullards satirized in *MacFlec-*

knoe (1682). In the nineteenth and twentieth centuries, Shirley suffered from his position as the last Renaissance dramatist writing at the end of a period generally seen as the decline of English drama before the close of the theaters. Like his contemporaries Ford, Massinger, and others, he was an inferior to Shakespeare and a scribe for a period marked by decadence and excess. Modern critics often characterize Shirley as a transitional figure who reuses the familiar tropes of earlier playwrights like Shakespeare and Jonson, but also hinting at the Restoration comedy of manners. Robert Forsythe, writing in the early twentieth century, describes the theatrical scene of Shirley's day as highly static, with little room for innovation. Forsythe credits Shirley with a talent for reshaping and combining old materials in a new way, answering the common criticism that Shirley's work is competent but derivative and unoriginal. Arthur Nason reaches a similar conclusion, describing Shirley as combining the methods and materials of Shakespeare, Jonson, and Fletcher to produce both realistic and romantic plays. After centuries spent in the valley between two dramatic golden ages, the playwright has benefited from more recent focus on the specific circumstances of the Caroline era. In that light, scholars have noted Shirley's ability to write for his audience, to please an elite coterie, and to critique the society he nevertheless dramatizes sympathetically. A pioneering study in this area is Stephen Orgel's *The Illusion of Power,* which discussed the close relationship between monarchical power and theatrical performance, including Shirley's masque *The Triumph of Peace.* Since Orgel's book, several critics have examined *The Triumph of Peace* in the context of the court of Charles I, including Shirley's French biographer George Bas and theater scholar Martin Butler. Butler also led the way in drawing attention to the political context of Caroline drama with the 1984 study *Theatre and Crisis,* which similarly shed new light on Shirley's plays. Even in the comedies, Butler emphasizes the political implications of Shirley's repeated motifs of liberty, courtesy, and courtship. The work of Orgel, Butler, and other historically minded scholars has led a re-evaluation of Shirley as a successful dramatist in his own right.

PRINCIPAL WORKS

Plays

Love Tricks 1625
The Brothers 1626
The Maid's Revenge 1626
The Wedding 1626-29
The Witty Fair One 1628
The Grateful Servant 1629

The Humorous Courtier 1631
Love's Cruelty 1631
The Traitor 1631
The Arcadia 1632
The Ball 1632
Changes, or Love in a Maze 1632
Hyde Park 1632
The Bird in a Cage 1632-33
The Gamester 1633
The Young Admiral 1633
The Example 1634
The Opportunity 1634
The Triumph of Peace 1634
The Coronation 1635
The Lady of Pleasure 1635
The Duke's Mistress 1636
The Royal Master 1637
The Constant Maid 1637-40
St. Patrick for Ireland 1637-40
The Doubtful Heir 1638
No Wit, No Help Like a Woman's 1638
The Gentleman of Venice 1639
The Politician 1639
The Tragedy of St. Albans c. 1639
The Imposture 1640
The Cardinal 1641
The Court Secret 1642
The Sisters 1642
The Triumph of Beauty 1646
Cupid and Death 1653
The Contention of Ajax and Ulysses for the Armor of Achilles 1658
Honoria and Mammon 1658

Other Major Works

Poems &c. by James Shirley (poetry) 1646
Via ad Latinam linguam complanata; The Way Made Plaine to the Latine Tongue, the Rules Composed in English and Latine Verse (textbook) 1649; republished as *Grammatica Anglo-Latina. An English and Latine Grammar,* 1651
An Ode upon the Happy Return of King Charles II. To His Languishing Nations, May 29, 1660 (poetry) 1660
The Rudiments of Grammar (textbook) 1656; enlarged as *Manductio; or, A Leading of Children by the Hand through the Principles of Grammar,* 1660

OVERVIEWS

Robert S. Forsythe (essay date 1914)

SOURCE: Forsythe, Robert S. "The General Characteristics of Shirley's Plays." In *The Relations of Shirley's Plays to Elizabethan Drama,* pp. 48-63. New York: Columbia University Press, 1914.

[*In the following excerpt, Forsythe enumerates the dominant characteristics of Shirley's works, describing him as a courtly playwright concerned with moral justice. He also notes that Shirley was an innovative adaptor writing at a time when dramatic conventions were deeply entrenched.*]

In the words of the author of the excellent article upon the Gifford-Dyce edition of Shirley in The Quarterly Review, XLIX, 14:

"When Shirley came on the stage, he might seem to succeed to a mine, of which the wealth had been completely exhausted—a land, of which every nook and corner had been explored and cultivated to its utmost height of productiveness. Every source from which dramatic invention had drawn its materials might seem dried up. The history of every country had been dramatized—every distinguished personage in ancient or modern times had appeared on the stage—even the novelists of Italy were well nigh run to their dregs; human nature itself might almost appear to have been worked out—every shade and modification of character had been variously combined, every incident placed in every possible light."

Not only were the sources for plays exhausted, but by reason of that very exhaustion, in part, the drama had become conventionalized "when Shirley came on the stage." The dramatic types which were to dominate the English stage until the closing of the theaters, and which were to exert a strong influence upon the drama of the Restoration, had been firmly established. The tragedies, tragi-comedies, and comedies of Fletcher and his school were to define the plays of 1625-42. The influence of Jonson, Shakespeare, and other playwrights still persisted, but in a less distinct form, or in minor writers, and in the case of Jonson, often intermingled with romantic elements from Fletcher.

Because of this very conventionalization of its elements, both in comedy and the more serious forms, and because of its subject-matter and treatment, the drama had drawn appreciably away from life and genuine realism. It had begun to receive its inspiration chiefly from earlier plays and from established convention rather than from the realism of observation or imagination. The drama was semi-literary, and therefore often dealt with life at second-hand. Two courses were open to the dramatist of this period: to carry on the established traditions or to seek out new material. Ford did the latter; almost all other dramatists did the former. As a result, we find Ford almost as far from real life as Carlell. One pictures the darkest and rarest emotions of the human heart (which earlier dramatists had never dared to portray); the other gives us wildly romantic plays "full of loue & the tryalls of louers."[1]

There is no unanimity among scholars as to what dramatist exerted the greater influence upon Shirley. Professor Thorndike considers that of Fletcher to be the strongest, as do Nissen (James Shirley, p. 2), Prölss (Das neuere Drama der Engländer, p. 210), Koeppel (Shakespeare's Wirkung, pp. 54-55). Ward intimates the same (Hist. Eng. Dram. Lit., III, 94), as does Neilson (Cam. Hist. Eng. Lit., VI, 223). On the other hand, Schipper (James Shirley, p. 345) and Schelling (Eliz. Dram., II, 323) consider Shirley either more a follower of Shakespeare or Jonson, or else more original than do other scholars generally. Prölss (as cited above) sees a strong influence of Webster and Ford upon Shirley's dramas. He is not far wrong in regard to certain plays, but there are no grounds for such a sweeping statement.

While it cannot be denied that to a certain extent Shirley follows Shakespeare and Jonson, still it seems that Fletcher, whose name was so often linked with that of Shirley in comparisons in their own century, was his real master. That this is the case, a study of the subject-matter and methods of treating it of the two dramatists will show. They handle the same situation in the same settings with the same characters too frequently to permit the forming of any other opinion.

It should not be supposed that Shirley followed Fletcher blindly; such is not the case. Not infrequently does he introduce original variations upon the Fletcherian incident; but he exhibits the influence as well of Shakespeare, Jonson, and others of the more important dramatists. Sometimes, too, he draws upon such obscure writers as Sharpham and Machin. Furthermore, he seems occasionally beyond doubt to have invented certain of his incidents. In any event, however, the sum of Shirley's borrowings from single plays is insignificant when compared with his general indebtedness to the great mass of extant dramatic material. *Most often his source is not a single play but the various groups of plays which employ in common with his dramas certain situations, incidents, devices, and characters.*

The plot of each of Shirley's plays—even to some degree those of *The Arcadia* and of *The Opportunity*—represents a combination of materials from various sources. As is shown in Chap. V, Shirley had no scruples about revising the plots which he borrowed. He not only changed their catastrophes to suit himself, but introduced new episodes, new incidents, new devices, new characters and new characterizations. These are new only in the sense that they are the playwright's addition, for in fact they often have many parallels in earlier plays. With scarcely an exception the incidents added by Shirley tend further to complicate the plot. The new characters fall in love and thus create new entanglements, and so on. Only in *The Young Admiral* do we find Shirley cutting down his original without introducing new complications in place of the expunged

incidents. It is true that he substitutes comic scenes for the unused passages, but they are very simple in structure, and do not add anything to the main plot. When there is no discoverable specific main source for the plot of a play of Shirley's, we are justified in asserting that he follows the same course, whether his original be merely unknown or whether the plot be of his own invention. The same process of combining anew old and conventionalized elements with perhaps slight variations or reversals of the characters concerned runs through all his plays from *Love Tricks* to *The Court Secret.* Let any play of Shirley's, save *The Arcadia,* be compared with fifty earlier dramas, and the poet will be judged an arrant plagiarist. Let, however, the Shirleian play be considered in its relations to the entire earlier Elizabethan drama, and its author will be seen in his true light as a conformer to things as they were whose originality lies not in his material, but in his use of it, and as a writer who preferred morality (in the Caroline sense) and some degree of probability to originality and novelty.

Before proceeding to a detailed consideration of the situations, incidents, devices and characters in Shirley's plays, there are some general characteristics which should be discussed. They serve either to relate the plays as wholes with the body of the Elizabethan drama, or to differentiate them from it.

Eighteen of Shirley's plays, not including *Chabot,* have scenes laid at court either in entirety or in part. This number includes all the tragedies save *The Maid's Revenge,* all eight tragicomedies, and all the romantic comedies except *The Brothers,* and *The Sisters,* in the latter of which a prince in disguise and a mock-court occur. The nearest approach in the realistic comedies to a court setting is the sham-court of *The Constant Maid.* However, pure realistic comedy is never laid at court, and save in chronicle plays sovereigns seldom take part in genuinely comic scenes.

The characters in the plays which deal with life at court are appropriate to the setting. Sovereigns, courtiers and court-ladies are among the chief figures. Personages of rank or of distinctly good birth figure in all the plays except *The Wedding.* The characters in that play, it must be noted, are by no means of the lowest orders.

Shirley usually shows no especial regard for the "divinity that doth hedge a King." Sciarrha in *The Traitor,* III, 2, makes his preparations for putting the Duke to death in spite of Amidea's recalling to him that person's rank. The attempted assassinations of *The Politician, The Duke's Mistress,* and *The Imposture* fail because of genuine loyalty on the part of a conspirator, not because of any trepidation engendered by the prospective victim's rank. Vittori in *The Young Admiral,* who is loyal at heart, is independent. *The Court Secret* is

Fletcherian in the great respect shown by Manuel for Prince Carlos' person, but even Manuel fights the Prince of Portugal in the course of the play without any compunctions. There is very little approach in Manuel or any other character of Shirley's to the abject loyalty of Amintor, *The Maid's Tragedy,* III, 1, of Valerio, A Wife for a Month, III, 3, or of Lucio, The Cruel Brother, V, 1.

What is practically a single plot is met with in several of Shirley's plays. **The Maid's Revenge, The Politician, The Cardinal, The Royal Master, The Court Secret,** The Humorous Courtier, and The Coronation have in reality only one action. In a number of the other plays the secondary plot is so closely interwoven with the main action and the characters of both are so closely connected that they are very nearly entitled to membership in the same group. The broadly comic scenes in Shirley are generally so very much subordinated to the more serious plot that often they need hardly be considered as forming a separate action. Frequently they are extremely episodic, as in **The Bird in a Cage,** and sometimes, as in **The Court Secret,** the characters figuring in them take an important part in the main action as well. We find but one comic scene in **The Maid's Revenge, The Traitor,** and **The Politician.** There is one entirely comic scene and a humorous dialogue in another scene in **Love's Cruelty.** Only a portion of one scene in **The Cardinal** is devoted to comedy. **The Coronation** is nearly devoid of any low comedy. This comparative lack of a farcical sub-plot tends to unify the play, of course, and, generally speaking, a well unified plot is a characteristic of Shirley's.

As Ward says, Shirley "displayed in tragic as well as comic actions a curious presentiment of the modern theatrical principle that everything depends on the success of one great scene (*la scène à faire*)" (D. N. B., LII, 128). In evidence we may cite **The Traitor,** III, 3, **Love's Cruelty,** IV, 1, **The Grateful Servant,** IV, 2, **The Example,** III, 1.

The love element is sometimes very much subordinated in Shirley's plays, as in **The Politician.** In **The Humorous Courtier** it is pretended love which is set to the front while genuine love is kept in the background. Rivalry in love is a prominent motive in most of the tragicomedies and some of the romantic and realistic comedies. Generally, in the first two classes the rivals are a prince or princess, and a mere gentleman or lady. **The Young Admiral, The Duke's Mistress, The Court Secret,** and **The Opportunity** are concerned with the love of a prince and a gentleman for the same lady. The last-named play also shows a princess and a lady as rivals for the hand of a private gentleman. In **The Royal Master,** and **The Imposture** we have a prince and a favorite as suitors to a princess. Two princely brothers are rivals for a lady's hand in St. Patrick for Ireland.

Apparent or real disparity of birth used as an obstacle to love is found in **The Royal Master, The Imposture, The Gentleman of Venice, The Bird in a Cage,** and **The Coronation.** Disparity of fortune figures as a hindrance to love in several realistic comedies, as in **The Wedding, The Witty Fair One,** and **Love in a Maze.**

True love and lust are contrasted in **The Traitor, Love's Cruelty, The Duke's Mistress, St. Patrick for Ireland, The Grateful Servant, The Arcadia, The Witty Fair One, Hyde Park, The Gamester,** and **The Example.** In several of these, however, the contrast is not carried through the play or is perhaps more a contrast of character than of action, as in **The Traitor.** In **The Example** a contrast is furnished by the conversion of a rake in the middle of the play. **St. Patrick for Ireland, The Witty Fair One,** and **The Gamester** are the most Fletcherian in their presentation of the contrast.

Heroic love, the sort of love which to possess its object will go to any extreme of violent or unusual action, is most nearly approached in **The Young Admiral, The Court Secret,** and **The Coronation.** As a modification of heroic love the renunciatory type of love as treated in the following chapter should be noted. Closely connected with heroic love are the conflicts of love and honor, love and friendship, and love and ambition. These conflicts are not very much emphasized by Shirley; he has frequently the opportunity for them, but generally does not utilize them. Love and honor enter into **The Maid's Revenge,** and **The Young Admiral,** love and friendship into **Love's Cruelty,** and love and ambition into **The Opportunity,** and **The Coronation.**

Inconstancy in love is not uncommon in Shirley's plays. We have not only the lover who forsakes his mistress and then returns to her to be forgiven and to be reconciled, but also the corresponding female figure—the fickle mistress,—and the errant husband or wife. The lovers who leave one mistress temporarily for another or who hesitate between two ladies but who return to their old loves or definitely choose one lady are Cesario in **The Young Admiral,** the Duke in **The Royal Master,** Carlo in **The Court Secret,** Alberto and Don Carlos (the latter of whom is finally unsuccessful as is Aurelio in **The Opportunity**) in **The Brothers,** the Duke in **The Grateful Servant** (a variation, as is Contarini in The Sisters), Arcadius in **The Coronation,** Thornay, Gerard, and Yongrave in **Love in a Maze.** To their number Ferdinand in **The Doubtful Heir** may be added, as far as his actions go; at heart he is faithful to Rosania, even though he marries Olivia.

The fickle mistress is exemplified in Selina in **Love Tricks,** Olivia in **The Doubtful Heir,** Maria in **The Court Secret,** Estefania in **The Brothers,** the Duchess and Cornelia in **The Opportunity,** Sophia in **The Coronation,** Chrysolina in **Love in a Maze,** and Julietta in

Hyde Park. Possibly Berinthia's being won away from Velasco by Antonio in *The Maid's Revenge* should be mentioned in this group, but Shirley does not emphasize her previous regard for Velasco. Certain of the characters above noted fall in this category as mistresses who merely transfer their love from one character to another. Selina, Maria, Estefania, Chrysolina, and Julietta are of this description.

The husband whose love for his wife is weakened for the time being by the charms of another lady is found in the persons of the King in *The Politician,* the Duke in *The Duke's Mistress,* Basilius in *The Arcadia,* Contarini in *The Humorous Courtier,* and Wilding in *The Gamester.* To these might be added the Duke in *The Traitor* (whose wife, a child of thirteen is mentioned *ibid.,* IV, 2) and Lodwick in *The Grateful Servant* whose infidelity is due to no particular lady. The Duke of Florence in the former play, it should be noted, is not finally reconciled with his wife.

The inconstant wife who finally returns to her husband is used four times by Shirley in uncollaborated plays, as Gynecia in *The Arcadia,* Mrs. Bonavent in *Hyde Park,* Lady Plot in *The Example,* and Lady Bornwell in The Lady of Pleasure. Lady Huntlove in the collaborated (?) *Captain Underwit* is a character of the same description. Mrs. Bonavent hardly belongs in this class since she remarries under the impression that her husband is dead. Clariana in *Love's Cruelty,* it must be remembered, is not won back by her husband.

Here then we have at least sixteen of Shirley's independent plays, to say nothing of one other in which he probably had a hand, which deal with errant affections that at last fix themselves upon the object to which they first were directed or that shift merely from one character to another. Not only do we have one case of this amorous instability in a single play, but even sometimes two or three, as in *The Opportunity, The Coronation,* or *Love in a Maze.*

Kingsley in Plays and Puritans has much to say concerning Shirley's immorality, which he asserts to be extreme. However, Kingsley has considered Shirley's plays apart from their own times and apart from the body of Elizabethan drama. In spite of his evident desire to make out a strong case against the Anglican priest turned papist and dramatist, Kingsley has actually missed the two really doubtfully moral plays—*The Example* and *The Lady of Pleasure* (*Captain Underwit* had not yet been connected with Shirley).

As a matter of fact, virtue is generally triumphant in Shirley's plays. When it is not, guilty and innocent fall together. Dramatic truth is sacrificed to the author's desire to reconcile his characters with virtue, as in the conversion of the Duke in *The Duke's Mistress.* In that

play and in *The Politician* we find the wicked characters all receiving their just deserts while the virtuous live happily forever after. It is certainly true that assaults upon innocence play a large part in Shirley's plays; but it is true also that only in *The Lady of Pleasure* (if by any extreme of courtesy Lady Bornwell may be called innocent) does a woman yield to her desires without paying the penalty. Even she seems to suffer from her conscience. Lady Plot in *The Example* is ready to yield were she attacked, but she has at least a little excuse for her actions in Sir Solitary's mania. Lady Huntlove in *Captain Underwit* is another character of the same general sort. Clariana in *Love's Cruelty* and Marpisa in *The Politician,* who are both adulteresses, die after torturing mental struggles, one at the hands of her former paramour, the other by self-administered poison. Juliana in *The Imposture,* whose life has not been spotless, is sentenced to finish her days in a nunnery.

It cannot be denied that in some plays Shirley, like nearly every other Elizabethan dramatist, shows a certain moral obtuseness or callousness. Lodwick in *The Grateful Servant,* Contarini in *The Humorous Courtier,* and Cornari in *The Gentleman of Venice* escape entirely too easily in every way the consequences of their variations upon the situation of *The Curious Impertinent.* Likewise, the horrible effrontery of Wilding in *The Gamester,* who would have his wife procure her kinswoman for him, certainly is not adequately punished. But in these four cases we must remember that the characters mentioned believe themselves cuckolds for a time and suffer accordingly. Doubtless their mental perturbation was made much more vivid on the stage than it is in cold type to us. Lady Bornwell suffers as a result of her transgression, but there seems no especial regret on the parts of Lady Plot and Lady Huntlove for their projected infidelity.

Shirley's habit of converting his wicked or licentious characters (in tragicomedy and comedy) during the course of a play has been mentioned before. His young profligates do not (with the exception of Luys in *The Brothers*) play various amusing but unexemplary pranks through a comedy and make their final exits unsubdued and fortunate besides. His Fowlers and Lodwicks, unlike Fletcher's Monsieur Thomases and Pinacs, finally are repentant. Unconvincing as some of the conversions are, being purely sops to the dramatist's conscience,[2] they are there in the plays and the fact of Shirley's use of them forces their consideration in any discussion of the dramatist's morality.

We find little grossness for its own sake in Shirley's plays. True, the discovery of Clariana and Hippolito in bed in *Love's Cruelty,* IV, 1, is a strong situation even for the Elizabethan stage, but it is not merely dragged in as being *risqué.* On the other hand, it heightens very much the effect of Bellamente's surprise of the guilty couple, and thus serves an important theatrical purpose. In *Love Tricks,* II, 2, III, 1, old Rufaldo gloats over the charms of his youthful bride. If we compare these two passages with Mrs. Behn's Lucky Chance, I, 3, we can see what possibilities lay there, and can readily appreciate the discretion and decency of Shirley. Only in *The Gentleman of Venice* is a prostitute a character, and only in *The Lady of Pleasure* is a bawd introduced. Juliana in *The Imposture* has merely gone astray, and the Nurse in *The Constant Maid* is not a professional procuress. In none of the comedies (or any of the other plays) do we find even an approach to the utter vileness of thought and language of such a play as, for instance, The Parson's Wedding. Indeed in spite of occasional lapses (which are to be found in the plays of every Elizabethan dramatist) it cannot be said that Shirley was by any means consistently immoral in conception or gross in language.

Even in *The Traitor* or *Love's Cruelty* we find no such almost totally unrelieved atmosphere of lust and horror as we encounter in The Revenger's Tragedy, King Lear, The White Devil, Thierry and Theodoret, The Unnatural Combat, Women Beware Women, Albovine, and 'Tis Pity She's a Whore. *The Traitor* has the nobility of Cosmo (which is, however, a trifle dulled by his prudence), as a relief, and *Love's Cruelty* has a comparatively bright spot in the Duke's penitence and his proposed match with Eubella. *The Cardinal,* which is more consistently gloomy than any of the other tragedies, has lust merely as an incident, not as a motive.

For a writer who was evidently conversant with much of the earlier drama, and who wrote at a time when sensation of some sort was nearly the prime necessity in a play, Shirley has kept singularly clear of that element, as far as theatrical devices go. We have indeed the old horror of kissing a corpse by mistake for a living woman in *The Traitor.* Lorenzo's stabbing the Duke's picture in the same play is a bit of uncalled-for clap-trap. Death by poison with its more or less gruesome accompaniments is introduced in *The Maid's Revenge, The Politician, The Cardinal,* and *St. Patrick for Ireland.* Assassinations take place on the stage in *The Maid's Revenge,*[3] *The Traitor, Love's Cruelty,* and *The Cardinal,* and are attempted in *The Politician,* and *The Imposture.* Duels are found in *The Maid's Revenge,*[4] *The Cardinal,* and *The Court Secret.* Deaths by violence are represented also in *The Duke's Mistress,* and *St. Patrick for Ireland.* Murder in a masque occurs only in *The Cardinal,* although masques are introduced in *The Maid's Revenge,* and *The Traitor.*

Illicit relationships exist only in *Love's Cruelty, The Politician,* and *The Lady of Pleasure,* and in the last two plays they are not especially emphasized. A sister in love with a brother is found in *The Court Secret* and

The Coronation. The same situation is made use of in *The Opportunity.* In the first two plays the relationship is discovered or the love is transferred before the matter has gone too far, and in the last-named the relationship is not an actual one, but feigned.

Revenge, as a motive, plays an important part in *The Maid's Revenge, The Traitor, Love's Cruelty, The Politician,* and *The Cardinal,* and enters into *The Duke's Mistress,* and *St. Patrick for Ireland. The Cardinal,* indeed, is strongly reminiscent of such plays as Hoffman, or Hamlet, for we have Columbo's revenge upon Alvarez, the revenge of Hernando and Rosaura upon Columbo and the Cardinal, and the revenge of the last upon them. Single revenges are found in the other plays mentioned above.

The family feud which is at the bottom of the action of The Bloody Brother, and Thierry and Theodoret, for instance, is utilized by Shirley only in *The Maid's Revenge, The Gentleman of Venice, The Court Secret,* and *The Coronation.* In the last two plays it is the result of the ignorance of the true identity of certain of the characters involved. Only in *The Maid's Revenge* does the feud assume anything like the proportions and the seriousness of those in some earlier plays, and there, as well as in *The Gentleman of Venice,* it is not laid at court.

Shirley possesses the fondness for surprises of the average dramatist of his time. Usually, they are well handled. Very seldom does he manage a sudden change in relationship as badly as the shift of Selina's affections from Rufaldo to Infortunio in *Love Tricks.* After her passion for the former has been emphasized, as it is, it is inadequate in the extreme to introduce her without warning as having fled from her father's house to avoid her impending marriage with Rufaldo. Some of Shirley's other plays into which surprise enters are *The Traitor, Love's Cruelty, The Politician, The Cardinal, The Duke's Mistress, St. Patrick for Ireland, The Doubtful Heir, The Gentleman of Venice, The Imposture, The Court Secret, The Brothers, The Grateful Servant, The Bird in a Cage, The Coronation, The Sisters, The Wedding, Hyde Park, The Gamester, The Example, The Constant Maid.* The sudden changes in some of these plays, like the conversion of Fitzavarice in *The Example,* are more or less mechanical. Nearly always they are short cuts to the happy ending of the play (as such devices often are). Thus the discovery of Giovanni's real parentage in *The Gentleman of Venice* removes the only obstacle to his marriage with Bellaura. Occasionally the surprise is used with excellent effect and with considerable originality, as in Julietta's breaking her engagement to Trier because of the test to which he has subjected her (*Hyde Park*).[5] Other circumstances of a novel nature (although not unparalleled) are the return of the Duke to the pursuit of Amidea in **The Traitor,** and the manner of the Cardinal's death in **The Cardinal.** Most frequently resurrections, repentances, and the explanation of actions as trials of one quality or another are Shirley's favorite means of injecting the unexpected into a play.

Shirley was fond of introducing deliberate contrasts of character; and sometimes he has done it very effectively. Berinthia and Catalina in the first four acts of **The Maid's Revenge** illustrate very well this practice of the dramatist's. Often the contrast is almost too obvious to be really striking. Thus the Duke and Cosmo in **The Traitor,** or Marpisa and Albina in **The Politician,** are too nearly the exact opposites of each other. As further examples of this Fletcherian device we may cite Eubella and Clariana, Sebastian and Bovaldo in **Love's Cruelty,** Domitilla and Theodosia in **The Royal Master,** Rosania and Olivia in **The Doubtful Heir,** Conan and Corybreus in **St. Patrick for Ireland,** Giovanni and Thomazo in **The Gentleman of Venice,** Manuel and Carlo in **The Court Secret,** the Duke and Lodwick, or Foscari and Lodwick in **The Grateful Servant,** Ursini and Aurelio in **The Opportunity,** Polidora and Sophia, Seleucus and Arcadius in **The Coronation,** Angelina and Paulina in **The Sisters,** Aimwell and Fowler in **The Witty Fair One,** Yongrave and Thornay in **Love in a Maze,** Beaumont and Wilding in **The Gamester,** Lady Peregrine and Lady Plot in **The Example,** and Celestina and Lady Bornwell in **The Lady of Pleasure.**

Notes

1. From a quaint MS. critical note by "Frances Wolverton" in Mead's Combat of Love and Friendship, Columbia University Library copy.

2. Malipiero, The Gentleman of Venice, V, 2, 4, Contarini, The Humorous Courtier, V, 3.

3. A sister slays her brother while he sleeps.

4. Two ladies, each of whom loves the other's brother, witness those same brothers engage in a duel which is fatal to one combatant.

5. There is a somewhat remote analogue in The Humorous Lieutenant, IV, 8 (see under Hyde Park, V, 2).

Bibliography

Koeppel, Emil, Ben Jonson's Wirkung auf zeitgenössische Dramatiker und andere Studien . . . *Anglistische Forschungen.* Heft 20. Heidelburg, 1906. (Ben Jonson's Wirkung). Quellen Studien zu den Dramen George Chapman's . . . Quellen und Forschungen . . . , LXXXII. (1897). (Quellen Studien). *Studien über Shakespeare's Wirkung auf zeitgenössische Dramatiker. Materialien zur Kunde des älteren Englischen Dramas,* IX. Louvain, 1905. (Shakespeare's Wirkung).

Neilson, W. A., Ford and Shirley. *Cambridge History of English Literature,* VI, 221 ff. New York, Cambridge, 1910. (Cam. Hist. Eng. Lit.).

Nissen, P., *James Shirley.* Hamburg, 1901.

Prölss, Robert, *Geschichte des neueren Dramas.* Band II, Hälfe 2. Leipzig, 1882.

Richard Morton (essay date 1966)

SOURCE: Morton, Richard. "Deception and Social Dislocation: An Aspect of James Shirley's Drama." *Renaissance Drama,* 9 (1966): 227-45.

[*In the following essay, Morton contends that scholarly interpretations of Shirley's plays have been limited by the tendency to focus on the playwright as a transitional figure between the Renaissance and the Restoration. Morton examines Shirley's use of deception or trickery—especially disguise and mistaken identity—in several plays, finding that this plot motif successfully dramatizes particular social issues of the Caroline era.*]

The temptation to classify minor literary figures as transitional can hardly be resisted in the case of James Shirley, who was born in 1596, the year of the second volume of *The Faerie Queene,* and died exactly 300 years ago, in 1666, Dryden's *Annus Mirabilis.* As a comic dramatist, he has frequently been identified as a link between Jonson and the Restoration playwrights, between the comedy of humours and the comedy of manners. There is much to support such a view. Forsythe's thorough documentation[1] has revealed Shirley's indebtedness to the Elizabethan and Jacobean stage. The regular appearance in his plays of courtly fashion and the Truewit-Witwoud-Witless ritual of outwitting,[2] so popular in the reign of Charles II, counters Dryden's celebrated rejection of his works as meaningless to the new age:

> Heywood and Shirley were but types of thee,
> Thou last great prophet of tautology.[3]

Pepys, for example, seems to have had some warm responses to his plays, which were among the more popular of the old dramas at the Restoration court.[4]

To concentrate on the transitional aspects of a playwright's works has some disadvantages; it tends to shatter the integrity of the individual pieces, to label one scene or character an echo of the past, another a prefiguration of the future. Shirley's plays have perhaps suffered too much from such scholastic mayhem. Ashley H. Thorndike typifies this approach in his generally admirable and perceptive pages:

> No earlier dramatist presents so many reminiscences of Shakespeare . . . and he often imitates Jonson. . . . But his plays in their main characteristics naturally

adapt themselves to the models of Fletcher and Massinger. . . . He is almost as close to the heroic play, the tragicomedy and the comedy of manners of the Restoration as to the romances and comedies of Fletcher.[5]

Shirley's plays are doubtless conventional, but they are independent works of art, achieving their effects by their intrinsic qualities rather than by their position in literary history. My purpose here is to notice one of those aspects of Shirley's plays which give them coherence and effectiveness.

I

The direction of comedy in general is toward reconciliation of discordant elements, and its method in Renaissance drama is most commonly the intrigue, in which, typically, the young outwit the old. The Jonsonian comedy of humours may show the reformation of the eccentric individual; the Restoration comedy of manners frequently shows the resolution of conflicting ways of life—a whole element of society is eccentric. Shirley's comic method has elements of both: he has many "humours" characters, and in his best plays he draws on the fluid and rapidly changing world of Caroline London to produce a comedy of conflicting social elements which seems, perhaps because of its source in a world of genuine social conflict, to have unique urgency and validity. Characteristically, the plot of a play by Shirley depends on a trick or a misunderstanding. As with Renaissance drama in general, the deception of husband by wife, father by daughter, suitor by witty mistress, and foolish citizen by elegant courtier is commonplace and easily anticipated. When, for example, in the delightful comedy *The Lady of Pleasure* we see Aretina fashionably kicking her heels in courtly London, flaunting her noble connections and wasting the estates of her husband, Bornwell, we may well expect him to expostulate fruitlessly in Act I and then, in Act II, to attempt subterfuge. Aretina's appropriate reformation, in Act V, is both timely and inevitable:

> Already
> I feel a cure upon my soul, and promise
> My after life to virtue.[6]

As Father Curry has neatly observed: "On the Elizabethan stage the race of dupes, both native and exotic, flourished in a prolific variety of breeds, and the hunting was both merry and determined."[7]

With Shirley's best plays the irony implicit in the deception situation, where one character misunderstands another or is deliberately duped, serves as more than a source of laughter at the foolishness of the gull. It illuminates the contrast between the viewpoints of the trickster and the tricked, reveals their difficulties of communication, and, when the differences are at a social level, demonstrates the conflicts within the society portrayed.

Shirley's plays show him to have been particularly aware of these conflicts. The well-known tensions between the servant and the master, the countryman and the townsman, the tradesman and the fop, are as staple to his plays as to those of his contemporaries, but he is unusually sophisticated in his perception of conflicts among the various groups of leisured city-dwellers.[8] The famous comedy, *The Ball,* devotes so much attention to documentation of distinctions between the higher levels of London life that the plot, for want of weeding, is confused and neglected. *The Constant Maid* puts on stage a neat abstract of the dramatist's London. Hartwell is a young descendant of the minor gentry, unwilling to hold the office by which his father had eked out an archaic, hospitable squire's existence. Playfair is a courtly gallant of elegant phrase and considerable means, which he devotes to the pursuit of intrigue. He is the nephew of Sir Clement, the somewhat old-fashioned justice in whose house the action takes place. Startup is a foolish rustic who inevitably becomes the rival suitor. A farcical plot, involving swapping of clothes and misidentification, puts into opposition these three typical figures of a fluctuating society. Decayed gentry, prosperous courtier, and *nouveau riche* farmer meet on approximately equal social terms but differ markedly in interests, attitudes, and behavior. Naturally, then, they live side by side but do not really understand or trust one another. Confusions, the basis for comedy, arise. Shirley's world of fashion is exclusive, intricate, formal, and slightly debauched; his gentry and mercantile classes are commonsensical, but they are frequently bewildered by the elaborate courtiers. So Julietta, in *Hyde Park,* a perfectly respectable gentlewoman of leisure, is explicit when she must entertain the courtly Lord Bonvile:

TRIER

> —Sweet lady, pray
> Assure his lordship he is welcome.

JULIETTA

> I want words.

LORD BONVILE

> Oh, sweet lady, your lip in silence
> Speaks the best language.

JULIETTA

> Your lordship's welcome to this humble roof.
>
> (II.iii; Gifford and Dyce, II, 481)

It is this failure to communicate easily across the bounds of social class which forms the basis for the tricks or misunderstandings so frequently found in the plays.

Conventionally, of course, the honest woman tempted by her superior reveals or feigns a modest failure to communicate or understand. So, in *The Traitor,* Sciarrha tests the honor of his sister, Amidea, by telling her of the Duke's lusts:

SCIARRHA

You must to court. Oh happiness!

AMIDEA

For what?

SCIARRHA

What do great ladies do at court, I pray?
Enjoy the pleasures of the world, dance, kiss
The amorous lords, and change court breath, sing
    loose
Belief of other heaven, tell wanton dreams,
Rehearse your sprightly bed scenes, and boast which
Hath most idolators, accuse all faces
That trust to the simplicity of nature,
Talk witty blasphemy,
Discourse their gaudy wardrobes, plot new pride,
Jest upon courtiers' legs, laugh at the wagging
Of their own feathers, and a thousand more
Delights which private ladies never think of.
. . . . .

AMIDEA

You make me wonder.
Pray speak that I may understand.

SCIARRHA

Why will you
Appear so ignorant? I speak the dialect
Of Florence to you.[9]

In this passage, as elsewhere in Shirley's plays, we have a richly documented description of the life of a certain social group. The influence of formal satire and the character books is clearly at work; the society Shirley draws requires a fine discrimination which would no doubt be appreciated by the leisured classes in his audience. In *Hyde Park* and *The Traitor* the contest is not between rich and poor, powerful and impotent; rather it is between the apparently closer levels of courtier and gentry. Shirley is not dealing with the extravagant and unlikely union of Fair 'Em and King William but with possible and plausible affairs such as that between Kenelm Digby and Venetia Stanley, which Professor Harbage feels may be dealt with explicitly in *The Wedding*.[10] The dramatic situation is rooted in the life of London and made particularly relevant to a court audience, for whom these matters of class relationships in the upper levels of society would inevitably be of major import.

The failure of comprehension between different groups is sometimes deliberately exploited in a trick, sometimes it grows spontaneously from the dramatic interplay of character. But in Shirley's plays it normally produces uncertainty, discomfiture, and, at last, when the misunderstanding is clarified, discovery and increased self-awareness. Aretina realizes that she cannot really understand or live in the extravagant fashionable world

and so, at the end, returns to a proper and decent position of subservience to her husband and the ideals of the minor gentry.

Shirley's devotion to the trick as a dramatic device is demonstrated by his best-known play, *The Cardinal,* which, while a revenge tragedy, opens with a deception more nearly allied to the comic. Although the action begins with a scene of ominous political discussion, stressing for the audience the solemnity of the play, the trick played on the stern soldier Columbo comes from the comedy of manners. In the lively chatter between Rosaura and her maids, he is castigated as uncourtly and uncouth. On stage he confirms this impression, using, as Professor Forker has aptly noted, "military metaphor for court etiquette"[11] in a way calculated to display his personality. The ladies in waiting, Valeria and Celinda, discourse of Columbo's valorous and noble figure in the language of Fletcher's court maidens; their witty dialogue, toying conceitedly with the concept of a soldier as a lover, neatly stimulates the audience's awareness of the distinction between the stiff general and the brilliant court.

When Columbo receives the Duchess' letter, his impatience with the messenger's romantic dialect stresses again the gulf between his manners and those of the Duchess. He interrupts the flood of eloquence with a curt "No Poetry" (II.i.124). His failure to understand the purpose of the letter arises from his incompetent attempt to think in the unaccustomed vein of a lover:

> [*Aside*] I have found it out, the Dutchess loves me
>   dearly,
> She exprest a trouble in her when I took
> My leave, and chid me with a sullen ey;
> 'Tis a device to hasten my return;
> Love has a thousand arts; I'l answer it,
> Beyond her expectation.
>
> (II.i.128-133)

His instinctive response—to reject the letter with fury—was the right one. He falls into Rosaura's trap because he tries to affect a habit of mind he does not possess. Thus this episode, the first step in a dark and bloody tragedy, is a variation of the gulling of the Witwoud, whose affectations lead him into pitfalls which his native good sense would have avoided.

Columbo's revenge for his injury is quite deliberately based on his awareness of the difference between his manners and those of the modish court. The murder of D'Alvarez in the midst of festivities and before royalty is, for the court as for the audience, above all else a shocking breach of decorum. It is his insulting and arrogant disregard of etiquette which the King finds most distressing:

This contempt
Of Majesty transcends my power to pardon,
And you shall feel my anger Sir.

(III.ii.229-231)

Professor Forker comments: "Note here the shabbiness of the King's motive, the selfishness implied by his capacity to look upon sudden murder (in the presence of the bereaved) as primarily a breach of court etiquette" (p. 63 n.). It may rather be thought that the focus on manners is inevitable in a play which marries tragedy and comedy of intrigue. Inevitably, the deception and the misunderstanding have comic overtones, but their principal purpose within the drama is surely to focus attention on the incompatibility of the characters and to stress the tension between the modes of life which they represent.

If the ritual of deception can be central to an effective tragedy, it is not surprising that Shirley can use it to a significant degree in his comedies, to lend clarity and coherence to their structure. Examples from some of Shirley's less well-known plays may show how he develops and refines the use of misunderstanding. In the early **Love Tricks** the conflicts and deceptions are farcical and entertaining but lack any coherence. In **The Gamester** the deceptions are more meaningfully related to character, and the plot has a genuine direction. In **The Example** and **The Opportunity** we can see the deceptions related significantly to character and to the patterns of society; these plays are consistent and valid analyses of social life, cast in the mode of comic drama.

II

Love Tricks, or The School of Compliment has a plot constructed around a complex series of deceits, which take various forms of gulling, disguise, masquerade, and self-deception. Much of the interest of the play comes from Shirley's skillful maintenance of a wide and dizzy range of confusions. The grotesque tricks played by Gorgon and Gasparo on the aged Rufaldo are conventionally farcical. The temporary irrationality of the beautiful Selina, who believes that she wishes to marry the old man, is a stranger love trick. Both Rufaldo and Selina realize that they have been deceived. Rufaldo rages at his tricksters, while Selina wonders at her folly and exiles herself to life in a pastoral landscape. But at the play's end they both come to self-awareness and accept their proper places. Rufaldo abandons his lusts and welcomes his daughter's wedding, and Selina marries her beloved Infortunio.

A series of similar episodes shows this basic pattern in the adventures of other characters: a movement from deception and blindness to anger or distress and then to eventual self-awareness. But Shirley seems to have no single theme in the play; it wanders amiably and loosely from episode to episode. The scenes at the School of Compliment, a witty series of parodies on books of polite instruction, do, however, show some social awareness. In this School, where the clownish come to learn sophistication, the fluid society of the 1620's reveals its many problems of behavior and communication for the new rich. The desire of Aretina in **The Lady of Pleasure** to make a great figure in the fashionable world is foreshadowed in the Oaf, who is brought to the School to receive polish and progresses so well that he can soon make a convincing imitation of the speech of a cynical fop:

> A younger brother, sir; born at the latter end of the week, and wane of the moon; put into the world to seek my own fortune; got a great estate of wealth by gaming and wenching, and so purchas'd unhappily this state of damnation you see me in.

(III.v; Gifford and Dyce, I, 54)

The School scenes demonstrate Shirley's interest in social affectation—an affectation which is the up-to-date form of the humour and consists of the improper and mistaken decision to behave in a way at odds with one's genuine personality. Rufaldo and Selina are basically sensible; temporarily they affect the lover and the martyr. Aretina and the Oaf affect a social class not properly theirs; the dramatic function of their eccentricities is not different from that of Rufaldo and Selina. Carol, the socially affected and flighty heroine of **Hyde Park,** is similar to the egregious Sir Gervase Simple in **Love in a Maze,** a Jonsonian rustic who is either dumb or incoherent in company. Carol flirts vivaciously and nervously; Sir Gervase loosens his tongue with alcohol. They both affect a competence they do not naturally have. The affected person inevitably falls into confusion and is ripe for deception.

The plot of intrigue and the rather static School scenes are not integrated in **Love Tricks,** but they show, side by side, Shirley's skill in manipulating affectations and portraying fashionable London. In his best comedies these elements come together.

The Gamester rapidly sets on stage the irreconcilable views of life which clash throughout the play, giving it a focus sharper than that of **Love Tricks.** Men of overnice honor devoted to the dangers and romance of swordplay are introduced; a wounded duelist, Delamore, is carried on, and his high-minded opponent and sometime friend, Beaumont, is arrested. Meanwhile, Wilding, who is so lacking in honor as to ask his wife's help in debauching his ward, cynically discusses dueling with Hazard, the gamester:

> Is't not a great deal safer, now, to skirmish
> With a petticoat, and touze a handsome wench
> In private, than be valiant in the streets,
> And kiss the gallows for't? Hang, hang this foolery!

(I.i; Gifford and Dyce, III, 194)

The audience is assured of a sharp contrast between the two groups shown on stage.

Throughout the play Shirley maintains consistently the tension between the romance of Delamore and Beaumont—in a subplot of supposed death and tearful reconciliation—and the cynicism of Wilding or, to a lesser degree, Hazard. As usual, the plot develops through a trick, but the deception practiced on Wilding is not a conventional device. It is exactly and shrewdly chosen to suit his personality—first to batten on his libertinism, then to force him to discover his own unworthiness and actively struggle to regain a way of life that is honorable in the Delamore sense. Believing himself to be cuckolded, he analyzes, in two involved soliloquies, his supposed position, attempts to work a way out, perceives his own villainy, and realizes the full implications of his predicament:

> I am justly punish'd now for all my tricks,
> And pride o' the flesh. I had ambition
> To make men cuckolds; now the devil has paid me.
> . . . . .
> And spight of [all] these tricks, am a Cornelius.
>
> (V.i,ii; Gifford and Dyce, III, 260, 272)

The libertine is reformed by jealousy, the vice of the man of honor, but logically irrelevant and meaningless to a Wilding. He is led into the trap, not because he is ambitious, lustful, or foolish; indeed, he is shown from the beginning of the play as sympathetic in some ways. Rather, his view of life is the result of an affection. Unable to sustain consistently the part he has chosen to play, he falls into self-contradiction and confusion. Wilding is not stupid; his mind, under the influence of the affection, just does not work in the same way as that of Mrs. Wilding, and consequently he cannot understand or communicate with her. The trick is designed to force an adjustment back to his proper view of life; the romantic subplot provides a symbol of the appropriate direction in which to move.

The Gamester is a neat and actable play, with some good scenes of London life, particularly those connected with the gambling tables; but the passages of realistic social comment are not meaningfully integrated into the main plot, and the play, while less diffuse than *Love Tricks,* is by no means completely unified.

The Gamester is built around conflicts between views of life. *The Example,* an excellent, fast-moving comedy, unfairly neglected, is built around the conflict between two different ways of life—that of the noble courtier and that of the old-fashioned gentry. Shirley is here able to incorporate his social awareness into the comic structure. The court is represented by Lord Fitzavarice, who mixes shrewd business dealing with arrogant libertinism and provides himself with a scrivener and a po-etaster, Confident Rapture, to manage the two sides of his destructive activities. The honest and upright gentry are represented by the Lady Peregrine, whose husband, Sir Walter, has been forced into exile as a debtor, and her uncle, Sir Solitary Plot, so paranoiac that he watches nervously through the night, convinced of the dangers of the modern world and dreaming of plots in everything. The servants, what with waiting on Lady Peregrine through the day and Sir Solitary through the night, are chronically incompetent from lack of sleep. The expected trick played on Sir Solitary has the effect of shaking him from his humour; Lord Fitzavarice is persuaded by Lady Peregrine's honesty and purity to reject his vicious way of life.

Significant is the way in which these two key characters, in their tensions and their eventual return to decent behavior, consistently speak of themselves and their manners in terms of their social status. The action occurs because of the problems created by the interaction of the different classes. Sir Solitary's fears arise from his terror of bravoes in the streets, with their lascivious intent, and from his distrust of the high, fashionable life of gambling and the ball. Fitzavarice's assaults on Lady Peregrine seem to him perfectly proper, in view of his nobility and her genteel penury. His page, we may notice, defines her scruples as uncourtly:

> You are the first
> Lady within my observation,
> That has took time to ask her conscience
> The meaning of a jewel, sent by a lord,
> A young and handsome lord too; 'tis a thing
> At court is not in fashion, and 'twere pity
> One with so good a face should be the precedent
> Of such superfluous modesty.
>
> (I.i; Gifford and Dyce, III, 291)

The actual courtship, whether by the proxy wit of Confident Rapture or by Fitzavarice himself, stresses the nobility of the wooer and assumes that his status deserves her submission.

Moreover, he is convinced that he can purchase her love by his promise to repair her husband's fortunes. This is the typical misunderstanding of a Wilding—an assumption that one's own desires (in this case, cupidity) are generally shared, in other words, an affection of consensus. But the courtship of Fitzavarice is more than the conventional nobleman's lust. He is governed by a sense of his own position, which forces him into continuing even after he regrets his precipitation:

> I must have
> Some way to enjoy her body for my credit;
> The world takes notice I have courted her,
> And if I mount her not, I lose my honour.
>
> (I.i; Gifford and Dyce, III, 296-297)

Most invincible; no temptation
Can fasten on her: would I had ne'er laid siege to her!
The taking of her province will not be
So much advantage to me, as the bare
Removing of my siege will lose me credit.

(II.i; Gifford and Dyce, III, 302)

Later he is forced into dueling with Sir Walter, against his wishes but impelled by a sense of his honor, which, he claims, is precarious in a world of malice. Lord Fitzavarice is indeed the courtier, dependent on the maintenance of a fragile reputation—as much a prisoner of his honor as Sir Solitary is of his timidity. Sir Walter's valid question, "Can lords / Be cowards?" (IV.iii; Gifford and Dyce, III, 344) is apt. It is the Lord's way of life, even his social status, that forces him into an intolerable position. Neither he nor Sir Solitary can comprehend the environment into which they fall; their actions are repugnant to common sense yet seem essential to them. Both are restored to society by a general rejection of their follies, and, as has been made clear throughout, both are in essence decent and sensible. The relief with which Lord Fitzavarice' wicked ways are abandoned is neatly suggested in a scene which shows his page returning to Lady Peregrine, this time on a proper errand:

I meet
Honest employments with more cheerfulness.
. . . . .
When I go upon
Lascivious errands, madam, I take money
There is no other benefit belongs to 'em;
But good ones pay themselves.

(III.i; Gifford and Dyce, III, 320)

By stressing a failure of understanding rather than of morality, by relating the failure to understand to the social environment, and by showing the eccentric behavior as a temporary affectation, Shirley has made convincing and even moving the reformation and reconciliation scenes at the end of the play. We do not suddenly see a rake turning angel in Act V; rather we have the discovery, by a basically sympathetic character, that his way of life has been misdirected. This is perhaps more clearly seen in an admirable passage in *The Witty Fair One.* Fowler has been attempting to trick Penelope by feigning sickness. She organizes an elaborate series of deceptions to confront him with his supposed death and funeral. At first the jest is lighthearted and witty; then Fowler gradually realizes the solemnity implicit in the device and laments his loose ways.

The problems inherent when one social group comes into contact with another are skillfully and imaginatively revealed in the romantic comedy *The Opportunity.* The theme of mistaken identification is ancient and conventional, though we might expect the love affairs which arise from the comedy of errors to be permanent. That

the transient soldiers, Aurelio and Pisauro, leave Urbino unattached, that their influence in the city is a temporary aberration, is made to seem inevitable as a result of the social contrast between their characters, as straightforward military men, and the intricate courtly environment into which they fall. Always in the background of the Duchess' affairs is the significance of her lofty political status. Lucio, a courtier, observes:

Although I honour Borgia [Aurelio],
And wish him heartily advanced, I would
Not kneel to him; my voice is for Ferrara,
He is a prince; I would not for my state
This should break off his treaty.

(II.ii; Gifford and Dyce, III, 393)

Pisauro becomes delighted with the prospect of power, and Aurelio himself is shown unromantically balancing political and amorous success:

Betwixt the duchess and Cornelia
My soul divides: I must not be a fool,
And for the fable of [mere] amorous love
Leave state that courts me with a glorious title.

(II.iii; Gifford and Dyce, III, 400)

The audience is not allowed to forget the implications of the action, nor does Shirley ignore the distinctions between the heroes and the courtiers around them. He uses the device of a trick to demonstrate this distinction. The Duchess has encouraged the diffident Aurelio by dictating a love letter which includes a broadly hinted assignation. Aurelio, uncertain if this is the opportunity he must grasp, happens on the Duke of Ferrara, who quotes what he had overheard on a previous occasion and persuades the unhappy soldier that the letter belongs in nobler hands. The Duke's trick works because Aurelio is out of his depth, confused in the courtly atmosphere around him. The nature of the deception and the Duke's easy and fluent dissimulation convince the audience that the traveling soldiers, while they may make a brief impression in Urbino, have really no proper place there. Aurelio's high hopes are an affectation, which the Duke's trick exposes.

A somewhat similar situation is found in *The Humorous Courtier,* where the ambitious courtier Contarini imagines that the Duchess is in love with him. He attributes his confusion, not entirely without reason, to the allusive nature of royal conversation:

'Tis great pity custom should make princes
So reserv'd in wooing.

(V.iii; Gifford and Dyce, IV, 606)

Typically, the Jacobean or Caroline romantic drama tends to be distant from reality; artifice and a fairy-tale atmosphere seem to deny any opportunity for social comment. Conversely, the realistic dramas of the day tend to submerge any general purpose beneath the details of everyday behavior and life in the London streets. Shirley's continuing interest in social status marks both romantic plays such as *The Opportunity* and realistic pieces such as *Hyde Park,* giving to the one a relevance and to the other a consistent theme. Romantic comedy with valid social comment, and realistic comedy with a firm dramatic focus, are Shirley's particular gifts to the theater of his time.

III

The failure of understanding, revealing the different modes of thought in differing social groups and forcing the rejection of affectation, is seen at its clearest and most sophisticated in the celebrated comedy *The Lady of Pleasure.* The central deception has an ironic inversion: Aretina is never found out by the fop she tricks. The comic movement toward understanding and reformation works here through a trick, but it is the successful trickster who undergoes the change. Aretina, who has ambitions to step into fashionable life, is unable to cope with the ways of that life. But her change of heart comes from the spontaneous collapse of her affectation following her moment of insight. Doubtless, Shirley's recognition of the essentially introspective nature of the self-discovery makes him have her withdraw from the stage to recover her composure behind the scenes.

The usual dramatic purpose of the comic trick is to reveal the character of the gull; in the case of Wilding and the others, the revelation is to themselves. In *The Lady of Pleasure* the trick reveals the true character of the fops to Aretina. The gull's character, as well as her own, is made plain; it is the trickster who, shocked at what she sees, reforms her behavior. The gull, Kickshaw, never learns the truth.

Critics have tended to be severe on Aretina. As Professor Knowland comments: "Aretina . . . having enjoyed her sin is 'converted' and left unpunished; but the awakened sense of guilt is just another theatrical trick."[12] But it is possible that a dramatist can show a convincing reformation without the external urges of public scorn or poetic justice. Aretina does indeed fall victim to the deception played by her husband, who pretends to be as devoted as she to a life of fashionable luxury and feigns riot to the point of apparent ruin. His miming of her affectations and extravagance acts as a comic mirror to show her the flaws in her own life, which she first sees vaguely and then, as his deception continues and bankruptcy threatens, perceives in full degree (V.i; Gifford and Dyce, IV, 82, 85).

Aretina's realization that the fashionable life is dangerous and inappropriate is illustrated by a number of excellent comic devices. The effect of her ambitions on her nephew, Frederick, is well shown. He first appears as a mild-mannered if rather oafish student, fresh from college in his *sub-fusc.* Determining to civilize him, she gives him over to her steward for tuition. Frederick proves a most apt pupil, becoming a fashion-obsessed buffoon and drunkard. When he attempts to court his aunt, she finally realizes the disastrous results of her educational experiment and packs him off again to the university. She is less able to undo the effects of her infatuation on her steward. He has first appeared as a typical old-fashioned retainer, and his greeting of Frederick shows him as a genuine friend of the family: "Welcome home, sweet master Frederick!" (II.i; Gifford and Dyce, IV, 24). But he rapidly sinks into the dissolute urban life, and the last we hear of him is Frederick's comment:

> Your steward has some pretty notions too,
> In moral mischief.

(IV.ii; Gifford and Dyce, IV, 71)

Through *The Lady of Pleasure* the audience is shown the true significance of the life of fashion. Throughout they are aware that Kickshaw and Littleworth are, as their names tell us, of no account. The portrait of the elegant Celestina, a more polished and witty figure, though scorned by Aretina and the fops, shows some of the true value of the high life.

Several passages explicitly contrast the life of fashion and the ideal life of the past, which Aretina has rejected. The play opens with her vivacious description of the country life she hates; while intentionally a rejection, the speech develops into an elaborate and splendid image of the old world, which conflicts with the similarly ornate invective against city luxury delivered by her husband. As their dialogue progresses, the imagery stresses the essentially destructive impact of luxury:

BORNWELL

> I could accuse the gaiety of your wardrobe,
> And prodigal embroideries, under which
> Rich satins, plushes, cloth of silver, dare
> Not shew their own complexions; your jewels,
> Able to burn out the spectators' eyes,
> And shew like bonfires on you by the tapers.

(I.i; Gifford and Dyce, IV, 8)

Such passages underline the falsity of Aretina's position in general moral terms. Elsewhere the dramatist skillfully shows the incompatibility of the lives of the gentry and the fops. In Act I, scene i, Kickshaw and Littleworth visit Aretina and are briefly entertained by Bornwell. All three try to be pleasant. Kickshaw and Littleworth are not arrogant Restoration beaux, Bornwell is no clownish squire. But they do not succeed in communicating with each other; their small talk dissolves into misunderstood compliment and unanswered question:

KICKSHAW AND LITTLEWORTH

        Save you, sir Thomas!

BORNWELL

    Save you, gentlemen!

KICKSHAW

          I kiss your hand.

BORNWELL

    What day is it abroad?

LITTLEWORTH

    The morning rises from your lady's eye:
    If she look clear, we take the happy omen
    Of a fair day.

BORNWELL

          She'll instantly appear,
    To the discredit of your complement;
    But you express your wit thus.

KICKSHAW

               And you modesty,
    Not to affect the praises of your own.

BORNWELL

    Leaving this subject, what game's now on foot?
    What exercise carries the general vote
    O' the town, now? nothing moves without your
      knowledge.

KICKSHAW

    The cocking now has all the noise; I'll have
    A hundred pieces on one battle.—Oh,
    These birds of Mars!

LITTLEWORTH

          Venus is Mars' bird too.

KICKSHAW

    Why, and the pretty doves are Venus's,
    To shew that kisses draw the chariot.

LITTLEWORTH

    I am for that skirmish.

BORNWELL

          When shall we have
    More booths and bagpipes upon Bansted downs?
    No mighty race is expected?—But my lady
    Returns!

             (I.i; Gifford and Dyce, IV, 12-13)

The passage is worth quoting at length to illustrate Shirley's skill in documenting embarrassment. Bornwell's simple questions, about the weather or about local news, attract witty extravagance and private jokes instead of replies. His final question about Banstead Downs elicits only stunned silence. Happily, Aretina appears, to set effective conversation again in motion. In this scene Shirley gives an abstract of his comic subject: the two levels of society exist, but they cannot meaningfully dwell together. The wealth and attractions of an Aretina may link the two groups for a time in courtship or intrigue, but, as discovered in *The Opportunity,* the liaison is temporary. A trick may recoil, a character may reconsider, and the persons in the play must return to their original, unaffected ways of life.

The comedy of intrigue generally suffers from the excessive virtuosity of its practitioners. Manipulation of a complex plot is more important than a single-minded dramatic purpose. Shirley's effective linking of the deception episode with a consistent view of English life permits him uniquely to turn the scampering plots of Renaissance theater into meaningful social commentaries.

Professor Knights quotes from a source in 1622:

> For nowadays most men live above their callings, and promiscuously step forth vice-versa into one another's ranks. The countryman's eye is upon the citizen: the citizen's upon the gentleman: the gentleman's upon the nobleman.[13]

In a period of rapid social change, inevitably a sense of dislocation will be felt by many individuals. The uncertainty of their position will be reflected in confused behavior, affectation, or an exaggerated awareness of status. The satirist and the comic writer will work effectively with the materials of snobbery and the stupidity of social ambition. James Shirley's contacts with the polite world of London and with the gentry of the provinces provided for him a rich experience of the uncertainties and foolishness of much contemporary society. His range is perhaps more limited than that of his predecessors, his wit less incisive than that of his successors; he may, to speak of him again as transitional, lack the variety of Jonson and the modish glitter of Etherege. But he is admirable in his grasp of the conflicts in the middle range of society and fruitful in his development and manipulation of the conventional intrigues. His use of the trick and the deception to illustrate the social situation of his comedy gives to his best pieces a consistency of purpose and a unity of plot not often met with in English comedy of the Jacobean and Caroline periods.

Notes

1. R. S. Forsythe, *The Relations of Shirley's Plays to the Elizabethan Drama* (New York, 1914).

2. Described in T. H. Fujimura, *The Restoration Comedy of Wit* (Princeton, 1952), pp. 65-66.

3. "MacFlecknoe," ll. 29-30.

4. See Eleanore Boswell, *The Restoration Court Stage* (Cambridge, 1932), pp. 105-106.

5. Ashley H. Thorndike, *English Comedy* (New York, 1929), p. 236.

6. Act V, scene i; James Shirley, *The Dramatic Works and Poems,* ed. William Gifford and Alexander Dyce (London, 1833), IV, 99. With the exception of passages from *The Traitor* and *The Cardinal,* which have recently been well edited, quotations are from the Gifford-Dyce edition, now available in a photographic reprint (New York: Russell & Russell, 1966).

7. John V. Curry, *Deception in Elizabethan Comedy* (Chicago, 1955), p. 6.

8. The best treatment of this aspect—indeed one of the best discussions of Shirley's art in general—is in Kathleen M. Lynch, *The Social Mode of Restoration Comedy* (New York, 1926), pp. 34-42.

9. James Shirley, *The Traitor,* ed. John Stewart Carter (Lincoln, 1965), II.i.182-194, 204-207.

10. Alfred Harbage, "James Shirley's *The Wedding* and the Marriage of Sir Kenelm Digby," *PQ,* XVI (January, 1937), 35-40.

11. James Shirley, *The Cardinal,* ed. Charles R. Forker (Bloomington, 1964), p. 18 n.

12. *Six Caroline Plays,* ed. A. S. Knowland (London, 1962), p. x.

13. L. C. Knights, *Drama and Society in the Age of Jonson* (London, 1937), p. 108.

Martin Butler (essay date 1984)

SOURCE: Butler, Martin. "City Comedies: Courtiers and Gentlemen." In *Theatre and Crisis, 1632-1642,* pp. 141-80. Cambridge: Cambridge University Press, 1984.

[*In the following excerpt, Butler examines the relationship between class and politics in Shirley's comedies, particularly as illustrated through the world of manners, drawing a close connection between the courtship behavior of Shirley's lovers and tensions in the Caroline court.*]

TOWN AND COUNTRY

In his intelligent and complex play [*The Weeding of Covent Garden*], Brome finds in Covent Garden, the symbol of the new permanent gentry presence (and crossness) in London, an occasion for defending the gentry's developing political character and for making a general critique of the personal rule. In turning to Shirley's town plays we find a society more confident in its own autonomy, and one of Shirley's main aims, consequently, is simply the elucidation of the new codes of manners as they act as internal standards to regulate and censure behaviour. But for Shirley as for Brome, these manners are resonant with political meanings; the problem is that these have been obscured by an obliquity of interpretation, a treatment of Caroline city comedy as largely either post-Jacobean or pre-Restoration. In fact, Shirley's preoccupations and anxieties rest on notions about the shape of society and the whereabouts of its points of tension different from those obtaining in both periods; we will not understand the significance of his comedies until we treat them as characteristically Caroline, and not merely adjunct to but fully distinct from both their predecessors and successors.

To conduct the kind of inquiry he wished for in *The Weeding of Covent Garden,* Brome adopted a deliberately old-fashioned style, playing the severe moralist in the Jonsonian mould, more concerned with humours than manners; his model is obviously *Bartholomew Fair.* Broadly speaking, Jacobean city comedy is moral rather than social, and takes greed and folly for its principal preoccupations; it also evinces little direct interest in the court. The main social antagonism with which it deals is between citizen and gentleman, Money and Land; London means the city, a place of legalism and sharp practice. This polarization did not greatly obsess the dramatists of our period. London in the 1630s implies the Strand, not Cheapside, and the motives to action are less commercial than amorous, so although London comedy is still a serious form, the vices it castigates are promiscuity and pride rather than greed, and its yardstick is civilized behaviour rather than human kindness. Moreover, as we have seen, many playgoers were making connections with the rich merchant classes, and the plays they saw rarely suggested that the city was out to destroy the gentry. I have argued elsewhere[1] that the great apparent exception, Massinger's *The City Madam* (1632) actually proves the rule; Massinger attacks civic avarice and social-climbing but from the standpoint of Sir John Frugal, a dignified citizen of aldermanic rank who associates with and counsels the nobleman, Lord Lacy, yet who is also a thrifty and highly successful businessman. Frugal cures the ladies of his family of pride above their station; nevertheless he still marries one daughter to a gentleman, the other to Lord Lacy's son.

Fletcher's city comedies begin to deal more obviously with London's leisured classes and develop an interest in 'wit' as a social value ('accomplishment' or 'breeding') as opposed to the 'wit' of Middleton's heroes which represents their capacity to swindle. However, his gallants are still footloose and their 'wit' is a nervous reaction, 'a flourish of indifference towards money'[2] and the obligations it brings with it; 'wit' rationalizes their rootlessness in terms of London's competitiveness, providing a weapon against insecurity. In *Wit Without Money* (c. 1614) Valentine, even though an elder brother, decides to live in London by his wits and attractively but outrageously parades his contempt of responsibility. His 'wit' converts his sense of displacement into aggression; Fletcher's plays are still largely without much sense of a communal social round such as becomes commonplace for the 1630s. Valentine walks the streets or visits taverns; in *Wit at Several Weapons* (c. 1609?) the clown kills time by wandering around 'the new River by Islington, there they shall have me looking upon the Pipes, and whistling'.[3] In Caroline plays people never simply lack anything to do but participate in an established and socially sanctioned Town. So although Shirley depicts 'wits', their *otium* is never, like Valentine's, radically at variance with their *negotium*. Caroline London plays continually demand that 'wit' be reconciled with more traditional notions of 'worth', and that it should cease to be the badge only of the *déclassé*.

It is more essential to distinguish Caroline comedy from its counterpart in the 1660s and 1670s because here critics have found the similarities most compelling (even though Shirley was felt to be out of date by 1667).[4] Restoration comedy spoke principally to a metropolitan audience accustoming itself to absenteeism and establishing permanent roots in London, itself rapidly becoming the only centre of political power. The centre of the stage has been taken over by the Town, and the criteria of behaviour have become urbanity and a cultivated and detached civility. 'Wit' has developed into an electric, sophisticated and sardonic mode of discourse entirely unlike anything in the 1630s (the nearest equivalent is the compliment, always regarded suspiciously by Caroline dramatists),[5] and marriage and romantic love are treated realistically and sceptically, perhaps fully for the first time. Clearly much has changed—including the attitudes to society and politics.

The precedence of the town in the 1660s and 1670s is established by a continual comparison with country dullness. This issue is examined most searchingly in Wycherley's *The Country Wife* (1675) in which, although the value of Margery Pinchwife's rural 'naturalness' is plain, her husband's error is to take it for something which is antithetical to the habits of the town. Her innocence exerts no positive pressure at all; it is simply lack of experience, and she quickly discovers it is as 'natural' for herself to prefer the town to the country as it is for any more sophisticated person ('how shou'd I help it, Sister').[6] 'Nature' is everywhere outraged in *The Country Wife*, but as a prescriptive system of value it hardly exists. Rather, in Wycherley's Hobbesian human zoo men are 'naturally' predatory

and pleasure-seeking, just as it is 'natural' for jealous husbands, like Pinchwife, to be cuckolded. Ironically, it is the town which best fulfils these conditions, and is witty man's 'state of nature'. In Etherege's plays, the country is similarly a place of dullness or sterility, the 'Wildness' of the heroine of *The Man of Mode* (1676)[7] is exactly that quality which allies her with the town against the country. Any suggestion that the town fulfils man's 'nature' or represents the sum of experience in this way is wholly alien to the 1630s.

Alongside this devaluation of the country is a shift in the political position of the town. The Cavalier-puritan polarity absent from the 1630s is much in evidence in the 1660s and 1670s. A main butt of Etherege's seminal comedy *The Comical Revenge* (1664) is 'Sir Nich'las Culley,* one whom *Oliver,* for the transcendent knavery and disloyalty of his Father, has dishonour'd with Knight-hood' and who therefore is allowed no serious qualities; the hero, Bruce, is a loyal Cavalier who has to vindicate himself from puritan slanders ('Look on your Friend; your drooping Country view; / And think how much they both expect from you').[8] The tendency of these comedies, even within a single play, to over- and under-seriousness reflects the self-images towards which the exiled courtiers were forced in the Interregnum, either heroic Prince Ruperts or debauched devil-may-cares. In Dryden's *Marriage-à-la-Mode* (1672), and many like it, the play world simply splits into two contrasting halves, one prose, one verse, which coexist yet barely interact except as versions of these extreme, alternating mentalities. The place of the town in this is quite evident. Sedley's *The Mulberry Garden* (1668) opens with an apparently objective debate on the freedom of town pleasures, recalling similar discussions in Caroline comedies, but its seriousness is suddenly undermined when the critic of the town is revealed as a puritan and hence a killjoy who in the overplot prevents his daughter from wedding a heroic Cavalier loyal to the exiled king. Throughout the play the puritan is satirized and humiliated, and the success of true love is signalled by the return of Charles II and the vindication of loyalty and the gaiety of the town. A comparable re-alignment is observable in more serious drama too.[9]

Evidently the experiences of 1642-60 have undermined the Town's independence and forced it into a close association with the court and into opposition to city, country and puritanism of any brand. Dryden formulated his criticisms of the drama of the previous age precisely in terms of its lack of courtliness. Accusing Jonson of 'meanness of thought', he complained that the wit of his contemporaries

> was not that of gentlemen; there was ever somewhat that was ill-bred and clownish in it, and which confessed the conversation of the authors . . . In the age wherein these poets lived, there was less of gal-

lantry than in ours; neither did they keep the best company of theirs . . . I cannot find that any of them were conversant in courts, except Ben Jonson: and his genius lay not so much that way as to make an improvement by it . . .

The present (1672) refinement he ascribed to the influence of 'the Court: and, in it, particularly to the King, whose example gives a law to it'; later (1679) he attacked Fletcher for allowing kings who were not usurpers to appear bad, and for failing to provide 'those royal marks which ought to appear in a lawful successor of the throne'.[10] There is a unity of artistic and political outlook here in which a dislike of 'lowness' in art reinforces a rejection of ungentlemanly behaviour in politics, and specifically of 'country' distrust of and opposition to the king. The dramatic equivalents of Dryden's precepts are Lady Woodvill in *The Man of Mode* (she being an absurd 'admirer of the Forms and Civility of the last Age') and Old Bellair whose ridiculous rustic obstinacy ('go, bid her dance no more, it don't become her, it don't become her, tell her I say so; a Dod I love her') is a deft parody of the deliberate stubbornness associated with the political idea of the 'country';[11] sixty years later, Chesterfield was quite certain about what the involvement of the Restoration dramatists with the court had meant for the political attitudes they had expressed.[12] It is this narrow courtliness in politics which it is tempting, but most misleading, to read back into the Town plays of the 1630s. These are the attitudes of a society purposefully retreating from serious political engagement, not of one moving towards it.

In several Caroline plays, the country is indeed ridiculed in a figure who has come to London and failed to reproduce society's good manners. However, the social pretender is always satirized not for his *rusticity* but for his *lowness* and his attempt to clamber into a higher rank than he deserves. In Shirley's *The Changes* (1632; pub. London, 1632) a country knight, Simple, finally returns to the provinces to sell his servant his 'Knighthood for halfe the mony it cost me, and turne Yeoman in the country agen' (p. 69). In *The Constant Maid* (c. 1637; pub. London, 1640), Startup, claiming gentility, admits 'my father was / A Yeoman . . . my Grandfather was a Nobleman['s] Foot-man, and indeed he [ran] his countrey; my father did outrun the Constable' (sig.C2ᵛ); he is contrasted with the dignified figure of a countryman whose daughter he has wronged. Other figures abused for their lack of gentility rather than urbanity are Brome's Tim Hoyden (in *The Sparagus Garden*, 1635) and Cavendish's Simpleton (in *The Variety, c.* 1641-42), the latter's attempted rape of the play's heroine making him a most undesirable character. The attitudes are social and moral, not anti-rural; rather, this feeling that rank ought to be answerable to a standard of worth seems to me to be a characteristically 'country' conviction.

I have been suggesting that the roots of Caroline high society were still firmly linked to the provinces, and the instinctive sympathy of Caroline city comedies (and Shirley's in particular) for the outlook and attitudes of the country is a feature which significantly distinguishes them from their Restoration successors. This sympathy is made explicit in Shirley's *The Witty Fair One* (London, 1633), written shortly before our main period (1628). The heroine's social placing is very carefully detailed:

> Her Father is a man who though he write
> Himselfe but Knight, keepes a warme house i'the
>   Countrey
> 'Mongst his Tenants, takes no Lordly pride
> To trauell with a Footman and a Page
> To *London,* humbly rides th old fashion
> With halfe a douzen wholesome Liueries,
> To whom he gives Christian wages and not counte-
>   nance
> Alone to liue on, can spend by th'yeare
> Eight hundred pounds, and put vp fine sleepes quietly
> Without dreaming on Morgages or Statutes
> Or such like curses on his Land, can number
> May be ten thousand pound in ready coyne
> Of's own, yet neuer bought an office for't
> Ha's plate no question, and Iewels too
> In's old Ladies cabinet, beside
> Other things worth an Inuentory, and all this
> His daughter is an heyre to . . .

(sig.B3ʳ)

Sir George Richley, described here, typifies the traditional country values—conservative, hospitable, plain yet wealthy, knowing his place yet independent of the court ('never bought an office'), and he is contrasted with the foolish Sir Nicholas Treedle who lacks love for his servants, pursues foreign fashions and is 'a Knight & no Gentleman' (sig.K1ᵛ). Although Richley opposes his daughter's match, the play exhibits considerable respect for the attitudes represented in this speech. The best characters are shown acting in a magnanimous, dignified manner, and their generous language matches their deeds. Typical are the scenes in which Richley's daughter's suitor is counselled by her uncle, or in which the subsidiary heroine is aided by two anonymous gentlemen to reform her rakish suitor:

2 Gᴇɴᴛʟᴇᴍᴀɴ.

> Gentle Lady
> And if it prove fortunate, the designe
> Will be your honour, and the deed it selfe
> Reward us in his benefit, he was ever wilde

1 Gᴇɴᴛʟᴇᴍᴀɴ.

> Assured your ends are noble, we are happy in'[t].

(sigs.I2ʳ⁻ᵛ)

The play is permeated with the values and speech of a gentry class moving to London yet conscious of its traditional duties of courtesy and responsibility, and this feeling for 'country' values continually recurs in London plays of the 1630s. For example, Shirley's **Constant Maid** opens with the hero bidding a sad farewell to the family retainers he can no longer support, one of whom refuses to leave him; and in Thomas May's *The Old Couple* (1636), the Jacobean city comedy motifs of usury and avarice have been imposed, with little sense of incongruity, on a story set amongst country gentry and emphasizing values of charity and neighbourliness.

Another feature distinguishing Caroline from Restoration comedy is that in the former the Town is not the only centre of attention, but the other localities of the realm are invoked besides and the behaviour of the metropolis is measured against them. The completest example is, again, Shirley's **Constant Maid** whose hero, we have seen, has a country background and who, at the nadir of his fortunes, leaves the town for the fields. The city is present in a usurer, Hornet, who opposes his daughter's marriage, and the court is represented in burlesque by a group of servants who dress up as courtiers to help fool Hornet out of his daughter. So although the town gallants triumph, the town is placed against a broad context of all the estates of the realm in a manner quite unlike Restoration comedy. In the ease with which the tyrannous Hornet is deceived by the fake courtiers' talk of monopolies and projects (and in his readiness to threaten the gallants with a prosecution in Star Chamber), Shirley seems to be associating city and court together as both unattractive and avaricious, whereas the gallants, with their dignity and resistance to parental attempts to force their affections, adopt a 'country' outspokenness and respect for free judgment and action. For example, one of the girls resists her mother's oppression indignantly:

> Though in imagination [i.e. in thought] I allow you
> The greatest woman in the earth, whose frowne
> Could kill . . . I durst tell you
> Though all your terrours were prepared to punish
> My bold defence; you were a tyrant . . .
> My soul's above your tyranny, and would
> From torturing flame, receive new fire of love.
>
> (sigs.G1ʳ⁻ᵛ)

Although in comedy parents traditionally oppose lovers' freedoms, the violence of this retort and its language of 'tyranny' (and the girl's insistence on her essential obedience and willingness to submit despite her speaking her mind) seem to me wholly characteristic of the tone of this drama with its instinctive feeling for the gentry's inviolable dignity and for the freedom due to their 'place'. This 'country' sense of *place* derives from the gentry's identity as the principal propertied class; it both defines their social position, and protects their independence from the encroachments of other ranks.

Country gentry in town, such as Sir Humphrey Mildmay and Sir Edward Dering, would have felt much

sympathy with these characters on the Caroline stage, and much continuity exists between the respect for gentility, responsibility and worth in these plays and the sentiments which are commonplace in the memoirs, letters and notebooks preserved by such people as Sir George Sondes, Sir John Oglander, the Verneys of Buckinghamshire and Oxindens of Kent, men deeply conscious of the traditions and responsibilities the ownership of land confers. Although this serious aspect of Caroline comedy has been dismissed by critics as an anticipation of Augustan sentimentality, or as 'dubious grace',[13] it is something that runs very deep in this period. It also carries a considerable political charge. There is, for instance, much common ground between the distaste for parental tyranny in **The Constant Maid** and the reflections on 'political nobilitie' made by the Kent gentleman Henry Oxinden. Oxinden felt that the aristocracy should be esteemed according to their behaviour, not their titles:[14]

> The knowledge and consideration whereof hath caused mee not to value anie man by having anie inward respect or conceite of him beefore another, beecause he excells in degrees of honour, but according to the concomitant ornaments, as vertue, riches, wisdom, power etc. etc.

> If I see a man of what low degree or quality soever that is vertuous, rich, wise or powerful, him will I preferre beefore the greatest Lord in the kingdome that comes short of him in these . . .

The implications for the political attitudes of the Caroline gentry of this respect for traditional dignities and valuation of virtue above title are worked out most fully in Shirley's two major comedies.

TOWN AND COURT

Shirley's **The Lady of Pleasure** (1635; pub. London, 1637) opens with an attack by Sir Thomas Bornwell (and his steward) on the extravagance of his wife, Aretina, which is destroying their wealth in the country, and the play is often read as if it were a moralistic rejection of the behaviour of the town from the point of view of a rural society outraged and threatened by it. Shirley's opening, though, must be balanced against the scene in the second act in which Bornwell visits the other 'lady of pleasure', Celestina, apparently also to 'test' her behaviour in town. After acting towards her in the bawdy manner of the gallants with whom his own wife consorts, he finds that her manners are not a blind for lascivious or over-liberal behaviour but a reflection of her true, virtuous nature, and he apologizes to her and praises her innocence. The scene acts as a norm of social behaviour which Shirley admires, and thereafter Bornwell associates with the 'good' lady of pleasure rather than with Aretina, in order to cure the latter's misbehaviour. Bornwell and Celestina are two prongs in one argument—country attack of the town's excess, and an example of what it should be. The play parallels the careers of Celestina and Aretina, demonstrating in the former that the achievement of a social code enshrines positive values and enables free social intercourse by defining its limits, and attacking in the latter those who misuse the social codes for ambition and lasciviousness.[15]

The main force of the Aretina plot is moral. Shirley attacks fashionable ladies for whom manners contradict morality ('Praying's forgot. / 'Tis out of fashion' (sig.C1ᵛ)), and the plot culminates with Aretina's re-awakening to virtue as she realizes the degeneracy of her lover and her nephew (whose attempted rape of her is the fruit of the fashionable dissipation to which she has encouraged him). But this moral failure is related in the first scene to a political failure. Aretina's extravagance is an attempt to make her household like the court, and she encourages her husband to use his wealth to procure offices:

> A narrow minded husband is a theefe
> To his owne fame, and his preferment too,
> He shuts his parts and fortunes from the world
> While from the popular vote and knowledge men
> Rise to imployment in the state.

BORNWELL.

> I have
> No great ambition to buy preferment
> At so deare rate.

(sig.B3ʳ)

'Deare' here implies expense to the pocket and to honour. Aretina is (quite literally) prostituting herself to the court, and Bornwell responds to this as to a subversion of his 'gentry' integrity. Her court-centred attitudes are realized in her language, for she justifies her actions, as Charles his prerogative rule, on the grounds of 'privilege':

> I finde you would intrench and wound the liberty
> I was borne with, were my desires unpriviledged
> By example . . .
> You ought not to oppose.

(sig.B3ʳ)

With this 'privilege' she subordinates Bornwell's freedom, keeping him in awe of her 'kinsmen great and powerfull, / It'h State', and he admits that if she does not have her will 'the house [will] be shooke with names / Of all her kindred, tis a servitude, / I may in time shake off' (sigs.B2ʳ, B3ᵛ). Her extravagance is related to court tyranny; Bornwell complains she makes gaming 'Not a Pastime but a tyrannie, and vexe / Your selfe and my estate by't' (sig.B2ᵛ). This distinction between court and town has been obscured by critics who have persistently referred to Sir Thomas Bornwell as 'Lord Bornwell'. There is, though, a clear correlation between Aretina's behaviour and her desertion to the court; she offends against the values of the town gentry morally, economically and politically.

Whereas Aretina's steward criticizes her expenditure, Celestina's questions her morals:

> tis not for
> My profit, that I manage your estate,
> And save expence, but for your honour Madam.

CELESTINA.

> How sir, my honour?

STEWARD.

> Though you heare it not
> Mens toungues are liberall in your character,
> Since you began to live thus high, I know
> Your fame is precious to you.

(sigs.C2ʳ⁻ᵛ)

The steward's suspicions reflect on his baseness, not Celestina's, and she strikes him for them. Such criticisms the play's action shows to be false, for Celestina is a town lady whose expense is the true image of her 'generosity'—both her financial openness and her dignified gentility (the word derives from *generosus,* meaning 'of high birth'). It does not compromise her modesty but marks the freedom proper to her 'place'; she and her women are resolved to possess

> Our pleasure with security of our honour,
> And that preservd, I welcome all the joyes
> My fancy can let in.

(sig.D3ʳ)

So although Celestina resists Bornwell's temptations, she rebukes one of her women for not freely returning a courteous kiss that she is given. Liberality is thus the outward sign of inner gentility, and suited to her social position. She is not, then, overbearing like Aretina, but her freedom is precisely that natural behaviour proper to a gentlewoman. She reverses Aretina's position, establishing herself in opposition to, not emulation of, the court; she will

> Be hospitable then, and spare no cost
> That may engage all *generous* report
> To trumpet forth my bounty and my braverie,
> Till the Court envie, and remove . . .

(sig.C2ᵛ, my italics)

Whereas the ridiculousness of the courtiers with whom Aretina consorts exposes them, Celestina herself satirizes the worthlessness of those who visit her. One she slyly guesses is a courtier 'by your confidence' (sig.C2ᵛ); another she characterizes as

> a wanton emissarie

Or scout for *Venus* wild [fowl], which made tame
He thinkes no shame to stand court centinell,
In hope of the reversion.

(sigs.D3^{r-v})

This implicit friction between court and town becomes explicit in the fourth act in which Celestina undergoes a test of courtesy with an unnamed lord.

The great court lord who is thrown Celestina's way is a platonic in love after the manner fashionable at Henrietta Maria's Whitehall in mid decade. When he first appears, he is professing an elaborate and rather pompous fidelity to a dead mistress, Bella Maria: he boasts of having 'a heart, 'bove all licentious flame' and of having loved Bella Maria for her beauty rather than her person, so that he claims now not merely to be mourning her loss but still to be in love with her 'Idea' as his 'Saint' (sigs.E4^{r-v}, I4^r). Celestina 'tests' the lord rather as Bornwell tested her and is pleased to find at first that his professions are matched by a real purity, and are not a merely fashionable courtly pose:

Nor will I thinke these noble thoughts grew first
From melancholy, for some femall losse,
As the phantasticke world beleeves, but from
Truth, and your love of Innocence . . .

(sig.H4^r)

However, in the final act he reverses his position and succumbs to Celestina's charms. As base as her steward, he now supposes that her personal openness indicates she has lascivious intentions like Aretina's:

These widowes are so full of circumstance,
Ile undertake in this time I ha courted
Your Ladiship for the toy, to ha broken ten,
Nay twenty colts, Virgins I meane, and taught em
The amble, or what pace I most affected.

(sig.K1^r)

He now disowns his earlier constancy as 'A noble folly' and offers her instead a platonic love that really is, like Aretina's manners, only the superficies of respectability, a mask for looser practices ('Your sexe doth hold it no dishonour / To become Mistris to a noble servant / In the now court, Platonicke way' (sig.I4^v)). He goes on to woo her with an elaborate flowery speech, perhaps intended to recall the language of Davenant's platonic plays. Celestina only regains him for virtue by narrating an exemplary fable about a social upstart who tried to purchase honour equivalent to his, implying his honour is worth no more than bought honour if not matched with personal integrity. Thus the town corrects the court, its virtue being shown to have a more solid foundation than the artificialities of courtly platonism, and Celestina's moral point is underlined (in a manner typical of Shirley) in the action immediately following in which a

minor courtier defends his gentility honourably and exposes the lack of gentility of another, merely fashionable, courtier (sigs.K1^v-2^r).

The lord's tactics are also tyrannous, like Aretina's. He appeals to his status, expecting that his position at court can validate his behaviour:

consider
Who tis that pleades to you, my birth, and present
Value can be no stain to your embrace . . .

(sig.I4^v)

Celestina admits that 'gay men have a priviledge', but warns the lord that by presuming on this privilege 'you doe forget / Your selfe and me' (sigs.K1^{r-v}). That is to say, in respecting the lord's privilege, she expects an answering respect for *her* privilege: the system of 'privilege' defines the freedom of behaviour appropriate to every rank within that system but its operation demands that the 'privilege' of each rank is as inviolable as that of the next. By assuming that because his privilege is courtly it is in some way superior to Celestina's, the lord invades and destroys her privilege—in the language of opposition to Charles, it is an *encroachment* on her rights. This too is the burden of the fable Celestina instructs the lord in, that the attempt of the parvenu to purchase honour like the lord's renders the system within which it operates meaningless and destroys the very basis of that honour. Privilege and honour are forces which determine social boundaries, but cannot be used to override them for that would turn them against themselves; the sanction of society's values, they are not strategies to exceed them. By disrespecting Celestina's privilege and resorting to *tyranny* the lord has destroyed the guarantee of his own freedom, the privilege which protects his rights as well as hers.

Clearly, this incident, and the fable with which Celestina corrects the lord, have far-reaching social and political implications. It is not merely that the lord is using the authority of his 'honour' dishonourably, but Celestina's rebuke reaches out impressively to imply a wide social system of checks and balances in which each man respects the freedom and integrity of those around him and in which the respect he can command is a guarantee of his own freedom. It is a mature, comprehensive picture of the workings of society, depending for its dynamic on the gentry sense of one's 'place', a position in which one can act and speak freely without encroaching on the freedoms of others. This has obvious continuities with the attitudes of Charles's critics in parliament whose anxiety for their liberty of life and person was bound up with a concern for their property rights, the security of the possession of their goods from court encroachment. Denzil Holles complained in 1641 that Charles's judges 'have removed our land marks, have taken away the bound stones of the Propriety of the subject, have left no *meum* and *tuum;* but he that had most might had most right and the law was sure to be of his side'.[16] Celestina, arguing that the privilege which gives the lord his freedom does not sanction his attempt to override her freedom, is anticipating Holles's argument.

Celestina's free speaking here is also a form of resistance to the court's centralizing tendencies. Her answer of course attacks the lord's notion that his status enables him to arbitrate all moral value according to his uncontrolled will. But on a different level, she is replying to the extremely flowery platonizing speech with which he tries to tempt her. It is a long, over-poetic description of the delights she can expect in his paradise of love, and she parodies it as 'linsey woolsie, to no purpose' (sig.K1[r]). But it does have a purpose—to overwhelm her resistance with a catalogue of sensual delights, subjugating her with a stream of all varieties of pleasure. Just as the court laid claim to a monopoly of authority, this speech shows the lord claiming a monopoly of experience, destroying value (and Celestina's freedom to act morally) by invoking all value. This is a common *topos* with Shirley. In *The Example* (1634; pub. London, 1637), Lord Fitzavarice (whose name suggests the economic encroachments which parallel his moral encroachments) tries to overwhelm the wife of an absent gentleman with extravagant poetry:

> consent, deere Ladie, to
> Be mine, and thou shat tast more happinesse,
> Then womans fierce ambition can persue;
> Shift more delights, then the warme-spring can boast
> Varietie of leaves, or wealthie harvest
> Graine from the teeming earth. Joy shall dry all
> Thy teares, and take his throne up, in thy eies,
> Where it shall sit, and blesse what e're they shine on.
> The night shall Sowe her pleasures in thy bosome,
> And morning shall rise only to salute thee.

> (sig.D1[r])

Fitzavarice's expressions suggest he can control all experience and hence all value, a monopoly of authority which destroys discrimination (his creature, Confident—Shirley's typical name for a courtier—claims that to inquire 'The meaning of a Jewell, sent by a Lord, / . . . 'tis a thing / At Court, is not in fashion' (sig.A4[v]). The tempted gentlewoman heroically resists this sensual assault:

> not your estate,
> Though multiplied to Kingdomes, and those wasted
> With your invention, to serue my pleasures,
> Have power to bribe my life away from him,
> To whose use I am bid to weare it . . .
> Ile rather choose to die
> Poore wife to *Peregrine,* then live a Kings
> Inglorious strumpet

> (sigs.D1[r v])

Shirley presents us again with another gentlewoman preserving her moral independence against a courtier who claims to control all value.[17] The blasphemous echoes in his speech ('Joy shall dry all / Thy teares . . .') recall the assertions that were being made about Charles's divinity in court masques, and in *Love's Cruelty* (1631) an explicit link is made by the courtier Hippolito who, instructed by the duke to seduce a gentlewoman for him, once more embarks on such another speech of the rapturous delights of the court which culminates in a description of the scenic wonders of Jonson's masque *Neptune's Triumph* (1624). Here Shirley penetrates to the heart of the court's ethos. The masque, a symbol of the king's power, shows all nature subjected to him and obedient to his magical will as the scenes range over all times and places. The masque is thus the highest expression of the court's imperialism,[18] making the king the lord of all possible experience and value, and it is this imperialism with which Shirley's courtiers try to tyrannize Celestina and her counterparts.

This pattern, in which the town criticizes and restrains the court's monopolizing tendencies, underlies all Shirley's major city plays with the exception of *The Gamester* (1633) which, significantly, he wrote specifically for court performance. It can be found in *Hyde Park, The Example,* the collaborative play *The Country Captain* (c. 1641) and, in modified form, *The Constant Maid.*[19] *The Ball* (1632) seems to follow the pattern, but it is ambiguous because of the alterations Shirley was forced, by court interference, to make in the play. One would dearly like to know more about those people 'personated so naturally, both of lords and others of the court' that Sir Henry Herbert insisted Shirley cut out.[20] Evidently the pattern represents for Shirley something very basic and challenging about the town's position in the social structure; nevertheless, he does not offer to present the town as replacing the court but balancing it, and modifying its excesses. The pattern shows the court being restrained from usurping the centre of value but equally prevents the town from doing the same (and in this Shirley's plays are typical of the broad perspective characteristic of Caroline city comedy in general). While Celestina's cautionary fable criticizes the court's misuse of its status, she has no quarrel with the system that grants it its privilege. She is not so much attacking the court as defending the *status quo* (the system of honour) which is unbalanced by the lord's exceeding of his place. The lord's failure to match his 'worth' to his 'status' (the two ideas suggested by 'honour') disrupts and nullifies the system; Celestina's riposte suggests that the system is prescriptive and that, to deserve his status, the lord must recognize the responsibilities, as well as the privileges, that it confers (this is the same argument that seemed so ineffective when advanced in Shirley's *The Duke's Mistress* (chapter 3 above). An admonition to the court to fulfil its proper social/political role carries a different pressure depending on the context in which it is made; the court's and town's conceptions of this role would not have been identical.)

It was exactly such a notion of a balanced system, the members of which sustain and restrain each other, to which the parliamentary leaders frequently appealed in defence of the rights which Charles's government seemed increasingly to be eroding. Pym argued in 1628 that the constitution was one of finely balanced 'mutual relation and intercourse'; the 'form of government is that which doth actuate and dispose every part and member of the state to the common good; and as those parts give strength and ornament to the whole, so they receive from it again strength and protection in their several stations and degrees'. If these degrees are exceeded, 'there should remain no more industry, no more justice, no more courage; for who will contend, who will endanger himself for that which is not his own?' Clarendon similarly urged in 1641 that if either king or parliament tried to increase its dominance, it hurt the very basis of its power: 'if the least branch of the prerogative was torn off, or parted with, the subject suffered by it, and . . . his right was impaired: and he [Clarendon] was as much troubled when the crown exceeded its just limits, and thought its prerogative hurt by it'. In 1647 his solution was that 'the frame and constitution of the Kingdom [should] be observed, and the known laws and bounds between the King's power and the Subjects' right'.[21] These are the constitutionalist sentiments of a gentry class concerned for the survival of their interests and wishing for reform but reluctant to provoke social revolution in the process. Similarly, Shirley reforms his stage-courtiers, but then puts his trust in their future good faith. In ***The Example,*** Fitzavarice is rebuked in the third act, and thereafter acts in a wholly noble way, even being allowed to defend his honour in a duel. He ends taking to wife the heroine's sister (though 'not for any titles' but 'for [his] noble nature' (sig.I2^v)). Once he acknowledges the responsibilities lying on him, he resumes his place in a properly reformed world, in which the checks and balances inherent in the system will ensure its just operation. Both court and gentry have their *place* in this order; but the gentry maintain their freedom and dignity by reminding the courtiers that they will only receive their dignity—their *place*—by respecting the dignity—the *place*—of others. 'Respect' and 'restraint' are the forces that bind together, and simultaneously distinguish, the various components of this society.

Shirley's completest account of this harmoniously balanced society is drawn in that beautifully achieved play ***Hyde Park*** (1632; pub. London, 1637).[22] The action follows three parallel courtships of three ladies, the spirited Carol, her suitor Fairfield's sister Julietta, and Mrs Bonavent, a merchant's wife and, supposedly, his widow. The Julietta plot presents another gentry-courtier contrast. Julietta is tested by her gallant, the aptly named

Trier, who exposes her to the dubious attentions of Lord Bonvile, having secretly assured Bonvile she is a courtesan. Her innocent openness to Bonvile is based on her understanding that her integrity will be protected by the social forms, giving Bonvile all respect since

> It is my duty, where the king has seal'd
> His favours, I should shew humility
> My best obedience to his act.

> (sig.H4^v)

The credit she allows Bonvile is that which answers his social position ('There's nothing in the verge of my command / That should not serve your Lordship' (sig.E2^r)), and she refuses to probe the sincerity of his behaviour for he is 'one it becomes not me to censure' (sig.E3^r). Such respectful, dignified language matches her ideal of civil, generous behaviour and clearly she expects Bonvile will treat her respectfully in return. But he is full of ambiguous compliments. Where her language has been that of 'plaine humilitie', his is dark, leading her to protest 'Ile not beleeve my Lord you meane so wantonly / As you professe' (sigs.E2$^{r\ v}$). In fact, he wishes simply to violate the proper boundaries of social place which her careful language acknowledges. Quite literally, he would approach her too closely:

LORD.

> Come, that [word] humble was
> But complement in you too.

JULIETTA.

> I wood not
> Be guilty of dissembling with your Lordship,
> I know [no] words have more proportion
> With my distance to your birth and fortune,
> Then humble servant.

LORD.

> I doe not love these distances.

> (sig.C2^r[=D2^r])

Julietta's faith in the protecting system of decorum is thus rendered useless by the lord who does not recognize the constraints of that system. He is another tyrannizing courtier, expecting absolute deference from all ranks beneath him (when Julietta offers her 'best obedience', he says, 'So should / All hansome women that will be good subjects' (sig.H4^v)). In a short episode after this initial seduction scene, Bonvile's page tries to rape Julietta's woman, spurred on by his master's example, Shirley implying that Bonvile's contempt for decorum causes similar disruption at all levels, and threatens the whole basis of society's order.

The plot culminates with another rebuking scene. Julietta tells Bonvile his disrespect for her dignity destroys his own dignity, and that true status is dependent on the hierarchy of virtue to which he, as much as any man, must submit:

> this addition
> Of vertue is above all shine of State,
> And will draw more admirers . . .
> Were every petty Mannor you possesse
> A Kingdome, and the bloud of many Princes
> Vnited in your veynes, with these had you
> A person that had more attraction
> Then Poesie can furnish, love withall,
> Yet I, I in such infinite distance am
> As much above you in my innocence.
>
> (sig.I1ʳ)

Julietta's defiant assertion echoes Henry Oxinden's regard for virtue above degree (p. 166 above). In her, the town criticizes the court from a standpoint of independent, disinterested judgment, while still reserving its essential duty ('Tis the first libertie / I ever tooke to speake my selfe' (sig.I1ʳ)), and desiring to see the order reformed, rather than overturned (Julietta admonishes Bonvile, 'Live my Lord to be / Your Countries honour and support' (sig.I1ʳ)). On the last page, Bonvile has his place and Julietta's respect, but it is based on his answering respect for her virtue, and, one feels, for the town's.

By contrast, Trier has been rejected as a suitable husband for her. His behaviour has travestied gentility. He has degraded her before Bonvile, and by thinking her virtue needed testing, he has shown his own baseness and lost her respect (Lord Bonvile rebukes him, 'Oh fie *Franke,* practice jealousie so soone, / Distrust the truth of her thou lov'st[?] suspect / Thy owne heart sooner' (sig.I3ᵛ)). He assents to the moral and social view of the unreformed Bonvile, allowing that 'his honour / May priviledge more sinnes' (sig.B2ᵛ). Having degraded Julietta he degrades himself before Bonvile, using the very basest compliments:

TRIER.

> If [you] knew Lady, what
> Perfection of honour dwels in him,
> You would be studious with all ceremony
> To entertaine him! beside, to me
> His Lordship's goodnes hath so flow'd, you cannot
> Study, what will oblige more then in his welcome!

LORD.

> Come, you Complement!
>
> (sig.C1ᵛ)

Of course he compliments! Not only is he being insincere and putting place above worth, he is compromising the integrity of the town as Aretina had done, making it a place of courtship rather than of true judgment.

This association of insincerity with ungentility is related to the play's main antithesis between nature and chance. Trier belongs with the other characters who are only game-players, uncommitted to anything but fortune, and seeing courtship only as an amusement to be dabbled in. In the first scene, Carol's suitors approach courtship as a game in which one will defeat the others; the widow's suitor sees her as a business venture, a 'voyage' he makes, or a 'bond' to be cashed (sig.B1ʳ). The supreme gamester, Carol, uses games to avoid commitment. Her freeness allies her with court rather than town, for it involves a tyranny of personal will:

> Keepe him [a lover] still to be your servant,
> Imitate me . . . I
> Dispose my frownes, and favours like a Princesse
> Deject, advance, undo, create againe
> It keepes the subjects in obedience,
> And teaches em to looke at me with distance.
>
> (sig.C3ᵛ)

The play shows her learning to put aside wilfulness, relinquishing games for a serious personal relationship. The mere gamesters and complimenters are rejected and 'nature' is allowed to triumph. Carol describes flattery of a mistress or a lord as offensive to man's 'natural' dignity:

> You neglect
> Your selves, the Nobleness of your birth and nature
> By servile flattery of this jigging,
> And that coy Mistresse[.] Keepe your priviledge
> Your Masculine property.

FAIRFIELD.

> Is there
> So great a happinesse in nature!
>
> (sig.C2ʳ)

This speech recommends an idea of *natural* 'privilege', man's freedom to be his dignified self, and the term 'property' here is close to Denzil Holles's notion of 'propriety' (p. 171 above), meaning that which is *proper* to each man, his by right of possession (with all its attendant political suggestions). Similarly, in the horse-racing and betting scenes of Act IV, Bonvile attributes his success to his belief in nature, not chance ('Won, won, I knew by instinct, / The mare would put some trick upon him' (sig.G4ᵛ)). In the third plot, the return of the widow's husband comes as the restoration of a deeper, natural order:

> Welcome to life agen, I see a providence
> In this, and I obey it.
>
> (sig.K1ʳ)

This sense of nature taking over is clearest in the bird calls of the central scenes. Nature greets the winners with the nightingale, the losers with the cuckoo, endorsing those who have chosen a respectful, responsible mode of loving, and in whom outward status is matched by nobility of mind.

It is thus in the park itself that man's natural condition—'the Nobleness . . . of birth and nature' to which Carol refers—can be most fully realized. Hyde Park, a green world in urban London, is both country and town, nature and art. It is a cultivated nature, expressing the dual character (of town and country) of the gentry who frequent it and who are 'cultivating' themselves. The agents of this cultivation are 'good manners', also simultaneously artificial yet natural to those for whom courteous deportment reflects inner respectfulness. The park is both the natural environment of this gentry and a symbol of their values, for enshrined in the manners of this high society are the ideals of decorum and balance, social and moral distance, which Julietta brings to bear against Bonvile. In Hyde Park and high society, England's political character is harmonized, for here the court and the country are brought into a mutually respectful, mutually beneficial relationship.[23]

So in exploring the manners of London's developing fashionable world, Shirley's city comedies are also concerned with the moral attitudes they protect and the political adjustments they make possible; the three are inextricably mixed, and the purely social ideal of respect acts as a key to the relationships which Shirley, and the genteel audience he addresses, would see obtaining between the political entities of court and country, nobleman and gentleman. Although this reinforces the structure of the system as Shirley finds it, it leaves the gentry in the key position in that structure, for it is precisely they, with their 'country' sense of responsibility and place, who are most aware when 'place' is being exceeded and may best act as the arbiters of this hierarchy of deference. Court and country do not exist in isolation, for each term implies the other; but it is the gentry, and their developing town midway between the two, who see themselves as reconciling and balancing the various constituents of the political nation.

There is a suggestively proto-Whiggish admixture in these plays of fashionable London life which makes them ideal vehicles for expressing the outlook of a landed but discontented class. The gentry (broadly speaking) may increasingly have felt politically excluded, yet nevertheless they were well and firmly entrenched socially and in so far as they can be said to have desired revolution, it was only revolution in their favour—change taking place within careful limits, and governed by a respect for traditional and constitutional forms and principles. I have tried to show that the admiration which distinctively marks these plays for balance and 'propriety' in manners and politics arises from a feeling for the sacredness of 'property'—a concern for secure enjoyment of one's liberties, protected by customary restraints from the depradations of arbitrary and irresponsible powers.[24] But not only the landed interest was spoken for from the Caroline stage. The popular stages were still active and, apparently,

successful, and on the more fashionable theatres they exerted an important and much underestimated influence. Alongside the comedies of manners another and more plebeian, varied and eclectic tradition of drama coexisted. Inevitably, the political sentiments to which it gave voice were far more disturbing and subversive of established values and hierarchies than the comedies of elegant society could possibly be.

Notes

1. In my 'Massinger's *The City Madam* and the Caroline audience' [*Renaissance Drama*, N.S. 13 (1982), 157-87].

2. I quote from the typescript of a forthcoming essay by L. G. Salingar, '"Wit" in Jacobean comedy'.

3. Fletcher, *Works* (ed. A Glover and A. R. Waller, 10 vols, Cambridge, 1905-12), IX, p. 119. Although probably by Middleton, this play was published as Fletcher's in 1639 and found its way into the folio of 1647.

4. See the prologue published with the third (1667) edition of his *The School of Compliments*.

5. E.g. *The Lady of Pleasure,* III.ii; *The Sparagus Garden,* IV.x.

6. Wycherley, *The Complete Plays* (ed. G. Weales, New York, 1967), p. 273.

7. Etherege, *The Dramatic Works* (ed. H. F. B. Brett-Smith, 2 vols, Oxford, 1927), III.i.4.

8. Ibid, I.ii.160, IV.iv.111. Another good instance is Aphra Behn's *The Rover* (1677) which is set among exiled royalists on the continent (ed. F. M. Link (London, 1967), I.ii.66-7, II.ii.22, V.i.510-11). The fool is a country squire and supporter of parliament (I.ii.50-8, 293).

9. For example, Edward Howard's *The Change of Crowns* (1667) often brings Habington's *Queen of Aragon* to mind, but operates within much narrower limits. Here political difficulties dissolve easily away before the force of true love, and the 'change of crowns' is much less radical than the title might suggest—the exchange takes place within a restricted and firmly royal circle, and raises none of the questions about hierarchy and authority which Habington pursued (significantly, the disguised hero's real name is Carolo). Yet this play was deemed scandalously subversive in 1667, and was prevented from reaching print.

10. J. Dryden, *Of Dramatic Poesy and Other Essays* (ed. G. Watson, 2 vols, London, 1962), I, pp. 180-1, 252.

11. In *Dramatic Works,* I.i.123, IV.i.6. Compare Brome's Crosswill, deliberately stubborn yet, in 1633, still sympathetic.

12. See his speech of 1737 on the Licensing Bill: 'in King *Charles* IId's Time . . . when we were out of *Humour* with *Holland, Dryden* the Laureat wrote his Play of the *Cruelty* of the *Dutch* at *Amboyna.* When the Affair of the *Exclusion Bill* was depending, he wrote his *Duke of Guise.* When the Court took offence at the Citizens . . . the Stage was employ'd to expose them as Fools, Cheats, Usurers, and to compleat their Characters, Cuckolds. The *Cavaliers* at that Time, who were to be *flattered,* tho' the worst of Characters, were always *very worthy honest Gentlemen;* and the *Dissenters,* who were *to be abused,* were always *Scoundrels* and *quaint mischievous Fellows*' (*The Gentleman's Magazine,* 7 (1737), 410).

13. D. Underwood, *Etherege and the Seventeenth-Century Comedy of Manners* (London, 1957), pp. 138-42.

14. Gardiner, *Oxinden Letters* (London, 1933), p. 279.

15. My argument here has been anticipated by G. Bas, 'Titre, thèmes et structure dans *The Lady of Pleasure* de James Shirley', *Annales de la Faculté des Lettres et Sciences Humaines de Nice,* 34 (1978), 97-107. There is a revealing contrast with Fletcher's *The Noble Gentleman* (1625) which initiates a parallel debate between the thrift of the country and the wastefulness of the court which Fletcher simply does not (or cannot) resolve. In *The Lady of Pleasure* the Town provides Shirley with a third term midway between Court and Country in which the conflicting claims of each are harmonized into an acceptable mean.

16. [W.J.) Jones, *Politics and the Bench* [London, 1971], p. 214. See also Sir John Eliot's speech on grievances, 24 March 1628 (Forster, *Eliot,* II, p. 125).

17. A similar overwhelming speech in Massinger's *Believe as You List* (1631) actually is spoken by a courtesan (IV.ii.184-204).

18. L. Barkan, 'The Imperialist arts of Inigo Jones', *Renaissance Drama,* N.S. 7 (1976), 257-85, *passim.*

19. As well as in Massinger's *The Picture* (1629) and *The City Madam* (1632), and Brome's *The Sparagus Garden* (1635).

20. Bentley, [*The Jacobean and Caroline Stage* (Oxford, 1941-68)], V, p. 1077.

21. J. P. Kenyon, *The Stuart Constitution 1603-1688* (Cambridge, 1966), pp. 16-18; [B.H.G.] Wormald, *Clarendon* [*: Politics, History and Religion* (Cambridge, 1951], pp. 11-12, 148.

22. There are recent discussions of *Hyde Park* by R. Levin, 'The triple plot of *Hyde Park*', *Modern Language Review,* 62 (1967), 17-27; and A. Wertheim, 'Games and courtship in James Shirley's *Hyde Park*', *Anglia,* 90 (1972), 71-91.

23. The country is also brought to the city in Brome's *The Sparagus Garden* and Nabbes's *Tottenham Court.* In each there is a similar association of a (cultivated) natural setting with 'country' criticism of courtiers.

24. The collocation of propriety in manners and politics (and aesthetics) is suggestively elaborated by Clarendon: 'Whatsoever is of Civility and good Manners, all that is of Art and Beauty, or of real and solid Wealth in the World, is the . . . child of beloved Propriety; and they who would strangle this Issue, desire to demolish all Buildings, eradicate all Plantations, to make the Earth barren, and man-kind to live again in Tents, and nourish his Cattle where the grass grows' (quoted in C. Hill, *Puritanism and Revolution* (London, 1958), p. 211).

Abbreviations

Bentley, *JCS:* G. E. Bentley, *The Jacobean and Caroline Stage* (7 vols, Oxford, 1941-68)

CSPD: Calendar of State Papers, Domestic Series

CSPV: Calendar of State Papers, Venetian Series

DNB: Dictionary of National Biography

ELH: ELH; formerly *Journal of English Literary History*

HMC: Historical Manuscripts Commission, *Report*

TLS: Times Literary Supplement

Sandra A. Burner (essay date 1988)

SOURCE: Burner, Sandra A. "The Gray's Inn Circle and the Professional Dramatists." In *James Shirley: A Study of Literary Coteries and Patronage in Seventeenth-Century England,* pp. 41-84. Lanham, Md: University Press of America, 1988.

[*In the following excerpt, Burner discusses the relationship between theater and audience in the development of new plays, noting that Shirley was among a select coterie of playwrights writing for private theaters and upper-class audiences.*]

The interrelationships among the people who comprised the Gray's Inn circle are apparent through the verses written for members who published within the group— poetry, drama, essays. Within this larger circle are the friends who also made up part of another group, the

Catholic Court coterie. One of the contributors to Shirley's published plays who bridges the two circles was Robert Stapleton, who arrived in London some time after 1625 when he left the Benedictine monastery at Douay, renounced his religion, and returned to England. Much of his known dramatic activity takes place after the Restoration, but he published several translations during the Caroline years, such as *The fourth booke of Virgils Aeneis,* entered for publication by a Shirley publisher, W. Cooke, in November 1634 with commendatory verses not surprisingly by a fellow Catholic, William Habington. Stapleton wrote verses not only for Shirley but also for the Beaumont and Fletcher Folio of 1647.[1]

Like Shirley's **The Grateful Servant** when it was published in 1630, Massinger's *The Roman Actor* on its publication in 1629 contained no less than six sets of commendatory verses, including two written by their mutual friends Ford and May. Some of these supporters were connected with the theatre as actors or playwrights; others, among them Shirley's friend Robert Harvey, were with the Inns of Court. In 1630 Massinger dedicated *The Picture* "To my Honored, and selected friends of the Noble society of the Inner Temple."[2]

By 1630, then, the larger literary group known as the Gray's Inn Circle was taking clear direction, and minor figures allied themselves with established writers and prominent courtiers in that group. What developed during these years was a fairly well knit circle of friends, familiar with each other's literary work and presumably serving as critics and advocates for one another. The Gray's Inn circle worked much like a merchant guild, functioning to protect and support its members, seeking to advance their careers. Certain members, such as Habington, undoubtedly opened the way to the courtier patrons connected with the Court and the Catholic coterie for Shirley and other dramatists, including Davenant. Ford and Massinger gave Shirley access to the established writers and their patrons, becoming the means by which he entered another group, the smaller coterie of professional dramatists. Many of Shirley's acquaintances during this time were simply young men studying at the Inns of Court and developing their interests in drama and playgoing. One such person, for example, probably was Will Atkins "of Gray's Inn" who wrote the only lines commending Shirley's **The Traitor** when it was published in 1635. Atkins had been admitted to the Inn in 1631 and before that had probably lived in the parish of St. Dunstan's in the West, next to Holborn, of which the Scavenger's Rate Assessments list his name along with those of the Catholic courtier Tobie Mathew and the author Izaac Walton for the years 1628-30.[3]

Writers with associations in the Inns of Court addressed a more exclusive audience than earlier authors had known. Expensive private theatres were attracting playgoers of the well-to-do middle class, the gentry, and the nobility, while for most of the year the general London citizenry frequented the public theatres. The Cockpit Theatre, for which Shirley wrote, stood near the town houses of the gentry on Drury Lane and drew much of its audience from the upperclass ladies and gentlemen who lived nearby as well as the Inns of Court students and lawyers.[4] Gerald Eades Bentley classifies the Cockpit as a coterie theatre along with the Salisbury Court Theatre, for which Richard Brome was the principal playwright.[5] The private theatre audience might also include gamesters, military men, city wives, and country gentlemen. All had special seating within the theatre, the exact position being dependent on the ability to pay a fee of sixpence for a seat in the top gallery to half a crown for a private box. A devotee could attend the theatre several times a week and see a different play every night. Most obnoxious to both playwright and players were the courtiers who paid 2/6d. to sit on a stool on stage, doing so simply to distract the audience, call attention to their dress, and make critical comments about the play being performed. Many of the Caroline gentry and aristocracy looked for resemblances between play characters and well known Londoners, whether intended by the playwright or not, and satirical references to specific well-to-do people were frequent.[6] Increasingly, the audience came to shape the subjects and styles of the drama; because it was a self-selected group, the private theatre audience could dictate what sorts of plays were produced and, by extension, who wrote them. Associations and affiliations became ever more important to professional dramatists.

By the early 1630's many playwrights were beginning to concentrate on writing comedies centering on familiar London scenes and situations in an attempt to appeal to the tastes of this audience. In 1632 Shirley's **Hyde Park** and **The Ball** and Brome's *The Weeding of Covent Garden* were staged, to be followed by other comedies set in familiar and popular areas frequented by the wits and gentry in the audience. Trading on the earlier city comedies of Jonson, Middleton, and Marston that illustrated a city changing economically from public market place to private shop, these dramatists continued the commercial theme, using terms having to do with exchange, buying and selling, and accumulation. Some city comedies raise serious questions about new wealth. Criticism most often is expressed in the exploration of relations between sex and money.[7] The theme of the commercialization of social life indicates the dramatists' dependence on London's mixed audiences; and the increased number of prologues and addresses to the reader of published dramas points to the uncertainty playwrights felt about the reception of plays that had to please patrons as well as courtiers, merchants as well as apprentices. Even for the relatively select audience of the private theatres, dramatists wrote plays which reflect the dual character of the city, if only to appeal to the gentry in the audience. Sharp commentary on the nou-veaux riches could be taken as expressing the mind of courtiers of old family in the audience. Yet though such people could have their haughty amusement at the recent arrivals, their Court was dependent on new money. The prologue to Shirley's ***The Doubtful Heir,*** which first was staged in Ireland as ***Rosania, or Love's Victory*** and later performed in the London public theatre, the Globe,[8] makes it clear that the play was intended for the private Blackfriars stage:

> . . . No shews, no dance,
> . . . here's no target-fighting
> Upon the stage, all work for cutlers barr'd
> No bawdry, nor no ballads; . . .
> But language clean; and, what affects you not,
> Without impossibilities the plot:
> No clown, no squibs, no devil in't. . . .
>
> (IV,279)

But there were vacation periods, usually beginning in July and lasting through September, when the Inns of Court men were not around and the gentry and nobility returned to their country estates. At this time, the private theatres depended on the city merchants, tradesmen, clerks, even apprentices—the "cits." And there is evidence that in every audience there was this element. Davenant in his prologue to *The Platonic Lovers* (1635) produced at the private Blackfriars Theatre and Brome in *The Court Beggar* (1639) performed at the private Cockpit Theatre refer to the city audience.[9] References to citizens and the mercantile class in Shirley's plays and those of many of his fellow dramatists restrict their satiric comment generally to Puritan merchants and to newly successful social climbers, separating the old, established guild citizenry from the newer group.

Dramatists liked to write for the private audience, for though it was developing a taste for lavish pageantry, it also was interested in logical plots and clever dialogue more than in the clowning and physical combat that appealed to many of the apprentices and citizens who frequented the public theatres. The witty dialogue in ***Hyde Park,*** for example, and in Shirley's other London comedies defines the taste of his audience. Dialogue that is more important than action and that depicts character is possible only with a sophisticated clientele, such as might also include playgoers trained in debate and casuistry as the Inns of Court men were. In the relative ease of his relationship with his audience, Shirley's London comedies anticipate the audience participation in analyzing a play; criticism had become a topic of polite conversation.[10]

But what serious playwrights had to say to this audience was not necessarily what it thought it was hearing. A useful division of the playgoers would be between old nobility and gentry and a composite London class made up of recent social arrivals: prosperous commercial citizens, some of them with purchased titles, along with a number of country gentlefolk trying to adjust to sophisticated urban life. A knowledgeable Carolinian, of course, could break down those categories into fine pieces. The rough dividing line is between people who were socially secure, and therefore tempted to be supercilious toward newcomers, and insecure people eager to take on the manners of the old families—an ancient and modern phenomenon particularly well marked in the elegant Court and theatre world of the seventeenth century. Attending a play critical of the gaucheries and the opportunism of the wealthy merchants or the naivete of country ladies and gentlemen, both the established set and the new were doubtless confident of being squarely of the same opinion as the playwright and enjoying his favor. Merchants and their wives basking in the friendliness of a Court that needed and sought new money could believe that they had fully arrived and were not at all like their cruder social cousins who merely thought that they had arrived; courtiers of old lineage could believe that they were sharing with the dramatist a private joke on the nouveaux in the audience.

But Shirley can be numbered among playwrights who were in fact commenting on all or much of Carolinian upper class behavior. Most obvious is the scolding of the newcomers for greed and pretension. But such a play as ***The Humorous Courtier*** or ***The Lady of Pleasure*** carries another message that should not have pleased the haughtier of the old families: that their claims and manners are not worth copying, that an honest citizen has all the nobility the human race can acquire. Moralist playwrights were also lecturing the monarchy, to which they were staunchly loyal, against its practice of selling titles and its dependence on quick money. The professional dramatists Philip Massinger, Richard Brome, and Shirley, then, wrote from somewhere just outside the current contented certainties even when their elegance and elevation of language gratified the taste that attended those certainties.[11]

The clearest indication of this ambivalence on the part of the professional playwrights toward their audience and its taste is seen in the prologues written for many plays. The prologue to Shirley's ***The Example*** (1634) complains about people who set themselves up as arbiters of taste:

> . . . the praise
> Of wit and judgment is not, now a days,
> Owing to them that write; but he that can
> Talk loud, and high, is held the witty man,
> And censures finely, rules the box, and strikes
> With his court nod consent to what he likes.
>
> . . . Nay, he that in the parish never was
> Thought fit to be o' the jury, has a place

Here, on the Bench, for sixpence; and dares sit,
And boast himself commissioner of wit:
Which though he want, he can condemn with oaths
  . . .

. . . This is a destiny to which we bow,
For all are innocent but the poets now;
Who suffer from their guilt of truth and arts, . . .
If any meet here, as some men i' the age
Who understand no sense, but from one stage,
And over partial, will entail, like land,
Upon heirs-male, all action, and command
Of voice and gesture, upon whom they love;
These, though call'd judges, may delinquents prove.

                             (III,282-83)

Shirley refers to the courtiers who sit on the stage, commenting loudly on the play, but he also seems to be referring to those who prefer only the type of performance that pleased the Court taste and, perhaps, only one particular theatre. Courtiers were becoming interested in developing the accomplishments admired in an elite society—dance, horsemanship, poetry, and drama. Encouraged by the queen, they began to write and produce their own plays. This encroachment on the craft, along with a genuine liking for the audience, moved playwrights to seek an exclusive relationship with discerning patrons. That the relationship was precarious is illustrated by the number of prologues and commendatory verses that complain about the audience and critics or defend them. Some of the complaints no doubt were part of a recognized convention. Dedications to groups of people, such as the dedication by Ford of *The Lover's Melancholy* to the "Noble Society of Gray's Inn," is one illustration of a special relationship with a large segment of an audience.[12] And in a prologue written to *The Imposture* six years later Shirley again comments on the prevailing taste—"A Prologue must have more wit than the play"—but then praises the gentlemen and reassures the ladies:

  . . . You, gentlemen, that sit
Our judges, great commissioners of wit,
  . . . for the author's sake,
I' the progress of his play, not to be such
Who'll understand too little, or too much;
But choose your way to judge.—To the ladies..
In all his poems you have been his care,
  . . . no fright
Shall strike chaste ears . . .
No innocence shall bleed in any scene . . .

                             (V,189)

Shirley's prologue to *The Duke's Mistress,* which was performed before the Court at St. James on February 22, 1636,[13] perhaps describes best the difficulty of pleasing the audience:

  So various are the palates of our age,
  That nothing is presented on the stage,
  Though ne'er so square, and apted to the laws

Of poesy, that can win full applause.
This likes a story, that a cunning plot;
This wit, that lines; here one, he knows not what.
But after all this looking several ways,
We do observe the general guests to plays
Must in opinion of two strains, that please,
Satire and wantonness; the last of these,
Though old, if in new dressing it appear,
Will move a smile from all,—but shall not here.

. . . For satire, they do know best what it means,
That dare apply; and if a poet's pen,
Aiming at general errors, note the men,
'Tis not his fault: . . .
But here we quit your fear of satire too, . . .

                             (IV,191)

Though Shirley here indirectly censures current taste for its satire and its "wantonness," he amply employs both in his plays, most notably his London comedies, **Hyde Park** and **The Lady of Pleasure.**

The plays of Shirley, Massinger, and Brome show a striking similarity in the preoccupation with the changing society and the values of various classes within it. These three professional dramatists illustrate the complexity of the larger Inns of Court circle, forming a small coterie within that circle, commenting on the interests, attitudes and manners of the Inns of Court itself, the larger London bourgeoisie, and the elite Court coterie.

Surely the dramatist who influenced Shirley most directly was Philip Massinger. Massinger had a long playwriting career, collaborating notably with Fletcher and, at Fletcher's death in 1625, becoming chief playwright for the Blackfriars Theatre. That Shirley found Massinger's acquaintance important to his own work is evident from the commendatory verses each wrote for the other. Massinger, prior to assuming the position of chief dramatist for Blackfriars, wrote a number of tragicomedies and comedies for Beeston's company at the Cockpit before and after Shirley began his long alliance with that theatre. Sometime between 1621 and 1625 *A New Way to Pay Old Debts,* perhaps Massinger's most scathing indictment of the new middle class, was produced by Beeston's players, and in 1627 they presented his *The Great Duke of Florence.*[14] The influence of the older dramatist on the younger playwright seeking to establish a working relationship with the Cockpit company is suggested by a number of similarities between them in dramatic technique and ideology.

Like Shirley, Massinger was fond of expressing his moral convictions in his plays and often weakened his plot by departing from the narrative to adapt the action to his moral theme. Massinger's moral commentary is more direct than Shirley's; he concentrated his views on politics, religion, and the relationship between the sexes. Despite his criticism of evil rulers in his plays, Massinger holds to a belief in the divine right of kings as in *The Roman Actor* and to the need of rulers to listen to frank advisers such as is depicted in *The Great Duke of Florence.* Frequent allusions to court affairs of his times always make some moral point. Some critics believe that George Villiers, the Duke of Buckingham, is the model for Fulgentio, the king's favorite in *The Maid of Honour,* and again for the admiral of the Carthaginian fleet in *The Bondman.* In *The Emperor of the East,* the playwright suggests through the character of Theodosius the prodigality of Charles I and his lack of grip. *The Picture* takes a sidelong glance at the court of Charles I; a king neglects his duties because he so dotes on his queen, and Massinger makes the point that a wife should not intrude her will or attitude on her husband's business. Massinger was concerned primarily with the changing society of London as a microcosm of the whole country. His criticism of the Court's nepotism, favoritism, and extravagance in such things as expensive masques goes with his concern about the country's unpreparedness for war and the poor treatment of former military men. He came close to equating heredity with virtue, believing the social integrity of the nobility threatened by the financial power of the wealthier tradesmen, and more than one play has this as its centering moral preoccupation.[15]

Massinger's indictment of a changing society is best expressed in *A New Way to Pay Old Debts,* probably written before 1625. The play's main character, Sir Giles Overreach, is generally agreed to be modeled on the character and career of Sir Giles Mompesson. Having received a patent from King James for the sole manufacture of gold and silver thread, Mompesson used copper instead, which resulted in laming, blindness, and death. Massinger's Overreach is struck down for betraying his obligations in a trust given him by the King and for trying to rise above his social position; he becomes the projection of the evil that will later be identified with capitalism. The character of Welborne embodies ancient right and rank; Timothy Tapwell represents the new accession of prestige without tradition.[16] The play argues that efforts to cross class barriers are dangerous and destructive of society as a whole.[17]

Lady Frugal and her daughters in *The City Madam* (1632) are additions to the argument. These women are made to look ridiculous in their attempts to act in dress and manner as the nobility; at the same time, Mr. Plenty as a representative of the nouveau riche remarks that he pays his tailor for his clothes when they are delivered, unlike men of title. But in the end title is all to Massinger; people are worthy only if they keep to their social place. In the same play he gently satirizes the

activities of fashionable ladies who want to be affiliated with the Court. Massinger contends that city women should move in their own spheres.[18]

Massinger undoubtedly influenced Shirley's more delicate treatment of the shift in social power. *The Lady of Pleasure* (1635), centering on London customs and places, illustrates Shirley's ambivalence toward country and city gentry and nobility. A wealthy couple representing the landed gentry comes to London to acquire the affectations and culture the city offers. Lord Bornwell speaks for the simple virtues of the landed gentry. It was more fashionable to cast slurs on the pastoral life as does Lady Bornwell, who represents a new monied class in its attempts to merge into the nobility of birth and breeding. Yet Shirley also comments on the sophistication of the aristocracy, superficial but hard and impenetrable to an outsider such as Lord Bornwell. He fares best in the outcome because he knows his place. Lady Bornwell, unfaithful to her marriage, is Shirley's gravest examination of the newly monied class in its quest for status and title. Shirley exhorts his audience to look not to social position but to the true nobility that comes from within. In *The Lady of Pleasure* as in other work that is most typical of him, Shirley's didacticism and correctional satire address more than one social class.[19] In *The Ball* (1632) Shirley takes a look at the pastimes of rising courtiers and their affectations. There are references to Sir Marmaduke's "patent for making vinegar" and his involvement in various citizens' projects—draining fens, operating iron mills, making buttons. The character of Bostock in the play serves as Shirley's critical and strongly partisan comment on those who claim honor through noble relatives or connections: ". . . for we inherit nothing truly / But what our actions make us worthy of" (III,63).

At times Massinger's plays, like Shirley's, were censored by Sir Henry Herbert, Master of the Revels, for making obvious dramatic allusions to Court figures and for incorporating current events into their plots. At a time when England and Spain were at peace, Massinger's *Believe as You List* (1631) was denied licensing because its plot referred to the deposing of the King of Portugal by the King of Spain. The play had to be rewritten, the setting changed to ancient Rome. King Charles read Massinger's now lost play, *The King and the Subject,* and in 1638 Herbert censored it at the King's direction since certain lines referred to the various methods the King used to raise taxes.[20]

Shirley had similar trouble. The Master of the Revels required him to revise *The Ball* and remove certain parts because "there were divers personated so naturally, both of lords and others of the Court. . . ."[21] What people at court the characters represent is mere conjecture, but Barker and Bostock perhaps were modeled on real people; so possibly was Lord Rainbow, the

"May Lord" and "bubble of Nobility" whose actions with the ladies are inconsistent with his words to Bostock on honor (III,63). Although Jack Freshwater is a stereotype, it may be that Monsieur le Frisk, the French dancing master, derives from one of Henrietta Maria's servants. Scholars have generally agreed that, although the printing of **The Ball** designates Chapman as co-author, the play is largely Shirley's creation, Chapman having been called in for revision of those offensive parts to which the Master of the Revels objected, and set to diffusing the identities of characters who were clearly parodies of court figures. If Chapman did revise and change names (Lord Loveall becomes Rainbow, Sir Lionel is changed to Marmaduke), he may have inserted the brief masque that defends the chaste activities of the balls. The revision is careful to use very few "noble" people in the altered cast but it is clear that all are of the upper class.[22]

Massinger and Shirley wished to instruct as well as entertain. But the courtly audience of the late 1620's and the 1630's, when it did not turn to mere show, was interested in the wit and humor afforded by the social pretensions of the changing middle class rather than in the effects of a strong merchant class on the economic and social future of the nation. Shirley took a middle course, commenting on the manners and morals of the various classes that made up the world of London, and perhaps more successfully than Massinger or Brome managing to establish with his theatre audience a spirit of cooperation in poking fun at those outside of its circle and coterie, allowing the audience to believe itself above and separate from the targets of the wit and humor, yet implicitly remarking on social climbing in a serious way.

Brome's plays, like Shirley's London comedies, are occupied with court abuses, political and social. They provided their fastidious and sophisticated but somewhat shallow audience with domineering women, intricate plots culminating in one big, sensational scene, and the use of names and places well known to their fashionable audiences. Brome is more critical of the Court and its indulgences than are Massinger and Shirley and has a more narrow and perhaps less philosophic view of London society.[23] More than Massinger and Shirley, he places his comedies in London, using an almost reportorial colloquial dialogue, and his plays capitalize on current events and places. Shirley's **Hyde Park** (1635), for example, offers without much critical comment an intimate glimpse of the interests and pleasures of a monied, leisure class. The debate between Fairfield and Carol is a piece of showmanship, designed to display wittily the typical pastimes of a young woman in that stratum: playing "gleek" (cards), attending plays, going to the foot races and horse races, being seen at Springgarden and the "Sparagus" (II,490). The independence that is desirable to a woman, a topic that would be of great interest to Restoration audiences,[24] Carol defines when she advises the widow Bonavent to keep her freedom: her pets, jewels, private tailor and doctor might be taken away if she remarries, and now she can talk as she likes at the table, dance, and go to bed when she pleases (II,475). The dominating woman in *A Mad Couple Well Matched* (1636), which has been described as Brome's closest anticipation of the Restoration comedy, is a subtle satire on the puritanic, strait-laced wife who is a conniving hypocrite; the friendship plot in the play can be viewed as a satire on the court's fad of the precieuse. Brome criticizes pretense, social climbing, and coterie affectation, the last in his "roaring boy" clubs, a lower-class parallel to a court coterie.[25] Both elements appear as well in Shirley. **The Humorous Courtier** (1631) is Shirley's most consistent attack on courtiers. Shirley's ridiculous courtier is a comment on the singleminded greed for power or status. Hypocrisy is played by the villain Orseolo, who affects misogyny. Greed appears in four variations through Volterre, Contarini, Comachio, and Depazzi. The theme smacks of Jonson's *Volpone*.

In 1629 Shirley's **The Wedding** was issued with a list of the cast naming parts for fourteen actors. In that same year, Massinger's *The Roman Actor* and Lodowick Carlell's *The Deserving Favourite* also published cast lists, and Ford's *Lover's Melancholy* included an actor list. Three of the four plays were presented by the King's Men at the Blackfriars Theatre; Shirley's play was acted by the Queen's Men at the Cockpit. Actor lists appeared in two more of Massinger's plays printed in 1630: *The Picture,* produced by the King's Men, and *The Renegado,* written for the Queen's Men. As Bentley points out, printing the actors' names and their roles with a play edition was a noteworthy departure from custom. He suggests that the inclusion of cast lists may have resulted from cooperation among the playwrights. That each was deeply interested in the works of his colleagues is evident from the verses that Ford, Massinger, and Shirley wrote for one another in the years 1629 and 1630.[26] The cooperation indicates a need to establish solidarity against attack. Another possibility is that the inclusion of actors' lists was a requirement imposed by the companies, who became the owners of the playwright's work.[27] In either case, professional playwrights were entering a defensive league with one another and with actors, for both were now under assault.

On the one side, the Puritans were denouncing them. The protection acting companies earned when King James I placed them under royal patronage in 1603 had raised their status. But Parliament in 1625 had been presented with *A Shorte Treatise against Stage-Playes;* Massinger's *The Roman Actor,* played in late 1626, is generally thought to be the profession's reply to this attack. Publishing cast lists was one way of legitimating the professions of dramatist and actor. Meanwhile the professional authors, in their solicitation of audiences of wealth and rank, were facing competition from amateur courtier dramatists writing at the urging of the queen. A theatre war between the two sets of authors put under siege the reputations of playwrights, theatre houses, and actors. Shirley's friends who wrote commendatory poems for the publication of *The Grateful Servant* all refer to literary attacks on the playwright. The number of verses is unusual, particularly for Shirley, whose publications seldom include any commendatory pieces.[28]

The differences between the two factions, both of which had members within the larger Gray's Inn circle, represent a growing division among playwrights and writers and their attitudes toward their craft, brought about in part by the changing tastes and interests of a Cavalier court. The private audience connected with the Court viewed attendance at plays as an opportunity to display the cultural refinement it cultivated as well as a diversion from the growing political unrest around it. While upper-class taste could find gratification in sophisticated plot and dialogue, and did so to Shirley's advantage, masque and pageantry were becoming the fashion. Courtiers began to write somewhat vapid but visually spectacular dramas that appealed to Queen Henrietta Maria. Davenant was most attuned to this taste, and his appointments of servant to the Queen and later of poet laureate confirm his ability to please.[29] Massinger's biographer T. A. Dunn writes of courtly authors, followers of Ben Jonson, who called themselves the Tribe of Ben.[30] Not all of the Tribe joined the courtier faction: Randolph was part of that group, and he allied himself with Shirley against his critics. After he suffered a stroke in 1628, Jonson was no longer the assertive influence on the drama he had been, but his followers, such as Davenant, Carew, and Suckling, carried on his critical tradition albeit with less experience and knowledge. Through their own works and their attacks on the established professional dramatists' plays produced at the leading private theatres, they attempted to make the drama conform to the fashionable masque-like presentations admired by the Court.[31] The uneasy relations between Ben Jonson and the architect and masque designer Inigo Jones as they collaborated in a series of court masques bespeak the clash in sensibility between serious writers—for both Jonson and Jones were serious—and the courtly audience for whom they wrote, responsive to the graceful word or movement rather than to genuine feeling or ideas.[32] The professionals disdained, even when they had to accommodate, the prettiness of Court and Cavalier taste, the contrived elevation of language, the expensive masques, the Platonic love fashion. And while partisans in both camps could look with hostility or with humorous condescension on the social climbing of new wealth, it was the professionals—more inclined to moral statement in any event—who were the more explicit in their condemnation, for the Court was drawing on new money for the dramatic presentations that offended the professional playwrights. In remarking about the professional dramatists' reaction to their audience, Clifford Leech refers to the "emotional refinement of Ford and Shirley, the compromises of Davenant, the sense of unease in Massinger, the constant impatience of Brome."[33] The rivalry among acting companies expressed these clashes in social attitudes and in concepts of craft. In the end the King's Men at Blackfriars was supreme after a brief period from 1628 to 1630 when the Cockpit and Red Bull enjoyed considerable popularity. Until 1636 when the theatres were closed once again by outbreaks of the plague and Shirley left for Ireland, the Cockpit stood second only to the Blackfriars in reputation, in part because of Shirley's productivity.[34]

Verses written by Thomas Carew for William Davenant's publication of *The Just Italian* contributed to the dispute. Carew wrote to praise Davenant's play, presented at Blackfriars in November of 1629 and printed very quickly in January 1630. It had not been well received on the stage. Shirley's *Grateful Servant,* presented in December of 1629 and printed in February of 1630, had been a resounding success. Carew's poem alludes to the Cockpit and Red Bull theatres, "where not a tong / Of th'untun'd Kennell, can a line repeat / Of serious sense: but like lips, meet like meat; Whilst the true brood of Actors, that alone / Keepe naturall vnstrayn'd Action in her throne . . ." at Blackfriars play to empty audiences.[35] It was a broadside attack on the actors, implicating playwrights and theatres as well and blaming audiences for poor judgment.

Georges Bas, in his study of Carew's verses and those written for Shirley, has noted that Thomas Craford's verses to Shirley for *The Grateful Servant* were a direct rebuttal to Carew's poem:[36]

> I doe not praise thy straines, in hope to see
> My verses read before thy Comedy;
> But for it selfe—that cunning I remit
> To the new tribe, and Mountebanks of wit
> That martyre ingenuity . . .
> And had that stage no other play, it might
> Have made the critticke blush at cock-pit flight,
> Who not discouering what pitch it flies
> His wit came down in pitty to his eyes
> And lent him a discourse of cocke and bull
> To make his other commendations full:
> But let such Momi pause, and give applause
> Among the brood of actors, in whose cause,
> As Champion he hath sweat . . .
> Let 'em vnkennell malice, yet thy praise
> Shall mount secure, hell cannot blast thy bayes.

(I,1xxx)

John Fox begins, "Present thy work unto the wiser few, / That can discern and judge; . . . be therefore boldly wise, / And scorn malicious censurers; . . . Because thou dost not swell with mighty rhymes, / Audacious metaphors; like verse, like times. / Let others bark; keep thou poetic laws, . . ." "Jo. Hall" remarks, "Who would write well for the abused stage, / When only swelling words do please the age, / And malice is thought wit? To make't appear / They judge, they misinterpret what they hear . . . Thee and thy strains I vindicate, whose pen / Wisely disdains to injure lines, or men: . . . Let purblind critics still endure this curse, / To see good plays, and ever like the worse." Referring perhaps to the Blackfriars' predominance, Charles Aleyn opens his verses, "Tush, I will not believe that judgment's light / Is fix'd but in one sphere, and that dull night / Muffles the rest; . . ." Thomas Randolph's poem begins with a stanza of grandiose verbiage, mocking the style of the critics of Shirley: "I cannot fulminate or tonitruate words, / To puzzle intellects . . ." and goes on: ". . . others with disturbed channels go, / And headlong, like Nile-cataracts, do fall / With a huge noise, and yet not heard at all. . . ." Robert Stapleton refers to flowery language and obfuscation: ". . . thy Muse . . . doth not use / To wear a mask or veil, which now a days / Is grown a fashion, . . ." Shirley's friend Habington hints that the playwright's adversaries lean on influential and prestigious supporters: "My name is free, and my rich clothes commend / No deform'd bounty of a looser friend, / Nor am I warm i' th'sunshine of great men, / By gilding their dark sins; . . ." Along with Randolph, Habington refers to the Cockpit specifically: ". . . thou'st given a name / To the English Phoenix, which by thy great flame / Will live in spite of malice to delight / Our nation, doing art and nature right. . . ." Massinger joins in the attack on the style of the opposing camp: ". . . I dare not raise / Giant hyperboles unto thy praise, / Or hope it can find credit in this age, . . . Here are no forc'd expressions, no rack'd phrase, / No Babel compositions, to amaze / The tortur'd reader, no believ'd defense / To strengthen the bold atheist's insolence, / No obscene syllable, that may compel / A blush from a chaste maid; . . ."[37]

Such a crowd of indignant defenses of Shirley undoubtedly had more to occasion it than Carew's remarks, which refer to the theatres and actors at the Cockpit and the Red Bull and their audiences' lack of taste rather than to a specific play or playwright. Bas suggests that the conflict was primarily over the contention that the King's Men were superior to the actors at the Cockpit and Red Bull.[38] Shirley's preface to *The Grateful Servant* defends the actors:

> I dare not owne their character of my selfe,
> or play, but I must ioyne with them that have
> written, to doe the Comedians iustice, among whom,
> some are held comparable with the best that are, and
> have beene in the world, and the most of them
> deseruing a name in the file of those that are eminent
> for gracefull and vnaffected action. Thus much Reader
> I thought meet to declare in this place, and if
> thou beest ingenuous, thou wilt accuse with me,

their bold seuerity, who for the offence of being modest
and not iustling others for the wall haue most
iniuriously thrust so many actors into the
Kennell—now—

Panduntur portae, I uvat ire—(II,5)

But Bas believes that the virtues of the playwrights were at issue as well. Davenant had his champions, Carew and Suckling, working as an advance guard to prepare the way for his success, while he aspired perhaps to replace Massinger at the Blackfriars. Yet his own play performed there was not liked and his earlier work, *Albovine* (1628), which he had printed in 1629, had never been performed.[39] Commendatory verses printed with *The Emperor of the East* in 1632 offer evidence that Massinger was receiving unfavorable commentary from the Blackfriars critics. Massinger's friends John Clavell, William Singleton, and Henry Parker defend him against "the gallants" in the audience who disliked the play.[40]

Shirley never developed a literary association with Davenant so far as is known. Perhaps each questioned the other's originality; Shirley was older than Davenant by about ten years, and might naturally resent rather than be complimented by a younger man eager to supplant him. The elevated verbiage that Shirley's friends attributed to his opponents is characteristic of Davenant's work.[41] His dialogue shifts from everyday conversational speech to stately and ornate hyperbole, particularly when he is attempting to depict the Platonic love cult popularized by Queen Henrietta Maria. More than most authors, Davenant aimed to please and to entertain. His *News from Plymouth* (1635) includes a conventional quarrel between masculine liberty and the female search for equality and freedom in marriage; a brief threat of tragic possibilities is soon dispelled in a lively and cheerful picture of seventeenth-century life. Whether he sincerely embraced the ideals of Platonic love (his malady, which ended in embarrassing disfigurement to his nose, announces that he did not practice them), Davenant became the leader of the fad, writing some six plays about it between 1634 and 1642.[42]

Both of Davenant's biographers describe him as a consummate opportunist. In a chapter entitled "The Search for Patrons," Arthur H. Nethercot writes: "His whole method of campaign, in fact, lay in this plan: to publicize himself; to become known to all the great people who could help him upward; to fight, to write, to carouse and discourse, to flatter and compliment, until he was accepted and welcomed in that bright world above him, which was so unlike that in which he had been reared."[43] What eventually paid off for Davenant was the support of two powerful patrons in the Court, Endymion Porter and Henry Jermyn. Alfred Harbage pictures Davenant as a young man "strongly attracted by the glamour of fashionable circles, sincerely devoted to poetry, but alert to find achievement whether as a poet, a soldier, or a courtier. Affable and vivacious, he was finding popularity in a widening circle of friends. Most of these friends were young men of his own age, better connected than he, but as yet of no more importance in the world. Unfortunately for him, they were inclined to set up as *bon vivants* as well as wits, and he shared their pleasures."[44]

Prominent among these new friends was John Suckling, who had been admitted to Gray's Inn in 1627.[45] Suckling was the supreme courtier; Harbage refers to him as "almost a symbol of the Cavalier legend."[46] He combined wealth (an inheritance he spent extravagantly), wit, a love of gambling and socializing, and a tendency toward ostentatious display tantamount to pageantry, particularly in demonstrating loyalty to his king. Best known of his exploits was his contribution to King Charles' cause in the Bishops' Wars of a troop of one hundred men, attired in white silk and mounted on splendid horses. Yet many of his contemporaries saw him as a coxcomb with little valor or virtue. And Suckling had produced slight literary work by 1630, although he was to have an elaborate production of his play, *Aglaura,* presented at Blackfriars in 1638. For the fifth act the company could choose between a tragic and a happy ending. Suckling spent several hundred pounds on costumes for the players and then gave them to the actors, a highly unusual and an extravagant gesture. This display occurred long after the appearance of the verses in **The Grateful Servant** that chronicle the controversy between cavalier critics and professional playwrights. Suckling's reputation had preceded his production by many years.[47]

Although he was not the gallant Suckling was, Davenant rode the coattails of the Sucklings and Carews and thus continued to be associated with the Court coterie. Such an association yielded him the poet laureateship in 1637. The following year, Brome in his prologue to *The Antipodes* announced:

> Opinion, which our Author cannot court,
>   . . . has, of late,
> From the old way of Playes possest a Sort
> Only to run to those, that carry state
> In Scene magnificent and language high;
> And Cloathes worth all the rest, except the Action,
> And such are only good those Leaders cry;
> And into that beleefs draw on a Faction,
> That must despise all sportive, merry Wit,
> Because some such great Play had none in it.[48]

It is clear that Davenant was angling for the control of a theatre and had for some time been interested in writing for one of the major acting companies. He wrote plays for the Blackfriars while Massinger was still principal playwright there in 1633 and 1634; Brome's

last play for that company can be dated 1632 or 1633. Davenant also was writing for the Cockpit in 1640 and 1641 when Brome returned to the Salisbury Court Theatre, although in May 1641 the Cockpit produced Brome's *Jovial Crew.*[49] The ever ambitious Davenant had adeptly used his position of poet laureate to secure permission to build a theatre, posing a direct threat to all of the established acting companies and the professional playwrights under contract with those companies. By October of 1639 Davenant had agreed to forego the privileges of his patent, probably because he saw a way to become manager of one of the established playhouses with the help of his powerful court friends. His failure to establish a new theatre could also be explained in part by probable opposition from the Lord Chamberlain, who held financial interests in the Salisbury Theatre, and from Sir Henry Herbert, Master of the Revels, who owned a share in the same theatre and presumably appealed to his kin, Philip Herbert, Lord Chamberlain to the King.[50]

In May 1640, Davenant seized upon his advantage. William Beeston, who had become manager of the Cockpit in 1638 after his father Christopher Beeston died, was in prison for having presented an unlicensed play which referred to political activities of the King regarding a journey he had made to the north. The management of the company was turned over to Davenant.[51] Now that he was in charge of a theatre, he could emphasize courtly interests and fashions on the stage, including the courtly love fad. And he could effectively control the jockeying for positions of principal playwright for one of the three major acting companies.

These events placed Brome in a difficult situation. He had been under contract as principal dramatist to the Salisbury Court Theatre but also furnished plays to the Cockpit company. Indeed, the offending play was likely Brome's *The Court Beggar,* acted at the Cockpit. It refers not only to the King's trip north but also to courtiers who contrive to secure patents or acquire monopolies or estates to be dissolved.[52] Brome was particularly antagonistic to Davenant's and Suckling's tendency to incorporate the interests of Platonic court ladies and Cavalier mannerisms into the theatre, and the play offers a sweeping blow at the courtier Davenant aspired to represent. It features a character named Court-Wit, who writes a masque for a lady of the Court and attempts as well to secure a patent to be instructor to all actors. A reference to building a theatre on barges on the Thames presumably refers to Davenant and his royal patent of March 1639, allowing him to build a theatre in Fleet Street. The location of that proposed theatre would have been painfully near both the Salisbury and the Cockpit theatres. All this, along with references to his diseased nose, confirms that Court-Wit is modeled on Davenant. Finally, a character named Sir Ferdinando appears to be a caricature of Suckling; he is depicted as a ladies' man, coward, gambler, and would-be soldier who gains unearned success at court.[53] Ten years after the first war of the theatres, Brome had scored his final coup in the intermittent and prolonged dispute between the courtiers and the professional dramatists. By 1640, when he finished *The Court Beggar,* the skirmishes had been joined by a more prevalent anti-Cavalier sentiment, a precursor to the coming Civil Wars.

Though Shirley's plays have their similarities with Brome's and with Massinger's, and all wrote primarily for private and select audiences in closed theatres, they differ in their attitudes toward the mercantile class and the aristocracy. Massinger had little tolerance for social newcomers. Brome, the pragmatist, is something of a muckraker of noble folk and merchants and dealt with political practices such as the abusive monopolies. Shirley is a critical commentator on both classes, concerned with universal values of honor and friendship, love and loyalty. He never fully dissociated himself from the mercantile class, yet he moved among the ruling classes. He satirized the merchants through his comments on city government increasingly dominated by wealthy Puritan merchants, and he ridiculed the social pretension of the wives and daughters of the merchants. His was the bias of the old established merchant guilds as they confronted the new individual tradesmen.

Shirley was able, unlike Massinger and Brome, to establish a form of drama that involved cooperation between author and audience, and the product of this cooperation anticipates the later comedy of manners. In a successful comedy of manners, there must be one group representing fashionable life and another composed of pretenders; the difficulty for Caroline playwrights, according to one critic, is that they could not count on a fixed status and makeup of either group or situation, for the society was continually changing.[54] Shirley's formal schooling and his intimate knowledge of the court gave him an advantage over both Brome and Massinger; manners and place were well established and formal at court, and pretenders could be clearly distinguished and could play their intrigues within conventions easily recognizable to them and to an audience. But this son of a draper, this curate and schoolteacher who twice married daughters of merchants and had two barber-surgeon sons, was gentler on commercial society than were his playwright colleagues. And he could be sharp with the upper classes. His comedies of manners are distinctive for the initial detachment he shows towards his characters. The impartiality of his observations makes his work in a way more pessimistic than that of either Massinger or Brome. And it is inseparable from his harshest characteristic: an appearance almost of disdainful aloofness from the concerns and interests of those who patronized him.

Notes

1. "Dido and Aeneas," *Virgilius Maro Publius.* Film 8018, Reel 1044, BM; Arber, *Stationers,* IV, 304; Williams, *Dedications,* p. 177; Bentley, *JCS,* V, 1186-87; Hugh Aveling, *Northern Catholics: The Catholic Recusants of the North Riding of Yorkshire, 1558-1700* (London, 1966), p. 251.

2. *The Plays and Poems of Philip Massinger,* ed. Philip Edwards and Colin Gibson (Oxford, 1976), I, xxi. Neither play was entered in the Stationer's Register, but *The Roman Actor* was licensed for the stage by Herbert in October 1626 and *The Picture* was licensed in June 1627. Herbert, *Dramatic Records,* pp. 31, 32. See also Bentley, *JCS,* IV, 815-16; T. A. Dunn, *Philip Massinger: The Man and the Playwright* (London, 1957), pp. 219-21.

3. Dyce, *Works,* I, lxxxii; "Scavenger's Rate Asessments 1628-1630," Parish Rate Assessments, St. Dunstan's West, Guildhall MS. 3783. According to Wood's *Fasti,* Will Atkins was created doctor of civil law in November 1642. Part II (1820), IV, col. 43; fol. 872, p. 192.

4. William A. Armstrong, "The Audience of the Elizabethan Private Theatres," *RES,* NS 10, No. 39 (1959), 234-38.

5. Bentley, *JCS,* III, 52-4; IV, 47-49, 61-62; VI, 192-93.

6. Armstrong, "The Audience of the Elizabethan Private Theatres," pp. 238-43, 245-47.

7. Herbert, *Dramatic Records,* p. 34; [Susan] Wells, "Jacobean City Comedy and the Ideology of the City," [*ELH,* 48, No. 2 (Spring 1981)] pp. 37-38, 48-50; Kathleen McLuskie, "Caroline Professionals: Brome and Shirley" in *The Revels History of Drama in English,* ed. Philip Edwards *et al.* (New York, 1981), IV (1613-1660), pp. 241-46, 252-55.

8. Bentley, *JCS,* V, 105-06; Dyce, *Works,* IV, 278-79. Quotations from Shirley's works in the text are generally from Dyce and are followed by a reference to volume and page. When later preferred editions of individual plays are used, footnotes contain the proper citations.

9. Kenneth Richards, "Theatre Audiences in Caroline and Early Restoration London: Continuity and Change," *Das Theater und Sein Publikum* (Vienna, 1977), pp. 167-70, 173, 175; see also [Andrew] Gurr, *The Shakespearean Stage* [Cambridge, 1970], p. 148.

10. Michael Neill, "'Wits most accomplished Senate': The Audience of the Caroline Private Theaters," *SEL,* 18 (1978), 342, 346, 351, 354.

11. Clifford Leech, "The Caroline Audience," *Shakespeare's Tragedies and Other Studies in Seventeenth Century Drama* (1950; rpt. London, 1961), pp. 161, 163-64, 170-73.

12. Neill, "'Wits most accomplished Senate' . . . ," pp. 342-47; Armstrong, "The Audience of the Elizabethan Private Theatres," pp. 242-43.

13. Herbert: *Dramatic Records,* pp. 37, 56.

14. Bentley argues that both dates are too late for Massinger to be writing for the Cockpit theatre. See *JCS,* IV, 781-88, 801-02. Earlier productions of these plays would place them during Shirley's years in St. Albans. Because Shirley makes no mention of Massinger in his introduction to the Beaumont and Fletcher folio, Massinger's biographer, T. A. Dunn, assumes they were not very close friends. *Massinger,* pp. 27-29.

15. Dunn, *Massinger,* pp. 147, 166-76. On Massinger's portrayal of women in his plays and his own religious beliefs, see Dunn, pp. 114-31, 176-91. See also Edwards, *Plays and Poems of Massinger,* I, xvi-xvii.

16. Edwards, *Plays and Poems of Massinger,* III, 517, n. 2; Michael Neill, "Massinger's Patriarchy: The Social Vision of *A New Way to Pay Old Debts,*" *Renaissance Drama,* 10 (1979), 187-89, 197.

17. S. Gorley Putt, "The Complacency of Philip Massinger, Gent," *English,* 30 (Summer 1981), 107.

18. Edwards, *Plays and Poems of Massinger,* IV, cf. Acts I, ii, iv; IV, iv; V, iii.

19. Richard Morton, "Deception and Social Dislocation: An Aspect of James Shirley's Drama," *Renaissance Drama,* 9 (1966), 242-44; *A Critical Edition of James Shirley's 'The Lady of Pleasure,'* ed. Marilyn J. Thorssen, Garland Series (New York, 1980), pp. 40-41, 45-47, 57-59, 63; Edgar L. Chapman, "The Comic Art of James Shirley: A Modern Evaluation of His Comedies," Diss. Brown University 1964, pp. 139-44, 148, 155-59, 162-63; Thomas Marc Parrott and Robert H. Ball, *A Short View of Elizabethan Drama* (New York, 1943), pp. 274-75; Kathleen M. Lynch, *The Social Mode of Restoration Comedy* (New York, 1926), pp. 36-40; Joe Lee Davis, *The Sons of Ben: Jonsonian Comedy in Caroline England* (Detroit, 1967), 87-90 and *passim.*

20. Herbert, *Dramatic Records,* pp. 19, 22, 33; Dunn, *Massinger,* pp. 43-44; [Gerald Eades] Bentley, *The Profession of Dramatist* [*in Shakespeare's Time* (Princeton, 1971], pp. 155, 167-68, 172-73.

21. Herbert, *Dramatic Records,* p. 19.

22. [Roberts.] Forsythe in *The Relation of Shirley's Plays to the Elizabethan Drama* [New York, 1914] (pp. 407-09) discusses the various critics and their theories. See also *The Ball,* ed. Thomas Marc Parrott in *The Plays and Poems of George Chapman: The Comedies* (London, 1914), pp. 869-87; F. G. Fleay, *A Biographical Chronicle of the English Drama, 1559-1642* (London, 1891), II, 238-39; Bentley, *JCS,* V, 1077-79; Dyce, *Works,* III, 3; Hunter, *Chorus Vatum,* V, 62; Dana McKinnon, "*The Ball* by George Chapman and James Shirley: A Critical Edition," Diss. Univ. of Illinois at Urbana 1965, Introduction, pp. ix-xl.

Shirley presumably did not know, for instance, the Earl of Newcastle at this time (the dedication of *The Traitor* in 1635 to him states that Shirley is ambitious to be known to Newcastle), but the character of Lord Bonvile in *Hyde Park* is suggestive: "Next to a woman, / He loves a running horse.—" See later references to Newcastle's interest in women and horses in *Mercurius Britannicus,* No. 13, 16 Nov.—23 Nov. 1643, p. 103, Thomason Tracts, BM E 75; *Cal. SP Ven.,* 23 (1632-36), No. 129, March 25, 1633, p. 87. See also F. S. Boas, *An Introduction to Stuart Drama* (London, 1946), pp. 356-57; Hanson T. Parlin, *A Study in Shirley's Comedies of London Life, Bulletin of the University of Texas,* No. 371 (Nov. 15, 1914), pp. 59, 62, 64.

23. R. J. Kaufman, *Richard Brome: Caroline Playwright* (New York, 1961), pp. 10-11, 13-15. See also C. E. Andrews, "Richard Brome," *Yale Studies in English,* 56 (1913), 55-64.

24. Dyce, *Works,* II, 457-541; Dale Underwood, *Etherege and the Seventeenth-Century Comedy of Manners* (New Haven, 1957), pp. 152-53; Theodore Miles, "Place Realism in a Group of Caroline Plays," *RES,* 18 (1942), 431-38.

25. Richard Jefferson, "Some Aspects of Richard Brome's Comedies of Manners: A Re-Interpretation," Diss. University of Wisconsin 1955, p. 164; Kaufman, *Richard Brome,* pp. 13-16. Kaufman asserts that Brome argues that one should not attempt to rise above his place in society (p. 15, n.20). See also Catherine Shaw, *Richard Brome,* (Boston, 1980), pp. 17, 31.

26. Bentley, *JCS,* I, 223-25, 246; III, 116, 449-50; IV, 809-10, 813-14, 816-17; V, 1165.

27. Stephen Orgel, "The Royal Theatre and the Role of King," *Patronage in the Renaissance,* ed. Guy F. Lytle and Stephen Orgel (Princeton, 1981), pp. 267, 270; Bentley, *The Profession of Dramatist,* pp. 82, 143, 264, 269-71; Gurr, *The Shakespearean Stage,* pp. 140-41.

28. Dyce, *Works,* I, lxxiii-lxxxi; Bentley, *JCS,* IV, 816; V, 115-18. Jack R. Ramsey gives the fullest and most convincing argument concerning the competition among professional playwrights. His detailed discussion shows that Shirley and Davenant carried on a ten-year rivalry, each seeking the favor of the prestigious private theatregoers and of the influential members of the Court coterie. That Davenant "won" is demonstrated by his appointment as poet laureate and his considerable success after the Restoration. See "A Critical Edition of James Shirley's *The Grateful Servant,*" Diss. University of Michigan 1971, pp. 102-30.

29. [Alfred Harbage, *Sir William Davenant: Poet Venturer* (1935; rpt. New York, 1971)], pp. 49-50, 64-65; Neill, "'Wits most accomplished Senate,'" pp. 344-47 and *passim;* [Arthur H. Nethercot, *Sir William Davenant: Poet Laureate and Playwright-Manager* (New York, 1938)], pp. 149-50, 166; Bentley, *JCS,* III, 194-95, 211-12, 216-18.

30. Dunn, *Massinger,* pp. 37-40; see also Davis, *The Sons of Ben,* pp. 8, 29-30.

31. Harbage, *Cavalier Drama,* pp. 156-57.

32. Roy Strong, "A Royalist Arcadia: Charles I," *Splendor at Court: Renaissance Spectacle and the Theater of Power* (Boston, 1973), pp. 213-18; D. J. Gordon, "Poet and Architect: the Intellectual Setting of the Quarrel between Ben Jonson and Inigo Jones," *Journal of the Warburg and Courtauld Institutes,* 12 (1949), 152-55, 157-58, 160-63, 165-67, 170-71, 175-76.

33. Clifford Leech, "The Caroline Audience," *Shakespeare's Tragedies,* p. 161; see also pp. 163, 172-74.

34. Bentley, *JCS,* I, 223-26.

35. Herbert, *Dramatic Records,* p. 33; Arber, *Stationers,* IV, 190; Greg, *Bibliography,* I, #429, pp. 579-80; Nethercot, *Davenant,* pp. 80-81, 84-85; Bentley, *JCS,* I, 224-25; III, 204-05; V, 1115-18.

36. Georges Bas, "James Shirley et 'Th' Untun'd Kennell' une petite guerre des theatres vers 1630," *EA,* 16 (1963), 11-14.

37. Dyce, *Works,* I, 1xxxiii-1xxxi.

38. Bas, "James Shirley . . . guerre des theatres vers 1630," pp. 20-22.

39. Bas, "James Shirley . . . guerre des theatres vers 1630," pp. 15-21.

40. Edwards, *Plays and Poems of Massinger,* I, Introduction, pp. xl-xli; Dunn, *Massinger,* pp. 31-33.

41. Yet these works show similarities. The role of Fredeline in Davenant's *The Temple of Love* (1635) is close to that of Lord A in Shirley's *Lady*

of Pleasure (1635), and her questionable ethics compare to those of Confident Rapture in *The Example* (1634). Lady Ample in *The Wits* (1634) by Davenant brings to mind Shirley's witty women in his realistic London comedies, such as *The Witty Fair One* (1628) and *Hyde Park* (1632). And Alteza in *The Just Italian* (1629) commits an indiscretion similar to that of Lady Bornwell in *The Lady of Pleasure.* See also Charles Squier, "The Comic Spirit of Sir William Davenant: A Critical Study of His Caroline Comedies," Diss. University of Michigan 1963, pp. 26, 49-50, 65, 87-90, 111, 123n.

42. Nethercot, *Davenant,* pp. 127-29.

43. Nethercot, *Davenant,* pp. 75-76.

44. Harbage, *Davenant,* p. 43; Ramsey, "A Critical Edition of James Shirley's *The Grateful Servant,*" pp. 121-22.

45. Foster, *Register: Gray's Inn,* p. 180.

46. Harbage, *Cavalier Drama,* p. 109.

47. Harbage, pp. 109-10; Bentley, *JCS,* I, 58; V, 1198.

48. *The Dramatic Works of Richard Brome: Containing Fifteen Comedies Now First Collected in Three Volumes,* ed. John Pearson (1873; rpt. New York, 1966), III; Kaufman, *Richard Brome,* p. 151; Edmund K. Broadus, *The Laureateship* (Oxford, 1921), p. 225.

49. John Freehafer, "Brome, Suckling, and Davenant's Theater Project of 1639," *Texas Studies in Literature and Language,* 10 (Fall, 1968), 370, 380-81; Bentley, *JCS,* III, 52, 71-72.

50. Kaufman, *Richard Brome,* pp. 151-52; Bentley, *JCS,* II, 421; Freehafer, "Brome, Suckling, and Davenant's Theater Project of 1639," p. 377.

51. Kaufman, *Richard Brome,* pp. 152-53.

52. Freehafer, "Brome, Suckling, and Davenant's Theater Project of 1639," pp. 367, 370, 374.

53. Kaufman, "Suckling and Davenant Satirized by Brome," *MLR,* 55 (1960), 335-44; Bentley, *JCS,* III, 61-65. See also Act IV. i, ii of Brome's *The Court Beggar* in *The Dramatic Works of Richard Brome,* I, ed. Pearson.

54. William H. Hickerson, "The Significance of Shirley's Realistic Plays in the History of English Comedy," Diss. University of Michigan 1932, p. 22; see also Kaufman, *Richard Brome,* pp. 10-15; Underwood, *Etherege,* pp. 152-53.

List of Works Frequently Cited

Arber, *Stationers A Transcript of the Registers of the Company of Stationers of London: 1554-1640,* ed. Edward Arber, 5 vols., 1875-94; rpt. New York, 1950.

Bentley, *JCS* Gerald Eades Bentley, *The Jacobean and Caroline Stage,* 7 vols., Princeton, 1941-68. [I, II (1941); III, IV, V (1956); VI, VII (1968)]

Cal. SP Ven. Calendar of State Papers, Venetian, ed. Rawdon Brown, G. C. Bentinck, H. F. Brown, and A. B. Hinds, 35 vols., London, 1864-1935.

Dyce, *Works The Dramatic Works and Poems of James Shirley,* eds. William Gifford and Alexander Dyce, 6 vols., 1833; rpt. New York, 1966.

Foster, *Register: Gray's Inn The Register of Admissions to Gray's Inn, 1521-1889,* ed. Joseph Foster, London, 1889.

Greg, *Bibliography* W. W. Greg, *A Bibliography of the English Printed Drama to the Restoration,* Bibliographical Society, 4 vols., Oxford, 1939-59. [II (1951), Plays 1617-1689, #350-836]

Herbert, *Dramatic Records The Dramatic Records of Sir Henry Herbert,* ed. Joseph Quincy Adams, New Haven, 1917.

Howarth, "Poems" Robert G. Howarth, "An Edition of the Poems of James Shirley," Non-Collegiate Thesis, 2 vols., Oxford, 1931.

Hunter, *Chorus Vatum* Joseph Hunter, *Chorus Vatum Anglicanorum,* 6 vols., BM Addl. MS. 24487 (I, 1838); 24488 (II, 1843); 24489 (III, 1845); 24490 (IV, 1848); 24491 (V, 1851); 24492 (VI, 1854).

Wood, *Fasti* Anthony à Wood, *Fasti Oxonienses or Annals of the University of Oxford,* ed. Philip Bliss, 3rd ed., 4 vols., Part I, London, 1815; Part II, London, 1820.

Ira Clark (essay date 1992)

SOURCE: Clark, Ira. "Shirley's Social Comedy of Adaptation to Degree." In *Professional Playwrights: Massinger, Ford, Shirley, and Brome,* pp. 112-54. Lexington: University Press of Kentucky, 1992.

[*In the following excerpt, Clark portrays Shirley as socially ambitious and loyal to Charles I, absolute monarchy, and class hierarchy.*]

SHIRLEY'S REVERENCE FOR DEGREE

"*I never affected the ways of flattery: some say I have lost my preferment, by not practising that Court sin.*"[1] So claimed Shirley in 1639, finally dedicating his second play and first tragedy, **The Maid's Revenge** (1626), "*come late to the impression.*" This oft-noted asseveration was made by a poet-playwright who could make some claim to privilege (far more than Brome, perhaps more than Massinger, distinctly less than Ford), enough to display a coat of arms. One wondrous season,

1633-34, he was identified as a gentleman, a member of Gray's Inn, and "one of the Valets of the Chamber of Queen Henrietta Maria"; he championed the court's interest in drama against William Prynne's diatribe, *Histriomastix;* he enjoyed the applause of the Master of the Revels when **The Young Admiral** was licensed and that of the king when the play was presented at the regal birthday celebration; with premier architect Inigo Jones and foremost composers William Lawes and Simon Ives he was commissioned by the inns of court to produce a lavish masque, **The Triumph of Peace,** in reconciliatory praise of and diplomatic advice to the monarch; and he based **The Gamester** on a plot supplied by the laudatory Charles I. He must have been considered a likely successor to aging laureate Ben Jonson. Instead it was William Davenant who was graced with "her majesty's servant" on title pages after *The Temple of Love* (1635), who produced the regal masques and the "state poem" *Madagascar* (1638) with its complement of commendations by courtiers, who maintained close relations with amateur courtly dramatists and was appointed theater manager by the crown, who was granted an annual pension of £100 and virtual laureateship by his royal master in December of 1638, and who was knighted. So it has been surmised that Shirley, by reflecting contemporary mores and personages in such amiably satiric plays as **The Humourous Courtier** (1631) and **The Ball** (1632) and by joining the Irish theater from 1636 until he came to the King's Men in 1640, parted ways with palace corruption and refused to seek court preferment.[2] This hypothesis fits neither some important dates nor the contour of Shirley's career. His career exhibits consistent veneration of degree and of court; it appears to have been a quest for courtly approval and support unmatched by any other Caroline professional playwright.

According to sketchy accounts, Shirley was prepared to pursue contacts among the courtly gentry and nobility. Born in 1596 to a middling London family, he was educated at the Merchant Taylors' School, perhaps a while at Oxford, and at St. Catherine's Cambridge. After his brief service as the pastor and schoolmaster at St. Alban's in Hertfordshire, in 1625 he began writing about two plays per year until the closing of the theaters in 1642. Then he served the royalist cause. Afterward he printed a volume of poetry (1646) and produced an occasional commendatory poem, preface, or school interlude; mainly, however, he resumed teaching (he wrote two elementary grammars) until he died in 1666.[3]

Many worthies to whom Shirley offered dedications or who commended him remain but tentatively identifiable beyond the status of esquire, knight, baronet, captain, barrister he assigned to them. At times initials, names, or abbreviations which duplicate those of identifiable social, poetic, or dramatic associates may conceal other people. Often those identified are barely characterized by their family heritages or their offices. Even so, enough is known to establish Shirley's pattern of esteeming and seeking preferment from those who were well placed. Indeed, in his 1652 dedication of *The Sisters* (1642) to one "MOST WORTHILY HONOURED" William Paulet, Esq., he laments that "*COMPOSITIONS of this nature have heretofore been graced by the acceptance and protection of the greatest nobility, (I may say princes;) but in this age, when the scene of dramatic poetry is changed into a wilderness, it is hard to find a patron to a legitimate muse.*" "*[i]n this unequal condition of the time*" the fortunes of many of his nation's betters have sunk beneath even the fortunes of poets. Fortunate worthies were more plentiful during Shirley's rise through the later 1620s and early 1630s. His elegies addressed the relatives and friends bereft by the deaths of Lord Abergavenny's eldest son, Sir John Beaumont's son, and the Viscount Savage; his verses praised the second Earl of Essex's daughter, portrayed the ideal beauty of the Countess of Ormonde, and blessed the marriage of the Earl of Thenot's daughter.

Shirley found noble dedicatees for many plays. One notable addressee was the wealthy, influential privy councillor Francis, the Earl of Rutland, a great grandson of Sir Philip Sidney; his protection Shirley begged in 1630 for *The Grateful* (or *Faithful*) *Servant* (1629). Another was George Lord Berkley, known for his learning as well as for his noble birth; to him Shirley offered the 1637 printing of *The Young Admiral* (1633). Abraham Wright, an Anglican divine who kept a notebook on Caroline productions, astutely observed more than the fact that *The Grateful Servant* has a "plot well contrived and smooth" and verses typically "full of complement": "I beeleeue [it was] purposely so studied by him for to take ye court."[4] Whether or not *The Young Admiral* was also designed to woo the court, Wright considered it "A very good play, both for lines and plot, ye last beeing excellent," and a modish one.

Shirley's efforts to win recognition from the elite were exceptionally well received. On licensing *The Young Admiral* for production, on 3 July 1633 the Master of the Revels, Sir Henry Herbert, praised the tragicomedy "for the improvement of the quality, which hath received some brushings of late. When Mr. Sherley hath read this approbation, I know it will encourage him to pursue this beneficial and cleanly way of poetry, and when other poetts heare and see his good success, I am confident they will imitate the original for their own credit, and make such copies in this harmless way, as shall speak them masters in their art, at the first sight, to all judicious spectators." Helping to assure the play's success, Herbert arranged for its presentation as part of the birthday celebration for Charles I; both the king and the queen liked it.[5] Later that season, on 6 February 1634, Charles found *The Gamester* "the best play he

had seen for seven years." His approbation is scarcely surprising since this comedy elaborated "a plot of the king's, given [Shirley] by mee" (Sir Henry Herbert).[6] Shirley's works were also hearalded by amateur courtly poets and playwrights bonded by their pursuit of advancement. Besides earning Massinger's commendation, *The Grateful Servant* gained the praise of William Habington, the acclaimed author of the *Castara* volume and *The Queen of Aragon,* an accomplished tragedy sumptuously mounted at Whitehall; of Thomas Randolph, a son of Ben whose plays won success at his university, Cambridge, and at court; and of Robert Stapylton, a playwright later knighted for loyalty to his king. Among the many commenders of *The Wedding* (played and printed in 1629) were Habington, Ford, the "king's poet" and playwright Thomas May, and a host of lesser would-be courtiers.

The climax of Shirley's wondrous season was the lavish production of *The Triumph of Peace.* This masque was presented by all the inns of court at Whitehall Banqueting House on the Duke of York's birthday, 3 February 1634, and again on the king's command at the Merchant Taylors' Hall on 13 February.[7] Its initial presentation was virtually mandated when Charles suggested that an "outward and splendid visible testimony of a Royal Masque" would demonstrate the legal establishment's loyal "affections" despite the infamous "*Vtter-Barrester of* Lincolnes Inne" who dedicated *Histriomastix* to the "4 famous Innes of Court." William Prynne's polemic must have seemed to be directed against the offended royal couple as well as against the stage. At least the Star Chamber condemned the Puritan for defaming the queen and her ladies in waiting, who in 1632 had taken roles in Walter Montague's trendsetting *The Shepherds' Paradise.* Because of Shirley's popularity with the benchers he was a likely choice to invent the masque. And he had positioned himself well by attacking Prynne in a commendatory poem for Ford's *Love's Sacrifice* and by sarcastically dedicating *The Bird in a Cage* (1633) to the prisoner in the Tower, before the Star Chamber issued its savage sentence.

Probably because the London theaters were closed, Shirley next joined the Master of the Revels for Dublin, John Ogilby, in trying to establish an Irish stage. This post was conspicuously involved with noble patronage. The impresario and the playwright tried to place dramatic productions at the center of a court culture surrounding the Earl of Strafford and Lord Deputy of Ireland, Sir Thomas Wentworth. Shirley honored his putative elite audience with poems and offerings. In 1638, for example, he dedicated *The Royal Master* (1637) to the Earl of Kildare, the most highly esteemed lord of Ireland. A host of commenders, apparently Irish as well as English and including Ogilby, graced this play's opening pages. And Shirley's special New Year's epilogue extolled Charles, the royal master of the realm, and Charles's most powerful lord, the "*never enough Honoured*" Strafford, the patron for whom Shirley and Ogilby produced *The Royal Master*. It was Strafford whom Shirley commemorated for recovering from dysentery and gout in 1640, and it was Strafford's son whom Shirley chose for the dedication of the "Never Acted" *The Court Secret* when it was printed in 1653. Shirley courted and exhorted the Irish gentry and nobility in the prologues to eight plays by others (including Fletcher, Jonson, and Middleton) that were produced while he was there. Once again begging a larger audience of elite patrons, he vents his frustrations and proclaims his hopes in "A Prologue there to the *Irish Gent*," addressing the gentry and nobility as well as naming the play. He opens frustrated about the failure of his hope that literature civilizes:

> We know at first, what black and generall curse
> Fell on the earth; but shall this Isle be worse?
> While others are repair'd, and grow refin'd
> By Arts, shall this onely to weeds be kinde?
> Let it not prove a storie of your time,
> And told abroad to staine this promising Clime,
> That wit, and soule-enriching Poesie,
> Transported hither must like Serpents dye.

Then he renews his hope of refining the manners of the isle through the small number of nobility who appreciate his stage:

> But truce Poetic rage, and let not what
> Concernes the Countrey, fall upon a spot
> Of it, a few here met to see a Play:
> All these are innocent; the better they
> To tell this fault abroad, that there may be,
> Some repaire done to injur'd Poesie.
>   Then we may grow, and this place by your raies,
>   Cherish'd, may turne into a Grove of Bayes.

In 1640, when Shirley returned to London as Massinger's successor with the King's Men he found theaters emptier than when he had left. Potential English audiences seemed as unappreciative as the Irish he had chastised in prologues to *The Toy* or *The Generall* for having "sickly . . . Palats" apter to pay for hobby horses than "Wits sacrifice." His puns on the dread "vacation" of the theaters and his esteem for the vanishing appreciative nobility were noted by at least two patrons, particularly after the closing of the theaters. In 1635 Shirley had dedicated *The Traitor* (1631) to William Cavendish, the Earl of Newcastle, whose "*general knowledge and excellent nature, both an ornament to your blood . . . [made him] the rare and justified example to our age.*" This exemplary patron of Jonson, of Ford, and of Brome as well as of Shirley was apparently seen by these different playwrights with different eyes. For Shirley, as well perhaps as for Ford, Cavendish appeared as the nostalgic model of Elizabethan knighthood.[8] During the early 1640s Shirley served in the royal forces under the command of this "great

Preserver of the King / And your owne honour." Shirley's brief ode eulogizes Newcastle for literary creation as well as for patriotism. According to Anthony à Wood, "Our author Shirley did also much assist his generous patron William duke of Newcastle in the composure of certain plays, which the duke afterwards published."[9] Shirley's patron in the mid-1640s was young Thomas Stanley, who apparently supported a coterie of budding poet/scholars around Shirley.[10] Besides the epithalamion for Stanley's wedding in 1648, Shirley contributed an appreciative verse commendation to Stanley's edition of "elegant" poems in 1647. In 1652 he dedicated *The Brothers* (1641) to Stanley in "*memory and contemplation of good offices received . . . [and] the greatness and number [of] favours*" which obliged his service. In "On a black Ribband" Shirley took the risk of commending Stanley's flaunted loyalty to the recaptured Charles; so Stanley's favors must have included uncommon moral and political as well as financial support.[11]

Through and beyond his dramatic career Shirley sought recognition and patronage from the gentry and the nobility. He did not seek them in vain, but won an elite audience. This fact has been accentuated by frequent quotation of the prologue to his public theater production in London of a play written for the private theater in Dublin under the title *Rosania, or Loves Victory* (1638?). "*A Prologue at the* Globe *to his Comedy call'd* The Doubtfull Heire, *which should have been presented at the* Black-Friers" opens,

> Gentlemen, I am onely sent to say
> Our Author did not calculate his Play,
> For this Meridian; The Bank-side he knowes
> Is far more skilful at the ebbes and flowes
> Of Water then of Wit.

It goes on to ask this public house audience o elevate their expectations above slapstick and bawdry and to conduct themselves with the decorum of the elite, "As you were now in the *Black-Friers* pit." More pointed than comments in previous years, these lines represent a late, dark mood.

Though Shirley's audience disappointed him from time to time, it had been drawn from the privileged caste ever since his first play. Before he moved to Ireland, all but one of his plays were produced at the Cock-pit or Phoenix, a "private House in Drury Lane," by Queen Henrietta's Men. Such a production was second in prestige only to the King's Men at Blackfriars. Moreover, the single exception, *The Changes, or Love in a Maze* (1632), "was presented at the Private House in Salisbury Court, by the Company of His Majesties Revels," the third among the elite theaters. In Ireland James Shirley "Gent." tried to help create a courtly theater modeled on the elite companies in London; this goal accounts for much of his didactic approach to that audience. And on his return to London he assumed the post of playwright to the King's Men. There he designed his plays, according to their title pages, exclusively for Blackfriars.

Perhaps tinged bitter, Shirley's late assessment of the genteel, noble, even royal audience he wooed and won seems accurate. He, of all the Caroline professional playwrights, most definitively severs his plays and their privileged audience from the despised crowd who came to demand the blameworthy plays which deserved the 1642 ban: *"Though the severity of the times took away those dramatic recreations, (whose language so much glorified the English scene,) and perhaps looking at some abuses of the common theatres, which were not so happily purged from scurrility and under-wit, (the only entertainment of vulgar capacities,) they have outed the more noble and ingenious actions of the eminent stages."* The *"many lovers of this exiled poesy left, who are great masters of reason, and that dare conscientiously own this musical part of human learning, when it is presented without the stains of impudence and profanation"* include the honorable Walter Moyle, esq., to whom Shirley dedicated ***The Politician*** (1639?) in 1655. In retirement Shirley continued to seek the elite patronage he had courted from the beginning of his dramatic career, that courtship which Abraham Wright astutely discerned. And their traditional sociopolitical values he, most like Ford among the Caroline professionals, extolled in his plays.

DEGREE'S PREROGATIVES, ABUSES, AND
STANDARDS

Rendering tribute in his introduction of the 1647 Beaumont and Fletcher folio, Shirley identified his social ends with those of fellow playwrights who valued drama for teaching by pleasing. Primarily he shows a predilection for modeling behavior. First he commends the social perspicacity of any dramatist, *"there being required in him a* Soule *miraculously knowing, and conversing with all mankind, inabling him to expresse not onely the Phlegme and folly of thick-skin'd men, but the strength and maturity of the wise, the Aire and insinuations of the* Court, *the discipline and Resolution of the Soldier, the Vertues and passions of every noble condition, nay the councells and characters of the greatest Princes."*[12] Praising the dramatist for universal empathy, Shirley acknowledges a task of correction but emphasizes the task of exemplification. So he spotlights the model behavior of the elite who most deserve to be imitated: the prudent members of martial, courtly, noble, and regal circles. The renowned dramatic collaborators are monumental for all ages and supreme among all literatures because *"the Authentick witt that made Blackfriars an Academy, where the three howers spectacle, while* Beaumont *and* Fletcher *were presented, were usually of more advantage to the hopefull young Heire then a costly, dangerous forraigne Travell."*

Shirley concludes this paragraph by combining his two primary concerns—drama's pleasurable presentation of exemplary noble behavior and drama's didactic potency: *"it cannot be denied but that the young spirits of the Time, whose birth & quality made them impatient of the sowrer wayes of education, have from the attentive hearing these pieces, got ground in point of wit and carriage of the most severely-employed Students, while these Recreations were digested into Rules, and the very Pleasure did edifie. How many passable discoursing dining witts stand yet in good credit upon the bare stock of two or three of these single Scenes."* Drama provides an alluring conduct book for gentlemen and ladies. Its crucial task is to represent effectively and so teach the elite how to model their behavior on courtly values and roles.

Only Shirley among the Caroline professional playwrights claims to mentor his privileged audience by delightful examples. His prologue to the Irish ***Rosania*** promises that "Not the least rude uncivill Language shall / Approach your ear, or make one cheek look pale" (27-28), a promise of "clean wit" he reiterates before ***The Doubtfull Heire,*** the play's London title. The prologue to ***The Imposture*** (1640, printed 1653) likewise pledges that no ladies will have to "wrinckle now that fair / Smooth Alablaster of your brow, no fright / Shall strike chast eares, or dye the harmless white / Of any cheek with blushes" (24-27). In this characteristically gentle satire he abides by the promise he made before the rougher ***The Duke's Mistress*** (1636, printed 1638), to chasten general errors and to cure. Rarely did Shirley commit himself so explicitly as when he labeled ***The Example*** (1634, printed 1637), a traditional didactic drama that presents genteel social behavior; yet his prologues imply and his plays reflect just such a commitment.

Shirley's contemporary reputation indicates that his declarations reflect a career-long goal of teaching civility. When Thomas May commended ***The Wedding*** for exalted passions and harmless mirth, delight for the soul as well as the eye, he recognized Shirley's commitment to a drama that depicts courtly manners. Commending the same play, William Habington initiates a virtual refrain about the chasteness of Shirley's Muse; the innocence and devotion of his verse oppose the "Atheisticke Rimes" of the rude contingent of courtiers. In honoring ***The Grateful Servant*** John Hall sings anew about Shirley's chaste Muse on a stage and in a society abused by malicious art. Maybe the most telling, surely the most memorable, testimony is Massinger's commendation of ***The Grateful Servant.*** Protesting his own reasoned moderation, Massinger honors Shirley's clear verse and social responsibility. In the play can be found

no beleeu'd defence
To strengthen the bold atheists insolence,

No obscene sillable, that may compell
  A blush from a chast maide, but all so well
Exprest and orderd, as wise men must say
  It is a gratefull Poem, a good play.

[17-22]

Grace and goodness seem to describe Shirley's civic didacticism and his civil style.

Perhaps a commitment to present the exemplars of his elite society caused Shirley to set over half his comedies, and only his comedies, in England but generally to place his troubled tragicomedies and tragedies in Italy. For comedies can especially reflect models for gentry and nobility while they criticize the flawed and the fraud. Perhaps such a commitment helps explain why in his comedies Shirley is prone to present the social institutions of the English elite, *The School of Compliment, The Ball,* the spring races at *Hyde Park.* Surely his commitment is largely responsible for the conventional sociopolitical stances he presents. Like Ford he promotes hierarchical status empowered by ascription, but he does not display the rigid idealism that typifies Ford's characteristic tragedy. Rather Shirley's plays present felicitous adaptations of strictly defined, privileged roles within a virtually unchallengeable elite hierarchy that exalts royalism, ascribed sociopolitical status, paternalism, and male dominion. His plays further exemplify social responsibilities as well as prerogatives within that structure, so that two groups fall to his censure: upstarts incapable of meeting his standard and failures unwilling to abide by it. At their most interesting his plays present elite role models that incorporate admirable variations on strict norms of noble behavior; they thereby allow adaptations in incidental matters as they ridicule the failures of adherence to polite norms.

Shirley affirmed absolute royal will as law. His military service for the king, his steadfast loyalty to the Wentworths and Stanley, and his risk of the 1646 publication of "On a black Ribband," which proclaims royalist loyalty and exhorts support of a forlorn Charles, seem incontrovertible evidence. His assumption of monarchical absolutism so pervades his plays and diction as to be unquestionable.[13] His first monarch is a Duke of Savoy whom all the exemplary society of *The Grateful Servant* strive to please. The self-sacrificing love of the title character, who disappears so his lady can marry their prince, is gauged by the rule that a prince commands all the allegiance and all the love of all his subjects. From *Love's Cruelty* (1631) to *The Court Secret* (unacted) statements reaffirm the divine right of monarchs; monarchs command fidelity because a loyalty to hierarchy appears as the only alternative to sociopolitical disarray. The principle holds despite weak and vacillating rulers, like the yielding king in the tragicomic *The Young Admiral,* or rulers misled by machiavels,

like princes in the tragedies, *The Traitor* and *The Politician,* or the tragicomedies, *The Royal Master* and *The Imposture.* Usually Shirley's corrupted monarchs get rehabilitated while their magistrates get blamed. The pattern of aberration followed by restoration is exemplified in *The Duke's Mistress.* In this tragicomedy a monarch forsakes his faithful wife to pursue an infatuation until, before its consummation, he is reconverted.[14]

While Shirley's support of the right of royal will is unimpeachable, his works can suggest a melioration of absolutism that might seem like Massinger's reforming accommodation. An instance of the questioning they invite is evident in interpretations of *The Triumph of Peace.* Charles attested to his pleasure with the masque when he made the rare command for its second performance. Yet Bulstrode Whitelocke provides a historical foundation for a different evaluation. So Orgel can judge that the masque is "diplomatically but unequivocally critical of royal policy" that elevated rex over lex, and Sharpe can decide that the entertainment is "'a successful vehicle for critical opinion'" about court practices. Their inferences follow from the masque's setting (a peace piazza), its presentation of the king's commoners in the antimasques, and its explanation of the necessity of Eunomia (Law) for Irene (Peace). Only after the union of Eunomia and Irene does Dice (Justice) join them: since "The world shall give prerogative to neither. / We cannot flourish but together" (560-61).[15] But there remains evidence for the contrary view, that the masque concludes favorably for Charles. The peace celebrated is attributed to Charles. Moreover, allusions in the antimasques promote Charles's policies of prohibiting the gentry from residing in London and of limiting their control over local affairs; the allusions also lend support to his grants of monopolies. So Lawrence Venuti can conclude, primarily from references in the antimasques, that the masque favors rex over lex and that it approves Charles's isolation and alarmist repression of political disgruntlement among some of the elite.[16]

These opposed stances of critique and approval of Charles's policies allow the opportunity to suggest mediation. So Martin Butler can deduce, mostly from the sociopolitical context of the performance, that the masque lauds Charles's reforms and finds common ground for agreement between Charles's advisers and the disaffected elite, mainly on Charles's turf.[17] Contention over *The Triumph of Peace* forms an interpretive paradigm of Shirley's political stance: he stands steadfast, foremost and finally, in favor of the prerogatives of royal will; but in between he shuffles so as to permit limited alleviation and to warn against the abuse of power. Sometimes a critic may discover in Shirley a reminder that kingship is based on upholding justice.[18] But Shirley's monarchs rarely need reminding; generally they are just by definition. Shirley's plays often reaffirm monarchical rights, along with the prerogatives of degree, when they reveal the concealed royal and noble bloodlines of characters whose behavior has confirmed rightful, i.e. inherited or ascribed, status.

The popular Caroline motif that bloodlines, like murder, will out recurs prominently through Shirley's plays. Pervasive in his later dramatic career, this theme first appears as a central motif in *The Coronation* (1635). This tragicomedy juxtaposes a machiavellian guardian's wrongful attempt to usurp an adolescent queen's power and a born prince's inalienable right to seize absolute rule despite his apparently lower station. All the characters, honoring Sophia's rights as God's representative, are preoccupied with attending to the well-being of their queen and thus of the body politic. But the discovery of the inherent regal rights of others establishes irresistible new allegiances. Since royalty will unto royalty, when Sophia chooses a noble husband she instinctively picks one of her unrecognized brothers, Demetrius. Then Seleucus's overweening rebellion is legitimized as he turns out to be the prime prince of the realm, Leonatus. He expounds to his newfound siblings,

> there were seeds
> Scattered upon my heart, that made it swell
> With thought of Empire, Princes, I see cannot
> Be totally eclipst, but wherefore stayes
> *Demetrius,* and *Sophia,* at whose names
> A gentle spirit walk'd upon my blood.
> . . . . .
> Nature has rectifi'd in me *Demetrius,*
> The wandrings of ambition.

[V.iii/537-38]

Shirley's ascription of absolute royal prerogatives to nature, here through Seleucus/Leonatus, recurs emphatically. Years before the start of his prince-and-pauper tale, *The Gentleman of Venice,* a wetnurse to the duke of Venice exchanged her son and the prince. Her Thomazo remains a lecherous, debauched rebel by nature despite his palatial nurture whereas Roberto proves regal by making the palace garden a court and by fighting nobly. The subplot confirms the importance of blood degree; it presents an impotent noble desperately trying to compel a paragon of courtiers to beget an heir for him so he can save his family line from the polluting succession of a dissolute nephew.[19] Characters from late in Shirley's career are often revealed by their deeds as either noble or peasant by birth well before their origins are corroborated by testimony: such include the regal presence of Ferdinand in *The Doubtful Heir,* the comeuppance of the vain, boorish "older sister" in *The Sisters* (1642), and the royal match of the discernible albeit concealed prince in *The Court Secret* (unperformed).

While the assumption of absolute royal prerogatives pervades his plays and the theme of bloodlines telling recurs throughout them, Shirley's plays pay special heed to the manners that identify the elite and degrade the presumptuous. Although all the Caroline professional playwrights are noteworthy for their attentiveness to manners and social codes, the degree of Shirley's preoccupation distinguishes him. Nor can such an interest be easily dismissed as an index of shallow decadence. Martin Butler has recently pressed the minority opinion advanced by such earlier scholars as Douglas Sedge and Richard Morton: significant political comments are embedded in social codes.[20] Moreover, social scientists have increasingly set forth the ways by which political and moral principles are created, enforced, and modified by social behavior. The roles played by Shirley's characters create their personalities, social types praiseworthy and blameworthy on the basis of moral and political principles that sustain and are sustained by types and society.

Shirley's plays exhibit a particular preoccupation with interactions between members of different estates, a preoccupation bracketed by a brief morality he wrote early in his dramatic career and expanded much later, perhaps after his dramatic career was over. *A Contention for Honour and Riches* was published in 1633; the augmented *Mammon and Honoria* appeared in 1658. In *A Contention* two pairs of suitors, representing estates and professions, vie for two ladies, Honour and Riches. Clod, a country gentleman whose native resources and bluff loyalty lay a foundation for the body politic, and Gettings, a citizen merchant whose business builds on that foundation, pursue Lady Riches; meanwhile a Courtier and a Soldier court Lady Honour. After self-promotions that eulogize the ideals and scoffs that satirize the failings of society's strata, Gettings wins Riches; but Ingenuity, a scholar, gains Lady Honour because she believes that he unites martial valor and courtly polish. In this interlude the betrothals seem to reconcile the strife between rival estates.

Mammon and Honoria expands *A Contention* by presenting a vision of what the commonweal might become if members of the estates played their given roles to perfection. Shirley's revisions emphasize citizen and country cowardice, isolate and banish other destructive elements in the society, and idealize the potential of the courtier, the officer, and the scholar. The didact's fantasy still grants Lady Honoria to the scholar, Alworth. But the merchant, Fulbank, surrenders Lady Mammon to Colonel Conquest. The problems Citizen Fulbank stores for the nation appear as well in his country counterpart, Maslin. The word *maslin,* a medley of grains, suggests the country gentleman's push toward strife over differences as well as his pull toward generous community. Martial braggadochio and waste are now laid to a Captain Squanderbag. Two other new characters show how a commonwealth can be damaged by self-ishness. Phantasm, Lady Mammon's gentleman usher, creates false expectations for the representative of each estate, disabuses him, then vanishes. Traverse, a lawyer, exacerbates and manages others' contentions for his own ends before he repents at having caused strife and promotes justice. In contrast, Lady Honoria praises Alamode's potential as a statesman who considers only the nation's prosperity, Conquest's promise as a guardian who defends the nation's achievements, and Alworth's achievement as a self-sacrificing if affected visionary who proclaims an ideal body politic in which each estate plays its part dutifully. Shirley's second version follows his typical resolution whereby military valor and courtly manner put upstarts in their proper places. In the comic plot of *The Doubtful Heir,* for example, a captain abuses and disciplines citizens as a courtier explains their rightful roles.

Shirley's principle—that the hierarchy's stratified roles, prerogatives, and duties deserve reverence—can be misconstrued as Massinger's accommodation. For it allows some variation, criticizes abuses, and sounds genial. But Shirley permits scant individuality within a rigid structure; characters who counter the system get marked as climbers. *The Ball* (1632) provides an instructive example, since it is cited to support claims that Shirley became critical of the Caroline court.[21] At one time this social satire identified some courtiers recognizably enough to earn Henry Herbert's censorship: "In the play of *The Ball,* written by Sherley, and acted by the Queens players, ther were divers personated so naturally, both of lords and others of the court, that I took it ill, and would have forbidden the play, but that Biston promiste many things which I found faulte withall should be left out."[22] *The Ball* roused enough interest that in *The Lady of Pleasure* Sir Thomas Bornwell can chastise his wife for so indulging in this faddish, reputedly promiscuous "subscription dance" that its playwright had to be "brib'd to a modest / Expression of your Anticke gambolls in't, / [lest] Some darkes had beene discover'd, and the deeds too" (I.i.124-26).[23]

This comedy defends the innocence of balls. It portrays a coterie who enjoy the pleasures of chaste love as celebrated in a final masque in honor of Diana with Venus. Moreover, this comedy explains away the ill repute of balls as envious slander-mongering, represented by the play's principal satirist. The aptly named Barker, masqued as a Satyr, decides to "traduce / Your Ball" when he gets rejected by Lady Honoria for thinking that she is loose-hilted instead of "loose-witted" (flirtatious). The play satirizes, in interlinked sets of fortune hunters, common stage butts adapted to the aspiring gentry who swirled round the Caroline court. One set, knights and relatives of nobility, quest after the fortune of the brilliant widow Lady Lucina; once rejected, they next seek acclaim and worldly goods, Ladies Honoria and Rosamond. The venturers: Sir Ambrose Lamount, who tries to mount any prize, Sir Marmaduke Travers, who traverses all terrain, and Colonel

Winfield, who wins the battle of the sexes. All seem kin to the last suitor, Bostock, who lives up to his name by bragging about his noble lineage, excusing his palpable cowardice as guaranteeing future generation, and dropping names. The second set, Honoria and Rosamond, compete for a pot of gold, Lord Rainbow, who supports Bostock and sponsors subscription balls. The scene is filled out by two affectations. A French dancing master, Monsieur Le Frisk, caricatures shallow, bawdy mimicry of the entourage, fashions, and demeanor imported by Queen Henrietta Maria. And an English traveler whose peregrinations are limited to his moniker, Freshwater, displays a motley of national stereotypes and mangled references to continental commonplaces. Typically, he sells his family estate to invest in capital markets, ineptly sharks exorbitant loans to the play's pretenders to privilege, then ends bankrupt at Gravesend.

The Ball ridicules the failings of social and economic climbers whose success might verify their pretensions to ascribed privilege. In a private conference with each of her suitors Lucina appears to have elected him; but she jeers when he reveals his complicity in some practice that drew contemporary complaints about marginal gentry. Her criticism is most relevant when she asks Travers about alleged projects to drain fens, construct iron mills, establish a foundry for brass buttons, or get a patent for vinegar during this "age / For men to look about them" (II.iii/28). Puzzled over how to respond, Travers follows a hunch about her "appetite" for commercial wealth and declares such ventures. Likely she has caught Travers managing business affairs a nobleman would despise; perhaps, though, she points to his decay resulting from neglect of the increasingly dominant cash commerce that a prudent nobleman would eye to improve his estate.[24] Lucina attacks Lamount for displaying his dancing legs and giving locks of his hair as love tokens, two lures when fishing for a marriage to an estate and increased status. She makes Bostock confess the spuriousness of his claim to the bloodlines he trades on. And she sneers at Winfield for campaigning for a petticoat fortune instead of waging war for maintenance.

At the same time that *The Ball* exposes social climbers, it presents an imitable privileged style. Shirley thereby admits the ease with which master impersonators could mime the manners of their betters while he disallows the legitimacy of their claims to higher rank. His critique holds true for cits, like the Barnacles who trade on the cycle of merchants aspiring to land and landholders seeking cash, and it holds for wits, like the Will Hazards who hunt rich widows and heiresses, through such plays as *The Gamester* (1633). It holds true for the greater gentry who come to town seeking entry into courtly circles, like Lady Aretina Bornwell, and it holds for the gallants who surround her in *The Lady of Pleasure* (1635). It holds for such lesser courtiers as the trio in *The Bird in a Cage* (1633) who aver that all anyone needs for success at court is wit plentiful enough to invent mischief and memory scant enough to forget debts, and for the greater councillors whom the Duchess of Mantua tests for the foolish and knavish ambition of trying to ascend to monarchy by way of her bed in *The Humorous Courtier* (1631). It holds just as truly for upwardly mobile gentlemen, like Aurelio Andreozzi, granted *The Opportunity* (1634), by a mistake, to marry into monarchy, as it does for servants, like his Pimponio who mistakes himself for a bully "natural prince." As Lucow observes, Shirley insists "that individual identity is best determined by birth and status. Individual fulfillment arises not from seizing opportunities to advance oneself beyond one's station, but from working faithfully and steadily within the limitations of one's class." Yet Lucow admits that Shirley shows how the imitation of elite styles can be effective for short periods.[25] Shirley seems aware of the problems that can be created by master mimics of privileged role models, but he keeps faith with the safeguards presumably transmitted by blood.

Shirley's awareness of such problems has led some critics to point to his dissatisfaction with individual Caroline courtiers and incidents.[26] They quote the familiar designs of the steward Jacomo in *The Grateful Servant* (1629): "Mee thinkes I talke, like a peremptorie Statesman already, I shall quickly learne to forget my selfe when I am in great office, I will oppresse the Subiect, flatter the Prince, take bribes a both sides, doe right to neyther, serue Heauen as farre as my profit will giue mee leaue, and tremble, only at the Summons of a Parliament" (II.i/25). And they describe the play's satire on sleazy, sycophantic climbers when Grimundo imitates them to cure the Duke of Savoy's wild brother. But critics are wrong to conclude from Shirley's satire of isolated instances of unworthy representatives of the caste system that he was inclined, like Massinger, to be disaffected with an absolute hierarchy based on heredity. Rather, like Ford, he supported it. His presentations are generally reassuring about the failure of threats by the ambitious machiavellian favorites who mislead or supplant princes: Lorenzo and his fidgety accomplice Depazzi in *The Traitor* (1631), Valerio in *The Duke's Mistress* (1636), Montalto in *The Royal Master* (1637), Gotharus in *The Politician* (1639?), Flaviano in *The Imposture* (1640), and Columbo's churchman brother in *The Cardinal* (1641). While the increasing incidence of such villains might indicate a growing uneasiness about heredity or alarm at the power of impersonation, Shirley's target is the perversion of posts not held by the right of bloodlines. The very failure of his villains to gain their unworthy ambitions signals the ultimate insufficiency of the subversive imitation of forms. It signals, too, Shirley's courtly stance.

Another way to rescue Shirley from absolute royalism and reverence for degree is ventured by Butler: "I shall later argue . . . that an upholding of 'place' and decorum was characteristic of 'gentry' attitudes to politics and was a very effective form of criticism when directed from those lower down in the hierarchy against those exceeding their 'place' above them (for example, in Shirley's own city comedies)." The thesis that some interrelated gentry and city families were poised as mediators between "court" and "country" is important. "But clearly," Butler acknowledges a problem, "this idea is not the same when advanced from above, in a court context, against critics from below, when it becomes merely a justification of the freedom of action of the constituted powers."[27] *The Lady of Pleasure, The Example,* and *Hyde Park* do not likely speak for mediation. These plays can, like *The Triumph of Peace,* be interpreted as critical of the court, but in the context of all of Shirley's works they seem finally to support it. Furthermore, to satirize those who abuse a system is one thing, to attack the inadequacies of a system is something altogether different. Shirley's corpus shows that, willing to allow some adaptation, he represented a hierarchy which permitted only a few eccentricities.

Much more than the tenet of a hierarchy based on degree, even more than the tenet of absolute monarchy, Shirley's tenet of patriarchy appears to form a fundamental assumption. The moderation suggested by a chastened and thus concerned father in his earliest known comedy, *Love Tricks,* and by a disastrously rigid father in his earliest known tragedy, *The Maid's Revenge,* disappears with *The Wedding* (1626-29). This comedy first presents his pattern in which patriarchs rightly employ their powers in seemingly obstructive but truly provident ways in such plays as *The Brothers* (a misnomer for the late *The Politic Father*?); such powers are also exercised by an occasional "lady mother," as in *The Constant Maid.*[28] More typically, when Shirley's fathers impede their children, the children, as in *The Witty Fair One* (1628), seek paternal blessings. Shirley honors filial piety from the gratified Gratiana of *The Wedding* to the martyred Haraldas in *The Politician.* Demands on children are often made so that interlocking authorities reinforce each other. The Duke of Mantua, for example, incarcerates princess Eugenia; thus *The Bird in a Cage* applies to her as well as to her disguised suitor. And the patriotism of the hero's father in *The Young Admiral* fosters his son's loyalty in spite of the wrongs done him by his prince. Shirley's portrayal of fathers virtually prohibits anything more than nonessential variations of his culture's patriarchal hierarchies.

Beyond that, Shirley's presentation of male superiority consistently reinforces and interlocks with his other hierarchical views. In *The Sisters* Angellina proves her nobility when her quiet manner, humility, and obedience win a prince; meanwhile her changeling sister, Paulina, reveals her commonness as her display, vanity, and social climbing earn her misalliance with a bandit. Shirley, less often and less forcefully than Massinger, criticizes the double standard, limits male prodigality, and allows women to speak up. So his presentation of traditional male dominion could be seen as melioration. But Shirley's women, more like Ford's, must acquiesce. As a wealthy widow, *The Ball*'s Lucina begins in the most independent status available to a Caroline woman. Falling for Winfield's ploy of inciting rival suitors to chastise her so he can make a chivalrous rescue, she ambushes the veteran campaigner by her condition for marriage: he must have been "honest of [his] body." Yet he, his stage society, and presumably his audience agree that no one could reasonably expect a gentleman of his breeding, parts, and profession to be so constrained. Since, then, she must pardon anything beyond his oath of freedom from infection, he cavalierly reciprocates. But his gesture is so empty that she lies transparently about a dozen dependent children; a *lady* is, of course, wealthy, landed, degreed, heirless—and chaste. His offer of equivalent sexual forgiveness is predicated on the inconceivability of her needing it. Shirley does not permit equivalent sexual activity to any lady other than the critically infamous Aretina Bornwell. And she repents mightily and is disciplined to traditional feminine virtue. "Tis a false glass," she moans while facing her mirror, "sure I am more deformed. / What have I done? My soule is miserable" (V.i. 287-88). Filled with self-loathing, she submits her higher station to her husband. For receiving a gigolo anonymously one time Lady Aretina suffers far greater remorse than Shirley's whole crowd of lecherous male prodigals who are forgiven—some scarcely repentant, few reformed.[29]

There has been conjecture that Charles and Henrietta Maria's celebrated fidelity promoted more equitable marital relations than heretofore. But Charles gave Shirley the plot for a blatantly male chauvinist play, *The Gamester*.[30] If the play is representative, Charles's and Shirley's interest in reforming social behavior is limited to curbing the double standard—after marriage—just as the prodigally lustful husband, aptly named Wilding, is tamed by his obediently faithful wife and her chaste ward, notably named Penelope. Motivated more by ego than by lust, Wilding arranges to bed Penelope and marry her off so as to conceal their liaison: he can be titillated by adultery; he can bully his obedient wife into abetting it; he can enjoy clever villainy; "mainly" he can revel in making a cuckold, "The only pleasure o' the world" "Which sweetens the rest" (III.i/225). But he is horrified to hear afterward that the night he, wanting to go on gambling, hired Hazard as his substitute at the assignation, his wife replaced Penelope. Imagining his humiliation popping out in a pair of horns, desperately covering his shame, and accusing his wife of being a whore, the cuckold maker suffers the anguish of

being cuckolded until he arranges a wedding settlement profitable for Hazard and Penelope. Then the women and Hazard convert the situation, Wilding, and the audience; they reveal that they recognized the bed trick in time to save everyone's virtue. Chastely faithful, obediently loving feminine virtue forgives the contrite transgressor so that the play reaffirms an old marriage and promises a new one. Charles and Shirley's plot remains strictly inside convention.[31] Wilding and virtue depend on women, yet he retains dominion. Early in the play he describes the lines of his power to Penelope: "my wife, I allow / Your kinswoman far off, to whom, a widow, / Your father left you, with a handsome fortune, / Which, by marriage, I have in possession, / And you too" (I.i/187). Late in the play he still controls Penelope's dowry and he presides over her marriage pact. Never mind his likely reversion or Hazard's occupation, gigolo.

In *The Example* (1634) Shirley, without royal prompting, proffered another version of his paradigm that features the conversion of a prodigal man by a chaste subordinate woman. While Shirley, as Nathan Cogan has recognized, was concerned about libertinage,[32] his solution depends on a premarital double standard and on the woman's responsibility for chastity despite enticement and duress. The rapacious Lord Fitzavarice seduces women for his "credit": "The world takes notice I have courted her, / And if I mount her not, I lose my honour" (I.i/297). Driven by ego, "honour," he lusts to "mould" each "wench" "into a wanton shape, / And quicken her to air by my own art . . . till she become / A glorified spirit, and acknowledge / She took her exaltation from me." The transformational techniques of the sexual alchemical master are scarcely mysteries: he offers a woman the honor of his station, bribes her with jewels, pledges his love to her, discounts her allegiance to a husband who is absent, accepts the blame (and the credit). Since Peregrine, the officer husband, wanders abroad to pay off his debts, Fitzavarice promises to cancel these on the sweetly lovable Bellamia's first surrender and to pay exorbitantly for each subsequent compliance. Spurned, he starts to force Bellamia until, recognizing her virtue, he converts. Or does he, realizing that force confesses failure, avoid shame? Whatever, the redeemed prodigal is granted Bellamia's younger sister, who has saved her chastity for a match that affords wealth, status, and honor (issuing in part from Fitzavarice's sexual repute). Shirley habitually retains this hierarchical gender status. Typically, the imitation of male sexual prerogatives by a Clariana leads to the tragic outcome of *Love's Cruelty* (1631). Habitually, maiden Penelopes, beginning with the heroine of *The Witty Fair One*, live up to her name by way of fabrications that save their Fowlers; and wives remain redeemingly loyal to actual philanderers (Astella to Lodwick in *The Grateful Servant*) or to would-be ones (the Duchess Euphemia to Farnese in *The Duke's*

Mistress). Often, as in these instances, wives are abetted by their husbands' supposedly loose but actually chaste prey.

Finally, though the independent wit of many of Shirley's heroines might suggest their enhanced status, that inference is delusive because women's free speech is restricted to minor adaptations of rigid role norms. The illusion of frankness by a Lucina in *The Ball* or a Violetta in *The Witty Fair One* can be seen in Shirley's most popular heroine, the heavenly, loveworthy Celestina, Lady Bellamour of *The Lady of Pleasure.* Butler argues that this rich, independent widow makes a socio-political contrast to Lady Aretina Bornwell, who is a caricature of the debasement, extravagance, and promiscuity among citified "country" gentry who imitate the corrupted pretensions, opulence, and license at court. In her assured behavior, liberal expenditures, and free talk Celestina exemplifies a "town" magnanimity proportioned from country, city, and court. She holds privileges that she inherited, but she must maintain them.[33] From this perspective she teaches two novices the "becomming fortitude" of virtuous acts and satiric wit aimed so as to "not lose my priviledge" of independence (II.ii.11, 21). But from another vantage she tutors them in every unattached woman's dependence on a marriage mart wherein birth and rich widowhood virtally supplant her personal attributes. This market Celestina plays by maintaining "thrift" in her "reward" to keep men devoted and to "preserve / Our selves in stocke" (II.ii.72-73), whereas less calculating ladies waste "prodigal" favors. By this barter economy she converts the lord of the play from two prominent love fashions: early, from an old-fashioned abstinent neoplatonic devotion to his dead lady and later from a libertine "now court Platonic way." The lord's courtship is doubly flawed. Celestina's economic exemplum confirms that the honor he would have her sacrifice is as precious to a lady and her family as a coat of arms is to him and his. And the lord's need for the gigolo "Scentlove" corroborates Littleworth's description of a debasement that depends on two ever-present attendants: a fool on a ship of fools and a pimp on a ladder descending from monarch through gentlemen. So Celestina, with shrewd wit, conforms to his "fair opinion" as he serves her. She plays another of Shirley's converting Penelopes. Moreover, she does not question but wholeheartedly trusts the court position and the vacillating lord on whom her worth now depends. *The Lady of Pleasure*'s resolution typifies Shirley's allegiance to courtly attitudes about manners and prerogatives.

Shirley's show of adaptability in political rights, in meritorious advancement, and in more independence for women and children might seem to resemble Massinger's accommodation. But Shirley, like Ford, restricts the viable options to rigid monarchical absolutism, position by blood degree, and the maintenance of traditional patriarchal status and family norms. His criticisms, which might seem to resemble Massinger's reforms, attack the debasement and abuse of traditional standards; so, like Ford's, they support a courtly value system. Shirley's works appeal, like his women, by using clever language to shape roles in slightly asymmetrical conformity to dominant social patterns. Celestina proves attractive when she one-ups Aretina's court French and puts down the gallants' sneers, when she exemplifies courtly conceits and employs "linseywoolsey" against fatuous, licentious conceits. Likewise, Shirley makes a winning appeal through a witty style that mainly displays role-constituting language, manners, and social occasions in support of the privileges, powers, and customs of the Caroline court as it apparently liked to be considered.

Notes

1. For Shirley's dedications I quote the original printed edition. Whenever a scholarly edition of a Shirley play is available I cite and quote it. When there is none I quote the original printed edition but cite the textually inadequate act.scene/page of *The Dramatic Works and Poems,* ed. William Gifford and Alexander Dyce. For poems, including prologues and epilogues to the plays, I cite and quote *The Poems,* ed. Ray Livingstone Armstrong. For dates of the plays and most bibliography I rely on Albert Wertheim's essay in Logan and Smith, *Later Jacobean and Caroline Dramatists,* 152-71.

2. See Marvin Morillo, "Shirley's 'Preferment' and the Court of Charles I."

3. Biographical data from Arthur Huntington Nason's doublecheck of Anthony à Wood's *Athenæ Oxoniensis* in *James Shirley, Dramatist: A Biographical and Critical Study,* 3-163, Albert C. Baugh's "Some New Facts about Shirley," Georges Bas's essays, particularly "Two Misrepresented Biographical Documents Concerning James Shirley," and William D. Wolf's "Some New Facts and Conclusions about James Shirley: Residences and Religion" have been comprehensively reviewed and extended in Sandra A. Burner's *James Shirley: A Study of Literary Coteries and Patronage in Seventeenth-Century England.* I am not persuaded by her presupposition of Shirley's Roman Catholic conversion and her hedged construal of what might then have happened. I agree with Bas and Wolf, who find this old hypothesis implausible, particularly since Shirley's children were baptized as Anglicans.

4. See Arthur C. Kirsch's full text of "A Caroline Commentary on the Drama," 257, as well as James G. McManaway's announcement and digest of the text in "Excerpta Quaedam per A. W. Adolescentem," 124.

5. For Wright, see Kirsch, "Caroline Commentary," 258. For Herbert I quote and cite *The Dramatic Records of Sir Henry Herbert, Master of the Revels, 1623-1673*, 19-20, 53.

6. Herbert, *Dramatic Records,* 54-55.

7. I draw information, quotations, and citations involving this masque from Stephen Orgel and Roy Strong's monumental *Inigo Jones: The Theatre of the Stuart Court* 2: 537-65.

8. For assessments in relation to Jonson see Anne Barton's *Ben Jonson, Dramatist,* 300-320 passim and David Rigg's *Ben Jonson: A Life,* 301-37 passim. For a view of Cavendish related to Brome, see my sketch of Brome's audience, below.

9. Wood, *Athenæ Oxoniensis,* 3:739. For an assessment of Shirley's possible contributions to Cavendish's *The Country Captain* see Harbage's *Cavalier Drama,* 74-77.

10. For speculation see Gerald Eades Bentley's "James Shirley and a Group of Unnoted Poems on the Wedding of Thomas Stanley"; for the poems with literary and biographical annotations, see Armstrong's edition.

11. For the text see Armstrong, 13; for R. G. Howarth's as well as Armstrong's full commentary see Armstrong, 66-67.

12. For all citations and quotations of the 1647 folio, where the text is available I use the ongoing *The Dramatic Works in the Beaumont and Fletcher Canon,* ed. Fredson Bowers. Where it is not I use *The Works of Francis Beaumont and John Fletcher,* ed. Arnold Glover and A. R. Waller. For this preface I quote the latter, 1:xi.

13. The political theme of Ben Lucow's *James Shirley* is Shirley's presentation of monarchical absolutism and a hierarchy by ascription. Note especially Lucow's argument, 18-20, and his impressive collection of Shirley's habitual political diction, 148-50.

14. For an interesting but implausible and unverifiable political placement of this play in Charles's court see Butler, *Theatre and Crisis,* 42-44.

15. See Orgel, *Illusion of Power,* 77-83 (the quotation is from 79) and Sharpe, *Criticism and Compliment,* 211-22 (the quotation is from 222). Sharpe here as elsewhere counters an undiscriminating broadside characteristic of Graham Parry's otherwise useful study of the era's noble patronage, *The Golden Age Restor'd: The Culture of the Stuart Court, 1603-42.*

16. Venuti, "The Politics of Allusion: The Gentry and Shirley's *The Triumph of Peace.*"

17. Butler, "Politics and the Masque: *The Triumph of Peace.*"

18. See Sedge, for example, on Alinda's speech in the middle of *The Doubtful Heir,* "Social and Ethical Concerns," 61-63.

19. Nason, *James Shirley,* 304-7 provides a typical example of critical moral disgust over the Cornari episodes; while Nason's maneuvers facilitate appreciation of Shirley's formal integration of plots, they deny access to Shirley's thematic parallels.

20. All Butler's work emphasizes this thesis; on Shirley see *Theatre and Crisis,* 158-59. Though he does not cite these earlier critics, he modifies and extends tendencies in Sedge's identification of passages and in Morton's "Deception and Social Dislocation: An Aspect of Shirley's Drama," a consideration of caste structure and conflict.

21. The most credible claimant is Morillo.

22. Herbert, *Dramatic Records,* 19. I follow Harbage in *Cavalier Drama,* 78, and especially Bentley in *Profession of Dramatist,* 190-91, in distributing Herbert's blame to the players as well as the playwright.

23. For *The Lady of Pleasure* I quote the critical edition by Marilyn J. Thorssen. For the circumstances of *The Ball* see Hanson T. Parlin, *A Study in Shirley's Comedies of London Life,* 59.

24. See Stone's *Crisis of the Aristocracy,* chapters six and seven, "Estate Management" and "Business."

25. Lucow, *James Shirley,* 93-94.

26. See Sedge, "Social and Ethical Concerns," 317ff. Besides Morillo's essay, see his introduction to *The Humorous Courtier,* especially 64-79.

27. Butler, *Theatre and Crisis,* 44. Butler's extended argument runs 166-80.

28. See Nason, *James Shirley,* 54-68.

29. For a listing of Shirley's prodigals, see the tabulations of Robert Stanley Forsythe in *The Relations of Shirley's Plays to the Elizabethan Drama,* 100-101. Only two ladies appear: besides Lady Aretina there is Lady Plot, an adulterous philanderer and treacherous go-between in *The Example.*

30. See Herbert, *Dramatic Records,* 54-55.

31. Although in *Criticism and Compliment* (44-47) Sharpe catalogs the rough satire in *The Gamester,* he elides my main issue: Shirley targets blatant abuses that draw attention away from some problems that were becoming evident in his traditional hierarchy; rather than defending it with Ford, testing it with Brome, or reforming it with Massinger, he assumes its righteousness.

32. See Cogan, "James Shirley's *The Example:* Some Reconsiderations," 317-31.

33. The persuasive center of Butler's discussion appears in *Theatre and Crisis,* 166-70; the concessions my argument builds on appear on 172-75, especially 174-75.

Works Cited

Barton, Anne. *Ben Jonson, Dramatist.* Cambridge: Cambridge Univ. Press, 1984.

Bas, Georges. "James Shirley et 'Th' Untun'd Kennel': Une petite guerre des théâtres vers 1630." *Etudes Anglaises* 16 (1963): 11-22.

————. "Two Misrepresented Biographical Documents Concerning James Shirley." *Review of English Studies* n.s. 27 (1976): 303-10.

Baugh, Albert C. "Some New Facts about Shirley." *Modern Language Review* 17 (1922): 228-35.

Beaumont, Francis, and John Fletcher. *The Dramatic Works in the Beaumont and Fletcher Canon.* Ed. Fredson Bowers. 6 vols. to date. Cambridge: Cambridge Univ. Press, 1966-.

————. *The Works of Francis Beaumont and John Fletcher.* Ed. Arnold Glover and A.R. Waller. 10 vols. Cambridge: Cambridge Univ. Press, 1905-12.

Bentley, Gerald Eades. "James Shirley and a Group of Unnoted Poems on the Wedding of Thomas Stanley." *Huntington Library Quarterly* 2 (1939): 219-31.

Burner, Sandra A. *James Shirley: A Study of Literary Coteries and Patronage in Seventeenth-Century England.* Lanham, Md.: Univ. Press of America, 1988.

Butler, Martin. "Politics and the Masque: *The Triumph of Peace.*" *Seventeenth Century* 2 (1987): 117-41.

————. *Theatre and Crisis, 1632-1642.* Cambridge: Cambridge Univ. Press, 1984.

Cogan, Nathan. "James Shirley's *The Example:* Some Reconsiderations." *Studies in English Literature, 1500-1900* 17 (1977): 317-31.

Forsythe, Robert Stanley. *The Relations of Shirley's Plays to the Elizabethan Drama.* New York: Columbia Univ. Press, 1914.

Harbage, Alfred. *Cavalier Drama.* New York: Modern Language Association, 1936.

Herbert, Sir Henry. *The Dramatic Records of Sir Henry Herbert, Master of the Revels, 1623-1673.* Ed. Joseph Quincy Adams. New Haven: Yale Univ. Press, 1917.

Kirsch, Arthur C. "A Caroline Commentary on the Drama." *Modern Philology* 66 (1969): 256-61.

Logan, Terence P., and Denzell S. Smith. *The Later Jacobean and Caroline Dramatists.* Lincoln: Univ. of Nebraska Press, 1978.

Lucow, Ben. *James Shirley.* Boston: Twayne, 1981.

McManaway, James G. "Excerpta Quaedam per A. W. Adolescentem." *Studies in Honor of DeWitt T. Starnes.* Ed. Thomas P. Harrison et al. Austin: Univ. of Texas, 1967. 117-29.

Morillo, Marvin. "Shirley's 'Preferment' and the Court of Charles I." *Studies in English Literature, 1500-1900* 1 (1961): 101-17.

Morton, Richard. "Deception and Social Dislocation: An Aspect of Shirley's Drama." *Renaissance Drama* 9 (1966): 227-45.

Nason, Arthur Huntington. *James Shirley, Dramatist: A Biographical and Critical Study.* University Heights, N.Y.: Nason, 1915.

Orgel, Stephen. *The Illusion of Power: Political Theatre in the English Renaissance.* Berkeley: Univ. of California Press, 1975.

————, and Roy Strong. *Inigo Jones: The Theatre of the Stuart Court.* 2 vols. London and Berkeley: Sotheby Parke Bernet and Univ. of California Press, 1973.

Parlin, Hanson T. *A Study in Shirley's Comedies of London Life.* Bulletin of the Univ. of Texas No. 371, Studies in English No. 2. Austin, 1914.

Parry, Graham. *The Golden Age Restor'd: The Culture of the Stuart Court, 1603-42.* New York: St. Martin's Press, 1981.

Riggs, David. *Ben Jonson: A Life.* Cambridge, Mass.: Harvard Univ. Press, 1989.

Sharpe, Kevin. *Criticism and Compliment: The Politics of Literature in the England of Charles I.* Cambridge: Cambridge Univ. Press, 1987.

Shirley, James. *The Dramatic Works and Poems of James Shirley.* Ed. William Gifford and Alexander Dyce. 6 vols. London: J. Murray, 1833. New York: Russell & Russell, 1966.

————. *The Humourous Courtier.* Ed. Marvin Morillo. New York: Garland, 1979.

————. *The Lady of Pleasure.* Ed. Marilyn J. Thorssen. New York: Garland, 1980.

————. *The Poems.* Ed. Ray Livingstone Armstrong. Morningside Heights, N.Y.: King's Crown Press, 1941.

Stone, Lawrence. *The Crisis of the Aristocracy, 1558-1641.* Oxford: Oxford Univ. Press, 1965.

Venuti, Lawrence. "The Politics of Allusion: The Gentry and Shirley's *The Triumph of Peace.*" *English Literary Renaissance* 16 (1986): 182-205.

Wolf, William D. "Some New Facts and Conclusions about James Shirley: Residences and Religion." *Notes and Queries* 29 (1982): 133-34.

Wood, Anthony à. *Athenæ Oxoniensis.* Ed. Philip Bliss. 4 vols. London, 1813-20.

HYDE PARK (1632)

PRODUCTION REVIEWS

Michael Billington (review date 17 April 1987)

SOURCE: Billington, Michael. "The Bright Side of the Park." *The Guardian (Manchester)* (17 April 1987): 16.

[*In the following review, Billington explores director Barry Kyle's production of* Hyde Park *at the Swan Theatre as a successful evocation of several literary periods: the Edwardian era of the Bloomsbury group, the witty Restoration, and the class-conscious Caroline age.*]

Barry Kyle's delightful production of James Shirley's **Hyde Park** at Stratford's Swan Theatre proves several things. One is that there is pleasure to be had from discovering a neglected work that is a fascinating social document rather than a blazing masterpiece. Another is that the Swan has really come of age now that a director feels free to update the action of a play by, in this case, three centuries.

Shirley's play, written in 1632, forms a missing link between the sweet melancholy of Shakespearean comedy and the sexual realism of the Restoration world. Its nominal subject is the courtship of three women by a group of sports, poseurs and rakes. But its underlying theme is the rise of a leisured, affluent class, based around the Strand and Covent Garden, who take to Hyde Park for recreation and self-discovery almost as if it were Shakespeare's Arden.

Shirley's strength is less dramatic structure than social reporting: much of the play's interest lies in its portrait of the Park not merely as a place of fashionable rendezvous but as a sports-venue where the toffs went to wager on horse-racing and foot-racing with the Irish pitted, as so often, against the English.

You could argue that by loosely updating the action to a between-the-wars world of ragtime, Attic fancy-dress parties and Fair Isle pull-overs, Mr Kyle blurs Shirley's

point. But I found no problem in seeing the play bifocally both as a Caroline comedy and as a comment on Bloomsbury on a bender. Mr Kyle's treatment also throws into sharp focus the central relationship between Fiona Shaw's Mistress Carol, an amorous sheep in Virginia Woolf's clothing, and Alex Jennings's prim suitor who, with his great-coat and loosely-knotted scarf, has the faintly fogeyish look of the young men who do architectural films on Saturday Review.

Ms Shaw's character, historically poised midway between Beatrice and Millamant, is that classic figure of English comedy: the wittily independent woman with suppressed romantic yearnings. And Ms Shaw matches her contradictions beautifully.

She uses her long body to great comic effect as she lunges through smart salons wearing a pith-helmet and clutching a stuffed monkey or taps out feminist aphorisms on her typewriter: equally, when she hurls herself on to a mossy Hyde Park bank, it is with the morose confusion of a woman unwillingly ensnared by love. She has, in fact, something of Maggie Smith's quality of being able to turn a line with asperity and display true feeling.

And Mr Jennings, as her suitor, is nicely dry and legalistic as he draws up a fake contract of separation that Congreve surely plagiarised when he wrote The Way of the World.

Shirley's sub-plot, in which a tortured lover puts his mistress on trial by offering her to a predatory aristo, also comes alive because it is given a precise economic and social context.

Mr Kyle makes the lover a painter dependent on his lordship for new commissions; and John Carlisle is excellent as his patron, a beaky seducer stalking his nervous prey (Felicity Dean) through the Park like a biggame hunter and then slowly stripping her in a drawing room before undergoing a change of heart.

What doesn't work (Shirley's fault) is the third plot in which a young woman, whose merchant-husband has been lost for seven years, decides to remarry. It is based on the staggering assumption that a woman would not recognise, after a seven-year gap, her old man.

But although there are odd thin patches, it makes for a pleasant evening because Mr Kyle has managed to reconcile the dappled sadness of Shakespearean comedy, the bargaining wit of the Restoration and a sense of modern aesthetes at play.

The production evokes several periods rather than one. Gerard Howland's set, converting a suspended chandelier into a grassy knoll, is also highly ingenious and

Jeremy Sams's music adds to the sense of diverting anachronism by suggesting that Scott Joplin worked Hyde Park in the spring.

Lois Potter (review date 1 May 1987)

SOURCE: Potter, Lois. "Caroline Courtships." *Times Literary Supplement* (1 May 1987): 464.

[*In the following review, Potter finds Shirley's* Hyde Park *banal and overly slight, despite fine performances by the actresses in the three lead female roles.*]

A play written for the spring opening of Hyde Park in 1632—comedy of manners with a dash of local colour—must have seemed an appropriate opening too for the new season at the Swan. But Shirley's play **Hyde Park** poses more problems than one might expect. It isn't very funny. Nor, though written in verse, is it poetic (Lord Bonvile's little aria, "Lady, you are welcome to the spring", on which John Carlisle lavishes his most dulcet tones, is a rare example of the "compliment" for which the author's contemporaries admired him). The dialogue is chiefly characterized by a rather colourless realism, with much of the vagueness, hesitation and banality of ordinary conversation. This makes it hard to follow. Shirley can find his way around Caroline society, but cannot tell a stranger how to get there.

The Park is only one of several settings for the intertwining courtships of several people of leisure. They watch foot and horse races, drink syllabub, and guess at their success in love (like Milton in an early sonnet) by whether they first hear the nightingale or the cuckoo. The cuckoo dominates, and a surprising number of men are left unpartnered at the end. But the women, however "wild" they claim to be, are all paired off. No one makes any real attempt to defy conventional morality. In fact, no one does anything much: apart from one unlucky competitor, the racing involves the cast only as spectators.

Though the programme is full of information about Caroline London, the only pointer it gives to the nature of Barry Kyle's production is a reference to the "Hyde Park Gate News" which Virginia Woolf edited at the age of eight. The play has been reset in arty Georgian London. Trier is a society painter; Fairfield and Carol look a bit like the young Rupert Brooke and the not-so-young Virginia Woolf. The stage is dominated at first by Trier's elegantly decorative portraits of the female characters. Then, in the final scene, when everyone brings wedding presents for Lacy and Mistress Bonavent, Lord Bonvile arrives with Van Dyck's "Charles I on Horseback". The portrait watches over the remaining action, except when Bonvile, interrupting his seduction attempt, turns it to the wall.

A joke, or a symbol of the return to chivalric values which war will soon bring? The women sometimes seem dimly aware of the coming change, but are powerless to bring it about. A suffragette approaches Mistress Bonavent and Carol in Hyde Park, presumably on her way to throw herself under a horse; one woman is disgusted, the other quizzically amused. Julietta, whose fiancé has had the bright idea of leaving her alone with Bonvile to see whether she can cope, is so frozen with horror when he starts taking her clothes off that she can only carry on moralizing, instead of dashing for the door. Her words, amazingly, are able to stop the ageing roué in his tracks. Even Felicity Dean's beautiful performance cannot explain how. Carol, who literally sums up the play—her name suggests birdsong, dance, and King Charles—is played by Fiona Shaw as a clever neurotic, badly in need of a room of her own, who takes out her frustration by tormenting her suitors. All three women eventually succumb to authority figures. Mistress Bonavent (touchingly played by Pippa Guard) unhesitatingly abandons the young man she has just married when her previous husband, a middle-aged army officer, turns up after seven years' absence. Julietta exchanges the weak-kneed Trier for the supposedly repentant Bonvile. Carol determines to marry the only man able to take a tough line with her contrariness.

Transplanting the play solves the problem of creating an atmosphere free from the associations of Jacobean and Restoration comedy. But it creates other problems. It is hard to watch a play about Bloomsbury while listening to one about Caroline London, especially when, as on the first night, the music drowns some crucial lines. Moreover, Kyle, though he uses a very full text, keeps slightly more information from the audience than Shirley did, for the sake of a more effective ending. (The programme text, incidentally, no longer indicates alterations.) More seriously, the intelligence that has obviously gone into this production is too much of a burden for the play to bear. Despite a sympathetic cast, with outstanding performances from three fine actresses, it remains an example rather than a critique of triviality. For a genuinely critical view of Caroline social and dramaturgical conventions, you have to go to Richard Brome. How about reviving *him* next year?

Edwin Wilson (review date 13 July 1987)

Wilson, Edwin. "Shirley and Shakespeare." *The Wall Street Journal* (13 July 1987): 20.

[*In the following review, Wilson admires the Swan Theatre production of* Hyde Park *for its intimate character and for its resurrection of a lost comedy of manners.*]

James Shirley, a 17th-century British dramatist whom no one except English professors ever heard of, would continue to be unknown, and certainly unproduced, were it not for the policy of the Swan Theater, the new venture of the Royal Shakespeare Company here in Stratford. The theater, one of the most attractive to open in recent memory, is dedicated to presenting not only rarely produced Shakespearean plays, but plays in "Shakespeare's context," that is, works by his contemporaries as well as those who came before and after him.

The theater itself is an accident of English weather, of which this June, the rainiest on record, was an excellent example. Spectators at the Royal Ascot Races sloshed through mud for four days and Wimbledon tennis began nearly two days late because of rain. On a typically wet English afternoon in 1982, Frederick R. Koch, an American philanthropist visiting Stratford, sought refuge from the weather in the RSC museum, where he saw a model of the Swan Theater developed by architect Michael Reardon. When he discovered that the theater had not been built due to a lack of funds, Mr. Koch quietly agreed to supply them. A 430-seat Jacobean-style playhouse, the Swan fills the gap between the large main theater and the 150-seat Other Place where small experimental productions are mounted.

Now in its second season, the theater is a resounding success. Three levels of galleries fronted by thin wooden rails encircle a large thrust stage in a space that is at once expansive and intimate. Both the ambiance and the acoustics are ideal for Elizabethan and Jacobean plays, as evidenced by the two productions I saw, one of which was James Shirley's *Hyde Park.* From 1625 until 1642, when London theaters were closed by the Puritans, Shirley wrote two plays a year as a house playwright for a series of companies. *Hyde Park,* a comedy of manners, first appeared in 1632. The plot involves three interlocking love stories. Trier (James Fleet) decides to test the love of Julietta (Felicity Dean) by turning her loose with the lecherous Lord Bonville (John Carlisle); if she withstands the latter's advances, Trier will marry her. Lacy (Richard McCabe) pursues Mistress Bonavent (Pippa Guard), whose husband disappeared seven years previously and who finally marries Lacy. Meanwhile, Julietta's brother, Fairfield (Alex Jennings), is in love with Mistress Carol (Fiona Shaw), an anti-romantic who spurns all advances from her many suitors.

At least two of the love stories end unconventionally. After Lacy has married Mistress Bonavent, her first husband turns up unexpectedly to reclaim her, and Julietta, rather than submitting to the lascivious Lord Bonville, converts him to virtue and agrees to marry him. The third couple, Fairfield and Carol, are in a line of witty layers that runs through English drama—from Beatrice and Benedick in "Much Ado About Nothing"

to characters in the plays of George Bernard Shaw. In fact, Carol is a perfect Shavian heroine: an outspoken feminist who eschews love but eventually falls hardest of all.

It's a marvelous part and it is played to perfection by Ms. Shaw, whose timing and offhand delivery, added to her charm, make her an irresistible comedienne. In Mr. Jennings she has an expert partner for her ripostes. Director Barry Kyle has kept the text intact, but has costumed the characters in clothes of the Edwardian era, a transformation that works admirably.

CRITICAL COMMENTARY

Richard Levin (essay date 1967)

SOURCE: Levin, Richard. "The Triple Plot of *Hyde Park.*" *Modern Language Review* 62 (1967): 17-27.

[*In the following essay, Levin emphasizes the importance of interpreting the action of* Hyde Park *as a unified play rather than as three disconnected plots.*]

Shirley's *Hyde Park* is one of the best known and most widely admired of that interesting group of plays, usually classified as his 'realistic comedies' or 'comedies of manners', produced in the five year period preceding his departure for Ireland; in fact, many students of the Caroline stage have ranked it second only to *The Lady of Pleasure,* which is regarded as his greatest achievement in this genre and is frequently coupled with *Hyde Park* in their discussions. Judging from these discussions, however, it would appear that their enthusiasm for the play is largely limited to the 'realism' of its 'manners'. Although few critics have gone as far as W. A. Neilson, who states flatly that 'The value of *Hide Parke* . . . is almost altogether in the minutely realistic study of fashionable life, especially of horse racing in the park',[1] most of them still centre their attention, and their praise, upon the portrayal of the amusements of the Park in the third and fourth acts.[2] But while these scenes undoubtedly provide an additional source of enjoyment for us, as they must have for the original audience, they are only meant to serve as a background to the action itself, which one would expect to be something more than an excuse for bringing runners and (in the Restoration revival) horses on to the stage. If the play has any real artistic merit, it should be possible to discover some sort of internal coherence in its over-all comic structure and, in the process, to demonstrate that the special environment of the Park is subordinated to this larger scheme of action, rather than the other way around. Moreover, since this basic structure is quite similar to that found in *The Lady of Pleasure* and the other comedies of this group, an attempt to examine *Hyde Park* in these terms should provide some insight into Shirley's general practice in this dramatic species.

Such an attempt is immediately faced with the problem that this comedy, like *The Ball, The Gamester,* and *The Lady of Pleasure,* is actually the product of three separate and very different comic plots: the first is concerned with the contest between Carol, a 'scornful lady', and her suitors, Fairfield, Venture, and Rider; the second with the consequences of Frank Trier's plan to test his intended bride, Julietta, by subjecting her to the advances of Lord Bonville; and the third with the marriage of Lacy to the supposed widow, Mistress Bonavent, and the return of her long-lost husband. These distinct actions are connected, most obviously, by means of the family ties of the chief characters of the main action, since Fairfield is the brother of Julietta, and Carol is related to, and living with, Mistress Bonavent. These relationships are used here, as they are in many other multiple-plot dramas of this period, to bring together members of the different plots at crucial points, notably in the two major ensemble scenes built around the celebration of the Lacy-Bonavent wedding (II.ii and V.ii), which serve as a kind of frame to the action proper; and they are also exploited to produce two brief moments of interaction between the first and second plots—in III.i, where Fairfield arouses Carol's jealousy by pretending to court his sister (who is not yet known to her), and in V.i, where Carol uses Julietta to arrange a meeting with her brother. But neither of these manœuvres has anything to do with Julietta's role in her own plot, nor are they, in any case, essential to the outcome (nothing results from Fairfield's trick, and Carol could easily have found another way to meet him). And the same can be said for Bonville's intervention, in IV.iii, to prevent a duel between Bonavent and Lacy. Actually, there are no meaningful causal links between plots here. Each action proceeds along its own line from beginning to end, without affecting, or being affected by, any event in the remaining two.

This does not mean, however, that our *response* to any one of these independent lines of action is not significantly affected by the others. The very fact that all three actions unfold before us in alternating scenes (and are even brought together at some critical junctures) invites us to draw certain comparisons that will inevitably condition our attitudes toward each of them and toward the drama as a whole. Moreover, this tendency to compare them is reinforced by a number of analogous relationships among the plots, relationships embedded in the original conception of the triple-plot structure and repeatedly underscored in the details of its execution. The combination of these three stories, in itself, seems to suggest an analogy, since each one is con-structed about a love-triangle involving a woman and two male rivals. (In the main plot there are three men, to be sure, but Venture and Rider really figure as a single dramatic entity; they are not differentiated in character and are treated as inseparable and interchangeable twins from their first appearance in I.i, when each discovers that Carol has given his gift to the other, to their last in V.ii, when they enter together reciting alternate lines of Venture's love letter to Carol, as if it had been their joint composition, and are both awarded the willow garlands symbolizing their failure to win her.) Furthermore, each story turns upon a complete and surprising reversal of the woman's initial position in this triangle: Carol began by emphatically rejecting all her suitors (I.ii), and ends by proposing to Fairfield; Julietta in her opening dialogue acknowledged her love for Trier (II.iii), and in her final lines indicates her readiness to accept Bonville; and Mistress Bonavent, who was first seen announcing her decision to marry Lacy (I.ii), is at the close reunited with Bonavent. Even more significant is the fact that in all three plots one of the men has, on his own initiative, entered into a compact with the woman which in effect surrenders his claim on her and thus gives her freedom of choice. In II.iv, Fairfield has Carol swear to grant him a boon, which he states as follows:

> by that oath
> I binde you, never to desire my company
> Hereafter, for no reason to affect me
>
> (Mermaid edition, p. 210)[3]

In the next scene, Trier, who had previously arranged a deliberate 'triall' of Julietta's chastity by introducing her to Bonville and urging her 'To entertain him' (II.iii; p. 201), explicitly promises not to interfere with their future meetings, after being reminded by her that

> you have
> Engag'd me to his conversation
>
> (III.i; p. 215)

And we are told by a servant of the agreement Bonavent made with his wife before he went to sea:

> at his departure he
> Engag'd her to a seven yeares expectation
> Which full expir'd this morning
>
> (II.i; pp. 196-7)

These compacts serve to precipitate the action in their respective stories, and so are further emphasized as parallel elements in the central analogy that seems to underly the triple-plot structure.

However, while these three plots share this basic situation, their treatments of it differ markedly with respect to all of the major variables involved, as though Shirley were working a series of systematic changes on his common theme. For one thing, there is an obvious contrast in the original status of the three women: at the outset Carol is completely free, Julietta is engaged, and Mistress Bonavent married. This, in turn, leads to an important difference in the nature of the peripeties that they were all seen to undergo during the course of the action. Carol's reversal goes from non-attachment to attachment, since she falls in love for the first time, and with a man she had previously scorned. Julietta's is from an old attachment to a new one; she breaks off her earlier engagement to commit herself to another man whom she had not known before. And Mistress Bonavent moves in the opposite direction by giving up her second husband to return to her first. There is a corresponding differentiation of the initial positions of the men, and of their relative responsibility for the changes brought about in those positions. The prospects of Carol's suitors seem equally hopeless at first, because of her declared aversion to love and marriage; but Fairfield, by his own cleverness, is able to surmount this and win her. Trier, on the other hand, begins with a definite advantage over Bonville, which he loses through his own mistake. And Lacy at the outset has apparently triumphed over the memory of his 'dead' rival, only to discover at the end that Bonavent actually held the advantage all along, although in this case no credit or blame attaches to either man.

This last differentiation is itself a reflexion of the contrasting roles of the three compacts in their respective actions. Although these 'engagements' all take the same form—in that they are deliberately framed to grant the woman her freedom—they do not have the same purposes or results. The agreement that Fairfield imposes upon Carol is a trick; he hopes she will break it and she does, with the outcome he anticipated, for it is by this agreement that he arouses her interest and, ultimately, wins her, as she confesses:

> In vaine I see I should dissemble w'ee,
> I must confesse y'ave caught me, had you still
> Pursued the common path, I had fled from you,
> You found the constitution of women
> In me, whose will, not reason is their law,
> Most apt to doe, what most they are forbidden,
> Impatient of curbes in their desires.
>
> (III.ii; p. 222)

The reverse is true of Trier's compact with Julietta. This was also a calculated manœuvre on his part, but he takes its terms most seriously; he wants her to keep them and she does, passing the test as he had hoped, yet the outcome is the exact opposite of his intention, for the test itself is the cause of his losing her. It has aroused her bitter resentment, as she informs him:

> Vnworthily you have suspected me,
> And cherish'd that bad humor, for which know

> You never must have hope to gaine my love,
> He that shall doubt my vertue, out of fancy,
> Merits my just suspition and disdaine.
>
> (V.ii; p. 254)

And it has, at the same time, by throwing her and Bonville together, made possible Bonville's reformation and the romance between them. The agreement that Bonavent made with his wife has a still different function. It was not a trick at all, but a completely straightforward contract, which was intended seriously by him and observed religiously by her. It also appears, at first, to be the cause of his losing her, since on the very day that it expires she marries Lacy; yet when Bonavent arrives on this same day, before the consummation of the marriage, we realize that this agreement has in fact preserved her for him and so given him his unqualified victory. However, it is clear that in this case the outcome is entirely dependent upon the coincidence of the timing, for the compact itself does not really alter any of the characters or their affections.

This difference in the roles of the three compacts results in yet another systematic variation within the basic analogy. While all three plots involve a triangular situation, each one emphasizes the relationship—always some kind of conflict—between just two of the characters; and since these conflicts, produced by the compacts, include a different pair in each case, they serve to exhaust all the possible combinations. In the main action the oath Fairfield extracts from Carol leads to an extended contest between them that becomes the central issue. But the test initiated by Trier necessarily removes him from the scene and so directs our attention to his rival and Julietta, whom it has brought together. And in the third plot, where the compact does not really involve the romantic attachments of the characters, only the two men come into collision, with Mistress Bonavent looking on as a more or less passive spectator.

This analysis would seem to be confirmed by the actual allocation of scenes to the various plots, and by the order of their arrangement, for it must be remembered that the audience does not experience these plots as separate entities already abstracted from the total context (which this analysis has done), but as they evolve in the single sequence of alternating scenes that constitutes the drama. It is evident that the principal episodes in the middle portion, or complication, of the three plots are built around the confrontations of these pairs of characters, and that the number of such confrontations corresponds to the relative importance of each action in the play as a whole. Thus the first plot is focused upon the four major clashes between Fairfield and Carol (in I.ii, II.iv, III.ii, and V.i), the second upon three episodes of this sort between Bonville and Julietta (II.iii, III.i, V.i), and the last upon the two scenes where Bonavent and Lacy are in direct conflict (II.ii and IV.iii).

The arrangement of these central episodes, and of the opening and closing sections of the comedy, demonstrates Shirley's skill in working out the analogies among the separate plots. The exposition in I.i introduces these stories in an ascending order of importance, proceeding from the third, to the second, to the first, which is given the most elaborate development. Except for Bonville's brief passage across the stage, the scene is devoted entirely to the future losers in the three triangles—Lacy, Trier, Venture, and Rider—to suggest their parallel roles; and the same technique is used in I.ii, where the emphatic contrast between Mistress Bonavent's promise to marry Lacy and Carol's disdainful rejection of Fairfield underscores the symmetrical opposition of these two women in their respective plots, and establishes the necessary bases for the reversals which in each case will follow. Act III presents the three compacts—again, in the same sequence—and thereby initiates the complications of all three plots, before sending everyone off to the Park: in II.i-ii Bonavent arrives at his wife's wedding on the day that his pact with her expired (as we learn here), and clashes with Lacy; in II.iii Trier decides to test Julietta by leaving her with Bonville; and in II.iv Fairfield and Carol formally conclude their agreement. This scene is immediately followed by the next episode of the second plot (III.i), in which Trier and Julietta make their parallel agreement, and then by the third confrontation of Fairfield and Carol (III.ii). The first scenes of Act IV mark a definite pause in this movement, just before the separate denouements, which are foreshadowed here by the notes of the nightingale and cuckoo, the convergence of the three women upon the lodge to drink a health to the men whom their 'thoughts preferre', and the horse race with its prophetic outcome. The next two scenes (IV.iii and V.i) bring each plot, in order, to its resolution: first Bonavent discloses his identity to his wife, then Bonville is 'converted' by Julietta, and, finally, Fairfield accepts Carol's proposal. After this, all that remains is to tell the other men of their bad fortune, so that the last scene (V.ii), in concentrating upon this expository function, and upon the four losers, seems to resemble the first. And the ceremonial crowning of these men with willow garlands at the close serves to draw together the three plots—this time in a descending sequence, the garlands going to Venture and Rider, then to Trier, then to Lacy—and to dramatize, in this symbolic ritual, their parallel structure.

We should also now be in a position to understand the role of the Park in this structure. No doubt one reason for introducing this locale was, quite simply, its independent interest as a kind of spectacle; in fact, it has been shown that the presentation of famous 'sights' of London and its vicinity became something of a theatrical vogue at this time, although the idea goes back at least as far as Jonson's *Barthomolew Fair*.[4] But this does not preclude the possibility that a superior

playwright could integrate the particular locale he is exploiting into his over-all artistic scheme; and I believe that Shirley has, to some extent, been able to do this. He certainly has not been as successful as Jonson, for while their excursion to Hyde Park clearly serves to develop, and to accelerate, the newly evolving relationships among the visitors, from all three plots, who come together there, the Park itself, unlike the Fair, does not directly alter their lives or their attitudes. Nor is this at all surprising, because the Park does not confront them with a radically different environment which can undermine their customary patterns of behaviour, as did Jonson's Fair and its denizens; it is, rather, an extension of their everyday genteel world, peopled with very pale and innocuous figures (a milkmaid, a jockey, a bagpiper) placed here for their amusement. It must be so, of course, if Shirley is to maintain the consistent social and ethical tone—the particular 'manners'—upon which his comedy depends. But given this limitation, he has managed to create a definite atmosphere in the Park that contributes to his dramatic effect. The characteristic activity here, as he portrays it, is the racing, and the still more prominent betting among the onlookers. He has made it the special domain of chance, the place where men gamble on an unpredictable contest, and unpredictably win or lose. But this is also, in effect, the situation of these same men in their courtships. The analogy between these two activities is enforced in a number of ways, primarily in the Park scenes but in others as well. Some of these connexions are made on the verbal level, such as the practice of calling suitors 'gamesters', and the word-play on 'sport' in IV.i (p. 226), where it is taken to mean both betting on the horses and making love. In the conversation on racing bets in III.i (p. 213), the track odds are applied to courting and the gambling terms 'venture' and 'lay' are used with a bawdy double-entendre, as are the terms of card games in III.i (p. 217) and IV.iii (p. 234.) We hear of men casting dice for a woman in I.i (p. 186), and in V.i (p. 246) of women drawing cuts for a man.[5] Trier, in describing Bonville's favourite 'recreations', says that 'next to a Woman / He loves a running horse' (I.i; p. 184); and when Rider is scornfully dismissed by Carol, he cries out,

> Fare you well gentlewoman, by this light a devill,
> Ile follow my old game of horse-rasing.

> (II.iv; p. 206)

This connexion emerges most clearly, however, in the action itself of the Park episode, which regularly alternates between the romances and the races. The progress of the three love stories is punctuated by the gambling, the cheers of the spectators, and the appearance of the runners and victorious jockey. On two occasions Bonville breaks off his pursuit of Julietta to attend to his bets; Lacy twice leaves his new bride for the same reason; and the horse race draws Venture and

Rider from Carol's side. Even the ladies interrupt their romantic talk and intrigues long enough to wager gloves and stockings on the events. The continuous juxtaposition of these two activities suggests that they are in some sense parallel, and this suggestion is considerably strengthened by the climactic horse race during the final scene in the Park, for its results are also applicable to the three plots. Venture is riding a 'disdainefull Mare' and seems to have won, only to be ignominiously thrown by her at the end, just as he is by Carol in Act I and again in Act V;[6] and the fortunes of the bettors correspond to their subsequent fates in the triangles: Bonville is the winner, while Venture, Rider, Trier, and probably Lacy[7] are all losers. Within the confines of this realm of chance, a man's luck in gambling foreshadows his luck in love.

This same conception is dramatized most effectively in the episode of the bird calls, which comes at the very centre of the two acts placed in the Park, during the significant pause in the action noted above. This, too, seems to be one of the Park's characteristic attractions, since some of the visitors are shown walking about there listening for the 'happy Augury' of the nightingale's song. Of course, the song is heard by those who will win out in the love triangles, while those doomed to failure hear the ominous notes of the cuckoo instead. And the order in which this occurs (like the order of passing out the willow garlands in V.ii) reflects the relative importance of the three plots: first the nightingale is heard by Carol and Fairfield, then by Julietta and Bonville, and last by Bonavent; but just before Bonavent appears, his wife and Lacy and Trier hear the cuckoo,[8] and so do Rider and Venture after he leaves. This charming sequence contributes to the analogical identification of the two main forms of activity, for some of the listeners apply the omen to the coming horse race, and the rest to their romances. But its principal function here is to suggest the dominance—in this little world of the Park, and, by extension, in the larger world of the drama—of a whimsical comic Fate whose irrational and irresistable operations constitute what the characters regard as their 'luck' or fortune.[9] They all enter this realm of chance, still with their original attachments, pursue their separate lines of action there (each plot has one major episode in the Park), and then return to the ordinary world, but now closer to realizing the startling reversals that were foretold and, in this special sense, determined within its confines. It is true that the Park itself does not actually produce any of these reversals, but in a subtle manner, through its crystallization of this power of Fate or luck,[10] it prepares us for them, and also indicates the general limits of our response to them.

This does not mean that these plots are pitched at the same emotional level; they are not all equally affected by the kind of external and capricious 'Fortune'

embodied in Hyde Park, and their difference in this respect reflects a contrast in their essential natures that places them at separate points along the comic scale. Indeed, this is the most important contrast of all, for while the system of symmetrical variation that has been traced here clearly demonstrates the author's ability to integrate a very complicated dramatic structure (an ability with which he is not often credited), it is evident that this purely formal scheme of relationships cannot be an end in itself. It explains, I believe, how these plots have been joined together, but not the significance of their combination, since that depends upon what is being combined. Each of these components has its own distinctive quality or tone which is developed by means of this carefully organized pattern and enters into the total effect of the play.

The Bonavent-Lacy plot is obviously the least serious of the three since, as was pointed out, it is wholly determined by chance (which may be the reason why it is the only plot to be resolved inside the Park). Bonavent's return on the day of the wedding is a sheer coincidence, and he need only reveal himself, whenever he pleases, in order to bring about a denouement that is actually imposed upon the characters—Mistress Bonavent automatically reverts to her original marital status without any hesitation, and Lacy has no choice but to acquiesce as gracefully as possible. However, the other two plots do require a radical alteration in one of the characters, and are to that extent more internalized and more serious. These alterations, in fact, are mirror images of each other: in the Fairfield-Carol action a man is reforming a woman who is too 'cruell to mankinde', while in the Bonville-Julietta plot a woman reforms a man who is too 'tender hearted' to the opposite sex; and this neat balance between them is enhanced by the juxtaposition of their two resolutions in a single scene (V.i). But it is a superficial balance which sets up a comparison in order to establish a much more basic difference, for the two reformations are not at all of the same order of experience. Carol's change of heart is the direct result of the compact that Fairfield exacted from her as part of a calculated plan to trick her into submission, which in turn leads her to react (once she realizes his purpose) with counter-manœuvres of the same sort. Their relationship, therefore, remains at the level of a sparkling battle of wits between adversaries attempting to manipulate each other by a series of external devices (his original pact and pretended courtship of his sister, her arrangement of the first meeting in the Park and subsequent use of Venture's letter); it is a kind of intellectual game that engages their feelings, to be sure, yet without raising any real moral issues. But it was shown that the equivalent trick in the second plot (Trier's test of Julietta) only brought the two main characters together and then ceased to operate. Julietta's ultimate effect on Bonville does not depend upon any deliberate scheme of hers, nor upon her cleverness, for she confronts him not in the intellectual but in the ethical realm, and it is her ingenuous and passionate adherence to her principles of 'honour', rather than any skill at intrigue, that finally wins him. As a result, the entire action is taken more seriously than the first.

This difference in emotional scale can be seen very clearly in the sequential arrangement of incidents within each plot. The four interviews between Fairfield and Carol are ordered in an oscillating pattern appropriate to their prolonged contest: in I.ii she defeats him, in II.iv he defeats her, in III.ii he seems to have won, until she discovers his trick and unexpectedly turns the tables, and then in V.i they fight each other to a draw and finally make peace. The key terms in this sequence, as might be expected, are those of tactical manœuvre against a foe—''twas a poore tricke in him', 'there is some tricke in't', 'You worke by stratagem and Ambuscado', 'I must confesse y'ave caught me', 'be a witnes of my triumph', 'But do not triumph in your conquest sir, / Be modest in your victory', 'Observe but how Ile triumph'—and it terminates, very fittingly, with Fairfield's recognition that they are 'Each others now by conquest'. The three main scenes of the second plot, however, proceed in a straight line, described by the increasing importunacy of Bonville's advances, and Julietta's very respectful attempts to parry them, up to the climactic moment when she turns upon him ('Tis the first libertie / I ever tooke to speake my selfe') and brings about his transformation; and the terms applied to this change in him are not those of conquest but of religious experience—'You may in time convert him', 'Ile bee a convertite', 'If I doe turne Carthusian, / And renounce flesh'—which he himself acknowledges in the closing speech of the play when he tells her,

> By thy cure
> I am now my selfe, yet dare call nothing mine,
> Till I be perfect blest in being thine.

Finally, the two major scenes of the third plot are organized, much like the first sequence, in terms of the alternating success of two adversaries: in II.ii Lacy forces Bonavent to dance against his will, and then in IV.iii Bonavent does the same to Lacy. But their conflict, unlike that between Fairfield and Carol, does not lead to the resolution of their plot, a resolution which has no necessary connexion to this preceding action, and which Lacy correctly attributes, not to anyone's defeat or conversion, but to 'fortune' and 'providence' (V.ii; p. 257). Moreover, this conflict is not a battle of wits, still less of moral principle; it is fought out in almost physical terms, and centres upon two amusing spectacles that approach the level of visual slapstick.

It appears, then, that this triple-plot structure has been designed to encompass three traditional species of comedy. The main plot is a sophisticated or 'high'

comedy of clever intrigue, appealing primarily to the intellect; the second is a sentimental comedy that is directed to our ethical sensibilities;[11] and the third a simple comedy of situation that depends mainly, like most other plots of this type, upon coincidence, disguise, and sheer spectacle. There is, also, at least the suggestion of a still lower comic level adumbrated here in the ludicrous activities of Venture and Rider, for while these two men technically belong to the main plot, as suitors of Carol, they are never really taken seriously in that role (by anyone except themselves), and certainly are not qualified to participate in the contest of wits that constitutes that plot, their most distinctive and obvious characteristic being, in fact, their utter witlessness. Rather, it would seem that they are developed independently, in the few brief episodes devoted to them, as a pair of blundering clowns who are to be regarded as operating in another comic world, in this case, the world of pure farce, which occupies a place somewhat below that of the Bonavent-Lacy action—although it, too, might well be classified in this same general comic species—and therefore provides a kind of elemental base for the dramatic hierarchy that is presented here. This hierarchy may appear to be unusually complicated, but it is not actually much more elaborate, in its broad outlines, than some of the structures created by Shirley's predecessors on the stage. A number of what are customarily called 'double-plot' plays of the Elizabethan and Jacobean periods also include another separable set of characters (often, as here, a pair of clowns) who are loosely connected to the main or subplot but function in more or less independent episodes evoking a third distinct level of dramatic interest, frequently through some sort of farcical analogy to the other two plots.[12] It is the order of these other two plots here that is most surprising, for we do not ordinarily find the more serious action in a subplot.[13] Yet Shirley seems to have been fond of this arrangement, employing it, in substantially the same fashion, throughout the group of plays to which **Hyde Park** belongs. In **The Ball,** for example, there is also a main action of clever intrigue, in which Colonel Winfield outwits and conquers the scornful Lady Lucina, an underplot where the philandering Lord Rainbow is converted (here by two ladies), and another farcical level that includes a separate minor action (Freshwater and Gudgeon), as well as Lucina's foolish suitors (Lamount, Travers, and Bostock). **The Gamester** uses somewhat different material and doubles the number of couples in the two chief actions, but its basic scheme is the same: a main plot of trickery and manipulation (Wilding, his wife, Hazard, and Penelope), a second plot of exalted moral sentiment (Leonora, Delamore, Violante, and Beaumont), and a third of slapstick clowning (Barnacle and his nephew). But **The Lady of Pleasure** is the play that most closely resembles **Hyde Park** in this respect. Here, once more, we see a main action devoted to a battle of wits wherein a man out-manœuvres and reforms a woman, and an idealized sentimental subplot which shows a woman reforming a man (only here the vices to be cured have changed gender—Lady Bornwell in the first plot is the profligate, while the nameless Lord in the second plot is the scorn-ful misogamist), and a third level of farce in the little sequence built around Frederick, and also in the antics of the comic gallants of the main plot, Kickshaw and Littleworth, whose role here is similar to that of Venture and Rider in **Hyde Park,** and Lamount, Travers, and Bostock in **The Ball.**

In these plays the over-all emotional effect must in some sense include all three kinds of comedy, but it is not a simple aggregate of the three. In **Hyde Park,** and in the rest to varying degrees, the separate comic levels are brought into a functional relationship by the analogi-cal scheme of comparisons and contrasts, so that our response to each of them is qualified by our response to the others. The witty situations of the main action are somehow brightened when seen against the more sombre background of the subplot, and are at the same time limited—'placed', as it were—since they are deliberately divorced from the realm of serious moral concern. And in a corresponding way the other two comic effects are both enhanced and circumscribed by the total dramatic environment. What we have here, then, is a genuine artistic composite, which cannot be appreciated fully without taking into account all of its ingredients, as well as the principle of their combina-tion. That is why the labels that have usually been ap-plied to it—'comedy of manners' and 'realistic comedy' and the like—have proved so unsatisfactory in describ-ing Shirley's characteristic achievement within this genre, or even in determining which of his plays the genre includes.[14] No single label, drawn from just one of the components, can be adequate. It is, rather, the complex triple structure itself that seems to be the formula through which we can define the special kind of drama Shirley has created, and at least begin to explain its unique comic quality.[15]

Notes

1. 'Ford and Shirley', *Cambridge History of English Literature,* VI (Cambridge, 1919), 202. See also A. W. Ward, *History of English Dramatic Litera-ture to the Death of Queen Anne* (1899), III, 106: 'Only in so far as it is descriptive of . . . the realities of contemporary life and manners . . . can any special interest be said to attach to the comedy of *Hyde Park*.'

2. Felix Schelling, for example, finds that '*Hyde Park* centers in the races' (*Elizabethan Drama* (Boston, 1908), II, 290), while Henry Wells says, 'The chief scenes present the races and other amusements of Hyde Park' (*Elizabethan and Ja-*

cobean Playwrights (New York, 1939), p. 185). See also Arthur Nason, *James Shirley, Dramatist* (New York, 1915), pp. 229-30; Algernon C. Swin-burne, *Contemporaries of Shakespeare* (1919), p. 292; Thomas Parrott and Robert Ball, *Short View of Elizabethan Drama* (New York, 1943), p. 273; and Frederick Boas, *Introduction to Stuart Drama* (1946), p. 355.

3. Since there is no satisfactory modern text, quota-tions are taken from the 1637 quarto; citations refer to the scene divisions and the page numbers of the Mermaid edition (edited by Edmund Gosse, 1888).

4. It has even been suggested that the publication of Jonson's play in 1631 may have inaugurated this vogue, which extended from about 1631 to 1635. See Richard Perkinson, 'Topographical Comedy in the Seventeenth Century', *ELH,* 3 (1936), 270-90, and Theodore Miles, 'Place-Realism in a Group of Caroline Plays', *Review of English Stud-ies,* 18 (1942), 428-40. Miles, in his discussion of *Hyde Park,* acknowledges that 'Shirley indubitably works the place into his play more gracefully than the others' who took part in this vogue (Marmion, Brome, and Nabbes); but the only explanation he provides is that 'he was the more graceful dramatist' and his rivals were 'less gifted' (see pp. 432, 440).

5. Shirley dramatized such a situation in *The Ball,* V.i. And in some of his other comedies these gambling terms are also applied in a sexual sense, but not, I think, as systematically as they are here.

6. There is a verbal parallel between Venture's two failures: in I.i (p. 184) he is so sure of winning Carol that he boasts, ''tis impossible / She should put any trick upon me', only to discover that she has; and after the race Bonville says, 'I knew by instinct, / The mare would put some tricke upon him' (IV.iii; p. 237). Note also the pervasive equestrian metaphor in II.iv (pp. 205-6), where Carol rejects Venture and Rider. (A very similar use is made of the steeplechase in *Anna Karenina,* II, xxv, where Vronsky breaks the back of the mare he is riding, and so foreshadows his ultimate effect upon Anna.)

7. In IV.iii (p. 236) Bonville bets against Rider, Trier, and a third man whose one speech here is prefixed *Fa.* (1637 quarto, G4^r), which the modern editors read as Fairfield. But there is good reason to believe that this is a misprint for *La.*, even aside from the analogy to their later fates, for Fairfield never shows any interest elsewhere in the races or in betting, while Lacy comments on this race a few lines below in a manner that suggests he is backing Venture, and at III.i (p. 217) he insisted

upon leaving his new bride, over her protests, because he 'must have a bet' on the runners.

8. We are told in IV.i (p. 227) that it is 'the first Bird' heard in the season that determines one's fortunes, so when Mistress Bonavent says, just before the cuckoo sings, that she heard a nightingale yesterday, we realize the ill omen does not apply to her, but only to Lacy and Trier.

9. See their comments in III.ii (p. 225) and IV.i (pp. 226-7).

10. In this very general sense, the Park resembles Jonson's Fair, which is dominated by 'Lucke and Saint *Bartholmew*' (V.i.1, *Works,* edited by Herford and Simpson); but the fortunes of Jonson's visitors are, at least in part, determined by their reactions to the pressures imposed by the Fair. On this point see my article, 'The Structure of *Bartholomew Fair*', *P.M.L.A.,* 80 (1965), 172-9, and compare the functions of the forests in *A Midsummer Night's Dream* and *As You Like It.*

11. When Robert Reed discusses *Hyde Park* as one of the forerunners of eighteenth-century sentimental comedy ('James Shirley, and the Sentimental Comedy', *Anglia,* 73 (1955), 149-70), he is really only concerned with this second plot, while Kathleen Lynch, in her study of Shirley's role in the evolution of the comedy of manners, concentrates upon the Fairfield-Carol action (*Social Mode of Restoration Comedy* (New York, 1926), pp. 36-42). Each critic abstracts from the composite whole the one component that fits his thesis.

12. Embryonic third plots of this type appear, for example, in *The Nice Valour, The Atheist's Tragedy, The Insatiate Countess, The Old Law, A Fair Quarrel, The Spanish Gipsy,* and *The Witch of Edmonton.*

13. Yet there are even some precedents for this, in such plays as Middleton's *Michaelmas Term, A Mad World, My Masters,* and *A Trick to Catch the Old One* (if the Dampit scenes there can be called a subplot). In all three the main action is an amoral comedy of clever intrigue (centring on money, rather than love), but the subordinate action raises serious moral issues, in one case actually producing two spiritual conversions.

14. Some commentators place just four of Shirley's comedies within this category (and not always the same four), others as many as ten; but very few have attempted to explain what these terms might mean as the definition of a dramatic genre (to some critics, apparently, they mean no more than that the plays are set in London). See Thomas Marc Parrott, *Comedies of George Chapman* (1914), pp. 872-3; Robert Forsythe, *Relations of*

Shirley's Plays to the Elizabethan Drama (New York, 1914), chapter IX; Felix Schelling, *Elizabethan Playwrights* (New York, 1925), p. 265; Ashley Thorndike, *English Comedy* (New York, 1929), pp. 240-1; Gerald E. Bentley, *Jacobean and Caroline Stage,* V (Oxford, 1956), 1108; Nason, pp. 387-92; Boas, pp. 353-9; and Reed, p. 155; among others. Some of these studies show that certain kinds of characters and incidents reappear in various plays in this group, but without relating them to the plot structure.

15. This article represents part of a study made possible by a fellowship awarded by the American Council of Learned Societies for 1963-4.

Sophie Eliza Tomlinson (essay date 1999)

SOURCE: Tomlinson, Sophie Eliza. "Too Theatrical? Female Subjectivity in Caroline and Interregnum Drama." *Women's Writing* 6, no. 1 (1999): 65-79.

[*In the following essay, Tomlinson compares Shirley's* Hyde Park *to a play written by aristocratic women to illuminate the issue of female subjectivity. She finds in Shirley's female characters a developing assertion of the female self and feminine will.*]

One of the funniest and most affecting moments in Emma Thompson's screen adaptation of Jane Austen's *Sense and Sensibility* (1995) occurs when Thompson, as Elinor Dashwood, bursts into what the novel describes as "tears of joy" on hearing from Edward Ferrars that he is yet unmarried. Thompson's performance of Elinor's overpowering emotion gains appreciably from its theatrical display as compared with its narration in the novel. As viewers we have witnessed Elinor's subduing of her feelings for Edward and her resignation to a state of unfulfilment. The sudden reversal of that expectation of unhappiness unleashes a show of feeling all the more cathartic for its worldlessness.

If I were to search for a comparable moment of unconstrained emotion in seventeenth-century drama, it would be the scene of Calantha's self-willed death in John Ford's Caroline tragedy *The Broken Heart* (1629). Paradoxically, the moment in which Calantha commands her heartstrings to crack is at once a display of supreme self-control and emotional abandon. Calantha's death is as immaculately orchestrated as Cleopatra's; the vital difference is the absence of an asp or human agent to bring it about. Ford's heroine dies from sheer intensity of grief: the spectacular breaking of her heart represents inward feeling made outward, subjectivity made theatrical.

Indeed, it was seventeenth-century drama, the immediate context of Renaissance drama by women, which allowed conceptions of female subjectivity to appear as fluid, shifting and most importantly, emergent.[1] A key reason for this development was the change in what was permissible on stage, namely the representation, that is the voicing and embodying, of female roles by women themselves. What had previously been hidden was made emphatically outward in a burst of theatrical display.[2]

With respect to Caroline drama in particular, I would argue that this shift in the conception of female subjectivity was attributable to the increasing cultural visibility of women, specifically in the domain of theatrical performance. Plays written for both court and commercial theatres manifest a concern with the issues of liberty, civility and agency that derive from a sympathetic interest in female selfhood. At the same time these plays demonstrate a new attitude towards female theatricality, hitherto a focus of ambivalence in Renaissance drama and English culture in general. In this new disposition, the theatrical woman is viewed sympathetically, her outward identity seen either as socially imposed or as a ruse to protect her emotional self. Interestingly, this depiction of femininity is anticipated in a work by a woman, Lady Mary Wroth's prose romance, the *Urania* (1621). Heather Weidemann argues that in the *Urania* Wroth represents women "not so much as spectacles as revelatory subjects; their appearances often point to a subjective female identity which is hidden but nonetheless authentic".[3] Significantly, this sympathetic construction of female theatricality also informs the work of Wroth's admirer, Ben Jonson: in his late comedy *The New Inn* (1629), Lady Frampul's "excellent acting" functions as a vehicle of self-discovery in her relationship with her suitor, Lovel; indeed, in this play, Jonson represents feigning as not merely a female vice (though it is that too) but as the means of reconstituting and reconciling an entire family.

Cultural change offers a means of accounting for shifts in the literary conception of subjectivity. Occasionally a text offers a glimpse of changing mores, allowing speculation about the porousness of social and ideological boundaries. Take the use of the word "theatrical" in this excerpt from Sir Francis Osborne's *Historical Memoires on the Reigns of Queen Elizabeth and King James* (1658), with reference to Elizabeth I's self-presentation:

> Her Sex *did beare out many* impertinencies in her words *and actions,* as her making Latin speeches in the Universities, *and professing her selfe in publique* a Muse, *then thought something too Theatrical for a virgine Prince.*[4]

Osborne constructs Elizabeth's theatricality as conflicting with her femininity, or her status as a "virgine Prince". Elizabeth's display of her learning and presentation of herself as a muse are forms of assertiveness which Osborne represents as "impertinencies" in respect of the Queen's gender. At the same time, Osborne's account of Elizabeth suggests a subtle shift of response towards this performative femininity: the Queen's behaviour, he writes, was "*then* thought something too Theatrical for a virgine Prince". His remark testifies to a shift of attitude, and an alteration of circumstance, taking place between Elizabeth's reign and the time of Osborne's writing shortly before the Stuart Restoration. While Elizabeth was extolled as a Phoenix, authoritative female self-fashioners from a later generation are more numerous: Queens Anna and Henrietta Maria, Margaret Cavendish, Duchess of Newcastle, and Katherine Philips, the "matchless Orinda", come immediately to mind. It was the innovative performances of the Danish Anna and the French Henrietta which made possible the appearance of women on the professional Restoration stage: a watershed in theatrical history and in seventeenth-century English culture.[5]

What changes were brought about, with regard to the dramatic representation of female subjectivity, by the presence of women on stage? And what was the relationship of women dramatists to the shifts in seventeenth-century theatrical culture I am describing? This article addresses the latter question by focusing on *The Concealed Fancies,* a comedy of courtship written by the sisters Lady Jane Cavendish and Lady Elizabeth Brackley in the mid-1640s. I approach this female-authored play via a discussion of the most sparkling social comedy of the preceding decade, James Shirley's **Hyde Park,** (1632, published 1637), together with the court drama performed by Henrietta Maria and her ladies in January 1633, Walter Montagu's *The Shepherd's Paradise* (published 1659). This may seem a strange yoking: a comedy of manners written for the London stage, a court pastoral and a provincial drama by two young women, which we have no definite knowledge was ever performed.[6] *The Concealed Fancies* offers a fascinating window onto women's perception of themselves as actors in a network of familial and social relations. I believe the view of femininity, and of female self-fashioning opened up by their text, increases in interest when read in the context of the Caroline drama of Montagu and Shirley, both of whom broach new conceptions of female subjectivity and its dynamic relationship with theatricality. By juxtaposing these plays I will show that in respect to courtship and marriage *The Concealed Fancies* exhibits a *savoir-faire* quite different from the emotionally revealing drama written for the professional theatres.[7]

In the same year that Shirley's **Hyde Park** was licensed, and probably performed by the Queen's Men at the Phoenix theatre, the lawyer Thomas Edgar published his emended and enlarged version of *The Lawes Resolution of Women's Rights or The Lawes Provision for*

Women (1632). Following his citation of God's cursing of Eve in the third chapter of *Genesis,* Edgar adds the following comment:

> See here the reason . . . that Women have no voyse in Parliament, They make no Lawes, they consent to none, they abrogate none. All of them are understood either married or to bee married and their desires or [are] subject to their husband, I know no remedy though some women can shift it well enough.[8]

The modification "though some women can shift it well enough" suggests the gap between ideology and practice, a gap borne out by legal and dramatic discourse and by numerous cases of individual women in the seventeenth century. Feminist scholars have observed that "the notion of the husband's legal right to a woman's body and mind was . . . being contested in the [Renaissance] period".[9] Evidence of some women's ability to "shift it", or to strategically secure a space for themselves in their domestic relationships may be found in the speech and actions of Maria, the heroine of *The Woman's Prize or The Tamer Tamed* (1611), John Fletcher's Jacobean riposte to Shakespeare's *The Taming of the Shrew* (1592).[10] Maria counters her sister's attempt to dissuade her from withholding her sexual delights from Petruchio with words which seriously undermine the concept of wifely subjection:

> A weaker subject
> Would shame the end I aime at: disobedience?
> You talk too tamely: By the faith I have
> In mine own Noble will, that childish woman
> That lives a prisoner to her husbands pleasure,
> Has lost her making, and becomes a beast,
> Created for his use, not fellowship.[11]

Buttressed by the Protestant ideal of equality in the state of marriage, Maria asserts a sense of herself as an independent being, encapsulated in the phrase "mine own Noble will". The feminist implications of Maria's assertion are toned down in the Epilogue's summary of the play's intent, it "being aptly meant / To teach both Sexes due equality; / And as they stand bound, to love mutually".[12] This has all the tones of early modern marriage guidance! Nevertheless, it is this affirmation of women's will, together with their capacity to judge and find men wanting, which forms the backbone of the new dimension of female subjectivity I will delineate in *Hyde Park* and *The Shepherd's Paradise*.[13]

In her attempts to fend off the sleazy and overbearing Lord Bonvile in *Hyde Park* Julietta vows ingenuous allegiance to the system of aristocratic privilege:

> It is my duty, where the king has sealed
> His favors, I should show humility,
> My best obedience, to his act.
>
> LORD B.
>
> So should
> All handsome women that will be good subjects.[14]

By disregarding Bonvile's tawdry innuendo, Julietta allows his sexualised reading of social obligation to sound discordantly against her testimonial of innocence:

> I must
> Be bold to tell you, sir, unless you prove
> A friend to virtue, were your honor centupled . . .
> Yet I, I in such infinite distance, am
> As much above you in my innocence.
>
> (V. 1. 130-140)

Julietta's emphatically doubled "I" testifies to her assertion of self, a boldness borne out by her protestation and defence of her discursive "liberty":

> 'Tis the first liberty
> I ever took to speak myself; I have been
> Bold in the comparison, but find not
> Wherein I have wronged virtue, pleading for it.
>
> (V. 1. 141-144)

Do Julietta's words carry a feminist valence? Recent critical approaches downplay or sidestep this issue. Martin Butler's reading of the play somewhat narrowly identifies Julietta with the "town": "In her, the town criticizes the court from a standpoint of independent, disinterested judgment, while still reserving its essential duty".[15] Ira Clark contends that the change wrought in Bonvile by Julietta "is no reformation but a reconversion to a set of standards already in place"; moreover, he stresses, "Julietta . . . remains subordinate, dependent for any leverage on marital brokerage".[16] But is it not the leverage afforded by an ethical and political voice which projects a glimpse of female subjectivity in earnest?

The graceful weave of comic registers in *Hyde Park* means that the notions of liberty, and of female subjectivity, are scrutinised from many different angles. The providential overtone of the plot involving Mistress Bonavent, her suitor Lacy and her husband who has been lost at sea for 7 years is offset by the satiric approach to liberty dramatised in the courtship of Fairfield and Mistress Carol. At the outset of the play Carol tells Fairfield:

> You neglect
> Your selves, the nobleness of your birth and nature,
> By servile flattery of this jigging,
> And that coy mistress; keep your privilege,
> Your masculine property.
>
> (I. 2. 88-92)

Martin Butler glosses the word "privilege" in Carol's speech as meaning "man's freedom to be his dignified self", and suggests further, "the term 'property' here is close to Denzil Holles's notion of 'propriety' . . . meaning that which is *proper* to each man, his by right of possession" (with all its attendant political suggestions).[17] This idea of integrity and property going hand in hand acquires a feminist emphasis in Carol's ironic discourse castigating her cousin Mistress Bonavent for her intention to marry: "You have / Too, too much liberty" (I. 2. 167-168). As Carol's speech wittily depicts, a leisured gentlewoman in charge of her own estate and household has much to lose "when husbands come to rule" (I. 2. 176). As defence against the plight of a *"femme covert"* Carol maintains the attitude of a Platonic mistress, holding absolute dominion over her servants:

> I
> Dispose my frowns and favors like a princess;
> Deject, advance, undo, create again;
> It keeps the subjects in obedience,
> And teaches 'em to look at me with distance.
>
> (I. 2. 188-192)

The dramatic interest in the courtship of Carol and Fairfield derives from the puncturing of this tyrannous relationship through Carol's inadvertent swearing of an oath never to solicit Fairfield's company. In dramatising Carol's subsequent pursuit of Fairfield, Shirley makes palpable her emotional susceptibility; for instance, in Carol's aside after she sees Fairfield with an unknown woman (in fact his sister, Julietta): "Keep in, great heart" (III. 1. 143). In the interview Carol procures with Fairfield her affected indifference prompts Fairfield to accuse her of overacting:

> O woman!
> How far thy tongue and heart do live asunder! . . .
> A little peevishness to save your credit
> Had not been much amiss, but this over-
> Over-doing the business . . .
>
> (III. 2. 51-58)

Shirley's sense of dramatic counterpoint will not let this cliché of female dissembling rest. Fairfield's boast to "see thy heart, and every thought within it" (III. 2. 55) invites Carol's answering ruse: offering to contract herself to Fairfield in front of a witness, she obstructs their union by posing as a moneylender to the witness he provides, frustrating Fairfield's expectations of victory and socially humiliating him. Carol's device upends Fairfield's complacency and highlights her independence as a woman of means. The comedy moves through another tonal shift when in spite of herself, Carol's jeering of Fairfield becomes abusive. Her asides convey her struggle to articulate her true feeling: "I'd fain speak kindly to him . . . I shall fool too much . . . it will not out" (III. 2. 142-147) The scene culminates in Fairfield's anger and sexual aggression triggered off by the call of the nightingale: "'Twas Philomel, they say; and thou wert one, / I should new ravish thee" (III. 2. 156-157).

Commenting on Carol's initial greeting of the nightingale as a sign of good luck, Ira Clark writes, "as [Fairfield] stomps away [Carol] lets him know that in private she will play her society's assignment of submissive woman".[18] Clark seems determined to construe Shirley's mapping of gender relations in as conservative a light as possible. In this instance, he overlooks the density of associations which Shirley weaves through Fairfield's allusion to Philomel. The myth of Philomel represents the ambivalence attached to women's speech; the raped and tongueless woman transformed into a songbird is at once an image of muteness and inarticulacy and of feminine eloquence.[19] Shirley uses this paradox to delineate the emotional impasse between Fairfield and Carol. Fairfield responds to Carol's attempted rapprochement with a derisory image of female loquaciousness: "When you are out of breath, / You will give over . . . stay you and practice with the bird" (III. 2. 151-156). Carol's words after Fairfield's heated departure convey her emotion, and its painful constriction by the public arena of Hyde Park:

> I must to the coach and weep; my heart will break
>   else.
> I'm glad he does not see me.
>
> (III. 2. 159-160)

At the last Fairfield forces an expression of love from Carol only by threatening to geld himself; clearly Carol has more interest in his "masculine property" than she has previously acknowledged! Shirley's scripting of Carol's speech after her declaration "I do love you" (V. 1. 287) is instructive:

> my thoughts
> Point on no sensuality; remit
> What's past, and I will meet your best affection.
> I know you love me still; do not refuse me.
> If I go once more back, you ne'er recover me.
>
> (V. 1. 294-298)

The difference between Carol and Cleopatra, to whom her suitor Rider compares her (I. 2. 170-172), could not be more apparent. While sharing the Egyptian Queen's histrionic caprice, Carol's love comes modestly girded. Sensuality is suppressed in the interest of feminine decorum. Shirley's ideal union is chaste and witty, with the volatility of a horse race and the elegance of a dance.

* * *

It is not only professional drama which articulates a concern with the rights of female subjects in relation to their superiors or sovereigns. *The Shepherd's Paradise* shows a heightened awareness of the loss of subjectivity incurred by women in the passage from courtship to marriage. The shepherd Melidoro and his mistress Camena debate the question of whether marriage entails a form of possession or "propriety" which weakens "Love's prerogative".[20] While Melidoro maintains that

marriage enlarges each partner's self-possession, Camena is wary of the self-loss that "nuptiall bonds" imply for women: "I cannot yet resolve to abate soe much from what I love so well, my selfe, as to submit to a propriety" (p. 52).[21]

The concern with female identity, which is expressed here through dialogue, also forms the focus of the song, "Presse me no more kind love", in which the Queen of the Shepherd's Paradise, Bellesa, acted by Henrietta Maria, confesses her love for the shepherd Moramente. After visiting the lovesick Moramente, Bellesa had expressed her disquiet at the stirrings of love: "I ne'er knew any thing yet so neer Love as the fear of it" (p. 85). Rather than a confession of love, Bellesa's song is a negotiation with Love about the terms on which she may disclose her emotions. Her conflict between the promptings of love and "virgin-shame" is expressed through the imagery of red and white, suggesting the onset of passion, offset by chastity:

> I find a glowing heat that turnes red hot
> My heart, but yet it doth not flame a jot.
> It doth but yet to such a colour turne,
> It seemes to me rather to blush than burne.
> You would perswade me that this flaming light
> Rising will change this colour into white,
> I would fain know if this whites inference
> Pretend pale guilt, or candid innocence.
>
> (p. 112)

Bellesa's song rehearses theatrically William Prynne's association between female speech and impudence, one meaning of which is "unblushing".[22] The song symbolises a form of bodily speech, imaging the distillation of a blush from red into white. Bellesa's anxiousness about disclosing her love derives piquancy from Henrietta's physical presence on stage, which belies Bellesa's appeal to Cupid, "Not to bring me to witnesse [her love] to men" (p. 112). By stressing her pudency and innocence, Bellesa's song neutralises the implications of immodesty in the Queen's display of her body and her freedom of public speech.[23]

Although the song focuses on the inner motions of Bellesa's heart, it ends with a request which recognises the pitfalls involved in giving that emotion social expression:

> Then take you care of me, a meane so rare
> Betwixt mens vanity, and their dispaire.
>
> (p. 112)

Bellesa's song answers the question put earlier by Melidoro to Camena as to whether Bellesa and the shepherdess Pantamora are affected by love: "Do you think, Camena, that Bellesa and Pantamora are not moved? do you think that women are like windes, that do not feel the storms they raise?" (p. 90). When Camena distin-

guishes between Pantamora's "restlesse humor" and Bellesa's serenity, Melidoro presses his question further: "Do you not beleeve *Camena*, that *Bellesa* doth act the Queens part more then her own, in this distancing of her selfe from any sense of *Moraments* love?" (p. 90).

Here Montagu spins subtle irony from the situation of coterie performance, exploiting his play's meshing of reality with dramatic role. Melidoro suggests that, in this case, for Bellesa/Henrietta to "act the Queen's part" is disingenuous: the Queen is adhering too much to her social-political persona. As a validation of that queenliness, Camena's response justifies Bellesa's behaviour as a model of decorum and naturalness:

> I do not know. Methinks she hath so equall and significant a liberty, as it speakes all things that she doth naturall, as I beleeve her the perfection of our sex. I cannot think her voyd of sense; but I beleeve it sinks no deeper then the face of that civility, where men do see it set, and make a returne to Moramente.
>
> (p. 90)

Camena represents Bellesa's agency as ambiguous, ascribing to her a "liberty" and "civility" that reside in the right of reply, rather than in voluntary self-expression.[24] Her praise discreetly avoids answering Melidoro's assertion that Bellesa's behaviour is too theatrical. Instead, Camena attributes to Bellesa a sense which remains on the "civil" side of sensuality, a sensibility represented in terms of surface rather than depth. This ideal female self is immaculate and inscrutable, defined by a woman and compelling the gaze of men.

Interestingly, *The Shepherd's Paradise* contains an Echo scene which theatricalises Bellesa's aural confession of love. In a wood called "Love's Cabinet" (p. 134), Bellesa questions the Echo, who counsels her to "Speake", "Love" and "Do", reassuring her of Moramente's "Constancy" and their mutual "Content". When Moramente finds her alone Bellesa tells him to speak to "Love's Counsellor" (p. 136) if he has any suit. To his query, "doth Bellesa love[?]", the Echo replies in the affirmative, "Love". When Moramente declares, "it is too much of a miracle to be beleeved from any voyce but yours", Bellesa affirms:

> It is my voyce *Moramente*, and I have let it loose from me, that it might not have so much as modesty to hold it back. Beleeve it. For if you put me to take it in againe, I have virgin cold that would not let it speake so cleare.
>
> (p. 137)

Here Bellesa represents her own voice as emanating from elsewhere; the female self she represents is disembodied, theatrical. Bellesa's ventriloquism negotiates the same trauma over female self-expression registered in her song. When Moramente pleads that Bellesa re-ingest her voice ("give me leave to begg for this kind voyce . . . that you would take it in againe", p. 137), Bellesa returns him an assurance which answers Camena's uncertainty as to whether she is "voyd of sense":

> I have had long a sense well fitted to your sufferings, and I have beleeved so well of you as I did not feare the seemingnesse of my indifferency would divert you from a meritorious persistency.

(p. 137)

Bellesa resolves her condition of doubleness, which she describes as "the seemingnesse of my indifferency", by dropping her queenly role: "Rise *Moramente,* unlesse you wish an answer from a Queen, and not *Bellesa*" (p. 137). Bellesa's "answering" of Moramente, like the Echo device itself, chimes with Camena's sense of "civility" as involving a feminine reciprocation of masculine feeling. In dialogue with the Echo, Bellesa had expressed her fear of Moramente proving either vain or inconstant (p. 135). In admitting that she has been "studying you all this while" (p. 137) Bellesa signals that she has surmounted those fears through patient perusal of Moramente's character. The full scope of Bellesa's "liberty" as a lover is in trying Moramente and finding him true.

The motif of women trying men in Caroline drama does not simply invert the literary tradition of men trying women's chastity. Rather than focusing on sexuality, the trials conducted by women in Montagu's and Shirley's plays centre on the ethical and moral dimensions of their lovers. In **Hyde Park,** Julietta parries her suitor Trier's statement that he has found her "right / And perfect gold" (V. 2. 7-8) by asserting her right to try, and reject, him: "I have tried you / And found you dross; nor do I love my heart / So ill, to change it with you" (V. 2. 9-11). Like Margaret Cavendish 20 years later, and Mary Wroth a decade earlier, Montagu and Shirley seriously entertain the possibility of women withholding themselves from sexual exchange. In Shirley's social comedy, this possibility is foreclosed by the reformation of Lord Bonvile, whose wish to "be a servant to [Julietta's] virtue" (V. 2. 126) looks likely to prefer him in the way of marriage. However, in Montagu's pastoral, with its aestheticising of solitude, the single woman has dramatic viability: in spite of the multiple couplings with which the play ends, Princess Miranda, alias Fidamira, remains as Queen of the Shepherd's Paradise, having made "a vow of chastity which is not in my power to recall" (p. 170). Exceptionally, Montagu represents female "Selfe-love" (p. 38) as a valid alternative to marriage.[25]

* * *

The Shepherd's Paradise struggles with the doubts and dilemmas of female subjectivity in a wholly new context of female performance. *The Concealed Fancies* by Lady Elizabeth Brackley and Lady Jane Cavendish presents yet another departure from and development of seventeenth-century theatrical and dramatic tradition. The sisters' experience of being besieged by parliamentary troops in their home of Welbeck Abbey in Nottinghamshire forms the backdrop for a comedy of courtship deriving from the drama of Shakespeare, Jonson, Fletcher and Shirley. Unlike the *Poems and Fancies* of their stepmother Margaret Cavendish, published in 1653, *The Concealed Fancies* was presented in manuscript form, constituting the last part of the volume entitled *Poems Songs a Pastorall and a Play,* signed by both women and presented to their father, "W. N.", William Cavendish, Earl, and later Duke, of Newcastle.[26]

One of the delightful aspects of *The Concealed Fancies* is the absorption of its female characters in theatrical self-invention. In one scene the three "Lady Cousins" vie for the part of bravely suffering heroine:

> —Pray, how did I look in the posture of a delinquent?
>
> —You mean how did you behave yourself in the posture of a delinquent? Faith, as though you thought the scene would change, and you would be happy—though you suffered misery for a time. And how did I look?
>
> —As yourself; that's great, though in misfortune.
>
> —So did you.
>
> —How should I do otherwise, for I practised Cleopatra when she was in her captivity, and could they have thought me worthy to have adorned their Triumphs I would have performed his gallant Tragedy, and so have made myself glorious for time to come.[27]

The enigmatically named "Sh." transforms the tedium of her captivity by practising Cleopatra, imitating the Egyptian Queen's resolution and imaginatively enacting her gallant death. The frisson created by Shakespeare's ironic disclosure of the transvestite boy-actor is succeeded in the Cavendishes's text by a salute to Cleopatra as the exemplar of noble feminine action. This fantasy of heroic performance pays tribute to Plutarch, to Shakespeare and perhaps also to Mary Sidney's translation of Robert Garnier's *Tragedy of Antonie* (1595).[28] It is hard to distinguish whether it is Shakespeare, Cleopatra or female performance *per se* that is depicted here as empowering.

The play, then, offers a view of theatrical self-fashioning that caters to female fantasy, and crucially, pragmatism. The distinction between the wit and fancy of the sisters Luceny and Tattiny, and duller female sensibilities is brought home in a dialogue between the chambermaid Pert and the gentlewoman Toy, servants of the upwardly aspiring Lady Tranquility. The focus of their chat is Toy's affair with her mistress's lover, Lord Calsindow.

Pert teases Toy, "I know some ladies that will be so much of the wench with their husband, that thou would prove at best but a cold mouldy pie". When Toy retorts she "would be the wife with that lady's husband, and make him fond that way", Pert exclaims:

> A pox of thy no wit, this lady that I mean will have her several scenes, now wife, then mistress, then my sweet Platonic soul, and then write in the like several changes of mistress not onely to confirm love, but provoke love, then dress themselves always as a pretty sweet wife or mistress.

(p. 148)

Pert's image of the theatrical woman confines her "infinite variety" to the boudoir or closet. The lady's role-play is the key to sustaining her husband's sexual interest, "confirm[ing] [and] provok[ing] love". This domestication of female acting resonates suggestively with the use of Cleopatra as "a signifier of domestic concord" in texts and visual images of the Renaissance and seventeenth century. Mary Hamer scrutinises the enclosure of Cleopatra in the conjugal family, coincident with the regularising of sexual behaviour within marriage undertaken by the agents of the Reformation. Sixty years after Shakespeare's "intensely conflicted representation of Cleopatra"[29], Dryden's *All for Love* (1677) presents her as just such a chastened figure, "a silly harmless, household dove".[30]

In place of Shakespeare's serpent and Dryden's dove, the Cavendishes posit the image of woman as monkey, mimicking the wifely role.[31] However, as Pert's collocation of "lady" and "wench" suggests, such feminine role-play transgresses the bounds of gentlewomanly conduct. The modern Caroline wife knows equally how to play the angel *and* the whore. Little wonder that Toy feels defeated by such competition: "I'll serve none of your she-wits" (p. 148).

While confined to the domestic sphere, the play's portrayal of theatrical femininity carries a political valence. The sisters view marriage as a social form "to join lovers", rather than a bond in which "husbands are the rod of authority" (p. 153). Rather than rebelling outright, Luceny and Tattiny wield their "fancies" as instruments of self-defence and seduction. In her post-nuptial account of her relationship with Presumption, Tattiny presents herself as balancing aggression with appeasement: when Presumption is angry, she is petulant; when he speaks "in company according to a discreet husband", she gives him "a modest return of wife, and yet appear[s] his mistress" (p. 153). Tattiny's calculated performance safeguards her "privilege", and strengthens what she describes as her "equal marriage".[32]

Thus far I have discussed the way that *The Concealed Fancies* draws on theatrical language to facilitate women's pleasurable and strategic manipulation of a "scene self" (p. 133).[33] But does the play represent women as anything more than canny performers; or to phrase the question differently: what do the Cavendish sisters have to say about women as subjects of feeling?

Consistent with the veiling gesture of the play's title, the emotional dimension of the women's lives is overtly focused on their family relationships, particularly on the sisters' longing for their absent father (the Lady Cousins' uncle), Lord Calsindow. Midway through the sexual sparring with which they pass away their captivity, Luceny and Tattiney become nuns, a transformation motivated ostensibly by their grief for their "loved, dear and absent friends" (p. 146). Yet the sisters' profound melancholy, expressed in the formal registers of verse and song, is not immune from histrionic excess. While their sadness is sympathetically evoked, their taking the veil stems as much from "fancy" as from forlornness. In one scene Colonel Free comments, "I wonder what fancy my wife will be possessed withal, for she can neither be nun, nor vestal, she hath so many children" (p. 144). After assuring Free that "the sweet lady will be in a consumption for your sake", Corpolant informs him that "our sweet young Stellows" (the sisters' brothers) are "very melancholy" (p. 144). Corpolant's suspicion that the Stellows' melancholy is due to their love for the "Lady Cousins" is set alongside, and reflects ironically upon, the state of their sisters as "nuns in melancholy" (p. 144). The play allows the possibility that the sisters' disguise is a further provocative deferral of their love for Courtly and Presumption. Their melodramatic role-play certainly prompts the men to greater seriousness, causing Presumption to abandon his antagonism and vow that were Tattiney his, he would "dedicated be / To her and give her leave for to be free" (p. 143).[34]

In a discussion with Presumption about methods of wife-taming, Courtly had earlier purported his ambition to gain, through love, Luceny's "observancy", which he defines in terms of reciprocal respect: "she shall love me so well, as she shall think me worthy of my freedom, and so we will continue the conversation and friendship of lovers, without knowing the words of man and wife" (p. 142). This ideal looks forward to the character of Congreve's Millamant in *The Way of the World* (1700), with her determination not to be called names after she is married, "as wife, spouse, my dear, joy, jewel, love, sweetheart, and the rest of that nauseous cant in which men and their wives are so fulsomely familiar".[35] It is a mark of the shrewdness of the Cavendish sisters that in the extended Epilogue Luceny reveals that Courtly's practice has fallen short of his ideal.

One reason why *The Concealed Fancies* appeals to female students in particular is its focus on courtship as a matter of gameswomanship and performance. The same facet of the text can be viewed as jejune: as one male student commented of the play, "there's no emotion". I believe that the Cavendish sisters were scoring a subtle point in the obliquity of their approach to female desire and affection. In naming their play, the sisters made use of a contemporary cliché about the behaviour of women in love. In his conduct book *The English Gentlewoman* (1631), Richard Braithwait extols the "pretty pleasing kinde of wooing drawne from a conceived but concealed Fancy".[36] In adopting his phrase the Cavendishes avoid Braithwait's stress on women's bashfulness, using "fancy" primarily in the sense of wit or caprice, and only hinting in their title at the sense of fondness or love.[37]

Yet if Luceny and Tattiney follow the path of discretion in their dealings with men, the play also represents the three cousins in one scene exploring their uncle's "cordials", and devising to "pick his cabinet locks" to see Lord Calsindow's "magazine of love" (p. 144). In this scene Sh. expresses the wish that her exiled uncle "saw us in a prospective", to which her sister replies, "'tis a great way for him to look in a prospective" (p. 143). Cerasano & Wynne-Davies offer the alternate glosses of a crystal ball and a telescope for the word "prospective" in this exchange.[38] This scene is one instance of the Cavendishes' intense awareness "of the constitutive and erotic power of the gaze".[39] In this scene that awareness not only highlights the self that is seen, but discloses the self that wishes to be seen, a female self defined by desire. It is this territory that Shirley and Montagu navigate with respective tact and *préciocité*. All three of the plays I have discussed here manifest a concern with women's social, political and emotional selves. The Cavendishes' fond depiction of female fantasy or women's "strong imagination" (p. 144) was perhaps only conceivable in drama composed within and for a close-knit family circle. But while Jane Cavendish and Elizabeth Brackley stay close to home in their writings, their youthful stepmother, and other women who followed her, would unleash their fancies to create "far other worlds and other seas".

Notes

Unless otherwise specified dates in brackets following films and plays refer to dates of known or estimated first performance/production. I would like to thank Marion Wynne-Davies for helpful editorial suggestions, and Sarah Shieff, Mark Houlahan, Stuart Young and Matt Mancini for commenting on drafts of this essay.

1. My argument here should be seen as a development of the feminist mode of analysis initiated by Catherine Belsey in her book, *The Subject of Tragedy: Identity and Difference in Renaissance Drama* (London: Methuen, 1985).

2. Elizabeth Howe's study, *The First English Actresses: Women and Drama 1660-1700* (Cambridge: Cambridge University Press, 1992) examines the shift in women's status as actors at the Restoration and its impact upon Restoration drama. On female performance in England before 1660 see my article "She that Plays the King; Henrietta Maria and the Threat of the Actress in Caroline Culture", in G. McMullan & J. Hope (Eds) *The Politics of Tragicomedy: Shakespeare and After* (London: Routledge, 1992) and Stephen Orgel, *Impersonations: the Performance of Gender in Shakespeare's England* (Cambridge: Cambridge University Press, 1996), pp. 1-11.

3. Heather L. Weidemann, "Theatricality and Female Identity in Mary Wroth's *Urania*", in Naomi J. Miller & Gary Waller (Eds) *Reading Mary Wroth Representing Alternatives in Early Modern England* (Knoxville: University of Tennessee Press, 1991), pp. 191-209 (p. 192).

4. Sir Francis Osborne, *Historical Memoires on the Reigns of Queen Elizabeth and King James* (1658), pp. 60-61 (Osborne's emphasis).

5. The shift I am describing was in no way absolute; theatricality in women, and in men, continued to pose a considerable threat to customary notions of identity and social stability throughout this period. Witness the upset caused by the Duke of Buckingham's impersonation of a fencing master in an anonymous Queen's masque of 1626, thought by many "too histrionical to become him"; cited in Stephen Orgel & Roy Strong, *Inigo Jones: The Theatre of the Stuart Court,* 2 vols (London: Sotheby Parke Bernet, 1973), I, p. 389.

6. On the possibility of a private performance of *The Concealed Fancies* see S. P. Cerasano & Marion Wynne-Davies (Eds) *Renaissance Drama by Women: Texts and Documents* (London: Routledge, 1996), p. 129. The editors suggest a date of composition *circa* 1645. See also the article by Alison Findlay, "'She gave you the civility of the house': Household Performance in *The Concealed Fancies*", in S. P. Cerasano & Marion Wynne-Davies, *Readings in Renaissance Women's Drama: Criticism, History and Performance 1594-1998* (London: Routledge, 1998).

7. A discussion of the play which complements my own, but omits to consider the changing context of female performance, is Lisa Hopkins, "Judith Shakespeare's Reading: Teaching *The Concealed Fancies*", *Shakespeare Quarterly,* 47 (1996), 4, pp. 396-406.

8. T. E., *The Lawes Resolution of Women's Rights: or, The Lawes Provision for Women* (1632), p. 6.

9. Kim Walker, *Women Writers of the English Renaissance* (New York: Twayne, 1996), p. 138.

10. See the *Oxford English Dictionary* (*OED*), second edition, prepared by J. A. Simpson & E. S. C. Weiner (Oxford: Oxford University Press, 1989): "shift", *sb,* 6b, c and d, and *v,* 5a and b, 6.

11. *The Dramatic Works in the Beaumont and Fletcher Canon,* General Editor, Fredson Bowers, (Cambridge: Cambridge University Press, 1966-96), vol. IV, I. 2. 133-138.

12. Bowers, Epilogue, lines 6-8.

13. *Hyde Park* was revived by the Royal Shakespeare Company in 1987 and produced at the Swan theatre, the Jacobean-style playhouse designed to showcase plays by Shakespeare's contemporaries. The production was given a Bloomsburyesque setting, with Fiona Shaw portraying the heroine, Mistress Carol, as a Virginia Woolf-inspired new woman. While this approach made *Hyde Park* attractive to modern feminism, the setting prevented the play from speaking on its own, Caroline, terms. *The Shepherd's Paradise* still awaits a modern revival.

14. Russell A. Fraser & Norman Rabkin (Eds), *Drama of the English Renaissance,* II, The Stuart Period (New York: Macmillan, 1976), V. 1. 116-119. All further quotations from *Hyde Park* refer to this edition and are incorporated in brackets in the text.

15. Martin Butler, *Theatre and Crisis 1632-1642* (Cambridge: Cambridge University Press, 1984), p. 177.

16. Ira Clark, *Professional Playwrights: Massinger, Ford, Shirley and Brome* (Lexington: University Press of Kentucky, 1992), p. 143.

17. Butler, *Theatre and Crisis,* pp. 178-179; see also pp. 170-171.

18. Clark, *Professional Playwrights,* p. 153; Clark interprets *Hyde Park* as a "social comedy of adaptation", arguing that Shirley's play reinforces "traditional hierarchies" (p. 153).

19. The same paradox is explored in a contemporary dramatic reworking of the Philomel myth, Timberlake Wertenbaker's, *The Love of the Nightingale* (1988).

20. Walter Montagu, *The Shepherd's Paradise* 1629 (*recte* 1659), p. 51. All further page references are incorporated in the text.

21. Camena's language has political and contractual resonances, which anticipate the exploration of women's condition within marriage in Restoration comedy.

22. *OED:* "impudent", *a.*1.wanting in shame or modesty; shameless, unblushing. See *Histrio-Mastix: The Players Scourge, or Actors Tragaedie*

(1633): "And dare then any Christian woman be so more then [*sic*] whorishly impudent, as to act, to speake publikely on a Stage", sig. 6R[4]^{r}.

23. Compare Posthumous's eroticised description of Imogen's innocence in Shakespeare's *Cymbeline* (1609): "Me of my lawful pleasure she restrain'd . . . did it with / A pudency so rosy, the sweet view on't / Might well have warm'd old Saturn", The Arden Shakespeare, ed. J. M. Nosworthy (London: Methuen, 1969), II. 4. 161-164.

24. It is possible to discern a political aura in Camena's linking of the epithets "equal" and "natural" with the concept of liberty; yet her discourse here seems to me more focused on social propriety than political liberty, more akin to Jane Austen than to Hugo Grotius or Thomas Hobbes.

25. In remaining wedded to chastity and herself, Montagu's Miranda mirrors the shepherdess Silvesta in Mary Wroth's unpublished pastoral comedy *Love's Victory* (c. 1620). See Margaret Anne Mclaren, "An Unknown Continent: Lady Mary Wroth's Forgotten Pastoral Drama, 'Loves Victorie'", in Anne M. Haselkorn & Betty S. Travitsky (Eds) *The Renaissance Englishwoman in Print: Counterbalancing the Canon* (Amherst: University of Massachusetts Press, 1990), pp. 276-294 (pp. 286-287).

26. *Poems Songs a Pastorall and a Play by the Right Honourable the Lady Jane Cavendish and Lady Elizabeth Brackley,* Bodleian, Rawlinson MS, Poet. 16. Margaret Ezell discusses the Duke of Newcastle's fostering of his daughters' literary production in "'To Be Your Daughter In Your Pen': The Social Functions of Literature in the Writings of Lady Elizabeth Brackley and Lady Jane Cavendish", *Huntington Library Quarterly,* 51 (1988), pp. 281-296.

27. Cerasano & Wynne-Davies, *Renaissance Drama by Women,* p. 143. All further page references to this edition are incorporated in the text.

28. As suggested by Lisa Hopkins: see her valuable discussion of this scene, "Judith Shakespeare's Reading", pp. 400-402 (p. 402).

29. Mary Hamer, *Signs of Cleopatra: History, Politics, Representation* (London: Routledge, 1993), pp. 25, 43.

30. "Nature meant me / A wife; a silly, harmless, household dove", *John Dryden: Selected Works* (San Francisco: Rinehart Press, 1971), IV. 1. 91-92.

31. Cerasano & Wynne-Davies, *Renaissance Drama by Women,* pp. 133, 151.

32. *The Concealed Fancies* forms part of a seventeenth-century feminist discourse on marriage represented by texts such as Mary More's

The Woman's Right, or her Power in a Greater Equality to her Husband proved than is allowed or practised in England (c. 1674) published as Appendix II in Margaret Ezell's, *The Patriarch's Wife: Literary Evidence and the History of the Family* (Chapel Hill: University of North Carolina Press, 1987).

33. The textual status of the phrase "scene self" must remain conjectural, as the word "self" appears to be a later insertion in the manuscript (*Poems Songs a Pastorall and a Play,* p. 91). I am grateful to Martin Butler for cautioning me on this matter.

34. Thomas Hobbes's definition of "a free man" is relevant here. To paraphrase Hobbes: "A FREE-WOMAN, is she, that in those things, which by her strength and wit she is able to do, is not hindred to doe what she has a will to". See *Leviathan,* ed. C. B. Macpherson (Harmondsworth: Penguin, 1981), p. 262.

35. William Congreve, *The Way of the World,* ed. Brian Gibbons, New Mermaids (London: Ernest Benn, 1979), IV.1.169-171.

36. Braithwait, *The English Gentlewoman* (1631), p. 131.

37. For the latter sense see *OED:* "fancy", sb., 8a and b.

38. Cerasano & Wynne-Davies, *Renaissance Drama by Women,* p. 212, n. 45.

39. Hopkins, "Judith Shakespeare's Reading", p. 404.

THE TRIUMPH OF PEACE (1632)

CRITICAL COMMENTARY

Stephen Orgel (essay date 1975)

SOURCE: Orgel, Stephen. "The Role of King." In *The Illusion of Power: Political Theater in the English Renaissance,* pp. 59-87. Berkeley: University of California Press, 1975.

[*In the following essay, Orgel interprets Jacobean and Caroline masques as a mirror reflecting the crown as it wanted to be seen. He asserts that for Charles I the masque was an expression of the strength of his royal will—even when, as in Shirley's The Triumph of Peace, it attempted to correct or advise the monarch.*]

Hostile critics saw in the royal histrionics only frivolity or hypocrisy, and even sympathic observers regularly referred to masques as "vanities." This, indeed, is Prospero's term for his own masque, "some vanity of mine art."[1] The description is exact and the charge irrefutable: these works are totally self-regarding. They are designed to be so. "All representations," wrote Ben Jonson, "especially those of this nature in court, public spectacles, either have been or ought to be the mirrors of man's life."[2] But mirrors, like so many Renaissance symbols, may be viewed in various and contradictory ways, and their moral implications lie in the eye of the beholder. They are emblems of worldliness and pride, frail glasses "which are as easy broke as they make forms."[3] They are also the way to self-knowledge. English didacticism in 1559 could do no better than provide a mirror for magistrates; and Hamlet's player holding the mirror up to nature is not encouraging her self-esteem. For the Jacobean translator of Ovid, the myth of Narcissus embodied the full ambiguity of the power of reflection. The youth's mother, reports George Sandys, *"enquiring whether he should live until he were old,* Tiresias *replied:* If he know not himselfe. *As strange as obscure; and seeming contradictory to that Oracle of* Apollo: To know a mans selfe is the chiefest knowledge. *The lacke hereof hath ruined many: but having it must needs ruine our beautiful* Narcissus: *who only is in love with his owne perfection."*[4] This is a paradigm for the Stuart court and the mirror of its theater.

Roles in plays, to Puritan observers, were impostures and lies. The very act of imitation, in drama as in art, usurped a divine prerogative, and theatrical productions were therefore often seen to be at the heart of the court's degeneracy and impiety. But from another point of view the parts we choose to play are not impersonations but ideals. They are what we wish to be, and they reveal not so much the way we want others to see us as the way we want to see ourselves.

Here are some ways in which the Stuart court wanted to see itself.

THE MASQUE OF QUEENS

In 1609 Ben Jonson and Inigo Jones created a heroic masque for Queen Anne and her ladies. *The Masque of Queens* provided a martial context for womanly virtue—whereas King James, we will recall, was an ardent and programmatic pacifist. The production opened on a coven of witches and an ugly hell; infernal dances and charms provided an elaborate and extended antimasque. Suddenly the hall was filled with a blast of loud music, "with which not only the hags themselves but the hell into which they ran quite vanished, and the whole face of the scene altered, scarce suffering the memory of such a thing. But in the place of it appeared a glorious and magnificent building figuring the House of Fame, in the top of which were discovered the twelve masquers sitting upon a throne triumphal erected in form of a pyramid and circled with all store of light."

Eleven of the masquers had the roles of warrior queens from history. In Jones's costume designs, the Amazonian qualities are expressed through a variety of details: an elegant bodice adapted from armor, a plumed helmet, masculine half-sleeves, bases, and instead of dancing pumps, light boots. For the twelfth queen, Anne of Denmark, Jonson invented the figure of Bel-Anna, Queen of the Ocean. Only the design for her headdress has survived. Jones has crowned her with an armillary sphere, a celestial globe. Just such a model as this had demonstrated to Ficino the power of human knowledge and the essential divinity of the mind.

Jones's drawing of the House of Fame is the earliest surviving design for stage machinery in England. The drawing shows the front of a hexagonal building; it has double doors within a huge central arch, above which sit the twelve masquers on their pyramidal throne. The figures on the roof are probably musicians; the two deities in the clouds on either side of the cornice are identified by Jonson as "eminent figures of Honor and Virtue." The façade is adorned with statues. Those on the lower tier represent "the most excellent poets, as Homer, Virgil, Lucan, etc., as being the substantial supporters of Fame," while those on the upper are "Achilles, Aeneas, Caesar, and those great heroes which these poets had celebrated." The conception, Jonson says, derives from Chaucer.

The architecture of the building is a characteristic amalgam of styles. It has certain Palladian elements—the central arch, the pilasters, the windows of the lower story—but the basic motif of the upper tier is the gothic trefoil. In the same way, the statuary on the façade pays homage to classical heroes, but the house itself is a realization of the work of the greatest English medieval poet. The union of classic and romantic, heroic and chivalric, was a continual ideal of James's reign, and Jones's setting is an architectural assertion of the success of the synthesis. But Jonson also makes it clear that in the House of Fame, heroism is a secondary virtue: the heroes are glorified not by their deeds alone, but by the enduring and transforming power of poetry. Every hero has his poet, and the building is inspired by Chaucer. The whole vision presents the Jacobean court with its own best image. Heroism is the royal consort; but the highest virtue is that of the pacific king, not a warrior, but a classical scholar and poet.

This was the setting for the entry of the masquers. The pyramidal throne suddenly turned around, and in its place the winged figure of Fame appeared. The great gates then opened, and the ladies were borne forth into the hall in three triumphant chariots, drawn respectively by "far-sighted eagles, to note Fame's sharp eye," griffins, "that design / Swiftness and strength," and, for the queen's carriage, lions, "that imply / The top of graces, state and majesty."

OBERON

Like his mother, Henry Prince of Wales was an ardent masquer, and like his father, an antiquarian and patron of the arts. For the two seasons following *The Masque of Queens,* 1610 and 1611, he commissioned from Jonson and Jones two entertainments designed to restore to life the world of ancient British chivalry. For the first, *Prince Henry's Barriers,* he chose a role from the Arthurian romances, Meliadus, lover of The Lady of the Lake. In Jonson's fiction, the young prince is summoned by Merlin and King Arthur to revitalize English knighthood—the production centered about feats of arms in which Henry distinguished himself. A contemporary spectator records that "the Prince performed this challenge with wondrous skill and courage, to the great joy and admiration of all the beholders, the Prince not being full sixteene yeeres of age."[5]

But the martial side of the prince's nature apparently disturbed King James, who vetoed a similar project for the next year. In honor of Henry's creation as Prince of Wales, Jonson and Jones devised instead the masque of *Oberon, The Fairy Prince.* Spenserian romance joins with classical myth to create a Britain that unites the traditions of chivalry with classical order. Silenus and his satyrs celebrate the accession of Oberon, heir of King Arthur—Greek and British mythology are, for Jonson, part of a single tradition. Indeed, in a gloss Jonson even suggests that the English word "fairy" is cognate with the Greek *féras,* a late form of *théras,* satyrs. The synthesis is again apparent in Jones's costume for the young prince. King James's heir is a medieval knight and Roman emperor combined; he also wears recognizable elements of contemporary dress. The Roman skirt, for example, has been transformed into Jacobean trunk hose. Oberon is not an impersonation, but a version of the true prince.

The palace Jones designed for Oberon is another synthesis, an anthology of architectural styles. A rusticated basement seems to grow out of the rocks. The parterre has a Palladian balustrade. A splendid pedimented archway fills the central façade, supported by grotesque Italian terms, and accented by Doric pilasters and Serlian windows. Crenellated English medieval turrets are topped with tiny baroque minarets; two pure Elizabethan chimneys frame an elegant dome in the style of Bramante.

Jones's inspiration here is not merely eclectic. Rather this design makes a programmatic visual statement about the national culture and the sources of its heroism. England becomes great through the imposition of classical order upon British nature; the rough native strength of the castle is remade according to the best models, civilized by the arts of design, by learning and taste. In the same way the Prince of Faery, the new Prince of Wales, comes out of the woods, tames the rough satyrs, and descends to salute his father, the real King James, in the Palladian architecture of the White-hall Banqueting House.

Such productions reveal a great deal about the age's sense of itself and its intense hopes for this young man. The king, for all his pacific policies (which in any case were not especially popular) was awkward and largely without charm. Henry's untimely death in 1612 robbed England not only of a patron for her poets and artists, but of a romantic hero as well.

NEPTUNE'S TRIUMPH FOR THE RETURN OF ALBION

In 1623 Prince Charles, the Duke of Buckingham, the prince's private secretary Sir Francis Cottington, and an odd assortment of others including the court dwarf Archibald Armstrong, went to Spain to negotiate the prince's marriage with the Infanta Maria, sister of Philip IV. The Spanish match was a favorite project of King James; it represented a major European alliance, and seemed to promise an eventual reconciliation with the Catholic faith and the powers that adhered to it. But it also involved large concessions to the Catholic cause in England, and was therefore understandably unpopular with the British public. The prince and his negotiators were eager for an agreement, and undertook to meet all conditions; but the Spanish court rightly felt that Charles's promises regarding the necessary changes in the English laws of religious conformity were unrealistic, and after almost a year of discussions the plan was abandoned. The prince's party sourly returned home in October 1624, to find their failure greeted with popular rejoicing. To the king, however, the whole episode must have seemed a galling fiasco, and the court provided no celebrations of its own.

Three months later Jonson and Jones prepared a long delayed welcome home. *Neptune's Triumph for the Return of Albion* does more than put the best face on a bad situation. It provides a context within which the fiasco may be seen as a victory. Jonson's fiction begins, like so many of his later masques, as fact: it opens in the Banqueting House itself. The stage presents nothing but two pillars dedicated to Neptune; the masque has not yet begun. A poet enters, ostensibly to distribute playbills; the court cook appears, and requests an account of the forthcoming entertainment. The poet expounds his allegory:

> The mighty Neptune, mighty in his styles,
> And large command of waters and of isles,

> Not as the lord and sovereign of the seas,
> But chief in the art of riding, late did please
> To send his Albion forth . . .
> Through Celtiberia; and to assist his course,
> Gave him his powerful Manager of Horse,
> With divine Proteus, father of disguise,
> To wait upon them with his counsels wise
> In all extremes. His great commands being done,
> And he desirous to review his son,
> He doth dispatch a floating isle from hence
> Unto the Hesperian shores to waft him thence.

In this allegory, King James is Neptune, Prince Charles Albion; Buckingham is visible under his title of Master of the King's Horse in the first of Albion's associates; and Cottington, who had served as a secret agent, is Proteus. The journey is "through Celtiberia" because their route took them first to Paris, but the reason for the expedition is carefully glossed over. The floating island is then described. The royal party will make its appearance enthroned beneath a mystical Tree of Harmony, the banyan, first planted in India by the sun himself. The tree becomes a symbol of the harmonious strength of the court; every one of its branches sends out roots, and becomes a new trunk supporting the whole.

The cook demands more entertainment, the comedy of an antimasque. The poet replies that his work is high art, addressed only to the intellect. But the cook then articulates Jonson's own concept of theater at court: these presentations speak to the whole man, and must satisfy all his senses; they are given in the Banqueting House because they are not merely poems but banquets, ravishing sights and sounds, sweet smells; they feed all parts of the observer's sensibility. And the cook himself then produces the comic dancers, in the form of meats and vegetables from his own gigantic cooking pot.

Now the poet's masque begins. The heavens open revealing Apollo and Mercury (patrons respectively of the poetry of the masque and the prose of the antimasque), accompanied by the muses and the goddess Harmony. To their music the floating island appears, and moves forward bearing the masquers. Jones's island is covered with an arbor, as the text requires; but it is an arbor of palms, not a banyan tree. In part, this doubtless reflects merely the architect's ignorance of Asian botany; however the choice of palms can hardly have been accidental. The all-powerful Neptune's island bears emblems of peace; the returning prince appears beneath the branches that heralded Christ's entry into Jerusalem.

The association of James's pacifism with the peace of God, and of his capital with the holy city, formed an important part of Jacobean official imagery from the very beginning of the reign, and as a way of justifying unpopular policies, particularly in ecclesiastical matters, it became increasingly insistent. James was regularly represented as Solomon (for example, he is so depicted by Rubens on the Banqueting House ceiling), and the Anglican church under the Stuart monarchy was held to preserve the pristine purity of Christ and the Apostles. The line of argument ran this way: England was converted by Joseph of Arimathea, long before Constantine and the conversion of Rome. The decay of Christianity began with the advent of Augustine and his popish monks, but the abolition of the English monasteries had allowed the ancient faith to flower again. All of this is implied in Jones's emblematic palms.

But the masque makes a more overt set of claims for the monarchy as well. James is explicitly represented, after all, not as Solomon but as Neptune. With the descent of the masquers the island disappears, and Jones's scene opens to reveal a marine palace. James's Palladian Banqueting House is now translated into the deep perspective of a maritime fantasy. Behind the allegorization of the king as Neptune lies a long tradition. In the same way, Sir Walter Ralegh had sung the Ocean's love to Cynthia, the moon, ruler of the sea; and Jonson and Jones in 1609 had presented Queen Anne not as the sovereign of the realm but as Bel-Anna, Queen of the Ocean. There is, of course, a simple military reality behind this: the strength of an island kingdom depends heavily on its navy. But there are mythographic realities as well that tell us a good deal more about the way the Stuart court saw itself. Neptune appears in the masque "Not as the lord and sovereign of the seas"—he is that in any case—"But chief in the art of riding."

The connection between these two aspects of the royal persona would not have seemed obscure to a Jacobean audience who knew that King James's favorite sport was riding. But Jonson's allusion goes deeper, to a myth in which Neptune was the creator and tamer of the embodiment of the ocean's energy, the horse. From Plato onward, horsemanship had served as a symbol for the imposition of reason upon the wildness of nature or the violence of the passions. This is why the implications of the term chivalry are so much more complex than its derivation—from *chevalerie,* horsemanship—would suggest. To bring the destructive energies of nature under control, both within and without, was the end of Renaissance education and science. Every gentleman was thus properly a type of Neptune; and on a larger scale, the myth provided a pattern for the relation between king and commonwealth.

That the pattern was unrealistic goes without saying. The only mind operating in Jonson's allegory is the monarch's. Albion's return is a triumph because it is executed at Neptune's command; the whole action is presented as a serene extension of the royal will. This is a political myth, an accurate record of the way James

viewed his government in his last years. His son's autocracy is only a step beyond. But the danger of political myths lies in their tendency to exclude political realities: the mirror of the king's mind allows him to know only himself. By 1624 the commonwealth, unlike the sea or the horse, had developed a very strong mind of its own. And indeed, in this penultimate year of his reign, political realities denied the king even his theatrical triumph. The French and Spanish ambassadors could not be invited to attend together, and each threatened the most dire diplomatic reprisals if the other were given priority. Within two days of the performance, James was forced to cancel the masque.

THE TRIUMPH OF PEACE AND *COELUM BRITANNICUM*

The development of Charles I's autocracy is one of the most extraordinary chapters in British legal history. In 1629, outraged by what he took to be continual inroads on the crown's authority, frustrated by inadequate revenues and the failure of numerous proposals for new taxes, the king dissolved Parliament and determined to rule without it. He managed to do so for the next eleven years. The 1630s saw the most complete consolidation of royal power in British history; by 1635 the king claimed the rights of direct taxation, the granting of monopolies in all industries, the control of all ecclesiastical offices including those in private households, the enforcement of absolute religious conformity—even the manufacture of soap was declared to be a royal prerogative. No area of the nation's life was too insignificant for Charles to want to regulate it: for example, by royal edict alehouses were forbidden to sell tobacco, and London inns to serve game. (The latter measure was conceived as a way of making town life so unpleasant for country gentlemen that they would be persuaded to return home to manage their estates.)

There were many challenges to the legality of the royal prerogatives. In every case, the basic question was whether laws could be made by royal fiat, without the assent of parliament. Gradually over the decade, usually by the barest possible majority, the courts came to support the king. By 1638, when the Star Chamber handed down its decision in the famous ship-money case[6] that *rex* was *lex,* that king was law, the British monarchy was *statutorily* the most powerful in Europe. The political realities were, of course, quite different. Only *authority* can derive from statute. A government's power depends on its ability to enforce its authority. The crown might impose taxes, but people increasingly refused to pay them; and if they could not be persuaded to do so by noble rhetoric and high ideals, the king's only recourse was an army that had to be paid out of uncollected taxes. Such realities produced in Charles only patient bafflement at the stubborn unregeneracy of so ungrateful a populace; he ruled according to a political theory that had the quality of a hermetic allegory. In a very profound way the stage at Whitehall was his truest kingdom, the masque the most accurate expression of his mind.

The legal profession was on the whole uncomfortable about royal prerogatives, and unsympathetic to the crucial principle of Divine Right, which made the king responsible only to God. In 1634 the Inns of Court took the remarkable step of retaining Inigo Jones and James Shirley in an attempt to speak to the king in his own language. The lawyers presented a masque at Whitehall that was, for all its courtly splendor, diplomatically but unequivocally critical of the royal policies, and undertook, through the power of poetry and the marvels of spectacle, to persuade the royal spectator to return to the rule of law.

The impulse to produce **The Triumph of Peace** came, oddly enough, from a royal command. William Prynne, author of *Histrio-Mastrix,* with its treasonable attack on court theatricals, had been indicted, and his trial was about to begin. The prisoner was a barrister of Lincoln's Inn, and had dedicated the offending volume to his fellow lawyers. Charles demanded that the legal fraternities definitively repudiate their colleague and publicly declare their loyalty to the crown. What gesture of loyalty could be more appropriate than the presentation of a lawyers' masque at court?

The Inns lavishly complied. Shirley composed his text in consultation with a committee of barristers; the subject of **The Triumph of Peace** was the relationship between the king and the law. The setting Jones provided for the masque's opening was an Italian piazza. In fact, Shirley had given the architect a choice; the text calls for a scene "representing the Forum or Piazza of Peace." Jones chose not a classical Roman forum, but the center of the life of an Italian Renaissance city-state, the architectural embodiment of republican principles. In contrast, two years earlier when Jones created a similar setting for the king's masque *Albion's Triumph,* the architecture had been a clear expression of imperial ideals.

The Roman analogy is carefully avoided in **The Triumph of Peace.** Extravagantly and with unparalleled splendor the legal profession asserted to the crown their joint responsibilities:

> The world shall give prerogative to neither;
> We cannot flourish but together.

Not surprisingly, considering the nature of the medium, the message failed to get across. The masque was a huge success; the royal solipsist saw in it nothing but adulation, and was graciously pleased to order it repeated.[7]

Two weeks later the king presented his own view of his place in the commonwealth. Thomas Carew's and Inigo Jones's *Coelum Britannicum* was the greatest theatrical expression of the Caroline autocracy. Carew's allegory is about the radical reformation of society, the purifying of the mind and passions, the power of language and apparitions to exorcise the rebellious spirit; it even undertakes to create a new body of poetic symbolism, as if to redeem through its imagery the imperfect nature that art imitates. The masque conceives the royal will as central to an unprecedented degree. In its fable, Jove has taken the Caroline court as a model for his own, and has banished licentiousness and ignoble passion from the heavens. The opening scene is a ruined city, the decadent civilization that is to be revitalized and ennobled. Its shutters part, and the gigantic figure of Atlas fills the stage. For the Renaissance, Atlas was the exemplar of cosmic wisdom. Jones's heroic figure, crowned and bearing the heavens on his shoulders, is the link between earth and heaven, an allegory of the monarch described in *Basilikon Doron.* The great globe opens, revealing the constellations, those glorifications of ancient lust and violence, the mythology of an outworn past. Each in its turn is deposed and extinguished, until heaven at last stands empty, ready to receive a chaste and heroic iconography.

The reformation then begins. Atlas and the sphere vanish and a mountainous landscape appears. From beneath the stage come ancient Britons, the kingdom's history restored to life. (They are the figures shown seated on the rocks.) Above, wild nature is framed by the palms of the royal peace. This setting is to open, revealing first a garden and a princely villa, and then an elegant pastoral perspective with Windsor Castle in the distance, while the heavens will part to show beneficent deities smiling on Charles's reign.

The grandiloquence of the masque's conception lay as much in its engineering as in its poetry. Carew's text gives a vivid sense of the spectator's experience:

> . . . there began to rise out of the earth the top of a hill, which by little and little grew to be a huge mountain that covered all the scene; the underpart of this was wild and craggy, and above somewhat more pleasant and flourishing; about the middle part of this mountain were seated the three kingdoms of England, Scotland and Ireland, all richly attired in regal habits appropriated to the several nations, with crowns on their heads, and each of them bearing the ancient arms of the kingdoms they represented. At a distance above these sat a young man in a white embroidered robe, upon his fair hair an olive garland, with wings at his shoulders, and holding in his hand a cornucopia filled with corn and fruits, representing the genius of these kingdoms. . . .

> At this the underpart of the rock opens, and out of a cave are seen to come the masquers, richly attired like ancient heroes; the colours yellow embroidered with silver, their antique helms curiously wrought, and great plumes on the top; before them a troop of young lords and noblemen's sons bearing torches of virgin wax; these were apparelled after the old British fashion in

white coats embroidered with silver, girt, and full gathered, cut square-collared, and round caps on their heads, with a white feather wreathen about them; first these dance with their lights in their hands, after which the masquers descend into the room and dance their entry.

The dance being past, there appears in the further part of the heaven coming down a pleasant cloud, bright and transparent, which coming softly downwards before the upper part of the mountain, embraceth the genius, but so as through it all his body is seen; and then rising again with a gentle motion bears up the genius of the three kingdoms, and being past the airy region, pierceth the heavens, and is no more seen. At that instant the rock with the three kingdoms on it sinks and is hidden in the earth. This strange spectacle gave great cause of admiration, but especially how so huge a machine, and of that great height, could come from under the stage, which was but six foot high.

The full force of Caroline idealism, the determination to purify, reorder, reform, reconceive a whole culture, is here fully realized in apparitions and marvelous machinery. The most complete expression of the royal will in the age lay not in the promulgation of edicts, erratically obeyed, nor in military power, inadequately furnished, but in Inigo Jones's ability to do the impossible.

Notes

1. *The Tempest* 4.1.41.

2. *Love's Triumph through Callipolis,* lines 1-3.

3. *Measure for Measure* 2.4.123-26.

4. *Ovid's Metamorphoses Englished* (Oxford, 1632), p. 103.

5. Stephen Orgel and Roy Strong, *Inigo Jones* (Berkeley, 1973), 1:159.

6. The king had revived an Elizabethan tax on coastal towns for the support of the navy. In 1633 the tax was extended to inland districts, and met with considerable resistance, the opponents arguing that the imposition of ship-money constituted taxation by royal fiat. The test case was Rex v. Hampden, 1637; the decision was overturned by Parliament in 1641.

7. For a detailed discussion of the masque's complex political context, and a full analysis of the allegory, see *Inigo Jones* 1:63-66.

Martin Butler (essay date July 1987)

SOURCE: Butler, Martin. "Politics and the Masque: *The Triumph of Peace.*" *The Seventeenth Century* 2, no. 2 (July 1987): 117-41.

[*In the following essay, Butler challenges the notion that Caroline masques were merely dramatic spectacles, arguing instead that court masques were one aspect of* Charles I's government by consensus. Focusing on Shirley's Triumph of Peace, *Butler analyzes how the production of a masque can generate multiple political meanings.*]

Recent years have seen much important and suggestive work on the court masque under the early Stuarts. The conditions that generated the masque have been fully documented and, especially, the function of the form as a vehicle of political statement is much better understood than in the past; the masque no longer seems to be inflated flattery but a complex fusion of counsel and compliment. A great deal of this work has come together in the books of Stephen Orgel and Roy Strong, particularly in their sumptuous joint enterprise, *Inigo Jones: The Theatre of the Stuart Court.*[1] However, a number of significant misconceptions remain, particularly in relation to the 1630s, a decade that was a culmination in every sense, artistic and political.

In particular, in spite of a widespread acknowledgement of the very considerable political capital that the masques provided, a tendency still remains to write down the court festivals of the 1630s as, in the long run, a kind of escapism; for all the substantial sophistication of their achievement, in the retrospective illumination of 1642 the masques still seem a distraction, naively over-confident, inevitably doomed. This is a view which powerfully colours the introduction to *Inigo Jones: The Theatre of the Stuart Court,* where the masques are presented against a background of political dissent and fragmentation which they themselves were helping to create. As England polarized steadily into court and country so, we are told, the masques could only be a 'profound irrelevance'. In the context of the approaching civil war, the illusions in which the masques traded became ironically precise symbols of the position of the crown: Charles I's Star Chamber decrees were 'as unreal as Inigo Jones's victory over gravity' (I, 72, 75). The same note is heard even more insistently in Roy Strong's chapter on Caroline culture in his *Splendour at Court,*[2] in which the Caroline masques are seen as 'little more than a postponement of disastrous troubles to come' (p.233). Charles placed much confidence in 'the effect of these spectacles in staving off the oncoming tide of disaster' (p.241), but the 'illusion of control' (p.219) which they allowed was belied by the actuality; Charles was left with only 'extravagant assertions of a mirage of power', while those who danced with him now seem not a little 'pathetic', or 'faintly comic' (pp.247-48). This view of the Caroline masque continues in Graham Parry's *The Golden Age Restor'd,*[3] in which the decade's masquing is said to culminate in 'the hollow symbolism of pretended victories'; the 'essential divinity of kings is confirmed', but only to the satisfaction of 'the enclosed world of the court' (pp.201-02).

Plainly, there is a contradiction here which has been only partially confronted. High claims are being advanced for the cultural importance of the court masque yet these are simultaneously contradicted by the political failure which the masque is assumed to have encouraged: the form is being represented as at once hermetically closed and incapable of closure. This contradiction in the masque form is repeated at the level of masque commentary: a considerable amount of Orgel and Strong's energies has gone into investigating the intellectual contexts of the masque, yet at the end of the day the form is still not granted full intellectual seriousness, but left very much as Francis Bacon dismissed it, an expensive toy.

A major problem here is the retrospective focus of much writing on the masque. For Orgel and Strong, the masque is symbolic of royal myopia before the civil war: Charles dances heedless of the political deterioration around him. The limitations of the masque form are coded into the exclusiveness of the court event: if the court was only talking to itself and only telling itself what it wanted to hear, little wonder that the political collapse at the end of the decade should have been so absolute. Clearly there is a great deal of truth in this position. The narrowness of the court's cultural sympathies goes a long way towards explaining the feelings of alienation from the court which became possible in the 1640s, while the magical transformations and sudden transitions of masque staging were designed to underpin an ideology of innate royal authority which could not survive a general loss of confidence in the crown. And yet the perception of these ironies depends on the prior historical assumption that such a loss of confidence was indeed going inevitably to come about, that England in the 1630s was already embarked on a 'highroad to civil war'[4] that had only one destination. Obviously, one of the factors that is operating here is a simple difficulty of historical perspective: it is impossible for us to erase our foreknowledge that the Caroline regime, for all its large pretensions, was not going to survive beyond 1642. But what also seems to be present in the language with which Orgel and Strong criticize the political inadequacies of the masque is a logical circularity which sounds suspiciously Whiggish and teleological: the masque was seeking to promulgate royal power; royal power was on the brink of collapse; therefore, the masque was ineffective and 'irrelevant'.

I have elsewhere expatiated at length on the dangers of an 'ex post facto' reading of the literature of the 1630s;[5] it is rather surprising (in view of the opinions quoted above) to find that so too has Roy Strong.[6] What is more to the point is that a large gap has long been present between perceptions of the decade in the minds of historians of politics and historians of the masque.[7] The historical model that underlies Orgel and Strong's accounts represents the 1630s as a single and accelerating divide between the crown and the crown's 'opponents', in which the court becomes increasingly embattled and isolated, marginalized by the steady advance of more powerful political forces. Against this background the masque is inevitably going to look fragile. But political historians have not represented the decade quite like this for some time; indeed, there is some justice in thinking of Charles in 1630 as being on the offensive, rather than in a posture of defence. One estimate goes like this:[8] after the fiasco of the 1629 parliament, Charles (who had begun his reign by doggedly holding four parliaments in five years) went into the 1630s intent on exploring such other options as were open to him. There ensued an attempt to tighten up government efficiency and consolidate the crown's fiscal powers. The privy council became the linch-pin of royal government and its business multiplied; the gentry were chivvied back to their roles as local governors; a stream of proclamations regulating all aspects of life began to issue from Whitehall. Finance was raised through channels that did not require parliamentary consent; by maintaining a non-interventionist posture on foreign affairs Charles avoided a prime burden that would seriously have strained his resources. Far from disappearing beneath a tide of 'opposition', Charles was endeavouring to adopt a style of government all too familiar from the other European monarchies, where parliaments were giving place to modern bureaucratic absolutisms. And simultaneous with this attempt to promote 'an ambitious renovation in church and state'[9] led by the court and depending on ideals of order, discipline and deference, there was developed a programme of masques, performed before an invited audience drawn from the political élites, to promulgate the wisdom, justice and stability of Stuart government, and to proclaim the value of peace in a Europe that everywhere else was being ruined by war. The masques may have idealized Charles's achievements but this alone does not make them 'escapist'. Rather, they were the necessary cultural counterpart to the court's attempt to take a radical political initiative.

Now clearly it is important not to underestimate the distrust with which Charles's religious policies and fiscal devices came to be regarded, nor to overstimate the strength of the financial resources to which, without summoning parliament, he was confined.[10] His freedom of movement was limited in that he could not afford to take steps which would alienate the political élites on whom he depended for money and support in the provinces (as the fiasco of the Scottish campaigns eventually demonstrated). The Caroline experiment in government promised more than it was finally able to perform, yet for as long as Charles's political élites continued to co-operate with his needs his power was not a mirage. Orgel and Strong represent royal power in such a way as to imply that it was inherently unstable and always destined ultimately to collapse, but while the gentry continued to collect Ship Money the court masques dramatized an ideology focussed on Whitehall that was daily being turned into political action.

A second problem with Orgel and Strong's position is that it represents early Stuart politics almost exclusively in terms of conflict. Modern historians, on the other hand, have increasingly come to emphasize that Caroline government rested on principles of consensus and co-operation, and exploited such channels of communication and 'points of contact'[11] as were open to it. A particularly pointed case of this is posed in *Inigo Jones: The Theatre of the Stuart Court* by the treatment of Attorney General Noy who had a hand in preparing **The Triumph of Peace.** Noy, a lawyer, had been prominent in the parliaments of the 1620s for his speeches criticizing the legality of patents and monopolies. Notwithstanding, he was offered the post of Attorney General in 1631 and thereafter his legal skills were employed on developing several of Charles's fiscal devices; the responsibility for Ship Money rests very largely with him. And yet he was involved in planning **The Triumph of Peace,** a masque which, as Orgel and Strong correctly perceive, is in some senses a critique of those very same devices. I shall be offering my own explanation of these curious 'facts' shortly. The reaction of Orgel and Strong is to throw up their hands in horror: 'Noy was a curious figure, a thoroughgoing opportunist and unabashed turncoat' to whom Charles had 'made it clear that it was to his advantage to change his allegiance' (I, 65). The problem with this comment is that its language projects a politics of conflict on to a situation remarkable for its consensus. Working on the assumption that there were two 'sides' in the 1630s and that the royal side was in a state of incipient collapse, Orgel and Strong cannot make sense of Noy except as an outrageous traitor to former loyalties shoring up a shoddy cause. But Noy's career was not an untypical one. We find other honourable men co-operating with the court in the 1630s who had been court critics only a few years before: men like Dudley Digges (arrested for seditious words in the 1626 parliament, proponent of the Petition of Right, then latterly Master of the Rolls) or John Selden (arrested 1629, to be found in 1635 compiling learned arguments in support of Ship Money). In parliament these men had represented themselves as critics of royal policies rather than royal power, and in the absence of parliament they naturally utilized their political skills in the only other way available to them, through the channels of the Caroline experiment in government. Orgel and Strong's accusation that Noy changed his 'allegiance' is frankly meaningless; with no parliaments in the 1630s there could be no parliamentary 'opposition' for him to betray.[12]

The consensual basis of Charles's personal government is well seen in the delegation of authority that took place, from privy council to lords lieutenant, to the provincial bench and thence to parish officialdom, but its most remarkable demonstration lies in this body of former court critics who in the 1630s chose actively to work with the court. Some, like John Pym, held minor offices in the localities. Others performed powerful and influential roles at the centre: most famously Thomas Wentworth, future Earl of Strafford, but also smaller men like Digges, Selden and Noy. The resources of loyalty on which the crown could still draw in the 1630s are well seen in Charles's ability to build bridges to people who, in different circumstances, might have been found in 'opposition'. It is precisely when it became impossible to work with such men, as happened in 1640-42, that Charles's position was rendered critical, and it is no coincidence that this was the historical moment at which the masques ceased to come. My contention in this paper is that the masque too could participate in this politics of consensus. Rather than being read as rearguard actions against an unpalatable 'reality', the finest masques can be understood as attempts at finding bridges, between the crown, the crown's supporters, and the crown's critics.

I have no wish to deny the basic truth that the loss of confidence in Charles in 1640 was reflected in, and partly generated by, the limitations of the culture which he sponsored: the masques of 1638-40 which register a consciousness of Charles's political problems in the crisis over the Scots do not embody an adequate response to those difficulties. What I am arguing, however, is that this retrospective consciousness has pervasively skewed understanding of the masques of the preceding years. On the one hand, the masques have not been granted full seriousness as political acts. Though on one level private entertainments, they were on another level spectacles of stage in which king and court together tested, defined, promulgated or outlawed current ideological values which outside the masque were being used to inform acts of power. On the other hand, the complexity with which the masques are sited in respect to social and political relations generally has been considerably underestimated. It is probably true to say that a complete hermeneutics of the masque has still to be written. Briefly, a masque constructs meaning from (at least) four variables: an author, a masquer, an audience, and a monarch. Sometimes the monarch may be the masquer; sometimes he may be, to all intents and purposes, the author. The formal complexities which these four generate are considerable. The masque may be read as a simple statement of royal intent. If the king is the spectator, it may be understood as a reflection of the king's meaning for the sake of the king, or it may be offered to the king as an act of homage or, more interestingly, persuasion. If the king is a masquer, it is possible that he is being made to perform roles which express what it is hoped he would be rather than what he is. Sometimes the audience's perception of the masque's meaning differs from the king's; sometimes the author's perception differs from both of these (as seems to have been the case with Jonson's *Masque of Metamorphosed Gipsies*).[13] Plainly, the meanings available in a masque are limited by the question of tact; it is not going to be possible to present meanings which the king cannot be made to tolerate. But within these limits there is still significant room for manoeuvre, manoeuvring which may have a real political function as an act of rapprochement, appeasement, or finding of 'points of contact'. The masque text is one corner in a dialogue the other corners of which are the audiences by which the masque is received and appropriated.

II

A text which usefully focuses these strictures is James Shirley's *The Triumph of Peace,* presented to the king in February 1634 by the gentlemen of the Inns of Court, and notorious for being the most expensive and widely-reported masque of the decade. *The Triumph of Peace* is useful because it appears to be anomalous: as Orgel and Strong point out, this masque is remarkable for the 'cautious but unmistakable critiques of Charles's policy' which it contains (I, 63). Most obviously, there is the antimasque which satirizes six 'projectors', racketeers who are seeking to gain from the king grants of monopoly for ludicrous inventions—perpetual motion machines, submarine suits, poultry diets and the like—which they will then operate to the royal profit but also, implicitly, to feather their own nests. This antimasque alludes quite explicitly to some of the more 'extraordinary courses' by which Charles was raising finance without parliament; in Bulstrode Whitelocke's account of the masque, the projectors 'pleased the Spectators the more, because by it an Information was covertly given to the King, of the unfitness and ridiculousness of these Projects against the Law'.[14] But more remarkably, the fable of the masque as a whole, performed by representatives of the kingdom's legal profession, was a statement about the dependence of Peace and Justice on the institution of Law, and constituted a tactful but firm caution about the necessity of governments acknowledging the constraints of legality.

The problem with all of this is that the masque represents itself as an act of homage to the king: royal hints had been dropped that after the offence given to the court by the rude remarks about despotic rulers in *Histriomastix* (1633), written by the lawyer William Prynne and dedicated to the Inns of Court, a public apology from the profession might be in order, and the preface to the printed text of *The Triumph of Peace* avows that its intention had been to celebrate 'the happiness of our kingdom, so blest in the present government and . . . our native Princes' (lines 3-5).[15] One might assume that the lawyers had taken the opportunity of an address to the king to make some assertions about

their point of view on the affair, were it not that the king and queen both expressed themselves 'exceeding well pleased with that Testimony which they lately gave us, of their great respect and affection to us',[16] and commanded that the whole show be restaged all over again ten days later at Merchant Taylors' Hall in the city.

Understandably, Orgel and Strong treat *The Triumph of Peace* as an appropriation of the masque form by the court's critics; it is an attempt to speak to the king in his own language. But if that is the case, the masque would appear to have failed; the king took its criticisms for compliments, so that Orgel and Strong are driven to conclude 'how exceedingly clumsy as a mode of political statement the form was' (I, 64). Thus we have here a plain instance of the critical contradiction which I described earlier: the finest Caroline masque is praised as a cultural achievement but written off as politically inept. However, that is plainly not the way that it appeared to contemporaries. My argument will be that the masque's political meanings have been inadequately grasped because its conditions of production have been incorrectly delineated.

Orgel and Strong's underlying assumption is that Charles's government was illegal, but in this period 'unparliamentary' and 'illegal' are not synonymous. Before the Triennial Act (1641), there was no statutory machinery by which a monarch could be compelled to rule with parliament. Parliament had great symbolic force as an icon of one kind of consensual government and the assumption that kings *ought* to call frequent parliaments was profoundly rooted, yet, as Charles reminded the 1626 parliament,

> parliaments are altogether in my power for their calling, sitting and dissolution; therefore as I find the fruits of them good or evil, they are to continue, or not to be.[17]

In early Stuart England parliaments were occasional events, called by kings to advise, grant finance and legislate. Charles (and his father before him) had little desire to legislate, and if he could raise finance by other means then he had no need for parliament. The political élites may have preferred more parliamentary contact, but there was nothing 'illegal' about this. Rather, in an age before the separation of powers between the executive and the judiciary, Charles's judges were also administrators, and his administrators were often judges.[18] The criteria by which parliament would or would not be called were not legal but financial and political.

Thus criticism of the illegality of Charles's rule does not mean resistance to non-parliamentary government (though in the absence of confidence in the king the argument might finally be stretched that far). What was at stake here were the strategies by which non-parliamentary government was being operated—not whether Charles was to rule but whether he was ruling with proper respect for the constraints of law—and here there were plenty of areas for disagreement. In the parliaments of the 1620s both James and Charles had faced critics who used legal arguments to challenge some of the unpopular sources of income on which the crown relied—such as patents and monopolies (attacked in 1621 and 1624), forced loans (1626) and tunnage and poundage (normally granted to the king as a matter of course but, for complex reasons, never fully authorized by Charles's early parliaments)[19]—but with the premature dissolution of the 1629 parliament these issues were left unresolved. Despairing of ever being able to achieve a working relationship with his turbulent assemblies, in the 1630s Charles began systematically to exploit dues and privileges which the crown held as of right. It is this development of 'projects and extraordinary courses' that forms the background to *The Triumph of Peace.*

Three areas are especially relevant. Firstly, I have already mentioned the attempt to tighten-up discipline and authority which was enforced across the country. The gentry were sent back to their localities; regulations were issued for governing protocol at court; a series of proclamations on vagrancy, poor relief, overcrowding in London, the export of grain, plague, the observance of Lent and so forth announced Charles's intention of implementing the full force of the statutes; a *Book of Orders* was sent to the magistracy in 1631 which complained of past laxity and demanded that they oversee the poor, idle and young, keep up public works, maintain employment and regulate alehouses and petty crime. The Privy Council threatened to enquire into the behaviour of local officers, monthly reports were demanded, the judges on circuit exhorted parish officials to be diligent. Charles was looking to implement an energetic reformation founded on the efficient running of the machinery of government: his personal influence was intended to be distilled to every level of the nation's life.[20]

Secondly, Charles set himself to realizing to the full any privileges which might have financial value to the crown. In particular, ancient rights which had long lain dormant or were virtually defunct were revived and rigorously implemented. For example, the obligation on all freeholders of £40 and above to proceed to the honour of knighthood was implemented, and a commission established for compounding with those who had failed to take up their knighthood at the coronation. By 1635 this had produced £165,000. Another commission was organized to compound with royal tenants whose titles to their land were defective or non-existent, and moved against people occupying reclaimed land, or who had enclosed or encroached upon commons and

wastes. Related to this was the vigorous revival of the feudal forest laws and the antiquarian scrutiny of the boundaries of royal forests. The relentless prosecution of the crown's forest rights promised huge returns but was particularly open to abuse; a forest court sitting at Gloucester in 1634 for the first time since the reign of Edward I fined two landowners £80,000 for cutting timber and declared that seventeen towns had encroached on the royal forest, while on another occasion the boundaries of Rockingham Forest were increased from six to sixty miles. The Court of Wards, which administered royal rights over minors and their estates, was another profitable institution producing a vastly augmented return in the 1630s.[21]

Thirdly, Charles's rule in the 1630s was increasingly reliant for its implementation on the courts connected with the prerogative powers of the crown, and especially the court of Star Chamber, through which royal proclamations were enforced. Star Chamber became notorious for the political trials which were conducted there (including those against William Prynne), but its more regular work involved the punishing of breaches of proclamations, unlawful residence in London, unlawful building of tenements, infringing of monopolies, hoarding of corn, the laxity of sheriffs and so forth. Increasingly, such prosecutions were conducted with an eye to compounding and the crown's financial interest; much the same goes for the Councils of the North and of the Marches.[22]

It is important to recognize the technical legality of all this activity. Orgel and Strong completely misunderstand the situation when they write (*apropos* of Ship Money) that the basic question 'was whether the King could make the law without consent of parliament' and that 'Noy had worked zealously to keep the issues out of the courts' (I, 63,65). The issue was not the making but the interpreting of law, and in many respects Charles's rule was excessively legalistic. Charles repeatedly consulted with the judges and was eager at every stage to test the validity of his powers in the courts; the 1630s have been well described as 'a decade of intense government by common lawyers'.[23] The problem was that as the decade progressed so the parade of legal correctness was increasingly placed in service to Charles's pressing financial needs. The punishment of breaches of proclamations with a hefty Star Chamber fine is a case in point. In the Long Parliament John Pym was to complain that the desire for profitability had undermined the intention of the law and that the law was being enforced only to be sold: 'Many great nuisances have been complained of, but when there hath been money given, and compositions made, then they are no more nuisances . . . the Star Chamber now is become a court of revenue'.[24] Similarly, Charles's commission of enquiry into the excessive fees and perquisites taken by court officials was reduced to absurdity by the pardons that were granted on payment of composition; abuses were being 'reformed' in order that they could be translated into cash. Gradually Charles's legalism came to be seen as a threat to the security of the subject's liberties and property: as it was said of the Court of Wards, many 'were exceedingly incensed . . . looking upon what the law had intended for their protection and preservation to be now applied to their destruction'.[25]

The ambiguity operating here was that the law was understood to uphold both the subject's liberties and the king's authority; Charles's father had been careful to establish that he was 'King by the common law of the land'.[26] From the point of view of the subject, however, as the crucial legal decisions all went in favour of the crown—most notoriously the Ship Money case—so the issue metamorphosed from a question of legality into one of politics. The alarm generated by these measures even among the more moderate of Charles's legally-minded gentry can be read in the account of Edward Hyde, former member of the Middle Temple, friend of poets and future leader of the Long Parliament's attack on the prerogative courts:

> the damage and mischief cannot be expressed, that the Crown and State sustained by the deserved reproach and infamy that attended the judges, by being made use of in this and the like acts of power; there being no possibility to preserve the dignity, reverence, and estimation of the laws themselves but by the integrity and innocency of the judges.[27]

The gentry were among those on whom Charles's measures fell hardest, and not only because they were expected to dig deep; a major grudge against the Star Chamber was to be that it had allowed sentences of mutilation to be carried out against gentlemen. The effect of this can be read in Clarendon's language, as it struggles to represent in legal terms what was at root essentially a political anxiety—for example, he objects to distraint of knighthood that 'though it had a foundation in right, yet, in the circumstances of proceeding, it was very grievous, and no less unjust', but also that it displeased 'all persons of quality, or indeed of any reasonable condition throughout the kingdom'.[28] Charles may have had legal correctness on his side but the crisis of 1640, as W. J. Jones tellingly puts it, marked 'that point when legal justification becomes politically unacceptable'.[29] Furthermore, in the 1640s the judges themselves were to pay for their willingness to prop up what had finally become a discredited regime. John Selden was to comment sardonically: 'The King's Oath is not security enough for our Property, for he swears to Govern according to Law; now the Judges they interpret the Law, and what Judges can be made to do we know'.[30]

III

This, however, is to anticipate, since the future bankruptcy of Caroline legalism could not be prophesied in 1634, though its underlying tendencies, and the poli-

cies which it was employed to support, could still be causes for concern. Of course anxiety about the king's policies does not in itself mean opposition to the king, though it may eventually come to that if the loss of confidence goes too far; what is remarkable about *The Triumph of Peace* is its open attempt to define common ground on a divisive issue.

We are fortunate to possess very full information about the preparation and audience of the masque, and here the co-operative nature of the enterprise is most in evidence.[31] The committee of lawyers that devised the masque embraced every possible strand of opinion. On the one hand there was Sir John Finch, a courtier through and through, the speaker in the 1629 parliament who had refused to allow Denzil Holles and Sir John Eliot to read their declaration, and who, as Lord Keeper and Chief Justice of the Common Pleas, was a prime mover in the notorious Star Chamber and High Commission cases of the 1630s; he was impeached by the Long Parliament in 1640 and fled the country. Also courtiers, though more moderate and with former 'opposition' credentials, were William Noy and Sir Edward Herbert. Herbert had been one of the managers of Buckingham's impeachment and defence counsel for Selden in his prosecution after the 1629 dissolution; in 1633 he defended the bishop of Lincoln against Laud in the altar-table controversy. However, in 1635 he was appointed the Queen's attorney-general, and proceeded via the solicitor-generalship to Noy's old post; it was he who in 1641 would charge the Five Members with high treason, for which he was impeached by the Commons. On the other hand, in Edward Hyde and John Selden the committee also included constitutionally-minded critics of the king, the former becoming in 1640-41 one of the most determined opponents of Ship Money but after 1642 one of Charles's most determined supporters, the latter an MP who chose to remain in parliament until 1649 but who was distrustful of the legality of both parliament's actions and the king's. As for Hyde's friend Bulstrode Whitelock, this Middle Templar was to be active in political life into the 1650s, ending up as a Privy Councillor on Cromwell's Council of State.

The same kind of bridging of gaps is notable in the performance of the masque. The event cost the lawyers an astonishing £5013, but often the services on which they were drawing were those of court musicians and costumers, while other service personnel that were involved were retainers from aristocratic households on loan to the lawyers.[32] More important is the fact that the masque was not only performed privately for the court but preceeded by a procession through the city streets in Whitehall. The masque was expected to generate interest, for some 3000 copies of the text were printed in anticipation, but it was the procession 'in the nature of a triumph' that really created the widest attention and was said to have 'attracted a great crowd, exciting the curiosity and applause of all the people'.[33] Normally masques were exclusive affairs and watched by only a narrow social and political élite, but the lawyers saw to it that their statement was addressed to a wider public: **The Triumph of Peace** is that unique object, a Caroline masque that reached both a courtly and a plebeian audience.[34] Nor was the audience at Whitehall devoid of its potential tensions, since we know that the masque attracted spectators whom we would not normally associate with royal festivities. The visitors from the Inns of Court included the King's Bench Justices Jones and Berkeley, who in 1638 were to give judgment in favour of Ship Money, but also George Croke, whose outspoken and uncompromising judgment against the same levy was to turn him into a puritan hero, and a coach was even hired for Simonds D'Ewes, the godly lawyer who would visit Prynne in prison, sit among the Presbyterian party in the Long Parliament and write in his autobiography a thunderous seven-page assault on the pernicious sin of Ship Money.[35] Amusingly, D'Ewes's puritan principles led him in retrospect to suppress from his autobiography any mention of his attendance at so frivolous an event as a masque. It may be worth mentioning also that the author, James Shirley, though he ridiculed Prynne in the preface to his play **The Bird in a Cage** (published 1633), was not in his other writings exactly an uncritical admirer of kings.[36]

In choosing to make their masque a triumph, the lawyers were borrowing the typical iconography of Whitehall: Charles had himself paraded as a Roman emperor in *Albion's Triumph,* two years before. But it is possible that they were also following the lead here of Thomas May's historical poem *The Reign of King Henry II* (1633) which included an extended passage contrasting the happy amity of Henry and his sons with the sight of a victorious military triumph:

> This sight more joy'd the hearts of people now,
> Then any triumph of a warre could doe.
> Nor could the greatest conquest, by the blood
> Of slaughter'd nations purchas'd, be so good.
> So did th'Italian youths follow in throngs
> Their laurell'd chariots with triumphant songs,
> When captive Kings were brought, when woefull
>   stories
> Of ruin'd lands were made their envy'd glories.
> Before this triumph no sad captives goe
> To waile in chaines their woefull overthrow;
> No pale dejected lookes, no hearts afraid
> Are found, no envy'd glories are display'd;
> But gentle peace does with a gracious eye
> Appeare, and leade the faire solemnity.
> Whose crowne of olive does more glorious show
> Then any victor's laurell wreath could doe.
>
>   (sig. K6ʳ)

May had himself a past connection with the Inns of Court, and his poem, dedicated to Charles, was full of improving political reflections. What may have caught

the lawyers' attention in this section was its theme of reconciliation. Henry's sons raise a rebellion against him, but eventually an accord is struck up again; they return to their duty and he attends to their grievances and, 'like a wise and noble Potentate, / To cure the sad diseases of his state . . . beginnes' (sig. K6ᵛ). Among the reforms involved in this appeasement is a substantial section praising Henry for instituting circuit judges and improving the law:

> Those mighty kings who by such specious deedes
> As founding towers or stately Pyramids
> Would raise their names, and by that vast expence
> Doe seeke the fame of high magnificence,
> Doe not deserve, by those proud workes they raise,
> So true an honour, nor such lasting praise,
> As he, whose wisedome to good manners drawes
> The mindes of men by founding wholesome lawes
> And planting perfect justice in a state.
>
>   (sig. K7ʳ)

Better, it seems, to be a legal than a princely king. In other respects the sentiments of the masque bring to mind the kinds of language and attitudes associated less with the court that with city pageants.

In its opening lines, Shirley's masque bridges one of the gaps of the 1630s. The text begins with Confidence and his friends Fancy, Jollity and Laughter welcoming to court Opinion and his family Novelty and Admiration. Confidence is a courtier, a 'gay man' (208) with slashed doublet, long hair and ribbons (35-39), while Opinion, it appears, is a country gentleman, wearing an 'old-fashioned doublet of black velvet and trunk hose' (33), carrying a 'grave' face (171) and inclined to 'like nothing' (280). Thus the show begins with the country coming up to court. The antimasques which these characters present are fanciful, but they refer in a general way to the social welfare programme which Charles had been seeking to implement. There is first a tavern, with its gamesters, wenches and beggars, and it is, beside, an irregular one, of the kind that Charles had recently been commanding his officers to bring within the control of a comprehensive licensing system:[37]

NOVELTY.

A spick and span new tavern.

ADMIRATION.

Wonderful, here was none within two minutes.

LAUGHTER.

No such wonder, lady, taverns are quickly up.
It is but hanging out a bush at a nobleman's door,
    or
an alderman's gate, and 'tis made instantly.

                                    (301-05)

Similarly, the beggars are members of the idle poor, who fake disabilities to earn charity, then throw away their crutches and dance at their success:

OPINION.

> I am glad they are off. Are these the effects of
> peace?
> Corruption, rather.

FANCY.

>   O, the beggars show
> The benefit of peace.

>   (328-30)

The gallants at the tavern are cheated, a merchant is nearly robbed in a grove by sturdy rogues, Confidence and his friends all become drunk: the antimasques genially but pointedly present images of peace as it is without benefit of law. When Irene (Peace) arrives and banishes the grotesque characters of the antimasques she calls for Eunomia (Law) to support her: 'Appear, appear, Eunomia . . . / Irene calls. / Like dew that falls / Into a stream, / I'm lost with them / That know not how to order me' (505-11). These antimasques would seem to be complimentary to Charles's reforming purposes, though the reforms they isolate for praise are the ones most likely to be welcomed by the conservatively-minded country gentry.

The fifth antimasque, which satirizes, in the persons of six eccentric inventors, the granting of crazy monopolies, is known to have been the brainchild of Attorney General Noy. This has created considerable confusion since Noy himself was responsible for licensing some of Charles's preferential economic projects, including the notorious patent for royal soap. Of course the granting of monopolies to favoured courtiers had been fiercely censured in the 1620s parliaments and was to come under attack again in 1640, but the position was not quite the one of blatant illegality which Orgel and Strong take it to have been. Rather, in the interests of industry and innovation, the 1624 statute had discriminated between different kinds of monopoly and excluded from condemnation monopolies held by corporations and, for limited periods, inventions. The characters in the antimasque are quite clearly described as 'Projectors' (339) who are seeking either to patent ludicrously unworkable inventions or to impose their whimsies upon the long-suffering public at large, like the jockey who, said Whitelocke, 'signified a Projector, who begged a Patent, that none in the Kingdom might ride their Horses, but with such Bits as they should buy of him'.[38] Obviously Noy's function at court was to get the best return for his royal master, but he had himself been a parliamentary critic of monopolies and at court in the 1630s he seems to have been attached to the opposition to Lord Treasurer Weston who *was* inclined to allow

mere racketeering.[39] His antimasque admonishes the king concerning his observation of the Statute of Monopolies, and warns against the countenancing of any far-fetched scheme for the sake of the revenue it promised, as indeed was already beginning to happen. Though Noy was not immune from his own satire here, he must have believed that the antimasque expressed what he *thought* he was doing, while on the other hand his contribution was warmly praised by Whitelocke (see p. 122 above) and would have pleased such a man as Edward Hyde who was openly disgusted with the 'projects of all kinds, many ridiculous, many scandalous, all very grievous . . . the envy and reproach of which came to the King, the profit to other men'.[40]

The main masque follows, the subject of which is the delicate relationship between Peace, Justice and Law, and the fable which the lawyers chose is one which carefully establishes the indispensability of law to government while remaining tactfully deferential and conciliatory towards the king. The antimasquers are dismissed by Peace as improper for the glorious presence of the King and Queen, but she is at pains to emphasize that what corrects the chaos of disordered peace is the controlling power of law. Descending alone, she laments her solitude, and complains that without Law she is 'lost' and distressed (510), and only when Law arrives to support her can the third deity, Justice (Dike or Astraea), descend. The relationship between Peace and Law is said to be equal, but Peace is markedly deferential to the blessings Law brings:

IRENE.

> Thou dost beautify increase,
> And chain security with peace.

EUNOMIA.

> Irene fair, and first divine,
> All my blessings spring from thine.

IRENE.

> I am but wild without thee, thou abhorrest
> What is rude, or apt to wound,
> Canst throw proud trees to the ground,
> And make a temple of a forest.

>   (529-36)

This fable is complimentary to the happiness of Caroline government but it carries its own particular emphasis: without Law, Peace will be wild or rude, and Justice will not descend to the earth. Peace is the spring, but Law is the sun that alone can ripen it (541-42).

The language of Charles's personal government is borrowed for the duet between Peace and Law:

EUNOMIA.

> No more, no more, but join
> Thy voice and lute with mine.

BOTH.

> The world shall give prerogative to neither.
> We cannot flourish but together.

                                        (537-40)

It is important to realize that this does not constitute, as Orgel and Strong claim, 'an argument against prerogative rule' (I, 66). Irene is not Charles's government, but Peace, an aspect of that government, while it is equally misleading to construe Eunomia, Law, as equivalent to parliament. But while it is not a parliamentary way of government which is being advocated here, the duet still announces a clear warning about the way that non-parliamentary government is conducted: Law *has* to be strict and even-handed:

> Irene enters like a perfum'd spring,
> Eunomia ripens everything
> And in the golden harvest leaves
> To every sickle his own sheaves.

                                        (541-44)

The harvest is golden because it respects the boundaries between mine and thine; this concluding couplet seems designed to voice discreetly but firmly the concern of Charles's propertied subjects that the law should not be manipulated to erode what they took to be their basic liberties. It is inconceivable that the law should operate in any other way than in the service of Charles's peace, but it must also regulate that peace to preserve the subject's rights and freedom: leaving to every sickle his own sheaves expresses precisely the political moral which the gentry and lawyers anxious about Ship Money and the forest laws were most concerned to emphasize. No disloyalty to the King is implied, but a statement about the nature and responsibilities of kingly government certainly is.

Orgel and Strong rightly praise the charged effect of the following action, in which Justice descends and addresses the King and Queen as Jove and Themis, 'the parents of us three' (581). It is difficult now to recover the impact of such a moment. Normally at Whitehall the king and queen danced in their own masques and were spoken of as if they possessed the attributes of the gods whose roles they played, but in *The Triumph of Peace* this element of impersonation was suspended since the lawyers who were shortly to appear really were the 'sons' of Peace, Law and Justice in whose roles they masqueraded. The lawyers' fiction enables them to make a gracious gesture of filial duty to 'Jove and Themis', but also to remind the king of the nature and identity of his 'grandchildren'. Moreover, in addressing them as Jove and Themis, Divine Power and Divine Law respectively, Justice was pressing home exactly that distinction which Edward Hyde would later blame Charles for having overlooked:

> In the wisdom of former times, when the prerogative went highest . . . never any court of law, very seldom any judge, or lawyer of reputation, was called upon to assist in an act of power; the Crown well knowing the moment of keeping those the objects of reverence and veneration with the people, and that though it might sometimes make sallies upon them by the prerogative, yet the law would keep the people from any invasion of it, and that the King could never suffer whilst the law and the judges were looked upon by the subject as the asyla for their liberties and security.[41]

In casting Charles and Henrietta Maria as power and law, Shirley is analysing royal authority even as he compliments it. The authority with which Charles rules is conceded, but so too is the separateness of the two principles which constitute his authority; the law not merely confirms the king's acts, it should be the guiding light by which power operates. Power must love law in emulation of the 'chaste embraces' (595) of Charles and Henrietta Maria.

The odd feature of the main masque entry which follows is the querulous tone in which the Genius identifies the masquers as the sons of Peace, Law and Justice:

> No foreign persons I make known
> But here present you with your own,
> The children of your reign and blood;
> Of age, when they are understood,
> Not seen by faction or owl's sight,
> Whose trouble is the clearest light;
> But treasures to their eye, and ear,
> That love good for itself, not fear.
> O smile on what yourselves have made . . .

                                        (630-38)

The Genius introduces the lawyers as if he were doubtful whether Jove would choose to recognize his relationship to them. His grandchildren wither without him, they are not 'of age' until they are 'understood', but it is only 'faction or owl's sight', that will interpret their behaviour maliciously. Indeed, Jove cannot but acknowledge the masquers, they are 'children of your reign and blood' and he must 'smile on what yourselves have made', and as if to prove the point the Genius attributes the sudden moving of the motionless masquers to the influence of his approving regard of them. Thus the speech represents as compliment and eulogy what must have seemed to the lawyers very like the enforcing of a political point, that it is not in Charles's interests, not in his nature even, to deny his affiliation to what they represent. The point is neatly made in the reveals that follow, as court and lawyers join together in dance.

So the masque sets out to build a bridge between the king, his advisers, and those with reservations about the tendency of his government; the deference of the lawyers' act of duty to their monarch is performed in such a way as to impose on to him a recognition of the complex and necessary interdependence of royal justice and law. Furthermore, in a striking and imaginative invention, Shirley builds this acknowledgement of consensus into the very fabric of the masque. Antimasques normally belonged to the early parts of the event, but in the middle of the main masque here 'there is heard a great noise and confusion of voices within' and 'a crack is heard in the works, as if there were some danger by some piece of the machines falling' (669-72). Into the main masque there tumble a carpenter, a painter, one of the black guard, a tailor and his wife, and the wives of an embroiderer, a feather-maker and a property man, each demanding to be allowed to see the dances, then, noticing the laughter and surprise of the people around them, they 'pretend' to be just another antimasque and go off in a dance. This moment must have been amusing and entertaining in performance, but its symbolic force is patent. These are all characters who have been involved in creating the masque yet excluded from its performance. Now they come to 'challenge a privilege' (694) and claim recognition for their contribution to the collective enterprise that a masque was: 'What though we be no ladies, we are Christians in these clothes, and the King's subjects, God bless us' (700-01). At the very centre of the masque was a deliberate violation of the illusion which presses the spectators to acknowledge that the apparently effortless magical effects were in fact achieved through an unseen but all-important act of collaboration. It is not exactly an affront to prerogative government, but a clear reminder, if any were needed, of the joint enterprise that alone made Charles's rule possible.

IV

About the reception of **The Triumph of Peace** we are, again, quite well-informed. Most directly, there is Whitelocke's long narrative of the performance which stresses both the inclusion of the satire against projectors and the king's gracious acquiescence in the whole enterprise: 'I cannot but give them thanks for it, and shall be ready upon all occasions, to manifest the good opinion I have of them, and to do them and you in particular any favour'.[42] Another suggestive pointer to the way that the masque was understood is the fact that when the king asked to see it a second time it was the city that offered to foot the bill. But before describing the direct contemporary comments that have come down to us, I should like to consider first two other texts which constitute themselves as indirect responses to **The Triumph of Peace**. Charles's public reply was to invite 120 lawyers to court five days later to see him dance Thomas Carew's masque *Coelum Britannicum*.[43] This had been in preparation at least since the beginning of the year, but essentially it addresses itself to the same theme as **The Triumph of Peace,** the Caroline *renovatio* of church and state. The masque opens with the arrival of Mercury at Whitehall to announce the

forthcoming reformation which is to be led by the example of the newly-disciplined English court, which even Jove himself emulates:

> Your exemplar life
> Hath not alone transfus'd a zealous heat
> Of imitation through your vertuous Court,
> By whose bright blaze your Pallace is become
> The envy'd patterns of this underworld,
> But the aspiring flame hath kindled heaven;
> Th'immortall bosomes burne with emulous fires,
> Jove rivalls your great vertues, Royall Sir,
> And Iuno, Madam, your attractive graces;
> He his wild lusts, her raging jealousies
> She layes aside, and through th'Olympique hall,
> As yours doth here, their great Example spreads.

(62-73)

Mercury stands before the ruins of a great Roman city, typifying the disorder which is to be returned to civility under King Charles; the various measures mentioned in the masque—proclamations for regulating taverns and the sale of tobacco, rectifying the 'sophistication of wares' (236), controlling commodities, commanding the gentry back to the country—correspond to proclamations which Charles himself had intensively put into practice around 1633-34.[44] So successful is this reformation of earthly discipline, says Mercury, that Jove has been moved to reform his heavens; the bad constellations will be removed and Charles and his heroic courtiers stellified in their place.

The interesting feature of this masque is Carew's inclusion, beside Mercury, of the scurrilous railing god Momus, who restates Mercury's idealized account of Caroline government in considerably less idealized terms. It has sometimes been supposed, most recently by Annabel Patterson,[45] that Momus's voice admits a radical ambiguity, a current of scepticism or parody which disallows the royal reformation even as it advances it. This, I hazard, is an overstatement which makes nonsense of Charles's sponsorship of the masque; rather, Momus might be better described as affectionately guying the inflated fable in which the whole elaborate enterprise is wrapped but which will (notwithstanding) be brought to a spectacular culmination later in the evening.

Momus is noteworthy for the legal language in which he specializes: the poets, he says, have a 'Patent' to draw down gods on masque nights (127), Jove presides over a 'convocation of the Superlunary Peers' (199), the constellations are dissolved 'by the authority aforesaid enacted' (213), incontinencies are punished in Jove's 'high Commission Court' (222), new orders are 'read in the Presence Chamber, by the Vi-President of *Pernassus*' (234-35), Jove is to redecorate his 'Starre-Chamber' (437), and so on. Momus's language is a direct reflection of his role as spokesman for the legal machinery by which the Caroline reformation is being enforced: his summary of Jove's declarations, he tells Mercury, is a quotation from 'a passage at a Counsell-table' (223-24), and when the constellations have been darkened he announces Jove's desire to replace them in a passage which pretends to be a royal proclamation:

> O yes, O yes, O yes,
> By the Father of the gods,
> and the King of Men,
>
> Whereas we having observed a very commendable practice taken into frequent use by Princes of these latter Ages . . .
>
> . . . Given at Our Palace in Olympus the first day of the first month, in the first yeare of the Reformation.
>
> (421-65)

This is a remarkable comic version of the public pronouncements that must have been all too familiar under the personal rule.

Potentially, then, Momus could well have projected the doubts of the lawyers in the audience about the legalism of Caroline government, and at first this truly seems to be his role for when announcing his name and function he says that he sits in heaven's 'Parliamentary Assemblies' and though he has 'no vote in the sanction of new lawes, I have yet a Praerogative of wresting the old to any whatsoever interpretation, whether it be to the behoofe, or prejudice, of *Iupiter* his Crowne and Dignity, for, or against the Rights of either house of Patrician or Plebeian gods' (146-52). This joke openly admits mention of the anxieties about the loss of traditional laws and liberties which lie behind *The Triumph of Peace,* but it seems clear that its thrust is basically reassuring: the fear is admitted in order to be acknowledged and so defused. And Momus's part is like this throughout the masque. The subject of his ironies is not the royal government but the fiction of the masque itself: it is Mercury whom he repeatedly twits, not the King. In effect, Momus concedes the point which was being urged in the late, unexpected antimasque in *The Triumph of Peace,* that the masque is not in itself a form of power but a symbolic elaboration of that power, that Mercury's fable projects not an image of what Charles's government is but what it aspires to be. Momus provides a bridge between the 'British Hercules' and his less dazzled observers, a safety-net against scepticism: in the final scene Carew can represent the Stuart dynasty as frankly transcendent having already admitted the less than transcendent measures by which this ideology is sustained.

Thus *Coelum Britannicum* responds to, and in some ways counters from the king's side the hesitations about confidence in Charles built into *The Triumph of Peace.* My second text, however, reworks Shirley's masque

from a perspective of almost completely forfeited trust. This is *The Tragedy of the Cruel War,* an anonymous pamphlet of 1643, recently re-discovered and found to be a revamping of Shirley's antimasques and the first three songs in a context of real internecine violence.[46] In this sad little squib, the antimasque characters have become symbolic of the woes that have overtaken the once peaceful land. Laughter, Fancy, Novelty and so on are all frivolous scoundrels who 'revive the drooping consciences of the Cavaliers and make them merry in their greatest cruelties' (53-55), the beggars and drunkards display the 'effects of warre and corruption' (136), the projectors have become either businessmen who are making money from the war or victims whom war has reduced to a deplorable condition. The last page reprints the songs of Irene and Eunomia with marginal notes that reinterpret them as a commentary on the relations of king and parliament: 'The world shall give / Prerogative to neither, / We cannot flourish but together' (211-13).

Whoever wrote this pamphlet, he was a neuter whose sympathies lay broadly on the parliamentary side: his pamphlet represents the Cavaliers as bloody, cruel and popish, but he still hopes that the king may be brought back to an accommodation with his parliament. His pamphlet is interesting for seizing as it does on the apparently contradictory resonances of Shirley's text. On the one hand the implied social criticism of the antimasques has become an open rebuke to the King's misdemeanours, on the other admonition to the King to take the path of conciliation has understandably become even more urgent. The distrust of Charles which is latent but always held in check in the masque can in 1643 be openly acknowledged.

All of which is enough to send us back to that aspect of the masque which I earlier mentioned in passing, that it is not one event but two, a private entertainment and a public triumph. Whatever the conciliatory noises of the performance at Whitehall, the parade of the lawyers through the city streets cannot have been devoid of tougher implications. Whitelocke was at pains to stress the magnificence of the show the lawyers mounted. The procession was led by twenty footmen; then followed a marshal and a hundred gentlemen on horseback, each with two lackeys and a page, heralded by trumpets and lit by a 'multitude of torches'; then came the antimasquers, each with their own music, then two huge open chariots and six, with figures in the habits of gods, torches and musicians, then the four chariots carrying the 'Grand Masquers', designed after 'the *Roman* Triumphant Chariots, as near as could be gathered by some old Prints', with footmen at the side and 'Torches and flaming huge Flamboys' that 'made it seem lightsom as at Noon-day'.[47] Each of the hundred gentlemen wore suits that cost above £100, so that the cost of the procession alone was in excess of £10000. To the King this was most gratifying, and he made them walk twice around the tiltyard, but one wonders whether the 'multitude of the Spectators in the streets' understood the message to be rather different. The triumphal procession was the single most important spectacle to be staged publicly in London in a reign that, through royal insolvency, had not even seen a coronation entry. To the King it meant compliment, but it seems quite likely to me that the citizens may have read it as a statement of the wealth and importance of one section of the gentry, England's parliamentary class.

This is certainly what some courtiers took it to mean. It was expected in advance that the masque was intended in some way as a show to rival what the court could mount; one courtier wrote in October 1633, 'The emulation that will be between the Inns of Court men and the courtiers you may easily imagine'.[48] Another courtier, George Garrard, was far from reassured by the event:

> Oh that they would once give over these Things, or lay them aside for a Time, and bend all their Endeavours to make the King Rich! For it gives me no Satisfaction, who am but a looker on, to see a rich Commonwealth, a rich People, and the Crown poor. God direct them to remedy this quickly.[49]

This comment is usually read as if it were a reflection on the escapism of masques, but Garrard is actually acknowledging *The Triumph of Peace* as a threat. It is not the occasion's extravagance that has upset him, but the political imbalance that it has revealed. He plainly has the lawyers' expertise and the masque's theme in mind when he supposes they could make the King rich if they would. For him the gesture simply has not been conciliatory enough, and much the same view was expressed retrospectively by a royalist historian in 1655 when he wrote 'This entertainment was very costly to the City, so dear was then, I say not this *King,* but their own vanity to them, and that this vanity was dearer to them than their King is evident, because some few years after, when they flourished, and he wanted most to re-presse the *Scottish-darings,* he could not obtain from them any the least pittance of supply'.[50] Another contemporary spelled out in the form of a poem on the procession implications which may have struck many minds:

> These are the sons of Charles's peaceful reign
> Whom yet if war's rude accents shall constrain
> To put on arms will quickly understand
> The laws of arms as well as of the land,
> And be as valiant in the midst of fight
> As they seemed glorious in the masque of night.[51]

This anonymous observer has patently read the event as a show of strength. The sons of peace may love Charles so much that they would go to war for him, but the only hopes for war that get expressed in the 1630s are

for a patriotic and godly campaign against the Habsburg to recapture the Palatinate and further true religion. It would have been an event that necessitated the recall of parliament and the implementation of a militant foreign policy: this is not a suggestion that would have especially gladdened Charles's heart.

V

This essay has been investigating ways in which the court masque, a seemingly 'decadent' form, can be understood to be participating in, rather than retreating from, the political and ideological shifts obtaining at its specific historical moment. It should be clear, I hope, that the relationships in which this masque is sited with respect to its circumstances of production were considerably more problematic than they have usually been understood to be, and that far from being a political 'irrelevance' *The Triumph of Peace* is a strenuous attempt at a meaningful political gesture—it advances counsel, it offers grounds for conciliation, it seeks to define an accommodation. Of course the freedom of manoeuvre of the masque is restricted by the necessity of offering homage of a conventional kind to the king, but within these limits the masque's political content is not minimal. Its interest (and our sense of its superiority to the general run of masques of the 1630s) lies in Shirley's attempt to negotiate between attitudes which, if not yet contradictory, were ultimately going to be found to be incompatible.

Since the participants in the masque were people who would eventually find themselves on opposite sides of the political divide, the masque can be said to be particularly revealing of the unrealised tensions imminent in its moment of production. It is apparent that the ability of both Charles and his future opponents to suppose that the masque spoke for them rests on two things. Firstly, there were contradictions and unconformities present in the political and legal ideologies of the decade which, before the breakdown in 1642, had not been fully articulated or brought to consciousness: it is easy to see how Charles may have *thought* that he was ruling as the lawyers were asking him to do, especially since he and the lawyers are still employing an ideology of consensus which obscures their actual disagreement concerning the operation of that consensus. Shirley has identified problems which are central to his age, but he lacks a language which would allow him fully to confront them (indeed, these are problems which the age would never satisfactorily resolve); even as he speaks of co-operation he admits contrary attitudes into his masque which are representative of tendencies that will eventually explode this dominant ideology from within.

Secondly, there is an equally important false consciousness coded into the circumstances of the masque which can only be extracted by a more complex hermeneutics than it has hitherto received; it is apparent that the masque voices different meanings depending on where you stand to watch it. To a considerable extent this is a feature which arises from the fact that the king is spectator rather than originator of *The Triumph of Peace,* but all masques must have been so affected, if not as markedly as this one. In this case, there are at least three audiences receiving and appropriating *The Triumph of Peace,* and they are all hearing significantly different things.

Of course *The Triumph of Peace* is anomalous, as I have already said. It is a masque presented to the court and not by it. But insofar as it is attempting to build bridges across gaps which in a matter of only a few years are going to be quite unbridgeable, it is performing from the outside-in a function the regular masques tried to do from the inside-out, and, in the absence of other public bridges in the 1630s (such as parliament), this function has very considerable importance. The willingness of subjects to participate in the royal culture and the ability of the King to comprehend the conditions of their participation are an exact index of the power of survival of the royal government. It is only when Charles suddenly finds that his masque audience is no longer listening that his difficulties really begin.

Notes

1. S. Orgel and R. Strong, *Inigo Jones: The Theatre of the Stuart Court,* 2 vols (London and Berkeley, California, 1973).

2. R. Strong, *Splendour at Court* (London, 1973).

3. G. Parry, *The Golden Age Restor'd* (Manchester, 1981).

4. Cf. G.R. Elton, *Studies in Tudor and Stuart Politics and Government,* 3 vols (Cambridge, 1974), II, 164-82.

5. See my *Theatre and Crisis 1632-1642* (Cambridge, 1984), pp. 7-11.

6. See his *Van Dyck: Charles I on Horseback* (London, 1972).

7. Exceptions to this generalization are Raymond A. Anselment, 'Thomas Carew and the "Harmlesse Pastimes" of Caroline peace', *Philological Quarterly,* 62 (1983), 201-19; and David Norbrook, 'The Reformation of the masque' in *The Court Masque,* edited by David Lindley (Manchester, 1984).

8. This paragraph is largely dependent on Kevin Sharpe, 'The personal rule of Charles I' in *Before the English Civil War,* edited by Howard Tomlinson (London, 1983), pp. 53-78. See also J. P. Kenyon, *Stuart England* (Harmondsworth, 1978);

John Morrill, *The Revolt of the Provinces* (London, 1976); and Conrad Russell, *Parliaments and English Politics 1621-1629* (Oxford, 1979).

9. Sharpe, 'The personal rule of Charles I', p.63.

10. For a critical view of the staying-power of Charles's personal government, see D. Hirst, *Authority and Conflict: England 1603-1658* (London, 1986), pp. 160-87.

11. See Elton, *Studies in Tudor and Stuart Politics and Government,* III, 3-57.

12. See, for example, Derek Hirst, 'Court, and country and politics before 1629' in *Faction and Parliament,* edited by Kevin Sharpe (Oxford, 1978), pp. 105-38; Morrill, *The Revolt of the Provinces,* pp. 14-17. On Noy, see especially W. J. Jones, '"The Great Gamaliel of the Law": Mr. Attorney Noye', *Huntington Library Quarterly,* 40 (1977), 197-226.

13. See D. B. J. Randall, *Jonson's Gipsies Unmasked* (Durham, N.C., 1975).

14. B. Whitelocke, *Memorials of the English Affairs* (London, 1682), p. 20.

15. I quote *The Triumph of Peace* from the text edited by Clifford Leech for *A Book of Masques in Honour of Allardyce Nicoll,* edited by T. J. B. Spencer and S. W. Wells (Cambridge, 1967), pp. 275-313.

16. Whitelocke, *Memorials,* p. 21.

17. J. P. Kenyon, *The Stuart Constitution* (Cambridge, 1966), p. 59.

18. See W. J. Jones, *Politics and the Bench* (London, 1971), p. 16.

19. Kenyon, *The Stuart Constitution,* pp. 60-61.

20. See especially L. M. Hill, 'County government in Caroline England' in *The Origins of the English Civil War,* edited by C. Russell (London, 1973), pp. 66-90; and also Sharpe, 'The personal rule of Charles I', pp. 58-63, and T. G. Barnes, *Somerset 1625-40* (London, 1961), *passim.*

21. See Jones, *Politics and the Bench,* pp. 95-103; Kenyon, *The Stuart Constitution,* pp. 86-89.

22. Jones, *Politics and the Bench,* pp. 103-08; Kenyon, *The Stuart Constitution,* pp. 117-20.

23. Jones, *Politics and the Bench,* p. 94.

24. Kenyon, *The Stuart Constitution,* pp. 201-02.

25. E. Hyde, *History of the Rebellion,* edited by W. D. Macray (Oxford, 1888), I, 199.

26. Jones, *Politics and the Bench,* p. 30.

27. Hyde, *History of the Rebellion,* I, 88.

28. Hyde, *History of the Rebellion,* I, 85.

29. Jones, *Politics and the Bench,* p.vii.

30. J. Selden, *Table Talk,* edited by R. Milward (London, 1689), p. 21.

31. See Whitelocke, *Memorials,* pp. 18-21; *Trois Masques à la Cour de Charles Ier d'Angleterre,* edited by M. Lefkowitz (Paris, 1970); and T. Orbison, 'The Middle Temple documents relating to James Shirley's *Triumph of Peace', Malone Society Collections,* 12 (1983), 31-84.

32. Orbison, 'Middle Temple documents', p. 41; Whitelocke, *Memorials,* p. 19.

33. G. E. Bentley, *The Jacobean and Caroline Stage,* 7 vols (Oxford, 1941-68), V, 1156, 1157.

34. In this respect the masque resembles other entertainments produced by the Inns of Court (such as *Gesta Grayorum,* 1594) in which the private revels were carried out into the city streets.

35. Orbison, 'Middle Temple documents', pp. 60, 70; S. D'Ewes, *The Autobiography and Correspondence,* edited by J. O. Halliwell, 2 vols (London, 1845), II, 105, 129-36.

36. See my *Theatre and Crisis,* pp. 163-79.

37. The antimasques are discussed in detail by Lawrence Venuti in 'The Politics of allusion: The gentry and Shirley's *Triumph of Peace', English Literary Renaissance,* 16 (1986), 182-205, an interesting essay which appeared too late for me to be able to make use of it in writing this article. Venuti explores the masque's allusions to Charles's local government initiative in greater detail than I do here; however, I cannot accept his argument that the masque is to be read as an attack by the lawyers, in the crown's behalf, on the gentry whom Charles was at that time attempting to compel back to their country estates. The categories of 'lawyer' and 'gentleman', while not coterminous, cannot be distinguished so rigidly in this period: into which category would he put Hyde, Whitelocke or D'Ewes? Similarly, many of the details of his interpretation of the antimasques seem to me to be forced. For example, he assumes that Opinion, the country gentleman, is made to praise the absurd inventions of the projectors, but his language is actually marked by amazement and hostility. So too he describes the fantastic knight (antimasque 11) as a country gentleman who foolishly aspires to nobility, yet in this episode it is the 'country gentleman' who beats him and sends him off lame for his folly (458). And again, he describes the bowlers (antimasque

12) as an allusion to gentlemen who throw away their money in gambling at bowling greens in London, yet this is one of the antimasques performed against the scene of a woody landscape, not a town setting; these country sports can only with difficulty be stretched into an attack on the gentry in town.

38. Whitelocke, *Memorials,* p. 20.

39. Jones, '"The Great Gamaliel of the Law"', *passim;* idem, *Politics and the Bench,* pp. 92-95.

40. Hyde, *History of the Rebellion,* I, 85.

41. Hyde, *History of the Rebellion,* I, 85.

42. Whitelocke, *Memorials,* p. 21.

43. Orbison, 'The Middle Temple documents', p. 34. I quote *Coelum Britannicum* from the edition of Rhodes Dunlap, *The Poems of Thomas Carew* (Oxford, 1949).

44. See Dunlap, *Poems of Carew,* pp. 278-79.

45. A. Patterson, *Censorship and Interpretation* (Madison, 1984), pp. 108-11.

46. I quote the text from J. Fuzier, 'English political dialogues 1641-1651: a suggestion for research, with a critical edition of *The Tragedy of the Cruell Warre', Cahiers Elisabéthains,* 14 (1978), 49-68. See also G. Bas, 'More about the anonymous *Tragedy of the Cruell Warre* and James Shirley's *The Triumph of Peace', Cahiers Elisabéthains,* 17 (1980), 43-57.

47. Whitelocke, *Memorials,* p. 20.

48. Historical Manuscripts Commission, *Report* 12 (Cowper MSS), ii, p. 34.

49. *The Earl of Strafford's Letters and Dispatches,* edited by W. Knowler, 2 vols (London, 1739), I, 177.

50. H. L'Estrange, *The Reign of King Charles,* second edition (London, 1656), pp. 133-34.

51. Quoted in M. B. Pickel, *Charles I as Patron of Poetry and Drama* (London, 1936), p. 147.

C. E. McGee (essay date 1991)

SOURCE: McGee, C. E. '"Strangest consequence from remotest cause': The Second Performance of *The Triumph of Peace.*" *Medieval and Renaissance Drama in England* 5 (1991): 309-19.

[*In the following essay, McGee discusses the political and financial details of a performance of* The Triumph of Peace *produced by the City of London, noting that it reflects and illuminates tense relations between Charles I and the city.*]

From Enid Welsford's *The Court Masque* (1927) to David Lindley and R. L. Smallwood's *The Court Masque* (1984), critics of the masque have worked, as many masquers danced and claimed they lived, within the sphere of the monarch.[1] Even masques performed neither at court nor in the presence of royalty—*Comus* for instance—found their way into such studies, as if the union of masque and court were indissoluble. Few would object to the match: the vast majority of these entertainments, whether at court or in the country, were danced by royalty or in their presence; and especially in the last decade of the reign of Charles I, the court-masque union made for a compelling story, the story of a privileged elite indulging and admiring itself while forces of revolution gathered. But recent criticism, suggesting other ways of characterizing masques, has at least complicated the understanding of the relationship between the court and that form of drama. Martin Butler has observed that "the early Stuart period saw the rise of one particular kind of provincial theatrical entertainment—the amateur masque or show, mounted at a great house privately within a circle of friends, family, and, possibly neighbors and tenants—which does demand some attention as a form novel in this period. . . ."[2] Counting fourteen such shows—a conservative estimate, as preliminary work on household accounts and aristocratic patronage is demonstrating[3]—Butler suggests that we need to consider not just the court masque, but also the country masque. Alan Somerset has pointed out yet another direction for masque criticism, most provocatively when he concluded that Milton's *Comus* was "not a private family performance" but "one of the civic occasions by which the town and the Lord President ceremonially greeted each other."[4] As such, *Comus* illustrates that the connections between masques and the communities in which they were performed (and by whose labors they were produced) need to be investigated. It is in this second direction, toward the city rather than the country, that I wish to proceed, and on the ground of some hitherto unpublished records of *The Triumph of Peace.*

Of all the masques that might be relevant to London, James Shirley's *The Triumph of Peace* is the best candidate. Both the triumphal parade and the masque were performed at Whitehall on 3 February 1634; their success led to a second performance at Merchant Taylors' Hall, a performance scheduled for 11 February, then postponed until the 13th of that month. The second performance created problems for the City, which was rebuked—or so Garrard reported to Strafford—by the Lord Chamberlain for the unfitting cash gift it proposed to give the King.[5] Moreover, Shirley made city life one of his themes both by alluding "to Charles' prohibition of the gentry's residence in London"[6] and by including an anti-masque of projectors—the very kind of entrepreneur who brought the Court, the City, and its companies into bitter conflict. Since these circumstances and concerns of *The Triumph of Peace* have been known for some time, it is somewhat surprising that the records of the Corporation of London have not been explored for additional information. (The fact that they have not is consistent, of course, with the predisposition to keep the masque at court.[7]) Put very generally, what the civic records indicate is that providing a feast for the King and Queen at the Lord Mayor's house, ensuring the safe and easy passage of the triumphal procession from the Inns of Court to Merchant Taylors' Hall, and playing host to King, Queen, lords, ladies, gentlemen of the Inns and their masque were part of a diplomatic effort by which the City hoped to build a secure, harmonious, profitable relationship with the Crown. In the backs of the minds of the city fathers as they prepared for the frivolity of a court masque were the "many questions and great suits . . . depending betweene his Ma<jes>ty and this Citty."[8]

The cause of the *first* performance of *The Triumph of Peace* seems clear enough: the gentlemen of the Inns of Court wanted to distance themselves "from Mr Prynne's new learning," "confute his *Histrio-Mastix* against interludes," and endorse *The King's Book of Sports,* which King Charles had reprinted in October 1633.[9] But what prompted the second performance? Contemporaries offered several rather different explanations: Bulstrode Whitelocke said that the Queen was so delighted by the show that "she desired to see it acted over again"; Mr. Garrard, writing to the Earl of Strafford, extended the desire to "both the King and Queen," so that they "invited themselves to supper at my Lord Mayor's within a Week after . . . ;" and the Venetian ambassador portrayed the second performance as an inexorable consequence of the success of the first, which, he says, excited "the curiosity and applause of all the people, and afforded particular gratification to their Majesties, so that they [the Inns of Court] had to repeat their procession and representation."[10]

To these reports, we can now add that of William Whiteway, merchant and capital burgess of Dorchester in Dorset, sometime MP, and, most important, someone *not* connected with the Court. His connections were with the City. He and the Lord Mayor, Ralph Freeman, may have done business, for both were involved in the cloth trade. Whiteway certainly had some contact with London officials at about this time, for the City Cash Book 1635-36 registered a payment to him of £36, interest on a loan of £900 for the outfitting of five ships.[11] His different sources made for a different story of the second performance of *The Triumph of Peace,* a story in which the soap-makers and laundresses of London are the remote cause of a strange, marvellous consequence, a lavish court-masque in a City company's hall:

> This maske cost the actors .17. M. pound and did so
> please the King, that he invited himselfe, the Queene &

Maskers to sup at the *Lord* Maiors, Sr Ralph Freemans the .13. february. Where the *Lord* Maior spent 3000ˢ to entertaine them, in pulling downe diuers houses betwen his house & Marchantailors Hall, & making a gallery for the King to passe through. The King invited himself to the *Lord* Maiors, to make him amends, for the sharp words he had lately giuen him, calling him old foole, for speaking in the behalfe of the Sopeboilers & Laundresses of London: which troubled him so that he kept his bed a whole moneth after it, & was like to dy, had not the *Kings* message reuiued him. The Queene dancing at the *Lord* Maiors, strained her foote & was like to haue taken much hurt.

(A. 20-35)

Whiteway focuses attention on political and economic conditions of the entertainment. To do so is typical of him: elsewhere in his diary he attributes the death of Dr. Butts, Vice-Chancellor of Cambridge University, to the King's displeasure with a play; teaching the lesson that the Lord's Day was not to be profaned by sports, he reports how a maypole being fetched on a Sunday crushed the head of one of the children involved; he notes that Dorchester refused to allow Mrs. Provoe and William Sands's puppeteers to perform in that city in spite of their warrants from higher authorities, the Master of the Revels in the case of the former and the King himself in the latter.[12] Whiteway's account of ***The Triumph of Peace,*** however, is longer than any other entry about drama in his diary and tighter than any other as a sequence of events with clear causes and precise effects. With its details of lavish and sudden expenditure, demolition and construction, and a marvellous cure, Whiteway's story seems too good to be true. The City records tell a similar one however, though in the pristine,[13] disjointed discourse of civic ordinances, official correspondence, and postings in the City Cash Books. To these Whiteway's account may stand as a coda.

3000ˢ (AND THEN SOME)

Calculated in shillings, the cost to the Lord Mayor seems impressive, and it may have been to a Dorchester merchant, but Ralph Freeman could well afford to pay. His will, apart from the evidence it gives of properties in London, Surrey, Kent, Devon, and Hertfordshire, included cash bequests totalling approximately £30,000.[14] His 3000 shillings are important as just one part of the total cost of the second performance of the masque. The Inns of Court paid for new torches, silk stockings, and an additional speech by James Shirley.[15] The Merchant Taylors made several payments to prepare their hall for the event, and presumably the Drapers had similar, but smaller, expenses in order to provide for the anti-masquers.[16] All these sums are dwarfed, however, by the expenditures of the Corporation of London, which spent about £5300 between 6 February, when the announcement of the second performance of the mas-

que was first entered in City records, and 14 February, when the Court of Alderman decided to give the King a diamond valued at £4000 for "the great and extraordinary favour and love of their Ma<jes>tys herein declared and manifested vnto this Citty" (B. 200-202). The total cost of the diamond and all was £300 more than "the grand total paid out by all four Inns,"[17] £1000 more than charges for a royal entry planned for the Spring of 1626.[18] The £1287.7.8.ob. for things other than the diamond is roughly equivalent, given inflation, to the £1061.5.1 that the Merchant Taylors spent on the entertainment of King James and Prince Henry in 1607, and comparable to the £1786 that the City spent for festivities at the Guildhall when Charles finally did make an official entry into London in 1641.[19] Spending such sums of money in such a short period of time—spending so much on provisions in a winter when the guilds were forbidden to hold "cuntry feasts" because of the scarcity of food[20]—reveals the readiness of the City both to do what the Crown expected of it and to invest in an entertainment as a way of advancing political and economic causes.

The practical steps the City took to prepare for the triumph and masque have this dual purpose. Repairing the streets along the route of the triumphal procession, clearing, cleaning, and lighting them not only enhanced the brilliance of the glittering cavalcade, but also demonstrated to the King and the court that the city fathers were capable of providing "the good government of this Cittie" (D. 621-622). The double watch and ward, especially in that it closed off cross-streets along the parade route, helped define that route and to exclude disorderly persons (D. 579-586); it dramatised at the same time the allegiance of London whose citizens stood, armed with halberts, ready to defend King Charles. Similarly, while outfitting Merchant Taylors' Hall with scaffolding, furniture, and lighting was necessary for the performance of the masque, adorning it with a cloth-covered walkway, tapestries, the king's arms, and his picture were ways of making a statement, a statement of the City's affection and respect for the monarch. The practicalities had to be well taken care of if an edifying ideal—the harmony of a loving and gracious monarch and an obedient and loving City—were to be acted out convincingly and efficaciously.[21]

A GALLERY FOR THE KING

William Whiteway reported that Mayor Freeman pulled down "diuers Houses betwen his house & Marchantailors Hall" and made "a gallery for the King to passe through" (A. 25-27). The City records say little of the demolition; they indicate only that "a way or passage was made" (C. 389-390) through the house of the late John Slany and that "the Brickwall betwixt Mʳ Slany his yard and the yard of the said merchantaylours hall . . . was broken downe for their Ma*jestes* passage thither . . ." (C. 516-518). It is hard to imagine that so conspicuous a feature of the preparations as the destruction of properties would have been invented by Whiteway or his informants. Perhaps the houses were Freeman's own, and cleared away at his own expense, for apart from his capital messuage in Cornhill, he owned "ten*ementes* lyeing nere or adioyning to the same situate lyeing and being in the parish of St. Michaell in Cornhill."²² The City Cash Book provides more details about the construction of the gallery, though not all the details needed to imagine the structure.²³ This "gallery or Scaffold" (C. 386) had two purposes: first, as it stood "in the streete in Cornhill," it was "for the passage of their Ma*jes*ties and their attendants from the said Lord Maiors house to the late dwelling house of Mr John Slany in Cornhill" (C. 386-389);²⁴ as it stood "before the Lord Maio*urs* gate," it served as a viewing stand for Charles and Henrietta Maria "to behold the Maskers . . . together with the Gentlemen Riders" (C. 406-408). The royal seat, the posts of which were covered with light blue baize, stood on a railed platform adorned with bright blue cloth and covered with rushes. Providing this gallery so that the royal couple could see the triumphal parade was certainly one way in which the City ensured the "good contentment" (B. 136) of the King and Queen. When *The Triumph of Peace* was first performed, King Charles managed to see the cavalcade three times: once at Salisbury House, a second time "from the long gallery at the upper end of the tilting yard" at Whitehall, and a third time there after asking "that the whole show might fetch a turn about the Tilt-yard, that their Majesties might have a double view of them."²⁵

Besides improving the sight lines of the royal party, the gallery made Charles and his consort the "observed of all observers." In the account of the entertainment in the minutes of the Court of Alderman, nothing is more important than this "privileged visibility"²⁶ of the royal couple: not the author of the masque, nor the architect (Inigo Jones), nor the title, nor the anti-masque's portrayal of seedy features of urban life, nor the main masque's critique of royal prerogative are mentioned. The thread running through the account of the event in the *Repertory* of the Court of Aldermen is that the King and Queen allowed themselves to be seen: they came to Freeman's house "in their open Chariott" (B. 179); they proceeded from there to Merchant Taylors' Hall "in publique view" (B. 190-191); and as spectators of the masque, "in the full aspect of the Aldermen their Ladies and wifes and many others of the Cheife Citizens men and women," Charles and Henrietta Maria were gracious enough "to shew themselves" (B. 194-197). What the records describe in conventionally grand terms as a manifestation of "the great and extraordinary favour and love of their Ma<jes>tys . . . vnto this Citty such as in the like manner hath not bine shewed . . . by any Prince" (B. 200-203) was (merely) the royal presence.

Sopeboilers & Laundresses

That King Charles and the Lord Mayor disagreed early in January about the Soapboilers dispute is surprising, because just before Christmas the conflict seemed to have been settled, temporarily at least.²⁷ On 6 December, in response to continual violations of the privileges granted the Soapmakers of Westminster and to complaints about the damage done by their new soap both to cloth and to the hands of the laundresses, a second test of the new soap was ordered. One of the authorities who conducted the public trial was "ye now Lord Maior of our Cittie of London who had longe traded with the former sopeboilers by ventinge vnto them the Whale oyle of Greenland wherein he is a principall old venturer."²⁸ On 24 December, Mayor Freeman endorsed the findings of the committee, that the new white soap made by the Westminster company did, "with very small difference," lather better and make the cloth, once dry, whiter and sweeter than that washed with the soap of the London company.²⁹ The King's new orders concerning the soap industry, "given at Courte at Whitehall the 26th day of Januarie,"³⁰ were proclaimed as law on 5 February, eight days before the second performance of *The Triumph of Peace.* And eight days after it, all but one of the soapboilers of London who had been imprisoned in the Fleet since May for their resistance to the Westminster monopoly were freed.³¹ In short, early in 1634 it seemed that at least a ceasefire, if not the triumph of peace, had been negotiated in the Soapboilers' dispute.

The conflict had been intense and rumors about it were undoubtedly in the air at the time of the masque. Perhaps William Whiteway, for the sake of a good plot, assigned one of these rumors, one based on a real disagreement between Charles and Freeman earlier in the fall, to the story of the Mayor's illness. On the other hand, perhaps, having conceded to the Soapmakers of Westminster their privileges, Freeman rekindled the King's anger by trying to negotiate on behalf of London soapboilers. One would expect this tactic of a businessman as successful as Freeman, and there is at least a little evidence that he would support pet projects of the Crown only on his own terms; he bequeathed £1000 to be used to complete the second half of the repairs of the west end of St. Paul's with the proviso that the first half be finished.³² Unfortunately, the records of the City never explicitly connect the Soapboilers dispute with the masque. The only connection they make is paratactical: in the *Journals* of the Court of Common Council, the transcription of King Charles's proclamation of 26 January follows immediately after the various orders passed by the Council by way of preparation for the masque.

Judging from the City records, one would conclude that the Soapboilers' dispute was but one of many conflicts straining the relationship between London and the

Crown. The King's visit to see the masque at Merchant Taylors' Hall was judged to be "especially" gracious and extraordinary "at this tyme, when as many questions and great suits are depending betweene his Ma<jes>ty and this Citty" (B. 203-205).[33] Among the questions were the City's rights under its charter of 23 Henry VI to certain fines and estreats, the Crown's proposed scheme for incorporating the suburbs, the corrupt practices of the royal commissioners for building and of the customs officers, and the threat posed by new, craft-based companies. to the financial power of London's livery companies. There were two worrisome suits as well: in the Court of Exchequer was an information attacking the Trustees of the Royal Contract Estates, and, potentially most costly to the City, hanging fire in the Court of Star Chamber was the charge against the City for mismanagement of the Londonderry plantation. The City, realizing that it had a lot to lose, tried to settle out of court. The aldermen petitioned Charles in March 1633 to intervene to protect the City against the number of suits brought against it. A month later, the City offered the Privy Council £20,000 to see that some of these charges were dropped. In January 1634, the City increased that offer to £30,000.[34] The decision in the Londonderry plantation case indicates how high the stakes were: the City was initially fined £70,000 and it forfeited the estates (which, for £125,000 more, it might redeem).[35] Faced with such potential losses, the city fathers might well have judged that spending £5300 entertaining King Charles himself was a good investment.

THE MAYOR'S ILLNESS AND THE KING'S CURE

Early in 1634 Mayor Freeman had cause for anxiety. As a clothworker, he cared about the cost of soap, the price of which was to rise as a consequence of the privileges granted the Westminster Soapmakers. He was a member of the Greenland Company and of the Merchant Adventurers. The former suffered because of the reduced demand for whale oil, which had been used in making soap until the founding of the Soapmakers of Westminster. The latter suffered because in 1630 the King gave the Eastland Company sole right to trade with the Baltic. Freeman had invested in a Haberdashers' plantation in Londonderry and owned Crown lands in several counties "late purchased of our nowe Soveraigne Lord King Charles."[36] His mayoralty had been marked from the very start by conflict with the Crown; in November 1633, "the lord mayor and aldermen were censured by the privy council both for the slovenly and irreverent manner in which they had taken their oaths on an official occasion and for returning home in coaches rather than on horseback in formal procession."[37] Add to this friction the stress generated by his mediation of the Soapboilers' dispute, which, as

Whiteway tells the story, culminated in an insulting royal rebuff, and the Lord Mayor's illness seems understandable.

The City records confirm both that Freeman fell ill about a month before the masque was first performed and that the masque restored him temporarily. The mayor led the civic party at the baptism of Prince Henry in November, participated in the public trial of the new soap, and chaired meetings of the Court of Aldermen until January 9, 1634, when the chairman was Sir Martin Lumley. Subsequent meetings dealing with the normal business of the court were all chaired by Lumley. However, when *The Triumph of Peace* was on the agenda, Freeman rose from his sick bed to conduct the meetings, which were held at his house on 6, 12, 14, and 18 February. He oversaw the preparations for the masque and, despite the physical strain on him, he played his role in the entertainment of the monarch, as Sir John Finet observed:

> At the Kyngs descent from his coach before the lord mayors doors, his lordship receyved him on his knee and wyth the sword borne by himself and the mace before him ushered him to his chamber. About the mydst of supper he came forth (sicke and weak as he then was) to present theyr Majestyes with a welcome and the lords with the lyke.[38]

Freeman saw to it that the King and Queen received a handsome gift by way of thanks for their visit, then retired from political activity. Meetings in February and March at which other payments for the masque were made were all chaired by Sir Martin Lumley.

The Triumph of Peace was Ralph Freeman's last business on the City's behalf, for the king's readiness to make amends produced no lasting cure. Freeman went into remission only briefly, and on 16 March 1634 he "departed this presente life betweene the houres of three and fower of the clock in the afternoone."[39] One of the only two lord mayors of that time not knighted, Ralph Freeman was remembered in an elegy by the Queen's poet, for which the City paid forty shillings more.[40]

Notes

1. Or, from Enid Welsford's seminal work *The Court Masque: A Study in the Relationship between Poetry & the Revels* (Cambridge: Cambridge University Press, 1927) to the most important recent collection of essays, edited by David Lindley and R. L. Smallwood, *The Court Masque* (Manchester: Manchester University Press, 1984).

2. "A Provincial Masque of Comus, 1636," *Renaissance Drama,* N.S. XVII (1986), 149.

3. Lynne Hulse of King's College, University of London is just completing "The Musical Patronage of the English Aristocracy, c. 1590-c. 1640," a

study based on the family papers of some twenty-five of the nobility. The first findings of some REED editors, such as those of John Wasson concerning Derbyshire magnates, Robert Alexander concerning the Percies, and Barbara Palmer concerning the Cliffords, have been presented at conferences, but not yet published.

4. "The Lords President, Their Activities and Companies: Evidence from Shropshire," *Elizabethan Theatre X* (1988), 96.

5. For Garrard's letter, dated 27 February 1634, see *The Earl of Strafforde's Letters and Despatches, with an essay towards his life,* ed. William Knowles (London: William Bowyer, 1739), 1, 207. A transcription from this volume of the final sentences of the letter, those dealing with the City's entertainment of the King and Queen, has been published by Elizabeth Hamilton, *Henrietta Maria* (New York: Coward, McCann & Geoghegan, Inc., 1976), p. 117.

6. Lawrence Venuti, "The Politics of Allusion: The Gentry and Shirley's *The Triumph of Peace,*" in *Renaissance Historicism: Selections from "English Literary Renaissance"*, ed. Arthur F. Kinney and Dan S. Collins (Amherst: The University of Massachusetts Press, 1987), p. 295.

7. The most striking illustration of this appears in Gerald Eades Bentley, *The Jacobean and Caroline Stage,* 7 vols. (Oxford: Clarendon Press, 1941-1968), V, 1158-1159, where everything but that part of Mr. Garrard's letter dealing with the mayor's illness and the City's gift has been reprinted. The letter in its entirety has been published in *The Dramatic Works and Poems of James Shirley,* ed. Alexander Dyce (1833; rpt. New York: Russell & Russell, 1966), I, xxvii, n. 7.

8. Appendix B, ll. 204-205; subsequent quotations from the manuscripts shall be identified by the Appendix letter and the line number(s) in parenthesis.

9. This formulation of the purpose is based primarily on Bulstrode Whitelocke, *Memorials of English Affairs* (1732), as reprinted in Murray Lefkowitz, *Trois Masques á la Cour de Charles I^{er}D'Angleterre: The Triumph of Peace, The Triumph of the Prince d'Amour, Britannia Triumphans* (Paris: Editions du Centre National de la Recherche Scientifique, 1970), p. 30; William Whiteway, Appendix A, ll. 35-36, alludes specifically to *The King's Book of Sports.* The most complete gathering of contemporary notices of the entertainment is that in Bentley, V, 1154-1163. Additional information on the triumphal proces-

sion has been published by Jerzy Limon in the *REED Newsletter,* 13, No. 2 (1988), 2-9; even more from the Bulstrode Whitelocke papers is forthcoming from Ruth Spalding and John R. Elliott.

10. Bulstrode Whitelocke, p. 35; Bentley, V, 1158-1159 and 1157. Sir John Finet concurs with Garrard; see *Ceremonies of Charles I: The Note Books of John Finet 1628-1641,* ed. Albert J. Loomie (New York: Fordham University Press, 1987), p. 149.

11. Corporation of London Record Office (CLRO), City of London Cash Books 1/2 (1635/36), f. 51^v.

12. British Library (BL) MS. Egerton 784, ff. 87, 102^v, 110, 79^v; this manuscript has been fully transcribed by Thomas Murphy, "The Diary of William Whiteway of Dorchester, County Dorset, From the Year 1618 to the Year 1635. With Notes and Introduction," (Diss: Yale University, 1939) and another transcription is soon to be published by the Dorset Record Society. Whiteway's commonplace book, Cambridge University Library MS. Dd.11.73, f. 148, has another story of this kind, an apocryphal story in which King James is manipulated by a "play-within-the-play" so that he authorizes a performance (of *Ignoramus* in this case) despite the Lord Chief Justice's objections. For a complete transcription of Whiteway's entries regarding *Ignoramus* and Dr. Butt's suicide, see "Stuart Kings and Cambridge University Drama," *Notes and Queries,* 233 (Dec., 1988), 494-496.

13. The City records of the seventeenth century often seem to be expurgated texts; they provide a useful record of decisions and resolutions, without giving a sense of discussion, debate, and disagreement leading to those resolutions. Recording what was done, not what was said, was certainly a labour- and money-saving device and perhaps a defensive measure against those who might use the City records against City fathers.

14. PRO, P.C.C. 29 Seagar July 3, 1633 (Reel 165), ff. 226-231^v.

15. Tucker Orbison, "The Middle Temple Documents Relating to James Shirley's *The Triumph of Peace,*" in Malone Society *Collections XII* (Oxford: Oxford University Press, 1983), items S70 and S72.

16. See Appendix E for the expenses of the Merchant Taylors; reimbursement of the Drapers for beer for the anti-masquers is entered in the City Cash Books, Appendix C. 524-529.

17. Tucker Orbison, p. 41.

18. David M. Bergeron, "Charles I's Royal Entries into London," *Guildhall Miscellany,* III (1970),

94; another £1000 might easily have been spent had this entry not been cancelled by King Charles.

19. *Ibid.,* 96, for information about the reception in 1641; for the Merchant Taylors' entertainment, see Charles M. Clode, *The Early History of the Guild of Merchant Taylors,* 2 vols. (London: Harrison & Sons, 1888), I, 317.

20. CLRO, Court of Aldermen, *Repertory* 48, f. 17.

21. Records of *The Triumph of Peace* also provide some evidence of the attempt to fashion the audience into an image of the ideal social hierarchy. This requires foregrounding certain classes, as the Privy Council tried to do in requiring for the first performance of the masque "a very good and carefull watch . . . by the Constables and *better sort of Citizens*" (CLRO, *Remembrancia,* VII, 106, in Bentley, 1156; italics mine). The ideal image also required the elimination of other groups of people; hence the order from the mayor "for cleeringe the streetes" not only of offal and filth, coaches and carts, but also of "all manner of vagrants and other loose & idle people" (D. 588-589).

22. PRO, P.C.C. 29 Seagar July 3, 1633 (Reel 165), f. 228^v.

23. One crucial piece of information that is still missing is the location of Ralph Freeman's house and the gate thereto. In his will Freeman says that his capital messuage in St. Michael's parish, Cornhill, was recently purchased from John Hawes, "Cittizen and Haberdasher of London." No deed for property in St. Michael's parish owned by Hawes or Freeman has been found among the collections of the Haberdashers, the Guildhall Library, or the PRO, but an exhaustive search of all the records that might help determine the location of the Lord Mayor's property (records of the parish, the Clothworkers, and the Haberdashers) needs to be made.

James Elmes, *A Topographical Dictionary of London and its Environs* (London: Whittaker, Teacher and Arnet, 1831), p. 198, notes a property called Freeman's Court, in Cornhill, which "is about six houses on the left hand from the Royal Exchange, going towards Leadenhall street." Called "Freeman's yard" in 1677 and 1679, this property included by that time at least three tenements, which rented for 60 s., 20 s., and 20 s. per annum (Guildhall Library MS 15619).

John Slany, Master of the Merchant Taylors in 1619, held the old hall of the Merchant Taylors along with its garden. Henry Lennox Hopkinson, *The History of Merchant Taylors' Hall* (Cambridge: Cambridge University Press, 1931), p. 60, says that this old hall "stood on the site of No. 4 Newman's Court" and that the garden is the

one now known as the "little garden" of the Merchant Taylors.

24. Sir John Finet confirms this use of the gallery and calls attention to one of its advantages; it provided the distinguished guests of the City with their own special route of access to Merchant Taylors' Hall; see *Ceremonies of Charles I,* p. 149.

25. Bentley, V, 1157; Bulstrode Whitelocke, p. 34.

26. Stephen Greenblatt, "Invisible Bullets: Renaissance Authority and its Subversion," *Glyph,* 8 (1981), 57.

27. A contemporary, anonymous, embittered account of the Soapboilers dispute is to be found among the Thomason tracts at the British Library: *A Short and true relation concerning the Soap-business* (London: for Nicholas Bourne, 1641), Wing *STC* S3555. See also George Unwin, *The Gilds and Companies of London* (1908; London: Frank Cass, 1966), pp. 293-325; and William Hyde Price, *The English Patents of Monopoly,* Harvard Economic Studies, Vol. I (Boston and New York: Houghton, Mifflin and Company, 1906), pp. 35-42. Stephen Orgel and Roy Strong, when discussing the antimasque of projectors in *The Triumph of Peace,* mention the Soapmakers of Westminster as the "most notorious" of the Caroline monopolies in *Inigo Jones: The Theatre of the Stuart Court,* 2 vols. (Berkeley and Los Angeles: University of California Press, 1973), I, 65.

28. CLRO, Court of Common Council, *Journal* 36, f. 222.

29. *Ibid.*

30. *Ibid.,* f. 218; *STC* 9008 is the printed text.

31. *A Short and true relation concerning the Soap-business,* p. 10.

32. PRO, P.C.C. 29 Seagar July 3, 1633 (Reel 165), f. 226.

33. The discussion of these questions and suits that follows is based on the work of Robert Ashton, *The City and the Court 1603-1643* (Cambridge and New York: Cambridge University Press, 1979), pp. 141-143, 157-176; of Valerie Pearl, *London and the Outbreak of the Puritan Revolution: City Government and National Politics, 1625-43* (London: Oxford University Press, 1961), pp. 79-91; and of Lawrence Stone, *The Causes of the English Revolution 1529-1642* (New York: Harper & Row, 1972), pp. 122-130.

34. Valerie Pearl, pp. 83-84; Robert Ashton, pp. 159-160.

35. T. W. Moody, *The Londonderry Plantation, 1609-1641* (Belfast: William Mullan & Son, 1939), p. 366. James Stevens Curl notes Ralph Freeman's

portion, arising from a legal dispute of 1632, in *The Londonderry Plantation 1609-1914* (Chichester: Phillimore, 1986), p. 315.For a glimpse of the importance of the Irish Estates to one livery company of London, see Arthur Henry Johnson, *The History of the Worshipful Company of the Drapers of London,* 4 vols. (Oxford: Clarendon Press, 1922), III, 123-139.

36. PRO, P.C.C. 29 Seagar July 3, 1633 (Reel 165), f. 228ᵛ.

37. Robert Ashton, p. 173.

38. *Ceremonies of Charles I,* pp. 149-150.

39. CLRO, Court of Aldermen, *Repertory* 48, f. 251ᵛ.

40. *Ibid.,* f. 276ᵛ.

THE LADY OF PLEASURE (1635)

CRITICAL COMMENTARY

George F. Sensabaugh (essay date 1952)

SOURCE: Sensabaugh, George F. "Platonic Love in Shirley's *The Lady of Pleasure.*" In *A Tribute to George Coffin Taylor: Studies and Essays, Chiefly Elizabethan,* edited by Arnold Williams, pp. 168-77. Chapel Hill: University of North Carolina Press, 1952.

[*In the following essay, Sensabaugh discusses* The Lady of Pleasure *in light of the courtly cult of platonic love popularized by Queen Henrietta Maria. Tracing the theme of platonic love in the relationship between Lord A and Celestina, Sensabaugh suggests that Shirley portrayed the platonic lovers sympathetically as part of his bid for advancement at court.*]

James Shirley, in *The Lady of Pleasure,* sharply satirized Caroline manners and morals in both town and court. Through Scentlove and Frederick, he made fun of fops and affected behavior; through the sordid assignation of Aretina and Kickshaw he laid bare lasciviousness in high quarters. Indeed, the main plot centers in Lord Bornwell's attempt to restrict Aretina's extravagance and looseness and is in itself an exposé of the foibles and sins of the age.[1] But to read *The Lady of Pleasure* as satire alone is to miss much of its meaning. It also presents, through Celestina and Lord A, love in the "court Platonic way" and contrasts this love with the sordid affair of Aretina and Kickshaw.[2] An examina-

tion of this love as it appeared in the court of Henrietta Maria, together with an analysis of how Shirley incorporated it into *The Lady of Pleasure,* should therefore not only illuminate the actions of Celestina and Lord A but also lend fresh meaning to the whole play.

What Platonic love meant to Henrietta Maria and her coterie in court may be quickly told.[3] It was, as James Howell described it in his letter of June 3, 1634, a "Love abstracted from all corporeal gross Impressions and sensual Appetite, but consists in Contemplations and Ideas of the Mind, not in any carnal Fruition".[4] Such a conception of love, stemming no doubt from the sonnets of Petrarch, sixteenth-century Italian pastorals, Spanish romances, French Renaissance poetry and prose, and even from tales of medieval chivalry, soon made itself manifest in the poetry of Habington, Suckling, Herbert of Cherbury, Cartwright, George Daniel, and Cowley, and in Waller's letters of compliment to Sacharissa, the wife of Lord Spencer. But the drama, more than any other one form of literature during the Caroline period, embodied in detail the rituals and tenets of the Queen's coterie. As early as 1629, for example, in Jonson's *The New Inn,* Lady Frances Frampul, one of the chief characters in the play, thinks nothing a felicity but to have a multitude of "servants" and to be called "mistress" by them;[5] Lovel explains that love is an affection most noble and pure, a desire for what is truly beautiful and fair, a yearning to make two persons one in spirit, the mind being affected before the flesh is aroused.[6] Somewhat later, Prudence, another character, designates this love as "Platonic" in the court where Lovel had explained the doctrine. Other plays, like Walter Montague's *The Shepheard's Paradise* and D'Avenant's *The Platonic Lovers,* are devoted almost entirely to an exposition of the practices and tenets of Platonic love as understood in the court.[7] In these plays devotees of the cult gather around a mistress to kiss her hand, praise her beauty and wit, and discuss in extravagant terms the meaning and purpose of true love.

It is not necessary here to present the rites of the cult in any detail, except to note that coterie members apparently followed a strict code of behavior and incorporated into their language and thought notions faintly reminiscent of Plato. One such notion, appearing again and again in court drama, was that beauty and goodness are one and the same, a beautiful body indicating a beautiful soul. In D'Avenant's *The Unfortunate Lovers,* for example, Rampino called attention to this relationship when, in speaking to Amaranta, he says:

> The beauty of her mind shines in her face:
> For she is good as fair. . . .[8]

Theander, in *The Platonic Lovers,* had in mind the same relationship when he described his mistress, Eurithea:

> And thou, my love, art sweeter far
> Than balmy incense in the purple smoke;
> Pure and unspotted, as the cleanly ermine ere
> The hunter sullies her with his pursuit;
> Soft as her skin, chaste as th' Arabian bird,
> That wants a sex to woo, or as the dead
> That are divorc'd from warmth, from objects,
> And from thought.[9]

Physical beauty thus became to these Platonic lovers a sign of inner purity and virtue, and it followed from this that possessors of beauty could never sin.

The notion that beautiful women could never sin led to many curious practices in courtship and love. In Henry Glapthorne's *The Ladies Privilege,* for example, Doria and Chrisea feel that their young love cannot "conceive a sinne" or commit a "lawless passion"; yet this innocent woman is wholly convinced that they may freely "entwine".[10] In *The Platonic Lovers,* D'Avenant gently satirized the absurdities the notion engendered. Ariola, whose hope of marriage in the first part of this play has denied her the joys of outward affection, now decides to think in a "cleaner sense" and to love according to Platonic doctrine. As a result, she may now take "All liberty" and make her greetings "More amorous and bold, though virtuous still".[11] In the same play, Theander, an avowed follower of the coterie code, chides Eurithea when she stays "too remote" and hence commands her to "Sit nearer!" so that they may realize more fully their spiritual love.[12] Once he pursues Eurithea to her own boudoir, where, after she unveils on her couch, he presses his suit with a vigor that seems quite remote from "Love abstracted from all corporeal gross Impressions and sensual Appetite," yet he claims it is chaste:

> Thou art not Eurithea, but my rose,
> My sober bashful flower, and I
> Thy wanton woodbine that must grow about
> Thee in embracements thus, until thou art
> Entangled with chaste courtesies of love.[13]

Platonic lovers thus enjoyed liberties in courtship not vouchsafed other, more mundane suitors; they indeed encircled what ordinarily passes for dalliance with a halo of purity so long as they followed coterie manners and morals and kept their minds free from marriage or from actual "carnal Fruition".

Now in Shirley's *The Lady of Pleasure* Celestina and Lord A exemplify in many ways Platonic love in the court of Henrietta Maria. Celestina's entrance, to be sure, shows her to be something of a calculating young widow, bent on the pleasures of a courtly society; and Lord A first gives an appearance of a jaded roué, awakening after a night of debauchery. But in Act II Celestina reveals to Mariana and Isabella her plans, which are very much like the aspirations of Lady

Frances Frampul in Jonson's *The New Inn.* She explains to them that she has no thought of leaving the "sweet freedom" she now possesses to court herself into "new marriage fetters"; instead, she will be merry, full of song and dancing, pleasant in language, but not lascivious in action.[14] Furthermore, she will exact from her suitors a strict compliance with the rules of courtesy, allowing them her lip and hand, but no more; for, she goes ahead to explain, ladies who go further soon have "nothing but / The naked sin left to reward their servants".[15] Therefore, Celestina concludes, she and Mariana and Isabella should be thrifty in their rewards in order to keep "Men long in their devotion" both to preserve themselves and to "encourage those that honour" them.[16] In this way, they can secure the freedom of their mirth and possess their "pleasures" with the "security" of their "honour".[17] In short, Celestina plans to set up a coterie with herself as the center of love so that she may enjoy the liberties of courtship accorded those whose aim is neither marriage nor carnal fruition. These plans match those expressed not only by Lady Frances Frampul but by nearly all lovers in Platonic drama.

Celestina can enjoy rightly such liberties in courtship without a taint of sin because she is a very paragon of beauty. Kickshaw, through whom Celestina first becomes known, tells of his evening at this remarkable lady's establishment. It would have been sin to have slept there, he reveals to Lady Bornwell,

> where so much
> Delight and beauty was to keep me waking.
> There is a lady, madam, will be worth
> Your free society; my conversation
> Ne'er knew so elegant and brave a soul,
> With most incomparable flesh and blood;[18]

and later, in speaking to Lord A, he says that he never saw "So sweet, so fair, so rich a piece of nature".[19] Scentlove, who also pays court to Celestina, adds that Lord A must, when he sees her, give her "victory, / And triumph, o'er all beauties past and living",[20] even though he knows full well that Lord A has sworn to be true to his deceased Bella Maria. Furthermore, when Lord Bornwell, to spite his wife's extravagances, begins to court Celestina, she calls to his attention that he is married and dares him to be virtuous, whereupon he replies:

> I dare,
> By this fair hand I dare; and ask a pardon,
> If my rude words offend your innocence,
> Which, in a form so beautiful, would shine
> To force a blush in them suspected it,
> And from the rest draw wonder.[21]

Even Lady Bornwell is compelled to comment upon Celestina's beauty, which she admits shines far above her own; and she is moved to say, when Lord Bornwell speaks of his courtship of Celestina, that Celestina possesses true beauty. Indeed, she becomes philosophical as she develops her theme:

> True beauty
> Is mocked when we compare thus, itself being
> Above what can be fetched to make it lovely;
> Or, could our thoughts reach something to declare
> The glories of a face, or body's elegance,
> That touches but our sense; when beauty spreads
> Over the soul, and calls up understanding
> To look what thence is offered, and admire.
> In both I must acknowledge Celestina
> Most excellently fair, fair above all
> The beauties I have seen, and one most worthy
> Man's love and wonder.[22]

Lady Bornwell brings her rhapsody to a close by saying that Celestina is a "piece" so "angelically moving" that she thinks

> Frailty excused to dote upon her form,
> And almost virtue to be wicked with her.[23]

In suggesting, through Lady Bornwell, that wickedness with Celestina might almost be virtuous, Shirley hardly goes as far as D'Avenant, who satirized such a notion, or as John Ford, who through Platonic arguments made virtue out of conventional sin, but he comes perilously near to both. Of importance, however, is not Shirley's fleeting speculation upon the implications of Platonic love as understood in the court but a presentation of its practice and a demonstration of its effects on those who worship at its shrine.

The effects of Platonic love become clear in the extended courtship of Lord A and Celestina. Lord A, something of a man of the world still doting on the memory of his deceased Bella Maria, confronts Celestina, only to be led away from what could have developed into a common assignation to the heights of spiritual love. Prepared through the offices of Scentlove, Lord A meets Celestina, who plans to test him and his intentions, as he indeed plans to show Kickshaw and Scentlove that no living woman can turn him away from the memory of his former love. When he first glimpses her, Lord A comments on her beauty in terms of courtly love:

> Though you could turn each place you move in to
> A temple, rather than a wall should hide
> So rich a beauty from the world, it were
> Less want to lose our piety and your prayer.
> A throne were fitter to present you to
> Our wonder, whence your eyes, more worth than all
> They look on, should chain every heart a prisoner.[24]

The ritual once started, Celestina becomes merry, even bawdy, in her conversation, leading Lord A on in order to sound out his intentions. She even speaks of Lord A's reputation with women, and of his recent restraint "against the imperial laws of love", forced on him by a mistress with whom he has buried his hopes; and as she warms to her task, she chides him in that he has lived in court "wherein / True beauty moves" and still mourns his lost love. She goes so far as to say that he must have turned surgeon and made an eunuch of himself, whereupon his blood leaps in reply:

> . . . I am man enough, but knew not where,
> Until this meeting, beauty dwelt. The court
> You talk of must be where the queen of love is,
> Which moves but with your person; in your eye
> Her glory shines, and only at that flame
> Her wanton boy doth light his quickening torch.[25]

When Celestina asks, "Can you return to do what love commands?" he kisses her, only to declare that he is now proof against all carnal temptation, having withstood her voice and beauty; and as he turns to depart, thinking that Celestina has actually tried to lead him from his pledge to Bella Maria, he remarks that she is a brave one if she is as chaste as she is fair. At this, Celestina reveals that she *is* chaste, that she has been only testing his honor, that if he had actually tried to sully her name through any wantonness, she would have scorned him. As the scene closes, Celestina ventures that Lord A's noble thoughts arose not from the memory of "some female loss" but from truth and his love of innocence, both of "which shine / So bright in the two royal luminaries / At court",[26] that is, in Queen Henrietta Maria and King Charles I. With such motivations and such examples of virtue Lord A could not lose his way to "chastity".

He almost loses his way, however. For a second view of Celestina makes Lord A think he should have rewarded "her amorous courtship / With manly freedom". With this aim, as well as with this misunderstanding of Celestina's true intent, he renews his suit, only to drop almost immediately into the ritual of Platonic love. When Celestina asks what kind of love he intends to present, he replies, "That which doth perfect both"; and when he declares that his heart has prepared a spacious dwelling for a mistress like Celestina, she asks: "Your mistress, my good lord?", to which he replies:

> Why, my good lady,
> Your sex doth hold it no dishonour
> To become mistress to a noble servant
> In the now court Platonic way.[27]

With this declaration, Lord A launches into a most extravagant suit, painting a picture of their idyllic love amidst flowers and song, where they can "Embrace and kiss, tell tales, and kiss again", and none but heaven be their rivals.[28] Celestina, following Lord A's lead, shifts their paradise to a grove of tall pines, from which they will descend into a valley "that shall shame / All the delights of Tempe". Here in this hallowed spot Graces shall be called to dance for their pleasure, until, with the sound in their ears of harmonious water dropping on pearl, they surfeit with joy. In the middle of this extravagant language, Celestina suddenly breaks off with something of a satiric note:

> And such love linsey woolsey, to no purpose.[29]

Such a note reminds Lord A of his earlier aim, whereupon he too changes his note, throwing off his affection of Platonic love by boasting how he could have, in the time thus spent with Celestina, broken ten, nay, twenty, virgins to run whatever pace he desired. Celestina rebukes this display of carnal desire with the story of an acquaintance of hers who would like to buy a coat of arms. This acquaintance, she goes on, would be willing to pay a good price; would Lord A be interested in selling his own honourable coat? When Lord A answers that he would sooner give his coat of arms to the hangman's axe, his head and heart to twenty executions than part with one atom of his good name, Celestina replies, in effect, that her honor is as dear to her as his coat of arms is to him. Then she chides him in that he was willing to ravish *her* honor yet not for any price would he sell the honor of *his* house. Lord A sees the meaning of her story, blushes, and returns to a Platonic plane. "From this / Minute I'll be a servant to your goodness", he exclaims. "A mistress in the wanton sense is common, / I'll honour you with chaste thoughts, and call you so".[30] Lord A and Celestina have thus achieved true love in the "court Platonic way"—a love "abstracted from all corporeal gross Impressions and sensual Appetite", consisting in "Contemplations and Ideas of the Mind, not in any carnal Fruition".

The Lady of Pleasure, then, is more than a satire upon manners and morals in town and court; it is also an exposition of Platonic love and its effects upon those who practice its rites and live by its tenets. This kind of love, however full of artificial posturing and questionable behavior, contrasts sharply with the lascivious assignation of Aretina and Kickshaw and the lecherous peregrinations of Madam Decoy. Though Shirley probably had little sympathy for what he saw in the court and at times seemed to have his tongue in his cheek when he described the courtship of Lord A and Celestina, as a dramatist he recognized that the contrast between Platonic love and open immorality would be extremely effective. As an ambitious playwright he perhaps also recognized that a contrast so favorable to Platonic love would enhance his position at court. In an age when royal approval meant so much it is not hard to believe that this was uppermost in his mind.

Notes

1. *The Lady of Pleasure* is usually considered a good example of a comedy of manners. See, for example, William Allan Neilson, *The Chief Elizabethan Dramatists* (New York, 1911), p. 860; and Arthur Huntington Nason, *James Shirley, Dramatist* (New York, 1915), pp. 276-80. Nason described the play as "a bitter but clever satire upon the wilder lords and ladies of the court; their extravagance, their gaming, their drunkenness, and their licentiousness".

2. In Act V, sc.1, Lord A makes love to Celestina in the "court Platonic way". Hanson T. Parlin, in *A Study in Shirley's Comedies of London Life* (Reprint from *The Bulletin of the University of Texas,* No. 371, November 15, 1914, p. 64) noted a suggestion of the doctrine of Platonic love in the "whole fabric of *The Lady of Pleasure*", but made it clear that Shirley is not "in any way satirizing the 'new religion in love'". Kathleen M. Lynch, however, in *The Social Mode of Restoration Comedy* (New York, 1926), p. 56, states that "Shirley gives no evidence of serious interest in the cult".

3. The description of Platonic love given here is an abridgment of a fuller account in *The Tragic Muse of John Ford* (Stanford University Press, 1944), pp. 105-51.

4. *Epistolae Ho-Elianae* (London, 1890), I, 317-18.

5. *The Works of Ben Jonson* (London, 1875), V, 304.

6. *Ibid.,* V, 366-68.

7. Most court drama took Platonic love seriously, but D'Avenant, in *The Platonic Lovers,* gently satirizes its manners and morals.

8. *The Dramatic Works of Sir William D'Avenant* (London, 1872-74), III, 17.

9. *Ibid.,* II, 34-35.

10. *The Ladies Priviledge* (London, 1640), sig. B3v.

11. D'Avenant, *op. cit.,* II, 77.

12. *Ibid.,* II, 58.

13. *Ibid.,* II, 34.

14. *James Shirley* (Mermaid Series, London, 1888), p. 288.

15. *Ibid.,* p. 289.

16. *Idem.*

17. *Idem.*

18. *Ibid.,* p. 272.

19. *Ibid.,* p. 303.

20. *Ibid.,* p. 305.

21. *Ibid.,* p. 296.

22. *Ibid.,* pp. 329-30.

23. *Ibid.,* p. 330.

24. *Ibid.*, p. 331.

25. *Ibid.*, p. 335.

26. *Ibid.*, p. 336.

27. *Ibid.*, p. 349.

28. *Ibid.*, p. 350.

29. *Ibid.*, p. 351.

30. *Ibid.*, p. 353.

Ronald Huebert (essay date 1981)

SOURCE: Huebert, Ronald. "The Staging of Shirley's *The Lady of Pleasure.*" In *The Elizabethan Theatre IX,* edited by G. R. Hibbard, pp. 41-59. Port Credit, Ontario, Canada: P. D. Meany, 1981.

[In the following essay, Huebert constructs a version of the original production of The Lady of Pleasure, *including blocking, casting, and set design. In doing so, he highlights Shirley's use of stagecraft to support the action and dialogue of the play.]*

The first performance of **The Lady of Pleasure** took place in late October or early November, 1635. The play was licensed for performance on 15 October,[1] and by 5 or 6 November it had attracted sufficient notice to deserve mention in John Greene's diary. Referring to the party of guests which gathered to celebrate his sister's wedding, Greene wrote as follows: "wee were at a play, some at cockpit, some at blackfriers. The play at cockpit was Lady of pleasure, at blackfriers the conspiracy."[2] A month later, on 8 December, Sir Humphrey Mildmay recorded in his account book the expenditure of 1 shilling for admission to the play, and in his diary he added the following description: "dined w[i]th Rob[ert] Dowgill wente to the La[dy] of pleasure & sawe that rare playe came home late Supped."[3]

Very little can be inferred with confidence from these laconic observations by members of Shirley's audience. Indeed, Greene may not have been a member of this audience at all, if he was among those wedding celebrants who chose to see *The Conspiracy* at Blackfriars rather than Shirley's play at the Cockpit. Still, Greene's notation confirms one fact and one assumption: it agrees with the title page of the quarto (1637) and with the Lord Chamberlain's list (10 August 1639)[4] in assigning **The Lady of Pleasure** to the Cockpit in Drury Lane, otherwise known as the Phoenix theatre; and it supports the view of some theatre historians that by 1635 the Cockpit and Blackfriars were theatrical institutions of virtually equal prestige.[5]

Mildmay's jottings, however cryptic, will reward more detailed inspection. First, the shilling which Mildmay spent on 8 December 1635 appears to have been the normal minimum price of admission for a cavalier gentleman. I doubt that Sir Humphrey would have been satisfied to pay the absolute minimum of sixpence, if by such thrift he were to risk the social opprobrium which Shirley attaches to unsophisticated spectators in the Prologue to **The Example** (1637):

> Nay, hee that in the Parish never was
> Thought fit to bee o'th jury, has a place
> Here, on the Bench for six pence, and dares sit
> And boast himself commissioner of wit.

> (sig. *2)

Indeed, in his recorded decade of playgoing, Mildmay never paid less than a shilling for a performance at a professional theatre.[6] He often paid exactly a shilling, as he did when he saw "a pretty & Merry Co[m]edy att the Cocke" (6 June 1633), or when he visited Blackfriars to see *The Wits* on one occasion (22 January 1633/ 4), *The Elder Brother* on another (25 April 1635). Frequently Mildmay paid more than a shilling: "a Newe play Called the spartan Lady" (1 May 1634) cost him a shilling and threepence, a "base play att the Cocke pitt" (20 March 1633/4) cost him one and six, and an unnamed play at the Globe (18 July 1633) one shilling ten. When he was "with company" Mildmay's expenditures reflected his hospitality, ranging from about three shillings up to eleven. On these occasions, no doubt, Mildmay wanted to be thought well of, to be "held the witty man, / [Who] censures finely, rules the Box, and strikes / With his court nod consent to what he likes."[7]

When he paid his shilling to see **The Lady of Pleasure,** then, Mildmay was doing what was typical and unpretentious for a person of his social class and theatrical tastes.[8] And, in attending the theatre between his midday meal (when he "dined") and his evening meal (when he "Supped"), Mildmay was engaging in perfectly normal behaviour both for himself and countless others. When he described **The Lady of Pleasure** as "that rare playe," however, Mildmay was breaking with his personal habits: though in the space of a decade he recorded sixty-one theatrical excursions, he seldom confided his judgment to the diary. On three occasions he expressed distaste for a play, and on three occasions he recorded approbation. In the eyes of its first critic, **The Lady of Pleasure** appears to have been an outstanding theatrical achievement.

The external stimulus provided by the assignment of editing **The Lady of Pleasure** is largely to blame for my interest in Mildmay's opinions, and indeed for my central concern in the pages which follow: namely, to recover some rough impression of the nature and quality of Sir Humphrey Mildmay's experience on the afternoon of 8 December 1635. Without being able to see what he saw or hear what he heard, it becomes necessary to rely on such historical evidence as may have a bearing on three principal subjects: the design of the playhouse which Mildmay visited, the talents of the theatrical company engaged in the performance, and the staging requirements of the play being performed. These, for purposes of clarity, will be the stages of my argument; in those few instances where I violate my own division, I ask for indulgence by appealing to the more exacting demands of an untidy and intractable world of external fact.

The playhouse in which *The Lady of Pleasure* was first performed came into being when Christopher Beeston, a prominent member of Queen Anne's company at the Red Bull, planned and sponsored the construction of the Cockpit in Drury Lane in 1616 and 1617. On 9 August 1616 he leased for thirty-one years

> All that edifices or building called the Cockpittes and the Cockhouses and the shedds thereunto adjoining . . . Togeather alsoe with one tenement or house and a little Garden therunto belonging next adjoyning to the said Cockpittes . . . and one part or parcell of ground behinde the said Cockpittes.[9]

Within seven months the buildings had been renovated and the new playhouse was in operation. But not for long. On Shrove Tuesday, 4 March 1616/17, an unusually vigorous apprentice riot interrupted Beeston's enterprise; one part of the mob,

> making for Drury Lane, where lately a newe playhouse is erected, . . . besett the house round, broke in, wounded divers of the players, broke open their trunkes, & what apparell, bookes, or other things they found, they burnt & cutt in peeces; & not content herewith, gott on the top of the house, & untiled it, & had not the Justices of the Peace & Sherife levied an aide, & hindred their purpose, they would have laid that house likewise even with the grownd.[10]

Undaunted by this disastrous beginning, Beeston set about having the damage repaired, and within three months (by 3 June 1617) the playhouse was ready to open again.[11] Perhaps the alternate name for the theatre, the Phoenix, was Beeston's attempt to make good publicity out of the near destruction and quick revival of his edifice. In any case, the public continued to prefer the traditional name, the Cockpit, as the remarks of Sir Humphrey Mildmay (already quoted) indicate. On this question of usage, I will follow Sir Humphrey's taste, so that "the Cockpit" (unqualified) may be understood as referring to Beeston's theatre, and should not be confused with the Cockpit-in-Court, of which more later.

No direct documentary evidence about the design of the Cockpit has been discovered. The earliest verbal description occurs in James Wright's *Historia Histrionica* (1699), cast in the form of a dialogue between Truman, an "Honest Old Cavalier" who remembers a great deal about the good old days before the closing of the theatres, and Lovewit, a persistent interrogator who today might be either the host of a talk-show on daytime TV or a Professor of Oral History. "What kind of Playhouses had they before the Wars?" asks the genial interviewer. Truman replies:

> The *Black-friers, Cockpit,* and *Salisbury-court,* were called Private Houses, and were very small to what we see now. The *Cockpit* was standing since the Restauration, and *Rhode's* Company Acted there for some time.

"I have seen that," Lovewit interposes, and the old gentleman continues:

> Then you have seen the other two, in effect; for they were all three Built almost exactly alike, for Form and Bigness. Here they had Pits for the Gentry, and Acted by Candle-light. The *Globe, Fortune* and *Bull,* were large Houses, and lay partly open to the Weather, and there they alwaies Acted by Daylight.[12]

Since a great many of Truman's assertions have been confirmed by modern scholarship, we ought to treat his claim about the resemblance between the Cockpit and the other "Private Houses" with some respect. If it is true that the "Bigness" of the Cockpit was roughly the same as that of Blackfriars, then we might suppose it to have occupied a space 46 feet by 66 feet with a seating capacity not much in excess of 500 spectators.[13] If it is true that the "Form" of the Cockpit resembled that of the other two, then we can suppose it contained a platform stage somewhat smaller than that specified in the Fortune contract (43 feet by 27 feet 6 inches);[14] that the stage was flanked on either side by high-priced gentleman's boxes; that opposite the stage was a pit, furnished with benches "for the Gentry" instead of a yard for the groundlings in the outdoor manner; and that the pit was surrounded on three sides by a U-shaped configuration of galleries, in either two or three tiers.[15] Some of these inferences by analogy can be confirmed by indirect evidence drawn from plays performed at the Cockpit. In the Prologue to *The Example,* quoted above, Shirley refers to the man of wit who "rules the Box" from which he observes the play, and contrasts him with a less officious spectator who "has a place / Here, on the Bench." The Prologue continues, in a passage not yet quoted, with a reference to a stagekeeper who "beares / Three-footed stooles in stead of Juory chaires" (sig. *2). This allusion to the practice, peculiar to the private houses, of allowing some spectators to sit on the edges of the stage, is consistent with other available evidence, like the imaginary portrait by Hemminges and Condell of a gallant who "sit[s] on the Stage at *Black-Friers,* or the *Cock-pit,* to arraigne Playes dailie."[16]

To return briefly to Wright's claims about the private houses, I should point out that in two respects his remarks are quite uncontroversial: he asserts indirectly that the private houses were indoor theatres, and directly that the stages were lit by candles. There is no reason to doubt the truth of either of these claims, or their pertinence to the design of the Cockpit.

But there is one highly controversial inference to be drawn from Wright, and I shall mention it without presuming to solve the problem it creates. If the Cockpit was anything like Blackfriars or Salisbury Court in "Form," then it should be visualized as a rectangular structure. No matter how diligently the Burbages renovated the Upper Frater of the Blackfriars monastery, the result must have been a rectangular auditorium. And since the builders of Salisbury Court began with a barn on a plot of ground measuring 42 feet by 140 feet, it is difficult to imagine them achieving anything but a rectangular playhouse.[17] Yet it has been a favourite belief among students of the Cockpit that they are dealing with a round or octagonal structure.[18] This belief is based on three separate kinds of evidence: first, the conventionally circular or polygonal shape of buildings used for cockfighting in the seventeenth century, and hence the plausible assumption that the cockpit leased by Beeston was also "round";[19] secondly, the hazardous assumption that Inigo Jones's drawing of the octagonal interior he designed for the Cockpit-in-Court bears a rough resemblance to the design of Beeston's Cockpit; and thirdly, the hasty supposition that references to "this sphere of love" in Cockpit plays can be understood as describing the shape of the galleries.[20] The second and third lines of argument are, without documentary support, little more than fanciful guesswork. The first hypothesis, based on what is known about the design of cockhouses, does bear on a crucial question: namely, what was Beeston up to when, in 1616 and 1617, he converted a plain ordinary cockpit into *the* Cockpit in Drury Lane?

In order to arrive at a possible answer to this question, I will begin by taking a brief detour along a road already travelled by members of this conference under the guidance of D.F. Rowan in 1969. I am referring, of course, to Rowan's discovery of the Jones/Webb theatre drawings (7B and 7C in the collection at Worcester College, Oxford) which, in one of the few ironies of theatre scholarship, can no longer be described as neglected.[21] After a thorough review of the evidence connected with the drawings themselves and some speculations about their significance, Rowan concludes that "there can be no doubt that they represent a real or proposed private 'professional' theatre."[22] This conclusion, though temporate enough to invite eager assent, is also decisive enough to affect in significant ways our interpretations of staging practices in the private houses. But this is a question to which I shall later return.

At present my concern is the ground-plan in the Jones/Webb project. This drawing shows a semicircular shape (housing the pit and galleries) combined with a square shape (housing the stage, boxes, and tiring-house). John Orrell has argued, on what is admittedly "circumstantial evidence," that this ground plan and the drawings which accompany it are in fact the designs for the Cockpit in Drury Lane.[23] If Orrell is right, then we have encountered a highly unusual compromise between the rectangle and the circle. The ground plan is in one sense a rectangle, with two of its corners rounded: enough of a rectangle, that is, to allow James Wright to compare its "Form" without qualification to Blackfriars and Salisbury Court. But the ground plan includes a semicircle as well: enough of a circle, that is, to betray the cockhouse origins of the edifice and to allow its galleries to be referred to as a "sphere." Still, to make the association between the Jones/Webb drawings and the Cockpit, though highly enticing, remains a temptation rather than a virtue, at least until there are further documentary witnesses.

Sir Humphrey Mildmay has paid his shilling and been seated, at last, probably on one of the fairly desirable benches in the pit or the first gallery (not on the stage, nor in a private box, nor in an upper gallery seat, I would suppose), and as he looks around him, he sees the interior of either a rectangular playhouse, or a circular playhouse, or a combination of both. More important, as he looks toward the stage, what does Sir Humphrey see? He sees a platform, a façade with doors, hangings, and an above; but these are features which I will discuss in connection with the staging requirements of *The Lady of Pleasure.* As soon as the play begins, he sees costumed actors; upon them will depend the success or failure of the performance, and it is to the players themselves that I should now like to turn.

Of the actors in Queen Henrietta Maria's company in 1635, at least twelve can be securely identified. Collectively, they possess all of the talents one would expect of a first-class company put together by a shrewd theatrical entrepreneur. The members include the sedate if ageing leading man, the fresh-faced adolescent already admired for his female roles, the former adolescent now being groomed for romantic leads, the veteran comedian who has never been averse to earning a laugh by exploiting his unusually skinny physique, and a sprinkling of character actors who habitually expend their energies on assorted merchants, dukes, old men, and servants. In short, Queen Henrietta's men were a repertory company in the best sense of the term: their well-balanced and amply diversified abilities must have been perfectly suited to a play like *The Lady of Pleasure,* which requires stylish collaboration among the actors who play the sixteen speaking roles, and which distributes responsibility rather evenly among the players who take the eight principal parts.

If the company had a star actor, it would be Richard Perkins (c. 1585-1650). I qualify his status in this way because, among the virtues attributed to Perkins by his contemporaries is the one which star performers shun: professional modesty. Perkins played Barabas in the Cockpit revival of Marlowe's *The Jew of Malta* (1633); in the Prologue which Heywood wrote for this occasion, Edward Alleyn is described as "peerless" in his creation of the original Jew for Lord Strange's men; Perkins is awarded the lesser laurel of "merit" which is said to be consistent with his own view of the matter: "nor is it his ambition / To exceed or equal [Alleyn], being of condition / More modest."[24] However surprising, Heywood's assertion should not be lightly dismissed, for his association with Perkins was of long standing, dating back more than thirty years to an earlier theatrical generation when Perkins, Heywood, and Christopher Beeston were all actors with the Earl of Worcester's men. The earliest known reference to Perkins' career, in Henslowe's *Diary,* is remarkable for its quaint anticipation of a professional friendship: "Lent unto Richard perkens the 4 of septemb[er] 1602 to bye thing[s] for thomas hewode playe . . . xvs."[25] Probably seventeen years of age, Perkins was obviously very much the apprentice in 1602. But a decade later he had acquired the skills to attract an unprecedented compliment from Webster. Now a member of Queen Anne's men at the Red Bull, Perkins had played in the first staging of *The White Devil:* a generally unsuccessful production, to judge by Webster's grumblings in the preliminary letter "To the Reader" of the published play. Whatever the causes of Webster's disappointment, the actors' performances were not among them, for he acknowledges their efforts in a note appended to the final scene, concluding his commendation as follows: "in particular I must remember the well approved industry of my friend Master Perkins, and confess the worth of his action did crown both the beginning and end."[26]

By 1635, at the age of fifty, Perkins was a veteran performer. His known roles, aside from Barabas, are Sir John Belfare in Shirley's *The Wedding* (c.1626), Captain Goodlack in the first part of Heywood's *The Fair Maid of the West* (c.1630), Fitzwater in Davenport's *King John and Matilda* (c.1634), and Hanno in Nabbes' *Hannibal and Scipio* (1635). All of these parts he played for Queen Henrietta's men, whom he joined in about 1626 and with whom he remained until their dispersion in 1637.[27] In one of them he earned a tribute from Andrew Pennycuicke, a man who claimed to be a fellow actor and whose edition of *King John and Matilda* (1655) informs us that the part of Fitzwater was played by "M[aster] Perkins, Whose action gave Grace to the Play."[28]

Of these roles, the one which most clearly concerned Shirley is that of Sir John Belfare in *The Wedding.* Here Perkins played the part of a dignified father, a man who behaves with surprising restraint in his dealings with his marriageable daughter, but who is nevertheless prepared to defend her honour with firmness and vigour. When Belfare makes comfortable allusions to his advancing age, or when he refers to his "gray hairs" (III. ii),[29] Shirley seems to be indulging in his habit of writing with even the personal appearance of a particular actor in mind. This impression can be confirmed by observing the attitude of candid confidence and whimsical frankness on the cavalier-style face in the only known portrait of Perkins (Dulwich College, no. 423).

When Shirley wrote *The Lady of Pleasure* he must have visualized Perkins in one of the principal roles. I believe Sir Thomas Bornwell to have been the only genuinely suitable part. His is the only "straight" role which could be effectively played by an actor of fifty. As the exceptionally tolerant husband of Aretina, Bornwell combines authority, good humour, and restraint in a manner quite reminiscent of Sir John Belfare in *The Wedding.* Since modesty, industry, and grace were characteristics apparently within Perkins' command, he would have been eminently qualified (both by experience and by nature) to take on Bornwell's part. It should not be surprising to find such easy compatibility between the player and his role in a company where, as in this case, the working relationship between star actor and leading dramatist extended over approximately nine years.

The outstanding comic among Queen Henrietta's men was William Robbins, evidently a professional thin man, who appears to have been generously assisted by William Sherlock, a professional fat man. In the *Historia Histrionica,* Wright names "*Robins* a Comedian" among "those of principal Note at the *Cockpit.*"[30] Shirley seems to have placed considerable confidence in his talents, for in *The Wedding* it is Robbins in the role of "Rawbone, *a thin citizen*" who remains on stage at the close to speak the Epilogue and ask for the spectators' applause. Physically emaciated and morally avaricious, Rawbone repeatedly draws attention to these comic faults, as do other characters, who refer to him as "a piece of folly! / A thing made up of parchment," or little more than "an anatomy" (I. iii).[31] Robbins' other known roles include "Carazie, *an Eunuch*" in *The Renegado*[32] and Antonio, the title role, in *The Changeling.*[33] William Sherlock appears in *The Wedding* as "Lodam, *a fat gentleman*" with a penchant for obvious lines, like "I have no stomach to your acquaintance" (II. iii) or "love is worse than a Lent to me, and fasting is a thing my flesh abhors" (III. ii).[34] His other roles include "Mr Ruffman, *a swaggering Gentleman*" in the first part of *The Fair Maid of the West.*[35]

This pair must have played two of the three principal comic roles in *The Lady of Pleasure*: Sir William Sentlove, Master Haircut, and Sir John Littleworth. Just which was which is a matter of speculation, but I am tempted—on grounds of girth—to cast Sherlock as Littleworth. In Act V, after an offstage dunking in the Thames, Littleworth enters "*wet*" (V. ii. 57.1) and complains that his "belly" has disgorged "a tun of water, beside wine" (V. ii. 61, 64).[36] Sir William Sentlove, the trickster and ringleader among the comedians, might well have been Robbins' role.

John Sumner, a regular though not a leading member of the company, would have been the obvious choice for the part of Alexander Kickshaw. He seems to have played roles demanding sexual charisma, like that of Marwood in **The Wedding** or Mustapha in *The Renegado*. In **The Wedding,** Beauford's jealousy is confirmed by his assessment of Marwood's masculinity: "He has a handsome presence and discourse, / Two subtle charms to tempt a woman's frailty" (II. ii).[37] These qualities are exactly what Kickshaw needs, if Aretina's behaviour in **The Lady of Pleasure** is to be credible.

Among the adolescent actors of the company, Ezekiel Fenn is the most likely candidate for one of the female leads. He played the pathos-laden parts of Sophonisba in *Hannibal and Scipio* (1635) and Winifride in a revival of *The Witch of Edmonton* (c. 1635). Since both of these demanding roles were probably acted in the same season as **The Lady of Pleasure,** we can assume that Fenn was at the height of his powers as a "woman actor" when Shirley's play was staged. At fifteen he was already experienced, and his voice must have broken late, for he played his first "mans part" four years later—an event celebrated by Glapthorne in the 1639 edition of his *Poems*.[38] Fenn would have played either Celestina or Aretina, but in the absence of other evidence, it is impossible to be more specific.

The speculative casting I have so far engaged in still leaves plenty of room for such journeymen actors as William Allen, Robert Axen, George Stutville, and Anthony Turner. There is also room for Michael Bowyer, who frequently played male romantic leads, but may have left the company before **The Lady of Pleasure** opened.[39] And there is additional room on both sides of the sexual divide for Theophilus Bird, Hugh Clark, and John Page, all of whom played women's parts, but all of whom may have been too old for anyone but Madam Decoy by 1635, when they were gradually taking on more and more responsibility as adult male actors. Michael Mohun, a boy actor already well known by 1637, may have joined the company in time to play one of the female leads.[40] But at this point speculation becomes rainbow-chasing. It is time to abjure the rough magic of conjecture to return to Sir Humphrey Mildmay as he watches a scene develop on the reliably substantial pageant of the Cockpit stage.

In order to place the actors into their customary environment, I wish to rely in part on four familiar specimens

of visual evidence: the elevation showing the stage in the series of Jones/Webb drawings already discussed, the frontispiece for *The Wits* (1662), and the two vignettes from the title pages of *Roxana* (1632) and *Messalina* (1640).[41] It is possible that none of these visual specimens represents the stage of the Cockpit in 1635, but let us assume that even indirect visual evidence can assist us where it corroborates or illuminates the evidence drawn from the stage directions of Cockpit plays.

My interpretation of the verbal evidence in particular is heavily indebted to William B. Markward's unpublished thesis, "A Study of the Phoenix Theatre in Druary Lane, 1617-1638" (University of Birmingham, 1953); to William A. Armstrong's published lecture, *The Elizabethan Private Theatres: Facts and Problems* (1958); to an article by T. J. King, "Staging of Plays at the Phoenix in Drury Lane, 1617-42" (*Theatre Notebook,* 19 [1964-65], 146-66); and to the compendious resources contained in the seven volumes of Gerald Eades Bentley's *The Jacobean and Caroline Stage*. The scholars just named would, in varying degrees, be at odds about how the available evidence should be treated. Markward's thesis, for example, is based on all of the conceivably relevant information: on the texts of plays written specifically for the Cockpit, those revived at the Cockpit, and on those possibly staged at the Cockpit though not published until the interregnum. I shall call this procedure a *promiscuous* treatment of the evidence. King's inquiry is based on a selection: that is, on plays incontrovertibly written for and staged at the Cockpit, whose texts or manuscript copies bear marks of association with performance in the theatre. By calling this a *chaste* interpretation of the evidence, I am admitting something about my own predilections. But I should add that, in the following attempt to visualize **The Lady of Pleasure** in performance, I have been guided not only by the scholar's obligation to test his evidence, but also by the editor's responsibility to make sense of a scene even where final proof is wanting.

The process of reconstructing the action and spectacle devised by Shirley for the Cockpit stage can safely begin with a platform, thrust forward from the tiring-house wall, and surrounded on three sides by spectators. The façade of the wall in all four of the visual specimens mentioned above is divided into two levels: a level contiguous with the stage and an above. The design of the above varies significantly from drawing to drawing, but on the evidence of the Cockpit plays we can infer that it was often used as an observation post from which one or more actors could look down on and comment upon the action on the platform below.[42] Three of the visual specimens show hangings covering all or part of the lower façade, and the presence of these is nowhere better confirmed than in Celestina's instructions to her Steward in **The Lady of Pleasure**:

CEL.

. . . What hangings have we here?

STEW.

They are arras, madam.

CEL.

Impudence, I know't.
I will have fresher and more rich, not wrought
With faces that may scandalise a Christian,
With Jewish stories stuffed with corn and camels;
. . . I say I will have other,
Good master steward, of a finer loom.
Some milk and silver, if your worship please
To let me be at so much cost.

(I. ii. 11-22)

In addition, though of the drawings only the Jones/ Webb project provides for them, the tiring-house façade required doors for entrances and exits. If Jones and Webb were designing the Cockpit, they certainly wanted three doors: two of normal size at either edge of the façade, and a larger arched doorway at upstage centre. Three doors are stipulated by Markward, who promiscuously exploits the possibly contaminated evidence offered by Nabbes' *Covent Garden* and Heywood's *The English Traveller.*[43] King's chaste analysis of the thirty pure Cockpit plays yields only two necessary doors. This debate could be prolonged by citation of and interpretation of stage directions. I propose to suspend it, for the present limited purposes, by leaving the left-hand and right-hand doors exactly where they are, and by drawing the hangings from either side of the stage façade neatly together until they meet, thus enclosing the arched aperture at upstage centre. Now, at least, we have accommodated the stage direction from *The English Traveller* (1633): "*Enter at one doore an* Usurer and his Man, *at the other,* Old Lionell *with his servant: In the midst* Reginald."[44] The compromise I propose has the advantage of giving Heywood credit for knowing the difference between a door and an aperture which is not a door. And an entrance "*In the midst*" can be visualized as nothing more serious than what is going on between the two panels of hangings in the frontispiece to *The Wits.*

The features of the Cockpit stage thus visualized are perfectly adequate for most scenes in *The Lady of Pleasure.* They are adequate even when stage directions are fairly elaborate, as in the opening of the third act: "*Enter* Lord *unready;* HAIRCUT *preparing his periwig, table, and looking-glass*" (III i. 0.1-2). I am fully aware that *unready* is an adjective meaning "not completely dressed" and that the stage direction requires the actor to finish his adornment onstage. But, since this nobleman has been given no proper name, I refer to him

throughout by the nickname "Lord Unready" in order to avoid verbal confusion with any other personages, terrestrial or celestial.

Before the scene in question opens, in the musical interval between Acts II and III, anonymous hirelings have, I presume, placed the specified table and the unspecified but necessary stool or chair into a reasonably prominent downstage position. The looking-glass may also have been placed in position on the table, perhaps by Master Haircut, who could enter during the final minute of the interval to ensure that all is well for the beginning of Act III. While the last bars of music are being played, Lord Unready enters by one of the two doors, crosses to the table, and sits. He adjusts the mirror to allow himself to watch Haircut arranging the wig to best advantage and completing the application of his cosmetic powers. Conversation begins, only to be interrupted by the Secretary's arrival at the other stage door to announce the approach of Madam Decoy. She now enters and requests a private audience; to oblige her, Lord Unready asks the Secretary and Haircut to "Wait i'th' next chamber till I call" (III. i. 13), upon which they go out through the door from which Decoy has just entered.

The rest of the scene can be managed in precisely the same way, though embellished with many hand-held properties. The Secretary must produce, perhaps from a hiding-place in the table, a pen, an inkwell, and a sheet of paper. He must sit while writing the letter which Lord Unready dictates, and must produce sealing-wax, melting it no doubt by using the nearest convenient candle. After Sentlove and Kickshaw enter, Lord Unready must produce a miniature of his dead mistress (Bella Maria) from a pocket in his costume, and Kickshaw will study the image with affected nonchalance. At the end of the scene, the stage will be cleared, though presumably the table and chair will remain in place until the end of the act.

The scene which follows immediately (III. ii) takes place in the lodgings of Bornwell and Aretina in the Strand. No changes of scenery are required, but a special problem arises in relation to exits, entrances, and eavesdropping. Near the beginning of the scene, Aretina extracts promises from Littleworth and Kickshaw to the effect that they will use their combined wits to humiliate Celestina, the Bornwells' guest. But, Aretina specifies, "Begin not, till I whisper you" (III. ii. 85). Now Bornwell, Celestina, Mariana, and Isabella enter, and a highly social conversation (much of it in French) ensues. Aretina's Steward and her nephew Frederick join the party, and after further badinage, a stage direction reads: "*Ex[eunt] all but* EEL[ESTINA], ALEX-[ANDER], *and* LITTLE[WORTH]" (III. ii. 201.1). At this point Aretina says, "Now, gentlemen" (201); that is, she gives the promised cue to Kickshaw and Littleworth.

The two gentlemen subject Celestina to verbal abuse which continues without a halt even after the stage direction, "*Enter* BORNWELL" (III. ii. 224.1). Bornwell's two brief lines—"How's this?" (224) and "A conspiracy!" (268)—have no effect whatever on some fifty lines of dialogue during which the flyting continues. At last he addresses Celestina as "Brave soul!" and vilifies her abusers as a "brace of horse-leeches" (283-84). Encouraged by Bornwell, Celestina takes the initiative, gains verbal revenge for some thirty lines, and then asks Bornwell: "How shall I / Acquit your lady's silence?" (321-22). After a brief exchange of graceful exit lines between Bornwell and Celestina, Aretina unexpectedly asks, "Is she gone?" (326).

Here there is confusion in plenty. How is it that Bornwell's presence fails to intrude on the action for fifty lines? Why does Celestina remark on Aretina's silence, if indeed she has been offstage for more than a hundred lines? Even more oddly, how can an absent Aretina suddenly resume her place in the dialogue without the stage direction, "*Enter* ARETINA"?

I believe the answers to these questions lie in the use of the above, even though there is no authority for such a notion in the quarto. We can be sure, from its specified function in eleven bona fide Cockpit plays, that the theatre had an above; and we can infer that communication between the platform and the above was remarkably rapid and easy. In the final act of Davenport's *A New Trick to Cheat the Devil* (1639), Master Changeable, after announcing that the Devil will soon appear, says to his Wife: "will you ascend and guide my Lord to a / Convenient place, where you may view this object?" The stage direction which follows is uncompromising: "*They ascend.*"[45] Eight lines of dialogue cover the ascent, after which the Wife and three other characters "*Enter above.*" At the climax of this scene the Wife offers to leap down to the platform below, but is warned that she may break her neck and advised that "The Stair-case will doe better."[46] This is presumably a permanent, backstage staircase which allowed the ascent to be made in the first place, and which allows the Wife to descend while twelve further lines of dialogue cover her actions.[47]

Once the above is allowed its normal function as an observation post, the apparently confusing action in *The Lady of Pleasure,* III. ii, falls readily into place. Aretina, after giving her instructions to Littleworth and Kickshaw, goes out with the general "*Ex*[eunt]" (III. ii. 201.1), leaving only Celestina and her two assailants on the platform. By a backstage route, Aretina ascends and reappears silently at the observation point, above. "*Enter* BORNWELL" (III. ii. 224.1) means that he appears on the platform, taking a position reasonably distant from the characters involved in the game of insults. From this position, his two brief lines (224, 268) can be spoken as

asides without interrupting the scene. But when Bornwell cries out "Brave soul!" (283) he attracts the attention of the other characters on the platform. While Celestina completes her verbal revenge, Bornwell approaches her in order to be quite near her when she inquires, "How shall I / Acquit your lady's silence?" (321-22). The reference, of course, is to the silent but visible Aretina at the observation point above. Now Aretina retreats and, retracing her backstage route, descends to the platform level. She enters just as Bornwell and Celestina go out, and hence addresses Littleworth and Kickshaw with the most natural question: "Is she gone?" (326).

In the two scenes which I have chosen to discuss, indeed in *The Lady of Pleasure* as a whole, the broad outlines of Shirley's theatre craft are remarkably clear. He allows actions of major significance to be played out on the platform, where the actors' voices and gestures will be most effective. He frequently calls for properties, but most of these are small hand-held articles which not only contribute to the action but also reveal the social circumstances or personal inclinations of his characters. Numerous asides, many of them not clearly marked in the quarto, and frequent references to goings-on in this or that chamber just offstage are among the techniques Shirley uses to build the conspiratorial atmosphere which characterizes the world of the play.

In selecting two scenes for analysis, I have necessarily slighted others, among them the crucial actions of Act IV, in which Kickshaw is led in "*blind[fold]ed*" (IV. i. 0.2), bribed by Madam Decoy, and bedded by Aretina. When Decoy presses her offer, showing Kickshaw "a prospect / Of the next chamber" and asking him to "observe / That bed" (IV. i. 84-90), I believe that the action has moved to upstage centre, where Decoy is enticing her confused client to enter Aretina's bedroom by going out through the gap between the hangings. If this is the case, then it is another instance of Shirley's shrewdness: if this unusual exit ("*in the midst*") is used at all, it is fitting that it should be used here, and used only once.

To follow Madam Decoy a single step further would be an error of crude self-indulgence. I shall resist, and I shall conclude by gathering a few indications of the quality of Shirley's theatrical style in *The Lady of Pleasure*. Something of Shirley's taste in this matter may be inferred from his address to the reader prefixed to *The Grateful Servant*. In response to adverse criticism from Blackfriars partisans, Shirley takes a stand which he hopes will "do the comedians justice, amongst whom, some are held comparable with the best that are, and have been in the world, and the most of them deserving a name in the file of those that are eminent for graceful and unaffected action."[48]

Just what actions will qualify as free of affectation is always open to question, especially in the theatre; but in this context it is fair to assume that, in the relatively small, indoor, artificially lighted Cockpit playhouse, an actor like Richard Perkins, whose background included the Hope and the Red Bull, would reduce the volume of his voice and the scale of his gestures in accordance with the modesty of his nature and the dimensions of his new environment. In doing so, Perkins would have increased his attractiveness in the eyes of a playwright who designed each scene with a special alertness to social nuance. An acknowledged runner-up in his re-creation of Marlowe's towering passions, Perkins may well have been "comparable with the best that are" when the script required ingenious adjustments of mood within an intricately balanced network of social relationships.

"Graceful . . . action," in Shirley's terms, was undoubtedly very considerable praise. A playwright who repeatedly places his characters into dance-like formations, and who thinks of a Lord as unready until he is armed with his periwig, is admitting a taste for elegance. And actors who deal in mirrors and miniatures rather than tankards and targets will need to be graceful in both bearing and speech. As the leading playwright of Queen Henrietta's men in 1635, Shirley knew the resources of his theatre, the talents of his actors, and the tastes of his audience. In response to these external influences, he created the "graceful and unaffected action" of **The Lady of Pleasure**: "that rare playe" by which he earned, in its first production, the admiration of Sir Humphrey Mildmay, and for which he is awarded, even today, "a name in the file of those that are eminent" for impeccably crafted comedy of social artifice.

Notes

1. *"The Lady of Pleasure,* by James Shirley, licensed" (*The Dramatic Records of Sir Henry Herbert,* ed. Joseph Quincy Adams [New Haven, 1917], p. 37).

2. See Gerald Eades Bentley, *The Jacobean and Caroline Stage* (Oxford, 1941-68), V, 1125.

3. Bentley, II, 677. Whenever I quote from old-spelling texts or manuscripts, usage of *i/j, u/v,* and long *s* is silently modernized.

4. Bentley, I, 330-31.

5. See William B. Markward, "A Study of the Phoenix Theatre in Drury Lane, 1617-1638" (Dissertation, University of Birmingham, 1953), p. 166; Bentley, I, 224-26: T. J. King, "Staging of Plays at the Phoenix in Drury Lane, 1617-42," *Theatre Notebook,* 19 (1964-65), 146; and Andrew Gurr, *The Shakespearean Stage, 1574-1642* (Cambridge, 1970), p. 43.

6. See the records printed in Bentley, II, 674-80. Two expenditures of sixpence each do not qualify as exceptions: the first pertains to a masque

performed at Whitehall (18 February 1633/4), the second "To a Playe of Warre" (16 November 1643) which took place after the closing of the theatres. Neither of these events is necessarily comparable to attendance at a professional theatre.

7. Prologue to *The Example,* sig. *2. It is disconcerting to find that, in the metaphor of the gallant who "censures finely" from his position "on the Bench" as if he were "commissioner of wit," Shirley is heavily indebted to Jonson; see the Induction to *Bartholomew Fair,* ed. E. A. Horsman, The Revels Plays (London, 1960), 11. 98-107: "It is also agreed, that every man here exercise his own judgement, and not censure by contagion, or upon trust, from another's voice, or face, that sits by him, be he never so first in the commission of wit: . . . and not to be brought about by any that sits on the bench with him, though they indict and arraign plays daily." Both passages, of course, are describing conventional behaviour which could have been as easily observed at the Hope in 1614 as at the Cockpit some twenty years later.

8. That a shilling should be treated as a normal charge for admission can be confirmed by citing the dedicatory verse (by W. B.) to *The Bondman* in *The Plays and Poems of Philip Massinger,* ed. Philip Edwards and Colin Gibson (Oxford, 1976), I, 314:

   > And (Reader) if you have disburs'd a shilling,
   > To see this worthy STORY, and are willing
   > To have a large encrease; (if rul'd by me)
   > You may a MARCHANT, and a POET be.
   > 'Tis granted for your twelve-pence you did sit,
   > And *See,* and *Heare,* and *Understand* not yet.
   > The AUTHOR (in a Christian pitty) takes
   > Care of your good, and Prints it for your sakes.
   > That such as will but venter Six-pence more,
   > May *Know,* what they but *Saw,* and *Heard* before.

   This play was licensed for performance at the Cockpit on 3 December 1623, and was printed in the following year. The bookseller must have been grateful to W. B. for pointing out that the cost of a printed quarto was only half of the normal admission charge at the theatre.

9. Bentley, VI, 48.

10. The account is contained in a letter by Edward Sherburne (8 March 1616/17), and is printed in Bentley, VI, 54.

11. Ibid., 56.

12. The relevant extracts are printed in Bentley, II, 694.

13. The dimensions are those given by Richard Hosley in his essay on "The Playhouses" in *The Revels History of Drama in English,* ed. Clifford Leech

and T. W. Craik, III (London, 1975), 206. Irwin Smith estimates the capacity of Blackfriars at 516 In *Shakespeare's Blackfriars Playhouse* (New York, 1964), p. 297. The highest known receipt for a single Blackfriars performance is £19 15s (see Bentley, VI, 22). At the putative average price of a shilling per admission, this would mean 395 spectators. But of course, on the occasion in question, the house may not have been full or even very near to full. The estimate of 516 would seem to be a safe maximum, if there is any truth in Wright's claim that the Caroline private houses were "very small" compared to Restoration playhouses; Wren's Drury Lane reputedly held about 600 to 800 spectators, or so Richard Southern claims in *The Revels History of Drama in English,* ed. T. W. Craik, V (London, 1976), 110.

14. For a review of the evidence concerning stage sizes, see Leonie Star, "The Middle of the Yard, Part II: The Calculation of Stage Sizes for English Renaissance Playhouses," *Theatre Notebook,* 30 (1976), 65-69. Star estimates the dimensions of the Blackfriars stage as 30 feet in width by something less than 30 feet in depth; this compares favourably with Hosley's calculations of 29 feet by 18 feet 6 inches (*Revels History,* III, 210) and with William A. Armstrong's observations about the relative smallness of the stage at Blackfriars (*The Elizabethan Private Theatres: Facts and Problems* [London, 1958], p. 5).

15. This is not the place to demonstrate that these features were common to both of the other private houses mentioned by Wright, but a good case could be made by comparing Hosley's carefully documented reconstruction of Blackfriars (*Revels History,* III, 205-17) with the evidence assembled by Bentley (VI, 86-115) pertaining to the Salisbury Court theatre.

16. From the address "To the Great Variety of Readers" prefixed to *Mr William Shakespeares Comedies, Histories, & Tragedies* (London, 1623), sig. A3.

17. See Bentley, VI, 88-92.

18. See Markward, pp. 182-83, 363-64; and Bentley, VI, 50.

19. For a review of the evidence, see John Orrell, "Inigo Jones at the Cockpit," *Shakespeare Survey* 30 (1977), 163-65.

20. See the Prologue to *The Coronation* in *The Dramatic Works and Poems of James Shirley,* ed. William Gifford and Alexander Dyce (London, 1833), III, 459.

21. See "A Neglected Jones/Webb Theatre Project, Part II: A Theatrical Missing Link," *The Elizabe-*

than Theatre II (1969), pp. 60-73. See also "A Neglected Jones/Webb Theatre Project: Barber-Surgeons Hall Writ Large," *New Theatre Magazine,* 9 (168-9), 6-15, and an abridgement of the same article in *Shakespeare Survey* 23 (1970), 125-29.

22. "Missing Link," pp. 72-73.

23. "Inigo Jones at the Cockpit," pp. 157-68.

24. *The Complete Plays of Christopher Marlowe,* ed. Irving Ribner (New York, 1963), p. 178.

25. *Henslowe's Diary,* ed. R. A. Foakes and R. T. Rickert (Cambridge, 1961), p. 213.

26. *The White Devil,* ed. John Russell Brown, The Revels Plays (London, 1960), p. 187. Brown infers that, only if Perkins were playing the part of Flamineo could he be described as crowning "both the beginning and end," since Bracciano dies long before the conclusion ("Introduction," p. xxiii).

27. See Bentley, II, 526-28.

28. See Bentley, II, 528.

29. Shirley, *Works,* I, 415.

30. Bentley, II, 693.

31. Shirley, *Works,* I, 366, 372, 375.

32. Massinger, *Plays,* II, 12.

33. Bentley, II, 401, 548.

34. Shirley, *Works,* I, 366, 393, 409.

35. Bentley, II, 572-73.

36. Citations from *The Lady of Pleasure* refer to my own edition, in preparation for The Revels Plays.

37. Shirley, *Works,* I, 385.

38. Bentley, II, 433-4.

39. See Bentley, II, 386-7.

40. Bentley, II, 511-12.

41. The last three illustrations are often reprinted, most conveniently in *The Riverside Shakespeare,* ed. G. Blakemore Evans et al. (Boston, 1974), pls. 8 and 10 following p. 494.

42. See King, pp. 159-60.

43. Markward, pp. 329-32.

44. Sig. F1^{v}.

45. Sig. K1.

46. Sig. K2.

47. In the spoken version of this paper I argued largely on the basis of this scene that the Cockpit was equipped with a visible, onstage staircase, but I

am no longer convinced that this was the case. Cf. Markward, who believes that the "rapid entrances" in *The English Traveller, A Tale of a Tub,* and *Claricilla* "seem to hint that there may have been an inner stairway leading from lower to upper stage situated very near one of the side doors" (p. 408). There is no reason to doubt that Queen Henrietta's men could have produced a staircase for any production that required one. The Lord Admiral's men, in an inventory of properties held on 10 March 1598/9, are said to have owned a "payer of stayers for Fayeton" (*Henslowe's Diary,* p. 319). But the logical step from a possibly to a necessarily visible staircase is a dangerous one, as I now realize, thanks to the convivial warnings issued by members of the Waterloo conference.

48. *Works,* II, 5.

Ronald Huebert (essay date 1986)

SOURCE: Huebert, Ronald. Introduction to *The Lady of Pleasure,* by James Shirley, pp. 1-49. Manchester: Manchester University Press, 1986.

[*In the following excerpt, Huebert characterizes* The Lady of Pleasure *as a dramatization of decadence, regarding which Shirley's own stance is unclear.*]

The first reader of ***The Lady of Pleasure*** to have recorded a critical response to the play is Abraham Wright, who at some time near the middle of the seventeenth century made the following notation in his commonplace book:

> Y^e best play of Shirleys for ye lines, but ye plot is as much as none. ye latter end of ye 4th act ye scene twixt Celestine and ye lord is good for ye humour of neete complement. Aretina, who is ye lady of pleasure a good part for y^e . . . expressing ye many waies of pleasure and expences. Celestine for ye same: both shewing ye pride and excesse in every thing of ye court ladies.[1]

Wright gives unusual prominence to Shirley, to judge by the space he allots in his commonplace book to quotations from and comments on eleven of Shirley's plays. By contrast, Beaumont and Fletcher are represented by six titles, Jonson and Shakespeare by two apiece. Thus Shirley's first literary critic is a sympathetic reader, and one whose standards of judgement are those common in his day rather than ours. *The Maid's Tragedy* is for Wright 'a very good play', better even than *A King and No King,* itself 'a good play . . . especially for ye plot wch is extraordinary'. *The White Devil* is 'but an indifferent play to reade, but for ye presentments I beeleeve good'; *A New Way to Pay Old Debts* is 'a silly play'; and *Hamlet* 'but an indifferent play, ye lines but meane'. However whimsical these judgements

may seem today, they are based on typical Caroline attitudes: a preference for tragicomedy over other dramatic forms, and a belief in the radical importance of plot.

STRUCTURE

Wright's claim that the plot of ***The Lady of Pleasure*** 'is as much as none' ranks as his most interesting observation about the play. What he means, no doubt, is that the play lacks a complicated intrigue, for this is what he praises in plays whose plots he admires. The plot of ***Hyde Park*** is, according to Wright, 'best at ye last act', and *The Duchess of Malfi* is to be commended 'especially for ye plot at ye latter end'. Wright clearly has a taste for the bizarre coincidences, reversals and contrivances which have disturbed many modern readers of these plays, and he misses these artificial devices in ***The Lady of Pleasure.***

More importantly, he overlooks by the narrowest of margins the structural axis which becomes apparent when the play is considered not merely as a series of narrative events but as a social artefact.[2] In drawing attention to Aretina's 'expences' and in commenting on 'ye pride and excesse in every thing of ye court ladies', Wright seems to be reaching towards a concept such as conspicuous consumption or, to use the language of the play itself, 'prodigality'. This impulse governs the social behaviour of the characters in the play with such alarming tyranny as to suggest that Shirley is observing and commenting on a pattern of life in the London society he intimately knew.

The signs of prodigality in ***The Lady of Pleasure*** have almost nothing to do with the mere satisfaction of primary human appetites. There is plenty of food in the world of the play, most of it made available in the offstage banquets, taverns and ordinaries which occupy a central place in the social lives of the gentry; but feasting in this play is an acquired art in which competitive social nuances have replaced gastronomical rumblings. When Alexander Kickshaw anticipates a tavern meal, he has in mind 'a dozen partridge in a dish' along with pheasants, quails and sturgeon (IV.ii.148-51). When he flatters himself with the prospect of dining at court, his desire is explicitly 'not for the table' (V.ii.104) but for the pleasure of making a favourable impression. The drinks which accompany such self-conscious meals may be sack or Rhenish or 'what strange wine else' (V.i.75), but never ale or beer. This is a world of sophisticated palates where Falstaff's traditional menus would be more likely to provoke derision than hunger.

The smells and savours associated with food in ***The Lady of Pleasure*** owe more to artifice than to nature. The appropriate symbol of refinement which alters and disguises natural food is the box of sugar-plums that Littleworth never tires of offering to the ladies. Equally telling is Kickshaw's resolution, on having discovered a lavish source of income, to 'forget there is a butcher' and rely instead on the advice of 'a witty epicure' in planning his meals (V.ii.105-7). Although food and talk about food are constantly crossing these characters' lips, there is nothing of the aromatic succulence which draws everyone in the direction of Ursula's passionately roasting pigs in *Bartholomew Fair*. Instead of simply appealing to the senses, food in **The Lady of Pleasure** is refined by art until it rivals the dreams of Sir Epicure Mammon.[3]

What is true about food holds even more conspicuously in the case of clothing. Here the extreme instance is that of Master Frederick, who arrives from the university in respectable academic dress only to discover that his aunt's fashionable pretensions have been mortified. Promptly consigned to the tutelage of Kickshaw and Littleworth, Master Frederick is transformed with great effort into a caricature of the over-dressed gallant. In a scene that amounts to a seventeenth-century fashion show (IV.ii), albeit one with a clumsy male model, Littleworth coaches Frederick in the conspicuous art of wearing his new clothes. The mundane considerations of comfort, cleanliness and utility are petulantly brushed aside in Littleworth's pursuit of pure ostentation. The wearer of truly fashionable clothing will find even his body altered, Littleworth claims: 'it is not / The cut of your apparel makes a gallant, / But the geometrical wearing of your clothes' (IV.ii.9-11). Good taste is hardly the point, and restraint is out of the question; the object of Littleworth's code of dress is flamboyance at any price.

The dressing of Master Frederick is only a slight exaggeration of what passes for normal elsewhere in the play. Lord Unready, whose name I have pilfered from Shirley's inadvertently appropriate stage direction,[4] makes his first two appearances while suffering the attentions of Master Haircut to such details of public life as his periwig. And Celestina, both wealth and youth on her side by virtue of being a widow at fifteen, broadens the principle of decorative ostentation to include her coach and sedan-chair. With an ingenuous honesty appropriate to her youth, Celestina admits that the purpose of lavish consumption is to be splendidly conspicuous: 'my balcony / Shall be the courtier's idol, and more gazed at / Than all the pageantry at Temple Bar' (I.ii.93-5). Celestina's desire to live in a world of 'silk and silver' (I.ii.21) may be shocking to her Steward, but it is simply the adolescent fantasy which corresponds to the values of her society at large.

Shirley's awareness of prodigality as more than an accident that happens to the rich—as a principle of human behaviour, in fact—can be deduced from his metaphori-

cal application of the idea to the sexual experience of his characters. Kickshaw would like to be thought of as a sexual gourmet: hence, in alluding euphemistically to his female quarry, he prefers the term 'pheasant' (III.i. 140) to such traditional alternatives as 'mutton'. The note of bravado in Kickshaw's attitude towards women is a false one in the sense that it has nothing to do with sheer appetite or high spirits; his idiom belongs not to the locker-room but to the wine-tasting salon. The morning after his first meeting with Celestina finds Kickshaw enumerating her qualities with something of the collector's emphasis on status and scarcity: 'Such a widow is not common', he concludes, 'And now she shines more fresh and tempting / Than any natural virgin' (I.i.264-6).

But Kickshaw must not bear exclusive blame for an artificial and ornamental tone which is characteristic of sexual encounters and attitudes in the play as a whole. Madam Decoy is the broker in charge of conspicuous sexual consumption, and she has taken the trouble to provide her house with 'artful chambers, / And pretty pictures to provoke the fancy' (III.ii.20-1). Littleworth subscribes to an elaborately hierarchical theory of pimping (IV.ii.75-82), a view which lends credence to the rumour that some of the gallants 'are often my lord's tasters' (II.ii.92). Celestina, however skilful she may be in preserving her honour, is perfectly aware of the terms which society will place on her slightest gesture of sexual approval or discouragement:

> Some ladies are so expensive in their graces
> To those that honour 'em, and so prodigal,
> That in a little time they have nothing but
> The naked sin left to reward their servants;
> Whereas a thrift in our rewards will keep
> Men long in their devotion, and preserve
> Our selves in stock, to encourage those that honour
>   us.
>
>   (II.ii.66-72)

This is the language of an accomplished flirt. Celestina gains a reputation for chastity precisely because she knows how to manipulate her suitors in order to provoke the maximum amount and the right kind of conspicuous sexual adulation.

That Shirley himself wishes the notion of prodigality to be invoked as a standard by which to judge the behaviour of his characters can be inferred from the opening scene, in which Bornwell rebukes his wife Aretina for taking up the fashionable patterns of town life with excessive and foolish enthusiasm. Bornwell is neither prudish nor avaricious; his case against the town rests partly on his instinctive preference for the life of a country squire, but it cannot be dismissed as mere special pleading. He opposes Aretina's adopted way of life because it is expensive, but this is only the surface of an argument which cuts deeper. Prodigality is also artificial, competitive and tyrannical. It is artificial in the sense that even the rich materials of Aretina's wardrobe 'dare / Not show their own complexions' (I.i.91-2) but are covered in layers of ornament. It is competitive in the sense that other fashionable women arouse in Aretina the fear of being 'eclipsed' (I.i.279). And it is tyrannical in the sense that Aretina does not have enough experience of high living to carry it off casually:

> You make play
> Not a pastime but a tyranny, and vex
> Yourself and my estate by't.

> (I.i.109-11)

Thus, Bornwell's metaphors of prodigality as a form of suffocation—an experience which can 'stifle' or which threatens 'chocking' (I.i.82, 86)—are fully justified. On the evidence before him, Bornwell believes that fashionable urban living is at odds with human sanity and integrity.

I am not proposing that Bornwell be taken as Shirley's moral mouthpiece in the play as whole. His view of events is restricted, his understanding incomplete. His decision to mimic Aretina's behaviour—to 'Repent in sack and prodigality', as he terms it (I.i.290)—amounts to a tactical ploy too shallow to qualify as moral wisdom. But in the opening confrontation with Aretina, Bornwell's arguments are cogent and persuasive, all the more so because they bear the stamp of personal conviction. That these arguments are placed near the beginning of the play is, I believe, Shirley's way of providing a vantage point from which prodigal indulgence can be seen for what it is.

The structural pattern which I have been outlining is in part the product of social forces which converged on the city of London during the reign of Charles I. In 1632 the king issued one in a series of Stuart proclamations designed to prevent the rural gentry from abandoning their estates in order to set up fashionable London residences, and listing among the consequences of current practice the expenditure of large sums of money 'in excess of apparel provided from foreign parts, to the enriching of other nations and unnecessary consumption of a great part of the treasure of his realm, and in other delights and expenses'.[5] This proclamation seems to have had about as much effect as attempts to restrict the economic behaviour of a privileged class by law normally do. What is important here is that, in the London of 1632, conspicuous consumption was a social problem of such magnitude that not even the king could ignore it.

The dimensions of the problem have been studied by Lawrence Stone, who argues that conspicuous consumers fell into roughly four overlapping but distinguish-able categories. The first group, represented in *The Lady of Pleasure* by the presence of Lord Unready, consisted of noblemen engaged in service to the crown and hence required by tradition to maintain a level of 'pomp and circumstance' consistent with their offices. The second group, of whom Haircut is a humble example, was composed of persons willing to risk 'the cost of attendance at Court in the hope of office'. Nearly everyone in the play would qualify for membership in 'the third and largest group', made up of 'those attracted to the pleasures and vanities of London, who entered into a round of dissipation which in time inevitably undermined both health and fortune'. The fourth group, represented in the play only by Bornwell, and imperfectly even then, 'were those who stuck to the old country ways under the new conditions'. These conservative gentlemen would need to spend lavishly on servants, retainers and household provisions if the standards of country hospitality were to be maintained, and thus they could ruin themselves by encountering the town, which required a second and unrelated mode of expenditure.[6] Bornwell, who has sold his country estate in order to accommodate Aretina's desire for urban life, remains temperamentally if not economically a member of this final group.

Shirley's attention to the pattern of prodigality would suggest that, in *The Lady of Pleasure,* he is a shrewd observer of London life, just as surely as Dekker is in *The Shoemaker's Holiday,* Middleton in *A Chaste Maid in Cheapside,* Jonson in *Bartholomew Fair,* or Massinger in *The City Madam.* But the London Shirley observes is a rather different one, as might be expected from a playwright who held the title—however temporary or nominal—of 'one of the Valets of the Chamber of Queen Henrietta Maria'. The wide gap which separates *The Lady of Pleasure* from its antecedents in this specialised genre can be underscored by observing that nobody in Shirley's play belongs to a profession (let alone a trade), and hence there is no such thing as an honest day's work. Dekker's world is filled with people of both sexes who make things, ranging from garments to garlands; Middleton's London is centred in Goldsmith's Row and includes, aside from Yellowhammer himself, an assortment of watermen, comfit-makers, nurses, and other employees of the commercial world. Jonson's characters, though inhabiting the holiday world of the fair, are if anything more busily occupied in searching for bargains or guarding their purses or selling their products than they would be on an ordinary working day. And for Massinger, the social and moral standing of apprentices, artisans, merchants and whores is largely dependent on the kind and quality of the work they do. In *The Lady of Pleasure* the closest approximation to productive work is, as Aretina remarks, the effort required in having one's portrait painted:

It does conclude
A lady's morning work: we rise, make fine,
Sit for our picture, and 'tis time to dine.

                                                   (I.i.321-3)

Shirley's contribution to the comedy of London life rests primarily on his ability to observe and record the behaviour of a segment of society for whom consumption was a business not confined to recreational hours but spread out conspicuously to fill the entire day.

Where, then, does Shirley stand in relation to the world he creates in *The Lady of Pleasure*? Is he presenting us with an ironic vision of a society gone astray? Or is he, like Aretina, rather too easily taken in by the glamour of a circle he has entered as an outsider? Is he too eager to court his audience of would-be conspicuous consumers with a favourable reflection of themselves? These questions are not easily answered, partly because Shirley has neither Dekker's benevolent optimism nor Jonson's satirical swagger. What he has instead is a reticence which is even harder to interpret than Middleton's habitual detachment. 'I will say nothing positive', Shirley writes in the Prologue to *The Cardinal;* 'you may / Think what you please'.[7] I believe, on the evidence provided by the structure of *The Lady of Pleasure* itself, that Shirley was keenly aware of the self-indulgent vanity of the society he created and of the audience he sought to entertain. This view is consistent with the arguments he gives to Bornwell in the opening scene. It is also consistent with Lord Unready's shocked rejection of the proposal that he might sell his armorial bearings (V.i.134-6); here at last is a stand taken on principle, in defiance of the ethic of prodigality, and we are meant to respond with admiration. That Shirley is willing to heap scorn on the comic *arriviste* characters—Sentlove, Kickshaw, Haircut and Littleworth—is readily deduced from the humiliations he prepares for them in the final act. But with characters drawn from the nobility or gentry he is—like Massinger—less candid, more insecure. In this sense Shirley was not a courageous artist; or, to put the matter more charitably, his was the tightrope-walker's courage, not the lion-tamer's.

THEME

The one crucial event in *The Lady of Pleasure,* which occurs offstage during Act IV, is the adulterous coupling of Aretina and Alexander Kickshaw. It is in relation to this act of infidelity that the implicit values or overt pronouncements of each principal character need to be assessed. And without claiming for Shirley a greatness that is beyond his reach, it is only fair to observe that his treatment of infidelity in this play is remarkable in at least three respects: in its resistance to the established conventions for dealing with infidelity in the drama; in its presentation of the theme from a point of view which allows the woman's side of the story to be told; and in its development of the subject as a private matter with specific emotional consequences rather than as a public scandal.

The quickest way of calling to mind the range of assumptions about infidelity which can be expected in Jacobean drama would be to listen to the characters in *Othello*. The men of Shakespeare's Venice—Brabantio, Cassio, Iago and Othello himself—become eloquent partisans whenever the subject is introduced. The women say nothing. Nothing, that is, until the quietly intimate undressing scene which precedes the catastrophe. Here we are allowed to overhear Desdemona and Emilia in casual conversation. The subject is one that of course would preoccupy them. 'O, these men, these men!' Desdemona begins:

> Dost thou in conscience think—tell me, Emilia—
> That there be women do abuse their husbands
> In such gross kind?

Emilia responds, cryptically, 'There be some such, no question'; but Desdemona presses forward, insisting on a personal answer.

DESDEMONA.

> Wouldst thou do such a deed for all the world?

EMILIA.

> The world's a huge thing; it is a great price for a small vice. . . . Marry, I would not do such a thing for a joint-ring, nor for measures of lawn, nor for gowns, petticoats, nor caps, nor any petty exhibition; but for all the whole world—'Ud's pity! who would not make her husband a cuckold to make him a monarch?

                                                   (IV.iii.58-75)

Still unconvinced, Desdemona disagrees in principle: 'Beshrew me if I would do such a wrong / For the whole world' (IV.iii.77-8).

The radical division of opinion represented by Desdemona's absolute 'no' and Emilia's provisional 'yes' is in general characteristic of attitudes taken towards infidelity in Jacobean drama. The absolute 'no', based overtly on idealistic perceptions of the meaning of chastity and linked indirectly to patterns of sexual paternalism, is the standard invoked by Jacobean tragic heroes in assessing the behaviour of their wives. Frankford's desire, in *A Woman Killed with Kindness,* to recall the impossible past 'that I might take her / As spotless as an angel in my arms'[8] is a paradigm case of masculine idealism. Similar attitudes are expressed, often less attractively, by many tragic husbands who fear betrayal: Sforza in Massinger's *The Duke of Milan,* Leantio in Middleton's *Women Beware Women,* and Caraffa in Ford's *Love's Sacrifice* have in common a sexual idealism too fragile for the experience they encounter. Husbands who countenance infidelity with a provisional 'yes' are by definition excluded from tragic action and relegated to satire. The most famous instance is Allwit in *A Chaste Maid in Cheapside,* for whom being a cuckold is 'The happiest state that ever man was born to!'[9] Most of the cuckolds in Jacobean satire fall short of such amicable adjustment; but the deflation of stature and esteem which accompanies cuckoldry is implied nonetheless by means of Harebrain's vapid cheerfulness in *A Mad World, My Masters,* Pietro's impotent posturings in *The Malcontent* or even Camillo's drunken resignation in *The White Devil.*

If the concern over infidelity seems obsessive by modern standards or the polarisation of attitudes artificial, it should be remembered that sixteenth- and seventeenth-century laws and customs allowed for detailed chaperoning of what went on in the bedrooms of the nation. To judge by surviving evidence from the county of Essex, any irregular sexual practice was likely to provoke a hearing in the ecclesiastical courts.[10] Persons found guilty of adultery were subjected to shame punishments such as those listed by William Harrison: 'carting, ducking, and doing of open penance in sheets, in churches and marketsteads'.[11] Although Harrison finds these modes of rebuke too lenient ('For what great smart is it to be turned out of an hot sheet into a cold . . . ?' he asks), the threat of humiliation must have been real enough for anyone who valued public opinion. Married women had more to fear from exposure for adultery than men, since legal conventions permitted a husband to repudiate an unfaithful wife and protected him in the event that he chose to vindicate his honour by killing her.[12]

The social context which clarifies the meaning of infidelity in the drama can be illustrated by referring to the story of Frances Coke, the younger daughter of Sir Edward Coke and Lady Elizabeth Hatton. In G. R. Hibbard's lively account of the principal events, Frances Coke is described as 'a very beautiful girl of fifteen' who was married in 1617, for all the wrong dynastic reasons, to Sir John Villiers, the elder brother of the Duke of Buckingham. Unable to endure a husband whose domestic routine included 'periodic fits of insanity', she abandoned him in favour of a secluded and adulterous life with Sir Robert Howard. In consequence, she was put on trial in 1627 and assigned the shame punishment of 'open penance in sheets', to use Harrison's phrase—a punishment she was able to evade thanks to personal ingenuity and the collusion of her lover. In the first instance she escaped the pursuit of her arresting officers by exchanging clothes with a pageboy. The law, having been made an ass, would show the persistence of a mule: in 1634, after a lapse of seven years, Frances Coke was arrested and imprisoned for her failure to perform penance as ordered. This time a

friend of her lover's provided another male disguise, a bribe for the prison officer, and a safe escort to France. Only after receiving the king's pardon, some six years later, was she able to return to England.[13]

Aretina's position in ***The Lady of Pleasure*** is unlike that of Frances Coke in all respects but one: like her contemporary in real life, Aretina is playing a very dangerous game. As modern readers, we are free to applaud her courage or to cringe at her folly, but we are not at liberty to regard her act of sexual indulgence as a casual and relatively harmless diversion. In fact, Aretina goes to great lengths to prevent the public consequences of infidelity, only to find that she is vulnerable to the private consequences instead.

From the beginning Aretina is a restless married woman who has come to London looking for adventure and (by implication) trouble. She challenges her husband's authority and asserts her personal freedom in words that recall Emilia's argument in *Othello* and anticipate the sentiments that would be spoken one day by Nora Helmer and Hedda Gabler:

> I take it great injustice
> To have my pleasures circumscribed and taught me.
> A narrow-minded husband is a thief
> To his own fame, and his preferment too.
>
> (I.i.143-6)

Clearly, Aretina is deliberately seeking pleasures other than the domestic comforts of marriage. She is not actively seeking adultery, but when she meets a man (Alexander Kickshaw) both attractive enough to please her erotic tastes and shallow enough to be readily controlled, she decides that she will try him. And it is here, in her decision, that she stands apart from the passive Anne Frankfords and befuddled Mistress Harebrains of dramatic tradition. Although he disapproves of her decision, Shirley has enough respect for Aretina to treat her as a moral agent: as a person responsible for her actions.

Having settled on Kickshaw as her choice, Aretina directs all of her energies toward ensuring absolute circumspection. This she accomplishes through the connivance of Madam Decoy, whose professional credit is dependent on the same code of secrecy which applies to espionage agents in hostile territory. Thus, Aretina gives Decoy her instructions in a confidential whisper (III.ii.13.1), and adds the solemn warning: 'He must not / Have the least knowledge of my name or person' (III.ii.25-6). Decoy's performance borders on the spectacular: Kickshaw is blindfolded and brought to a darkened room where Decoy persuades him, with the rhetoric of gold pieces, to enter an offstage chamber and make love to someone he believes to be a witch in one of her more attractive metamorphoses. In every technical point, Aretina has achieved her purpose; scandal has been avoided, her husband is none the wiser, and her sexual partner is prevented by his ignorance from betraying her.

Shirley's real achievement in writing the part of Aretina rests on his understanding of how she would behave on the morning after this ambivalent encounter. The occasion of her next appearance is Frederick's transformation into a clothes-horse, which she handles with approval and poise. Then Kickshaw enters, also dressed in new clothes, and Aretina must admit, 'Now he looks brave and lovely' (IV.ii.143). After an appropriately brief social conversation, she can reassure herself: 'I am confident he knows me not, and I were worse than mad to be my own betrayer' (IV.ii.172-3). The need for circumspection, still uppermost in Aretina's mind, continues to govern every nuance of her social behaviour.

Her husband is the first to notice that Aretina's bearing is uncharacteristically 'melancholy' (IV.ii.181). And in private conversation between husband and wife, Aretina strikes a philosophical key which has not been hers before. She distinguishes between 'True beauty' which pertains to the soul and superficial charm 'That touches but our sense' (IV.ii.194-9), and although she is overtly using the distinction to praise Celestina, her mood suggests that she is introspectively concerned with her own recent actions. Shirley avoids the stereotypical alternatives which men prepare for unfaithful wives: Aretina does not melt into guilty incoherence, nor does she turn into a brazen strumpet of limitless appetite. Instead, she remains what she was—a morally cogent human being—though her sense of self now includes a new and disturbing set of experiences.

Careful as she has been to avert public shame, Aretina cannot forestall private humiliation. In her next encounter with Kickshaw she has the opportunity of speaking with him privately, and what she learns is devastating to her pride. Not only does Kickshaw swagger impertinently at the thought of continuing to exploit his new source of revenue, but he remains convinced that he has slept with 'an old witch, a strange ill-favoured hag' (V.ii.146), 'a most insatiate, abominable devil with a tail thus long' (V.ii.157-8). To hear herself described—however callously or unwittingly—in these terms is enough to reduce Aretina to tears. It is in this condition that her husband finds her in the final scene, at which point the two of them withdraw for 'ten minutes' (V.iii.10) and return publicly reconciled. For the first time Aretina takes a submissive stance in relation to Bornwell: 'I throw my own will off', she announces, 'And now in all things obey yours' (V.iii.176-7). This resolution, though morally satisfying to the orthodox, is dramatically specious for reasons I shall hold in reversion for the moment, since they have more to do with Bornwell's character than with Aretina's.

I have chosen to concentrate on Shirley's treatment of one character in the adulterous triangle—the unfaithful wife—because it is in the sensitive revelation of Aretina's nature that he is at his best. Kickshaw, as I have repeatedly implied, is a fairly stupid fop who fancies himself a genuine libertine. The part could be flamboyantly arresting if played by the right actor, but hardly more than that. With Bornwell Shirley has created problems that require better solutions than he has given them, particularly in the final scene of the play.

From the outset Bornwell has been an attractive figure: a husband whose heart is in the country but who is willing to tolerate the city for his wife's sake, a man of settled habits who is willing to risk adventure if that is what society requires. The action of the play has made him a cuckold. But the consequences of this deeply personal affront, both for Bornwell's own estimate of himself and for the relationship between husband and wife, Shirley chooses to ignore. At Aretina's tearful request Bornwell follows her offstage, and on their return his rhetorical stance is too pompous to be genuinely reassuring. 'Dearer now / Than ever to my bosom', he says to Aretina, 'thou shalt please / Me best to live at thy own choice' (V.iii.179-81). Are we to assume that Aretina has told him the whole truth, and that he feels the injury no more deeply than this? Or must we believe that Aretina, though presenting herself as 'A penitent' (V.iii.176), has been prudently selective in her confession? The play provides no adequate answers to these questions; the truth is that we can never know.[14] If Shirley took special pains to insist on the emotional complexity of Aretina's experience, he seems to have glossed over the corresponding emotions in the case of Bornwell for the purpose of concluding the play on a note of domestic tranquillity. And the price for achieving this purpose is a heavy one. Just where the audience is expecting a confrontation which will resolve at last the conflict between Aretina's assertion of liberty and Bornwell's insistence on responsibility, Shirley remains enigmatically silent. There is a point at which reticence becomes evasion, and Shirley is dangerously close to it; what appears to be simply a technical fault in dramatic construction is also a failure of nerve.

In complementary opposition to the adulterous meeting between Aretina and Kickshaw, Shirley presents the Platonic relationship between Celestina and Lord Unready. In the early scenes, the contrast between Aretina and Celestina is handled with considerable adroitness. Both women are engaged in the game of indulging in prodigality while keeping appearances unruffled. As the widow of someone called Bellamour, Celestina has a freedom from personal obligations which she enjoys exploiting perhaps beyond the limits of good taste but never farther than modesty permits. While Aretina is growing impatient with the restrictions of married life, Celestina is expertly avoiding the 'new marriage fetters' (II.ii.47) which any number of suitors would wish to impose. When Lord Unready appears we learn that he too has suffered bereavement; the death of someone called Bella Maria has deprived him of domestic bliss but not of an ideal of human perfection which he continues to worship.

All that remains is to bring these two lovelorn aristocrats together—a procedure which Shirley manages at exceeding length. Their first meeting begins with exchanges of mutual praise that border on idolatry, and appears to be moving quickly towards a seduction, when Lord Unready abruptly announces that he has withstood temptation and remains true to Bella Maria. Celestina now reports that, had her seducer been in earnest, she would have rewarded his 'wanton flame' not with compliance but with 'scorn' (IV.iii.175). Their second encounter follows a similar pattern: Lord Unready proposes that Celestina become his mistress in 'the now court Platonic way' (V.iii.54), she appears to accept and then scoffs at his offer, he becomes petulant, she rebukes him, and at length both agree to a stand-off in which they will celebrate one another 'with chaste thoughts' (V.iii.159) as if nothing whatever had occurred. It is hard to believe that Shirley had in mind in these scenes anything more than an extended allusion to the courtly cult of Platonic love,[15] for in any other terms the relationship is a shambles. True, nobody wants to praise a fugitive and cloistered virtue, but this is the opposite extreme. It is difficult to credit as ideal chastity a pattern of behaviour which Swinburne described in another context as 'obscene abstinence'.[16]

Still, if Shirley failed in the noble attempt to dramatise the highest reaches of moral idealism, he failed in distinguished company. What remains valuable in *The Lady of Pleasure* is the sensitive interpretation of imperfect humanity, especially in the character of Aretina. And here the interpretation is a sensitive one, because Shirley has gone beneath the surfaces of historical custom and literary convention to reveal what is fundamentally an act of betrayal which impinges partly on another person but principally on the self.

LANGUAGE

The most vigorous attack on Shirley's abilities as a poet is tucked away, almost as a digression, in an essay entitled 'Variation in Shakespeare and Others' by C. S. Lewis.[17] The attack depends on a subtle argument about the poetic habits of Elizabethan and later dramatists, all of whom, Lewis claims, relied on the 'method of variation'. As opposed to the method of construction, by means of which a poet such as Milton builds a logical sequence of ideas and images to a point of apparently inevitable completion, the method of variation allows the poet greater freedom and flexibility. He can bring together a dozen different images, all of them

experimentally related to a particular idea, none of them presented as definitive. The master of this second technique is Shakespeare, but 'it is shared by all the Elizabethan dramatists'.

The method of variation is especially attractive to playwrights in that it allows the actor to speak, even in moments of great rhetorical splendour, with an apparently unrehearsed tentativeness, as if the character's own sensibility (and not the poet's craft) were proposing the multifarious perceptions of experience. Among the examples which Lewis draws from Marlowe, Jonson, Middleton, Ford and Shakespeare is the following speech from *Antony and Cleopatra*:

> His legs bestrid the ocean: his reared arm
> Crested the world: his voice was propertied
> As all the tunèd spheres, and that to friends;
> But when he meant to quail and shake the orb,
> He was as rattling thunder. For his bounty,
> There was no winter in't: an autumn 'twas
> That grew the more by reaping: his delights
> Were dolphin-like. . . .
>
>   (V.ii.82-9)

The coherence of this speech depends on Cleopatra's feeling for Antony, and is hence beyond question. And the poetic technique, to use Lewis's metaphor, is like the darting of a swallow: the music of the spheres, the rattling thunder, the autumn harvest and the dolphin are all genuine glimpses though none of these alternatives offers a point of rest from which one might compose a full portrait.

In Shirley's verse, Lewis argues, all the 'peculiar vices' of this method are 'painfully visible'. These vices consist of imaginative infertility, implied by Shirley's 'unfailing' reliance on the single resource of variation, and dramatic immobility, the result of Shirley's willingness to sacrifice the progressive movement of a scene for 'endless change of language'.

Believing he has observed these vices in the argument between Bornwell and Aretina in the opening scene, Lewis closes his case against Shirley with words that beguile:

> On the strictly dramatic side he has nothing to say that could not have been said in six lines. 'Why are you angry?' asks Bornwell. 'Because you stint me,' retorts the lady. 'I don't. On the contrary I allow you to spend far too much,' says Bornwell. 'Well, I still think you're mean,' says Lady Bornwell. That is the whole scene, as drama. What swells it to its 130 odd lines is pure *variation* on the theme 'you spend too much' put into the mouth of Bornwell. During this the dramatic situation stands still. 'Have you done, Sir?' Lady Bornwell asks at the end of her husband's first speech; at the end of his third she is sill asking, 'Have you concluded your lecture?' The angry husband and the scornful wife remain dramatically immobile and the play ceases to

go forward while the waves of variation roll over the audience. In other words, what Shirley has here to say as a dramatist is extremely little; and to convert that little into something that should seem richer he has to call in variation.

These are serious charges, powerfully asserted, and I have quoted them at length because they deserve to be seriously answered.

To begin, Lewis's commentary on the scene between Bornwell and Aretina requires some comment in its own right. His remarks owe their amusing charm to a technique that many experienced lecturers find irresistible: the technique of speeding up the pace of a scene or a plot in the retelling so as to produce a caricature. The effect is the same as that produced by an old piece of newsreel played back at twice the intended speed. In itself this is a harmless diversion, but it provides a very bad basis for judging anything. The same technique could be applied, with hilarious results, to the long expository scene between Prospero and Miranda in *The Tempest* (I.ii.1-185).

Readers who are willing to take the opening scene of **The Lady of Pleasure** at a less breathtaking pace will notice a great many subtleties of dramatic language which caricature cannot reproduce. Before Bornwell enters (I.i.45.1), Aretina has already told her Steward that she is glad to have put behind her the provincial boredom of country living. Bornwell's first words are solicitous: 'How now? What's the matter? . . . Angry, sweet heart?' (ll. 46-7). Aretina's response is beautifully evasive: 'I am angry with myself, / To be so miserably restrained' (ll. 47-8). For the moment her sense of decorum prevents her from admitting that the Steward and Bornwell are the real objects of her anger, and part of the dramatic purpose of the argument as a whole is to show Aretina's genuine dissatisfaction breaking through the surface of well-bred poise.

Bornwell appeals to his own generosity, arguing that Aretina should at least give him credit for his willingness to placate her by moving to the town; but this gets him nowhere, so he rebukes her extravagance in a series of speeches which do depend on rhetorical variation. Among the targets of Bornwell's aversion are the following:

> Your change of gaudy furniture, and pictures
> Of this Italian master and that Dutchman's;
> Your mighty looking-glasses, like artillery,
> Brought home on engines . . .
>
> (ll. 74-7)

The appeal to good taste (in 'gaudy') is intended to nettle Aretina, and the nonchalance about her art collection is deliberately dismissive. But Bornwell remains good-humoured: there is a mock-heroic levity in his

inflation of 'looking-glasses' into 'artillery', transported on military 'engines'. As Pope recommends, Bornwell is 'using a vast force to lift a *feather*'.[18]

Aretina's impatience is progressively revealed. She tries the ironic parry—'I like / Your homily of thrift' (ll. 98-9)—but when this merely provokes further accusations she lets Bornwell know she finds him 'tedious' (l. 133) and 'avaricious' (l. 136). Then she retorts with her own lecture, which includes the reproof of Bornwell, quoted earlier, for behaving as only 'a narrow-minded husband' would (l. 145).

If the actors who play this scene are at all sensitive to what Shirley has given them, they will want to avoid at all cost the suggestion that this is a normal conversation which occurs every other day in the Bornwell household. To give in to caricature in this way would reduce the couple to Dagwood and Blondie, or to 'the angry husband and the scornful wife' of C. S. Lewis's description. What Shirley gives the actors is the chance to develop a series of delicate emotional adjustments between husband and wife—adjustments which occur because of the recent and decisive changes in their pattern of social living. The language he writes for them is not in itself brilliant, but it is full of dramatic possibilities which the actors can exploit and enrich.

I trust that Shirley has been cleared from suspicion on the charge of dramatic immobility. But the question of imaginative infertility remains, and here my defence will be qualified in certain crucial respects. First, however, I should like to offer Shirley the opportunity of defending himself, in the following impressive example of variation spoken by Celestina:

> You two, that have not 'twixt you both the hundredth
> Part of a soul, coarse woollen-witted fellows
> Without a nap, with bodies made for burdens;
> You that are only stuffings for apparel
> (As you were made but engines for your tailors
> To frame their clothes upon and get them custom)
> Until men see you move, yet then you dare not,
> Out of your guilt of being the ignobler beast,
> But give a horse the wall (whom you excel
> Only in dancing of the brawl, because
> The horse was not taught the French way). . . .
> . . . . . But I waste time
> And stain my breath in talking to such tadpoles.
> Go home and wash your tongues in barley-water,
> Drink clean tobacco, be not hot i'th' mouth,
> And you may 'scape the beadle; so I leave you
> To shame and your own garters.
>
> (III.ii.293-319)

This is Shirley at his satiric best: precise yet conversational, inventive but under control. In a series of variations nearly twice as long as that reproduced in the quotation, Celestina is deflating Kickshaw and Littleworth in response to the verbal abuse which they have directed at her. She begins by improvising on a clothing metaphor ('woollen-witted') until she has transformed her assailants into dancing mannequins. She turns the slander of her accusers back on them in the form of foul, unwashed, tobacco-stained breath. And she concludes with a brilliant adaptation of a proverb which recommends hanging in one's own garters as a last resort for fools.[19] The passage as a whole indicates what Shirley owes to his 'acknowledged master, learned JONSON',[20] though in Jonson the fools would have less to fear from a verbal opponent than from the deflating ironies of their own rhetorical habits.

Although Shirley's reliance on variation is not the mechanical and sterile reflex which Lewis's description implies, there are two special respects in which his limited imagination does detract from his ability as a poet. The first of these is a narrowness of range, the result of a virtually exclusive concentration on the social and verbal behaviour of the middle and upper levels of society.[21] Instead of a wide spectrum of languages, ranging as in Jonson from the courtly inanities of Sir Amorous La Foole to the sensual vulgarity of Ursula the pig-woman, Shirley confines himself to the idiom of cultivated speakers of English, and uses their speech as the norm in judging such relatively minor aberrations as pretension (in Haircut's case) or effusion (in Lord Unready's). This constricted verbal register brings with it a second weakness: the inability to provide each character with a distinctively personal style of speaking.[22] Celestina's shrewd wit, in the passage quoted above, is not so much a personal idiom as a particularly agile exercise in a verbal mode which all of the characters in *The Lady of Pleasure* either claim or would like to claim as their own. I am not asserting that all of the characters are equally witty, but rather that all of them would subscribe to the same standard of wit. And though Celestina is a brilliant success by this standard, and Littleworth a dismal failure, there is not in Shirley the close relationship between a character and his or her language which, in the case of greater playwrights, identifies a turn of speech as indelible Mosca or vintage Falstaff.

Shirley's abilities as a poet and playwright are, in the last analysis, those of a highly skilled professional. D. J. Enright's discerning assessment of Shirley is consistent, in large measure, with the arguments I have been advancing:

> Though he had no original genius, the range of his reference is wider than that of later comedy. His is a neat, fluent, easy, and rather colourless style, yet simple rather than insipid. The emotional pressure is never very high, and the metaphorical tension so slack that obviously he wrote in verse only because it was the tradition. Yet this makes for a healthier atmosphere than we find in much of Beaumont and Fletcher; after them we welcome Shirley's lack of pretension. He is

concerned with a polite society which has not yet grown altogether complacent about the rest of the world.[23]

No purpose would be served by quarrelling over minor matters of emphasis in this basically sound evaluation. I should like to add only that Shirley's claim on a modern reader's attention rests not exclusively on his literary merits, but also on his performance as a theatrical craftsman.

Notes

1. 'Excerpta Quaedam per A. W. Adolescentem', British Library Add. MS 22608, fol. 101v. This and subsequent quotations from Wright's manuscript are taken from the transcription by Arthur C. Kirsch in 'A Caroline Commentary on the Drama', *Modern Philology*, LXVI (1968-9), 256-9. Wright's commonplace book is discussed and dated not earlier than 1639 by James G. McManaway in 'Excerpta Quaedam per A. W. Adolescentem', *Studies in Honor of Dewitt T. Starnes*, ed. Thomas P. Harrison *et al.* (Austin, Texas, 1967), pp. 117-26.

2. Of indirect relevance to the structure of the play is Shirley's procedure of writing, evidently, with no specific narrative or dramatic sources in mind. Forsythe nominates Fletcher's *The Noble Gentleman* and Davenant's *The Just Italian* as plays which seem to have influenced *The Lady of Pleasure* (p. 372), but the strongest claim to be made for them is consignment to the dubious rank of analogues. That Shirley's imagination was a virtual storehouse of situations, characters and phrases drawn from the dramatic repertoire of his day is beyond question. But the raw material which went into the making of *The Lady of Pleasure* is the social world of Caroline London (see Papousek, pp. 66-9).

3. The symbolic nature of food in Jonson has been discussed by Jonas A. Barish, who remarks on the one hand that in *Bartholomew Fair* 'the ubiquitous word "belly" focuses our attention on the center of appetite, the stomach' (*Ben Jonson and the Language of Prose Comedy*, Cambridge, Mass., 1960, p. 227), and observes elsewhere that 'Jonsonian cuisine' can appeal to the sophisticated palate as well, notably in *The Alchemist* where the menu includes 'the dolphin's milk butter in which Sir Epicure Mammon's shrimps will swim' ('Feasting and Judging in Jonsonian Comedy', *Renaissance Drama*, n.s. V, 1972, 6).

4. See III.i.0.1 and the note at this point, in which my decision to christen Lord Unready is explained.

5. The text of the proclamation is quoted by Papousek, as Appendix A of her edition (pp. 278-81).

6. *The Crisis of the Aristocracy, 1558-1641* (Oxford, 1965), pp. 186-8.

7. *Wks,* V, 275.

8. Heywood, *A Woman Killed with Kindness,* ed. R. W. Van Fossen (London, 1961), xiii.61-2.

9. Middleton, *A Chaste Maid in Cheapside,* ed. R. B. Parker (London, 1969), I.ii.21.

10. See F. G. Emmison, *Elizabethan Life: Morals and the Church Courts* (Chelmsford, Essex, 1973), pp. 1-2: 'nearly 10,000 men and women were summoned on sexual charges by the Elizabethan Essex spiritual courts', a number which amounts to about one in seven of the adult population. For their concern with regulating sexual conduct, the church courts 'became known in vulgar parlance throughout England as the Bawdy Courts'.

11. *The Description of England,* ed. Georges Edelen (Ithaca, New York, 1968), p. 189.

12. See Keith Thomas, 'The Double Standard', *Journal of the History of Ideas,* XX (1959), 200-1; and Van Fossen's Introduction to *A Woman Killed with Kindness,* pp. xxx-xxxi.

13. See G. R. Hibbard, 'Love, Marriage and Money in Shakespeare's Theatre and Shakespeare's England', *The Elizabethan Theatre,* VI (1975), 140-2.

14. On this point I am in substantial agreement with Nathan Franklin Cogan's analysis of Bornwell's character in 'The London Comedies of James Shirley, 1625-1635: The Dramatic Context of *The Lady of Pleasure*' (Ph.D. thesis, University of California, Berkeley, 1971), pp. 213-15.

15. See G. F. Sensabaugh, 'Platonic Love in Shirley's *The Lady of Pleasure*', *A Tribute to George Coffin Taylor,* ed. Arnold Williams (Chapel Hill, North Carolina, 1952), pp. 168-77.

16. Swinburne uses this phrase, in *Essays and Studies,* 3rd ed. (London, 1888), pp. 287-8, to characterise the relationship between Fernando and Bianca in Ford's *Love's Sacrifice.*

17. The essay appears in *Rehabilitations and Other Essays* (Oxford, 1939), pp. 161-80.

18. See the Postscript to the *Odyssey,* in *The Poems of Alexander Pope,* ed. John Butt *et al.* (New Haven, 1939-69), X, 387.

19. Tilley, G 42. See also III.ii.319n.

20. See the Dedication to *The Grateful Servant* (Shirley, *Wks,* II, 3).

21. See Richard Morton, 'Deception and Social Dislocation: An Aspect of James Shirley's Drama', *Renaissance Drama,* IX (1966), 245.

22. See Juliet McGrath, 'James Shirley's Uses of Language', *Studies in English Literature, 1500-1900,* VI (1966), 332: 'only rarely are linguistic extremes displayed, and the language spoken by the majority of the characters seems to have a pronounced sameness almost regardless of the character who is speaking'.

23. 'Elizabethan and Jacobean Comedy', in *The Age of Shakespeare,* vol. II of *A Guide to English Literature,* ed. Boris Ford (Harmondsworth, Middlesex, 1955), p. 427.

Abbreviations

EDITIONS COLLATED

Papousek: Marilyn D. Papousek, 'A Critical Edition of James Shirley's *The Lady of Pleasure*' (Ph.D. thesis, University of Iowa, 1971).

WORKS OF REFERENCE, ETC.

Forsythe: Robert Stanley Forsythe, *The Relations of Shirley's Plays to the Elizabethan Drama* (New York, 1914).

Shirley, *Wks: The Dramatic Works and Poems of James Shirley,* ed. William Gifford and Alexander Dyce, 6 vols. (London, 1833).

Tilley: Morris Palmer Tilley, *A Dictionary of the Proverbs in England in the Sixteenth and Seventeenth Centuries* (Ann Arbor, 1950).

THE CARDINAL (1641)

CRITICAL COMMENTARY

Arthur Huntington Nason (essay date 1915)

SOURCE: Nason, Arthur Huntington. "The Cardinal." In *James Shirley, Dramatist,* pp. 344-61. New York: Arthur H. Nason, 1915.

[*In the following excerpt, Shirley's early twentieth-century biographer, Arthur Nason describes* The Cardinal *as a romantic tragedy and one of the playwright's best works, noting especially the strength of Shirley's character development, particularly in the female lead role.*]

Foremost among the later plays of Shirley, and among the greatest that Shirley ever wrote, is ***The Cardinal,*** licensed November 25, 1641. In plot, this romantic tragedy is a struggle between the duchess Rosaura on the one hand and the cardinal on the other: the duchess being supported by a colonel named Hernando, and the cardinal being in alliance with his nephew Don Columbo. Opening in a struggle concerning the marriage of the duchess, the play concludes as a struggle for revenge.

The cardinal, for the strengthening of his own power, has persuaded the king to bestow the hand of the duchess upon Don Columbo. While Columbo is absent defending the kingdom against Arragon, the duchess writes him, demanding her release. Columbo, supposing it but a hint to hasten home, gives her her freedom. The duchess shows his letter to the king; and, on the strength of it, she secures the king's assent to her marriage with her long-time lover, Count d'Alvarez. Columbo returns upon their wedding night, stabs with his own hand Count d'Alvarez, and stays to justify his crime. His victory over Arragon pleads in his behalf; and this, by the cardinal's influence, wipes out all memory of the assassination. Columbo forces himself upon the duchess, and vows that, should she ever think to wed again, he will slay the next bridegroom as he has the last.

With this, the duchess accepts as her champion one Hernando, a colonel who has also personal grounds for hating both Columbo and the cardinal. In the duel that follows, Hernando slays Columbo. The duchess, meanwhile, seemingly insane, is made the cardinal's ward. He resolves to take revenge upon her by violating and then poisoning her. When, however, he attempts assault upon her, Hernando, concealed behind the arras, rushes to her rescue, stabs the cardinal, and then stabs himself and dies. To the king and court, the wounded cardinal confesses his treachery; and, in token of his penitence, he begs the duchess to accept an antidote for a poison which, he alleges, he administered to her at supper. In token of his good faith, he takes a portion of the antidote before her. She drinks, and finds it poison. He rejoices in the success of his deceit—and then learns that his own wound was not mortal. The cardinal and the duchess die together. Both have their revenge.

Upon and around this central story, Shirley has grouped a succession of strong and brilliant scenes. The departure of Columbo and the immediate meeting of d'Alvarez and the duchess;[1] the council of war, with Columbo's quarrel with Hernando, his receipt of the duchess's letter, and his answer;[2] her successful appeal to the king and resulting quarrel with the cardinal;[3] the celebration of the duchess's wedding to d'Alvarez, the "revels" by the unknown maskers, their murder of d'Alvarez, the unmasking of Columbo, his bold confession and defiance, and the duchess's cry for justice;[4] her subsequent meetings with Columbo, with Hernando, and with the cardinal;[5] the duel between Hernando and Columbo with their respective seconds, from which

Hernando is the sole survivor;[6] the visit of Hernando and of the cardinal to the supposedly insane duchess, and the resulting deaths of all three:[7] all these scenes tell swiftly and vividly the story from which the remaining scenes—such as the comic episode of the servants dressing for the play, and the hinted amours of Columbo and Celinda—are but slight digressions. As a combination of emotional unity in each individual scene with intellectual unity in the play taken as a whole, *The Cardinal* stands first among Shirley's tragedies.

The Cardinal is notable, however, not solely for management of plot and for the high effectiveness of particular scenes; it is notable also for the interest of its characters. The duchess, Columbo, Hernando, and the cardinal: each is a powerful personality, powerfully conceived; each different from the others, and each finely delineated.

Most difficult of delineation was the character of the duchess Rosaura. Her, Shirley must present as guilty of the initial overt act that divorced her from her affianced lover, married her to that lover's rival, and led on to the assassination of d'Alvarez, the death of Columbo and two others in the resulting duel, the suicide of Hernando, and the death by poison of the cardinal and herself; and yet Shirley must so present the duchess that, from first to last, our sympathy shall be with her— the all but helpless soul struggling for life amid the cardinal's toils. This sympathy, Shirley skilfully builds up from scene to scene: he shows us how the anger of the lords runs high against the cardinal; how the love of the duchess for d'Alvarez antedated her forced alliance with the cardinal's nephew, Don Columbo; how, against the united power of the mighty general, the mightier cardinal, and the pliant king, naught could avail the duchess but a woman's stratagem; how, widowed on her wedding night, she cried in vain for justice against the murderer of her lord; how Columbo, more firm than ever in the king's support, drove her, by his threats, to desperation, and forced upon her, not for revenge or justice only, but even for self-preservation, her alliance with Hernando for the death of Columbo and the cardinal. Perhaps the finest touch—coming as it does between the death of Columbo in the duel and that of the cardinal by his own poison—is the scene in which the duchess, seemingly insane, receives her champion, Hernando:

HERNANDO.

> Dear madam, do not weep.

DUCHESS.

> You're very welcome.
> I have done. I will not shed a tear more
> Till I meet Alvarez; then I'll weep for joy.
> He was a fine young gentleman, and sung sweetly.
> An you had heard him but the night before

We were married, you would have sworn he had been
A swan, and sung his own sad epitaph.
But we'll talk of the Cardinal.

HER.

                                    Would his death
Might ransom your fair sense! he should not live
To triumph in the loss. Beshrew my manhood,
But I begin to melt.

DUCH.

                              I pray, sir, tell me,
For I can understand, although they say
I have lost my wits; but they are safe enough,
And I shall have them when the Cardinal dies;
Who had a letter from his nephew, too,
Since he was slain.

HER.

                              From whence?

DUCH.

I do not know where he is. But in some bower
Within a garden he is making chaplets.
And means to send me one. But I 'll not take it.
I have flowers enough, I thank him, while I live.

HER.

But do you love your governor?

DUCH.

Yes, but I'll never marry him; I am promis'd
Already.

HER.

To whom, madam?

DUCH.

                              Do not you
Blush when you ask me that? Must not you be
My husband? I know why, but that's a secret.
Indeed, if you believe me, I do love
No man alive so well as you. The Cardinal
Shall never know't; he'll kill us both; and yet
He says he loves me dearly, and has promis'd
To make me well again; but I'm afraid,
One time or other, he will give me poison.

HER.

Prevent him, madam, and take nothing from him.

DUCH.

Why, do you think 'twill hurt me?

HER.

                              It will kill you.

DUCH.

I shall but die, and meet my dear-loved lord,
Whom, when I have kiss'd, I'll come again and work
A bracelet of my hair for you to carry him,
When you are going to heaven. The poesy shall
Be my own name, in little tears that I
Will weep next winter, which, congeal'd i' the frost,
Will show like seed-pearl. You'll deliver it?
I know he'll love and wear it for my sake.

HER.

She is quite lost.

DUCH.

                              Pray give me, sir, your
pardon;
I know I talk not wisely; but if you had
The burthen of my sorrow, you would miss
Sometimes your better reason. Now I'm well.
What will you do when the Cardinal comes?
He must not see you for the world.

HER.

                              He shall not;
I'll take my leave before he comes.

DUCH.

                              Nay, stay;
I shall have no friend left me when you go.
He will but sup; he shall not stay to lie with me;
I have the picture of my lord abed;
Three are too much this weather.
                    Enter PLACENTIA.

PLA.

                              Madam, the Cardinal.

HER.

He shall sup with the devil.

DUCH.

                              I dare not stay;
The red cock will be angry. I'll come again.[8]

By such devices as this does Shirley maintain our sympathy for the duchess Rosaura; but, besides picturing a character that holds our sympathy, he has here—contrary to his custom—pictured a character that grows. From a timorous maiden, hiding her heart from Columbo and the world, she becomes first the woman that dares demand her freedom, appeal to the king, and hurl defiance at the cardinal, and then, widowed of d'Alvarez and crushed beneath the threefold power, the woman that dares to draw Hernando to her aid against Columbo and, by feigned insanity, so to entrap the cardinal that she may "be Alvarez' justicer."

Strongly contrasted with the intriguing duchess on the one hand and with the intriguing cardinal on the other are the two bold, outspoken soldiers, Hernando and Columbo—the former calmly, the latter passionately brave. In Columbo, Shirley has depicted a commander that makes his very impetuosity a means to victory, and that thinks to take a wife as he would take a town—by storm. That the vanquished have rights, he cannot comprehend; nor can he comprehend the fine nobility of Count d'Alvarez. Against a valiant swordsman, he scorns a base advantage; yet he is on the point of resenting the message of the duchess by slaying the duchess's messenger, and he vents his rage upon the duchess with the same brutality as his revenge upon d'Alvarez. He is perhaps most nearly magnificent in the scene of the assassination at the wedding, when he stays to justify his deed; yet more characteristic is his subsequent visit to the duchess:

PLACENTIA.

> Madam, here's Don Columbo says he must
> Speak with your grace.

DUCHESS.

>   But he must not, I charge you.
> None else wait? Is this well done,
> To triumph in his tyranny? . . .

ANTONIO.

> Sir, you must not see her.

COLUMBO.

> Not see her? Were she cabled up above
> The search of bullet or of fire, were she
> Within her grave, and that the toughest mine
> That ever nature teem'd and groan'd withal,
> I would force some way to see her.—Do not fear
> I come to court your madam; you are not worth
> The humblest of my kinder thoughts. I come
> To show the man you have provok'd, and lost,
> And tell you what remains of my revenge.
> Live, but never presume again to marry.
> I'll kill the next at the altar, and quench all
> The smiling tapers with his blood. If after,
> You dare provoke the priest and heaven so much,
> To take another, in thy bed I'll cut him from
> Thy warm embrace, and throw his heart to ravens.

CELINDA.

> This will appear an unexampled cruelty.

COLUMBO.

> Your pardon, madam; rage and my revenge
> Not perfect took away my eyes. You are
> A noble lady; this not worth your eye-beam,
> One of so slight a making and so thin
> An autumn leaf is of too great a value
> To play which shall be soonest lost i' the air.
> Be pleased to own me by some name, in your
> Assurance; I despise to be receiv'd

> There. Let her witness that I call you mistress;
> Honour me to make these pearls your carkanet.[9]

Against this valiant brutality of Columbo, Shirley paints the valiant nobility of Hernando. He pictures Hernando's wisdom at the council-board, his self-control in the face of Columbo's accusation, his brave devotion to the dead d'Alvarez and to the living duchess, his victory in the duel, his rescue of the duchess from the cardinal, and his self-inflicted death. Any of these scenes would be worth quoting; but, for the sake of illustrating at once the directness of Hernando and the indirection—or, perhaps, the crescent bravery—of the duchess, I select his meeting with her after d'Alvarez' death:

HERNANDO.

> I know not how your grace will censure so
> Much boldness, when you know the affairs I come
>   for.

DUCHESS.

> My servant has prepar'd me to receive it,
> If it concern my dead lord.

HER.

>   Can you name
> So much of your Alvarez in a breath,
> Without one word of your revenge? O, madam,
> I come to chide you, and repent my great
> Opinion of your virtue, that can walk,
> And spend so many hours in naked solitude;
> As if you thought that no arrears were due
> To his death, when you had paid his funeral charges,
> Made your eyes red, and wet a handkerchief.
> I come to tell you that I saw him bleed;
> I, that can challenge nothing in his name
> And honour, saw his murder'd body warm,
> And panting with the labour of his spirits,
> Till my amazed soul shrunk and hid itself:
> While barbarous Columbo grinning stood,
> And mock'd the weeping wounds. It is too much
> That you should keep your heart alive so long
> After this spectacle, and not revenge it.

DUCH.

> You do not know the business of my heart,
> That censure me so rashly; yet I thank you:
> And, if you be Alvarez' friend, dare tell
> Your confidence, that I despise my life,
> But know not how to use it in a service,
> To speak me his revenger. This will need
> No other proof than that to you, who may
> Be sent with cunning to betray me, I
> Have made this bold confession. I so much
> Desire to sacrifice to that hovering ghost
> Colombo's life, that I am not ambitious
> To keep my own two minutes after it.

HER.

> If you will call me coward, which is equal
> To think I am a traitor, I forgive it,

For this brave resolution, which time
And all the destinies must aid. I beg
That I may kiss your hand for this; and may
The soul of angry honour guide it—

Duch.

                                        Whither?

Her.

To Don Columbo's heart.

Duch.

                        It is too weak, I fear, alone.

Her.

Alone? Are you in earnest? Why, will it not
Be a dishonour to your justice, madam,
Another arm should interpose? But that
It were a saucy act to mingle with you,
I durst, nay, I am bound in the revenge
Of him that's dead, (since the whole world has inter-
     est
In every good man's loss,) to offer it:
Dare you command me, madam?

Duch.

                        Not command;
But I should more than honour such a truth
In man, that durst, against so mighty odds,
Appear Alvarez' friend and mine. The Cardinal—

Her.

Is for the second course; Columbo must
Be first cut up; his ghost must lead the dance:
Let him die first.

Duch.

                        But how?

Her.

How! with a sword; and, if I undertake it,
I will not lose so much of my own honour,
To kill him basely.

Duch.

                        How shall I reward
This infinite service? 'Tis not modesty,
While now my husband groans beneath his tomb,
And calls me to his marble bed, to promise
What this great act might well deserve, myself,
If you survive the victor. But if thus
Alvarez' ashes be appeas'd, it must
Deserve an honourable memory;
And though Columbo (as he had all power,
And grasp'd the fates) has vowed to kill the man
That shall succeed Alvarez—

Her.

                        Tyranny!

Duch.

                                        Yet, if ever
I entertain a thought of love hereafter,
Hernando from the world shall challenge it;
Till when, my prayers and fortune shall wait on
     you.

Her.

This is too mighty recompense.

Duch.

                                'Tis all just.

Her.

If I outlive Columbo, I must not
Expect security at home.

Duch.

                                Thou canst
Not fly where all my fortunes and my love
Shall not attend to guard thee.

Her.

                                If I die—

Duch.

                                Thy memory
Shall have a shrine, the next within my heart
To my Alvarez.

Her.

                        Once again your hand.
Your cause is so religious you need not
Strengthen it with your prayers; trust it to me.

Placentia.

Madam, the Cardinal.

Duch.

                        Will you appear?

Her.

An he had all the horror of the devil
In's face, I would not baulk him.[10]

Last comes the cardinal; a subtle statesman subtly drawn. Shirley shows us but little of his doings: his means we know not; but we feel his might. How the cardinal forced the betrothal of the duchess to his nephew, and how, after the bold assassination, he secured that nephew's pardon—or, better still, release without a pardon—we are not told; we know only that the thing is done; we marvel and we fear. And just as Shirley makes us feel the cardinal's power without letting us behold its operation, so Shirley makes us feel the cardinal's wickedness almost without specific crime. With the exception of that portion of the final scene in which the cardinal endeavors to betray the duchess, he is ever the reverend churchman, full of regret at the evil he beholds. His hypocritical remorse before his death is typical of his life; his needless self-destruction, a dramatic master-stroke of irony:

CARDINAL.

>I have deserv'd you should turn from me, sir:
>My life hath been prodigiously wicked;
>My blood is now the kingdom's balm. Oh, sir,
>I have abus'd your ear, your trust, your people,
>And my own sacred office; my conscience
>Feels now the sting. Oh, shew your charity
>And with your pardon, like a cool soft gale,
>Fan my poor sweating soul, that wanders through
>Unhabitable climes and parched deserts.—
>But I am lost, if the great world forgive me,
>Unless I find your mercy for a crime
>You know not, madam, yet, against your life,
>I must confess, more than my black intents
>Upon your honour; you're already poisoned.

KING.

>By whom?

CAR.

>   By me,
>In the revenge I ow'd Columbo's loss;
>With your last meat was mix'd a poison, that
>By subtle and by sure degrees must let
>In death.

KING.

>Look to the duchess, our physicians!

CAR.

>   Stay.
>I will deserve her mercy, though I cannot
>Call back the deed. In proof of my repentance,
>If the last breath of a now dying man
>May gain your charity and belief, receive
>This ivory box; in it an antidote
>'Bove that they boast the great magistral medicine:
>That powder, mix'd with wine, by a most rare
>And quick access to the heart, will fortify it
>Against the rage of the most nimble poison.
>I am not worthy to present her with it.
>Oh, take it, and preserve her innocent life.

1 LORD.

>Strange, he should have a good thing in such readi-
>   ness.

CAR.

>'Tis that which in my jealousy and state,
>Trusting to false predictions of my birth,
>That I should die by poison, I preserv'd
>For my own safety. Wonder not, I made
>That my companion was to be my refuge.
>   *Enter* SERVANT, *with a bowl of wine.*

1 LORD.

>Here is some touch of grace.

CAR.

>In greater proof of my pure thoughts, I take
>This first, and with my dying breath confirm
>My penitence; it may benefit her life,
>But not my wounds. Oh, hasten to preserve her;
>And though I merit not her pardon, let not
>Her fair soul be divorced.
>   *The* DUCHESS *takes the bowl and drinks.*

KING.

>This is some charity; may it prosper, madam!

VALERIA.

>How does your grace?

DUCH.

>And I must owe my life to him whose death
>Was my ambition? Take this free acknowledgment;
>I had intent, this night, with my own hand
>To be Alvarez' justicer.

KING.

>   You were mad,
>And thought past apprehension of revenge.

DUCH.

>That shape I did usurp, great sir, to give
>My art more freedom and defence; but when
>Hernando came to visit me, I thought
>I might defer my execution;
>Which his own rage supplied without my guilt,
>And, when his lust grew high, met with his blood.

1 LORD.

>The Cardinal smiles.

CAR.

>   Now my revenge has met
>With you, my nimble duchess! I have took
>A shape to give my act more freedom too,
>And now I am sure she's poison'd with that dose
>I gave her last.

KING.

>   Thou'rt not so horrid!

DUCH.

>Ha! some cordial.

CAR.

>   Alas, no preservative
>Hath wings to overtake it. Were her heart
>Lock'd in a quarry, it would search, and kill
>Before the aids can reach it. I am sure
>You shall not now laugh at me.

KING.

How came you by that poison?

CAR.

                              I prepar'd it,
Resolving, when I had enjoy'd her, which
The colonel prevented, by some art
To make her take it, and by death conclude
My last revenge. You have the fatal story.

KING.

This is so great a wickedness, it will
Exceed belief.

CAR.

                    I knew I could not live.

SURG.

Your wounds, sir, were not desperate.

CAR.

Not mortal? Ha! Were they not mortal?

SURG.

If I have skill in surgery.

CAR.

Then I have caught myself in my own engine.

2 LORD.

It was your fate, you said, to die by poison.

CAR.

That was my own prediction, to abuse
Your faith; no human art can now resist it;
I feel it knocking at the seat of life;
It must come in; I have wreck'd all my own,
To try your charities: now it would be rare,—
If you but waft me with a little prayer;
My wings that flag may catch the wind; but 'tis
In vain; the mist is risen, and there's none
To steer my wand'ring bark.[11]

In the creation and delineation of character, as in the mastery of plot and scene, we have found reason highly to commend the work of Shirley in **The Cardinal.** Were we likewise to discuss its language—its poetic form—we might add a commendation more; indeed, the frequent beauty of its verse must be already evident from incidental illustration. To say all this of a play that attempted, in the year 1641, to present once more the Websterian round of revenge, depravity, and rape, is no small praise. Shirley was correct in his opinion that this play might "rival with his best."[12] Save for his own modesty, he might have added that, even when measured with the best work of his contemporaries, Shirley's **The Cardinal** must be accounted a notable romantic tragedy.

Notes

1. *The Cardinal,* I, ii.

2. *Ibid.,* II, i.

3. *Ibid.,* II, iii.

4. *Ibid.,* III, ii.

5. *Ibid.,* IV, ii.

6. *Ibid.,* IV, iii.

7. *Ibid.,* V, iii.

8. *The Cardinal,* V, iii; [*Dramatic Works and Poems,* ed. Alexander Dyce (London, 1833)], V, 341-343.

9. *The Cardinal,* IV, ii; *Works,* V, 320-321.

10. *The Cardinal.* IV, ii; *Works,* V, 322-325.

11. *The Cardinal,* V, iii; *Works,* V, 348-351.

12. Prologue to *The Cardinal; Works,* V, 275.

Catherine Belsey (essay date 1981)

SOURCE: Belsey, Catherine. "Tragedy, Justice, and the Subject." In *1642: Literature and Power in the Seventeenth Century,* edited by Francis Barker, pp. 166-86. Colchester, England: Department of Literature, University of Essex, 1981.

[*In the following essay, Belsey examines* The Cardinal *in the contexts of Renaissance revenge tragedy and changing perceptions of political authority.*]

1

Shirley's tragedy, **The Cardinal,** was performed by the King's Men in 1641. **The Cardinal** is the revenge play to end all revenge plays (literally, I want to argue). Most obviously, it combines motifs from *Hamlet, The Spanish Tragedy, The Duchess of Malfi* and *The White Devil.* Less obviously, at least to bourgeois criticism in quest of the essential coherence of the text, **The Cardinal** spectacularly gives way under the pressure of precisely those contradictions which are held in precarious balance in earlier revenge plays.

'Revenge tragedy' is a modern category with no Renaissance authority.[1] It was produced by and has produced a mode of criticism which focused on psychology and motive—the state of mind of the revenger—and the history of ideas—the moral status of revenge in the period. On those counts we have probably got as far as can be expected: revengers are well-intentioned but unbalanced; seventeenth century audiences knew that private revenge was contrary to Christian morality ('Vengeance is mine; I will repay, saith the Lord'),[2] but they probably had a tendency to sympathise with revengers all the same. The banality of those conclusions may suggest the inadequacy of the original classification.

The word which insists most vehemently throughout *The Cardinal* is 'justice', and it is at the moment when justice is announced, defined and installed that the point of collapse is reached. On the wedding day of the Duchess Rosaura to D'Alvarez, the bridegroom is murdered in a masque by his rival, Columbo. The King, who is present and in control, promises justice and imprisons Columbo. As Act III ends, guards escort Columbo from the stage, and the Duchess declares, 'This shows like justice' (III, ii, 247).[3] Immediately afterwards, at the beginning of Act IV, Columbo is at large and vowing to kill at the altar any future bridegroom of the Duchess. The King is conspicuously absent at this point, and he remains so until the final scene, when he reappears at the climactic moment, authoritatively interrogates all those present, encourages the innocent Duchess to take poison by mistake, expresses amazement at the extraordinary wickedness of the Cardinal (V, iii, 270-71), and concludes that Kings should be more careful (V, iii, 299).

Whether or not the Machiavellian Cardinal himself was identified by contemporary audiences as Archbishop Laud, misleader of Charles I, there is no doubt that this is a royalist play. There is one explicit reference to the extra-textual events of the period: the Duchess urges the Cardinal to reform his ways, 'before the short hair'd men / Do crowd and call for justice' (II, iii, 165-66). But the royalist project is most readily apparent in the displacement of the revenger, Hernando, by the figure of the King. Hernando has a relatively minor role in the play; he is apparently killed by the Cardinal's servants before the final scene (V, iii, 181 S.D.); and although he kills Columbo and wounds the Cardinal, he does not dominate the play at its climax in the manner of Hamlet, Hieronimo or Vindice. On the contrary, the dominant figure at the high points of the action is the King.

The two symmetrically placed scenes of violence, the murder of D'Alvarez and the murder of the Duchess (III, ii and V, iii, 184 ff.), are conducted in the presence of the King and centre in each case on an appeal to him for justice. The King's response each time is prompt, authoritative, confident and entirely ineffectual. It is clear that the sovereign is the only source of justice, that he acts with the authority of heaven, that he must be just 'Or be no king' (III, ii, 205) and that his failure to impose justice is the pivot of the tragedy.

There are several ways of accounting for the radical incoherence of the play (without resorting to the inanity, simply contradicted by the emphatic, authoritative parataxis of his key speeches, that the King is to be seen as a weak character).[4] Reflectionist criticism would

find the play a precise mirror of the problems of the period, with Charles I's heroic, confident, stubborn blindness central among them. Alternatively, we can find here a collision between the ideological project of the play—to show that kings, because they are the source of justice, must be vigilant—and the interest of the narrative, which necessitates that justice is withheld so that revenge becomes imperative. If the King's promise of justice had stood uncontradicted, the play would have had to end with Act III. In order to be a play about revenge, *The Cardinal* has to become a play about a crisis of justice. But because the ideological project foregrounds the figure of the King, the crisis of justice is not merely the context of an act of revenge: on the contrary, it is at the centre of the play.

2

Our commitment to our own classifications tends to suppress the preoccupation with justice in the plays of the Renaissance. *Measure for Measure,* a problem play interpreted in relation to *All's Well* and *Troilus,* is only secondarily seen as posing the problem of the just administration of the law. *Measure for Measure* is rarely linked with *The Merchant of Venice* and *The Tempest,* which quite overtly propose related debates about the nature of justice and the right to inflict punishment. Similar questions reverberate through the political plays of Shakespeare and Ben Jonson, and the so-called revenge plays of Chapman and Marston. But they ring out in the speeches of the earliest revengers: Hieronimo ripping the bowels of the earth with his dagger, and begging for 'Justice, O justice, justice, gentle king' (*The Spanish Tragedy,* III, xii, 63);[5] and Titus Andronicus, urging his kinsmen to dig a passage to Pluto's region, with a petition 'for justice and for aid' (*Titus Andronicus,* IV, iii, 15).[6]

The problems posed in these plays are never fully resolved, and the chronic interrogation of justice in the drama of the period becomes critical in certain of the revenge plays. Hieronimo and Titus, like Vindice in *The Revenger's Tragedy,* act unjustly in the interests of justice and are justly destroyed in consequence. When 'the world's justice fails' (*The Cardinal,* V, iii, 78), they act *against* the will of God, on behalf of an earthly justice which is *consistent with* the will of God. There is no closure in these plays, no obvious position of final knowingness for the audience, because neither the ordering of the discourses within the texts themselves nor the colliding planes of their intelligibility permit the spectators to know whether Hieronimo, Titus and Vindice—or Hamlet, or Hernando in *The Cardinal*—are, simply, right or wrong.

No closure is possible in that that question cannot be resolved, and this in turn is because the terms in which the question is posed prevent the possibility of resolution. It is my hypothesis that there is a radical discontinuity between medieval justice and the form of justice brought into being by the English revolution, and that **The Cardinal** is the last in a succession of plays which are themselves the site of this discontinuity, instances of a discourse of justice in crisis. I do not want to seem to privilege drama, nor in any way to diminish the well-documented struggles being fought out within and between the institutions of the law, the monarchy and parliament. I want to argue that the discourse of the theatre and these institutional struggles converge in the 'theatricals' of the trial and execution of Charles I, and that this is the moment at which the Renaissance contradictions, crystallised and made visible in the tragedy of the period, finally precipitate a bourgeois justice, guaranteed by and guaranteeing the existence of the bourgeois subject. In consequence, tragedy itself begins to give way to classic realism, the dominant mode of bourgeois fiction. To substantiate this I need to move some way from 1642.

3

Medieval justice is divine and offence against it is sin. Its paradigm is the Last Judgment and its guarantee is the presence of God as judge. At the end of *The Castle of Perseverance* (c. 1400) the Four Daughters of God participate in the trial of Mankind's soul after his death. Righteousness and Truth as prosecution hold that he is damned for his sins; Mercy and Peace in his defence plead for clemency. God pronounces sentence from his throne above the playing area. Mankind is to be saved because he cast himself on God's mercy, but God utters a solemn warning to the audience:

'Lytyl and mekyl, the more and the les,
All the statys of the werld is at myn renoun; [control]
To me schal the yeue acompt at my dygne des.
Whanne Myhel hys horn blowyth at my dred dom
. . .'

(ll.3614-17)[7]

Medieval justice haunts the Renaissance. Macbeth's murder of Duncan is performed in the shadow of the Last Judgment:

'this Duncan
Hath borne his faculties so meek, hath been
So clear in his great office, that his virtues
Will plead like angels, trumpet-tongu'd, against
The deep damnation of his taking-off.'

(*Macbeth,* I, vii, 16-20)

The soul of Desdemona will confront Othello in that high court of justice:

'When we shall meet at compt,
This look of thine will hurl my soul from heaven,
And friends will snatch at it.'

(*Othello,* V, ii, 276-78)

The will of God is not constrained by any external, abstract measure of justice. On the contrary, the divine will is itself the source and guarantee of justice: 'God must first will a thing before it can be just'.[8] God's justice is absolute, and the divine sovereignty is displayed in the tortures of hell, where each sin has its just penalty:

'Where usurers are chok'd with melting gold,
And wantons are embrac'd with ugly snakes,
And murderers groan with never-killing wounds,
And perjur'd wights scalded in boiling lead,
And all foul sins with torments overwhelm'd.'

(*The Spanish Tragedy,* I, i, 67-71)

This justice descends vertically from heaven to earth. Its order is one and continuous, from God to the individual soul, and its intermediaries, whether these are the church, the sovereign or conscience, are links in a chain of command. In the medieval moralities this vertical order is evident in the ironic mode of the plays, where an uncomprehending protagonist chooses between good and evil at the instigation of counsellors marked as knowing, while the audience, equally knowing, watches the hero stumble towards the inevitable Judgment. Whatever contradictions may be present in the medieval morality plays, they are not here, in the ordering of justice.

The institutional practices of feudal law maintain the vertical system of control. The abandonment of trial by ordeal in 1215 meant that God no longer exercised his judgment in a direct way. But the medieval judicial system identified justice with power, and progressively centralised both in the hands of the sovereign.[9] By the sixteenth century the sovereign, as God's representative on earth, has become the guardian of earthly justice, in the interest of the common weal, which, as Foucault points out, defines 'a state of affairs where all the subjects without exception obey the laws, accomplish the tasks expected of them, practise the trade to which they are assigned, and respect the established order so far as this order conforms to the laws imposed by God on nature and men'.[10] This circular justice finds its guarantee in the delegation of power from God to princes 'that sit in the throne of God', and in the analogy between God's will and the will of the sovereign:

'It is atheism and blasphemy to dispute what God can do; good Christians content themselves with His Will revealed in His Word: so it is presumption and high contempt in a subject to dispute what a King can do, or say that a King cannot do this or that, but rest with that which is the King's revealed will in his law.'[11]

When in **The Cardinal** the Duchess appeals to the King for justice, she identifies crime with sin, law with the law of God, and faith in sovereignty with Christian faith:

'If you do think there is a Heaven, or pains
To punish such black crimes i' th' other world,
Let me have swift and such exemplar justice
As shall become this great assassinate.
You will take off our faith else, and if here
Such innocence must bleed and you look on,
Poor men that call you gods on earth will doubt
To obey your laws; may, practise to be devils,
As fearing, if such monstrous sins go on,
The saints will not be safe in Heaven.'

The King's reply is emphatic, authoritative and comes from the heart of Stuart ideology: 'You shall, / You shall have justice' (III, ii, 102-12).

By 1641, of course, this ideology is itself in crisis, but the challenge to it begins to emerge much earlier in sixteenth century glimpses of a new and broadly horizontal order of justice. The Protestant reformers could not praise a fugitive and cloistered virtue. The dissolution of the monasteries ensured that the world became the arena of the Protestant struggle for the practice of charity, and sin began to have consequences for the social body as well as for the soul. In *The Castle of Perseverance* Mankind's avarice is evidence of a misplaced sense of values, but in *Enough is as Good as a Feast,* a morality of the 1560's, Worldly Man's surrender to the persuasions of Covetous precipitates the appearance on stage of three representative social types, Tenant, Servant and Hireling, with a petition against rack-renting and exploitation.

No redress is available to these pathetic figures except the conviction that God will punish Worldly Man when the time comes:

'No more shall it prevail him, the Scripture saith
  indeed,
To ask mercy of the Lord when he standeth in need.'

(ll.1155-56)[12]

In *The Longer Thou Livest, the More Fool Thou Art,* also in the 1560's, the complaint of People is similarly pathetic and similarly without relief in the world:

'For remedy we wot not whither to go
To have our calamity redressed.
Unto God only we refer our cause;
Humbly we commit all to his judgment.'

(ll.1737-40)

Divine justice acts more swiftly in this instance, when God's Judgment, 'with a terrible visure', arrests the offending hero and strikes him with the sword of vengeance (l.1791).[13]

Divine justice here is purely retributive: it does not undertake to cure the ills of the social body. The hero is damned, but God does not intervene to avert the sufferings of People. A gap begins to appear between divine retribution and earthly justice. Once the arena of the struggle for salvation is the world, justice in the world becomes an issue, and so does the question of action to secure it. God wills the world to be just and brands injustice a sin which is to be punished. But God as the only source of justice does not undertake to bring it about in a fallen world. On the contrary, the vertical order of justice withholds *authority* to act from human beings who are nonetheless *required* to act in the interests of justice precisely because the divine order does not guarantee it. Vengeance is God's, but God may defer it till doomsday, and in the meantime human beings are committed to an ideal of justice in the world.[14]

This is the problem of Hieronimo, who seeks justice in the earth and cannot find it, and of Titus, who shoots arrows at the gods soliciting them 'to send down Justice for to wreak our wrongs' (IV, iii, 51). But Astraea, goddess of justice, left the earth when the golden age came to an end, and she has ceased to intervene in human affairs (*Titus Andronicus,* IV, iii, 4; *The Spanish Tragedy,* III, xiii, 140).[15]

Revenge is not justice. Titus is a man 'so just that he will not revenge' (IV, i, 129). Revenge is an act of will, devoid of grace, contrary to the will of God and the authority of the sovereign. But revengers may act as instruments of God's judgment, in the same way that the devils enact divine justice by tormenting the damned in hell. The bloody masques and Thyestean banquets of the plays originate in hell, but they have the effect in each case of securing divine retribution and purging a corrupt social body. Revenge is an (as yet unauthorised) assertion of the individual in the interests of social justice.

4

In *The Longer Thou Livest* (c.1560), the instrument of divine retribution was a personified abstraction, God's Judgment. Stage revengers are human beings who are entitled to be instruments but not agents of justice. The discontinuity in the concept of justice is matched by a parallel discontinuity in the concept of the subject, and the same group of plays which show justice in crisis are also instances of a discourse of subjectivity in crisis.

The protagonist of *The Castle of Perseverance* is a subject-in-fragments. The circular playing area shown on the stage-plan as surrounded by water is the *world* in which Mankind makes a series of critical choices which will determine his eternal future.[16] It is also the *little world* of man, the microcosm, peopled by virtues and vices which together constitute Mankind's nature, his being in the world. The play shows the cosmic struggles between God and the Devil duplicated in the conflict within the protagonist. He is perplexed, torn, wavering, confused, invited to co-operate with the fragments of his own being, to *subject* himself to their promises, arguments, lies. Control is divided between these knowing fragments and the bewildered figure who, nonetheless, is required to choose. He has no power of himself to help himself, and is saved only in consequence of the will of God, the Absolute Subject.

In the tradition of the psychomachia these fragments are abstract spiritual qualities, but the distinction between physical and psychological properties is a modern one. In the 'little world, made cunningly / Of elements', where the blend of humours defines disposition, the physical and the psychological are continuous. The repentant Everyman greets his own Beauty, Strength and Five Senses, as well as Discretion and Knowledge, only to be parted from them all as he crawls into his grave.

In 1637 Prynne and two others had their ears cut off for libel. It is the humanist concept of the subject as a unit to be trained, disciplined, rendered docile, which makes punishment by mutilation a scandal. Titus cuts off his hand and Hieronimo bites out his tongue, reproducing the medieval subject-in-fragments. In Book V of *The Faerie Queene* Talus, with more obviously allegorical implications, executes justice by cutting off Munera's hands and feet (V, ii, 26).

Lady Macbeth's invocation to cruelty displays the nature of the Renaissance subject:

> 'Come, you spirits
> That tend on mortal thoughts, unsex me here;
> And fill me, from the crown to the toe, top-full
> Of direst cruelty. Make thick my blood,
> Stop up th' access and passage to remorse,
> That no compunctious visitings of nature
> Shake my fell purpose nor keep peace between
> Th' effect and it. Come to my woman's breasts,
> And take my milk for gall, you murd'ring ministers,
> Wherever in your sightless substances
> You wait on nature's mischief. Come, thick night,
> And pall thee in the dunnest smoke of hell,
> That my keen knife see not the wound it makes,
> Nor heaven peep through the blanket of the dark
> To cry "Hold, hold".'

> (*Macbeth*, I, v, 37-51)

The personified abstractions of the moralities have given way to fictional human beings in the Renaissance theatre, and the speaker, the subject of the enunciation, is visible on the stage, there before us as a unity, performing the invocation. But it is noticeable that the subject of the *énoncé*, the 'I' of discourse, is barely present in the speech. It is not the grammatical subject of the actions, and the moment it appears (as 'me') in the text, it is divided into crown, toe, cruelty, blood, remorse, nature, breasts, milk. The speech concludes with the opposition between heaven and hell, reproduc-

ing the morality pattern of the subject as a battleground between cosmic forces duplicated in its own being, autonomous only to the point of choosing between them.

Hieronimo's 'eyes, no eyes, but fountains fraught with tears' (III, ii, 1) constitutes a modest instance of fragmentation compared with the whole text of *Titus Andronicus*, where messengers deliver heads and hands with calm mockery (III, i, 234-40) and bones are ground with blood to make pastry (V, ii, 187-8). The discourse of subjectivity in *Titus* incorporates the mutilation of the narrative to produce a high degree of instability, a series of slides between unity and a fragmentation which borders on disintegration (Titus' madness). Here is an instance:

> 'Marcus, unknit that sorrow-wreathen knot;
> Thy niece and I, poor creatures, want our hands,
> And cannot passionate our tenfold grief
> With folded arms. This poor right hand of mine
> Is left to tyrannize upon my breast;
> Who, when my heart, all mad with misery,
> Beats in this hollow prison of my flesh,
> Then thus I thump it down.'

> (III, ii, 4-11)

Folded arms are signifiers of grief (ll.4-7), but breast-beating becomes the signified of a tangle of signifiers ('This poor right hand . . . is left . . .') in which the grammatical subject shifts from 'hand' (l.7) to 'I' (l.11) by means of a 'who' (l.9) which has no obvious antecedent.

Titus is an extreme case, but vestiges of the subject-in-fragments survive even in ***The Cardinal*** in the exchanges between the Duchess and Hernando, at the precise moment when Hernando becomes a revenger on her behalf. He urges the Duchess not to keep her *heart* alive without vengeance; her *hand* should be guided by *honour* to Columbo's *heart;* her *hand* is too weak alone, and another *arm* must interpose (IV, ii, 135-60). (If the fragmentation here has begun to sound figurative, a formal and rhetorical use of synecdoche, this is a measure of the imminence in 1641 of the unitary bourgeois subject).

The choice of action once made, however, the fragments must be assembled, brought under control. Macbeth exclaims, 'I . . . bend up / Each corporal agent to this terrible feat' (I, vii, 79-80). Hieronimo tells himself,

> 'thou must enjoin
> Thine eyes to observation, and thy tongue
> To milder speeches than thy spirit affords,
> Thy heart to patience, and thy hands to rest,
> Thy cap to courtesy and thy knee to bow,
> Till to revenge thou know, when, where and how.'

> (III, xiii, 39-44)

Thus unified, in defiance of nature, the subject appropriates an imaginary autonomy, claims a false authority, fails to observe a proper subjection to the will of God which is justice, and acts unjustly, however good the cause.

5

The revenger performs a heroic act of injustice on behalf of justice, inviting the audience to pose (without answering) the question, 'Whether 'tis nobler in the mind to suffer / The slings and arrows of outrageous fortune, / Or to take arms . . .'. *Hamlet,* as always, is a special case, and deserves special treatment. The other plays I have focused on (*Titus Andronicus, The Spanish Tragedy, The Revenger's Tragedy*) avoid the collapse which occurs in **The Cardinal** by holding in precarious balance distinct and sometimes contradictory planes of intelligibility.

The clearest case is *The Spanish Tragedy,* where G. K. Hunter has identified an ironic relationship between divine justice, represented in the framing dialogue between Andrea and Revenge, and the blind human attempts to secure justice which constitute the main plot of the play. Thus, he argues, Hieronimo and the other figures on the stage are not perceived by the audience as autonomous subjects, but as puppets of a divine justice they do not understand.[17] There is in the play a hierarchy of discourses in which only the discourse of Revenge is fully knowing, and the human figures merely *think* they know, from Andrea himself, who cannot see where the action is leading, down to Pedringano, who *thinks* on the scaffold that Lorenzo has placed his reprieve in the box which the audience knows to be empty.

The ironic mode here traces a direct descent from the morality plays. The difference, however, is that while the allegorical mode of the moralities insists on the subject-in-fragments, the quasi-realism of Elizabethan drama permits us to perceive the protagonist as a unity. However much the speeches may deal in fragments, they are uttered by a subject of the enunciation who appears autonomous: '*I will* revenge his death' (*The Spanish Tragedy,* III, xiii, 20; my italics).

The Spanish Tragedy is about divine justice; it is also about a human quest for earthly justice. The murder of Horatio is a sin which incurs divine vengeance. But the murders of Horatio, Serberine and Pedringano, and Lorenzo's deception of the King, the fountainhead of justice on earth, are evidence of corruption in the social body. Hieronimo invokes divine vengeance and royal justice, apparently in vain. When the vertical order of justice fails, he turns to the horizontal (and incipient bourgeois) scheme of human action on behalf of earthly justice, and purges the corruption of the social body. He

thus becomes an *instrument* of divine vengeance—and an *agent* of hell. Hieronimo is poised at the intersection of the feudal scheme of justice and a newly glimpsed, but not yet authoritative, bourgeois order in which the individual acts on behalf of society. He is poised also at the intersection of two orders of subjectivity: he is both instrument and agent, ironic and heroic, subject-in-fragments and Cartesian unity. These orders are held in balance within the play by the intersection of two modes: the medieval, allegorical, divine comedy of the Andrea-Revenge dialogue; and the quasi-realist tragedy of Hieronimo's revenge.

In *Titus Andronicus* the relationship between the two modes is differently ordered. Like Hieronimo, Titus as revenger is mad, located in an unauthorised order of subjectivity. In his madness he promises to embrace Tamora, who is disguised as a personification of revenge (V, ii, 67-69). Tamora is a human being: her adoption of the role of Revenge is a device to delude Titus. At the same time, Tamora, barbaric Gothic queen, brings revenge to Rome and initiates the series of acts of vengeance which constitutes the narrative. An emblematic reading of this extremely emblematic play would see Tamora as, precisely, a personification of Revenge. Titus is not really deluded:

'I knew them all, though they suppos'd me mad,
And will o'erreach them in their own devices.'

(V, ii, 142-43)

He falls in with Tamora's scheme only with a view to inviting her to dine on her children. At the same time, it is in the moment that he promises to embrace Tamora that he is appropriated by revenge. In this episode the human being of the realist mode momentarily becomes a morality fragment without ceasing to be a human subject.

In *The Revenger's Tragedy* Vindice is both human figure and fragment simultaneously. The entire action is intelligible on two distinct planes. In his opening speech, Vindice addresses himself direct to vengeance:

'Vengeance, thou murder's quit-rent, and whereby
Thou show'st thyself tenant to Tragedy . . .'

(I, i, 39-40)[18]

On one plane he is a wronged man, holding the skull of his murdered love and invoking vengeance; on another he *is* vengeance, as his name implies, addressing *himself* as abstract participant in the tragic order of divine justice. But it is as human subject that Vindice is required to pay the tragic price of his actions. At the end of the play Antonio summarily despatches the avenger of his wife's death to execution. The new, just ruler, justly installed as sovereign by the unjust actions of the human hero, has the hero justly punished.

'Vengeance is mine; I will repay, saith the Lord'. Vindice as abstraction brings a series of vices (Lussurioso, Spurio, Ambitioso, etc.) to divine retribution; Vindice as human subject takes vengeance on a corrupt court dominated by corrupt human beings (Lussurioso, Spurio, Ambitioso, etc.). In doing so Vindice arrogates the vengeance which belongs to God, and himself merits divine retribution. The play achieves its precarious coherence by signifying on these two planes simultaneously, but the planes are brought into direct collision in the judicial execution of the protagonist.

In *The Cardinal* the pressure of the tragic contradictions of revenge is such that the play collapses into incoherence. The absolutist project of the text is unable to generate a narrative, and in the gap between the ideological and the formal constraints there insists the continuing crisis of justice which in 1641 remains unresolved.

6

In 1637, when Prynne's ears were cut off 'against all law and justice',[19] he did not flinch 'even to the astonishment of all the beholders'.[20] Prynne's Christian martyrdom promptly became part of the popular mythology of Puritanism.[21] In 1649 Charles I met his death 'with the saint-like behaviour of a blessed martyr'.[22] Divine justice had reached a point of impasse when each side invoked it against the other. The collision precipitated a new form of justice.

Prynne claimed that his illegal sentence was an encroachment on the liberties of the people of England:

> 'Alas! poor England, what will become of thee if thou look not the sooner into thine own privileges, and maintainest not thine own lawful liberty? Christian people, I beseech you all, stand firm, and be zealous for the cause of God and His true Religion, to the shedding of your dearest blood, otherwise you will bring yourselves and all your posterities into perpetual bondage and slavery.'[23]

Charles I at his trial protested against the illegality of the court, in the name of the liberties of the people of England:

> 'and do you pretend what you will, I stand more for their liberties, for if power without Law may make laws, may alter the fundamental laws of the Kingdom, I do not know what subject he is in England that can be sure of his life or anything that he calls his own.'[24]

But there is no contradiction. For Charles I the liberty of the people consists in having a government which guarantees law and order. 'It is not for having a share in Government, Sirs; that is nothing pertaining to them. A subject and a sovereign are clean different things . . .'.[25]

Meanwhile, in 1642 Henry Parker, a lawyer of Lincoln's Inn, called for the supremacy of the people through their representatives in parliament.[26] In January 1649 the House of Commons declared 'that the People under God are the original of all just Power'.[27] God is included here but the grammatical subject, the presence which is the source and guarantee of just power, is the people. Parliament went on to declare 'that the Commons of England assembled in Parliament, being chosen by and representing the People, have the supreme Authority of this Nation'.[28] A fortnight later, the Lord President addressed the King:

> '. . . the Commons of England . . . according to the debt they did owe to God, to justice, the Kingdom and themselves, and according to that fundamental power that is vested, and trust reposed in them by the people . . . have . . . constituted this Court of Justice before which you are now brought, where you are to hear your charge, upon which the Court will proceed according to justice.'[29]

Charles I was tried and executed in the name of the People of England, represented by the House of Commons. The real content of these phrases is, of course, male forty-shilling freeholders represented by a severely purged Commons. In 1649 Britain officially became, as it largely remains, a politically managed patriarchal democracy where property is power. Nevertheless, the vertical scheme of authority has been supplanted by a broadly horizontal one in which individuals, including the sovereign, are accountable to the social body. Charles I's assertion that 'a subject and a sovereign are clean different things' takes on a new meaning unknown to him. The people are now sovereign, and the way is open for their subjection to that sovereignty.

Their sovereignty is the natural heritage of the people, 'being originally and naturally in every one of them, and unitedly in them all'.[30] In consequence:

> 'the power of kings and magistrates is nothing else but what is only derivative, transferred, and committed to them in trust from the people to the common good of them all, in whom the power yet remains fundamentally and cannot be taken from them without a violation of their natural birthright.'[31]

Law and order is now firmly grounded in *human nature* and guaranteed by *civil society*. The opposition is no longer between heavenly justice and earthly justice, nor between monarch and people, but between the individual and society. Liberal humanism is installed, and with it the autonomous, unified bourgeois subject, subject to and subjected by new and more ruthless mechanisms of power.

The crisis of justice, confronted but not resolved in a series of tragedies, is settled by the production of a new order of justice out of institutional collision. Ironically, this collision itself, a clash between the 'just' Cromwell and the king's 'helpless right', culminated in the dramatic spectacle of the 'royal actor' on the 'tragic scaffold', 'While round the armed bands / Did clap their bloody hands'.[32] Charles I, unlike the revengers, submitted to earthly justice, accepting it without defiance as the will of God. His death was the death of an entire order of justice and of subjectivity.

7

It was also the beginning of the slow death of tragedy. In Otway's *Venice Preserved* (1682) the driving motive of the hero, Jaffeir, is revenge, but the emphasis of the play is on his individual, psychological instability. There is no serious interest in the problem of justice.

Jaffeir is an impoverished gentleman who holds the Venetian Senate responsible in some undefined way for the loss of his fortunes, and is persuaded under the stress of financial desperation to join a conspiracy to overthrow them. Thus isolated from the social body, Jaffeir is induced by his virtuous wife to confess all to the Senate. In consequence, he is cast out by the conspirators too. The only means by which he is able to reassert his integrity is by killing himself, after stabbing to death his friend, Pierre, to save him from being broken on the wheel as a conspirator. Both Pierre and Jaffeir thus die nobly, unfragmented, as individuals (literally, undivided).

The key concerns of *Venice Preserved* are psychological error, social obligation and personal integrity. Jaffeir is anti-social:

> 'I hate this Senate, am a foe to Venice;
> A friend to none but men resolved like me,
> To push on mischief.'

> (II, iii, 141-43)[33]

He is thus a deviant. But social isolation is intolerable to him. He chooses conspiracy under pressure of friendship, and chooses to betray it under pressure of love. His final act of heroism—killing his friend and himself—is both a recognition of the right of the social body to punish deviants and an assertion of the autonomy of the subject. The two are not in contradiction: Jaffeir acts as an individual on behalf of the social interest and this constitutes an act of justice. *Venice Preserved* points forwards to *The Searchers* rather than backwards to **The Cardinal** and *The Revenger's Tragedy*.

Venice Preserved displays most of the features of classic realism. There are no abstract figures, no distinct planes of the action. The play takes place in a self-contained fictional world and the diegesis is not fractured. The play moves from enigma to closure, offering the audience a clear position from which it is ethically intelligible. Correspondingly, the Restoration theatre which is its setting contains the world of the fiction by a proscenium arch, and stands its characters against a perspective backdrop, offering a single place from which the coherence of its world is visible. From the position of the audience, relations between characters on the stage, and between characters and their context, are seen to be both internally coherent and consistent with relations in the world outside the theatre. The stage itself contains a microcosmic reflection of the social body, becomes a little world of society, resolving the contradictions and simultaneously displacing the grandeur of the little world of man.

Restoration heroes, for all their deference to the classical proprieties of heroic drama, are not grand. The autonomous subject of classic realism is a more subjected being than the subject-in-fragments, because bourgeois ideology provides no space for the microcosm which defies the macrocosm, and does so in the *imagery* of the macrocosm with which it is continuous and which is duplicated in its own being. The final location of the revenge tradition is the classic western, where the central figure acts justly, conforming to the true interest of a God-fearing society. This mode of heroism calls for skill, judgment, authority and independence—the true bourgeois virtues—but not for grandeur.

Tragedy thrives on grandeur and on contradiction. It is dispelled by the provision for the spectator of a unitary position of transcendent knowingness. Renaissance tragedy is produced by the crises of a period of discontinuity between one social order and another.

In the Restoration period, Renaissance tragedy (particularly Shakespeare) was re-*written*, smoothed out, rendered coherent and intelligible to the spectator of classic realism. In the nineteenth century, Shakespeare was re-*read* as analysing erring individual subjectivity. Titus' problem of justice has been dissolved into the psychological problems of his 'character'; Lady Macbeth's fragments have been reassembled to make her intelligible as perversely feminine. Coleridge, Hazlitt and Bradley between them reduced Renaissance tragedy to the novelistic. Meanwhile, twentieth century criticism systematically dissipates the contradictions of **The Cardinal** in the character of the King, and recuperates the crises of *The Spanish Tragedy* and *The Revenger's Tragedy* as authorial incompetence. In doing so the critical apparatus performs an act of injustice which demonstrates its subjection to an order of justice and of subjectivity which badly needs to be brought into crisis once more.

Notes

1. Fredson Bowers, *Elizabethan Revenge Tragedy 1587-1642* (Princeton, 1966), pp.62, 259.

2. Romans xii, 19.

3. James Shirley, *The Cardinal,* in R. G. Lawrence, ed., *Jacobean and Caroline Tragedies* (London, 1974). References are to this edition.

4. Lawrence, p.187.

5. Thomas Kyd, *The Spanish Tragedy,* ed. Philip Edwards (London, 1959; The Revels Plays). References are to this edition.

6. Shakespeare references are to the one-volume edition of Peter Alexander (London, 1951).

7. Mark Eccles, ed., *The Macro Plays* (London, 1969; EETS, O.S. 262).

8. William Perkins, *Works* (3 vols.), Vol.1 (Cambridge, 1612), p.288.

9. See S. F. C. Milson, *Historical Foundations of the Common Law* (London, 1969), pp.3-22.

10. Michel Foucault, 'Governmentality', in *Ideology and Consciousness,* 6, 1979, 5-21, p.12.

11. James I, quoted in Stuart E. Prall, *The Agitation for Law Reform during the Puritan Revolution 1640-1660* (The Hague, 1966), p.9.

12. W. Wager, *The Longer Thou Livest* and *Enough is as Good as a Feast,* ed. R. Mark Benbow (London, 1968; Regents Renaissance Drama Series). References to both plays are to this edition.

13. These representatives of the oppressed become standard figures on the late morality stage: see George Wapull, *The Tide Tarrieth no Man* (printed 1576); Thomas Lupton, *All for Money* (1560's or 70's); Robert Greene and Thomas Lodge, *A Looking Glass for London and England* (c.1590); anon, *A Knack to Know a Knave* (1592).

14. For Calvinism the contradiction is finally resolved only with the coming of the Kingdom of God on earth: 'In completing the redemption of man God will restore order to the present confusion of earth . . . We are content with the simple doctrine that such measure and order will prevail in the world as will exclude all distortion and destruction.'. Calvin, *Commentary* on Romans v, 21, quoted in David Little, *Religion, Order and Law* (Oxford, 1970), p.63. (This did not absolve Calvinists, of course, of the need to be just).

15. For the other instances see Frances Yates, 'Queen Elizabeth I as Astraea', in *Astraea, the Imperial Theme in the Sixteenth Century* (London, 1975), pp.29-87.

16. See Catherine Belsey, 'The Stage-Plan of *The Castle of Perseverance*', in *Theatre Notebook,* 28, 1974, pp.124-32.

17. G. K. Hunter, 'Ironies of Justice in *The Spanish Tragedy*', in *Dramatic Identities and Cultural Tradition* (Liverpool, 1978), pp.214-29.

18. Cyril Tourneur, *The Revenger's Tragedy,* ed. R. A. Foakes (London, 1966; The Revels Plays).

19. William Lamont and Sybil Oldfield, *Politics, Religion and Literature in the Seventeenth Century* (London, 1975), p.51.

20. *Ibid,* p.53.

21. *Ibid,* p.53 ff.

22. *Ibid,* p.142.

23. *Ibid,* p.52.

24. Roger Lockyer, ed., *The Trial of Charles I* (London, 1974), p.88.

25. *Ibid,* p.135.

26. Prall, p.17.

27. Lockyer, p.76.

28. *Ibid.*

29. *Ibid,* pp.81-2.

30. John Milton, 'The Tenure of Kings and Magistrates' (1649), *Prose Writings* (London, 1958), p.191.

31. *Ibid,* p.192. Milton cites in his support Christopher Goodman, who fled to Geneva from the Marian persecutions a hundred years earlier. The differences between them are as revealing as the similarities. In the earlier text vengeance belongs to God and it can be executed against a sovereign only when all right to sovereignty has been forfeited: 'When kings or rulers become blasphemers of God, oppressors and murderers of their subjects, they ought *no more to be accounted kings* or lawful magistrates, but as *private men* to be examined, accused, condemned and punished *by the law of God,* and being convicted and punished by that law, it is *not man's but God's doing*' (my italics). It is God who acts, and the people are his instruments: 'When magistrates cease to do their duty, the people are as it were without magistrates; yea worse, and then God giveth the sword into the people's hand, and he himself is become immediately their head' (p.203).

32. Andrew Marvell, 'An Horatian Ode upon Cromwell's Return from Ireland', in *The Complete Poems,* ed. Elizabeth Story Donno (Harmondsworth, 1972).

33. Thomas Otway, *Venice Preserved,* ed. Malcolm Kelsall (London, 1969; Regents Restoration Drama Series).

Ben Lucow (essay date 1981)

SOURCE: Lucow, Ben. "'Seeds of Honour': *The Lady of Pleasure* and *The Cardinal*." In *James Shirley*, pp. 123-36. Boston: Twayne Publishers, 1981.

[*In the following excerpt, Lucow downplays topical analyses of* The Cardinal *and instead emphasizes its debt to the revenge-tragedy tradition. Lucow contends that although Shirley considered* The Cardinal *his best play, it fails to rise to the quality of his best comedies.*]

Some of the scholarly interest in **The Cardinal** arises from its supposed historical and biographical parallels. Shirley's cryptic Prologue does suggest ("keep your fancy active," "Think what you please") and almost simultaneously disowns ("'tis nothing so," "I will say nothing positive") a parallel between the characters of the play and contemporary public figures. The "short-haird men" about whom the Duchess Rosaura warns the Cardinal (II.iii), in an attempt to get him to change his high-handed ways, may very well be Spanish counterparts of the Roundheads, the English Puritans critical of the Anglican Church in the 1630s and 1640s. But there is no other internal evidence of the play's alleged topicality or occasional intent. Rather, **The Cardinal** represents Shirley's last attempt to write a great play in the revenge-tragedy tradition; its setting and action were possibly suggested by John Webster's *The Duchess of Malfi*.

The atmosphere of the royal court in **The Cardinal** is dangerous. Discretion and caution guide discussion of court affairs, as in the opening scene, where two unnamed lords deliver most of the exposition. The powerful have spies everywhere ("Take heed, the Cardinal holds Intelligence / With every bird i'th'air"), near the beginning of the play; near the end, "But do not talk too loud, we are not all / Honest i' the house, some are the Cardinals creatures" (V.ii). The King enjoys absolute sovereignty, which cannot be disputed. The King's favorite, the Cardinal, exercises his will unchecked ("Death on his purple pride, / He governs all" [I.i]).

The immediate issue in the first scene is the widowed Duchess Rosaura's impending marriage to the Cardinal's nephew, Columbo, although she loves the Count d'Alvarez. Alvarez and Rosaura are ideally suited to each other ("*Hymen* cannot tie / A knot of two more equall hearts and blood"), but the wise and honorable Alvarez has deferred to the Cardinal's, and thus the King's, wishes through "Wisdom," not "Fear." In the wayward currents of court life dominated by such a powerful intriguer as the Cardinal, noble souls struggle to steer straight in an honorable direction. Images of stream, storm, and wind in the opening scene of **The Cardinal** insist upon the turbulent nature of the King of Navarre's court and upon the heroic effort required to maintain integrity in an unstable atmosphere.

The second scene, with attunements to female sensibility peculiar to Shirley, presents a paragon of courtly grace whose physical beauty is an essential attribute. On her first appearance in the play the Duchess Rosaura is addressed by one of her ladies-in-waiting as "the noblest frame / Of beauty that this Kingdom ever boasted" (I.ii). Rosaura's state of mind, which affects her appearance unfavorably, causes concern for her painful adjustment to widowhood. Rosaura is still mourning her late husband, while her attendants would have her anticipating a second marriage joyfully, in accord with her "New dress, and smiling garment." Rosaura resolves to create an untroubled appearance for the court, with the proviso that ladies-in-waiting Valeria and Celinda do not mention her grief or advise her to forget it. Not fear or awe, but deference to superior sensibility dictates the caution with which noble men and women sometimes share intimate confidences with royalty. Valeria asks permission of Rosaura to be bold; Rosaura bids her speak freely. Such freedom is a sign of favor, and at their best those closest to majesty recognize the special privilege they enjoy at the pleasure of their superiors.

After she has listened to Valeria and Celinda's frank opinions, which she had solicited and licensed, Rosaura, alone, complains of the constraints on her own freedom. What good does it do her to be "born above these Ladies"? She has not the greatness of the King; she is, paradoxically, enslaved by her greatness; Valeria and Celinda are free to love whom they choose, she says. Of course, in several plays, characters like Rosaura or her King often arrange marriages for women like Valeria and Celinda; marriage to men they love would appear to be a happy accident. Shirley does not hint at irony in his depiction of Rosaura's sentiments here; her pity for herself should be shared by his audience. Perhaps Rosaura's unwillingness to confide in Valeria and Celinda entitles her to sympathy; what she really thinks and feels she keeps to herself. She struggles to behave like a duchess and to be true, at the same time, to herself. She will muster her courage, "assume / The privilege I was born with," and tell the King that "he hath no power nor art / To steer a Lovers Soul."

Antonio, her secretary, whom she had sent to Alvarez, tells her he is waiting to see her, and also advises her of an impending war. Rosaura's hopes rise. Antonio's news gives her some reason for thinking there is a way out of the arranged marriage to Columbo, for the Cardinal's nephew is to lead the troops of Navarre against Aragon. She wishes him dead, but orders Antonio not to tell anyone what she has said. Antonio predicts that Columbo's scheduled departure will bring him quickly to Rosaura, and he leaves. Rosaura, again alone, impatient to say goodbye to Columbo, rejoins Valeria and Celinda, who have been talking to each other apart. They welcome her smiles, genuine this time, although they do not suspect their sinister cause. Rosaura's elation here represents a perversion of noble sentiment. She is now rather enjoying her need to conceal her true feelings.

Valeria and Celinda opened the second scene with remarks about Rosaura's appearance; first genuinely sad, she later pretends to be cheerful, then positively gleeful, but not for the reason her ladies-in-waiting think she is. Now Rosaura remarks on Columbo's happiness. And he is genuinely happy to have been appointed general of the army. He will win his victory before he marries Rosaura. Columbo feels exactly the way he says he does. He is aware, from the indulgent smiles of Valeria and Celinda, that his attempt at courtly address to Rosaura reveals that he is no adept at "Court tacticks." Rosaura tells him that the King is cruel to separate them and to risk Columbo's life. Columbo replies that the opportunity to fight is a greater gift than Rosaura's beauty. Antonio reenters to announce the King and the Cardinal. The King promises a splendid marriage on Columbo's return; the Cardinal approves of Rosaura's "sadness" at parting from Columbo. Rosaura bids farewell to the general, who leaves with the King, the Cardinal, and several lords. She dismisses Valeria and Celinda. For the third time alone on stage, she is not conscience-stricken by her dissimulation, for she is being true to Alvarez, to whom she pledged her love: "Forgive me virtue that I have dissembled, / And witness with me, I have not a thought / To tempt or to betray him, but secure / The promise I first made to love and honour" (I.ii). Antonio enters to announce Alvarez. Alone again for a moment, Rosaura wonders how she ought to behave.

Her ladies-in-waiting, still unmarried, are not yet answered for. Valeria's shift of preference from Alvarez to Columbo indicates the latter's superior attractiveness, not capriciousness in her. Rosaura loves Alvarez and has pledged herself to him; honor in love makes it impossible for her to obey the King and accept Columbo. Alvarez is ready to obey Rosaura's commands, but she will not command where she once promised love. She reminds him of the sacredness of their "mutual vows"—perhaps he doubts his own faith? But he takes orders from the King, and he urges Rosaura not to let him be a millstone round her neck. She must "Preserve [her] greatness." Rosaura deplores her higher station and insists that Alvarez's blood is as noble as that of kings. He reminds her that there are other considerations, such as the King's displeasure if they should not obey. A threat arises from the Cardinal's "Plot to advance" Columbo, himself no one to be trifled with. Any of them or all three could ruin Alvarez and Rosaura. She wants to know if Alvarez is afraid. He is, but only for her. He is ready to suffer; his "single tragedy" would be minor, for he is so much beneath

her. Rosaura wants to know what he would do if Columbo should die in battle or give her up. It would be like heaven, he says. But he has reconciled himself to losing her, and he leaves. Alone again, Rosaura resolves to have Alvarez, one way or another. Honor and concern for Rosaura lead Alvarez to accept, however reluctantly, the impediment to fulfillment of their love. Honor in love leads Rosaura to choose her contrary course of action. She is not a passive heroine.

Meanwhile, Columbo is pleased with the morale of his military council outside the town taken by the Aragonians, who have not destroyed the wealthy city in the course of helping themselves to everything there they wanted. Colonel Hernando of Columbo's army advises a waiting period, until the army of occupation becomes soft. A "First Colonel" disagrees. Waiting means fear, conquest increases courage, and news of the success of Aragon will attract more men to its army. Hernando points out that the Navarre army is smaller and untrained; Alphonso puts his faith in the men's spirit. Columbo accuses Hernando of cowardice or treason; Hernando resigns. Alphonso and the First Colonel reassure Hernando that he is valiant. Columbo sends him with a letter to the King saying that Columbo is going to attack: "A pretty Court way / Of dismissing an Officer" (II.i), according to Hernando. Hernando leaves; Columbo challenges those who remain to risk death and to ask the same of their men. He has a plan of action for that night. Antonio enters with letters from Rosaura, asking for her release from their engagement. Columbo is deeply insulted and draws a pistol to kill Antonio, who tells him Rosaura did not look angry when she gave him the letter. Columbo now thinks Rosaura wants him to test her, so he answers her letter "Beyond her expectation" to "put / Her soul to a noble test." Antonio congratulates himself, in an aside, on getting out of a difficult situation. His description of Rosaura's manner when she gave him the letter has led Columbo to believe that she is testing *him.* Inexperienced as a courtier, the soldierly Columbo confidently believes that "Love has a thousand arts." While he writes, his officers discuss the loyalty of his men, his prospective marriage, and the early demise of Rosaura's first husband, who left her a virgin (they had been married before either of them was old enough to consummate the marriage). Columbo gives Antonio his reply and sends his officers to their posts.

His uncle, the Cardinal, intends to visit Rosaura daily during Columbo's absence. Rosaura apologizes for her inability to entertain him as he deserves. The Cardinal assures her of his favor. The two politely exchange compliments, but, in the light of Rosaura's earlier revelation of her true feelings and intentions, her references to his power can be understood as at least ironic. The Cardinal takes them as evidence of her bounteous nobility. Alone once again, Rosaura admits she is playing a dangerous game. She dare not anger the Cardinal until she knows how Columbo reacts to her letter. She trusts that the "greatness of his soul" will not allow him to take a wife who "comes with murmur" (II.ii), that is, with reservations, demurrers—if he understands her letter. Antonio returns with Columbo's reply. Rosaura does not realize that Columbo thinks he is playing her game of testing, and joy replaces her fear. She rewards Antonio and leaves, saying, "*Columbo* now is noble."

The King attributes the breach between Columbo and Hernando to Columbo's quick temper, which subsides as quickly as it flares up. He orders Hernando to return to the front. Two lords advise Hernando not to submit and to wait until Columbo discovers his error in dismissing him. They warn him to beware the Cardinal's plots, which he says do not bother him. His loyalty to the King cannot be shaken. He means to obey the command to return. Alvarez admits to the King that Rosaura and he have been in love, but that now he defers to her honor and to the King's election. When Rosaura shows the King Columbo's letter, he consents to her marrying Alvarez. The Cardinal is puzzled and angry, chastising Rosaura for rushing to a meaner man. They exchange rather harsh words, she accusing him of partiality, he her of "licence"—and Alvarez of "effeminacy." Rosaura defies him; he plans "action and revenge" to "calm her fury" (II.iii).

Valeria and Celinda are puzzled by Columbo's release of Rosaura, the more so when they learn of his victory and imminent return to court. They leave on the entrance of the Cardinal, who is discontented about the marriage of Rosaura and Alvarez. He cannot understand what Columbo has done. In the next scene he does, when Columbo clarifies his behavior, bloodily. A "company of Cavaliers" led by Columbo, all masked, invite Alvarez off stage. The masquers return with the dead body of Alvarez and leave, except for Columbo, who removes his mask. Rosaura demands justice, and the King promises her she shall have it. A servant enters to report the masquers' flight. Columbo gives Rosaura's letter to the King, who appears to be looking for a way to exonerate the murderer but is still angry with him for killing Alvarez in his presence. Columbo pleads his record of service, displeasing the King with rash remarks about dependence on soldiers in crisis and neglect in peacetime. The King orders him arrested. Columbo is guilty of a breach of etiquette (*lèse-majesté*) in displaying Alvarez's corpse in the royal presence. Not the murder, but the manner, arouses the King's greater displeasure.

Later, Hernando and others wonder at Columbo's exoneration, and they broach the possibility of a resumption of negotiations for marriage to Rosaura. Hernando, meaning to kill the Cardinal, goes to consult with Rosaura. Also on his way to see her is the Cardinal himself, whom the King is sending to comfort her. Rosaura is determined to get revenge. To carry out her plan, she feigns madness. The Cardinal will not kill her while she is mad, for then she would not suffer the full force of his punishment. He means to rape and poison her. In the last act, dialogue between Rosaura and Hernando makes it intriguingly difficult to tell whether or not she is really mad. Certainly Hernando thinks so. When the Cardinal begins his sexual assault on her, he finds, with his first kiss, that he is falling in love with her. She calls for help. Hernando rushes in to kill the Cardinal. Rosaura leaves; Antonio rouses the court; he recognizes Hernando, who kills himself; the King, Rosaura, Valeria, and various lords and guards enter; Hernando dies;[1] Rosaura appears to have recovered her wits; the Cardinal begs mercy and warns Rosaura that she is poisoned; he offers an antidote, which is actually poison; Rosaura drinks it; he reveals his duplicity and dies; Rosaura dies.

The action of *The Cardinal* is rendered in a style best described in relation to a distinctive pattern of imagery, a contained imagery developed by pervasive reference to the color cardinal. "I would have't a Comedie, / For all the purple in the name," says Shirley in the prologue, and, he might have added, for all the purple in the play. In the first act an anonymous lord at the court of the King of Navarre takes the first step on the purple path of *The Cardinal* by cursing the title character with "Death on his purple pride" (I.i). Columbo postpones his wedding for a war, "the purple field of glory" (I.ii). Elsewhere the Cardinal or his dress are referred to in such expressions as "the purple gownman" and "Your reverend purples," while the reference to his nephew ("his soul is purpled o'er") links the Cardinal imagery directly to references to "blood" (in its various meanings), to "bloody," and to "bleeding": "I would not shrink to bleed," "envious blood," "The gloss of blood and merit," "partial where your blood runs," "innocence must bleed," "cool bloods," "a common man, whose blood has no / Ingredient of honour," vindication of Columbo's honor that "might have been / Less bloody," "guilt of blood," "Alvarez' blood," and twenty-two other "bloody" phrases, not to mention related terms: "Ambition and scarlet sins," "holy blushes," "the Church's wounds," "crimson penitence," "red eyes," "weeping wounds," "arteries," and "guilty flowings"; the Cardinal described as a "red cock"; "hot veins," and a dozen more references to "wound," "blush," and "scarlet." The iteration makes for a consistent but monochromatic verbal texture. One need not prefer Webster's more diffusely colored image patterns, with their affinity to the excesses of his sensational plots, to find Shirley's design less evocative than it is "neat."

The coolness, even cold-bloodedness, of Shirley's distancing from the action of *The Cardinal* neutralizes passionate conflict, much as the King's abstract, all-embracing moral comment at the end on the resolution of that conflict neutralizes the horror of the mutual destruction of all the leading characters. The nobility of Rosaura, Columbo, and Hernando becomes a reflection of a fixed attitude toward birth and honor, not a nobility experienced. The depravity of the Cardinal, culminating in an attempted rape and a successful poisoning, becomes an aberration, not a consequence of a high-born churchman's preoccupation with family pride, reputation, and political power. *The Cardinal,* like many of Shirley's plays, is artfully structured, but unlike several, lifeless and essentially undramatic. Yet Shirley considered *The Cardinal* his best play (Dedication). In the prologue he moderates his judgment to "this play / Might rival with his best." Some commentators on *The Cardinal* have agreed with him.[2]

Notes

1. He may not have killed himself: "'*Her.* I'd make you al some sports,—So, now we are even' could mean he's challenging Antonelli and the Cardinal's servants, and is killed after some sword-play. Gifford-Dyce added the stage-direction 'stabs himself.'" Frank Manley, "The Death of Hernando in Shirley's *The Cardinal,*" *N&Q* 12 (1965): 342-43.

2. Not all: among those who have dismissed *The Cardinal* as a worthy postscript to earlier seventeenth-century tragedy is Irving Ribner, *Jacobean Tragedy: The Quest for Moral Order* (New York: Barnes and Noble, 1962): "A play like Shirley's *The Cardinal,* although brilliantly constructed and no doubt extremely effective upon the stage, is merely the shallow imitation of only some external features of Webster's Italian tragedies" (p. 18). See also, for a general indictment of Shirley's tragedies, L. C. Knights, *Drama and Society in the Age of Jonson* (London: Chatto and Windus, 1957): Knights lists Shirley among those playwrights whose work shows "that progressive narrowing of the scope of drama that leads from *Lear* to *Aureng-Zebe*" (p. 300).

E. M. Yearling (essay date 1986)

SOURCE: Yearling, E. M. Introduction to *The Cardinal,* by James Shirley, pp. 1-42. Manchester: Manchester University Press, 1986.

[*In the following excerpt, Yearling emphasizes Shirley's simple style in* The Cardinal, *but cautions against reading the play as a stripped-down revenge tragedy. Though Yearling discounts a strong connection to Archbishop Laud in the character of the Cardinal, she asserts that the key themes of the play are political.*]

The sources suggested bear out R. S. Forsythe's description of Shirley as unoriginal in his materials but original in his organisation of those materials (p. 149). No play appears to be the single source of *The Cardinal*'s action. Plot-devices come from the obscurest and from the greatest of Shirley's predecessors. He was a literary playwright whose plays bulge with memories of other men's words and of his own, with incidents and characters drawn, like the masque properties of III.ii, from stock.[1] Yet it has been argued that for the name character of this play we should look to contemporary politics. Forker follows F. S. Boas in suspecting allusions to Archbishop Laud, and develops the comparison between Shirley's villain and Charles's unpopular adviser. He cites attacks on Laud which resemble Rosaura's tirade against the Cardinal (II.iii.139-68); he outlines Laud's character and activities, and explains why Shirley, a firm loyalist, might criticise the archbishop.[2] It is difficult not to see some reflection of Caroline politics in Shirley's portrayal of an absolutist king dependent on a powerful adviser. Not only was Laud regularly accused of popery but the prologue's allusion to Richelieu (ll. 2-3) could have turned men's thoughts, even in court circles, to Laud, who had already been compared with Richelieu. In 1635, Sir Thomas Roe wrote about the archbishop to Elizabeth of Bohemia: 'Being now so great he cannot be eminent and show it to the world by treading in beaten paths and the exploded steps of others. But he must choose and make new ways, to show he knows and can do more than others; and this only hath made the Cardinal Richelieu so glorious.' He then urges Elizabeth to show Laud 'the way to make himself the Richelieu of England', by helping her.[3] The King of Navarre, threatened by an uprising in Aragon, can be roughly paralleled with Charles, menaced by the Scots in 1641, although Shirley's king, unlike Charles, easily defeats the invaders. And in the month before *The Cardinal* appeared on stage the Irish rebelled. Furthermore Rosaura's use of 'the short-haired men' as bogeymen enforces contemporary application, and Laud's presence would help to explain the play's lurking references to treason and to give contours to the Cardinal's rather nebulous aura of corruption.

The link should not be overstressed. *The Cardinal* is not primarily a political play. It would in any case have been too late to provide a warning against Laud, who was already imprisoned in the Tower—although earlier the suspicion of an attack on someone so influential could not have escaped the censure of the Master of the Revels. And besides the resemblance to Laud, this Cardinal has a good deal of the wicked adviser and unscrupulous favourite found in earlier plays, and repeatedly in Shirley's own.[4] The mixture of topical reference and stock character suggests that Shirley again blends his sources, drawing on Laud for some of the Cardinal's characteristics but not focusing on the archbishop. Although *The Cardinal* is not without political theory,[5] the play's ultimate emphasis is not on constitutional matters but on individuals engaged in a conflict which, despite their exalted status, is essentially domestic. The villain's crime is not the oppression and pillage of a nation but the murder and attempted rape of his ward.

Besides possible literary and historical sources, a strong influence on Shirley was his audience. Clifford Leech judges the theatre's patrons as partly responsible for drama's decline during Charles's reign. He characterises the Caroline audience as genteel, unreceptive of ideas, and disliking difficulty, especially in verse.[6] Shirley's prologue to *The Imposture,* licensed a year before *The Cardinal,* glories in emasculation:

> To the ladies, one
> Address from the author, and the Prologue's done:—
> In all his poems you have been his care,
> Nor shall you need to wrinkle now that fair
> Smooth alabaster of your brow; no fright
> Shall strike chaste ears, or dye the harmless white
> Of any cheek with blushes: by this pen,
> No innocence shall bleed in any scene.
>
>   (V, 181)

The prospect is uninviting. Prologues of the period demonstrate that the Caroline audience was vociferous in its criticism, and only the most stubborn—or financially independent—dramatist would be likely to stand firm against its values. *The Imposture*'s prologue begins by confessing Shirley's anxiety about the play's reception by its 'judges'. Michael Neill thinks that the willingness to criticise indicates a rather different audience from Leech's collection of genteel dummies. He claims that its members were highly sophisticated, a leisured class which emulated courtiers and their accomplishments. They enjoyed and evaluated plays. In response, the dramatists became more self-conscious and tried to appeal to the mind.[7] We know that Caroline theatre-goers were not all fools. Sir Humphrey Mildmay shows his discrimination in a liking for 'that rare playe', *The Lady of Pleasure,* and Abraham Wright combines his enjoyment of Shirley with brief critical analyses. He prefers an elaborate plot. *The Grateful Servant* is 'well contrived' whereas *The Bird in a Cage* is 'indifferent' because the plot, although new, is not intricate. Yet plot is not all. *Hyde Park* is let down by 'ordinary' lines, and *The Lady of Pleasure* is praised for its style despite a plot which fails to please. In play after play Wright adjudicates on plot and lines, criteria which show that his pleasure in the theatre was more intellectual than emotional.[8]

Leech implies that the language of Caroline dramatists is plain and straightforward because the audience was inattentive to complexities of sound. Neill explains things differently. He thinks that Caroline dramatists

taught their audience to appreciate clear pure language.[9] The plain style had long been extolled but not always adopted, especially in drama where high emotion was frequently accompanied by elaborately figurative language. Marston attacks verbal extravagance but himself resorts to rant; other Jacobeans, especially Webster and Tourneur, are far from plain. Shirley however writes without much decoration. His plays include occasional overblown speeches but his writing is notable for being, as he promises in the prologue to *The Brothers,* 'clearly understood' (I, 191).[10] His style might well suit an audience which preferred not to think too hard, but his plainness could appeal equally to the cognoscenti for whom plainness was intellectually popular.

THE PLAY

Wright's stress on the plots and lines of plays tells us what a Caroline spectator might look for in *The Cardinal.* In his prologue, Shirley gives primacy to the action: 'A poet's art is to lead on your thought / Through subtle paths and workings of a plot' (ll. 7-8).[11] With a nice touch of self-conscious humour he shares his opinion with the comic servant who criticises the Duchess's wedding play: 'Under the rose, and would this cloth of silver doublet might never come off again, if there be any more plot than you see in the back of my hand' (III.ii.44-6). It is as a craftsman that Shirley is most likely to be praised by later critics: he is 'competent and estimable' in tragedy, excellent in exposition.[12] Swinburne, even in censorious mood, finds him achieving at worst 'passable craftsmanship and humble merit'.[13] Yet Bas, Shirley's most recent biographer, chooses to condemn the importance of plot: *The Cardinal*'s formal economy is linked with superficiality (p. 188); 'personnages et idées sont sacrifiés à l'action pure' (p. 200); the interest is in what happens, rather than in why it happens (p. 426).[14] We tend now to devalue—even to avoid—coherent and capable plotting and yet in a literary world which included Rawlins and Harding it is not to be sneered at. And 'what happens' is not in this play entirely a shallow matter.

Shirley's last tragedy is a revenge play shorn of many of the macabre accretions of the Jacobean imagination: no skulls, no poisoned helmets or pictures, no exulting in horrible deaths. With unJacobean simplicity, *The Cardinal* presents a series of events culminating in a murder which is followed by the execution of revenge on the murderer and his patron by their weaker opponents. For the action, Swinburne has undiluted praise: 'a model of composition, simple and lucid and thoroughly well sustained in its progress towards a catastrophe remarkable for tragic originality and power of invention'.[15] There is little digression but much commentary. Scenes in which the action progresses alternate with recapitulation of salient facts; characters freely discuss the past deeds of others and their own intentions. Two anonymous lords and the Duchess's secretary, Antonio, talk about the Duchess Rosaura and her relationship to Columbo and Count D'Alvarez, whose warlike and courtly natures they contrast. They mutter about the Cardinal's power and are interrupted by news of invasion. After this exposition the Duchess appears in the melancholy mood already described, and her ladies, Valeria and Celinda, repeat the distinction between Columbo and Alvarez. Again news comes of the impending war, and with it the first movement onwards—Columbo will be general in the war, and the Duchess hopes for his death. Columbo's farewell and departure to the front advance the action, but in the main his and Alvarez's interviews with the Duchess recall and expand their antithetical characters. In the act's last moments, the Duchess hints at a plan for persuading Columbo to release her.

Act I is largely talk. The Duchess's quandary is clear, the action minimal. Act II moves rapidly as Rosaura bestirs herself. She writes to Columbo. She receives a reply and when she takes this to the king we learn that Columbo has set her free. She then claims Alvarez, her more attractive suitor, for a husband. Some significant events prepare for later action. At a council of war, Columbo falls out with one of his colonels, Hernando, and dismisses him. The Cardinal is an unwelcome visitor to the Duchess. They round on each other and eventually the Cardinal, left alone, promises revenge. The play's main battle-lines are drawn up. Yet in the midst of this act's developments, two colonels and two captains repeat what we already know about the Duchess and Columbo (II.i.139-50). If the interest lies in what happens, there is still time to anticipate and recapitulate.

In Act III, the courtiers continue to gossip about recent events. We hear of Columbo's victory and while we wait for his return, the Duchess's servants talkatively prepare a play. Then, during the more formal masque which the Duchess has chosen, Alvarez is murdered by Columbo. Again narrative takes over while Columbo tells the court about the Duchess's letter which, as we must have guessed, requested freedom. With Columbo's arrest the action could be complete, but in the interval between Acts III and IV the king pardons Columbo. We are not told how this has come about, although the Cardinal is manifestly responsible. What matters is that Columbo is free and that honest men react with wonder and horror. Act IV resembles Act I in pattern.[16] Hernando and two lords discuss the Duchess, the Cardinal, and Columbo. Shortly afterwards the Duchess again displays a grief which has already been reported, and again receives contrasting visitors, one unwelcome, one welcome. The wrathful Columbo is this time followed by Hernando, who offers pity and help and is, like Alvarez, promised the Duchess's love. Further action is anticipated: Rosaura and Hernando plot the deaths of

their opponents, and the Duchess decides to disarm suspicion by feigning madness. Very soon Hernando kills Columbo.

The gossiping lords introduce the last act; they tell us what we know already and a little that we do not know. Now an earlier side-issue, Celinda's bawdy talk, becomes relevant. A series of scenes shows us Antonio and Antonelli stalking Celinda. In such an atmosphere the Cardinal's plan to rape the Duchess before murdering her seems less extraordinary. She has after all been linked with four men—Mendoza, Columbo, Alvarez and Hernando—although Shirley does not mention her sexual allure before the last scene. Hernando's return to court leads to the Cardinal's expected death. His repentance and confession that he has poisoned the Duchess are plausible, for Shirley's wicked characters often repent,[17] and he had earlier planned to poison Rosaura (V.i.92). His offer to save her parallels— ominously—Edmund's dying reparation in *King Lear.* The antidote which he provides and drinks himself is one of intrigue drama's drugs of convenience. But in the end there is a sting. The remorse is feigned, the antidote a poison, the Duchess a dead woman. The Cardinal's wounds are pronounced 'not fatal' so that he can be hoist with his own petard. In truth, the audience cannot have been much surprised. The revenge tradition was by 1641 too familiar for Rosaura's death to come as a shock. Yet the delayed poisoning of the Duchess is still an effective final stroke.[18] In Shirley's previous tragedy, *The Imposture,* the innocent had survived.

I have dwelt on the plot not simply because Shirley himself considered a play's action important but because it illustrates his customary lucidity and one source of that lucidity—the repeating and discussing of information. There are however some local defects. The major plot weakness is the Duchess's letter to Columbo. She gambles either on his death in battle or on his complaisance, and she is easily exposed. We are too aware that, as Columbo guesses, ''Tis a device' (II.i.128).[19] I am not so sure that the hiatus between Acts III and IV is a failing: Bas thinks we should witness how the Cardinal engineers Columbo's release (p. 206). Yet we know the Cardinal can sway the king. That he can sway him in such a serious matter is 'wondrous' but since the focus is on the king's failure of justice it is appropriate that we should share the courtiers' astonishment without hearing the debate which explains away the king's strange decision. We do see what happens without quite seeing why but the effect is not necessarily weak. A further objection comes from Boas. The plot demands a change in the Cardinal's character; at first merely a cunning intriguer, he becomes in the last act a monster who plans rape and murder.[20] But it is only when Columbo dies that the Cardinal is encumbered with the task of revenge, and his capacity for evil has been indicated by an almost universal mistrust and the

Duchess's direct accusations. The flaw lies rather in his sketchily drawn revenge plot. Shirley does not make it clear whether the visit from the court coquette, Celinda, is what makes him think of rape. In his soliloquy after her departure (V.i.86-99) the Cardinal reveals what he has decided but not how he has come to his decision. And we do not learn whether Celinda is, as Bas assumes (p. 188), the Cardinal's accomplice. In V.ii she draws off Antonio, leaving the Duchess without her usual male protector, but Shirley does not suggest that the Cardinal has put her up to it. The ending too is marred, this time by careful morality. After the Cardinal has confessed to poisoning Rosaura and has produced his antidote, the Duchess unexpectedly confesses:

> And must I owe my life to him whose death
> Was my ambition? Take this free acknowledgement,
> I had intent this night with my own hand
> To be Alvarez' justicer.
>
> (V.iii.243-6)

The only reason she owes her life to anyone is because the Cardinal has poisoned her—or so everyone believes. Hers is an oversensitive conscience, given to her so that she also can admit to a kind of guilt, and we can acquiesce more willingly in her death.[21] Shirley provides the guilty avenger required by revenge tragedy, thereby stretching probability to accommodate what is expected. Yet whatever its deficiencies, the plot of *The Cardinal* moves clearly and directly to its end, without the convolutions of some of its predecessors.

Shirley, like Wright, felt strongly about 'lines'. Apart from his remarks in the prologue of *The Brothers,* he frequently allows one character to tax another with obscurity: 'your language / Is not so clear as it was wont' (*The Traitor,* I.i; II, 100); 'your language, / . . . is dark and mystical' (*The Gamester,* II.iii; III, 221); 'I know not how to interpret, sir, your language' (*The Opportunity,* IV.i; III, 419). Plain language is often set against the rhetoric of a devious court:

> you talk too fine a language
> For me to understand; we are far from court,
> Where, though you may speak truth, you clothe it with
> Such trim and gay apparel, we, that only
> Know her in plainness and simplicity,
> Cannot tell how to trust our ears, or know
> When men dissemble.
>
> (*The Sisters,* II.ii; V, 377)

In liking plainness and clarity, Shirley was at one with his times. The sixteenth-century abuse of style with elaborate tropes and figures—which Gabriel Harvey had called 'curls and curling-irons'—had been remedied by returning to the 'perspicuitie' advocated by Ben Jonson and many others.[22] It was for simplicity, clarity and elegance that Shirley's contemporaries praised him.[23]

Modern critics who, unlike Shirley's contemporaries, are not implicitly congratulating themselves on having struggled free of the previous century's stylistic tangles, are less impressed by a style whose major virtue is clarity.[24] Juliet McGrath thinks Shirley's distrust of verbal artifice explains why his plays lack 'linguistic vitality and variety'. She finds in his 'stress on clear, concrete language' the cause of his alleged shallowness: 'his emphasis on the limitations of language renders him unable either to define intellectual depth in character or to indicate consistently the conceptual motivation behind action'.[25] Bas, in a detailed account of Shirley's writing finds worse faults. He demolishes the dramatist's style, accusing it of 'paresse et . . . pauvreté' (p. 376), and singles out *The Cardinal* for its second-hand imagery (p. 383). If, like Bas, we pick phrases or sentences out of *The Cardinal* and assess the sprightliness of the English we may agree with him, but if we look at speeches in context, and the play in its social and linguistic setting, we understand some of the reasons for that 'pauvreté'. And we begin to see that this play is not simply the last Jacobean revenge play: its style is part of a difference which sets it apart from its predecessors.

The basic style of *The Cardinal* is clear but stiff. Shirley is likely to use verb-noun phrases where an honest verb would be less stodgy. Alvarez fears that ''Tis not a name that makes / Our separation' (I.ii.208-9), although 'separates us' would express his fear more vividly and reduce our impression that his lines have been written for him. Perhaps in contrast, the first colonel's 'While we have tameness to expect' (II.i.25) fits what it says, but shortly afterwards keenness is unforgivably blunted: 'The men are forward in their arms, and take / The use with avarice of fame' (II.i.34-5). The Duchess instead of seeming disturbed 'expressed a trouble' (II.i.126); the Cardinal will 'perform a visit' (II.ii.1). Often these phrases depend on a neutral verb—'make', 'have', 'take', 'express', 'perform', words which contribute nothing to the life of a passage and make the lines seem static. Even verbs of motion or anticipation, such as 'advance' or 'expect', lose their impetus through overuse in phrases. Sometimes the vocabulary is not only predictable but careless. Shirley's ear seems deaf to repetitions. During the play preparations both a servant and the scenery for a masque are troublesome (III.ii.13 and 36). The Duchess's 'Expect me in the garden' (I.ii.150) is awkwardly picked up in 'This is above all expectation happy' (I.ii.151).

The repetitions sound casual, as if Shirley has a particular word fixed in his head for a while. The stiff and formal language is a different matter. The language of a play, more than that of a novel or a poem, needs to be considered not just in the context of literary language, but in terms of the language used by its audience. At the beginning of the century Sir William Corn-wallis complained about his countrymen's false eloquence, and fabricated as an instance, 'O *Signiour*, the starre that governs my life in contentment give me leave to interre my selfe in your armes.'[26] And the complaints continued. Over fifty years later Dorothy Osborne told of a servant who believed 'putting pen to paper was much better then plaine writeing'.[27] Jacobean and Caroline letter-writing preserves, amongst much that is refreshingly direct and colloquial, a more pretentious style. Dr John Bowle, seeking preferment from the Marquis of Buckingham, 'could not by any level taken frome my poore indeavors have measured the favor which your Honor graced mee withall'. 'I am embowldened to entreat yow to doe me soe much favour as to take some . . . oportunety' wrote the Earl of Cork to Sir Edmund Verney. Edward Peyton offered up a letter to his sister, Mrs Anne Oxinden, 'at the alter of your clemency', and Sir Simonds D'Ewes wrote to Sir Henry Willoughby 'to implore your favour in vouchsafing mee liberty' to 'addresse . . . affection' to his daughter.[28]

Several of these examples illustrate the fondness for replacing a verb with a weaker verb and noun. Yet the last few are from letters whereas Shirley's characters *talk* in stiff phrases. There is plenty of evidence that social climbers in seventeenth-century England were taught not just to write but to speak formally. The letter-writing textbooks of the late sixteenth and early seventeenth centuries were accompanied by conversation manuals. Benvenuto Italian's *The Passenger* was published in 1612. It provides model dialogues in parallel English and Italian texts. 'Doe me the favour', the courteous Alatheus asks his friend, 'to accept of my intentive desire to serve you' (p. 371). Eutrapelus is stricken with nouns: 'the debility of my condition should indeede rather reverence you with a divote silence, then in an outward demonstration of words' (p. 389). More nearly contemporary with *The Cardinal* is *The Academy of Complements*[29] which presents as suitable address to a great lord, 'it will be an addition unto my felicity, if I may approve this present opportunity, to make tender of my service' (p. 61); a lady is begged 'to excuse my audacity, and to pardon my temerity' (p. 77). Nouns proliferate.

Seventeenth-century comments about bombastic style; the more formal passages of upper-class letters; conversation manuals; these all suggest that a stodgy diction, overendowed with nouns, and with phrases instead of single-word verbs, was associated with courtly and polite society and aspired to by its imitators. Compliments were readily linked with the court.[30] As my examples show, this formal style was not unique to the Caroline period, but there does seem to be an upsurge of critical concentration on compliment in the 1620's, notably in Shirley's own first play, *Love Tricks* (1625), in Thomas Randolph's *The Drinking Academy* (?1626), and in some of Ford's plays. The trouble with

The Cardinal is that it reflects, without criticising, the formal mode of genteel Englishmen of the time.[31] Some of their favourite words are in the play—'protestation', 'vouchsafe', 'oblige', 'commend'. What is worse, Bas argues that the play contains some of Shirley's most persistently stiff and flat writing. But if we turn to *The Cardinal* we shall have to modify the impression that Shirley wrote unthinkingly in the bland manner of cultivated Englishmen.

Extended wordy stretches occur in formal passages, such as the exchange between Alvarez and the king (II.iii.17-29), which the king ends with a promise, not to 'recompense' Alvarez but to 'find / A compensation'. IV.i includes a stiff little conversation between king and Cardinal:

KING.

> Commend us to the Duchess, and employ
> What language you think fit and powerful,
> To reconcile her to some peace. My lords.

CARDINAL.

> Sir, I possess all for your sacred uses.

> (ll. 51-4)

Here are three main features of the bland style: fashionable vocabulary—'commend'; a phrase for a verb—'employ / . . . language'; and meaningless compliment in the Cardinal's line. Such diction prevails in *The Cardinal* because there is so much courtly conversation. But the play is not uniformly written in this public mode.[32] The formal language provides a base from which rise heightened passages. When the characters are disturbed or move into action, either the writing becomes livelier and more figurative or words are pared right down. The most vivid passages come in several of Hernando's speeches, in the Duchess's attack on the Cardinal where she accuses him of winding courtiers' tongues 'Like clocks, to strike at the just hour you please' (II.iii.151), and in Antonio's delight when the vengeful Hernando arrives:

> I would this soldier had the Cardinal
> Upon a promontory, with what a spring
> The churchman would leap down; it were a spectacle
> Most rare to see him topple from the precipice,
> And souse in the salt water with a noise
> To stun the fishes; and if he fell into
> A net, what wonder would the simple sea-gulls
> Have, to draw up the o'ergrown lobster,
> So ready boiled! He shall have my good wishes.

> (V.ii.105-13)

The formal base is still there—'what wonder . . . / Have'—but it is overlaid with lively imagery and strong verbs: 'leap', 'topple', 'souse', 'stun'.

At the other extreme, Shirley's narrative manner is an efficient vehicle for the action. Here his main aim is to subordinate words to facts, and so his style features compact grammatical devices. In Columbo's description of how he was deceived, zeugma, ellipsis and apposition all help to compress information:

> Read there how you were cozened, sir,
> Your power affronted, and my faith, her smiles
> A juggling witchcraft.
>
> (III.ii.133-5)

Parenthesis adds a vital detail in the following passage:

> I sent
> That paper, which her wickedness, not justice,
> Applied, what I meant trial, her divorce.
>
> (III.ii.163-65)

The Act I exposition is concise; only 'Alas poor lady' breaks into the initial parade of facts. Moreover, although the first lord's ignorance is artificial, the first scene of the play seems a model of normal conversation when set against the efforts of some of Shirley's contemporaries. There is none of the larding with 'Thou knowest' and 'it is true' which encumbers the opening lines of Carlell's *The Deserving Favourite* (between 1622 and 1629); and in nineteen lines Shirley summarises relationships more complex than his fellow professional Glapthorne describes in the sixty lines of bombast which open *Argalus and Parthenia* (between 1632 and 1638). At the very least Shirley's writing is a craft of which many Caroline dramatists, amateur and professional, knew little.

Shirley also cuts words away in a crisis. Alvarez's murderers act in silence. They enter as masquers and summon their victim; meanwhile a brief conversation among the watchers threatens danger.

KING.

> Do you know the masquers, madam?

DUCHESS.

> Not I, sir.

CARDINAL.

> [*Aside*] There's one, but that my nephew is abroad,
> And has more soul than thus to jig upon
> Their hymeneal night, I should suspect
> 'Twere he.
>
> (III.ii.87-91)

'Has . . . soul', another grouping of neutral verb and noun, is countered by the jolliness of 'jig'. The climax which follows is largely visual. Columbo and the masquers '*bring in* ALVAREZ *dead*' and when the king asks where he is, '*Columbo points to the body.*' The onlookers react at first with questions and exclamations, keeping words to a minimum. Language here is unobtrusive, so that the spectator concentrates on what he sees.

If the wordy style of which Bas complains is never far away, it is accompanied both by a simpler narrative manner and by a more vigorous, figurative diction. Occasionally however the heightened passages may seem overstated. In Act II, Rosaura receives Columbo's reply to her letter. Antonio's description of Columbo's angry response to the Duchess's message (II.ii.28-33) teases Rosaura, creating a spurious excitement. He motivates, but does not entirely justify the *frisson* of horror in her reaction:

> My soul doth bathe itself in a cold dew;
> Imagine I am opening of a tomb, [*Opens the letter.*]
> Thus I throw off the marble to discover
> What antic posture death presents in this
> Pale monument to fright me—
>
> (II.ii.39-43)

Columbo has released the Duchess. The extended imagery of death and the tomb creates an atmosphere of imminent and real disaster and seems gratuitously melodramatic, but with hindsight we may find it has prepared us for Columbo's menace and the death he brings. Similar imagery features in Hernando's soliloquy before the denouement (V.iii.56-83). Since Hernando, concealed in the Duchess's chamber, expects the Cardinal's entry and a chance for vengeance, images of death—hearse-cloth, mourners, ashes, ghost—are not inconsistent with events. The speech modulates successfully between Hernando's thoughts and his feelings and has a strong emotional unity which overcomes the stock diction.[33]

In general, Bas is right about Shirley's style. His commitment to the noun and to inert verbs results in a rather static verse. But Bas's selective method gives a flatter impression of Shirley's style than the dramatist deserves. If we attend to speaker and occasion we meet a variety of modes appropriate to the events of the plot. We are also driven to consider larger issues of tone. In this play a remarkable amount of the dialogue is talk by courtiers and about courtiers. Whereas the Jacobeans—in particular Webster—presented abnormal events taking place in a diseased and abnormal society, Shirley depicts an ordered court peopled in the main by well-intentioned, morally sane, if rather passive characters. Forker accuses the court of 'vacillation and polite cynicism' (p. lxvii) but his judgement ignores the attitudes of the two lords and the loyalty of Placentia and of Antonio, whose questionable jokes are excused as a reaction to the depressing atmosphere of the Duchess's household and whose seduction by Celinda shows his lack of sophistication. The language reflects the difference between Shirley and most of the Jacobeans. Jonson believed that 'Wheresoever, manners, and fashions are corrupted, Language is' (*Wks.,* VIII, 593). Webster developed a vein of rich, dark, obsessive imagery for his rich, dark, obsessive characters. Shirley's society is not on the moral alert but neither is it especially corrupt and its speech is fittingly undynamic but clear, neither perverse nor inspired. There is however one strong Jacobean connection—with Beaumont and Fletcher. They also use everyday language and Fletcher in particular has a 'command of the courtier's conversation'.[34] Undoubtedly they anticipated and influenced Shirley's Caroline mode. Yet there is a difference of tone. Beaumont and Fletcher lay more stress than Shirley on evil and unnatural passions; they create with their 'emotional rhetoric' 'a world apart', a world of extremes.[35] Shirley's catastrophe erupts with unexpected horror into an ordinary world and it is because evil is not the norm that *what* happens is significant. It may not even be too rash to note that in contemporary England terrible and inconceivable events had begun to strike a comfortable and sophisticated court.

Shirley's skilful plotting has been generally acknowledged; his contemporaries praised his language and even his detractors admit its clarity. But his virtues in plot and style are closely related to his alleged defects. Character is at times a function of the plot; the plain style does not achieve the depth and complexity for which Shakespeare is admired. Shirley seems to be weak in just those areas where the great Elizabethans and Jacobeans are most powerful: characterisation, imagery and theme. The people are often types; the weak king, the villainous favourite, the blunt soldier, the courtier, the virtuous heroine—the latter frequently set against a lady of easier morals. The imagery is competently marshalled from the Jacobean store but does little to stir the mind or the emotions. Muriel Bradbrook complains that Shirley borrows 'the whole of the Revenge convention except that living core which was its justification, the imagery, the peculiar tone, the poetry'.[36] And as a revenge play *The Cardinal* is little more than an action. Shirley does not make us think about the morality of revenge or about its effect on the avengers. One of the harshest comments on this play comes from Clifford Leech who, after praising Shirley's competence, cites *The Cardinal* as an example of 'the nullity of Caroline tragedy'.[37]

If we accept all these negatives we are bound to consider *The Cardinal* not worth reading or seeing twice. Yet if again we look at what happens in this play, instead of treating it as an anaemic Jacobean tragedy, we may find more to interest us. Bowers argues that *The Cardinal* does consider the ethics of revenge (p. 231), but it is rather late in the revenge tradition to expect much further illumination of the morality of vengeance, an ambiguous topic even in its heyday. Shir-

ley deploys the plot-motifs of revenge, the masque of death, the lustful villain, the devious poisoning, but despite its four avengers his play's themes and ideas have little to do with vengeance. Instead, Shirley touches on political issues. Current political thought was inevitably much occupied with monarchs and their advisers. One of the most powerful scenes in *The Cardinal* tackles the Cardinal's misuse of his authority. In Act II, scene iii, the Cardinal in disappointed rage attacks the Duchess and is in turn anatomised. Rosaura's denunciation is sincere and purposeful. She directs the Cardinal to begin his correction 'at home' and lists his villainies. An enemy of the people, a corrupter of the king and his court, he even injures the church he was installed to defend:

> 'tis your
> Ambition and scarlet sins that rob
> Her altar of the glory, and leave wounds
> Upon her brow; which fetches grief and paleness
> Into her cheeks; making her troubled bosom
> Pant with her groans, and shroud her holy blushes
> Within your reverend purples.

> (ll. 157-63)

She begs him to reform 'before the short-haired men / Do crowd and call for justice' (ll. 167-8). The pressure of contemporary events reinforces the Duchess's pleading but her speeches already have a strength and eloquence which deepen the play's effect. For a moment her personal battle spreads to the world outside. Critics have found in Shirley a 'serious attitude toward life and . . . severe morality',[38] and these speeches reveal a man deeply and movingly affected by wrong. Even the Cardinal, who has come to domineer, stays to applaud the Duchess's spirit.

Elsewhere Shirley draws attention to the king's role. Catherine Belsey has argued that 'in order to be a play about revenge, *The Cardinal* has to become a play about a crisis of justice'. The play is royalist, and presents the king as absolute, as the source of justice; he dominates in the key scenes (III.ii and the second half of V.iii) and cannot be considered a weak character since his behaviour is confident, his main speeches authoritative. The plot demands that his justice fail, since without Columbo's release there would be no need for revenge; Hernando undertakes a personal struggle for social justice in a world deserted by the divine justice which should have emanated from the king. Yet at the end of the play the king replaces Hernando as the dominant figure and blithely reminds us that kings must be on their guard. The action and the royalist theme are at odds.[39] I agree that the king is prominent in this play but I am not persuaded that plot confounds theme. The king's divine right is invoked in III.ii.108 and III.ii.196 although the second allusion is the Cardinal's and sounds like ironic flattery. If the king's power is absolute, his bent is conciliatory. The second lord's reaction to the Aragonian aggression is to wonder 'What have they, but the sweetness of the king, / To make a crime?' (I.i.62-3). When the king speaks to Hernando of the quarrel with Columbo he insists that 'we must have / You reconciled' (II.iii.1-2); he plans to compensate Alvarez for giving up Rosaura (II.iii.27-9); and he asks the Cardinal to forgive the Duchess: 'I heard you had a controversy with / The Duchess, I will have you friends' (III.i.49-50). Once Alvarez is dead, the king again sends the Cardinal to the Duchess 'To reconcile her to some peace' (IV.i.53). His initial reaction to the murderer is merciful:

> We thought to have put your victory and merits
> In balance with Alvarez' death, which while
> Our mercy was to judge, had been your safety.
>
> (III.ii.235-7)

He uses his authority, sensibly enough, to smooth over offences to others, but what he cannot ignore is an affront to himself. He may forgive Alvarez's murder but not 'the offence, / That with such boldness struck at me' (III.ii.207-8). Thus in his central speeches of judgement against Columbo, the king becomes syntactically both subject and object (III.ii.182-91, 200-205, 206-15, 235-40); he is both judge and victim. Forker accuses him of accepting evil 'with a rebuke to violated etiquette' (p. lxvii) but his reaction is not as morally frivolous as Forker's charge implies for, as Lawrence Stone explains (p. 232), physical attack at court was regarded as 'an exceptionally grave offence' since it could so easily put the monarch himself at risk. Columbo's imprisonment is for an assault on majesty, and thus his release is a defeat of the king's absolute authority, a defeat befitting a king whose favour is in his own words 'indulgence' (III.ii.209, V.iii.295). His final speech in the play once more centres on his own injury, not on the Duchess's death:

> How much are kings abused by those they take
> To royal grace! Whom, when they cherish most
> By nice indulgence, they do often arm
> Against themselves.
>
> (V.iii.293-6)

Here there is an interesting pattern as kings move from the passive ('are kings abused') to the active mode ('they take', 'they cherish', 'they . . . arm') to suffering object ('Against themselves'). In this context the banal last line, *None have more need of perspectives than kings*', becomes more relevant. Again the syntax makes its own point; the sentence is about kings but 'kings' is not unequivocally the grammatical subject. The absolutism is qualified, and for good reason. The king's misjudgements in enforcing the engagement to Columbo (III.ii.182-91), in freeing Columbo and in trusting the Cardinal as Rosaura's guardian precipitate the tragedy. He is indeed more important in this play than are the justicers in many earlier revenge plays, but his significance is not blurred by the plot. The central story is of the Duchess but she is destroyed because the king lacks 'perspectives'. Her fate illustrates on the private, personal level the political theme which informs the play, that of all people an absolute monarch cannot afford to be wrong.[40]

Such thematic material as *The Cardinal* contains has more to do with politics and justice than with revenge. Yet although the atmosphere is not that of the Jacobean revenge plays, there are some signs of a more disordered world which seem to belong to the darker settings of Shirley's predecessors. Not only does the play have a background of military strife but there are warnings of treason. Early in the play, the first lord remarks of the Aragonian offensive.

> This flame has breath at home to cherish it;
> There's treason in some hearts, whose faces are
> Smooth to the state.
>
> (I.i.70-2)

We expect the treachery in court to have some link with the smooth faces and plotting hearts of the main plot, but the hints are not taken up, although treason, treachery and betrayal lurk in the play. The Cardinal is believed to control spies (I.i.19-20). Columbo accuses Hernando of being either a coward or a traitor (II.i.36-7), and the accusation rankles. Hernando later tells the Duchess: 'If you will call me coward, which is equal / To think I am a traitor, I forgive it' (IV.ii.150-1). The Duchess suspects she may be betrayed (IV.ii.144-5), and Hernando fears betrayal (V.ii.77, V.iii.123), but both use the term in a weakened, personal sense. Treason is part of the metaphoric structure which supports Shirley's plot.

It is not misleading to speak of a metaphoric structure since, despite the plainness and lack of poetic richness, Shirley uses his imagery thematically to point up the play's main oppositions and connections. Appropriately in a play which begins with the topics of love and war, Shirley applies the standard comparison between them. Columbo is first characterised as 'The darling of the war, whom victory / Hath often courted' (I.i.23-4), Valeria remarks that 'war and grim- / Faced honour are his mistresses' (I.ii.55-6), and he himself thinks of kissing women as 'court tactics' (I.ii.107). Military imagery accompanies him through the play, whereas the Duchess is forced to play a passive role. Publicly she speaks of 'A peace concluded 'twixt my grief and me', while privately regretting that 'I must counterfeit a peace, when all / Within me is at mutiny' (I.ii.16 and 27-8). Even after planning revenge she pretends, to protect herself, that the Cardinal has given her 'sorrow so much truce' (IV.ii.304).

There are many allusions to the bleeding wounds of love and war; the strong characters actively inflict bloody wounds and their opponents bleed. For Alvarez, who protests that he 'would not shrink to bleed / Out [his] warm stock of life' (II.iii.25-6), hyperbole becomes fact. In contrast Columbo sheds blood, dealing out 'bloody execution' (III.ii.213); his soul 'is purpled o'er, and reeks with innocent blood' (IV.ii.45). Relationship is defined in terms of blood (II.iii.106) as too is rank (I.ii.201), and even the colour of blood is significant. In the Cardinal's red-robed presence is figured the blood which spills from his ambitious plans. There must be a strong temptation to any designer to exploit the play's dominant red and purple.[41]

The imagery enhances the play's emotional antitheses. The Duchess's side stands for love and peace. There are metaphors of growth: 'Now the king / Hath planted us, methinks we grow already' (II.iii.60-1). A comparison may derive from religion—the Duchess's fame 'stands upon an innocence as clear / As the devotions you pay to heaven' (II.iii.117-18); or from natural beauty—the Duchess is 'Serene, as I / Have seen the morning rise upon the spring' (II.i.117-18). Opposing the gentle vein are warfare and violence, the spilling of blood, disease, fire, storm and devilry. Yet despite their appeal to the feelings, the images ultimately have an intellectual rather than an imaginative effect. The allusions to the devil, for instance, lack resonance. This is because the Cardinal, to whom they usually apply (as at III.i.74 and V.iii.54), is a limited embodiment of evil. 'Devil' tells us what to think of him, but his 'cloven foot' (V.iii.165) does not chill us as does Iago's. The metaphorical world of *The Cardinal* does not stretch our imaginations, nor does it provoke a gut response to good and evil; it works as an aid to moral clarity, providing a coherent figurative background to the plot and characters.

The characters are, in many of Shirley's plays, his weakest point but in *The Cardinal* we come across some unexpected variation. Richard Gerber writes of a grand style being given to tiny people, of villains who are villains in a small way.[42] Initially this criticism seems true of the Cardinal. His pride is repeatedly stressed; he is disliked and distrusted; but his prime aim in the early parts of the play is to advance his family by marrying his nephew to a fortune. The complaints about his pride and villainy are inadequately borne out by his actions, although his practice of lurking in the background when he enters a room may substantiate the accusations of spying. When he turns rapist and murderer, he is motivated by the straightforward desire to avenge his nephew. Yet as he moves from venial plotting to an intellectual pleasure in planning rape only to find himself sensually aroused by his own vengeance, we may detect once again this play's atmosphere of disturbance and evil rising out of the ordinary. The Cardinal's moment of lust contrasts with the mental control of a man whose reaction to his nephew's crime

is 'Now to come off were brave' (III.ii.112), and who reacts in the same way to his own death:

> now it would be rare,
> If you but waft me with a little prayer,
> My wings that flag may catch the wind.
>
> (V.iii.279-81)

His main opponent seems for much of the play a firm character. The Duchess is burdened with our memories of the Duchess of Malfi and of Bel-Imperia but she has a considerable presence. She stage-manages her release by Columbo; she confronts the Cardinal boldly, sending a nervous Alvarez to wait in the garden; she turns the Cardinal's attention from her own follies by denouncing his crimes. Although her feigned madness alternating with apparently genuine insanity derives from Hamlet, Shirley gives it his own gentle, rather pretty stamp. But the plot works against the Duchess's characterisation. She who was so positive becomes passive, dependent on Hernando's help. The change is highlighted by the structural similarity between I.ii and IV.ii: in I.ii, the Duchess is in control during her interviews with Columbo and Alvarez; in IV.ii, she is weak and defeated. Columbo hectors her and Hernando takes over her task of revenge. Although the Cardinal grows in villainy he is matched with no mighty opposite, for as he begins to show his 'cloven foot' the Duchess, who had earlier displayed a spirit 'to tame the devil's' (II.iii.170), crumples. Her collapse removes tension from the central conflict. Yet the combination of submission and insistence on choosing her own husband is interesting. Three years after *The Cardinal,* Lady Anne Halkett began a struggle to be matched with the man of her choice but eventually, Stone records, 'made a practical prosaic match of the most traditional kind'. Stone regards her story as typical of the seventeenth century—a woman caught between the tradition of female submissiveness and new ideas of independence and personal decision.[43] The Duchess is not unlike Anne Halkett.

The Duchess's choice in marriage is puzzling. Alvarez is a courtier, a type often criticised by Shirley.[44] Columbo and the Cardinal make an issue of his courtliness. Columbo despises this 'curlèd minion' (III.ii.137), and the Cardinal compares the two suitors:

> Because Alvarez has a softer cheek,
> Can like a woman trim his wanton hair,
> Spend half a day with looking in the glass
> To find a posture to present himself,
> And bring more effeminacy than man
> Or honour to your bed; must he supplant him?
>
> (II.iii.109-14)

Although prejudiced, these remarks must exaggerate the truth; they are unlikely to be a flat lie. Interestingly, the Restoration cast list preserved in the Leeds University copy of Octavo shows that in the early 1660s Alvarez was played by Kynaston shortly after that actor had given up the female roles for which he was famous. Less biased commentators also hint at Alvarez's weakness. The first lord praises his wisdom in not insisting on his prior claim to the Duchess, but the other lord is doubtful. Alvarez has 'tamely' renounced the Duchess (I.i.30): 'If wisdom, not inborn fear, make him compose, / I like it' (I.i.43-4). Alvarez confirms his suspicions. In his first interview with the Duchess, he outlines the dangers, from king, Cardinal, and Columbo, that confront himself and Rosaura. 'Then you do look on these with fear', she responds (I.ii.217). He protests that his concern is for her, but he does fear. In II.iii, he watches with trepidation the Cardinal's approach. 'Take no notice of his presence', advises the Duchess, 'Leave me to meet and answer it' (ll. 66-7). He obeys. She is the dominant partner in birth and personality. Here we *are* reminded of the Duchess of Malfi. Alvarez's submission and lack of eagerness to stand by her make us uneasy, especially when his offer to give her up to Columbo is preceded by thoughts of himself:

I am a man on whom but late the king
Has pleased to cast a beam, which was not meant
To make me proud, but wisely to direct
And light me to my safety.

(I.ii.188-91)

The Duchess is not thinking of safety, nor later is Hernando, who leaves his 'own security' to avenge Alvarez (V.iii.67). Even Valeria's no doubt politic praise of Alvarez's sweet composition, speaking eyes and natural black curls (I.ii.37 and 39-42), accords with the Cardinal's criticism. So does Alvarez's speech. His first appearance is marked by impersonal compliment (I.ii.161-3) and a balanced and antithetical syntax redolent of courtliness and cautious premeditation (I.ii.167-71 and 177-9). He is an unusual choice for one of Shirley's heroines. Does Shirley here couple courtliness with timidity, and hint that the Duchess loves unworthily?

Consider the man she rejects. Columbo is a blunt soldier, a type favoured by Shirley, and often set to his advantage against a courtly foil. Shirley breaks down the usual associations by setting Columbo against Hernando, another soldier, as well as against Alvarez. At first he seems stock. Valeria's remark that 'His talk will fright a lady' (I.ii.55) promises someone resembling Beaumont and Fletcher's Memnon in *The Mad Lover,* but when Columbo appears he breaks that mould:

Madam, he kisseth your white hand, that must
Not surfeit in this happiness—and ladies,
I take your smiles for my encouragement;
I have not long to practise these court tactics.

(I.ii.104-7)

This is polished enough, with a touch of old-fashioned formality in the inflected ending of 'kisseth'. Celinda admires his expert embrace.[45] Columbo is not a villain. The first lord praises him, finding even his pride appropriate (I.i.23-7), and even after Alvarez's murder, the same lord is prepared to make excuses for Columbo (IV.i.38-9). He has the stage soldier's hasty temper, as one of his own colonels concedes (II.i.140), and yet he does not seem wholly unjustified in attacking Hernando as a coward since Hernando's strategy is to sit tight until the enemy eat and drink themselves into a stupor. His summoning of a council of war implies deviousness since he already knows of a plot to betray the city they are menacing and thus he needs no advice. But the council is less a test of Columbo's supporters than a device prompted by the plot's demand for a quarrel with Columbo which will give Hernando a personal motive for revenge. In the same scene Columbo's brusque 'No poetry' in response to Antonio's fanciful description of the Duchess (II.i.117-20) is the kind of reaction Shirley usually gives to favoured characters.

In the context of Shirley's attitudes to courtiers and soldiers, Columbo and Alvarez reward scrutiny; the courtier plays the juvenile lead, the uncourtly soldier is a 'villain'. The contrast is not thoroughly worked out. Alvarez is too empty to interest us for long, Columbo is not a bad man. Yet there is just enough complexity, intended or not, to make us wonder about the Duchess's judgement in choosing Alvarez, and her justification for treating Columbo as she does. His revenge becomes vindictive when he threatens to destroy all future lovers but he has perhaps some grounds for his murderous reaction against Alvarez. We do begin to question our assumptions about avengers and their victims. Although Shirley does not concentrate our attention on the moral issues of revenge we are left with some thinking to do.

The play which Shirley reckoned 'the best of my flock' (Dedication, l. 11) has ever since had a mixed reception. In 1671, Edward Howard ranked it among 'the highest of our English Tragedies', but a century later Charles Dibdin found it 'a very dull thing'. Praise of *The Cardinal* is, on the whole, qualified: the play 'can hold its own with any but the greatest masterpieces of that age' (Parrott and Ball); it is 'a notable romantic tragedy' (Nason); in 'construction and actability' it is one of the best of the Elizabethan revenge plays (Bowers). Schelling points to what may be the dramatist's main drawback when he comments that Shirley has 'the shortcomings of the moderate man'.[46] For *The Cardinal* could be seen as the work of a man too much in control, perhaps even with too sane and untroubled a mind.[47] Shirley is an elegant craftsman; a swift, well-organised plot progresses with the help of a clear style, a competent varying of register and a simple but coherent structure of imagery. Theme, characterisation and images lack the imaginative excitement of the Jacobeans. Yet the ambiguous treatment of Rosaura's lovers and the embryonic political themes of the play invite an intellectual response, and our feelings as well as our minds are impressed by this representation of sudden disastrous events exploding in a relatively civilised and well-behaved court. For all its Jacobean ingredients, *The Cardinal* is a tragedy of its own times.

ORIGINAL STAGING AND THEATRE HISTORY

Although we have no contemporary drawing or description of the Blackfriars Theatre, enough detail of its location and dimensions is revealed in legal documents for several recent researchers to have evolved precise, if conflicting, ideas of the theatre's size and structure.[48] The plays known to have been performed at Blackfriars give us some evidence about the stage equipment.[49] *The Cardinal,* like other Blackfriars plays, calls for relatively simple staging. The entrances at the beginning of Act I indicate two doors in the back of the stage; two lords enter 'at one door', Antonio 'at the other'. The theatre could accommodate flights, and entrances through a trapdoor, but *The Cardinal* makes no use of such spectacle although the servants discuss whether a masque complete with descending throne would be preferable to their play. Hernando's eavesdropping in Act V needs hangings for concealment, and the theatre's bell rouses the court at the catastrophe. The play makes no special demands, though T. J. King considers a tree necessary for the garden (p. 77). John Freehafer argues that by 1635 the private theatres were occasionally using perspective scenery but none of his evidence comes from Shirley's plays.[50]

The simple staging is not primitive staging. The King's Men were a sophisticated company, used to performing at court, and their dramatist was the author of *The Triumph of Peace,* the most spectacular masque of the Caroline period. *The Cardinal* shows some signs of spectacle deliberately avoided. Alvarez is killed during a masque, but by masquers whose entertainment is rudimentary, who lead their prey offstage, and who return bearing his body. Instead of focusing on the murder, Shirley shows reactions to the murder. He does include an onstage duel and Hernando's rescue of the Duchess from rape but he stages the final deaths unflamboyantly. Neither the Cardinal nor the Duchess seems to suffer much from taking poison. Their deaths are rapid and quiet. There is no stage direction to describe Hernando's death and so we can only speculate about whether his is a quick suicide or a more spectacular struggle. Suicide seems not to be in character, and Hernando's reference to 'sport' (V.iii.181) echoes his pleasure in the duel (IV.iii.16). His opponents are the foppish Antonelli and the Cardinal's servants, whom we may expect to overwhelm him with numbers rather than spirited sword-play. Shirley does not always seize opportunities for display. Disaster comes swiftly and sud-

denly. The stagecraft, as does the language, presents a fairly normal world with brief intrusions of violence. Indeed for a dramatist whose main output was Fletcherian tragicomedy the comparative calm of *The Cardinal*'s moments of crisis is notable.

The play's later stage history is patchy. The existence of an alternative prologue which, with its allusion to the court's sojourn in York, could not have belonged to the original performance, suggests a revival in 1642.[51] After the Restoration, *The Cardinal* seems to have been popular for a while, perhaps—G. E. Bentley suggests (V, 1087)—because of the actor Hart, who had earlier gained his reputation in the part of Rosaura. Sir Henry Herbert records a performance on 23 July 1662 by the King's Company.[52] The cast for this revival—or for the performance on 2 October 1662—may well be that recorded in the copy of Octavo held in the Brotherton Library at Leeds University; the list includes Theophilus Bird (Second Lord) who was dead by 1663, and Walter Clun (Antonio) who was murdered in 1664. Several of the cast were boy actors before 1642. Charles Hart now played Hernando, one of a long series of major roles which included Mosca, Hotspur, Brutus, and Othello, a part which he took over from Nicholas Burt (the Cardinal). Columbo was given to Michael Mohun, who was later to play Volpone, Face, and Iago; Alvarez was Edward Kynaston, who had recently graduated from female roles. William Wintershall, noted as a comedian, took the minor part of First Lord, and the remaining roles attributed went to less well-known actors: Blagden (King), Marmaduke Watson (Alphonso), Bateman (Antonelli). Shortly afterwards we hear from Pepys, for whom the play seems to have improved on acquaintance. On 2 October 1662 he was cool about *The Cardinal*: 'a tragedy I had never seen before, nor is there any great matter in it'. 24 August 1667 found him won over with the help of the acting: 'After dinner, we to a play and there saw *The Cardinall* at the King's House, wherewith I am mightily pleased; but above all with Becke Marshall.' And on 27 April 1668 his approval was unqualified: at the King's playhouse he 'saw most of *The Cardinall,* a good play'.[53]

The great gap that follows is interrupted by a play on which *The Cardinal* had a small influence, Sophia Lee's *Almeyda, Queen of Granada,* performed at the Theatre Royal in Drury Lane on 20 April 1796.[54] The advertisement tells us: 'The story of ALMEYDA is wholly a fiction; and the incident which produces the catastrophe the only one not my own.—The deep impression made on me, long since, by a similar denouement, in an old play of JAMES SHIRLEY's, determined me to apply it.'[55] There are hints of other ingredients from *The Cardinal.* The Moorish Almeyda, who has been hostage to the King of Castile and loves his son, is returned as heir to Granada on her father's death. She has to rejoin the Moors while her lover Alonzo is at war. Abdallah her uncle plans to force her to marry his son Orasmyn. Alonzo is captured while secretly visiting Almeyda and she, mistakenly believing him dead, runs mad. Abdallah tries to persuade her to abdicate but is led to confess his own crimes. When Almeyda then faints, Abdallah, pretending she is poisoned, sends for an antidote which he drinks first. Abdallah, unlike the Cardinal, has knowingly killed himself in destroying his victim.

There have been few twentieth-century productions. The New York Public Library holds a programme for a performance by senior students at the Feagin School of Drama and Radio, in November 1948. For four performances *The Cardinal* hit Fifth Avenue. More important is the 1970 production at Farnham's Castle Theatre, the predecessor of the Redgrave Theatre. Malcolm Griffiths's production of *The Cardinal* with Maev Alexander as the Duchess and Brendan Barry as the Cardinal roused conflicting reactions. At worst Shirley was described as a dramatist who wrote 'at the fag end of a blood-and-thunder tradition'; at best came claims that the play had 'the violence of Marlowe, the robustness of Jonson and the poetry of Shakespeare'.[56] What the critics pitched on was the very element of spectacle which I have argued is played down; the duel, attempted rape, suicide and most notably the murder of Alvarez.[57] There are two reasons for such an emphasis. In the context of other revenge tragedies Shirley's seems subdued but as one play in a season of calmer productions it is bound to seem typically bloodthirsty. Also stage effect was accentuated by one major peculiarity of the production. Alvarez's death did not occur offstage. Instead, during the wedding entertainment, he was invited to stand in a magician's vanishing box. He did not vanish but was apparently electrocuted. Presumably this coup de théâtre was added because the play was felt not to be startling enough in its first catastrophe, but inevitably its inclusion affects not just one scene but the tone of the whole play. My own memory of this production is of an honest revival which did not quite test the play's own merits. It would have been interesting to see whether Shirley's central scene, with the emphasis less on the murder than on its aftermath, was strong enough in its original form.

The most recent appearance of *The Cardinal* is also the most unexpected. In January 1979, the Magic Theatre of San Francisco staged *The Red Snake* by Michael McLure, who updated 'a near-forgotten, unplayable late Renaissance play by James Shirley called *The Cardinal.*'[58] Michael McLure, John Lion the director, and Peter Coyote, who played the Cardinal, are all prominent in experimental and controversial theatre; the Magic Theatre Company specialises in new works, often by new dramatists. What did this group of modern talents do with *The Cardinal*? The play seems to have been pared to its plot. Cardinal, king, Duchess, Columbo

and Alvarez (the last two shortened to Collum and Dalv)[59] are bound in the same basic relationships except that the play 'begins and ends with' the Cardinal's 'erotic advances on the equally calculating Duchess' who has 'a will to power that equals any of the men's' and 'a healthy, well-indulged sexual appetite'.[60] Modern slang is substituted for Shirley's dialogue, not with entire success. Bernard Weiner complains about the uneasy blend of styles: 'McLure's characters are often into spouting philosophy and poetic observations about love, death and everything in between, so that their constant descent into scatology seems forced, overworked and, on several occasions, ludicrous.'[61] The theatre's press release of 20 December 1978 suggests a stronger political and social intent than emerges from Shirley's play: *The Red Snake* 'examines the brutality and corruption of sex, religion, politics, money and war'. These themes were reinforced by the setting, described by Weiner as an 'abstract icy cave' which gradually became blood-stained, and the costumes, at first white, later black and red. Although McLure fundamentally altered *The Cardinal* it says much for Shirley's play that a modern dramatist could find himself so 'greatly attracted to Shirley's play' that it inspired a new direction in his own writing.[62]

Notes

1. See Forsythe and the notes to the present edition. The other five of Shirley's *Six New Playes* are full of anticipations and memories of *The Cardinal.*

2. Boas, p. 376; Forker, pp. xxxvii-xlvii. Forker notes the possible influence of *H8,* II.iv and III.i, where Wolsey confronts Katherine.

3. *C.S.P.D.,* 1635, pp. viii-ix. In the years preceding the writing of *The Cardinal* many cases are recorded of men arraigned for accusing Laud of popery, e.g. 's 1633-4, p. 207; 1634-5, p. 22; 1638-9, pp. 213-14. For a general study of Caroline drama's interest in politics see Frank Occhiogrosso, 'Sovereign and Subject in Caroline Tragedy' (unpublished doctoral dissertation, Johns Hopkins University, 1969).

4. See Forsythe, pp. 96-7. Official reaction against *The Cardinal's Conspiracy* in 1639 (Bentley, *Profession,* pp. 180-1) indicates why Shirley could not earlier have risked this particular villain.

5. See pp. 19-20.

6. *Shakespeare's Tragedies and Other Studies in Seventeenth Century Drama* (London, 1950), pp. 161 and 178.

7. '"Wits most accomplished Senate"; The Audience of the Caroline Private Theaters', *S.E.L.,* XVIII (1978), 341-60.

8. G. E. Bentley, 'The Diary of a Caroline Theater-goer', *M.P.*, XXXV (1937-8), 61-72 (p. 72); Arthur C. Kirsch, 'A Caroline Commentary on the drama', *M.P.*, LXVI (1968-9), 256-61.

9. Leech, p. 178; Neill, p. 356.

10. See pp. 11-12.

11. For Shirley's comments on his plots, see prologues to *The Brothers* and *The Doubtful Heir* (I, 191; IV, 279).

12. Alfred Harbage, *Cavalier Drama*, (New York 1936), p. 165; Jakob Schipper, *James Shirley. Sein Leben und Seine Werke* (Vienna and Leipzig, 1911), p. 355. See also Bas, pp. 187-9, and Forker, pp. lxii-lxv.

13. *The Complete Works of Algernon Charles Swinburne,* ed. Edmund Gosse and Thomas Wise, 20 vols. (London, 1925-7), XII, 340. In 1885, Swinburne discouraged A. C. Bullen from editing Shirley's plays (*The Swinburne Letters,* ed. Cecil Y. Lang, 6 vols., New Haven, 1959-62, V, 95, 96, and 118).

14. See also *Love's Cruelty,* ed. John F. Nims, Garland Renaissance Drama (New York and London, 1980), p. lxi.

15. *Complete Works,* XII, 363.

16. Emrys Jones (*Scenic Form in Shakespeare,* Oxford, 1971, p. 69) cites the argument that this kind of twofold structure was common in Elizabethan drama.

17. See Forsythe, p. 71.

18. Flaviano pretends conversion in *The Imposture,* II.i (Forsythe, p. 71), but in the earlier play the audience is alerted to falsehood. Cf. Dekker's *Match Me in London,* III.i (Forker): Don John eats grapes with Valasco, pretends to be poisoned and sends for an antidote. Valasco drinks and falls—but Don John has himself been deceived with a sleeping potion instead of poison.

19. A 'disingenuous' stratagem, review of Gifford, *The American Quarterly Review,* XVI (1834), 103-66, p. 163; see also Boas, p. 375.

20. Boas, p. 377; also Bas, p. 252.

21. Shirley liked to save the truly innocent—Albina in *The Politician,* Eubella in *Love's Cruelty.*

22. Harvey, *Ciceronianus,* introd. H. S. Wilson, trans. C. A. Forbes, Studies in the Humanities, 4 (Lincoln, Nebraska, 1945), p. 63. Jonson (*Wks.,* VIII, 622) echoes John Hoskins's *Directions for Speech and Style* (1590), ed. H. H. Hudson (Princeton, 1935), p. xxvii.

23. See the verses by Edmund Colles, John Fox, Philip Massinger, and John Jackson (Gifford, I, lxix, lxxiii, lxxix, and lxxxviii-lxxxix). *The Cardinal* does however have some murky patches (Gifford, V, 300n.).

24. But see Felix E. Schelling, *Elizabethan Drama 1558-1642,* 2 vols. (Boston and New York, 1908), II, 326 ('limpid and perspicuous'); W. H. Williams, *Specimens of the Elizabethan Drama* (Oxford, 1905), p. 418 ('graceful, fluent, and perspicuous').

25. 'James Shirley's Uses of *Language*', *S.E.L.,* VI (1966), 323-39 (pp. 332 and 339). Cf. Nason's praise of *The Cardinal*'s intellectual unity (p. 346).

26. 'Of Complements', *Essayes* (1600-1), ed. Don Cameron Allen (Baltimore, Md., 1946), pp. 90-1.

27. *The Letters of Dorothy Osborne to William Temple,* ed. G. C. Moore Smith (Oxford, 1928), p. 91 (September 1653).

28. *The Fortescue Papers,* ed. Samuel R. Gardiner, Camden Society (London, 1871), p. 128 (May 1620); *Letters and Papers of the Verney Family,* ed. John Bruce, Camden Society (London, 1853), p. 125 (July 1626); *The Oxinden Letters, 1607-1642,* ed. Dorothy Gardiner (London, 1933), p. 105 (July 1635); *The Autobiography and Correspondence of Sir Simonds D'Ewes,* ed. James O. Halliwell, 2 vols. (London, 1845), II, 294 (July 1642).

29. Philomusus (John Gough), augmented 7th ed. (1646).

30. Ralph Verney's tutor wrote to his protégé in 1633: 'what else the court may alter in others, it hath not made you soe little reall as to measure a friend by a compliment', *Memoirs of the Verney Family During the Civil War,* ed. Frances P. Verney, 2 vols. (London, 1892), I, 124-5.

31. Shirley may himself have perpetrated a compliment book. *Wits Labyrinth* by 'J. S.' (1648) was tentatively attributed by Malone (in his copy, now in the Bodleian Library) to Shirley.

32. One counter to the formality is Shirley's characteristic colloquial contraction (wo', sho', 'em). See Cyrus Hoy, 'The Shares of Fletcher and his Collaborators in the Beaumont and Fletcher Canon (IV)', *S.B.,* XII (1959), 91-116 (p. 109); Ronald M. Huebert, 'On Detecting John Ford's Hand: A Fallacy', *The Library,* XXVI (1971), 256-9.

33. Forker, p. lxix, and George Saintsbury (*A History of English Prosody,* 3 vols., London, 1906-10, II, 308) praise Hernando's speech.

34. Clifford Leech, *The John Fletcher Plays* (London, 1962), p. 137.

35. Eugene M. Waith, *The Pattern of Tragicomedy in Beaumont and Fletcher* (New Haven, 1952), pp. 24-5.

36. *Themes and Conventions of Elizabethan Tragedy* (Cambridge, 1935), p. 266; see also Baskerville, p. 1577.

37. *Shakespeare's Tragedies and Other Studies in Seventeenth Century Drama*, p. 40.

38. Nason, writing of Shirley's London comedies, p. 287; see also S. J. Radtke, *James Shirley: His Catholic Philosophy of Life* (Washington, D.C., 1929).

39. 'Tragedy, Justice and the Subject', *1642: Literature and Power in the Seventeenth Century*, ed. Francis Barker and others (Colchester, 1981), pp. 166-86.

40. See pp. 5-6 for some contemporary historical parallels.

41. See the account of *The Red Snake* on pp. 29-30.

42. *James Shirley, Dramatiker der Decadenz*, Swiss Studies in English, XXX (Berne, 1952), p. 58.

43. *The Family, Sex and Marriage in England, 1500-1800* (London, 1977), p. 307.

44. For instance in *Honoria and Mammon*.

45. But Columbo's revenge offends court etiquette (Richard Morton, 'Deception and Social Dislocation: An Aspect of James Shirley's Drama', *Renaissance Drama*, IX, 1966, 227-45, p. 233).

46. Howard, preface to *The Womens Conquest*, sig. A3v; Dibdin, *A Complete History of the English Stage*, 5 vols. (London, 1797-1800), IV, 45; Thomas M. Parrott and Robert H. Ball, *A Short View of Elizabethan Drama* (New York, 1943), p. 277; Nason, p. 361; Bowers, p. 230; Schelling, *Elizabethan Drama*, II, 428.

47. Bas, p. 341, thinks Shirley was too fundamentally optimistic and orthodox about man and his destiny to write tragedy.

48. Richard Hosley, 'A Reconstruction of the Second Blackfriars', *The Elizabethan Theatre I*, ed. David Galloway (Toronto, 1969), pp. 74-88, thinks the stage was relatively small. See the counter-argument in David Whitmarsh-Knight, 'The Second Blackfriars: The Globe Indoors', *T.N.*, XXVII (1972-3), 94-8.

49. See T. J. King, *Shakespearean Staging, 1599-1642* (Cambridge, Mass., 1971). King queries the methods and findings of Irwin Smith, *Shakespeare's Blackfriars Playhouse* (London, 1966).

50. 'Perspective Scenery and the Caroline Playhouses', *T.N.*, XXVII (1972-3), 98-113.

51. The prologue is assigned to *The Cardinal* in Shirley's *Poems, etc.* (1646) but attached to *The Sisters* in *Six New Playes*. See Appendix II.

52. Herbert, p. 118. The details of the actors who may have played in this production are taken from E. Nungezer, *A Dictionary of Actors* (New Haven, 1929), and John Downes, *Roscius Anglicanus*, ed. Montague Summers (London, n.d.). The Leeds copy also names, in a different hand, eight Caroline actors, but since three of those named (John Rice, Nicholas Tooley and John Honyman) had either left the company or were dead by 1636 the list must simply be an uninformed guess. The other actors listed are Robert Benfield, Thomas Pollard, John Lowin, Joseph Taylor, and Richard Robinson. Oct. records that Thomas Pollard spoke the epilogue.

53. *The Diary of Samuel Pepys*, ed. R. C. Latham and W. Matthews (London, 1970-83), III, 211-12; VIII, 399; IX, 177.

54. Genest, *The English Stage, 1660-1830*, 10 vols. (Bath, 1832), VII, 238-40.

55. London, 1796.

56. Eric Shorter, *Daily Telegraph,* February 1970; *Farnham Herald,* February 1970.

57. *Daily Telegraph, Surrey and Hants. Newsletter, Farnham Herald,* all February 1970.

58. Doug Shaffer, *San Francisco Bay Guardian,* 1 February 1979.

59. Valeria becomes Val, Celinda Seely, and Hernando Hern.

60. *San Francisco Bay Guardian,* 1 February 1979.

61. *San Francisco Chronicle,* 15 January 1979.

62. *San Francisco Chronicle,* 8 January 1979.

Abbreviations

Sʜɪʀʟᴇʏ: Eᴅɪᴛɪᴏɴs Cᴏʟʟᴀᴛᴇᴅ

Gifford: *The Dramatic Works and Poems of James Shirley,* ed. William Gifford and Alexander Dyce, 6 vols. (London, 1833).

Gosse: *James Shirley,* ed. Edmund Gosse, Mermaid Series (London, 1888).

Forker: *The Cardinal,* ed. Charles R. Forker (Bloomington, Ind., 1964).

Oᴛʜᴇʀ

Bas: Georges Bas, *James Shirley (1596-1666): Dramaturge Caroléen* (Lille, 1973).

Beaumont and Fletcher, *Wks.: The Works of Francis Beaumont and John Fletcher,* ed. A. Glover and A. R. Waller, 10 vols. (Cambridge, 1905-12).

Bentley: Gerald E. Bentley, *The Jacobean and Caroline Stage,* 7 vols. (Oxford, 1941-68).

Bentley, *Profession:* Gerald E. Bentley, *The Profession of Dramatist in Shakespeare's Time, 1590-1642* (Princeton, 1971).

Boas: F. S. Boas, *An Introduction to Stuart Drama* (London, 1946).

Bowers: Fredson Bowers, *Elizabethan Revenge Tragedy, 1587-1642* (Princeton, 1940).

C.S.P.D.: Calendar of State Papers, Domestic Series.

Forsythe: Robert S. Forsythe, *The Relations of Shirley's Plays to the Elizabethan Drama* (New York, 1914).

Herbert: *The Dramatic Records of Sir Henry Herbert,* ed. Joseph Q. Adams (New Haven, 1917).

Jonson, *Wks.: Ben Jonson,* ed. C. H. Herford and Percy and Evelyn Simpson, 11 vols. (Oxford, 1925-52).

Nason: Arthur H. Nason, *James Shirley, Dramatist* (New York, 1915).

FURTHER READING

Criticism

Bas, George. "More about the Anonymous *Tragedy of the Cruell Warre* and James Shirley's *The Triumph of Peace.*" *Cahiers Élisabéthans* 17 (April 1980): 43-57.
>   Examines the anonymous pamphlet as an adaptation of Shirley's masque into anti-Cavalier, anti-Catholic propaganda

Cogan, Nathan. "James Shirley's *The Example* (1634): Some Reconsiderations." *SEL* 17, no. 2 (spring 1977): 317-31.
>   Revisits *The Example,* deemed the best of Shirley's work by Victorian critics but generally ignored in the twentieth-century, and examines the play's place in the development of Shirley's city comedies.

Keller, James R. "James Shirley's *The Politician* and the Demand for Responsible Government in the Court of Charles I." *Journal of the Rocky Mountain Medieval and Renaissance Association* 18 (1997): 179-99.
>   Suggests that in this work Shirley treats the tension between the infallibility of the king and the argument that a king could be mislead by his advisors, discussing the impeachment of the Duke of Buckingham as context.

McGrath, Juliet. "James Shirley's Use of Language." *SEL* 6, no. 2 (spring 1966): 323-40.
>   Discusses Shirley's use of the word "language" in several plays, noting his distrust of its reliability.

McKinnen, Dana G. "A Description of a Restoration Promptbook of Shirley's *The Ball.*" *Restoration and Eighteenth-Century Theatre Research* 20, no. 2 (May 1971): 25-28.
>   Examines text notes from a Restoration production of *The Ball* that suggest that the play had a longer stage history than previously thought.

Milhous, Judith and Robert D. Hume. "A 1660s Promptbook of Shirley's *Loves Cruelty.*" *Theatre Research International* 11, no. 1 (spring 1986): 1-13.
>   Notes casting information and significant cuts made to religious and bawdy sections of the text of a 1660s production of *Love's Cruelty.*

Morillo, Marvin. "Shirley's 'Preferment' and the Court of Charles I." *SEL* 1, no. 2 (spring 1961): 101-18.
>   Attributes Shirley's declining status within the Caroline court to the playwright's criticism of licentiousness at court, his lack of interest in Platonic romance, and to the rise of the highly ambitious playwright William Davenant.

Radtke, Stephen J. *James Shirley: His Catholic Philosophy of Life.* Washington, D.C.: Catholic University of America, 1929, 113 p.
>   Analyzes the influence of Catholic principles in Shirley's works, citing the playwright's treatment of marriage, confession, and prayer as examples.

Randall, Dale B. J. "Mungrell Masques and Their Kin." In *Winter Fruit: English Drama, 1642-1660,* pp. 157-83. Lexington: University Press of Kentucky, 1995.
>   Examines performances of masques during the Commonwealth, beginning with Shirley's lesser known *Triumph of Beauty* and *Cupid and Death.*

Sharpe, Kevin. "The Caroline Court Masque." In *Criticism and Compliment: The Politics of Literature in the England of Charles I,* pp. 179-64. Cambridge: Cambridge University Press, 1987.
>   Looks at *The Triumph of Peace* as an instance of the masque's potential for both praise and careful dissent.

Spinrad, Phoebe S. "James Shirley: Decadent or Realist?" *English Language Notes* 35, no. 4 (June 1988): 24-32.
>   Defends Shirley from characterization as a decadent whose plays mark the decline of Renaissance drama and argues that his realism reflects his tumultuous era.

Venuti, Lawrence. "The Politics of Allusion: The Gentry and Shirley's *The Triumph of Peace*." *English Literary Renaissance* 16, no. 1 (winter 1986): 182-205.

Focuses on Shirley's allusion to Charles I's prohibition of the gentry's residence in London in *The Triumph of Peace*.

Walker, Kim. "*New Prison*: Representing the Female Actor in Shirley's *The Bird in a Cage*." *English Literary Renaissance* 21, no. 3 (autumn 1991): 385-400.

Interprets Shirley's play in the context of the controversy over William Prynne's anti-theatrical polemic *Histriomastix* and Queen Henrietta-Maria's participation in court theatricals.

Wertheim, Albert. "Games and Courtship in James Shirley's *Hyde Park*." *Anglia* 90 (1972): 71-91.

Examines the connection between setting and theme of *Hyde Park*. Wertheim draws an analogy between horse racing in Hyde Park and competition among suitors for the love of the heroines.

————. "James Shirley and the Caroline Masques of Ben Jonson." *Theatre Notebook* 27, no. 4 (summer 1973): 157-61.

Analyzes Shirley's descriptions of Jonson's court masques as an effort to promote Jonson.

Additional coverage of Shirley's life and career is contained in the following sources published by Thomson Gale: *Dictionary of Literary Biography,* **Vol. 58;** *Literature Criticism from 1400 to 1800,* **Vol. 96;** *Literature Resource Center;* **and** *Reference Guide to English Literature,* **Ed. 2.**

How to Use This Index

The main references

> **Calvino, Italo**
>   1923-1985 .... CLC 5, 8, 11, 22, 33, 39,
>   73; SSC 3, 48

list all author entries in the following Gale Literary Criticism series:

AAL = *Asian American Literature*
BG = *The Beat Generation: A Gale Critical Companion*
BLC = *Black Literature Criticism*
BLCS = *Black Literature Criticism Supplement*
CLC = *Contemporary Literary Criticism*
CLR = *Children's Literature Review*
CMLC = *Classical and Medieval Literature Criticism*
DC = *Drama Criticism*
HLC = *Hispanic Literature Criticism*
HLCS = *Hispanic Literature Criticism Supplement*
HR = *Harlem Renaissance: A Gale Critical Companion*
LC = *Literature Criticism from 1400 to 1800*
NCLC = *Nineteenth-Century Literature Criticism*
NNAL = *Native North American Literature*
PC = *Poetry Criticism*
SSC = *Short Story Criticism*
TCLC = *Twentieth-Century Literary Criticism*
WLC = *World Literature Criticism, 1500 to the Present*
WLCS = *World Literature Criticism Supplement*

The cross-references

> See also CA 85-88, 116; CANR 23, 61;
> DAM NOV; DLB 196; EW 13; MTCW 1, 2;
> RGSF 2; RGWL 2; SFW 4; SSFS 12

list all author entries in the following Gale biographical and literary sources:

AAYA = *Authors & Artists for Young Adults*
AFAW = *African American Writers*
AFW = *African Writers*
AITN = *Authors in the News*
AMW = *American Writers*
AMWR = *American Writers Retrospective Supplement*
AMWS = *American Writers Supplement*
ANW = *American Nature Writers*
AW = *Ancient Writers*
BEST = *Bestsellers*
BPFB = *Beacham's Encyclopedia of Popular Fiction: Biography and Resources*
BRW = *British Writers*
BRWS = *British Writers Supplement*
BW = *Black Writers*
BYA = *Beacham's Guide to Literature for Young Adults*
CA = *Contemporary Authors*
CAAS = *Contemporary Authors Autobiography Series*
CABS = *Contemporary Authors Bibliographical Series*
CAD = *Contemporary American Dramatists*
CANR = *Contemporary Authors New Revision Series*
CAP = *Contemporary Authors Permanent Series*
CBD = *Contemporary British Dramatists*
CCA = *Contemporary Canadian Authors*
CD = *Contemporary Dramatists*
CDALB = *Concise Dictionary of American Literary Biography*
CDALBS = *Concise Dictionary of American Literary Biography Supplement*
CDBLB = *Concise Dictionary of British Literary Biography*

CMW = *St. James Guide to Crime & Mystery Writers*

CN = *Contemporary Novelists*

CP = *Contemporary Poets*

CPW = *Contemporary Popular Writers*

CSW = *Contemporary Southern Writers*

CWD = *Contemporary Women Dramatists*

CWP = *Contemporary Women Poets*

CWRI = *St. James Guide to Children's Writers*

CWW = *Contemporary World Writers*

DA = *DISCovering Authors*

DA3 = *DISCovering Authors 3.0*

DAB = *DISCovering Authors: British Edition*

DAC = *DISCovering Authors: Canadian Edition*

DAM = *DISCovering Authors: Modules*

   DRAM: *Dramatists Module;* **MST:** *Most-studied Authors Module;*

   MULT: *Multicultural Authors Module;* **NOV:** *Novelists Module;*

   POET: *Poets Module;* **POP:** *Popular Fiction and Genre Authors Module*

DFS = *Drama for Students*

DLB = *Dictionary of Literary Biography*

DLBD = *Dictionary of Literary Biography Documentary Series*

DLBY = *Dictionary of Literary Biography Yearbook*

DNFS = *Literature of Developing Nations for Students*

EFS = *Epics for Students*

EXPN = *Exploring Novels*

EXPP = *Exploring Poetry*

EXPS = *Exploring Short Stories*

EW = *European Writers*

FANT = *St. James Guide to Fantasy Writers*

FW = *Feminist Writers*

GFL = *Guide to French Literature,* Beginnings to 1789, 1798 to the Present

GLL = *Gay and Lesbian Literature*

HGG = *St. James Guide to Horror, Ghost & Gothic Writers*

HW = *Hispanic Writers*

IDFW = *International Dictionary of Films and Filmmakers: Writers and Production Artists*

IDTP = *International Dictionary of Theatre: Playwrights*

LAIT = *Literature and Its Times*

LAW = *Latin American Writers*

JRDA = *Junior DISCovering Authors*

MAICYA = *Major Authors and Illustrators for Children and Young Adults*

MAICYAS = *Major Authors and Illustrators for Children and Young Adults Supplement*

MAWW = *Modern American Women Writers*

MJW = *Modern Japanese Writers*

MTCW = *Major 20th-Century Writers*

NCFS = *Nonfiction Classics for Students*

NFS = *Novels for Students*

PAB = *Poets: American and British*

PFS = *Poetry for Students*

RGAL = *Reference Guide to American Literature*

RGEL = *Reference Guide to English Literature*

RGSF = *Reference Guide to Short Fiction*

RGWL = *Reference Guide to World Literature*

RHW = *Twentieth-Century Romance and Historical Writers*

SAAS = *Something about the Author Autobiography Series*

SATA = *Something about the Author*

SFW = *St. James Guide to Science Fiction Writers*

SSFS = *Short Stories for Students*

TCWW = *Twentieth-Century Western Writers*

WLIT = *World Literature and Its Times*

WP = *World Poets*

YABC = *Yesterday's Authors of Books for Children*

YAW = *St. James Guide to Young Adult Writers*

Cumulative Author Index

Allan, Sydney
  See Hartmann, Sadakichi
Allard, Janet .... **CLC 59**
Allen, Edward 1948- .... **CLC 59**
Allen, Fred 1894-1956 .... **TCLC 87**
Allen, Paula Gunn 1939- ..... **CLC 84; NNAL**
  See also AMWS 4; CA 112; 143; CANR
  63, 130; CWP; DA3; DAM MULT; DLB
  175; FW; MTCW 1; RGAL 4
Allen, Roland
  See Ayckbourn, Alan
Allen, Sarah A.
  See Hopkins, Pauline Elizabeth
Allen, Sidney H.
  See Hartmann, Sadakichi
Allen, Woody 1935- .... **CLC 16, 52, 195**
  See also AAYA 10, 51; CA 33-36R; CANR
  27, 38, 63, 128; DAM POP; DLB 44;
  MTCW 1
Allende, Isabel 1942- ... **CLC 39, 57, 97, 170;
  HLC 1; SSC 65; WLCS**
  See also AAYA 18; CA 125; 130; CANR
  51, 74, 129; CDWLB 3; CLR 99; CWW
  2; DA3; DAM MULT, NOV; DLB 145;
  DNFS 1; EWL 3; FW; HW 1, 2; INT CA-
  130; LAIT 5; LAWS 1; LMFS 2; MTCW
  1, 2; NCFS 1; NFS 6, 18; RGSF 2;
  RGWL 3; SSFS 11, 16; WLIT 1
Alleyn, Ellen
  See Rossetti, Christina (Georgina)
Alleyne, Carla D. .... **CLC 65**
Allingham, Margery (Louise)
  1904-1966 .... **CLC 19**
  See also CA 5-8R; 25-28R; CANR 4, 58;
  CMW 4; DLB 77; MSW; MTCW 1, 2
Allingham, William 1824-1889 ...... **NCLC 25**
  See also DLB 35; RGEL 2
Allison, Dorothy E. 1949- .... **CLC 78, 153**
  See also AAYA 53; CA 140; CANR 66, 107;
  CSW; DA3; FW; MTCW 1; NFS 11;
  RGAL 4
Alloula, Malek .... **CLC 65**
Allston, Washington 1779-1843 .... **NCLC 2**
  See also DLB 1, 235
Almedingen, E. M. .... **CLC 12**
  See Almedingen, Martha Edith von
  See also SATA 3
Almedingen, Martha Edith von 1898-1971
  See Almedingen, E. M.
  See also CA 1-4R; CANR 1
Almodovar, Pedro 1949(?)- .... **CLC 114;
  HLCS 1**
  See also CA 133; CANR 72; HW 2
Almqvist, Carl Jonas Love
  1793-1866 .... **NCLC 42**
**al-Mutanabbi, Ahmad ibn al-Husayn Abu
  al-Tayyib al-Jufi al-Kindi**
  915-965 .... **CMLC 66**
  See also RGWL 3
Alonso, Damaso 1898-1990 .... **CLC 14**
  See also CA 110; 131; 130; CANR 72; DLB
  108; EWL 3; HW 1, 2
Alov
  See Gogol, Nikolai (Vasilyevich)
al'Sadaawi, Nawal
  See El Saadawi, Nawal
  See also FW
Al Siddik
  See Rolfe, Frederick (William Serafino
  Austin Lewis Mary)
  See also GLL 1; RGEL 2
Alta 1942- .... **CLC 19**
  See also CA 57-60
Alter, Robert B(ernard) 1935- .... **CLC 34**
  See also CA 49-52; CANR 1, 47, 100
Alther, Lisa 1944- .... **CLC 7, 41**
  See also BPFB 1; CA 65-68; CAAS 30;
  CANR 12, 30, 51; CN 7; CSW; GLL 2;
  MTCW 1

Althusser, L.
  See Althusser, Louis
Althusser, Louis 1918-1990 .... **CLC 106**
  See also CA 131; 132; CANR 102; DLB
  242
Altman, Robert 1925- .... **CLC 16, 116**
  See also CA 73-76; CANR 43
Alurista .... **HLCS 1**
  See Urista (Heredia), Alberto (Baltazar)
  See also DLB 82; LLW 1
Alvarez, A(lfred) 1929- .... **CLC 5, 13**
  See also CA 1-4R; CANR 3, 33, 63, 101,
  134; CN 7; CP 7; DLB 14, 40
Alvarez, Alejandro Rodriguez 1903-1965
  See Casona, Alejandro
  See also CA 131; 93-96; HW 1
Alvarez, Julia 1950- .... **CLC 93; HLCS 1**
  See also AAYA 25; AMWS 7; CA 147;
  CANR 69, 101, 133; DA3; DLB 282;
  LATS 1:2; LLW 1; MTCW 1; NFS 5, 9;
  SATA 129; WLIT 1
Alvaro, Corrado 1896-1956 .... **TCLC 60**
  See also CA 163; DLB 264; EWL 3
Amado, Jorge 1912-2001 ... **CLC 13, 40, 106;
  HLC 1**
  See also CA 77-80; 201; CANR 35, 74;
  CWW 2; DAM MULT, NOV; DLB 113,
  307; EWL 3; HW 2; LAW; LAWS 1;
  MTCW 1, 2; RGWL 2, 3; TWA; WLIT 1
Ambler, Eric 1909-1998 .... **CLC 4, 6, 9**
  See also BRWS 4; CA 9-12R; 171; CANR
  7, 38, 74; CMW 4; CN 7; DLB 77; MSW;
  MTCW 1, 2; TEA
Ambrose, Stephen E(dward)
  1936-2002 .... **CLC 145**
  See also AAYA 44; CA 1-4R; 209; CANR
  3, 43, 57, 83, 105; NCFS 2; SATA 40,
  138
Amichai, Yehuda 1924-2000 .. **CLC 9, 22, 57,
  116; PC 38**
  See also CA 85-88; 189; CANR 46, 60, 99,
  132; CWW 2; EWL 3; MTCW 1
Amichai, Yehudah
  See Amichai, Yehuda
Amiel, Henri Frederic 1821-1881 .... **NCLC 4**
  See also DLB 217
Amis, Kingsley (William)
  1922-1995 ...... **CLC 1, 2, 3, 5, 8, 13, 40,
  44, 129**
  See also AITN 2; BPFB 1; BRWS 2; CA
  9-12R; 150; CANR 8, 28, 54; CDBLB
  1945-1960; CN 7; CP 7; DA; DA3; DAB;
  DAC; DAM MST, NOV; DLB 15, 27,
  100, 139; DLBY 1996; EWL 3; HGG;
  INT CANR-8; MTCW 1, 2; RGEL 2;
  RGSF 2; SFW 4
Amis, Martin (Louis) 1949- .... **CLC 4, 9, 38,
  62, 101**
  See also BEST 90:3; BRWS 4; CA 65-68;
  CANR 8, 27, 54, 73, 95, 132; CN 7; DA3;
  DLB 14, 194; EWL 3; INT CANR-27;
  MTCW 1
Ammianus Marcellinus c. 330-c.
  395 .... **CMLC 60**
  See also AW 2; DLB 211
Ammons, A(rchie) R(andolph)
  1926-2001 ...... **CLC 2, 3, 5, 8, 9, 25, 57,
  108; PC 16**
  See also AITN 1; AMWS 7; CA 9-12R;
  193; CANR 6, 36, 51, 73, 107; CP 7;
  CSW; DAM POET; DLB 5, 165; EWL 3;
  MTCW 1, 2; PFS 19; RGAL 4
Amo, Tauraatua i
  See Adams, Henry (Brooks)
Amory, Thomas 1691(?)-1788 .... **LC 48**
  See also DLB 39
Anand, Mulk Raj 1905-2004 ...... **CLC 23, 93**
  See also CA 65-68; CANR 32, 64; CN 7;
  DAM NOV; EWL 3; MTCW 1, 2; RGSF
  2

Anatol
  See Schnitzler, Arthur
Anaximander c. 611B.C.-c.
  546B.C. .... **CMLC 22**
Anaya, Rudolfo A(lfonso) 1937- ...... **CLC 23,
  148; HLC 1**
  See also AAYA 20; BYA 13; CA 45-48;
  CAAS 4; CANR 1, 32, 51, 124; CN 7;
  DAM MULT, NOV; DLB 82, 206, 278;
  HW 1; LAIT 4; LLW 1; MTCW 1, 2; NFS
  12; RGAL 4; RGSF 2; WLIT 1
Andersen, Hans Christian
  1805-1875 .... **NCLC 7, 79; SSC 6, 56;
  WLC**
  See also AAYA 57; CLR 6; DA; DA3;
  DAB; DAC; DAM MST, POP; EW 6;
  MAICYA 1, 2; RGSF 2; RGWL 2, 3;
  SATA 100; TWA; WCH; YABC 1
Anderson, C. Farley
  See Mencken, H(enry) L(ouis); Nathan,
  George Jean
Anderson, Jessica (Margaret) Queale
  1916- .... **CLC 37**
  See also CA 9-12R; CANR 4, 62; CN 7
Anderson, Jon (Victor) 1940- .... **CLC 9**
  See also CA 25-28R; CANR 20; DAM
  POET
Anderson, Lindsay (Gordon)
  1923-1994 .... **CLC 20**
  See also CA 125; 128; 146; CANR 77
Anderson, Maxwell 1888-1959 .... **TCLC 2,
  144**
  See also CA 105; 152; DAM DRAM; DFS
  16, 20; DLB 7, 228; MTCW 2; RGAL 4
Anderson, Poul (William)
  1926-2001 .... **CLC 15**
  See also AAYA 5, 34; BPFB 1; BYA 6, 8,
  9; CA 1-4R; 181; 199; CAAE 181; CAAS
  2; CANR 2, 15, 34, 64, 110; CLR 58;
  DLB 8; FANT; INT CANR-15; MTCW 1,
  2; SATA 90; SATA-Brief 39; SATA-Essay
  106; SCFW 2; SFW 4; SUFW 1, 2
Anderson, Robert (Woodruff)
  1917- .... **CLC 23**
  See also AITN 1; CA 21-24R; CANR 32;
  DAM DRAM; DLB 7; LAIT 5
Anderson, Roberta Joan
  See Mitchell, Joni
Anderson, Sherwood 1876-1941 .. **SSC 1, 46;
  TCLC 1, 10, 24, 123; WLC**
  See also AAYA 30; AMW; AMWC 2; BPFB
  1; CA 104; 121; CANR 61; CDALB
  1917-1929; DA; DA3; DAB; DAC; DAM
  MST, NOV; DLB 4, 9, 86; DLBD 1; EWL
  3; EXPS; GLL 2; MTCW 1, 2; NFS 4;
  RGAL 4; RGSF 2; SSFS 4, 10, 11; TUS
Andier, Pierre
  See Desnos, Robert
Andouard
  See Giraudoux, Jean(-Hippolyte)
Andrade, Carlos Drummond de ..... **CLC 18**
  See Drummond de Andrade, Carlos
  See also EWL 3; RGWL 2, 3
Andrade, Mario de .... **TCLC 43**
  See de Andrade, Mario
  See also DLB 307; EWL 3; LAW; RGWL
  2, 3; WLIT 1
Andreae, Johann V(alentin)
  1586-1654 .... **LC 32**
  See also DLB 164
Andreas Capellanus fl. c. 1185- .... **CMLC 45**
  See also DLB 208
Andreas-Salome, Lou 1861-1937 ... **TCLC 56**
  See also CA 178; DLB 66
Andreev, Leonid
  See Andreyev, Leonid (Nikolaevich)
  See also DLB 295; EWL 3
Andress, Lesley
  See Sanders, Lawrence

Arnold, Matthew 1822-1888 ..... NCLC 6, 29, 89, 126; PC 5; WLC
See also BRW 5; CDBLB 1832-1890; DA; DAB; DAC; DAM MST, POET; DLB 32, 57; EXPP; PAB; PFS 2; TEA; WP

Arnold, Thomas 1795-1842 .... NCLC 18
See also DLB 55

Arnow, Harriette (Louisa) Simpson
1908-1986 .... CLC 2, 7, 18
See also BPFB 1; CA 9-12R; 118; CANR 14; DLB 6; FW; MTCW 1, 2; RHW; SATA 42; SATA-Obit 47

Arouet, Francois-Marie
See Voltaire

Arp, Hans
See Arp, Jean

Arp, Jean 1887-1966 .... CLC 5; TCLC 115
See also CA 81-84; 25-28R; CANR 42, 77; EW 10

Arrabal
See Arrabal, Fernando

Arrabal, Fernando 1932- ... CLC 2, 9, 18, 58
See Arrabal (Teran), Fernando
See also CA 9-12R; CANR 15; EWL 3; LMFS 2

Arrabal (Teran), Fernando 1932-
See Arrabal, Fernando
See also CWW 2

Arreola, Juan Jose 1918-2001 .... CLC 147; HLC 1; SSC 38
See also CA 113; 131; 200; CANR 81; CWW 2; DAM MULT; DLB 113; DNFS 2; EWL 3; HW 1, 2; LAW; RGSF 2

Arrian c. 89(?)-c. 155(?) .... CMLC 43
See also DLB 176

Arrick, Fran .... CLC 30
See Gaberman, Judie Angell
See also BYA 6

Arrley, Richard
See Delany, Samuel R(ay), Jr.

Artaud, Antonin (Marie Joseph)
1896-1948 .... DC 14; TCLC 3, 36
See also CA 104; 149; DA3; DAM DRAM; DLB 258; EW 11; EWL 3; GFL 1789 to the Present; MTCW 1; RGWL 2, 3

Arthur, Ruth M(abel) 1905-1979 ..... CLC 12
See also CA 9-12R; 85-88; CANR 4; CWRI 5; SATA 7, 26

Artsybashev, Mikhail (Petrovich)
1878-1927 .... TCLC 31
See also CA 170; DLB 295

Arundel, Honor (Morfydd)
1919-1973 .... CLC 17
See also CA 21-22; 41-44R; CAP 2; CLR 35; CWRI 5; SATA 4; SATA-Obit 24

Arzner, Dorothy 1900-1979 .... CLC 98

Asch, Sholem 1880-1957 .... TCLC 3
See also CA 105; EWL 3; GLL 2

Ascham, Roger 1516(?)-1568 .... LC 101
See also DLB 236

Ash, Shalom
See Asch, Sholem

Ashbery, John (Lawrence) 1927- .. CLC 2, 3, 4, 6, 9, 13, 15, 25, 41, 77, 125; PC 26
See Berry, Jonas
See also AMWS 3; CA 5-8R; CANR 9, 37, 66, 102, 132; CP 7; DA3; DAM POET; DLB 5, 165; DLBY 1981; EWL 3; INT CANR-9; MTCW 1, 2; PAB; PFS 11; RGAL 4; WP

Ashdown, Clifford
See Freeman, R(ichard) Austin

Ashe, Gordon
See Creasey, John

Ashton-Warner, Sylvia (Constance)
1908-1984 .... CLC 19
See also CA 69-72; 112; CANR 29; MTCW 1, 2

Asimov, Isaac 1920-1992 ..... CLC 1, 3, 9, 19, 26, 76, 92
See also AAYA 13; BEST 90:2; BPFB 1; BYA 4, 6, 7, 9; CA 1-4R; 137; CANR 2, 19, 36, 60, 125; CLR 12, 79; CMW 4; CPW; DA3; DAM POP; DLB 8; DLBY 1992; INT CANR-19; JRDA; LAIT 5; LMFS 2; MAICYA 1, 2; MTCW 1, 2; RGAL 4; SATA 1, 26, 74; SCFW 2; SFW 4; SSFS 17; TUS; YAW

Askew, Anne 1521(?)-1546 .... LC 81
See also DLB 136

Assis, Joaquim Maria Machado de
See Machado de Assis, Joaquim Maria

Astell, Mary 1666-1731 .... LC 68
See also DLB 252; FW

Astley, Thea (Beatrice May)
1925-2004 .... CLC 41
See also CA 65-68; 229; CANR 11, 43, 78; CN 7; DLB 289; EWL 3

Astley, William 1855-1911
See Warung, Price

Aston, James
See White, T(erence) H(anbury)

Asturias, Miguel Angel 1899-1974 .... CLC 3, 8, 13; HLC 1
See also CA 25-28; 49-52; CANR 32; CAP 2; CDWLB 3; DA3; DAM MULT, NOV; DLB 113, 290; EWL 3; HW 1; LAW; LMFS 2; MTCW 1, 2; RGWL 2, 3; WLIT 1

Atares, Carlos Saura
See Saura (Atares), Carlos

Athanasius c. 295-c. 373 .... CMLC 48

Atheling, William
See Pound, Ezra (Weston Loomis)

Atheling, William, Jr.
See Blish, James (Benjamin)

Atherton, Gertrude (Franklin Horn)
1857-1948 .... TCLC 2
See also CA 104; 155; DLB 9, 78, 186; HGG; RGAL 4; SUFW 1; TCWW 2

Atherton, Lucius
See Masters, Edgar Lee

Atkins, Jack
See Harris, Mark

Atkinson, Kate 1951- .... CLC 99
See also CA 166; CANR 101; DLB 267

Attaway, William (Alexander)
1911-1986 .... BLC 1; CLC 92
See also BW 2, 3; CA 143; CANR 82; DAM MULT; DLB 76

Atticus
See Fleming, Ian (Lancaster); Wilson, (Thomas) Woodrow

Atwood, Margaret (Eleanor) 1939- ... CLC 2, 3, 4, 8, 13, 15, 25, 44, 84, 135; PC 8; SSC 2, 46; WLC
See also AAYA 12, 47; AMWS 13; BEST 89:2; BPFB 1; CA 49-52; CANR 3, 24, 33, 59, 95, 133; CN 7; CP 7; CWP; DA; DA3; DAB; DAC; DAM MST, NOV, POET; DLB 53, 251; EWL 3; EXPN; FW; INT CANR-24; LAIT 5; MTCW 1, 2; NFS 4, 12, 13, 14, 19; PFS 7; RGSF 2; SATA 50; SSFS 3, 13; TWA; WWE 1; YAW

Aubigny, Pierre d'
See Mencken, H(enry) L(ouis)

Aubin, Penelope 1685-1731(?) .... LC 9
See also DLB 39

Auchincloss, Louis (Stanton) 1917- .. CLC 4, 6, 9, 18, 45; SSC 22
See also AMWS 4; CA 1-4R; CANR 6, 29, 55, 87, 130; CN 7; DAM NOV; DLB 2, 244; DLBY 1980; EWL 3; INT CANR-29; MTCW 1; RGAL 4

Auden, W(ystan) H(ugh) 1907-1973 . CLC 1, 2, 3, 4, 6, 9, 11, 14, 43, 123; PC 1; WLC
See also AAYA 18; AMWS 2; BRW 7; BRWR 1; CA 9-12R; 45-48; CANR 5, 61, 105; CDBLB 1914-1945; DA; DA3; DAB; DAC; DAM DRAM, MST, POET; DLB 10, 20; EWL 3; EXPP; MTCW 1, 2; PAB; PFS 1, 3, 4, 10; TUS; WP

Audiberti, Jacques 1899-1965 .... CLC 38
See also CA 25-28R; DAM DRAM; EWL 3

Audubon, John James 1785-1851 . NCLC 47
See also ANW; DLB 248

Auel, Jean M(arie) 1936- .... CLC 31, 107
See also AAYA 7, 51; BEST 90:4; BPFB 1; CA 103; CANR 21, 64, 115; CPW; DA3; DAM POP; INT CANR-21; NFS 11; RHW; SATA 91

Auerbach, Erich 1892-1957 .... TCLC 43
See also CA 118; 155; EWL 3

Augier, Emile 1820-1889 .... NCLC 31
See also DLB 192; GFL 1789 to the Present

August, John
See De Voto, Bernard (Augustine)

Augustine, St. 354-430 .... CMLC 6; WLCS
See also DA; DA3; DAB; DAC; DAM MST; DLB 115; EW 1; RGWL 2, 3

Aunt Belinda
See Braddon, Mary Elizabeth

Aunt Weedy
See Alcott, Louisa May

Aurelius
See Bourne, Randolph S(illiman)

Aurelius, Marcus 121-180 .... CMLC 45
See Marcus Aurelius
See also RGWL 2, 3

Aurobindo, Sri
See Ghose, Aurabinda

Aurobindo Ghose
See Ghose, Aurabinda

Austen, Jane 1775-1817 ...... NCLC 1, 13, 19, 33, 51, 81, 95, 119; WLC
See also AAYA 19; BRW 4; BRWC 1; BRWR 2; BYA 3; CDBLB 1789-1832; DA; DA3; DAB; DAC; DAM MST, NOV; DLB 116; EXPN; LAIT 2; LATS 1:1; LMFS 1; NFS 1, 14, 18, 20; TEA; WLIT 3; WYAS 1

Auster, Paul 1947- .... CLC 47, 131
See also AMWS 12; CA 69-72; CANR 23, 52, 75, 129; CMW 4; CN 7; DA3; DLB 227; MTCW 1; SUFW 2

Austin, Frank
See Faust, Frederick (Schiller)
See also TCWW 2

Austin, Mary (Hunter) 1868-1934 . TCLC 25
See Stairs, Gordon
See also ANW; CA 109; 178; DLB 9, 78, 206, 221, 275; FW; TCWW 2

Averroes 1126-1198 .... CMLC 7
See also DLB 115

Avicenna 980-1037 .... CMLC 16
See also DLB 115

Avison, Margaret (Kirkland) 1918- .. CLC 2, 4, 97
See also CA 17-20R; CANR 134; CP 7; DAC; DAM POET; DLB 53; MTCW 1

Axton, David
See Koontz, Dean R(ay)

Ayckbourn, Alan 1939- ..... CLC 5, 8, 18, 33, 74; DC 13
See also BRWS 5; CA 21-24R; CANR 31, 59, 118; CBD; CD 5; DAB; DAM DRAM; DFS 7; DLB 13, 245; EWL 3; MTCW 1, 2

Aydy, Catherine
See Tennant, Emma (Christina)

Barbour, John c. 1316-1395 .... **CMLC 33**
See also DLB 146
Barbusse, Henri 1873-1935 .... **TCLC 5**
See also CA 105; 154; DLB 65; EWL 3;
RGWL 2, 3
Barclay, Alexander c. 1475-1552 .... **LC 109**
See also DLB 132
Barclay, Bill
See Moorcock, Michael (John)
Barclay, William Ewert
See Moorcock, Michael (John)
Barea, Arturo 1897-1957 .... **TCLC 14**
See also CA 111; 201
Barfoot, Joan 1946- .... **CLC 18**
See also CA 105
Barham, Richard Harris
1788-1845 .... **NCLC 77**
See also DLB 159
Baring, Maurice 1874-1945 .... **TCLC 8**
See also CA 105; 168; DLB 34; HGG
Baring-Gould, Sabine 1834-1924 ... **TCLC 88**
See also DLB 156, 190
Barker, Clive 1952- .... **CLC 52; SSC 53**
See also AAYA 10, 54; BEST 90:3; BPFB
1; CA 121; 129; CANR 71, 111, 133;
CPW; DA3; DAM POP; DLB 261; HGG;
INT CA-129; MTCW 1, 2; SUFW 2
Barker, George Granville
1913-1991 .... **CLC 8, 48**
See also CA 9-12R; 135; CANR 7, 38;
DAM POET; DLB 20; EWL 3; MTCW 1
Barker, Harley Granville
See Granville-Barker, Harley
See also DLB 10
Barker, Howard 1946- .... **CLC 37**
See also CA 102; CBD; CD 5; DLB 13,
233
Barker, Jane 1652-1732 .... **LC 42, 82**
See also DLB 39, 131
Barker, Pat(ricia) 1943- ...... **CLC 32, 94, 146**
See also BRWS 4; CA 117; 122; CANR 50,
101; CN 7; DLB 271; INT CA-122
Barlach, Ernst (Heinrich)
1870-1938 .... **TCLC 84**
See also CA 178; DLB 56, 118; EWL 3
Barlow, Joel 1754-1812 .... **NCLC 23**
See also AMWS 2; DLB 37; RGAL 4
Barnard, Mary (Ethel) 1909- .... **CLC 48**
See also CA 21-24R; CAP 2
Barnes, Djuna 1892-1982 .... **CLC 3, 4, 8, 11,
29, 127; SSC 3**
See Steptoe, Lydia
See also AMWS 3; CA 9-12R; 107; CAD;
CANR 16, 55; CWD; DLB 4, 9, 45; EWL
3; GLL 1; MTCW 1, 2; RGAL 4; TUS
Barnes, Jim 1933- .... **NNAL**
See also CA 108, 175; CAAE 175; CAAS
28; DLB 175
Barnes, Julian (Patrick) 1946- . **CLC 42, 141**
See also BRWS 4; CA 102; CANR 19, 54,
115; CN 7; DAB; DLB 194; DLBY 1993;
EWL 3; MTCW 1
Barnes, Peter 1931-2004 .... **CLC 5, 56**
See also CA 65-68; CAAS 12; CANR 33,
34, 64, 113; CBD; CD 5; DFS 6; DLB
13, 233; MTCW 1
Barnes, William 1801-1886 .... **NCLC 75**
See also DLB 32
Baroja (y Nessi), Pio 1872-1956 .... **HLC 1;
TCLC 8**
See also CA 104; EW 9
Baron, David
See Pinter, Harold
Baron Corvo
See Rolfe, Frederick (William Serafino
Austin Lewis Mary)

Barondess, Sue K(aufman)
1926-1977 .... **CLC 8**
See Kaufman, Sue
See also CA 1-4R; 69-72; CANR 1
Baron de Teive
See Pessoa, Fernando (Antonio Nogueira)
Baroness Von S.
See Zangwill, Israel
Barres, (Auguste-)Maurice
1862-1923 .... **TCLC 47**
See also CA 164; DLB 123; GFL 1789 to
the Present
Barreto, Afonso Henrique de Lima
See Lima Barreto, Afonso Henrique de
Barrett, Andrea 1954- .... **CLC 150**
See also CA 156; CANR 92
Barrett, Michele .... **CLC 65**
Barrett, (Roger) Syd 1946- .... **CLC 35**
Barrett, William (Christopher)
1913-1992 .... **CLC 27**
See also CA 13-16R; 139; CANR 11, 67;
INT CANR-11
Barrie, J(ames) M(atthew)
1860-1937 .... **TCLC 2**
See also BRWS 3; BYA 4, 5; CA 104; 136;
CANR 77; CDBLB 1890-1914; CLR 16;
CWRI 5; DA3; DAB; DAM DRAM; DFS
7; DLB 10, 141, 156; EWL 3; FANT;
MAICYA 1, 2; MTCW 1; SATA 100;
SUFW; WCH; WLIT 4; YABC 1
Barrington, Michael
See Moorcock, Michael (John)
Barrol, Grady
See Bograd, Larry
Barry, Mike
See Malzberg, Barry N(athaniel)
Barry, Philip 1896-1949 .... **TCLC 11**
See also CA 109; 199; DFS 9; DLB 7, 228;
RGAL 4
Bart, Andre Schwarz
See Schwarz-Bart, Andre
Barth, John (Simmons) 1930- ... **CLC 1, 2, 3,
5, 7, 9, 10, 14, 27, 51, 89; SSC 10**
See also AITN 1, 2; AMW; BPFB 1; CA
1-4R; CABS 1; CANR 5, 23, 49, 64, 113;
CN 7; DAM NOV; DLB 2, 227; EWL 3;
FANT; MTCW 1; RGAL 4; RGSF 2;
RHW; SSFS 6; TUS
Barthelme, Donald 1931-1989 ... **CLC 1, 2, 3,
5, 6, 8, 13, 23, 46, 59, 115; SSC 2, 55**
See also AMWS 4; BPFB 1; CA 21-24R;
129; CANR 20, 58; DA3; DAM NOV;
DLB 2, 234; DLBY 1980, 1989; EWL 3;
FANT; LMFS 2; MTCW 1, 2; RGAL 4;
RGSF 2; SATA 7; SATA-Obit 62; SSFS
17
Barthelme, Frederick 1943- ...... **CLC 36, 117**
See also AMWS 11; CA 114; 122; CANR
77; CN 7; CSW; DLB 244; DLBY 1985;
EWL 3; INT CA-122
Barthes, Roland (Gerard)
1915-1980 .... **CLC 24, 83; TCLC 135**
See also CA 130; 97-100; CANR 66; DLB
296; EW 13; EWL 3; GFL 1789 to the
Present; MTCW 1, 2; TWA
Bartram, William 1739-1823 .... **NCLC 145**
See also ANW; DLB 37
Barzun, Jacques (Martin) 1907- ..... **CLC 51,
145**
See also CA 61-64; CANR 22, 95
Bashevis, Isaac
See Singer, Isaac Bashevis
Bashkirtseff, Marie 1859-1884 .... **NCLC 27**
Basho, Matsuo
See Matsuo Basho
See also PFS 18; RGWL 2, 3; WP
Basil of Caesaria c. 330-379 .... **CMLC 35**
Basket, Raney
See Edgerton, Clyde (Carlyle)

Bass, Kingsley B., Jr.
See Bullins, Ed
Bass, Rick 1958- .... **CLC 79, 143; SSC 60**
See also ANW; CA 126; CANR 53, 93;
CSW; DLB 212, 275
Bassani, Giorgio 1916-2000 .... **CLC 9**
See also CA 65-68; 190; CANR 33; CWW
2; DLB 128, 177, 299; EWL 3; MTCW 1;
RGWL 2, 3
Bastian, Ann .... **CLC 70**
Bastos, Augusto (Antonio) Roa
See Roa Bastos, Augusto (Antonio)
Bataille, Georges 1897-1962 .... **CLC 29;
TCLC 155**
See also CA 101; 89-92; EWL 3
Bates, H(erbert) E(rnest)
1905-1974 .... **CLC 46; SSC 10**
See also CA 93-96; 45-48; CANR 34; DA3;
DAB; DAM POP; DLB 162, 191; EWL
3; EXPS; MTCW 1, 2; RGSF 2; SSFS 7
Bauchart
See Camus, Albert
Baudelaire, Charles 1821-1867 . **NCLC 6, 29,
55; PC 1; SSC 18; WLC**
See also DA; DA3; DAB; DAC; DAM
MST, POET; DLB 217; EW 7; GFL 1789
to the Present; LMFS 2; PFS 21; RGWL
2, 3; TWA
Baudouin, Marcel
See Peguy, Charles (Pierre)
Baudouin, Pierre
See Peguy, Charles (Pierre)
Baudrillard, Jean 1929- .... **CLC 60**
See also DLB 296
Baum, L(yman) Frank 1856-1919 .. **TCLC 7,
132**
See also AAYA 46; BYA 16; CA 108; 133;
CLR 15; CWRI 5; DLB 22; FANT; JRDA;
MAICYA 1, 2; MTCW 1, 2; NFS 13;
RGAL 4; SATA 18, 100; WCH
Baum, Louis F.
See Baum, L(yman) Frank
Baumbach, Jonathan 1933- .... **CLC 6, 23**
See also CA 13-16R; CAAS 5; CANR 12,
66; CN 7; DLBY 1980; INT CANR-12;
MTCW 1
Bausch, Richard (Carl) 1945- .... **CLC 51**
See also AMWS 7; CA 101; CAAS 14;
CANR 43, 61, 87; CSW; DLB 130
Baxter, Charles (Morley) 1947- . **CLC 45, 78**
See also CA 57-60; CANR 40, 64, 104, 133;
CPW; DAM POP; DLB 130; MTCW 2
Baxter, George Owen
See Faust, Frederick (Schiller)
Baxter, James K(eir) 1926-1972 .... **CLC 14**
See also CA 77-80; EWL 3
Baxter, John
See Hunt, E(verette) Howard, (Jr.)
Bayer, Sylvia
See Glassco, John
Baynton, Barbara 1857-1929 .... **TCLC 57**
See also DLB 230; RGSF 2
Beagle, Peter S(oyer) 1939- .... **CLC 7, 104**
See also AAYA 47; BPFB 1; BYA 9, 10,
16; CA 9-12R; CANR 4, 51, 73, 110;
DA3; DLBY 1980; FANT; INT CANR-4;
MTCW 1; SATA 60, 130; SUFW 1, 2;
YAW
Bean, Normal
See Burroughs, Edgar Rice
Beard, Charles A(ustin)
1874-1948 .... **TCLC 15**
See also CA 115; 189; DLB 17; SATA 18
Beardsley, Aubrey 1872-1898 .... **NCLC 6**
Beattie, Ann 1947- ..... **CLC 8, 13, 18, 40, 63,
146; SSC 11**
See also AMWS 5; BEST 90:2; BPFB 1;
CA 81-84; CANR 53, 73, 128; CN 7;
CPW; DA3; DAM NOV, POP; DLB 218,
278; DLBY 1982; EWL 3; MTCW 1, 2;
RGAL 4; RGSF 2; SSFS 9; TUS

Benford, Gregory (Albert) 1941- ..... **CLC 52**
See also BPFB 1; CA 69-72, 175; CAAE
175; CAAS 27; CANR 12, 24, 49, 95,
134; CSW; DLBY 1982; SCFW 2; SFW
4

Bengtsson, Frans (Gunnar)
1894-1954 .... **TCLC 48**
See also CA 170; EWL 3

Benjamin, David
See Slavitt, David R(ytman)

Benjamin, Lois
See Gould, Lois

Benjamin, Walter 1892-1940 .... **TCLC 39**
See also CA 164; DLB 242; EW 11; EWL
3

Ben Jelloun, Tahar 1944-
See Jelloun, Tahar ben
See also CA 135; CWW 2; EWL 3; RGWL
3; WLIT 2

Benn, Gottfried 1886-1956 .. **PC 35; TCLC 3**
See also CA 106; 153; DLB 56; EWL 3;
RGWL 2, 3

Bennett, Alan 1934- .... **CLC 45, 77**
See also BRWS 8; CA 103; CANR 35, 55,
106; CBD; CD 5; DAB; DAM MST;
MTCW 1, 2

Bennett, (Enoch) Arnold
1867-1931 .... **TCLC 5, 20**
See also BRW 6; CA 106; 155; CDBLB
1890-1914; DLB 10, 34, 98, 135; EWL 3;
MTCW 2

Bennett, Elizabeth
See Mitchell, Margaret (Munnerlyn)

Bennett, George Harold 1930-
See Bennett, Hal
See also BW 1; CA 97-100; CANR 87

Bennett, Gwendolyn B. 1902-1981 .... **HR 2**
See also BW 1; CA 125; DLB 51; WP

Bennett, Hal .... **CLC 5**
See Bennett, George Harold
See also DLB 33

Bennett, Jay 1912- .... **CLC 35**
See also AAYA 10; CA 69-72; CANR 11,
42, 79; JRDA; SAAS 4; SATA 41, 87;
SATA-Brief 27; WYA; YAW

Bennett, Louise (Simone) 1919- .... **BLC 1;
CLC 28**
See also BW 2, 3; CA 151; CDWLB 3; CP
7; DAM MULT; DLB 117; EWL 3

Benson, A. C. 1862-1925 .... **TCLC 123**
See also DLB 98

Benson, E(dward) F(rederic)
1867-1940 .... **TCLC 27**
See also CA 114; 157; DLB 135, 153;
HGG; SUFW 1

Benson, Jackson J. 1930- .... **CLC 34**
See also CA 25-28R; DLB 111

Benson, Sally 1900-1972 .... **CLC 17**
See also CA 19-20; 37-40R; CAP 1; SATA
1, 35; SATA-Obit 27

Benson, Stella 1892-1933 .... **TCLC 17**
See also CA 117; 154, 155; DLB 36, 162;
FANT; TEA

Bentham, Jeremy 1748-1832 .... **NCLC 38**
See also DLB 107, 158, 252

Bentley, E(dmund) C(lerihew)
1875-1956 .... **TCLC 12**
See also CA 108; DLB 70; MSW

Bentley, Eric (Russell) 1916- .... **CLC 24**
See also CA 5-8R; CAD; CANR 6, 67;
CBD; CD 5; INT CANR-6

ben Uzair, Salem
See Horne, Richard Henry Hengist

Beranger, Pierre Jean de
1780-1857 .... **NCLC 34**

Berdyaev, Nicolas
See Berdyaev, Nikolai (Aleksandrovich)

Berdyaev, Nikolai (Aleksandrovich)
1874-1948 .... **TCLC 67**
See also CA 120; 157

Berdyayev, Nikolai (Aleksandrovich)
See Berdyaev, Nikolai (Aleksandrovich)

Berendt, John (Lawrence) 1939- ...... **CLC 86**
See also CA 146; CANR 75, 93; DA3;
MTCW 1

Beresford, J(ohn) D(avys)
1873-1947 .... **TCLC 81**
See also CA 112; 155; DLB 162, 178, 197;
SFW 4; SUFW 1

Bergelson, David (Rafailovich)
1884-1952 .... **TCLC 81**
See Bergelson, Dovid
See also CA 220

Bergelson, Dovid
See Bergelson, David (Rafailovich)
See also EWL 3

Berger, Colonel
See Malraux, (Georges-)Andre

Berger, John (Peter) 1926- .... **CLC 2, 19**
See also BRWS 4; CA 81-84; CANR 51,
78, 117; CN 7; DLB 14, 207

Berger, Melvin H. 1927- .... **CLC 12**
See also CA 5-8R; CANR 4; CLR 32;
SAAS 2; SATA 5, 88; SATA-Essay 124

Berger, Thomas (Louis) 1924- .. **CLC 3, 5, 8,
11, 18, 38**
See also BPFB 1; CA 1-4R; CANR 5, 28,
51, 128; CN 7; DAM NOV; DLB 2;
DLBY 1980; EWL 3; FANT; INT CANR-
28; MTCW 1, 2; RHW; TCWW 2

Bergman, (Ernst) Ingmar 1918- ...... **CLC 16,
72**
See also CA 81-84; CANR 33, 70; CWW
2; DLB 257; MTCW 2

Bergson, Henri(-Louis) 1859-1941 . **TCLC 32**
See also CA 164; EW 8; EWL 3; GFL 1789
to the Present

Bergstein, Eleanor 1938- .... **CLC 4**
See also CA 53-56; CANR 5

Berkeley, George 1685-1753 .... **LC 65**
See also DLB 31, 101, 252

Berkoff, Steven 1937- .... **CLC 56**
See also CA 104; CANR 72; CBD; CD 5

Berlin, Isaiah 1909-1997 .... **TCLC 105**
See also CA 85-88; 162

Bermant, Chaim (Icyk) 1929-1998 ... **CLC 40**
See also CA 57-60; CANR 6, 31, 57, 105;
CN 7

Bern, Victoria
See Fisher, M(ary) F(rances) K(ennedy)

Bernanos, (Paul Louis) Georges
1888-1948 .... **TCLC 3**
See also CA 104; 130; CANR 94; DLB 72;
EWL 3; GFL 1789 to the Present; RGWL
2, 3

Bernard, April 1956- .... **CLC 59**
See also CA 131

Bernard of Clairvaux 1090-1153 .. **CMLC 71**
See also DLB 208

Berne, Victoria
See Fisher, M(ary) F(rances) K(ennedy)

Bernhard, Thomas 1931-1989 ..... **CLC 3, 32,
61; DC 14**
See also CA 85-88; 127; CANR 32, 57; CD-
WLB 2; DLB 85, 124; EWL 3; MTCW 1;
RGWL 2, 3

Bernhardt, Sarah (Henriette Rosine)
1844-1923 .... **TCLC 75**
See also CA 157

Bernstein, Charles 1950- .... **CLC 142,**
See also CA 129; CAAS 24; CANR 90; CP
7; DLB 169

Bernstein, Ingrid
See Kirsch, Sarah

Berriault, Gina 1926-1999 .... **CLC 54, 109;
SSC 30**
See also CA 116; 129; 185; CANR 66; DLB
130; SSFS 7,11

Berrigan, Daniel 1921- .... **CLC 4**
See also CA 33-36R, 187; CAAE 187;
CAAS 1; CANR 11, 43, 78; CP 7; DLB 5

Berrigan, Edmund Joseph Michael, Jr.
1934-1983
See Berrigan, Ted
See also CA 61-64; 110; CANR 14, 102

Berrigan, Ted .... **CLC 37**
See Berrigan, Edmund Joseph Michael, Jr.
See also DLB 5, 169; WP

Berry, Charles Edward Anderson 1931-
See Berry, Chuck
See also CA 115

Berry, Chuck .... **CLC 17**
See Berry, Charles Edward Anderson

Berry, Jonas
See Ashbery, John (Lawrence)
See also GLL 1

Berry, Wendell (Erdman) 1934- ... **CLC 4, 6,
8, 27, 46; PC 28**
See also AITN 1; AMWS 10; ANW; CA
73-76; CANR 50, 73, 101, 132; CP 7;
CSW; DAM POET; DLB 5, 6, 234, 275;
MTCW 1

Berryman, John 1914-1972 ... **CLC 1, 2, 3, 4,
6, 8, 10, 13, 25, 62**
See also AMW; CA 13-16; 33-36R; CABS
2; CANR 35; CAP 1; CDALB 1941-1968;
DAM POET; DLB 48; EWL 3; MTCW 1,
2; PAB; RGAL 4; WP

Bertolucci, Bernardo 1940- ...... **CLC 16, 157**
See also CA 106; CANR 125

Berton, Pierre (Francis Demarigny)
1920-2004 .... **CLC 104**
See also CA 1-4R; CANR 2, 56; CPW;
DLB 68; SATA 99

Bertrand, Aloysius 1807-1841 .... **NCLC 31**
See Bertrand, Louis oAloysiusc

Bertrand, Louis oAloysiusc
See Bertrand, Aloysius
See also DLB 217

Bertran de Born c. 1140-1215 .... **CMLC 5**

Besant, Annie (Wood) 1847-1933 ..... **TCLC 9**
See also CA 105; 185

Bessie, Alvah 1904-1985 .... **CLC 23**
See also CA 5-8R; 116; CANR 2, 80; DLB
26

Bestuzhev, Aleksandr Aleksandrovich
1797-1837 .... **NCLC 131**
See also DLB 198

Bethlen, T. D.
See Silverberg, Robert

Beti, Mongo .... **BLC 1; CLC 27**
See Biyidi, Alexandre
See also AFW; CANR 79; DAM MULT;
EWL 3; WLIT 2

Betjeman, John 1906-1984 ...... **CLC 2, 6, 10,
34, 43**
See also BRW 7; CA 9-12R; 112; CANR
33, 56; CDBLB 1945-1960; DA3; DAB;
DAM MST, POET; DLB 20; DLBY 1984;
EWL 3; MTCW 1, 2

Bettelheim, Bruno 1903-1990 .... **CLC 79;
TCLC 143**
See also CA 81-84; 131; CANR 23, 61;
DA3; MTCW 1, 2

Betti, Ugo 1892-1953 .... **TCLC 5**
See also CA 104; 155; EWL 3; RGWL 2, 3

Betts, Doris (Waugh) 1932- ..... **CLC 3, 6, 28;
SSC 45**
See also CA 13-16R; CANR 9, 66, 77; CN
7; CSW; DLB 218; DLBY 1982; INT
CANR-9; RGAL 4

Bevan, Alistair
See Roberts, Keith (John Kingston)

Bobette
See Simenon, Georges (Jacques Christian)

Boccaccio, Giovanni 1313-1375 ... **CMLC 13, 57; SSC 10**
See also EW 2; RGSF 2; RGWL 2, 3; TWA

Bochco, Steven 1943- .... **CLC 35**
See also AAYA 11; CA 124; 138

Bode, Sigmund
See O'Doherty, Brian

Bodel, Jean 1167(?)-1210 .... **CMLC 28**

Bodenheim, Maxwell 1892-1954 .... **TCLC 44**
See also CA 110; 187; DLB 9, 45; RGAL 4

Bodenheimer, Maxwell
See Bodenheim, Maxwell

Bodker, Cecil 1927-
See Bodker, Cecil

Bodker, Cecil 1927- .... **CLC 21**
See also CA 73-76; CANR 13, 44, 111; CLR 23; MAICYA 1, 2; SATA 14, 133

Boell, Heinrich (Theodor)
1917-1985 ..... **CLC 2, 3, 6, 9, 11, 15, 27, 32, 72; SSC 23; WLC**
See Boll, Heinrich
See also CA 21-24R; 116; CANR 24; DA; DA3; DAB; DAC; DAM MST, NOV; DLB 69; DLBY 1985; MTCW 1, 2; SSFS 20; TWA

Boerne, Alfred
See Doeblin, Alfred

Boethius c. 480-c. 524 .... **CMLC 15**
See also DLB 115; RGWL 2, 3

Boff, Leonardo (Genezio Darci)
1938- .... **CLC 70; HLC 1**
See also CA 150; DAM MULT; HW 2

Bogan, Louise 1897-1970 .... **CLC 4, 39, 46, 93; PC 12**
See also AMWS 3; CA 73-76; 25-28R; CANR 33, 82; DAM POET; DLB 45, 169; EWL 3; MAWW; MTCW 1, 2; PFS 21; RGAL 4

Bogarde, Dirk
See Van Den Bogarde, Derek Jules Gaspard Ulric Niven
See also DLB 14

Bogosian, Eric 1953- .... **CLC 45, 141**
See also CA 138; CAD; CANR 102; CD 5

Bograd, Larry 1953- .... **CLC 35**
See also CA 93-96; CANR 57; SAAS 21; SATA 33, 89; WYA

Boiardo, Matteo Maria 1441-1494 .... **LC 6**

Boileau-Despreaux, Nicolas 1636-1711 . **LC 3**
See also DLB 268; EW 3; GFL Beginnings to 1789; RGWL 2, 3

Boissard, Maurice
See Leautaud, Paul

Bojer, Johan 1872-1959 .... **TCLC 64**
See also CA 189; EWL 3

Bok, Edward W(illiam)
1863-1930 .... **TCLC 101**
See also CA 217; DLB 91; DLBD 16

Boker, George Henry 1823-1890 . **NCLC 125**
See also RGAL 4

Boland, Eavan (Aisling) 1944- .. **CLC 40, 67, 113; PC 58**
See also BRWS 5; CA 143, 207; CAAE 207; CANR 61; CP 7; CWP; DAM POET; DLB 40; FW; MTCW 2; PFS 12

Boll, Heinrich
See Boell, Heinrich (Theodor)
See also BPFB 1; CDWLB 2; EW 13; EWL 3; RGSF 2; RGWL 2, 3

Bolt, Lee
See Faust, Frederick (Schiller)

Bolt, Robert (Oxton) 1924-1995 .... **CLC 14**
See also CA 17-20R; 147; CANR 35, 67; CBD; DAM DRAM; DFS 2; DLB 13, 233; EWL 3; LAIT 1; MTCW 1

Bombal, Maria Luisa 1910-1980 .... **HLCS 1; SSC 37**
See also CA 127; CANR 72; EWL 3; HW 1; LAW; RGSF 2

Bombet, Louis-Alexandre-Cesar
See Stendhal

Bomkauf
See Kaufman, Bob (Garnell)

Bonaventura .... **NCLC 35**
See also DLB 90

Bond, Edward 1934- .... **CLC 4, 6, 13, 23**
See also AAYA 50; BRWS 1; CA 25-28R; CANR 38, 67, 106; CBD; CD 5; DAM DRAM; DFS 3, 8; DLB 13; EWL 3; MTCW 1

Bonham, Frank 1914-1989 .... **CLC 12**
See also AAYA 1; BYA 1, 3; CA 9-12R; CANR 4, 36; JRDA; MAICYA 1, 2; SAAS 3; SATA 1, 49; SATA-Obit 62; TCWW 2; YAW

Bonnefoy, Yves 1923- . **CLC 9, 15, 58; PC 58**
See also CA 85-88; CANR 33, 75, 97; CWW 2; DAM MST, POET; DLB 258; EWL 3; GFL 1789 to the Present; MTCW 1, 2

Bonner, Marita .... **HR 2**
See Occomy, Marita (Odette) Bonner

Bonnin, Gertrude 1876-1938 .... **NNAL**
See Zitkala-Sa
See also CA 150; DAM MULT

Bontemps, Arna(ud Wendell)
1902-1973 ..... **BLC 1; CLC 1, 18; HR 2**
See also BW 1; CA 1-4R; 41-44R; CANR 4, 35; CLR 6; CWRI 5; DA3; DAM MULT, NOV, POET; DLB 48, 51; JRDA; MAICYA 1, 2; MTCW 1, 2; SATA 2, 44; SATA-Obit 24; WCH; WP

Boot, William
See Stoppard, Tom

Booth, Martin 1944-2004 .... **CLC 13**
See also CA 93-96, 188; 223; CAAE 188; CAAS 2; CANR 92

Booth, Philip 1925- .... **CLC 23**
See also CA 5-8R; CANR 5, 88; CP 7; DLBY 1982

Booth, Wayne C(layson) 1921- .... **CLC 24**
See also CA 1-4R; CAAS 5; CANR 3, 43, 117; DLB 67

Borchert, Wolfgang 1921-1947 .... **TCLC 5**
See also CA 104; 188; DLB 69, 124; EWL 3

Borel, Petrus 1809-1859 .... **NCLC 41**
See also DLB 119; GFL 1789 to the Present

Borges, Jorge Luis 1899-1986 ... **CLC 1, 2, 3, 4, 6, 8, 9, 10, 13, 19, 44, 48, 83; HLC 1; PC 22, 32; SSC 4, 41; TCLC 109; WLC**
See also AAYA 26; BPFB 1; CA 21-24R; CANR 19, 33, 75, 105, 133; CDWLB 3; DA; DA3; DAB; DAC; DAM MST, MULT; DLB 113, 283; DLBY 1986; DNFS 1, 2; EWL 3; HW 1, 2; LAW; LMFS 2; MSW; MTCW 1, 2; RGSF 2; RGWL 2, 3; SFW 4; SSFS 17; TWA; WLIT 1

Borowski, Tadeusz 1922-1951 .... **SSC 48; TCLC 9**
See also CA 106; 154; CDWLB 4; DLB 215; EWL 3; RGSF 2; RGWL 3; SSFS 13

Borrow, George (Henry)
1803-1881 .... **NCLC 9**
See also DLB 21, 55, 166

Bosch (Gavino), Juan 1909-2001 ..... **HLCS 1**
See also CA 151; 204; DAM MST, MULT; DLB 145; HW 1, 2

Bosman, Herman Charles
1905-1951 .... **TCLC 49**
See Malan, Herman
See also CA 160; DLB 225; RGSF 2

Bosschere, Jean de 1878(?)-1953 ... **TCLC 19**
See also CA 115; 186

Boswell, James 1740-1795 ... **LC 4, 50; WLC**
See also BRW 3; CDBLB 1660-1789; DA; DAB; DAM MST; DLB 104, 142; TEA; WLIT 3

Bottomley, Gordon 1874-1948 ..... **TCLC 107**
See also CA 120; 192; DLB 10

Bottoms, David 1949- .... **CLC 53**
See also CA 105; CANR 22; CSW; DLB 120; DLBY 1983

Boucicault, Dion 1820-1890 .... **NCLC 41**

Boucolon, Maryse
See Conde, Maryse

Bourdieu, Pierre 1930-2002 .... **CLC 198**
See also CA 130; 204

Bourget, Paul (Charles Joseph)
1852-1935 .... **TCLC 12**
See also CA 107; 196; DLB 123; GFL 1789 to the Present

Bourjaily, Vance (Nye) 1922- .... **CLC 8, 62**
See also CA 1-4R; CAAS 1; CANR 2, 72; CN 7; DLB 2, 143

Bourne, Randolph S(illiman)
1886-1918 .... **TCLC 16**
See also AMW; CA 117; 155; DLB 63

Bova, Ben(jamin William) 1932- ...... **CLC 45**
See also AAYA 16; CA 5-8R; CAAS 18; CANR 11, 56, 94, 111; CLR 3, 96; DLBY 1981; INT CANR-11; MAICYA 1, 2; MTCW 1; SATA 6, 68, 133; SFW 4

Bowen, Elizabeth (Dorothea Cole)
1899-1973 . **CLC 1, 3, 6, 11, 15, 22, 118; SSC 3, 28, 66; TCLC 148**
See also BRWS 2; CA 17-18; 41-44R; CANR 35, 105; CAP 2; CDBLB 1945-1960; DA3; DAM NOV; DLB 15, 162; EWL 3; EXPS; FW; HGG; MTCW 1, 2; NFS 13; RGSF 2; SSFS 5; SUFW 1; TEA; WLIT 4

Bowering, George 1935- .... **CLC 15, 47**
See also CA 21-24R; CAAS 16; CANR 10; CP 7; DLB 53

Bowering, Marilyn R(uthe) 1949- .... **CLC 32**
See also CA 101; CANR 49; CP 7; CWP

Bowers, Edgar 1924-2000 .... **CLC 9**
See also CA 5-8R; 188; CANR 24; CP 7; CSW; DLB 5

Bowers, Mrs. J. Milton 1842-1914
See Bierce, Ambrose (Gwinett)

Bowie, David .... **CLC 17**
See Jones, David Robert

Bowles, Jane (Sydney) 1917-1973 ..... **CLC 3, 68**
See Bowles, Jane Auer
See also CA 19-20; 41-44R; CAP 2

Bowles, Jane Auer
See Bowles, Jane (Sydney)
See also EWL 3

Bowles, Paul (Frederick) 1910-1999 . **CLC 1, 2, 19, 53; SSC 3**
See also AMWS 4; CA 1-4R; 186; CAAS 1; CANR 1, 19, 50, 75; CN 7; DA3; DLB 5, 6, 218; EWL 3; MTCW 1, 2; RGAL 4; SSFS 17

Bowles, William Lisle 1762-1850 . **NCLC 103**
See also DLB 93

Box, Edgar
See Vidal, (Eugene Luther) Gore
See also GLL 1

Boyd, James 1888-1944 .... **TCLC 115**
See also CA 186; DLB 9; DLBD 16; RGAL 4; RHW

Boyd, Nancy
See Millay, Edna St. Vincent
See also GLL 1

Boyd, Thomas (Alexander)
1898-1935 .... **TCLC 111**
See also CA 111; 183; DLB 9; DLBD 16

Boyd, William 1952- .... **CLC 28, 53, 70**
See also CA 114; 120; CANR 51, 71, 131;
CN 7; DLB 231

Boyesen, Hjalmar Hjorth
1848-1895 .... **NCLC 135**
See also DLB 12, 71; DLBD 13; RGAL 4

Boyle, Kay 1902-1992 .... **CLC 1, 5, 19, 58,
121; SSC 5**
See also CA 13-16R; 140; CAAS 1; CANR
29, 61, 110; DLB 4, 9, 48, 86; DLBY
1993; EWL 3; MTCW 1, 2; RGAL 4;
RGSF 2; SSFS 10, 13, 14

Boyle, Mark
See Kienzle, William X(avier)

Boyle, Patrick 1905-1982 .... **CLC 19**
See also CA 127

Boyle, T. C.
See Boyle, T(homas) Coraghessan
See also AMWS 8

Boyle, T(homas) Coraghessan
1948- .... **CLC 36, 55, 90; SSC 16**
See Boyle, T. C.
See also AAYA 47; BEST 90:4; BPFB 1;
CA 120; CANR 44, 76, 89, 132; CN 7;
CPW; DA3; DAM POP; DLB 218, 278;
DLBY 1986; EWL 3; MTCW 2; SSFS 13,
19

Boz
See Dickens, Charles (John Huffam)

Brackenridge, Hugh Henry
1748-1816 .... **NCLC 7**
See also DLB 11, 37; RGAL 4

Bradbury, Edward P.
See Moorcock, Michael (John)
See also MTCW 2

Bradbury, Malcolm (Stanley)
1932-2000 .... **CLC 32, 61**
See also CA 1-4R; CANR 1, 33, 91, 98;
CN 7; DA3; DAM NOV; DLB 14, 207;
EWL 3; MTCW 1, 2

Bradbury, Ray (Douglas) 1920- .... **CLC 1, 3,
10, 15, 42, 98; SSC 29, 53; WLC**
See also AAYA 15; AITN 1, 2; AMWS 4;
BPFB 1; BYA 4, 5, 11; CA 1-4R; CANR
2, 30, 75, 125; CDALB 1968-1988; CN
7; CPW; DA; DA3; DAB; DAC; DAM
MST, NOV, POP; DLB 2, 8; EXPN;
EXPS; HGG; LAIT 3, 5; LATS 1:2;
LMFS 2; MTCW 1, 2; NFS 1; RGAL 4;
RGSF 2; SATA 11, 64, 123; SCFW 2;
SFW 4; SSFS 1, 20; SUFW 1, 2; TUS;
YAW

Braddon, Mary Elizabeth
1837-1915 .... **TCLC 111**
See also BRWS 8; CA 108; 179; CMW 4;
DLB 18, 70, 156; HGG

Bradfield, Scott (Michael) 1955- .... **SSC 65**
See also CA 147; CANR 90; HGG; SUFW
2

Bradford, Gamaliel 1863-1932 .... **TCLC 36**
See also CA 160; DLB 17

Bradford, William 1590-1657 .... **LC 64**
See also DLB 24, 30; RGAL 4

Bradley, David (Henry), Jr. 1950- .... **BLC 1;
CLC 23, 118**
See also BW 1, 3; CA 104; CANR 26, 81;
CN 7; DAM MULT; DLB 33

Bradley, John Ed(mund, Jr.) 1958- . **CLC 55**
See also CA 139; CANR 99; CN 7; CSW

Bradley, Marion Zimmer
1930-1999 .... **CLC 30**
See Chapman, Lee; Dexter, John; Gardner,
Miriam; Ives, Morgan; Rivers, Elfrida
See also AAYA 40; BPFB 1; CA 57-60; 185;
CAAS 10; CANR 7, 31, 51, 75, 107;
CPW; DA3; DAM POP; DLB 8; FANT;
FW; MTCW 1, 2; SATA 90, 139; SATA-
Obit 116; SFW 4; SUFW 2; YAW

Bradshaw, John 1933- .... **CLC 70**
See also CA 138; CANR 61

Bradstreet, Anne 1612(?)-1672 ...... **LC 4, 30;
PC 10**
See also AMWS 1; CDALB 1640-1865;
DA; DA3; DAC; DAM MST, POET; DLB
24; EXPP; FW; PFS 6; RGAL 4; TUS;
WP

Brady, Joan 1939- .... **CLC 86**
See also CA 141

Bragg, Melvyn 1939- .... **CLC 10**
See also BEST 89:3; CA 57-60; CANR 10,
48, 89; CN 7; DLB 14, 271; RHW

Brahe, Tycho 1546-1601 .... **LC 45**
See also DLB 300

Braine, John (Gerard) 1922-1986 . **CLC 1, 3,
41**
See also CA 1-4R; 120; CANR 1, 33; CD-
BLB 1945-1960; DLB 15; DLBY 1986;
EWL 3; MTCW 1

Braithwaite, William Stanley (Beaumont)
1878-1962 .... **BLC 1; HR 2; PC 52**
See also BW 1; CA 125; DAM MULT; DLB
50, 54

Bramah, Ernest 1868-1942 .... **TCLC 72**
See also CA 156; CMW 4; DLB 70; FANT

Brammer, William 1930(?)-1978 ...... **CLC 31**
See also CA 77-80

Brancati, Vitaliano 1907-1954 .... **TCLC 12**
See also CA 109; DLB 264; EWL 3

Brancato, Robin F(idler) 1936- .... **CLC 35**
See also AAYA 9; BYA 6; CA 69-72; CANR
11, 45; CLR 32; JRDA; MAICYA 2;
MAICYAS 1; SAAS 9; SATA 97; WYA;
YAW

Brand, Dionne 1953- .... **CLC 192**
See also BW 2; CA 143; CWP

Brand, Max
See Faust, Frederick (Schiller)
See also BPFB 1; TCWW 2

Brand, Millen 1906-1980 .... **CLC 7**
See also CA 21-24R; 97-100; CANR 72

Branden, Barbara .... **CLC 44**
See also CA 148

Brandes, Georg (Morris Cohen)
1842-1927 .... **TCLC 10**
See also CA 105; 189; DLB 300

Brandys, Kazimierz 1916-2000 .... **CLC 62**
See also EWL 3

Branley, Franklyn M(ansfield)
1915-2002 .... **CLC 21**
See also CA 33-36R; 207; CANR 14, 39;
CLR 13; MAICYA 1, 2; SAAS 16; SATA
4, 68, 136

Brant, Beth (E.) 1941- .... **NNAL**
See also CA 144; FW

Brathwaite, Edward Kamau
1930- .... **BLCS; CLC 11; PC 56**
See also BW 2, 3; CA 25-28R; CANR 11,
26, 47, 107; CDWLB 3; CP 7; DAM
POET; DLB 125; EWL 3

Brathwaite, Kamau
See Brathwaite, Edward Kamau

Brautigan, Richard (Gary)
1935-1984 .... **CLC 1, 3, 5, 9, 12, 34, 42;
TCLC 133**
See also BPFB 1; CA 53-56; 113; CANR
34; DA3; DAM NOV; DLB 2, 5, 206;
DLBY 1980, 1984; FANT; MTCW 1;
RGAL 4; SATA 56

Brave Bird, Mary .... **NNAL**
See Crow Dog, Mary (Ellen)

Braverman, Kate 1950- .... **CLC 67**
See also CA 89-92

Brecht, (Eugen) Bertolt (Friedrich)
1898-1956 ..... **DC 3; TCLC 1, 6, 13, 35;
WLC**
See also CA 104; 133; CANR 62; CDWLB
2; DA; DA3; DAB; DAC; DAM DRAM,
MST; DFS 4, 5, 9; DLB 56, 124; EW 11;
EWL 3; IDTP; MTCW 1, 2; RGWL 2, 3;
TWA

Brecht, Eugen Berthold Friedrich
See Brecht, (Eugen) Bertolt (Friedrich)

Bremer, Fredrika 1801-1865 .... **NCLC 11**
See also DLB 254

Brennan, Christopher John
1870-1932 .... **TCLC 17**
See also CA 117; 188; DLB 230; EWL 3

Brennan, Maeve 1917-1993 ... **CLC 5; TCLC
124**
See also CA 81-84; CANR 72, 100

Brent, Linda
See Jacobs, Harriet A(nn)

Brentano, Clemens (Maria)
1778-1842 .... **NCLC 1**
See also DLB 90; RGWL 2, 3

Brent of Bin Bin
See Franklin, (Stella Maria Sarah) Miles
(Lampe)

Brenton, Howard 1942- .... **CLC 31**
See also CA 69-72; CANR 33, 67; CBD;
CD 5; DLB 13; MTCW 1

Breslin, James 1930-
See Breslin, Jimmy
See also CA 73-76; CANR 31, 75; DAM
NOV; MTCW 1, 2

Breslin, Jimmy .... **CLC 4, 43**
See Breslin, James
See also AITN 1; DLB 185; MTCW 2

Bresson, Robert 1901(?)-1999 .... **CLC 16**
See also CA 110; 187; CANR 49

Breton, Andre 1896-1966 .. **CLC 2, 9, 15, 54;
PC 15**
See also CA 19-20; 25-28R; CANR 40, 60;
CAP 2; DLB 65, 258; EW 11; EWL 3;
GFL 1789 to the Present; LMFS 2;
MTCW 1, 2; RGWL 2, 3; TWA; WP

Breytenbach, Breyten 1939(?)- .. **CLC 23, 37,
126**
See also CA 113; 129; CANR 61, 122;
CWW 2; DAM POET; DLB 225; EWL 3

Bridgers, Sue Ellen 1942- .... **CLC 26**
See also AAYA 8, 49; BYA 7, 8; CA 65-68;
CANR 11, 36; CLR 18; DLB 52; JRDA;
MAICYA 1, 2; SAAS 1; SATA 22, 90;
SATA-Essay 109; WYA; YAW

Bridges, Robert (Seymour)
1844-1930 .... **PC 28; TCLC 1**
See also BRW 6; CA 104; 152; CDBLB
1890-1914; DAM POET; DLB 19, 98

Bridie, James .... **TCLC 3**
See Mavor, Osborne Henry
See also DLB 10; EWL 3

Brin, David 1950- .... **CLC 34**
See also AAYA 21; CA 102; CANR 24, 70,
125, 127; INT CANR-24; SATA 65;
SCFW 2; SFW 4

Brink, Andre (Philippus) 1935- . **CLC 18, 36,
106**
See also AFW; BRWS 6; CA 104; CANR
39, 62, 109, 133; CN 7; DLB 225; EWL
3; INT CA-103; LATS 1:2; MTCW 1, 2;
WLIT 2

Brinsmead, H. F(ay)
See Brinsmead, H(esba) F(ay)

Brinsmead, H. F.
See Brinsmead, H(esba) F(ay)

Brinsmead, H(esba) F(ay) 1922- ...... **CLC 21**
See also CA 21-24R; CANR 10; CLR 47;
CWRI 5; MAICYA 1, 2; SAAS 5; SATA
18, 78

Brittain, Vera (Mary) 1893(?)-1970 . **CLC 23**
See also BRWS 10; CA 13-16; 25-28R;
CANR 58; CAP 1; DLB 191; FW; MTCW
1, 2

Broch, Hermann 1886-1951 .... **TCLC 20**
See also CA 117; 211; CDWLB 2; DLB 85,
124; EW 10; EWL 3; RGWL 2, 3

Brock, Rose
See Hansen, Joseph
See also GLL 1

Brod, Max 1884-1968 .... **TCLC 115**
See also CA 5-8R; 25-28R; CANR 7; DLB 81; EWL 3

Brodkey, Harold (Roy) 1930-1996 .. **CLC 56; TCLC 123**
See also CA 111; 151; CANR 71; CN 7; DLB 130

Brodsky, Iosif Alexandrovich 1940-1996
See Brodsky, Joseph
See also AITN 1; CA 41-44R; 151; CANR 37, 106; DA3; DAM POET; MTCW 1, 2; RGWL 2, 3

Brodsky, Joseph . **CLC 4, 6, 13, 36, 100; PC 9**
See Brodsky, Iosif Alexandrovich
See also AMWS 8; CWW 2; DLB 285; EWL 3; MTCW 1

Brodsky, Michael (Mark) 1948- .... **CLC 19**
See also CA 102; CANR 18, 41, 58; DLB 244

Brodzki, Bella ed. .... **CLC 65**

Brome, Richard 1590(?)-1652 .... **LC 61**
See also BRWS 10; DLB 58

Bromell, Henry 1947- .... **CLC 5**
See also CA 53-56; CANR 9, 115, 116

Bromfield, Louis (Brucker)
1896-1956 .... **TCLC 11**
See also CA 107; 155; DLB 4, 9, 86; RGAL 4; RHW

Broner, E(sther) M(asserman)
1930- .... **CLC 19**
See also CA 17-20R; CANR 8, 25, 72; CN 7; DLB 28

Bronk, William (M.) 1918-1999 .... **CLC 10**
See also CA 89-92; 177; CANR 23; CP 7; DLB 165

Bronstein, Lev Davidovich
See Trotsky, Leon

Bronte, Anne 1820-1849 ..... **NCLC 4, 71, 102**
See also BRW 5; BRWR 1; DA3; DLB 21, 199; TEA

Bronte, (Patrick) Branwell
1817-1848 .... **NCLC 109**

Bronte, Charlotte 1816-1855 ...... **NCLC 3, 8, 33, 58, 105; WLC**
See also AAYA 17; BRW 5; BRWC 2; BRWR 1; BYA 2; CDBLB 1832-1890; DA; DA3; DAB; DAC; DAM MST, NOV; DLB 21, 159, 199; EXPN; LAIT 2; NFS 4; TEA; WLIT 4

Bronte, Emily (Jane) 1818-1848 ... **NCLC 16, 35; PC 8; WLC**
See also AAYA 17; BPFB 1; BRW 5; BRWC 1; BRWR 1; BYA 3; CDBLB 1832-1890; DA; DA3; DAB; DAC; DAM MST, NOV, POET; DLB 21, 32, 199; EXPN; LAIT 1; TEA; WLIT 3

Brontes
See Bronte, Anne; Bronte, Charlotte; Bronte, Emily (Jane)

Brooke, Frances 1724-1789 .... **LC 6, 48**
See also DLB 39, 99

Brooke, Henry 1703(?)-1783 .... **LC 1**
See also DLB 39

Brooke, Rupert (Chawner)
1887-1915 ..... **PC 24; TCLC 2, 7; WLC**
See also BRWS 3; CA 104; 132; CANR 61; CDBLB 1914-1945; DA; DAB; DAC; DAM MST, POET; DLB 19, 216; EXPP; GLL 2; MTCW 1, 2; PFS 7; TEA

Brooke-Haven, P.
See Wodehouse, P(elham) G(renville)

Brooke-Rose, Christine 1926(?)- ..... **CLC 40, 184**
See also BRWS 4; CA 13-16R; CANR 58, 118; CN 7; DLB 14, 231; EWL 3; SFW 4

Brookner, Anita 1928- .. **CLC 32, 34, 51, 136**
See also BRWS 4; CA 114; 120; CANR 37, 56, 87, 130; CN 7; CPW; DA3; DAB; DAM POP; DLB 194; DLBY 1987; EWL 3; MTCW 1, 2; TEA

Brooks, Cleanth 1906-1994 . **CLC 24, 86, 110**
See also AMWS 14; CA 17-20R; 145; CANR 33, 35; CSW; DLB 63; DLBY 1994; EWL 3; INT CANR-35; MTCW 1, 2

Brooks, George
See Baum, L(yman) Frank

Brooks, Gwendolyn (Elizabeth)
1917-2000 ... **BLC 1; CLC 1, 2, 4, 5, 15, 49, 125; PC 7; WLC**
See also AAYA 20; AFAW 1, 2; AITN 1; AMWS 3; BW 2, 3; CA 1-4R; 190; CANR 1, 27, 52, 75, 132; CDALB 1941-1968; CLR 27; CP 7; CWP; DA; DA3; DAC; DAM MST, MULT, POET; DLB 5, 76, 165; EWL 3; EXPP; MAWW; MTCW 1, 2; PFS 1, 2, 4, 6; RGAL 4; SATA 6; SATA-Obit 123; TUS; WP

Brooks, Mel .... **CLC 12**
See Kaminsky, Melvin
See also AAYA 13, 48; DLB 26

Brooks, Peter (Preston) 1938- .... **CLC 34**
See also CA 45-48; CANR 1, 107

Brooks, Van Wyck 1886-1963 .... **CLC 29**
See also AMW; CA 1-4R; CANR 6; DLB 45, 63, 103; TUS

Brophy, Brigid (Antonia)
1929-1995 .... **CLC 6, 11, 29, 105**
See also CA 5-8R; 149; CAAS 4; CANR 25, 53; CBD; CN 7; CWD; DA3; DLB 14, 271; EWL 3; MTCW 1, 2

Brosman, Catharine Savage 1934- ..... **CLC 9**
See also CA 61-64; CANR 21, 46

Brossard, Nicole 1943- .... **CLC 115, 169**
See also CA 122; CAAS 16; CCA 1; CWP; CWW 2; DLB 53; EWL 3; FW; GLL 2; RGWL 3

Brother Antoninus
See Everson, William (Oliver)

The Brothers Quay
See Quay, Stephen; Quay, Timothy

Broughton, T(homas) Alan 1936- ..... **CLC 19**
See also CA 45-48; CANR 2, 23, 48, 111

Broumas, Olga 1949- .... **CLC 10, 73**
See also CA 85-88; CANR 20, 69, 110; CP 7; CWP; GLL 2

Broun, Heywood 1888-1939 .... **TCLC 104**
See also DLB 29, 171

Brown, Alan 1950- .... **CLC 99**
See also CA 156

Brown, Charles Brockden
1771-1810 .... **NCLC 22, 74, 122**
See also AMWS 1; CDALB 1640-1865; DLB 37, 59, 73; FW; HGG; LMFS 1; RGAL 4; TUS

Brown, Christy 1932-1981 .... **CLC 63**
See also BYA 13; CA 105; 104; CANR 72; DLB 14

Brown, Claude 1937-2002 ... **BLC 1; CLC 30**
See also AAYA 7; BW 1, 3; CA 73-76; 205; CANR 81; DAM MULT

Brown, Dee (Alexander)
1908-2002 .... **CLC 18, 47**
See also AAYA 30; CA 13-16R; 212; CAAS 6; CANR 11, 45, 60; CPW; CSW; DA3; DAM POP; DLBY 1980; LAIT 2; MTCW 1, 2; NCFS 5; SATA 5, 110; SATA-Obit 141; TCWW 2

Brown, George
See Wertmueller, Lina

Brown, George Douglas
1869-1902 .... **TCLC 28**
See Douglas, George
See also CA 162

Brown, George Mackay 1921-1996 ... **CLC 5, 48, 100**
See also BRWS 6; CA 21-24R; 151; CAAS 6; CANR 12, 37, 67; CN 7; CP 7; DLB 14, 27, 139, 271; MTCW 1; RGSF 2; SATA 35

Brown, (William) Larry 1951-2004 . **CLC 73**
See also CA 130; 134; CANR 117; CSW; DLB 234; INT CA-134

Brown, Moses
See Barrett, William (Christopher)

Brown, Rita Mae 1944- .... **CLC 18, 43, 79**
See also BPFB 1; CA 45-48; CANR 2, 11, 35, 62, 95; CN 7; CPW; CSW; DA3; DAM NOV, POP; FW; INT CANR-11; MTCW 1, 2; NFS 9; RGAL 4; TUS

Brown, Roderick (Langmere) Haig-
See Haig-Brown, Roderick (Langmere)

Brown, Rosellen 1939- .... **CLC 32, 170**
See also CA 77-80; CAAS 10; CANR 14, 44, 98; CN 7

Brown, Sterling Allen 1901-1989 ...... **BLC 1; CLC 1, 23, 59; HR 2; PC 55**
See also AFAW 1, 2; BW 1, 3; CA 85-88; 127; CANR 26; DA3; DAM MULT, POET; DLB 48, 51, 63; MTCW 1, 2; RGAL 4; WP

Brown, Will
See Ainsworth, William Harrison

Brown, William Hill 1765-1793 .... **LC 93**
See also DLB 37

Brown, William Wells 1815-1884 ...... **BLC 1; DC 1; NCLC 2, 89**
See also DAM MULT; DLB 3, 50, 183, 248; RGAL 4

Browne, (Clyde) Jackson 1948(?)- ... **CLC 21**
See also CA 120

Browne, Thomas 1605-1682 .... **LC 111**
See also BW 2; DLB 151

Browning, Elizabeth Barrett
1806-1861 ... **NCLC 1, 16, 61, 66; PC 6; WLC**
See also BRW 4; CDBLB 1832-1890; DA; DA3; DAB; DAC; DAM MST, POET; DLB 32, 199; EXPP; PAB; PFS 2, 16; TEA; WLIT 4; WP

Browning, Robert 1812-1889 . **NCLC 19, 79; PC 2, 61; WLCS**
See also BRW 4; BRWC 2; BRWR 2; CDBLB 1832-1890; CLR 97; DA; DA3; DAB; DAC; DAM MST, POET; DLB 32, 163; EXPP; LATS 1:1; PAB; PFS 1, 15; RGEL 2; TEA; WLIT 4; WP; YABC 1

Browning, Tod 1882-1962 .... **CLC 16**
See also CA 141; 117

Brownmiller, Susan 1935- .... **CLC 159**
See also CA 103; CANR 35, 75; DAM NOV; FW; MTCW 1, 2

Brownson, Orestes Augustus
1803-1876 .... **NCLC 50**
See also DLB 1, 59, 73, 243

Bruccoli, Matthew J(oseph) 1931- ... **CLC 34**
See also CA 9-12R; CANR 7, 87; DLB 103

Bruce, Lenny .... **CLC 21**
See Schneider, Leonard Alfred

Bruchac, Joseph III 1942- .... **NNAL**
See also AAYA 19; CA 33-36R; CANR 13, 47, 75, 94; CLR 46; CWRI 5; DAM MULT; JRDA; MAICYA 2; MAICYAS 1; MTCW 1; SATA 42, 89, 131

Bruin, John
See Brutus, Dennis

Brulard, Henri
See Stendhal

Brulls, Christian
See Simenon, Georges (Jacques Christian)

Castellanos, Rosario 1925-1974 .... **CLC 66;**
HLC 1; SSC 39, 68
See also CA 131; 53-56; CANR 58; CD-
WLB 3; DAM MULT; DLB 113, 290;
EWL 3; FW; HW 1; LAW; MTCW 1;
RGSF 2; RGWL 2, 3

Castelvetro, Lodovico 1505-1571 .... **LC 12**

Castiglione, Baldassare 1478-1529 ...... **LC 12**
See Castiglione, Baldesar
See also LMFS 1; RGWL 2, 3

Castiglione, Baldesar
See Castiglione, Baldassare
See also EW 2

Castillo, Ana (Hernandez Del)
1953- .... **CLC 151**
See also AAYA 42; CA 131; CANR 51, 86,
128; CWP; DLB 122, 227; DNFS 2; FW;
HW 1; LLW 1; PFS 21

Castle, Robert
See Hamilton, Edmond

Castro (Ruz), Fidel 1926(?)- .... **HLC 1**
See also CA 110; 129; CANR 81; DAM
MULT; HW 2

Castro, Guillen de 1569-1631 .... **LC 19**

Castro, Rosalia de 1837-1885 ... **NCLC 3, 78;**
PC 41
See also DAM MULT

Cather, Willa (Sibert) 1873-1947 . **SSC 2, 50;**
TCLC 1, 11, 31, 99, 132, 152; WLC
See also AAYA 24; AMW; AMWC 1;
AMWR 1; BPFB 1; CA 104; 128; CDALB
1865-1917; CLR 98; DA; DA3; DAB;
DAC; DAM MST, NOV; DLB 9, 54, 78,
256; DLBD 1; EWL 3; EXPN; EXPS;
LAIT 3; LATS 1:1; MAWW; MTCW 1,
2; NFS 2, 19; RGAL 4; RGSF 2; RHW;
SATA 30; SSFS 2, 7, 16; TCWW 2; TUS

Catherine II
See Catherine the Great
See also DLB 150

Catherine the Great 1729-1796 .... **LC 69**
See Catherine II

Cato, Marcus Porcius
234B.C.-149B.C. .... **CMLC 21**
See Cato the Elder

Cato, Marcus Porcius, the Elder
See Cato, Marcus Porcius

Cato the Elder
See Cato, Marcus Porcius
See also DLB 211

Catton, (Charles) Bruce 1899-1978 . **CLC 35**
See also AITN 1; CA 5-8R; 81-84; CANR
7, 74; DLB 17; SATA 2; SATA-Obit 24

Catullus c. 84B.C.-54B.C. .... **CMLC 18**
See also AW 2; CDWLB 1; DLB 211;
RGWL 2, 3

Cauldwell, Frank
See King, Francis (Henry)

Caunitz, William J. 1933-1996 .... **CLC 34**
See also BEST 89:3; CA 125; 130; 152;
CANR 73; INT CA-130

Causley, Charles (Stanley)
1917-2003 .... **CLC 7**
See also CA 9-12R; 223; CANR 5, 35, 94;
CLR 30; CWRI 5; DLB 27; MTCW 1;
SATA 3, 66; SATA-Obit 149

Caute, (John) David 1936- .... **CLC 29**
See also CA 1-4R; CAAS 4; CANR 1, 33,
64, 120; CBD; CD 5; CN 7; DAM NOV;
DLB 14, 231

Cavafy, C(onstantine) P(eter) .... **PC 36;**
TCLC 2, 7
See Kavafis, Konstantinos Petrou
See also CA 148; DA3; DAM POET; EW
8; EWL 3; MTCW 1; PFS 19; RGWL 2,
3; WP

Cavalcanti, Guido c. 1250-c.
1300 .... **CMLC 54**
See also RGWL 2, 3

Cavallo, Evelyn
See Spark, Muriel (Sarah)

Cavanna, Betty .... **CLC 12**
See Harrison, Elizabeth (Allen) Cavanna
See also JRDA; MAICYA 1; SAAS 4;
SATA 1, 30

Cavendish, Margaret Lucas
1623-1673 .... **LC 30**
See also DLB 131, 252, 281; RGEL 2

Caxton, William 1421(?)-1491(?) .... **LC 17**
See also DLB 170

Cayer, D. M.
See Duffy, Maureen

Cayrol, Jean 1911- .... **CLC 11**
See also CA 89-92; DLB 83; EWL 3

Cela (y Trulock), Camilo Jose
See Cela, Camilo Jose
See also CWW 2

Cela, Camilo Jose 1916-2002 .... **CLC 4, 13,**
59, 122; HLC 1; SSC 71
See Cela (y Trulock), Camilo Jose
See also BEST 90:2; CA 21-24R; 206;
CAAS 10; CANR 21, 32, 76; DAM
MULT; DLBY 1989; EW 13; EWL 3; HW
1; MTCW 1, 2; RGSF 2; RGWL 2, 3

Celan, Paul .... **CLC 10, 19, 53, 82; PC 10**
See Antschel, Paul
See also CDWLB 2; DLB 69; EWL 3;
RGWL 2, 3

Celine, Louis-Ferdinand .. **CLC 1, 3, 4, 7, 9,**
15, 47, 124
See Destouches, Louis-Ferdinand
See also DLB 72; EW 11; EWL 3; GFL
1789 to the Present; RGWL 2, 3

Cellini, Benvenuto 1500-1571 .... **LC 7**

Cendrars, Blaise .... **CLC 18, 106**
See Sauser-Hall, Frederic
See also DLB 258; EWL 3; GFL 1789 to
the Present; RGWL 2, 3; WP

Centlivre, Susanna 1669(?)-1723 .... **DC 25;**
LC 65
See also DLB 84; RGEL 2

Cernuda (y Bidon), Luis 1902-1963 . **CLC 54**
See also CA 131; 89-92; DAM POET; DLB
134; EWL 3; GLL 1; HW 1; RGWL 2, 3

Cervantes, Lorna Dee 1954- ..... **HLCS 1; PC**
35
See also CA 131; CANR 80; CWP; DLB
82; EXPP; HW 1; LLW 1

Cervantes (Saavedra), Miguel de
1547-1616 .... **HLCS; LC 6, 23, 93; SSC**
12; WLC
See also AAYA 56; BYA 1, 14; DA; DAB;
DAC; DAM MST, NOV; EW 2; LAIT 1;
LATS 1:1; LMFS 1; NFS 8; RGSF 2;
RGWL 2, 3; TWA

Cesaire, Aime (Fernand) 1913- .... **BLC 1;**
CLC 19, 32, 112; DC 22; PC 25
See also BW 2, 3; CA 65-68; CANR 24,
43, 81; CWW 2; DA3; DAM MULT;
POET; EWL 3; GFL 1789 to the Present;
MTCW 1, 2; WP

Chabon, Michael 1963- ... **CLC 55, 149; SSC**
59
See also AAYA 45; AMWS 11; CA 139;
CANR 57, 96, 127; DLB 278; SATA 145

Chabrol, Claude 1930- .... **CLC 16**
See also CA 110

Chairil Anwar
See Anwar, Chairil
See also EWL 3

Challans, Mary 1905-1983
See Renault, Mary
See also CA 81-84; 111; CANR 74; DA3;
MTCW 2; SATA 23; SATA-Obit 36; TEA

Challis, George
See Faust, Frederick (Schiller)
See also TCWW 2

Chambers, Aidan 1934- .... **CLC 35**
See also AAYA 27; CA 25-28R; CANR 12,
31, 58, 116; JRDA; MAICYA 1, 2; SAAS
12; SATA 1, 69, 108; WYA; YAW

Chambers, James 1948-
See Cliff, Jimmy
See also CA 124

Chambers, Jessie
See Lawrence, D(avid) H(erbert Richards)
See also GLL 1

Chambers, Robert W(illiam)
1865-1933 .... **TCLC 41**
See also CA 165; DLB 202; HGG; SATA
107; SUFW 1

Chambers, (David) Whittaker
1901-1961 .... **TCLC 129**
See also CA 89-92; DLB 303

Chamisso, Adelbert von
1781-1838 .... **NCLC 82**
See also DLB 90; RGWL 2, 3; SUFW 1

Chance, James T.
See Carpenter, John (Howard)

Chance, John T.
See Carpenter, John (Howard)

Chandler, Raymond (Thornton)
1888-1959 .... **SSC 23; TCLC 1, 7**
See also AAYA 25; AMWC 2; AMWS 4;
BPFB 1; CA 104; 129; CANR 60, 107;
CDALB 1929-1941; CMW 4; DA3; DLB
226, 253; DLBD 6; EWL 3; MSW;
MTCW 1, 2; NFS 17; RGAL 4; TUS

Chang, Diana 1934- .... **AAL**
See also CA 228; CWP; EXPP

Chang, Eileen 1921-1995 .... **AAL; SSC 28**
See Chang Ai-Ling; Zhang Ailing
See also CA 166

Chang, Jung 1952- .... **CLC 71**
See also CA 142

Chang Ai-Ling
See Chang, Eileen
See also EWL 3

Channing, William Ellery
1780-1842 .... **NCLC 17**
See also DLB 1, 59, 235; RGAL 4

Chao, Patricia 1955- .... **CLC 119**
See also CA 163

Chaplin, Charles Spencer
1889-1977 .... **CLC 16**
See Chaplin, Charlie
See also CA 81-84; 73-76

Chaplin, Charlie
See Chaplin, Charles Spencer
See also DLB 44

Chapman, George 1559(?)-1634 . **DC 19; LC**
22
See also BRW 1; DAM DRAM; DLB 62,
121; LMFS 1; RGEL 2

Chapman, Graham 1941-1989 .... **CLC 21**
See Monty Python
See also CA 116; 129; CANR 35, 95

Chapman, John Jay 1862-1933 .... **TCLC 7**
See also AMWS 14; CA 104; 191

Chapman, Lee
See Bradley, Marion Zimmer
See also GLL 1

Chapman, Walker
See Silverberg, Robert

Chappell, Fred (Davis) 1936- .... **CLC 40, 78,**
162
See also CA 5-8R; 198; CAAE 198; CAAS
4; CANR 8, 33, 67, 110; CN 7; CP 7;
CSW; DLB 6, 105; HGG

Char, Rene(-Emile) 1907-1988 .... **CLC 9, 11,**
14, 55; PC 56
See also CA 13-16R; 124; CANR 32; DAM
POET; DLB 258; EWL 3; GFL 1789 to
the Present; MTCW 1, 2; RGWL 2, 3

Charby, Jay
See Ellison, Harlan (Jay)

Churchill, Charles 1731-1764 .... **LC 3**
 See also DLB 109; RGEL 2
Churchill, Chick
 See Churchill, Caryl
 See also CD 5
Churchill, Sir Winston (Leonard Spencer)
 1874-1965 .... **TCLC 113**
 See also BRW 6; CA 97-100; CDBLB
 1890-1914; DA3; DLB 100; DLBD 16;
 LAIT 4; MTCW 1, 2
Chute, Carolyn 1947- .... **CLC 39**
 See also CA 123; CANR 135
Ciardi, John (Anthony) 1916-1986 . **CLC 10,**
 40, 44, 129
 See also CA 5-8R; 118; CAAS 2; CANR 5,
 33; CLR 19; CWRI 5; DAM POET; DLB
 5; DLBY 1986; INT CANR-5; MAICYA
 1, 2; MTCW 1, 2; RGAL 4; SAAS 26;
 SATA 1, 65; SATA-Obit 46
Cibber, Colley 1671-1757 .... **LC 66**
 See also DLB 84; RGEL 2
Cicero, Marcus Tullius
 106B.C.-43B.C. .... **CMLC 3**
 See also AW 1; CDWLB 1; DLB 211;
 RGWL 2, 3
Cimino, Michael 1943- .... **CLC 16**
 See also CA 105
Cioran, E(mil) M. 1911-1995 .... **CLC 64**
 See also CA 25-28R; 149; CANR 91; DLB
 220; EWL 3
Cisneros, Sandra 1954- .... **CLC 69, 118, 193;**
 HLC 1; PC 52; SSC 32, 72
 See also AAYA 9, 53; AMWS 7; CA 131;
 CANR 64, 118; CWP; DA3; DAM MULT;
 DLB 122, 152; EWL 3; EXPN; FW; HW
 1, 2; LAIT 5; LATS 1:2; LLW 1; MAI-
 CYA 2; MTCW 2; NFS 2; PFS 19; RGAL
 4; RGSF 2; SSFS 3, 13; WLIT 1; YAW
Cixous, Helene 1937- .... **CLC 92**
 See also CA 126; CANR 55, 123; CWW 2;
 DLB 83, 242; EWL 3; FW; GLL 2;
 MTCW 1, 2; TWA
Clair, Rene .... **CLC 20**
 See Chomette, Rene Lucien
Clampitt, Amy 1920-1994 .... **CLC 32; PC 19**
 See also AMWS 9; CA 110; 146; CANR
 29, 79; DLB 105
Clancy, Thomas L., Jr. 1947-
 See Clancy, Tom
 See also CA 125; 131; CANR 62, 105;
 DA3; INT CA-131; MTCW 1, 2
Clancy, Tom .... **CLC 45, 112**
 See Clancy, Thomas L., Jr.
 See also AAYA 9, 51; BEST 89:1, 90:1;
 BPFB 1; BYA 10, 11; CANR 132; CMW
 4; CPW; DAM NOV, POP; DLB 227
Clare, John 1793-1864 .. **NCLC 9, 86; PC 23**
 See also DAB; DAM POET; DLB 55, 96;
 RGEL 2
Clarin
 See Alas (y Urena), Leopoldo (Enrique
 Garcia)
Clark, Al C.
 See Goines, Donald
Clark, (Robert) Brian 1932- .... **CLC 29**
 See also CA 41-44R; CANR 67; CBD; CD
 5
Clark, Curt
 See Westlake, Donald E(dwin)
Clark, Eleanor 1913-1996 .... **CLC 5, 19**
 See also CA 9-12R; 151; CANR 41; CN 7;
 DLB 6
Clark, J. P.
 See Clark Bekederemo, J(ohnson) P(epper)
 See also CDWLB 3; DLB 117
Clark, John Pepper
 See Clark Bekederemo, J(ohnson) P(epper)
 See also AFW; CD 5; CP 7; RGEL 2

Clark, Kenneth (Mackenzie)
 1903-1983 .... **TCLC 147**
 See also CA 93-96; 109; CANR 36; MTCW
 1, 2
Clark, M. R.
 See Clark, Mavis Thorpe
Clark, Mavis Thorpe 1909-1999 ...... **CLC 12**
 See also CA 57-60; CANR 8, 37, 107; CLR
 30; CWRI 5; MAICYA 1, 2; SAAS 5;
 SATA 8, 74
Clark, Walter Van Tilburg
 1909-1971 .... **CLC 28**
 See also CA 9-12R; 33-36R; CANR 63,
 113; DLB 9, 206; LAIT 2; RGAL 4;
 SATA 8
Clark Bekederemo, J(ohnson) P(epper)
 1935- .... **BLC 1; CLC 38; DC 5**
 See Clark, J. P.; Clark, John Pepper
 See also BW 1; CA 65-68; CANR 16, 72;
 DAM DRAM, MULT; DFS 13; EWL 3;
 MTCW 1
Clarke, Arthur C(harles) 1917- .... **CLC 1, 4,**
 13, 18, 35, 136; SSC 3
 See also AAYA 4, 33; BPFB 1; BYA 13;
 CA 1-4R; CANR 2, 28, 55, 74, 130; CN
 7; CPW; DA3; DAM POP; DLB 261;
 JRDA; LAIT 5; MAICYA 1, 2; MTCW 1,
 2; SATA 13, 70, 115; SCFW; SFW 4;
 SSFS 4, 18; YAW
Clarke, Austin 1896-1974 .... **CLC 6, 9**
 See also CA 29-32; 49-52; CAP 2; DAM
 POET; DLB 10, 20; EWL 3; RGEL 2
Clarke, Austin C(hesterfield) 1934- .. **BLC 1;**
 CLC 8, 53; SSC 45
 See also BW 1; CA 25-28R; CAAS 16;
 CANR 14, 32, 68; CN 7; DAC; DAM
 MULT; DLB 53, 125; DNFS 2; RGSF 2
Clarke, Gillian 1937- .... **CLC 61**
 See also CA 106; CP 7; CWP; DLB 40
Clarke, Marcus (Andrew Hislop)
 1846-1881 .... **NCLC 19**
 See also DLB 230; RGEL 2; RGSF 2
Clarke, Shirley 1925-1997 .... **CLC 16**
 See also CA 189
Clash, The
 See Headon, (Nicky) Topper; Jones, Mick;
 Simonon, Paul; Strummer, Joe
Claudel, Paul (Louis Charles Marie)
 1868-1955 .... **TCLC 2, 10**
 See also CA 104; 165; DLB 192, 258; EW
 8; EWL 3; GFL 1789 to the Present;
 RGWL 2, 3; TWA
Claudian 370(?)-404(?) .... **CMLC 46**
 See also RGWL 2, 3
Claudius, Matthias 1740-1815 .... **NCLC 75**
 See also DLB 97
Clavell, James (duMaresq)
 1925-1994 .... **CLC 6, 25, 87**
 See also BPFB 1; CA 25-28R; 146; CANR
 26, 48; CPW; DA3; DAM NOV, POP;
 MTCW 1, 2; NFS 10; RHW
Clayman, Gregory .... **CLC 65**
Cleaver, (Leroy) Eldridge
 1935-1998 .... **BLC 1; CLC 30, 119**
 See also BW 1, 3; CA 21-24R; 167; CANR
 16, 75; DA3; DAM MULT; MTCW 2;
 YAW
Cleese, John (Marwood) 1939- .... **CLC 21**
 See Monty Python
 See also CA 112; 116; CANR 35; MTCW 1
Cleishbotham, Jebediah
 See Scott, Sir Walter
Cleland, John 1710-1789 .... **LC 2, 48**
 See also DLB 39; RGEL 2
Clemens, Samuel Langhorne 1835-1910
 See Twain, Mark
 See also CA 104; 135; CDALB 1865-1917;
 DA; DA3; DAB; DAC; DAM MST, NOV;
 DLB 12, 23, 64, 74, 186, 189; JRDA;
 LMFS 1; MAICYA 1, 2; NCFS 4; NFS
 20; SATA 100; SSFS 16; YABC 2

Clement of Alexandria
 150(?)-215(?) .... **CMLC 41**
Cleophil
 See Congreve, William
Clerihew, E.
 See Bentley, E(dmund) C(lerihew)
Clerk, N. W.
 See Lewis, C(live) S(taples)
Cleveland, John 1613-1658 .... **LC 106**
 See also DLB 126; RGEL 2
Cliff, Jimmy .... **CLC 21**
 See Chambers, James
 See also CA 193
Cliff, Michelle 1946- .... **BLCS; CLC 120**
 See also BW 2; CA 116; CANR 39, 72; CD-
 WLB 3; DLB 157; FW; GLL 2
Clifford, Lady Anne 1590-1676 .... **LC 76**
 See also DLB 151
Clifton, (Thelma) Lucille 1936- .... **BLC 1;**
 CLC 19, 66, 162; PC 17
 See also AFAW 2; BW 2, 3; CA 49-52;
 CANR 2, 24, 42, 76, 97; CLR 5; CP 7;
 CSW; CWP; CWRI 5; DA3; DAM MULT,
 POET; DLB 5, 41; EXPP; MAICYA 1, 2;
 MTCW 1, 2; PFS 1, 14; SATA 20, 69,
 128; WP
Clinton, Dirk
 See Silverberg, Robert
Clough, Arthur Hugh 1819-1861 ... **NCLC 27**
 See also BRW 5; DLB 32; RGEL 2
Clutha, Janet Paterson Frame 1924-2004
 See Frame, Janet
 See also CA 1-4R; 224; CANR 2, 36, 76,
 135; MTCW 1, 2; SATA 119
Clyne, Terence
 See Blatty, William Peter
Cobalt, Martin
 See Mayne, William (James Carter)
Cobb, Irvin S(hrewsbury)
 1876-1944 .... **TCLC 77**
 See also CA 175; DLB 11, 25, 86
Cobbett, William 1763-1835 .... **NCLC 49**
 See also DLB 43, 107, 158; RGEL 2
Coburn, D(onald) L(ee) 1938- .... **CLC 10**
 See also CA 89-92
Cocteau, Jean (Maurice Eugene Clement)
 1889-1963 ...... **CLC 1, 8, 15, 16, 43; DC**
 17; TCLC 119; WLC
 See also CA 25-28; CANR 40; CAP 2; DA;
 DA3; DAB; DAC; DAM DRAM, MST,
 NOV; DLB 65, 258; EW 10; EWL 3; GFL
 1789 to the Present; MTCW 1, 2; RGWL
 2, 3; TWA
Codrescu, Andrei 1946- .... **CLC 46, 121**
 See also CA 33-36R; CAAS 19; CANR 13,
 34, 53, 76, 125; DA3; DAM POET;
 MTCW 2
Coe, Max
 See Bourne, Randolph S(illiman)
Coe, Tucker
 See Westlake, Donald E(dwin)
Coen, Ethan 1958- .... **CLC 108**
 See also AAYA 54; CA 126; CANR 85
Coen, Joel 1955- .... **CLC 108**
 See also AAYA 54; CA 126; CANR 119
The Coen Brothers
 See Coen, Ethan; Coen, Joel
Coetzee, J(ohn) M(axwell) 1940- ..... **CLC 23,**
 33, 66, 117, 161, 162
 See also AAYA 37; AFW; BRWS 6; CA 77-
 80; CANR 41, 54, 74, 114, 133; CN 7;
 DA3; DAM NOV; DLB 225; EWL 3;
 LMFS 2; MTCW 1, 2; WLIT 2; WWE 1
Coffey, Brian
 See Koontz, Dean R(ay)
Coffin, Robert P(eter) Tristram
 1892-1955 .... **TCLC 95**
 See also CA 123; 169; DLB 45

Cooper, James Fenimore
1789-1851 .... **NCLC 1, 27, 54**
See also AAYA 22; AMW; BPFB 1;
CDALB 1640-1865; DA3; DLB 3, 183,
250, 254; LAIT 1; NFS 9; RGAL 4; SATA
19; TUS; WCH

Cooper, Susan Fenimore
1813-1894 .... **NCLC 129**
See also ANW; DLB 239, 254

Coover, Robert (Lowell) 1932- ...... **CLC 3, 7,**
15, 32, 46, 87, 161; SSC 15
See also AMWS 5; BPFB 1; CA 45-48;
CANR 3, 37, 58, 115; CN 7; DAM NOV;
DLB 2, 227; DLBY 1981; EWL 3;
MTCW 1, 2; RGAL 4; RGSF 2

Copeland, Stewart (Armstrong)
1952- .... **CLC 26**

Copernicus, Nicolaus 1473-1543 .... **LC 45**

Coppard, A(lfred) E(dgar)
1878-1957 .... **SSC 21; TCLC 5**
See also BRWS 8; CA 114; 167; DLB 162;
EWL 3; HGG; RGEL 2; RGSF 2; SUFW
1; YABC 1

Coppee, Francois 1842-1908 .... **TCLC 25**
See also CA 170; DLB 217

Coppola, Francis Ford 1939- ... **CLC 16, 126**
See also AAYA 39; CA 77-80; CANR 40,
78; DLB 44

Copway, George 1818-1869 .... **NNAL**
See also DAM MULT; DLB 175, 183

Corbiere, Tristan 1845-1875 .... **NCLC 43**
See also DLB 217; GFL 1789 to the Present

Corcoran, Barbara (Asenath)
1911- .... **CLC 17**
See also AAYA 14; CA 21-24R, 191; CAAE
191; CANR 11, 28, 48; CLR
50; DLB 52; JRDA; MAICYA 2; MAIC-
YAS 1; RHW; SAAS 20; SATA 3, 77;
SATA-Essay 125

Cordelier, Maurice
See Giraudoux, Jean(-Hippolyte)

Corelli, Marie .... **TCLC 51**
See Mackay, Mary
See also DLB 34, 156; RGEL 2; SUFW 1

Corinna c. 225B.C.-c. 305B.C. ...... **CMLC 72**

Corman, Cid .... **CLC 9**
See Corman, Sidney
See also CAAS 2; DLB 5, 193

Corman, Sidney 1924-2004
See Corman, Cid
See also CA 85-88; 225; CANR 44; CP 7;
DAM POET

Cormier, Robert (Edmund)
1925-2000 .... **CLC 12, 30**
See also AAYA 3, 19; BYA 1, 2, 6, 8, 9;
CA 1-4R; CANR 5, 23, 76, 93; CDALB
1968-1988; CLR 12, 55; DA; DAB; DAC;
DAM MST, NOV; DLB 52; EXPN; INT
CANR-23; JRDA; LAIT 5; MAICYA 1,
2; MTCW 1, 2; NFS 2, 18; SATA 10, 45,
83; SATA-Obit 122; WYA; YAW

Corn, Alfred (DeWitt III) 1943- .... **CLC 33**
See also CA 179; CAAE 179; CAAS 25;
CANR 44; CP 7; CSW; DLB 120, 282;
DLBY 1980

Corneille, Pierre 1606-1684 ... **DC 21; LC 28**
See also DAB; DAM MST; DLB 268; EW
3; GFL Beginnings to 1789; RGWL 2, 3;
TWA

Cornwell, David (John Moore)
1931- .... **CLC 9, 15**
See le Carre, John
See also CA 5-8R; CANR 13, 33, 59, 107,
132; DA3; DAM POP; MTCW 1, 2

Cornwell, Patricia (Daniels) 1956- . **CLC 155**
See also AAYA 16, 56; BPFB 1; CA 134;
CANR 53, 131; CMW 4; CPW; CSW;
DAM POP; DLB 306; MSW; MTCW 1

Corso, (Nunzio) Gregory 1930-2001 . **CLC 1,**
11; PC 33
See also AMWS 12; BG 2; CA 5-8R; 193;
CANR 41, 76, 132; CP 7; DA3; DLB 5,
16, 237; EWL 3; LMFS 2; MTCW 1, 2; WP

Cortazar, Julio 1914-1984 ... **CLC 2, 3, 5, 10,**
13, 15, 33, 34, 92; HLC 1; SSC 7, 76
See also BPFB 1; CA 21-24R; CANR 12,
32, 81; CDWLB 3; DA3; DAM MULT,
NOV; DLB 113; EWL 3; EXPS; HW 1,
2; LAW; MTCW 1, 2; RGSF 2; RGWL 2,
3; SSFS 3, 20; TWA; WLIT 1

Cortes, Hernan 1485-1547 .... **LC 31**

Corvinus, Jakob
See Raabe, Wilhelm (Karl)

Corwin, Cecil
See Kornbluth, C(yril) M.

Cosic, Dobrica 1921- .... **CLC 14**
See also CA 122; 138; CDWLB 4; CWW
2; DLB 181; EWL 3

Costain, Thomas B(ertram)
1885-1965 .... **CLC 30**
See also BYA 3; CA 5-8R; 25-28R; DLB 9;
RHW

Costantini, Humberto 1924(?)-1987 . **CLC 49**
See also CA 131; 122; EWL 3; HW 1

Costello, Elvis 1954- .... **CLC 21**
See also CA 204

Costenoble, Philostene
See Ghelderode, Michel de

Cotes, Cecil V.
See Duncan, Sara Jeannette

Cotter, Joseph Seamon Sr.
1861-1949 .... **BLC 1; TCLC 28**
See also BW 1; CA 124; DAM MULT; DLB
50

Couch, Arthur Thomas Quiller
See Quiller-Couch, Sir Arthur (Thomas)

Coulton, James
See Hansen, Joseph

Couperus, Louis (Marie Anne)
1863-1923 .... **TCLC 15**
See also CA 115; EWL 3; RGWL 2, 3

Coupland, Douglas 1961- .... **CLC 85, 133**
See also AAYA 34; CA 142; CANR 57, 90,
130; CCA 1; CPW; DAC; DAM POP

Court, Wesli
See Turco, Lewis (Putnam)

Courtenay, Bryce 1933- .... **CLC 59**
See also CA 138; CPW

Courtney, Robert
See Ellison, Harlan (Jay)

Cousteau, Jacques-Yves 1910-1997 .. **CLC 30**
See also CA 65-68; 159; CANR 15, 67;
MTCW 1; SATA 38, 98

Coventry, Francis 1725-1754 .... **LC 46**

Coverdale, Miles c. 1487-1569 .... **LC 77**
See also DLB 167

Cowan, Peter (Walkinshaw)
1914-2002 .... **SSC 28**
See also CA 21-24R; CANR 9, 25, 50, 83;
CN 7; DLB 260; RGSF 2

Coward, Noel (Peirce) 1899-1973 . **CLC 1, 9,**
29, 51
See also AITN 1; BRWS 2; CA 17-18; 41-
44R; CANR 35, 132; CAP 2; CDBLB
1914-1945; DA3; DAM DRAM; DFS 3,
6; DLB 10, 245; EWL 3; IDFW 3, 4;
MTCW 1, 2; RGEL 2; TEA

Cowley, Abraham 1618-1667 .... **LC 43**
See also BRW 2; DLB 131, 151; PAB;
RGEL 2

Cowley, Malcolm 1898-1989 .... **CLC 39**
See also AMWS 2; CA 5-8R; 128; CANR
3, 55; DLB 4, 48; DLBY 1981, 1989;
EWL 3; MTCW 1, 2

Cowper, William 1731-1800 ..... **NCLC 8, 94;**
PC 40
See also BRW 3; DA3; DAM POET; DLB
104, 109; RGEL 2

Cox, William Trevor 1928-
See Trevor, William
See also CA 9-12R; CANR 4, 37, 55, 76,
102; DAM NOV; INT CANR-37; MTCW
1, 2; TEA

Coyne, P. J.
See Masters, Hilary

Cozzens, James Gould 1903-1978 . **CLC 1, 4,**
11, 92
See also AMW; BPFB 1; CA 9-12R; 81-84;
CANR 19; CDALB 1941-1968; DLB 9,
294; DLBD 2; DLBY 1984, 1997; EWL
3; MTCW 1, 2; RGAL 4

Crabbe, George 1754-1832 .... **NCLC 26, 121**
See also BRW 3; DLB 93; RGEL 2

Crace, Jim 1946- .... **CLC 157; SSC 61**
See also CA 128; 135; CANR 55, 70, 123;
CN 7; DLB 231; INT CA-135

Craddock, Charles Egbert
See Murfree, Mary Noailles

Craig, A. A.
See Anderson, Poul (William)

Craik, Mrs.
See Craik, Dinah Maria (Mulock)
See also RGEL 2

Craik, Dinah Maria (Mulock)
1826-1887 .... **NCLC 38**
See Craik, Mrs.; Mulock, Dinah Maria
See also DLB 35, 163; MAICYA 1, 2;
SATA 34

Cram, Ralph Adams 1863-1942 ..... **TCLC 45**
See also CA 160

Cranch, Christopher Pearse
1813-1892 .... **NCLC 115**
See also DLB 1, 42, 243

Crane, (Harold) Hart 1899-1932 .... **PC 3;**
TCLC 2, 5, 80; WLC
See also AMW; AMWR 2; CA 104; 127;
CDALB 1917-1929; DA; DA3; DAB;
DAC; DAM MST, POET; DLB 4, 48;
EWL 3; MTCW 1, 2; RGAL 4; TUS

Crane, R(onald) S(almon)
1886-1967 .... **CLC 27**
See also CA 85-88; DLB 63

Crane, Stephen (Townley)
1871-1900 ...... **SSC 7, 56, 70; TCLC 11,**
17, 32; WLC
See also AAYA 21; AMW; AMWC 1; BPFB
1; BYA 3; CA 109; 140; CANR 84;
CDALB 1865-1917; DA; DA3; DAB;
DAC; DAM MST, NOV, POET; DLB 12,
54, 78; EXPN; EXPS; LAIT 2; LMFS 2;
NFS 4, 20; PFS 9; RGAL 4; RGSF 2;
SSFS 4; TUS; WYA; YABC 2

Cranmer, Thomas 1489-1556 .... **LC 95**
See also DLB 132, 213

Cranshaw, Stanley
See Fisher, Dorothy (Frances) Canfield

Crase, Douglas 1944- .... **CLC 58**
See also CA 106

Crashaw, Richard 1612(?)-1649 .... **LC 24**
See also BRW 2; DLB 126; PAB; RGEL 2

Cratinus c. 519B.C.-c. 422B.C. ..... **CMLC 54**
See also LMFS 1

Craven, Margaret 1901-1980 .... **CLC 17**
See also BYA 2; CA 103; CCA 1; DAC;
LAIT 5

Crawford, F(rancis) Marion
1854-1909 .... **TCLC 10**
See also CA 107; 168; DLB 71; HGG;
RGAL 4; SUFW 1

Crawford, Isabella Valancy
1850-1887 .... **NCLC 12, 127**
See also DLB 92; RGEL 2

Dalton, Roque 1935-1975(?) ..... **HLCS 1; PC 36**
See also CA 176; DLB 283; HW 2

Daly, Elizabeth 1878-1967 .... **CLC 52**
See also CA 23-24; 25-28R; CANR 60; CAP 2; CMW 4

Daly, Mary 1928- .... **CLC 173**
See also CA 25-28R; CANR 30, 62; FW; GLL 1; MTCW 1

Daly, Maureen 1921- .... **CLC 17**
See also AAYA 5, 58; BYA 6; CANR 37, 83, 108; CLR 96; JRDA; MAICYA 1, 2; SAAS 1; SATA 2, 129; WYA; YAW

Damas, Leon-Gontran 1912-1978 .... **CLC 84**
See also BW 1; CA 125; 73-76; EWL 3

Dana, Richard Henry Sr.
1787-1879 .... **NCLC 53**

Daniel, Samuel 1562(?)-1619 .... **LC 24**
See also DLB 62; RGEL 2

Daniels, Brett
See Adler, Renata

Dannay, Frederic 1905-1982 .... **CLC 11**
See Queen, Ellery
See also CA 1-4R; 107; CANR 1, 39; CMW 4; DAM POP; DLB 137; MTCW 1

D'Annunzio, Gabriele 1863-1938 ... **TCLC 6, 40**
See also CA 104; 155; EW 8; EWL 3; RGWL 2, 3; TWA

Danois, N. le
See Gourmont, Remy(-Marie-Charles) de

Dante 1265-1321 .... **CMLC 3, 18, 39, 70; PC 21; WLCS**
See also DA; DA3; DAB; DAC; DAM MST, POET; EFS 1; EW 1; LAIT 1; RGWL 2, 3; TWA; WP

d'Antibes, Germain
See Simenon, Georges (Jacques Christian)

Danticat, Edwidge 1969- .... **CLC 94, 139**
See also AAYA 29; CA 152, 192; CAAE 192; CANR 73, 129; DNFS 1; EXPS; LATS 1:2; MTCW 1; SSFS 1; YAW

Danvers, Dennis 1947- .... **CLC 70**

Danziger, Paula 1944-2004 .... **CLC 21**
See also AAYA 4, 36; BYA 6, 7, 14; CA 112; 115; 229; CANR 37, 132; CLR 20; JRDA; MAICYA 1, 2; SATA 36, 63, 102, 149; SATA-Brief 30; WYA; YAW

Da Ponte, Lorenzo 1749-1838 .... **NCLC 50**

Dario, Ruben 1867-1916 .... **HLC 1; PC 15; TCLC 4**
See also CA 131; CANR 81; DAM MULT; DLB 290; EWL 3; HW 1, 2; LAW; MTCW 1, 2; RGWL 2, 3

Darley, George 1795-1846 .... **NCLC 2**
See also DLB 96; RGEL 2

Darrow, Clarence (Seward)
1857-1938 .... **TCLC 81**
See also CA 164; DLB 303

Darwin, Charles 1809-1882 .... **NCLC 57**
See also BRWS 7; DLB 57, 166; LATS 1:1; RGEL 2; TEA; WLIT 4

Darwin, Erasmus 1731-1802 .... **NCLC 106**
See also DLB 93; RGEL 2

Daryush, Elizabeth 1887-1977 ...... **CLC 6, 19**
See also CA 49-52; CANR 3, 81; DLB 20

Das, Kamala 1934- .... **CLC 191; PC 43**
See also CA 101; CANR 27, 59; CP 7; CWP; FW

Dasgupta, Surendranath
1887-1952 .... **TCLC 81**
See also CA 157

Dashwood, Edmee Elizabeth Monica de la Pasture 1890-1943
See Delafield, E. M.
See also CA 119; 154

da Silva, Antonio Jose
1705-1739 .... **NCLC 114**

Daudet, (Louis Marie) Alphonse
1840-1897 .... **NCLC 1**
See also DLB 123; GFL 1789 to the Present; RGSF 2

d'Aulnoy, Marie-Catherine c.
1650-1705 .... **LC 100**

Daumal, Rene 1908-1944 .... **TCLC 14**
See also CA 114; EWL 3

Davenant, William 1606-1668 .... **LC 13**
See also DLB 58, 126; RGEL 2

Davenport, Guy (Mattison, Jr.)
1927-2005 .... **CLC 6, 14, 38; SSC 16**
See also CA 33-36R; CANR 23, 73; CN 7; CSW; DLB 130

David, Robert
See Nezval, Vitezslav

Davidson, Avram (James) 1923-1993
See Queen, Ellery
See also CA 101; 171; CANR 26; DLB 8; FANT; SFW 4; SUFW 1, 2

Davidson, Donald (Grady)
1893-1968 .... **CLC 2, 13, 19**
See also CA 5-8R; 25-28R; CANR 4, 84; DLB 45

Davidson, Hugh
See Hamilton, Edmond

Davidson, John 1857-1909 .... **TCLC 24**
See also CA 118; 217; DLB 19; RGEL 2

Davidson, Sara 1943- .... **CLC 9**
See also CA 81-84; CANR 44, 68; DLB 185

Davie, Donald (Alfred) 1922-1995 .... **CLC 5, 8, 10, 31; PC 29**
See also BRWS 6; CA 1-4R; 149; CAAS 3; CANR 1, 44; CP 7; DLB 27; MTCW 1; RGEL 2

Davie, Elspeth 1919-1995 .... **SSC 52**
See also CA 120; 126; 150; DLB 139

Davies, Ray(mond Douglas) 1944- ... **CLC 21**
See also CA 116; 146; CANR 92

Davies, Rhys 1901-1978 .... **CLC 23**
See also CA 9-12R; 81-84; CANR 4; DLB 139, 191

Davies, (William) Robertson
1913-1995 .... **CLC 2, 7, 13, 25, 42, 75, 91; WLC**
See Marchbanks, Samuel
See also BEST 89:2; BPFB 1; CA 33-36R; 150; CANR 17, 42, 103; CN 7; CPW; DA; DA3; DAB; DAC; DAM MST, NOV, POP; DLB 68; EWL 3; HGG; INT CANR-17; MTCW 1, 2; RGEL 2; TWA

Davies, Sir John 1569-1626 .... **LC 85**
See also DLB 172

Davies, Walter C.
See Kornbluth, C(yril) M.

Davies, William Henry 1871-1940 ... **TCLC 5**
See also CA 104; 179; DLB 19, 174; EWL 3; RGEL 2

Da Vinci, Leonardo 1452-1519 ..... **LC 12, 57, 60**
See also AAYA 40

Davis, Angela (Yvonne) 1944- .... **CLC 77**
See also BW 2, 3; CA 57-60; CANR 10, 81; CSW; DA3; DAM MULT; FW

Davis, B. Lynch
See Bioy Casares, Adolfo; Borges, Jorge Luis

Davis, Frank Marshall 1905-1987 ...... **BLC 1**
See also BW 2, 3; CA 125; 123; CANR 42, 80; DAM MULT; DLB 51

Davis, Gordon
See Hunt, E(verette) Howard, (Jr.)

Davis, H(arold) L(enoir) 1896-1960 . **CLC 49**
See also ANW; CA 178; 89-92; DLB 9, 206; SATA 114

Davis, Rebecca (Blaine) Harding
1831-1910 .... **SSC 38; TCLC 6**
See also CA 104; 179; DLB 74, 239; FW; NFS 14; RGAL 4; TUS

Davis, Richard Harding
1864-1916 .... **TCLC 24**
See also CA 114; 179; DLB 12, 23, 78, 79, 189; DLBD 13; RGAL 4

Davison, Frank Dalby 1893-1970 ..... **CLC 15**
See also CA 217; 116; DLB 260

Davison, Lawrence H.
See Lawrence, D(avid) H(erbert Richards)

Davison, Peter (Hubert) 1928- .... **CLC 28**
See also CA 9-12R; CAAS 4; CANR 3, 43, 84; CP 7; DLB 5

Davys, Mary 1674-1732 .... **LC 1, 46**
See also DLB 39

Dawson, (Guy) Fielding (Lewis)
1930-2002 .... **CLC 6**
See also CA 85-88; 202; CANR 108; DLB 130; DLBY 2002

Dawson, Peter
See Faust, Frederick (Schiller)
See also TCWW 2, 2

Day, Clarence (Shepard, Jr.)
1874-1935 .... **TCLC 25**
See also CA 108; 199; DLB 11

Day, John 1574(?)-1640(?) .... **LC 70**
See also DLB 62, 170; RGEL 2

Day, Thomas 1748-1789 .... **LC 1**
See also DLB 39; YABC 1

Day Lewis, C(ecil) 1904-1972 . **CLC 1, 6, 10; PC 11**
See Blake, Nicholas
See also BRWS 3; CA 13-16; 33-36R; CANR 34; CAP 1; CWRI 5; DAM POET; DLB 15, 20; EWL 3; MTCW 1, 2; RGEL 2

Dazai Osamu .... **SSC 41; TCLC 11**
See Tsushima, Shuji
See also CA 164; DLB 182; EWL 3; MJW; RGSF 2; RGWL 2, 3; TWA

de Andrade, Carlos Drummond
See Drummond de Andrade, Carlos

de Andrade, Mario 1892(?)-1945
See Andrade, Mario de
See also CA 178; HW 2

Deane, Norman
See Creasey, John

Deane, Seamus (Francis) 1940- ...... **CLC 122**
See also CA 118; CANR 42

de Beauvoir, Simone (Lucie Ernestine Marie Bertrand)
See Beauvoir, Simone (Lucie Ernestine Marie Bertrand) de

de Beer, P.
See Bosman, Herman Charles

de Brissac, Malcolm
See Dickinson, Peter (Malcolm de Brissac)

de Campos, Alvaro
See Pessoa, Fernando (Antonio Nogueira)

de Chardin, Pierre Teilhard
See Teilhard de Chardin, (Marie Joseph) Pierre

Dee, John 1527-1608 .... **LC 20**
See also DLB 136, 213

Deer, Sandra 1940- .... **CLC 45**
See also CA 186

De Ferrari, Gabriella 1941- .... **CLC 65**
See also CA 146

de Filippo, Eduardo 1900-1984 ... **TCLC 127**
See also CA 132; 114; EWL 3; MTCW 1; RGWL 2, 3

Defoe, Daniel 1660(?)-1731 .... **LC 1, 42, 108; WLC**
See also AAYA 27; BRW 3; BRWR 1; BYA 4; CDBLB 1660-1789; CLR 61; DA; DA3; DAB; DAC; DAM MST, NOV;

Elliott, William
See Bradbury, Ray (Douglas)

Ellis, A. E. .... **CLC 7**

Ellis, Alice Thomas .... **CLC 40**
See Haycraft, Anna (Margaret)
See also DLB 194; MTCW 1

Ellis, Bret Easton 1964- ...... **CLC 39, 71, 117**
See also AAYA 2, 43; CA 118; 123; CANR 51, 74, 126; CN 7; CPW; DA3; DAM POP; DLB 292; HGG; INT CA-123; MTCW 1; NFS 11

Ellis, (Henry) Havelock
1859-1939 .... **TCLC 14**
See also CA 109; 169; DLB 190

Ellis, Landon
See Ellison, Harlan (Jay)

Ellis, Trey 1962- .... **CLC 55**
See also CA 146; CANR 92

Ellison, Harlan (Jay) 1934- ... **CLC 1, 13, 42, 139; SSC 14**
See also AAYA 29; BPFB 1; BYA 14; CA 5-8R; CANR 5, 46, 115; CPW; DAM POP; DLB 8; HGG; INT CANR-5; MTCW 1, 2; SCFW 2; SFW 4; SSFS 13, 14, 15; SUFW 1, 2

Ellison, Ralph (Waldo) 1914-1994 .... **BLC 1; CLC 1, 3, 11, 54, 86, 114; SSC 26; WLC**
See also AAYA 19; AFAW 1, 2; AMWC 2; AMWR 2; AMWS 2; BPFB 1; BW 1, 3; BYA 2; CA 9-12R; 145; CANR 24, 53; CDALB 1941-1968; CSW; DA; DA3; DAB; DAC; DAM MST, MULT, NOV; DLB 2, 76, 227; DLBY 1994; EWL 3; EXPN; EXPS; LAIT 4; MTCW 1, 2; NCFS 3; NFS 2; RGAL 4; RGSF 2; SSFS 1, 11; YAW

Ellmann, Lucy (Elizabeth) 1956- ..... **CLC 61**
See also CA 128

Ellmann, Richard (David)
1918-1987 .... **CLC 50**
See also BEST 89:2; CA 1-4R; 122; CANR 2, 28, 61; DLB 103; DLBY 1987; MTCW 1, 2

Elman, Richard (Martin)
1934-1997 .... **CLC 19**
See also CA 17-20R; 163; CAAS 3; CANR 47

Elron
See Hubbard, L(afayette) Ron(ald)

El Saadawi, Nawal 1931- .... **CLC 196**
See al'Sadaawi, Nawal; Sa'adawi, al-Nawal; Saadawi, Nawal El; Sa'dawi, Nawal al-
See also CA 118; CAAS 11; CANR 44, 92

Eluard, Paul .... **PC 38; TCLC 7, 41**
See Grindel, Eugene
See also EWL 3; GFL 1789 to the Present; RGWL 2, 3

Elyot, Thomas 1490(?)-1546 .... **LC 11**
See also DLB 136; RGEL 2

Elytis, Odysseus 1911-1996 .... **CLC 15, 49, 100; PC 21**
See Alepoudelis, Odysseus
See also CA 102; 151; CANR 94; CWW 2; DAM POET; EW 13; EWL 3; MTCW 1, 2; RGWL 2, 3

Emecheta, (Florence Onye) Buchi
1944- .... **BLC 2; CLC 14, 48, 128**
See also AFW; BW 2, 3; CA 81-84; CANR 27, 81, 126; CDWLB 3; CN 7; CWRI 5; DA3; DAM MULT; DLB 117; EWL 3; FW; MTCW 1, 2; NFS 12, 14; SATA 66; WLIT 2

Emerson, Mary Moody
1774-1863 .... **NCLC 66**

Emerson, Ralph Waldo 1803-1882 . **NCLC 1, 38, 98; PC 18; WLC**
See also AAYA 60; AMW; ANW; CDALB 1640-1865; DA; DA3; DAB; DAC; DAM MST, POET; DLB 1, 59, 73, 183, 223, 270; EXPP; LAIT 2; LMFS 1; NCFS 3; PFS 4, 17; RGAL 4; TUS; WP

Eminescu, Mihail 1850-1889 .. **NCLC 33, 131**

Empedocles 5th cent. B.C.- .... **CMLC 50**
See also DLB 176

Empson, William 1906-1984 ... **CLC 3, 8, 19, 33, 34**
See also BRWS 2; CA 17-20R; 112; CANR 31, 61; DLB 20; EWL 3; MTCW 1, 2; RGEL 2

Enchi, Fumiko (Ueda) 1905-1986 ..... **CLC 31**
See Enchi Fumiko
See also CA 129; 121; FW; MJW

Enchi Fumiko
See Enchi, Fumiko (Ueda)
See also DLB 182; EWL 3

Ende, Michael (Andreas Helmuth)
1929-1995 .... **CLC 31**
See also BYA 5; CA 118; 124; 149; CANR 36, 110; CLR 14; DLB 75; MAICYA 1, 2; MAICYAS 1; SATA 61, 130; SATA-Brief 42; SATA-Obit 86

Endo, Shusaku 1923-1996 ..... **CLC 7, 14, 19, 54, 99; SSC 48; TCLC 152**
See Endo Shusaku
See also CA 29-32R; 153; CANR 21, 54, 131; DA3; DAM NOV; MTCW 1, 2; RGSF 2; RGWL 2, 3

Endo Shusaku
See Endo, Shusaku
See also CWW 2; DLB 182; EWL 3

Engel, Marian 1933-1985 .... **CLC 36; TCLC 137**
See also CA 25-28R; CANR 12; DLB 53; FW; INT CANR-12

Engelhardt, Frederick
See Hubbard, L(afayette) Ron(ald)

Engels, Friedrich 1820-1895 .. **NCLC 85, 114**
See also DLB 129; LATS 1:1

Enright, D(ennis) J(oseph)
1920-2002 .... **CLC 4, 8, 31**
See also CA 1-4R; 211; CANR 1, 42, 83; CP 7; DLB 27; EWL 3; SATA 25; SATA-Obit 140

Enzensberger, Hans Magnus
1929- .... **CLC 43; PC 28**
See also CA 116; 119; CANR 103; CWW 2; EWL 3

Ephron, Nora 1941- .... **CLC 17, 31**
See also AAYA 35; AITN 2; CA 65-68; CANR 12, 39, 83

Epicurus 341B.C.-270B.C. .... **CMLC 21**
See also DLB 176

Epsilon
See Betjeman, John

Epstein, Daniel Mark 1948- .... **CLC 7**
See also CA 49-52; CANR 2, 53, 90

Epstein, Jacob 1956- .... **CLC 19**
See also CA 114

Epstein, Jean 1897-1953 .... **TCLC 92**

Epstein, Joseph 1937- .... **CLC 39**
See also AMWS 14; CA 112; 119; CANR 50, 65, 117

Epstein, Leslie 1938- .... **CLC 27**
See also AMWS 12; CA 73-76, 215; CAAE 215; CAAS 12; CANR 23, 69; DLB 299

Equiano, Olaudah 1745(?)-1797 . **BLC 2; LC 16**
See also AFAW 1, 2; CDWLB 3; DAM MULT; DLB 37, 50; WLIT 2

Erasmus, Desiderius 1469(?)-1536 ..... **LC 16, 93**
See also DLB 136; EW 2; LMFS 1; RGWL 2, 3; TWA

Erdman, Paul E(mil) 1932- .... **CLC 25**
See also AITN 1; CA 61-64; CANR 13, 43, 84

Erdrich, Louise 1954- .... **CLC 39, 54, 120, 176; NNAL; PC 52**
See also AAYA 10, 47; AMWS 4; BEST 89:1; BPFB 1; CA 114; CANR 41, 62, 118; CDALBS; CN 7; CP 7; CPW; CWP; DA3; DAM MULT, NOV, POP; DLB 152, 175, 206; EWL 3; EXPP; LAIT 5; LATS 1:2; MTCW 1; NFS 5; PFS 14; RGAL 4; SATA 94, 141; SSFS 14; TCWW 2

Erenburg, Ilya (Grigoryevich)
See Ehrenburg, Ilya (Grigoryevich)

Erickson, Stephen Michael 1950-
See Erickson, Steve
See also CA 129; SFW 4

Erickson, Steve .... **CLC 64**
See Erickson, Stephen Michael
See also CANR 60, 68; SUFW 2

Erickson, Walter
See Fast, Howard (Melvin)

Ericson, Walter
See Fast, Howard (Melvin)

Eriksson, Buntel
See Bergman, (Ernst) Ingmar

Eriugena, John Scottus c.
810-877 .... **CMLC 65**
See also DLB 115

Ernaux, Annie 1940- .... **CLC 88, 184**
See also CA 147; CANR 93; NCFS 3, 5

Erskine, John 1879-1951 .... **TCLC 84**
See also CA 112; 159; DLB 9, 102; FANT

Eschenbach, Wolfram von
See Wolfram von Eschenbach
See also RGWL 3

Eseki, Bruno
See Mphahlele, Ezekiel

Esenin, Sergei (Alexandrovich)
1895-1925 .... **TCLC 4**
See Yesenin, Sergey
See also CA 104; RGWL 2, 3

Eshleman, Clayton 1935- .... **CLC 7**
See also CA 33-36R, 212; CAAE 212; CAAS 6; CANR 93; CP 7; DLB 5

Espriella, Don Manuel Alvarez
See Southey, Robert

Espriu, Salvador 1913-1985 .... **CLC 9**
See also CA 154; 115; DLB 134; EWL 3

Espronceda, Jose de 1808-1842 ..... **NCLC 39**

Esquivel, Laura 1951(?)- ... **CLC 141; HLCS 1**
See also AAYA 29; CA 143; CANR 68, 113; DA3; DNFS 2; LAIT 3; LMFS 2; MTCW 1; NFS 5; WLIT 1

Esse, James
See Stephens, James

Esterbrook, Tom
See Hubbard, L(afayette) Ron(ald)

Estleman, Loren D. 1952- .... **CLC 48**
See also AAYA 27; CA 85-88; CANR 27, 74; CMW 4; CPW; DA3; DAM NOV, POP; DLB 226; INT CANR-27; MTCW 1, 2

Etherege, Sir George 1636-1692 . **DC 23; LC 78**
See also BRW 2; DAM DRAM; DLB 80; PAB; RGEL 2

Euclid 306B.C.-283B.C. .... **CMLC 25**

Eugenides, Jeffrey 1960(?)- .... **CLC 81**
See also AAYA 51; CA 144; CANR 120

Euripides c. 484B.C.-406B.C. .... **CMLC 23, 51; DC 4; WLCS**
See also AW 1; CDWLB 1; DA; DA3; DAB; DAC; DAM DRAM, MST; DFS 1, 4, 6; DLB 176; LAIT 1; LMFS 1; RGWL 2, 3

Evan, Evin
See Faust, Frederick (Schiller)

Evans, Caradoc 1878-1945 ... **SSC 43; TCLC 85**
See also DLB 162

Ferguson, Niall 1964- .... **CLC 134**
See also CA 190

Ferguson, Samuel 1810-1886 .... **NCLC 33**
See also DLB 32; RGEL 2

Fergusson, Robert 1750-1774 .... **LC 29**
See also DLB 109; RGEL 2

Ferling, Lawrence
See Ferlinghetti, Lawrence (Monsanto)

Ferlinghetti, Lawrence (Monsanto)
1919(?)- .... **CLC 2, 6, 10, 27, 111; PC 1**
See also CA 5-8R; CANR 3, 41, 73, 125;
CDALB 1941-1968; CP 7; DA3; DAM
POET; DLB 5, 16; MTCW 1, 2; RGAL 4;
WP

Fern, Fanny
See Parton, Sara Payson Willis

Fernandez, Vicente Garcia Huidobro
See Huidobro Fernandez, Vicente Garcia

Fernandez-Armesto, Felipe .... **CLC 70**

Fernandez de Lizardi, Jose Joaquin
See Lizardi, Jose Joaquin Fernandez de

Ferre, Rosario 1938- ...... **CLC 139; HLCS 1;
SSC 36**
See also CA 131; CANR 55, 81, 134; CWW
2; DLB 145; EWL 3; HW 1, 2; LAWS 1;
MTCW 1; WLIT 1

Ferrer, Gabriel (Francisco Victor) Miro
See Miro (Ferrer), Gabriel (Francisco
Victor)

Ferrier, Susan (Edmonstone)
1782-1854 .... **NCLC 8**
See also DLB 116; RGEL 2

Ferrigno, Robert 1948(?)- .... **CLC 65**
See also CA 140; CANR 125

Ferron, Jacques 1921-1985 .... **CLC 94**
See also CA 117; 129; CCA 1; DAC; DLB
60; EWL 3

Feuchtwanger, Lion 1884-1958 .... **TCLC 3**
See also CA 104; 187; DLB 66; EWL 3

Feuerbach, Ludwig 1804-1872 ..... **NCLC 139**
See also DLB 133

Feuillet, Octave 1821-1890 .... **NCLC 45**
See also DLB 192

Feydeau, Georges (Leon Jules Marie)
1862-1921 .... **TCLC 22**
See also CA 113; 152; CANR 84; DAM
DRAM; DLB 192; EWL 3; GFL 1789 to
the Present; RGWL 2, 3

Fichte, Johann Gottlieb
1762-1814 .... **NCLC 62**
See also DLB 90

Ficino, Marsilio 1433-1499 .... **LC 12**
See also LMFS 1

Fiedeler, Hans
See Doeblin, Alfred

Fiedler, Leslie A(aron) 1917-2003 ..... **CLC 4,
13, 24**
See also AMWS 13; CA 9-12R; 212; CANR
7, 63; CN 7; DLB 28, 67; EWL 3; MTCW
1, 2; RGAL 4; TUS

Field, Andrew 1938- .... **CLC 44**
See also CA 97-100; CANR 25

Field, Eugene 1850-1895 .... **NCLC 3**
See also DLB 23, 42, 140; DLBD 13; MAI-
CYA 1, 2; RGAL 4; SATA 16

Field, Gans T.
See Wellman, Manly Wade

Field, Michael 1915-1971 .... **TCLC 43**
See also CA 29-32R

Field, Peter
See Hobson, Laura Z(ametkin)
See also TCWW 2

Fielding, Helen 1958- .... **CLC 146**
See also CA 172; CANR 127; DLB 231

Fielding, Henry 1707-1754 .... **LC 1, 46, 85;
WLC**
See also BRW 3; BRWR 1; CDBLB 1660-
1789; DA; DA3; DAB; DAC; DAM
DRAM, MST, NOV; DLB 39, 84, 101;
NFS 18; RGEL 2; TEA; WLIT 3

Fielding, Sarah 1710-1768 .... **LC 1, 44**
See also DLB 39; RGEL 2; TEA

Fields, W. C. 1880-1946 .... **TCLC 80**
See also DLB 44

Fierstein, Harvey (Forbes) 1954- ..... **CLC 33**
See also CA 123; 129; CAD; CD 5; CPW;
DA3; DAM DRAM, POP; DFS 6; DLB
266; GLL

Figes, Eva 1932- .... **CLC 31**
See also CA 53-56; CANR 4, 44, 83; CN 7;
DLB 14, 271; FW

Filippo, Eduardo de
See de Filippo, Eduardo

Finch, Anne 1661-1720 .... **LC 3; PC 21**
See also BRWS 9; DLB 95

Finch, Robert (Duer Claydon)
1900-1995 .... **CLC 18**
See also CA 57-60; CANR 9, 24, 49; CP 7;
DLB 88

Findley, Timothy (Irving Frederick)
1930-2002 .... **CLC 27, 102**
See also CA 25-28R; 206; CANR 12, 42,
69, 109; CCA 1; CN 7; DAC; DAM MST;
DLB 53; FANT; RHW

Fink, William
See Mencken, H(enry) L(ouis)

Firbank, Louis 1942-
See Reed, Lou
See also CA 117

Firbank, (Arthur Annesley) Ronald
1886-1926 .... **TCLC 1**
See also BRWS 2; CA 104; 177; DLB 36;
EWL 3; RGEL 2

Fish, Stanley
See Fish, Stanley Eugene

Fish, Stanley E.
See Fish, Stanley Eugene

Fish, Stanley Eugene 1938- .... **CLC 142**
See also CA 112; 132; CANR 90; DLB 67

Fisher, Dorothy (Frances) Canfield
1879-1958 .... **TCLC 87**
See also CA 114; 136; CANR 80; CLR 71,;
CWRI 5; DLB 9, 102, 284; MAICYA 1,
2; YABC 1

Fisher, M(ary) F(rances) K(ennedy)
1908-1992 .... **CLC 76, 87**
See also CA 77-80; 138; CANR 44; MTCW
1

Fisher, Roy 1930- .... **CLC 25**
See also CA 81-84; CAAS 10; CANR 16;
CP 7; DLB 40

Fisher, Rudolph 1897-1934 .... **BLC 2; HR 2;
SSC 25; TCLC 11**
See also BW 1, 3; CA 107; 124; CANR 80;
DAM MULT; DLB 51, 102

Fisher, Vardis (Alvero) 1895-1968 .... **CLC 7;
TCLC 140**
See also CA 5-8R; 25-28R; CANR 68; DLB
9, 206; RGAL 4; TCWW 2

Fiske, Tarleton
See Bloch, Robert (Albert)

Fitch, Clarke
See Sinclair, Upton (Beall)

Fitch, John IV
See Cormier, Robert (Edmund)

Fitzgerald, Captain Hugh
See Baum, L(yman) Frank

FitzGerald, Edward 1809-1883 .... **NCLC 9**
See also BRW 4; DLB 32; RGEL 2

Fitzgerald, F(rancis) Scott (Key)
1896-1940 ... **SSC 6, 31, 75; TCLC 1, 6,
14, 28, 55, 157; WLC**
See also AAYA 24; AITN 1; AMW; AMWC
2; AMWR 1; BPFB 1; CA 110; 123;
CDALB 1917-1929; DA; DA3; DAB;
DAC; DAM MST, NOV; DLB 4, 9, 86,
219, 273; DLBD 1, 15, 16; DLBY 1981,
1996; EWL 3; EXPN; EXPS; LAIT 3;
MTCW 1, 2; NFS 2, 19, 20; RGAL 4;
RGSF 2; SSFS 4, 15; TUS

Fitzgerald, Penelope 1916-2000 . **CLC 19, 51,
61, 143**
See also BRWS 5; CA 85-88; 190; CAAS
10; CANR 56, 86, 131; CN 7; DLB 14,
194; EWL 3; MTCW 2

Fitzgerald, Robert (Stuart)
1910-1985 .... **CLC 39**
See also CA 1-4R; 114; CANR 1; DLBY
1980

FitzGerald, Robert D(avid)
1902-1987 .... **CLC 19**
See also CA 17-20R; DLB 260; RGEL 2

Fitzgerald, Zelda (Sayre)
1900-1948 .... **TCLC 52**
See also AMWS 9; CA 117; 126; DLBY
1984

Flanagan, Thomas (James Bonner)
1923-2002 .... **CLC 25, 52**
See also CA 108; 206; CANR 55; CN 7;
DLBY 1980; INT CA-108; MTCW 1;
RHW

Flaubert, Gustave 1821-1880 .... **NCLC 2, 10,
19, 62, 66, 135; SSC 11, 60; WLC**
See also DA; DA3; DAB; DAC; DAM
MST, NOV; DLB 119, 301; EXPS;
GFL 1789 to the Present; LAIT 2; LMFS
1; NFS 14; RGSF 2; RGWL 2, 3; SSFS
6; TWA

Flavius Josephus
See Josephus, Flavius

Flecker, Herman Elroy
See Flecker, (Herman) James Elroy

Flecker, (Herman) James Elroy
1884-1915 .... **TCLC 43**
See also CA 109; 150; DLB 10, 19; RGEL
2

Fleming, Ian (Lancaster) 1908-1964 . **CLC 3,
30**
See also AAYA 26; BPFB 1; CA 5-8R;
CANR 59; CDBLB 1945-1960; CMW 4;
CPW; DA3; DAM POP; DLB 87, 201;
MSW; MTCW 1, 2; RGEL 2; SATA 9;
TEA; YAW

Fleming, Thomas (James) 1927- ...... **CLC 37**
See also CA 5-8R; CANR 10, 102; INT
CANR-10; SATA 8

Fletcher, John 1579-1625 .... **DC 6; LC 33**
See also BRW 2; CDBLB Before 1660;
DLB 58; RGEL 2; TEA

Fletcher, John Gould 1886-1950 .... **TCLC 35**
See also CA 107; 167; DLB 4, 45; LMFS
2; RGAL 4

Fleur, Paul
See Pohl, Frederik

Flieg, Helmut
See Heym, Stefan

Flooglebuckle, Al
See Spiegelman, Art

Flora, Fletcher 1914-1969
See Queen, Ellery
See also CA 1-4R; CANR 3, 85

Flying Officer X
See Bates, H(erbert) E(rnest)

Fo, Dario 1926- .... **CLC 32, 109; DC 10**
See also CA 116; 128; CANR 68, 114, 134;
CWW 2; DA3; DAM DRAM; DLBY
1997; EWL 3; MTCW 1, 2

Fogarty, Jonathan Titulescu Esq.
See Farrell, James T(homas)

Follett, Ken(neth Martin) 1949- .... **CLC 18**
See also AAYA 6, 50; BEST 89:4; BPFB 1;
CA 81-84; CANR 13, 33, 54, 102; CMW
4; CPW; DA3; DAM NOV, POP; DLB
87; DLBY 1981; INT CANR-33; MTCW
1

Fondane, Benjamin 1898-1944 ..... **TCLC 159**

Fontane, Theodor 1819-1898 .... **NCLC 26**
See also CDWLB 2; DLB 129; EW 6;
RGWL 2, 3; TWA

Fontenot, Chester .... **CLC 65**

Fonvizin, Denis Ivanovich
1744(?)-1792 .... **LC 81**
See also DLB 150; RGWL 2, 3

Foote, Horton 1916- .... **CLC 51, 91**
See also CA 73-76; CAD; CANR 34, 51,
110; CD 5; CSW; DA3; DAM DRAM;
DFS 20; DLB 26, 266; EWL 3; INT
CANR-34

Foote, Mary Hallock 1847-1938 .. **TCLC 108**
See also DLB 186, 188, 202, 221

Foote, Samuel 1721-1777 .... **LC 106**
See also DLB 89; RGEL 2

Foote, Shelby 1916- .... **CLC 75**
See also AAYA 40; CA 5-8R; CANR 3, 45,
74, 131; CN 7; CPW; CSW; DA3; DAM
NOV, POP; DLB 2, 17; MTCW 2; RHW

Forbes, Cosmo
See Lewton, Val

Forbes, Esther 1891-1967 .... **CLC 12**
See also AAYA 17; BYA 2; CA 13-14; 25-
28R; CAP 1; CLR 27; DLB 22; JRDA;
MAICYA 1, 2; RHW; SATA 2, 100; YAW

Forche, Carolyn (Louise) 1950- .... **CLC 25,
83, 86; PC 10**
See also CA 109; 117; CANR 50, 74; CP 7;
CWP; DA3; DAM POET; DLB 5, 193;
INT CA-117; MTCW 1; PFS 18; RGAL 4

Ford, Elbur
See Hibbert, Eleanor Alice Burford

Ford, Ford Madox 1873-1939 ... **TCLC 1, 15,
39, 57**
See Chaucer, Daniel
See also BRW 6; CA 104; 132; CANR 74;
CDBLB 1914-1945; DA3; DAM NOV;
DLB 34, 98, 162; EWL 3; MTCW 1, 2;
RGEL 2; TEA

Ford, Henry 1863-1947 .... **TCLC 73**
See also CA 115; 148

Ford, Jack
See Ford, John

Ford, John 1586-1639 .... **DC 8; LC 68**
See also BRW 2; CDBLB Before 1660;
DA3; DAM DRAM; DFS 7; DLB 58;
IDTP; RGEL 2

Ford, John 1895-1973 .... **CLC 16**
See also CA 187; 45-48

Ford, Richard 1944- .... **CLC 46, 99**
See also AMWS 5; CA 69-72; CANR 11,
47, 86, 128; CN 7; CSW; DLB 227; EWL
3; MTCW 1; RGAL 4; RGSF 2

Ford, Webster
See Masters, Edgar Lee

Foreman, Richard 1937- .... **CLC 50**
See also CA 65-68; CAD; CANR 32, 63;
CD 5

Forester, C(ecil) S(cott) 1899-1966 . **CLC 35;
TCLC 152**
See also CA 73-76; 25-28R; CANR 83;
DLB 191; RGEL 2; RHW; SATA 13

Forez
See Mauriac, Francois (Charles)

Forman, James
See Forman, James D(ouglas)

Forman, James D(ouglas) 1932- .... **CLC 21**
See also AAYA 17; CA 9-12R; CANR 4,
19, 42; JRDA; MAICYA 1, 2; SATA 8,
70; YAW

Forman, Milos 1932- .... **CLC 164**
See also CA 109

Fornes, Maria Irene 1930- .... **CLC 39, 61,
187; DC 10; HLCS 1**
See also CA 25-28R; CAD; CANR 28, 81;
CD 5; CWD; DLB 7; HW 1, 2; INT
CANR-28; LLW 1; MTCW 1; RGAL 4

Forrest, Leon (Richard)
1937-1997 .... **BLCS; CLC 4**
See also AFAW 2; BW 2; CA 89-92; 162;
CAAS 7; CANR 25, 52, 87; CN 7; DLB
33

Forster, E(dward) M(organ)
1879-1970 ...... **CLC 1, 2, 3, 4, 9, 10, 13,
15, 22, 45, 77; SSC 27; TCLC 125;
WLC**
See also AAYA 2, 37; BRW 6; BRWR 2;
BYA 12; CA 13-14; 25-28R; CANR 45;
CAP 1; CDBLB 1914-1945; DA; DA3;
DAB; DAC; DAM MST, NOV; DLB 34,
98, 162, 178, 195; DLBD 10; EWL 3;
EXPN; LAIT 3; LMFS 1; MTCW 1, 2;
NCFS 1; NFS 3, 10, 11; RGEL 2; RGSF
2; SATA 57; SUFW 1; TEA; WLIT 4

Forster, John 1812-1876 .... **NCLC 11**
See also DLB 144, 184

Forster, Margaret 1938- .... **CLC 149**
See also CA 133; CANR 62, 115; CN 7;
DLB 155, 271

Forsyth, Frederick 1938- .... **CLC 2, 5, 36**
See also BEST 89:4; CA 85-88; CANR 38,
62, 115; CMW 4; CN 7; CPW; DAM
NOV, POP; DLB 87; MTCW 1, 2

Forten, Charlotte L. 1837-1914 .... **BLC 2;
TCLC 16**
See Grimke, Charlotte L(ottie) Forten
See also DLB 50, 239

Fortinbras
See Grieg, (Johan) Nordahl (Brun)

Foscolo, Ugo 1778-1827 .... **NCLC 8, 97**
See also EW 5

Fosse, Bob .... **CLC 20**
See Fosse, Robert Louis

Fosse, Robert Louis 1927-1987
See Fosse, Bob
See also CA 110; 123

Foster, Hannah Webster
1758-1840 .... **NCLC 99**
See also DLB 37, 200; RGAL 4

Foster, Stephen Collins
1826-1864 .... **NCLC 26**
See also RGAL 4

Foucault, Michel 1926-1984 . **CLC 31, 34, 69**
See also CA 105; 113; CANR 34; DLB 242;
EW 13; EWL 3; GFL 1789 to the Present;
GLL 1; LMFS 2; MTCW 1, 2; TWA

**Fouque, Friedrich (Heinrich Karl) de la
Motte** 1777-1843 .... **NCLC 2**
See also DLB 90; RGWL 2, 3; SUFW 1

Fourier, Charles 1772-1837 .... **NCLC 51**

Fournier, Henri-Alban 1886-1914
See Alain-Fournier
See also CA 104; 179

Fournier, Pierre 1916- .... **CLC 11**
See Gascar, Pierre
See also CA 89-92; CANR 16, 40

Fowles, John (Robert) 1926- . **CLC 1, 2, 3, 4,
6, 9, 10, 15, 33, 87; SSC 33**
See also BPFB 1; BRWS 1; CA 5-8R;
CANR 25, 71, 103; CDBLB 1960 to
Present; CN 7; DA3; DAB; DAC; DAM
MST; DLB 14, 139, 207; EWL 3; HGG;
MTCW 1, 2; RGEL 2; RHW; SATA 22;
TEA; WLIT 4

Fox, Paula 1923- .... **CLC 2, 8, 121**
See also AAYA 3, 37; BYA 3, 8; CA 73-76;
CANR 20, 36, 62, 105; CLR 1, 44, 96;
DLB 52; JRDA; MAICYA 1, 2; MTCW
1; NFS 12; SATA 17, 60, 120; WYA;
YAW

Fox, William Price (Jr.) 1926- .... **CLC 22**
See also CA 17-20R; CAAS 19; CANR 11;
CSW; DLB 2; DLBY 1981

Foxe, John 1517(?)-1587 .... **LC 14**
See also DLB 132

Frame, Janet .. **CLC 2, 3, 6, 22, 66, 96; SSC
29**
See Clutha, Janet Paterson Frame
See also CN 7; CWP; EWL 3; RGEL 2;
RGSF 2; TWA

France, Anatole .... **TCLC 9**
See Thibault, Jacques Anatole Francois
See also DLB 123; EWL 3; GFL 1789 to
the Present; MTCW 1; RGWL 2, 3;
SUFW 1

Francis, Claude .... **CLC 50**
See also CA 192

Francis, Richard Stanley 1920- ... **CLC 2, 22,
42, 102**
See also AAYA 5, 21; BEST 89:3; BPFB 1;
CA 5-8R; CANR 9, 42, 68, 100; CDBLB
1960 to Present; CMW 4; CN 7; DA3;
DAM POP; DLB 87; INT CANR-9;
MSW; MTCW 1, 2

Francis, Robert (Churchill)
1901-1987 .... **CLC 15; PC 34**
See also AMWS 9; CA 1-4R; 123; CANR
1; EXPP; PFS 12

Francis, Lord Jeffrey
See Jeffrey, Francis
See also DLB 107

Frank, Anne(lies Marie)
1929-1945 .... **TCLC 17; WLC**
See also AAYA 12; BYA 1; CA 113; 133;
CANR 68; CLR 101; DA; DA3; DAB;
DAC; DAM MST; LAIT 4; MAICYA 2;
MAICYAS 1; MTCW 1, 2; NCFS 2;
SATA 87; SATA-Brief 42; WYA; YAW

Frank, Bruno 1887-1945 .... **TCLC 81**
See also CA 189; DLB 118; EWL 3

Frank, Elizabeth 1945- .... **CLC 39**
See also CA 121; 126; CANR 78; INT CA-
126

Frankl, Viktor E(mil) 1905-1997 ...... **CLC 93**
See also CA 65-68; 161

Franklin, Benjamin
See Hasek, Jaroslav (Matej Frantisek)

Franklin, Benjamin 1706-1790 .... **LC 25;
WLCS**
See also AMW; CDALB 1640-1865; DA;
DA3; DAB; DAC; DAM MST; DLB 24,
43, 73, 183; LAIT 1; RGAL 4; TUS

**Franklin, (Stella Maria Sarah) Miles
(Lampe)** 1879-1954 .... **TCLC 7**
See also CA 104; 164; DLB 230; FW;
MTCW 2; RGEL 2; TWA

Fraser, Antonia (Pakenham) 1932- . **CLC 32,
107**
See also AAYA 57; CA 85-88; CANR 44,
65, 119; CMW; DLB 276; MTCW 1, 2;
SATA-Brief 32

Fraser, George MacDonald 1925- ...... **CLC 7**
See also AAYA 48; CA 45-48, 180; CAAE
180; CANR 2, 48, 74; MTCW 1; RHW

Fraser, Sylvia 1935- .... **CLC 64**
See also CA 45-48; CANR 1, 16, 60; CCA
1

Frayn, Michael 1933- . **CLC 3, 7, 31, 47, 176**
See also BRWC 2; BRWS 7; CA 5-8R;
CANR 30, 69, 114, 133; CBD; CD 5; CN
7; DAM DRAM, NOV; DLB 13, 14, 194,
245; FANT; MTCW 1, 2; SFW 4

Fraze, Candida (Merrill) 1945- .... **CLC 50**
See also CA 126

Frazer, Andrew
See Marlowe, Stephen

Frazer, J(ames) G(eorge)
1854-1941 .... **TCLC 32**
See also BRWS 3; CA 118; NCFS 5

Frazer, Robert Caine
See Creasey, John
Frazer, Sir James George
See Frazer, J(ames) G(eorge)
Frazier, Charles 1950- .... **CLC 109**
See also AAYA 34; CA 161; CANR 126;
CSW; DLB 292
Frazier, Ian 1951- .... **CLC 46**
See also CA 130; CANR 54, 93
Frederic, Harold 1856-1898 .... **NCLC 10**
See also AMW; DLB 12, 23; DLBD 13;
RGAL 4
Frederick, John
See Faust, Frederick (Schiller)
See also TCWW 2
Frederick the Great 1712-1786 .... **LC 14**
Fredro, Aleksander 1793-1876 .... **NCLC 8**
Freeling, Nicolas 1927-2003 .... **CLC 38**
See also CA 49-52; 218; CAAS 12; CANR
1, 17, 50, 84; CMW 4; CN 7; DLB 87
Freeman, Douglas Southall
1886-1953 .... **TCLC 11**
See also CA 109; 195; DLB 17; DLBD 17
Freeman, Judith 1946- .... **CLC 55**
See also CA 148; CANR 120; DLB 256
Freeman, Mary E(leanor) Wilkins
1852-1930 .... **SSC 1, 47; TCLC 9**
See also CA 106; 177; DLB 12, 78, 221;
EXPS; FW; HGG; MAWW; RGAL 4;
RGSF 2; SSFS 4, 8; SUFW 1; TUS
Freeman, R(ichard) Austin
1862-1943 .... **TCLC 21**
See also CA 113; CANR 84; CMW 4; DLB
70
French, Albert 1943- .... **CLC 86**
See also BW 3; CA 167
French, Antonia
See Kureishi, Hanif
French, Marilyn 1929- .. **CLC 10, 18, 60, 177**
See also BPFB 1; CA 69-72; CANR 3, 31,
134; CN 7; CPW; DAM DRAM, NOV,
POP; FW; INT CANR-31; MTCW 1, 2
French, Paul
See Asimov, Isaac
Freneau, Philip Morin 1752-1832 .. **NCLC 1,
111**
See also AMWS 2; DLB 37, 43; RGAL 4
Freud, Sigmund 1856-1939 .... **TCLC 52**
See also CA 115; 133; CANR 69; DLB 296;
EW 7; EWL 3; LATS 1:1; MTCW 1, 2;
NCFS 3; TWA
Freytag, Gustav 1816-1895 .... **NCLC 109**
See also DLB 129
Friedan, Betty (Naomi) 1921- .... **CLC 74**
See also CA 65-68; CANR 18, 45, 74; DLB
246; FW; MTCW 1, 2; NCFS 5
Friedlander, Saul 1932- .... **CLC 90**
See also CA 117; 130; CANR 72
Friedman, B(ernard) H(arper)
1926- .... **CLC 7**
See also CA 1-4R; CANR 3, 48
Friedman, Bruce Jay 1930- ...... **CLC 3, 5, 56**
See also CA 9-12R; CAD; CANR 25, 52,
101; CD 5; CN 7; DLB 2, 28, 244; INT
CANR-25; SSFS 18
Friel, Brian 1929- .... **CLC 5, 42, 59, 115; DC
8; SSC 76**
See also BRWS 5; CA 21-24R; CANR 33,
69, 131; CBD; CD 5; DFS 11; DLB 13;
EWL 3; MTCW 1; RGEL 2; TEA
Friis-Baastad, Babbis Ellinor
1921-1970 .... **CLC 12**
See also CA 17-20R; 134; SATA 7
Frisch, Max (Rudolf) 1911-1991 ... **CLC 3, 9,
14, 18, 32, 44; TCLC 121**
See also CA 85-88; 134; CANR 32, 74; CD-
WLB 2; DAM DRAM, NOV; DLB 69,
124; EW 13; EWL 3; MTCW 1, 2; RGWL
2, 3

Fromentin, Eugene (Samuel Auguste)
1820-1876 .... **NCLC 10, 125**
See also DLB 123; GFL 1789 to the Present
Frost, Frederick
See Faust, Frederick (Schiller)
See also TCWW 2
Frost, Robert (Lee) 1874-1963 .. **CLC 1, 3, 4,
9, 10, 13, 15, 26, 34, 44; PC 1, 39;
WLC**
See also AAYA 21; AMW; AMWR 1; CA
89-92; CANR 33; CDALB 1917-1929;
CLR 67; DA; DA3; DAB; DAC; DAM
MST, POET; DLB 54, 284; DLBD 7;
EWL 3; EXPP; MTCW 1, 2; PAB; PFS 1,
2, 3, 4, 5, 6, 7, 10, 13; RGAL 4; SATA
14; TUS; WP; WYA
Froude, James Anthony
1818-1894 .... **NCLC 43**
See also DLB 18, 57, 144
Froy, Herald
See Waterhouse, Keith (Spencer)
Fry, Christopher 1907- .... **CLC 2, 10, 14**
See also BRWS 3; CA 17-20R; CAAS 23;
CANR 9, 30, 74, 132; CBD; CD 5; CP 7;
DAM DRAM; DLB 13; EWL 3; MTCW
1, 2; RGEL 2; SATA 66; TEA
Frye, (Herman) Northrop
1912-1991 .... **CLC 24, 70**
See also CA 5-8R; 133; CANR 8, 37; DLB
67, 68, 246; EWL 3; MTCW 1, 2; RGAL
4; TWA
Fuchs, Daniel 1909-1993 .... **CLC 8, 22**
See also CA 81-84; 142; CAAS 5; CANR
40; DLB 9, 26, 28; DLBY 1993
Fuchs, Daniel 1934- .... **CLC 34**
See also CA 37-40R; CANR 14, 48
Fuentes, Carlos 1928- .. **CLC 3, 8, 10, 13, 22,
41, 60, 113; HLC 1; SSC 24; WLC**
See also AAYA 4, 45; AITN 2; BPFB 1;
CA 69-72; CANR 10, 32, 68, 104; CD-
WLB 3; CWW 2; DA; DA3; DAB; DAC;
DAM MST, MULT, NOV; DLB 113;
DNFS 2; EWL 3; HW 1, 2; LAIT 3; LATS
1:2; LAW; LAWS 1; LMFS 2; MTCW 1,
2; NFS 8; RGSF 2; RGWL 2, 3; TWA;
WLIT 1
Fuentes, Gregorio Lopez y
See Lopez y Fuentes, Gregorio
Fuertes, Gloria 1918-1998 .... **PC 27**
See also CA 178, 180; DLB 108; HW 2;
SATA 115
Fugard, (Harold) Athol 1932- . **CLC 5, 9, 14,
25, 40, 80; DC 3**
See also AAYA 17; AFW; CA 85-88; CANR
32, 54, 118; CD 5; DAM DRAM; DFS 3,
6, 10; DLB 225; DNFS 1, 2; EWL 3;
LATS 1:2; MTCW 1; RGEL 2; WLIT 2
Fugard, Sheila 1932- .... **CLC 48**
See also CA 125
Fukuyama, Francis 1952- .... **CLC 131**
See also CA 140; CANR 72, 125
Fuller, Charles (H.), (Jr.) 1939- .... **BLC 2;
CLC 25; DC 1**
See also BW 2; CA 108; 112; CAD; CANR
87; CD 5; DAM DRAM, MULT; DFS 8;
DLB 38, 266; EWL 3; INT CA-112;
MTCW 1
Fuller, Henry Blake 1857-1929 .... **TCLC 103**
See also CA 108; 177; DLB 12; RGAL 4
Fuller, John (Leopold) 1937- .... **CLC 62**
See also CA 21-24R; CANR 9, 44; CP 7;
DLB 40
Fuller, Margaret
See Ossoli, Sarah Margaret (Fuller)
See also AMWS 2; DLB 183, 223, 239
Fuller, Roy (Broadbent) 1912-1991 ... **CLC 4,
28**
See also BRWS 7; CA 5-8R; 135; CAAS
10; CANR 53, 83; CWRI 5; DLB 15, 20;
EWL 3; RGEL 2; SATA 87

Fuller, Sarah Margaret
See Ossoli, Sarah Margaret (Fuller)
Fuller, Sarah Margaret
See Ossoli, Sarah Margaret (Fuller)
See also DLB 1, 59, 73
Fuller, Thomas 1608-1661 .... **LC 111**
See also DLB 151
Fulton, Alice 1952- .... **CLC 52**
See also CA 116; CANR 57, 88; CP 7;
CWP; DLB 193
Furphy, Joseph 1843-1912 .... **TCLC 25**
See Collins, Tom
See also CA 163; DLB 230; EWL 3; RGEL
2
Fuson, Robert H(enderson) 1927- .... **CLC 70**
See also CA 89-92; CANR 103
Fussell, Paul 1924- .... **CLC 74**
See also BEST 90:1; CA 17-20R; CANR 8,
21, 35, 69, 135; INT CANR-21; MTCW
1, 2
Futabatei, Shimei 1864-1909 .... **TCLC 44**
See Futabatei Shimei
See also CA 162; MJW
Futabatei Shimei
See Futabatei, Shimei
See also DLB 180; EWL 3
Futrelle, Jacques 1875-1912 .... **TCLC 19**
See also CA 113; 155; CMW 4
Gaboriau, Emile 1835-1873 .... **NCLC 14**
See also CMW 4; MSW
Gadda, Carlo Emilio 1893-1973 ...... **CLC 11;
TCLC 144**
See also CA 89-92; DLB 177; EWL 3
Gaddis, William 1922-1998 ... **CLC 1, 3, 6, 8,
10, 19, 43, 86**
See also AMWS 4; BPFB 1; CA 17-20R;
172; CANR 21, 48; CN 7; DLB 2, 278;
EWL 3; MTCW 1, 2; RGAL 4
Gaelique, Moruen le
See Jacob, (Cyprien-)Max
Gage, Walter
See Inge, William (Motter)
Gaiman, Neil (Richard) 1960- .... **CLC 195**
See also AAYA 19, 42; CA 133; CANR 81,
129; DLB 261; HGG; SATA 85, 146;
SFW 4; SUFW 2
Gaines, Ernest J(ames) 1933- .. **BLC 2; CLC
3, 11, 18, 86, 181; SSC 68**
See also AAYA 18; AFAW 1, 2; AITN 1;
BPFB 2; BW 2, 3; BYA 6; CA 9-12R;
CANR 6, 24, 42, 75, 126; CDALB 1968-
1988; CLR 62; CN 7; CSW; DA3; DAM
MULT; DLB 2, 33, 152; DLBY 1980;
EWL 3; EXPN; LAIT 5; LATS 1:2;
MTCW 1, 2; NFS 5, 7, 16; RGAL 4;
RGSF 2; RHW; SATA 86; SSFS 5; YAW
Gaitskill, Mary (Lawrence) 1954- .... **CLC 69**
See also CA 128; CANR 61; DLB 244
Gaius Suetonius Tranquillus
See Suetonius
Galdos, Benito Perez
See Perez Galdos, Benito
See also EW 7
Gale, Zona 1874-1938 .... **TCLC 7**
See also CA 105; 153; CANR 84; DAM
DRAM; DFS 17; DLB 9, 78, 228; RGAL
4
Galeano, Eduardo (Hughes) 1940- . **CLC 72;
HLCS 1**
See also CA 29-32R; CANR 13, 32, 100;
HW 1
Galiano, Juan Valera y Alcala
See Valera y Alcala-Galiano, Juan
Galilei, Galileo 1564-1642 .... **LC 45**
Gallagher, Tess 1943- .... **CLC 18, 63; PC 9**
See also CA 106; CP 7; CWP; DAM POET;
DLB 120, 212, 244; PFS 16

Gorky, Maxim .... **SSC 28; TCLC 8; WLC**
  See Peshkov, Alexei Maximovich
  See also DAB; DFS 9; DLB 295; EW 8;
  EWL 3; MTCW 2; TWA

Goryan, Sirak
  See Saroyan, William

Gosse, Edmund (William)
  1849-1928 .... **TCLC 28**
  See also CA 117; DLB 57, 144, 184; RGEL
  2

Gotlieb, Phyllis (Fay Bloom) 1926- .. **CLC 18**
  See also CA 13-16R; CANR 7, 135; DLB
  88, 251; SFW 4

Gottesman, S. D.
  See Kornbluth, C(yril) M.; Pohl, Frederik

Gottfried von Strassburg fl. c.
  1170-1215 .... **CMLC 10**
  See also CDWLB 2; DLB 138; EW 1;
  RGWL 2, 3

Gotthelf, Jeremias 1797-1854 .... **NCLC 117**
  See also DLB 133; RGWL 2, 3

Gottschalk, Laura Riding
  See Jackson, Laura (Riding)

Gould, Lois 1932(?)-2002 .... **CLC 4, 10**
  See also CA 77-80; 208; CANR 29; MTCW
  1

Gould, Stephen Jay 1941-2002 .... **CLC 163**
  See also AAYA 26; BEST 90:2; CA 77-80;
  205; CANR 10, 27, 56, 75, 125; CPW;
  INT CANR-27; MTCW 1, 2

Gourmont, Remy(-Marie-Charles) de
  1858-1915 .... **TCLC 17**
  See also CA 109; 150; GFL 1789 to the
  Present; MTCW 2

Gournay, Marie le Jars de
  See de Gournay, Marie le Jars

Govier, Katherine 1948- .... **CLC 51**
  See also CA 101; CANR 18, 40, 128; CCA
  1

Gower, John c. 1330-1408 .... **LC 76; PC 59**
  See also BRW 1; DLB 146; RGEL 2

Goyen, (Charles) William
  1915-1983 .... **CLC 5, 8, 14, 40**
  See also AITN 2; CA 5-8R; 110; CANR 6,
  71; DLB 2, 218; DLBY 1983; EWL 3;
  INT CANR-6

Goytisolo, Juan 1931- .... **CLC 5, 10, 23, 133;
  HLC 1**
  See also CA 85-88; CANR 32, 61, 131;
  CWW 2; DAM MULT; EWL 3; GLL 2;
  HW 1, 2; MTCW 1, 2

Gozzano, Guido 1883-1916 .... **PC 10**
  See also CA 154; DLB 114; EWL 3

Gozzi, (Conte) Carlo 1720-1806 .... **NCLC 23**

Grabbe, Christian Dietrich
  1801-1836 .... **NCLC 2**
  See also DLB 133; RGWL 2, 3

Grace, Patricia Frances 1937- .... **CLC 56**
  See also CA 176; CANR 118; CN 7; EWL
  3; RGSF 2

Gracian y Morales, Baltasar
  1601-1658 .... **LC 15**

Gracq, Julien .... **CLC 11, 48**
  See Poirier, Louis
  See also CWW 2; DLB 83; GFL 1789 to
  the Present

Grade, Chaim 1910-1982 .... **CLC 10**
  See also CA 93-96; 107; EWL 3

Graduate of Oxford, A
  See Ruskin, John

Grafton, Garth
  See Duncan, Sara Jeannette

Grafton, Sue 1940- .... **CLC 163**
  See also AAYA 11, 49; BEST 90:3; CA 108;
  CANR 31, 55, 111, 134; CMW 4; CPW;
  CSW; DA3; DAM POP; DLB 226; FW;
  MSW

Graham, John
  See Phillips, David Graham

Graham, Jorie 1951- .... **CLC 48, 118; PC 59**
  See also CA 111; CANR 63, 118; CP 7;
  CWP; DLB 120; EWL 3; PFS 10, 17

Graham, R(obert) B(ontine) Cunninghame
  See Cunninghame Graham, Robert
  (Gallnigad) Bontine
  See also DLB 98, 135, 174; RGEL 2; RGSF
  2

Graham, Robert
  See Haldeman, Joe (William)

Graham, Tom
  See Lewis, (Harry) Sinclair

Graham, W(illiam) S(idney)
  1918-1986 .... **CLC 29**
  See also BRWS 7; CA 73-76; 118; DLB 20;
  RGEL 2

Graham, Winston (Mawdsley)
  1910-2003 .... **CLC 23**
  See also CA 49-52; 218; CANR 2, 22, 45,
  66; CMW 4; CN 7; DLB 77; RHW

Grahame, Kenneth 1859-1932 .... **TCLC 64,
  136**
  See also BYA 5; CA 108; 136; CANR 80;
  CLR 5; CWRI 5; DA3; DAB; DLB 34,
  141, 178; FANT; MAICYA 1, 2; MTCW
  2; NFS 20; RGEL 2; SATA 100; TEA;
  WCH; YABC 1

Granger, Darius John
  See Marlowe, Stephen

Granin, Daniil 1918- .... **CLC 59**
  See also DLB 302

Granovsky, Timofei Nikolaevich
  1813-1855 .... **NCLC 75**
  See also DLB 198

Grant, Skeeter
  See Spiegelman, Art

Granville-Barker, Harley
  1877-1946 .... **TCLC 2**
  See Barker, Harley Granville
  See also CA 104; 204; DAM DRAM;
  RGEL 2

Granzotto, Gianni
  See Granzotto, Giovanni Battista

Granzotto, Giovanni Battista
  1914-1985 .... **CLC 70**
  See also CA 166

Grass, Guenter (Wilhelm) 1927- ... **CLC 1, 2,
  4, 6, 11, 15, 22, 32, 49, 88; WLC**
  See Grass, Gunter (Wilhelm)
  See also BPFB 2; CA 13-16R; CANR 20,
  75, 93, 133; CDWLB 2; DA; DA3; DAB;
  DAC; DAM MST, NOV; DLB 75, 124;
  EW 13; EWL 3; MTCW 1, 2; RGWL 2,
  3; TWA

Grass, Gunter (Wilhelm)
  See Grass, Guenter (Wilhelm)
  See also CWW 2

Gratton, Thomas
  See Hulme, T(homas) E(rnest)

Grau, Shirley Ann 1929- .... **CLC 4, 9, 146;
  SSC 15**
  See also CA 89-92; CANR 22, 69; CN 7;
  CSW; DLB 2, 218; INT CA-89-92;
  CANR-22; MTCW 1

Gravel, Fern
  See Hall, James Norman

Graver, Elizabeth 1964- .... **CLC 70**
  See also CA 135; CANR 71, 129

Graves, Richard Perceval
  1895-1985 .... **CLC 44**
  See also CA 65-68; CANR 9, 26, 51

Graves, Robert (von Ranke)
  1895-1985 .. **CLC 1, 2, 6, 11, 39, 44, 45;
  PC 6**
  See also BPFB 2; BRW 7; BYA 4; CA 5-8R;
  117; CANR 5, 36; CDBLB 1914-1945;
  DA3; DAB; DAC; DAM MST, POET;

DLB 20, 100, 191; DLBD 18; DLBY
  1985; EWL 3; LATS 1:1; MTCW 1, 2;
  NCFS 2; RGEL 2; RHW; SATA 45; TEA

Graves, Valerie
  See Bradley, Marion Zimmer

Gray, Alasdair (James) 1934- .... **CLC 41**
  See also BRWS 9; CA 126; CANR 47, 69,
  106; CN 7; DLB 194, 261; HGG; INT
  CA-126; MTCW 1, 2; RGSF 2; SUFW 2

Gray, Amlin 1946- .... **CLC 29**
  See also CA 138

Gray, Francine du Plessix 1930- ..... **CLC 22,
  153**
  See also BEST 90:3; CA 61-64; CAAS 2;
  CANR 11, 33, 75, 81; DAM NOV; INT
  CANR-11; MTCW 1, 2

Gray, John (Henry) 1866-1934 ...... **TCLC 19**
  See also CA 119; 162; RGEL 2

Gray, Simon (James Holliday)
  1936- .... **CLC 9, 14, 36**
  See also AITN 1; CA 21-24R; CAAS 3;
  CANR 32, 69; CD 5; DLB 13; EWL 3;
  MTCW 1; RGEL 2

Gray, Spalding 1941-2004 .... **CLC 49, 112;
  DC 7**
  See also CA 128; 225; CAD; CANR 74;
  CD 5; CPW; DAM POP; MTCW 2

Gray, Thomas 1716-1771 .... **LC 4, 40; PC 2;
  WLC**
  See also BRW 3; CDBLB 1660-1789; DA;
  DA3; DAB; DAC; DAM MST; DLB 109;
  EXPP; PAB; PFS 9; RGEL 2; TEA; WP

Grayson, David
  See Baker, Ray Stannard

Grayson, Richard (A.) 1951- .... **CLC 38**
  See also CA 85-88; 210; CAAE 210; CANR
  14, 31, 57; DLB 234

Greeley, Andrew M(oran) 1928- ...... **CLC 28**
  See also BPFB 2; CA 5-8R; CAAS 7;
  CANR 7, 43, 69, 104; CMW 4; CPW;
  DA3; DAM POP; MTCW 1, 2

Green, Anna Katharine
  1846-1935 .... **TCLC 63**
  See also CA 112; 159; CMW 4; DLB 202,
  221; MSW

Green, Brian
  See Card, Orson Scott

Green, Hannah
  See Greenberg, Joanne (Goldenberg)

Green, Hannah 1927(?)-1996 .... **CLC 3**
  See also CA 73-76; CANR 59, 93; NFS 10

Green, Henry .... **CLC 2, 13, 97**
  See Yorke, Henry Vincent
  See also BRWS 2; CA 175; DLB 15; EWL
  3; RGEL 2

Green, Julien (Hartridge) 1900-1998
  See Green, Julian
  See also CA 21-24R; 169; CANR 33, 87;
  CWW 2; DLB 4, 72; MTCW 1

Green, Julian .... **CLC 3, 11, 77**
  See Green, Julien (Hartridge)
  See also EWL 3; GFL 1789 to the Present;
  MTCW 2

Green, Paul (Eliot) 1894-1981 .... **CLC 25**
  See also AITN 1; CA 5-8R; 103; CANR 3;
  DAM DRAM; DLB 7, 9, 249; DLBY
  1981; RGAL 4

Greenaway, Peter 1942- .... **CLC 159**
  See also CA 127

Greenberg, Ivan 1908-1973
  See Rahv, Philip
  See also CA 85-88

Greenberg, Joanne (Goldenberg)
  1932- .... **CLC 7, 30**
  See also AAYA 12; CA 5-8R; CANR 14,
  32, 69; CN 7; SATA 25; YAW

Greenberg, Richard 1959(?)- .... **CLC 57**
  See also CA 138; CAD; CD 5

Harvey, Caroline
See Trollope, Joanna

Harvey, Gabriel 1550(?)-1631 .... **LC 88**
See also DLB 167, 213, 281

Harwood, Ronald 1934- .... **CLC 32**
See also CA 1-4R; CANR 4, 55; CBD; CD
5; DAM DRAM, MST; DLB 13

Hasegawa Tatsunosuke
See Futabatei, Shimei

Hasek, Jaroslav (Matej Frantisek)
1883-1923 .... **SSC 69; TCLC 4**
See also CA 104; 129; CDWLB 4; DLB
215; EW 9; EWL 3; MTCW 1, 2; RGSF
2; RGWL 2, 3

Hass, Robert 1941- ... **CLC 18, 39, 99; PC 16**
See also AMWS 6; CA 111; CANR 30, 50,
71; CP 7; DLB 105, 206; EWL 3; RGAL
4; SATA 94

Hastings, Hudson
See Kuttner, Henry

Hastings, Selina .... **CLC 44**

Hathorne, John 1641-1717 .... **LC 38**

Hatteras, Amelia
See Mencken, H(enry) L(ouis)

Hatteras, Owen .... **TCLC 18**
See Mencken, H(enry) L(ouis); Nathan,
George Jean

Hauptmann, Gerhart (Johann Robert)
1862-1946 .... **SSC 37; TCLC 4**
See also CA 104; 153; CDWLB 2; DAM
DRAM; DLB 66, 118; EW 8; EWL 3;
RGSF 2; RGWL 2, 3; TWA

Havel, Vaclav 1936- ..... **CLC 25, 58, 65, 123;
DC 6**
See also CA 104; CANR 36, 63, 124; CD-
WLB 4; CWW 2; DA3; DAM DRAM;
DFS 10; DLB 232; EWL 3; LMFS 2;
MTCW 1, 2; RGWL 3

Haviaras, Stratis .... **CLC 33**
See Chaviaras, Strates

Hawes, Stephen 1475(?)-1529(?) .... **LC 17**
See also DLB 132; RGEL 2

Hawkes, John (Clendennin Burne, Jr.)
1925-1998 .. **CLC 1, 2, 3, 4, 7, 9, 14, 15,
27, 49**
See also BPFB 2; CA 1-4R; 167; CANR 2,
47, 64; CN 7; DLB 2, 7, 227; DLBY
1980, 1998; EWL 3; MTCW 1, 2; RGAL
4

Hawking, S. W.
See Hawking, Stephen W(illiam)

Hawking, Stephen W(illiam) 1942- . **CLC 63,
105**
See also AAYA 13; BEST 89:1; CA 126;
129; CANR 48, 115; CPW; DA3; MTCW
2

Hawkins, Anthony Hope
See Hope, Anthony

Hawthorne, Julian 1846-1934 .... **TCLC 25**
See also CA 165; HGG

Hawthorne, Nathaniel 1804-1864 ... **NCLC 2,
10, 17, 23, 39, 79, 95; SSC 3, 29, 39;
WLC**
See also AAYA 18; AMW; AMWC 1;
AMWR 1; BPFB 2; BYA 3; CDALB
1640-1865; DA; DA3; DAB; DAC; DAM
MST, NOV; DLB 1, 74, 183, 223, 269;
EXPN; EXPS; HGG; LAIT 1; NFS 1, 20;
RGAL 4; RGSF; SSFS 1, 7, 11, 15;
SUFW 1; TUS; WCH; YABC 2

Haxton, Josephine Ayres 1921-
See Douglas, Ellen
See also CA 115; CANR 41, 83

Hayaseca y Eizaguirre, Jorge
See Echegaray (y Eizaguirre), Jose (Maria
Waldo)

Hayashi, Fumiko 1904-1951 .... **TCLC 27**
See Hayashi Fumiko
See also CA 161

Hayashi Fumiko
See Hayashi, Fumiko
See also DLB 180; EWL 3

Haycraft, Anna (Margaret) 1932-
See Ellis, Alice Thomas
See also CA 122; CANR 85, 90; MTCW 2

Hayden, Robert E(arl) 1913-1980 ..... **BLC 2;
CLC 5, 9, 14, 37; PC 6**
See also AFAW 1, 2; AMWS 2; BW 1, 3;
CA 69-72; 97-100; CABS 2; CANR 24,
75, 82; CDALB 1941-1968; DA; DAC;
DAM MST, MULT, POET; DLB 5, 76;
EWL 3; EXPP; MTCW 1, 2; PFS 1;
RGAL 4; SATA 19; SATA-Obit 26; WP

Haydon, Benjamin Robert
1786-1846 .... **NCLC 146**
See also DLB 110

Hayek, F(riedrich) A(ugust von)
1899-1992 .... **TCLC 109**
See also CA 93-96; 137; CANR 20; MTCW
1, 2

Hayford, J(oseph) E(phraim) Casely
See Casely-Hayford, J(oseph) E(phraim)

Hayman, Ronald 1932- .... **CLC 44**
See also CA 25-28R; CANR 18, 50, 88; CD
5; DLB 155

Hayne, Paul Hamilton 1830-1886 . **NCLC 94**
See also DLB 3, 64, 79, 248; RGAL 4

Hays, Mary 1760-1843 .... **NCLC 114**
See also DLB 142, 158; RGEL 2

Haywood, Eliza (Fowler)
1693(?)-1756 .... **LC 1, 44**
See also DLB 39; RGEL 2

Hazlitt, William 1778-1830 ...... **NCLC 29, 82**
See also BRW 4; DLB 110, 158; RGEL 2;
TEA

Hazzard, Shirley 1931- .... **CLC 18**
See also CA 9-12R; CANR 4, 70, 127; CN
7; DLB 289; DLBY 1982; MTCW 1

Head, Bessie 1937-1986 ...... **BLC 2; CLC 25,
67; SSC 52**
See also AFW; BW 2, 3; CA 29-32R; 119;
CANR 25, 82; CDWLB 3; DA3; DAM
MULT; DLB 117, 225; EWL 3; EXPS;
FW; MTCW 1, 2; RGSF 2; SSFS 5, 13;
WLIT 2; WWE 1

Headon, (Nicky) Topper 1956(?)- ..... **CLC 30**

Heaney, Seamus (Justin) 1939- ..... **CLC 5, 7,
14, 25, 37, 74, 91, 171; PC 18; WLCS**
See also BRWR 1; BRWS 2; CA 85-88;
CANR 25, 48, 75, 91, 128; CDBLB 1960
to Present; CP 7; DA3; DAB; DAM
POET; DLB 40; DLBY 1995; EWL 3;
EXPP; MTCW 1, 2; PAB; PFS 2, 5, 8,
17; RGEL 2; TEA; WLIT 4

Hearn, (Patricio) Lafcadio (Tessima Carlos)
1850-1904 .... **TCLC 9**
See also CA 105; 166; DLB 12, 78, 189;
HGG; RGAL 4

Hearne, Samuel 1745-1792 .... **LC 95**
See also DLB 99

Hearne, Vicki 1946-2001 .... **CLC 56**
See also CA 139; 201

Hearon, Shelby 1931- .... **CLC 63**
See also AITN 2; AMWS 8; CA 25-28R;
CANR 18, 48, 103; CSW

Heat-Moon, William Least .... **CLC 29**
See Trogdon, William (Lewis)
See also AAYA 9

Hebbel, Friedrich 1813-1863 . **DC 21; NCLC
43**
See also CDWLB 2; DAM DRAM; DLB
129; EW 6; RGWL 2, 3

Hebert, Anne 1916-2000 .... **CLC 4, 13, 29**
See also CA 85-88; 187; CANR 69, 126;
CCA 1; CWP; CWW 2; DA3; DAC;
DAM MST, POET; DLB 68; EWL 3; GFL
1789 to the Present; MTCW 1, 2; PFS 20

Hecht, Anthony (Evan) 1923-2004 .... **CLC 8,
13, 19**
See also AMWS 10; CA 9-12R; CANR 6,
108; CP 7; DAM POET; DLB 5, 169;
EWL 3; PFS 6; WP

Hecht, Ben 1894-1964 ..... **CLC 8; TCLC 101**
See also CA 85-88; DFS 9; DLB 7, 9, 25,
26, 28, 86; FANT; IDFW 3, 4; RGAL 4

Hedayat, Sadeq 1903-1951 .... **TCLC 21**
See also CA 120; EWL 3; RGSF 2

Hegel, Georg Wilhelm Friedrich
1770-1831 .... **NCLC 46**
See also DLB 90; TWA

Heidegger, Martin 1889-1976 .... **CLC 24**
See also CA 81-84; 65-68; CANR 34; DLB
296; MTCW 1, 2

Heidenstam, (Carl Gustaf) Verner von
1859-1940 .... **TCLC 5**
See also CA 104

Heidi Louise
See Erdrich, Louise

Heifner, Jack 1946- .... **CLC 11**
See also CA 105; CANR 47

Heijermans, Herman 1864-1924 .... **TCLC 24**
See also CA 123; EWL 3

Heilbrun, Carolyn G(old)
1926-2003 .... **CLC 25, 173**
See Cross, Amanda
See also CA 45-48; 220; CANR 1, 28, 58,
94; FW

Hein, Christoph 1944- .... **CLC 154**
See also CA 158; CANR 108; CDWLB 2;
CWW 2; DLB 124

Heine, Heinrich 1797-1856 .... **NCLC 4, 54,
147; PC 25**
See also CDWLB 2; DLB 90; EW 5; RGWL
2, 3; TWA

Heinemann, Larry (Curtiss) 1944- .. **CLC 50**
See also CA 110; CAAS 21; CANR 31, 81;
DLBD 9; INT CANR-31

Heiney, Donald (William) 1921-1993
See Harris, MacDonald
See also CA 1-4R; 142; CANR 3, 58; FANT

Heinlein, Robert A(nson) 1907-1988 . **CLC 1,
3, 8, 14, 26, 55; SSC 55**
See also AAYA 17; BPFB 2; BYA 4, 13;
CA 1-4R; 125; CANR 1, 20, 53; CLR 75;
CPW; DA3; DAM POP; DLB 8; EXPS;
JRDA; LAIT 5; LMFS 2; MAICYA 1, 2;
MTCW 1, 2; RGAL 4; SATA 9, 69;
SATA-Obit 56; SCFW; SFW 4; SSFS 7;
YAW

Helforth, John
See Doolittle, Hilda

Heliodorus fl. 3rd cent. - .... **CMLC 52**

Hellenhofferu, Vojtech Kapristian z
See Hasek, Jaroslav (Matej Frantisek)

Heller, Joseph 1923-1999 . **CLC 1, 3, 5, 8, 11,
36, 63; TCLC 131, 151; WLC**
See also AAYA 24; AITN 1; AMWS 4;
BPFB 2; BYA 1; CA 5-8R; 187; CABS 1;
CANR 8, 42, 66, 126; CN 7; CPW; DA;
DA3; DAB; DAC; DAM MST, NOV,
POP; DLB 2, 28, 227; DLBY 1980, 2002;
EWL 3; EXPN; INT CANR-8; LAIT 4;
MTCW 1, 2; NFS 1; RGAL 4; TUS; YAW

Hellman, Lillian (Florence)
1906-1984 .. **CLC 2, 4, 8, 14, 18, 34, 44,
52; DC 1; TCLC 119**
See also AAYA 47; AITN 1, 2; AMWS 1;
CA 13-16R; 112; CAD; CANR 33; CWD;
DA3; DAM DRAM; DFS 1, 3, 14; DLB
7, 228; DLBY 1984; EWL 3; FW; LAIT
3; MAWW; MTCW 1, 2; RGAL 4; TUS

Helprin, Mark 1947- .... **CLC 7, 10, 22, 32**
See also CA 81-84; CANR 47, 64, 124;
CDALBS; CPW; DA3; DAM NOV, POP;
DLBY 1985; FANT; MTCW 1, 2; SUFW
2

Hill, Geoffrey (William) 1932- ...... **CLC 5, 8, 18, 45**
See also BRWS 5; CA 81-84; CANR 21, 89; CDBLB 1960 to Present; CP 7; DAM POET; DLB 40; EWL 3; MTCW 1; RGEL 2

Hill, George Roy 1921-2002 .... **CLC 26**
See also CA 110; 122; 213

Hill, John
See Koontz, Dean R(ay)

Hill, Susan (Elizabeth) 1942- ...... **CLC 4, 113**
See also CA 33-36R; CANR 29, 69, 129; CN 7; DAB; DAM MST, NOV; DLB 14, 139; HGG; MTCW 1; RHW

Hillard, Asa G. III .... **CLC 70**

Hillerman, Tony 1925- ..... **CLC 62, 170**
See also AAYA 40; BEST 89:1; BPFB 2; CA 29-32R; CANR 21, 42, 65, 97, 134; CMW 4; CPW; DA3; DAM POP; DLB 206, 306; MSW; RGAL 4; SATA 6; TCWW 2; YAW

Hillesum, Etty 1914-1943 .... **TCLC 49**
See also CA 137

Hilliard, Noel (Harvey) 1929-1996 ... **CLC 15**
See also CA 9-12R; CANR 7, 69; CN 7

Hillis, Rick 1956- .... **CLC 66**
See also CA 134

Hilton, James 1900-1954 .... **TCLC 21**
See also CA 108; 169; DLB 34, 77; FANT; SATA 34

Hilton, Walter (?)-1396 .... **CMLC 58**
See also DLB 146; RGEL 2

Himes, Chester (Bomar) 1909-1984 .. **BLC 2; CLC 2, 4, 7, 18, 58, 108; TCLC 139**
See also AFAW 2; BPFB 2; BW 2; CA 25-28R; 114; CANR 22, 89; CMW 4; DAM MULT; DLB 2, 76, 143, 226; EWL 3; MSW; MTCW 1, 2; RGAL 4

Hinde, Thomas .... **CLC 6, 11**
See Chitty, Thomas Willes
See also EWL 3

Hine, (William) Daryl 1936- .... **CLC 15**
See also CA 1-4R; CAAS 15; CANR 1, 20; CP 7; DLB 60

Hinkson, Katharine Tynan
See Tynan, Katharine

Hinojosa(-Smith), Rolando (R.) 1929- .... **HLC 1**
See Hinojosa-Smith, Rolando
See also CA 131; CAAS 16; CANR 62; DAM MULT; DLB 82; HW 1, 2; LLW 1; MTCW 2; RGAL 4

Hinton, S(usan) E(loise) 1950- .. **CLC 30, 111**
See also AAYA 2, 33; BPFB 2; BYA 2, 3; CA 81-84; CANR 32, 62, 92, 133; CDALBS; CLR 3, 23; CPW; DA; DA3; DAB; DAC; DAM MST, NOV; JRDA; LAIT 5; MAICYA 1, 2; MTCW 1, 2; NFS 5, 9, 15, 16; SATA 19, 58, 115; WYA; YAW

Hippius, Zinaida (Nikolaevna) .... **TCLC 9**
See Gippius, Zinaida (Nikolaevna)
See also DLB 295; EWL 3

Hiraoka, Kimitake 1925-1970
See Mishima, Yukio
See also CA 97-100; 29-32R; DA3; DAM DRAM; GLL 1; MTCW 1, 2

Hirsch, E(ric) D(onald), Jr. 1928- .... **CLC 79**
See also CA 25-28R; CANR 27, 51; DLB 67; INT CANR-27; MTCW 1

Hirsch, Edward 1950- .... **CLC 31, 50**
See also CA 104; CANR 20, 42, 102; CP 7; DLB 120

Hitchcock, Alfred (Joseph) 1899-1980 .... **CLC 16**
See also AAYA 22; CA 159; 97-100; SATA 27; SATA-Obit 24

Hitchens, Christopher (Eric) 1949- .... **CLC 157**
See also CA 152; CANR 89

Hitler, Adolf 1889-1945 .... **TCLC 53**
See also CA 117; 147

Hoagland, Edward 1932- .... **CLC 28**
See also ANW; CA 1-4R; CANR 2, 31, 57, 107; CN 7; DLB 6; SATA 51; TCWW 2

Hoban, Russell (Conwell) 1925- ... **CLC 7, 25**
See also BPFB 2; CA 5-8R; CANR 23, 37, 66, 114; CLR 3, 69; CN 7; CWRI 5; DAM NOV; DLB 52; FANT; MAICYA 1, 2; MTCW 1, 2; SATA 1, 40, 78, 136; SFW 4; SUFW 2

Hobbes, Thomas 1588-1679 .... **LC 36**
See also DLB 151, 252, 281; RGEL 2

Hobbs, Perry
See Blackmur, R(ichard) P(almer)

Hobson, Laura Z(ametkin) 1900-1986 .... **CLC 7, 25**
See Field, Peter
See also BPFB 2; CA 17-20R; 118; CANR 55; DLB 28; SATA 52

Hoccleve, Thomas c. 1368-c. 1437 ...... **LC 75**
See also DLB 146; RGEL 2

Hoch, Edward D(entinger) 1930-
See Queen, Ellery
See also CA 29-32R; CANR 11, 27, 51, 97; CMW 4; DLB 306; SFW 4

Hochhuth, Rolf 1931- .... **CLC 4, 11, 18**
See also CA 5-8R; CANR 33, 75; CWW 2; DAM DRAM; DLB 124; EWL 3; MTCW 1, 2

Hochman, Sandra 1936- .... **CLC 3, 8**
See also CA 5-8R; DLB 5

Hochwaelder, Fritz 1911-1986 .... **CLC 36**
See Hochwalder, Fritz
See also CA 29-32R; 120; CANR 42; DAM DRAM; MTCW 1; RGWL 3

Hochwalder, Fritz
See Hochwaelder, Fritz
See also EWL 3; RGWL 2

Hocking, Mary (Eunice) 1921- .... **CLC 13**
See also CA 101; CANR 18, 40

Hodgins, Jack 1938- .... **CLC 23**
See also CA 93-96; CN 7; DLB 60

Hodgson, William Hope 1877(?)-1918 .... **TCLC 13**
See also CA 111; 164; CMW 4; DLB 70, 153, 156, 178; HGG; MTCW 2; SFW 4; SUFW 1

Hoeg, Peter 1957- .... **CLC 95, 156**
See also CA 151; CANR 75; CMW 4; DA3; DLB 214; EWL 3; MTCW 2; NFS 17; RGWL 3; SSFS 18

Hoffman, Alice 1952- .... **CLC 51**
See also AAYA 37; AMWS 10; CA 77-80; CANR 34, 66, 100; CN 7; CPW; DAM NOV; DLB 292; MTCW 1, 2

Hoffman, Daniel (Gerard) 1923- . **CLC 6, 13, 23**
See also CA 1-4R; CANR 4; CP 7; DLB 5

Hoffman, Eva 1945- .... **CLC 182**
See also CA 132

Hoffman, Stanley 1944- .... **CLC 5**
See also CA 77-80

Hoffman, William 1925- .... **CLC 141**
See also CA 21-24R; CANR 9, 103; CSW; DLB 234

Hoffman, William M(oses) 1939- ..... **CLC 40**
See Hoffman, William M.
See also CA 57-60; CANR 11, 71

Hoffmann, E(rnst) T(heodor) A(madeus) 1776-1822 .... **NCLC 2; SSC 13**
See also CDWLB 2; DLB 90; EW 5; RGSF 2; RGWL 2, 3; SATA 27; SUFW 1; WCH

Hofmann, Gert 1931- .... **CLC 54**
See also CA 128; EWL 3

Hofmannsthal, Hugo von 1874-1929 ... **DC 4; TCLC 11**
See also CA 106; 153; CDWLB 2; DAM DRAM; DFS 17; DLB 81, 118; EW 9; EWL 3; RGWL 2, 3

Hogan, Linda 1947- ..... **CLC 73; NNAL; PC 35**
See also AMWS 4; ANW; BYA 12; CA 120, 226; CAAE 226; CANR 45, 73, 129; CWP; DAM MULT; DLB 175; SATA 132; TCWW 2

Hogarth, Charles
See Creasey, John

Hogarth, Emmett
See Polonsky, Abraham (Lincoln)

Hogg, James 1770-1835 .... **NCLC 4, 109**
See also BRWS 10; DLB 93, 116, 159; HGG; RGEL 2; SUFW 1

Holbach, Paul Henri Thiry Baron 1723-1789 .... **LC 14**

Holberg, Ludvig 1684-1754 .... **LC 6**
See also DLB 300; RGWL 2, 3

Holcroft, Thomas 1745-1809 .... **NCLC 85**
See also DLB 39, 89, 158; RGEL 2

Holden, Ursula 1921- .... **CLC 18**
See also CA 101; CAAS 8; CANR 22

Holderlin, (Johann Christian) Friedrich 1770-1843 .... **NCLC 16; PC 4**
See also CDWLB 2; DLB 90; EW 5; RGWL 2, 3

Holdstock, Robert
See Holdstock, Robert P.

Holdstock, Robert P. 1948- .... **CLC 39**
See also CA 131; CANR 81; DLB 261; FANT; HGG; SFW 4; SUFW 2

Holinshed, Raphael fl. 1580- .... **LC 69**
See also DLB 167; RGEL 2

Holland, Isabelle (Christian) 1920-2002 .... **CLC 21**
See also AAYA 11; CA 21-24R; 205; CAAE 181; CANR 10, 25, 47; CLR 57; CWRI 5; JRDA; LAIT 4; MAICYA 1, 2; SATA 8, 70; SATA-Essay 103; SATA-Obit 132; WYA

Holland, Marcus
See Caldwell, (Janet Miriam) Taylor (Holland)

Hollander, John 1929- .... **CLC 2, 5, 8, 14**
See also CA 1-4R; CANR 1, 52; CP 7; DLB 5; SATA 13

Hollander, Paul
See Silverberg, Robert

Holleran, Andrew 1943(?)- .... **CLC 38**
See Garber, Eric
See also CA 144; GLL 1

Holley, Marietta 1836(?)-1926 .... **TCLC 99**
See also CA 118; DLB 11

Hollinghurst, Alan 1954- .... **CLC 55, 91**
See also BRWS 10; CA 114; CN 7; DLB 207; GLL 1

Hollis, Jim
See Summers, Hollis (Spurgeon, Jr.)

Holly, Buddy 1936-1959 .... **TCLC 65**
See also CA 213

Holmes, Gordon
See Shiel, M(atthew) P(hipps)

Holmes, John
See Souster, (Holmes) Raymond

Holmes, John Clellon 1926-1988 ...... **CLC 56**
See also BG 2; CA 9-12R; 125; CANR 4; DLB 16, 237

Holmes, Oliver Wendell, Jr. 1841-1935 .... **TCLC 77**
See also CA 114; 186

Holmes, Oliver Wendell 1809-1894 .... **NCLC 14, 81**
See also AMWS 1; CDALB 1640-1865; DLB 1, 189, 235; EXPP; RGAL 4; SATA 34

Hughes, Edward James
  See Hughes, Ted
  See also DA3; DAM MST, POET
Hughes, (James Mercer) Langston
  1902-1967 ..... **BLC 2; CLC 1, 5, 10, 15,**
    35, 44, 108; DC 3; HR 2; PC 1, 53;
    SSC 6; WLC
  See also AAYA 12; AFAW 1, 2; AMWR 1;
    AMWS 1; BW 1, 3; CA 1-4R; 25-28R;
    CANR 1, 34, 82; CDALB 1929-1941;
    CLR 17; DA; DA3; DAB; DAC; DAM
    DRAM, MST, MULT, POET; DFS 6, 18;
    DLB 4, 7, 48, 51, 86, 228; EWL 3; EXPP;
    EXPS; JRDA; LAIT 3; LMFS 2; MAI-
    CYA 1, 2; MTCW 1, 2; PAB; PFS 1, 3, 6,
    10, 15; RGAL 4; RGSF 2; SATA 4, 33;
    SSFS 4, 7; TUS; WCH; WP; YAW
Hughes, Richard (Arthur Warren)
  1900-1976 .... **CLC 1, 11**
  See also CA 5-8R; 65-68; CANR 4; DAM
    NOV; DLB 15, 161; EWL 3; MTCW 1;
    RGEL 2; SATA 8; SATA-Obit 25
Hughes, Ted 1930-1998 . **CLC 2, 4, 9, 14, 37,**
    119; PC 7
  See Hughes, Edward James
  See also BRWC 2; BRWR 2; BRWS 1; CA
    1-4R; 171; CANR 1, 33, 66, 108; CLR 3;
    CP 7; DAB; DAC; DLB 40, 161; EWL 3;
    EXPP; MAICYA 1, 2; MTCW 1, 2; PAB;
    PFS 4, 19; RGEL 2; SATA 49; SATA-
    Brief 27; SATA-Obit 107; TEA; YAW
Hugo, Richard
  See Huch, Ricarda (Octavia)
Hugo, Richard F(ranklin)
  1923-1982 .... **CLC 6, 18, 32**
  See also AMWS 6; CA 49-52; 108; CANR
    3; DAM POET; DLB 5, 206; EWL 3; PFS
    17; RGAL 4
Hugo, Victor (Marie) 1802-1885 .... **NCLC 3,**
    10, 21; PC 17; WLC
  See also AAYA 28; DA; DA3; DAB; DAC;
    DAM DRAM, MST, NOV, POET; DLB
    119, 192, 217; EFS 2; EW 6; EXPN; GFL
    1789 to the Present; LAIT 1, 2; NFS 5,
    20; RGWL 2, 3; SATA 47; TWA
Huidobro, Vicente
  See Huidobro Fernandez, Vicente Garcia
  See also DLB 283; EWL 3; LAW
Huidobro Fernandez, Vicente Garcia
  1893-1948 .... **TCLC 31**
  See Huidobro, Vicente
  See also CA 131; HW 1
Hulme, Keri 1947- .... **CLC 39, 130**
  See also CA 125; CANR 69; CN 7; CP 7;
    CWP; EWL 3; FW; INT CA-125
Hulme, T(homas) E(rnest)
  1883-1917 .... **TCLC 21**
  See also BRWS 6; CA 117; 203; DLB 19
Humboldt, Wilhelm von
  1767-1835 .... **NCLC 134**
  See also DLB 90
Hume, David 1711-1776 .... **LC 7, 56**
  See also BRWS 3; DLB 104, 252; LMFS 1;
    TEA
Humphrey, William 1924-1997 .... **CLC 45**
  See also AMWS 9; CA 77-80; 160; CANR
    68; CN 7; CSW; DLB 6, 212, 234, 278;
    TCWW 2
Humphreys, Emyr Owen 1919- .... **CLC 47**
  See also CA 5-8R; CANR 3, 24; CN 7;
    DLB 15
Humphreys, Josephine 1945- ..... **CLC 34, 57**
  See also CA 121; 127; CANR 97; CSW;
    DLB 292; INT CA-127
Huneker, James Gibbons
  1860-1921 .... **TCLC 65**
  See also CA 193; DLB 71; RGAL 4
Hungerford, Hesba Fay
  See Brinsmead, H(esba) F(ay)

Hungerford, Pixie
  See Brinsmead, H(esba) F(ay)
Hunt, E(verette) Howard, (Jr.)
  1918- .... **CLC 3**
  See also AITN 1; CA 45-48; CANR 2, 47,
    103; CMW 4
Hunt, Francesca
  See Holland, Isabelle (Christian)
Hunt, Howard
  See Hunt, E(verette) Howard, (Jr.)
Hunt, Kyle
  See Creasey, John
Hunt, (James Henry) Leigh
  1784-1859 .... **NCLC 1, 70**
  See also DAM POET; DLB 96, 110, 144;
    RGEL 2; TEA
Hunt, Marsha 1946- .... **CLC 70**
  See also BW 2, 3; CA 143; CANR 79
Hunt, Violet 1866(?)-1942 .... **TCLC 53**
  See also CA 184; DLB 162, 197
Hunter, E. Waldo
  See Sturgeon, Theodore (Hamilton)
Hunter, Evan 1926- .... **CLC 11, 31**
  See McBain, Ed
  See also AAYA 39; BPFB 2; CA 5-8R;
    CANR 5, 38, 62, 97; CMW 4; CN 7;
    CPW; DAM POP; DLB 306; DLBY 1982;
    INT CANR-5; MSW; MTCW 1; SATA
    25; SFW 4
Hunter, Kristin
  See Lattany, Kristin (Elaine Eggleston)
    Hunter
Hunter, Mary
  See Austin, Mary (Hunter)
Hunter, Mollie 1922- .... **CLC 21**
  See McIlwraith, Maureen Mollie Hunter
  See also AAYA 13; BYA 6; CANR 37, 78;
    CLR 25; DLB 161; JRDA; MAICYA 1,
    2; SAAS 7; SATA 54, 106, 139; SATA-
    Essay 139; WYA; YAW
Hunter, Robert (?)-1734 .... **LC 7**
Hurston, Zora Neale 1891-1960 .... **BLC 2;**
    CLC 7, 30, 61; DC 12; HR 2; SSC 4;
    TCLC 121, 131; WLCS
  See also AAYA 15; AFAW 1, 2; AMWS 6;
    BW 1, 3; BYA 12; CA 85-88; CANR 61;
    CDALBS; DA; DA3; DAC; DAM MST,
    MULT, NOV; DFS 6; DLB 51, 86; EWL
    3; EXPN; EXPS; FW; LAIT 3; LATS 1:1;
    LMFS 2; MAWW; MTCW 1, 2; NFS 3;
    RGAL 4; RGSF 2; SSFS 1, 6, 11, 19;
    TUS; YAW
Husserl, E. G.
  See Husserl, Edmund (Gustav Albrecht)
Husserl, Edmund (Gustav Albrecht)
  1859-1938 .... **TCLC 100**
  See also CA 116; 133; DLB 296
Huston, John (Marcellus)
  1906-1987 .... **CLC 20**
  See also CA 73-76; 123; CANR 34; DLB
    26
Hustvedt, Siri 1955- .... **CLC 76**
  See also CA 137
Hutten, Ulrich von 1488-1523 .... **LC 16**
  See also DLB 179
Huxley, Aldous (Leonard)
  1894-1963 .... **CLC 1, 3, 4, 5, 8, 11, 18,**
    35, 79; SSC 39; WLC
  See also AAYA 11; BPFB 2; BRW 7; CA
    85-88; CANR 44, 99; CDBLB 1914-1945;
    DA; DA3; DAB; DAC; DAM MST, NOV;
    DLB 36, 100, 162, 195, 255; EWL 3;
    EXPN; LAIT 5; LMFS 2; MTCW 1, 2;
    NFS 6; RGEL 2; SATA 63; SCFW 2;
    SFW 4; TEA; YAW
Huxley, T(homas) H(enry)
  1825-1895 .... **NCLC 67**
  See also DLB 57; TEA

Huysmans, Joris-Karl 1848-1907 ... **TCLC 7,**
    69
  See also CA 104; 165; DLB 123; EW 7;
    GFL 1789 to the Present; LMFS 2; RGWL
    2, 3
Hwang, David Henry 1957- .... **CLC 55, 196;**
    DC 4, 23
  See also CA 127; 132; CAD; CANR 76,
    124; CD 5; DA3; DAM DRAM; DFS 11,
    18; DLB 212, 228; INT CA-132; MTCW
    2; RGAL 4
Hyde, Anthony 1946- .... **CLC 42**
  See Chase, Nicholas
  See also CA 136; CCA 1
Hyde, Margaret O(ldroyd) 1917- ..... **CLC 21**
  See also CA 1-4R; CANR 1, 36; CLR 23;
    JRDA; MAICYA 1, 2; SAAS 8; SATA 1,
    42, 76, 139
Hynes, James 1956(?)- .... **CLC 65**
  See also CA 164; CANR 105
Hypatia c. 370-415 .... **CMLC 35**
Ian, Janis 1951- .... **CLC 21**
  See also CA 105; 187
Ibanez, Vicente Blasco
  See Blasco Ibanez, Vicente
Ibarbourou, Juana de
  1895(?)-1979 .... **HLCS 2**
  See also DLB 290; HW 1; LAW
Ibarguengoitia, Jorge 1928-1983 ..... **CLC 37;**
    TCLC 148
  See also CA 124; 113; EWL 3; HW 1
Ibn Battuta, Abu Abdalla
  1304-1368(?) .... **CMLC 57**
  See also WLIT 2
Ibn Hazm 994-1064 .... **CMLC 64**
Ibsen, Henrik (Johan) 1828-1906 .... **DC 2;**
    TCLC 2, 8, 16, 37, 52; WLC
  See also AAYA 46; CA 104; 141; DA; DA3;
    DAB; DAC; DAM DRAM, MST; DFS 1,
    6, 8, 10, 11, 15, 16; EW 7; LAIT 2; LATS
    1:1; RGWL 2, 3
Ibuse, Masuji 1898-1993 .... **CLC 22**
  See Ibuse Masuji
  See also CA 127; 141; MJW; RGWL 3
Ibuse Masuji
  See Ibuse, Masuji
  See also CWW 2; DLB 180; EWL 3
Ichikawa, Kon 1915- .... **CLC 20**
  See also CA 121
Ichiyo, Higuchi 1872-1896 .... **NCLC 49**
  See also MJW
Idle, Eric 1943- .... **CLC 21**
  See Monty Python
  See also CA 116; CANR 35, 91
Idris, Yusuf 1927-1991 .... **SSC 74**
  See also AFW; EWL 3; RGSF 2, 3; RGWL
    3; WLIT 2
Ignatow, David 1914-1997 .... **CLC 4, 7, 14,**
    40; PC 34
  See also CA 9-12R; 162; CAAS 3; CANR
    31, 57, 96; CP 7; DLB 5; EWL 3
Ignotus
  See Strachey, (Giles) Lytton
Ihimaera, Witi (Tame) 1944- .... **CLC 46**
  See also CA 77-80; CANR 130; CN 7;
    RGSF 2; SATA 148
Ilf, Ilya .... **TCLC 21**
  See Fainzilberg, Ilya Arnoldovich
  See also EWL 3
Illyes, Gyula 1902-1983 .... **PC 16**
  See also CA 114; 109; CDWLB 4; DLB
    215; EWL 3; RGWL 2, 3
Imalayen, Fatima-Zohra
  See Djebar, Assia
Immermann, Karl (Lebrecht)
  1796-1840 .... **NCLC 4, 49**
  See also DLB 133
Ince, Thomas H. 1882-1924 .... **TCLC 89**
  See also IDFW 3, 4

Kane, Paul
See Simon, Paul (Frederick)

Kanin, Garson 1912-1999 .... **CLC 22**
See also AITN 1; CA 5-8R; 177; CAD;
CANR 7, 78; DLB 7; IDFW 3, 4

Kaniuk, Yoram 1930- .... **CLC 19**
See also CA 134; DLB 299

Kant, Immanuel 1724-1804 ..... **NCLC 27, 67**
See also DLB 94

Kantor, MacKinlay 1904-1977 .... **CLC 7**
See also CA 61-64; 73-76; CANR 60, 63;
DLB 9, 102; MTCW 2; RHW; TCWW 2

Kanze Motokiyo
See Zeami

Kaplan, David Michael 1946- .... **CLC 50**
See also CA 187

Kaplan, James 1951- .... **CLC 59**
See also CA 135; CANR 121

Karadzic, Vuk Stefanovic
1787-1864 .... **NCLC 115**
See also CDWLB 4; DLB 147

Karageorge, Michael
See Anderson, Poul (William)

Karamzin, Nikolai Mikhailovich
1766-1826 .... **NCLC 3**
See also DLB 150; RGSF 2

Karapanou, Margarita 1946- .... **CLC 13**
See also CA 101

Karinthy, Frigyes 1887-1938 .... **TCLC 47**
See also CA 170; DLB 215; EWL 3

Karl, Frederick R(obert)
1927-2004 .... **CLC 34**
See also CA 5-8R; 226; CANR 3, 44

Karr, Mary 1955- .... **CLC 188**
See also AMWS 11; CA 151; CANR 100;
NCFS 5

Kastel, Warren
See Silverberg, Robert

Kataev, Evgeny Petrovich 1903-1942
See Petrov, Evgeny
See also CA 120

Kataphusin
See Ruskin, John

Katz, Steve 1935- .... **CLC 47**
See also CA 25-28R; CAAS 14, 64; CANR
12; CN 7; DLBY 1983

Kauffman, Janet 1945- .... **CLC 42**
See also CA 117; CANR 43, 84; DLB 218;
DLBY 1986

Kaufman, Bob (Garnell) 1925-1986 . **CLC 49**
See also BG 3; BW 1; CA 41-44R; 118;
CANR 22; DLB 16, 41

Kaufman, George S. 1889-1961 ...... **CLC 38;**
DC 17
See also CA 108; 93-96; DAM DRAM;
DFS 1, 10; DLB 7; INT CA-108; MTCW
2; RGAL 4; TUS

Kaufman, Sue .... **CLC 3, 8**
See Barondess, Sue K(aufman)

Kavafis, Konstantinos Petrou 1863-1933
See Cavafy, C(onstantine) P(eter)
See also CA 104

Kavan, Anna 1901-1968 .... **CLC 5, 13, 82**
See also BRWS 7; CA 5-8R; CANR 6, 57;
DLB 255; MTCW 1; RGEL 2; SFW 4

Kavanagh, Dan
See Barnes, Julian (Patrick)

Kavanagh, Julie 1952- .... **CLC 119**
See also CA 163

Kavanagh, Patrick (Joseph)
1904-1967 .... **CLC 22; PC 33**
See also BRWS 7; CA 123; 25-28R; DLB
15, 20; EWL 3; MTCW 1; RGEL 2

Kawabata, Yasunari 1899-1972 ..... **CLC 2, 5,**
9, 18, 107; SSC 17
See Kawabata Yasunari
See also CA 93-96; 33-36R; CANR 88;
DAM MULT; MJW; MTCW 2; RGSF 2;
RGWL 2, 3

Kawabata Yasunari
See Kawabata, Yasunari
See also DLB 180; EWL 3

Kaye, M(ary) M(argaret)
1908-2004 .... **CLC 28**
See also CA 89-92; 223; CANR 24, 60, 102;
MTCW 1, 2; RHW; SATA 62; SATA-Obit
152

Kaye, Mollie
See Kaye, M(ary) M(argaret)

Kaye-Smith, Sheila 1887-1956 .... **TCLC 20**
See also CA 118; 203; DLB 36

Kaymor, Patrice Maguilene
See Senghor, Leopold Sedar

Kazakov, Iurii Pavlovich
See Kazakov, Yuri Pavlovich
See also DLB 302

Kazakov, Yuri Pavlovich 1927-1982 . **SSC 43**
See Kazakov, Iurii Pavlovich; Kazakov,
Yury
See also CA 5-8R; CANR 36; MTCW 1;
RGSF 2

Kazakov, Yury
See Kazakov, Yuri Pavlovich
See also EWL 3

Kazan, Elia 1909-2003 .... **CLC 6, 16, 63**
See also CA 21-24R; 220; CANR 32, 78

Kazantzakis, Nikos 1883(?)-1957 .... **TCLC 2,**
5, 33
See also BPFB 2; CA 105; 132; DA3; EW
9; EWL 3; MTCW 1, 2; RGWL 2, 3

Kazin, Alfred 1915-1998 ..... **CLC 34, 38, 119**
See also AMWS 8; CA 1-4R; CAAS 7;
CANR 1, 45, 79; DLB 67; EWL 3

Keane, Mary Nesta (Skrine) 1904-1996
See Keane, Molly
See also CA 108; 114; 151; CN 7; RHW

Keane, Molly .... **CLC 31**
See Keane, Mary Nesta (Skrine)
See also INT CA-114

Keates, Jonathan 1946(?)- .... **CLC 34**
See also CA 163; CANR 126

Keaton, Buster 1895-1966 .... **CLC 20**
See also CA 194

Keats, John 1795-1821 ...... **NCLC 8, 73, 121;**
PC 1; WLC
See also AAYA 58; BRW 4; BRWR 1; CD-
BLB 1789-1832; DA; DA3; DAB; DAC;
DAM MST, POET; DLB 96, 110; EXPP;
LMFS 1, PAB; PFS 1, 2, 3, 9, 17; RGEL
2; TEA; WLIT 3; WP

Keble, John 1792-1866 .... **NCLC 87**
See also DLB 32, 55; RGEL 2

Keene, Donald 1922- .... **CLC 34**
See also CA 1-4R; CANR 5, 119

Keillor, Garrison .... **CLC 40, 115**
See Keillor, Gary (Edward)
See also AAYA 2; BEST 89:3; BPFB 2;
DLBY 1987; EWL 3; SATA 58; TUS

Keillor, Gary (Edward) 1942-
See Keillor, Garrison
See also CA 111; 117; CANR 36, 59, 124;
CPW; DA3; DAM POP; MTCW 1, 2

Keith, Carlos
See Lewton, Val

Keith, Michael
See Hubbard, L(afayette) Ron(ald)

Keller, Gottfried 1819-1890 .... **NCLC 2; SSC**
26
See also CDWLB 2; DLB 129; EW; RGSF
2; RGWL 2, 3

Keller, Nora Okja 1965- .... **CLC 109**
See also CA 187

Kellerman, Jonathan 1949- .... **CLC 44**
See also AAYA 35; BEST 90:1; CA 106;
CANR 29, 51; CMW 4; CPW; DA3;
DAM POP; INT CANR-29

Kelley, William Melvin 1937- .... **CLC 22**
See also BW 1; CA 77-80; CANR 27, 83;
CN 7; DLB 33; EWL 3

Kellogg, Marjorie 1922- .... **CLC 2**
See also CA 81-84

Kellow, Kathleen
See Hibbert, Eleanor Alice Burford

Kelly, M(ilton) T(errence) 1947- ...... **CLC 55**
See also CA 97-100; CAAS 22; CANR 19,
43, 84; CN 7

Kelly, Robert 1935- .... **SSC 50**
See also CA 17-20R; CAAS 19; CANR 47;
CP 7; DLB 5, 130, 165

Kelman, James 1946- .... **CLC 58, 86**
See also BRWS 5; CA 148; CANR 85, 130;
CN 7; DLB 194; RGSF 2; WLIT 4

Kemal, Yasar
See Kemal, Yashar
See also CWW 2; EWL 3

Kemal, Yashar 1923(?)- .... **CLC 14, 29**
See also CA 89-92; CANR 44

Kemble, Fanny 1809-1893 .... **NCLC 18**
See also DLB 32

Kemelman, Harry 1908-1996 .... **CLC 2**
See also AITN 1; BPFB 2; CA 9-12R; 155;
CANR 6, 71; CMW 4; DLB 28

Kempe, Margery 1373(?)-1440(?) ... **LC 6, 56**
See also DLB 146; RGEL 2

Kempis, Thomas a 1380-1471 .... **LC 11**

Kendall, Henry 1839-1882 .... **NCLC 12**
See also DLB 230

Keneally, Thomas (Michael) 1935- ... **CLC 5,**
8, 10, 14, 19, 27, 43, 117
See also BRWS 4; CA 85-88; CANR 10,
50, 74, 130; CN 7; CPW; DA3; DAM
NOV; DLB 289, 299; EWL 3; MTCW 1,
2; NFS 17; RGEL 2; RHW

Kennedy, A(lison) L(ouise) 1965- ... **CLC 188**
See also CA 168, 213; CAAE 213; CANR
108; CD 5; CN 7; DLB 271; RGSF 2

Kennedy, Adrienne (Lita) 1931- .... **BLC 2;**
CLC 66; DC 5
See also AFAW 2; BW 2, 3; CA 103; CAAS
20; CABS 3; CANR 26, 53, 82; CD 5;
DAM MULT; DFS 9; DLB 38; FW

Kennedy, John Pendleton
1795-1870 .... **NCLC 2**
See also DLB 3, 248, 254; RGAL 4

Kennedy, Joseph Charles 1929-
See Kennedy, X. J.
See also CA 1-4R, 201; CAAE 201; CANR
4, 30, 40; CP 7; CWRI 5; MAICYA 2;
MAICYAS 1; SATA 14, 86, 130; SATA-
Essay 130

Kennedy, William 1928- ... **CLC 6, 28, 34, 53**
See also AAYA 1; AMWS 7; BPFB 2; CA
85-88; CANR 14, 31, 76, 134; CN 7;
DA3; DAM NOV; DLB 143; DLBY 1985;
EWL 3; INT CANR-31; MTCW 1, 2;
SATA 57

Kennedy, X. J. .... **CLC 8, 42**
See Kennedy, Joseph Charles
See also CAAS 9; CLR 27; DLB 5; SAAS
22

Kenny, Maurice (Francis) 1929- ..... **CLC 87;**
NNAL
See also CA 144; CAAS 22; DAM MULT;
DLB 175

Kent, Kelvin
See Kuttner, Henry

Kenton, Maxwell
See Southern, Terry

Kenyon, Jane 1947-1995 .... **PC 57**
See also AMWS 7; CA 118; 148; CANR
44, 69; CP 7; CWP; DLB 120; PFS 9, 17;
RGAL 4

Kenyon, Robert O.
See Kuttner, Henry

Kivi, Aleksis 1834-1872 .... **NCLC 30**
Kizer, Carolyn (Ashley) 1925- ... **CLC 15, 39, 80**
See also CA 65-68; CAAS 5; CANR 24, 70, 134; CP 7; CWP; DAM POET; DLB 5, 169; EWL 3; MTCW 2; PFS 18
Klabund 1890-1928 .... **TCLC 44**
See also CA 162; DLB 66
Klappert, Peter 1942- .... **CLC 57**
See also CA 33-36R; CSW; DLB 5
Klein, A(braham) M(oses)
1909-1972 .... **CLC 19**
See also CA 101; 37-40R; DAB; DAC; DAM MST; DLB 68; EWL 3; RGEL 2
Klein, Joe
See Klein, Joseph
Klein, Joseph 1946- .... **CLC 154**
See also CA 85-88; CANR 55
Klein, Norma 1938-1989 .... **CLC 30**
See also AAYA 2, 35; BPFB 2; BYA 6, 7, 8; CA 41-44R; 128; CANR 15, 37; CLR 2, 19; INT CANR-15; JRDA; MAICYA 1, 2; SAAS 1; SATA 7, 57; WYA; YAW
Klein, T(heodore) E(ibon) D(onald)
1947- .... **CLC 34**
See also CA 119; CANR 44, 75; HGG
Kleist, Heinrich von 1777-1811 ...... **NCLC 2, 37; SSC 22**
See also CDWLB 2; DAM DRAM; DLB 90; EW 5; RGSF 2; RGWL 2, 3
Klima, Ivan 1931- .... **CLC 56, 172**
See also CA 25-28R; CANR 17, 50, 91; CDWLB 4; CWW 2; DAM NOV; DLB 232; EWL 3; RGWL 3
Klimentev, Andrei Platonovich
See Klimentov, Andrei Platonovich
Klimentov, Andrei Platonovich
1899-1951 .... **SSC 42; TCLC 14**
See Platonov, Andrei Platonovich; Platonov, Andrey Platonovich
See also CA 108
Klinger, Friedrich Maximilian von
1752-1831 .... **NCLC 1**
See also DLB 94
Klingsor the Magician
See Hartmann, Sadakichi
Klopstock, Friedrich Gottlieb
1724-1803 .... **NCLC 11**
See also DLB 97; EW 4; RGWL 2, 3
Kluge, Alexander 1932- .... **SSC 61**
See also CA 81-84; DLB 75
Knapp, Caroline 1959-2002 .... **CLC 99**
See also CA 154; 207
Knebel, Fletcher 1911-1993 .... **CLC 14**
See also AITN 1; CA 1-4R; 140; CAAS 3; CANR 1, 36; SATA 36; SATA-Obit 75
Knickerbocker, Diedrich
See Irving, Washington
Knight, Etheridge 1931-1991 ... **BLC 2; CLC 40; PC 14**
See also BW 1, 3; CA 21-24R; 133; CANR 23, 82; DAM POET; DLB 41; MTCW 2; RGAL 4
Knight, Sarah Kemble 1666-1727 .... **LC 7**
See also DLB 24, 200
Knister, Raymond 1899-1932 .... **TCLC 56**
See also CA 186; DLB 68; RGEL 2
Knowles, John 1926-2001 ... **CLC 1, 4, 10, 26**
See also AAYA 10; AMWS 12; BPFB 2; BYA 3; CA 17-20R; 203; CANR 40, 74, 76, 132; CDALB 1968-1988; CLR 98; CN 7; DA; DAC; DAM MST, NOV; DLB 6; EXPN; MTCW 1, 2; NFS 2; RGAL 4; SATA 8, 89; SATA-Obit 134; YAW
Knox, Calvin M.
See Silverberg, Robert
Knox, John c. 1505-1572 .... **LC 37**
See also DLB 132

Knye, Cassandra
See Disch, Thomas M(ichael)
Koch, C(hristopher) J(ohn) 1932- .... **CLC 42**
See also CA 127; CANR 84; CN 7; DLB 289
Koch, Christopher
See Koch, C(hristopher) J(ohn)
Koch, Kenneth (Jay) 1925-2002 .... **CLC 5, 8, 44**
See also CA 1-4R; 207; CAD; CANR 6, 36, 57, 97, 131; CD 5; CP 7; DAM POET; DLB 5; INT CANR-36; MTCW 2; PFS 20; SATA 65; WP
Kochanowski, Jan 1530-1584 .... **LC 10**
See also RGWL 2, 3
Kock, Charles Paul de 1794-1871 . **NCLC 16**
Koda Rohan
See Koda Shigeyuki
Koda Rohan
See Koda Shigeyuki
See also DLB 180
Koda Shigeyuki 1867-1947 .... **TCLC 22**
See Koda Rohan
See also CA 121; 183
Koestler, Arthur 1905-1983 ... **CLC 1, 3, 6, 8, 15, 33**
See also BRWS 1; CA 1-4R; 109; CANR 1, 33; CDBLB 1945-1960; DLBY 1983; EWL 3; MTCW 1, 2; NFS 19; RGEL 2
Kogawa, Joy Nozomi 1935- ...... **CLC 78, 129**
See also AAYA 47; CA 101; CANR 19, 62, 126; CN 7; CWP; DAC; DAM MST, MULT; FW; MTCW 2; NFS 3; SATA 99
Kohout, Pavel 1928- .... **CLC 13**
See also CA 45-48; CANR 3
Koizumi, Yakumo
See Hearn, (Patricio) Lafcadio (Tessima Carlos)
Kolmar, Gertrud 1894-1943 .... **TCLC 40**
See also CA 167; EWL 3
Komunyakaa, Yusef 1947- .. **BLCS; CLC 86, 94; PC 51**
See also AFAW 2; AMWS 13; CA 147; CANR 83; CP 7; CSW; DLB 120; EWL 3; PFS 5, 20; RGAL 4
Konrad, George
See Konrad, Gyorgy
Konrad, Gyorgy 1933- .... **CLC 4, 10, 73**
See also CA 85-88; CANR 97; CDWLB 4; CWW 2; DLB 232; EWL 3
Konwicki, Tadeusz 1926- .... **CLC 8, 28, 54, 117**
See also CA 101; CAAS 9; CANR 39, 59; CWW 2; DLB 232; EWL 3; IDFW 3; MTCW 1
Koontz, Dean R(ay) 1945- .... **CLC 78**
See also AAYA 9, 31; BEST 89:3, 90:2; CA 108; CANR 19, 36, 52, 95; CMW 4; CPW; DA3; DAM NOV, POP; DLB 292; HGG; MTCW 1; SATA 92; SFW 4; SUFW 2; YAW
Kopernik, Mikolaj
See Copernicus, Nicolaus
Kopit, Arthur (Lee) 1937- ...... **CLC 1, 18, 33**
See also AITN 1; CA 81-84; CABS 3; CD 5; DAM DRAM; DFS 7, 14; DLB 7; MTCW 1; RGAL 4
Kopitar, Jernej (Bartholomaus)
1780-1844 .... **NCLC 117**
Kops, Bernard 1926- .... **CLC 4**
See also CA 5-8R; CANR 84; CBD; CN 7; CP 7; DLB 13
Kornbluth, C(yril) M. 1923-1958 .... **TCLC 8**
See also CA 105; 160; DLB 8; SFW 4
Korolenko, V. G.
See Korolenko, Vladimir Galaktionovich
Korolenko, Vladimir
See Korolenko, Vladimir Galaktionovich

Korolenko, Vladimir G.
See Korolenko, Vladimir Galaktionovich
Korolenko, Vladimir Galaktionovich
1853-1921 .... **TCLC 22**
See also CA 121; DLB 277
Korzybski, Alfred (Habdank Skarbek)
1879-1950 .... **TCLC 61**
See also CA 123; 160
Kosinski, Jerzy (Nikodem)
1933-1991 .... **CLC 1, 2, 3, 6, 10, 15, 53, 70**
See also AMWS 7; BPFB 2; CA 17-20R; 134; CANR 9, 46; DA3; DAM NOV; DLB 2, 299; DLBY 1982; EWL 3; HGG; MTCW 1, 2; NFS 12; RGAL 4; TUS
Kostelanetz, Richard (Cory) 1940- .. **CLC 28**
See also CA 13-16R; CAAS 8; CANR 38, 77; CN 7; CP 7
Kostrowitzki, Wilhelm Apollinaris de
1880-1918
See Apollinaire, Guillaume
See also CA 104
Kotlowitz, Robert 1924- .... **CLC 4**
See also CA 33-36R; CANR 36
Kotzebue, August (Friedrich Ferdinand) von
1761-1819 .... **NCLC 25**
See also DLB 94
Kotzwinkle, William 1938- ..... **CLC 5, 14, 35**
See also BPFB 2; CA 45-48; CANR 3, 44, 84, 129; CLR 6; DLB 173; FANT; MAI-CYA 1, 2; SATA 24, 70, 146; SFW 4; SUFW 2; YAW
Kowna, Stancy
See Szymborska, Wislawa
Kozol, Jonathan 1936- .... **CLC 17**
See also AAYA 46; CA 61-64; CANR 16, 45, 96
Kozoll, Michael 1940(?)- .... **CLC 35**
Kramer, Kathryn 19(?)- .... **CLC 34**
Kramer, Larry 1935- .... **CLC 42; DC 8**
See also CA 124; 126; CANR 60, 132; DAM POP; DLB 249; GLL 1
Krasicki, Ignacy 1735-1801 .... **NCLC 8**
Krasinski, Zygmunt 1812-1859 .... **NCLC 4**
See also RGWL 2, 3
Kraus, Karl 1874-1936 .... **TCLC 5**
See also CA 104; 216; DLB 118; EWL 3
Kreve (Mickevicius), Vincas
1882-1954 .... **TCLC 27**
See also CA 170; DLB 220; EWL 3
Kristeva, Julia 1941- .... **CLC 77, 140**
See also CA 154; CANR 99; DLB 242; EWL 3; FW; LMFS 2
Kristofferson, Kris 1936- .... **CLC 26**
See also CA 104
Krizanc, John 1956- .... **CLC 57**
See also CA 187
Krleza, Miroslav 1893-1981 .... **CLC 8, 114**
See also CA 97-100; 105; CANR 50; CD-WLB 4; DLB 147; EW 11; RGWL 2, 3
Kroetsch, Robert 1927- .. **CLC 5, 23, 57, 132**
See also CA 17-20R; CANR 8, 38; CCA 1; CN 7; CP 7; DAC; DAM POET; DLB 53; MTCW 1
Kroetz, Franz
See Kroetz, Franz Xaver
Kroetz, Franz Xaver 1946- .... **CLC 41**
See also CA 130; CWW 2; EWL 3
Kroker, Arthur (W.) 1945- .... **CLC 77**
See also CA 161
Kropotkin, Peter (Aleksieevich)
1842-1921 .... **TCLC 36**
See Kropotkin, Petr Alekseevich
See also CA 119; 219
Kropotkin, Petr Alekseevich
See Kropotkin, Peter (Aleksieevich)
See also DLB 277
Krotkov, Yuri 1917-1981 .... **CLC 19**
See also CA 102

Landwirth, Heinz 1927-
    See Lind, Jakov
    See also CA 9-12R; CANR 7

Lane, Patrick 1939- .... **CLC 25**
    See also CA 97-100; CANR 54; CP 7; DAM
    POET; DLB 53; INT CA-97-100

Lang, Andrew 1844-1912 .... **TCLC 16**
    See also CA 114; 137; CANR 85; CLR 101;
    DLB 98, 141, 184; FANT; MAICYA 1, 2;
    RGEL 2; SATA 16; WCH

Lang, Fritz 1890-1976 .... **CLC 20, 103**
    See also CA 77-80; 69-72; CANR 30

Lange, John
    See Crichton, (John) Michael

Langer, Elinor 1939- .... **CLC 34**
    See also CA 121

Langland, William 1332(?)-1400(?) ..... **LC 19**
    See also BRW 1; DA; DAB; DAC; DAM
    MST, POET; DLB 146; RGEL 2; TEA;
    WLIT 3

Langstaff, Launcelot
    See Irving, Washington

Lanier, Sidney 1842-1881 . **NCLC 6, 118; PC
50**
    See also AMWS 1; DAM POET; DLB 64;
    DLBD 13; EXPP; MAICYA 1; PFS 14;
    RGAL 4; SATA 18

Lanyer, Aemilia 1569-1645 .... **LC 10, 30, 83;
PC 60**
    See also DLB 121

Lao-Tzu
    See Lao Tzu

Lao Tzu c. 6th cent. B.C.-3rd cent.
    B.C. .... **CMLC 7**

Lapine, James (Elliot) 1949- .... **CLC 39**
    See also CA 123; 130; CANR 54, 128; INT
    CA-130

Larbaud, Valery (Nicolas)
    1881-1957 .... **TCLC 9**
    See also CA 106; 152; EWL 3; GFL 1789
    to the Present

Lardner, Ring
    See Lardner, Ring(gold) W(ilmer)
    See also BPFB 2; CDALB 1917-1929; DLB
    11, 25, 86, 171; DLBD 16; RGAL 4;
    RGSF 2

Lardner, Ring W., Jr.
    See Lardner, Ring(gold) W(ilmer)

Lardner, Ring(gold) W(ilmer)
    1885-1933 .... **SSC 32; TCLC 2, 14**
    See Lardner, Ring
    See also AMW; CA 104; 131; MTCW 1, 2;
    TUS

Laredo, Betty
    See Codrescu, Andrei

Larkin, Maia
    See Wojciechowska, Maia (Teresa)

Larkin, Philip (Arthur) 1922-1985 ... **CLC 3,
5, 8, 9, 13, 18, 33, 39, 64; PC 21**
    See also BRWS 1; CA 5-8R; 117; CANR
    24, 62; CDBLB 1960 to Present; DA3;
    DAB; DAM MST, POET; DLB 27; EWL
    3; MTCW 1, 2; PFS 3, 4, 12; RGEL 2

La Roche, Sophie von
    1730-1807 .... **NCLC 121**
    See also DLB 94

La Rochefoucauld, Francois
    1613-1680 .... **LC 108**

**Larra (y Sanchez de Castro), Mariano Jose
de** 1809-1837 .... **NCLC 17, 130**

Larsen, Eric 1941- .... **CLC 55**
    See also CA 132

Larsen, Nella 1893(?)-1963 .... **BLC 2; CLC
37; HR 3**
    See also AFAW 1, 2; BW 1; CA 125; CANR
    83; DAM MULT; DLB 51; FW; LATS
    1:1; LMFS 2

Larson, Charles R(aymond) 1938- ... **CLC 31**
    See also CA 53-56; CANR 4, 121

Larson, Jonathan 1961-1996 .... **CLC 99**
    See also AAYA 28; CA 156

La Sale, Antoine de c. 1386-1460(?) . **LC 104**
    See also DLB 208

Las Casas, Bartolome de
    1474-1566 .... **HLCS; LC 31**
    See Casas, Bartolome de las
    See also LAW

Lasch, Christopher 1932-1994 .... **CLC 102**
    See also CA 73-76; 144; CANR 25, 118;
    DLB 246; MTCW 1, 2

Lasker-Schueler, Else 1869-1945 ... **TCLC 57**
    See Lasker-Schuler, Else
    See also CA 183; DLB 66, 124

Lasker-Schuler, Else
    See Lasker-Schueler, Else
    See also EWL 3

Laski, Harold J(oseph) 1893-1950 . **TCLC 79**
    See also CA 188

Latham, Jean Lee 1902-1995 .... **CLC 12**
    See also AITN 1; BYA 1; CA 5-8R; CANR
    7, 84; CLR 50; MAICYA 1, 2; SATA 2,
    68; YAW

Latham, Mavis
    See Clark, Mavis Thorpe

Lathen, Emma .... **CLC 2**
    See Hennissart, Martha; Latsis, Mary J(ane)
    See also BPFB 2; CMW 4; DLB 306

Lathrop, Francis
    See Leiber, Fritz (Reuter, Jr.)

Latsis, Mary J(ane) 1927-1997
    See Lathen, Emma
    See also CA 85-88; 162; CMW 4

Lattany, Kristin
    See Lattany, Kristin (Elaine Eggleston)
    Hunter

Lattany, Kristin (Elaine Eggleston) Hunter
    1931- .... **CLC 35**
    See also AITN 1; BW 1; BYA 3; CA 13-
    16R; CANR 13, 108; CLR 3; CN 7; DLB
    33; INT CANR-13; MAICYA 1, 2; SAAS
    10; SATA 12, 132; YAW

Lattimore, Richmond (Alexander)
    1906-1984 .... **CLC 3**
    See also CA 1-4R; 112; CANR 1

Laughlin, James 1914-1997 .... **CLC 49**
    See also CA 21-24R; 162; CAAS 22; CANR
    9, 47; CP 7; DLB 48; DLBY 1996, 1997

Laurence, (Jean) Margaret (Wemyss)
    1926-1987 . **CLC 3, 6, 13, 50, 62; SSC 7**
    See also BYA 13; CA 5-8R; 121; CANR
    33; DAC; DAM MST; DLB 53; EWL 3;
    FW; MTCW 1, 2; NFS 11; RGEL 2;
    RGSF 2; SATA-Obit 50; TCWW 2

Laurent, Antoine 1952- .... **CLC 50**

Lauscher, Hermann
    See Hesse, Hermann

Lautreamont 1846-1870 .. **NCLC 12; SSC 14**
    See Lautreamont, Isidore Lucien Ducasse
    See also GFL 1789 to the Present; RGWL
    2, 3

Lautreamont, Isidore Lucien Ducasse
    See Lautreamont
    See also DLB 217

Lavater, Johann Kaspar
    1741-1801 .... **NCLC 142**
    See also DLB 97

Laverty, Donald
    See Blish, James (Benjamin)

Lavin, Mary 1912-1996 . **CLC 4, 18, 99; SSC
4, 67**
    See also CA 9-12R; 151; CANR 33; CN 7;
    DLB 15; FW; MTCW 1; RGEL 2; RGSF
    2

Lavond, Paul Dennis
    See Kornbluth, C(yril) M.; Pohl, Frederik

Lawler, Ray
    See Lawler, Raymond Evenor
    See also DLB 289

Lawler, Raymond Evenor 1922- .... **CLC 58**
    See Lawler, Ray
    See also CA 103; CD 5; RGEL 2

Lawrence, D(avid) H(erbert Richards)
    1885-1930 .... **PC 54; SSC 4, 19, 73;
    TCLC 2, 9, 16, 33, 48, 61, 93; WLC**
    See Chambers, Jessie
    See also BPFB 2; BRW 7; BRWR 2; CA
    104; 121; CANR 131; CDBLB 1914-
    1945; DA; DA3; DAB; DAC; DAM MST,
    NOV, POET; DLB 10, 19, 36, 98, 162,
    195; EWL 3; EXPP; EXPS; LAIT 2, 3;
    MTCW 1, 2; NFS 18; PFS 6; RGEL 2;
    RGSF 2; SSFS 2, 6; TEA; WLIT 4; WP

Lawrence, T(homas) E(dward)
    1888-1935 .... **TCLC 18**
    See Dale, Colin
    See also BRWS 2; CA 115; 167; DLB 195

Lawrence of Arabia
    See Lawrence, T(homas) E(dward)

Lawson, Henry (Archibald Hertzberg)
    1867-1922 .... **SSC 18; TCLC 27**
    See also CA 120; 181; DLB 230; RGEL 2;
    RGSF 2

Lawton, Dennis
    See Faust, Frederick (Schiller)

Layamon fl. c. 1200- .... **CMLC 10**
    See La3amon
    See also DLB 146; RGEL 2

Laye, Camara 1928-1980 ..... **BLC 2; CLC 4,
38**
    See Camara Laye
    See also AFW; BW 1; CA 85-88; 97-100;
    CANR 25; DAM MULT; MTCW 1, 2;
    WLIT 2

Layton, Irving (Peter) 1912- .... **CLC 2, 15,
164**
    See also CA 1-4R; CANR 2, 33, 43, 66,
    129; CP 7; DAC; DAM MST, POET;
    DLB 88; EWL 3; MTCW 1, 2; PFS 12;
    RGEL 2

Lazarus, Emma 1849-1887 ...... **NCLC 8, 109**

Lazarus, Felix
    See Cable, George Washington

Lazarus, Henry
    See Slavitt, David R(ytman)

Lea, Joan
    See Neufeld, John (Arthur)

Leacock, Stephen (Butler)
    1869-1944 .... **SSC 39; TCLC 2**
    See also CA 104; 141; CANR 80; DAC;
    DAM MST; DLB 92; EWL 3; MTCW 2;
    RGEL 2; RGSF 2

Lead, Jane Ward 1623-1704 .... **LC 72**
    See also DLB 131

Leapor, Mary 1722-1746 .... **LC 80**
    See also DLB 109

Lear, Edward 1812-1888 .... **NCLC 3**
    See also AAYA 48; BRW 5; CLR 1, 75;
    DLB 32, 163, 166; MAICYA 1, 2; RGEL
    2; SATA 18, 100; WCH; WP

Lear, Norman (Milton) 1922- .... **CLC 12**
    See also CA 73-76

Leautaud, Paul 1872-1956 .... **TCLC 83**
    See also CA 203; DLB 65; GFL 1789 to the
    Present

Leavis, F(rank) R(aymond)
    1895-1978 .... **CLC 24**
    See also BRW 7; CA 21-24R; 77-80; CANR
    44; DLB 242; EWL 3; MTCW 1, 2;
    RGEL 2

Leavitt, David 1961- .... **CLC 34**
    See also CA 116; 122; CANR 50, 62, 101,
    134; CPW; DA3; DAM POP; DLB 130;
    GLL 1; INT CA-122; MTCW 2

Leblanc, Maurice (Marie Emile)
    1864-1941 .... **TCLC 49**
    See also CA 110; CMW 4

Lermontov, Mikhail Iur'evich
    See Lermontov, Mikhail Yuryevich
    See also DLB 205
Lermontov, Mikhail Yuryevich
    1814-1841 .... **NCLC 5, 47, 126; PC 18**
    See Lermontov, Mikhail Iur'evich
    See also EW 6; RGWL 2, 3; TWA
Leroux, Gaston 1868-1927 .... **TCLC 25**
    See also CA 108; 136; CANR 69; CMW 4;
    NFS 20; SATA 65
Lesage, Alain-Rene 1668-1747 .... **LC 2, 28**
    See also EW 3; GFL Beginnings to 1789;
    RGWL 2, 3
Leskov, N(ikolai) S(emenovich) 1831-1895
    See Leskov, Nikolai (Semyonovich)
Leskov, Nikolai (Semyonovich)
    1831-1895 .... **NCLC 25; SSC 34**
    See Leskov, Nikolai Semenovich
Leskov, Nikolai Semenovich
    See Leskov, Nikolai (Semyonovich)
    See also DLB 238
Lesser, Milton
    See Marlowe, Stephen
Lessing, Doris (May) 1919- ... **CLC 1, 2, 3, 6,**
    10, 15, 22, 40, 94, 170; SSC 6, 61;
    WLCS
    See also AAYA 57; AFW; BRWS 1; CA
    9-12R; CAAS 14; CANR 33, 54, 76, 122;
    CD 5; CDBLB 1960 to Present; CN 7;
    DA; DA3; DAB; DAC; DAM MST, NOV;
    DFS 20; DLB 15, 139; DLBY 1985; EWL
    3; EXPS; FW; LAIT 4; MTCW 1, 2;
    RGEL 2; RGSF 2; SFW 4; SSFS 1, 12,
    20; TEA; WLIT 2, 4
Lessing, Gotthold Ephraim 1729-1781 . **LC 8**
    See also CDWLB 2; DLB 97; EW 4; RGWL
    2, 3
Lester, Richard 1932- .... **CLC 20**
Levenson, Jay .... **CLC 70**
Lever, Charles (James)
    1806-1872 .... **NCLC 23**
    See also DLB 21; RGEL 2
Leverson, Ada Esther
    1862(?)-1933(?) .... **TCLC 18**
    See Elaine
    See also CA 117; 202; DLB 153; RGEL 2
Levertov, Denise 1923-1997 .. **CLC 1, 2, 3, 5,**
    8, 15, 28, 66; PC 11
    See also AMWS 3; CA 1-4R, 178; 163;
    CAAE 178; CAAS 19; CANR 3, 29, 50,
    108; CDALBS; CP 7; CWP; DAM POET;
    DLB 5, 165; EWL 3; EXPP; FW; INT
    CANR-29; MTCW 1, 2; PAB; PFS 7, 17;
    RGAL 4; TUS; WP
Levi, Carlo 1902-1975 .... **TCLC 125**
    See also CA 65-68; 53-56; CANR 10; EWL
    3; RGWL 2, 3
Levi, Jonathan .... **CLC 76**
    See also CA 197
Levi, Peter (Chad Tigar)
    1931-2000 .... **CLC 41**
    See also CA 5-8R; 187; CANR 34, 80; CP
    7; DLB 40
Levi, Primo 1919-1987 ...... **CLC 37, 50; SSC**
    12; TCLC 109
    See also CA 13-16R; 122; CANR 12, 33,
    61, 70, 132; DLB 177, 299; EWL 3;
    MTCW 1, 2; RGWL 2, 3
Levin, Ira 1929- .... **CLC 3, 6**
    See also CA 21-24R; CANR 17, 44, 74;
    CMW 4; CN 7; CPW; DA3; DAM POP;
    HGG; MTCW 1, 2; SATA 66; SFW 4
Levin, Meyer 1905-1981 .... **CLC 7**
    See also AITN 1; CA 9-12R; 104; CANR
    15; DAM POP; DLB 9, 28; DLBY 1981;
    SATA 21; SATA-Obit 27
Levine, Norman 1924- .... **CLC 54**
    See also CA 73-76; CAAS 23; CANR 14,
    70; DLB 88

Levine, Philip 1928- .. **CLC 2, 4, 5, 9, 14, 33,**
    118; PC 22
    See also AMWS 5; CA 9-12R; CANR 9,
    37, 52, 116; CP 7; DAM POET; DLB 5;
    EWL 3; PFS 8
Levinson, Deirdre 1931- .... **CLC 49**
    See also CA 73-76; CANR 70
Levi-Strauss, Claude 1908- .... **CLC 38**
    See also CA 1-4R; CANR 6, 32, 57; DLB
    242; EWL 3; GFL 1789 to the Present;
    MTCW 1, 2; TWA
Levitin, Sonia (Wolff) 1934- .... **CLC 17**
    See also AAYA 13, 48; CA 29-32R; CANR
    14, 32, 79; CLR 53; JRDA; MAICYA 1,
    2; SAAS 2; SATA 4, 68, 119, 131; SATA-
    Essay 131; YAW
Levon, O. U.
    See Kesey, Ken (Elton)
Levy, Amy 1861-1889 .... **NCLC 59**
    See also DLB 156, 240
Lewes, George Henry 1817-1878 ... **NCLC 25**
    See also DLB 55, 144
Lewis, Alun 1915-1944 .... **SSC 40; TCLC 3**
    See also BRW 7; CA 104; 188; DLB 20,
    162; PAB; RGEL 2
Lewis, C. Day
    See Day Lewis, C(ecil)
Lewis, C(live) S(taples) 1898-1963 .... **CLC 1,**
    3, 6, 14, 27, 124; WLC
    See also AAYA 3, 39; BPFB 2; BRWS 3;
    BYA 15, 16; CA 81-84; CANR 33, 71,
    132; CDBLB 1945-1960; CLR 3, 27;
    CWRI 5; DA; DA3; DAB; DAC; DAM
    MST, NOV, POP; DLB 15, 100, 160, 255;
    EWL 3; FANT; JRDA; LMFS 2; MAI-
    CYA 1, 2; MTCW 1, 2; RGEL 2; SATA
    13, 100; SCFW; SFW 4; SUFW 1; TEA;
    WCH; WYA; YAW
Lewis, Cecil Day
    See Day Lewis, C(ecil)
Lewis, Janet 1899-1998 .... **CLC 41**
    See Winters, Janet Lewis
    See also CA 9-12R; 172; CANR 29, 63;
    CAP 1; CN 7; DLBY 1987; RHW;
    TCWW 2
Lewis, Matthew Gregory
    1775-1818 .... **NCLC 11, 62**
    See also DLB 39, 158, 178; HGG; LMFS
    1; RGEL 2; SUFW
Lewis, (Harry) Sinclair 1885-1951 . **TCLC 4,**
    13, 23, 39; WLC
    See also AMW; AMWC 1; BPFB 2; CA
    104; 133; CANR 132; CDALB 1917-
    1929; DA; DA3; DAB; DAC; DAM MST,
    NOV; DLB 9, 102, 284; DLBD 1; EWL
    3; LAIT 3; MTCW 1, 2; NFS 15, 19;
    RGAL 4; TUS
Lewis, (Percy) Wyndham
    1884(?)-1957 .. **SSC 34; TCLC 2, 9, 104**
    See also BRW 7; CA 104; 157; DLB 15;
    EWL 3; FANT; MTCW 2; RGEL 2
Lewisohn, Ludwig 1883-1955 .... **TCLC 19**
    See also CA 107; 203; DLB 4, 9, 28, 102
Lewton, Val 1904-1951 .... **TCLC 76**
    See also CA 199; IDFW 3, 4
Leyner, Mark 1956- .... **CLC 92**
    See also CA 110; CANR 28, 53; DA3; DLB
    292; MTCW 2
Lezama Lima, Jose 1910-1976 .... **CLC 4, 10,**
    101; HLCS 2
    See also CA 77-80; CANR 71; DAM
    MULT; DLB 113, 283; EWL 3; HW 1, 2;
    LAW; RGWL 2, 3
L'Heureux, John (Clarke) 1934- ...... **CLC 52**
    See also CA 13-16R; CANR 23, 45, 88;
    DLB 244
Li Ch'ing-chao 1081(?)-1141(?) .... **CMLC 71**
Liddell, C. H.
    See Kuttner, Henry

Lie, Jonas (Lauritz Idemil)
    1833-1908(?) .... **TCLC 5**
    See also CA 115
Lieber, Joel 1937-1971 .... **CLC 6**
    See also CA 73-76; 29-32R
Lieber, Stanley Martin
    See Lee, Stan
Lieberman, Laurence (James)
    1935- .... **CLC 4, 36**
    See also CA 17-20R; CANR 8, 36, 89; CP
    7
Lieh Tzu fl. 7th cent. B.C.-5th cent.
    B.C. .... **CMLC 27**
Lieksman, Anders
    See Haavikko, Paavo Juhani
Li Fei-kan 1904-
    See Pa Chin
    See also CA 105; TWA
Lifton, Robert Jay 1926- .... **CLC 67**
    See also CA 17-20R; CANR 27, 78; INT
    CANR-27; SATA 66
Lightfoot, Gordon 1938- .... **CLC 26**
    See also CA 109
Lightman, Alan P(aige) 1948- .... **CLC 81**
    See also CA 141; CANR 63, 105
Ligotti, Thomas (Robert) 1953- ...... **CLC 44;**
    SSC 16
    See also CA 123; CANR 49, 135; HGG;
    SUFW 2
Li Ho 791-817 .... **PC 13**
Li Ju-chen c. 1763-c. 1830 .... **NCLC 137**
Lilar, Francoise
    See Mallet-Joris, Francoise
Liliencron, (Friedrich Adolf Axel) Detlev
    von 1844-1909 .... **TCLC 18**
    See also CA 117
Lille, Alain de
    See Alain de Lille
Lilly, William 1602-1681 .... **LC 27**
Lima, Jose Lezama
    See Lezama Lima, Jose
Lima Barreto, Afonso Henrique de
    1881-1922 .... **TCLC 23**
    See Lima Barreto, Afonso Henriques de
    See also CA 117; 181; LAW
Lima Barreto, Afonso Henriques de
    See Lima Barreto, Afonso Henrique de
    See also DLB 307
Limonov, Edward 1944- .... **CLC 67**
    See also CA 137
Lin, Frank
    See Atherton, Gertrude (Franklin Horn)
Lin, Yutang 1895-1976 .... **TCLC 149**
    See also CA 45-48; 65-68; CANR 2; RGAL
    4
Lincoln, Abraham 1809-1865 .... **NCLC 18**
    See also LAIT 2
Lind, Jakov .... **CLC 1, 2, 4, 27, 82**
    See Landwirth, Heinz
    See also CAAS 4; DLB 299; EWL 3
Lindbergh, Anne (Spencer) Morrow
    1906-2001 .... **CLC 82**
    See also BPFB 2; CA 17-20R; 193; CANR
    16, 73; DAM NOV; MTCW 1, 2; SATA
    33; SATA-Obit 125; TUS
Lindsay, David 1878(?)-1945 .... **TCLC 15**
    See also CA 113; 187; DLB 255; FANT;
    SFW 4; SUFW 1
Lindsay, (Nicholas) Vachel
    1879-1931 .... **PC 23; TCLC 17; WLC**
    See also AMWS 1; CA 114; 135; CANR
    79; CDALB 1865-1917; DA; DA3; DAC;
    DAM MST, POET; DLB 54; EWL 3;
    EXPP; RGAL 4; SATA 40; WP
Linke-Poot
    See Doeblin, Alfred

Mamet, David (Alan) 1947- .. **CLC 9, 15, 34, 46, 91, 166; DC 4, 24**
See also AAYA 3, 60; AMWS 14; CA 81-84; CABS 3; CANR 15, 41, 67, 72, 129; CD 5; DA3; DAM DRAM; DFS 2, 3, 6, 12, 15; DLB 7; EWL 3; IDFW 4; MTCW 1, 2; RGAL 4

Mamoulian, Rouben (Zachary)
1897-1987 .... **CLC 16**
See also CA 25-28R; 124; CANR 85

Mandelshtam, Osip
See Mandelstam, Osip (Emilievich)
See also EW 10; EWL 3; RGWL 2, 3

Mandelstam, Osip (Emilievich)
1891(?)-1943(?) .... **PC 14; TCLC 2, 6**
See Mandelshtam, Osip
See also CA 104; 150; MTCW 2; TWA

Mander, (Mary) Jane 1877-1949 ... **TCLC 31**
See also CA 162; RGEL 2

Mandeville, Bernard 1670-1733 .... **LC 82**
See also DLB 101

Mandeville, Sir John fl. 1350- ...... **CMLC 19**
See also DLB 146

Mandiargues, Andre Pieyre de .... **CLC 41**
See Pieyre de Mandiargues, Andre
See also DLB 83

Mandrake, Ethel Belle
See Thurman, Wallace (Henry)

Mangan, James Clarence
1803-1849 .... **NCLC 27**
See also RGEL 2

Maniere, J.-E.
See Giraudoux, Jean(-Hippolyte)

Mankiewicz, Herman (Jacob)
1897-1953 .... **TCLC 85**
See also CA 120; 169; DLB 26; IDFW 3, 4

Manley, (Mary) Delariviere
1672(?)-1724 .... **LC 1, 42**
See also DLB 39, 80; RGEL 2

Mann, Abel
See Creasey, John

Mann, Emily 1952- .... **DC 7**
See also CA 130; CAD; CANR 55; CD 5; CWD; DLB 266

Mann, (Luiz) Heinrich 1871-1950 ... **TCLC 9**
See also CA 106; 164, 181; DLB 66, 118; EW 8; EWL 3; RGWL 2, 3

Mann, (Paul) Thomas 1875-1955 .... **SSC 5, 70; TCLC 2, 8, 14, 21, 35, 44, 60; WLC**
See also BPFB 2; CA 104; 128; CANR 133; CDWLB 2; DA; DA3; DAB; DAC; DAM MST; NOV; DLB 66; EW 9; EWL 3; GLL 1; LATS 1:1; LMFS 1; MTCW 1, 2; NFS 17; RGSF 2; RGWL 2, 3; SSFS 4, 9; TWA

Mannheim, Karl 1893-1947 .... **TCLC 65**
See also CA 204

Manning, David
See Faust, Frederick (Schiller)
See also TCWW 2

Manning, Frederic 1882-1935 .... **TCLC 25**
See also CA 124; 216; DLB 260

Manning, Olivia 1915-1980 .... **CLC 5, 19**
See also CA 5-8R; 101; CANR 29; EWL 3; FW; MTCW 1; RGEL 2

Mano, D. Keith 1942- .... **CLC 2, 10**
See also CA 25-28R; CAAS 6; CANR 26, 57; DLB 6

Mansfield, Katherine . **SSC 9, 23, 38; TCLC 2, 8, 39; WLC**
See Beauchamp, Kathleen Mansfield
See also BPFB 2; BRW 7; DAB; DLB 162; EWL 3; EXPS; FW; GLL 1; RGEL 2; RGSF; SSFS 2, 8, 10, 11; WWE 1

Manso, Peter 1940- .... **CLC 39**
See also CA 29-32R; CANR 44

Mantecon, Juan Jimenez
See Jimenez (Mantecon), Juan Ramon

Mantel, Hilary (Mary) 1952- .... **CLC 144**
See also CA 125; CANR 54, 101; CN 7; DLB 271; RHW

Manton, Peter
See Creasey, John

Man Without a Spleen, A
See Chekhov, Anton (Pavlovich)

Manzoni, Alessandro 1785-1873 ... **NCLC 29, 98**
See also EW 5; RGWL 2, 3; TWA

Map, Walter 1140-1209 .... **CMLC 32**

Mapu, Abraham (ben Jekutiel)
1808-1867 .... **NCLC 18**

Mara, Sally
See Queneau, Raymond

Maracle, Lee 1950- .... **NNAL**
See also CA 149

Marat, Jean Paul 1743-1793 .... **LC 10**

Marcel, Gabriel Honore 1889-1973 . **CLC 15**
See also CA 102; 45-48; EWL 3; MTCW 1, 2

March, William 1893-1954 .... **TCLC 96**
See also CA 216

Marchbanks, Samuel
See Davies, (William) Robertson
See also CCA 1

Marchi, Giacomo
See Bassani, Giorgio

Marcus Aurelius
See Aurelius, Marcus
See also AW 2

Marguerite
See de Navarre, Marguerite

Marguerite d'Angouleme
See de Navarre, Marguerite
See also GFL Beginnings to 1789

Marguerite de Navarre
See de Navarre, Marguerite
See also RGWL 2, 3

Margulies, Donald 1954- .... **CLC 76**
See also AAYA 57; CA 200; DFS 13; DLB 228

Marie de France c. 12th cent. - ..... **CMLC 8; PC 22**
See also DLB 208; FW; RGWL 2, 3

Marie de l'Incarnation 1599-1672 ...... **LC 10**

Marier, Captain Victor
See Griffith, D(avid Lewelyn) W(ark)

Mariner, Scott
See Pohl, Frederik

Marinetti, Filippo Tommaso
1876-1944 .... **TCLC 10**
See also CA 107; DLB 114, 264; EW 9; EWL 3

Marivaux, Pierre Carlet de Chamblain de
1688-1763 .... **DC 7; LC 4**
See also GFL Beginnings to 1789; RGWL 2, 3; TWA

Markandaya, Kamala .... **CLC 8, 38**
See Taylor, Kamala (Purnaiya)
See also BYA 13; CN 7; EWL 3

Markfield, Wallace 1926-2002 .... **CLC 8**
See also CA 69-72; 208; CAAS 3; CN 7; DLB 2, 28; DLBY 2002

Markham, Edwin 1852-1940 .... **TCLC 47**
See also CA 160; DLB 54, 186; RGAL 4

Markham, Robert
See Amis, Kingsley (William)

Markoosie .... **NNAL**
See Patsauq, Markoosie
See also CLR 23; DAM MULT

Marks, J.
See Highwater, Jamake (Mamake)

Marks, J
See Highwater, Jamake (Mamake)

Marks-Highwater, J
See Highwater, Jamake (Mamake)

Marks-Highwater, J.
See Highwater, Jamake (Mamake)

Markson, David M(errill) 1927- .... **CLC 67**
See also CA 49-52; CANR 1, 91; CN 7

Marlatt, Daphne (Buckle) 1942- .... **CLC 168**
See also CA 25-28R; CANR 17, 39; CN 7; CP 7; CWP; DLB 60; FW

Marley, Bob .... **CLC 17**
See Marley, Robert Nesta

Marley, Robert Nesta 1945-1981
See Marley, Bob
See also CA 107; 103

Marlowe, Christopher 1564-1593 . **DC 1; LC 22, 47; PC 57; WLC**
See also BRW 1; BRWR 1; CDBLB Before 1660; DA; DA3; DAB; DAC; DAM DRAM, MST; DFS 1, 5, 13; DLB 62; EXPP; LMFS 1; RGEL 2; TEA; WLIT 3

Marlowe, Stephen 1928- .... **CLC 70**
See Queen, Ellery
See also CA 13-16R; CANR 6, 55; CMW 4; SFW 4

Marmion, Shakerley 1603-1639 .... **LC 89**
See also DLB 58; RGEL 2

Marmontel, Jean-Francois 1723-1799 .. **LC 2**

Maron, Monika 1941- .... **CLC 165**
See also CA 201

Marquand, John P(hillips)
1893-1960 .... **CLC 2, 10**
See also AMW; BPFB 2; CA 85-88; CANR 73; CMW 4; DLB 9, 102; EWL 3; MTCW 2; RGAL 4

Marques, Rene 1919-1979 .. **CLC 96; HLC 2**
See also CA 97-100; 85-88; CANR 78; DAM MULT; DLB 305; EWL 3; HW 1, 2; LAW; RGSF 2

Marquez, Gabriel (Jose) Garcia
See Garcia Marquez, Gabriel (Jose)

Marquis, Don(ald Robert Perry)
1878-1937 .... **TCLC 7**
See also CA 104; 166; DLB 11, 25; RGAL 4

Marquis de Sade
See Sade, Donatien Alphonse Francois

Marric, J. J.
See Creasey, John
See also MSW

Marryat, Frederick 1792-1848 .... **NCLC 3**
See also DLB 21, 163; RGEL 2; WCH

Marsden, James
See Creasey, John

Marsh, Edward 1872-1953 .... **TCLC 99**

Marsh, (Edith) Ngaio 1895-1982 .. **CLC 7, 53**
See also CA 9-12R; CANR 6, 58; CMW 4; CPW; DAM POP; DLB 77; MSW; MTCW 1, 2; RGEL 2; TEA

Marshall, Garry 1934- .... **CLC 17**
See also AAYA 3; CA 111; SATA 60

Marshall, Paule 1929- .. **BLC 3; CLC 27, 72; SSC 3**
See also AFAW 1, 2; AMWS 11; BPFB 2; BW 2, 3; CA 77-80; CANR 25, 73, 129; CN 7; DA3; DAM MULT; DLB 33, 157, 227; EWL 3; LATS 1:2; MTCW 1, 2; RGAL 4; SSFS 15

Marshallik
See Zangwill, Israel

Marsten, Richard
See Hunter, Evan

Marston, John 1576-1634 .... **LC 33**
See also BRW 2; DAM DRAM; DLB 58, 172; RGEL 2

Martel, Yann 1963- .... **CLC 192**
See also CA 146; CANR 114

Martha, Henry
See Harris, Mark

Marti, Jose
See Marti (y Perez), Jose (Julian)
See also DLB 290

Middleton, Stanley 1919- .... **CLC 7, 38**
See also CA 25-28R; CAAS 23; CANR 21, 46, 81; CN 7; DLB 14

Middleton, Thomas 1580-1627 ...... **DC 5; LC 33**
See also BRW 2; DAM DRAM, MST; DFS 18; DLB 58; RGEL 2

Migueis, Jose Rodrigues 1901-1980 . **CLC 10**
See also DLB 287

Mikszath, Kalman 1847-1910 .... **TCLC 31**
See also CA 170

Miles, Jack .... **CLC 100**
See also CA 200

Miles, John Russiano
See Miles, Jack

Miles, Josephine (Louise)
1911-1985 .... **CLC 1, 2, 14, 34, 39**
See also CA 1-4R; 116; CANR 2, 55; DAM POET; DLB 48

Militant
See Sandburg, Carl (August)

Mill, Harriet (Hardy) Taylor
1807-1858 .... **NCLC 102**
See also FW

Mill, John Stuart 1806-1873 .... **NCLC 11, 58**
See also CDBLB 1832-1890; DLB 55, 190, 262; FW 1; RGEL 2; TEA

Millar, Kenneth 1915-1983 .... **CLC 14**
See Macdonald, Ross
See also CA 9-12R; 110; CANR 16, 63, 107; CMW 4; CPW; DA3; DAM POP; DLB 2, 226; DLBD 6; DLBY 1983; MTCW 1, 2

Millay, E. Vincent
See Millay, Edna St. Vincent

Millay, Edna St. Vincent 1892-1950 ..... **PC 6, 61; TCLC 4, 49; WLCS**
See Boyd, Nancy
See also AMW; CA 104; 130; CDALB 1917-1929; DA; DA3; DAB; DAC; DAM MST, POET; DLB 45, 249; EWL 3; EXPP; MAWW; MTCW 1, 2; PAB; PFS 3, 17; RGAL 4; TUS; WP

Miller, Arthur 1915- ...... **CLC 1, 2, 6, 10, 15, 26, 47, 78, 179; DC 1; WLC**
See also AAYA 15; AITN 1; AMW; AMWC 1; CA 1-4R; CABS 3; CAD; CANR 2, 30, 54, 76, 132; CD 5; CDALB 1941-1968; DA; DA3; DAB; DAC; DAM DRAM, MST; DFS 1, 3, 8; DLB 7, 266; EWL 3; LAIT 1, 4; LATS 1:2; MTCW 1, 2; RGAL 4; TUS; WYAS 1

Miller, Henry (Valentine)
1891-1980 .... **CLC 1, 2, 4, 9, 14, 43, 84; WLC**
See also AMW; BPFB 2; CA 9-12R; 97-100; CANR 33, 64; CDALB 1929-1941; DA; DA3; DAB; DAC; DAM MST, NOV; DLB 4, 9; DLBY 1980; EWL 3; MTCW 1, 2; RGAL 4; TUS

Miller, Hugh 1802-1856 .... **NCLC 143**
See also DLB 190

Miller, Jason 1939(?)-2001 .... **CLC 2**
See also AITN 1; CA 73-76; 197; CAD; CANR 130; DFS 12; DLB 7

Miller, Sue 1943- .... **CLC 44**
See also AMWS 12; BEST 90:3; CA 139; CANR 59, 91, 128; DA3; DAM POP; DLB 143

Miller, Walter M(ichael, Jr.)
1923-1996 .... **CLC 4, 30**
See also BPFB 2; CA 85-88; CANR 108; DLB 8; SCFW; SFW 4

Millett, Kate 1934- .... **CLC 67**
See also AITN 1; CA 73-76; CANR 32, 53, 76, 110; DA3; DLB 246; FW; GLL 1; MTCW 1, 2

Millhauser, Steven (Lewis) 1943- .... **CLC 21, 54, 109; SSC 57**
See also CA 110; 111; CANR 63, 114, 133; CN 7; DA3; DLB 2; FANT; INT CA-111; MTCW 2

Millin, Sarah Gertrude 1889-1968 ... **CLC 49**
See also CA 102; 93-96; DLB 225; EWL 3

Milne, A(lan) A(lexander)
1882-1956 .... **TCLC 6, 88**
See also BRWS 5; CA 104; 133; CLR 1, 26; CMW 4; CWRI 5; DA3; DAB; DAC; DAM MST; DLB 10, 77, 100, 160; FANT; MAICYA 1, 2; MTCW 1, 2; RGEL 2; SATA 100; WCH; YABC 1

Milner, Ron(ald) 1938-2004 ..... **BLC 3; CLC 56**
See also AITN 1; BW 1; CA 73-76; CAD; CANR 24, 81; CD 5; DAM MULT; DLB 38; MTCW 1

Milnes, Richard Monckton
1809-1885 .... **NCLC 61**
See also DLB 32, 184

Milosz, Czeslaw 1911- ...... **CLC 5, 11, 22, 31, 56, 82; PC 8; WLCS**
See also CA 81-84; CANR 23, 51, 91, 126; CDWLB 4; CWW 2; DA3; DAM MST, POET; DLB 215; EW 13; EWL 3; MTCW 1, 2; PFS 16; RGWL 2, 3

Milton, John 1608-1674 ..... **LC 9, 43, 92; PC 19, 29; WLC**
See also BRW 2; BRWR 2; CDBLB 1660-1789; DA; DA3; DAB; DAC; DAM MST, POET; DLB 131, 151, 281; EFS 1; EXPP; LAIT 1; PAB; PFS 3, 17; RGEL 2; TEA; WLIT 3; WP

Min, Anchee 1957- .... **CLC 86**
See also CA 146; CANR 94

Minehaha, Cornelius
See Wedekind, (Benjamin) Frank(lin)

Miner, Valerie 1947- .... **CLC 40**
See also CA 97-100; CANR 59; FW; GLL 2

Minimo, Duca
See D'Annunzio, Gabriele

Minot, Susan 1956- .... **CLC 44, 159**
See also AMWS 6; CA 134; CANR 118; CN 7

Minus, Ed 1938- .... **CLC 39**
See also CA 185

Mirabai 1498(?)-1550(?) .... **PC 48**

Miranda, Javier
See Bioy Casares, Adolfo
See also CWW 2

Mirbeau, Octave 1848-1917 .... **TCLC 55**
See also CA 216; DLB 123, 192; GFL 1789 to the Present

Mirikitani, Janice 1942- .... **AAL**
See also CA 211; RGAL 4

Mirk, John (?)-c. 1414 .... **LC 105**
See also DLB 146

Miro (Ferrer), Gabriel (Francisco Victor)
1879-1930 .... **TCLC 5**
See also CA 104; 185; EWL 3

Misharin, Alexandr .... **CLC 59**

Mishima, Yukio ... **CLC 2, 4, 6, 9, 27; DC 1; SSC 4**
See Hiraoka, Kimitake
See also AAYA 50; BPFB 2; GLL 1; MJW; MTCW 2; RGSF 2; RGWL 2, 3; SSFS 5, 12

Mistral, Frederic 1830-1914 .... **TCLC 51**
See also CA 122; 213; GFL 1789 to the Present

Mistral, Gabriela
See Godoy Alcayaga, Lucila
See also DLB 283; DNFS 1; EWL 3; LAW; RGWL 2, 3; WP

Mistry, Rohinton 1952- ... **CLC 71, 196; SSC 73**
See also BRWS 10; CA 141; CANR 86, 114; CCA 1; CN 7; DAC; SSFS 6

Mitchell, Clyde
See Ellison, Harlan (Jay)

Mitchell, Emerson Blackhorse Barney
1945- .... **NNAL**
See also CA 45-48

Mitchell, James Leslie 1901-1935
See Gibbon, Lewis Grassic
See also CA 104; 188; DLB 15

Mitchell, Joni 1943- .... **CLC 12**
See also CA 112; CCA 1

Mitchell, Joseph (Quincy)
1908-1996 .... **CLC 98**
See also CA 77-80; 152; CANR 69; CN 7; CSW; DLB 185; DLBY 1996

Mitchell, Margaret (Munnerlyn)
1900-1949 .... **TCLC 11**
See also AAYA 23; BPFB 2; BYA 1; CA 109; 125; CANR 55, 94; CDALBS; DA3; DAM NOV, POP; DLB 9; LAIT 2; MTCW 1, 2; NFS 9; RGAL 4; RHW; TUS; WYAS 1; YAW

Mitchell, Peggy
See Mitchell, Margaret (Munnerlyn)

Mitchell, S(ilas) Weir 1829-1914 .... **TCLC 36**
See also CA 165; DLB 202; RGAL 4

Mitchell, W(illiam) O(rmond)
1914-1998 .... **CLC 25**
See also CA 77-80; 165; CANR 15, 43; CN 7; DAC; DAM MST; DLB 88

Mitchell, William (Lendrum)
1879-1936 .... **TCLC 81**
See also CA 213

Mitford, Mary Russell 1787-1855 ... **NCLC 4**
See also DLB 110, 116; RGEL 2

Mitford, Nancy 1904-1973 .... **CLC 44**
See also BRWS 10; CA 9-12R; DLB 191; RGEL 2

Miyamoto, (Chujo) Yuriko
1899-1951 .... **TCLC 37**
See Miyamoto Yuriko
See also CA 170, 174

Miyamoto Yuriko
See Miyamoto, (Chujo) Yuriko
See also DLB 180

Miyazawa, Kenji 1896-1933 .... **TCLC 76**
See Miyazawa Kenji
See also CA 157; RGWL 3

Miyazawa Kenji
See Miyazawa, Kenji
See also EWL 3

Mizoguchi, Kenji 1898-1956 .... **TCLC 72**
See also CA 167

Mo, Timothy (Peter) 1950(?)- ... **CLC 46, 134**
See also CA 117; CANR 128; CN 7; DLB 194; MTCW 1; WLIT 4; WWE 1

Modarressi, Taghi (M.) 1931-1997 ... **CLC 44**
See also CA 121; 134; INT CA-134

Modiano, Patrick (Jean) 1945- .... **CLC 18**
See also CA 85-88; CANR 17, 40, 115; CWW 2; DLB 83, 299; EWL 3

Mofolo, Thomas (Mokopu)
1875(?)-1948 .... **BLC 3; TCLC 22**
See also AFW; CA 121; 153; CANR 83; DAM MULT; DLB 225; EWL 3; MTCW 2; WLIT 2

Mohr, Nicholasa 1938- .... **CLC 12; HLC 2**
See also AAYA 8, 46; CA 49-52; CANR 1, 32, 64; CLR 22; DAM MULT; DLB 145; HW 1, 2; JRDA; LAIT 5; LLW 1; MAICYA 2; MAICYAS 1; RGAL 4; SAAS 8; SATA 8, 97; SATA-Essay 113; WYA; YAW

Moi, Toril 1953- .... **CLC 172**
See also CA 154; CANR 102; FW

Morris, Bill 1952- .... **CLC 76**
See also CA 225
Morris, Julian
See West, Morris L(anglo)
Morris, Steveland Judkins 1950(?)-
See Wonder, Stevie
See also CA 111
Morris, William 1834-1896 . **NCLC 4; PC 55**
See also BRW 5; CDBLB 1832-1890; DLB
18, 35, 57, 156, 178, 184; FANT; RGEL
2; SFW 4; SUFW
Morris, Wright 1910-1998 .. **CLC 1, 3, 7, 18,
37; TCLC 107**
See also AMW; CA 9-12R; 167; CANR 21,
81; CN 7; DLB 2, 206, 218; DLBY 1981;
EWL 3; MTCW 1, 2; RGAL 4; TCWW 2
Morrison, Arthur 1863-1945 .... **SSC 40;
TCLC 72**
See also CA 120; 157; CMW 4; DLB 70,
135, 197; RGEL 2
Morrison, Chloe Anthony Wofford
See Morrison, Toni
Morrison, James Douglas 1943-1971
See Morrison, Jim
See also CA 73-76; CANR 40
Morrison, Jim .... **CLC 17**
See Morrison, James Douglas
Morrison, Toni 1931- ..... **BLC 3; CLC 4, 10,
22, 55, 81, 87, 173, 194**
See also AAYA 1, 22; AFAW 1, 2; AMWC
1; AMWS 3; BPFB 2; BW 2, 3; CA 29-
32R; CANR 27, 42, 67, 113, 124; CDALB
1968-1988; CLR 99; CN 7; CPW; DA;
DA3; DAB; DAC; DAM MST, MULT,
NOV, POP; DLB 6, 33, 143; DLBY 1981;
EWL 3; EXPN; FW; LAIT 2, 4; LATS
1:2; LMFS 2; MAWW; MTCW 1, 2; NFS
1, 6, 8, 14; RGAL 4; RHW; SATA 57,
144; SSFS 5; TUS; YAW
Morrison, Van 1945- .... **CLC 21**
See also CA 116; 168
Morrissy, Mary 1957- .... **CLC 99**
See also CA 205; DLB 267
Mortimer, John (Clifford) 1923- ..... **CLC 28,
43**
See also CA 13-16R; CANR 21, 69, 109;
CD 5; CDBLB 1960 to Present; CMW 4;
CN 7; CPW; DA3; DAM DRAM, POP;
DLB 13, 245, 271; INT CANR-21; MSW;
MTCW 1, 2; RGEL 2
Mortimer, Penelope (Ruth)
1918-1999 .... **CLC 5**
See also CA 57-60; 187; CANR 45, 88; CN
7
Mortimer, Sir John
See Mortimer, John (Clifford)
Morton, Anthony
See Creasey, John
Morton, Thomas 1579(?)-1647(?) .... **LC 72**
See also DLB 24; RGEL 2
Mosca, Gaetano 1858-1941 .... **TCLC 75**
Moses, Daniel David 1952- .... **NNAL**
See also CA 186
Mosher, Howard Frank 1943- .... **CLC 62**
See also CA 139; CANR 65, 115
Mosley, Nicholas 1923- .... **CLC 43, 70**
See also CA 69-72; CANR 41, 60, 108; CN
7; DLB 14, 207
Mosley, Walter 1952- .... **BLCS; CLC 97, 184**
See also AAYA 57; AMWS 13; BPFB 2;
BW 2; CA 142; CANR 57, 92; CMW 4;
CPW; DA3; DAM MULT, POP; DLB
306; MSW; MTCW 2
Moss, Howard 1922-1987 . **CLC 7, 14, 45, 50**
See also CA 1-4R; 123; CANR 1, 44; DAM
POET; DLB 5
Mossgiel, Rab
See Burns, Robert

Motion, Andrew (Peter) 1952- .... **CLC 47**
See also BRWS 7; CA 146; CANR 90; CP
7; DLB 40
Motley, Willard (Francis)
1909-1965 .... **CLC 18**
See also BW 1; CA 117; 106; CANR 88;
DLB 76, 143
Motoori, Norinaga 1730-1801 .... **NCLC 45**
Mott, Michael (Charles Alston)
1930- .... **CLC 15, 34**
See also CA 5-8R; CAAS 7; CANR 7, 29
Mountain Wolf Woman 1884-1960 . **CLC 92;
NNAL**
See also CA 144; CANR 90
Moure, Erin 1955- .... **CLC 88**
See also CA 113; CP 7; CWP; DLB 60
Mourning Dove 1885(?)-1936 .... **NNAL**
See also CA 144; CANR 90; DAM MULT;
DLB 175, 221
Mowat, Farley (McGill) 1921- .... **CLC 26**
See also AAYA 1, 50; BYA 2; CA 1-4R;
CANR 4, 24, 42, 68, 108; CLR 20; CPW;
DAC; DAM MST; DLB 68; INT CANR-
24; JRDA; MAICYA 1, 2; MTCW 1, 2;
SATA 3, 55; YAW
Mowatt, Anna Cora 1819-1870 ..... **NCLC 74**
See also RGAL 4
Moyers, Bill 1934- .... **CLC 74**
See also AITN 2; CA 61-64; CANR 31, 52
Mphahlele, Es'kia
See Mphahlele, Ezekiel
See also AFW; CDWLB 3; DLB 125, 225;
RGSF 2; SSFS 11
Mphahlele, Ezekiel 1919- ... **BLC 3; CLC 25,
133**
See Mphahlele, Es'kia
See also BW 2, 3; CA 81-84; CANR 26,
76; CN 7; DA3; DAM MULT; EWL 3;
MTCW 2; SATA 119
Mqhayi, S(amuel) E(dward) K(rune Loliwe)
1875-1945 .... **BLC 3; TCLC 25**
See also CA 153; CANR 87; DAM MULT
Mrozek, Slawomir 1930- .... **CLC 3, 13**
See also CA 13-16R; CAAS 10; CANR 29;
CDWLB 4; CWW 2; DLB 232; EWL 3;
MTCW 1
Mrs. Belloc-Lowndes
See Lowndes, Marie Adelaide (Belloc)
Mrs. Fairstar
See Horne, Richard Henry Hengist
M'Taggart, John M'Taggart Ellis
See McTaggart, John McTaggart Ellis
Mtwa, Percy (?)- .... **CLC 47**
Mueller, Lisel 1924- .... **CLC 13, 51; PC 33**
See also CA 93-96; CP 7; DLB 105; PFS 9,
13
Muggeridge, Malcolm (Thomas)
1903-1990 .... **TCLC 120**
See also AITN 1; CA 101; CANR 33, 63;
MTCW 1, 2
Muhammad 570-632 .... **WLCS**
See also DA; DAB; DAC; DAM MST
Muir, Edwin 1887-1959 . **PC 49; TCLC 2, 87**
See Moore, Edward
See also BRWS 6; CA 104; 193; DLB 20,
100, 191; EWL 3; RGEL 2
Muir, John 1838-1914 .... **TCLC 28**
See also AMWS 9; ANW; CA 165; DLB
186, 275
Mujica Lainez, Manuel 1910-1984 ... **CLC 31**
See Lainez, Manuel Mujica
See also CA 81-84; 112; CANR 32; EWL
3; HW 1
Mukherjee, Bharati 1940- ..... **AAL; CLC 53,
115; SSC 38**
See also AAYA 46; BEST 89:2; CA 107;
CANR 45, 72, 128; CN 7; DAM NOV;
DLB 60, 218; DNFS 1; EWL 3; FW;
MTCW 1, 2; RGAL 4; RGSF 2; SSFS 7;
TUS; WWE 1

Muldoon, Paul 1951- .... **CLC 32, 72, 166**
See also BRWS 4; CA 113; 129; CANR 52,
91; CP 7; DAM POET; DLB 40; INT CA-
129; PFS 7
Mulisch, Harry (Kurt Victor)
1927- .... **CLC 42**
See also CA 9-12R; CANR 6, 26, 56, 110;
CWW 2; DLB 299; EWL 3
Mull, Martin 1943- .... **CLC 17**
See also CA 105
Muller, Wilhelm .... **NCLC 73**
Mulock, Dinah Maria
See Craik, Dinah Maria (Mulock)
See also RGEL 2
Munday, Anthony 1560-1633 .... **LC 87**
See also DLB 62, 172; RGEL 2
Munford, Robert 1737(?)-1783 .... **LC 5**
See also DLB 31
Mungo, Raymond 1946- .... **CLC 72**
See also CA 49-52; CANR 2
Munro, Alice 1931- .... **CLC 6, 10, 19, 50, 95;
SSC 3; WLCS**
See also AITN 2; BPFB 2; CA 33-36R;
CANR 33, 53, 75, 114; CCA 1; CN 7;
DA3; DAC; DAM MST, NOV; DLB 53;
EWL 3; MTCW 1, 2; RGEL 2; RGSF 2;
SATA 29; SSFS 5, 13, 19; WWE 1
Munro, H(ector) H(ugh) 1870-1916 .... **WLC**
See Saki
See also AAYA 56; CA 104; 130; CANR
104; CDBLB 1890-1914; DA; DA3;
DAB; DAC; DAM MST, NOV; DLB 34,
162; EXPS; MTCW 1, 2; RGEL 2; SSFS
15
Murakami, Haruki 1949- .... **CLC 150**
See Murakami Haruki
See also CA 165; CANR 102; MJW; RGWL
3; SFW 4
Murakami Haruki
See Murakami, Haruki
See also CWW 2; DLB 182; EWL 3
Murasaki, Lady
See Murasaki Shikibu
Murasaki Shikibu 978(?)-1026(?) ... **CMLC 1**
See also EFS 2; LATS 1:1; RGWL 2, 3
Murdoch, (Jean) Iris 1919-1999 ... **CLC 1, 2,
3, 4, 6, 8, 11, 15, 22, 31, 51**
See also BRWS 1; CA 13-16R; 179; CANR
8, 43, 68, 103; CDBLB 1960 to Present;
CN 7; CWD; DA3; DAB; DAC; DAM
MST, NOV; DLB 14, 194, 233; EWL 3;
INT CANR-8; MTCW 1, 2; NFS 18;
RGEL 2; TEA; WLIT 4
Murfree, Mary Noailles 1850-1922 .. **SSC 22;
TCLC 135**
See also CA 122; 176; DLB 12, 74; RGAL
4
Murnau, Friedrich Wilhelm
See Plumpe, Friedrich Wilhelm
Murphy, Richard 1927- .... **CLC 41**
See also BRWS 5; CA 29-32R; CP 7; DLB
40; EWL 3
Murphy, Sylvia 1937- .... **CLC 34**
See also CA 121
Murphy, Thomas (Bernard) 1935- ... **CLC 51**
See also CA 101
Murray, Albert L. 1916- .... **CLC 73**
See also BW 2; CA 49-52; CANR 26, 52,
78; CSW; DLB 38
Murray, James Augustus Henry
1837-1915 .... **TCLC 117**
Murray, Judith Sargent
1751-1820 .... **NCLC 63**
See also DLB 37, 200
Murray, Les(lie Allan) 1938- .... **CLC 40**
See also BRWS 7; CA 21-24R; CANR 11,
27, 56, 103; CP 7; DAM POET; DLB 289;
DLBY 2001; EWL 3; RGEL 2

Murry, J. Middleton
See Murry, John Middleton
Murry, John Middleton
1889-1957 .... **TCLC 16**
See also CA 118; 217; DLB 149
Musgrave, Susan 1951- .... **CLC 13, 54**
See also CA 69-72; CANR 45, 84; CCA 1;
CP 7; CWP
Musil, Robert (Edler von)
1880-1942 .... **SSC 18; TCLC 12, 68**
See also CA 109; CANR 55, 84; CDWLB
2; DLB 81, 124; EW 9; EWL 3; MTCW
2; RGSF 2; RGWL 2, 3
Muske, Carol .... **CLC 90**
See Muske-Dukes, Carol (Anne)
Muske-Dukes, Carol (Anne) 1945-
See Muske, Carol
See also CA 65-68, 203; CAAE 203; CANR
32, 70; CWP
Musset, (Louis Charles) Alfred de
1810-1857 .... **NCLC 7**
See also DLB 192, 217; EW 6; GFL 1789
to the Present; RGWL 2, 3; TWA
Mussolini, Benito (Amilcare Andrea)
1883-1945 .... **TCLC 96**
See also CA 116
Mutanabbi, Al-
See al-Mutanabbi, Ahmad ibn al-Husayn
Abu al-Tayyib al-Jufi al-Kindi
My Brother's Brother
See Chekhov, Anton (Pavlovich)
Myers, L(eopold) H(amilton)
1881-1944 .... **TCLC 59**
See also CA 157; DLB 15; EWL 3; RGEL
2
Myers, Walter Dean 1937- .. **BLC 3; CLC 35**
See also AAYA 4, 23; BW 2; BYA 6, 8, 11;
CA 33-36R; CANR 20, 42, 67, 108; CLR
4, 16, 35; DAM MULT, NOV; DLB 33;
INT CANR-20; JRDA; LAIT 5; MAICYA
1, 2; MAICYAS 1; MTCW 2; SAAS 2;
SATA 41, 71, 109; SATA-Brief 27; WYA;
YAW
Myers, Walter M.
See Myers, Walter Dean
Myles, Symon
See Follett, Ken(neth Martin)
Nabokov, Vladimir (Vladimirovich)
1899-1977 .... **CLC 1, 2, 3, 6, 8, 11, 15,
23, 44, 46, 64; SSC 11; TCLC 108;
WLC**
See also AAYA 45; AMW; AMWC 1;
AMWR 1; BPFB 2; CA 5-8R; 69-72;
CANR 20, 102; CDALB 1941-1968; DA;
DA3; DAB; DAC; DAM MST, NOV;
DLB 2, 244, 278; DLBD 3; DLBY 1980,
1991; EWL 3; EXPS; LATS 1:2; MTCW
1, 2; NCFS 4; NFS 9; RGAL 4; RGSF 2;
SSFS 6, 15; TUS
Naevius c. 265B.C.-201B.C. .... **CMLC 37**
See also DLB 211
Nagai, Kafu .... **TCLC 51**
See Nagai, Sokichi
See also DLB 180
Nagai, Sokichi 1879-1959
See Nagai, Kafu
See also CA 117
Nagy, Laszlo 1925-1978 .... **CLC 7**
See also CA 129; 112
Naidu, Sarojini 1879-1949 .... **TCLC 80**
See also EWL 3; RGEL 2
Naipaul, Shiva(dhar Srinivasa)
1945-1985 .... **CLC 32, 39; TCLC 153**
See also CA 110; 112; 116; CANR 33;
DA3; DAM NOV; DLB 157; DLBY 1985;
EWL 3; MTCW 1, 2

Naipaul, V(idiadhar) S(urajprasad)
1932- .... **CLC 4, 7, 9, 13, 18, 37, 105,
199; SSC 38**
See also BPFB 2; BRWS 1; CA 1-4R;
CANR 1, 33, 51, 91, 126; CDBLB 1960
to Present; CDWLB 3; CN 7; DA3; DAB;
DAC; DAM MST, NOV; DLB 125, 204,
207; DLBY 1985, 2001; EWL 3; LATS
1:2; MTCW 1, 2; RGEL 2; RGSF 2;
TWA; WLIT 4; WWE 1
Nakos, Lilika 1903(?)-1989 .... **CLC 29**
Napoleon
See Yamamoto, Hisaye
Narayan, R(asipuram) K(rishnaswami)
1906-2001 . **CLC 7, 28, 47, 121; SSC 25**
See also BPFB 2; CA 81-84; 196; CANR
33, 61, 112; CN 7; DA3; DAM NOV;
DNFS 1; EWL 3; MTCW 1, 2; RGEL 2;
RGSF 2; SATA 62; SSFS 5; WWE 1
Nash, (Frediric) Ogden 1902-1971 . **CLC 23;
PC 21; TCLC 109**
See also CA 13-14; 29-32R; CANR 34, 61;
CAP 1; DAM POET; DLB 11; MAICYA
1, 2; MTCW 1, 2; RGAL 4; SATA 2, 46;
WP
Nashe, Thomas 1567-1601(?) .... **LC 41, 89**
See also DLB 167; RGEL 2
Nathan, Daniel
See Dannay, Frederic
Nathan, George Jean 1882-1958 .... **TCLC 18**
See Hatteras, Owen
See also CA 114; 169; DLB 137
Natsume, Kinnosuke
See Natsume, Soseki
Natsume, Soseki 1867-1916 .... **TCLC 2, 10**
See Natsume Soseki; Soseki
See also CA 104; 195; RGWL 2, 3; TWA
Natsume Soseki
See Natsume, Soseki
See also DLB 180; EWL 3
Natti, (Mary) Lee 1919-
See Kingman, Lee
See also CA 5-8R; CANR 2
Navarre, Marguerite de
See de Navarre, Marguerite
Naylor, Gloria 1950- ..... **BLC 3; CLC 28, 52,
156; WLCS**
See also AAYA 6, 39; AFAW 1, 2; AMWS
8; BW 2, 3; CA 107; CANR 27, 51, 74,
130; CN 7; CPW; DA; DA3; DAC; DAM
MST, MULT, NOV, POP; DLB 173; EWL
3; FW; MTCW 1, 2; NFS 4, 7; RGAL 4;
TUS
Neff, Debra .... **CLC 59**
Neihardt, John Gneisenau
1881-1973 .... **CLC 32**
See also CA 13-14; CANR 65; CAP 1; DLB
9, 54, 256; LAIT 2
Nekrasov, Nikolai Alekseevich
1821-1878 .... **NCLC 11**
See also DLB 277
Nelligan, Emile 1879-1941 .... **TCLC 14**
See also CA 114; 204; DLB 92; EWL 3
Nelson, Willie 1933- .... **CLC 17**
See also CA 107; CANR 114
Nemerov, Howard (Stanley)
1920-1991 .... **CLC 2, 6, 9, 36; PC 24;
TCLC 124**
See also AMW; CA 1-4R; 134; CABS 2;
CANR 1, 27, 53; DAM POET; DLB 5, 6;
DLBY 1983; EWL 3; INT CANR-27;
MTCW 1, 2; PFS 10, 14; RGAL 4
Neruda, Pablo 1904-1973 .. **CLC 1, 2, 5, 7, 9,
28, 62; HLC 2; PC 4; WLC**
See also CA 19-20; 45-48; CANR 131; CAP
2; DA; DA3; DAB; DAC; DAM MST,
MULT, POET; DLB 283; DNFS 2; EWL
3; HW 1; LAW; MTCW 1, 2; PFS 11;
RGWL 2, 3; TWA; WLIT 1; WP

Nerval, Gerard de 1808-1855 ... **NCLC 1, 67;
PC 13; SSC 18**
See also DLB 217; EW 6; GFL 1789 to the
Present; RGSF 2; RGWL 2, 3
Nervo, (Jose) Amado (Ruiz de)
1870-1919 .... **HLCS 2; TCLC 11**
See also CA 109; 131; DLB 290; EWL 3;
HW 1; LAW
Nesbit, Malcolm
See Chester, Alfred
Nessi, Pio Baroja y
See Baroja (y Nessi), Pio
Nestroy, Johann 1801-1862 .... **NCLC 42**
See also DLB 133; RGWL 2, 3
Netterville, Luke
See O'Grady, Standish (James)
Neufeld, John (Arthur) 1938- .... **CLC 17**
See also AAYA 11; CA 25-28R; CANR 11,
37, 56; CLR 52; MAICYA 1, 2; SAAS 3;
SATA 6, 81, 131; SATA-Essay 131; YAW
Neumann, Alfred 1895-1952 .... **TCLC 100**
See also CA 183; DLB 56
Neumann, Ferenc
See Molnar, Ferenc
Neville, Emily Cheney 1919- .... **CLC 12**
See also BYA 2; CA 5-8R; CANR 3, 37,
85; JRDA; MAICYA 1, 2; SAAS 2; SATA
1; YAW
Newbound, Bernard Slade 1930-
See Slade, Bernard
See also CA 81-84; CANR 49; CD 5; DAM
DRAM
Newby, P(ercy) H(oward)
1918-1997 .... **CLC 2, 13**
See also CA 5-8R; 161; CANR 32, 67; CN
7; DAM NOV; DLB 15; MTCW 1; RGEL
2
Newcastle
See Cavendish, Margaret Lucas
Newlove, Donald 1928- .... **CLC 6**
See also CA 29-32R; CANR 25
Newlove, John (Herbert) 1938- .... **CLC 14**
See also CA 21-24R; CANR 9, 25; CP 7
Newman, Charles 1938- .... **CLC 2, 8**
See also CA 21-24R; CANR 84; CN 7
Newman, Edwin (Harold) 1919- ...... **CLC 14**
See also AITN 1; CA 69-72; CANR 5
Newman, John Henry 1801-1890 . **NCLC 38,
99**
See also BRWS 7; DLB 18, 32, 55; RGEL
2
Newton, (Sir) Isaac 1642-1727 ...... **LC 35, 53**
See also DLB 252
Newton, Suzanne 1936- .... **CLC 35**
See also BYA 7; CA 41-44R; CANR 14;
JRDA; SATA 5, 77
New York Dept. of Ed. .... **CLC 70**
Nexo, Martin Andersen
1869-1954 .... **TCLC 43**
See also CA 202; DLB 214; EWL 3
Nezval, Vitezslav 1900-1958 .... **TCLC 44**
See also CA 123; CDWLB 4; DLB 215;
EWL 3
Ng, Fae Myenne 1957(?)- .... **CLC 81**
See also BYA 11; CA 146
Ngema, Mbongeni 1955- .... **CLC 57**
See also BW 2; CA 143; CANR 84; CD 5
Ngugi, James T(hiong'o) . **CLC 3, 7, 13, 182**
See Ngugi wa Thiong'o
Ngugi wa Thiong'o
See Ngugi wa Thiong'o
See also DLB 125; EWL 3
Ngugi wa Thiong'o 1938- ... **BLC 3; CLC 36,
182**
See Ngugi, James T(hiong'o); Ngugi wa
Thiong'o
See also AFW; BRWS 8; BW 2; CA 81-84;
CANR 27, 58; CDWLB 3; DAM MULT,
NOV; DNFS 2; MTCW 1, 2; RGEL 2;
WWE 1

Niatum, Duane 1938- .... **NNAL**
    See also CA 41-44R; CANR 21, 45, 83;
    DLB 175

Nichol, B(arrie) P(hillip) 1944-1988 . **CLC 18**
    See also CA 53-56; DLB 53; SATA 66

Nicholas of Cusa 1401-1464 .... **LC 80**
    See also DLB 115

Nichols, John (Treadwell) 1940- .... **CLC 38**
    See also AMWS 13; CA 9-12R, 190; CAAE
    190; CAAS 2; CANR 6, 70, 121; DLBY
    1982; LATS 1:2; TCWW 2

Nichols, Leigh
    See Koontz, Dean R(ay)

Nichols, Peter (Richard) 1927- .... **CLC 5, 36,
    65**
    See also CA 104; CANR 33, 86; CBD; CD
    5; DLB 13, 245; MTCW 1

Nicholson, Linda ed. .... **CLC 65**

Ni Chuilleanain, Eilean 1942- .... **PC 34**
    See also CA 126; CANR 53, 83; CP 7;
    CWP; DLB 40

Nicolas, F. R. E.
    See Freeling, Nicolas

Niedecker, Lorine 1903-1970 ..... **CLC 10, 42;
    PC 42**
    See also CA 25-28; CAP 2; DAM POET;
    DLB 48

Nietzsche, Friedrich (Wilhelm)
    1844-1900 .... **TCLC 10, 18, 55**
    See also CA 107; 121; CDWLB 2; DLB
    129; EW 7; RGWL 2, 3; TWA

Nievo, Ippolito 1831-1861 .... **NCLC 22**

Nightingale, Anne Redmon 1943-
    See Redmon, Anne
    See also CA 103

Nightingale, Florence 1820-1910 ... **TCLC 85**
    See also CA 188; DLB 166

Nijo Yoshimoto 1320-1388 .... **CMLC 49**
    See also DLB 203

Nik. T. O.
    See Annensky, Innokenty (Fyodorovich)

Nin, Anais 1903-1977 ..... **CLC 1, 4, 8, 11, 14,
    60, 127; SSC 10**
    See also AITN 2; AMWS 10; BPFB 2; CA
    13-16R; 69-72; CANR 22, 53; DAM
    NOV, POP; DLB 2, 4, 152; EWL 3; GLL
    2; MAWW; MTCW 1, 2; RGAL 4; RGSF
    2

Nisbet, Robert A(lexander)
    1913-1996 .... **TCLC 117**
    See also CA 25-28R; 153; CANR 17; INT
    CANR-17

Nishida, Kitaro 1870-1945 .... **TCLC 83**

Nishiwaki, Junzaburo
    See Nishiwaki, Junzaburo
    See also CA 194

Nishiwaki, Junzaburo 1894-1982 .... **PC 15**
    See Nishiwaki, Junzaburo; Nishiwaki
    Junzaburo
    See also CA 194; 107; MJW; RGWL 3

Nishiwaki Junzaburo
    See Nishiwaki, Junzaburo
    See also EWL 3

Nissenson, Hugh 1933- .... **CLC 4, 9**
    See also CA 17-20R; CANR 27, 108; CN
    7; DLB 28

Nister, Der
    See Der Nister
    See also EWL 3

Niven, Larry .... **CLC 8**
    See Niven, Laurence Van Cott
    See also AAYA 27; BPFB 2; BYA 10; DLB
    8; SCFW 2

Niven, Laurence Van Cott 1938-
    See Niven, Larry
    See also CA 21-24R, 207; CAAE 207;
    CAAS 12; CANR 14, 44, 66, 113; CPW;
    DAM POP; MTCW 1, 2; SATA 95; SFW
    4

Nixon, Agnes Eckhardt 1927- .... **CLC 21**
    See also CA 110

Nizan, Paul 1905-1940 .... **TCLC 40**
    See also CA 161; DLB 72; EWL 3; GFL
    1789 to the Present

Nkosi, Lewis 1936- .... **BLC 3; CLC 45**
    See also BW 1, 3; CA 65-68; CANR 27,
    81; CBD; CD 5; DAM MULT; DLB 157,
    225; WWE 1

Nodier, (Jean) Charles (Emmanuel)
    1780-1844 .... **NCLC 19**
    See also DLB 119; GFL 1789 to the Present

Noguchi, Yone 1875-1947 .... **TCLC 80**

Nolan, Christopher 1965- .... **CLC 58**
    See also CA 111; CANR 88

Noon, Jeff 1957- .... **CLC 91**
    See also CA 148; CANR 83; DLB 267;
    SFW 4

Norden, Charles
    See Durrell, Lawrence (George)

Nordhoff, Charles Bernard
    1887-1947 .... **TCLC 23**
    See also CA 108; 211; DLB 9; LAIT 1;
    RHW 1; SATA 23

Norfolk, Lawrence 1963- .... **CLC 76**
    See also CA 144; CANR 85; CN 7; DLB
    267

Norman, Marsha 1947- . **CLC 28, 186; DC 8**
    See also CA 105; CABS 3; CAD; CANR
    41, 131; CD 5; CSW; CWD; DAM
    DRAM; DFS 2; DLB 266; DLBY 1984;
    FW

Normyx
    See Douglas, (George) Norman

Norris, (Benjamin) Frank(lin, Jr.)
    1870-1902 .... **SSC 28; TCLC 24, 155**
    See also AAYA 57; AMW; AMWC 2; BPFB
    2; CA 110; 160; CDALB 1865-1917; DLB
    12, 71, 186; LMFS 2; NFS 12; RGAL 4;
    TCWW 2; TUS

Norris, Leslie 1921- .... **CLC 14**
    See also CA 11-12; CANR 14, 117; CAP 1;
    CP 7; DLB 27, 256

North, Andrew
    See Norton, Andre

North, Anthony
    See Koontz, Dean R(ay)

North, Captain George
    See Stevenson, Robert Louis (Balfour)

North, Captain George
    See Stevenson, Robert Louis (Balfour)

North, Milou
    See Erdrich, Louise

Northrup, B. A.
    See Hubbard, L(afayette) Ron(ald)

North Staffs
    See Hulme, T(homas) E(rnest)

Northup, Solomon 1808-1863 ...... **NCLC 105**

Norton, Alice Mary
    See Norton, Andre
    See also MAICYA 1; SATA 1, 43

Norton, Andre 1912- .... **CLC 12**
    See Norton, Alice Mary
    See also AAYA 14; BPFB 2; BYA 4, 10,
    12; CA 1-4R; CANR 68; CLR 50; DLB
    8, 52; JRDA; MAICYA 2; MTCW 1;
    SATA 91; SUFW 1, 2; YAW

Norton, Caroline 1808-1877 .... **NCLC 47**
    See also DLB 21, 159, 199

Norway, Nevil Shute 1899-1960
    See Shute, Nevil
    See also CA 102; 93-96; CANR 85; MTCW
    2

Norwid, Cyprian Kamil
    1821-1883 .... **NCLC 17**
    See also RGWL 3

Nosille, Nabrah
    See Ellison, Harlan (Jay)

Nossack, Hans Erich 1901-1978 .... **CLC 6**
    See also CA 93-96; 85-88; DLB 69; EWL 3

Nostradamus 1503-1566 .... **LC 27**

Nosu, Chuji
    See Ozu, Yasujiro

Notenburg, Eleanora (Genrikhovna) von
    See Guro, Elena (Genrikhovna)

Nova, Craig 1945- .... **CLC 7, 31**
    See also CA 45-48; CANR 2, 53, 127

Novak, Joseph
    See Kosinski, Jerzy (Nikodem)

Novalis 1772-1801 .... **NCLC 13**
    See also CDWLB 2; DLB 90; EW 5; RGWL
    2, 3

Novick, Peter 1934- .... **CLC 164**
    See also CA 188

Novis, Emile
    See Weil, Simone (Adolphine)

Nowlan, Alden (Albert) 1933-1983 ... **CLC 15**
    See also CA 9-12R; CANR 5; DAC; DAM
    MST; DLB 53; PFS 12

Noyes, Alfred 1880-1958 ...... **PC 27; TCLC 7**
    See also CA 104; 188; DLB 20; EXPP;
    FANT; PFS 4; RGEL 2

Nugent, Richard Bruce 1906(?)-1987 ... **HR 3**
    See also BW 1; CA 125; DLB 51; GLL 2

Nunn, Kem .... **CLC 34**
    See also CA 159

Nwapa, Flora (Nwanzuruaha)
    1931-1993 .... **BLCS; CLC 133**
    See also BW 2; CA 143; CANR 83; CD-
    WLB 3; CWRI 5; DLB 125; EWL 3;
    WLIT 2

Nye, Robert 1939- .... **CLC 13, 42**
    See also BRWS 10; CA 33-36R; CANR 29,
    67, 107; CN 7; CP 7; CWRI 5; DAM
    NOV; DLB 14, 271; FANT; HGG; MTCW
    1; RHW; SATA 6

Nyro, Laura 1947-1997 .... **CLC 17**
    See also CA 194

Oates, Joyce Carol 1938- .. **CLC 1, 2, 3, 6, 9,
    11, 15, 19, 33, 52, 108, 134; SSC 6, 70;
    WLC**
    See also AAYA 15, 52; AITN 1; AMWS 2;
    BEST 89:2; BPFB 2; BYA 11; CA 5-8R;
    CANR 25, 45, 74, 113, 129; CDALB
    1968-1988; CN 7; CP 7; CPW; CWP; DA;
    DA3; DAB; DAC; DAM MST, NOV,
    POP; DLB 2, 5, 130; DLBY 1981; EWL
    3; EXPS; FW; HGG; INT CANR-25;
    LAIT 4; MAWW; MTCW 1, 2; NFS 8;
    RGAL 4; RGSF 2; SSFS 17; SUFW 2;
    TUS

O'Brian, E. G.
    See Clarke, Arthur C(harles)

O'Brian, Patrick 1914-2000 .... **CLC 152**
    See also AAYA 55; CA 144; 187; CANR
    74; CPW; MTCW 2; RHW

O'Brien, Darcy 1939-1998 .... **CLC 11**
    See also CA 21-24R; 167; CANR 8, 59

O'Brien, Edna 1932- ..... **CLC 3, 5, 8, 13, 36,
    65, 116; SSC 10, 77**
    See also BRWS 5; CA 1-4R; CANR 6, 41,
    65, 102; CDBLB 1960 to Present; CN 7;
    DA3; DAM NOV; DLB 14, 231; EWL 3;
    FW; MTCW 1, 2; RGSF 2; WLIT 4

O'Brien, Fitz-James 1828-1862 ..... **NCLC 21**
    See also DLB 74; RGAL 4; SUFW

O'Brien, Flann .... **CLC 1, 4, 5, 7, 10, 47**
    See O Nuallain, Brian
    See also BRWS 2; DLB 231; EWL 3;
    RGEL 2

O'Brien, Richard 1942- .... **CLC 17**
    See also CA 124

Ortega y Gasset, Jose 1883-1955 ...... **HLC 2; TCLC 9**
See also CA 106; 130; DAM MULT; EW 9; EWL 3; HW 1, 2; MTCW 1, 2

Ortese, Anna Maria 1914-1998 .... **CLC 89**
See also DLB 177; EWL 3

Ortiz, Simon J(oseph) 1941- .... **CLC 45; NNAL; PC 17**
See also AMWS 4; CA 134; CANR 69, 118; CP 7; DAM MULT, POET; DLB 120, 175, 256; EXPP; PFS 4, 16; RGAL 4

Orton, Joe ...... **CLC 4, 13, 43; DC 3; TCLC 157**
See Orton, John Kingsley
See also BRWS 5; CBD; CDBLB 1960 to Present; DFS 3, 6; DLB 13; GLL 1; MTCW 2; RGEL 2; TEA; WLIT 4

Orton, John Kingsley 1933-1967
See Orton, Joe
See also CA 85-88; CANR 35, 66; DAM DRAM; MTCW 1, 2

Orwell, George ...... **SSC 68; TCLC 2, 6, 15, 31, 51, 128, 129; WLC**
See Blair, Eric (Arthur)
See also BPFB 3; BRW 7; BYA 5; CDBLB 1945-1960; CLR 68; DAB; DLB 15, 98, 195, 255; EWL 3; EXPN; LAIT 4, 5; LATS 1:1; NFS 3, 7; RGEL 2; SCFW 2; SFW 4; SSFS 4; TEA; WLIT 4; YAW

Osborne, David
See Silverberg, Robert

Osborne, George
See Silverberg, Robert

Osborne, John (James) 1929-1994 .... **CLC 1, 2, 5, 11, 45; TCLC 153; WLC**
See also BRWS 1; CA 13-16R; 147; CANR 21, 56; CDBLB 1945-1960; DA; DAB; DAC; DAM DRAM, MST; DFS 4, 19; DLB 13; EWL 3; MTCW 1, 2; RGEL 2

Osborne, Lawrence 1958- .... **CLC 50**
See also CA 189

Osbourne, Lloyd 1868-1947 .... **TCLC 93**

Osgood, Frances Sargent
1811-1850 .... **NCLC 141**
See also DLB 250

Oshima, Nagisa 1932- .... **CLC 20**
See also CA 116; 121; CANR 78

Oskison, John Milton
1874-1947 .... **NNAL; TCLC 35**
See also CA 144; CANR 84; DAM MULT; DLB 175

Ossian c. 3rd cent. - .... **CMLC 28**
See Macpherson, James

Ossoli, Sarah Margaret (Fuller)
1810-1850 .... **NCLC 5, 50**
See Fuller, Margaret; Fuller, Sarah Margaret
See also CDALB 1640-1865; FW; LMFS 1; SATA 25

Ostriker, Alicia (Suskin) 1937- .... **CLC 132**
See also CA 25-28R; CAAS 24; CANR 10, 30, 62, 99; CWP; DLB 120; EXPP; PFS 19

Ostrovsky, Aleksandr Nikolaevich
See Ostrovsky, Alexander
See also DLB 277

Ostrovsky, Alexander 1823-1886 .. **NCLC 30, 57**
See Ostrovsky, Aleksandr Nikolaevich

Otero, Blas de 1916-1979 .... **CLC 11**
See also CA 89-92; DLB 134; EWL 3

O'Trigger, Sir Lucius
See Horne, Richard Henry Hengist

Otto, Rudolf 1869-1937 .... **TCLC 85**

Otto, Whitney 1955- .... **CLC 70**
See also CA 140; CANR 120

Otway, Thomas 1652-1685 ... **DC 24; LC 106**
See also DAM DRAM; DLB 80; RGEL 2

Ouida .... **TCLC 43**
See De la Ramee, Marie Louise (Ouida)
See also DLB 18, 156; RGEL 2

Ouologuem, Yambo 1940- .... **CLC 146**
See also CA 111; 176

Ousmane, Sembene 1923- ... **BLC 3; CLC 66**
See Sembene, Ousmane
See also BW 1, 3; CA 117; 125; CANR 81; CWW 2; MTCW 1

Ovid 43B.C.-17 .... **CMLC 7; PC 2**
See also AW 2; CDWLB 1; DA3; DAM POET; DLB 211; RGWL 2, 3; WP

Owen, Hugh
See Faust, Frederick (Schiller)

Owen, Wilfred (Edward Salter)
1893-1918 ... **PC 19; TCLC 5, 27; WLC**
See also BRW 6; CA 104; 141; CDBLB 1914-1945; DA; DAB; DAC; DAM MST, POET; DLB 20; EWL 3; EXPP; MTCW 2; PFS 10; RGEL 2; WLIT 4

Owens, Louis (Dean) 1948-2002 .... **NNAL**
See also CA 137; 179; 207; CAAE 179; CAAS 24; CANR 71

Owens, Rochelle 1936- .... **CLC 8**
See also CA 17-20R; CAAS 2; CAD; CANR 39; CD 5; CP 7; CWD; CWP

Oz, Amos 1939- ...... **CLC 5, 8, 11, 27, 33, 54; SSC 66**
See also CA 53-56; CANR 27, 47, 65, 113; CWW 2; DAM NOV; EWL 3; MTCW 1, 2; RGSF 2; RGWL 3

Ozick, Cynthia 1928- .... **CLC 3, 7, 28, 62, 155; SSC 15, 60**
See also AMWS 5; BEST 90:1; CA 17-20R; CANR 23, 58, 116; CN 7; CPW; DA3; DAM NOV, POP; DLB 28, 152, 299; DLBY 1982; EWL 3; EXPS; INT CANR-23; MTCW 1, 2; RGAL 4; RGSF 2; SSFS 3, 12

Ozu, Yasujiro 1903-1963 .... **CLC 16**
See also CA 112

Pabst, G. W. 1885-1967 .... **TCLC 127**

Pacheco, C.
See Pessoa, Fernando (Antonio Nogueira)

Pacheco, Jose Emilio 1939- .... **HLC 2**
See also CA 111; 131; CANR 65; CWW 2; DAM MULT; DLB 290; EWL 3; HW 1, 2; RGSF 2

Pa Chin .... **CLC 18**
See Li Fei-kan
See also EWL 3

Pack, Robert 1929- .... **CLC 13**
See also CA 1-4R; CANR 3, 44, 82; CP 7; DLB 5; SATA 118

Padgett, Lewis
See Kuttner, Henry

Padilla (Lorenzo), Heberto
1932-2000 .... **CLC 38**
See also AITN 1; CA 123; 131; 189; CWW 2; EWL 3; HW 1

Page, James Patrick 1944-
See Page, Jimmy
See also CA 204

Page, Jimmy 1944- .... **CLC 12**
See Page, James Patrick

Page, Louise 1955- .... **CLC 40**
See also CA 140; CANR 76; CBD; CD 5; CWD; DLB 233

Page, P(atricia) K(athleen) 1916- ...... **CLC 7, 18; PC 12**
See Cape, Judith
See also CA 53-56; CANR 4, 22, 65; CP 7; DAC; DAM MST; DLB 68; MTCW 1; RGEL 2

Page, Stanton
See Fuller, Henry Blake

Page, Stanton
See Fuller, Henry Blake

Page, Thomas Nelson 1853-1922 .... **SSC 23**
See also CA 118; 177; DLB 12, 78; DLBD 13; RGAL 4

Pagels, Elaine Hiesey 1943- .... **CLC 104**
See also CA 45-48; CANR 2, 24, 51; FW; NCFS 4

Paget, Violet 1856-1935
See Lee, Vernon
See also CA 104; 166; GLL 1; HGG

Paget-Lowe, Henry
See Lovecraft, H(oward) P(hillips)

Paglia, Camille (Anna) 1947- .... **CLC 68**
See also CA 140; CANR 72; CPW; FW; GLL 2; MTCW 2

Paige, Richard
See Koontz, Dean R(ay)

Paine, Thomas 1737-1809 .... **NCLC 62**
See also AMWS 1; CDALB 1640-1865; DLB 31, 43, 73, 158; LAIT 1; RGAL 4; RGEL 2; TUS

Pakenham, Antonia
See Fraser, Antonia (Pakenham)

Palamas, Costis
See Palamas, Kostes

Palamas, Kostes 1859-1943 .... **TCLC 5**
See Palamas, Kostis
See also CA 105; 190; RGWL 2, 3

Palamas, Kostis
See Palamas, Kostes
See also EWL 3

Palazzeschi, Aldo 1885-1974 .... **CLC 11**
See also CA 89-92; 53-56; DLB 114, 264; EWL 3

Pales Matos, Luis 1898-1959 .... **HLCS 2**
See Pales Matos, Luis
See also DLB 290; HW 1; LAW

Paley, Grace 1922- .. **CLC 4, 6, 37, 140; SSC 8**
See also AMWS 6; CA 25-28R; CANR 13, 46, 74, 118; CN 7; CPW; DA3; DAM POP; DLB 28, 218; EWL 3; EXPS; FW; INT CANR-13; MAWW; MTCW 1, 2; RGAL 4; RGSF 2; SSFS 3, 20

Palin, Michael (Edward) 1943- .... **CLC 21**
See Monty Python
See also CA 107; CANR 35, 109; SATA 67

Palliser, Charles 1947- .... **CLC 65**
See also CA 136; CANR 76; CN 7

Palma, Ricardo 1833-1919 .... **TCLC 29**
See also CA 168; LAW

Pamuk, Orhan 1952- .... **CLC 185**
See also CA 142; CANR 75, 127; CWW 2

Pancake, Breece Dexter 1952-1979
See Pancake, Breece D'J
See also CA 123; 109

Pancake, Breece D'J .... **CLC 29; SSC 61**
See Pancake, Breece Dexter
See also DLB 130

Panchenko, Nikolai .... **CLC 59**

Pankhurst, Emmeline (Goulden)
1858-1928 .... **TCLC 100**
See also CA 116; FW

Panko, Rudy
See Gogol, Nikolai (Vasilyevich)

Papadiamantis, Alexandros
1851-1911 .... **TCLC 29**
See also CA 168; EWL 3

Papadiamantopoulos, Johannes 1856-1910
See Moreas, Jean
See also CA 117

Papini, Giovanni 1881-1956 .... **TCLC 22**
See also CA 121; 180; DLB 264

Paracelsus 1493-1541 .... **LC 14**
See also DLB 179

Parasol, Peter
See Stevens, Wallace

Pardo Bazan, Emilia 1851-1921 .... **SSC 30**
See also EWL 3; FW; RGSF 2; RGWL 2, 3

Porter, William Sydney 1862-1910
See Henry, O.
See also CA 104; 131; CDALB 1865-1917;
DA; DA3; DAB; DAC; DAM MST; DLB
12, 78, 79; MTCW 1, 2; TUS; YABC 2

Portillo (y Pacheco), Jose Lopez
See Lopez Portillo (y Pacheco), Jose

Portillo Trambley, Estela 1927-1998 .. HLC 2
See Trambley, Estela Portillo
See also CANR 32; DAM MULT; DLB
209; HW 1

Posey, Alexander (Lawrence)
1873-1908 .... NNAL
See also CA 144; CANR 80; DAM MULT;
DLB 175

Posse, Abel .... CLC 70

Post, Melville Davisson
1869-1930 .... TCLC 39
See also CA 110; 202; CMW 4

Potok, Chaim 1929-2002 ... CLC 2, 7, 14, 26,
112
See also AAYA 15, 50; AITN 1, 2; BPFB 3;
BYA 1; CA 17-20R; 208; CANR 19, 35,
64, 98; CLR 92; CN 7; DA3; DAM NOV;
DLB 28, 152; EXPN; INT CANR-19;
LAIT 4; MTCW 1, 2; NFS 4; SATA 33,
106; SATA-Obit 134; TUS; YAW

Potok, Herbert Harold -2002
See Potok, Chaim

Potok, Herman Harold
See Potok, Chaim

Potter, Dennis (Christopher George)
1935-1994 .... CLC 58, 86, 123
See also BRWS 10; CA 107; 145; CANR
33, 61; CBD; DLB 233; MTCW 1

Pound, Ezra (Weston Loomis)
1885-1972 .. CLC 1, 2, 3, 4, 5, 7, 10, 13,
18, 34, 48, 50, 112; PC 4; WLC
See also AAYA 47; AMW; AMWR 1; CA
5-8R; 37-40R; CANR 40; CDALB 1917-
1929; DA; DA3; DAB; DAC; DAM MST,
POET; DLB 4, 45, 63; DLBD 15; EFS 2;
EWL 3; EXPP; LMFS 2; MTCW 1, 2;
PAB; PFS 2, 8, 16; RGAL 4; TUS; WP

Povod, Reinaldo 1959-1994 .... CLC 44
See also CA 136; 146; CANR 83

Powell, Adam Clayton, Jr.
1908-1972 .... BLC 3; CLC 89
See also BW 1, 3; CA 102; 33-36R; CANR
86; DAM MULT

Powell, Anthony (Dymoke)
1905-2000 .... CLC 1, 3, 7, 9, 10, 31
See also BRW 7; CA 1-4R; 189; CANR 1,
32, 62, 107; CDBLB 1945-1960; CN 7;
DLB 15; EWL 3; MTCW 1, 2; RGEL 2;
TEA

Powell, Dawn 1896(?)-1965 .... CLC 66
See also CA 5-8R; CANR 121; DLBY 1997

Powell, Padgett 1952- .... CLC 34
See also CA 126; CANR 63, 101; CSW;
DLB 234; DLBY 01

Powell, (Oval) Talmage 1920-2000
See Queen, Ellery
See also CA 5-8R; CANR 2, 80

Power, Susan 1961- .... CLC 91
See also BYA 14; CA 160; CANR 135; NFS
11

Powers, J(ames) F(arl) 1917-1999 ..... CLC 1,
4, 8, 57; SSC 4
See also CA 1-4R; 181; CANR 2, 61; CN
7; DLB 130; MTCW 1; RGAL 4; RGSF
2

Powers, John J(ames) 1945-
See Powers, John R.
See also CA 69-72

Powers, John R. .... CLC 66
See Powers, John J(ames)

Powers, Richard (S.) 1957- .... CLC 93
See also AMWS 9; BPFB 3; CA 148;
CANR 80; CN 7

Pownall, David 1938- .... CLC 10
See also CA 89-92, 180; CAAS 18; CANR
49, 101; CBD; CD 5; CN 7; DLB 14

Powys, John Cowper 1872-1963 ... CLC 7, 9,
15, 46, 125
See also CA 85-88; CANR 106; DLB 15,
255; EWL 3; FANT; MTCW 1, 2; RGEL
2; SUFW

Powys, T(heodore) F(rancis)
1875-1953 .... TCLC 9
See also BRWS 8; CA 106; 189; DLB 36,
162; EWL 3; FANT; RGEL 2; SUFW

Prado (Calvo), Pedro 1886-1952 ... TCLC 75
See also CA 131; DLB 283; HW 1; LAW

Prager, Emily 1952- .... CLC 56
See also CA 204

Pratchett, Terry 1948- .... CLC 197
See also AAYA 19, 54; BPFB 3; CA 143;
CANR 87, 126; CLR 64; CN 7; CPW;
CWRI 5; FANT; SATA 82, 139; SFW 4;
SUFW 2

Pratolini, Vasco 1913-1991 .... TCLC 124
See also CA 211; DLB 177; EWL 3; RGWL
2, 3

Pratt, E(dwin) J(ohn) 1883(?)-1964 . CLC 19
See also CA 141; 93-96; CANR 77; DAC;
DAM POET; DLB 92; EWL 3; RGEL 2;
TWA

Premchand .... TCLC 21
See Srivastava, Dhanpat Rai
See also EWL 3

Preseren, France 1800-1849 .... NCLC 127
See also CDWLB 4; DLB 147

Preussler, Otfried 1923- .... CLC 17
See also CA 77-80; SATA 24

Prevert, Jacques (Henri Marie)
1900-1977 .... CLC 15
See also CA 77-80; 69-72; CANR 29, 61;
DLB 258; EWL 3; GFL 1789 to the
Present; IDFW 3, 4; MTCW 1; RGWL 2,
3; SATA-Obit 30

Prevost, (Antoine Francois)
1697-1763 .... LC 1
See also EW 4; GFL Beginnings to 1789;
RGWL 2, 3

Price, (Edward) Reynolds 1933- ... CLC 3, 6,
13, 43, 50, 63; SSC 22
See also AMWS 6; CA 1-4R; CANR 1, 37,
57, 87, 128; CN 7; CSW; DAM NOV;
DLB 2, 218, 278; EWL 3; INT CANR-
37; NFS 18

Price, Richard 1949- .... CLC 6, 12
See also CA 49-52; CANR 3; DLBY 1981

Prichard, Katharine Susannah
1883-1969 .... CLC 46
See also CA 11-12; CANR 33; CAP 1; DLB
260; MTCW 1; RGEL 2; RGSF 2; SATA
66

Priestley, J(ohn) B(oynton)
1894-1984 .... CLC 2, 5, 9, 34
See also BRW 7; CA 9-12R; 113; CANR
33; CDBLB 1914-1945; DA3; DAM
DRAM, NOV; DLB 10, 34, 77, 100, 139;
DLBY 1984; EWL 3; MTCW 1, 2; RGEL
2; SFW 4

Prince 1958- .... CLC 35
See also CA 213

Prince, F(rank) T(empleton)
1912-2003 .... CLC 22
See also CA 101; 219; CANR 43, 79; CP 7;
DLB 20

Prince Kropotkin
See Kropotkin, Peter (Alekseievich)

Prior, Matthew 1664-1721 .... LC 4
See also DLB 95; RGEL 2

Prishvin, Mikhail 1873-1954 .... TCLC 75
See Prishvin, Mikhail Mikhailovich

Prishvin, Mikhail Mikhailovich
See Prishvin, Mikhail
See also DLB 272; EWL 3

Pritchard, William H(arrison)
1932- .... CLC 34
See also CA 65-68; CANR 23, 95; DLB
111

Pritchett, V(ictor) S(awdon)
1900-1997 ... CLC 5, 13, 15, 41; SSC 14
See also BPFB 3; BRWS 3; CA 61-64; 157;
CANR 31, 63; CN 7; DA3; DAM NOV;
DLB 15, 139; EWL 3; MTCW 1, 2;
RGEL 2; RGSF 2; TEA

Private 19022
See Manning, Frederic

Probst, Mark 1925- .... CLC 59
See also CA 130

Prokosch, Frederic 1908-1989 ...... CLC 4, 48
See also CA 73-76; 128; CANR 82; DLB
48; MTCW 2

Propertius, Sextus c. 50B.C.-c.
16B.C. .... CMLC 32
See also AW 2; CDWLB 1; DLB 211;
RGWL 2, 3

Prophet, The
See Dreiser, Theodore (Herman Albert)

Prose, Francine 1947- .... CLC 45
See also CA 109; 112; CANR 46, 95, 132;
DLB 234; SATA 101, 149

Proudhon
See Cunha, Euclides (Rodrigues Pimenta)
da

Proulx, Annie
See Proulx, E(dna) Annie

Proulx, E(dna) Annie 1935- ...... CLC 81, 158
See also AMWS 7; BPFB 3; CA 145;
CANR 65, 110; CN 7; CPW 1; DA3;
DAM POP; MTCW 2; SSFS 18

Proust, (Valentin-Louis-George-Eugene)
Marcel 1871-1922 ..... SSC 75; TCLC 7,
13, 33; WLC
See also AAYA 58; BPFB 3; CA 104; 120;
CANR 110; DA; DA3; DAB; DAC; DAM
MST, NOV; DLB 65; EW 8; EWL 3; GFL
1789 to the Present; MTCW 1, 2; RGWL
2, 3; TWA

Prowler, Harley
See Masters, Edgar Lee

Prus, Boleslaw 1845-1912 .... TCLC 48
See also RGWL 2, 3

Pryor, Richard (Franklin Lenox Thomas)
1940- .... CLC 26
See also CA 122; 152

Przybyszewski, Stanislaw
1868-1927 .... TCLC 36
See also CA 160; DLB 66; EWL 3

Pteleon
See Grieve, C(hristopher) M(urray)
See also DAM POET

Puckett, Lute
See Masters, Edgar Lee

Puig, Manuel 1932-1990 .... CLC 3, 5, 10, 28,
65, 133; HLC 2
See also BPFB 3; CA 45-48; CANR 2, 32,
63; CDWLB 3; DA3; DAM MULT; DLB
113; DNFS 1; EWL 3; GLL 1; HW 1, 2;
LAW; MTCW 1, 2; RGWL 2, 3; TWA;
WLIT 1

Pulitzer, Joseph 1847-1911 .... TCLC 76
See also CA 114; DLB 23

Purchas, Samuel 1577(?)-1626 .... LC 70
See also DLB 151

Purdy, A(lfred) W(ellington)
1918-2000 .... CLC 3, 6, 14, 50
See also CA 81-84; 189; CAAS 17; CANR
42, 66; CP 7; DAC; DAM MST, POET;
DLB 88; PFS 5; RGEL 2

Purdy, James (Amos) 1923- .... **CLC 2, 4, 10, 28, 52**
See also AMWS 7; CA 33-36R; CAAS 1; CANR 19, 51, 132; CN 7; DLB 2, 218; EWL 3; INT CANR-19; MTCW 1; RGAL 4

Pure, Simon
See Swinnerton, Frank Arthur

Pushkin, Aleksandr Sergeevich
See Pushkin, Alexander (Sergeyevich)
See also DLB 205

Pushkin, Alexander (Sergeyevich)
1799-1837 .... **NCLC 3, 27, 83; PC 10; SSC 27, 55; WLC**
See Pushkin, Aleksandr Sergeevich
See also DA; DA3; DAB; DAC; DAM DRAM, MST, POET; EW 5; EXPS; RGSF 2; RGWL 2, 3; SATA 61; SSFS 9; TWA

P'u Sung-ling 1640-1715 .... **LC 49; SSC 31**

Putnam, Arthur Lee
See Alger, Horatio, Jr.

Puzo, Mario 1920-1999 .... **CLC 1, 2, 6, 36, 107**
See also BPFB 3; CA 65-68; 185; CANR 4, 42, 65, 99, 131; CN 7; CPW; DA3; DAM NOV, POP; DLB 6; MTCW 1, 2; NFS 16; RGAL 4

Pygge, Edward
See Barnes, Julian (Patrick)

Pyle, Ernest Taylor 1900-1945
See Pyle, Ernie
See also CA 115; 160

Pyle, Ernie .... **TCLC 75**
See Pyle, Ernest Taylor
See also DLB 29; MTCW 2

Pyle, Howard 1853-1911 .... **TCLC 81**
See also AAYA 57; BYA 2, 4; CA 109; 137; CLR 22; DLB 42, 188; DLBD 13; LAIT 1; MAICYA 1, 2; SATA 16, 100; WCH; YAW

Pym, Barbara (Mary Crampton)
1913-1980 .... **CLC 13, 19, 37, 111**
See also BPFB 3; BRWS 2; CA 13-14; 97-100; CANR 13, 34; CAP 1; DLB 14, 207; DLBY 1987; EWL 3; MTCW 1, 2; RGEL 2; TEA

Pynchon, Thomas (Ruggles, Jr.)
1937- ...... **CLC 2, 3, 6, 9, 11, 18, 33, 62, 72, 123, 192; SSC 14; WLC**
See also AMWS 2; BEST 90:2; BPFB 3; CA 17-20R; CANR 22, 46, 73; CN 7; CPW 1; DA; DA3; DAB; DAC; DAM MST, NOV, POP; DLB 2, 173; EWL 3; MTCW 1, 2; RGAL 4; SFW 4; TUS

Pythagoras c. 582B.C.-c. 507B.C. . **CMLC 22**
See also DLB 176

Q
See Quiller-Couch, Sir Arthur (Thomas)

Qian, Chongzhu
See Ch'ien, Chung-shu

Qian, Sima 145B.C.-c. 89B.C. .... **CMLC 72**

Qian Zhongshu
See Ch'ien, Chung-shu
See also CWW 2

Qroll
See Dagerman, Stig (Halvard)

Quarrington, Paul (Lewis) 1953- ..... **CLC 65**
See also CA 129; CANR 62, 95

Quasimodo, Salvatore 1901-1968 .... **CLC 10; PC 47**
See also CA 13-16; 25-28R; CAP 1; DLB 114; EW 12; EWL 3; MTCW 1; RGWL 2, 3

Quatermass, Martin
See Carpenter, John (Howard)

Quay, Stephen 1947- .... **CLC 95**
See also CA 189

Quay, Timothy 1947- .... **CLC 95**
See also CA 189

Queen, Ellery .... **CLC 3, 11**
See Dannay, Frederic; Davidson, Avram (James); Deming, Richard; Fairman, Paul W.; Flora, Fletcher; Hoch, Edward D(entinger); Kane, Henry; Lee, Manfred B(ennington); Marlowe, Stephen; Powell, (Oval) Talmage; Sheldon, Walter J(ames); Sturgeon, Theodore (Hamilton); Tracy, Don(ald Fiske); Vance, John Holbrook
See also BPFB 3; CMW 4; MSW; RGAL 4

Queen, Ellery, Jr.
See Dannay, Frederic; Lee, Manfred B(ennington)

Queneau, Raymond 1903-1976 ..... **CLC 2, 5, 10, 42**
See also CA 77-80; 69-72; CANR 32; DLB 72, 258; EW 12; EWL 3; GFL 1789 to the Present; MTCW 1, 2; RGWL 2, 3

Quevedo, Francisco de 1580-1645 .... **LC 23**

Quiller-Couch, Sir Arthur (Thomas)
1863-1944 .... **TCLC 53**
See also CA 118; 166; DLB 135, 153, 190; HGG; RGEL 2; SUFW 1

Quin, Ann (Marie) 1936-1973 .... **CLC 6**
See also CA 9-12R; 45-48; DLB 14, 231

Quincey, Thomas de
See De Quincey, Thomas

Quindlen, Anna 1953- .... **CLC 191**
See also AAYA 35; CA 138; CANR 73, 126; DA3; DLB 292; MTCW 2

Quinn, Martin
See Smith, Martin Cruz

Quinn, Peter 1947- .... **CLC 91**
See also CA 197

Quinn, Simon
See Smith, Martin Cruz

Quintana, Leroy V. 1944- ...... **HLC 2; PC 36**
See also CA 131; CANR 65; DAM MULT; DLB 82; HW 1, 2

Quiroga, Horacio (Sylvestre)
1878-1937 .... **HLC 2; TCLC 20**
See also CA 117; 131; DAM MULT; EWL 3; HW 1; LAW; MTCW 1; RGSF 2; WLIT 1

Quoirez, Francoise 1935- .... **CLC 9**
See Sagan, Francoise
See also CA 49-52; CANR 6, 39, 73; MTCW 1, 2; TWA

Raabe, Wilhelm (Karl) 1831-1910 . **TCLC 45**
See also CA 167; DLB 129

Rabe, David (William) 1940- .. **CLC 4, 8, 33; DC 16**
See also CA 85-88; CABS 3; CAD; CANR 59, 129; CD 5; DAM DRAM; DFS 3, 8, 13; DLB 7, 228; EWL 3

Rabelais, Francois 1494-1553 .... **LC 5, 60; WLC**
See also DA; DAB; DAC; DAM MST; EW 2; GFL Beginnings to 1789; LMFS 1; RGWL 2, 3; TWA

Rabinovitch, Sholem 1859-1916
See Aleichem, Sholom
See also CA 104

Rabinyan, Dorit 1972- .... **CLC 119**
See also CA 170

Rachilde
See Vallette, Marguerite Eymery; Vallette, Marguerite Eymery
See also EWL 3

Racine, Jean 1639-1699 .... **LC 28**
See also DA3; DAB; DAM MST; DLB 268; EW 3; GFL Beginnings to 1789; LMFS 1; RGWL 2, 3; TWA

Radcliffe, Ann (Ward) 1764-1823 ... **NCLC 6, 55, 106**
See also DLB 39, 178; HGG; LMFS 1; RGEL 2; SUFW 1; WLIT 3

Radclyffe-Hall, Marguerite
See Hall, (Marguerite) Radclyffe

Radiguet, Raymond 1903-1923 ...... **TCLC 29**
See also CA 162; DLB 65; EWL 3; GFL 1789 to the Present; RGWL 2, 3

Radnoti, Miklos 1909-1944 .... **TCLC 16**
See also CA 118; 212; CDWLB 4; DLB 215; EWL 3; RGWL 2, 3

Rado, James 1939- .... **CLC 17**
See also CA 105

Radvanyi, Netty 1900-1983
See Seghers, Anna
See also CA 85-88; 110; CANR 82

Rae, Ben
See Griffiths, Trevor

Raeburn, John (Hay) 1941- .... **CLC 34**
See also CA 57-60

Ragni, Gerome 1942-1991 .... **CLC 17**
See also CA 105; 134

Rahv, Philip .... **CLC 24**
See Greenberg, Ivan
See also DLB 137

Raimund, Ferdinand Jakob
1790-1836 .... **NCLC 69**
See also DLB 90

Raine, Craig (Anthony) 1944- .. **CLC 32, 103**
See also CA 108; CANR 29, 51, 103; CP 7; DLB 40; PFS 7

Raine, Kathleen (Jessie) 1908-2003 .. **CLC 7, 45**
See also CA 85-88; 218; CANR 46, 109; CP 7; DLB 20; EWL 3; MTCW 1; RGEL 2

Rainis, Janis 1865-1929 .... **TCLC 29**
See also CA 170; CDWLB 4; DLB 220; EWL 3

Rakosi, Carl .... **CLC 47**
See Rawley, Callman
See also CA 228; CAAS 5; CP 7; DLB 193

Ralegh, Sir Walter
See Raleigh, Sir Walter
See also BRW 1; RGEL 2; WP

Raleigh, Richard
See Lovecraft, H(oward) P(hillips)

Raleigh, Sir Walter 1554(?)-1618 .... **LC 31, 39; PC 31**
See Ralegh, Sir Walter
See also CDBLB Before 1660; DLB 172; EXPP; PFS 14; TEA

Rallentando, H. P.
See Sayers, Dorothy L(eigh)

Ramal, Walter
See de la Mare, Walter (John)

Ramana Maharshi 1879-1950 .... **TCLC 84**

Ramoacn y Cajal, Santiago
1852-1934 .... **TCLC 93**

Ramon, Juan
See Jimenez (Mantecon), Juan Ramon

Ramos, Graciliano 1892-1953 .... **TCLC 32**
See also CA 167; DLB 307; EWL 3; HW 2; LAW; WLIT 1

Rampersad, Arnold 1941- .... **CLC 44**
See also BW 2, 3; CA 127; 133; CANR 81; DLB 111; INT CA-133

Rampling, Anne
See Rice, Anne
See also GLL 2

Ramsay, Allan 1686(?)-1758 .... **LC 29**
See also DLB 95; RGEL 2

Ramsay, Jay
See Campbell, (John) Ramsey

Ramuz, Charles-Ferdinand
1878-1947 .... **TCLC 33**
See also CA 165; EWL 3

Rand, Ayn 1905-1982 ...... **CLC 3, 30, 44, 79; WLC**
See also AAYA 10; AMWS 4; BPFB 3; BYA 12; CA 13-16R; 105; CANR 27, 73; CDALBS; CPW; DA; DA3; DAC; DAM MST, NOV, POP; DLB 227, 279; MTCW 1, 2; NFS 10, 16; RGAL 4; SFW 4; TUS; YAW

Randall, Dudley (Felker) 1914-2000 . **BLC 3; CLC 1, 135**
See also BW 1, 3; CA 25-28R; 189; CANR 23, 82; DAM MULT; DLB 41; PFS 5

Randall, Robert
See Silverberg, Robert

Ranger, Ken
See Creasey, John

Rank, Otto 1884-1939 .... **TCLC 115**

Ransom, John Crowe 1888-1974 .. **CLC 2, 4, 5, 11, 24; PC 61**
See also AMW; CA 5-8R; 49-52; CANR 6, 34; CDALBS; DA3; DAM POET; DLB 45, 63; EWL 3; EXPP; MTCW 1, 2; RGAL 4; TUS

Rao, Raja 1909- .... **CLC 25, 56**
See also CA 73-76; CANR 51; CN 7; DAM NOV; EWL 3; MTCW 1, 2; RGEL 2; RGSF 2

Raphael, Frederic (Michael) 1931- ... **CLC 2, 14**
See also CA 1-4R; CANR 1, 86; CN 7; DLB 14

Ratcliffe, James P.
See Mencken, H(enry) L(ouis)

Rathbone, Julian 1935- .... **CLC 41**
See also CA 101; CANR 34, 73

Rattigan, Terence (Mervyn) 1911-1977 .... **CLC 7; DC 18**
See also BRWS 7; CA 85-88; 73-76; CBD; CDBLB 1945-1960; DAM DRAM; DFS 8; DLB 13; IDFW 3, 4; MTCW 1, 2; RGEL 2

Ratushinskaya, Irina 1954- .... **CLC 54**
See also CA 129; CANR 68; CWW 2

Raven, Simon (Arthur Noel) 1927-2001 .... **CLC 14**
See also CA 81-84; 197; CANR 86; CN 7; DLB 271

Ravenna, Michael
See Welty, Eudora (Alice)

Rawley, Callman 1903-2004
See Rakosi, Carl
See also CA 21-24R; CANR 12, 32, 91

Rawlings, Marjorie Kinnan 1896-1953 .... **TCLC 4**
See also AAYA 20; AMWS 10; ANW; BPFB 3; BYA 3; CA 104; 137; CANR 74; CLR 63; DLB 9, 22, 102; DLBD 17; JRDA; MAICYA 1, 2; MTCW 2; RGAL 4; SATA 100; WCH; YABC 1; YAW

Ray, Satyajit 1921-1992 .... **CLC 16, 76**
See also CA 114; 137; DAM MULT

Read, Herbert Edward 1893-1968 ..... **CLC 4**
See also BRW 6; CA 85-88; 25-28R; DLB 20, 149; EWL 3; PAB; RGEL 2

Read, Piers Paul 1941- .... **CLC 4, 10, 25**
See also CA 21-24R; CANR 38, 86; CN 7; DLB 14; SATA 21

Reade, Charles 1814-1884 .... **NCLC 2, 74**
See also DLB 21; RGEL 2

Reade, Hamish
See Gray, Simon (James Holliday)

Reading, Peter 1946- .... **CLC 47**
See also BRWS 8; CA 103; CANR 46, 96; CP 7; DLB 40

Reaney, James 1926- .... **CLC 13**
See also CA 41-44R; CAAS 15; CANR 42; CD 5; CP 7; DAC; DAM MST; DLB 68; RGEL 2; SATA 43

Rebreanu, Liviu 1885-1944 .... **TCLC 28**
See also CA 165; DLB 220; EWL 3

Rechy, John (Francisco) 1934- ...... **CLC 1, 7, 14, 18, 107; HLC 2**
See also CA 5-8R, 195; CAAE 195; CAAS 4; CANR 6, 32, 64; CN 7; DAM MULT; DLB 122, 278; DLBY 1982; HW 1, 2; INT CANR-6; LLW 1; RGAL 4

Redcam, Tom 1870-1933 .... **TCLC 25**

Reddin, Keith .... **CLC 67**
See also CAD

Redgrove, Peter (William) 1932-2003 .... **CLC 6, 41**
See also BRWS 6; CA 1-4R; 217; CANR 3, 39, 77; CP 7; DLB 40

Redmon, Anne .... **CLC 22**
See Nightingale, Anne Redmon
See also DLBY 1986

Reed, Eliot
See Ambler, Eric

Reed, Ishmael 1938- ..... **BLC 3; CLC 2, 3, 5, 6, 13, 32, 60, 174**
See also AFAW 1, 2; AMWS 10; BPFB 3; BW 2, 3; CA 21-24R; CANR 25, 48, 74, 128; CN 7; CP 7; CSW; DA3; DAM MULT; DLB 2, 5, 33, 169, 227; DLBD 8; EWL 3; LMFS 2; MSW; MTCW 1, 2; PFS 6; RGAL 4; TCWW 2

Reed, John (Silas) 1887-1920 .... **TCLC 9**
See also CA 106; 195; TUS

Reed, Lou .... **CLC 21**
See Firbank, Louis

Reese, Lizette Woodworth 1856-1935 . **PC 29**
See also CA 180; DLB 54

Reeve, Clara 1729-1807 .... **NCLC 19**
See also DLB 39; RGEL 2

Reich, Wilhelm 1897-1957 .... **TCLC 57**
See also CA 199

Reid, Christopher (John) 1949- .... **CLC 33**
See also CA 140; CANR 89; CP 7; DLB 40; EWL 3

Reid, Desmond
See Moorcock, Michael (John)

Reid Banks, Lynne 1929-
See Banks, Lynne Reid
See also AAYA 49; CA 1-4R; CANR 6, 22, 38, 87; CLR 24; CN 7; JRDA; MAICYA 1, 2; SATA 22, 75, 111; YAW

Reilly, William K.
See Creasey, John

Reiner, Max
See Caldwell, (Janet Miriam) Taylor (Holland)

Reis, Ricardo
See Pessoa, Fernando (Antonio Nogueira)

Reizenstein, Elmer Leopold
See Rice, Elmer (Leopold)
See also EWL 3

Remarque, Erich Maria 1898-1970 . **CLC 21**
See also AAYA 27; BPFB 3; CA 77-80; 29-32R; CDWLB 2; DA; DA3; DAB; DAC; DAM MST, NOV; DLB 56; EWL 3; EXPN; LAIT 3; MTCW 1, 2; NFS 4; RGWL 2, 3

Remington, Frederic 1861-1909 ..... **TCLC 89**
See also CA 108; 169; DLB 12, 186, 188; SATA 41

Remizov, A.
See Remizov, Aleksei (Mikhailovich)

Remizov, A. M.
See Remizov, Aleksei (Mikhailovich)

Remizov, Aleksei (Mikhailovich) 1877-1957 .... **TCLC 27**
See Remizov, Alexey Mikhaylovich
See also CA 125; 133; DLB 295

Remizov, Alexey Mikhaylovich
See Remizov, Aleksei (Mikhailovich)
See also EWL 3

Renan, Joseph Ernest 1823-1892 . **NCLC 26, 145**
See also GFL 1789 to the Present

Renard, Jules(-Pierre) 1864-1910 .. **TCLC 17**
See also CA 117; 202; GFL 1789 to the Present

Renault, Mary .... **CLC 3, 11, 17**
See Challans, Mary
See also BPFB 3; BYA 2; DLBY 1983; EWL 3; GLL 1; LAIT 1; MTCW 2; RGEL 2; RHW

Rendell, Ruth (Barbara) 1930- .. **CLC 28, 48**
See Vine, Barbara
See also BPFB 3; BRWS 9; CA 109; CANR 32, 52, 74, 127; CN 7; CPW; DAM POP; DLB 87, 276; INT CANR-32; MSW; MTCW 1, 2

Renoir, Jean 1894-1979 .... **CLC 20**
See also CA 129; 85-88

Resnais, Alain 1922- .... **CLC 16**

Revard, Carter (Curtis) 1931- .... **NNAL**
See also CA 144; CANR 81; PFS 5

Reverdy, Pierre 1889-1960 .... **CLC 53**
See also CA 97-100; 89-92; DLB 258; EWL 3; GFL 1789 to the Present

Rexroth, Kenneth 1905-1982 .... **CLC 1, 2, 6, 11, 22, 49, 112; PC 20**
See also BG 3; CA 5-8R; 107; CANR 14, 34, 63; CDALB 1941-1968; DAM POET; DLB 16, 48, 165, 212; DLBY 1982; EWL 3; INT CANR-14; MTCW 1, 2; RGAL 4

Reyes, Alfonso 1889-1959 .... **HLCS 2; TCLC 33**
See also CA 131; EWL 3; HW 1; LAW

Reyes y Basoalto, Ricardo Eliecer Neftali
See Neruda, Pablo

Reymont, Wladyslaw (Stanislaw) 1868(?)-1925 .... **TCLC 5**
See also CA 104; EWL 3

Reynolds, John Hamilton 1794-1852 .... **NCLC 146**
See also DLB 96

Reynolds, Jonathan 1942- .... **CLC 6, 38**
See also CA 65-68; CANR 28

Reynolds, Joshua 1723-1792 .... **LC 15**
See also DLB 104

Reynolds, Michael S(hane) 1937-2000 .... **CLC 44**
See also CA 65-68; 189; CANR 9, 89, 97

Reznikoff, Charles 1894-1976 .... **CLC 9**
See also AMWS 14; CA 33-36; 61-64; CAP 2; DLB 28, 45; WP

Rezzori (d'Arezzo), Gregor von 1914-1998 .... **CLC 25**
See also CA 122; 136; 167

Rhine, Richard
See Silverstein, Alvin; Silverstein, Virginia B(arbara Opshelor)

Rhodes, Eugene Manlove 1869-1934 .... **TCLC 53**
See also CA 198; DLB 256

R'hoone, Lord
See Balzac, Honore de

Rhys, Jean 1890-1979 .... **CLC 2, 4, 6, 14, 19, 51, 124; SSC 21, 76**
See also BRWS 2; CA 25-28R; 85-88; CANR 35, 62; CDBLB 1945-1960; CD-WLB 3; DA3; DAM NOV; DLB 36, 117, 162; DNFS 2; EWL 3; LATS 1:1; MTCW 1, 2; RGEL 2; RGSF 2; RHW; TEA; WWE 1

Ribeiro, Darcy 1922-1997 .... **CLC 34**
See also CA 33-36R; 156; EWL 3

Ribeiro, Joao Ubaldo (Osorio Pimentel) 1941- .... **CLC 10, 67**
See also CA 81-84; CWW 2; EWL 3

Ribman, Ronald (Burt) 1932- .... **CLC 7**
See also CA 21-24R; CAD; CANR 46, 80; CD 5

Ricci, Nino (Pio) 1959- .... **CLC 70**
See also CA 137; CANR 130; CCA 1

Robinson, Lloyd
See Silverberg, Robert

Robinson, Marilynne 1944- ...... **CLC 25, 180**
See also CA 116; CANR 80; CN 7; DLB 206

Robinson, Mary 1758-1800 .... **NCLC 142**
See also DLB 158; FW

Robinson, Smokey .... **CLC 21**
See Robinson, William, Jr.

Robinson, William, Jr. 1940-
See Robinson, Smokey
See also CA 116

Robison, Mary 1949- .... **CLC 42, 98**
See also CA 113; 116; CANR 87; CN 7; DLB 130; INT CA-116; RGSF 2

Rochester
See Wilmot, John
See also RGEL 2

Rod, Edouard 1857-1910 .... **TCLC 52**

Roddenberry, Eugene Wesley 1921-1991
See Roddenberry, Gene
See also CA 110; 135; CANR 37; SATA 45; SATA-Obit 69

Roddenberry, Gene .... **CLC 17**
See Roddenberry, Eugene Wesley
See also AAYA 5; SATA-Obit 69

Rodgers, Mary 1931- .... **CLC 12**
See also BYA 5; CA 49-52; CANR 8, 55, 90; CLR 20; CWRI 5; INT CANR-8; JRDA; MAICYA 1, 2; SATA 8, 130

Rodgers, W(illiam) R(obert)
1909-1969 .... **CLC 7**
See also CA 85-88; DLB 20; RGEL 2

Rodman, Eric
See Silverberg, Robert

Rodman, Howard 1920(?)-1985 .... **CLC 65**
See also CA 118

Rodman, Maia
See Wojciechowska, Maia (Teresa)

Rodo, Jose Enrique 1871(?)-1917 .... **HLCS 2**
See also CA 178; EWL 3; HW 2; LAW

Rodolph, Utto
See Ouologuem, Yambo

Rodriguez, Claudio 1934-1999 .... **CLC 10**
See also CA 188; DLB 134

Rodriguez, Richard 1944- .... **CLC 155; HLC 2**
See also AMWS 14; CA 110; CANR 66, 116; DAM MULT; DLB 82, 256; HW 1, 2; LAIT 5; LLW 1; NCFS 3; WLIT 1

Roelvaag, O(le) E(dvart) 1876-1931
See Rolvaag, O(le) E(dvart)
See also CA 117; 171

Roethke, Theodore (Huebner)
1908-1963 .... **CLC 1, 3, 8, 11, 19, 46, 101; PC 15**
See also AMW; CA 81-84; CABS 2; CDALB 1941-1968; DA3; DAM POET; DLB 5, 206; EWL 3; EXPP; MTCW 1, 2; PAB; PFS 3; RGAL 4; WP

Rogers, Carl R(ansom)
1902-1987 .... **TCLC 125**
See also CA 1-4R; 121; CANR 1, 18; MTCW 1

Rogers, Samuel 1763-1855 .... **NCLC 69**
See also DLB 93; RGEL 2

Rogers, Thomas Hunton 1927- .... **CLC 57**
See also CA 89-92; INT CA-89-92

Rogers, Will(iam Penn Adair)
1879-1935 .... **NNAL; TCLC 8, 71**
See also CA 105; 144; DA3; DAM MULT; DLB 11; MTCW 2

Rogin, Gilbert 1929- .... **CLC 18**
See also CA 65-68; CANR 15

Rohan, Koda
See Koda Shigeyuki

Rohlfs, Anna Katharine Green
See Green, Anna Katharine

Rohmer, Eric .... **CLC 16**
See Scherer, Jean-Marie Maurice

Rohmer, Sax .... **TCLC 28**
See Ward, Arthur Henry Sarsfield
See also DLB 70; MSW; SUFW

Roiphe, Anne (Richardson) 1935- .. **CLC 3, 9**
See also CA 89-92; CANR 45, 73; DLBY 1980; INT CA-89-92

Rojas, Fernando de 1475-1541 ... **HLCS 1, 2; LC 23**
See also DLB 286; RGWL 2, 3

Rojas, Gonzalo 1917- .... **HLCS 2**
See also CA 178; HW 2; LAWS 1

Roland, Marie-Jeanne 1754-1793 .... **LC 98**

Rolfe, Frederick (William Serafino Austin Lewis Mary) 1860-1913 .... **TCLC 12**
See Al Siddik
See also CA 107; 210; DLB 34, 156; RGEL 2

Rolland, Romain 1866-1944 .... **TCLC 23**
See also CA 118; 197; DLB 65, 284; EWL 3; GFL 1789 to the Present; RGWL 2, 3

Rolle, Richard c. 1300-c. 1349 ...... **CMLC 21**
See also DLB 146; LMFS 1; RGEL 2

Rolvaag, O(le) E(dvart) .... **TCLC 17**
See Roelvaag, O(le) E(dvart)
See also DLB 9, 212; NFS 5; RGAL 4

Romain Arnaud, Saint
See Aragon, Louis

Romains, Jules 1885-1972 .... **CLC 7**
See also CA 85-88; CANR 34; DLB 65; EWL 3; GFL 1789 to the Present; MTCW 1

Romero, Jose Ruben 1890-1952 .... **TCLC 14**
See also CA 114; 131; EWL 3; HW 1; LAW

Ronsard, Pierre de 1524-1585 . **LC 6, 54; PC 11**
See also EW 2; GFL Beginnings to 1789; RGWL 2, 3; TWA

Rooke, Leon 1934- .... **CLC 25, 34**
See also CA 25-28R; CANR 23, 53; CCA 1; CPW; DAM POP

Roosevelt, Franklin Delano
1882-1945 .... **TCLC 93**
See also CA 116; 173; LAIT 3

Roosevelt, Theodore 1858-1919 ..... **TCLC 69**
See also CA 115; 170; DLB 47, 186, 275

Roper, William 1498-1578 .... **LC 10**

Roquelaure, A. N.
See Rice, Anne

Rosa, Joao Guimaraes 1908-1967 ... **CLC 23; HLCS 1**
See Guimaraes Rosa, Joao
See also CA 89-92; DLB 113, 307; EWL 3; WLIT 1

Rose, Wendy 1948- . **CLC 85; NNAL; PC 13**
See also CA 53-56; CANR 5, 51; CWP; DAM MULT; DLB 175; PFS 13; RGAL 4; SATA 12

Rosen, R. D.
See Rosen, Richard (Dean)

Rosen, Richard (Dean) 1949- .... **CLC 39**
See also CA 77-80; CANR 62, 120; CMW 4; INT CANR-30

Rosenberg, Isaac 1890-1918 .... **TCLC 12**
See also BRW 6; CA 107; 188; DLB 20, 216; EWL 3; PAB; RGEL 2

Rosenblatt, Joe .... **CLC 15**
See Rosenblatt, Joseph

Rosenblatt, Joseph 1933-
See Rosenblatt, Joe
See also CA 89-92; CP 7; INT CA-89-92

Rosenfeld, Samuel
See Tzara, Tristan

Rosenstock, Sami
See Tzara, Tristan

Rosenstock, Samuel
See Tzara, Tristan

Rosenthal, M(acha) L(ouis)
1917-1996 .... **CLC 28**
See also CA 1-4R; 152; CAAS 6; CANR 4, 51; CP 7; DLB 5; SATA 59

Ross, Barnaby
See Dannay, Frederic

Ross, Bernard L.
See Follett, Ken(neth Martin)

Ross, J. H.
See Lawrence, T(homas) E(dward)

Ross, John Hume
See Lawrence, T(homas) E(dward)

Ross, Martin 1862-1915
See Martin, Violet Florence
See also DLB 135; GLL 2; RGEL 2; RGSF 2

Ross, (James) Sinclair 1908-1996 ... **CLC 13; SSC 24**
See also CA 73-76; CANR 81; CN 7; DAC; DAM MST; DLB 88; RGEL 2; RGSF 2; TCWW 2

Rossetti, Christina (Georgina)
1830-1894 .... **NCLC 2, 50, 66; PC 7; WLC**
See also AAYA 51; BRW 5; BYA 4; DA; DA3; DAB; DAC; DAM MST, POET; DLB 35, 163, 240; EXPP; LATS 1:1; MAICYA 1, 2; PFS 10, 14; RGEL 2; SATA 20; TEA; WCH

Rossetti, Dante Gabriel 1828-1882 . **NCLC 4, 77; PC 44; WLC**
See also AAYA 51; BRW 5; CDBLB 1832-1890; DA; DAB; DAC; DAM MST, POET; DLB 35; EXPP; RGEL 2; TEA

Rossi, Cristina Peri
See Peri Rossi, Cristina

Rossi, Jean-Baptiste 1931-2003
See Japrisot, Sebastien
See also CA 201; 215

Rossner, Judith (Perelman) 1935- . **CLC 6, 9, 29**
See also AITN 2; BEST 90:3; BPFB 3; CA 17-20R; CANR 18, 51, 73; CN 7; DLB 6; INT CANR-18; MTCW 1, 2

Rostand, Edmond (Eugene Alexis)
1868-1918 .... **DC 10; TCLC 6, 37**
See also CA 104; 126; DA; DA3; DAB; DAC; DAM DRAM, MST; DFS 1; DLB 192; LAIT 1; MTCW 1; RGWL 2, 3; TWA

Roth, Henry 1906-1995 ..... **CLC 2, 6, 11, 104**
See also AMWS 9; CA 11-12; 149; CANR 38, 63; CAP 1; CN 7; DA3; DLB 28; EWL 3; MTCW 1, 2; RGAL 4

Roth, (Moses) Joseph 1894-1939 ... **TCLC 33**
See also CA 160; DLB 85; EWL 3; RGWL 2, 3

Roth, Philip (Milton) 1933- ... **CLC 1, 2, 3, 4, 6, 9, 15, 22, 31, 47, 66, 86, 119; SSC 26; WLC**
See also AMWR 2; AMWS 3; BEST 90:3; BPFB 3; CA 1-4R; CANR 1, 22, 36, 55, 89, 132; CDALB 1968-1988; CN 7; CPW 1; DA; DA3; DAB; DAC; DAM MST, NOV, POP; DLB 2, 28, 173; DLBY 1982; EWL 3; MTCW 1, 2; RGAL 4; RGSF 2; SSFS 12, 18; TUS

Rothenberg, Jerome 1931- .... **CLC 6, 57**
See also CA 45-48; CANR 1, 106; CP 7; DLB 5, 193

Rotter, Pat ed. .... **CLC 65**

Roumain, Jacques (Jean Baptiste)
1907-1944 .... **BLC 3; TCLC 19**
See also BW 1; CA 117; 125; DAM MULT; EWL 3

Rourke, Constance Mayfield
1885-1941 .... **TCLC 12**
See also CA 107; 200; YABC 1

Sahgal, Nayantara (Pandit) 1927- .... CLC 41
  See also CA 9-12R; CANR 11, 88; CN 7
Said, Edward W. 1935-2003 .... CLC 123
  See also CA 21-24R; 220; CANR 45, 74,
  107, 131; DLB 67; MTCW 2
Saint, H(arry) F. 1941- .... CLC 50
  See also CA 127
St. Aubin de Teran, Lisa 1953-
  See Teran, Lisa St. Aubin de
  See also CA 118; 126; CN 7; INT CA-126
Saint Birgitta of Sweden c.
  1303-1373 .... CMLC 24
Sainte-Beuve, Charles Augustin
  1804-1869 .... NCLC 5
  See also DLB 217; EW 6; GFL 1789 to the
  Present
Saint-Exupery, Antoine (Jean Baptiste
  Marie Roger) de 1900-1944 .... TCLC 2,
  56; WLC
  See also BPFB 3; BYA 3; CA 108; 132;
  CLR 10; DA3; DAM NOV; DLB 72; EW
  12; EWL 3; GFL 1789 to the Present;
  LAIT 3; MAICYA 1, 2; MTCW 1, 2;
  RGWL 2, 3; SATA 20; TWA
St. John, David
  See Hunt, E(verette) Howard, (Jr.)
St. John, J. Hector
  See Crevecoeur, Michel Guillaume Jean de
Saint-John Perse
  See Leger, (Marie-Rene Auguste) Alexis
  Saint-Leger
  See also EW 10; EWL 3; GFL 1789 to the
  Present; RGWL 2
Saintsbury, George (Edward Bateman)
  1845-1933 .... TCLC 31
  See also CA 160; DLB 57, 149
Sait Faik .... TCLC 23
  See Abasiyanik, Sait Faik
Saki .... SSC 12; TCLC 3
  See Munro, H(ector) H(ugh)
  See also BRWS 6; BYA 11; LAIT 2; MTCW
  2; RGEL 2; SSFS 1; SUFW
Sala, George Augustus 1828-1895 . NCLC 46
Saladin 1138-1193 .... CMLC 38
Salama, Hannu 1936- .... CLC 18
  See also EWL 3
Salamanca, J(ack) R(ichard) 1922- .. CLC 4,
  15
  See also CA 25-28R, 193; CAAE 193
Salas, Floyd Francis 1931- .... HLC 2
  See also CA 119; CAAS 27; CANR 44, 75,
  93; DAM MULT; DLB 82; HW 1, 2;
  MTCW 2
Sale, J. Kirkpatrick
  See Sale, Kirkpatrick
Sale, Kirkpatrick 1937- .... CLC 68
  See also CA 13-16R; CANR 10
Salinas, Luis Omar 1937- ... CLC 90; HLC 2
  See also AMWS 13; CA 131; CANR 81;
  DAM MULT; DLB 82; HW 1, 2
Salinas (y Serrano), Pedro
  1891(?)-1951 .... TCLC 17
  See also CA 117; DLB 134; EWL 3
Salinger, J(erome) D(avid) 1919- .. CLC 1, 3,
  8, 12, 55, 56, 138; SSC 2, 28, 65; WLC
  See also AAYA 2, 36; AMW; AMWC 1;
  BPFB 3; CA 5-8R; CANR 39, 129;
  CDALB 1941-1968; CLR 18; CN 7; CPW
  1; DA; DA3; DAB; DAC; DAM MST,
  NOV, POP; DLB 2, 102, 173; EWL 3;
  EXPN; LAIT 4; MAICYA 1, 2; MTCW
  1, 2; NFS 1; RGAL 4; RGSF 2; SATA 67;
  SSFS 17; TUS; WYA; YAW
Salisbury, John
  See Caute, (John) David
Sallust c. 86B.C.-35B.C. .... CMLC 68
  See also AW 2; CDWLB 1; DLB 211;
  RGWL 2, 3

Salter, James 1925- .. CLC 7, 52, 59; SSC 58
  See also AMWS 9; CA 73-76; CANR 107;
  DLB 130
Saltus, Edgar (Everton) 1855-1921 . TCLC 8
  See also CA 105; DLB 202; RGAL 4
Saltykov, Mikhail Evgrafovich
  1826-1889 .... NCLC 16
  See also DLB 238:
Saltykov-Shchedrin, N.
  See Saltykov, Mikhail Evgrafovich
Samarakis, Andonis
  See Samarakis, Antonis
  See also EWL 3
Samarakis, Antonis 1919-2003 .... CLC 5
  See Samarakis, Andonis
  See also CA 25-28R; 224; CAAS 16; CANR
  36
Sanchez, Florencio 1875-1910 .... TCLC 37
  See also CA 153; DLB 305; EWL 3; HW 1;
  LAW
Sanchez, Luis Rafael 1936- .... CLC 23
  See also CA 128; DLB 305; EWL 3; HW 1;
  WLIT 1
Sanchez, Sonia 1934- .... BLC 3; CLC 5, 116;
  PC 9
  See also BW 2, 3; CA 33-36R; CANR 24,
  49, 74, 115; CLR 18; CP 7; DA3; DAM
  DA3; DAM MULT; DLB 41; DLBD 8;
  EWL 3; MAICYA 1, 2; MTCW 1, 2;
  SATA 22, 136; WP
Sancho, Ignatius 1729-1780 .... LC 84
Sand, George 1804-1876 ..... NCLC 2, 42, 57;
  WLC
  See also DA; DA3; DAB; DAC; DAM
  MST, NOV; DLB 119, 192; EW 6; FW;
  GFL 1789 to the Present; RGWL 2, 3;
  TWA
Sandburg, Carl (August) 1878-1967 . CLC 1,
  4, 10, 15, 35; PC 2, 41; WLC
  See also AAYA 24; AMW; BYA 1, 3; CA
  5-8R; 25-28R; CANR 35; CDALB 1865-
  1917; CLR 67; DA; DA3; DAB; DAC;
  DAM MST, POET; DLB 17, 54, 284;
  EWL 3; EXPP; LAIT 2; MAICYA 1, 2;
  MTCW 1, 2; PAB; PFS 3, 6, 12; RGAL
  4; SATA 8; TUS; WCH; WP; WYA
Sandburg, Charles
  See Sandburg, Carl (August)
Sandburg, Charles A.
  See Sandburg, Carl (August)
Sanders, (James) Ed(ward) 1939- .... CLC 53
  See Sanders, Edward
  See also BG 3; CA 13-16R; CAAS 21;
  CANR 13, 44, 78; CP 7; DAM POET;
  DLB 16, 244
Sanders, Edward
  See Sanders, (James) Ed(ward)
  See also DLB 244
Sanders, Lawrence 1920-1998 .... CLC 41
  See also BEST 89:4; BPFB 3; CA 81-84;
  165; CANR 33, 62; CMW 4; CPW; DA3;
  DAM POP; MTCW 1
Sanders, Noah
  See Blount, Roy (Alton), Jr.
Sanders, Winston P.
  See Anderson, Poul (William)
Sandoz, Mari(e Susette) 1900-1966 .. CLC 28
  See also CA 1-4R; 25-28R; CANR 17, 64;
  DLB 9, 212; LAIT 2; MTCW 1, 2; SATA
  5; TCWW 2
Sandys, George 1578-1644 .... LC 80
  See also DLB 24, 121
Saner, Reg(inald Anthony) 1931- .... CLC 9
  See also CA 65-68; CP 7
Sankara 788-820 .... CMLC 32
Sannazaro, Jacopo 1456(?)-1530 .... LC 8
  See also RGWL 2, 3

Sansom, William 1912-1976 . CLC 2, 6; SSC
  21
  See also CA 5-8R; 65-68; CANR 42; DAM
  NOV; DLB 139; EWL 3; MTCW 1;
  RGEL 2; RGSF 2
Santayana, George 1863-1952 .... TCLC 40
  See also AMW; CA 115; 194; DLB 54, 71,
  246, 270; DLBD 13; EWL 3; RGAL 4;
  TUS
Santiago, Danny .... CLC 33
  See James, Daniel (Lewis)
  See also DLB 122
Santillana, Íñigo López de Mendoza,
  Marqués de 1398-1458 .... LC 111
  See also DLB 286
Santmyer, Helen Hooven
  1895-1986 .... CLC 33; TCLC 133
  See also CA 1-4R; 118; CANR 15, 33;
  DLBY 1984; MTCW 1; RHW
Santoka, Taneda 1882-1940 .... TCLC 72
Santos, Bienvenido N(uqui)
  1911-1996 ... AAL; CLC 22; TCLC 156
  See also CA 101; 151; CANR 19, 46; DAM
  MULT; EWL; RGAL 4; SSFS 19
Sapir, Edward 1884-1939 .... TCLC 108
  See also CA 211; DLB 92
Sapper .... TCLC 44
  See McNeile, Herman Cyril
Sapphire
  See Sapphire, Brenda
Sapphire, Brenda 1950- .... CLC 99
Sappho fl. 6th cent. B.C.- ... CMLC 3, 67; PC
  5
  See also CDWLB 1; DA3; DAM POET;
  DLB 176; PFS 20; RGWL 2, 3; WP
Saramago, Jose 1922- ..... CLC 119; HLCS 1
  See also CA 153; CANR 96; CWW 2; DLB
  287; EWL 3; LATS 1:2
Sarduy, Severo 1937-1993 .... CLC 6, 97;
  HLCS 2
  See also CA 89-92; 142; CANR 58, 81;
  CWW 2; DLB 113; EWL 3; HW 1, 2;
  LAW
Sargeson, Frank 1903-1982 .... CLC 31
  See also CA 25-28R; 106; CANR 38, 79;
  EWL 3; GLL 2; RGEL 2; RGSF 2; SSFS
  20
Sarmiento, Domingo Faustino
  1811-1888 .... HLCS 2
  See also LAW; WLIT 1
Sarmiento, Felix Ruben Garcia
  See Dario, Ruben
Saro-Wiwa, Ken(ule Beeson)
  1941-1995 .... CLC 114
  See also BW 2; CA 142; 150; CANR 60;
  DLB 157
Saroyan, William 1908-1981 ... CLC 1, 8, 10,
  29, 34, 56; SSC 21; TCLC 137; WLC
  See also CA 5-8R; 103; CAD; CANR 30;
  CDALBS; DA; DA3; DAB; DAC; DAM
  DRAM, MST, NOV; DFS 17; DLB 7, 9,
  86; DLBY 1981; EWL 3; LAIT 4; MTCW
  1, 2; RGAL 4; RGSF 2; SATA 23; SATA-
  Obit 24; SSFS 14; TUS
Sarraute, Nathalie 1900-1999 .... CLC 1, 2, 4,
  8, 10, 31, 80; TCLC 145
  See also BPFB 3; CA 9-12R; 187; CANR
  23, 66, 134; CWW 2; DLB 83; EW 12;
  EWL 3; GFL 1789 to the Present; MTCW
  1, 2; RGWL 2, 3
Sarton, (Eleanor) May 1912-1995 ..... CLC 4,
  14, 49, 91; PC 39; TCLC 120
  See also AMWS 8; CA 1-4R; 149; CANR
  1, 34, 55, 116; CN 7; CP 7; DAM POET;
  DLB 48; DLBY 1981; EWL 3; FW; INT
  CANR-34; MTCW 1, 2; RGAL 4; SATA
  36; SATA-Obit 86; TUS

Sartre, Jean-Paul 1905-1980 . **CLC 1, 4, 7, 9, 13, 18, 24, 44, 50, 52; DC 3; SSC 32; WLC**
See also CA 9-12R; 97-100; CANR 21; DA; DA3; DAB; DAC; DAM DRAM, MST, NOV; DFS 5; DLB 72, 296; EW 12; EWL 3; GFL 1789 to the Present; LMFS 2; MTCW 1, 2; RGSF 2; RGWL 2, 3; SSFS 9; TWA

Sassoon, Siegfried (Lorraine) 1886-1967 .... **CLC 36, 130; PC 12**
See also BRW 6; CA 104; 25-28R; CANR 36; DAB; DAM MST, NOV, POET; DLB 20, 191; DLBD 18; EWL 3; MTCW 1, 2; PAB; RGEL 2; TEA

Satterfield, Charles
See Pohl, Frederik

Satyremont
See Peret, Benjamin

Saul, John (W. III) 1942- .... **CLC 46**
See also AAYA 10; BEST 90:4; CA 81-84; CANR 16, 40, 81; CPW; DAM NOV, POP; HGG; SATA 98

Saunders, Caleb
See Heinlein, Robert A(nson)

Saura (Atares), Carlos 1932-1998 .... **CLC 20**
See also CA 114; 131; CANR 79; HW 1

Sauser, Frederic Louis
See Sauser-Hall, Frederic

Sauser-Hall, Frederic 1887-1961 ...... **CLC 18**
See Cendrars, Blaise
See also CA 102; 93-96; CANR 36, 62; MTCW 1

Saussure, Ferdinand de 1857-1913 .... **TCLC 49**
See also DLB 242

Savage, Catharine
See Brosman, Catharine Savage

Savage, Richard 1697(?)-1743 .... **LC 96**
See also DLB 95; RGEL 2

Savage, Thomas 1915-2003 .... **CLC 40**
See also CA 126; 132; 218; CAAS 15; CN 7; INT CA-132; SATA-Obit 147; TCWW 2

Savan, Glenn 1953-2003 .... **CLC 50**
See also CA 225

Sax, Robert
See Johnson, Robert

Saxo Grammaticus c. 1150-c. 1222 .... **CMLC 58**

Saxton, Robert
See Johnson, Robert

Sayers, Dorothy L(eigh) 1893-1957 . **SSC 71; TCLC 2, 15**
See also BPFB 3; BRWS 3; CA 104; 119; CANR 60; CDBLB 1914-1945; CMW 4; DAM POP; DLB 10, 36, 77, 100; MSW; MTCW 1, 2; RGEL 2; SSFS 12; TEA

Sayers, Valerie 1952- .... **CLC 50, 122**
See also CA 134; CANR 61; CSW

Sayles, John (Thomas) 1950- .... **CLC 7, 10, 14, 198**
See also CA 57-60; CANR 41, 84; DLB 44

Scammell, Michael 1935- .... **CLC 34**
See also CA 156

Scannell, Vernon 1922- .... **CLC 49**
See also CA 5-8R; CANR 8, 24, 57; CP 7; CWRI 5; DLB 27; SATA 59

Scarlett, Susan
See Streatfeild, (Mary) Noel

Scarron 1847-1910
See Mikszath, Kalman

Schaeffer, Susan Fromberg 1941- ..... **CLC 6, 11, 22**
See also CA 49-52; CANR 18, 65; CN 7; DLB 28, 299; MTCW 1, 2; SATA 22

Schama, Simon (Michael) 1945- ..... **CLC 150**
See also BEST 89:4; CA 105; CANR 39, 91

Schary, Jill
See Robinson, Jill

Schell, Jonathan 1943- .... **CLC 35**
See also CA 73-76; CANR 12, 117

Schelling, Friedrich Wilhelm Joseph von 1775-1854 .... **NCLC 30**
See also DLB 90

Scherer, Jean-Marie Maurice 1920-
See Rohmer, Eric
See also CA 110

Schevill, James (Erwin) 1920- .... **CLC 7**
See also CA 5-8R; CAAS 12; CAD; CD 5

Schiller, Friedrich von 1759-1805 ...... **DC 12; NCLC 39, 69**
See also CDWLB 2; DAM DRAM; DLB 94; EW 5; RGWL 2, 3; TWA

Schisgal, Murray (Joseph) 1926- .... **CLC 6**
See also CA 21-24R; CAD; CANR 48, 86; CD 5

Schlee, Ann 1934- .... **CLC 35**
See also CA 101; CANR 29, 88; SATA 44; SATA-Brief 36

Schlegel, August Wilhelm von 1767-1845 .... **NCLC 15, 142**
See also DLB 94; RGWL 2, 3

Schlegel, Friedrich 1772-1829 .... **NCLC 45**
See also DLB 90; EW 5; RGWL 2, 3; TWA

Schlegel, Johann Elias (von) 1719(?)-1749 .... **LC 5**

Schleiermacher, Friedrich 1768-1834 .... **NCLC 107**
See also DLB 90

Schlesinger, Arthur M(eier), Jr. 1917- .... **CLC 84**
See also AITN 1; CA 1-4R; CANR 1, 28, 58, 105; DLB 17; INT CANR-28; MTCW 1, 2; SATA 61

Schlink, Bernhard 1944- .... **CLC 174**
See also CA 163; CANR 116

Schmidt, Arno (Otto) 1914-1979 ...... **CLC 56**
See also CA 128; 109; DLB 69; EWL 3

Schmitz, Aron Hector 1861-1928
See Svevo, Italo
See also CA 104; 122; MTCW 1

Schnackenberg, Gjertrud (Cecelia) 1953- .... **CLC 40; PC 45**
See also CA 116; CANR 100; CP 7; CWP; DLB 120, 282; PFS 13

Schneider, Leonard Alfred 1925-1966
See Bruce, Lenny
See also CA 89-92

Schnitzler, Arthur 1862-1931 ..... **DC 17; SSC 15, 61; TCLC 4**
See also CA 104; CDWLB 2; DLB 81, 118; EW 8; EWL 3; RGSF 2; RGWL 2, 3

Schoenberg, Arnold Franz Walter 1874-1951 .... **TCLC 75**
See also CA 109; 188

Schonberg, Arnold
See Schoenberg, Arnold Franz Walter

Schopenhauer, Arthur 1788-1860 .. **NCLC 51**
See also DLB 90; EW 5

Schor, Sandra (M.) 1932(?)-1990 ..... **CLC 65**
See also CA 132

Schorer, Mark 1908-1977 .... **CLC 9**
See also CA 5-8R; 73-76; CANR 7; DLB 103

Schrader, Paul (Joseph) 1946- .... **CLC 26**
See also CA 37-40R; CANR 41; DLB 44

Schreber, Daniel 1842-1911 .... **TCLC 123**

Schreiner, Olive (Emilie Albertina) 1855-1920 .... **TCLC 9**
See also AFW; BRWS 2; CA 105; 154; DLB 18, 156, 190, 225; EWL 3; FW; RGEL 2; TWA; WLIT 2; WWE 1

Schulberg, Budd (Wilson) 1914- .. **CLC 7, 48**
See also BPFB 3; CA 25-28R; CANR 19, 87; CN 7; DLB 6, 26, 28; DLBY 1981, 2001

Schulman, Arnold
See Trumbo, Dalton

Schulz, Bruno 1892-1942 .. **SSC 13; TCLC 5, 51**
See also CA 115; 123; CANR 86; CDWLB 4; DLB 215; EWL 3; MTCW 2; RGSF 2; RGWL 2, 3

Schulz, Charles M(onroe) 1922-2000 .... **CLC 12**
See also AAYA 39; CA 9-12R; 187; CANR 6, 132; INT CANR-6; SATA 10; SATA-Obit 118

Schumacher, E(rnst) F(riedrich) 1911-1977 .... **CLC 80**
See also CA 81-84; 73-76; CANR 34, 85

Schumann, Robert 1810-1856 ...... **NCLC 143**

Schuyler, George Samuel 1895-1977 .... **HR 3**
See also BW 2; CA 81-84; 73-76; CANR 42; DLB 29, 51

Schuyler, James Marcus 1923-1991 .. **CLC 5, 23**
See also CA 101; 134; DAM POET; DLB 5, 169; EWL 3; INT CA-101; WP

Schwartz, Delmore (David) 1913-1966 ... **CLC 2, 4, 10, 45, 87; PC 8**
See also AMWS 2; CA 17-18; 25-28R; CANR 35; CAP 2; DLB 28, 48; EWL 3; MTCW 1, 2; PAB; RGAL 4; TUS

Schwartz, Ernst
See Ozu, Yasujiro

Schwartz, John Burnham 1965- .... **CLC 59**
See also CA 132; CANR 116

Schwartz, Lynne Sharon 1939- .... **CLC 31**
See also CA 103; CANR 44, 89; DLB 218; MTCW 2

Schwartz, Muriel A.
See Eliot, T(homas) S(tearns)

Schwarz-Bart, Andre 1928- .... **CLC 2, 4**
See also CA 89-92; CANR 109; DLB 299

Schwarz-Bart, Simone 1938- . **BLCS; CLC 7**
See also BW 2; CA 97-100; CANR 117; EWL 3

Schwerner, Armand 1927-1999 .... **PC 42**
See also CA 9-12R; 179; CANR 50, 85; CP 7; DLB 165

Schwitters, Kurt (Hermann Edward Karl Julius) 1887-1948 .... **TCLC 95**
See also CA 158

Schwob, Marcel (Mayer Andre) 1867-1905 .... **TCLC 20**
See also CA 117; 168; DLB 123; GFL 1789 to the Present

Sciascia, Leonardo 1921-1989 .. **CLC 8, 9, 41**
See also CA 85-88; 130; CANR 35; DLB 177; EWL 3; MTCW 1; RGWL 2, 3

Scoppettone, Sandra 1936- .... **CLC 26**
See Early, Jack
See also AAYA 11; BYA 8; CA 5-8R; CANR 41, 73; GLL 1; MAICYA 2; MAICYAS 1; SATA 9, 92; WYA; YAW

Scorsese, Martin 1942- .... **CLC 20, 89**
See also AAYA 38; CA 110; 114; CANR 46, 85

Scotland, Jay
See Jakes, John (William)

Scott, Duncan Campbell 1862-1947 .... **TCLC 6**
See also CA 104; 153; DAC; DLB 92; RGEL 2

Scott, Evelyn 1893-1963 .... **CLC 43**
See also CA 104; 112; CANR 64; DLB 9, 48; RHW

Scott, F(rancis) R(eginald) 1899-1985 .... **CLC 22**
See also CA 101; 114; CANR 87; DLB 88; INT CA-101; RGEL 2

Scott, Frank
See Scott, F(rancis) R(eginald)

Scott, Joan .... **CLC 65**

Scott, Joanna 1960- .... **CLC 50**
    See also CA 126; CANR 53, 92

Scott, Paul (Mark) 1920-1978 ...... **CLC 9, 60**
    See also BRWS 1; CA 81-84; 77-80; CANR
    33; DLB 14, 207; DLB 3; MTCW 1;
    RGEL 2; RHW; WWE 1

Scott, Ridley 1937- .... **CLC 183**
    See also AAYA 13, 43

Scott, Sarah 1723-1795 .... **LC 44**
    See also DLB 39

Scott, Sir Walter 1771-1832 .... **NCLC 15, 69,**
    110; PC 13; SSC 32; WLC
    See also AAYA 22; BRW 4; BYA 2; CD-
    BLB 1789-1832; DA; DAB; DAC; DAM
    MST, NOV, POET; DLB 93, 107, 116,
    144, 159; HGG; LAIT 1; RGEL 2; RGSF
    2; SSFS 10; SUFW 1; TEA; WLIT 3;
    YABC 2

Scribe, (Augustin) Eugene 1791-1861 . **DC 5;**
    NCLC 16
    See also DAM DRAM; DLB 192; GFL
    1789 to the Present; RGWL 2, 3

Scrum, R.
    See Crumb, R(obert)

Scudery, Georges de 1601-1667 .... **LC 75**
    See also GFL Beginnings to 1789

Scudery, Madeleine de 1607-1701 .. **LC 2, 58**
    See also DLB 268; GFL Beginnings to 1789

Scum
    See Crumb, R(obert)

Scumbag, Little Bobby
    See Crumb, R(obert)

Seabrook, John
    See Hubbard, L(afayette) Ron(ald)

Seacole, Mary Jane Grant
    1805-1881 .... **NCLC 147**
    See also DLB 166

Sealy, I(rwin) Allan 1951- .... **CLC 55**
    See also CA 136; CN 7

Search, Alexander
    See Pessoa, Fernando (Antonio Nogueira)

Sebald, W(infried) G(eorg)
    1944-2001 .... **CLC 194**
    See also BRWS 8; CA 159; 202; CANR 98

Sebastian, Lee
    See Silverberg, Robert

Sebastian Owl
    See Thompson, Hunter S(tockton)

Sebestyen, Igen
    See Sebestyen, Ouida

Sebestyen, Ouida 1924- .... **CLC 30**
    See also AAYA 8; BYA 7; CA 107; CANR
    40, 114; CLR 17; JRDA; MAICYA 1, 2;
    SAAS 10; SATA 39, 140; WYA; YAW

Sebold, Alice 1963(?)- .... **CLC 193**
    See also AAYA 56; CA 203

Second Duke of Buckingham
    See Villiers, George

Secundus, H. Scriblerus
    See Fielding, Henry

Sedges, John
    See Buck, Pearl S(ydenstricker)

Sedgwick, Catharine Maria
    1789-1867 .... **NCLC 19, 98**
    See also DLB 1, 74, 183, 239, 243, 254;
    RGAL 4

Seelye, John (Douglas) 1931- .... **CLC 7**
    See also CA 97-100; CANR 70; INT CA-
    97-100; TCWW 2

Seferiades, Giorgos Stylianou 1900-1971
    See Seferis, George
    See also CA 5-8R; 33-36R; CANR 5, 36;
    MTCW 1

Seferis, George .... **CLC 5, 11**
    See Seferiades, Giorgos Stylianou
    See also EW 12; EWL 3; RGWL 2, 3

Segal, Erich (Wolf) 1937- .... **CLC 3, 10**
    See also BEST 89:1; BPFB 3; CA 25-28R;
    CANR 20, 36, 65, 113; CPW; DAM POP;
    DLBY 1986; INT CANR-20; MTCW 1

Seger, Bob 1945- .... **CLC 35**

Seghers, Anna .... **CLC 7**
    See Radvanyi, Netty
    See also CDWLB 2; DLB 69; EWL 3

Seidel, Frederick (Lewis) 1936- .... **CLC 18**
    See also CA 13-16R; CANR 8, 99; CP 7;
    DLBY 1984

Seifert, Jaroslav 1901-1986 . **CLC 34, 44, 93;**
    PC 47
    See also CA 127; CDWLB 4; DLB 215;
    EWL 3; MTCW 1, 2

Sei Shonagon c. 966-1017(?) .... **CMLC 6**

Sejour, Victor 1817-1874 .... **DC 10**
    See also DLB 50

Sejour Marcou et Ferrand, Juan Victor
    See Sejour, Victor

Selby, Hubert, Jr. 1928-2004 ..... **CLC 1, 2, 4,**
    8; SSC 20
    See also CA 13-16R; 226; CANR 33, 85;
    CN 7; DLB 2, 227

Selzer, Richard 1928- .... **CLC 74**
    See also CA 65-68; CANR 14, 106

Sembene, Ousmane
    See Ousmane, Sembene
    See also AFW; EWL 3; WLIT 2

Senancour, Etienne Pivert de
    1770-1846 .... **NCLC 16**
    See also DLB 119; GFL 1789 to the Present

Sender, Ramon (Jose) 1902-1982 ...... **CLC 8;**
    HLC 2; TCLC 136
    See also CA 5-8R; 105; CANR 8; DAM
    MULT; EWL 3; HW 1; MTCW 1; RGWL
    2, 3

Seneca, Lucius Annaeus c. 4B.C.-c.
    65 .... **CMLC 6; DC 5**
    See also AW 2; CDWLB 1; DAM DRAM;
    DLB 211; RGWL 2, 3; TWA

Senghor, Leopold Sedar 1906-2001 ... **BLC 3;**
    CLC 54, 130; PC 25
    See also AFW; BW 2; CA 116; 125; 203;
    CANR 47, 74, 134; CWW 2; DAM
    MULT, POET; DNFS 2; EWL 3; GFL
    1789 to the Present; MTCW 1, 2; TWA

Senior, Olive (Marjorie) 1941- .... **SSC 78**
    See also BW 3; CA 154; CANR 86, 126;
    CN 7; CP 7; CWP; DLB 157; EWL 3;
    RGSF 2

Senna, Danzy 1970- .... **CLC 119**
    See also CA 169; CANR 130

Serling, (Edward) Rod(man)
    1924-1975 .... **CLC 30**
    See also AAYA 14; AITN 1; CA 162; 57-
    60; DLB 26; SFW 4

Serna, Ramon Gomez de la
    See Gomez de la Serna, Ramon

Serpieres
    See Guillevic, (Eugene)

Service, Robert
    See Service, Robert W(illiam)
    See also BYA 4; DAB; DLB 92

Service, Robert W(illiam)
    1874(?)-1958 .... **TCLC 15; WLC**
    See Service, Robert
    See also CA 115; 140; CANR 84; DA;
    DAC; DAM MST, POET; PFS 10; RGEL
    2; SATA 20

Seth, Vikram 1952- .... **CLC 43, 90**
    See also BRWS 10; CA 121; 127; CANR
    50, 74, 131; CN 7; CP 7; DA3; DAM
    MULT; DLB 120, 271, 282; EWL 3; INT
    CA-127; MTCW 2; WWE 1

Seton, Cynthia Propper 1926-1982 .. **CLC 27**
    See also CA 5-8R; 108; CANR 7

Seton, Ernest (Evan) Thompson
    1860-1946 .... **TCLC 31**
    See also ANW; BYA 3; CA 109; 204; CLR
    59; DLB 92; DLBD 13; JRDA; SATA 18

Seton-Thompson, Ernest
    See Seton, Ernest (Evan) Thompson

Settle, Mary Lee 1918- .... **CLC 19, 61**
    See also BPFB 3; CA 89-92; CAAS 1;
    CANR 44, 87, 126; CN 7; CSW; DLB 6;
    INT CA-89-92

Seuphor, Michel
    See Arp, Jean

Sevigne, Marie (de Rabutin-Chantal)
    1626-1696 .... **LC 11**
    See Sevigne, Marie de Rabutin Chantal
    See also GFL Beginnings to 1789; TWA

Sevigne, Marie de Rabutin Chantal
    See Sevigne, Marie de Rabutin-Chantal)
    See also DLB 268

Sewall, Samuel 1652-1730 .... **LC 38**
    See also DLB 24; RGAL 4

Sexton, Anne (Harvey) 1928-1974 ..... **CLC 2,**
    4, 6, 8, 10, 15, 53, 123; PC 2; WLC
    See also AMWS 2; CA 1-4R; 53-56; CABS
    2; CANR 3, 36; CDALB 1941-1968; DA;
    DA3; DAB; DAC; DAM MST, POET;
    DLB 5, 169; EWL 3; EXPP; FW;
    MAWW; MTCW 1, 2; PAB; PFS 4, 14;
    RGAL 4; SATA 10; TUS

Shaara, Jeff 1952- .... **CLC 119**
    See also CA 163; CANR 109

Shaara, Michael (Joseph, Jr.)
    1929-1988 .... **CLC 15**
    See also AITN 1; BPFB 3; CA 102; 125;
    CANR 52, 85; DAM POP; DLBY 1983

Shackleton, C. C.
    See Aldiss, Brian W(ilson)

Shacochis, Bob .... **CLC 39**
    See Shacochis, Robert G.

Shacochis, Robert G. 1951-
    See Shacochis, Bob
    See also CA 119; 124; CANR 100; INT CA-
    124

Shaffer, Anthony (Joshua)
    1926-2001 .... **CLC 19**
    See also CA 110; 116; 200; CBD; CD 5;
    DAM DRAM; DFS 13; DLB 13

Shaffer, Peter (Levin) 1926- .. **CLC 5, 14, 18,**
    37, 60; DC 7
    See also BRWS 1; CA 25-28R; CANR 25,
    47, 74, 118; CBD; CD 5; CDBLB 1960 to
    Present; DA3; DAB; DAM DRAM, MST;
    DFS 5, 13; DLB 13, 233; EWL 3; MTCW
    1, 2; RGEL 2; TEA

Shakespeare, William 1564-1616 .... **WLC**
    See also AAYA 35; BRW 1; CDBLB Before
    1660; DA; DA3; DAB; DAC; DAM
    DRAM, MST, POET; DFS 20; DLB 62,
    172, 263; EXPP; LAIT 1; LATS 1:1;
    LMFS 1; PAB; PFS 1, 2, 3, 4, 5, 8, 9;
    RGEL 2; TEA; WLIT 3; WP; WS; WYA

Shakey, Bernard
    See Young, Neil

Shalamov, Varlam (Tikhonovich)
    1907-1982 .... **CLC 18**
    See also CA 129; 105; DLB 302; RGSF 2

Shamloo, Ahmad
    See Shamlu, Ahmad

Shamlou, Ahmad
    See Shamlu, Ahmad

Shamlu, Ahmad 1925-2000 .... **CLC 10**
    See also CA 216; CWW 2

Shammas, Anton 1951- .... **CLC 55**
    See also CA 199

Shandling, Arline
    See Berriault, Gina

Sigourney, Lydia H.
See Sigourney, Lydia Howard (Huntley)
See also DLB 73, 183
Sigourney, Lydia Howard (Huntley)
1791-1865 .... NCLC 21, 87
See Sigourney, Lydia H.; Sigourney, Lydia Huntley
See also DLB 1
Sigourney, Lydia Huntley
See Sigourney, Lydia Howard (Huntley)
See also DLB 42, 239, 243
Siguenza y Gongora, Carlos de
1645-1700 .... HLCS 2; LC 8
See also LAW
Sigurjonsson, Johann
See Sigurjonsson, Johann
Sigurjonsson, Johann 1880-1919 ... TCLC 27
See also CA 170; DLB 293; EWL 3
Sikelianos, Angelos 1884-1951 .... PC 29;
TCLC 39
See also EWL 3; RGWL 2, 3
Silkin, Jon 1930-1997 .... CLC 2, 6, 43
See also CA 5-8R; CAAS 5; CANR 89; CP 7; DLB 27
Silko, Leslie (Marmon) 1948- .... CLC 23, 74,
114; NNAL; SSC 37, 66; WLCS
See also AAYA 14; AMWS 4; ANW; BYA 12; CA 115; 122; CANR 45, 65, 118; CN 7; CP 7; CPW 1; CWP; DA; DA3; DAC; DAM MST, MULT, POP; DLB 143, 175, 256, 275; EWL 3; EXPP; EXPS; LAIT 4; MTCW 2; NFS 4; PFS 9, 16; RGAL 4; RGSF 2; SSFS 4, 8, 10, 11
Sillanpaa, Frans Eemil 1888-1964 ... CLC 19
See also CA 129; 93-96; EWL 3; MTCW 1
Sillitoe, Alan 1928- .. CLC 1, 3, 6, 10, 19, 57,
148
See also AITN 1; BRWS 5; CA 9-12R, 191; CAAE 191; CAAS 2; CANR 8, 26, 55; CDBLB 1960 to Present; CN 7; DLB 14, 139; EWL 3; MTCW 1, 2; RGEL 2; RGSF 2; SATA 61
Silone, Ignazio 1900-1978 .... CLC 4
See also CA 25-28; 81-84; CANR 34; CAP 2; DLB 264; EW 12; EWL 3; MTCW 1; RGSF 2; RGWL 2, 3
Silone, Ignazione
See Silone, Ignazio
Silver, Joan Micklin 1935- .... CLC 20
See also CA 114; 121; INT CA-121
Silver, Nicholas
See Faust, Frederick (Schiller)
See also TCWW 2
Silverberg, Robert 1935- .... CLC 7, 140
See also AAYA 24; BPFB 3; BYA 7, 9; CA 1-4R, 186; CAAE 186; CAAS 3; CANR 1, 20, 36, 85; CLR 59; CN 7; CPW; DAM POP; DLB 8; INT CANR-20; MAICYA 1, 2; MTCW 1, 2; SATA 13, 91; SATA-Essay 104; SCFW 2; SFW 4; SUFW 2
Silverstein, Alvin 1933- .... CLC 17
See also CA 49-52; CANR 2; CLR 25; JRDA; MAICYA 1, 2; SATA 8, 69, 124
Silverstein, Shel(don Allan)
1932-1999 .... PC 49
See also AAYA 40; BW 3; CA 107; 179; CANR 47, 74, 81; CLR 5, 96; CWRI 5; JRDA; MAICYA 1, 2; MTCW 2; SATA 33, 92; SATA-Brief 27; SATA-Obit 116
Silverstein, Virginia B(arbara Opshelor)
1937- .... CLC 17
See also CA 49-52; CANR 2; CLR 25; JRDA; MAICYA 1, 2; SATA 8, 69, 124
Sim, Georges
See Simenon, Georges (Jacques Christian)
Simak, Clifford D(onald) 1904-1988 . CLC 1,
55
See also CA 1-4R; 125; CANR 1, 35; DLB 8; MTCW 1; SATA-Obit 56; SFW 4

Simenon, Georges (Jacques Christian)
1903-1989 .... CLC 1, 2, 3, 8, 18, 47
See also BPFB 3; CA 85-88; 129; CANR 35; CMW 4; DA3; DAM POP; DLB 72; DLBY 1989; EW 12; EWL 3; GFL 1789 to the Present; MSW; MTCW 1, 2; RGWL 2, 3
Simic, Charles 1938- .... CLC 6, 9, 22, 49, 68,
130
See also AMWS 8; CA 29-32R; CAAS 4; CANR 12, 33, 52, 61, 96; CP 7; DA3; DAM POET; DLB 105; MTCW 2; PFS 7; RGAL 4; WP
Simmel, Georg 1858-1918 .... TCLC 64
See also CA 157; DLB 296
Simmons, Charles (Paul) 1924- .... CLC 57
See also CA 89-92; INT CA-89-92
Simmons, Dan 1948- .... CLC 44
See also AAYA 16, 54; CA 138; CANR 53, 81, 126; CPW; DAM POP; HGG; SUFW 2
Simmons, James (Stewart Alexander)
1933- .... CLC 43
See also CA 105; CAAS 21; CP 7; DLB 40
Simms, William Gilmore
1806-1870 .... NCLC 3
See also DLB 3, 30, 59, 73, 248, 254; RGAL 4
Simon, Carly 1945- .... CLC 26
See also CA 105
Simon, Claude (Eugene Henri)
1913-1984 .... CLC 4, 9, 15, 39
See also CA 89-92; CANR 33, 117; CWW 2; DAM NOV; DLB 83; EW 13; EWL 3; GFL 1789 to the Present; MTCW 1
Simon, Myles
See Follett, Ken(neth Martin)
Simon, (Marvin) Neil 1927- ... CLC 6, 11, 31,
39, 70; DC 14
See also AAYA 32; AITN 1; AMWS 4; CA 21-24R; CANR 26, 54, 87, 126; CD 5; DA3; DAM DRAM; DFS 2, 6, 12, 18; DLB 7, 266; LAIT 4; MTCW 1, 2; RGAL 4; TUS
Simon, Paul (Frederick) 1941(?)- ..... CLC 17
See also CA 116; 153
Simonon, Paul 1956(?)- .... CLC 30
Simonson, Rick ed. .... CLC 70
Simpson, Harriette
See Arnow, Harriette (Louisa) Simpson
Simpson, Louis (Aston Marantz)
1923- .... CLC 4, 7, 9, 32, 149
See also AMWS 9; CA 1-4R; CAAS 4; CANR 1, 61; CP 7; DAM POET; DLB 5; MTCW 1, 2; PFS 7, 11, 14; RGAL 4
Simpson, Mona (Elizabeth) 1957- ... CLC 44,
146
See also CA 122; 135; CANR 68, 103; CN 7; EWL 3
Simpson, N(orman) F(rederick)
1919- .... CLC 29
See also CA 13-16R; CBD; DLB 13; RGEL 2
Sinclair, Andrew (Annandale) 1935- . CLC 2,
14
See also CA 9-12R; CAAS 5; CANR 14, 38, 91; CN 7; DLB 14; FANT; MTCW 1
Sinclair, Emil
See Hesse, Hermann
Sinclair, Iain 1943- .... CLC 76
See also CA 132; CANR 81; CP 7; HGG
Sinclair, Iain MacGregor
See Sinclair, Iain
Sinclair, Irene
See Griffith, D(avid Lewelyn) W(ark)
Sinclair, Mary Amelia St. Clair 1865(?)-1946
See Sinclair, May
See also CA 104; HGG; RHW

Sinclair, May .... TCLC 3, 11
See Sinclair, Mary Amelia St. Clair
See also CA 166; DLB 36, 135; EWL 3; RGEL 2; SUFW
Sinclair, Roy
See Griffith, D(avid Lewelyn) W(ark)
Sinclair, Upton (Beall) 1878-1968 ..... CLC 1,
11, 15, 63; WLC
See also AMWS 5; BPFB 3; BYA 2; CA 5-8R; 25-28R; CANR 7; CDALB 1929-1941; DA; DA3; DAB; DAC; DAM MST, NOV; DLB 9; EWL 3; INT CANR-7; LAIT 3; MTCW 1, 2; NFS 6; RGAL 4; SATA 9; TUS; YAW
Singe, (Edmund) J(ohn) M(illington)
1871-1909 .... WLC
Singer, Isaac
See Singer, Isaac Bashevis
Singer, Isaac Bashevis 1904-1991 .. CLC 1, 3,
6, 9, 11, 15, 23, 38, 69, 111; SSC 3, 53;
WLC
See also AAYA 32; AITN 1, 2; AMW; AMWR 2; BPFB 3; BYA 1, 4; CA 1-4R; 134; CANR 1, 39, 106; CDALB 1941-1968; CLR 1; CWRI 5; DA; DA3; DAB; DAC; DAM MST, NOV; DLB 6, 28, 52, 278; DLBY 1991; EWL 3; EXPS; HGG; JRDA; LAIT 3; MAICYA 1, 2; MTCW 1, 2; RGAL 4; RGSF 2; SATA 3, 27; SATA-Obit 68; SSFS 2, 12, 16; TUS; TWA
Singer, Israel Joshua 1893-1944 .... TCLC 33
See also CA 169; EWL 3
Singh, Khushwant 1915- .... CLC 11
See also CA 9-12R; CAAS 9; CANR 6, 84; CN 7; EWL 3; RGEL 2
Singleton, Ann
See Benedict, Ruth (Fulton)
Singleton, John 1968(?)- .... CLC 156
See also AAYA 50; BW 2, 3; CA 138; CANR 67, 82; DAM MULT
Siniavskii, Andrei
See Sinyavsky, Andrei (Donatevich)
See also CWW 2
Sinjohn, John
See Galsworthy, John
Sinyavsky, Andrei (Donatevich)
1925-1997 .... CLC 8
See Siniavskii, Andrei; Sinyavsky, Andrey Donatovich; Tertz, Abram
See also CA 85-88; 159
Sinyavsky, Andrey Donatovich
See Sinyavsky, Andrei (Donatevich)
See also EWL 3
Sirin, V.
See Nabokov, Vladimir (Vladimirovich)
Sissman, L(ouis) E(dward)
1928-1976 .... CLC 9, 18
See also CA 21-24R; 65-68; CANR 13; DLB 5
Sisson, C(harles) H(ubert)
1914-2003 .... CLC 8
See also CA 1-4R; 220; CAAS 3; CANR 3, 48, 84; CP 7; DLB 27
Sitting Bull 1831(?)-1890 .... NNAL
See also DA3; DAM MULT
Sitwell, Dame Edith 1887-1964 ..... CLC 2, 9,
67; PC 3
See also BRW 7; CA 9-12R; CANR 35; CDBLB 1945-1960; DAM POET; DLB 20; EWL 3; MTCW 1, 2; RGEL 2; TEA
Siwaarmill, H. P.
See Sharp, William
Sjoewall, Maj 1935- .... CLC 7
See Sjowall, Maj
See also CA 65-68; CANR 73
Sjowall, Maj
See Sjoewall, Maj
See also BPFB 3; CMW 4; MSW

Skelton, John 1460(?)-1529 ..... **LC 71; PC 25**
See also BRW 1; DLB 136; RGEL 2

Skelton, Robin 1925-1997 .... **CLC 13**
See Zuk, Georges
See also AITN 2; CA 5-8R; 160; CAAS 5;
CANR 28, 89; CCA 1; CP 7; DLB 27, 53

Skolimowski, Jerzy 1938- .... **CLC 20**
See also CA 128

Skram, Amalie (Bertha)
1847-1905 .... **TCLC 25**
See also CA 165

Skvorecky, Josef (Vaclav) 1924- ...... **CLC 15,
39, 69, 152**
See also CA 61-64; CAAS 1; CANR 10,
34, 63, 108; CDWLB 4; CWW 2; DA3;
DAC; DAM NOV; DLB 232; EWL 3;
MTCW 1, 2

Slade, Bernard .... **CLC 11, 46**
See Newbound, Bernard Slade
See also CAAS 9; CCA 1; DLB 53

Slaughter, Carolyn 1946- .... **CLC 56**
See also CA 85-88; CANR 85; CN 7

Slaughter, Frank G(ill) 1908-2001 ... **CLC 29**
See also AITN 2; CA 5-8R; 197; CANR 5,
85; INT CANR-5; RHW

Slavitt, David R(ytman) 1935- .... **CLC 5, 14**
See also CA 21-24R; CAAS 3; CANR 41,
83; CP 7; DLB 5, 6

Slesinger, Tess 1905-1945 .... **TCLC 10**
See also CA 107; 199; DLB 102

Slessor, Kenneth 1901-1971 .... **CLC 14**
See also CA 102; 89-92; DLB 260; RGEL
2

Slowacki, Juliusz 1809-1849 .... **NCLC 15**
See also RGWL 3

Smart, Christopher 1722-1771 . **LC 3; PC 13**
See also DAM POET; DLB 109; RGEL 2

Smart, Elizabeth 1913-1986 .... **CLC 54**
See also CA 81-84; 118; DLB 88

Smiley, Jane (Graves) 1949- ...... **CLC 53, 76,
144**
See also AMWS 6; BPFB 3; CA 104;
CANR 30, 50, 74, 96; CN 7; CPW 1;
DA3; DAM POP; DLB 227, 234; EWL 3;
INT CANR-30; SSFS 19

Smith, A(rthur) J(ames) M(arshall)
1902-1980 .... **CLC 15**
See also CA 1-4R; 102; CANR 4; DAC;
DLB 88; RGEL 2

Smith, Adam 1723(?)-1790 .... **LC 36**
See also DLB 104, 252; RGEL 2

Smith, Alexander 1829-1867 .... **NCLC 59**
See also DLB 32, 55

Smith, Anna Deavere 1950- .... **CLC 86**
See also CA 133; CANR 103; CD 5; DFS 2

Smith, Betty (Wehner) 1904-1972 .... **CLC 19**
See also BPFB 3; BYA 3; CA 5-8R; 33-
36R; DLBY 1982; LAIT 3; RGAL 4;
SATA 6

Smith, Charlotte (Turner)
1749-1806 .... **NCLC 23, 115**
See also DLB 39, 109; RGEL 2; TEA

Smith, Clark Ashton 1893-1961 .... **CLC 43**
See also CA 143; CANR 81; FANT; HGG;
MTCW 2; SCFW 2; SFW 4; SUFW

Smith, Dave .... **CLC 22, 42**
See Smith, David (Jeddie)
See also CAAS 7; DLB 5

Smith, David (Jeddie) 1942-
See Smith, Dave
See also CA 49-52; CANR 1, 59, 120; CP
7; CSW; DAM POET

Smith, Florence Margaret 1902-1971
See Smith, Stevie
See also CA 17-18; 29-32R; CANR 35;
CAP 2; DAM POET; MTCW 1, 2; TEA

Smith, Iain Crichton 1928-1998 .... **CLC 64**
See also BRWS 9; CA 21-24R; 171; CN 7;
CP 7; DLB 40, 139; RGSF 2

Smith, John 1580(?)-1631 .... **LC 9**
See also DLB 24, 30; TUS

Smith, Johnston
See Crane, Stephen (Townley)

Smith, Joseph, Jr. 1805-1844 .... **NCLC 53**

Smith, Lee 1944- .... **CLC 25, 73**
See also CA 114; 119; CANR 46, 118;
CSW; DLB 143; DLBY 1983; EWL 3;
INT CA-119; RGAL 4

Smith, Martin
See Smith, Martin Cruz

Smith, Martin Cruz 1942- .. **CLC 25; NNAL**
See also BEST 89:4; BPFB 3; CA 85-88;
CANR 6, 23, 43, 65, 119; CMW 4; CPW;
DAM MULT, POP; HGG; INT CANR-
23; MTCW 2; RGAL 4

Smith, Patti 1946- .... **CLC 12**
See also CA 93-96; CANR 63

Smith, Pauline (Urmson)
1882-1959 .... **TCLC 25**
See also DLB 225; EWL 3

Smith, Rosamond
See Oates, Joyce Carol

Smith, Sheila Kaye
See Kaye-Smith, Sheila

Smith, Stevie .... **CLC 3, 8, 25, 44; PC 12**
See Smith, Florence Margaret
See also BRWS 2; DLB 20; EWL 3; MTCW
2; PAB; PFS 3; RGEL 2

Smith, Wilbur (Addison) 1933- .... **CLC 33**
See also CA 13-16R; CANR 7, 46, 66, 134;
CPW; MTCW 1, 2

Smith, William Jay 1918- .... **CLC 6**
See also AMWS 13; CA 5-8R; CANR 44,
106; CP 7; CSW; CWRI 5; DLB 5; MAI-
CYA 1, 2; SAAS 22; SATA 2, 68, 154;
SATA-Essay 154

Smith, Woodrow Wilson
See Kuttner, Henry

Smith, Zadie 1976- .... **CLC 158**
See also AAYA 50; CA 193

Smolenskin, Peretz 1842-1885 .... **NCLC 30**

Smollett, Tobias (George) 1721-1771 ... **LC 2,
46**
See also BRW 3; CDBLB 1660-1789; DLB
39, 104; RGEL 2; TEA

Snodgrass, W(illiam) D(e Witt)
1926- .... **CLC 2, 6, 10, 18, 68**
See also AMWS 6; CA 1-4R; CANR 6, 36,
65, 85; CP 7; DAM POET; DLB 5;
MTCW 1, 2; RGAL 4

Snorri Sturluson 1179-1241 .... **CMLC 56**
See also RGWL 2, 3

Snow, C(harles) P(ercy) 1905-1980 ... **CLC 1,
4, 6, 9, 13, 19**
See also BRW 7; CA 5-8R; 101; CANR 28;
CDBLB 1945-1960; DAM NOV; DLB 15,
77; DLBD 17; EWL 3; MTCW 1, 2;
RGEL 2; TEA

Snow, Frances Compton
See Adams, Henry (Brooks)

Snyder, Gary (Sherman) 1930- . **CLC 1, 2, 5,
9, 32, 120; PC 21**
See also AMWS 8; ANW; BG 3; CA 17-
20R; CANR 30, 60, 125; CP 7; DA3;
DAM POET; DLB 5, 16, 165, 212, 237,
275; EWL 3; MTCW 2; PFS 9, 19; RGAL
4; WP

Snyder, Zilpha Keatley 1927- .... **CLC 17**
See also AAYA 15; BYA 1; CA 9-12R;
CANR 38; CLR 31; JRDA; MAICYA 1,
2; SAAS 2; SATA 1, 28, 75, 110; SATA-
Essay 112; YAW

Soares, Bernardo
See Pessoa, Fernando (Antonio Nogueira)

Sobh, A.
See Shamlu, Ahmad

Sobh, Alef
See Shamlu, Ahmad

Sobol, Joshua 1939- .... **CLC 60**
See Sobol, Yehoshua
See also CA 200

Sobol, Yehoshua 1939-
See Sobol, Joshua
See also CWW 2

Socrates 470B.C.-399B.C. .... **CMLC 27**

Soderberg, Hjalmar 1869-1941 ...... **TCLC 39**
See also DLB 259; EWL 3; RGSF 2

Soderbergh, Steven 1963- .... **CLC 154**
See also AAYA 43

Sodergran, Edith (Irene) 1892-1923
See Soedergran, Edith (Irene)
See also CA 202; DLB 259; EW 11; EWL
3; RGWL 2, 3

Soedergran, Edith (Irene)
1892-1923 .... **TCLC 31**
See Sodergran, Edith (Irene)

Softly, Edgar
See Lovecraft, H(oward) P(hillips)

Softly, Edward
See Lovecraft, H(oward) P(hillips)

Sokolov, Alexander V(sevolodovich) 1943-
See Sokolov, Sasha
See also CA 73-76

Sokolov, Raymond 1941- .... **CLC 7**
See also CA 85-88

Sokolov, Sasha .... **CLC 59**
See Sokolov, Alexander V(sevolodovich)
See also CWW 2; DLB 285; EWL 3; RGWL
2, 3

Solo, Jay
See Ellison, Harlan (Jay)

Sologub, Fyodor .... **TCLC 9**
See Teternikov, Fyodor Kuzmich
See also EWL 3

Solomons, Ikey Esquir
See Thackeray, William Makepeace

Solomos, Dionysios 1798-1857 .... **NCLC 15**

Solwoska, Mara
See French, Marilyn

Solzhenitsyn, Aleksandr I(sayevich)
1918- .. **CLC 1, 2, 4, 7, 9, 10, 18, 26, 34,
78, 134; SSC 32; WLC**
See Solzhenitsyn, Aleksandr Isaevich
See also AAYA 49; AITN 1; BPFB 3; CA
69-72; CANR 40, 65, 116; DA; DA3;
DAB; DAC; DAM MST, NOV; DLB 302;
EW 13; EXPS; LAIT 4; MTCW 1, 2; NFS
6; RGSF 2; RGWL 2, 3; SSFS 9; TWA

Solzhenitsyn, Aleksandr Isaevich
See Solzhenitsyn, Aleksandr I(sayevich)
See also CWW 2; EWL 3

Somers, Jane
See Lessing, Doris (May)

Somerville, Edith Oenone
1858-1949 .... **SSC 56; TCLC 51**
See also CA 196; DLB 135; RGEL 2; RGSF
2

Somerville & Ross
See Martin, Violet Florence; Somerville,
Edith Oenone

Sommer, Scott 1951- .... **CLC 25**
See also CA 106

Sommers, Christina Hoff 1950- ...... **CLC 197**
See also CA 153; CANR 95

Sondheim, Stephen (Joshua) 1930- . **CLC 30,
39, 147; DC 22**
See also AAYA 11; CA 103; CANR 47, 67,
125; DAM DRAM; LAIT 4

Sone, Monica 1919- .... **AAL**

Song, Cathy 1955- .... **AAL; PC 21**
See also CA 154; CANR 118; CWP; DLB
169; EXPP; FW; PFS 5

Sontag, Susan 1933- .... **CLC 1, 2, 10, 13, 31, 105, 195**
See also AMWS 3; CA 17-20R; CANR 25, 51, 74, 97; CN 7; CPW; DA3; DAM POP; DLB 2, 67; EWL 3; MAWW; MTCW 1, 2; RGAL 4; RHW; SSFS 10

Sophocles 496(?)B.C.-406(?)B.C. .... **CMLC 2, 47, 51; DC 1; WLCS**
See also AW 1; CDWLB 1; DA; DA3; DAB; DAC; DAM DRAM, MST; DFS 1, 4, 8; DLB 176; LAIT 1; LATS 1:1; LMFS 1; RGWL 2, 3; TWA

Sordello 1189-1269 .... **CMLC 15**

Sorel, Georges 1847-1922 .... **TCLC 91**
See also CA 118; 188

Sorel, Julia
See Drexler, Rosalyn

Sorokin, Vladimir .... **CLC 59**
See Sorokin, Vladimir Georgievich

Sorokin, Vladimir Georgievich
See Sorokin, Vladimir
See also DLB 285

Sorrentino, Gilbert 1929- .. **CLC 3, 7, 14, 22, 40**
See also CA 77-80; CANR 14, 33, 115; CN 7; CP 7; DLB 5, 173; DLBY 1980; INT CANR-14

Soseki
See Natsume, Soseki
See also MJW

Soto, Gary 1952- ... **CLC 32, 80; HLC 2; PC 28**
See also AAYA 10, 37; BYA 11; CA 119; 125; CANR 50, 74, 107; CLR 38; CP 7; DAM MULT; DLB 82; EWL 3; EXPP; HW 1, 2; INT CA-125; JRDA; LLW 1; MAICYA 2; MAICYAS 1; MTCW 2; PFS 7; RGAL 4; SATA 80, 120; WYA; YAW

Soupault, Philippe 1897-1990 .... **CLC 68**
See also CA 116; 147; 131; EWL 3; GFL 1789 to the Present; LMFS 2

Souster, (Holmes) Raymond 1921- .... **CLC 5, 14**
See also CA 13-16R; CAAS 14; CANR 13, 29, 53; CP 7; DA3; DAC; DAM POET; DLB 88; RGEL 2; SATA 63

Southern, Terry 1924(?)-1995 .... **CLC 7**
See also AMWS 11; BPFB 3; CA 1-4R; 150; CANR 1, 55, 107; CN 7; DLB 2; IDFW 3, 4

Southerne, Thomas 1660-1746 .... **LC 99**
See also DLB 80; RGEL 2

Southey, Robert 1774-1843 .... **NCLC 8, 97**
See also BRW 4; DLB 93, 107, 142; RGEL 2; SATA 54

Southwell, Robert 1561(?)-1595 .... **LC 108**
See also DLB 167; RGEL 2; TEA

Southworth, Emma Dorothy Eliza Nevitte 1819-1899 .... **NCLC 26**
See also DLB 239

Souza, Ernest
See Scott, Evelyn

Soyinka, Wole 1934- .. **BLC 3; CLC 3, 5, 14, 36, 44, 179; DC 2; WLC**
See also AFW; BW 2, 3; CA 13-16R; CANR 27, 39, 82; CD 5; CDWLB 3; CN 7; CP 7; DA; DA3; DAB; DAC; DAM DRAM, MST, MULT; DFS 10; DLB 125; EWL 3; MTCW 1, 2; RGEL 2; TWA; WLIT 2; WWE 1

Spackman, W(illiam) M(ode) 1905-1990 .... **CLC 46**
See also CA 81-84; 132

Spacks, Barry (Bernard) 1931- .... **CLC 14**
See also CA 154; CANR 33, 109; CP 7; DLB 105

Spanidou, Irini 1946- .... **CLC 44**
See also CA 185

Spark, Muriel (Sarah) 1918- ..... **CLC 2, 3, 5, 8, 13, 18, 40, 94; SSC 10**
See also BRWS 1; CA 5-8R; CANR 12, 36, 76, 89, 131; CDBLB 1945-1960; CN 7; CP 7; DA3; DAB; DAC; DAM MST, NOV; DLB 15, 139; EWL 3; FW; INT CANR-12; LAIT 4; MTCW 1, 2; RGEL 2; TEA; WLIT 4; YAW

Spaulding, Douglas
See Bradbury, Ray (Douglas)

Spaulding, Leonard
See Bradbury, Ray (Douglas)

Speght, Rachel 1597-c. 1630 .... **LC 97**
See also DLB 126

Spelman, Elizabeth .... **CLC 65**

Spence, J. A. D.
See Eliot, T(homas) S(tearns)

Spencer, Anne 1882-1975 .... **HR 3**
See also BW 2; CA 161; DLB 51, 54

Spencer, Elizabeth 1921- .... **CLC 22; SSC 57**
See also CA 13-16R; CANR 32, 65, 87; CN 7; CSW; DLB 6, 218; EWL 3; MTCW 1; RGAL 4; SATA 14

Spencer, Leonard G.
See Silverberg, Robert

Spencer, Scott 1945- .... **CLC 30**
See also CA 113; CANR 51; DLBY 1986

Spender, Stephen (Harold) 1909-1995 .... **CLC 1, 2, 5, 10, 41, 91**
See also BRWS 2; CA 9-12R; 149; CANR 31, 54; CDBLB 1945-1960; CP 7; DA3; DAM POET; DLB 20; EWL 3; MTCW 1, 2; PAB; RGEL 2; TEA

Spengler, Oswald (Arnold Gottfried) 1880-1936 .... **TCLC 25**
See also CA 118; 189

Spenser, Edmund 1552(?)-1599 ..... **LC 5, 39; PC 8, 42; WLC**
See also AAYA 60; BRW 1; CDBLB Before 1660; DA; DA3; DAB; DAC; DAM MST, POET; DLB 167; EFS 2; EXPP; PAB; RGEL 2; TEA; WLIT 3; WP

Spicer, Jack 1925-1965 .... **CLC 8, 18, 72**
See also BG 3; CA 85-88; DAM POET; DLB 5, 16, 193; GLL 1; WP

Spiegelman, Art 1948- .... **CLC 76, 178**
See also AAYA 10, 46; CA 125; CANR 41, 55, 74, 124; DLB 299; MTCW 2; SATA 109; YAW

Spielberg, Peter 1929- .... **CLC 6**
See also CA 5-8R; CANR 4, 48; DLBY 1981

Spielberg, Steven 1947- .... **CLC 20, 188**
See also AAYA 8, 24; CA 77-80; CANR 32; SATA 32

Spillane, Frank Morrison 1918-
See Spillane, Mickey
See also CA 25-28R; CANR 28, 63, 125; DA3; MTCW 1, 2; SATA 66

Spillane, Mickey .... **CLC 3, 13**
See Spillane, Frank Morrison
See also BPFB 3; CMW 4; DLB 226; MSW; MTCW 2

Spinoza, Benedictus de 1632-1677 .. **LC 9, 58**

Spinrad, Norman (Richard) 1940- ... **CLC 46**
See also BPFB 3; CA 37-40R; CAAS 19; CANR 20, 91; DLB 8; INT CANR-20; SFW 4

Spitteler, Carl (Friedrich Georg) 1845-1924 .... **TCLC 12**
See also CA 109; DLB 129; EWL 3

Spivack, Kathleen (Romola Drucker) 1938- .... **CLC 6**
See also CA 49-52

Spoto, Donald 1941- .... **CLC 39**
See also CA 65-68; CANR 11, 57, 93

Springsteen, Bruce (F.) 1949- .... **CLC 17**
See also CA 111

Spurling, (Susan) Hilary 1940- .... **CLC 34**
See also CA 104; CANR 25, 52, 94

Spyker, John Howland
See Elman, Richard (Martin)

Squared, A.
See Abbott, Edwin A.

Squires, (James) Radcliffe 1917-1993 .... **CLC 51**
See also CA 1-4R; 140; CANR 6, 21

Srivastava, Dhanpat Rai 1880(?)-1936
See Premchand
See also CA 118; 197

Stacy, Donald
See Pohl, Frederik

Stael
See Stael-Holstein, Anne Louise Germaine Necker
See also EW 5; RGWL 2, 3

Stael, Germaine de
See Stael-Holstein, Anne Louise Germaine Necker
See also DLB 119, 192; FW; GFL 1789 to the Present; TWA

Stael-Holstein, Anne Louise Germaine Necker 1766-1817 .... **NCLC 3, 91**
See Stael; Stael, Germaine de

Stafford, Jean 1915-1979 .. **CLC 4, 7, 19, 68; SSC 26**
See also CA 1-4R; 85-88; CANR 3, 65; DLB 2, 173; MTCW 1, 2; RGAL 4; RGSF 2; SATA-Obit 22; TCWW 2; TUS

Stafford, William (Edgar) 1914-1993 .... **CLC 4, 7, 29**
See also AMWS 11; CA 5-8R; 142; CAAS 3; CANR 5, 22; DAM POET; DLB 5, 206; EXPP; INT CANR-22; PFS 2, 8, 16; RGAL 4; WP

Stagnelius, Eric Johan 1793-1823 . **NCLC 61**

Staines, Trevor
See Brunner, John (Kilian Houston)

Stairs, Gordon
See Austin, Mary (Hunter)
See also TCWW 2

Stalin, Joseph 1879-1953 .... **TCLC 92**

Stampa, Gaspara c. 1524-1554 .... **PC 43**
See also RGWL 2, 3

Stampflinger, K. A.
See Benjamin, Walter

Stancykowna
See Szymborska, Wislawa

Standing Bear, Luther 1868(?)-1939(?) .... **NNAL**
See also CA 113; 144; DAM MULT

Stannard, Martin 1947- .... **CLC 44**
See also CA 142; DLB 155

Stanton, Elizabeth Cady 1815-1902 .... **TCLC 73**
See also CA 171; DLB 79; FW

Stanton, Maura 1946- .... **CLC 9**
See also CA 89-92; CANR 15, 123; DLB 120

Stanton, Schuyler
See Baum, L(yman) Frank

Stapledon, (William) Olaf 1886-1950 .... **TCLC 22**
See also CA 111; 162; DLB 15, 255; SFW 4

Starbuck, George (Edwin) 1931-1996 .... **CLC 53**
See also CA 21-24R; 153; CANR 23; DAM POET

Stark, Richard
See Westlake, Donald E(dwin)

Staunton, Schuyler
See Baum, L(yman) Frank

Stow, (Julian) Randolph 1935- ... **CLC 23, 48**
　See also CA 13-16R; CANR 33; CN 7;
　DLB 260; MTCW 1; RGEL 2

Stowe, Harriet (Elizabeth) Beecher
　1811-1896 .... **NCLC 3, 50, 133; WLC**
　See also AAYA 53; AMWS 1; CDALB
　1865-1917; DA; DA3; DAB; DAC; DAM
　MST, NOV; DLB 1, 12, 42, 74, 189, 239,
　243; EXPN; JRDA; LAIT 2; MAICYA 1,
　2; NFS 6; RGAL 4; TUS; YABC 1

Strabo c. 64B.C.-c. 25 .... **CMLC 37**
　See also DLB 176

Strachey, (Giles) Lytton
　1880-1932 .... **TCLC 12**
　See also BRWS 2; CA 110; 178; DLB 149;
　DLBD 10; EWL 3; MTCW 2; NCFS 4

Stramm, August 1874-1915 .... **PC 50**
　See also CA 195; EWL 3

Strand, Mark 1934- .... **CLC 6, 18, 41, 71**
　See also AMWS 4; CA 21-24R; CANR 40,
　65, 100; CP 7; DAM POET; DLB 5; EWL
　3; PAB; PFS 9, 18; RGAL 4; SATA 41

Stratton-Porter, Gene(va Grace) 1863-1924
　See Porter, Gene(va Grace) Stratton
　See also ANW; CA 137; CLR 87; DLB 221;
　DLBD 14; MAICYA 1, 2; SATA 15

Straub, Peter (Francis) 1943- ... **CLC 28, 107**
　See also BEST 89:1; BPFB 3; CA 85-88;
　CANR 28, 65, 109; CPW; DAM POP;
　DLBY 1984; HGG; MTCW 1, 2; SUFW
　2

Strauss, Botho 1944- .... **CLC 22**
　See also CA 157; CWW 2; DLB 124

Strauss, Leo 1899-1973 .... **TCLC 141**
　See also CA 101; 45-48; CANR 122

Streatfeild, (Mary) Noel
　1897(?)-1986 .... **CLC 21**
　See also CA 81-84; 120; CANR 31; CLR
　17, 83; CWRI 5; DLB 160; MAICYA 1,
　2; SATA 20; SATA-Obit 48

Stribling, T(homas) S(igismund)
　1881-1965 .... **CLC 23**
　See also CA 189; 107; CMW 4; DLB 9;
　RGAL 4

Strindberg, (Johan) August
　1849-1912 ... **DC 18; TCLC 1, 8, 21, 47;
　WLC**
　See also CA 104; 135; DA; DA3; DAB;
　DAC; DAM DRAM, MST; DFS 4, 9;
　DLB 259; EW 7; EWL 3; IDTP; LMFS
　2; MTCW 2; RGWL 2, 3; TWA

Stringer, Arthur 1874-1950 .... **TCLC 37**
　See also CA 161; DLB 92

Stringer, David
　See Roberts, Keith (John Kingston)

Stroheim, Erich von 1885-1957 ..... **TCLC 71**

Strugatskii, Arkadii (Natanovich)
　1925-1991 .... **CLC 27**
　See Strugatsky, Arkadii Natanovich
　See also CA 106; 135; SFW 4

Strugatskii, Boris (Natanovich)
　1933- .... **CLC 27**
　See Strugatsky, Boris (Natanovich)
　See also CA 106; SFW 4

Strugatsky, Arkadii Natanovich
　See Strugatskii, Arkadii (Natanovich)
　See also DLB 302

Strugatsky, Boris (Natanovich)
　See Strugatskii, Boris (Natanovich)
　See also DLB 302

Strummer, Joe 1953(?)- .... **CLC 30**

Strunk, William, Jr. 1869-1946 ...... **TCLC 92**
　See also CA 118; 164; NCFS 5

Stryk, Lucien 1924- .... **PC 27**
　See also CA 13-16R; CANR 10, 28, 55,
　110; CP 7

Stuart, Don A.
　See Campbell, John W(ood, Jr.)

Stuart, Ian
　See MacLean, Alistair (Stuart)

Stuart, Jesse (Hilton) 1906-1984 ... **CLC 1, 8,
　11, 14, 34; SSC 31**
　See also CA 5-8R; 112; CANR 31; DLB 9,
　48, 102; DLBY 1984; SATA 2; SATA-
　Obit 36

Stubblefield, Sally
　See Trumbo, Dalton

Sturgeon, Theodore (Hamilton)
　1918-1985 .... **CLC 22, 39**
　See Queen, Ellery
　See also AAYA 51; BPFB 3; BYA 9, 10;
　CA 81-84; 116; CANR 32, 103; DLB 8;
　DLBY 1985; HGG; MTCW 1, 2; SCFW;
　SFW 4; SUFW

Sturges, Preston 1898-1959 .... **TCLC 48**
　See also CA 114; 149; DLB 26

Styron, William 1925- .... **CLC 1, 3, 5, 11, 15,
　60; SSC 25**
　See also AMW; AMWC 2; BEST 90:4;
　BPFB 3; CA 5-8R; CANR 6, 33, 74, 126;
　CDALB 1968-1988; CN 7; CPW; CSW;
　DA3; DAM NOV, POP; DLB 2, 143, 299;
　DLBY 1980; EWL 3; INT CANR-6;
　LAIT 2; MTCW 1, 2; NCFS 1; RGAL 4;
　RHW; TUS

Su, Chien 1884-1918
　See Su Man-shu
　See also CA 123

Suarez Lynch, B.
　See Bioy Casares, Adolfo; Borges, Jorge
　Luis

Suassuna, Ariano Vilar 1927- .... **HLCS 1**
　See also CA 178; DLB 307; HW 2; LAW

Suckert, Kurt Erich
　See Malaparte, Curzio

Suckling, Sir John 1609-1642 . **LC 75; PC 30**
　See also BRW 2; DAM POET; DLB 58,
　126; EXPP; PAB; RGEL 2

Suckow, Ruth 1892-1960 .... **SSC 18**
　See also CA 193; 113; DLB 9, 102; RGAL
　4; TCWW 2

Sudermann, Hermann 1857-1928 .. **TCLC 15**
　See also CA 107; 201; DLB 118

Sue, Eugene 1804-1857 .... **NCLC 1**
　See also DLB 119

Sueskind, Patrick 1949- .... **CLC 44, 182**
　See Suskind, Patrick

Suetonius c. 70-c. 130 .... **CMLC 60**
　See also AW 2; DLB 211; RGWL 2, 3

Sukenick, Ronald 1932-2004 ..... **CLC 3, 4, 6,
　48**
　See also CA 25-28R; 209; 229; CAAE 209;
　CAAS 8; CANR 32, 89; CN 7; DLB 173;
　DLBY 1981

Suknaski, Andrew 1942- .... **CLC 19**
　See also CA 101; CP 7; DLB 53

Sullivan, Vernon
　See Vian, Boris

Sully Prudhomme, Rene-Francois-Armand
　1839-1907 .... **TCLC 31**
　See also GFL 1789 to the Present

Su Man-shu .... **TCLC 24**
　See Su, Chien
　See also EWL 3

Sumarokov, Aleksandr Petrovich
　1717-1777 .... **LC 104**
　See also DLB 150

Summerforest, Ivy B.
　See Kirkup, James

Summers, Andrew James 1942- .... **CLC 26**

Summers, Andy
　See Summers, Andrew James

Summers, Hollis (Spurgeon, Jr.)
　1916- .... **CLC 10**
　See also CA 5-8R; CANR 3; DLB 6

Summers, (Alphonsus Joseph-Mary
　Augustus) Montague
　1880-1948 .... **TCLC 16**
　See also CA 118; 163

Sumner, Gordon Matthew .... **CLC 26**
　See Police, The; Sting

Sun Tzu c. 400B.C.-c. 320B.C. ...... **CMLC 56**

Surrey, Henry Howard 1517-1574 ...... **PC 59**
　See also BRW 1; RGEL 2

Surtees, Robert Smith 1805-1864 .. **NCLC 14**
　See also DLB 21; RGEL 2

Susann, Jacqueline 1921-1974 .... **CLC 3**
　See also AITN 1; BPFB 3; CA 65-68; 53-
　56; MTCW 1, 2

Su Shi
　See Su Shih
　See also RGWL 2, 3

Su Shih 1036-1101 .... **CMLC 15**
　See Su Shi

Suskind, Patrick .... **CLC 182**
　See Sueskind, Patrick
　See also BPFB 3; CA 145; CWW 2

Sutcliff, Rosemary 1920-1992 .... **CLC 26**
　See also AAYA 10; BYA 1, 4; CA 5-8R;
　139; CANR 37; CLR 1, 37; CPW; DAB;
　DAC; DAM MST, POP; JRDA; LATS
　1:1; MAICYA 1, 2; MAICYAS 1; RHW;
　SATA 6, 44, 78; SATA-Obit 73; WYA;
　YAW

Sutro, Alfred 1863-1933 .... **TCLC 6**
　See also CA 105; 185; DLB 10; RGEL 2

Sutton, Henry
　See Slavitt, David R(ytman)

Suzuki, D. T.
　See Suzuki, Daisetz Teitaro

Suzuki, Daisetz T.
　See Suzuki, Daisetz Teitaro

Suzuki, Daisetz Teitaro
　1870-1966 .... **TCLC 109**
　See also CA 121; 111; MTCW 1, 2

Suzuki, Teitaro
　See Suzuki, Daisetz Teitaro

Svevo, Italo .... **SSC 25; TCLC 2, 35**
　See Schmitz, Aron Hector
　See also DLB 264; EW 8; EWL 3; RGWL
　2, 3

Swados, Elizabeth (A.) 1951- .... **CLC 12**
　See also CA 97-100; CANR 49; INT CA-
　97-100

Swados, Harvey 1920-1972 .... **CLC 5**
　See also CA 5-8R; 37-40R; CANR 6; DLB
　2

Swan, Gladys 1934- .... **CLC 69**
　See also CA 101; CANR 17, 39

Swanson, Logan
　See Matheson, Richard (Burton)

Swarthout, Glendon (Fred)
　1918-1992 .... **CLC 35**
　See also AAYA 55; CA 1-4R; 139; CANR
　1, 47; LAIT 5; SATA 26; TCWW 2; YAW

Swedenborg, Emanuel 1688-1772 ..... **LC 105**

Sweet, Sarah C.
　See Jewett, (Theodora) Sarah Orne

Swenson, May 1919-1989 ...... **CLC 4, 14, 61,
　106; PC 14**
　See also AMWS 4; CA 5-8R; 130; CANR
　36, 61, 131; DA; DAB; DAC; DAM MST,
　POET; DLB 5; EXPP; GLL 2; MTCW 1,
　2; PFS 16; SATA 15; WP

Swift, Augustus
　See Lovecraft, H(oward) P(hillips)

Swift, Graham (Colin) 1949- ...... **CLC 41, 88**
　See also BRWC 2; BRWS 5; CA 117; 122;
　CANR 46, 71, 128; CN 7; DLB 194;
　MTCW 2; NFS 18; RGSF 2

Teresa de Jesus, St. 1515-1582 .... **LC 18**

Terkel, Louis 1912-
See Terkel, Studs
See also CA 57-60; CANR 18, 45, 67, 132;
DA3; MTCW 1, 2

Terkel, Studs .... **CLC 38**
See Terkel, Louis
See also AAYA 32; AITN 1; MTCW 2; TUS

Terry, C. V.
See Slaughter, Frank G(ill)

Terry, Megan 1932- .... **CLC 19; DC 13**
See also CA 77-80; CABS 3; CAD; CANR
43; CD 5; CWD; DFS 18; DLB 7, 249;
GLL 2

Tertullian c. 155-c. 245 .... **CMLC 29**

Tertz, Abram
See Sinyavsky, Andrei (Donatevich)
See also RGSF 2

Tesich, Steve 1943(?)-1996 .... **CLC 40, 69**
See also CA 105; 152; CAD; DLBY 1983

Tesla, Nikola 1856-1943 .... **TCLC 88**

Teternikov, Fyodor Kuzmich 1863-1927
See Sologub, Fyodor
See also CA 104

Tevis, Walter 1928-1984 .... **CLC 42**
See also CA 113; SFW 4

Tey, Josephine .... **TCLC 14**
See Mackintosh, Elizabeth
See also DLB 77; MSW

Thackeray, William Makepeace
1811-1863 .... **NCLC 5, 14, 22, 43; WLC**
See also BRW 5; BRWC 2; CDBLB 1832-
1890; DA; DA3; DAB; DAC; DAM MST,
NOV; DLB 21, 55, 159, 163; NFS 13;
RGEL 2; SATA 23; TEA; WLIT 3

Thakura, Ravindranatha
See Tagore, Rabindranath

Thames, C. H.
See Marlowe, Stephen

Tharoor, Shashi 1956- .... **CLC 70**
See also CA 141; CANR 91; CN 7

Thelwell, Michael Miles 1939- .... **CLC 22**
See also BW 2; CA 101

Theobald, Lewis, Jr.
See Lovecraft, H(oward) P(hillips)

Theocritus c. 310B.C.- .... **CMLC 45**
See also AW 1; DLB 176; RGWL 2, 3

Theodorescu, Ion N. 1880-1967
See Arghezi, Tudor
See also CA 116

Theriault, Yves 1915-1983 .... **CLC 79**
See also CA 102; CCA 1; DAC; DAM
MST; DLB 88; EWL 3

Theroux, Alexander (Louis) 1939- .... **CLC 2, 25**
See also CA 85-88; CANR 20, 63; CN 7

Theroux, Paul (Edward) 1941- ..... **CLC 5, 8, 11, 15, 28, 46**
See also AAYA 28; AMWS 8; BEST 89:4;
BPFB 3; CA 33-36R; CANR 20, 45, 74,
133; CDALBS; CN 7; CPW 1; DA3;
DAM POP; DLB 2, 218; EWL 3; HGG;
MTCW 1, 2; RGAL 4; SATA 44, 109;
TUS

Thesen, Sharon 1946- .... **CLC 56**
See also CA 163; CANR 125; CP 7; CWP

Thespis fl. 6th cent. B.C.- .... **CMLC 51**
See also LMFS 1

Thevenin, Denis
See Duhamel, Georges

Thibault, Jacques Anatole Francois
1844-1924
See France, Anatole
See also CA 106; 127; DA3; DAM NOV;
MTCW 1, 2; TWA

Thiele, Colin (Milton) 1920- .... **CLC 17**
See also CA 29-32R; CANR 12, 28, 53,
105; CLR 27; DLB 289; MAICYA 1, 2;
SAAS 2; SATA 14, 72, 125; YAW

Thistlethwaite, Bel
See Wetherald, Agnes Ethelwyn

Thomas, Audrey (Callahan) 1935- .... **CLC 7, 13, 37, 107; SSC 20**
See also AITN 2; CA 21-24R; CAAS 19;
CANR 36, 58; CN 7; DLB 60; MTCW 1;
RGSF 2

Thomas, Augustus 1857-1934 .... **TCLC 97**

Thomas, D(onald) M(ichael) 1935- . **CLC 13, 22, 31, 132**
See also BPFB 3; BRWS 4; CA 61-64;
CAAS 11; CANR 17, 45, 75; CDBLB
1960 to Present; CN 7; CP 7; DA3; DLB
40, 207, 299; HGG; INT CANR-17;
MTCW 1, 2; SFW 4

Thomas, Dylan (Marlais) 1914-1953 .... **PC 2, 52; SSC 3, 44; TCLC 1, 8, 45, 105; WLC**
See also AAYA 45; BRWS 1; CA 104; 120;
CANR 65; CDBLB 1945-1960; DA; DA3;
DAB; DAC; DAM DRAM, MST, POET;
DLB 13, 20, 139; EWL 3; EXPP; LAIT
3; MTCW 1, 2; PAB; PFS 1, 3, 8; RGEL
2; RGSF 2; SATA 60; TEA; WLIT 4; WP

Thomas, (Philip) Edward 1878-1917 . **PC 53; TCLC 10**
See also BRW 6; BRWS 3; CA 106; 153;
DAM POET; DLB 19, 98, 156, 216; EWL
3; PAB; RGEL 2

Thomas, Joyce Carol 1938- .... **CLC 35**
See also AAYA 12, 54; BW 2, 3; CA 113;
116; CANR 48, 114, 135; CLR 19; DLB
33; INT CA-116; JRDA; MAICYA 1, 2;
MTCW 1, 2; SAAS 7; SATA 40, 78, 123,
137; SATA-Essay 137; WYA; YAW

Thomas, Lewis 1913-1993 .... **CLC 35**
See also ANW; CA 85-88; 143; CANR 38,
60; DLB 275; MTCW 1, 2

Thomas, M. Carey 1857-1935 .... **TCLC 89**
See also FW

Thomas, Paul
See Mann, (Paul) Thomas

Thomas, Piri 1928- .... **CLC 17; HLCS 2**
See also CA 73-76; HW 1; LLW 1

Thomas, R(onald) S(tuart)
1913-2000 .... **CLC 6, 13, 48**
See also CA 89-92; 189; CAAS 4; CANR
30; CDBLB 1960 to Present; CP 7; DAB;
DAM POET; DLB 27; EWL 3; MTCW 1;
RGEL 2

Thomas, Ross (Elmore) 1926-1995 .. **CLC 39**
See also CA 33-36R; 150; CANR 22, 63;
CMW 4

Thompson, Francis (Joseph)
1859-1907 .... **TCLC 4**
See also BRW 5; CA 104; 189; CDBLB
1890-1914; DLB 19; RGEL 2; TEA

Thompson, Francis Clegg
See Mencken, H(enry) L(ouis)

Thompson, Hunter S(tockton)
1937(?)- .... **CLC 9, 17, 40, 104**
See also AAYA 45; BEST 89:1; BPFB 3;
CA 17-20R; CANR 23, 46, 74, 77, 111,
133; CPW; CSW; DA3; DAM POP; DLB
185; MTCW 1, 2; TUS

Thompson, James Myers
See Thompson, Jim (Myers)

Thompson, Jim (Myers)
1906-1977(?) .... **CLC 69**
See also BPFB 3; CA 140; CMW 4; CPW;
DLB 226; MSW

Thompson, Judith .... **CLC 39**
See also CWD

Thomson, James 1700-1748 .... **LC 16, 29, 40**
See also BRWS 3; DAM POET; DLB 95;
RGEL 2

Thomson, James 1834-1882 .... **NCLC 18**
See also DAM POET; DLB 35; RGEL 2

Thoreau, Henry David 1817-1862 .. **NCLC 7, 21, 61, 138; PC 30; WLC**
See also AAYA 42; AMW; ANW; BYA 3;
CDALB 1640-1865; DA; DA3; DAB;
DAC; DAM MST; DLB 1, 183, 223, 270,
298; LAIT 2; LMFS 1; NCFS 3; RGAL
4; TUS

Thorndike, E. L.
See Thorndike, Edward L(ee)

Thorndike, Edward L(ee)
1874-1949 .... **TCLC 107**
See also CA 121

Thornton, Hall
See Silverberg, Robert

Thorpe, Adam 1956- .... **CLC 176**
See also CA 129; CANR 92; DLB 231

Thubron, Colin (Gerald Dryden)
1939- .... **CLC 163**
See also CA 25-28R; CANR 12, 29, 59, 95;
CN 7; DLB 204, 231

Thucydides c. 455B.C.-c. 395B.C. . **CMLC 17**
See also AW 1; DLB 176; RGWL 2, 3

Thumboo, Edwin Nadason 1933- .... **PC 30**
See also CA 194

Thurber, James (Grover)
1894-1961 .. **CLC 5, 11, 25, 125; SSC 1, 47**
See also AAYA 56; AMWS 1; BPFB 3;
BYA 5; CA 73-76; CANR 17, 39; CDALB
1929-1941; CWRI 5; DA; DA3; DAB;
DAC; DAM DRAM, MST, NOV; DLB 4,
11, 22, 102; EWL 3; EXPS; FANT; LAIT
3; MAICYA 1, 2; MTCW 1, 2; RGAL 4;
RGSF 2; SATA 13; SSFS 1, 10, 19;
SUFW; TUS

Thurman, Wallace (Henry)
1902-1934 .... **BLC 3; HR 3; TCLC 6**
See also BW 1, 3; CA 104; 124; CANR 81;
DAM MULT; DLB 51

Tibullus c. 54B.C.-c. 18B.C. .... **CMLC 36**
See also AW 2; DLB 211; RGWL 2, 3

Ticheburn, Cheviot
See Ainsworth, William Harrison

Tieck, (Johann) Ludwig
1773-1853 .... **NCLC 5, 46; SSC 31**
See also CDWLB 2; DLB 90; EW 5; IDTP;
RGSF 2; RGWL 2, 3; SUFW

Tiger, Derry
See Ellison, Harlan (Jay)

Tilghman, Christopher 1946- .... **CLC 65**
See also CA 159; CANR 135; CSW; DLB
244

Tillich, Paul (Johannes)
1886-1965 .... **CLC 131**
See also CA 5-8R; 25-28R; CANR 33;
MTCW 1, 2

Tillinghast, Richard (Williford)
1940- .... **CLC 29**
See also CA 29-32R; CAAS 23; CANR 26,
51, 96; CP 7; CSW

Timrod, Henry 1828-1867 .... **NCLC 25**
See also DLB 3, 248; RGAL 4

Tindall, Gillian (Elizabeth) 1938- ...... **CLC 7**
See also CA 21-24R; CANR 11, 65, 107;
CN 7

Tiptree, James, Jr. .... **CLC 48, 50**
See Sheldon, Alice Hastings Bradley
See also DLB 8; SCFW 2; SFW 4

Tirone Smith, Mary-Ann 1944- .... **CLC 39**
See also CA 118; 136; CANR 113; SATA
143

Tirso de Molina 1580(?)-1648 .... **DC 13; HLCS 2; LC 73**
See also RGWL 2, 3

Titmarsh, Michael Angelo
See Thackeray, William Makepeace

Ways, C. R.
See Blount, Roy (Alton), Jr.

Waystaff, Simon
See Swift, Jonathan

Webb, Beatrice (Martha Potter)
1858-1943 .... **TCLC 22**
See also CA 117; 162; DLB 190; FW

Webb, Charles (Richard) 1939- .... **CLC 7**
See also CA 25-28R; CANR 114

Webb, Frank J. .... **NCLC 143**
See also DLB 50

Webb, James H(enry), Jr. 1946- ...... **CLC 22**
See also CA 81-84

Webb, Mary Gladys (Meredith)
1881-1927 .... **TCLC 24**
See also CA 182; 123; DLB 34; FW

Webb, Mrs. Sidney
See Webb, Beatrice (Martha Potter)

Webb, Phyllis 1927- .... **CLC 18**
See also CA 104; CANR 23; CCA 1; CP 7;
CWP; DLB 53

Webb, Sidney (James) 1859-1947 .. **TCLC 22**
See also CA 117; 163; DLB 190

Webber, Andrew Lloyd .... **CLC 21**
See Lloyd Webber, Andrew
See also DFS 7

Weber, Lenora Mattingly
1895-1971 .... **CLC 12**
See also CA 19-20; 29-32R; CAP 1; SATA
2; SATA-Obit 26

Weber, Max 1864-1920 .... **TCLC 69**
See also CA 109; 189; DLB 296

Webster, John 1580(?)-1634(?) ...... **DC 2; LC
33, 84; WLC**
See also BRW 2; CDBLB Before 1660; DA;
DAB; DAC; DAM DRAM, MST; DFS
17, 19; DLB 58; IDTP; RGEL 2; WLIT 3

Webster, Noah 1758-1843 .... **NCLC 30**
See also DLB 1, 37, 42, 43, 73, 243

Wedekind, (Benjamin) Frank(lin)
1864-1918 .... **TCLC 7**
See also CA 104; 153; CANR 121, 122;
CDWLB 2; DAM DRAM; DLB 118; EW
8; EWL 3; LMFS 2; RGWL 2, 3

Wehr, Demaris .... **CLC 65**

Weidman, Jerome 1913-1998 .... **CLC 7**
See also AITN 2; CA 1-4R; 171; CAD;
CANR 1; DLB 28

Weil, Simone (Adolphine)
1909-1943 .... **TCLC 23**
See also CA 117; 159; EW 12; EWL 3; FW;
GFL 1789 to the Present; MTCW 2

Weininger, Otto 1880-1903 .... **TCLC 84**

Weinstein, Nathan
See West, Nathanael

Weinstein, Nathan von Wallenstein
See West, Nathanael

Weir, Peter (Lindsay) 1944- .... **CLC 20**
See also CA 113; 123

Weiss, Peter (Ulrich) 1916-1982 .. **CLC 3, 15,
51; TCLC 152**
See also CA 45-48; 106; CANR 3; DAM
DRAM; DFS 3; DLB 69, 124; EWL 3;
RGWL 2, 3

Weiss, Theodore (Russell)
1916-2003 .... **CLC 3, 8, 14**
See also CA 9-12R; 189; 216; CAAE 189;
CAAS 2; CANR 46, 94; CP 7; DLB 5

Welch, (Maurice) Denton
1915-1948 .... **TCLC 22**
See also BRWS 8, 9; CA 121; 148; RGEL
2

Welch, James (Phillip) 1940-2003 ..... **CLC 6,
14, 52; NNAL**
See also CA 85-88; 219; CANR 42, 66, 107;
CN 7; CP 7; CPW; DAM MULT, POP;
DLB 175, 256; LATS 1:1; RGAL 4;
TCWW 2

Weldon, Fay 1931- . **CLC 6, 9, 11, 19, 36, 59,
122**
See also BRWS 4; CA 21-24R; CANR 16,
46, 63, 97; CDBLB 1960 to Present; CN
7; CPW; DAM POP; DLB 14, 194; EWL
3; FW; HGG; INT CANR-16; MTCW 1,
2; RGEL 2; RGSF 2

Wellek, Rene 1903-1995 .... **CLC 28**
See also CA 5-8R; 150; CAAS 7; CANR 8;
DLB 63; EWL 3; INT CANR-8

Weller, Michael 1942- .... **CLC 10, 53**
See also CA 85-88; CAD; CD 5

Weller, Paul 1958- .... **CLC 26**

Wellershoff, Dieter 1925- .... **CLC 46**
See also CA 89-92; CANR 16, 37

Welles, (George) Orson 1915-1985 .. **CLC 20,
80**
See also AAYA 40; CA 93-96; 117

Wellman, John McDowell 1945-
See Wellman, Mac
See also CA 166; CD 5

Wellman, Mac .... **CLC 65**
See Wellman, John McDowell; Wellman,
John McDowell
See also CAD; RGAL 4

Wellman, Manly Wade 1903-1986 ... **CLC 49**
See also CA 1-4R; 118; CANR 6, 16, 44;
FANT; SATA 6; SATA-Obit 47; SFW 4;
SUFW

Wells, Carolyn 1869(?)-1942 .... **TCLC 35**
See also CA 113; 185; CMW 4; DLB 11

Wells, H(erbert) G(eorge) 1866-1946 . **SSC 6,
70; TCLC 6, 12, 19, 133; WLC**
See also AAYA 18; BPFB 3; BRW 6; CA
110; 121; CDBLB 1914-1945; CLR 64;
DA; DA3; DAB; DAC; DAM MST, NOV;
DLB 34, 70, 156, 178; EWL 3; EXPS;
HGG; LAIT 3; LMFS 2; MTCW 1, 2;
NFS 17, 20; RGEL 2; RGSF 2; SATA 20;
SCFW; SFW 4; SSFS 3; SUFW; TEA;
WCH; WLIT 4; YAW

Wells, Rosemary 1943- .... **CLC 12**
See also AAYA 13; BYA 7, 8; CA 85-88;
CANR 48, 120; CLR 16, 69; CWRI 5;
MAICYA 1, 2; SAAS 1; SATA 18, 69,
114; YAW

Wells-Barnett, Ida B(ell)
1862-1931 .... **TCLC 125**
See also CA 182; DLB 23, 221

Welsh, Irvine 1958- .... **CLC 144**
See also CA 173; DLB 271

Welty, Eudora (Alice) 1909-2001 .. **CLC 1, 2,
5, 14, 22, 33, 105; SSC 1, 27, 51; WLC**
See also AAYA 48; AMW; AMWR 1; BPFB
3; CA 9-12R; 199; CABS 1; CANR 32,
65, 128; CDALB 1941-1968; CN 7; CSW;
DA; DA3; DAB; DAC; DAM MST, NOV;
DLB 2, 102, 143; DLBD 12; DLBY 1987,
2001; EWL 3; EXPS; HGG; LAIT 3;
MAWW; MTCW 1, 2; NFS 13, 15; RGAL
4; RGSF 2; RHW; SSFS 2, 10; TUS

Wen I-to 1899-1946 .... **TCLC 28**
See also EWL 3

Wentworth, Robert
See Hamilton, Edmond

Werfel, Franz (Viktor) 1890-1945 ... **TCLC 8**
See also CA 104; 161; DLB 81, 124; EWL
3; RGWL 2, 3

Wergeland, Henrik Arnold
1808-1845 .... **NCLC 5**

Wersba, Barbara 1932- .... **CLC 30**
See also AAYA 2, 30; BYA 6, 12, 13; CA
29-32R, 182; CAAE 182; CANR 16, 38;
CLR 3, 78; DLB 52; JRDA; MAICYA 1,
2; SAAS 2; SATA 1, 58; SATA-Essay 103;
WYA; YAW

Wertmueller, Lina 1928- .... **CLC 16**
See also CA 97-100; CANR 39, 78

Wescott, Glenway 1901-1987 .. **CLC 13; SSC
35**
See also CA 13-16R; 121; CANR 23, 70;
DLB 4, 9, 102; RGAL 4

Wesker, Arnold 1932- .... **CLC 3, 5, 42**
See also CA 1-4R; CAAS 7; CANR 1, 33;
CBD; CD 5; CDBLB 1960 to Present;
DAB; DAM DRAM; DLB 13; EWL 3;
MTCW 1; RGEL 2; TEA

Wesley, John 1703-1791 .... **LC 88**
See also DLB 104

Wesley, Richard (Errol) 1945- .... **CLC 7**
See also BW 1; CA 57-60; CAD; CANR
27; CD 5; DLB 38

Wessel, Johan Herman 1742-1785 .... **LC 7**
See also DLB 300

West, Anthony (Panther)
1914-1987 .... **CLC 50**
See also CA 45-48; 124; CANR 3, 19; DLB
15

West, C. P.
See Wodehouse, P(elham) G(renville)

West, Cornel (Ronald) 1953- .... **BLCS; CLC
134**
See also CA 144; CANR 91; DLB 246

West, Delno C(loyde), Jr. 1936- .... **CLC 70**
See also CA 57-60

West, Dorothy 1907-1998 .. **HR 3; TCLC 108**
See also BW 2; CA 143; 169; DLB 76

West, (Mary) Jessamyn 1902-1984 ... **CLC 7,
17**
See also CA 9-12R; 112; CANR 27; DLB
6; DLBY 1984; MTCW 1, 2; RGAL 4;
RHW; SATA-Obit 37; TCWW 2; TUS;
YAW

West, Morris
See West, Morris L(anglo)
See also DLB 289

West, Morris L(anglo) 1916-1999 ..... **CLC 6,
33**
See West, Morris
See also BPFB 3; CA 5-8R; 187; CANR
24, 49, 64; CN 7; CPW; MTCW 1, 2

West, Nathanael 1903-1940 .. **SSC 16; TCLC
1, 14, 44**
See also AMW; AMWR 2; BPFB 3; CA
104; 125; CDALB 1929-1941; DA3; DLB
4, 9, 28; EWL 3; MTCW 1, 2; NFS 16;
RGAL 4; TUS

West, Owen
See Koontz, Dean R(ay)

West, Paul 1930- .... **CLC 7, 14, 96**
See also CA 13-16R; CAAS 7; CANR 22,
53, 76, 89; CN 7; DLB 14; INT CANR-
22; MTCW 2

West, Rebecca 1892-1983 ... **CLC 7, 9, 31, 50**
See also BPFB 3; BRWS 3; CA 5-8R; 109;
CANR 19; DLB 36; DLBY 1983; EWL
3; FW; MTCW 1, 2; NCFS 4; RGEL 2;
TEA

Westall, Robert (Atkinson)
1929-1993 .... **CLC 17**
See also AAYA 12; BYA 2, 6, 7, 8, 9, 15;
CA 69-72; 141; CANR 18, 68; CLR 13;
FANT; JRDA; MAICYA 1, 2; MAICYAS
1; SAAS 2; SATA 23, 69; SATA-Obit 75;
WYA; YAW

Westermarck, Edward 1862-1939 . **TCLC 87**

Westlake, Donald E(dwin) 1933- . **CLC 7, 33**
See also BPFB 3; CA 17-20R; CAAS 13;
CANR 16, 44, 65, 94; CMW 4; CPW;
DAM POP; INT CANR-16; MSW;
MTCW 2

Westmacott, Mary
See Christie, Agatha (Mary Clarissa)

Weston, Allen
See Norton, Andre

Wetcheek, J. L.
See Feuchtwanger, Lion

Williams, Charles
See Collier, James Lincoln
Williams, Charles (Walter Stansby)
1886-1945 .... **TCLC 1, 11**
See also BRWS 9; CA 104; 163; DLB 100,
153, 255; FANT; RGEL 2; SUFW 1
Williams, Ella Gwendolen Rees
See Rhys, Jean
Williams, (George) Emlyn
1905-1987 .... **CLC 15**
See also CA 104; 123; CANR 36; DAM
DRAM; DLB 10, 77; IDTP; MTCW 1
Williams, Hank 1923-1953 .... **TCLC 81**
See Williams, Hiram King
Williams, Helen Maria
1761-1827 .... **NCLC 135**
See also DLB 158
Williams, Hiram Hank
See Williams, Hank
Williams, Hiram King
See Williams, Hank
See also CA 188
Williams, Hugo (Mordaunt) 1942- ... **CLC 42**
See also CA 17-20R; CANR 45, 119; CP 7;
DLB 40
Williams, J. Walker
See Wodehouse, P(elham) G(renville)
Williams, John A(lfred) 1925- . **BLC 3; CLC**
5, 13
See also AFAW 2; BW 2, 3; CA 53-56, 195;
CAAE 195; CAAS 3; CANR 6, 26, 51,
118; CN 7; CSW; DAM MULT; DLB 2,
33; EWL 3; INT CANR-6; RGAL 4; SFW
4
Williams, Jonathan (Chamberlain)
1929- .... **CLC 13**
See also CA 9-12R; CAAS 12; CANR 8,
108; CP 7; DLB 5
Williams, Joy 1944- .... **CLC 31**
See also CA 41-44R; CANR 22, 48, 97
Williams, Norman 1952- .... **CLC 39**
See also CA 118
Williams, Sherley Anne 1944-1999 ... **BLC 3;**
CLC 89
See also AFAW 2; BW 2, 3; CA 73-76; 185;
CANR 25, 82; DAM MULT; POET; DLB
41; INT CANR-25; SATA 78; SATA-Obit
116
Williams, Shirley
See Williams, Sherley Anne
Williams, Tennessee 1911-1983 . **CLC 1, 2, 5,**
7, 8, 11, 15, 19, 30, 39, 45, 71, 111; DC
4; WLC
See also AAYA 31; AITN 1, 2; AMW;
AMWC 1; CA 5-8R; 108; CABS 3; CAD;
CANR 31, 132; CDALB 1941-1968; DA;
DA3; DAB; DAC; DAM DRAM, MST;
DFS 17; DLB 7; DLBD 4; DLBY 1983;
EWL 3; GLL 1; LAIT 4; LATS 1:2;
MTCW 1, 2; RGAL 4; TUS
Williams, Thomas (Alonzo)
1926-1990 .... **CLC 14**
See also CA 1-4R; 132; CANR 2
Williams, William C.
See Williams, William Carlos
Williams, William Carlos
1883-1963 .... **CLC 1, 2, 5, 9, 13, 22, 42,**
67; PC 7; SSC 31
See also AAYA 46; AMW; AMWR 1; CA
89-92; CANR 34; CDALB 1917-1929;
DA; DA3; DAB; DAC; DAM MST,
POET; DLB 4, 16, 54, 86; EWL 3; EXPP;
MTCW 1, 2; NCFS 4; PAB; PFS 1, 6, 11;
RGAL 4; RGSF 2; TUS; WP
Williamson, David (Keith) 1942- ..... **CLC 56**
See also CA 103; CANR 41; CD 5; DLB
289

Williamson, Ellen Douglas 1905-1984
See Douglas, Ellen
See also CA 17-20R; 114; CANR 39
Williamson, Jack .... **CLC 29**
See Williamson, John Stewart
See also CAAS 8; DLB 8; SCFW 2
Williamson, John Stewart 1908-
See Williamson, Jack
See also CA 17-20R; CANR 23, 70; SFW 4
Willie, Frederick
See Lovecraft, H(oward) P(hillips)
Willingham, Calder (Baynard, Jr.)
1922-1995 .... **CLC 5, 51**
See also CA 5-8R; 147; CANR 3; CSW;
DLB 2, 44; IDFW 3, 4; MTCW 1
Willis, Charles
See Clarke, Arthur C(harles)
Willy
See Colette, (Sidonie-Gabrielle)
Willy, Colette
See Colette, (Sidonie-Gabrielle)
See also GLL 1
Wilmot, John 1647-1680 .... **LC 75**
See Rochester
See also BRW 2; DLB 131; PAB
Wilson, A(ndrew) N(orman) 1950- .. **CLC 33**
See also BRWS 6; CA 112; 122; CN 7;
DLB 14, 155, 194; MTCW 2
Wilson, Angus (Frank Johnstone)
1913-1991 . **CLC 2, 3, 5, 25, 34; SSC 21**
See also BRWS 1; CA 5-8R; 134; CANR
21; DLB 15, 139, 155; EWL 3; MTCW 1,
2; RGEL 2; RGSF 2
Wilson, August 1945- ... **BLC 3; CLC 39, 50,**
63, 118; DC 2; WLCS
See also AAYA 16; AFAW 2; AMWS 8; BW
2, 3; CA 115; 122; CAD; CANR 42, 54,
76, 128; CD 5; DA; DA3; DAB; DAC;
DAM DRAM, MST, MULT; DFS 3, 7,
15, 17; DLB 228; EWL 3; LAIT 4; LATS
1:2; MTCW 1, 2; RGAL 4
Wilson, Brian 1942- .... **CLC 12**
Wilson, Colin 1931- .... **CLC 3, 14**
See also CA 1-4R; CAAS 5; CANR 1, 22,
33, 77; CMW 4; CN 7; DLB 14, 194;
HGG; MTCW 1; SFW 4
Wilson, Dirk
See Pohl, Frederik
Wilson, Edmund 1895-1972 .. **CLC 1, 2, 3, 8,**
24
See also AMW; CA 1-4R; 37-40R; CANR
1, 46, 110; DLB 63; EWL 3; MTCW 1, 2;
RGAL 4; TUS
Wilson, Ethel Davis (Bryant)
1888(?)-1980 .... **CLC 13**
See also CA 102; DAC; DAM POET; DLB
68; MTCW 1; RGEL 2
Wilson, Harriet
See Wilson, Harriet E. Adams
See also DLB 239
Wilson, Harriet E.
See Wilson, Harriet E. Adams
See also DLB 243
Wilson, Harriet E. Adams
1827(?)-1863(?) .... **BLC 3; NCLC 78**
See Wilson, Harriet; Wilson, Harriet E.
See also DAM MULT; DLB 50
Wilson, John 1785-1854 .... **NCLC 5**
Wilson, John (Anthony) Burgess 1917-1993
See Burgess, Anthony
See also CA 1-4R; 143; CANR 2, 46; DA3;
DAC; DAM NOV; MTCW 1, 2; NFS 15;
TEA
Wilson, Lanford 1937- .. **CLC 7, 14, 36, 197;**
DC 19
See also CA 17-20R; CABS 3; CAD; CANR
45, 96; CD 5; DAM DRAM; DFS 4, 9,
12, 16, 20; DLB 7; EWL 3; TUS

Wilson, Robert M. 1941- .... **CLC 7, 9**
See also CA 49-52; CAD; CANR 2, 41; CD
5; MTCW 1
Wilson, Robert McLiam 1964- .... **CLC 59**
See also CA 132; DLB 267
Wilson, Sloan 1920-2003 .... **CLC 32**
See also CA 1-4R; 216; CANR 1, 44; CN 7
Wilson, Snoo 1948- .... **CLC 33**
See also CA 69-72; CBD; CD 5
Wilson, William S(mith) 1932- .... **CLC 49**
See also CA 81-84
Wilson, (Thomas) Woodrow
1856-1924 .... **TCLC 79**
See also CA 166; DLB 47
Wilson and Warnke eds. .... **CLC 65**
Winchilsea, Anne (Kingsmill) Finch
1661-1720
See Finch, Anne
See also RGEL 2
Windham, Basil
See Wodehouse, P(elham) G(renville)
Wingrove, David (John) 1954- .... **CLC 68**
See also CA 133; SFW 4
Winnemucca, Sarah 1844-1891 .... **NCLC 79;**
NNAL
See also DAM MULT; DLB 175; RGAL 4
Winstanley, Gerrard 1609-1676 .... **LC 52**
Wintergreen, Jane
See Duncan, Sara Jeannette
Winters, Janet Lewis .... **CLC 41**
See Lewis, Janet
See also DLBY 1987
Winters, (Arthur) Yvor 1900-1968 .... **CLC 4,**
8, 32
See also AMWS 2; CA 11-12; 25-28R; CAP
1; DLB 48; EWL 3; MTCW 1; RGAL 4
Winterson, Jeanette 1959- .... **CLC 64, 158**
See also BRWS 4; CA 136; CANR 58, 116;
CN 7; CPW; DA3; DAM POP; DLB 207,
261; FANT; FW; GLL 1; MTCW 2; RHW
Winthrop, John 1588-1649 .... **LC 31, 107**
See also DLB 24, 30
Wirth, Louis 1897-1952 .... **TCLC 92**
See also CA 210
Wiseman, Frederick 1930- .... **CLC 20**
See also CA 159
Wister, Owen 1860-1938 .... **TCLC 21**
See also BPFB 3; CA 108; 162; DLB 9, 78,
186; RGAL 4; SATA 62; TCWW 2
Wither, George 1588-1667 .... **LC 96**
See also DLB 121; RGEL 2
Witkacy
See Witkiewicz, Stanislaw Ignacy
Witkiewicz, Stanislaw Ignacy
1885-1939 .... **TCLC 8**
See also CA 105; 162; CDWLB 4; DLB
215; EW 10; EWL 3; RGWL 2, 3; SFW 4
Wittgenstein, Ludwig (Josef Johann)
1889-1951 .... **TCLC 59**
See also CA 113; 164; DLB 262; MTCW 2
Wittig, Monique 1935(?)-2003 .... **CLC 22**
See also CA 116; 135; 212; CWW 2; DLB
83; EWL 3; FW; GLL 1
Wittlin, Jozef 1896-1976 .... **CLC 25**
See also CA 49-52; 65-68; CANR 3; EWL
3
Wodehouse, P(elham) G(renville)
1881-1975 . **CLC 1, 2, 5, 10, 22; SSC 2;**
TCLC 108
See also AITN 2; BRWS 3; CA 45-48; 57-
60; CANR 3, 33; CDBLB 1914-1945;
CPW 1; DA3; DAB; DAC; DAM NOV;
DLB 34, 162; EWL 3; MTCW 1, 2;
RGEL 2; RGSF 2; SATA 22; SSFS 10
Woiwode, L.
See Woiwode, Larry (Alfred)
Woiwode, Larry (Alfred) 1941- ... **CLC 6, 10**
See also CA 73-76; CANR 16, 94; CN 7;
DLB 6; INT CANR-16

Yeats, William Butler 1865-1939 . **PC 20, 51; TCLC 1, 11, 18, 31, 93, 116; WLC**
    See also AAYA 48; BRW 6; BRWR 1; CA 104; 127; CANR 45; CDBLB 1890-1914; DA; DA3; DAB; DAC; DAM DRAM, MST, POET; DLB 10, 19, 98, 156; EWL 3; EXPP; MTCW 1, 2; NCFS 3; PAB; PFS 1, 2, 5, 7, 13, 15; RGEL 2; TEA; WLIT 4; WP

Yehoshua, A(braham) B. 1936- .. **CLC 13, 31**
    See also CA 33-36R; CANR 43, 90; CWW 2; EWL 3; RGSF 2; RGWL 3

Yellow Bird
    See Ridge, John Rollin

Yep, Laurence Michael 1948- .... **CLC 35**
    See also AAYA 5, 31; BYA 7; CA 49-52; CANR 1, 46, 92; CLR 3, 17, 54; DLB 52; FANT; JRDA; MAICYA 1, 2; MAICYAS 1; SATA 7, 69, 123; WYA; YAW

Yerby, Frank G(arvin) 1916-1991 ..... **BLC 3; CLC 1, 7, 22**
    See also BPFB 3; BW 1, 3; CA 9-12R; 136; CANR 16, 52; DAM MULT; DLB 76; INT CANR-16; MTCW 1; RGAL 4; RHW

Yesenin, Sergei Alexandrovich
    See Esenin, Sergei (Alexandrovich)

Yesenin, Sergey
    See Esenin, Sergei (Alexandrovich)
    See also EWL 3

Yevtushenko, Yevgeny (Alexandrovich) 1933- ...... **CLC 1, 3, 13, 26, 51, 126; PC 40**
    See Evtushenko, Evgenii Aleksandrovich
    See also CA 81-84; CANR 33, 54; DAM POET; EWL 3; MTCW 1

Yezierska, Anzia 1885(?)-1970 .... **CLC 46**
    See also CA 126; 89-92; DLB 28, 221; FW; MTCW 1; RGAL 4; SSFS 15

Yglesias, Helen 1915- .... **CLC 7, 22**
    See also CA 37-40R; CAAS 20; CANR 15, 65, 95; CN 7; INT CANR-15; MTCW 1

Yokomitsu, Riichi 1898-1947 .... **TCLC 47**
    See also CA 170; EWL 3

Yonge, Charlotte (Mary) 1823-1901 .... **TCLC 48**
    See also CA 109; 163; DLB 18, 163; RGEL 2; SATA 17; WCH

York, Jeremy
    See Creasey, John

York, Simon
    See Heinlein, Robert A(nson)

Yorke, Henry Vincent 1905-1974 ..... **CLC 13**
    See Green, Henry
    See also CA 85-88; 49-52

Yosano Akiko 1878-1942 .... **PC 11; TCLC 59**
    See also CA 161; EWL 3; RGWL 3

Yoshimoto, Banana .... **CLC 84**
    See Yoshimoto, Mahoko
    See also AAYA 50; NFS 7

Yoshimoto, Mahoko 1964-
    See Yoshimoto, Banana
    See also CA 144; CANR 98; SSFS 16

Young, Al(bert James) 1939- ... **BLC 3; CLC 19**
    See also BW 2, 3; CA 29-32R; CANR 26, 65, 109; CN 7; CP 7; DAM MULT; DLB 33

Young, Andrew (John) 1885-1971 ...... **CLC 5**
    See also CA 5-8R; CANR 7, 29; RGEL 2

Young, Collier
    See Bloch, Robert (Albert)

Young, Edward 1683-1765 .... **LC 3, 40**
    See also DLB 95; RGEL 2

Young, Marguerite (Vivian) 1909-1995 .... **CLC 82**
    See also CA 13-16; 150; CAP 1; CN 7

Young, Neil 1945- .... **CLC 17**
    See also CA 110; CCA 1

Young Bear, Ray A. 1950- ... **CLC 94; NNAL**
    See also CA 146; DAM MULT; DLB 175

Yourcenar, Marguerite 1903-1987 ... **CLC 19, 38, 50, 87**
    See also BPFB 3; CA 69-72; CANR 23, 60, 93; DAM NOV; DLB 72; DLBY 1988; EW 12; EWL 3; GFL 1789 to the Present; GLL 1; MTCW 1, 2; RGWL 2, 3

Yuan, Chu 340(?)B.C.-278(?)B.C. . **CMLC 36**

Yurick, Sol 1925- .... **CLC 6**
    See also CA 13-16R; CANR 25; CN 7

Zabolotsky, Nikolai Alekseevich 1903-1958 .... **TCLC 52**
    See Zabolotsky, Nikolay Alekseevich
    See also CA 116; 164

Zabolotsky, Nikolay Alekseevich
    See Zabolotsky, Nikolai Alekseevich
    See also EWL 3

Zagajewski, Adam 1945- .... **PC 27**
    See also CA 186; DLB 232; EWL 3

Zalygin, Sergei -2000 .... **CLC 59**

Zalygin, Sergei (Pavlovich) 1913-2000 .... **CLC 59**
    See also DLB 302

Zamiatin, Evgenii
    See Zamyatin, Evgeny Ivanovich
    See also RGSF 2; RGWL 2, 3

Zamiatin, Evgenii Ivanovich
    See Zamyatin, Evgeny Ivanovich
    See also DLB 272

Zamiatin, Yevgenii
    See Zamyatin, Evgeny Ivanovich

Zamora, Bernice (B. Ortiz) 1938- .. **CLC 89; HLC 2**
    See also CA 151; CANR 80; DAM MULT; DLB 82; HW 1, 2

Zamyatin, Evgeny Ivanovich 1884-1937 .... **TCLC 8, 37**
    See Zamiatin, Evgenii; Zamiatin, Evgenii Ivanovich; Zamyatin, Yevgeny Ivanovich
    See also CA 105; 166; EW 10; SFW 4

Zamyatin, Yevgeny Ivanovich
    See Zamyatin, Evgeny Ivanovich
    See also EWL 3

Zangwill, Israel 1864-1926 ... **SSC 44; TCLC 16**
    See also CA 109; 167; CMW 4; DLB 10, 135, 197; RGEL 2

Zappa, Francis Vincent, Jr. 1940-1993
    See Zappa, Frank
    See also CA 108; 143; CANR 57

Zappa, Frank .... **CLC 17**
    See Zappa, Francis Vincent, Jr.

Zaturenska, Marya 1902-1982 ..... **CLC 6, 11**
    See also CA 13-16R; 105; CANR 22

Zayas y Sotomayor, Maria de 1590-c. 1661 .... **LC 102**
    See also RGSF 2

Zeami 1363-1443 .... **DC 7; LC 86**
    See also DLB 203; RGWL 2, 3

Zelazny, Roger (Joseph) 1937-1995 . **CLC 21**
    See also AAYA 7; BPFB 3; CA 21-24R; 148; CANR 26, 60; CN 7; DLB 8; FANT; MTCW 1, 2; SATA 57; SATA-Brief 39; SCFW; SFW 4; SUFW 1, 2

Zhang Ailing
    See Chang, Eileen
    See also CWW 2; RGSF 2

Zhdanov, Andrei Alexandrovich 1896-1948 .... **TCLC 18**
    See also CA 117; 167

Zhukovsky, Vasilii Andreevich
    See Zhukovsky, Vasily (Andreevich)
    See also DLB 205

Zhukovsky, Vasily (Andreevich) 1783-1852 .... **NCLC 35**
    See Zhukovsky, Vasilii Andreevich

Ziegenhagen, Eric .... **CLC 55**

Zimmer, Jill Schary
    See Robinson, Jill

Zimmerman, Robert
    See Dylan, Bob

Zindel, Paul 1936-2003 ...... **CLC 6, 26; DC 5**
    See also AAYA 2, 37; BYA 2, 3, 8, 11, 14; CA 73-76; 213; CAD; CANR 31, 65, 108; CD 5; CDALBS; CLR 3, 45, 85; DA; DA3; DAB; DAC; DAM DRAM, MST, NOV; DFS 12; DLB 7, 52; JRDA; LAIT 5; MAICYA 1, 2; MTCW 1, 2; NFS 14; SATA 16, 58, 102; SATA-Obit 142; WYA; YAW

Zinn, Howard 1922- .... **CLC 199**
    See also CA 1-4R; CANR 2, 33, 90

Zinov'Ev, A. A.
    See Zinoviev, Alexander (Aleksandrovich)

Zinov'ev, Aleksandr (Aleksandrovich)
    See Zinoviev, Alexander (Aleksandrovich)
    See also DLB 302

Zinoviev, Alexander (Aleksandrovich) 1922- .... **CLC 19**
    See Zinov'ev, Aleksandr (Aleksandrovich)
    See also CA 116; 133; CAAS 10

Zizek, Slavoj 1949- .... **CLC 188**
    See also CA 201

Zoilus
    See Lovecraft, H(oward) P(hillips)

Zola, Emile (Edouard Charles Antoine) 1840-1902 ...... **TCLC 1, 6, 21, 41; WLC**
    See also CA 104; 138; DA; DA3; DAB; DAC; DAM MST, NOV; DLB 123; EW 7; GFL 1789 to the Present; IDTP; LMFS 1, 2; RGWL 2; TWA

Zoline, Pamela 1941- .... **CLC 62**
    See also CA 161; SFW 4

Zoroaster 628(?)B.C.-551(?)B.C. ... **CMLC 40**

Zorrilla y Moral, Jose 1817-1893 .... **NCLC 6**

Zoshchenko, Mikhail (Mikhailovich) 1895-1958 .... **SSC 15; TCLC 15**
    See also CA 115; 160; EWL 3; RGSF 2; RGWL 3

Zuckmayer, Carl 1896-1977 .... **CLC 18**
    See also CA 69-72; DLB 56, 124; EWL 3; RGWL 2, 3

Zuk, Georges
    See Skelton, Robin
    See also CCA 1

Zukofsky, Louis 1904-1978 ... **CLC 1, 2, 4, 7, 11, 18; PC 11**
    See also AMWS 3; CA 9-12R; 77-80; CANR 39; DAM POET; DLB 5, 165; EWL 3; MTCW 1; RGAL 4

Zweig, Paul 1935-1984 .... **CLC 34, 42**
    See also CA 85-88; 113

Zweig, Stefan 1881-1942 .... **TCLC 17**
    See also CA 112; 170; DLB 81, 118; EWL 3

Zwingli, Huldreich 1484-1531 .... **LC 37**
    See also DLB 179

Literary Criticism Series
Cumulative Topic Index

This index lists all topic entries in Gale's *Children's Literature Review* (CLR), *Classical and Medieval Literature Criticism* (CMLC), *Contemporary Literary Criticism* (CLC), *Drama Criticism* (DC), *Literature Criticism from 1400 to 1800* (LC), *Nineteenth-Century Literature Criticism* (NCLC), *Short Story Criticism* (SSC), and *Twentieth-Century Literary Criticism* (TCLC). The index also lists topic entries in the Gale Critical Companion Collection, which includes the following publications: *The Beat Generation* (BG), and *Harlem Renaissance* (HR).

Topic Index

Topic Index

Topic Index

Topic Index

DC Cumulative Nationality Index

ALGERIAN
Camus, Albert **2**

AMERICAN
Albee, Edward (Franklin III) **11**
Baldwin, James (Arthur) **1**
Baraka, Amiri **6**
Brown, William Wells **1**
Bullins, Ed **6**
Chase, Mary (Coyle) **1**
Childress, Alice **4**
Chin, Frank (Chew Jr.) **7**
Elder, Lonne III **8**
Edson, Margaret **24**
Fornés, Mariá Irene **10**
Fuller, Charles (H. Jr.) **1**
Glaspell, Susan **10**
Gordone, Charles **8**
Gray, Spalding **7**
Guare, John **20**
Hansberry, Lorraine (Vivian) **2**
Hellman, Lillian (Florence) **1**
Henley, Beth **6, 14**
Hughes, (James) Langston **3**
Hurston, Zora Neale **12**
Hwang, David Henry **4, 23**
Kaufman, George S. **17**
Kennedy, Adrienne (Lita) **5**
Kramer, Larry **8**
Kushner, Tony **10**
Mamet, David (Alan) **4, 24**
Mann, Emily **7**
Miller, Arthur **1**
Moraga, Cherríe **22**
Norman, Marsha **8**
Odets, Clifford **6**
O'Neill, Eugene **20**
Parks, Suzan-Lori **23**
Rabe, David (William) **16**
Shange, Ntozake **3**
Shepard, Sam **5**
Simon, (Marvin) Neil **14**
Sondheim, Stephen **22**
Stein, Gertrude **19**
Terry, Megan **13**
Valdez, Luis (Miguel) **10**
Vogel, Paula **19**
Wasserstein, Wendy **4**
Wilder, Thornton (Niven) **1, 24**
Williams, Tennessee **4**
Wilson, August **2**
Wilson, Lanford **19**
Zindel, Paul **5**

AUSTRIAN
Bernhard, Thomas **14**
Grillparzer, Franz **14**
Handke, Peter **17**
Hofmannsthal, Hugo von **4**
Schnitzler, Arthur **17**

BARBADIAN
Kennedy, Adrienne (Lita) **5**

BELGIAN
Ghelderode, Michel de **15**

CANADIAN
Pollock, Sharon **20**

CUBAN
Fornés, Mariá Irene **10**

CZECH
Chapek, Karel **1**
Havel, Václav **6**

DUTCH
Bernhard, Thomas **14**

ENGLISH
Ayckbourn, Alan **13**
Beaumont, Francis **6**
Beddoes, Thomas Lovell **15**
Behn, Aphra **4**
Byron, Lord (George Gordon Noel) **24**
Centlivre, Susanna **25**
Chapman, George **19**
Churchill, Caryl **5**
Congreve, William **2**
Dekker, Thomas **12**
Dryden, John **3**
Etherege, George **23**
Fletcher, John **6**
Ford, John **8**
Jonson, Ben(jamin) **4**
Kyd, Thomas **3**
Lyly, John **7**
Marlowe, Christopher **1**
Middleton, Thomas **5**
Orton, Joe **3**
Otway, Thomas **24**
Pinter, Harold **15**
Rattigan, Terence (Mervyn) **18**
Shaffer, Peter (Levin) **7**
Shaw, George Bernard **23**
Sheridan, Richard Brinsley **1**
Shirley, James **25**
Stoppard, Tom **6**
Webster, John **2**
Wilde, Oscar **17**

FRENCH
Anouilh, Jean (Marie Lucien Pierre) **8, 21**
Artaud, Antonin (Marie Joseph) **14**
Beaumarchais, Pierre-Augustin Caron de **4**
Beckett, Samuel **22**
Becque, Henri **21**
Camus, Albert **2**
Cocteau, Jean **17**
Corneille, Pierre **21**
Dumas, Alexandre (fils) **1**
Genet, Jean **25**
Ionesco, Eugène **12**
Joyce, James (Augustine Aloysius) **16**
Marivaux, Pierre Carlet de Chamblain de **7**
Molière **13**
Rostand, Edmond (Eugene Alexis) **10**
Séjour, Victor **10**
Sartre, Jean-Paul **3**
Scribe, (Augustin) Eugène **5**

GERMAN
Brecht, (Eugen) Bertolt (Friedrich) **3**
Goethe, Johann Wolfgang von **20**
Hebbel, Friedrich **21**
Schiller, Friedrich von **12**

GREEK
Aeschylus **8**
Aristophanes **2**
Euripides **4**
Menander **3**
Sophocles **1**

IRISH
Friel, Brian **8**
Goldsmith, Oliver **8**
O'Casey, Sean **12**
Sheridan, Richard Brinsley **1**
Synge, (Edmund) J(ohn) M(illington) **2**

ITALIAN
Fo, Dario **10**
Machiavelli, Niccolò **16**
Pirandello, Luigi **5**
Plautus **6**

JAPANESE
Mishima, Yukio **1**
Zeami **7**

MARTINICAN
Césaire, Aimé **22**

NIGERIAN
Clark Bekedermo, J(ohnson) P(epper) **5**
Soyinka, Wole **2**

DC Cumulative Title Index

Title Index

ISBN 0-7876-8109-1